Online and Matching-Based Market Design

The rich, multi-faceted, and multi-disciplinary field of matching-based market design is active and important owing to its highly successful applications, with economic and sociological impact. Its home is economics but with intimate connections to algorithm design and operations research. With chapters contributed by over 50 top researchers from all three disciplines, this volume is unique in its breadth and depth while still giving a cohesive and unified picture of the field, suitable for the uninitiated as well as the expert. It explains the dominant ideas from computer science and economics underlying the most important results on market design and introduces the main algorithmic questions and combinatorial structures. Methodologies and applications from both the pre-Internet and post-Internet eras are covered in detail. Key chapters discuss the basic notions of efficiency, fairness, and incentives and the way in which market design seeks solutions guided by normative criteria borrowed from social choice theory.

Federico Echenique is a Professor of Economics at the University of California at Berkeley. He has published articles in the *American Economic Review*, *Econometrica*, *Journal of Political Economy*, *Quarterly Journal of Economics*, *Journal of Economic Theory*, and *Theoretical Economics*. He is a fellow of the Econometric Society, and co-editor of *Theoretical Economics*. Echenique was Program Co-chair of EC 2021.

Nicole Immorlica is a Principal Researcher at the Microsoft Research New England Laboratory. She has published more than 80 scholarly articles, surveys, and book chapters on topics including algorithmic game theory, market design, social networks, theoretical computer science, and economics. Her honors include the Harvard Excellence in Teaching Award, a Sloan Fellowship, and an NSF Career Award. Immorlica is Chair of SIGecom, former Vice Chair of SIGACT, Associate Editor of *ACM Transactions on Economics and Computing*, and was Program Co-chair for EC 2019.

Vijay V. Vazirani is Distinguished Professor in the Computer Science Department at the University of California, Irvine. He is one of the founders of algorithmic game theory, focusing on the computability of market equilibria. He is an ACM Fellow, a Guggenheim Fellow, and the recipient of the 2022 INFORMS John von Neumann Theory Prize. His previous books include *Approximation Algorithms* and (co-edited) *Algorithmic Game Theory*.

The cover image is meant to be a caricature of the housing market of Shapley and Shubik, appearing in Chapter 3. The picture portrays a comparison of the value of a house to that of a rock. In this case, the rock wins!

Online and Matching-Based Market Design

Edited by

Federico Echenique

University of California, Berkeley

Nicole Immorlica

Microsoft Research New England

Vijay V. Vazirani

University of California, Irvine

With a Foreword by Alvin E. Roth

Stanford University, California

CAMBRIDGE
UNIVERSITY PRESS

Shaftesbury Road, Cambridge CB2 8EA, United Kingdom

One Liberty Plaza, 20th Floor, New York, NY 10006, USA

477 Williamstown Road, Port Melbourne, VIC 3207, Australia

314–321, 3rd Floor, Plot 3, Splendor Forum, Jasola District Centre, New Delhi – 110025, India

103 Penang Road, #05–06/07, Visioncrest Commercial, Singapore 238467

Cambridge University Press is part of Cambridge University Press & Assessment, a department of the University of Cambridge.

We share the University's mission to contribute to society through the pursuit of education, learning and research at the highest international levels of excellence.

www.cambridge.org
Information on this title: www.cambridge.org/9781108831994
DOI: 10.1017/9781108937535

First published 2023

Printed in the United Kingdom by TJ Books Limited, Padstow Cornwall

A catalogue record for this publication is available from the British Library.

A Cataloging-in-Publication data record for this book is available from the Library of Congress.

ISBN 978-1-108-83199-4 Hardback

Cambridge University Press & Assessment has no responsibility for the persistence or accuracy of URLs for external or third-party internet websites referred to in this publication and does not guarantee that any content on such websites is, or will remain, accurate or appropriate.

Electronic version password: OMBMD_CUP

Contents

List of Contributors   *page xiii*
Foreword   xvii
Preface   xxi

PART ONE   FOUNDATIONS OF MARKET DESIGN

1   Two-Sided Markets: Stable Matching   **3**
Federico Echenique, Nicole Immorlica, and Vijay V. Vazirani
   1.1   Introduction   3
   1.2   The Gale–Shapley Deferred Acceptance Algorithm   4
   1.3   Incentive Compatibility   13
   1.4   The Lattice of Stable Matchings   18
   1.5   Linear Programming Formulation   29
   1.6   Exercises   31
   1.7   Bibliographic Notes   35
   References   35

2   One-Sided Matching Markets   **37**
Federico Echenique, Nicole Immorlica, and Vijay V. Vazirani
   2.1   Introduction   37
   2.2   Preliminaries   38
   2.3   Random Priority and Probabilistic Serial: Ordinal, No
            Endowments   39
   2.4   Top Trading Cycle: Ordinal, Endowments   44
   2.5   Hylland–Zeckhauser: Cardinal, No Endowments   46
   2.6 ϵ-Approximate ADHZ: Cardinal, Endowments   48
   2.7   Online Bipartite Matching   50
   2.8   Exercises   62
   2.9   Bibliographic Notes   64
   References   64

3   Matching Markets with Transfers and Salaries   **66**
Federico Echenique, Nicole Immorlica, and Vijay V. Vazirani
   3.1   Introduction   66

3.2 The Core Studied in a Paradigmatic Setting 67
3.3 Approximate Core for the General Graph Matching Game 76
3.4 Many-to-One Matching With Salaries 82
3.5 Matching with Contracts 85
3.6 Exercises 86
3.7 Bibliographic Notes 88
References 88

4 Objectives 90
Federico Echenique, Nicole Immorlica, and Vijay V. Vazirani
4.1 Introduction 90
4.2 Preliminaries: Individual Choice 90
4.3 A General Model of Social Choice 92
4.4 Normative Desiderata 94
4.5 Preference Aggregation 95
4.6 Pareto Optimality and Weighted Utilitarianism 98
4.7 Partial Equilibrium Analysis and Quasilinear Utility 99
4.8 Incentives 101
4.9 Bibliographical Notes 105
References 105

PART TWO   APPLICATIONS (MODERN AND TRADITIONAL)

5 Applications of Online Matching 109
Zhiyi Huang and Thorben Tröbst
5.1 Introduction 109
5.2 Models for Online Advertising 109
5.3 Arrival Models for Other Applications 120
5.4 Exercises 127
5.5 Bibliographic Notes 128
References 128

6 Online Matching in Advertisement Auctions 130
Nikhil R. Devanur and Aranyak Mehta
6.1 Introduction 130
6.2 The AdWords Problem 132
6.3 A Family of Algorithms 133
6.4 Adversarial Model 135
6.5 Stochastic Models 137
6.6 Packing Mixed Integer Linear Programs 143
6.7 Autobidding: A Decentralized Approach to Matching 144
6.8 The Design of Sponsored Search Auctions 149
6.9 Bibliographic Notes 152
References 153

7   Spectrum Auctions from the Perspective of Matching   **155**
Paul Milgrom and Andrew Vogt
  7.1   Introduction   155
  7.2   Spectrum Auction Algorithms   157
  7.3   Bidder Incentives and Regulator Objectives   161
  7.4   Substitutes and Complements   163
  7.5   Descending Clock Auctions   166
  7.6   Conclusion   177
  7.7   Bibliographic Notes   177
  References   178

8   School Choice   **180**
Atila Abdulkadiroğlu and Aram Grigoryan
  8.1   Introduction   180
  8.2   School Choice Problem   181
  8.3   School Choice Problem with Indifferences   186
  8.4   Controlled School Choice Problem   192
  8.5   Exercises   198
  8.6   Bibliographic Notes   199
  References   199

9   Kidney Exchange   **201**
Itai Ashlagi
  9.1   Introduction   201
  9.2   Preliminaries: The Exchange Pool   202
  9.3   Individually Rational Mechanisms   202
  9.4   Market Thickness in Static Exchange Pools   204
  9.5   Optimization   206
  9.6   Collaboration and Free Riding   207
  9.7   Dynamic Matching   210
  9.8   Bibliographic Notes   214
  References   214

PART THREE   THEORY

**10 Normative Properties for Object Allocation Problems: Characterizations
and Trade-Offs**   **219**
Lars Ehlers Bettina Klaus
  10.1 Introduction   219
  10.2 The Basic Model   220
  10.3 Top Trading Cycles Rules   221
  10.4 Serial Dictatorship Rules   224
  10.5 Endowment Inheritance Rules   226
  10.6 Deferred Acceptance Rules   230
  10.7 Relationships Between Classes of Rules   232
  10.8 Exercises   234

10.9 Bibliographic Notes 235
References 236

11 Choice and Market Design 238
Samson Alva and Battal Doğan
11.1 Introduction 238
11.2 Modeling Choice Behavior 239
11.3 Revealed Preference and Choice Behavior 244
11.4 Combinatorial Choice Behavior 248
11.5 Path-Independent Choice 249
11.6 Combinatorial Choice from Priorities and Capacities 253
11.7 Choice and Deferred Acceptance 257
11.8 Exercises 260
11.9 Bibliographic Notes 262
References 262

12 Combinatorics of Stable Matchings 264
Tamás Fleiner
12.1 Introduction 264
12.2 The Edge Removal Lemma 265
12.3 Bipartite Stable Matchings 270
12.4 Applications 273
12.5 Stable *b*-Matchings 277
12.6 Exercises 279
12.7 Bibiographic Notes 280
References 282

13 Algorithmics of Matching Markets 283
Jiehua Chen and David Manlove
13.1 Introduction 283
13.2 Preliminaries 285
13.3 Stable Marriage with Ties and Incomplete Lists 287
13.4 Stable Roommates without Ties:
Two Parameterized Algorithms 294
13.5 Selected Open Questions 299
13.6 Bibliographic Notes 300
References 301

14 Generalized Matching: Contracts and Networks 303
John William Hatfield, Ravi Jagadeesan, Scott Duke Kominers,
Alexandru Nichifor, Michael Ostrovsky, Alexander Teytelboym,
and Alexander Westkamp
14.1 Introduction 303
14.2 The Framework 304
14.3 Two-Sided Matching with Contracts 305
14.4 Supply Chains and Trading Networks 313
14.5 Transfers 317
14.6 Exercises 319
References 319

15 Complementarities and Externalities   **323**
Thành Nguyen and Rakesh Vohra
15.1 Introduction   323
15.2 Existence of Stable Matching, Revisited   324
15.3 Couples Matching   329
15.4 Complementarity via Constraints   332
15.5 Other Methods   338
15.6 Open Questions   339
15.7 Bibliographic Notes   340
References   340

16 Large Matching Markets   **343**
Jacob D. Leshno
16.1 Random Matching Markets and the Puzzle for the Proposing
Side   344
16.2 Continuum Matching Markets   351
16.3 Exercises   357
16.4 Bibliographic Notes   358
References   359

17 Pseudomarkets   **361**
Marek Pycia
17.1 Introduction   361
17.2 Preliminaries: Walrasian Equilibria in Discrete Settings   361
17.3 Eliciting Agents' Utilities   365
17.4 Efficiency   369
17.5 Fairness, Multiple-Unit Demand, Priorities, and Constraints   375
17.6 Exercises   377
17.7 Bibliographic Notes   378
References   379

18 Dynamic Matching   **381**
Mariagiovanna Baccara and Leeat Yariv
18.1 Introduction   381
18.2 Dynamic One-Sided Allocations   382
18.3 Dynamic Two-Sided Matching   387
18.4 Bibliographic Notes   399
References   400

19 Matching with Search Frictions   **402**
Hector Chade and Philipp Kircher
19.1 Introduction   402
19.2 Benchmark: Frictionless Case   402
19.3 Search Frictions: Some Modeling Choices   405
19.4 Directed Search   406
19.5 Random Search   413

19.6 Bibliographical Notes   424
References   425

20 Unraveling   **428**
Guillaume Haeringer and Hanna Halaburda
20.1 Introduction   428
20.2 Stable Mechanisms Are Not Enough to Prevent Unraveling   430
20.3 Market Timing and the Nature of Offers   432
20.4 Uncertainty as a Source of Unraveling   434
20.5 Structural Conditions   441
20.6 Information Disclosure and Unraveling   443
20.7 Bibliographic Notes   446
References   446

21 Investment in Matching Markets   **448**
Matthew Elliott and Eduard Talamàs
21.1 Introduction   448
21.2 Motivating Example   449
21.3 Model   449
21.4 Private Investment Incentives   451
21.5 Efficient Investments   455
21.6 Proofs of the Main Results   458
21.7 Discussion   461
21.8 Final Remarks   463
21.9 Exercises   463
References   465

22 Signaling in Two-Sided Matching Markets   **467**
Soohyung Lee
22.1 Introduction   467
22.2 Setting   467
22.3 Lessons from Theoretical Analyses   472
22.4 Signaling in Practice   476
22.5 Concluding Remarks   479
22.6 Bibliographic Notes   480
References   481

23 Two-Sided Markets and Matching Design   **484**
Renato Gomes and Alessandro Pavan
23.1 Introduction   484
23.2 General Setup   484
23.3 Pricing in Two-Sided Markets   486
23.4 Unknown Preference Distribution   492
23.5 Matching Design   496
23.6 Conclusions   506
23.7 Bibliographical Notes   507
References   507

PART FOUR EMPIRICS

24 Matching Market Experiments — **511**
Yan Chen
24.1 Introduction — 511
24.2 Laboratory Experiments — 512
24.3 Lab-in-the-Field Experiments — 521
24.4 Field Experiments — 523
24.5 Bibliographic Notes — 527
References — 527

25 Empirical Models of Non-Transferable Utility Matching — **530**
Nikhil Agarwal and Paulo Somaini
25.1 Introduction — 530
25.2 Empirical Model — 531
25.3 Analysis Using Final Matches and Stability — 534
25.4 Analysis Using Reported Preferences — 543
25.5 Applications, Extensions, and Open Questions — 546
25.6 Conclusion — 548
References — 549

26 Structural Estimation of Matching Markets with Transferable Utility — **552**
Alfred Galichon and Bernard Salanié
26.1 Matching with Unobserved Heterogeneity — 553
26.2 Identification — 558
26.3 Estimation — 560
26.4 Computation — 565
26.5 Other Implementation Issues — 566
26.6 Bibliographic Notes — 567
References — 570

PART FIVE RELATED TOPICS

27 New Solution Concepts — **575**
Shengwu Li and Irene Lo
27.1 Introduction — 575
27.2 Obvious Strategy-Proofness — 576
27.3 Stability under Incomplete Information — 582
27.4 Exercises — 588
27.5 Bibliographic Notes — 589
References — 589

28 Machine Learning for Matching Markets — **591**
Zhe Feng, David C. Parkes, and Sai Srivatsa Ravindranath

28.1 Introduction   591
28.2 Artificial Neural Networks   591
28.3 Optimal Auction Design   593
28.4 Two-Sided Matching   600
28.5 Discussion   610
28.6 Bibliographic Notes   611
References   612

29 Contract Theory   **614**
Gabriel Carroll
29.1 Introduction   614
29.2 Hidden-Action Models   614
29.3 Hidden-Information Models   626
29.4 Exercises   632
29.5 Bibliographic Notes   634
References   634

30 Secretaries, Prophets, and Applications to Matching   **635**
Michal Feldman and Brendan Lucier
30.1 Introduction to Sequential Online Decision-Making   635
30.2 The Secretary Problem   636
30.3 The Prophet Inequality   640
30.4 Application: Online Weighted Matching   642
30.5 Exercises   652
30.6 Bibliographic Notes   653
References   654

31 Exploration and Persuasion   **655**
Aleksandrs Slivkins
31.1 Motivation and Problem Formulation   656
31.2 Connection to Multi-Armed Bandits   658
31.3 Connection with Bayesian Persuasion   662
31.4 How Much Information to Reveal?   665
31.5 "Hidden Persuasion" for the General Case   667
31.6 Incentivized Exploration via "Hidden Persuasion"   670
31.7 A Necessary and Sufficient Assumption on the Prior   671
31.8 Bibliographic Notes   672
References   674

32 Fairness in Prediction and Allocation   **676**
Jamie Morgenstern and Aaron Roth
32.1 Introduction   676
32.2 The Need to Choose   681
32.3 Fairness in a Dynamic Model   683
32.4 Preserving Information Before Decisions   688
32.5 Bibliographic Notes   691
References   691

Index   694

Contributors

Nikhil Agarwal
Massachusetts Institute of Technology

Samson Alva
University of Texas at San Antonio

Itai Ashlagi
Stanford University

Mariagiovanna Baccara
Washington University in St. Louis

Atila Abdulkadiroğlu
Duke University

Gabriel Carroll
University of Toronto

Hector Chade
Arizona State University

Jiehua Chen
Vienna University of Technology

Yan Chen
University of Michigan

Nikhil R. Devanur
Amazon Co.

Battal Doğan
University of Bristol

Federico Echenique
University of California, Berkeley

Lars Ehlers
Université de Montréal

Matthew Elliott
University of Cambridge

Michal Feldman
Tel Aviv University

Zhe Feng
Google Research Mountain View

Tamás Fleiner
Budapest University of Technology and Economics

Alfred Galichon
New York University

Renato Gomes
Toulouse School of Economics

Aram Grigoryan
University of California, San Diego

Guillaume Haeringer
Baruch College

Hanna Halaburda
New York University

John William Hatfield
The University of Texas at Austin

Zhiyi Huang
University of Hong Kong

Ravi Jagadeesan
Stanford University

Philipp Kircher
Cornell University and
Catholic University of Louvain, Belgium

Bettina Klaus
University of Lausanne

Scott Duke Kominers
Harvard University

Nicole Immorlica
Microsoft Research New England

Soohyung Lee
Seoul National University

Jacob D. Leshno
University of Chicago Booth School of Business

Shengwu Li
Harvard University

Irene Lo
Stanford University

Brendan Lucier
Microsoft Research New England

David Manlove
University of Glasgow

Aranyak Mehta
Google Research

Paul Milgrom
Stanford University

Jamie Morgenstern
University of Washington

Thành Nguyen
Purdue University

Alexandru Nichifor
University of Melbourne

Michael Ostrovsky
Stanford University

David C. Parkes
Harvard University

Alessandro Pavan
Northwestern University

Marek Pycia
University of Zurich

Alvin E. Roth
Stanford University

Aaron Roth
University of Pennsylvania

Bernard Salanié
Columbia University

Aleksandrs Slivkins
Microsoft Research NYC

Paulo Somaini
Stanford University

Sai Srivatsa Ravindranath
Harvard University

Eduard Talamàs
IESE Business School

Alexander Teytelboym
University of Oxford

Thorben Tröbst
University of California, Irvine

Vijay V. Vazirani
University of California, Irvine

Andrew Vogt
Auctionomics

Rakesh Vohra
University of Pennsylvania

Alexander Westkamp
University of Cologne

Leeat Yariv
Princeton University

Foreword

This volume is a tribute to the interdisciplinarity (if that's a word) of matching markets and market design. It is also an invitation to pursue the many important open questions concerning theory, computation, and practical market design that are surveyed here from the perspectives of economics, computer science, and operations research.

Two of the founding papers of this literature are due to Gale and Shapley [3] and Shapley and Scarf [11]. Both demonstrated algorithms, for two crisply defined discrete models, that showed constructively that the core of the game – the set of outcomes that can't be disrupted by dissatisfied coalitions – is non-empty. That is, both papers demonstrated algorithms that could use information about the preferences of participants to identify outcomes with desirable efficiency and stability properties.

Gale and Shapley introduced what has become a canonical model of two-sided matching, which they called the marriage problem, involving two disjoint sets of players (e.g., "men" and "women"), each of whom has preferences over players on the other side. (They also sketched a many-to-one generalization that they called the college admissions problem.) An outcome of the game is a matching of men and women. They defined stable matchings as those that no man – woman pair not matched to each other, and no unhappily matched individual, would prefer to disrupt and introduced the deferred acceptance algorithm, which finds a stable matching with respect to any preferences. Under the rules that any willing pair of players from opposite sides may be matched to one another if and only if they both agree, the set of stable matchings is the core of the resulting game. But the set of stable matchings has proved of great interest even in models in which it differs from the core. And the deferred acceptance algorithm has sparked a literature of its own, not least in computer science, where it became well known following Donald Knuth's 1976 monograph in French, *Mariages Stables*.[1]

Shapley and Scarf introduced a model in which each agent initially possesses a single unit of an indivisible good, which they called a house. Agents have preferences over all the houses, which can be traded. But no money can be used: trades have to be house swaps, among cycles of any length. They introduced the top trading cycles algorithm (which they attributed to David Gale) and showed that, for any preferences over houses, it produces an allocation in the core of the game, i.e., one that no coalition can improve upon by trading among its own members. This is a

---

[1] For the English translation, see [5].

"one-sided" model: any player can trade with any other (unlike the case of the two-sided marriage model). Another way in which this and other models are one-sided rather than two-sided is that players (who have preferences, and for whom we have welfare concerns) are matched to objects, not to other players.

While both of these foundational papers were boundary-busting in how they combined game theory with algorithms, they both started from the point of view of cooperative game theory. The object of cooperative game theory (which was thought of as the study of a class of games in which players could reach binding agreements) was to identify desirable or likely outcomes of the games studied, whose rules were specified in terms of what coalitions could achieve by agreement, not in terms of what specific actions individual players could take. In contrast, non-cooperative game theory was thought of as studying games in which no binding agreements could be reached, and rules were specified in terms of the strategies that individuals could independently employ.

It seemed natural to think of Gale – Shapley and Shapley – Scarf as suggesting the designs of centralized clearinghouses, which would use information about the market to suggest market outcomes to participants. But while data on participants and resources could be observed and incorporated into the design of a clearinghouse, preferences are the private information of individuals. If we were interested in actually designing a centralized clearinghouse built around the deferred acceptance algorithm or top trading cycles, how would we obtain the preferences needed as inputs? In Roth [6], [7] I began to study when it would be safe for participants who were asked to state their preferences to state them truthfully. In game-theoretic terms, I was studying what was then thought of as part of non-cooperative game theory, namely when and for whom it could be made a *dominant strategy* to state preferences truthfully. I found that the top trading cycles algorithm makes it a dominant strategy to state preferences truthfully in the Shapley and Scarf model, but that no mechanism that always produces stable matchings can make the truthful revelation of preferences a dominant strategy for all players in the marriage model. However, it is possible to make it a dominant strategy for one side of the marriage market to state true preferences, and this has in some applications been sufficient, particularly in light of many subsequent results on the difficulty and low prevalence of profitable opportunities for agents on the other side to misrepresent their preferences in naturally occurring markets.[2]

These approaches showed that matching markets can be thought of both as cooperative games and as non-cooperative games, and today we no longer think of those two kinds of game theory as necessarily studying different games. Rather, coalitional models from cooperative game theory and strategic models from non-cooperative game theory answer different kinds of market design questions about a given market (see Roth and Wilson [10]). For example, the papers Roth [8] and Roth and Peranson [10] each studied the clearinghouse for new American doctors from the point of view of when stable matchings exist, and when truthful preferences can be safely elicited.

In the years since those beginnings, market design has continued to break boundaries, including those between theory, computation, and application. Market design has become an engineering discipline, in which game theory, computation,

---

[2] Dubins and Freedman [2] and Bergstrom and Manning [1] independently investigated closely related questions about the marriage model.

optimization, observation, and a healthy dose of trial and error combine to create new designs, which have had some notable practical successes in being implemented and maintained.

This volume opens up a window on much that has been accomplished so far. For readers new to the field, it provides an easy entryway, and the introductory essays by the editors provide helpful orientation. And (if my own experience is any indication) even grizzled veterans will find much to learn here, in the chapters on theory, on empirics and design, and on new boundaries to cross. This is a volume to read and study, and to let yourself be invited and recruited into the theory of matching and the practice of market design.

Alvin E. Roth

References

[1] Bergstrom, Ted, and Manning, Richard. 1983. Can courtship be cheatproof?, https://escholarship.org/uc/item/5dg0f759.

[2] Dubins, Lester E., and Freedman, David A. 1981. Machiavelli and the Gale–Shapley algorithm. *American Mathematical Monthly*, **88**(7), 485–494.

[3] Gale, David, and Shapley, Lloyd S. 1962. College admissions and the stability of marriage. *American Mathematical Monthly*, **69**(1), 9–15.

[4] Knuth, Donald Ervin. 1976. *Mariages Stables et Leurs Relations avec d'Autres Problemes Combinatoires: Introduction a l'Analysis Mathematique des Algorithmes.* Les Presses de l'Université de Montréal.

[5] Knuth, Donald Ervin. 1997. *Stable Marriage and Its Relation to Other Combinatorial Problems: An Introduction to the Mathematical Analysis of Algorithms.* vol. 10, American Mathematical Society.

[6] Roth, Alvin E. 1982a. Incentive compatibility in a market with indivisible goods. *Economics Lett.*, **9**, 127–132.

[7] Roth, Alvin E. 1082b. The economics of matching: Stability and incentives, *Mathematics of Operations Research*, **7**, 617–628.

[8] Roth, Alvin E. 1984. The evolution of the labor market for medical interns and residents: A case study in game theory. *J. Political Econ.*, **92**(6), 991–1016.: 991–1016.

[9] Roth, Alvin E., Peranson, Elliott. 1999. The redesign of the matching market for American physicians: Some engineering aspects of economic design. *American Economic Review*, **89**(4), 748–780.

[10] Roth, Alvin E., and Wilson, Robert B. 2019. How market design emerged from game theory: A mutual interview. *Journal of Economic Perspectives*, **33**(3), 118–143.

[11] Shapley, Lloyd, and Scarf, Herbert. 1974. On cores and indivisibility. *Journal of Mathematical Economics*, **1**(1), 23–37.

Preface

The topic of this book is the rich, multi-faceted, and multi-disciplinary field of matching-based market design. Although the home discipline of this field is economics, it has been intimately connected to the discipline of algorithm design right from its birth[3] and also shares boundaries with operations research. With chapters contributed by over 50 top researchers, from all three disciplines, this volume is unique in its breadth and depth of coverage while still retaining the feel of a cohesive, unified textbook.

The importance of this field arises from its highly successful applications, having economic as well as sociological impact. From the viewpoint of applications and algorithmic methodology, the field consists of two distinct eras – pre-Internet and post-Internet. Methodologies and applications from both eras are covered in detail in this book.

The book covers the dominant ideas from computer science and economics that underlie the most important results on market design. It introduces readers to the main algorithmic questions raised by matching markets, as well as to the key combinatorial structures that underlie such questions. It discusses the basic notions of efficiency, fairness, and incentives and the way in which market design seeks solutions that are guided by normative criteria borrowed from social choice theory. Because of its broad sweep of introductory as well as advanced topics, it will be valuable for the uninitiated as well as the expert.

The text is suitable for use in a wide variety of courses across several disciplines, as will be described next. A basic semester-long course on the topics of the book, suitable for upper-level undergraduates and beginning graduate students, would cover the four chapters of Part One, most of the chapters from Part Two, and a selection of the rest, based on the instructor's preferences. For a graduate course in economics, the book offers cutting-edge results on the most important areas of research on these topcis today, e.g., school choice, the AdWords and other online marketplaces, the organ donation market, large markets, and machine learning and pseudo-markets. A course on the economic theories of market design would concentrate on Parts One and Three, against a backdrop of other relevant topics. Readers interested in experimental economics, applied economics, or operations research will find relevant material in Parts Two and Four, and Part Five will appeal to those interested in new directions and advanced topics.

---

[3] The main result of the 1962 paper of Gale and Shapley, which initiated this field, was an *efficient algorithm* for the stable matching problem, obtained three years before polynomial time solvability was formally defined!

Because of the groundswell of fundamental algorithmic ideas, presented from first principles, this book is also suitable for use as a supplementary text in basic undergraduate and graduate courses on algorithm design. The first three chapters of Part One are particularly suitable for this.

Multiple thanks are due. First, to the chapter authors for producing very high quality chapters in a timely manner. Second, to Simons Institute for running a program on the same topic as the title of the book, in Fall 2019; it provided a scintillating environment in which the detailed structure of this book evolved. Third, to Lauren Cowles for her expert advice throughout the two years in which this book took shape.

We hope this book will contribute to the rapid growth of this field, not only as a pedagogic tool but also via the large number of open problems and issues discussed in the more advanced chapters. It is our intention that it will be in active use for several decades to come.

Federico Echenique
Nicole Immorlica
Vijay V. Vazirani

PART ONE

Foundations of Market Design

CHAPTER ONE

Two-Sided Markets: Stable Matching

Federico Echenique, Nicole Immorlica, and Vijay V. Vazirani

1.1 Introduction

The field of matching markets was initiated by the seminal work of Gale and Shapley on stable matching. Stable matchings have remarkably deep and pristine structural properties, which have led to polynomial time algorithms for numerous computational problems as well as quintessential game-theoretic properties. In turn, these have opened up the use of stable matching to a host of important applications.

This chapter will deal with the following four aspects:

1. Gale and Shapley's deferred acceptance algorithm for computing a stable matching; we will sometimes refer to it as the DA algorithm;
2. the incentive compatibility properties of this algorithm;
3. the fact that the set of all stable matchings of an instance forms a finite, distributive lattice, and the rich collection of structural properties associated with this fact;
4. the linear programing approach to computing stable matchings.

A general setting. A setting of the stable matching problem which is particularly useful in applications is the following (this definition is quite complicated because of its generality, and can be skipped on the first reading).

> **Definition 1.1.** Let W be a set of n workers and F a set of m firms. Let c be a *capacity function* $c\colon F \to \mathbb{Z}_+$ giving the maximum number of workers that can be matched to a firm; each worker can be matched to at most one firm. Also, let $G = (W, F, E)$ be a bipartite graph on vertex sets W, F and edge set E. For a vertex v in G, let $N(v)$ denote the set of its neighbors in G. Each worker w provides a strict preference list $l(w)$ over the set $N(w)$ and each firm f provides a strict preference list $l(f)$ over the set $N(f)$. We will adopt the convention that each worker and firm prefers being matched to one of its neighbors to remaining unmatched, and it prefers remaining unmatched to being matched to a non-neighbor.[1] If a worker or firm remains unmatched, we will say that it is matched to $\perp$.

---

[1] An alternative way of defining preference lists, which we will use in Section 1.3.2 is the following. Each worker w has a preference list over $F \cup \{\perp\}$, with firms in $N(w)$ listed in the preference order of w, followed by $\perp$, followed by $(F \setminus N(w))$ listed in arbitrary order. Similarly, each firm f's preference list is over $W \cup \{\perp\}$.

We wish to study all four aspects stated for this setting. However, it would be quite unwise and needlessly cumbersome to study the aspects directly in this setting. It turns out that the stable matching problem offers a natural progression of settings, hence allowing us to study the aspects gradually in increasing generality.

1. **Setting I.** Under this setting $n = m$, the capacity of each firm is one and graph G is a complete bipartite graph. Thus in this setting each side, consisting of workers or firms, has a total order over the other side. This simple setting will be used for introducing the core ideas.
2. **Setting II.** Under this setting n and m are not required to be equal and G is arbitrary; however, the capacity of each firm is still one. The definition of stability becomes more elaborate, hence making all four aspects more difficult in this setting. Relying on the foundation laid in Setting I, we will present only the additional ideas needed.
3. **Setting III.** This is the general setting defined in Definition 1.1. We will give a reduction from this setting to Setting II, so that the algorithm and its consequences carry over without additional work.

1.2 The Gale–Shapley Deferred Acceptance Algorithm

In this section we will define the notion of a stable matching for all three settings and give an efficient algorithm for finding it.

1.2.1 The DA Algorithm for Setting I

In this setting, the number of workers and firms is equal, i.e., $n = m$, and each firm has unit capacity. Furthermore, each worker and each firm has a total order over the other side.

Notation. If *worker w prefers firm f to f'* then we represent this as $f \succ_w f'$; a similar notation is used for describing the preferences of a firm.

We next recall a key definition from graph theory. Let $G = (W, F, E)$ be a graph with equal numbers of workers and firms, i.e., $|W| = |F|$. Then, $\mu \subseteq E$ is a *perfect matching* in G if each vertex of G has exactly one edge of μ incident at it. If so, μ can also be viewed as a bijection between W to F. If $(w, f) \in \mu$ then we will say that μ *matches w to f* and use the notation $\mu(w) = f$ and $\mu(f) = w$.

> **Definition 1.2.** Worker w and firm f form a *blocking pair* with respect to a perfect matching μ, if they prefer each other over their partners in μ, i.e., $w \succ_f \mu(f)$ and $f \succ_w \mu(w)$.

If (w, f) form a blocking pair with respect to perfect matching μ then they have an incentive to secede from matching μ and pair up by themselves. The significance of the notion of stable matching, defined next, is that no worker–firm pair has an incentive to secede from this matching. Hence such matchings lie in the *core* of the particular instance; this key notion will be introduced in Chapter 3. For now, recall from cooperative game theory that the core consists of solutions under which no subset of the agents can gain more (i.e., with each agent gaining at least as much and at least one agent gaining strictly more) by seceding from the grand coalition. Additionally, in Chapter 3 we will also establish that stable matchings are efficient and individually rational.

Definition 1.3. A perfect matching μ with no blocking pairs is called a *stable matching*.

It turns out that every instance of the stable matching problem with complete preference lists has at least one stable matching. Interestingly enough, this fact follows as a corollary of the deferred acceptance algorithm, which finds in polynomial time one stable matching among the $n!$ possible perfect matchings in G.

Example 1.4. Let I be an instance of the stable matching problem with three workers and three firms and the following preference lists:

$$w_1 : f_2, f_1, f_3 \qquad f_1 : w_1, w_2, w_3$$
$$w_2 : f_2, f_3, f_1 \qquad f_2 : w_1, w_2, w_3$$
$$w_3 : f_1, f_2, f_3 \qquad f_3 : w_1, w_3, w_2$$

Figure 1.1 shows three perfect matchings in instance I. The first matching is unstable, with blocking pair (w_1, f_2), and the last two are stable (this statement is worth verifying).

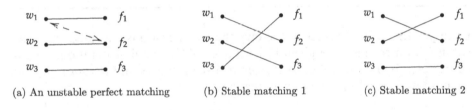

(a) An unstable perfect matching   (b) Stable matching 1   (c) Stable matching 2

Figure 1.1

We next present the deferred acceptance algorithm[2] for Setting I, described in Algorithm 1.8. The algorithm operates iteratively, with one side proposing and the other side acting on the proposals received. We will assume that workers propose to firms. The initialization involves each worker marking each firm in its preference list as *uncrossed*.

Each iteration consists of three steps. First, each worker proposes to the best uncrossed firm on its list. Second, each firm that got proposals tentatively accepts the best proposal it received and rejects all other proposals. Third, each worker who was rejected by a firm crosses that firm off its list. If in an iteration each firm receives a proposal, we have a perfect matching, say μ, and the algorithm terminates.

The following observations lead to a proof of correctness and running time.

Observation 1.5. *If a firm gets a proposal in a certain iteration, it will keep getting at least one proposal in all subsequent iterations.*

---

[2] The reason for this name is provided in Remark 1.11.

Observation 1.6. *As the iterations proceed, for each firm the following holds: once it receives a proposal, it tentatively accepts a proposal from the same or a better worker, according to its preference list.*

Lemma 1.7. *Algorithm 1.8 terminates in at most n^2 iterations.*

Proof In every iteration other than the last, at least one worker will cross a firm off its preference list. Consider iteration number $n^2 - n + 1$, assuming the algorithm has not terminated so far. Since the total size of the n preference lists is n^2, there is a worker, say w, who will propose to the last firm on its list in this iteration. Therefore by this iteration w has proposed to every firm and every firm has received a proposal. Hence, by Observation 1.5, in this iteration every firm will get a proposal and the algorithm will terminate with a perfect matching. □

Algorithm 1.8. Deferred acceptance algorithm

Until all firms receive a proposal, do:

1. $\forall w \in W$: w proposes to its best uncrossed firm.
2. $\forall f \in F$: f tentatively accepts its best proposal and rejects the rest.
3. $\forall w \in W$: If w got rejected by firm f, it crosses f off its list.

Output the perfect matching, and call it μ.

Example 1.9. The Figures 1.2 shows the two iterations executed by Algorithm 1.8 on the instance given in Example 1.4. In the first iteration, w_2 will get rejected by f_2 and will cross it from its list. In the second iteration, w_2 will propose to f_3, resulting in a perfect matching.

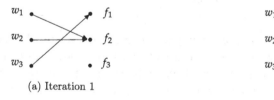

(a) Iteration 1   (b) Iteration 2

Figure 1.2

Theorem 1.10. *The perfect matching found by the DA algorithm is stable.*

Proof For the sake of contradiction assume that μ is not stable and let (w, f') be a blocking pair. Assume that $\mu(w) = f$ and $\mu(f') = w'$ as shown in Figure 1.3. Since (w, f') is a blocking pair, w prefers f' to f and therefore must have proposed to f' and been rejected in some iteration, say i, before eventually proposing to f. In iteration i, f' must have tentatively accepted the proposal from a worker it likes better than w. Therefore, by Observation 1.6, at the termination of the algorithm, $w' \succ_{f'} w$. This contradicts the assumption that (w, f') is a blocking pair. $\qquad\square$

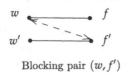

Blocking pair (w, f')

Figure 1.3 Blocking pair (w, f').

Remark 1.11. The Gale–Shapley algorithm is called the *deferred acceptance algorithm* because firms do not immediately accept proposals received by them – they defer them and accept only at the end of the algorithm when a perfect matching is found. In contrast, under the immediate acceptance algorithm, each firm immediately accepts the best proposal it has received; see Chapter 3.

Our next goal is to prove that the DA algorithm, with workers proposing, leads to a matching that is favorable for workers and unfavorable for firms. We first formalize the terms "favorable" and "unfavorable."

Definition 1.12. Let S be the set of all stable matchings over (W, F). For each worker w, the *realm of possibilities* $R(w)$ is the set of all firms to which w is matched in S, i.e., $R(w) = \{f \mid \exists \mu \in S \text{ s.t. } (w, f) \in \mu\}$. The *optimal firm* for w is the best firm in $R(w)$ with respect to w's preference list; it will be denoted by optimal(w). The *pessimal firm* for w is the worst firm in $R(w)$ with respect to w's preference list and will be denoted by pessimal(w). The definitions of these terms for firms are analogous.

Lemma 1.13. *Two workers cannot have the same optimal firm, i.e., each worker has a unique optimal firm.*

Proof Suppose that this is not the case and suppose that two workers w and w' have the same optimal firm, f. Assume without loss of generality that f prefers w' to w. Let μ be a stable matching such that $(w, f) \in \mu$ and let f' be the firm matched to w' in μ. Since $f = \text{optimal}(w')$ and w' is matched to f' in a stable matching, it must be the case that $f \succ_{w'} f'$. Then (w', f) forms a blocking pair with respect to μ, leading to a contradiction. See Figure 1.4. $\qquad\square$

Blocking pair (w', f) with respect to μ.

Figure 1.4 Blocking pair (w', f) with respect to μ.

Corollary 1.14. *Matching each worker to its optimal firm results in a perfect matching, say μ_W.*

Lemma 1.15. *The matching μ_W is stable.*

Proof Suppose that this is not the case and let (w,f') be a blocking pair with respect to μ_W, where $(w,f), (w',f') \in \mu_W$. Then $f' \succ_w f$ and $w \succ_{f'} w'$.

Since optimal$(w') = f'$, there is a stable matching, say μ', s.t. $(w',f') \in \mu'$. Assume that w is matched to firm f'' in μ'. Now since optimal$(w) = f, f \succ_w f''$. This together with $f' \succ_w f$ gives $f' \succ_w f''$. Then (w,f') is a blocking pair with respect to μ', giving a contradiction. See Figure 1.5. □

$$w \quad \overset{}{\longleftarrow} \quad f \qquad\qquad\qquad w' \quad \overset{}{\longrightarrow} \quad f'$$
$$w' \quad \overset{}{\longrightarrow} \quad f' \qquad\qquad\qquad w \quad \overset{}{\longleftarrow} \quad f''$$

(a) Blocking pair (w,f') with respect to μ_W (b) Blocking pair (w,f') with respect to μ'

Figure 1.5

Proofs similar to those of Lemmas 1.13 and 1.15 show that each worker has a unique pessimal firm and the perfect matching that matches each worker to its pessimal firm is also stable.

Definition 1.16. The perfect matching that matches each worker to its optimal (pessimal) firm is called the *worker-optimal (-pessimal) stable matching*. The notions of *firm-optimal (-pessimal) stable matching* are analogous. The worker and firm optimal stable matchings will be denoted by μ_W and μ_F, respectively.

Theorem 1.17. *The worker-proposing DA algorithm finds the worker-optimal stable matching.*

Proof Suppose that this is not the case; then there must be a worker who is rejected by its optimal firm before proposing to a firm it prefers less. Consider the first iteration in which a worker, say w, is rejected by its optimal firm, say f. Let w' be the worker that firm f tentatively accepts in this iteration; clearly, $w' \succ_f w$. By Lemma 1.13, optimal$(w') \neq f$ and, by the assumption made in the first sentence of this proof, w' has not yet been rejected by its optimal firm (and perhaps never will be). Therefore, w' has not yet proposed to its optimal firm; let the latter be f'. Since w' has already proposed to f, we have that $f \succ_{w'} f'$. Now consider the worker-optimal stable matching μ; clearly, (w,f), $(w',f') \in \mu$. Then (w',f) is a blocking pair with respect to μ, giving a contradiction. See Figure 1.6. □

Blocking pair (w',f) with respect to μ

Figure 1.6 Blocking pair (w',f) with respect to μ.

Lemma 1.18. *The worker-optimal stable matching is also firm pessimal.*

Proof Let μ be the worker-optimal stable matching and suppose that it is not firm pessimal. Let μ' be a firm-pessimal stable matching. Now, for some $(w,f) \in \mu$, pessimal$(f) \neq w$. Let pessimal$(f) = w'$; clearly, $w \succ_f w'$. Let $w =$ pessimal(f'); then $(w,f'), (w',f) \in \mu'$. Since optimal$(w) = f$ and w is matched to f' in a stable matching, $f \succ_w f'$. Then (w,f) forms a blocking pair with respect to μ', giving a contradiction. $\qquad\square$

1.2.2 Extension to Setting II

Recall that in this setting each worker and firm has a total preference order over only its neighbors in the graph $G = (W, F, E)$ and $\bot$, with $\bot$ the least preferred element in each list; matching a worker or firm to $\bot$ is equivalent to leaving it unmatched.

In this setting, a stable matching may not be a perfect matching in G even if the number of workers and firms is equal; however, it will be a maximal matching. Recall that a matching $\mu \subseteq E$ is *maximal* if it cannot be extended with an edge from $E - \mu$. As a result of these changes, in going from Setting I to Setting II, the definition of stability also needs to be enhanced.

Definition 1.19. Let μ be any maximal matching in $G = (W, F, E)$. Then the pair (w,f) forms a *blocking pair* with respect to μ if $(w,f) \in E$ and one of the following holds:

- **Type 1.** w, f are both matched in μ and prefer each other to their partners in μ.
- **Type 2a.** w is matched to f', f is unmatched, and $f \succ_w f'$.
- **Type 2b.** w is unmatched, f is matched to w', and $w \succ_f w'$.

Observe that, since $(w,f) \in E$, w and f prefer each other to remaining unmatched. Therefore they cannot both be unmatched in μ – this follows from the maximality of the matching.

The only modification needed to Algorithm 1.8 is to the termination condition; the modification is as follows. Every worker is either tentatively accepted by a firm or has crossed off all firms from its list. When this condition is reached, each worker in the first category is matched to the firm that tentatively accepted it and the rest remain unmatched. Let μ denote this matching. We will still call this the deferred acceptance algorithm. It is easy to see that Observations 1.5 and 1.6 still hold and that Lemma 1.7 holds with a bound nm on the number of iterations.

Lemma 1.20. *The deferred acceptance algorithm outputs a maximal matching in G.*

Proof Assume that $(w,f) \in E$ but that so far worker w and firm f are both unmatched in the matching found by the algorithm. During the algorithm, w must have proposed to f and been rejected. Now, by Observation 1.5, f must be matched, giving a contradiction. $\qquad\square$

Theorem 1.21. *The maximal matching found by the deferred acceptance algorithm is stable.*

Proof We need to prove that neither type of blocking pair exists with respect to μ. For the first type, the proof is identical to that in Theorem 1.10 and is omitted. Assume that (w, f) is a blocking pair of the second type. There are two cases:

Case 1. w is matched, f is not, and w prefers f to its match, say f'. Clearly w will propose to f before proposing to f'. Now, by Observation 1.5, f must be matched in μ, giving a contradiction.

Case 2. f is matched, w is not, and f prefers w to its match, say w'. Clearly w will propose to f during the algorithm. Since f prefers w to w', it will not reject w in favor of w', hence giving a contradiction. □

Notation. If worker w or firm f is unmatched in μ then we will denote this as $\mu(w) = \perp$ or $\mu(f) = \perp$. We will denote the sets of workers and firms matched under μ by $W(\mu)$ and $F(\mu)$, respectively.

Several of the definitions and facts given in Setting I carry over with small modifications; we summarize these next. The definition of the *realm of possibilities* of workers and firms remains the same as before; however, note that in Setting II, some of these sets could be the singleton set $\{\perp\}$. The definitions of *optimal and pessimal firms for a worker* also remain the same, with the change that they will be $\perp$ if the realm of possibilities is the set $\{\perp\}$. Let $W' \subseteq W$ be the set of workers whose realm of possibilities is non-empty. Then, via a proof similar to that of Lemma 1.13, it is easy to see that two workers in W' cannot have the same optimal firm, i.e., every worker in W' has a unique optimal firm.

Next, match each worker in W' to its optimal firm, leaving the remaining workers unmatched. This is defined to be the *worker-optimal matching*; we will denote it by μ_W. Similarly, define the *firm-optimal matching*; this will be denoted by μ_F. Using ideas from the proof of Lemma 1.15, it is easy to show that the worker-optimal matching is stable. Furthermore, using Theorem 1.17 one can show that the deferred acceptance algorithm finds this matching. Finally, using Lemma 1.18, one can show that the worker-optimal stable matching is also firm pessimal.

Lemma 1.22. *The numbers of workers and firms matched in all stable matchings are the same.*

Proof Each worker w prefers being matched to one of the firms that is its neighbor in G over remaining unmatched. Therefore, all workers who are unmatched in μ_W will be unmatched in all other stable matchings as well. Hence for an arbitrary stable matching μ we have $W(\mu_W) \supseteq W(\mu) \supseteq W(\mu_F)$. Thus $|W(\mu_W)| \geq |W(\mu)| \geq |W(\mu_F)|$. A similar statement for firms is $|F(\mu_W)| \leq |F(\mu)| \leq |F(\mu_F)|$. Since the number of workers and firms matched in any stable matching is equal, $|W(\mu_W)| = |F(\mu_W)|$ and $|W(\mu_F)| = |F(\mu_F)|$. Therefore the cardinalities of all sets given above are equal, hence establishing the lemma. □

Finally, we present the *rural hospital theorem*[3] for Setting II.

Theorem 1.23. *The set of workers matched is the same under all stable matchings; similarly for firms.*

Proof As observed in the proof of Lemma 1.22, $W(\mu_W) \supseteq W(\mu) \supseteq W(\mu_F)$. By Lemma 1.22 these sets are of equal cardinality. Hence they must all be the same set as well. □

1.2.3 Reduction from Setting III to Setting II

We will first give a definition of a blocking pair that is appropriate for Setting III. We will then give a reduction from this setting to Setting II, thereby allowing us to carry over the algorithm and its consequences to this setting directly. Finally, we will prove the rural hospital theorem for Setting III.

Definition 1.24. Given a graph $G = (V, E)$ and an upper bound function $b \colon V \to \mathbb{Z}_+$, a set $\mu \subseteq E$ is a *b-matching* if the number of edges of μ incident at each vertex $v \in V$ is at most $b(v)$. Furthermore, μ is a *maximal b-matching* if μ cannot be extended to a valid b-matching by adding an edge from $E - \mu$.

In Setting III, firms have capacities given by $c \colon F \to \mathbb{Z}_+$. For the graph $G = (W, F, E)$ specified in the instance given in Setting III, define an upper bound function $b \colon W \cup F \to \mathbb{Z}_+$ as follows. For $w \in W$, $b(w) = 1$ and for $f \in F$, $b(f) = c(f)$. Let μ be a maximal b-matching in $G = (W, F, E)$ with upper bound function b. We will say that firm f is *matched to capacity* if the number of workers matched to f is exactly $c(f)$ and it is *not matched to capacity* if f is matched to fewer than $c(f)$ workers. Furthermore, if a set $S \subseteq W$ of workers is matched to firm f under μ, with $|S| \leq c(f)$, then we will use the notation $\mu(f) = S$ and for each $w \in S$, $\mu(w) = f$.

Definition 1.25. Let μ be a maximal b-matching in $G = (W, F, E)$ with upper bound function b. For $w \in W$ and $f \in F$, (w, f) forms a *blocking pair* with respect to μ if $(w, f) \in E$ and one of the following hold:

- **Type 1.** f is matched to capacity, w is matched to f', and there is a worker w' that is matched to f such that $w \succ_f w'$ and $f \succ_w f'$.
- **Type 2a.** f is not matched to capacity, w is matched to f', and $f \succ_w f'$.
- **Type 2b.** w is unmatched, w' is matched to f, and $w \succ_f w'$.

Reduction to Setting II. Given an instance I of Setting III, we show below how to reduce it in polynomial time to an instance I' of Setting II in such a way that there

---

[3] The name of this theorem has its origins in the application of stable matching to the problem of matching residents to hospitals. The full scope of the explanation given next is best seen in the context of the extension of this theorem to Setting III, given in Section 1.2.3. In this application it was found that certain hospitals received very poor matches and even remained underfilled; moreover, this persisted even when a hospital-optimal stable matching was used. It turned out that these unsatisfied hospitals were mostly in rural areas and were preferred least by most residents. The question arose whether there was a "better" way of finding an allocation. The rural hospital theorem clarified that *every* stable matching would treat underfilled hospitals in the same way, i.e., give the same allocation.

is a bijection ϕ between the sets of stable matchings of I and I' such that ϕ and ϕ^{-1} can be computed in polynomial time.

Let I be given by (W, F, E, c) together with preference lists $l(w), \forall w \in W$ and $l(f), \forall f \in F$. Instance I' will be given by (W', F', E') together with preference lists $l'(w), \forall w \in W'$, and $l'(f), \forall f \in F'$, where:

- $W' = W$.
- $F' = \cup_{f \in F} \{f^{(1)}, \ldots, f^{(c(f))}\}$; i.e., corresponding to firm $f \in I$, I' will have $c(f)$ firms, namely $f^{(1)}, \ldots, f^{(c(f))}$.
- Corresponding to each edge $(w, f) \in E$, E' has edges $(w, f^{(i)})$ for each $i \in [1 \ldots c(f)]$.
- $\forall w \in W'$, $l'(w)$ is obtained by replacing each firm, say f, in $l(w)$ by the ordered list $f^{(1)}, \ldots, f^{(c(f))}$. More formally, if $f \succ_w f'$ then for all $1 \leq i \leq c(i)$ and $1 \leq j \leq c(j)$ we have $f^{(i)} \succ_w f'^{(j)}$ and for all $1 \leq i < j \leq c(i)$ we have $f^{(i)} \succ_w f^{(j)}$.
- $\forall f \in F$ and $i \in [1 \ldots c(f)]$, $l'(f^{(i)})$ is the same as $l(f)$.

Lemma 1.26. *Let μ be a stable matching for instance I of Setting III. Then the following hold:*

- *If firm f is matched to $k < c(f)$ workers then $f^{(1)}, \ldots, f^{(k)}$ must be matched and $f^{(k+1)}, \ldots, f^{(c(f))}$ must remain unmatched.*
- *If $(f^{(i)}, w), (f^{(j)}, w') \in \mu$ with $i < j$ then $w \succ_f w'$.*

Proof For contradiction assume that $f^{(i)}$ is unmatched and $f^{(j)}$ is matched, to w say, in μ, where $i < j$. Clearly, $f^{(i)} \succ_w f^{(j)}$ and $w \succ_{f^{(i)}} \bot$. Therefore $(w, f^{(i)})$ is a blocking pair; see Figure 1.7.

The proof of the second statement is analogous, with $\bot$ replaced by w'. $\square$

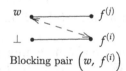

Blocking pair $\left(w, f^{(i)}\right)$

Figure 1.7 Blocking pair $\left(w, f^{(i)}\right)$.

Theorem 1.27. *There is a bijection between the sets of stable matchings of I and I'.*

Proof We will first define a mapping ϕ from the first set to the second and then prove that it is a bijection.

Let μ be a stable matching of instance I. Assume that a set $S \subseteq W$ of workers is matched in μ to firm f and worker $w \in S$ and w is the ith most preferred worker in S with respect to $l(f)$. Then, under $\phi(\mu)$ we will match w to $f^{(i)}$. This defines $\phi(\mu)$ completely.

For contradiction assume that $\phi(\mu)$ is not stable and let $(w, f^{(i)})$ be a blocking pair with respect to $\phi(\mu)$. Assume that $f^{(i)}$ is matched to w', where either $w' \in W'$ or $w' = \bot$. Clearly $f^{(i)}$ prefers w to w'; therefore, by construction, if w is matched to $f^{(j)}$ then $j < i$, contradicting the fact that $(w, f^{(i)})$ is a blocking pair. Hence w is either unmatched or is matched to $f'^{(k)}$ for some $f' \neq f$ and some k.

In the first case, under μ, w is unmatched, w' is matched to f, $w \succ_f w'$, and $f \succ_w \perp$. In the second case, under μ, w is matched to f', w' is matched to f, $w \succ_f w'$, and $f \succ_w f'$. Therefore, in both cases (w, f) is a blocking pair with respect to μ, giving a contradiction.

Finally we observe that ϕ has an inverse map $\phi^{-1}(\phi(\mu)) = \mu$. Let μ' be a stable matching of instance I'. If $\mu'(w) = f^{(i)}$ then $\phi^{-1}(\mu')$ matches w to f. The stability of $\phi^{-1}(\mu')$ is easily shown, in particular, because each f has the same preference lists as $f^{(i)}$ for $i \in [1, \ldots, c(f)]$. □

As a consequence of Theorem 1.27, we can transform the given instance I to an instance I' of Setting II, run the deferred acceptance algorithm on it, and transform the solution back to obtain a stable matching for I. Clearly, all notions established in Setting II following the algorithm, such as the realm of possibilities and the worker-optimal and firm-optimal stable matchings, also carry over to the current setting.

Finally, we present the rural hospital theorem for Setting III.

Theorem 1.28. *The following hold for an instance in Setting III:*

1. *Over all the stable matchings of the given instance the set of matched workers is the same and the number of workers matched to each firm is also the same.*
2. *Assume that firm f is not matched to capacity in the stable matchings. Then, the set of workers matched to f is the same over all stable matchings.*

Proof 1. Let us reduce the given instance, say I, to an instance I' in Setting II and apply Theorem 1.23. Then we obtain that the set of matched workers is the same over all the stable matchings of I', hence yielding the same statement for I as well. We also obtain that the set of matched firms is the same over all the stable matchings of I'. Applying the bijection ϕ^{-1} to I' we find that the number workers matched to each firm is also the same over all stable matchings.

2. Let μ_W and μ_F be the worker-optimal and firm-optimal stable matchings for instance I, respectively. Assume for contradiction that firm f is not filled to capacity and $\mu_W(f) \neq \mu_F(f)$. Then there is a worker w who is matched to f in μ_W but not in μ_F. Since μ_W is worker optimal, w prefers f to its match in μ_F. Since f is not filled to capacity, (w, f) forms a blocking pair of Type 2a (see Definition 1.25) with respect to μ_F, giving a contradiction. □

1.3 Incentive Compatibility

In this section we will study incentive compatibility properties of the deferred acceptance algorithm for all three settings. Theorem 1.17 shows that if workers propose to firms, then the matching computed is worker optimal in the sense that each worker is matched to the best firm in its realm of possibilities. However, for an individual worker this "best" firm may be very low in the worker's preference list; see end-of-chapter Exercise 1.7. If so, the worker may have an incentive to cheat, i.e., to manipulate its preference list in order to get a better match.

A surprising fact about the DA algorithm is that this worker will not be able to get a better match by falsifying its preference list. Hence its best strategy is to report its true preference list. Moreover, this holds no matter what preference lists the rest of the workers report. Thus the worker-proposing DA algorithm is *dominant-strategy incentive compatible (DSIC)* for workers.

This ground-breaking result on incentive compatibility opened up the DA algorithm to a host of consequential applications. An example is its use for matching students to public schools in big cities, such as New York and Boston, with hundreds of thousands of students seeking admission each year into hundreds of schools. Previously, Boston was using the immediate acceptance algorithm, which did not satisfy incentive compatibility. It therefore led to much guessing and gaming, making the process highly stressful for the students and their parents. With the use of the student-proposing DA algorithm, each student is best off simply reporting her true preference list. For further details on this application, see Chapter 8.

The proof of Theorem 1.32, showing that Setting I is DSIC, is quite non-trivial and intricate, and more complexity is introduced in Setting II. In this context, the advantage of partitioning the problem into the three proposed settings should become evident.

The rest of the picture for the incentive compatibility of the DA algorithm is as follows. In Setting I, the worker-proposing DA algorithm is not DSIC for firms; see Exercise 1.7. The picture is identical in Settings II and III for the worker-proposing DA algorithm. However, Setting III is asymmetrical for workers and firms, since firms have maximum capacities. For this setting, Theorem 1.35 will establish that there is no mechanism that is DSIC for firms.

1.3.1 Proof of DSIC for Setting I

The following lemma will be critical to proving Theorem 1.32; it guarantees a blocking pair with respect to an arbitrary perfect matching μ. Observe that the blocking pair involves a worker who does not improve its match in going from μ_W to μ.

Lemma 1.29 (Blocking lemma). *Let μ_W be the worker-optimal stable matching under preferences $\succ$ and let μ be an arbitrary perfect matching, not necessarily stable. Further, let W' be the set of workers who prefer their match under μ to their match under μ_W, i.e., $W' = \{w \in W \mid \mu(w) \succ_w \mu_W(w)\}$, and assume that $W' \neq \varnothing$. Then $W' \neq W$ and there exist $w \in (W \setminus W')$ and $f \in \mu(W')$ such that (w, f) is a blocking pair for μ.*

Proof   Clearly, for $w \in (W \setminus W'), \mu_W(w) \succeq_w \mu(w)$. Two cases arise naturally: whether the workers in W' get better matches in μ over μ_W by simply trading partners, i.e., whether $\mu(W') = \mu_W(W')$ or not. We will study the two cases separately.

Case 1. $\mu(W') \neq \mu_W(W')$. Since $|\mu(W')| = |\mu_W(W')| = |W'|$ and $(\mu(W') \setminus \mu_W(W')) \neq \varnothing$, therefore $W' \neq W$. Pick any $f \in (\mu(W') \setminus \mu_W(W'))$ and let $w = \mu_W(f)$. Now $w \in (W \setminus W')$, since if $f \notin \mu_W(W')$ then $\mu_W(f) \notin W'$. We will show that (w, f) is a blocking pair for μ. To this end, we will identify several other workers and firms.

Let $w' = \mu(f)$; since $f \in \mu(W'), w' \in W'$. Let $f'' = \mu_W(w')$; clearly, $f'' \in \mu_W(W')$. Finally let $f' = \mu(w)$; since $w \in (W \setminus W'), f' \in (F \setminus \mu(W'))$. Figure 1.8 should be helpful in visualizing the situation.

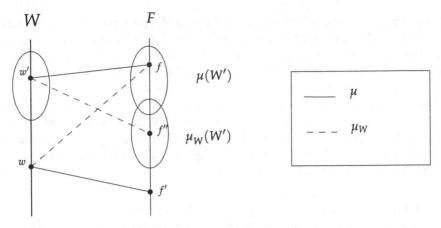

Figure 1.8 Blocking pair $\left(w,\, f^{(i)}\right)$.

Finally we need to show that $f \succ_w f'$ and $w \succ_f w'$. The first assertion follows on observing that $w \in (W \setminus W')$ and $f \neq f'$. Assume that the second assertion is false, i.e., that $w' \succ_f w$. Now $f \succ_{w'} f''$, since $w' \in W'$, $f = \mu(w')$, and $f'' = \mu_W(w')$. But this implies that (w', f) is a blocking pair for stable matching μ_W. The contradiction proves that $w \succ_f w'$. Hence (w, f) is a blocking pair for μ.

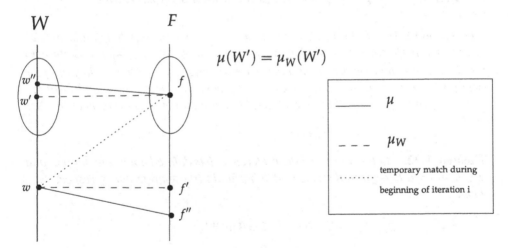

Figure 1.9

Case 2. $\mu(W') = \mu_W(W')$. In this case, unlike the previous one, we will crucially use the fact that μ_W is the matching produced by the DA algorithm with workers proposing. Let i be the last iteration of the DA algorithm in which a worker, say $w' \in W'$, first proposes to its eventual match; let the latter be $f \in \mu_W(W')$. Let $w'' = \mu(f)$. Since $f \in \mu(W')$, $w'' \in W'$.

By the definition of W', $f = \mu(w'') \succ_{w''} \mu_W(w'')$. Therefore, w'' must have proposed to f before iteration i and subsequently moved on to its eventual match under μ_W no later than iteration i. Now, by Observation 1.5, f must keep getting proposals in each iteration after w'' proposed to it. In particular, assume that at the end of iteration $i-1$, f had tentatively accepted the proposal of worker w. In iteration i, f will reject w and w will propose to its eventual match in iteration $i+1$ or later. Since w' is the last worker in W' to propose to its eventual match, $w \notin W'$. Therefore $W' \neq W$. We will show that (w,f) is a blocking pair for μ. Figure 1.9 visualizes the situation.

Since f must have rejected w'' before tentatively accepting the proposal of w, $w \succ_f w''$. Let $f' = \mu_W(w)$ and $f'' = \mu(w)$. In the DA algorithm, w had proposed to f before being finally matched to f', therefore $f \succ_w f'$. Since $w \in (W \setminus W')$, $f' \succeq_w f''$. Therefore $f \succ_w f''$. Together with the assertion $w \succ_f w''$, we get that (w,f) is a blocking pair for μ. $\qquad \square$

Notation 1.30. *Assume that a worker w reports a modified list; let us denote it by $\succ_w'$. Also assume that all other workers and all firms report their true preference lists. Define, for all $x \in F \cup W$,*

$$\succ_x' = \begin{cases} \succ_x & \text{if } x \in F \text{ or } x \in W \setminus \{w\}, \\ \succ_w' & \text{if } x = w. \end{cases}$$

Let μ_W and μ_W' be the worker-optimal stable matchings under the preferences $\succ$ and $\succ'$, respectively. We will use these notions to state and prove Theorem 1.32. However, first we will give the following straightforward observation.

Observation 1.31. *Let $(W, F, \succ)$ be an instance of stable matching and consider alternative preference lists $\succ_w'$ for every worker $w \in W$ and $\succ_f'$ for every firm $f \in F$. Assume that we are given a perfect matching μ which has a blocking pair (w,f) with respect to the preferences $\succ'$. Moreover, assume that w and f satisfy $\succ_w' = \succ_w$ and $\succ_f' = \succ_f$. Then (w,f) is a blocking pair in μ with respect to $\succ$ as well.*

Theorem 1.32. *Let $\succ$ and $\succ'$ be the preference lists defined above and let μ_W and μ_W' be the worker-optimal stable matchings under these preferences, respectively. Then*

$$\mu_W(w) \succeq_w \mu_W'(w),$$

i.e., the match of worker w, with respect to its original preference list, does not improve if it misrepresents its list as $\succ_w'$.

Proof We will invoke Lemma 1.29; for this purpose, denote μ_W' by μ. Suppose that w prefers its match in μ to its match in μ_W. Let $W' = \{w \in W \mid \mu(w) \succ_w \mu_W(w)\}$; clearly $w \in W'$ and therefore $W' \neq \varnothing$. Now, by Lemma 1.29, there is a blocking pair (w',f) for μ with respect to the preferences $\succ$, with $w' \notin W'$; clearly, $w' \neq w$.

Since $\succ'$ and $\succ$ differ only for w, by Observation 1.31 (w',f) is a blocking pair for μ with respect to $\succ'$ as well. This contradicts the fact that μ is a stable matching with respect to $\succ'$. $\qquad \square$

1.3.2 DSIC for Setting II

While studying incentive compatibility for the case of incomplete preference lists, we will allow a worker w not only to alter its preference list over its neighbors in graph G but also to alter its set of neighbors, i.e., to alter G itself. For this reason, it will be more convenient to define the preference list of each worker over the set $F \cup \{\bot\}$ and of each firm over the set $W \cup \{\bot\}$, as stated in footnote 1 in Section 1.1.

Let $\succ$ denote the original preference lists of workers and firms and let μ_W denote the worker-optimal stable matching under preferences $\succ$. The definition of a *blocking pair* with respect to a matching μ is changed in one respect only, namely $\mu(w) = \bot$ or $\mu(f) = \bot$ is allowed. Thus (w, f) is a blocking pair if and only if $(w, f) \notin \mu$, $\mu(w) \succ_w f$, and $\mu(f) \succ_f w$.

The only change needed to the statement of the blocking lemma, stated as Lemma 1.29 for Setting I, is that μ is an arbitrary matching, i.e., it is not necessarily perfect. Once again, the proof involves the same two cases presented in Lemma 1.29. The proof of the first case changes substantially and is given below.

Proof Case 1: $\mu(W') \neq \mu_W(W')$. For $w \in W'$, $\mu(w) \succ_w \mu_W(w)$, therefore $\mu(w) \neq \bot$. However, $\mu_W(w) = \bot$ is allowed. Therefore $|\mu(W')| = |W'| \geq |\mu_W(W')|$. Hence, $\mu(W') \not\subset \mu_W(W')$ and, since $\mu(W') \neq \mu_W(W')$, we obtain $(\mu(W') \setminus \mu_W(W')) \neq \oslash$. Pick any $f \in (\mu(W') \setminus \mu_W(W'))$. Clearly $\mu(f) \neq \bot$; let $w' = \mu(f)$. Let $\mu_W(w') = f''$, where $f'' = \bot$ is possible. By definition of W', $f \succ_{w'} f'' = \mu_W(w')$.

Assume for contradiction that $\mu_W(f) = \bot$. Since $\mu(f) = w'$, $w' \succ_f \bot$. Therefore we obtain $w' \succ_f \mu_W(f)$. If so, (w', f) is a blocking pair for μ_W, leading to a contradiction. Therefore $\mu_W(f) \neq \bot$. Let $\mu_W(f) = w$. Clearly, $w \notin W'$. Hence $W' \neq W$. Let $\mu(w) = f'$, where $f' = \bot$ is possible. Clearly, $f \neq f'$ and $f \succ_w f'$. This, together with the assertion $w \succ_f w'$, gives us that (w, f) is a blocking pair for μ. $\qquad\square$

Now consider Case 2, namely $\mu(W') = \mu_W(W')$. Since, for each $w \in W'$, we have $\mu(w) \succ_w \mu_W(w)$, w cannot be unmatched under μ. Therefore, in this case, $\forall w \in W'$, w is matched in both μ and μ_W. The rest of the proof is identical to that of Lemma 1.29, other than the fact that $f' = \bot$ and $f'' = \bot$ are allowed. We will not repeat the proof here. This establishes the blocking lemma for Setting II.

As in Setting I, presented in Section 1.3.1, we will adopt the notation $\succ$ and $\succ'$ given in Notation 1.30. Let μ'_W be the worker-optimal stable matchings under the preferences $\succ'$. Note that Observation 1.6 still holds. Finally, the statement of Theorem 1.32 carries over without change to this setting and its proof is also identical, provided one uses the slightly modified statement of the blocking lemma.

1.3.3 DSIC for Setting III

For Setting III, the DSIC algorithm for workers follows easily using the reduction from Setting II to Setting III, given in Section 1.2.3, and the fact that the worker-proposing DA algorithm is DSIC for workers. However, this setting is asymmetric for workers and firms, since firms can match to multiple workers. Therefore, we need to study the incentive compatibility of the firm-proposing DA algorithm as well.

The answer is quite surprising: not only is this algorithm not DSIC, but in fact no mechanism can be DSIC for this setting.

Example 1.33. Let the set of workers be $W = \{w_1, w_2, w_3, w_4\}$ and the set of firms be $F = \{f_1, f_2, f_3\}$. Suppose that firm f_1 has capacity 2 and firms f_2 and f_3 have unit capacities. Preferences are given by:

$$f_1: w_1 \succ w_2 \succ w_3 \succ w_4$$
$$f_2: w_1 \succ w_2 \succ w_3 \succ w_4$$
$$f_3: w_3 \succ w_1 \succ w_2 \succ w_4$$
$$w_1: f_3 \succ f_1 \succ f_2$$
$$w_2: f_2 \succ f_1 \succ f_3$$
$$w_3: f_1 \succ f_3 \succ f_2$$
$$w_4: f_1 \succ f_2 \succ f_3$$

Consider the instance given in Example 1.33. If firms propose to workers, the resulting stable matching, μ_F, assigns $\mu_F(f_1) = \{w_3, w_4\}$, $\mu_F(f_2) = \{w_2\}$, and $\mu_F(f_3) = \{w_1\}$.

Next consider matching μ with $\mu(f_1) = \{w_2, w_4\}$, $\mu(f_2) = \{w_1\}$, and $\mu(f_3) = \{w_3\}$. This matching is strictly preferred by all firms but it is not stable since (w_1, f_1) and (w_3, f_1) are both blocking pairs. However, if f_1 misrepresents its preferences as

$$f_1: w_2 \succ' w_4 \succ' w_1 \succ' w_3,$$

then μ becomes stable and firm optimal. Hence we get:

Lemma 1.34. *For the instance given in Example 1.33, there exists a matching μ which is not stable and which all firms strictly prefer to the firm-optimal stable matching μ_F. Moreover, there is a way for one firm to misrepresent its preferences so that μ becomes stable.*

The next theorem follows.

Theorem 1.35. *For the stable matching problem in Setting III with capacitated firms, there is no mechanism that is DSIC for firms.*

1.4 The Lattice of Stable Matchings

The notions of worker-optimal and worker-pessimal stable matchings, defined in Section 1.2.1, indicate that the set of all stable matchings of an instance has structure. It turns out that these notions form only the tip of the iceberg! Below we will define the notion of a *finite distributive lattice* and will prove that the set of stable matchings of an instance forms such a lattice. Together with the non-trivial notion of *rotation* and Birkhoff's representation theorem, this leads to an extremely rich collection of structural properties and efficient algorithms which find a use in important applications.

1.4.1 The Lattice for Setting I

Definition 1.36. Let S be a finite set, $\geq$ be a reflexive, anti-symmetric, transitive relation on S and $\pi = (S, \geq)$ be the corresponding partially ordered set. For any two elements $a, b \in S$, $u \in S$ is said to be an *upper bound* of a and b if $u \geq a$ and $u \geq b$. Further, u is said to be a *least upper bound* of a and b if $u' \geq u$ for any upper bound u' of a and b. The notion of the *(greatest) lower bound* of two elements is analogous. The partial order π is said to be a *lattice* if any two elements $a, b \in S$ have a unique least upper bound and a unique greatest lower bound. If so, these will be called the *join* and *meet* of a and b and will be denoted by $a \vee b$ and $a \wedge b$, respectively, and the partial order will typically be denoted by $\mathcal{L}$. Finally, $\mathcal{L}$ is said to be a *finite distributive lattice*, abbreviated *FDL*, if for any three elements $a, b, c \in S$, the distributive property holds, i.e.,

$$a \vee (b \wedge c) = (a \vee b) \wedge (a \vee c) \quad \text{and} \quad a \wedge (b \vee c) = (a \wedge b) \vee (a \wedge c).$$

Birkhoff's representation theorem, mentioned above, holds for FDLs. We next define a natural partial order on the set of stable matchings of an instance and show that it forms such a lattice.

Definition 1.37. Let S_μ be the set of stable matchings of a given instance in Setting I. Define a relation $\geq$ on S_μ as follows: for $\mu, \mu' \in S_\mu$, $\mu \geq \mu'$ if and only if every worker w weakly prefers her match in μ to her match in μ', i.e.,

$$\forall w \in W : \mu(w) \succeq_w \mu'(w).$$

Theorem 1.41 will show that the partial order $\mathcal{L}_\mu = (S_\mu, \geq)$ is a finite distributive lattice; $\mathcal{L}_\mu$ will be called the *stable matching lattice* for the given instance.

Let μ and μ' be two stable matchings. We define the following four operations. For worker w, $\max\{\mu(w), \mu'(w)\}$ is the firm that w weakly prefers among $\mu(w)$ and $\mu'(w)$, and $\min\{\mu(w), \mu'(w)\}$ is the firm that w weakly dislikes, where "dislikes" is the opposite of the relation "prefers". For a firm f, $\max\{\mu(f), \mu'(f)\}$ and $\min\{\mu(f), \mu'(f)\}$ are analogously defined.

Define two maps $M_W : W \to F$ and $M_F : F \to W$ as follows:

$$\forall w \in W : M_W(w) = \max\{\mu(w), \mu'(w)\} \quad \text{and} \quad \forall f \in F : M_F(f) = \min\{\mu(f), \mu'(f)\}.$$

Lemma 1.38. $\forall w \in W$, if $M_W(w) = f$ then $M_F(f) = w$.

Proof Assume $\mu(w) \neq \mu'(w)$, since otherwise the proof is obvious. Let $\mu(w) = f$ and $\mu'(w) = f'$, and without loss of generality assume that $f \succeq_w f'$. Let $\mu'(f) = w'$; clearly $w \neq w'$. Now if $w \succeq_f w'$ then (w, f) is a blocking pair for μ', leading to a contradiction. Therefore, $w' \succeq_f w$ and hence $M_F(f) = w$; see Figure 1.10 for an illustration. $\square$

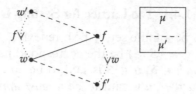

Figure 1.10 Illustration of the Figure for proof of Lemma 1.38.

Corollary 1.39. M_W and M_F are both bijections, and $M_W = M_F^{-1}$.

As a consequence of Corollary 1.39, M_W is a perfect matching on $W \cup F$; denote it by μ_1. Analogously, mapping each worker w to $\min \{\mu(w), \mu'(w)\}$ gives another perfect matching; denote it by μ_2. Observe that μ_2 matches each firm f to $\max \{\mu(f), \mu'(f)\}$; see Figure 1.11.

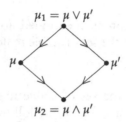

Figure 1.11 The meet and join of μ and μ'.

Lemma 1.40. *The matchings μ_1 and μ_2 are both stable.*

Proof Assume that (w, f) is a blocking pair for μ_1. Let $\mu(w) = f'$ and $\mu'(w) = f''$ and assume without loss of generality that $f' \succeq_w f''$. Then $\mu_1(w) = \max \{\mu(w), \mu'(w)\} = f'$.

Let $\mu(f) = w'$ and $\mu'(f) = w''$. By the definition of map M_F, $w'' \succeq_f w'$ and $\mu_1(f) = w'$; observe that $w \neq w'$. Since (w, f) is a blocking pair for μ_1, we have $w \succeq_f w'$. This implies that (w, f) is a blocking pair for μ, leading to a contradiction. Hence μ_1 is stable. An analogous argument shows that μ_2 is also stable; see Figure 1.12 for an illustration. $\square$

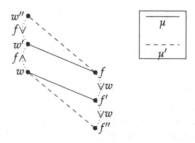

Figure 1.12 Illustration of the proof of Lemma 1.40.

Now consider the partial order $\mathcal{L}_\mu = (S_\mu, \geq)$ defined in Definition 1.37. Clearly, μ_1 and μ_2 are an upper bound and a lower bound of μ and μ', respectively. It is easy to see that they are also the unique lowest upper bound and the unique greatest lower bound of μ and μ'. Therefore $\mathcal{L}_\mu$ supports the operations of meet and join given by

$$\mu \vee \mu' = \mu_1 \quad \text{and} \quad \mu \wedge \mu' = \mu_2,$$

Finally, it is easy to show that the operations of meet and join satisfy the distributive property; see Exercise 1.8. Hence we get:

Theorem 1.41. *The partial order $\mathcal{L}_\mu = (S_\mu, \geq)$ is a finite distributive lattice.*

Remark 1.42. If $\mu, \mu' \in S_\mu$ with $\mu > \mu'$ then, by definition, workers get weakly better matches in μ than in μ'. The discussion presented above implies that firms get weakly worse matches.

Using the finiteness of $\mathcal{L}_\mu$, it is easy to show that there are two special matchings, say $\mu_\top, \mu_\perp \in S_\mu$, which we will call *top* and *bottom* matchings, respectively, such that, $\forall \mu \in S_\mu$, $\mu_\top \geq \mu$ and $\mu \geq \mu_\perp$. These stable matchings were already singled out in Section 1.2.1: $\mu_\top$ is the worker-optimal and firm-pessimal matching and $\mu_\perp$ is the firm-optimal and worker-pessimal matching; see Figure 1.13.

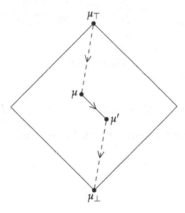

Figure 1.13 A path from the worker-optimal matching, $\mu_\top$, to the firm-optimal matching, $\mu_\perp$, in the lattice $\mathcal{L}_\mu$. The edge (μ, μ') indicates that $\mu' = \rho(\mu)$, for a rotation ρ with respect to μ.

1.4.1.1 Rotations, and Their Use for Traversing the Lattice

Several applications require stable matchings which are not as "extreme" as $\mu_\top$ and $\mu_\perp$, i.e., they treat the two sets W and F more equitably. These stable matchings can be found in the rest of the lattice. In this subsection we will define the notion of a rotation, which helps to traverse the lattice. In particular, we will prove that rotations help to traverse paths from $\mu_\top$ to $\mu_\perp$, as illustrated in Figure 1.13, with intermediate "vertices" on such a path being stable matchings and an "edge" (μ, μ') indicating that $\mu > \mu'$; see Lemma 1.45 and Corollary 1.46. By Remark 1.42, the intermediate matchings on any such path will gradually become better for firms and worse for workers. For an example of the use of rotations, see Exercise 1.13, which develops an efficient algorithm for finding a stable matching that treats workers and firms more equitably.

Definition 1.43. Fix a stable matching $\mu \neq \mu_\perp$ and define the function next: $W \to F \cup \{\boxtimes\}$ as follows: for a worker w, find its most preferred firm, say f, such that f prefers w to $\mu(f)$. If such a firm exists then next$(w) = f$ and otherwise next$(w) = \boxtimes$. A *rotation* ρ with respect to μ is an ordered sequence of pairs $\rho = \{(w_0, f_0), (w_1, f_1), \ldots, (w_{r-1}, f_{r-1})\}$ such that, for $0 \leq i \leq r - 1$:

- $(w_i, f_i) \in \mu$, and
- next$(w_i) = f_{(i+1) \,(\mathrm{mod}\, r)}$

By *applying rotation ρ to μ* we mean switching the matching of $w_0, \ldots, w_{r-2}, w_{r-1}$ to $f_1, \ldots, f_{r-1}, f_0$, respectively, and leaving the rest of μ unchanged. Clearly this results in a perfect matching; let us denote it by μ'. We will denote this operation as $\mu' = \rho(\mu)$. For example, in Figure 1.14, the rotation $\{(1, 1), (2, 2), (3, 4), (4, 5)\}$ applied to μ yields μ'. Observe that the matched edge $(5, 3)$ is not in the rotation and remains unchanged in going from μ to μ'.

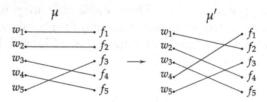

Figure 1.14

Lemma 1.44. *Let ρ be a rotation with respect to μ and let $\mu' = \rho(\mu)$. Then:*

1. *Workers get weakly worse matches and firms get weakly better matches in going from μ to μ'.*
2. *μ' is a stable matching.*
3. *$\mu > \rho(\mu)$.*

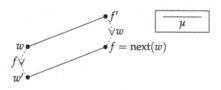

Figure 1.15

Proof 1. Suppose that next$(w) = f$; clearly $\mu(f) \neq w$. Let $\mu(w) = f'$ and $\mu(f) = w'$. By the definition of the operator next, $w \succ_f w'$. Observe that $f \succ_w f'$ is not possible, since then (w, f) would be a blocking pair for μ. Therefore $f' \succ_w f$. Hence, after the rotation, the matching of f is improved and that of w becomes worse. Clearly, this holds for all workers and firms in the rotation; see Figure 1.15.

2. Assume that μ' has a blocking pair, namely (w, f), where $\mu'(w) = f'$ and $\mu'(f) = w'$. From this blocking pair, we can infer that $w \succ_f w'$ and $f \succ_w f'$. Now there are two cases:

Case (a). $\mu(w) = f'$. Assume that $\mu(f) = w''$; by part (1) of this lemma we have $w' \succ_f w''$. Since $w \succ_f w'$, we get that $w \succ_f w''$, hence showing that (w, f) is a blocking pair for μ and leading to a contradiction; see Figure 1.16.

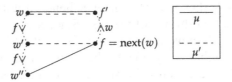

Figure 1.16 Illustration of proof of Case (a) in Lemma 1.44.

Case (b). $\mu(w) \neq f'$. If $\mu(f) \neq w'$ then let $\mu(f) = w''$. Since f improves its match after the rotation, we have $w' \succeq_f w''$ and, and since $w \succ_f w''$, we get that $w \succeq_f w''$. Therefore, whether or not $\mu(f) = w'$, we have that $w \succ \mu(f)$. Clearly, $\text{next}(w) = f'$. Since f prefers w to its match in μ and $f \neq \text{next}(w)$, we get that $f' \succ_w f$, hence contradicting the above-stated assertion that $f \succ_w f'$; see Figure 1.17.

3. This follows from the previous two statements. Assume that $\text{next}(w) \neq \bot$, i.e., $\text{next}(w)$ is a firm. We note that this does not guarantee that w will be in a rotation; see Exercise 1.10. For that to happen, the "cycle must close", i.e., for some r, $\text{next}(w_{r-1}) = f_0$. □

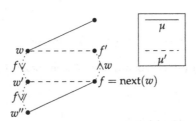

Figure 1.17 Illustration of the proof of Case (b) in Lemma 1.44.

The next lemma will justify Figure 1.13 via Corollary 1.46.

Lemma 1.45. *Let $\mu > \mu'$. Then there exists a rotation ρ with respect to μ such that $\mu > \rho(\mu) \geq \mu'$.*

Proof Define a map $g \colon W \to W \cup \{\boxtimes\}$ as follows:

$$g(w) = \begin{cases} \mu(\text{next}(w)) & \text{if } \text{next}(w) \in F, \\ \boxtimes & \text{otherwise.} \end{cases}$$

Let $W' = \{w \in W \mid \mu(w) \succ \mu'(w)\}$. We will prove that the range of g when restricted to W' is W' and, for $w \in W'$, $g(w) \neq w$.

Let $w \in W'$. We will first prove that $\text{next}(w) \in F$, hence showing that $g(w) \in W$. Let $\mu'(w) = f'$ and $\mu(f') = w''$. Since $\mu > \mu'$, μ is weakly better than μ' for workers. Therefore $f' \succ_{w''} \mu'(w'')$. If $w'' \succ_{f'} w$ then (w'', f') will be a blocking pair for μ', leading to a contradiction. Therefore, $w \succ_{f'} w''$. Hence there is a firm that likes w better than its own match under μ. Among such firms, let f be one that w prefers most. Then $\text{next}(w) = f$ and $g(w) = \mu(f) = w'$, say.

Next, we will show that $\mu(w') \succ \mu'(w')$, hence obtaining $w' \in W'$; see Figure 1.18. Suppose that this is not the case. Since $\mu > \mu'$ and μ is not strictly better than μ' for w', we must have that $\mu'(w') = \mu(w') = f$. Let $\mu'(w) = f'$. Since $\mu > \mu'$, we have that $w \succ_{f'} \mu(f')$. Therefore f' is a firm that prefers w to its match under μ. However, since f is the most preferred such firm for worker w, we get $f \succ_w f'$. Furthermore, since $\mu(f) = w'$, $w \succ_f w'$. Therefore (w, f) is a blocking pair for μ', leading to a contradiction. Therefore, $\mu(w') \succ \mu'(w')$ and hence $w' \in W'$. Clearly w' is distinct from w, hence giving $g(w) \neq w$.

Finally, we will use the map $g: W' \to W'$ to complete the proof. Start with any worker $w \in W'$ and repeatedly apply g until a worker is encountered for a second time. This gives us a "cycle", i.e., a sequence of workers $w_0, w_1, \ldots, w_{r-1}$ such that, for $0 \leq i \leq r - 1$, $g(w_i) = w_{i+1(\text{mod } r)}$. Then $\rho = \{(w_0, f_0), (w_1, f_1), \ldots, (w_{r-1}, f_{r-1})\}$ is a rotation with respect to μ, where $f_i = \mu(w_i)$ for $0 \leq i \leq r - 1$. Clearly, $\mu > \rho(\mu) \geq \mu'$. $\qquad\square$

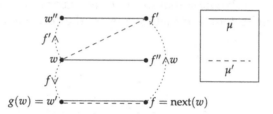

Figure 1.18 Illustration of why $w' \in W'$ in the proof of Lemma 1.45.

Corollary 1.46. *The following hold:*

1. *Let μ be a stable matching such that $\mu \neq \mu_\perp$. Then there is a rotation ρ with respect to μ.*
2. *Start with $\mu_\top$ as the "current matching" and keep applying an arbitrary rotation with respect to the current matching. This process will terminate at $\mu_\perp$.*

Let $G_\mu = (S_\mu, E_\mu)$ be a directed graph with vertex set S_μ and $(\mu, \mu') \in E_\mu$ if and only if there is a rotation ρ with respect to μ such that $\rho(\mu) = \mu'$. Then any path from $\mu_\top$ to $\mu_\perp$ is obtained by the process given in Corollary 1.46.

Definition 1.47. Let ρ be a rotation with respect to a stable matching μ and let $\rho(\mu) = \mu'$. Then the inverse of the map ρ is denoted by ρ^{-1}. We will call ρ^{-1} the *inverse rotation* with respect to the stable matching μ'. Clearly, $\rho^{-1}(\mu') = \mu$.

Inverse rotations help traverse paths from $\mu_\perp$ to $\mu_\top$ in G_μ, and a combination of rotations and inverse rotations suffices to find a path from any one matching to any other matching in G_μ.

1.4.1.2 Rotations Correspond to Join-Irreducible Stable Matchings

Definition 1.48. A stable matching μ is said to be *join-irreducible* if $\mu \neq \mu_\perp$ and μ is not the join of any two stable matchings. Let μ and μ' be two stable matchings. We will say that μ' is the *direct successor* of μ if $\mu > \mu'$ and there is no stable matching μ'' such that $\mu > \mu'' > \mu'$; if so, we will denote this by $\mu \rhd \mu'$.

Let μ be a join-irreducible stable matching. By Lemma 1.44 and Corollary 1.46 there is a unique rotation ρ with respect to μ. Let $\rho(\mu) = \mu'$. Clearly μ' is the unique stable matching such that $\mu \rhd \mu'$.

Lemma 1.49. *Let ρ_1 and ρ_2 be two distinct rotations with respect to the stable matching μ, and let $\mu_1 = \rho_1(\mu)$ and $\mu_2 = \rho_2(\mu)$. Then the following hold:*

1. *ρ_1 and ρ_2 cannot contain the same worker–firm pair.*
2. *ρ_1 and ρ_2 are rotations with respect to μ_2 and μ_1, respectively.*

Proof 1. Clearly, $\mu > \mu_1$ and $\mu > \mu_2$. Consider the set W' and the map $g\colon W' \to W'$ defined in the proof of Lemma 1.45. It is easy to see that ρ_1 and ρ_2 correspond to two disjoint "cycles" in this map, hence giving the lemma.

2. Since ρ_1 and ρ_2 correspond to disjoint "cycles", applying one results in a matching to which the other can be applied. $\quad\square$

Notation 1.50. *We will denote the set of all rotations used in a lattice $\mathcal{L}_\mu$ by $\mathcal{R}_\mu$, and the set of join-irreducible stable matchings of $\mathcal{L}_\mu$ by $\mathcal{J}_\mu$.*

Lemma 1.51. *Let $\rho \in \mathcal{R}_\mu$. Then there is a join-irreducible stable matching, say μ, such that ρ is the unique rotation with respect to μ.*

Proof Let $S_\rho = \{v \in S_\mu \mid \rho$ is a rotation with respect to $v\}$. Let μ be the meet of all matchings in S_ρ. Clearly $\mu \in S_\rho$ and hence ρ is a rotation with respect to μ. Suppose that μ is not join-irreducible and let ρ' be another rotation with respect to μ. By the second part of Lemma 1.49, ρ is a rotation with respect to $\rho'(\mu)$, therefore $\rho'(\mu) \in S_\rho$. This implies that $\rho'(\mu) \geq \mu$. But $\mu > \rho'(\mu)$, giving a contradiction. Uniqueness follows from the fact that μ is join-irreducible. $\quad\square$

Lemma 1.52. *Two rotations ρ and ρ' cannot contain the same worker–firm pair.*

Proof Suppose that rotations ρ and ρ' do both contain the same worker–firm pair, say (w,f). By Lemma 1.51, there are two join-irreducible stable matchings μ and v such that ρ and ρ' are rotations with respect to these matchings. Let $\mu \rhd \mu'$ and $v \rhd v'$.

Consider the matching $\mu \vee v$. Since $(w,f) \in \mu$ and $(w,f) \in v$, we have $(w,f) \in (\mu \vee v)$. On the other hand, since (w,f) is in rotations ρ and ρ', w is matched to a worse firm than f in μ' and in ν'. Therefore w is matched to a worse firm than f in $\mu' \vee \nu'$. But since μ and ν are join-irreducible, $(\mu' \vee \nu') = (\mu \vee \nu)$, leading to a contradiction. Hence ρ and ρ' cannot contain the same worker–firm pair. $\quad\square$

Lemmas 1.51 and 1.52, together with the facts that there are n^2 worker–firm pairs and each rotation has at least two worker–firm pairs, give:

Corollary 1.53. *The following hold:*

1. *There is a bijection $f: \mathcal{J}_\mu \to \mathcal{R}_\mu$ such that if $f(\mu) = \rho$ then ρ is the unique rotation with respect to μ.*
2. $|\mathcal{R}_\mu| \leq n^2/2$.

1.4.1.3 Birkhoff's Representation Theorem

Finite distributive lattices arise in diverse settings; Definition 1.54 below gives perhaps the simplest of these. A consequence of Birkhoff's representation theorem is that each FDL is isomorphic to a canonical FDL. In this section we will prove this for stable matching lattices; the general statement follows along similar lines.

Definition 1.54. Let S be a finite set and $\mathcal{F}$ be a family of subsets of S which is closed under union and intersection. Denote the partial order $(\mathcal{F}, \supseteq)$ by $\mathcal{L}_\mathcal{F}$. Then $\mathcal{L}_\mathcal{F}$ is an FDL with meet and join given by

$$A \wedge B = A \cap B \quad \text{and} \quad A \vee B = A \cup B,$$

for any two sets $A, B \in \mathcal{F}$; $\mathcal{L}_\mathcal{F}$ will be called a *canonical finite distributive lattice*.

Definition 1.55. The projection of $\mathcal{L}_\mu$ onto $\mathcal{J}_\mu$ is called a *join-irreducible partial order* and is denoted by $\pi_\mu = (\mathcal{J}_\mu, \geq)$. We will say that $S \subseteq \mathcal{J}_\mu$ is a *lower set of π_μ* if it satisfies the following: if $\mu \in S$ and $\mu > \mu'$ then $\mu' \in S$.

Let $\mathcal{F}_\pi$ be the family of subsets of $\mathcal{J}_\mu$ consisting of all lower sets of π_μ. It is easy to see that $\mathcal{F}_\pi$ is closed under union and intersection, and therefore that $\mathcal{L}_\pi = (\mathcal{F}_\mu, \supseteq)$ is a canonical FDL.

Theorem 1.56. *The lattice $\mathcal{L}_\mu$ is isomorphic to $\mathcal{L}_\pi$, i.e., there is a bijection $f_\mu: S_\mu \to \mathcal{F}_\pi$ such that $\mu \succeq \mu'$ if and only if $f_\mu(\mu) \supseteq f_\mu(\mu')$.*

Proof Define a function $f_\mu: S_\mu \to \mathcal{F}_\pi$ as follows. For $\mu \in S_\mu$, $f(\mu)$ is the set of all join-irreducible stable matchings ν such that $\mu \succ \nu$; let this set be S. Then S is a lower set of π_μ since if $\mu_1, \mu_2 \in \mathcal{J}_\mu$, with $\mu_1 \in S$ and $\mu_1 \succ \mu_2$ then $\mu \succ \mu_2$, therefore giving that $\mu_2 \in S$. Hence $S \in \mathcal{F}_\pi$. Next define a function $g: \mathcal{F}_\pi \to S_\mu$ as follows. For a lower set S of π_μ, $g(S)$ is the join of all join-irreducibles $\nu \in S$.

We first show that the compositions $g \bullet f$ and $f \bullet g$ both give the identity function, thereby showing that f and g are both bijections. Then $f_\mu = f$ is the required bijection.

Let $\mu \in S_\mu$ and let $f(\mu) = S$. For the first composition, we need to show that $g(S) = \mu$. There exist $j_1, \ldots, j_k$, join-irreducibles of $\mathcal{L}_\mu$, such that $\mu = (j_1 \vee \cdots \vee j_k)$.[4] Clearly, $j_1, \ldots, j_k \in S$ and therefore $g(S) \succeq (j_1 \vee \ldots \vee j_k)$. Furthermore, $\mu \succeq g(S)$. Therefore, $\mu \succeq g(S) \succeq (j_1 \vee \ldots \vee j_k) = \mu$. Hence $g(S) = \mu$.

Let S be a lower set of π_μ, let $j_1, \ldots, j_k$ be the join-irreducible stable matchings in S, and let μ be $g(S)$, i.e., the join of these join-irreducibles. Let j be a join-irreducible of $\mathcal{L}_\mu$ such that $\mu \succeq j$. For the second composition, we need to show that $j \in S$, since then $f(\mu) = S$. Now,

$$j \wedge \mu = j \wedge (j_1 \vee \cdots \vee j_k) = (j \wedge j_1) \vee \cdots \vee (j \wedge j_k),$$

where the second equality follows from the distributive property. Since j is a join-irreducible, it cannot be the join of two or more elements. Therefore $j = j \wedge j_i$ for some i. But then $j_i \succeq j$, therefore giving $j \in S$.

Finally, the definitions of f and g give that $\mu \succeq \mu'$ if and only if $f_\mu(\mu) \supseteq f_\mu(\mu')$. $\qquad\qquad\square$

Observe that an instance may have exponentially many, in n, stable matchings, hence leading to an exponentially large lattice. On the other hand, by Corollary 1.53 it follows that π_μ, which encodes this lattice, has a polynomial sized description. The precise way in which π_μ encodes $\mathcal{L}_\mu$ is clarified in Exercise 1.11.

Corollary 1.57. *There is a succinct description of the stable matching lattice.*

1.4.2 The Lattice for Settings II and III

The entire development on the lattice of stable matchings for Setting I, presented in Section 1.4.1, can be easily ported to Setting II with the help of the rural hospital theorem, Theorem 1.23, which proves that the sets of workers and firms that have been matched are the same in all stable matchings.

Let these sets be $W' \subseteq W$ and $F' \subseteq F$. Let $w \in W'$. Clearly, it suffices to restrict the preference list of w to F' only. If this list is not complete over F', simply add the missing firms of F' at the end; since w is never matched to these firms, their order does not matter. Applying this process to each worker and each firm yields an instance of stable matching over W' and F' which is in Setting I. The lattice for this instance is also the lattice for the original instance in Setting II.

The lattice for Setting III requires a reduction from Setting III to Setting II, given in Section 1.2.3, and the Rural Hospital theorem for Setting III, given in Theorem 1.28. The latter proves that if a firm is not matched to capacity in a stable matching then it is matched to the same set of workers in all stable matchings. However, a firm that is matched to capacity may be matched to different sets of workers in different stable matchings.

---

[4] Observe that every $\mu \in S_\mu$ can be written as the join of a set of join-irreducible stable matching as follows: If μ is a join-irreducible stable matchings, there is nothing to prove. Otherwise, it is the join of two or more matchings. Continue the process on each of those matchings.

Assume that firm f is matched to capacity in μ_1 and μ_2. A new question that arises is the following: which of these two matchings does f prefer? Observe that questions of this sort have natural answers for workers and firms in the previous settings (and for workers in Setting III) and that these answers were a key to formulating the lattice structure. The new difficulty is the following: if the two sets $\mu_1(f)$ and $\mu_2(f)$ are interleaved in complicated ways, when viewed with respect to the preference order of f we will have no grounds for declaring one matching better than the other. Lemma 1.60 shows that if μ_1 and μ_2 are stable matchings then such complications do not arise.

Definition 1.58. Fix a firm f. For $W' \subseteq W$, define $\min(W')$ to be the worker whom f prefers the least among the workers in W'. For $W_1 \subseteq W$ and $W_2 \subseteq W$, we will say that f *prefers* W_1 to W_2 if f prefers every worker in W_1 to every worker in W_2 and we will denote this as $W_1 \gg_f W_2$. Thus

$$W_1 = \{w \in W \mid \mu_1(w) \succ_w \mu_2(w)\} \quad \text{and} \quad W_2 = \{w \in W \mid \mu_2(w) \succ_w \mu_1(w)\}.$$

Also let

$$F_1 = \{f \in F \mid \min(\mu_2(f) - \mu_1(f)) \gg_f \min(\mu_1(f) - \mu_2(f))\} \quad \text{and}$$
$$F_2 = \{f \in F \mid \min(\mu_1(f) - \mu_2(f)) \gg_f \min(\mu_2(f) - \mu_1(f))\}.$$

Lemma 1.59. *Let* $(w,f) \in (\mu_1 - \mu_2)$. *Then*

1. $w \in W_1 \implies f \in F_1$
2. $w \in W_2 \implies f \in F_2$.

Lemma 1.60. *Let* μ_1 *and* μ_2 *be two stable matchings and* f *be a firm that is matched to capacity in both matchings. Then one of these possibilities must hold:*

1. $\mu_1(f) - \mu_2(f) \gg_f \mu_2(f)$ *(see Figure 1.19) or*
2. $\mu_2(f) - \mu_1(f) \gg_f \mu_1(f)$.

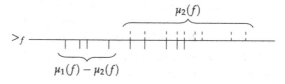

Figure 1.19 Illustration of the first possibility in Lemma 1.60. The horizontal line indicates the preference list of f, in decreasing order from left to right. The markings below the line indicate workers in set $\mu_1(f)$ and the dashed markings above the line indicate workers in $\mu_2(f)$.

Definition 1.61. Let μ_1 and μ_2 be two stable matchings and f be a firm that is matched to capacity in both matchings. Then f prefers μ_1 to μ_2 if the first possibility in Lemma 1.60 holds and it prefers μ_2 to μ_1 otherwise. We will denote these as $\mu_1 \succ_f \mu_2$ and $\mu_2 \succ_f \mu_1$, respectively.

Using Definition 1.61, whose validity is based on Lemma 1.60, we obtain a partial order on the set of stable matchings for Setting III. Using the reduction stated above and facts from Section 1.4.1, this partially ordered set forms an FLD.

1.5 Linear Programming Formulation

The stable matching problem in Setting I admits a linear programming formulation in which the polyhedron defined by the constraints has integer optimal vertices, i.e., the vertices of this polyhedron are stable matchings. This yields an alternative way of computing a stable matching in polynomial time using well-known ways of solving linear programs (LPs). Linear programs for Settings II and III follow using the rural hospital theorem 1.23 and the reduction from Setting III to Setting II given in Section 1.2.3, respectively.

1.5.1 LP for Setting I

A sufficient condition for a worker–firm pair, (w, f) to not form a blocking pair with respect to a matching μ is that if w is matched to firm f' such that $f \succ_w f'$ then f should be matched to a worker w' such that $w' \succ_f w$. The fractional version of this condition appears in the third constraint of LP (1.1); see also Exercise 1.15. The first two constraints ensure that each worker and each firm are fully matched. Observe that the objective function in the LP given below is simply 0:

$$\max \quad 0$$

$$\text{s.t.} \qquad \sum_w x_{wf} = 1 \quad \forall w \in W,$$

$$\sum_f x_{wf} = 1 \quad \forall f \in F,$$

$$\sum_{f \succ_w f'} x_{wf'} - \sum_{w' \succ_f w} x_{w'f} \leq 0 \quad \forall w \in W, \forall f \in F,$$

$$x_{wf} \geq 0 \quad \forall w \in W, \forall f \in F. \tag{1.1}$$

By the first two constraints, every integral feasible solution to LP (1.1) is a perfect matching on $W \cup F$ and, by the third constraint, it has no blocking pairs. It is therefore a stable matching.

Taking α_w, β_f, and γ_{wf} to be the dual variables for the first, second, and third constraints of LP (1.1), respectively, we obtain the dual LP:

$$\min \quad \sum_{w \in W} \alpha_w + \sum_{f \in F} \beta_f$$

$$\text{s.t.} \quad \alpha_w + \beta_f + \sum_{f' \succ_w f} \gamma_{wf'} + \sum_{w \succ_f w'} \gamma_{w'f} \geq 1 \quad \forall w \in W, \forall f \in F,$$

$$\gamma_{wf} \geq 0 \quad \forall w \in W, \forall f \in F. \tag{1.2}$$

Lemma 1.62. *If x is a feasible solution to LP (1.1) then $\alpha = 0$, $\beta = 0$, $\gamma = x$ is an optimal solution to LP (1.2). Furthermore, if $x_{wf} > 0$ then*

$$\sum_{f \succ_w f'} x_{wf'} = \sum_{w' \succ_f w} x_{w'f}.$$

Proof The feasibility of (α, β, γ) follows from the feasibility of x. The objective function value of this dual solution is 0, i.e., the same as that of the primal. Therefore, this solution is also optimal. For the solution since $\gamma = x$ is an optimal solution, if $x_{wf} > 0$ then $\gamma_{wf} > 0$. Now the desired equality follows by applying the complementary slackness condition to the third constraint of LP (1.1). $\qquad\square$

Next, we will work towards proving Theorem 1.65 and Corollary 1.66 below. Let x be a feasible solution to LP (1.1). Corresponding to x, we will define $2n$ unit intervals, I_w and I_f, one corresponding to each worker w and one corresponding to each firm f, as follows. For each worker w, we have $\sum_{f \in F} x_{wf} = 1$. Order the firms according to w's preference list; for simplicity, assume it is $f_1 \succ_w f_2 \succ_w \cdots \succ_w f_n$. Partition I_w into n ordered subintervals such that the ith interval has length x_{wf_i}; if this quantity is zero, the length of the interval is also zero. Next, for each firm f, we have $\sum_w x_{wf} = 1$. Now, order the workers according to f's preference list but in reverse order; assume it is $w_1 \prec_f w_2 \prec_w \cdots \prec_w w_n$, and partition I_f into n ordered subintervals such that the ith interval has length $x_{w_i f}$.

Pick θ with uniform probability in the interval $[0, 1]$ and, for each worker w, determine which subinterval of the interval I_w contains θ. The probability that any of these n subintervals is of zero length is zero, so we may assume that this event does not occur. Define a perfect matching μ_θ as follows: if the subinterval of I_w containing θ corresponds to firm f, then define $\mu_\theta(w) = f$.

Lemma 1.63. *If $\mu_\theta(w) = f$ then the subinterval of I_f containing θ corresponds to worker w.*

Proof Assume that the subinterval containing θ in I_w is $[a, b]$, where $a, b \in [0, 1]$; since it corresponding to f, $b - a = x_{wf}$. Since $x_{wf} > 0$, by the second part of Lemma 1.62 the subinterval corresponding to w in I_f is also $[a, b]$. Clearly, it contains θ. $\qquad\square$

Lemma 1.64. *For each $\theta \in [0, 1]$, the perfect matching μ_θ is stable.*

Proof Assume that $\mu_\theta(w) \neq f$. Let $\mu_\theta(w) = f'$ and $\mu_\theta(f) = w'$, where $f \succ_w f'$. We will show that $w' \succ_f w$, thereby proving that (w, f) is not a blocking pair. Extending this conclusion to all worker–firm pairs that are not matched by μ_θ, we obtain that μ_θ is a stable matching.

Since $\mu_\theta(w) = f'$, θ lies in the subinterval corresponding to f' in I_w. In Figure 1.20, this subinterval is marked as $[a, b]$. The number θ also lies in the subinterval corresponding to w' in I_f; this subinterval is marked as $[c, d]$ in Figure 1.20. Let p_f and p_w denote the larger endpoints of the subintervals containing f and w in I_w and I_f, respectively. By the third constraint of LP (1.1), the subinterval $[p_w, 1]$ of I_f is at least as large as the subinterval $[p_f, 1]$ of I_w.

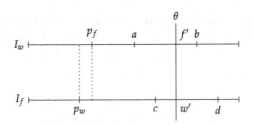

Figure 1.20

Since $f \succ_w f'$, θ lies in $[p_f, 1]$ and therefore it also lies in $[p_w, 1]$. Therefore, $w' \succ_f w$ and the lemma follows. $\square$

Theorem 1.65. *Every feasible solution to LP (1.1) is a convex combination of stable matchings.*

Proof The feasible solution x of LP (1.1) has at most $O(n^2)$ positive variables x_{wf} and therefore there are $O(n^2)$ non-empty subintervals corresponding to these variables in the intervals I_w and I_f. Hence $[0, 1]$ can be partitioned into at most $O(n^2)$ non-empty subintervals, say $I_1, \ldots, I_k$, in such a way that none of these subintervals straddles the subintervals corresponding to the positive variables. For $1 \le i \le k$, each $\theta \in I_i$ corresponds to the same stable matching $\mu_i = \mu_\theta$. Let the length of I_i be α_i; clearly $\sum_{i=1}^{k} \alpha_i = 1$. Then we have

$$x = \sum_{i=1}^{k} \alpha_i \mu_i.$$

The theorem follows. $\square$

Corollary 1.66. *The polyhedron defined by the constraints of LP (1.1) has integral optimal vertices; these are stable matchings.*

1.5.2 LPs for Settings II and III

For Setting II, by the rural hospital theorem 1.23, the sets of workers and firms matched in all stable matchings are the same. Let these sets be W' and F', respectively. Clearly, it suffices to work with the primal LP (1.1) restricted to these sets only.

For Setting III, we will use the reduction from Setting III to Setting II given in Section 1.2.3.

1.6 Exercises

Exercise 1.1 In Setting I, let M be a perfect matching which matches each worker $w \in W$ to a firm $f \in F$ such that $f \in R(w)$, i.e., f lies in the realm of possibilities of w. Prove or disprove that M is a stable matching.

Exercise 1.2 In Setting I, we will say that a perfect matching μ is *Pareto optimal* if there is no perfect matching $\mu' \neq \mu$ under which each agent is weakly better off, i.e., for each agent $a \in W \cup F$, $\mu(a) \succeq_a \mu'(a)$. Prove that every stable matching is Pareto optimal. Is the converse true? Give a proof or a counterexample.

Exercise 1.3 Define a *preferred couple* in Setting I to be a worker–firm pair such that each is the most preferred in the other's preference list.
  (a) Prove that if an instance has a preferred couple (w, f) then, in any stable matching, w and f must be matched to each other.
  (b) Prove that if in an instance with n workers and n firms there are n disjoint preferred couples then there is a unique stable matching.
  (c) Prove that the converse of the previous situation does not hold, i.e., there is an instance which does not have n disjoint preferred couples yet has a unique stable marriage.

Exercise 1.4 Construct an instance of Setting I that has exponentially many stable matchings.

Exercise 1.5 Design a polynomial time algorithm which, given an instance of Setting I, finds an unstable perfect matching, i.e., one having a blocking pair.

Exercise 1.6 In Setting II, let us add a second termination condition to the algorithm, namely terminate when every firm receives at least one proposal. If this condition holds, match every firm to its best proposal, leaving the rest of the workers unmatched. Give a counterexample to show that this matching is not stable.

Exercise 1.7 The following exercises are on the issue of incentive compatibility.
  (a) Find an instance $(W, F, \succ)$ in which some worker is matched to the last firm with respect to its preference list in the worker-optimal stable matching. How many such workers can there be in a instance?
  (b) For Setting I, find an instance in which a firm can improve its match in the worker-optimal stable matching by misreporting its preference list.
  (c) For Setting I, find an instance in which two workers can collude, i.e., both work together, in such a way that one of them does better and the other does no worse than in the worker-optimal stable matching.

Exercise 1.8 Use the fact that the operations of min and max on two-element sets satisfy the distributive property to prove that the operations of meet and join for the lattice of stable matching also satisfy this property.

Exercise 1.9 [2] Prove that lattices arising from instances of stable matching form a *complete set of finite distributive lattices*, i.e., every FDL is isomorphic to some stable matching lattice.

Exercise 1.10 The following exercises are on rotations.
  (a) Give an example of a stable matching μ such that $\text{next}(w) \neq \perp$ and yet w is not in a rotation with respect to μ.

(b) Let ρ be a rotation with respect to the stable matching μ. Obtain ρ' by permuting the sequence of pairs in ρ. Show that if the permutation is a cyclic shift then $\rho'(\mu) = \rho(\mu)$ but otherwise the matching $\rho'(\mu)$ is not stable.

(c) Let ρ be a rotation with respect to the stable matching μ and let $\rho(\mu) = \mu'$. Prove that μ' is a direct successor of μ, i.e., $\mu \rhd \mu'$.

(d) Show that any path in G_μ from $\mu_\top$ to $\mu_\bot$ involves applying each rotation in $\mathcal{R}_\mu$ exactly once. Use this fact to give a polynomial time algorithm for finding all rotations in $\mathcal{R}_\mu$.

(e) Give a polynomial time algorithm for the following problem: given a rotation $\rho \in \mathcal{R}_\mu$, find the join-irreducible matching to which it corresponds.

Exercise 1.11 The following exercises are on Birkhoff's theorem.

(a) Give a polynomial time algorithm for computing the succinct description of lattice $\mathcal{L}_\mu$ promised in Corollary 1.53, i.e., π_μ.

(b) Let S be a lower set of π_μ and let S_ρ be the set of rotations corresponding to the join-irreducibles in S. Let τ be any topological sort of the rotations in S_ρ that is consistent with the partial order π_μ. Show that, if starting with the matching $\mu_\bot$, the inverses of the rotations in S_ρ are applied in the order given by τ then the matching obtained in $\mathcal{L}_\mu$ will be $f_\mu^{-1}(S)$. Use this fact to show that $f_\mu^{-1}(S)$ can be computed in polynomial time for any lower set S of π_μ.

Exercise 1.12 For any positive integer n, let S_n denote the set of divisors of n. Define a partial order $\pi_n = (S_n, \succeq)$ as follows: for $a, b \in S_n$, $a \succeq b$ if $b|a$. Prove that π_n is an FDL with the meet and join of two elements $a, b \in S_n$ being the gcd and lcm of a and b, respectively. Figure 1.21 shows the lattice for $n = 60$. Give a characterization of the join-irreducible matchings of π_{60} and find the projection of π_{60} onto the join-irreducible matchings of this lattice. Do the set of lattices $\{\pi_n \mid n \in \mathbb{Z}_+\}$ form a complete set of FDLs, as defined in Exercise 1.9? Prove or disprove your answer.

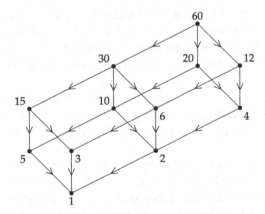

Figure 1.21 The lattice of divisors of 60.

Exercise 1.13 [6] For a stable matching μ in Setting I, define its *value* as follows. Assume $\mu(w) = f$, and that f is the jth firm on w's preference list and w is the kth worker on f's list; if so, define the value of the match (w, f) to be $k + j$. Define the value of μ to be the sum of the values of all matches in μ. Define an *equitable stable matching* to be one that minimizes the value. Give a polynomial time algorithm for finding such a matching.

Hint: Use the algorithms developed in Exercise 1.11. Also note that the problem of finding a minimum-weight lower set of π_μ is solvable in polynomial time, assuming that integer weights (positive, negative, or zero) are assigned to the elements of $\mathcal{J}_\mu$. The weight of a lower set S is defined to be the sum of weights of the elements in S.

Exercise 1.14 Prove Lemma 1.59 and use it to prove Lemma 1.60.

Hint: For the first part of Lemma 1.59, use a blocking pair argument, and, for the second part, first prove that

$$|W_1| + |W_2| = \sum_{f \in F_1} n_1(f) + \sum_{f \in F_2} n_2(f),$$

where $n_1(f) = |\mu_1(f) - \mu_2(f)|$ and $n_2(f) = |\mu_2(f) - \mu_1(f)|$.

Exercise 1.15 The LP (1.1) for the stable matching problem was derived from a sufficient condition, given in Section 1.5.1, which ensures that a worker–firm pair (w, f) does not form a blocking pair with respect to a matching μ. Another sufficient condition is that if f is matched to worker w' in such a way that $w \succ_f w'$ then w is matched to a firm f' such that $f' \succ_w f$. The fractional version of this condition is

$$\forall w \in W, \forall f \in F: \sum_{w \succ_f w'} x_{w'f} - \sum_{f' \succ_w f} x_{wf'} \le 0.$$

Show that this condition holds for any feasible solution x to LP (1.1).

Exercise 1.16 [13] Suppose that an instance of stable matching in Setting I has an odd number, k, of stable matchings. For each worker w, order its k matches, with multiplicity, according to its preference list and do the same for each firm f. Match w to the median element in its list. Let us call this the *median matching*. This exercise eventually helps to show that not only is this matching perfect but it is also stable. Moreover, it matches each firm to the median element in its list.

First, let $\mu_1, \ldots, \mu_l$ be any l stable matchings, not necessarily distinct, for an instance of stable matching in Setting I. For each worker–firm pair (w, f) let $n(w, f)$ be the number of these matchings in which w is matched to f and let $x_{wf} = (1/l)n(w, f)$.

Show that x is a feasible solution to LP (1.1), i.e., it is a fractional stable matching. For any k such that $1 \le k \le l$, let $\theta = (k/l) - \epsilon$, where $\epsilon > 0$ is smaller than $1/l$. Consider the stable matching μ_θ as defined by the procedure given in Section 1.5.1 for writing a fractional stable matching as a convex combination of stable matchings. Show that matching μ_θ matches each worker w to the kth firm in the ordered list of the l firms, not necessarily distinct, in which w is matched to under $\mu_1, \ldots, \mu_l$. Furthermore, show that μ_θ matches each firm f to the $(l - k + 1)$th worker in the ordered list of the l workers to which f is matched.

Using this fact, prove the assertions made above about median matching.

1.7 Bibliographic Notes

The seminal paper [5] introduced the stable matching problem and gave the deferred acceptance algorithm. For basic books on this problem and related topics see [4], [12], [8], and [9].

Theorem 1.32, proving that the worker-proposing DA algorithm is DSIC for workers, is due to Dubins and Freedman [3] (see also [10]). This ground-breaking result was instrumental in opening up the DA algorithm to highly consequential applications, such as school choice; for a discussion of the latter, see Chapter 8. Theorem 1.35, showing that there is no DSIC mechanism for firms in Setting III, is due to Roth [10].

John Conway proved that the set of stable matchings of an instance forms a finite distributive lattice; see [8]. The notion of rotation is due to Irving and Leather [6] and Theorem 1.56 is due to Birkhoff [1]. The LP formulation for stable matching was given by Vande Vate [14]; the proof given in Section 1.5.1 is due to Teo and Sethuraman [13].

References

[1] Birkhoff, Garrett. 1937. Rings of sets. *Duke Mathematical Journal*, **3**(3), 443–454.

[2] Blair, Charles. 1984. Every finite distributive lattice is a set of stable matchings. *Journal of Combinatorial Theory, Series A*, **37**(3), 353–356.

[3] Dubins, L. E., and Freedman, D. A. 1981. Machiavelli and the Gale–Shapley algorithm. *American Mathematical Monthly*, **88**(7), 485–494. www.jstor.org/stable/2321753.

[4] Gusfield, Dan, and Irving, Robert W. 1989. *The Stable Marriage Problem: Structure and Algorithm*. The MIT Press.

[5] Gale, David, and Shapley, Lloyd S. 1962. College admissions and the stability of marriage. *American Mathematical Monthly*, **69**(1), 9–15.

[6] Irving, Robert W., and Leather, Paul. 1986. The complexity of counting stable marriages. *SIAM Journal on Computing*, **15**(3), 655–667.

[7] Irving, Robert W., Leather, Paul, and Gusfield, Dan. 1987. An efficient algorithm for the "optimal" stable marriage. *Journal of the ACM*, **34**(3), 532–543.

[8] Knuth, Donald Ervin. 1997. *Stable Marriage and Its Relation to Other Combinatorial Problems: An Introduction to the Mathematical Analysis of Algorithms*. American Mathematical Society.

[9] Manlove, David. 2013. Algorithmics of Matching Under Preferences. World Scientific.

[10] Roth, A. E. 1982. The economics of matching: Stability and incentives. *Mathematics of Operations Research*, **7**(4), 617–628.

[11] Roth, A. E. 1985. The college admissions problem is not equivalent to the marriage problem. *Journal of Economic Theory*, **36**(2), 277–288. www.sciencedirect.com/science/article/pii/0022053185901061.

[12] Roth, Alvin E., and Sotomayor, Marilda. 1992. *Two-Sided Matching: A Study in Game-Theoretic Modeling and Analysis*. Econometric Society Monographs.

[13] Teo, Chung-Piaw, and Sethuraman, Jay. 1998. The geometry of fractional stable matchings and its applications. *Mathematics of Operations Research*, **23**(4), 874–891.

[14] Vande Vate, John H. 1989. Linear programming brings marital bliss. *Operations Research Letters*, **8**(3), 147–153.

CHAPTER TWO

One-Sided Matching Markets

Federico Echenique, Nicole Immorlica, and Vijay V. Vazirani

2.1 Introduction

A *one-sided matching allocation problem* consists of a set A of n agents, a set G of n indivisible goods, and the preferences of agents over goods The problem asks for a matching of each agent to a distinct good so as to ensure desirable normative properties, such as Pareto optimality, individual rationality, and envy-freeness. A market mechanism is often used to address this problem; such a mechanism should have game-theoretic properties such as strategy-proofness and core stability. Additionally, in the interest of usability of this mechanism in real-world applications, the mechanism needs to run in polynomial time.

One-sided matching markets can be classified in two dimensions: the nature of the utility functions of agents and whether agents have initial endowments. As stated in Chapter 4, utility functions may have either just an ordinal component, i.e., they are modeled via preference relations, or a cardinal component as well. Thus we get four possibilities, which are summarized below, together with the most well-known mechanism(s) for each.

1. *(ordinal, no endowments)* random priority and probabilistic serial
2. *(ordinal, endowments)* top trading cycle
3. *(cardinal, no endowments)* Hylland–Zeckhauser
4. *(cardinal, endowments)* ϵ-approximate ADHZ (Arrow–Debreu extension of Hylland–Zeckhauser)

The two types of utility functions described above have their individual pros and cons, and neither dominates the other. Whereas the former are easier to elicit, the latter are more expressive, enabling an agent not only to report whether she prefers one good to another but also by how much, thereby producing higher-quality allocations, as illustrated below in Example 2.20.

In recent decades, fundamental computer science revolutions regarding the Internet and mobile computing have led to the introduction of several novel and impactful market places which are based on one-sided matching markets. Several of these applications naturally lend themselves to the *online model of computation*, in which buyers arrive online, one at a time, and need to be matched instantaneously and irrevocably to goods, without knowledge of future arrivals. The matching produced by a mechanism for this setting will be compared with the optimal matching computed with full knowledge of all arrivals.

In Section 2.7, we present a paradigm-setting problem for such matching markets, namely online bipartite matching, as well an optimal mechanism, called RANKING, for it. Internet-based applications using these ideas are studied in Chapters 5 and 6; the first considers mobile-computing-based applications and the second studies ad auctions, e.g., the AdWords marketplace of Google.

2.2 Preliminaries

A *precedence relation* of agent $i \in A$ is a total order $\succ_i$ over the goods in G. The *ex post* allocation produced by the one-sided matching allocation problem is a one-to-one mapping of the n agents to the n goods. However, *ex ante* it may be a *random allocation* in which each good is viewed as one unit of probability shares and each agent's allocation is a total of one unit of probability shares over all goods, i.e., it is an $n \times n$ doubly stochastic matrix.

One way to view the random allocation is as a way for agents to time-share the goods. Alternatively, using the Birkhoff–von Neumann theorem, this *ex ante* allocation is equivalent to a probability distribution over *ex post* mappings of agents to goods.

Over the set of all possible random allocations that can be made to agent i, there exists a natural partial order but no total order. The partial order is defined below. Let x be an *ex ante* random allocation to all agents. Then x_i will denote the allocation made to agent i.

Definition 2.1. Let x and y be two random allocations. Assume that the components of x_i and y_i are ordered by $\succ_i$. Then x_i *stochastically dominates* y_i if

$$\forall k \in \{1, \ldots, n\} : \sum_{j=1}^{k} x_{ij} \geq \sum_{j=1}^{k} y_{ij}.$$

We will denote this relation by $x_i \succeq_i^{sd} y_i$. Furthermore, x_i *strictly stochastically dominates* y_i if x_i stochastically dominates y_i and, for some k, with $1 \leq k < n$, $\sum_{j=1}^{k} x_{ij} > \sum_{j=1}^{k} y_{ij}$. We will denote this by $x_i \succ_i^{sd} y_i$. Given two random allocations x and y, we will say that y is *stochastically dominated by x* if, for each agent i, $x_i \succeq_i^{sd} y_i$ and, for at least one agent j, $x_j \succ_j^{sd} y_j$.

For *ex ante* random allocations, the "correct" notion of efficiency is *ordinal efficiency* as defined below.

Definition 2.2. A random allocation x is said to be *envy-free* if for any two agents i and j, agent i's allocation stochastically dominates agent j's, i.e., $x_i \succeq_i^{sd} x_j$. The allocation x is *ordinally efficient* if x is not stochastically dominated by another random allocation x'.

Definition 2.3. Let x be the random allocation produced by a mechanism according to which agent i reports her preference relation truthfully and the rest report whatever they wish. Let x' be the random allocation produced when agent i misreports her preference relation and the rest do they know about the former? We will say that the mechanism is *strategyproof* if $x_i \succeq_i^{sd} x_i'$.

Definition 2.4. Let x and y be two *ex post* allocations, i.e., mappings of agents to goods. We will say that y *dominates* x if, for each agent i, $y_i \succeq_i x_i$ and, for at least one agent j, $y_j \succ_j x_j$; we will denote this as $y \succ x$. We will say that x is *ex post Pareto efficient* if there is no mapping of agents to goods y such that $y \succ x$.

2.3 Random Priority and Probabilistic Serial: Ordinal, No Endowments

The two mechanisms presented in this section have different pros and cons, and neither dominates the other.

2.3.1 Random Priority (RP)

As a prelude to random priority, we present the following particularly simple deterministic mechanism, which assigns goods in an integer way.

The priority mechanism. This mechanism is also called *serial dictatorship*. Initially, all n goods are declared available. Pick an ordering π of the n agents and, in the ith iteration, let the agent $\pi(i)$ pick her most preferred good among the currently available goods; declare the chosen good unavailable.

The priority mechanism is not envy–free: if several agents have as their first preference the same good, the one earliest in π will get it.

Lemma 2.5. *The priority mechanism is strategy-proof and the allocation produced by it is Pareto optimal.*

Proof Strategy-proofness is straightforward. In each iteration, the active agent has the opportunity of obtaining the best available good, according to her preference list. Therefore, misreporting preferences can only lead to a suboptimal allocation.

We next show Pareto optimality. Let μ be the allocation produced by the priority mechanism. For contradiction, assume that μ' is an allocation that dominates μ. Let i be the first index such that $\mu'(\pi(i)) \succ_{\pi(i)} \mu(\pi(i))$. Clearly, for $j < i$, agent $\pi(j)$ is assigned the same good under μ and μ'. Therefore, in the ith iteration, agent $\pi(i)$ has the available good $\mu'(\pi(i))$. Since $\pi(i)$ picks the best available good we have $\mu(\pi(i)) \succeq_{\pi(i)} \mu'(\pi(i))$, leading to a contradiction. $\qquad\square$

The priority mechanism suffers from the obvious drawback of not being fair since agents at the top of the list π have the opportunity of choosing their favorite goods while those at the bottom get the left-overs. Random priority corrects this as follows.

The RP mechanism. This mechanism is also called *random serial dictatorship*. It iterates over all $n!$ orderings of the n agents. For each ordering π, it runs the priority mechanism and when an agent chooses a good, it assigns a $(1/n!)$th share of the good to the agent. Clearly, at the end of the process, each agent has been assigned a total of one unit of probability shares, over all goods.

Lemma 2.6. *RP is strategy-proof and ex post Pareto optimal.*

Proof By Lemma 2.5, in each of the $n!$ iterations, truth-revealing is the best strategy of an agent. Therefore, RP is strategy-proof.

We next argue that the random allocation output of RP can be decomposed into a convex combination of perfect matchings of agents to goods such that the allocation made by each perfect matching is Pareto optimal. This is obvious if we choose the $n!$ perfect matchings corresponding to the $n!$ orderings of agents. Clearly, two different orderings may yield the same perfect matching; therefore the convex combination may be over fewer than $n!$ perfect matchings. Therefore, RP is *ex post* Pareto optimal. □

The reader may have surmised that, by similar reasoning to that in the proof of Lemma 2.6, the Pareto optimality of the priority mechanism would lead to ordinal efficiency of RP. Interestingly enough, that is not the case, as shown in Example 2.7. Even worse, RP is not envy–free despite the fact that the reason for generalizing from priority to RP was to introduce fairness; see Example 2.8.

Although the priority mechanism runs efficiently, RP takes exponential time, making it impractical, for all but very small values of n, to obtain the *ex ante* random allocation which is useful for the time-sharing of the goods. However, if an *integral* matching of agents to goods is desired then picking one ordering of agents at random suffices; clearly this is time-efficient.

Example 2.7. Let $n = 4$, $A = \{1, 2, 3, 4\}$, and $G = \{a, b, c, d\}$. Let the preferences of the agents be as follows:

$$
\begin{array}{ccccc}
1, & a & b & c & d \\
2, & a & b & c & d \\
3, & b & a & d & c \\
4, & b & a & d & c \\
\end{array}
$$

Then RP will return the random allocation in Table 2.1.

Table 2.1

Agent	a	b	c	d
1	5/12	1/12	5/12	1/12
2	5/12	1/12	5/12	1/12
3	1/12	5/12	1/12	5/12
4	1/12	5/12	1/12	5/12

However, it is stochastically dominated by the random allocation in Table 2.2.

Table 2.2

Agent	a	b	c	d
1	1/2	0	1/2	0
2	1/2	0	1/2	0
3	0	1/2	0	1/2
4	0	1/2	0	1/2

Example 2.8. Let $n = 3$, $A = \{1, 2, 3\}$, and $G = \{a, b, c\}$. Let the preferences of the agents be as follows:

$$
\begin{array}{cccc}
1, & a & b & c \\
2, & b & a & c \\
3, & b & c & a
\end{array}
$$

Then RP will return the allocation in Table 2.3.

Table 2.3

Agent	a	b	c
1	5/6	0	1/6
2	1/6	3/6	2/6
3	0	3/6	3/6

Since the total allocation of the two goods a and b to agents 1 and 2 is 5/6 and 4/6, respectively, agent 2's allocation does not stochastically dominate agent 1's allocation.

2.3.2 Probabilistic Serial (PS) Mechanism

With respect to the four properties studied above for RP, PS behaves in exactly the opposite manner; it is time-efficient, ordinally efficient, and envy-free but not strategy-proof.

The PS mechanism. As before, we will view each good as one unit of probability shares. Furthermore, for ease of presentation, let us think of probability as a fluid which can be "poured" at the rate of one unit per hour. In one hour PS will assign one unit of probability shares to each agent, using the following continuous process. Initially, each agent is allocated probability from her most preferred good; clearly, if m agents are simultaneously being allocated good j then j is getting depleted at the rate of m units per hour. As soon as an agent's preferred good is fully allocated to other agents, she moves on to her next most preferred good that is still available.

Since each agent has a total order over all n goods, at the end of one hour each agent will get a unit of allocation and all goods will be fully allocated. By iteratively computing the time at which a good becomes exhausted, this continuous process can be discretized. It is easy to see that the allocation computed can be written using rational numbers and the mechanism runs in polynomial time.

Lemma 2.9. *The allocation computed by PS is envy-free.*

Proof At each point in the algorithm, each agent is obtaining a probability share of her favorite good. Therefore, at any time in the algorithm, agent i cannot prefer agent j's current allocation to her own. Hence PS is envy-free. □

For showing that the random allocation computed by PS is ordinally efficient, we will appeal to the following property of stochastic dominance, which follows directly from its definition. Assume that x and y are two allocations made to agent i having equal total probability shares; let $t \le 1$ be this total. Assume that $x \succeq_i^{sd} y$. Let $\alpha < t$ and remove an amount α of the least desirable probability shares from each of x and y, to obtain x' and y', respectively. Then $x' \succeq_i^{sd} y'$.

Lemma 2.10. *The random allocation computed by PS is ordinally efficient.*

Proof During the running of PS on the given instance, let $t_0 = 0, t_1, \ldots, t_m = 1$ be the times at which some agent exhausts the good she is currently being allocated. By induction on k, we will prove that at time t_k, the partial allocation computed by PS is ordinally efficient among all allocations which give an amount t_k of probability shares to each agent.

The induction basis, for $k = 0$, is obvious since the empty allocation is vacuously ordinally efficient. Let A^k denote the allocation at time t_k and let A_i^k denote the allocation made to agent i under A^k. Assume the induction hypothesis, namely that the assertion holds for k, i.e., A^k is ordinally efficient.

For the induction step, we need to show that A^{k+1} is ordinally efficient. Suppose this is not the case, and let it be stochastically dominated by random allocation P. Let $\alpha = t_{k+1} - t_k$. For each agent i, remove an amount α of the least desirable probability shares from P_i to obtain P_i'. Since $P_i \succeq_i^{sd} A_i^{k+1}$, by the property stated above we have $P_i' \succeq_i^{sd} A_i^k$. By the induction hypothesis, $A_i^k \succeq_i^{sd} P_i'$ as well. Therefore $P_i' = A_i^k$. In the time period between t_k and t_{k+1}, each agent obtains α units of probability shares of her remaining most preferred good. Therefore, $A_i^{k+1} \succeq_i^{sd} P_i$, leading to a contradiction. □

To prove that a mechanism is strategy-proof, we would need to show that x_i stochastically dominates x_i', where x and x' are the allocations when i reports preferences truthfully and when it misreports, respectively. Example 2.11 shows that this does not hold for PS.

Example 2.11. Let $n = 3$, $A = \{1, 2, 3\}$, and $G = \{a, b, c\}$. Let the preferences of the agents be as follows:

$$
\begin{array}{cccc}
1, & a & b & c \\
2, & a & c & b \\
3, & b & a & c
\end{array}
$$

PS will return the allocation in Table 2.4.

Table 2.4

Agent	a	b	c
1	1/2	1/4	1/4
2	1/2	0	1/2
3	0	3/4	1/4

However, if Agent 3 lies and reports her preference list as $a \succ b \succ c$, then PS will return the allocation in Table 2.5.

Table 2.5

Agent	a	b	c
1	1/3	1/2	1/6
2	1/3	0	4/6
3	1/3	1/2	1/6

Therefore, by lying, agent 3 obtains 5/6 units of her favorite two goods, instead of only 3/4 units.

Finally, we provide an example in which RP and PS are Pareto incomparable in the sense that different agents prefer different allocations.

Example 2.12. Let $n = 4$, $A = \{1, 2, 3, 4\}$ and $G = \{a, b, c, d\}$. Let the preferences of the agents be as follows:

$$1, \quad a \quad b \quad c \quad d$$
$$2, \quad a \quad b \quad d \quad c$$
$$3, \quad b \quad a \quad c \quad d$$
$$4, \quad c \quad d \quad a \quad b$$

RP will return the allocation in Table 2.6.

Table 2.6

Agent	a	b	c	d
1	1/2	1/6	1/12	1/4
2	1/2	1/6	0	1/3
3	0	2/3	1/12	1/4
4	0	0	5/6	1/6

PS will return the allocation in Table 2.7.

Table 2.7

Agent	a	b	c	d
1	1/2	1/6	1/9	2/9
2	1/2	1/6	0	1/3
3	0	2/3	1/9	2/9
4	0	0	7/9	2/9

Agents 1 and 3 prefer the PS allocation, agent 4 prefers the RP allocation, and agent 2 is indifferent.

2.4 Top Trading Cycle: Ordinal, Endowments

For this section, we assume that the goods in G are individual houses owned by the n agents in A. The house owned by agent i is her initial endowment and will be called i. Each agent i has a total preference list $\succ_i$ over all n houses, including her own. The mechanism *top trading cycle (TTC)* presented below is iterative and, in each iteration, it constructs a directed graph $H = (U, E)$ where U is the set of unallocated agents. Each agent $i \in U$ has one out-edge (i,j), where j is the best available house under i's preference list; E consists of precisely these edges. In particular, if i's best available house is i, then E contains the self-loop (i, i).

The TTC mechanism. Initially, all houses are *available* and all agents are *unallocated*. An iteration is executed as follows. Construct the graph $H = (U, E)$ defined above. Pick a cycle in H, say C, and *allocate the cycle*: for each edge $(i,j) \in C$, allocate house j to i. All agents in C are declared *allocated* and houses in C are declared *unavailable*. The mechanism terminates when $U = \oslash$.

Since every node of H has one outgoing edge, H must contain a cycle. Therefore, the step "pick a cycle in H" will be successful. When C is allocated, the houses declared unavailable are those owned by agents in C. Therefore, in each iteration the available houses are precisely the initial endowments of agents in U.

In any iteration, H contains a set of disjoint cycles. Each vertex that is not in a cycle is on a directed path that ends at one of these cycles. Suppose that $(i,j) \in E$ with j in cycle C and $i \notin C$. When C gets allocated, i will point to another vertex, say k. This will lead to the formation of a new cycle if there is a path from k to i. Observe that once a cycle gets formed in H, it remains unchanged until it is allocated. Therefore the output of the algorithm is independent of the order in which it allocates cycles. Moreover, we can also allocate all cycles simultaneously in each iteration.

If in some iteration i's best house is i then, in this or a future iteration, i will be allocated house i. Therefore, no agent will be allocated a house which she prefers less than her own and hence the allocation computed is individually rational. On the other hand, TTC is not envy-free: if i and i' both like house j best then at most one of them will be given j.

We next define the fundamental cooperative game-theoretic solution concept of the core.

Definition 2.13. An allocation μ of houses to all agents is said to be in the *core* if, for any set $S \subseteq A$, when the agents in S exchange houses among themselves via an allocation, say μ', it cannot be the case that all agents of S are as happy under μ' as under μ and at least one agent is strictly happier.

Next we will show that the allocation found by TTC is core stable, i.e., it lies in the core; this is stronger than Pareto optimality. In the two-sided matching market model studied in Chapter 1, core stability is equivalent to stability because only pairs of agents can generate value.

Theorem 2.14. *Mechanism TTC is core stable, i.e., S cannot do better under μ' than μ, in the following sense:*

$$\forall i \in S, \; \mu'(i) \succeq_i \mu(i) \quad and \quad \exists j \in S \; s.t. \; \mu'(j) \succ_j \mu(j).$$

Proof Assume for contradiction that the above statement holds. Consider the first iteration of TTC, in which an agent in S is allocated a house, and let C be the cycle formed. If C contains an agent from $A \setminus S$ then there is an edge $(i,j) \in C$ such that $i \in S$ and $j \in (A \setminus S)$. Clearly, i prefers j to any house in S, $\mu(i) = j$, and $\mu'(i) \in S$. Therefore $\mu(i) \succ_i \mu'(i)$, leading to a contradiction.

Therefore, C is entirely within S. But then μ will assign each agent i in C her best house in S. Therefore $\mu(i) \succeq_i \mu'(i)$, hence giving $\mu(i) = \mu'(i)$. On removing all agents of C from S and applying the argument to the remaining set, we obtain that there is no agent $j \in S$ s.t. $\mu'(j) \succ_j \mu(j)$, leading to another contradiction. The theorem follows. $\qquad\square$

Theorem 2.15. *Mechanism TTC is strategy-proof.*

Proof Let R and R' denote the runs of the mechanism if agent i reports her preferences truthfully and if she does not, respectively. Suppose for contradiction that i is matched to house i' under R and to house j under R', where $j \succ_i i'$. For simplicity, assume that the algorithm allocates all cycles simultaneously in each iteration. Assume that, in run R', i is allocated in iteration k. We will show that i will be allocated house j in run R as well, hence leading to a contradiction.

Under R', if edge (i, l) for $l \neq j$, in the first k iterations this edge is inconsequential to the output of the algorithm; the only edge that is consequential is (i, j). Since there is a cycle C containing (i, j) in iteration k, there is a path from j to i by iteration k. There are two cases: j is demoted or promoted in going from i's true preferences to i's untrue preferences. In the first case, edge (i, j) is added to H earlier under run R than under run R'. Clearly, the path from j to i will eventually be formed under run R, and therefore cycle C will be formed and i will be allocated j. In the second case, edge (i, j) is added to H later under run R than under run R'. By the time that edge (i, j) is added to H, there is already a path from j to i. Therefore, cycle C will be formed in this case as well, and i will be allocated house j. $\square$

2.5 Hylland–Zeckhauser: Cardinal, No Endowments

The Hylland–Zeckhauser (HZ) solution uses the power of a pricing mechanism to arrive at equilibrium prices and allocations. Consequently, prices reflect the relative importance of goods on the basis of the utilities declared by buyers, thereby making allocations as equitable as possible. Furthermore, a pricing mechanism helps prevent an artificial scarcity of goods and ensures that scarce goods are allocated to agents who have the most utility for them. The allocation produced by the HZ solution is Pareto optimal and the scheme is incentive-compatible in the large.

The agents provide their preferences for goods by stating their von Neumann–Mogenstern utilities. Let u_{ij} represent the utility of agent i for good j. Each agent has one dollar with which she buys probability shares. As in RP and PS, the HZ mechanism also views each good as one unit of probability shares, and the allocation forms a *fractional perfect matching* in the complete bipartite graph over vertex sets A and G. Let p_j denote the price of good j. Let x_{ij} be the probability share that agent i receives of good j. Then $\sum_j u_{ij} x_{ij}$ is the *expected utility* accrued by agent i.

Definition 2.16. Let x and p denote arbitrary (non-negative) allocations and prices of goods. By the *size, cost, and value* of agent i's bundle we mean

$$\sum_{j \in G} x_{ij}, \quad \sum_{j \in G} p_j x_{ij}, \quad \text{and} \quad \sum_{j \in G} u_{ij} x_{ij},$$

respectively. We will denote these by $\text{size}_x(i)$, $\text{cost}_x(i)$, and $\text{value}_x(i)$, respectively.

Definition 2.17 (HZ equilibrium). The allocations and prices (x, p) form an *equilibrium* for the one-sided matching market stated above if:

1. The *market clears*, namely the total probability share of each good j is one unit, i.e., $\sum_i x_{ij} = 1$.
2. The size of each agent i's allocation is 1, i.e., $\text{size}_x(i) = 1$.
3. The cost of the bundle of each agent is *at most* one dollar; observe that an agent need not spend her entire dollar.
4. Subject to constraints 2 and 3, each agent i maximizes her expected utility, i.e., maximizes $\text{value}_x(i)$, subject to $\text{size}_x(i) = 1$ and $\text{cost}_x(i) \le 1$.

Equilibrium prices are invariant under the operation of *scaling the difference of prices from 1* in the following sense. Let (x, p) be an equilibrium and fix any $r > 0$. Let p' be such that $\forall j \in G$, $p'_j - 1 = r(p_j - 1)$. Then (x, p') is also an equilibrium; see Exercise 2.3.

A standard way of fixing the scale is to enforce that the minimum price of a good is zero – this leads to simplicity in certain situations. Observe that the main goal of the HZ mechanism is to yield the "correct" allocations to agents; the prices are simply a vehicle in the market mechanism to achieve this. Hence arbitrarily fixing the scale does not change the essential nature of the problem.

Using Kakutani's fixed point theorem, the following can be shown:

Theorem 2.18. *Every instance of the one-sided market defined above admits an equilibrium.*

In addition to the conditions stated in Definition 2.17, imposing the following condition ensures that every equilibrium allocation will be Pareto optimal. Each agent is allocated a utility-maximizing bundle of minimum cost, in the case when there are several. This *minimum cost condition* is used in the proof of Lemma 2.19; see Exercise 2.2 for an illustrative example.

Lemma 2.19. *Every HZ equilibrium allocation satisfying the minimum cost condition is Pareto optimal.*

Proof Let (x, p) be the equilibrium allocations and prices and assume for contradiction that x is not Pareto optimal. Let x' be an allocation which is at least as good as x for each agent and better for at least one agent, say i. Since i must have been allocated a utility-maximizing bundle of goods costing at most one dollar in the equilibrium, it must be the case that the allocation of i under x' costs more than one dollar with respect to the prices p.

Now, the total allocation of each good under x and under x' is one unit. Therefore, the total cost of the entire allocation x equals the total cost of x', with respect to the prices p. Therefore there must be an agent, say k, such that the cost of her bundle under allocation x' is less than the cost of her bundle under x. Since k obtains a utility-maximizing bundle of least cost in the equilibrium, k must accrue less utility under x' than under x, leading to a contradiction. $\square$

Finally, if this "market" is large enough, no individual agent will be able to improve her allocation by misreporting utilities nor will she be able to manipulate prices. For this reason, the HZ mechanism is incentive-compatible in the large.

The next example illustrates how, by using cardinal utilities, the HZ mechanism produces higher-quality allocations than any mechanism using ordinal utilities. For a detailed discussion of the notions of ordinal and cardinal utility functions, see Chapter 4.

Example 2.20. An instance has three types of goods, T_1, T_2, T_3, and these goods are present in the proportions (1%, 97%, 2%). On the basis of their utility functions, the agents are partitioned into two sets A_1 and A_2, where A_1 constitutes 1% of the agents and A_2, 99%. The utility functions of the agents in A_1 and A_2 for the three types of goods are $(1, \epsilon, 0)$ and $(1, 1 - \epsilon, 0)$, respectively, for a small number $\epsilon > 0$. The main point is that whereas the agents in A_2 marginally prefer T_1 to T_2, those in A_1 overwhelmingly prefer T_1 to T_2. Clearly, the ordinal utilities of all agents in $A_1 \cup A_2$ are the same. Therefore, a mechanism based on such utilities will not be able to make a distinction between the two types of agents. On the other hand, the HZ mechanism, which uses cardinal utilities, will fix the price of goods in T_3 to be zero and those in T_1 and T_2 appropriately, so that by and large the bundles of A_1 and A_2 consist of goods from T_1 and T_2, respectively.

2.6 ϵ-Approximate ADHZ: Cardinal, Endowments

What follows is an extension of the Hylland–Zeckhauser model to the setting in which agents have initial endowments.

Definition 2.21 (ADHZ equilibrium[1]). We require that the initial endowments form a fractional perfect matching in the complete bipartite graph over agents and goods. For given prices p of goods, each agent i sells her initial endowment to obtain a budget, say b_i; we will enhance HZ by allowing agents to have different amounts of money. Then (p, x) is an *ADHZ equilibrium* if (p, x) is an HZ equilibrium assuming budgets b_i. If so, observe that any positive scaling of p also leads to an equilibrium.

It turns out that not every instance of ADHZ admits an equilibrium; see Example 2.22 and Exercise 2.6

Example 2.22. Consider an ADHZ instance with $n = 3$, agents $A = \{a_1, a_2, a_3\}$, goods $G = \{g_1, g_2, g_3\}$, and utilities as given in Table 2.8. Observe that goods g_2 and g_3 are identical and a_1 and a_2 have identical utilities. The initial endowments of all agents are identical and contain 1/3 units of each good.

Lemma 2.23. *The ADHZ instance given in Example 2.22 does not admit an equilibrium.*

---

[1] A market model with cardinal utilities in which agents have initial endowments of goods is called an exchange, Walrasian, or Arrow–Debreu model; hence the name ADHZ.

Table 2.8 Agents' utilities.

	g_1	g_2	g_3
a_1	1	0	0
a_2	1	0	0
a_3	0	1	1

Proof Assume for contradiction that an equilibrium exists and let p and q be the equilibrium prices of goods g_1 and g_2 and g_3, respectively. Consider these two cases:

Case 1: $q > 0$. Without loss of generality assume that $q = 1$. If $p \leq 1$, a_1 and a_2 will both demand one unit of g_1, leading to a contradiction. Therefore $p > 1$ and the budget of each agent is $p/3 + 2/3$. With this price structure, a_3 will not buy g_1 at all and therefore g_1 is only bought by a_1 and a_2. Additionally, these two agents must together buy one unit total of g_2 and g_3, costing a total of $p + 1$. Therefore $2(p/3 + 2/3) = p + 1$, implying that $p = 1$ and leading to a contradiction.

Case 2: $q = 0$ and $p > 0$. Now a_3 buys one unit from g_2 and g_3, and g_1 is shared by a_1 and a_2. However, with a budget of $p/3$ each, a_1 and a_2 cannot afford to buy one total unit of g_1, leading to a contradiction.

Therefore the instance does not admit an equilibrium. $\qquad\square$

One solution to the lack of an equilibrium in the ADHZ model is the following hybrid between the HZ and ADHZ models.

Definition 2.24 (α-slack equilibrium). Let α be a fixed number with $\alpha \in (0, 1]$. As in ADHZ, agents have initial endowments of goods. For given prices p of goods, the budget of agent i is $m_i = \alpha + (1 - \alpha)b_i$, where b_i is the value of i's initial endowment. Then (p, x) is an *α-slack equilibrium* if (p, x) is an HZ equilibrium assuming budgets m_i.

A non-trivial proof, using the Kakutani fixed point theorem, gives:

Theorem 2.25. *For any α, with $\alpha \in (0, 1]$, an α-slack equilibrium always exists.*

Another possibility is to use the notion of an approximate equilibrium. This notion has been very successfully used in the study of equilibria, both market and Nash, within computer science. Besides retaining the market as a pure exchange model, this alternative also leads to better computational properties.

Definition 2.26 (ϵ-approximate ADHZ equilibrium). Let $1 > \epsilon > 0$ be a fixed number. As in ADHZ, agents have initial endowments of goods. For given prices p of goods, fix the budget of agent i to be m_i, where

$$(1 - \epsilon)b_i \leq m_i \leq \epsilon + b_i;$$

here b_i is the value of i's initial endowment. Then (p, x) is an ϵ-*approximate ADHZ equilibrium* if (p, x) is an HZ equilibrium assuming budgets m_i. Furthermore, we require that any two agents which have the same endowments also have the same budgets.

In Definition 2.26, the additive error term in the upper bound is needed since otherwise the counterexample given in Example 2.22 would still work, and the multiplicative term in the lower bound is useful for ensuring approximate individual rationality.

We note that individual rationality fundamentally clashes with envy-freeness in both ADHZ and ϵ-approximate ADHZ models, as the following example illustrates. Consider the case $n = 2$ with the initial endowments of agents 1 and 2 being two distinct goods, 1 and 2, respectively. Assume both agents prefer good 1 to good 2. Then individual rationality entails that agent 1 should get good 1. However, this allocation is not envy-free. For this reason, we define the notion of *equal-type envy-freeness* in exchange markets: it demands envy-freeness only for agents with the same initial endowment.

Theorem 2.27. *For any ϵ with $1 > \epsilon > 0$, an ϵ-approximate ADHZ equilibrium exists. It is Pareto optimal, approximately individually rational, and equal-type envy-free.*

Proof Since an α-slack equilibrium is also an α-approximate ADHZ equilibrium, we get the existence of the latter by Theorem 2.25. Since an ϵ-approximate ADHZ equilibrium is an HZ equilibrium for budgets defined in a certain way, Pareto optimality of the former follows the Pareto optimality of the latter. Since every agent has a budget of at least $1 - \epsilon$ times the cost of her initial endowment, her utility can decrease by at most a factor $1 - \epsilon$. As a result, approximate individual rationality follows. Equal-type envy-freeness follows immediately from the condition that agents with the same endowment have the same budget. □

2.7 Online Bipartite Matching

Let B be a set of n buyers and S a set of n goods. A bipartite graph $G = (B, S, E)$ is specified on vertex sets B and S and edge set E, where, for $i \in B$ and $j \in S$, $(i, j) \in E$ if and only if buyer i *likes* good j. The graph G is assumed to have a perfect matching and therefore each buyer can be given a unique good that she likes. The graph is revealed in the following manner. The n goods are known up-front and the buyers arrive one at a time. When buyer i arrives, the edges incident at i are revealed.

We are required to design an *online algorithm*[2] $\mathcal{A}$ in the following sense. At the moment a buyer i is revealed, the algorithm needs to match i to one of its unmatched neighbors, if any; if i's neighbors are all matched, i remains unmatched. The difficulty is that the algorithm does not "know" the edges incident at buyers which will arrive

---

[2] In the field of algorithm design, a distinction is made between *offline and online algorithms*: whereas the former assumes that the entire input is presented up-front, the latter assumes that the input is provided piecemeal to the algorithm, which is required to make irrevocable decisions about the arriving input without "knowing" highly relevant information that may arrive in the future.

in the future, and yet the size of the matching produced by the algorithm will be compared with the best *off-line matching*; the latter is a perfect matching, of course. The formal measure for the algorithm is defined below.

2.7.1 The Competitive Ratio of Online Algorithms

Definition 2.28. Let $G = (B, S, E)$ be a bipartite graph as specified above. The *competitive ratio* of a deterministic algorithm $\mathcal{A}$ for the online bipartite matching problem is defined to be

$$c(\mathcal{A}) = \min_{G=(B,S,E)} \min_{\rho(B)} \frac{\mathcal{A}(G, \rho(B))}{n},$$

where $\rho(B)$ is a specific order of arrival of vertices in B, and $\mathcal{A}(G, \rho(B))$ denotes the size of the matching produced by algorithm $\mathcal{A}$ when run on G under the order of arrival of vertices in B given by $\rho(B)$.

Remark 2.29. The assumption that G has a perfect matching is made for the sake of simplicity. It is easy to see that the entire ensuing discussion holds even if n were taken to be the size of a maximum matching in G.

Observe that the competitive ratio measures the "worst-case" performance of algorithm $\mathcal{A}$. A convenient way of talking about the worst case is to assume that the graph and the order of arrival of buyers are chosen by an *adversary* who has full knowledge of our algorithm.

We have assumed that $\mathcal{A}$ is *greedy*, i.e., if, on arrival, buyer i is incident at an unmatched good then $\mathcal{A}$ will definitely match i to one of them. This is without loss of generality since by leaving i unmatched, $\mathcal{A}$ can reap an extra advantage of at most one edge later; however, it has definitely lost an edge now. As a result, $\mathcal{A}$ produces a *maximal matching*, i.e., a matching that cannot be extended to a valid matching by adding any edge of G. Since the size of a maximal matching is at least half that of a maximum matching, $c(\mathcal{A}) \geq \frac{1}{2}$; furthermore, any deterministic algorithm can be forced by the adversary to produce a matching of this size; see Exercise 2.7. Therefore, a ratio of $\frac{1}{2}$ is *tight for any deterministic algorithm*.

To do better, we will resort to randomization. We first extend the definition of *competitive ratio for the randomized setting*:

$$c(\mathcal{A}) = \min_{G=(B,S,E)} \min_{\rho(B)} \frac{\mathbb{E}[\mathcal{A}(G, \rho(B))]}{n},$$

where $\mathbb{E}[\mathcal{A}(G, \rho(B))]$ is the expected size of matching produced by $\mathcal{A}$; the expectation is over the random bits used by $\mathcal{A}$.

Once again, we may assume that the worst-case graph and the order of arrival of buyers are chosen by an adversary who knows the algorithm. It is important to note that the algorithm provides random bits *after* the adversary makes its choices. This leads to a qualitative contrast between deterministic and randomized online algorithms: whereas in the former the adversary can effectively change the graph midway, in the latter it cannot since it cannot simulate the random bits in advance.

Perhaps the simplest idea using randomization is the following: match buyer i to a random unmatched neighbor. We will call this algorithm RANDOM. Example 2.31 gives a graph and an order of arrival of buyers such that the expected size of matching produced by RANDOM is $n/2 + O(\log n)$, i.e., it is only marginally better than the worst-case performance of a deterministic algorithm.

Algorithm 2.30 Algorithm RANKING.

---

1. **Initialization:** Pick a random permutation, π, of the goods in S.
2. **Online buyer arrival:** When a buyer, say i, arrives, match her to the first unmatched good she likes in the order π; if she likes none, leave i unmatched.

Output the matching, M, found.

Example 2.31. A bipartite graph $G = (B, S, E)$ over n buyers and n goods can be specified via its $n \times n$ adjacency matrix, say M_G. Assume n is even and let M_G have ones on the diagonal as well as in the $\frac{n}{2} \times \frac{n}{2}$ upper right-hand corner, i.e., the entries (i, j) for $i \in \{1, \ldots, \frac{n}{2}\}$ and $j \in \{(\frac{n}{2} + 1), \ldots, n\}$. The rest of the entries are 0; see Figure 2.1. The goods will correspond to the rows of M_G and the buyers to the columns. The adversarial order of arrival of buyers, i.e., the columns, is $n, (n - 1), (n - 2), \ldots, 2, 1$. We will divide the arrival of columns into two epochs: the arrival of the columns $n, (n - 1), \ldots, (\frac{n}{2} + 1)$ will be called Epoch 1 and that of columns $\frac{n}{2}, \ldots, 2, 1$, Epoch 2.

Observe that G has a perfect matching, namely the edges of the diagonal entries of M_G. Furthermore, any greedy online algorithm definitely matches all columns in Epoch 1; let j be one of these columns. We will say that column j has a *good match* if it is matched to row j and a *bad match* otherwise. If there are k good matches then the size of matching produced is $\frac{n}{2} + k$ because at the end of Epoch 1 there will be k unmatched rows from the top $\frac{n}{2}$ rows of M_G and they will be matched in Epoch 2.

Observe that in Epoch 1 the top right corner of M_G acts like a "trap" for RANDOM: columns have a high probability of being matched to a row

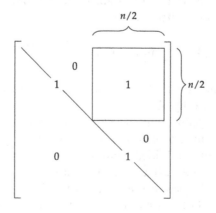

Figure 2.1 The matrix M_G.

in the "trap" and a low probability of obtaining a good match. Formally, $\mathbb{E}[k] = O(\log n)$; Exercise 2.8 gives a way of proving this bound. Therefore, the competitive ratio of RANDOM is $\frac{1}{2} + O(\frac{\log n}{n})$.

2.7.2 The Algorithm RANKING

A significantly better randomized algorithm is called RANKING and is given as Algorithm 2.30. Note that this algorithm picks a random permutation of goods only once; indeed, if it were to randomly permute goods with each buyer-arrival, it would be identical to RANDOM. Its competitive ratio is $1 - \frac{1}{e}$, as will be shown in Theorem 2.39. Furthermore, as will be shown in Theorem 2.45, it is an *optimal online bipartite matching algorithm*: no randomized algorithm can do better, up to an $o(1)$ term.

Why is RANKING so much better than RANDOM? In order to arrive at an intuitive reason, let us see why the "trap" of Example 2.31 is no longer effective. A run of the algorithm involves choosing a random permutation of rows, π; this choice fixes the rest of the outcomes. We will modify the notion of a *good match*, given in Example 2.31, by defining it with respect to each run. The argument given in Example 2.31 again shows that if in a run there are k good matches then the size of matching produced is $\frac{n}{2} + k$.

When does column j, which arrives in Epoch 1, get a good match? Assume that there are l rows, with indices in $[1, 2, \ldots, \frac{n}{2}]$, that are above row j under π. Clearly, none of the columns arriving before j can be matched to row j. Observe that column j will get a good match if and only if there are at least l bad matches before the arrival of column j,[3] since they will help to match the l rows above row j. Thus each bad match improves the probability of a good match later in the algorithm! This "self-correcting" property has a lot to do with the good performance of RANKING.

In order to prove Theorem 2.42, we will cast the online bipartite matching problem into an economic setting and restate RANKING as Algorithm 2.33, which operates as follows. Before the execution of Step (1), the adversary will determine the order in which buyers will arrive, say $\rho(B)$. In Step (1), all goods are assigned *prices* via the specified randomized process. Observe that, for each good j, $p_j \in [1/e, 1]$. In Step (2), buyers will arrive in the order $\rho(B)$ and will be matched to the cheapest available good.

Remark 2.32. In Step 1 of Algorithm 2.33, p_j is taken to be $e^{w_j - 1}$, where w_j is picked uniformly from $[0, 1]$. The optimality of the function $e^{w_j - 1}$ for obtaining the best bound on RANKING is established in Section 5.2.1.1 of Chapter 5; see also Exercise 2.9.

Algorithm 2.33 relies on picking a random real number in $[0, 1]$ corresponding to each good. For this reason, it is not suitable for the standard (fixed-precision) Turing machine model of computation. On the other hand, with probability 1 all n prices are distinct, and sorting the goods by increasing prices results in a random permutation. Furthermore, since Algorithm 2.33 uses this sorted order only and is oblivious of the actual prices, it is equivalent to Algorithm 2.30. As we will see, the

---

[3] A necessary condition on π for this to happen is that $n - j \geq l$.

random variables representing actual prices are crucially important as well in the analysis.

The *economic setting* is as follows: each buyer i has *unit–demand* and 0–1 *valuations* over the goods she likes, i.e., she accrues unit utility from each good she likes, and she wishes to obtain at most one of them. The latter set is precisely the set of neighbors of i in G. If on arrival of i there are several of these which are still unmatched, i will pick the one having the smallest price. As stated above, with probability 1 there are no ties.[4] Therefore the buyers will maximize their utility as defined below.

2.7.3 Analysis of RANKING

Henceforth, we will call Algorithm 2.33 by the name RANKING as well, since it is equivalent to Algorithm 2.30. For analyzing this algorithm we will define two sets of random variables, u_i for $i \in B$ and r_j for $j \in S$. These will be called the *utility of buyer i* and the *revenue of good j*, respectively. Each run of RANKING defines these random variables as follows. If RANKING matches buyer i to good j, then define $u_i = 1 - p_j$ and $r_j = p_j$, where p_j is the price of good j in this run of RANKING. Clearly, p_j is also a random variable, which is defined by Step (1) of the algorithm. If i remains unmatched, define $u_i = 0$, and if j remains unmatched, define $r_j = 0$. Observe that, for each good j, $p_j \in [1/e, 1]$ and for each buyer i, $u_i \in [0, 1 - 1/e]$.

In this setting, the *consumer surplus* and *producer surplus* are

$$\mathbb{E}\left[\sum_i^n u_i\right] \quad \text{and} \quad \mathbb{E}\left[\sum_j^n r_j\right], \quad \text{respectively,}$$

where the expectations are over the randomization in Step (1) of the algorithm. Let M be the matching produced by RANKING and let random variable $|M|$ denote its size. Then the *total surplus* created by RANKING is $\mathbb{E}[|M|]$.

Algorithm 2.33 Algorithm RANKING: economic viewpoint.

1. **Initialization:** $\forall j \in S$, pick w_j independently and uniformly from $[0, 1]$. Set price $p_j \leftarrow e^{w_j - 1}$.
2. **Online buyer arrival:** When a buyer, say i, arrives, match her to the cheapest unmatched good she likes; if there are none that she likes, leave i unmatched.

Output the matching, M, that has been found.

A key idea in the analysis of Algorithm 2.33 is a new random variable, u_e, for each edge $e \in E$ of graph G. This is called the *threshold for edge e* and is given in Definition 2.37. This random variable can be brought into play once we separate the contribution of each matched edge (i, j) into the utility of buyer i and the revenue of good j; this is done in Lemma 2.34. Next, using the threshold, we establish in Lemma 2.37 that, for each edge (i, j) in the graph, the total expected contribution of u_i and r_j is at least $1 - 1/e$. Then, the linearity of the expectation operator allows us

---

[4] Of course, in practice we will use Algorithm 2.30, which has no ambiguity.

to reassemble the $2n$ terms on the right-hand side of Lemma 2.34 in such a way that they are aligned with a perfect matching in G, and this yields Theorem 2.39.

Lemma 2.34. *The following holds:*

$$\mathbb{E}[|M|] = \sum_i^n \mathbb{E}[u_i] + \sum_j^n \mathbb{E}[r_j].$$

Proof By definition of the random variables,

$$\mathbb{E}[|M|] = \mathbb{E}\left[\sum_{i=1}^n u_i + \sum_{j=1}^n r_j\right] = \sum_i^n \mathbb{E}[u_i] + \sum_j^n \mathbb{E}[r_j],$$

where the first equality follows from the fact that if $(i,j) \in M$ then $u_i + r_j = 1$ and the second equality follows from the linearity of expectation. ☐

While running Algorithm 2.33, assume that the adversary has picked the order of arrival of buyers, say $\rho(B)$, and Step (1) has been executed. We next define several ways of executing Step (2). Let $\mathcal{R}$ denote the run of Step (2) on the entire graph G. Corresponding to each good j, let G_j denote graph G with vertex j removed. Define $\mathcal{R}_j$ to be the run of Step (2) on graph G_j.

Lemma 2.35 and Corollary 2.36 below establish a relationship between the sets of available goods for a buyer i in the two runs $\mathcal{R}$ and $\mathcal{R}_j$; the latter is crucially used in the proof of Lemma 2.38. For ease of notation in proving these two facts, let us renumber the buyers so that their order of arrival under $\rho(B)$ is $1, 2, \ldots, n$. Let $T(i)$ and $T_j(i)$ denote the sets of unmatched goods at the time of arrival of buyer i (i.e., just before buyer i gets matched) in the graphs G and G_j, in runs $\mathcal{R}$ and $\mathcal{R}_j$, respectively. Similarly, let $S(i)$ and $S_j(i)$ denote the set of unmatched goods that buyer i is incident to in G and G_j, in runs $\mathcal{R}$ and $\mathcal{R}_j$, respectively. We have assumed that Step (1) of Algorithm 2.33 has already been executed and a price p_k has been assigned to each good k. With probability 1, the prices are all distinct. Let L denote the set containing $(1 - p_k)$ for each good k, i.e., $L = \{1 - p_k | k \in A\}$. Let L_1 and L_2 be subsets of L containing goods k such that $1 - p_k > 1 - p_j$ and $1 - p_k < 1 - p_j$, respectively.

Lemma 2.35. *For each i, $1 \le i \le n$, the following hold:*

1. $(T_j(i) \cap L_1) = (T(i) \cap L_1)$.
2. $(T_j(i) \cap L_2) \subseteq (T(i) \cap L_2)$.

Proof Clearly, in both runs, $\mathcal{R}$ and $\mathcal{R}_j$, any buyer i having an available good in L_1 will match to the most profitable one of these, leaving the rest of the goods untouched. Since $j \in L_1$, the two runs behave in an identical manner on the set L_1, thereby proving the first statement.

The proof of the second statement is by induction on i. The base case is trivially true since $j \in L_2$.

Assume that the statement is true for $i = k$ and let us prove it for $i = k + 1$. By the first statement, the available goods for the $(k + 1)$th buyer in L_1 in the runs $\mathcal{R}$ and $\mathcal{R}_j$ are identical and if there are such goods, the second statement is obviously true. Next assume that there are no such goods. Assume that in run $\mathcal{R}_j$, the buyer gets matched to good l; if she remains unmatched, we will take l to be null. Clearly, l is the most profitable good she is incident to in $T_j(k)$. Therefore, the most profitable good she is incident to in run $\mathcal{R}$ is the better of l, the most profitable good in $T(k) - T_j(k)$, and j, if it is available. In each of these cases, the induction step holds. □

Corollary 2.36. *For each i, $1 \le i \le n$, the following hold:*

1. $(S_j(i) \cap L_1) = (S(i) \cap L_1)$.
2. $(S_j(i) \cap L_2) \subseteq (S(i) \cap L_2)$.

Next we define a new random variable, u_e, for each edge $e = (i, j)$ E. This is called the *threshold* for edge e and is given in Definition 2.37. It is critically used in the proofs of Lemmas 2.38 and 2.40.

Definition 2.37. Let $e = (i, j) \in E$ be an arbitrary edge in G. Define a new random variable, u_e, called the *threshold for edge e*, to be the utility of buyer i in run $\mathcal{R}_j$. Clearly, $u_e \in [0, 1 - 1/e]$.

Lemma 2.38. *Corresponding to each edge $(i, j) \in E$, the following hold.*

1. $u_i \ge u_e$, *where u_i and u_e are the utilities of buyer i in runs $\mathcal{R}$ and $\mathcal{R}_j$, respectively.*
2. *Let $z \in [0, 1 - 1/e]$. Conditioned on $ue = z$, if $p_j < 1$ then j will definitely be matched in run $\mathcal{R}_j$.*

Proof **1.** By Corollary 2.36, i has more options in run $\mathcal{R}$ as compared with run $\mathcal{R}_j$, and therefore $u_i \ge u_e$.

2. In run $\mathcal{R}$, if j is already matched when i arrives, there is nothing to prove. So assume that j is not matched. The crux of the matter is to prove that i does not have any option that is better than j. Since $p_j < 1 - z$, $S_j(i) \cap L_1 = 0$ and therefore $S(i) \cap L_1 = 0$. Finally, since buyer i gets more utility from j than from any good available to her in L_2, she must get matched to j. □

Remark 2.39. The random variable u_e is called the threshold because of the second statement in Lemma 2.38. It defines a value such that whenever p_j is smaller than this value, j is definitely matched in run $\mathcal{R}$.

The intuitive reason for the next, and most crucial, lemma is the following. The smaller u_e is, the larger is the range of values for p_j, namely $[0, 1 - u_e)$, over which (i, j) will be matched and j will accrue revenue p_j. Integrating p_j over this range, and adding $\mathbb{E}[u_i]$ to it, gives the desired bound. Crucial to this argument is the fact that p_j is independent of u_e. This follows from the fact that u_e is determined by run $\mathcal{R}_j$ on graph G_j, which does not contain vertex j.

Lemma 2.40. *Corresponding to each edge $(i, j) \in E$,*

$$\mathbb{E}[u_i + r_j] \ge 1 - \frac{1}{e}.$$

Proof By the first part of Lemma 2.38, $\mathbb{E}[u_i] \ge \mathbb{E}[u_e]$.

Next, we will lower-bound $\mathbb{E}[r_j]$. Let $z \in [0, 1 - 1/e]$, and let us condition on the event $u_e = z$. The critical observation is that u_e is determined by run $\mathcal{R}_j$. This is conducted on graph G_j, which does not contain vertex j. Therefore u_e is independent of p_j. By the second part of Lemma 2.38, $r_j = p_j$ whenever $p_j < 1 - z$. We will ignore the contribution to $\mathbb{E}[r_j]$ when $p_j \geq 1 - z$. Let w be such that $e^{w-1} = 1 - z$.

When $p_j < 1 - z$, the random variable r_j is defined as follows: pick x uniformly at random from $[0, w)$ and let r_j be e^{x-1}. Therefore,

$$\mathbb{E}[r_j \mid u_e = z] \geq \int_0^w e^{x-1}\, dx = e^{w-1} - \frac{1}{e} = 1 - \frac{1}{e} - z.$$

Let $f_{u_e}(z)$ be the probability density function of u_e; clearly, $f_{u_e}(z) = 0$ for $z \notin [0, 1 - 1/e]$. Therefore,

$$\mathbb{E}[r_j] = \mathbb{E}[\mathbb{E}[r_j \mid u_e]] = \int_{z=0}^{1-1/e} \mathbb{E}[r_j \mid u_e = z] f_{u_e}(z) dz$$

$$\geq \int_{z=0}^{1-1/e} \left(1 - \frac{1}{e} - z\right) f_{u_e}(z) dz = 1 - \frac{1}{e} - \mathbb{E}[u_e],$$

where the first equality follows from the law of total expectation and the inequality follows from the fact that we have ignored the contribution to $\mathbb{E}[r_j \mid u_e]$ when $p_j \geq 1 - z$. Hence we get

$$\mathbb{E}[u_i + r_j] = \mathbb{E}[u_i] + \mathbb{E}[r_j] \geq 1 - \frac{1}{e}. \qquad \square$$

Remark 2.41. Observe that Lemma 2.40 is a statement that is not about i and j being matched to each other, but about the utility accrued by i and the revenue accrued by j by being matched to various goods and buyers, respectively, over the randomization executed in Step (1) of Algorithm 2.33.

Theorem 2.42. *The competitive ratio of RANKING is at least* $1 - 1/e$.

Proof Let P denote a perfect matching in G. The expected size of the matching produced by RANKING is

$$\mathbb{E}[|M|] = \sum_i^n \mathbb{E}[u_i] + \sum_j^n \mathbb{E}[r_j] = \sum_{(i,j) \in P} \mathbb{E}[u_i + r_j] \geq n\left(1 - \frac{1}{e}\right),$$

where the first equality uses Lemma 2.34, the second follows from the linearity of expectation, and the inequality follows from Lemma 2.40 and the fact that $|P| = n$. The theorem follows. See Figure 2.2. $\qquad \square$

2.7.4 Upper-Bounding the Performance of Any Randomized Algorithm

In this section we will show, using the power of Von Neumann's minimax theorem (in particular Lemma 2.44, which is derived from the minimax theorem), that the competitive ratio of *any* randomized online matching algorithm is bounded by

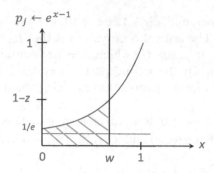

Figure 2.2 The shaded area is a lower bound on $\mathbb{E}[r_j | u_e = z]$.

$(1 - 1/e) + o(1)$, thereby showing that RANKING is the optimal algorithm up to an $o(1)$ term.

2.7.4.1 Sets of Algorithms and Inputs

Let I denote an input, involving n buyers and n goods, to RANKING. We will assume that the buyers in I have been ordered in the order of arrival dictated by the adversary. Algorithm 2.30 is randomized, i.e., it uses the flips of a fair coin to execute its steps. In particular, when run on input I, this algorithm uses the coin flips to randomly permute the n goods. Let $\mathcal{A}$ denote the deterministic part of this algorithm and, for each permutation π on $\{1, \ldots, n\}$, let $(\mathcal{A}, \pi)$ denote the algorithm which permutes the n goods according to π before running $\mathcal{A}$ on the given instance.

Consider the collection of $n!$ deterministic algorithms $(\mathcal{A}, \pi)$ for all possible permutations π. Let $\mathcal{A}_1, \ldots, \mathcal{A}_m$, for $m = n!$, be an arbitrary numbering of these deterministic algorithms. Clearly, the expected performance of Algorithm 2.30 on I is the same as the expected performance of an algorithm picked from the uniform probability distribution over this collection on I.

Consider the collection of all possible graphs in which n buyers and n goods have a perfect matching. We will assume that the buyers have been renumbered so that the adversarial order of arrival is $1, \ldots, n$. This is the set of all possible inputs of size n. Let k be its cardinality and let the set be $\{I_1, \ldots, I_k\}$.

2.7.4.2 Von Neumann's Minimax Theorem and Its Useful Consequence

In this subsection we will introduce *two-player zero-sum games* using the sets defined in Section 2.7.4.1. Let A denote a $k \times m$ matrix with non-negative real entries; A is called the *payoff matrix* of the game. The rows of A represent inputs the $I_1, \ldots, I_k$ and its columns represent the algorithms $\mathcal{A}_1, \ldots, \mathcal{A}_m$. The (i, j)th entry of A, $A(i, j)$, is the size of matching computed when algorithm $\mathcal{A}_j$ is run on instance I_i.

The two players of the game are the *row player* and the *column player*; they can be thought of as the *adversary* and the *algorithm designer*, respectively. The *pure strategy* of the row (column) player are to pick one of the rows (columns) of A. If the row player picks row i and the column player picks column j then the row player will pay $A(i, j)$ to the column player.

The column player's goal is to maximize her payoff and the row player's goal is to minimize the amount he pays. The name "zero-sum" refers sto the fact that the amount won by the column player is precisely the amount lost by the row player.

Observe that the row player should be prepared to pay the maximum entry in row i, since the column player can pick a column having such an entry. Therefore in order to minimize the amount he pays, the row player should pick that row in which the maximum entry is as small as possible, i.e., $\min_i \max_j A(i,j)$.

Similarly, in any column j the column player is guaranteed only the minimum entry, since the row player has the option of picking such a row. Therefore, the column player should pick that column j in which the smallest entry is as large as possible, i.e., $\max_j \min_i A(i,j)$. In general, $\min_i \max_j A(i,j) \neq \max_j \min_i A(i,j)$; see Exercise 2.10.

We next introduce the notion of mixed strategies, under which equality is guaranteed. A real-valued vector will be called a *probability vector* if its entries are non-negative and add up to 1. A *mixed strategy* of the row (column) player is a probability vector of dimension k (m); henceforth, these will be denoted by p and q, respectively. Thus the row player will pick a row, say i, from distribution p and the column player will pick a column, say j, from distribution q. If so, the *expected payoff* to the column player is $p^T A q$. The central fact about zero-sum games is the following.

Theorem 2.43 (Von Neumann's minimax theorem). *The minimax theorem states that*

$$\min_p \max_q p^T A q = \max_q \min_p p^T A q.$$

The quantity on either side of the equality in Theorem 2.43 is called the *value of game A* and will be denoted by $v(A)$. Once the row player has picked strategy p, the payoff $p^T A q$ is a linear function of the entries of q and hence is optimized by picking q to be a specific column. A similar remark applies to the choice of p, once q has been picked by the column player. Hence we get the following simpler form:

$$\min_p \max_j p^T A e_j = \max_q \min_i e_i^T A q,$$

where e_i and e_j are k- and m-dimensional unit vectors having ones in the ith and jth components, respectively.

Next assume that p and q are *arbitrary* probability vectors of dimensions k and m, respectively. Then clearly

$$\max_j p^T A e_j \;\geq\; v(A) \;\geq\; \min_i e_i^T A q. \tag{2.1}$$

We will use inequality (2.1) to upper-bound the performance of RANKING. We will take q to be the uniform probability distribution on the algorithms $\mathcal{A}_1, \ldots, \mathcal{A}_m$. This is equivalent to picking π at random, i.e., it is equivalent to running RANKING on the given input. Therefore, the right-hand side is the expected size of matching produced by RANKING on the worst input. This is precisely the quantity we wish to upper-bound.

To this end, we have the freedom of choosing a probability distribution p over all possible inputs of size n. Once we choose p, we need to determine the best algorithm, say $\mathcal{A}_j$, for an input picked from this distribution. Then, according to inequality (2.1), the expected performance of $\mathcal{A}_j$ on this input provides an upper bound. The distribution p is given below in Section 2.7.4.3.

For now, let us extract a general statement from inequality (2.1) so that it can be used for upper-bounding the performance of an arbitrary randomized algorithm. As for RANKING, a randomized algorithm can be viewed as a distribution over a suitable collection of deterministic algorithms. Let q represent this distribution and $\mathcal{M}_q$ represent the randomized algorithm we are studying. Then $\mathbb{E}[\mathcal{M}_q(I_i)]$ is the performance of this algorithm on input I_i.

In order to upper-bound this performance, we need to pick a suitable distribution p over the inputs such that the performance of the best algorithm, $\mathcal{M}_j$, on this distribution can be ascertained. The upper bound we obtain as a consequence is $\mathbb{E}[\mathcal{M}_j(I_p)]$. This is encapsulated in Lemma 2.44, whose proof follows from inequality (2.1).

Lemma 2.44 (Yao's lemma). *Let $\mathcal{M}_q$ and p be the randomized algorithm and probability distribution over inputs defined above. Then*

$$\max_j \ \mathbb{E}[\mathcal{M}_j(I_p)] \ \geq \ \min_i \ \mathbb{E}[\mathcal{M}_q(I_i)],$$

i.e., the expected performance of the best deterministic algorithm on an input picked from the chosen distribution is an upper bound on the worst-case performance of randomized algorithm $\mathcal{M}_q$.

2.7.4.3 Upper-Bounding the Performance of RANDOM

In this subsection we will give the distribution p on inputs promised above as well as the best deterministic algorithm for inputs chosen from p. For the distribution given below, it turns out that *every* deterministic greedy algorithm has optimal performance, making the second task fairly simple.

Let T denote an $n \times n$ *upper triangular matrix* such that $T(i,j) = 1$ if $i \leq j$ and 0 otherwise. For each permutation, π, let (T, π) denote the instance in which the rows of T are permuted according to π, and let q denote the uniform distribution on these $n!$ instances. We will assume that for any instance picked from this distribution, the adversarial order of arrival of columns is $n, n-1, \ldots, 1$. We will associate the notion of discrete *time* with the arrival of columns. It will be convenient to assume that the time starts at n and goes down to 1, i.e., it flows in the order $n, n-1, \ldots, 1$.

Consider a run of a greedy deterministic algorithm on an instance picked from distribution p and consider the set of rows to which column t can be matched. Clearly, this is the subset of the first t rows of T which are unmatched at time t; observe that T is the unpermuted upper triangular matrix. We will call this the *set of eligible rows at time t*.

The proof of the next lemma follows via an easy induction.

Lemma 2.45. *Consider a run of a greedy deterministic algorithm on inputs from distribution p and a run of RANDOM on T. Then:*

1. *In both the runs, at each time t, if the set of eligible rows has cardinality k then these rows are equally likely to be any k of the first t rows of T.*
2. *At each time t, the probability that the set of eligible rows has cardinality k is the same for both runs.*

The proof of the next lemma is left as Exercise 2.11.

Lemma 2.46. *The performance of any greedy deterministic algorithm on an instance drawn from distribution p is the same as that of RANDOM on T.*

Lemma 2.47. *The expected size of the matching found by RANDOM when run on instance T is at most $(1 - 1/e)n + o(n)$.*

Proof Let $c(t)$ and $r(t)$ be random variables representing the numbers of eligible columns and rows, respectively, at time t in a run of RANDOM on T. Observe that both random variables will monotonically decrease with decreasing t, and at the first time when $r(t) = 0$, the remaining columns cannot be matched and the algorithm stops. Until this time, the expected change in $c(t)$ is

$$\Delta(c) = c(t) - c(t+1) = -1,$$

since the column arriving at time t becomes ineligible.

Next, let us obtain an expression for the expected change in $r(t)$ until $r(t) = 0$ is reached. We have $\Delta(r) = r(t) - r(t+1)$. The number of eligible rows decreases for two reasons. First, it decreases because the row that is matched to column t becomes ineligible.

An additional decrease takes place if, at time t, row t is eligible and is not matched to column t; if so, row t also becomes ineligible. By the first fact given in Lemma 2.45, the eligible rows at time t are equally likely to be any $r(t)$ out of the first $c(t)$ rows. Therefore the probability that they include row t is $r(t)/c(t)$. Since the algorithm matches column t to a random eligible row, the conditional probability that it matches column t to a row different from t, given that row t is eligible, is $r(t) - 1/r(t)$. Taking the product of these two gives the expected additional decrease in $r(t)$. Therefore,

$$\mathbb{E}[\Delta(r)] = -1 - \frac{r(t)}{c(t)} \frac{(r(t) - 1)}{r(t)}.$$

Taking a ratio of expectations we get

$$\frac{\mathbb{E}[\Delta(r)]}{\mathbb{E}[\Delta(c)]} = 1 + \frac{r(t) - 1}{c(t)}.$$

Applying Kurtz' theorem, we find that as n tends to infinity, with probability tending to 1 the solution to this difference equation is closely approximated by the solution to the following differential equation with initial condition $c(n) = n$ and $r(n) = n$:

$$\frac{dr}{dc} = 1 + \frac{r(t) - 1}{c(t)}.$$

The solution to this differential equation is

$$r = 1 + c \left(\frac{n-1}{n} + \ln \frac{c}{n} \right).$$

It is easy to see that when $r(t) = 1$, $c(t) = n/e + o(n)$. The lemma follows. $\square$

Finally, Theorem 2.42 and Lemmas 2.44, 2.46, and 2.47 give:

Theorem 2.48. *RANKING is an optimal online bipartite matching algorithm up to an $o(1)$ term.*

Remark 2.49. The expected sizes of the matchings found by RANKING and RANDOM are the same for the instance T; see Exercise 2.12. Therefore, if one could show that T is the worst instance for RANKING, then Lemmas 2.44 and 2.46 would directly prove the optimality of RANKING.

2.8 Exercises

Exercise 2.1 [10] Observe that, under ordinal utilities, stochastic dominance leads only to a partial order over the set of possible allocations to one agent. Instead, if we compare allocations using lexicographic preferences, we obtain a total order. Let $x = (x_1, \ldots, x_n)$ and $y = (y_1, \ldots, y_n)$ be two allocations for agent i, where the goods have been ordered according to i's preference list. We will say that x is *lexicographically better* than y if $x_k > y_k$ where k is the first index j for which $x_j \neq y_j$. Show that, with respect to lexicographic preferences, PS enjoys all four properties of time-efficiency, Pareto optimality, envy-freeness and strategy-proofness.

    Hint: For strategyproofness, show and use the fact that for any false preference list given by agent i there is some good j that is *sacrificed*, in the sense that i obtains less of j in the false run than in the true run, thereby obtaining a lexicographically inferior allocation.

Exercise 2.2 Consider the following instance of HZ: it has $n = 2$ and utility functions $u_{11} = u_{21} = u_{22} = 1$ and $u_{12} = 0$. The prices $(2, 0)$ and the allocation $x_{11} = x_{12} = x_{21} = x_{22} = 0.5$ form an equilibrium. However, observe that agent 1 is not allocated a minimum-cost utility-maximizing bundle. Find an equilibrium in which the latter property also holds. Then compute the utilities accrued and thereby show that the above-stated allocation is not Pareto optimal.

    Hint: Let the prices be $(1, p)$, for any $p \in [0, 1]$.

Exercise 2.3 [13] Let (x, p) be an equilibrium for an HZ instance I. Prove that an HZ equilibrium is invariant under the following operations.

(a) *Scaling the difference of prices from 1.* Fix $r > 0$ and obtain p' from p as follows: $\forall j \in G, p'_j - 1 = r(p_j - 1)$. Then (x, p') is also an equilibrium.

(b) *Affine transformation of the utility function of any agent.* Let i's utility function be $u_i = \{u_{i1}, u_{i12}, \ldots, u_{in}\}$. For any two numbers $s > 0$ and $h \geq 0$, define $u'_i = \{u'_{i1}, u'_{i12}, \ldots, u'_{in}\}$ as follows: $\forall j \in G, u'_{ij} = su_{ij} + h$. Let I' be the instance obtained by replacing u_i by u'_i in I. Then (p, x) is an equilibrium for I if and only if it is an equilibrium for I'.

    Hint: Start by writing an LP whose optimal solutions capture optimal bundles to an agent i for given prices p.

Remark 2.50. Observe the fundamentally different ways in which an HZ equilibrium and a Nash bargaining solution change under an affine transformation of the utilities of agents.

Exercise 2.4 [13] Define a *bivalued utilities case* of HZ as follows. For each agent i, consider a set $\{a_i, b_i\}$, where $0 \leq a_i < b_i$, and the utilities u_{ij}, $\forall j \in G$, are picked from this set. The *dichotomous utilities case* is a special case of the bivalued utilities case in which, for each agent i, $a_i = 0$ and $b_i = 1$. Use Exercise 2.3 to give a reduction from the bivalued utilities case to the dichotomous utilities case of HZ.

Exercise 2.5 Recall that Example 2.22 gives an instance of ADHZ which does not admit an equilibrium. Another natural extension of HZ worth studying is a two-sided matching market under cardinal utilities and using a pricing mechanism. Give a suitable model for such a market and define the notion of equilibrium for it. Does your model admit an equilibrium? Give a proof or a counterexample.

Exercise 2.6 [5] For an exchange market, the *demand graph* is a directed graph with agents as vertices and with an edge (i,j) if for a good k which agent j has in her initial endowment, $u_{ik} > 0$. In the case of an Arrow–Debreu market with linear utilities, a sufficiency condition for the existence of equilibrium is that this graph be strongly connected. Is this condition sufficient to overcome counterexamples to the existence of an equilibrium in ADHZ as well? Via a counterexample, provide a negative answer to this question. Additionally, ensure that the counterexample has dichotomous utilities, i.e., 0/1 utilities.

Exercise 2.7 Prove that in a bipartite graph, the size of a maximal matching is at least half that of a maximum matching. Via an example, show that the bound one-half is tight.

Let $\mathcal{A}$ be any deterministic online bipartite matching algorithm. Show that the adversary can produce a bipartite graph $G = (B, S, E)$ and an order of arrival of buyers $\rho(B)$ on which $\mathcal{A}$ finds a matching of size exactly half the perfect matching.

Exercise 2.8 Consider the following $n/2$ experiments and random variables: for $1 \leq i \leq n/2$, pick a random element from the set $\{0, 1, \ldots, i\}$ and define X_i to be 1 if 0 is picked and 0 otherwise. Prove that

$$\mathbb{E}[k] \leq \sum_{i=1}^{n/2} \mathbb{E}[X_i] = O(\log n),$$

where k was defined in Example 2.31.

Exercise 2.9 In Step 1 of Algorithm 2.33, try other distributions for the prices of goods, e.g., the uniform distribution on $[0, 1]$. Is there a distribution that yields a ratio larger than $(1 - 1/e)$ by a small amount, i.e., $o(1)$?

Exercise 2.10 Let A be the $k \times m$ payoff matrix of a zero-sum game in which the row player is attempting to minimize the amount he pays and the column player is maximizing the amount she gets.
(a) Prove that $\min_i \max_j A(i,j) \geq \max_j \min_i A(i,j)$.
(b) Give an example of a game in which $\min_i \max_j A(i,j) > \max_j \min_i A(i,j)$.
(c) Prove the minimax theorem using the LP-duality theorem.

Exercise 2.11 Prove Lemma 2.46 by using the two facts given in Lemma 2.45.

Exercise 2.12 Prove that the expected size of matching found by RANKING and RANDOM is the same for the instance T, i.e., the complete upper triangular matrix.

2.9 Bibliographic Notes

The mechanisms RP and PS are due to [1], HZ is due to [6], α-Slack is due to [4], and ϵ-approximate ADHZ is due to [5]. The TTC mechanism was discovered by David Gale and reported in [9]. Example 2.22 is from [6].

The result presented in Section 2.7 is due to [8]. The analysis of RANKING presented here is due to [11]; it draws on ideas due to [2] and [3]. The minimax theorem is due to [12], and Lemma 2.44, which builds on the minimax theorem, is due to [14]. Kurtz's theorem is from [7].

References

[1] Bogomolnaia, Anna, and Moulin, Hervé. 2001. A new solution to the random assignment problem. *Journal of Economic Theory*, **100**(2), 295–328.

[2] Devanur, Nikhil R., Jain, Kamal, and Kleinberg, Robert D. 2013. Randomized primal–dual analysis of ranking for online bipartite matching. In: *Proc. 24th Annual ACM-SIAM Symposium on Discrete Algorithms*, pages 101–107. SIAM.

[3] Eden, Alon, Feldman, Michal, Fiat, Amos, and Segal, Kineret. 2021. An economic-based analysis of ranking for online bipartite matching. In: *Proc. SIAM Symposium on Simplicity in Algorithms*.

[4] Echenique, Federico, Miralles, Antonio, and Zhang, Jun. 2019. Constrained pseudo-market equilibrium. *arXiv preprint arXiv:1909.05986*.

[5] Garg, Jugal, Trobst, Thorben, and Vazirani, Vijay V. 2020. One-sided matching markets with endowments: Equilibria and algorithms. In *Proc. International Conference on Autonomous Agents and Multi-agent Systems (AAMAS)* (2022).

[6] Hylland, Aanund, and Zeckhauser, Richard. 1979. The efficient allocation of individuals to positions. *Journal of Political Economy*, **87**(2), 293–314.

[7] Kurtz, Thomas G. 1970. Solutions of ordinary differential equations as limits of pure jump markov processes. *Journal of Applied Probability*, **7**(1), 49–58.

[8] Karp, Richard M., Vazirani, Umesh V., and Vazirani, Vijay V. An optimal algorithm for on-line bipartite matching. In: *Proc. 22nd Annual ACM Symposium on Theory of Computing*, pages 352–358.

[9] Shapley, Lloyd, and Scarf, Herbert. 1974. On cores and indivisibility. *Journal of Mathematical Economics*, **1**(1), 23–37.

[10] Schulman, Leonard J., and Vazirani, Vijay V., 2015. Allocation of divisible goods under lexicographic preferences. In: *Proc. Conference on Foundations of Software Technology and Theoretical Computer Science*.

[11] Vazirani, Vijay V. 2022. Online bipartite matching and adwords. In *47th International Symposium on Mathematical Foundations of Computer Science*.

[12] von Neumann, John. 1928. Zur Theorie der Gesellschaftsspiele. *Mathematische Annalen*, **100**(1), 295–320, 1928.

[13] Vazirani, Vijay V. and Yannakakis, Mihalis. 2020. Computational complexity of the Hylland–Zeckhauser scheme for one-sided matching markets. In: *Proc. Conference on Innovations in Theoretical Computer Science*.

[14] Yao, Andrew C. C., 1977. Probabilistic computations: Towards a unified measure of complexity. In: *Proc. 18th Annual IEEE Symposium on Foundations of Computer Science*, pages 222–227.

CHAPTER THREE

Matching Markets with Transfers and Salaries

Federico Echenique, Nicole Immorlica, and Vijay V. Vazirani

3.1 Introduction

In the previous two chapters we studied how matches are made in matching markets based only on the preferences of agents over other agents or objects; in particular, a transfer of money is not involved in these markets. They are called *non-transferable utility (NTU) markets*. In contrast, there are fundamental matching markets, such as the labor market, in which monetary transfers, in the form of salaries, prices, or other terms (e.g., benefits) form an integral part of each match. These are called *transferable utility (TU) markets* and are the subject of this chapter. In most of this chapter we will assume that the utilities of the agents are stated in monetary terms and that side payments are allowed in transactions.

The *core* is a quintessential solution concept in this theory. It captures all possible ways of distributing the total worth of a game among individual agents so that the grand coalition remains intact, i.e., a sub-coalition will not be able to generate more profits by itself and therefore has no incentive to secede from the grand coalition. The core provides profound insights into the negotiating power of individuals and sub-coalitions. In particular, under a core imputation, the profit allocated to an agent is consistent with their negotiating power, i.e., their worth, see Section 3.2.3, and therefore the core is viewed as a "fair" profit-sharing mechanism.

In this chapter, we will study the core in the context of the *assignment game*, using in particular the setting of a housing market. The pristine structural properties of this game make it a paradigmatic setting for studying the intricacies of this solution concept, with a view to tackling profit-sharing in real-life situations. We will analyze the core of the assignment game using ideas from matching theory, LP-duality theory, and their non-trivial interplay.

The results given in Section 3.2 naturally raise the question of viewing core imputations through the lens of complementarity; this is done in Section 3.2.1. It yields a relationship between the competitiveness of individuals and teams of agents and the amount of profit they accrue, where by *competitiveness* we mean whether an individual or a team is matched in every, some, or no maximum matching. This viewpoint also sheds light on the phenomenon of *degeneracy* in assignment games, i.e., the situation when the maximum weight matching is not unique.

The generalization of the assignment game to general graphs, which include bipartite as well as non-bipartite graphs, is called the *general graph-matching game*. Whereas the core of this game is always non-empty, that of the general graph-matching game can indeed be empty. In Section 3.3, we show how to deal with this situation by using the notion of an approximate core.

In Section 3.4, we consider a many-to-one matching market, which may be interpreted as a labor market where monetary transfers represent salaries paid to workers. We first consider the case in which transfers are constrained to a discrete grid. Then, by taking the limit of an ever-finer discrete grid, we obtain a result for the model with a continuum of transfers. In Section 3.5, we introduce a model of matching with contracts in which the terms of employment between a firm and its workers may involve more than just salaries; in particular, it could involve benefits, medical leave, etc.

3.2 The Core Studied in a Paradigmatic Setting

We will study the *housing market* in the following setting. Let B be a set of n buyers and R a set of m sellers. Each seller $j \in R$ is attempting to sell her house, which she values at c_j dollars. Each buyer i has a valuation of h_{ij} dollars for house j. If $h_{ij} \geq c_j$ then there is a price at which this trade can happen in such a way that both agents are satisfied. Specifically, any p_j such that $c_j \leq p_j \leq h_{ij}$ is such a price, and it results in a *gain* or *profit* to agents i and j of:

$$v_i = h_{ij} - p_j \quad \text{or} \quad u_j = p_j - c_j,$$

respectively. If $h_{ij} < c_j$ then i and j will not be involved in this trade. If an agent does not trade at all, his/her gain will be zero. This motivates the following definition.

Definition 3.1. For $i \in B$ and $j \in R$, define the *worth w* of the coalition $\{i,j\}$ to be the total gain from this possible trade, i.e.,

$$w(\{i,j\}) = a_{ij} = \max\{0, h_{ij} - c_j\}.$$

We will extend this definition to the worth of an arbitrary coalition $S \subseteq (B \cup R)$; intuitively, it is the maximum gain possible via trades made within the set S. Clearly, if $|S| \leq 1$, no trades are possible and therefore $v(S) = 0$. For the same reason, if $S \subseteq B$ or $S \subseteq R$, $v(S) = 0$.

Definition 3.2. Let $S \subseteq (B \cup R)$ be a coalition and let $k = \min(|S \cap B|, |S \cap R|)$. Find k disjoint pairs $(i_1, j_1), \ldots, (i_k, j_k)$ of buyers and sellers from S such that the total gain from these k trades, i.e., $a_{i_1 j_1} + \cdots + a_{i_k j_k}$, is maximized. Then the *worth of S*, $w(S)$, is defined to be this total gain, and $w: 2^{B \cup R} \to \mathcal{R}_+$ is the *characteristic function* of the housing game.

Among the possible coalitions, the most important one is of course $B \cup R$; this is called *the grand coalition*. A important problem in economics is the following.

what are "good" ways of dividing the worth of the grand coalition among its agents? A quintessential solution concept in this respect is that of the *core*, which consists of ways of dividing the worth in such a way that no smaller coalition will have the incentive to secede and trade on its own.

However, before studying this concept, let us state explicitly some assumptions made in the housing game; these are implicit in the setting defined above. Despite these assumptions, the game still has a fair amount of flexibility, e.g., in the number of buyers and sellers participating and whether there is product differentiation. The assumptions are as follows.

1. The utilities of the agents are stated in monetary terms.
2. Side payments are allowed, in the form of prices.
3. The objects to be traded are indivisible.
4. The supply and demand functions are inflexible: each buyer wants at most one house and each seller has one house to sell.

The first two assumptions make this a *transferable utility (TU) market*. Recall that in the previous two chapters we studied the notion of the core in the context of NTU markets. We start by defining the core for the given TU setting.

Definition 3.3. An *imputation* for dividing the worth of the game, $w(B \cup R)$, among the agents consists of two non-negative vectors v and u specifying the gains conferred on agents, namely v_i for $i \in B$ and u_j for $j \in R$. An imputation (v, u) is said to be in the *core of the housing game* if for any coalition $S \subseteq (B \cup R)$, there is no way of dividing $w(S)$ among the agents in S in such a way that all agents are at least as well off and at least one agent is strictly better off than in the imputation (v, u).

An *assignment game* is defined as follows. Let $G = (B, R, E)$ be the complete bipartite graph over vertex sets B and R. The edge set E consists of edges (i, j) for all pairs $i \in B$ and $j \in R$. Let the weight function on E be given by a, i.e., the weight of (i, j) is a_{ij}. Finally, $w(B \cup R)$ is the weight of a maximum-weight matching in G. The assignment game asks for an imputation in the core.

Equation (3.1) below gives the LP-relaxation of the problem of finding a maximum-weight matching. In this program, the variable x_{ij} indicates the number of times that edge (i, j) is picked in the solution. The problem is as follows:

$$\max \quad \sum_{i \in B, j \in R} a_{ij} x_{ij}$$

$$\text{s.t.} \quad \sum_j x_{ij} \le 1 \quad \forall i \in B,$$

$$\sum_i x_{ij} \le 1 \quad \forall j \in R,$$

$$x_{ij} \ge 0 \quad \forall i \in B, \forall j \in R. \tag{3.1}$$

Taking v_i and u_j to be the dual variables for the first and second constraints of (3.1), we obtain the dual LP:

$$\min \quad \sum_{i \in B} v_i + \sum_{j \in R} u_j$$

$$\text{s.t.} \quad v_i + u_j \geq a_{ij} \quad \forall i \in B, \forall j \in R,$$

$$v_i \geq 0 \quad \forall i \in B,$$

$$u_j \geq 0 \quad \forall j \in R. \tag{3.2}$$

Theorem 3.4. *The imputation (v, u) is in the core of the assignment game if and only if it is an optimal solution to the dual LP (3.2).*

Proof It is well known that the LP-relaxation of the bipartite graph maximum-weight matching problem, namely (3.1), always has an optimal solution that is integral, i.e., there is always an optimal solution to this LP that has a maximum-weight matching in G. Let W be the weight of such a matching; clearly, $W = w(B, R)$.

Let (v, u) be an optimal solution to the dual LP (3.2). Then, by the LP-duality theorem,

$$\sum_{i \in B} v_i + \sum_{j \in R} u_j = W.$$

Therefore (v, u) is an imputation for distributing the worth of this game among the agents. Let $S \subseteq (B \cup R)$ and let $k = \min(|S \cap B|, |S \cap R|)$. By Definition 3.2, there are k disjoint buyer–seller pairs from S, say $(i_1, j_1), \ldots (i_k, j_k)$, such that $w(S) = (a_{i_1 j_1} + \cdots + a_{i_k j_k})$. By the first constraint of the dual LP, we have $v_{i_l} + u_{j_l} \geq a_{i_l j_l}$, for $1 \leq l \leq k$. Therefore, under the imputation (v, u), the total gain of agents in S is given by

$$\sum_{i \in S} v_i + \sum_{j \in S} u_j \geq (a_{i_1 j_1} + \cdots + a_{i_k j_k}) = w(S).$$

Therefore the agents in S cannot improve on their gain under (v, u) by trading among themselves. Hence (v, u) is in the core.

Next, let (v, u) be in the core of this game. By the definition of the core, for the coalition $\{i, j\}$, $i \in B$ and $j \in R$, we have $v_i + u_j \geq w(\{i, j\}) = a_{ij}$. Therefore (v, u) is a feasible solution to the dual LP. Again by the definition of the core, the total gain of the grand coalition is

$$\sum_{i \in B} v_i + \sum_{j \in R} u_j \geq w(B \cup R) = W.$$

Therefore (v, u) is an optimal solution to the dual LP. $\qquad \square$

3.2.1 The Core via the Lens of Complementarity

The worth of an assignment game is determined by an optimal solution to the primal LP (3.1) and each core imputation distributes it using an optimal solution to the dual LP (3.2). This fact naturally raises the question of viewing core imputations through the lens of complementarity.[1] This yields a relationship between the competitiveness of individuals and teams of agents and the amount of profit they accrue in imputations that lie in the core, where by *competitiveness* we mean whether an individual or a team is matched in every, some, or no optimal assignment. Additionally, it sheds light on the phenomenon of degeneracy in assignment games, i.e., the situation when the maximum-weight matching is not unique.

Observe that, in the housing market, the price at which a house is sold is completely determined by the core imputation that is chosen. In this section, we will use the following simpler setting to study the core of the assignment game. Suppose a tennis club has sets U and V of women and men players, respectively, who can participate in an upcoming mixed doubles tournament. Assume $|U| = m$ and $|V| = n$, where m, n are arbitrary. Let $G = (U, V, E)$ be a bipartite graph whose vertices are the women and men players and where an edge (u, v) represents the fact that agents $u \in U$ and $v \in V$ are eligible to participate as a mixed doubles team in the tournament. Let w be an edge-weight function for G, where $w_{uv} > 0$ represents the expected earnings if u and v do participate as a team in the tournament. The total worth of the game is the weight of a maximum-weight matching in G.

Assume that the club picks such a matching for the tournament. The question is how to distribute the total profit among the agents – strong players, weak players, and unmatched players – so that no subset of players feel they will be better off seceding and forming their own tennis club.

Definition 3.5. By a *team* we mean an edge in G; a generic team will be denoted as $e = (u, v)$. We will say that e is:

1. *essential* if e is matched in every maximum-weight matching in G;
2. *viable* if there is a maximum-weight matching M such that $e \in M$ and another, M', such that $e \notin M'$;
3. *subpar* if, for every maximum-weight matching M in G, $e \notin M$.

Definition 3.6. Let y be an imputation in the core of the game. We will say that e is *fairly paid in* y if $y_u + y_v = w_e$ and *overpaid* if $y_u + y_v > w_e$.[2] Finally, we will say that e is *always fairly paid* if it is fairly paid in every imputation in the core.

Definition 3.7. A generic player in $U \cup V$ will be denoted by q. We will say that q is:

1. *essential* if q is matched in every maximum-weight matching in G;
2. *viable* if there is a maximum-weight matching M such that q is matched in M and another, M', such that q is not matched in M';
3. *subpar* if, for every maximum-weight matching M in G, q is not matched in M.

Definition 3.8. Let y be an imputation in the core. We will say that *q gets paid in* y if $y_q > 0$ and *does not get paid* otherwise. Furthermore, q is *paid sometimes*

---

[1] Recall that the complementary slackness conditions for a primal–dual pair of LPs relate primal variables with dual constraints and dual variables with primal constraints.

[2] Observe that by the first constraint of the dual LP (3.2), these are the only possibilities.

if there is at least one imputation in the core under which q gets paid, and it is *never paid* if it is not paid under any imputation.

Theorem 3.9. *The following hold.*

1. *For every team $e \in E$:*

$$e \text{ is always paid fairly} \iff e \text{ is viable or essential.}$$

2. *For every player $q \in (U \cup V)$:*

$$q \text{ is paid sometimes} \iff q \text{ is essential.}$$

Proof The proofs of the two statements follow by applying complementary slackness conditions and strict complementarity to the primal LP (3.1) and dual LP (3.2). We will use Theorem 3.4, which states that the set of imputations in the core of the game is precisely the set of optimal solutions to the dual LP.

1. Let x and y be optimal solutions to LP (3.1) and LP (3.2), respectively. By the complementary slackness theorem, for each $e = (u, v) \in E$ we have $x_e(y_u + y_v - w_e) = 0$.

Suppose e is viable or essential. Then there is an optimal solution to the primal, say x, under which it is matched, i.e., $x_e > 0$. Let y be an arbitrary optimal dual solution. Then, by the complementary slackness theorem, $y_u + y_v = w_e$. Varying y over all optimal dual solutions, we find that e is always paid fairly. This proves the forward direction.

For the reverse direction, we will use strict complementarity. This implies that, corresponding to each team e, there is a pair of optimal primal and dual solutions x, y such that either $x_e = 0$ or $y_u + y_v = w_e$ but not both.

For team e, assume that the right-hand side of the first statement holds and that x, y is a pair of optimal solutions for which strict complementarity holds for e. Since $y_u + y_v = w_e$ it must be the case that $x_e > 0$. Now, since the polytope defined by the constraints of the primal LP (3.1) has integral optimal vertices, there is a maximum-weight matching under which e is matched. Therefore e is viable or essential and the left-hand side of the first statement holds.

2. The proof is along the same lines and will be stated more succinctly. Again, let x and y be optimal solutions to LP (3.1) and LP (3.2), respectively. By the complementary slackness theorem, for each $q \in (U \cup V)$ we have that $y_q(x(\delta(q)) - 1) = 0$. Suppose q is paid sometimes. Then, there is an imputation in the core, say y, such that $y_q > 0$. Therefore, for every primal optimal solution x, $x(\delta(q)) = 1$ and, in every maximum-weight matching in G, q is matched. Hence q is essential, proving the reverse direction.

Strict complementarity implies that, corresponding to each player q, there is a pair of optimal primal and dual solutions x, y such that either $y_q = 0$ or $x(\delta(q)) = 1$ but not both. Since we have already established that the second condition must hold for x, we obtain $y_q > 0$ and hence q is paid sometimes. $\square$

3.2.2 Consequences of Theorem 3.9

In this section, we will derive several useful consequences of Theorem 3.9.

1. Negating both sides of the first statement proved in Theorem 3.9 we get the following double implication. For every team $e \in E$,

$$e \text{ is subpar} \iff e \text{ is sometimes overpaid.}$$

Clearly, this statement is equivalent to the first statement of Theorem 3.9 and hence contains no new information. However, it may provide a new viewpoint. These two equivalent statements yield the following assertion, which at first sight seems incongruous with what we desire from the notion of the core and the just manner in which it allocates profits:

> *Whereas viable and essential teams are always paid fairly, subpar teams are sometimes overpaid.*

How can the core favor subpar teams over viable and essential teams? Here is an explanation. Even though u and v are strong players, the team (u, v) may be subpar because u and v do not play well together. On the one hand, u and v are allocated high profits since they generate large earnings while playing with other players. On the other hand, w_{uv} is small. Thus, this subpar team does not get overpaid while playing together but by teaming up with others.

2. The second statement of Theorem 3.9 is equivalent to the following: for every player $q \in (U \cup V)$,

$$q \text{ is never paid} \iff q \text{ is not essential.}$$

Thus core imputations pay only essential players. Since we have assumed that the weight of each edge is positive, so is the worth of the game, and all of it goes to essential players. This gives the next conclusion: in contrast, the set of essential teams may be empty, as is the case in Examples 3.13 and 3.14 in Section 3.2.3.

Corollary 3.10. *In the assignment game, the set of essential players is non-empty and, in every imputation, the entire worth of the game is distributed among the essential players.*

Corollary 3.10 is of much consequence: it tells us that the players who are allocated profits are precisely those who always play, i.e., independently of which sets of teams the tennis club picks. Furthermore, the identification of these players, and the exact manner in which the total profit is divided up among them, follows the negotiating process described in Section 3.2.3, in which each player ascertains his/her negotiating power on the basis of all possible sub-coalitions in which he/she participates.

Thus, by Theorem 3.4, each possible outcome of this very real process is captured by an inanimate object, namely an optimal solution to the dual LP (3.2). This is perhaps the most remarkable aspect of this theorem.

3. Clearly the worth of the game is generated by teams that do play. Assume that (u, v) is such a team in an optimal assignment. Since $x_{uv} > 0$, by complementary slackness we get that $y_u + y_v = w_{uv}$, where y is a core imputation. Thus core imputations distribute the worth generated by a team among its players only. In contrast, the two-thirds-approximate core imputation for the general graph matching game given in Section 3.3 distributes the worth generated by teams that play to non-playing agents as well, thereby making more use of the transferable utility (TU) aspect.

4. Next we use Theorem 3.9 to get insights into degeneracy. Examples 3.12 and 3.15 give a degenerate and a non-degenerate assignment game, respectively. Clearly, if an assignment game is non-degenerate then every team, and every player, is either always matched or always unmatched in the set of maximum=weight matchings in G, i.e., there are no viable teams or players. The next corollary characterizes the manner in which imputations in the core deal with players and teams in the presence of degeneracy.

Corollary 3.11. *In the presence of degeneracy, imputations in the core of an assignment game treat:*

- *viable and essential teams in the same way, namely they are always fairly paid.*
- *viable and subpar players in the same way, namely they are never paid.*

Example 3.12. An instance has $n = 3$ and $m = 2$. Table 3.1 gives the gains accrued by the various pairs of agents. This instance is degenerate; it has two maximum-weight matchings: $\{(b_1, r_1), (b_3, r_2)\}$ and $\{(b_2, r_1), (b_3, r_2)\}$, both of weight 190.

Table 3.1 Gains from all possible trades.

	r_1	r_2
b_1	100	0
b_2	100	70
b_3	0	90

3.2.3 Insights Provided by the Core into the Negotiating Power of Agents

Example 3.13. Consider an assignment game whose bipartite graph has two edges, $(u, v_1), (u, v_2)$, joining the three agents u, v_1, v_2. Clearly, one of v_1 and v_2 will be left out in any matching. First assume that the weight of both edges is 1. If so, the unique imputation in the core gives zero to v_1 and v_2, and 1 to u. Next assume that the weights of the two edges are 1 and $1 + \epsilon$ respectively, for a small $\epsilon > 0$. If so, the unique imputation in the core gives $0, \epsilon$, and 1 to v_1, v_2, and u, respectively.

How fair are the imputations given in Example 3.13? As stated in the Introduction to this chapter, imputations in the core have much to do with the negotiating power of individuals and sub-coalitions. Let us argue that when the imputations given above are viewed from this angle, they are fair in that the profit allocated to an agent is consistent with his/her negotiating power, i.e., his/her worth. In the first case, whereas u has alternatives, v_1 and v_2 do not. As a result, u will squeeze out all profits from whoever she plays with, by threatening to partner with the other player. Therefore v_1 and v_2 have to be content with no rewards! In the second case, u can always threaten to match up with v_2. Therefore v_1 has to be content with a profit of ϵ only.

In an arbitrary assignment game $G = (U, V, E), w$, we have by Theorem 3.9 that

$$q \text{ is never paid} \iff q \text{ is not essential}$$

Thus core imputations reward only those agents who always play. This raises the following question: can't a non-essential player, say q, team up with another player, say p, and secede, by promising p almost all the resulting profit? The answer is "No", because the dual (3.2) has the constraint $y_q + y_p \geq w_{qp}$. Therefore, if $y_q = 0$ then $y_p \geq w_{qp}$, i.e., p will not gain by seceding together with q.

Example 3.14. Next, consider an assignment game whose bipartite graph has four edges, $(u_1, v_1), (u_1, v_2), (u_2, v_2), (u_2, v_3)$ joining the five agents u_1, u_2, v_1, v_2, v_3. Let the wights of these four edges be $1, 1.1, 1.1$, and 1, respectively. The worth of this game is clearly 2.1.

In Example 3.14, at first sight v_2 looks like the dominant player since he has two choices of partners, namely u_1 and u_2, and because teams involving him have the biggest earnings, namely 1.1 as opposed to 1. Yet, the unique core imputation in the core awards 1, 1, 0, 0.1, 0 to agents u_1, u_2, v_1, v_2, v_3, respectively.

The question arises: "Why is v_2 allocated only 0.1? Can't v_2 negotiate a higher profit, given its favorable circumstance?" The answer is "No". The reason is that u_1 and u_2 are in an even stronger position than v_2, since both of them have a ready partner available, namely v_1 and v_3, respectively, with whom each can earn 1. Therefore, the core imputation awards 1 to each of them, giving the leftover profit of 0.1 to v_2. Hence the core imputation has indeed allocated profits according to the negotiating power of each agent.

3.2.4 Extreme Imputations in the Core

In this subsection, we will build on Theorem 3.4 to characterize the extreme imputations that belong to the core of the housing game. First, observe that each imputation completely pins down the prices of all houses, since for each $j \in R$, $p_j = c_j + u_j$. Therefore, the prices contain no extra information and will be typically dropped from the discussion.

If i and j do trade then $v_i + u_j = a_{ij}$. Consequently, v_i and u_j both belong to the interval $[0, a_{ij}]$. The first question that arises is whether v_i, and therefore u_j, can take every value in this interval. The answer turns out to be very interesting, namely, it

Table 3.2 Buyers' valuations for houses.

	r_1	r_2
b_1	900	770
b_2	845	710

Table 3.3 Gains from all possible trades.

	r_1	r_2
b_1	100	70
b_2	45	10

depends on the other options that i and j have available, even if those options are not good trades and therefore i or j may never be able to exercise such options. Example 3.15 illustrates this phenomenon.

Example 3.15. An instance has $n = m = 2$, with $c_1 = 800$ and $c_2 = 700$. The buyers' valuations for houses are given in Table 3.2. For the purpose of understanding the core of this game, the key information is contained in Table 3.3, which gives the gains accrued by the various pairs of agents from all possible trades.

It is easy to see that the trades that yield the maximum total gain are (b_1, r_2) and (b_2, r_1), with a total gain of 115. Since (b_1, r_2) and (b_2, r_1) are good trades, by Theorem 3.9,

$$b_1 + r_2 = 70 \quad \text{and} \quad b_2 + r_1 = 45.$$

Therefore $b_1 \leq 70$ and $r_1 \leq 45$. Additionally, we have

$$b_1 + r_1 \geq 100 \quad \text{and} \quad b_2 + r_2 \geq 10.$$

Combining with the previous facts we get $b_1 \geq 55$ and $r_1 \geq 30$. These give $b_2 \leq 15$ and $r_2 \leq 15$.

The interesting conclusion is that b_1 and r_1 are tightly constrained, with $b_1 \in [55, 70]$ and $r_1 \in [30, 45]$. The constraints on b_2 and r_2 are $b_2 \in [0, 15]$ and $r_2 \in [0, 15]$. Observe that the trade (b_1, r_1) will not happen. Yet, the threat of this possible trade gives b_1 and r_1 negotiating power, which ensures that they cannot be forced into zero gains; in fact the lower bounds on their gains are 55 and 30, respectively. On the other hand, the alternative trade which b_2 and r_2 have available is not competitive, thereby giving them little negotiating power and constraining their profits to intervals with upper bounds of 15 only.

Now we will show that the core contains two extreme imputations, one is maximally advantageous to buyers and the other to sellers; furthermore, the first is maximally disadvantageous to sellers and the second to buyers. For $i \in B$, let v_i^h and v_i^l denote the highest and lowest profits that i accrues among all imputations in the core. Similarly, for $j \in R$, let u_j^h and u_j^l denote the highest and lowest profits that j accrues in the core. Let v^h and v^l denote the vectors whose components are v_i^h and v_i^l, respectively. Similarly, let u^h and u^l denote vectors whose components are u_j^h and u_j^l, respectively. The following is a formal statement regarding the extreme imputations.

Theorem 3.16. *The two extreme imputations in the core are (v^h, u^l) and (v^l, u^h).*

We will start by proving Lemma 3.17 below. Let (q, r) and (s, t) be two imputations in the core. For each $i \in B$, let

$$\underline{v}_i = \min(q_i, s_i) \quad \text{and} \quad \bar{v}_i = \max(q_i, s_i).$$

Further, for each $j \in R$, let

$$\underline{u}_j = \min(r_j, t_j) \quad \text{and} \quad \bar{u}_j = \max(r_j, t_j).$$

Lemma 3.17. $(\underline{v}, \bar{u})$ *and* $(\bar{v}, \underline{u})$ *are imputations in the core.*

Proof Consider the first imputation. We will show that, for each $i \in B$ and $j \in R$, $\underline{v}_i + \bar{u}_j \geq a_{ij}$. Thus we write

$$\underline{v}_i = \min(q_i, s_i) \geq \min(a_{ij} - r_j, a_{ij} - t_j) = a_{ij} - \max(r_j, t_j) = a_{ij} - \bar{u}_j.$$

Next, we need to show that the sum of the profits of all agents under this imputation equals the total worth of $(B \cup R)$. By renaming agents, we may assume that each pair in the maximum-weight matching is of the form (l, l), for $l \in B$ and $l \in R$. Then, $q_l + r_l = a_{ll}$ and $s_l + t_l = a_{ll}$. Therefore, we get

$$\underline{v}_i = \min(q_i, s_i) = \min(a_{ij} - r_j, a_{ij} - t_j) = a_{ij} - \max(r_j, t_j) = a_{ij} - \bar{u}_j,$$

giving $\underline{v}_l + \bar{u}_l = a_{ll}$. Therefore, imputation $(\underline{v}, \bar{u})$ is in the core. An analogous statement about the second imputation follows in a similar manner. $\square$

Let us use the term *mating* to describe the process of obtaining imputations $(\underline{v}, \bar{u})$ and $(\bar{v}, \underline{u})$ from imputations (q, r) and (s, t). To obtain the extreme imputations promised in Theorem 3.16, we will start with an arbitrary imputation and keep mating it with an imputation that has v_i^l or u_j^h, for each value of i and j. This will give us (v^l, u^h). An analogous process will give us (v^h, u^l).

The extreme imputations in the core for Example 3.12 are $(0, 0, 0)$, $(100, 90)$ and $(0, 0, 20)$, $(100, 70)$, and those for Example 3.15 are $(55, 0)$, $(45, 15)$ and $(70, 15)$, $(30, 0)$.

3.3 Approximate Core for the General Graph Matching Game

The general graph matching game has numerous applications. Its underlying features are nicely captured in the following setting. Suppose that a tennis club has a set V of players who can play in an upcoming doubles tournament. Let $G = (V, E)$ be a graph whose vertices are the players and whose edges (i, j) represent the fact that players i and j are compatible doubles partners. Let w be an edge-weight function for G, where w_{ij} represents the expected earnings if i and j partner in the tournament. Then the total worth of the agents in V is the weight of a maximum weight matching in G. Assume that the club picks such a matching M for the tournament. The question is how to distribute the total profit among the agents – strong players, weak players, and unmatched players – in such a way that no subset of players feel they would be better off seceding and forming their own tennis club.

Definition 3.18. The *general graph matching game* consists of an undirected graph $G = (V, E)$ and an edge-weight function w. The vertices $i \in V$ are the agents and an edge (i, j) represents the fact that agents i and j are eligible for an activity; for concreteness, let us say that they are eligible to participate as a doubles team in a tournament. If $(i, j) \in E$ then w_{ij} represents the profit generated if

i and j play in the tournament. The *worth* of a coalition $S \subseteq V$ is defined to be the maximum profit that can be generated by teams within S and is denoted by $p(S)$. Formally, $p(S)$ is defined to be the weight of a maximum weight matching in the graph G restricted to vertices in S only. The *characteristic function* of the matching game is defined to be $p: 2^V \rightarrow \mathcal{R}_+$.

Among the possible coalitions, the most important one is of course V, the *grand coalition*.

Definition 3.19. An *imputation* gives a way of dividing the worth of the game, $p(V)$, among the agents. Formally, it is a function $v: V \rightarrow \mathcal{R}_+$ such that $\sum_{i \in V} v(i) = p(V)$. An imputation t is said to be in the *core of the matching game* if, for any coalition $S \subseteq V$, there is no way of dividing $p(S)$ among the agents in S in such a way that all agents are at least as well off and at least one agent is strictly better off than in the imputation t.

The core of a non-bipartite game may be empty, as will be shown in Example 3.20.

Example 3.20. Consider the graph K_3, i.e., a clique on three vertices, i, j, k, with a weight of 1 on each edge. Any maximum matching in K_3 has only one edge, and therefore the worth of this game is 1. Suppose that there is an imputation v which lies in the core. Consider all three two-agent coalitions. Then, we must have

$$v(i) + v(j) \geq 1, \quad v(j) + v(k) \geq 1, \quad \text{and} \quad v(i) + v(k) \geq 1.$$

This implies that $v(i) + v(j) + v(k) \geq 3/2$, which exceeds the worth of the game, giving a contradiction.

Observe, however, that if we distribute the worth of this game as follows, we get a 2/3-approximate core allocation: $v(i) = v(j) = v(k) = 1/3$. Now each edge is covered to the extent of 2/3 of its weight. In Section 3.3.1 we will show that such an approximate core allocation can always be obtained for the general graph matching game.

Definition 3.21. Let $p: 2^V \rightarrow \mathcal{R}_+$ be the characteristic function of a game and let $1 \geq \alpha > 0$. An imputation $t: V \rightarrow \mathcal{R}_+$ is said to be in the *α-approximate core* of the game if the following hold:

1. The total profit allocated by t is at most the worth of the game, i.e.,

$$\sum_{i \in V} t_i \leq p(V).$$

2. The total profit accrued by agents in a sub-coalition $S \subseteq V$ is at least α fraction of the profit which S can generate by itself, i.e.,

$$\forall S \subseteq V : \sum_{i \in S} t_i \geq \alpha p(S).$$

If imputation t is in the α-approximate core of a game, then the ratio of the total profit of any sub-coalition on seceding from the grand coalition and its profit while in the grand coalition is bounded by a factor of at most $1/\alpha$.

3.3.1 A Two-Thirds-Approximate Core for the Matching Game

We will work with the following LP-relaxation of the maximum weight matching problem, equation (3.3) below. This relaxation always has an integral optimal solution if G is bipartite, but not for general graphs. In the latter case, its optimal solution is a maximum-weight fractional matching in G. The LP problem is given as

$$\max \quad \sum_{(i,j)\in E} w_{ij} x_{ij}$$
$$\text{s.t.} \quad \sum_{(i,j)\in E} x_{ij} \leq 1 \quad \forall i \in V,$$
$$x_{ij} \geq 0 \quad \forall (i,j) \in E. \tag{3.3}$$

Taking v_i to be dual variables for the first constraint of (3.3), we obtain LP (3.4) below. Any feasible solution to this LP is called a *cover* of G since, for each edge (i,j), v_i and v_j cover edge (i,j) in the sense that $v_i + v_j \geq w_{ij}$. An optimal solution to this LP is a *minimum cover*. We will say that v_i is the *profit* of vertex i. The LP problem is now given as

$$\min \quad \sum_{i\in V} v_i$$
$$\text{s.t.} \quad v_i + v_j \geq w_{ij} \quad \forall (i,j) \in E,$$
$$v_i \geq 0 \quad \forall i \in V, \tag{3.4}$$

We will say that a solution x to LP (3.3) is *half-integral* if, for each edge (i,j), x_{ij} is 0, 1/2, or 1. By the LP duality theorem, the weight of a maximum weight fractional matching equals the total profit of a minimum cover. If for a graph G, LP (3.3) has an integral optimal solution then it is easy to see that an optimal dual solution gives a way of allocating the total worth that lies in the core; see the related Exercise 3.8. Otherwise, LP (3.3) must have a half-integral optimal solution, as will be shown next.

Transform $G = V, E)$ with edge weights w to a graph $G' = (V', E')$ with edge weights w' as follows. Corresponding to each $i \in V$, V' has vertices i' and i'' and, corresponding to each edge $(i,j) \in E$, E' has edges (i',j'') and (i'',j') each having weight $w_{ij}/2$.

Since each cycle of length k in G is transformed to a cycle of length $2k$ in G', the latter graph has only even-length cycles and is bipartite. A maximum weight matching and a minimum cover for G' can be computed in polynomial time; let them be x' and v', respectively. Next, let

$$x_{ij} = \frac{1}{2}(x_{i'j''} + x_{i''j'}) \quad \text{and} \quad v_i = v_{i'} + v_{i''}.$$

It is easy to see that the weight of x equals the value of v, thereby implying that v is an optimal cover.

Lemma 3.22. *It holds that x is a maximum weight half-integral matching and v is an optimal cover in G.*

Proof We will first use the fact that v' is a feasible cover for G' to show that v is a feasible cover for G. Corresponding to each edge (i, j) in G, we have two edges in G', satisfying

$$v'_{i'} + v'_{j''} \geq \frac{1}{2} w_{ij} \quad \text{and} \quad v'_{i''} + v'_{j'} \geq \frac{1}{2} w_{ij}.$$

Therefore, in G, $v_i + v_j \geq w_{ij}$, implying the feasibility of v.

By the LP-duality theorem, the weight of x' equals the value of v' in G'. Corresponding to each edge (i, j) in G, we have:

$$x_{ij} w_{ij} = \left(\frac{1}{2} (x_{i'j''} + x_{i''j'}) \right) w_{ij} = x_{i'j''} w'_{ij} + x_{i''j'} w'_{ij}.$$

Summing over all edges, we get that the weight of x in G equals the weight of x' in G'. Furthermore, the profit of i equals the sum of profits of i' and i''. Therefore the value of v in G equals the value of v' in G'.

Putting it a together, we get that the weight of w equals the value of v, implying the optimality of both. Clearly, x is half-integral. The lemma follows. $\square$

Edges that are set to one half in x form connected components which are either paths or cycles. For any such path, consider the two matchings obtained by picking alternate edges. The half-integral solution for this path is a convex combination of these two integral matchings. Therefore both these matchings must be of equal weight, since otherwise we could obtain a heavier matching. Pick either of them. Similarly, if a cycle is of even length, pick alternate edges and match them. This transforms x to a maximum weight half-integral matching in which all edges that are set to one half form disjoint odd cycles. Henceforth we will assume that x satisfies this property.

Let C be a half-integral odd cycle in x of length $2k + 1$, with consecutive vertices $i_1, \ldots, i_{2k+1}$. Let $w_C = w_{i_1, i_2} + w_{i_2, i_3} + \cdots + w_{i_{2k+1}, i_1}$ and $v_C = v_{i_1} + \cdots + v_{i_{2k+1}}$. On removing any one vertex, say i_j, with its two edges, from C, we are left with a path of length $2k - 1$. Let M_j be the matching consisting of the k alternate edges of this path and let $w(M_j)$ be the weight of this matching.

Lemma 3.23. *The odd cycle C satisfies:*

1. $w_C = 2v_C$;
2. *C has a unique cover $v_{i_j} = v_C - w(M_j)$, for $1 \leq j \leq 2k + 1$.*

Proof 1. We will use the fact that x and v are optimal solutions to the LPs (3.3) and (3.4), respectively. By the primal complementary slackness condition, for $1 \leq j \leq 2k + 1$ we have $w_{i_j, i_{j+1}} = v_{i_j} + v_{i_{j+1}}$, where addition in the subindices is done modulo $2k + 1$; this follows from the fact that $x_{i_j, i_{j+1}} > 0$. Adding over all vertices of C we get $w_C = 2v_C$.

2. By the equalities established in the proof of the first part, we obtain that, for $1 \leq j \leq 2k + 1$, $v_C = v_{i_j} + w(M_j)$. Rearranging terms gives the lemma. $\square$

Let M' be heaviest matching among M_j, for $1 \leq j \leq 2k + 1$.

Lemma 3.24.

$$w(M') \geq \frac{2k}{2k + 1} v_C.$$

Proof Adding the equality established in the second part of Lemma 3.23 for all $2k + 1$ values of j we get

$$\sum_{j=1}^{2k+1} w(M_j) = (2k)v_C.$$

Since M' is the heaviest of the $2k + 1$ matchings in the summation, the lemma follows. □

Now modify the half-integral matching x to obtain an integral matching T in G as follows. First pick all edges (i, j) such that $x_{ij} = 1$ in T. Next, for each odd cycle C, find the heaviest matching M' as described above and pick all its edges.

Definition 3.25. Let $1 > \alpha > 0$. A function $c: V \to \mathcal{R}_+$ is said to be an *α-approximate cover* for G if

$$\forall (i, j) \in E: \quad c_i + c_j \geq \alpha w_{ij}.$$

Define a function $f: V \to [\frac{2}{3}, 1]$ as follows. For all $i \in V$,

$$f(i) = \begin{cases} \dfrac{2k}{2k + 1} & \text{if } i \text{ is in a half-integral cycle of length } 2k + 1, \\ 1 & \text{if } i \text{ is not in a half-integral cycle.} \end{cases}$$

Next, modify the cover v to obtain an approximate cover c as follows: $\forall i \in V$: $c_i = f(i)v_i$.

Lemma 3.26. *The function c is a $\frac{2}{3}$-approximate cover for G.*

Proof Consider edge $(i, j) \in E$. Then

$$c_i + c_j = f(i)v_i + f(j)\,v_j \geq \frac{2}{3}(v_i + v_j) \geq \frac{2}{3}w_{ij},$$

where the first inequality follows from the fact that, $\forall i \in V$, $f(i) \geq 2/3$ and the second follows from the fact that v is a cover for G. □

The mechanism for obtaining an imputation c is summarized as Algorithm 3.27.

Algorithm 3.27 (Two-thirds-approximate core imputation).

1. Compute x and v, optimal solutions to LPs (3.3) and (3.2), where x is half-integral.
2. Modify x so that all half-integral edges form odd cycles.
3. $\forall i \in V$, compute

$$f(i) = \begin{cases} \dfrac{2k}{2k+1} & \text{if } i \text{ is in a half-integral cycle of length } 2k+1, \\ 1 & \text{otherwise.} \end{cases}$$

4. $\forall i \in V$: $c_i \leftarrow f(i)v_i$.
   Output c.

Theorem 3.28. *The imputation c is in the 2/3 approximate core of the general graph matching game.*

Proof We need to show that c satisfies the two conditions given in Definition 3.21, for $\alpha = 2/3$.

1. By Lemma 3.24, the weight of the matched edges picked in T from a half-integral odd cycle C of length $2k+1$ is $\geq f(k)v_C = \sum_{i \in C} c(i)$. Now remove all half-integral odd cycles from G to obtain G'. Let x' and v' be the projections of x and v onto G'.

By the first part of Lemma 3.23, the total decrease in weight in going from x to x' equals the total decrease in value in going from v to v'. Therefore, the weight of x' equals the total value of v'. Finally, observe that in G', T picks an edge (i,j) if and only if $x'_{ij} = 1$ and $\forall i \in G'$, $c_i = v'_i$.

Adding the weight of the matching and the value of the imputation c over G' and all half-integral odd cycles we get $w(T) \geq \sum_{i \in V} c_i$.

2. Consider a coalition $S \subseteq V$. Then $p(S)$ is the weight of a maximum weight matching in G restricted to S. Assume this matching is $(i_1,j_1),\ldots,(i_k,j_k)$, where $i_1,\ldots,i_k$ and $j_1,\ldots,j_k \in S$. Then $p(S) = w_{i_1j_1} + \cdots + w_{i_kj_k}$. By Lemma 3.26,

$$c_{i_l} + c_{j_l} \geq \frac{2}{3}w_{i_l,j_l}, \quad \text{for } 1 \leq l \leq k.$$

Adding all k terms we get

$$\sum_{i \in S} c_i \geq \frac{2}{3}p(S). \qquad \square$$

Because of Example 3.20, the factor 2/3 cannot be improved. Observe that, for the purposes of Lemma 3.26, we could have defined $f \forall i \in V$ simply as $f(i) = 2/3$. However, in general this would have left a good fraction of the worth of the game unallocated. The definition of f given above improves the allocation for agents who are in large odd cycles and those who are not in odd cycles with respect to the matching x. As a result, the gain of a typical sub-coalition on seceding will be less than a factor 3/2, giving it less incentive to secede.

3.4 Many-to-One Matching With Salaries

We now turn to the study of a many-to-one labor market with salaries. Instead of houses, the agents buy and sell heterogeneous labor services. The set B of n buyers of labor services is now called a set of *firms*. The set R of m sellers is a set of *workers*. Each firm i has a *valuation* h_i, a function that takes subsets of workers as arguments. If firm i hires a set of workers $A \subset R$, paying them salaries s_j (for $j \in A$), then its payoff is

$$h_i(A) - \sum_{j \in A} s_j.$$

Suppose that $h_i(\varnothing) = 0$ and that h_i is strictly monotonically increasing in the set of workers (so that a firm would always like to add a worker at a salary of zero). With these definitions in place, we can talk about the *demand function* for firm i:

$$d_i(s) = \operatorname{argmax}\{h_i(A) - \sum_{j \in A} s_j : A \subset R\},$$

for any vector $s \in \Re_+^R$ of salaries. Note that $d_i(s)$ may contain more than one set of workers.

A worker j who is employed by firm i suffers a loss, say $c_{j,i}$, from surrendering her labor services. This loss may depend on the identity of her employer because different firms require workers to perform different tasks, under different conditions. For example, assume that the workers are academics and the firms are universities. One university may demand a higher teaching load than another, or it may be located in a city that is more desirable to worker j than another. When worker j is employed by firm i at salary s, she obtains a utility, or payoff, $s - c_{j,i}$.

We need to make two assumptions. The first is relatively innocuous: it says that any firm would be willing to hire a worker at a salary that would compensate the worker for the disutility of working at the firm. Formally, suppose that, for any set of workers A,

$$h_i(A \cup \{j\}) - c_{j,i} \geq h_i(A \setminus \{j\}).$$

Call this assumption *acceptance*.

The second assumption is more substantive and will severely restrict the functions h_i that are allowed. The idea is that if a firm hires worker i at some given vector of salaries, the reason cannot be that i is part of a team of complementary workers. In particular, even if other workers' salaries are increased (and presumably some of those workers are laid off), worker i must continue to be employed by the firm. Formally, say that h_i satisfies the *substitutability* condition if whenever $A \in d_i(s)$ and $s \leq s'$ then there is an $A' \in d_i(s')$ such that A' contains all workers in A that have the same salary in s as in s'.[3]

The model determines a market outcome, which describes who works for whom and the salaries earned by each of the workers. A *matching* is a function $\mu : R \to B \cup R$ with the property that $\mu(j) \in B \cup \{j\}$, so that a worker is either employed by

---

[3] Substitutability implies that the valuation is submodular, but it is a strictly stronger property than submodularity. One characterization of substitutability uses the indirect utility function defined by h_i – the function mapping each salary vector to the highest profit attainable by the firm at those salaries. Substitutability is equivalent to the submodularity of indirect utility.

firm $\mu(j) \in B$ or unemployed, which we denote as $\mu(j) = j$. A *market outcome* is a pair (μ, s), where μ is a matching and $s \in \Re_+^R$ is a vector of salaries.

We shall restrict the set of possible salaries to lie on a discrete grid. Suppose, in particular, that the set of possible salaries is $\mathbb{Z}_+$. Suppose also for convenience that each $c_{j,i} \in \mathbb{Z}_+$.

Finally, the firms and the workers in the model have some individual agency to opt out of the market. They have an *outside option* available. A worker can choose not to be employed, and perhaps to take up another occupation, while firms can always opt to shut down operations. We assume that the utility of such an outside option is always zero.

Definition 3.29. We are interested in outcomes that leave no agent worse off than their outside option, where no recontracting is desirable.

- An outcome (μ, s) is *individually rational* if, for all workers i, $s_i \geq c_{\mu(i),i}$ and, for all firms j,

$$h_j(\mu^{-1}(j)) - \sum_{i \in \mu^{-1}(j)} s_i \geq 0.$$

- A firm i and a set of workers A *block* an outcome (μ, s) if there are salaries $(\hat{s}_j)_{j \in A}$ such that i would strictly prefer to hire the workers in A at salaries $(\hat{s}_j)_{j \in A}$ rather than the workers $\mu(i)$ at salaries $(s_j)_{j \in A}$, and all the workers $j \in A$ would strictly prefer to work for i at salaries $\hat{s}_j$ instead of for $\mu(j)$ at salary s_j.

Individual rationality provides workers with an option to stay out of the market if they are not minimally compensated for their employment, and firms with the option to shut down: i.e., to employ no workers and pay no salaries. Blocking, in turn, refers to a mutually beneficial recontracting between a firm and a set of workers. We have seen in Section 3.2 an instance of this phenomenon, where it is sufficient to be concerned about recontracting by limited subsets of agents – the only sets of agents that can generate value in the model.

Definition 3.30. An outcome is in the *core* if it is individually rational and there is no firm and set of workers that blocks it.

3.4.1 The Salary Adjustment Process

We propose a variation of the deferred acceptance algorithm that we term the *salary adjustment process*. The algorithm operates iteratively, with firms proposing employment to a set of workers at certain fixed salaries.

Initialize the algorithm by setting the salary offered by firm i to worker j at $s_{i,j}(0) = c_{j,i}$. In each iteration k of the algorithm, the algorithm carries out these steps:

1. Each firm offers employment to a set of workers $A \in d_i((s_{i,j}(k))_{j \in R})$, as long as A contains all the workers to whom i offered employment to the previous iteration of the algorithm and whose salaries did not change between iterations.
2. Each worker tentatively accepts the best offer that they have received, rejecting all others.

3. If a worker rejects an offer from a firm then the salary proposed by that firm increases by 1. So, if firm i made an offer to worker j, and j accepted another offer, then $s_{i,j}(k+1) = s_{i,j}(k) + 1$.

The algorithm ends when no worker rejects any more offers. The outcome of the algorithm is a matching, determined by the last accepted offers by each worker and a salary for each worker defined as the last salary that was proposed and accepted.
   Observe that:

• The algorithm asks firms to keep their offers to workers who did not reject them in prior rounds, and for whom salaries have been kept the same. This is made possible by the substitutability assumption.
• We may without loss of generality assume that, in the first iteration of the algorithm, all firms make an offer to all workers. Indeed, by our acceptance assumption, no firm makes any losses by including worker j at salary $c_{j,i}$.

Note also that, at each step of the algorithm, whenever some offer is rejected, the salary of some worker increases. By the nature of firms' profits, salaries can become high enough that no worker is hired. So it is also clear that the algorithm stops after a finite number of steps (a number of steps bounded by $m \times \bar{w}$, where $\bar{w}$ is a *choke salary* at which $d_i(\bar{w}, \ldots, \bar{w}) = \oslash$).
   When the algorithm starts, we may define $\mu(j)$ to be the last firm whose offer worker j tentatively accepted and set s_j to be the salary that was offered (so if the algorithm stopped in iteration k, $s_j = s_{\mu(j),j}(k)$). Let (μ, s) be the outcome of the salary adjustment process.

Theorem 3.31. *The outcome of the salary adjustment process is in the core.*

Proof First, it is clear that the outcome is individually rational. Indeed, offers start at salaries that compensate workers for the disutility involved in accepting the offer; firms, in turn, only make offers to sets of workers that maximize their profits. So they would never make an offer that is worse than shutting the firm down.
   Second, let us establish that there are no blocks. Suppose that worker j would rather work for firm i at salary $\hat{s}_i$, over the terms of her employment at the outcome of the salary adjustment process. Since all firms make an offer to each worker in the initial round of the algorithm, j would have made i an offer at all salaries (in the grid $\mathbb{Z}_+$) from $s_{j,i}(0)$ and up to some $s'_i < \hat{s}_i$. This offer must have been rejected by j.
   Now, suppose that A is a set of workers in this situation and $(\hat{s}_i)_{i \in A}$ the salaries at which they would prefer to work for firm j. Then we have that

$$h_i(\mu^{-1}(i)) - \sum_{l \in \mu^{-1}(i)} s_i \geq h_i(A) - \sum_{i \in A} s_i \geq h_i(A) - \sum_{i \in A} \hat{s}_i.$$

Thus the set of workers A together with firm j do not constitute a block. □

3.4.2 A Model with a Continuum of Salaries

We have taken salaries to be in a discrete grid, but it is easy to see that the argument we have laid out implies the existence of core outcomes for a model with continuum salaries. In the rest of our discussion we shall be somewhat informal, but the ideas are very simple.

First, as an exercise, we invite the reader to modify the description of the model to allow salaries to take any value in the compact interval $[0, \bar{\omega}]$. The model remains essentially the same, but salaries are allowed to take any real values in this interval. Note that $\bar{\omega} > 0$ should be chosen large enough to accommodate all values of $c_{j,i}$ and larger than the choke salary for all firms (so, large enough to make employment unprofitable at such high salaries).

Now, it should be easy to see that the argument proving Theorem 3.31 does not depend on the grid being $\mathbb{Z}_+$. Indeed, for any n we may consider the finite grid $W_n = \{0, \bar{\omega}/n, 2\bar{\omega}/n, \ldots, \bar{\omega}\} \cup \{c_{j,i} : j \in B, i \in R\}$. The salary adjustment process determines an outcome (μ^n, s^n) that is in the core of the appropriate discrete version of the model. By the compactness of $[0, \bar{\omega}]$, there is, after going to a subsequence, $(\mu, s) = \lim_{n \to \infty}(\mu^n, s^n)$. We leave the next result as an exercise.

Theorem 3.32. *The outcome (μ, s) is in the core of the continuum salary many-to-one market.*

3.5 Matching with Contracts

We next turn to a generalization of the model with salaries. Again we shall focus on many-to-one matchings between workers and firms, but now instead of a simple salary we shall allow for complex terms of employment. In addition to a salary, a firm may offer its workers health insurance, day-care, or a retirement plan. Such additional terms are captured through an abstract model of contracts.

Suppose that, as before, R is the set of workers and B the set of firms. The finite set X contains all possible contracts. Each contract $x \in X$ specifies a unique worker $x_R \in R$ and firm $x_B \in B$, the idea being that these are the two parties to the contract. There will generally be many contracts in X available to each worker–firm pair, and we can interpret the model as one of multilateral bargaining over terms of employment. Workers and firms interact with contracts in somewhat different ways.

First, we will restrict attention to many-to-one matching, which means that workers can sign at most one contract. Indeed, for worker i and a set of contracts X', we let $c_i(X')$ be the contract most preferred by worker i out of the set X'. The function c_i is a *choice function*. There are some implicit assumptions here that we should mention. The worker has a strict preference over contracts, and when we write "most preferred" we have this preference in mind. The worker always has the option of refusing all contracts in X', which is denoted as $c_i(X') = \emptyset$. Finally, obviously the chosen contract must involve worker i.

Firms can choose a set of contracts, each involving different workers. So firm j when facing a set X' of contracts will choose $c_j(X') \subseteq X'$ as its most preferred set of contracts. As for workers, these contracts must all involve j, and when j refuses all contracts in the set we shall write $c_j(X') = \emptyset$. Firms are assumed to have a strict preference over sets of contracts, so that $c_j(X')$ is the most preferred set of contracts involving firm j, out of all the contracts in X'. Finally, there can be no ambiguity in the terms of employment, so any two different contracts contained in $c_j(X')$ must involve two different workers.

In the model of matching with contracts, an *outcome* is a set of contracts such that each worker is involved in at most one contract. Clearly such an outcome specifies a matching between workers and firms because it describes with which firm any worker who holds a contract is employed. Workers who hold no contracts are unemployed. Moreover, for each employed worker, the terms of employment are determined by the unique contract that she holds.

For succinctness, let us denote by X'_a the set of contracts in X_a that involve agent a, who may be a worker or a firm. In an allocation, for a worker i, X'_i is either a single contract or $\oslash$.

Definition 3.33. We are interested in outcomes that leave no agent worse off than with their outside option, and where no recontracting is desirable.

- An outcome X' is *individually rational* if $c_a(X') = X'_a$ for all $a \in R \cup B$.
- A firm j and a set of workers A *block* an outcome X' if there is a set of contracts $X'' \neq X'$ for which $X'' = c_j(X' \cup X'')$ and $X''_i = c_i(X' \cup X'')$ for all $i \in A$.

Individual rationality here gives workers and firms agency to unilaterally turn down a contract. So a set of contracts respects individual rationality when no worker or firm prefers to drop one or more of the contracts in the outcome.

Blocking captures, as before, the idea of recontracting. The existence of a block means that a firm, together with a set of workers, using the vehicle of an alternative set of contracts can all be made better off. Note that we allow for some workers to receive the same contract in X' and in X'', so that they are not made strictly better off.

Definition 3.34. An outcome is *stable* if it is individually rational and admits no blocks.

Similarly to the model of matching with salaries, we shall rule out that firms regard workers as complements. Specifically, we say that a choice function c_j for firm j satisfies *substitutability* if, for any set of contracts $X' \subseteq X''$, if $x \in c_j(X'')$ and $x \in X'$ then $x \in c_j(X')$. In words, x cannot be chosen in X'' owing to the presence of some complementary contracts that are absent from X'.

Theorem 3.35. *There exists a stable outcome.*

3.6 Exercises

Exercise 3.1 [7] Let $S \subseteq (B \cup R)$ and q, r be agents not in S. We will say that q and r are of the same type if they are both buyers or both sellers, and that they are of different types otherwise. Let $S \cup \{q\}$ be denoted by S^q. Define the *marginal value of agent q* to S to be $w(S^q) - w(S)$, and denote it by $m(q, S)$. Prove that:
(a) If q and r are of the same type then $m(r, S^q) \leq m(r, S)$.

(b) If q and r are of different types then $m(r, S^q) \geq m(r, S)$.

Exercise 3.2 Give an efficient algorithm for checking the following. Given an instance of the housing market and an imputation (v, u), is it in the core?

Exercise 3.3 Consider an instance of a housing market with $n = m = 4$ and gains of pairs of agents given in Table 3.1; blanks represent zeros.

Table 3.4 Gains from all possible trades.

	r_1	r_2	r_3	r_4
b_1	100	100	51	
b_2	80	100		51
b_3	50			
b_4		50		

Show that the total profit distributed to agents b_3, b_4, r_3, r_4 by any imputation in the core is 2, even though they are matched in every maximum weight matching. What are the extreme imputations in the core?

Exercise 3.4 In the instance of Example 3.12, assume that edge (b_3, r_1) has weight 120, keeping all other weights the same. How many maximum weight matchings are there now and how many imputations are there in the core?

Exercise 3.5 [10] The maximum b-matching problem is a generalization of the assignment problem in which in addition to the bipartite graph $G = (B, R, E)$ and weights a on edges, we are given a function $b : (U \cup V) \rightarrow Z_+$ specifying the maximum number of matched edges that can be incident on a vertex of the graph. Subject to this constraint, edges can be matched a multiple number of times. The problem is to find a maximum weight b-matching.
(a) Write the LP-relaxation and dual for the maximum b-matching problem. Analogous to the assignment problem, this LP also has integral optimal solutions.
(b) Define the b-matching game; its worth is the weight of a maximum b-matching in the graph. Define the notion of core imputation for this game.
(c) Consider the special case of the b-matching game in which b is the constant function. Extend Theorem 3.4 to this case, i.e., show that core imputations are precisely optimal solutions to the dual.

Exercise 3.6 [10] For the assignment game, prove that there is a core imputation satisfying:
(a) a player $q \in U \cup V$ gets paid if and only if q is essential.
(b) a team $e \in E$ gets overpaid if and only if e is subpar.

Exercise 3.7 [1] Consider an instance of the housing market in which there is no product differentiation, i.e., all houses are identical for all buyers. However, different buyers have different values for a house. Also, different sellers have a different value for their own house. Find a way of computing the worth of this game via a process that is easier than computing a maximum weight matching. Also, prove that there is a uniform market price for all houses. Find the interval in which this price lies.

Exercise 3.8 [2] Prove that the core of the general graph matching game is non-empty if and only if LP (3.1) has an integral optimal solution.

Exercise 3.9 One way of formally stating an improved factor beyond that given in Theorem 3.28 is the following. Assume that the underlying graph G has no odd cycles of length less than $2k + 1$. Then imputation c computed by Algorithm 3.27 is in the $2k/2k + 1$-approximate core of the matching game for G. Prove this statement.

Exercise 3.10 Formalize the model in Section 3.4.2 and the proof of Theorem 3.32.

Exercise 3.11 [10] For a given instance of the assignment game, let $A = B \cup R$ denote its set of agents and let C denote its set of core imputations. An imputation $p \in C$ is said to be a *min-max fair core imputaton* if it satisfies:

$$p \in \arg\min_{q \in C} \left\{ \max_{a \in A} \{q(a)\} \right\},$$

where $q(a)$ is the profit of agent a under imputation q. Show how to modify the dual LP (3.2) to obtain an LP that yields a min-max core imputation for the assignment game.

3.7 Bibliographic Notes

Theorems 3.4 and 3.16 are from the classic paper of Shapley and Shubik [7] on the core of the assignment game. Theorems 3.9 and 3.28 are due to Vazirani and are taken from [8] and [9], respectively.

Section 3.4.1 is due to [5], while the model of matching with contracts was developed in [4], in part as a generalization of matching markets with salaries. Under the assumptions in that article, however, the two models turn out to be equivalent; see [3] for a discussion. An early model of matching with contracts was given in [6].

References

[1] Eugen von Böhm-Bawerk. The positive theory of capital, volume 2. GE Stechert & Company, reprint, 1923.

[2] Deng, Xiaotie, Ibaraki, Toshihide, and Nagamochi, Hiroshi. 1997. Algorithms and complexity in combinatorial optimization games. In: *Proc. 8th ACM Symposium on Discrete Algorithms*.

[3] Echenique, Federico, 2012. Contracts versus salaries in matching. *American Economic Review*, **102**(1), 594–601.

[4] Hatfield, John William, and Milgrom, Paul R. 2005. Matching with contracts. *American Economic Review*, **95**(4), 913–935.

[5] Kelso, Alexander S., and Crawford, Vincent P. 1982. Job matching, coalition formation, and gross substitutes. *Econometrica*, **50**(6), 1483–1504.

[6] Roth, Alvin E. 1984. Stability and polarization of interests in job matching. *Econometrica*, **52**(1), 47–57.

[7] Shapley, Lloyd S., and Shubik, Martin. 1971. The assignment game I: The core. *International Journal of Game Theory*, **1**(1), 111–130.

[8] Vijay V. Vazirani. 2022. The general graph matching game: Approximate core. *Games and Economic Behavior*, **132**, 478–486.

[9] Vijay V. Vazirani. 2022. New characterizations of core imputations of matching and *b*-matching games. In: *Foundations of Software Technology and Theoretical Computer Science*.

[10] Vijay V. Vazirani. LP-duality theory and the cores of games. arXiv preprint arXiv:2302.07627, 2023.

CHAPTER FOUR

Objectives

Federico Echenique, Nicole Immorlica, and Vijay V. Vazirani

4.1 Introduction

We describe the basic objectives that guide many solutions used in matching theory and mechanism design. The focus is on the basic principles of neoclassical economics that guide the choice of an objective. We seek, in particular, to clarify the ideas implicit in the utilitarian objective and the meaning of welfare maximization. After reading this chapter, we hope that readers will clearly understand the differences between efficiency, the utilitarian objective, and welfare (or surplus) maximization.

Many researchers adopt a utilitarian objective, which relies on ideas that can be controversial. We hope to clarify that the standard positive theory of economic choice, a theory that tries to explain economic agents' choices, does not naturally justify objectives that rely on the cardinal information contained in agents' utility functions. In contrast, we lay out a characterization of utilitarianism that clearly describes what sorts of cardinal comparisons are needed. A brief discussion of the egalitarian lexi-min criterion is included, mainly as a contrast with utilitarianism.

We touch on models with "money" and the resulting criterion of surplus maximization. We discuss the meaning of money in a model of economic resource allocation, and how it connects to the basic criterion of efficiency.

The chapter concludes with an overview of the role of incentives. We lay out the abstract notion of dominant strategy incentive compatibility, which is basic to much of the content of the book.

4.2 Preliminaries: Individual Choice

Economic models postulate the presence of humans with agency to make choices: economic agents. The idea is that these humans know how to choose among objects in some set X of alternatives or outcomes. An agent's choice behavior is often (but not exclusively) modeled through a *preference relation*, a complete and transitive binary relation $\succeq$ on X. We say that the agent prefers x to y, and write this as $x \succeq y$, when they would choose x out of the set $\{x, y\}$. This language is sometimes interpreted as a statement about the subject's subjective evaluation of x and y, that they "like" x more than y, but such interpretations are not what the neoclassical economists had in mind when they formulated the theory. In the neoclassical formulation of the model, only choice behavior can be observed and therefore $\succeq$ should be interpreted only as a summary of the agent's choice behavior. No psychological notion of well being can be inferred from an agent who consumes x rather than y.

Under some assumptions on X and $\succeq$ there is a representation of $\succeq$ using a *utility function* $u\colon X \to \mathbf{R}$.[1] This means that $x \succeq y$ if and only if $u(x) \geq u(y)$. With the utility function u in mind, the possibilities (one could say the dangers) of interpreting $u(x)$ as a measure of well-being are even greater than when we have access only to the agent's preference – indeed the word "utility" was originally meant to signify such a measure of well-being.[2]

The neoclassical interpretation of u is that it is solely a convenient representation of the agent's choice behavior, i.e., of the preference $\succeq$. If u represents $\succeq$, and $f\colon \mathbf{R} \to \mathbf{R}$ is strictly monotonically increasing, then $f \circ u$ also represents $\succeq$. The properties of u that depend only on the preference that u represents are termed *ordinal*. In consequence, the ordinal properties of u are shared by $u' = f \circ u$, for any strictly monotonically increasing $f\colon \mathbf{R} \to \mathbf{R}$. The remaining properties of u, those that are not preserved by such transformations f, are termed *cardinal*.

Example 4.1. Consider an agent choosing among vectors in $\mathbf{R}_+^2$, with utility function $u(x_1, x_2) = x_1 x_2$. This agent's preference is the same as for the utility function $u'(x_1, x_2) = \sqrt{x_1 x_2}$: these two utility functions have the same ordinal properties. Moreover, the utility for u of $(1, 1)$ is 25% of the utility of $(2, 2)$, but this is a cardinal property of u and is not shared by u'.

To summarize, traditional neoclassical economics is founded on a model of ordinal preferences and individual choice. Economics is an empirical discipline, and traditionally economists regard choices as empirically observable. Purely cardinal statements are not observable, and therefore are discounted.[3] The neoclassical upshot is that the theory should be grounded in preferences, the ordinal information contained in a utility function.

4.2.1 Quasilinear Utility

We turn to the most important special class of utility functions for this book: quasilinear utility functions.

Suppose that $X = Y \times \mathbf{R}$, so that an agent consumes objects of the form (y, t). Here y can represent any class of good, or outcome, while t is a real number and is called a *transfer*. We often think of the transfer as a "monetary" quantity and interpret it as the amount of money involved in $x = (y, t)$. A utility function $u\colon X \to \mathbf{R}$ is

---

[1] There exists a utility function representing $\succeq$ on X if and only if there is a countable set $Z \subseteq X$ with the property that whenever $x \succ y$ there is a $z \in Z$ with $x \succeq z$ and $z \succeq y$.

[2] Utility as a tool for making ethical judgements arose through utilitarianism, a nineteenth-century philosophical school that sought to measure the societal well-being associated with different outcomes. The utilitarian objective to be discussed later in this chapter is a particular incarnation of this school of thought.

[3] There is a debate among some economists on the possibility of using psychometrics and neuroeconomics to, essentially, observe utility. The promise of this approach is to ground utility in an empirical science. It is fair to say that the debate has not yet been settled.

quasilinear if there is a function $v\colon Y \to \mathbf{R}$ such that u represents the same preference as the utility function $(y, t) \mapsto v(y) + t$.

Note that the utility function $v(y) + t$ is expressed in units of "money," so the comments made above about the meaning of utilities become relevant. With quasilinear utility we can interpret, for example, the difference-in-v utility $v(y) - v(y')$ as the amount of money t that would leave the agent indifferent between consuming $(y, 0)$ and (y', t). In other words, the v component of the agent's utility has a cardinal meaning.

4.3 A General Model of Social Choice

All the models in this book can be thought of as solving a social choice problem. To this end, we present a very general model of social choice that will allow us to describe the broad objectives that one may want to pursue in solving and analyzing such problems.

An n-agent social choice environment is a tuple $(X, u^1, \ldots, u^n)$, in which

- X is a non-empty set of *outcomes*,
- $u_i\colon X \to \mathbf{R}$ is a *utility function* for each $i \in [n]$.

We proceed to illustrate the general setup with two important families of economic environments. Allocation problems are those where there is some quantity of goods that has to be divided among agents for their *private consumption*. Public goods problems are about deciding on the kind, or quantity, of public good to provide, the challenge being that all agents have to consume the same amount of public good.

4.3.1 Allocation

An n-agent *allocation problem* is an n-agent social choice environment $(X, u_1, \ldots, u_n)$ in which there exists a finite set of d *goods* and, for each agent i, a consumption space $X_i \subseteq \mathbf{R}_+^d$, so that $X = \times_{i=1}^n X_i$. Then an outcome $x \in X$ can be written as a vector $x = (x_i)_{i=1}^n \in \mathbf{R}^{nd}$, with agent i receiving, or consuming, x_i. The vector x_i specifies the quantity of each good that i consumes, their *private consumption*.

In an allocation problem there exists a vector $\bar{\omega} \in \mathbf{R}^d$ which specifies the total amount of each good that is to be allocated to the agents. We have then that

$$X = \{(x_i)_{i=1}^n \in \times_{i=1}^n X_i : \sum_{i=1}^n x_i \leq \bar{\omega}\}.$$

Agents' utilities only depend on their own private consumption, hence we write $u_i(x_i)$.

Example 4.2. An *exchange economy* witn n consumers and d goods is described by a tuple $(\omega_i, u_i)_{i=1}^n$, with $u_i\colon \mathbf{R}_+^d \to \mathbf{R}$ and $\omega_i \in \mathbf{R}_+^d$. Each (ω_i, u_i) describes a consumer, where $\omega_i \in \mathbf{R}_+^d$ specifies the consumer's initial *endowment* of each of the d goods and u_i is the consumer's utility function. Here $X_i = \mathbf{R}_+^d$ and $\bar{\omega} = \sum_{i=1}^n \omega_i$.

Example 4.3. A single-object *auction environment* is described by a collection (v_i) of functions $v_i : [0, 1] \to \mathbf{R}$. Here there is a single indivisible object that is to be allocated among the n agents. Let $y_i \in [0, 1]$ denote the probability that i gets the good, and let t_i be the monetary transfer to agent i. This is an allocation problem where $d = 2$, $X_i = [0, 1] \times \mathbf{R}$, and $\bar{\omega} = (1, 0)$. An outcome is $x = (y_i, t_i)_{i=1}^n$, and $u_i(y_i, t_i) = v_i(y_i) + t_i$.

4.3.2 Public Goods

In contrast with allocation problems, in a *public good* environment, there is no product structure to X because all agents must consume the same quantity of a public good. Often the model has some private consumption, such as transfers, which constitute the private consumption of money. The main object of the analysis is the public good, a good that is commonly consumed. A *pure public good* problem is one where there is no private consumption whatsoever. This happens, for example, when all agents' preferences over outcomes are strict (if there is some private consumption then agents $j \neq i$ are indifferent over outcomes that only differ in i's private consumption).

Example 4.4 (Facility location). Imagine deciding where a public library should be located in a city. The social choice problem is to select $x \in X = \mathbf{R}^2$, where x describes the geographical location of the library (its longitude and latitude). Each agent lives in the city, and would suffers a cost that is equal to the distance from their house to the library. Let agent i's house be located at $\theta_i \in X$, so that the cost for i of having the library located in x is the Euclidean distance $\|x - \theta_i\|$. Here, then, we have $X = \mathbf{R}^2$ and $u_i(x) = -\|x - \theta_i\|$.

Example 4.5 (Two-sided matching). Consider a set of n workers W and a set of m firms F. A *matching* is a set $\mu \subseteq W \times F$ that describes a bipartite graph with edge set μ. Suppose that each agent (worker or firm) $i \in W \cup F$ has at most one neighbor in μ. Let X be the set of all matchings, and suppose that $u_i : X \to \mathbf{R}$ describes agent i's preferences over matchings. It is reasonable to assume that i's preferences are solely derived from the agent to whom they are matched, if any. In that case we may think of two-sided matching as an instance of private consumption.

Public good problems are often analyzed in models with quasilinear utility and transfers (as the jargon goes, "with money"). For example, suppose that outcomes $x \in X$ are composed of a quantity $y \in Y \subseteq \mathbf{R}$ of a public good that all agents consume in identical quantities, and of a transfer t_i for each agent i. Thus $X = Y \times \mathbf{R}^n$.

In this case, assuming quasilinear utility as in an auction environment, we may write

$$u_i(x, (t_1, \ldots, t_n)) = v_i(y) + t_i.$$

4.4 Normative Desiderata

Economic objectives rest typically on two normative desiderata: efficiency and fairness. The word normative here means prescriptive: a desideratum that serves as the basis for formulating economic policies.

4.4.1 Efficiency

Outcomes are efficient when it is not possible to find alternative outcomes that improve some agents without making other agents worse off. Formally, an outcome $x \in X$ is *Pareto dominated* by an outcome x' if $u_i(x) \leq u_i(x')$ for all $i \in [n]$ and $u_i(x) < u_i(x')$ for at least one $i \in [n]$. The implicit idea is that no agent would object to an outcome that is better for someone else, as long as they are not harmed. An outcome is *Pareto optimal,* or *efficient*, if it is not Pareto dominated by any other outcome. Note that Pareto optimal outcomes may have questionable distributive properties: they say nothing about fairness or property rights. For example, for many allocative problems, one can give all the goods to one agent in a Pareto optimal outcome.

An outcome $x \in X$ is strongly Pareto dominated by an outcome x' if $u_i(x) < u_i(x')$ for all $i \in [n]$. An outcome is *weakly Pareto optimal* if it is not strongly Pareto dominated by any other outcome. In an allocation environment in which $X_i = \mathbf{R}_+^d$ and each utility function u_i is continuous and strictly increasing, an allocation is weakly Pareto optimal if and only if it is strongly Pareto optimal. The same is true of environments with quasi-linear utilities.

4.4.2 Fairness

Fairness can be discussed as a property of a particular outcome or as a property of a rule that chooses an outcome in all environments within a class.

There are many ways to conceptualize fairness, but, to be concrete, consider a notion of fairness for outcomes in an allocative environment. Specifically, imagine that we are allocating d goods among two agents, Alice and Bob. Suppose that we consider an efficient outcome $x = (x_A, x_B)$ in which Alice prefers x_B over x_A. The utility of Alice would be strictly greater at x_B than at x_A. She *envies* Bob. Such a consideration does not depend on the utility functions of all agents, it depends on performing a counterfactual evaluation of Alice's utility function. For allocative environments, a fair allocation is one in which no agent envies another: fairness equals *envy-freeness*. (There are other possible notions of fairness, such as "equal treatment of equals", but envy-freeness stands out.)

When we study a rule, fairness can take on additional meaning because we ask how the rule would treat Alice if she were to have Bob's role in society. The most basic, abstract, notion of fairness and equity results from imposing that outcomes be chosen without regard for the identity of the agents. We provide a formal definition later in this chapter. Suffice it to say here that the *anonymity* criterion translates into an invariance under the permutation of agents' names (or labels). To be concrete, fix a general n-agent social choice environment, and consider the use of majority voting to choose between x and x'. The decision is solely based on how many agents rank one alternative over the other, not on who they are. So, majority voting is anonymous and therefore fair. In contrast, if all decisions are based on what agent $i = 17$ prefers, this agent would be a *dictator*. A dictatorship is neither fair nor equitable.

4.5 Preference Aggregation

Consider an n-agent social choice environment $(X, u_1, \ldots, u_n)$. How do we choose between an outcome x, which results in the profile of utilities $(u_1(x), \ldots, u_n(x))$, and an outcome x', which results in $(u_1(x'), \ldots, u_n(x'))$? Do we count the number of agents that are better off in x than in x'? Do we take into account by how much agents' utilities change? We proceed with a discussion of some basic principles that can guide us in devising a system for making social choices. Suppose, for the sake of this discussion, that X is a finite set of cardinality at least three.[4]

Social choices can be made by means of a preference aggregation rule: a function $(u_1, \ldots, u_n) \mapsto \succeq(u_1, \ldots, u_n)$ that selects a "social" preference for each profile of utility functions. The idea here to use the social preference to make social choice (or, if you recall the discussion at the beginning of the chapter, preferences encode choices). The social preference should be complete and transitive, thus ensuring that a well-defined choice will be made from any set of alternatives.

The first consideration is *ordinality*. Social choices should depend only on the ordinal content $\succeq_i$ in u_i. If agent i were to choose an outcome in X, her choice would depend only on the ordinal information contained in her utility. This means that i's choice between x and x' depends only on the preference relation $\succeq_i$ represented by u_i. It stands to reason that the social choice should then depend only on $\succeq_i$, i.e., the ordinal content of the agents' utilities.

Ordinality. *If u_i and u'_i represent the same preference, for all $i \in [n]$, then $\succeq(u_1, \ldots, u_n) = \succeq(u'_1, \ldots, u'_n)$.*

Simply put, ordinality rules out interpersonal comparisons of utility because there is no scope for saying that one agent's preference for x over x' is stronger, or more intense, than another agent's preference for x' over x.

Our next axiom reduces the problem of choosing between x and x' to how individual agents would choose between them.

Independence of irrelevant alternatives. *If $\{i \in [n] : u_i(x) > u_i(x')\} = \{i \in [n] : u'_i(x) > u'_i(x')\}$ then $x \succeq(u_1, \ldots, u_n) x'$ iff $x \succeq(u'_1, \ldots, u'_n) x'$.*

The independence of irrelevant alternatives (IIA) says that, in comparing outcomes x and x', all that matters is how agents compare x and x': specifically, who would choose one over the other. This axiom says that the decision between x and x' should not be influenced by how agents compare outcomes that are not x or x'.

Observe that IIA implies ordinality.

Pareto. *If x is strongly Pareto dominated by x' for utilities $(u_1, \ldots, u_n)$, then $x' \succ(u_1, \ldots, u_n) x$.*

---

[4] The case when X has only two elements is special, in that simple majority voting yields a satisfactory solution.

The Pareto axiom (also called unanimity) forces social choices to be weakly efficient. If all agents strictly rank x' over x then the social choice from the set $\{x, x'\}$ should be x'.

Let L be the set of injective utility functions on X; that is, those that represent a strict preference. Let R be the set of all preference relations on X: all complete and transitive binary relations. Note that elements of R may express indifference among outcomes in X. Formally, then, a *preference aggregation rule* is a function $\succeq : L^n \to R$. If the preference aggregation rule satisfies ordinality then $\succeq(u_1, \ldots, u_n) = \succeq(u'_1, \ldots, u'_n)$ when each u_i represents the same preference as u'_i. Note that, by insisting on strict preferences, we are restricting attention to pure public goods problems.

Arrow's theorem. *Suppose that $|X| \geq 3$. A preference aggregation rule satisfies the Pareto axiom and the independence of irrelevant alternatives iff there exists an agent i for which, for all $(u_1, \ldots, u_n) \in L^n$, $\succ(u_1, \ldots, u_n)$ represents u_i.*

When the conclusion of Arrow's theorem holds, we say that i is a *dictator*.

Much can be said (and has!) about Arrow's theorem. Suffice it to write here that it exhibits a basic tension between efficiency, as captured by the Pareto axiom, and fairness – in the sense that a dictatorship is a violation of the most basic fairness criteria. For our purposes, however, it will be useful to emphasize ordinality, which is captured by IIA. We shall see that, by relaxing ordinality and allowing some cardinal information contained in utility functions to play a role, we are on our way to avoiding the dictatorial conclusion.

Specifically, consider the next property.

Independence of individual origins of utilities (IOU). *If there are scalars α_i and $\beta > 0$ such that $u'_i = \alpha_i + \beta u_i$ then $\succeq(u_1, \ldots, u_n) = \succeq(u'_1, \ldots, u'_n)$.*

Compare IOU with ordinality: IOU is also an invariance property, but a much weaker one. It says that the preference aggregation rule must treat two profiles in the same way whenever one is obtained from the other by means of an affine transformation $u'_i = \alpha_i + \beta u_i$, with a *common* scale factor $\beta > 0$. The IOU property means that agents' utilities are measured on a "partially common" scale, one that may only differ on the meaning of zero. In consequence, *changes* in utility are comparable across agents, while utility *levels* for different agents remain upcomparable.

The following axioms should be easy to grasp. First, we rule out dictatorships. Indeed, we impose anonymity as a fairness property: agents' names should play no role in social choice.

Anonimity. *If $\sigma : [n] \to [n]$ is a permutation then $\succeq(u_1, \ldots, u_n) = \succeq(u_{\sigma(1)}, \ldots, u_{\sigma(n)})$.*

The next two axioms are variations of Pareto and IIA. In them, we strengthen Pareto and impose a cardinal formulation of IIA.

Strong Pareto. *If x is Pareto dominated by x' for utilities $(u_1, \ldots, u_n)$ then $x' \succeq(u_1, \ldots, u_n) \, x$, and if x is strongly Pareto dominated by x' for utilities $(u_1, \ldots, u_n)$ then $x' \succ(u_1, \ldots, u_n) \, x$.*

Strong Pareto says that an outcome must be strictly preferred to any outcome that makes at least one agent worse off and no agent better off.

IIA'. *If $u_i(x) = u_i'(x)$ and $u_i(x') = u_i'(x')$ for all i then $x \succeq (u_1, \ldots, u_n) x'$ iff $x \succeq (u_1', \ldots, u_n') x'$.*

Recall that IIA imposes that the ranking between two alternatives must be the same for any profile of utilities in which individual ranks of the two alternatives do not change. The IIA' axiom avoids ordinality and says that the ranking must be the same for any profile of utilities in which agents' obtain the same utility values from the two alternatives. In this sense, it is a cardinal formulation of IIA.

As a result of these axioms, not only do we avoid the dictatorial conclusion of Arrow's theorem; we obtain a justification for utilitarianism.

Theorem 4.6. *A preference aggregation rule is anonymous, satisfies strong Pareto, IIA', and IOU iff it is utilitarian:*

$$x \succeq (u_1, \ldots, u_n) x' \text{ iff } \sum_{i=1}^{n} u_i(x) \geq \sum_{i=1}^{n} u_i(x').$$

The message of Theorem 4.6 is that, when we use the utilitarian criterion, we are buying into the axioms of anonymity, strong Pareto, IIA', and IOU. When using the utilitarian criterion, we are rejecting the axioms behind Arrow's theorem. Theorem 4.6 details the set of axioms that we are embracing instead.[5]

4.5.1 The Egalitarian Lexi-Min Rule

Utilitarianism relies on allowing the type of interpersonal comparisons of utilities that are consistent with IOU. As remarked above, IOU captures interpersonal comparisons of *utility changes*, not of utility levels. If we do entertain interpersonal comparisons of levels of utility then we are en route to a very strong (and very well known) egalitarian criterion. Specifically, consider the following.

Extremism. *For all $i, j \in [n]$ and $x, x' \in X$, whenever $u_h(x) = u_h(x')$ for all $h \in [n]$, $h \neq i, j$, we have that*

$$u_i(x) < u_i(x') < u_j(x') < u_j(x) \text{ implies } x' \succeq (u_1, \ldots, u_n) x.$$

Extremism says that, in choosing between x and x', we should favor the agent who is worse off. All agents other than i and j are indifferent, while i and j hold opposite preferences. Extremism rests on comparing the utilities of i and j at the two alternatives, and favoring the choice of the agent with the lower level of utility – lower regardless of the choice between x and x'.

Given $u = (u_1, \ldots, u_n)$ and $x \in X$, let $(v_1(u, x), \ldots, v_n(u, x))$ be a rearrangement of the vector $(u_1(x), \ldots, u_n(x))$ such that $v_i(u, x) \leq v_{i+1}(u, x)$. Moreover, denote

---

[5] One of the best known justifications for utilitarianism is Harsanyi's model of "behind the veil of ignorance" ethics. We have chosen not to include a formal discussion of Harsanyi's justification as it is probably less important for market design. Instead, we have emphasized a characterization that makes the role of interpersonal comparisons explicit.

the lexicographic ordering on $\mathbf{R}^n$ by $\leq_{lex}$: for any two vectors $\theta, \theta' \in \mathbf{R}^n$, say that $\theta \leq_{lex} \theta'$ when there exists h with $\theta_i = \theta'_i$ for all $i < h$ and $\theta_h < \theta'_h$.

Theorem 4.7. *A preference aggregation rule is anonymous, satisfies strong Pareto and extremism if and only if it is lexi-min:*

$$x \succeq (u_1, \ldots, u_n) \, x' \text{ iff } (v_1(u, x), \ldots, v_n(u, x)) \leq_{lex} (v_1(u, x'), \ldots, v_n(u, x')).$$

While the lexi-min rule rests on interpersonal comparisons of utility, it is not a fully cardinal rule. Lexi-min satisfies the next axiom, which is natural, and is worth contrasting with ordinality and IOU.

Co-ordinality. *If there exists a strictly monotone increasing $f: \mathbf{R} \to \mathbf{R}$ such that $u'_i = f \circ u_i$ for all $i \in [n]$ then $\succeq (u_1, \ldots, u_n) = \succeq (u'_1, \ldots, u'_n)$.*

Contrast co-ordinality with ordinality. The latter requires that the preference aggregation rule be invariant under individual ordinal transformations: $\succeq (u_1, \ldots, u_n) = \succeq (u'_1, \ldots, u'_n)$ whenever there exists, for all i, an ordinal (i.e., strictly increasing) transformation $f_i: \mathbf{R} \to \mathbf{R}$ such that $u'_i = f_i \circ u_i$. Co-ordinality requires invariance with respect to common ordinal transformations; IOU, in turn, focuses on affine utility transformations but does not impose a common transformation across agents.

4.5.2 Social Welfare Functions and Utilitarianism

We briefly touch on another foundation for utilitarianism, based on the idea of social welfare functions, a general device for making social choices. A *social welfare function* is a strictly increasing function $W: \mathbf{R}^n \to \mathbf{R}$. The idea is to choose x over x' when $W(u_1(x), \ldots, u_n(x)) > W(u_1(x'), \ldots, u_n(x'))$. Of course, for making choices, only the ordinal information contained in W matters; specifically, the composition of W with individual utilities orders the alternatives in X.

A social welfare function takes utility levels as its arguments, not the full utility function as does a preference aggregation rule. We use tildes, as in $\tilde{u}$, to denote levels of utility.

Origin independence. $W(\tilde{u}) \geq W(\tilde{u}')$ *implies that* $W(\tilde{u} + \tilde{v}) \geq W(\tilde{u}' + \tilde{v})$.

Theorem 4.8. *A continuous social choice function satisfies origin independence if and only if the following holds:*

$$W(\tilde{u}) \geq W(\tilde{u}') \text{ if and only if } \sum_{i=1}^{n} \tilde{u}_i \geq \sum_{i=1}^{n} \tilde{u}'_i.$$

4.6 Pareto Optimality and Weighted Utilitarianism

It should be clear that Pareto optimality, the basic notion of economic efficiency, is respected by the utilitarian rule. In most economic models, maximizing the utilitarian objective results in a Pareto optimal outcome. So it is natural to ask about

Pareto optimal outcomes that are not achieved by maximizing a particular utilitarian objective. We shall briefly describe the answer for allocative models. Specifically, fix an allocative environment with n agents. Recall that $X = \{(x_1, \ldots, x_n) : x_i \in \mathbf{R}^d_+, \sum_i x_i \le \bar{\omega}\}$ denotes the set of all allocations.

Given a vector $\lambda = (\lambda_1, \ldots, \lambda_n) \in \mathbf{R}^n_+$ of *welfare weights,* consider the *weighted utilitarian maximization* problem

$$P(\lambda) \colon \max_{x \in X} \sum_{i=1}^{n} \lambda_i u_i(x).$$

Observation 4.9. *If $\lambda_i > 0$ for all i then any solution to $P(\lambda)$ must be Pareto optimal.*

The *utility possibility set* for a social choice environment is

$$\mathcal{U} = \{(u_1(x), \ldots, u_n(x)) : x \in X\}.$$

Observation 4.10. *Consider an allocative environment in which X is compact and each utility function is continuous. If the set of $v \in \mathbf{R}^n$ for which there exists $v' \in \mathcal{U}$ with $v \le v'$ is convex then, for any Pareto optimal $x \in X$, there exist welfare weights λ for which x solves $P(\lambda)$.*

We say that $x \in X$ is a *utilitarian solution* if it solves the weighted utilitarian maximization problem with equal weights on all agents. The importance of Observation 4.10 is that there may be nothing special about the utilitarian solution. With non-uniform weights on utilities, any other Pareto optimal outcome is obtained. Uniform weights, in turn, only make sense if utilities are somehow measured on a common scale.

4.7 Partial Equilibrium Analysis and Quasilinear Utility

Think of an exchange economy as in Example 4.2, with d goods. Suppose that we are interested in the analysis of $L < d$ goods. Then we may imagine treating the remaining $d - L$ goods as a composite good termed "money." An agent then consumes a vector (y_i, t_i), where $y_i \in \mathbf{R}^L_+$ is a bundle of the L goods of interest and the scalar t_i represents consumption of the remaining goods. If preferences over (y_i, t_i) take a quasilinear form, we can carry out the analysis of the L goods in isolation: so-called *partial equilibrium analysis.*

Formally, consider a n-agent social choice environment in which $X = Y \times \mathbf{R}^n$. We consider allocative environments in which Y is the set of all vectors $(y_1, \ldots, y_n) \in \mathbf{R}^{nL}_+$ with $\sum_i y_i \le \bar{\omega}$. This is an economy with $L + 1$ goods, the last good being "money." We use quotation marks because this good may not have any of the properties that we identify with cash.[6] Suppose that the utilities are quasilinear and that $u_i((y_1, \ldots, y_n), (t_1, \ldots, t_n)) = v_i(y_i) + t_i$.

Imagine that agent i chooses (y_i, t_i) to maximize their utility, at some given prices. In fact we can normalize the price of money to be 1. Let $p \in \mathbf{R}^L_+$ be the vector of prices, and suppose that $I_i > 0$ is i's income. Then agent i solves the problem

---

[6] Actual money is created by a bank, usually a central bank such as the Federal Reserve, as a liability to the bank. Monetary economics is the area that studies the role of money in an economy: why agents use it, and its role in economic policy.

$$\max_{(y_i, t_i)} v_i(y_i) + t_i \text{ s.t } py_i + t_i \leq I_i.$$

We assume for simplicity that v_i is continuous, monotone, and strictly quasiconcave. The agent's optimization problem has then a unique solution. We allow agent i to consume negative quantities of money, so that at a solution to i's problem we must have $t_i = I_i - py_i$. Thus i's problem becomes

$$\max_{y_i \in \mathbf{R}_+^L} v_i(y_i) - py_i.$$

A solution $y_i = d_i(p)$ to this problem is termed i's *demand function* for y. Thanks to quasilinearity, d_i does not depend on i's income. This represents a tremendous simplification in comparison with general equilibrium models, which require a careful consideration of income effects. For example, in the exchange economy model of Example 4.2, when taxing the market for apples we need to worry about its effects on the market for oranges and grapes. Then we need to worry about the feedback loop: the effect of what happens to oranges and grapes on the market for apples. Quasilinear utility breaks the feedback loop and allows us to study the market for apples in isolation.

The magnitude $v_i(y_i) - py_i$ deserves the name *consumer's surplus*: the consumer would have been willing to pay $v_i(y_i)$ for the goods in the vector y_i, but they paid only py_i.

Continuing with our justification for the terminology that we shall use, imagine that there is a producer who earns revenue py_i from i's purchases. This producer earns then a total revenue $\sum_i py_i$, which (in the absence of costs) can be termed the producers' surplus.

Combining these ideas, we arrive at

$$\text{Total surplus} = \sum_{i=1}^{n} v_i(y_i) = \underbrace{\sum_{i=1}^{n} [v_i(y_i) - py_i]}_{\text{Consumers' surplus}} + \underbrace{\sum_{i=1}^{n} py_i}_{\text{Producers' surplus}}$$

In this economy, the set $Z = \{(y_i) \in \mathbf{R}_+^{nL} : \sum_i y_i \leq \bar{\omega}\}$ represents all the vectors of L goods that can be allocated among the agents. In addition to these goods, there is money. We say then that an allocation $(y, t_1, \ldots, t_n) \in Z \times \mathbf{R}^n$ is *Pareto optimal* if there is no $(y', \tau_1, \ldots, \tau_n) \in Z \times \mathbf{R}^n$ with $v_i(y_i) + t_i < v_i(y_i') + \tau_i$ and $\sum_i t_i \geq \sum_i \tau_i$. In other words, the allocation is Pareto optimal if there is no alternative allocation and a reassignment of the consumption of money that leaves everyone better off without using outside money.[7]

Finally, $(y_1, \ldots y_n)$ is *surplus-maximizing* if it solves the problem

$$\max_{(y_i) \in Z} \sum_{i=1}^{n} v_i(y_i).$$

Observation 4.11. *An outcome $(y_i, t_i)_{i=1}^{n}$ is Pareto optimal iff $(y_i)_{i=1}^{n}$ is surplus-maximizing.*

---

[7] We could define strong Pareto optimality separately, but the notions of Pareto and strong Pareto are the same in this model.

Proof Suppose that (y_i, t_i) is not Pareto optimal. Then there is (z_i, τ_i) with $(z_i) \in Z$ and $v_i(z_i) + \tau_i > v_i(y_i) + t_i$ for all i. Hence $\sum_i v_i(z_i) + \sum_i \tau_i > \sum_i v_i(y_i) + \sum_i t_i$. Now, $\sum_i \tau_i \leq \sum_i t_i$ implies that $\sum_i v_i(y_i) < \sum_i v_i(z_i)$; hence y is not surplus-maximizing.

Conversely, suppose that y is not surplus-maximizing. Then there is $(z_i) \in Z$ such that $\sum_i v_i(y_i) < \sum_i v_i(z_i)$. Let β_i be such that $\sum_i \beta_i = \sum_i v_i(z_i)$ and $\beta_i > v_i(y_i)$ for all $i \in [n]$. Set τ_i such that $v_i(z_i) + \tau_i = \beta_i + t_i > v_i(y_i) + t_i$. Then

$$\sum_i \tau_i = \sum_i \beta_i - \sum_i v_i(z_i) + \sum_i t_i = \sum_i t_i. \qquad \square$$

4.8 Incentives

We now turn to situations where individual agents hold a piece of information that is not commonly known. We are still looking for a desirable outcome, but what exactly that outcome is depends on information that each agent has. It may not be in their best interest to reveal this information to us.

Imagine allocating a piece of candy among three kids: Alice, Bob, and Carol. You are a believer in the utilitarian rule, which means that you want to give the candy to the kid who likes it the most. If you ask Alice, she will tell you that the candy is worth more to her than to Bob and Carol. The other two will say the same. It is impossible to find out how much the candy is worth to these kids. So, even though you are persuaded by the axioms behind utilitarianism, incentive problems prevent you from carrying out your objective.

To capture the information held by each agent, we introduce "types" into the model.

A n-agent *social choice environment* is a tuple $(X, (\Theta_i, u_i)_{i=1}^n)$ where

- X is a set of *outcomes*;
- for each i, Θ_i is a set of *types* and

$$u_i \colon \Theta_i \times X \to \mathbf{R}$$

is the *utility function* of agent i.

Denote by $\Theta = \Theta_1 \times \cdots \times \Theta_n$ be the set of *type profiles* $\theta = (\theta_1, \ldots, \theta_n)$. A function $f \colon \Theta \to X$ is a *social choice function*.

4.8.1 Mechanisms

Definition 4.12. A tuple $(M_1, \ldots, M_n, g)$ is a *mechanism* for the n-agent environment $(X, (\Theta_i, u_i)_{i=1}^n)$ if each M_i is a non-empty set of messages and

$$g \colon \times_{i=1}^n M_i \to X.$$

We use the following notation. A message *profile* is an element

$$m = (m_1, \ldots, m_n) \in M = \times_{i=1}^n M_i.$$

We write message profiles as $m = (m_i, m_{-i})$ for $m_i \in M_i$ and

$$m_{-i} = (m_1, \ldots, m_{i-1}, m_{i+1}, \ldots, m_n) \in \times_{j \neq i} M_j.$$

Example 4.13. Here is a public good example. Imagine two roommates who have to decide whether to buy a new air conditioning (AC) unit. The AC unit is consumed by both roommates in the same amount: it is a *public good*. Suppose that the new AC costs $c \in (0, 1)$. Public goods give rise to incentives to free-ride. If Agent 1 buys the AC, then Agent 2 will be able to enjoy it at no cost. This translates into incentives for revealing how much installing a new AC is worth to each of the agents. If, for example, we ask each agent to contribute an amount that is proportional to how much the good is worth to them, each agent may declare that the AC is worth less than it really is.

Formally the situation can be modeled as a two-agent social choice environment. Let $n = 2$ and X be the set of all tuples (y, t_1, t_2) such that $y \in \{0, 1\}$ and $t_i \in \mathbf{R}$ for $i = 1, 2$. Let $\Theta_i = [0, 1]$ and $u_i((y, t_1, t_2), \theta_i) = \theta_i y - t_i$.

In this environment, one example of a mechanism is (M_1^1, M_2^1, g^1), where each agent declares a message that is a non-negative real number: $m_i \in \mathbf{R}_+ = M_i^1$. If both m_1 and m_2 are strictly below c then $g^1(m_1, m_2) = (0, 0, 0)$. If at least one of m_1, m_2 exceeds c then $g^1(m_1, m_2) = (1, t_1^1(m_1, m_2), t_2^1(m_1, m_2))$, with

$$t_i^1(m_1, m_2) = \begin{cases} c & \text{if } m_i \geq c > m_{3-i}, \\ 0 & \text{if } m_i < c, \\ c/2 & \text{if } \min\{m_1, m_2\} \geq c. \end{cases}$$

Another mechanism for the same example has (M_1^2, M_2^2, g^2) with $M_i^2 = \mathbf{R}_+$ as above, but where

$$g^2(m_1, m_2) = \begin{cases} (0, 0, 0) & \text{if } m_1 + m_2 < c, \\ (1, t_1^2(m), t_2^2(m)) & \text{if } m_1 + m_2 \geq c, \end{cases}$$

where

$$t_i^2(m) = c \frac{m_i}{m_1 + m_2}$$

if $m_1 + m_2 \geq c$. Recall that $m = (m_1, m_2)$ denotes a message pair.

Finally, consider a mechanism (M_1^3, M_2^3, g^3) with $M_i^3 = \{0, 1\}$ and $g^3(m) = (1, c, 0)$ if $m_1 = 1$ and $g(m) = (0, 0, 0)$ otherwise.

4.8.1.1 Dominant Strategies

Let (M, g) be a mechanism in an n-agent environment $(X, (\Theta_i, u_i)_{i=1}^n)$. The mechanism and the environment give rise to a *game* in which each agent (or player) chooses a message simultaneously and without knowing the messages that the rest of the agents are choosing. In principle, to understand what message a agent will choose, we need to understand what she believes the other agents are going to choose. This is usually analyzed though game-theoretical equilibrium notions. Here, we are going to focus on particularly simple situations in which a message is optimal regardless of what the agent thinks that the other agents are going to choose.

A message is dominant for agent i at type θ_i if there is no other message she could send that would result in higher utility (when her type is θ_i), no matter what message the remaining agents send. Formally, a message $m_i \in M_i$ is *dominant* for agent i at $\theta_i \in \Theta_i$ if

$$u_i(\theta_i, g(m_i', m_{-i}')) \leq u_i(\theta_i, g(m_i, m_{-i}'))$$

for all $m'_i \in M_i$ and for all $m'_{-i} \in M_{-i}$. When a message is dominant, the agent in question has no reason to choose an alternative message, regardless of what she thinks the other agents will choose.[8]

Now, the agent needs to choose a message for each particular type that she may have. This type-dependent choice is summarized through the notion of a strategy. A *strategy* for player i is a function $s_i \colon \Theta_i \to M_i$.

A strategy s_i for player i is a *dominant strategy* if, for all $\theta_i \in \Theta_i$, $s_i(\theta_i) \in M_i$ is a dominant message for i at θ_i. So a strategy s_i is dominant if, for all $\theta_i \in \Theta_i$,

$$ u_i(\theta_i, g(m'_i, m'_{-i})) \le u_i(\theta_i, g(s_i(\theta_i), m'_{-i})) $$

for all $m'_i \in M_i$ and $m'_{-i} \in M_{-i}$.

A strategy profile $s = (s_1, \dots, s_n)$ is a *dominant-strategy equilibrium* if s_i is a dominant strategy for every i. Dominant strategies are desirable because we can trust that agents will behave as prescribed by the strategy, regardless of how they believe that other players are going to behave in the mechanism. If we design a mechanism with a particular outcome in mind (the ultimate purpose of the current discussion), then we can advertise among the agents that a particular strategy profile is a dominant-strategy equilibrium. The agents have no reason not to comply with the prescribed behavior. It is in their interest to act as the strategy prescribes, regardless of what they think the rest of the agents will do.

Consider the public good example we discussed above. The first two mechanisms have no dominant strategy equilibria. In the first mechanism (M^1, M^1, g^1), for an agent with a low value of θ_i it is dominant to set m_i very low, so as to never contribute to the public good. But, for higher levels of θ_i, the optimal decision depends on the messages sent by the other agents. The same is true in (M^2, M^2, g^2). The third mechanism has a dominant-strategy equilibrium in which agent 1 funds the public good on his own whenever it is worthwhile for him to do so.

4.8.2 Dominant-Strategy Implementation

Let f be a social choice function (scf). A mechanism $(M_1, \dots, M_n, g)$ *implements f in dominant strategies* if there is a dominant-strategy equilibrium s such that

$$ g(s(\theta)) = f(\theta) $$

for all $\theta \in \Theta$. We say that an scf f is *dominant-strategy implementable* if there exists a mechanism that implements it in dominant strategies.

Given an scf f, the *direct-revelation mechanism* defined by f is the mechanism in which each agent's message space is her type space: she is restricted to stating her type. The outcome function is simply the scf f. In symbols, the direct-revelation mechanism defined by f is $(\Theta_1, \dots, \Theta_n, f)$.

An scf is *truthfully implementable in dominant strategies* (or *strategy-proof*, or *dominant-strategy incentive compatible*) if the strategy profile s given by $s_i(\theta_i) = \theta_i$ for all $\theta_i \in \Theta_i$ is a dominant-strategy equilibrium of the direct revelation mechanism defined by f.

---

[8] Game theory distinguishes between weak and strong dominance, but we shall not do so here.

4.8.3 Revelation Principle

Our next result is important because it says that in investigating dominant-strategy implementable social choice functions, it is enough to check whether the function is truthfully implementable. The problem of finding an implementable scf, and verifying whether a particular scf is implementable, is therefore greatly simplified.

Proposition 4.14. *An scf is dominant-strategy implementable if and only if it is truthfully implementable.*

Proof One direction is obvious. So suppose that an scf is dominant-strategy implementable. Let $(M_1, \ldots, M_n, g)$ be a mechanism that dominant-strategy implements it, and let s be the relevant dominant-strategy equilibrium. Let $\theta_i, \theta_i' \in \Theta_i$ and let $\theta_{-i} \in \Theta_{-i}$. Then, if we let $m_i = s_i(\theta_i)$, $m_i' = s_i(\theta_i')$), and $m_{-i} = s_{-i}(\theta_{-i})$, we obtain that

$$u_i(\theta_i, f(\theta)) = u_i(\theta_i, g(s(\theta))) = u_i(\theta_i, g(m_i, m_{-i}))$$
$$\geq u_i(\theta_i, g(m_i', m_{-i}))$$
$$= u_i(\theta_i, g(s_i(\theta_i'), s_{-i}(\theta_{-i})))$$
$$= u_i(\theta_i, f(\theta_i', \theta_{-i})).$$

Thus f is truthfully implementable. $\qquad\square$

Example 4.15. This example involves the immediate acceptance mechanism.[9] Consider an environment in which there is a set of children and a set of schools. The children have preferences over the schools, and each school has a ranking over the children: a priority list. The scf is described through an algorithm. First, each child "applies" to his or her top-ranked school. Each school admits the best children (in terms of the school's ranking) that have applied, up to their unfilled capacity. The algorithm iterates this step as children are rejected.

Suppose that there are three children $\{k_1, k_2, k_3\}$ and three schools, $\{x_1, x_2, x_3\}$. All schools rank the children in the order k_1, k_2, k_3 and each has exactly one place available.

The childrens' preferences over schools are as described in Table 4.1.

Table 4.1

k_1	k_2	k_3
x_1	x_1	x_2
x_2	x_2	x_3
x_3	x_3	x_1

If k_2 has submitted her preferences truthfully, she "applies" first to school x_1 and is rejected. In second place she applies to school x_2, which has already accepted k_3's application in the first round of the algorithm. If, instead, k_2 lies and applies first to school x_2 (for example submitting the ranking x_2, x_1, x_3)

---

[9] Also known as the Boston mechanism.

then she competes with k_3 for school x_2 in the first round of the algorithm, Since k_2 has the higher priority at school x_2, she is accepted. Thus it is beneficial to child k_2 to lie about her preferences.

An scf function f is *dictatorial* if there is an agent i such that f always chooses an optimal outcome for i: for all $\theta \in \Theta$ and $x \in X$,

$$u_i(\theta_i, f(\theta)) \geq u_i(\theta_i, x).$$

An environment is *unrestricted* if for every possible ranking of X there is a $\theta_i \in \Theta_i$ such that $u_i(\theta_i, x)$ represents that ranking.

Gibbard–Sattherthwaite theorem. *Let $(X, (\Theta_i, u_i)_{i=1}^n)$ be an unrestricted environment containing at least three elements, and let f be an scf with $f(\Theta) = X$ (so that f is onto.) Then f is dominant-strategy implementable iff it is dictatorial.*

4.9 Bibliographical Notes

Arrow's theorem is taken from [1]. See [4] for an exposition. Theorems 4.6 and 4.7 were drawn from [2]. Partial equilibrium analysis is treated in detail in [3].

References

[1] Arrow, Kenneth J. 2012. *Social Choice and Individual Values*, vol. 12. Yale University Press.
[2] d'Aspremont, Claude, and Gevers, Louis. 1977. Equity and the informational basis of collective choice. *Review of Economic Studies*, **44**(2), 199–209.
[3] Mas-Colell, Andreu, Whinston, Michael Dennis, Green, Jerry R., 1995. *Microeconomic theory*, vol. 1. Oxford University Press.
[4] Moulin, Hervé. 1991. *Axioms of Cooperative Decision Making*, vol. 15. Cambridge University Press.

PART TWO

Applications (Modern and Traditional)

CHAPTER FIVE

Applications of Online Matching

Zhiyi Huang and Thorben Tröbst

5.1 Introduction

Building on three decades of research, online matching has evolved into a rich theory at the intersection of economics, operations research, and computer science. This development has been due in large part to many applications that have arisen from the evolution of the Internet and mobile computing: Google matches search queries to advertisers, Uber matches drivers to riders, Upwork matches employers to freelancers, Tinder matches people to other people, etc.

This chapter will present online matching models for these applications, and will study the corresponding algorithms from the economic viewpoint introduced in Chapter 2. Section 5.2 covers models inspired by online advertising. Section 5.3 focuses on more general arrival models motivated by other problems such as ride sharing. We will assume familiarity with the online bipartite matching problem and its associated notions defined in Chapter 2.

5.2 Models for Online Advertising

The online matching models that we will study in this section are a substantial abstraction of advertisement (ad) auctions that take place on search engines and other websites every day.

Example 5.1. Consider a search engine provider which shows ads to users when they perform searches. The offline vertices in this case are advertisements, e.g., 100 ads for a new book, 200 ads for a new chair, etc. The online vertices are search requests by users of the search engine.[1] Each time a user performs a search, an ad relevant to their search terms should be displayed instantaneously; relevance corresponds to edges in the graph.

The example leaves open how the advertisers pay the search engine provider. If each ad is worth the same amount, the algorithm and analysis from Chapter 2 apply. This section will consider more complex compensation schemes.

---

[1] In the terminology of Chapter 2, search requests would be *buyers* and advertisers *goods* even though their "real" roles in the ad market are the exact opposite.

Remark 5.2. In this chapter we will generally take a worst-case approach. However, in practice one may sometimes make certain additional assumptions such as requiring that search requests are sampled from a fixed distribution or that advertisers are able to pay for a large number of ads. Models with these additional assumptions are studied in Chapter 2.

5.2.1 RANKING with Vertex Weights

We start by studying a slight generalization of the online bipartite matching problem in which each good j has *value* $v_j \geq 0$, and the goal is to maximize the value of matched goods. This means that in Example 5.1 advertisers pay different rates to have their ads displayed.

Recall RANKING and its analysis from the economic viewpoint introduced in Chapter 2. We will make two changes to the algorithm: the price of good j is scaled by its value, and buyers buy goods maximizing their utility, i.e., the difference between a goods value and its price. Formally this is Algorithm 5.1.

Algorithm 5.1 RANKING with vertex weights.

---
1 **for** $j \in S$ **do**
2   ⌊ Set price $p_j \leftarrow v_j e^{w_j - 1}$ where $w_j \in [0, 1]$ is sampled uniformly.
3 **for** *each buyer i who arrives* **do**
4   │ Let $N(i)$ be the unmatched neighbors of i.
5   │ **if** $N(i) \neq \emptyset$ **then**
6   │   ⌊ Match i to $j \in N(i)$ maximizing $v_j - p_j$.

Definition 5.3. For good $j \in S$, the revenue r_j is p_j if it is sold and 0 otherwise. For buyer $i \in B$, the utility u_i is $v_j - p_j$ if it buys the good j and 0 otherwise.

The analysis of the vertex-weighted RANKING algorithm remains largely the same as in Chapter 2. For the sake of completeness, we will state the necessary lemmas and sketch their proofs. As before we consider a random variable u_e which represents the utility of buyer i if edge $e = (i, j)$ is removed from the graph.

Lemma 5.4. *Let $(i, j) \in E$ be arbitrary. Then:*

1. $u_i \geq u_e$.
2. If $p_j < v_j - u_e$ then j will be matched.

Proof 1. Having an additional edge can only increase the utility of buyer i since i is free to not choose it.

    2. If j has not been matched when i arrives then j will be matched to i.   □

Lemma 5.5. *Let $(i, j) \in E$ be arbitrary. Then $\mathbb{E}\left[u_i + r_j\right] \geq (1 - 1/e)v_j$.*

Proof As in Chapter 2, the idea is to condition on the value of u_e. By Lemma 5.4, we know that $\mathbb{E}[u_i] \geq \mathbb{E}[u_e]$. Moreover, for any $z \in [0, (1 - 1/e)v_j]$ let w be such that $v_j e^{w-1} = v_j - z$. Then, by Lemma 5.4,

$$\mathbb{E}\left[r_j \mid u_e = z\right] \geq \int_0^w v_j e^{x-1} \, dx$$

$$= \left(1 - \frac{1}{e}\right) v_j - z.$$

Note that this inequality holds trivially also if $z > (1 - 1/e)v_j$.

Finally, by the law of total expectation we know that

$$\mathbb{E}\left[r_j\right] = \mathbb{E}_z\left[\mathbb{E}\left[r_j \mid u_e = z\right]\right] = \left(1 - \frac{1}{e}\right) v_j - \mathbb{E}\left[u_e\right]$$

and thus $\mathbb{E}\left[u_i + r_j\right] \geq (1 - 1/e)v_j$ by the linearity of expectation. □

Theorem 5.6. *Algorithm 5.1 is $(1 - 1/e)$-competitive.*

Proof Let M be a matching in G which maximizes the total value of the matched goods. The value matched by RANKING is exactly $\sum_{i \in B} u_i + \sum_{j \in S} r_j$. Further, by Lemma 5.5 and the linearity of expectation we get

$$\mathbb{E}\left[\sum_{i \in B} u_i + \sum_{j \in S} r_j\right] \geq \sum_{(i,j) \in M} \mathbb{E}\left[u_i + r_j\right]$$

$$\geq \sum_{(i,j) \in M} \left(1 - \frac{1}{e}\right) v_j.$$

□

Chapter 2 showed that the factor $1 - 1/e$ is optimal, even in the case of unit values. Thus, RANKING provides an optimal online algorithm for the vertex-weighted online bipartite matching problem.

Remark 5.7. Readers familiar with primal–dual algorithms will recognize this type of argument: what we have essentially shown is that the variables $\mathbb{E}\left[u_i\right]$ and $\mathbb{E}\left[v_j\right]$ form an $(1 - 1/e)$-approximately feasible solution to the dual of the matching problem. This primal–dual viewpoint on online matching is equivalent to the economic viewpoint presented in this chapter.

5.2.1.1 Deriving the Optimal Prices

In the previous subsection we used the functions $g_j(x) := v_j e^{x-1}$ to assign prices $p_j \leftarrow g_j(w_j)$ to the goods j. But how did we know that these are the right prices? The idea is to carry out the analysis of Algorithm 5.1 via generic functions g_j and to try to maximize the bound on the competitive ratio.

Lemma 5.4 is unaffected by the choice of g_j but in Lemma 5.5 our goal is to prove that $\mathbb{E}\left[u_i + r_j\right] \geq \Gamma v_j$ for the largest possible Γ. In the proof we assumed that g_j is increasing and that its range contains $[(1 - \Gamma)v_j, v_j]$.

Under these assumptions, we then observed in the proof of Lemma 5.5 that

$$\mathbb{E}\left[r_j \mid u_e = z\right] \geq \int_0^w g_j(x)\, dx$$

where $z \in [0, \Gamma v_j]$ and w is such that $g_j(w) = v_j - z$. In order to finish the proof we need to use

$$\int_0^w g_j(x)\, dx \geq \Gamma v_j - z = \Gamma v_j - v_j + g_j(w).$$

So our goal is to find some g_j such that Γ can be chosen as large as possible. Let us assume that for optimal g_j and maximal Γ we have equality, i.e.,

$$v_j - g_j(w) + \int_0^w g_j(x)\, dx = \Gamma v_j. \tag{5.1}$$

Taking the derivative with respect to w of both sides yields the elementary differential equation $-g_j'(w) + g_j(w) = 0$, which is solved by functions of the form $g_j(x) = Ce^x$. Substituting this back into (5.1) yields $v_j - C = \Gamma v_j$, and so we would like to make C as small as possible. But since the range of g_j should include v_j, the minimum choice for C is v_j/e, which yields $g_j(x) = v_j e^{x-1}$ and $\Gamma = 1 - 1/e$.

5.2.2 Fractional and Multi-Matching Models

Aside from RANKING, there is another framework for solving online matching problems. If we allow matching multiple buyers to a single good, an effective strategy is to *balance* the number of buyers to which each good is matched. Depending on whether buyers are matched fractionally or in an integer way to the goods, the algorithms based on this idea are called WATER-FILLING or BALANCE.

5.2.2.1 WATER-FILLING

As a warm-up, we first introduce WATER-FILLING and its analysis in the online bipartite matching problem. In this setting, each buyer i is matched fractionally when it arrives, i.e., the algorithm determines non-negative values $(x_{i,j})_{(i,j)\in E}$ subject to $\sum_{j\in N(i)} x_{i,j} \leq 1$ and, for any good j, $\sum_{i\in N(j)} x_{i,j} \leq 1$. The goal is to maximize $\sum_{(i,j)\in E} x_{i,j}$.

Remark 5.8. Allowing fractional matchings makes the problem strictly easier. By a classical result in matching theory, in any bipartite graph, the size of a maximum *fractional* matching equals the size of a maximum *integral* matching.

The WATER-FILLING algorithm is inspired by the following physical metaphor. Imagine that each buyer brings a watering can filled with one unit of water and each good corresponds to a tank that holds at most one unit of water. How should we distribute each buyer's water into their neighboring tanks such that the total amount of water is maximized? The intuitive answer is that each buyer should pour water into the tanks with the lowest water level so as to equalize the water levels in the tanks. See Figure 5.1 for an example.

As with RANKING, we will take an economic viewpoint on WATER-FILLING. Each good will have a price e^{w-1}, similar to that in RANKING but this time it

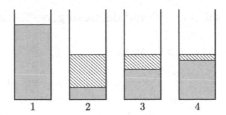

Figure 5.1 Shown is an iteration of WATER-FILLING with four "tanks" (offline vertices). The gray region represents the water level at the beginning of the iteration whereas the shaded regions represent an additional unit of water.

depends on the "water level" w, i.e., how much of the good has been matched so far. When buyer i arrives, it buys fractional edges $x_{i,j}$ from its neighbors $N(i)$ so as to maximize the total utility. Formally, let $w_j := \sum_{i' \in N(i)} x_{i',j}$ be the total amount of good j which has been sold so far. Buyer i solves the convex program

$$\max_{(x_{i,j})_{j \in N(i)}} \sum_{j \in N(i)} \int_{w_j}^{w_j + x_{i,j}} \left(1 - e^{w-1}\right) dw$$

$$\text{s.t.} \quad \sum_{j \in N(i)} x_{i,j} \leq 1,$$

$$x_{i,j} \geq 0 \qquad \forall j \in N(i) \tag{5.2}$$

which is equivalent to the aforementioned continuous process of water-filling.

Accordingly, buyer i pays $\int_{w_j}^{w_j + x_{i,j}} e^{w-1} dw$ for each good j. We remark that the utility $1 - e^{w-1}$ ensures that the water levels do not exceed 1. This results in Algorithm 5.2 (the payments are only required for the analysis).

Algorithm 5.2 WATER-FILLING for the online fractional bipartite matching problem

---

1 **for** *each buyer i who arrives* **do**
2 $\quad$ Compute an optimum solution $(x_{i,j})_{j \in N(i)}$ to the problem (5.2).

Under this economic interpretation of WATER-FILLING, its analysis follows the same framework as the analysis of RANKING presented in Chapter 2 and in the previous subsection. Let r_j be the total revenue of good j, i.e., the sum of all payments made for fractions of j by the buyers. Let u_i be the utility of buyer i, i.e., the objective function value of (5.2) in buyer i's iteration.

Lemma 5.9. *Let $(i, j) \in E$ be arbitrary. Then $r_j + u_i \geq 1 - 1/e$.*

Proof On the one hand, let w^* be the water level of good j at the end of Algorithm 5.2. Then $r_j = \int_0^{w^*} e^{w-1} dw$.

On the other hand, let w_j be the amount of good j which is allocated before buyer i arrives. Then u_i is the objective function value of (5.2) and thus must be at least $1 - e^{w_j + x_{i,j} - 1}$, otherwise the solution could be improved by increasing

$x_{i,j}$ by some suitably small $\epsilon > 0$ and decreasing $x_{i,j'}$ for some other $j' \in N(i)$ to maintain that $\sum_{k \in N(i)} x_{i,k} \leq 1$.

Finally, using $w_j + \Delta x_{i,j} \leq w^*$, we get

$$r_j + u_i \geq \int_0^{w^*} e^{w-1} \, dw + 1 - e^{w_j + \Delta x_{i,j} - 1}$$

$$\geq e^{w^*-1} - \frac{1}{e} + 1 - e^{w^*-1} = 1 - \frac{1}{e}. \qquad \square$$

Theorem 5.10. *Algorithm 5.2 is $(1 - 1/e)$-competitive.*

Proof It is clear from the updates of $x_{i,j}$, r_j, and u_i during the algorithm that

$$\sum_{(i,j) \in E} x_{i,j} = \sum_{j \in S} r_j + \sum_{i \in B} u_i.$$

On the other hand, let $(y_{i,j})_{(i,j) \in E}$ be any other fractional matching. Then

$$\sum_{(i,j) \in E} y_{i,j} \leq \frac{1}{1 - 1/e} \sum_{(i,j) \in E} y_{i,j}(r_j + u_i)$$

$$\leq \frac{1}{1 - 1/e} \left(\sum_{j \in S} r_j + \sum_{i \in B} u_i \right)$$

where we have used that $\sum_{j \in S} y_{i,j} \leq 1$ for all i and with a similar relation when we sum over buyers. Together with the previous equality this shows that the total size of the fractional matching x is at least a fraction $1 - 1/e$ of any fractional matching. $\qquad \square$

As previously discussed, the online fractional bipartite matching problem is easier than the integral problem, which also admits a $(1 - 1/e)$-competitive algorithm. The main improvement here is that WATER-FILLING is deterministic whereas RANK-ING is randomized. There is also a matching upper bound of $1 - 1/e$ for the fractional problem, and thus WATER-FILLING is optimal; see Exercise 5.3 at the end of the chapter.

5.2.2.2 BALANCE

WATER-FILLING is applicable only when fractional allocations are allowed, which is rarely the case in practice. Nonetheless, a rounded variant of WATER-FILLING called BALANCE works well for problems in which the offline vertices may be matched many times. Importantly, it includes the online advertising in Example 5.1 since advertisers typically want their ads displayed thousands or even millions of times.

Formally, the online bipartite b-matching problem is a variant of online bipartite matching in which each good may be matched up to $b \in \mathbb{N}$ times.[2] A natural approach for this problem is to match each online vertex to a neighboring offline vertex which is currently the least matched. From an economic viewpoint, it means that the price of a good increases monotonically with the fill level. The optimal choice

---

[2] The algorithm and analysis generalize to the case where there are distinct b_j for different goods j.

for the pricing function turns out to be $(1 + 1/b)^{w-b}$ where w is the number of buyers matched to the given good. When b is large, it is approximately $e^{w/b-1}$, i.e., the pricing function in WATER-FILLING. See Algorithm 5.3.

Algorithm 5.3 BALANCE for the online bipartite b-matching problem

---

1   Initialize the price p_j of each good j to $(1 + 1/b)^{-b}$.
2   **for** *each buyer i who arrives* **do**
3   Let $N(i)$ be the neighbors of i.
4   Match i to $j := \arg\min_{j \in N(i)} p_j$.
5      $p_j \leftarrow p_j (1 + 1/b)$

As before, let r_j be the total revenue collected by good j and let u_i be the utility obtained by buyer i.

Lemma 5.11. *Let $(i,j) \in E$ be arbitrary. Then $r_j/b + u_i \geq 1 - (1 + 1/b)^{-b}$.*

Proof   Let w be the total number of buyers who end up buying good j. Then

$$r_j = \sum_{k=0}^{w-1} \left(1 + \frac{1}{b}\right)^{k-b}$$

$$= b\left(\left(1 + \frac{1}{b}\right)^{w-b} - \left(1 + \frac{1}{b}\right)^{-b}\right).$$

On the other hand, the price of good j was at most $(1 + 1/b)^{w-b}$ when i arrived, and so $u_i \geq 1 - (1 + 1/b)^{w-b}$. Thus $r_j/b + u_i \geq 1 - (1 + 1/b)^{-b}$. $\square$

Theorem 5.12. *Algorithm 5.3 is $(1 - (1 + 1/b)^{-b})$-competitive.*

Proof   Let M be a maximal b-matching in G. Then

$$|M| \leq \sum_{(i,j) \in M} \frac{r_j/b + u_i}{1 - (1 + 1/b)^{-b}}$$

$$\leq \frac{1}{1 - (1 + 1/b)^{-b}} \left(\sum_{j \in S} r_j + \sum_{i \in B} u_i\right).$$

Since the sum of revenues and utilities is the size of the matching generated by the algorithm, this concludes the proof. $\square$

Because $(1 + 1/b)^{-b}$ converges to $1/e$ as $b \to \infty$, the competitive ratio converges to $1 - 1/e$ for large capacities. There is a matching lower bound of $1 - (1 + 1/b)^{-b}$ for *deterministic* algorithms in the online bipartite b-matching problem. Of course, if we consider randomized algorithms, RANKING is $(1 - 1/e)$-competitive.

5.2.3 Edge-Weighted Online Matching with Free Disposal

We will now turn to the edge-weighted online bipartite matching problem, in which the value of a good may also depend on the buyer to which it is matched, i.e., each edge $(i, j) \in E$ has a value $v_{i,j} \geq 0$. This is relevant in the modern markets of *targeted* advertising. Advertisers are willing to pay more if an ad is shown to a user from its target demographic. For example, a restaurant will be willing to pay more for having its ads shown to users that live close by. This is also known as the display ads problem.

Theorem 5.13. *There is no constant-factor-competitive online algorithm for the edge-weighted online bipartite matching problem.*

Proof Consider a family of instances that consist of a single good and n buyers. For any $1 \leq k \leq n$ and some $V > 1$, let there be an instance in which the first k buyers have values $1, V, V^2, \ldots, V^{k-1}$ for the good, and the remaining buyers have value 0. Suppose that the algorithm assigns the good to buyer i with probability p_i when $k \geq i$. Then $\sum_{i=1}^n p_i \leq 1$. Hence, there is some i such that $p_i \leq \frac{1}{n}$. But then the algorithm's expected value for the instance $k = i$ is at most $\frac{1}{n} V^{k-1} + \frac{n-1}{n} V^{k-2}$. Comparing with the optimal value V^{k-1}, the competitive ratio is at most $\frac{1}{n} + \frac{n-1}{nV}$, which tends to 0 as n and V tend to infinity. $\qquad\square$

Theorem 5.13 necessitates an additional assumption if we want to make the edge-weighted problem tractable. Observe that the constraint of displaying an advertiser's ad at most once is artificial. An advertiser would be happy to have their ad displayed multiple times if the extra displays were free. Hence, we consider a relaxed model where an offline vertex (i.e., an advertiser) can be matched more than once but only the most valuable one counts in the objective. Equivalently, it can be stated as the *free disposal* assumption: offline vertices may drop edges to previous online vertices in favor of better edges or matchings? It allows us to design constant competitive online algorithms; see e.g. Exercise 5.4 for a greedy approach.

We will modify the WATER-FILLING algorithm from Section 5.2.2 for the fractional setting by changing the prices of goods suitably. In particular, even if a good is already fully matched, it might continue getting matched to better and better edges. Thus the price can no longer depend only on the current fill-level of the good; it must further take into account the values of the edges along which it is matched.

To keep track of this, we define a function $w_{x,j} \colon \mathbb{R}_{\geq 0} \to [0, 1]$ for any fractional matching x and any good $j \in S$. The value of $w_{x,j}(t)$ represents the fraction of good j which is assigned in x on edges of value at least t, i.e.,

$$w_{x,j}(t) := \sum_{i : v_{i,j} \geq t} x_{i,j}.$$

Consider now what happens when buyer i arrives and wishes to buy good j. Assume that j is already fully matched to various buyers and let i' be the buyer with the least value. We can then think of i as filling up the rectangle $[v_{i',j}, v_{i,j}] \times [0, 1]$ with the graph of $w_{x,j}(t)$. See Figure 5.2.

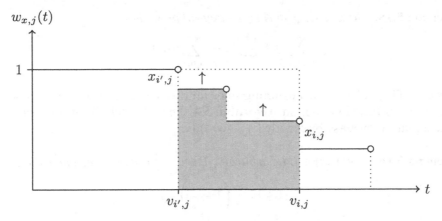

Figure 5.2 Shown is the function $w_{x,j}(t)$ for some fixed good j and assignment x. Switching some of the allocation from buyer i' to buyer i increases the level of $w_{x,j}(t)$ everywhere between the values of $v_{i',j}$ and $v_{i,j}$.

This motivates a price of the form $\int_{v_{i',j}}^{v_{i,j}} g(w_{x,j}(t)) \, dt$ and it turns out that setting $g(w) := e^{w-1}$ is optimal, as it was for WATER-FILLING. Matching j fractionally to i, however, will also unmatch the same amount of j from i'. Hence, to keep the utility of i' unchanged, an additional price of $v_{i',j}$ is necessary to "pay off" buyer i'. Thus the total price per unit of the edge (i, j) should be

$$v_{i'j} + \int_{v_{i'j}}^{v_{i,j}} e^{w_{x,j}(t)-1} \, dt = \int_0^{v_{i,j}} e^{w_{x,j}(t)-1} \, dt$$

resulting in Algorithm 5.4.

Algorithm 5.4 WATER-FILLING with edge weights and free disposal.

1 Match all goods j fully to dummy buyers along value-0 edges.
2 **for** *each buyer i who arrives* **do**
3   Let the price p_j of each good j be $\int_0^{v_{i,j}} e^{w_{x,j}(t)-1} \, dt$.
4   **while** *i is not fully matched and there is at least one good j with $v_{i,j} > p_j$* **do**
5   Let $j = \arg\max_{j \in S} v_{i,j} - p_j$ and let i' be a buyer of j along a least-value edge.
6   Reallocate an infinitesimal fraction of j by setting $x_{i,j} \leftarrow x_{i,j} + dx$ and $x_{i'j} \leftarrow x_{i'j} - dx$.

Remark 5.14. We are using the word "algorithm" loosely here to describe a continuous process. It is possible to use convex programming as in WATER-FILLING or other approximation methods to give an actual algorithm.

Revenues r_j and utilities u_i are defined as in the previous subsection. When the matching is adjusted by dx in line 6 of Algorithm 5.4, we interpret this as buyer i paying $(p_j - v_{i'j})dx$ to good j and $v_{i'j}dx$ to buyer i' so that $u_{i'}$ remains unchanged. Thus r_j increases by $(p_j - v_{i'j})dx$ and u_i increases by $(v_{i,j} - p_j)dx$.

Lemma 5.15. *At any stage during the algorithm, we have*

$$\sum_{j \in S} r_j + \sum_{i \in B} u_i = \sum_{(i,j) \in E} x_{i,j} v_{i,j}.$$

Proof This holds at the beginning since all variables are zero. Consider some iteration of the while loop in Algorithm 5.4. Then, by definition both sides of the equation increase by exactly $(v_{i,j} - v_{i',j})dx$. □

Lemma 5.16. *Let $(i,j) \in E$ be arbitrary. Then, at the end of the algorithm,*

$$r_j + u_i \geq \left(1 - \frac{1}{e}\right) v_{i,j}.$$

Proof Let x be the final allocation. Then during the iteration in which buyer i arrived, the price p_j would have been at most $\int_0^{v_{i,j}} e^{w_{x,j}(t)-1} \, dt$ since the prices are non-decreasing during the algorithm. Thus the utility of buyer i at the end of this iteration (which is the same as this buyer's utility at the end of the algorithm) must be at least $u_i \geq v_{i,j} - \int_0^{v_{i,j}} e^{w_{x,j}(t)-1} \, dt$.

On the other hand, the total revenue r_j collected by good j during the algorithm is

$$\int_0^\infty \int_0^{w_{x,j}(t)} e^{s-1} \, ds \, dt = \int_0^\infty \left(e^{w_{x,j}(t)-1} - \frac{1}{e}\right) dt.$$

Thus

$$r_j + u_i \geq v_{i,j} - \int_0^{v_{i,j}} e^{w_{x,j}(t)-1} \, dt + \int_0^\infty \left(e^{w_{x,j}(t)-1} - \frac{1}{e}\right) dt$$

$$\geq v_{i,j} - \int_0^{v_{i,j}} \frac{1}{e} \, dt = \left(1 - \frac{1}{e}\right) v_{i,j}.$$

□

Theorem 5.17. *Algorithm 5.4 is $(1 - 1/e)$-competitive.*

Proof This follows in the same way as the proofs of Theorems 5.6, 5.10, and 5.12. □

5.2.4 Online Matching with Stochastic Rewards

In the previous models, the revenue of an ad depended only on whether the user was *shown* the ad. However, advertisers are more interested in whether a user actually *clicked* on the ad. This has led to the *pay-per-click* model in online advertising, in which the reward for making a match depends on some external source – the users.

The online bipartite matching problem with stochastic rewards assumes stochastic user behaviors. When an algorithm attempts to match buyer i to good j, this will succeed with some probability $p_{i,j} \in [0, 1]$, which we assume to be known to the algorithm. The goal is to maximize the expected number of successfully matched edges.

The previous subsections analyzed the competitive ratios of online algorithms with respect to the optimal matching in G in hindsight; this is the best that an offline algorithm can do. This benchmark, however, is no longer suitable in the presence of stochasticity; see Exercise 5.5. Instead, we define the competitive ratio by comparing the expected size of the algorithm's matching to the solution of the budgeted allocation problem (see Chapter 6), which we will refer to as OPT:

$$\max_{(x_{i,j})_{(i,j)\in E}} \sum_{(i,j)\in E} p_{i,j}x_{i,j}$$

$$\text{s.t.} \quad \sum_{(i,j)\in E} p_{i,j}x_{i,j} \le 1 \quad \forall j \in S,$$

$$\sum_{(i,j)\subset E} x_{i,j} \le 1 \quad \forall i \in B,$$

$$x \ge 0.$$

We shall think of $x_{i,j}$ as the probability that the algorithm tries to match edge (i,j). Let $L_j := \sum_{i\in B} p_{i,j}x_{i,j}$ denote the *load* of any offline vertex $j \in S$.

Lemma 5.18. *The expected size of a matching computed by any algorithm $\mathcal{A}$ is at most OPT.*

Proof For any $i \in B$, $\sum_{j\in S} x_{i,j}$ is the expected number of $\mathcal{A}$'s attempts to match i, and is therefore at most 1. Moreover, the load L_j measures the expected number of successful matches to the vertex j, which is at most 1. Thus x is a feasible solution to the budgeted allocation problem. Finally, the expected size of $\mathcal{A}$'s matching is $\sum_{(i,j)\in E} p_{i,j}x_{i,j}$, and thus is at most OPT. $\qquad\square$

We now focus on *vanishing and equal probabilities*, i.e., all $p_{i,j}$ are equal to some p which tends to zero. Besides the ideas in the previous subsections, the main additional insight required to handle stochastic rewards is to view the matching process from an alternative angle.

Fix any online algorithm $\mathcal{A}$ and any instance of the online bipartite matching problem with stochastic rewards. Consider a stochastic process in which $\mathcal{A}$ is shown online vertices one by one and attempts to match them. There are now two different perspectives on who "decides" whether an attempted match (i,j) is successful. First, one might imagine that the online vertex i flips a coin to decide whether the match is successful. On the other hand, one could also imagine that the offline vertex j has already flipped a coin ahead of time for each matching attempt to determine whether it will be successful.

In the latter case, there is a $k \in \mathbb{N}$ for each good j such that j will be matched successfully if and only if $\mathcal{A}$ attempts at least k matches to j. Moreover, k is distributed geometrically, i.e., $\mathbb{P}[k = l] = p(1-p)^{l-1}$ for any $l \in \mathbb{N}$. As $p \to 0$, the distribution of the total load pk that can be assigned to j before a successful match is an exponential distribution. As a result we get the following theorem.

Theorem 5.19. *As $p \to 0$, the online bipartite matching problem with stochastic rewards becomes equivalent to the online bipartite matching problem with stochastic budgets, a variant of the online bipartite b-matching problem, in which the b-value of each good is unknown to the algorithm and independently sampled from an exponential distribution.*

A variant of BALANCE works well in this setting. This is Algorithm 5.5.

Algorithm 5.5 STOCHASTIC BALANCE for the online bipartite matching problem with stochastic budgets.

---

1 **for** *each online vertex i which arrives* **do**
2   Let $N(i)$ be neighbors of i that have not yet exceeded their budgets.
3   Match i to a neighbor $j \in N(i)$ that has the least number of match attempts thus far.

Unfortunately, bounding the competitive ratio of STOCHASTIC BALANCE is rather involved and lies beyond the scope of this chapter.

Theorem 5.20. *Algorithm 5.5 is $\frac{1}{2}(1+(1-p)^{2/p})$-competitive for the online bipartite matching problem with stochastic budgets and is thus $\frac{1}{2}(1 + e^{-2})$-competitive for the online bipartite matching problem with stochastic rewards as $p \to 0$.*

Unlike the simpler settings which we studied in the previous sections, these competitive ratios are not tight. In particular, they are taken with respect to the solution to the budgeted allocation problem. It is possible to define better benchmarks, and to improve the competitive ratio in this way.

5.3 Arrival Models for Other Applications

We now turn to other applications such as ride-sharing. These settings call for more general arrival models of vertices and edges, and in some cases involve non-bipartite graphs.

5.3.1 Fully Online Matching

The fully online matching problem is a generalization of the online bipartite matching problem. Here we are given a (potentially non-bipartite) graph $G = (V, E)$, which is unknown to the algorithm initially. Notably, there are no offline vertices that are known at the start. Two kinds of events occur in some order:

- *Arrival of a vertex i:* Vertex i and its incident edges with existing vertices are revealed. This is the earliest time at which i can be matched.
- *Deadline of a vertex i:* This is the latest time at which i can be matched. We assume that all neighbors of i arrive before its deadline.

The goal is as usual to compute a matching of maximum size.

Example 5.21. Consider a ride-sharing platform. Each rider specifies the pickup location and destination and remains on the platform for several minutes. Two riders can be paired up to share a ride if their pickup locations and destinations are near and their requests have overlapping time windows. We may use vertices to represent riders and edges to denote the pairs of riders that can share rides.

As usual a greedy approach yields a $\frac{1}{2}$-competitive algorithm; see Exercise 5.6. Both RANKING and WATER-FILLING from Section 5.2 generalize to the integral and fractional variants of the fully online matching problem, respectively.

5.3.1.1 RANKING

The main difference compared with Chapter 2 and Section 5.2 is the lack of an a priori classification of the vertices into buyers and goods. When a vertex arrives, it first acts as a good, i.e. a price is randomly sampled and the vertex passively waits for someone to buy it. Once it reaches the deadline, however, it will act as a buyer, immediately buying the cheapest neighboring vertex which has not yet been matched. Formally this is Algorithm 5.6.

Algorithm 5.6 RANKING for the fully online matching problem

---

1 **for** *each vertex i which arrives* **do**
2 $\quad$ Set price $p_i \leftarrow e^{w_i-1}$ where $w_i \in [0, 1]$ is sampled uniformly.
3 **for** *each vertex i which departs* **do**
4 $\quad$ Let $N(i)$ be the unmatched neighbors of i. **if** $N(i) \neq \emptyset$ **then**
5 $\quad\quad$ Match i to $j \in N(i)$ minimizing p_j.

When an edge (i, j), where i has the earlier deadline, is added to the matching by Algorithm 5.6, where i has the earlier deadline, i acts as a buyer and j acts as a good. Accordingly, the *gain* of i is $g_i = e^{w_i-1}$ and the gain of j is $g_j = 1 - e^{w_i-1}$ (corresponding to revenue and utility respectively).

Definition 5.22. The *marginal price* p_i^* of a vertex i with respect to the fixed prices of the other vertices is the highest price below which i would be bought before its deadline. The *marginal rank*, denoted as w_i^*, satisfies $e^{w_i^*-1} = p_i^*$. If i always acts as a good, define $p_i^* = w_i^* = 1$.

Next focus on an arbitrary edge $(i, j) \in E$, where i has an earlier deadline.

Lemma 5.23. *Either i acts as a good and gains e^{w_i-1}, or it gains at least $1 - p_j^*$.*

Proof The statement holds trivially in the boundary case when $p_j^* = w_j^* = 1$.
$\quad$ If $p_j > p_j^*$, j is unmatched by its deadline, which is after i's deadline. The claim holds because otherwise i should have chosen j at i's deadline.
$\quad$ Finally consider $p_j < p_j^*$. Compare the matching with the case where $p_j > p_j^*$ up to i's deadline. By induction, the set of vertices on j's side is always a superset of the previous case by at most one extra vertex. Hence, if a vertex on i's side has a different match, the reason is that either the extra vertex on j's

---

side buys it, or it buys the extra vertex on j's side owing to the cheaper price. In particular, this holds for vertex i and proves the lemma. $\qquad\square$

One can use this machinery of marginal prices to show that RANKING beats the greedy algorithm. The proof of this result is rather involved, however, and again lies beyond the scope of this chapter.

Theorem 5.24. *The competitive ratio of* RANKING *in fully online matching on general graphs is at least* 0.521.

Now we will restrict our attention to bipartite graphs. This is relevant in ride hailing, in which users act as either drivers or passengers.

Theorem 5.25. RANKING *is* 0.554-*competitive for the fully online bipartite matching problem.*

Proof Consider any edge (i, j) in the optimal matching, where i's deadline is earlier. By the definitions of j's marginal price p_j^* and marginal rank w_j^*, the expected gain of j is at least $\int_0^{w_j^*} e^{w_i - 1} \, dw_j$. By Lemma 5.23, on the other hand, we have $g_i \geq \min \left\{ e^{w_i - 1}, 1 - p_j^* \right\}$.

If $e^{w_i - 1} \geq 1 - p_j^*$, the analysis is similar to the analysis for the online bipartite matching problem:

$$ g_i + \mathsf{E}[g_j] \geq 1 - e^{w_j^* - 1} + \int_0^{w_j^*} e^{w_j - 1} \, dw_j = 1 - \frac{1}{e}. $$

Otherwise, we have $g_i \geq e^{w_i - 1}$. Taking expectation over w_j, a simple calculation now shows that

$$ \mathsf{E}[g_i] + \mathsf{E}[g_j] \geq \int_0^1 \min \left\{ 1 - \frac{1}{e}, e^{w_j - 1} \right\} \, dw_j \approx 0.55418. $$

Therefore, the expected size of the matching by RANKING is at least

$$ \sum_{i \in V} \mathsf{E}[g_i] \geq \sum_{(i,j) \in \text{OPT}} \left(\mathsf{E}[g_i] + \mathsf{E}[g_j] \right) \geq 0.554 \, |\text{OPT}|. \qquad\square $$

Finally, we remark that a similar yet more involved analysis gives the tight competitive ratio $\Omega \approx 0.567$ of RANKING in the fully online bipartite matching problem, where Ω is the unique solution to $\Omega e^{\Omega} = 1$.

5.3.1.2 WATER-FILLING

We can extend the WATER-FILLING approach to the fully online fractional Matching problem in a similar way as we did for RANKING: each vertex i acts as a good until its deadline at which point it acts as a buyer. The price of a neighboring good $j \in N(i)$ is then $p(w_j) := \frac{1}{\sqrt{2}} w_j + 1 - \frac{1}{\sqrt{2}}$ where w_j measures how much of j has been matched so far. Accordingly, each buyer will solve the convex program (CP)

$$\max_{(\Delta x_{i,j})_{j \in N(i)}} \sum_{j \in N(i)} \left(\Delta x_{i,j} - \int_{w_j}^{w_j + \Delta x_{i,j}} p(w) \, dw \right)$$

$$\text{s.t.} \quad \sum_{j \in N(i)} \Delta x_{i,j} \leq 1 - w_i,$$

$$\Delta x_{i,j} \geq 0 \quad \forall j \in N(i), \tag{5.3}$$

to maximize his/her utility and will pay $\int_{w_j}^{w_j + \Delta x_{i,j}} p(w) \, dw$ to each neighbor $j \in N(i)$; see Algorithm 5.7.

Remark 5.26. This is the first time that we have met a situation where the prices do not depend exponentially on the fill level w. The exact price function is, as always, chosen to yield an optimal analysis.

Algorithm 5.7 WATER-FILLING for the fully online fractional matching problem

---

1 **for** *each buyer i who departs* **do**
2   Compute an optimum solution $(\Delta x_{i,j})_{j \in N(i)}$ to the CP (5.3).
3   $x \leftarrow x + \Delta x$

As in Section 5.3.1.1, we let g_i be the *gain* of vertex i, i.e., the sum of its revenue while acting as a good and its utility while acting as a buyer.

Lemma 5.27. *Let $(i, j) \in E$ be arbitrary and let i's deadline be earlier. Then, at the end of Algorithm 5.7, we have $g_i + g_j \geq 2 - \sqrt{2}$.*

Proof Consider the matched levels w_i and w_j directly after i's deadline. Either $w_i = 1$ or $w_j = 1$; otherwise, i could have been matched more to j during its departure. Note that if $w_j = 1$, we have $g_j = \int_0^1 p(w) \, dw = 2 - \sqrt{2}$, proving the above inequality.

Now assume $w_i = 1$ and $w_j < 1$. Further, consider the matched level w_i' directly before i's deadline, i.e., consider how much of i was bought while it was acting as a good. Vertex i gains $\int_0^{w_i'} p(w) \, dw$ in revenue from those previous matches. In addition, i gains at least $1 - p(w_j)$ per unit of good that it buys on departure, as it could have always bought j instead. Thus

$$g_i \geq \int_0^{w_i'} p(w) \, dw + (1 - w_i')(1 - p(w_j)).$$

Further, by $g_j = \int_0^{w_j} p(w) \, dw$ and the choice of price $p(w) = \frac{1}{\sqrt{2}} w + 1 - \frac{1}{\sqrt{2}}$ we have

$$g_i + g_j \geq \int_0^{w_i'} p(w) \, dw + (1 - w_i')(1 - p(w_j)) + \int_0^{w_j} p(w) \, dw$$

$$= \frac{1}{2\sqrt{2}} (w_i' + w_j - 2 + \sqrt{2})^2 + 2 - \sqrt{2} \geq 2 - \sqrt{2}. \qquad \square$$

As a corollary we immediately obtain the following theorem.

Theorem 5.28. *The competitive ratio of* WATER-FILLING *for the fully online fractional matching problem is* $2 - \sqrt{2} \approx 0.585$.

Unlike for the online biparite matching problem, we have thus established a better competitive ratio for WATER-FILLING than for RANKING. One might conjecture that both algorithms ultimately end up being $(1 - 1/e)$-competitive, as is the case in many other settings we have studied so far. However, it is known that there is no 0.6317-competitive algorithm (note that $1 - 1/e \approx 0.6321$), even for the fully online fractional matching problem.

5.3.2 General Vertex Arrivals

The model of general vertex arrivals is similar to the fully online setting in that it also lets all vertices arrive online and allows non-bipartite graphs. However, matches must be made when the vertices *arrive* and there is no notion of departing.

This arrival model is even more difficult to handle, and the analysis of algorithms with competitive ratios strictly above $1/2$ is beyond the scope of this chapter. However, we will outline a proof that WATER-FILLING can once again be used to beat the greedy algorithm for the fractional variant of this problem.

The algorithm is mostly the same as Algorithm 5.7 except that vertices are matched on arrival and the price function $p \colon [0, 1] \to [0, 1]$ has to take on a more complicated form. For now we will just assume that p is non-decreasing and satisfies $p(1) = 1$.

In addition, if vertex i buys fractional edges $(\Delta_{i,j})_{j \in N(i)}$ then we require that

$$\sum_{j \in N(i)} \left(\Delta_{i,j} - \int_{w_j}^{w_j + x_{i,j}} p(w)\, \mathrm{d}w \right) \geq \int_0^{w_i + \sum_{j \in N(i)} \Delta x_{i,j}} p(w)\, \mathrm{d}w.$$

In other words, the gain (in the form of utility) that i achieves by buying other vertices should never be less than the gain (in the form of revenue) that it would have made if it had been matched to the same level later. This may simply be added as a constraint to the convex program (5.3).

Lemma 5.29. *For any vertex i, we have $g_i \geq \int_0^{w_i} p(w)\mathrm{d}w$.*

Proof Assume that upon arrival i was matched to level w_i' and then later to w_i.

The total utility it achieved during its arrival must have been at least $\int_0^{w_i'} p(w)\mathrm{d}w$ by assumption. Moreover, the total revenue it made later would have been exactly $\int_{w_i'}^{w_i} p(w)\mathrm{d}w$. Taking both facts together, the claim follows. $\square$

Lemma 5.30. *For any edge $(i, j) \in E$ where i arrives before j, we have $g_j \geq w_j(1 - p(w_i))$ after j arrives.*

Proof Since j fractionally matches its neighbors to maximize its gain and p is non-decreasing, j gets at least $1 - p(w_i)$ in utility per unit of match on its arrival. $\square$

To analyze the competitive ratio of WATER-FILLING, assume that there exists an auxiliary non-increasing function $f \colon [0, 1] \to [0, 1]$ with $f(1) = 0$, such that, for any $w^* \in [0, 1]$,

$$\int_0^{f(w^*)} p(w)\mathrm{d}w \le f(w^*)\big(1 - p(w^*)\big). \tag{5.4}$$

Lemma 5.31. *For any edge $(i, j) \in E$ where i arrives before j, $w_i = 1$ or $w_j \ge f(w_i)$ after j arrives.*

Proof The lemma is trivially true if $w_i = 1$ or $w_j = 1$. Since f is non-increasing, we may restrict ourselves to the time just after j arrives and assume that $w_i, w_j < 1$. Then we must have $g_j = \int_0^{w_j} p(w)\, \mathrm{d}w$ and $w_j > 0$ as otherwise j could have bought more of i.

Together with Lemma 5.30, this implies that

$$\int_0^{w_j} p(w)\mathrm{d}w \ge w_j\big(1 - p(w_i)\big).$$

Since p is non-decreasing, (5.4) implies that $x_j \ge f(x_i)$. $\qquad\square$

Theorem 5.32. *There is a price function p such that the competitive ratio of* WATER-FILLING *is at least 0.523.*

Proof Consider any edge $(i, j) \in E$, where i arrives before j. By Lemmas 5.29–5.31, the total gain of i and j is at least

$$\alpha_i + \alpha_j \ge \int_0^{w_i} p(w)\mathrm{d}w + f(w_i)\big(1 - p(w_i)\big).$$

Hence, we wish to find a non-decreasing p and non-increasing f that maximize

$$\Gamma := \min_{w_i \in [0,1]} \left(\int_0^{w_i} p(w)\mathrm{d}w + f(w_i)\big(1 - p(w_i)\big) \right).$$

Note that this would imply a Γ-competitive algorithm.

Unfortunately, we do not know of a simple closed-form solution for which it is easy to show that $\Gamma > \frac{1}{2}$. Nonetheless, by appropriately discretizing f and p, it is possible to solve for both functions numerically while optimizing Γ. Using this approach one can find numerical solutions with $\Gamma \ge 0.523$. $\qquad\square$

5.3.3 Edge Arrivals

Finally, let us briefly touch on the most general model of edge arrivals. The vertices are now entirely offline and, instead, it is the edges which arrive in adversarial order. Once an edge is revealed to the algorithm, it must decide whether it wants to include it in the matching or discard it forever.

The greedy algorithm remains $\frac{1}{2}$-competitive even with edge arrivals. Unlike the other models, however, no algorithm can do any better.

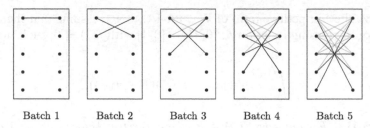

| Batch 1 | Batch 2 | Batch 3 | Batch 4 | Batch 5 |

Figure 5.3 Shown is a hard instance for edge arrivals with 10 vertices. The edges arrive in 5 separate batches.

Theorem 5.33. *The competitive ratio of any algorithm is at best $\frac{1}{2}$ under edge arrivals, even for bipartite graphs.*

Proof For a sufficiently large n, consider a bipartite graph $G = (B, S, E)$ with n vertices on each side. Let $B = \{b_1, b_2, \ldots, b_n\}$ and $S = \{s_1, s_2, \ldots, s_n\}$. The edges arrive in n batches. The first batch has only one edge (b_1, s_1). The second batch has two edges (b_1, s_2) and (b_2, s_1). Generally, the kth batch has k edges $(b_1, s_k), (b_2, s_{k-1}), \ldots, (b_k, s_1)$ for $k \leq n$. We consider a family of n instances, by following the above construction up to k batches for any $k \leq n$.

Observe that, for any $k \leq n$, the graph consisting of the first k batches has a unique perfect matching that consists entirely of the edges in the kth batch. Therefore, the algorithm faces a dilemma in every state: it needs to choose enough edges in the current stage to ensure a competitive ratio should it end right away; should the instance continue, however, all these chosen edges would hurt the final matching size.

Concretely, for any $i, j \leq n$ such that $i + j \leq n + 1$, let $x_{i,j}$ denote the probability that edge (b_i, s_j) is chosen by the algorithm. Assume that the algorithm is Γ-competitive for some constant $\Gamma \geq 1/2$; then (x, Γ) is a feasible solution of the following LP:

$$\max_{(x_{i,j})_{(i,j)\in E}, \Gamma} \quad \Gamma \tag{5.5a}$$

$$\text{s.t.} \quad \sum_{j \in N(i)} x_{i,j} \leq 1 \qquad \forall i \leq n, \tag{5.5b}$$

$$\sum_{i \in N(j)} x_{i,j} \leq 1 \qquad \forall j \leq n, \tag{5.5c}$$

$$\sum_{i=1}^{k} \sum_{j=1}^{k+1-i} x_{i,j} \geq \Gamma k \qquad \forall k \leq n, \tag{5.5d}$$

$$x_{i,j} \geq 0 \quad \forall (i, j) \in E. \tag{5.5e}$$

Constraint (5.5d) expresses the fact that the algorithm needs to be Γ-competitive even if we stop after the kth batch.

———— **126** ————

To prove the claim it suffices to show that this LP is bounded by $1/2$ as $n \to \infty$. Consider the dual LP:

$$\min_{(\alpha_i)_{i=1}^n, (\beta_j)_{j=1}^n, (\gamma_k)_{k=1}^n} \sum_{i=1}^n \alpha_i + \sum_{j=1}^n \beta_j$$

$$\text{s.t.} \quad \alpha_i + \beta_j \geq \sum_{k=i+j}^n \gamma_k \quad \forall i \leq n, j \in N(i),$$

$$\sum_{k=1}^n k\gamma_k \geq 1,$$

$$\alpha_i, \beta_j, \gamma_k \geq 0 \qquad \forall i, j, k \leq n.$$

By weak duality, we can bound (5.5a) and thus the competitive ratio Γ by providing a feasible dual assignment. For all i, j, k, set

$$\alpha_i := \beta_i := \begin{cases} \frac{n - 2(i-1)}{n(n+1)} & \text{if } i \leq \frac{n}{2} + 1, \\ 0 & \text{otherwise,} \end{cases}$$

$$\gamma_k := \frac{2}{n(n+1)}.$$

Then one may check that the dual objective function is $1/2 + O(1/n)$. $\qquad \square$

5.4 Exercises

Exercise 5.1 Give a complete proof of Lemma 5.4. In particular, carry out the proof by induction mentioned in the proof sketch.

Exercise 5.2 Give a deterministic WATER-FILLING algorithm for the online fractional vertex-weighted bipartite matching problem and show that it is $(1 - 1/e)$-competitive. *Hint:* The prices should be scaled in the same way as we did for RANKING in Section 5.2.1.

Exercise 5.3 Show that the family of upper-triangular graphs used in Chapter 2 to show the $1 - 1/e$ bound on the competive ratio for the online bipartite matching problem also yields a $1 - 1/e$ bound for the online fractional bipartite matching problem.

Exercise 5.4 Show that a variant of the greedy algorithm is $\frac{1}{2}$-competitive for the online edge-weighted bipartite matching problem with free disposal. Specifically, this greedy algorithm should match buyer i to good j maximizing $v_{i,j} - v_{i',j}$ where i' is the buyer to which j is currently matched.

Exercise 5.5 Give a family of bipartite graphs $G = (S, B, E)$, edge probabilities $p_{i,j}$, and an arrival order of the online vertices B such that the ratio between the best online algorithm with stochastic rewards and the expected size of a maximum matching in the graph tends to 0. *Hint:* It suffices to consider a single arriving vertex.

Exercise 5.6 Give greedy algorithms for the fully online matching problem and the online biparite matching problem with edge arrivals and show that they are $\frac{1}{2}$-competitive.

5.5 Bibliographic Notes

Online matching was first introduced in the seminal work [9]. The analysis of the algorithms in this chapter is largely based on [2] and the economic viewpoint on this analysis is given in [4]. Ranking with vertex weights was introduced in [1] and our proof is based on [12]. The article [8] gave the BALANCE algorithm for b-matching, which becomes equivalent to WATER-FILLING as b tends to infinity. The analysis of the online edge-weighted bipartite matching problem with free disposal is based on [3]. In [10] the setting with stochastic rewards was defined and the results covered in this chapter were proved.

The papers [6] and [7] introduced the fully online matching model and analyzed both RANKING and WATER-FILLING in this setting, proving the results from Section 5.3.1. In [13] the general vertex arrival model was given. The primal algorithm and analysis shown here is due to [11]. Lastly, in [5] the hardness result for the edge arrival model, Theorem 5.33, was proven.

References

[1] Aggarwal, Gagan, Goel, Gagan, Karande, Chinmay, and Mehta, Aranyak. 2011. Online vertex-weighted bipartite matching and single-bid budgeted allocations. Pages 1253–1264 of: *Proc. 22nd Annual ACM-SIAM Symposium on Discrete Algorithms*. SIAM.

[2] Devanur, Nikhil R., Jain, Kamal, and Kleinberg, Robert D. 2013. Randomized primal–dual analysis of ranking for online bipartite matching. Pages 101–107 of: *Proc. 24th Annual ACM-SIAM Symposium on Discrete algorithms*. SIAM.

[3] Devanur, Nikhil R., Huang, Zhiyi, Korula, Nitish, Mirrokni, Vahab S, and Yan, Qiqi. 2016. Whole-page optimization and submodular welfare maximization with online bidders. *ACM Transactions on Economics and Computation*, **4**(3), 1–20.

[4] Eden, Alon, Feldman, Michal, Fiat, Amos, and Segal, Kineret. 2021. An economics-based analysis of RANKING for online bipartite matching. Pages 107–110 of: Le, Hung Viet, and King, Valerie (eds.), *Proc. 4th Symposium on Simplicity in Algorithms*. SIAM.

[5] Gamlath, Buddhima, Kapralov, Michael, Maggiori, Andreas, Svensson, Ola, and Wajc, David. 2019. Online matching with general arrivals. Pages 26–37 of: *Proc. 60th Annual IEEE Symposium on Foundations of Computer Science*. IEEE.

[6] Huang, Zhiyi, Kang, Ning, Tang, Zhihao Gavin, Wu, Xiaowei, Zhang, Yuhao, and Zhu, Xue. 2018. How to match when all vertices arrive online. Pages 17–29 of: *Proc. 50th Annual ACM SIGACT Symposium on Theory of Computing*. ACM.

[7] Huang, Zhiyi, Peng, Binghui, Tang, Zhihao Gavin, Tao, Runzhou, Wu, Xiaowei, and Zhang, Yuhao. 2019. Tight competitive ratios of classic matching algorithms in the fully online model. Pages 2875–2886 of: *Proc. 30th Annual ACM-SIAM Symposium on Discrete Algorithms*. SIAM.

[8] Kalyanasundaram, Bala, and Pruhs, Kirk R. 2000. An optimal deterministic algorithm for online b-matching. *Theoretical Computer Science*, **233**(1), 319–325.

[9] Karp, Richard M., Vazirani, Umesh V., and Vazirani, Vijay V. 1990. An optimal algorithm for on-line bipartite matching. Pages 352–358 of: *Proc. 22nd Annual ACM Symposium on Theory of Computing*. ACM.

[10] Mehta, Aranyak, and Panigrahi, Debmalya. 2012. Online matching with stochastic rewards. Pages 728–737 of: *Proc. 53rd IEEE Annual Symposium on Foundations of Computer Science*. IEEE.

[11] Tang, Zhihao Gavin. 2020. Personal communication.

[12] Vazirani, Vijay V. 2022. Online bipartite matching and adwords. In: *Proc. 47th International Symposium on Mathematical Foundations of Computer Science*.

[13] Wang, Yajun, and Wong, Sam Chiu-wai. 2015. Two-sided online bipartite matching and vertex cover: Beating the greedy algorithm. Pages 1070–1081 of: *Proc. International Colloquium on Automata, Languages, and Programming*. Springer.

CHAPTER SIX

Online Matching in Advertisement Auctions

Nikhil R. Devanur and Aranyak Mehta

6.1 Introduction

Advertising has become a large source of revenue for many internet services, and at the same time internet technologies have completely transformed advertising. At the time of writing, worldwide digital advertising spend is estimated to be close to half a trillion dollars per year and accounts for a majority of all media ad spending. It is the ad revenue that allows internet services companies to offer *free* invaluable services such as search, social media, news, video, email, maps, operating systems, and all kinds of apps.

Among the different channels in internet advertising, search advertising deserves special mention. When a user issues a search query with the intent to look for certain goods or services, the platform matches the user to firms selling those goods or services, by displaying the relevant ads. Thus, firms are more certain to have their advertising budget spent on opportunities which are likely to result in a good return. Indeed, payment from an advertiser to a search engine is usually per click, since a click is already a strong indication that the user has found the ad useful. Even display and video advertising have moved to a world of real-time bidding, which allows sophisticated algorithms to evaluate differentially every single ad opportunity. Whenever user activity generates an ad-slot, ads compete in a fully automated auction to win that slot.

Given the size of the ad market and its importance to online commerce, deeper understanding and optimization of the underlying mechanisms has an outsize impact. In this chapter, we will describe an important aspect of this market design, namely that of online matching in the auction context.

Auctions. Being a market of a highly heterogeneous set of goods (e.g., the huge range of possible queries in search advertising), ads are sold via auctions rather than fixed prices. For each new ad-slot, retrieval and machine learning systems find the relevant ad candidates with their bids and quality scores, and an auction determines which ad gets shown and how much the advertiser pays. Indeed, the design of sponsored search auctions is itself a topic of considerable interest and practical impact. While we do not need to know the details of the auction design when considering the topic of online matching, we will return to the topic in Section 6.8.

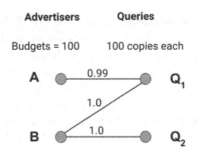

Figure 6.1 A bad instance of the straightforward auction approach.

Online matching. As such, auctions for any two ad-slots are independent of each other. However, demand constraints from the advertisers connect the different auctions. A very commonly used demand constraint is the budget: Besides a per-click bid for each ad-slot (expressed via keywords), an advertiser can also express an overall budget, denoting the maximum they are willing to pay in a time period (typically a day). Consequently, decisions taken in one auction affect other auctions. The obvious way for the platform to deal with budgets is to run a simple auction in which each ad-slot goes to the highest bidder and to remove advertisers from consideration as they finish their budgets. However, this approach is not ideal: advertisers would end up finishing their budgets early in the day, giving them a biased sample of ad opportunities. Further, this would lead to uneven competition in the auctions, with the competition thinning out later in the day. This dynamic can be clearly seen in the following extreme example.

Example 6.1. There are two advertisers (A and B) and 200 queries (see Figure 6.1). The advertisers have the same budget, $B_A = B_B = 100$. The first 100 queries Q_1 are identical (e.g., they could be ad-slots for the keyword "flowers") for which A and B both bid similarly: $b_{Aj} = 0.99, b_{Bj} = 1, \forall j \in Q_1$. The second 100 queries Q_2 are also identical (suppose that the keyword is "gifts"), with only B interested in them: $b_{Aj} = 0, b_{Bj} = 1, \forall j \in Q_2$. The straightforward auction approach matches all $j \in Q_1$ to B, at which point spend$_B = B_B$ (for simplicity assume the first price). Now when queries in Q_2 arrive, B can no longer matched, while A bids 0 for them. This results in a revenue of 100. An *optimal matching* instead matches all $j \in Q_1$ to A and all $j \in Q_2$ to B, with a revenue of 199.

Thus, running a straightforward auction and simply imposing the budget constraints leads to suboptimal efficiency and revenue; we need to explicitly consider the interactions across auctions and pace the spend over the day. This leads to an *online bipartite matching* formulation: the two sides of the bipartite graph are the demand (advertisers) and the supply (ad-slots), edges codify the bids and quality scores, and the budgets place constraints on each advertiser vertex. Note that the problem is necessarily online, i.e., each ad-slot needs to be matched to an advertiser as soon as it arrives, without knowledge of the future. We clarify here that we use the term matching in the more general sense of an allocation, determining which ads are shown for which queries; e.g., we are not necessarily constrained to match each advertiser vertex to exactly one neighbor.

Centralized vs. decentralized solutions. There are two different approaches to solving this matching problem. A *centralized approach* treats the problem as an (online) optimization problem and makes the matching decisions in each auction. We begin this chapter with a focus on the centralized approach, describing the problem, algorithms, and results. A *decentralized approach* considers the problem from a bidding perspective, in which each advertiser changes its bids under its budget constraints to optimize for itself. This raises the question of what happens when all advertisers bid in this way. What kind of matching would result? We will discuss this approach in Section 6.7.

6.2 The AdWords Problem

We formulate the centralized matching question as the following online budgeted allocation problem, referred to in the literature as the AdWords problem.

Definition 6.2. In the *AdWords problem*, there is a bipartite graph of n advertisers and m queries. Advertiser i has a budget of B_i for its total spend. The bid of advertiser i for query j is denoted by b_{ij}, which can be considered as the weight of the edge (i, j). Consider a matching M of queries to advertisers, where $M(i)$ denotes the set of queries matched to advertiser i. The total reward of M (we will also refer to this as the *revenue*) is defined as

$$\sum_{i \in [n]} \min\{B_i, \sum_{j \in M(i)} b_{ij}\}. \tag{6.1}$$

The algorithm starts off knowing only the set of advertisers and their budgets, but not the set of queries, which arrive sequentially, nor the potential bids. When a query j arrives, the algorithm reveals the bids b_{ij}, for all i, and has to immediately decide to match j to one advertiser (or leave j unmatched), irrevocably. The goal is to maximize the reward (6.1) at the end of the sequence.

We can also define the problem *iteratively* as follows. Initially, the *spend* of each advertiser i, spend_i, is 0. When a query j arrives, if possible the algorithm matches it to some advertiser i with $\text{spend}_i < B_i$. The algorithm accrues a reward of $\min\{b_{ij}, B_i - \text{spend}_i\}$, and spend_i increases by the same amount.

Remark 6.3. Note that the AdWords problem as defined above is quite general. For example, if we set every budget B_i to 1 and every bid b_{ij} to either 0 or 1 then we recover the online bipartite matching problem from Chapter 2. The general problem is hard to solve exactly even in an *offline* setting, i.e., when we know the entire graph in advance: it is NP-hard to approximate the optimal solution with a multiplicative approximation factor better than 15/16.

Competitive analysis. We evaluate an algorithm by its competitive ratio, which is the minimum ratio (over all instances of the problem) of the reward obtained by the algorithm to the optimal achievable reward in hindsight, i.e., if we knew the entire graph. We will refer to the latter as OPT throughout.

Let us recall the straightforward strategy of picking the highest bidder among those with a remaining budget.

Highest-bidder. Match the arriving query j to the advertiser i with the highest value of $\min\{b_{ij}, B_i - \text{spend}_i\}$.

In Example 6.1, we saw that this strategy achieves no more than half the optimal matching in hindsight (to be precise, we arrive at one half by increasing the value of the budgets and the length of the query sequences). This means the competitive ratio of Highest-bidder is no more than $1/2$; in fact it is precisely $1/2$ as it can be shown that it achieves at least half of OPT in every instance.

In light of this example, the goal is to find an algorithm with a competitive ratio strictly better than one half. It turns out that this is a very difficult problem in general, and the first such algorithm, achieving a slightly improved ratio of 0.5016, was discovered only very recently. Instead, we make the following reasonable practical assumption, which results in a much more tractable problem that allows for an algorithm with a much improved competitive ratio and also yields an heuristic with significant impact in practice.

Definition 6.4. Let $\rho = \max_{i \in [n], j \in [m]} b_{ij}/B_i$. In the *small-bids assumption*, we assume that ρ is small, i.e., every bid is much smaller than the corresponding budget. The performance of the algorithms is evaluated as $\rho \to 0$.

Remark 6.5. With this assumption, the AdWords problem no longer captures the online bipartite matching problem. Further, the offline version becomes much more approximable: solving the corresponding linear program optimally yields an almost integral solution, and the few fractional matches can be discarded without any significant loss in reward.

Remark 6.6 (Arrival models). We have not assumed anything about the query sequence in Definition 6.2. In the most general model, the *adversarial* model, the sequence is allowed to be completely arbitrary (as in Example 6.1; we consider this model in Section 6.4). We will also consider *stochastic* models of the query sequence (in Section 6.5), in which we can find algorithms with a competitive ratio close to 1.

6.3 A Family of Algorithms

In this section we introduce a family of algorithms that are simple, intuitive, and often give near-optimal competitive ratios.

Definition 6.7 (Auction-based algorithms). These algorithms have an interpretation as an auction, where a query j is allocated to the advertiser with the highest *normalized* bid $v_i b_{ij}$. Each advertiser i maintains a *bid normalizer* v_i, which we may update after each query is matched. The algorithms in this family differ on how the normalizers are initialized, and how they are updated. The spend of the advertiser is still incremented by the original bid b_{ij}. The normalized bid is used only to make the allocation decision.

For the sake of simplicity, if we match query j to advertiser i where $b_{ij} > B_i - \text{spend}_i > 0$, we are assuming that the algorithm's reward is b_{ij}. This may result in at most a difference ρ in the competitive ratio, because these extra credits may account for at most a fraction ρ of the algorithm's revenue. Since we have made the small-bids assumption, this difference is not significant.

Intuition. Auction-based algorithms have a simple intuition. The bid normalizers provide a simple lever to make the budget of an advertiser last longer: the lower the normalizer of an advertiser, the fewer the queries matched to the advertiser, and the longer the budget lasts. They allow us to trade off an immediate gain of b_{ij} with a future advantage of keeping the budget of advertiser i alive.

We can interpret such algorithms as a generalization of the algorithm in Chapter 2, where the value generated from a match is broken down into a revenue component and a utility component. In this context, the advertiser can be thought of as making an offer of $v_i b_{ij}$ (the revenue component) to the query, and the query chooses the advertiser with the highest offer.

Linear programming (LP) duality. The family of auction-based algorithms is not too restrictive because there exist fixed normalizers for each advertiser such that the resulting algorithm is almost optimal. This fact follows from the theory of *strong LP duality*, but we will not prove it here.[1] We use only what is called *weak LP duality* to get an upper bound on OPT: The following is an LP relaxation of the problem, and its dual:

Primal: $\max \sum_{i,j} b_{ij} x_{ij}$ s.t.

$$\forall i, \sum_j b_{ij} x_{ij} \leq B_i,$$

$$\forall j, \sum_i x_{ij} \leq 1,$$

$$\forall i, j, x_{ij} \geq 0.$$

Dual: $\min \sum_i \alpha_i B_i + \sum_j \beta_j$ s.t.

$$\forall i, j, \alpha_i b_{ij} + \beta_j \geq b_{ij},$$

$$\forall i, j, \alpha_i, \beta_j \geq 0.$$

$$(6.2)$$

It is easy to see that the optimal allocation gives a feasible solution to the primal LP, by letting $x_{ij} = 1$ if and only if query j is matched to advertiser i. This gives us the following instantiation of weak LP duality, i.e., that any feasible dual solution gives an upper bound on the primal optimal.

Theorem 6.8. *For any feasible solution to the dual LP, the dual objective function, $\sum_i \alpha_i B_i + \sum_j \beta_j$, is an upper bound on the primal optimal, which itself is an upper bound on OPT.*

The connection between this pair of LPs and auction-based algorithms is via the *primal complementary slackness* condition:

$$x_{ij} > 0 \Rightarrow \alpha_i b_{ij} + \beta_j = b_{ij}.$$

Rewriting this as $\beta_j = b_{ij}(1 - \alpha_i)$, and the constraint in the dual LP as $\beta_j \geq b_{ij}(1 - \alpha_i)$, we see that $x_{ij} > 0$ implies that i must maximize $b_{ij}(1 - \alpha_i)$ over all advertisers. This is exactly the allocation in an auction-based algorithm if we set

$$v_i = 1 - \alpha_i. \tag{6.3}$$

---

[1] The argument involves some delicate tie-breaking in degenerate cases, and would be a digression here.

Lagrangian relaxation. Auction-based algorithms are also equivalent to the algorithms you get using the technique of *Lagrangian relaxation*. This technique relaxes a constrained optimization problem to an unconstrained optimization problem, by moving the constraints into the objective function. A constraint such as $f(x) < c$ in a maximization problem goes into the objective function as $\lambda(c - f(x))$; thus, violating a constraint is penalized. The parameter λ is called the Lagrangian multiplier, and it is equivalent to the dual variable α_i in our formulation. The objective function of this unconstrained optimization problem is called the Lagrangian function. We will do a partial Lagrangian relaxation, where we move only the budget constraints into the objective function; this gives the Lagrangian function

$$L(\mathbf{x}, \alpha) = \sum_{i,j} b_{ij} x_{ij} + \sum_i \alpha_i \left(B_i - \sum_j b_{ij} x_{ij} \right) = \sum_{i,j} b_{ij} x_{ij} (1 - \alpha_i) + \sum_i \alpha_i B_i. \quad (6.4)$$

For a fixed α, this Lagrangian function is now separable over the queries. An auction-based algorithm with normalizers $v_i = 1 - \alpha_i$ maximizes this Lagrangian function for each query j, subject to the constraint $\sum_i x_{ij} \leq 1$.

Our problem is online, and we don't know the optimal α_i values; therefore our algorithms will update the α_i as we go along.

6.4 Adversarial Model

The classic model of query arrival is the *adversarial* or *worst-case* model. Here, the algorithm has no advance knowledge about the query side of the bipartite graph, and an adversary who knows the algorithm constructs the worst query sequence. In fact, for a deterministic algorithm like the one we will describe, one can even imagine the adversary generating each query after seeing the previous decisions of the algorithm.

The MSVV algorithm. We present an auction-based algorithm called MSVV which has the optimal performance in this model. Recall from Section 6.3 that in order to specify an auction-based algorithm for the AdWords problem, we need to define the bid normalizers v_i, for each advertiser i, over time as the query sequence unfolds. At any time t, let spend$_i$ denote the current spend of advertiser i. The algorithm takes the normalizer v_i at time t as a function of the spend and its budget B_i, as follows:

$$v_i := 1 - e^{-(1 - \text{spend}_i / B_i)} \quad (6.5)$$

The algorithm allocates the incoming query j to the advertiser i which maximizes $v_i b_{ij}$. After query j gets allocated (say to advertiser i), spend$_i$ increases by b_{ij} and consequently v_i gets reduced correspondingly. The algorithm does not allocate the query to any advertiser if all $v_i b_{ij} = 0$.

Intuition. Note that initially, $\forall i$, spend$_i = 0$ and therefore $v_i = 1 - 1/e$. Thus the very first query j to arrive will be allocated to the advertiser i with the highest bid b_{ij}. Over time, advertisers who have spent a greater fraction of their budget will have a lower normalizer and would have to bid much more highly to get allocated in comparison with advertisers who have not spent much of their budget. This trades off the immediate reward from a high bid with the goal of keeping advertiser budgets available for future queries in which some advertiser may have a high bid. Once an advertiser i finishes its entire budget, $v_i = 0$ and hence it is not allocated any further queries. From a *pricing* or a *bidding* perspective, one can interpret the algorithm as saying that the offer price or bid of an advertiser is shaded down dynamically on the basis of the fraction of its budget spent at that time.

One can prove that no matter what the query sequence is, MSVV achieves a revenue no worse than $1 - 1/e \simeq 0.63$ of OPT.

Theorem 6.9. *The algorithm MSVV achieves a competitive ratio of $1-1/e$, and this ratio is optimal among all algorithms, including randomized algorithms.*

Proof We will follow the primal–dual LP framework from Section 6.3. Recall that we do not know the LPs in advance; instead, they are gradually revealed to us. We begin with the primal and dual solutions x, α, β all set to 0. As we allocate the queries to advertisers using the algorithm's rule, we update the primal and dual solutions in a way such that three invariants hold throughout:

Invariant 1. x is a feasible solution for the (partial) primal LP.
Invariant 2. α, β form a feasible solution for the (partial) dual LP.
Invariant 3. The increase in the primal objective function is a fraction $1 - 1/e$ of the increase in the dual objective.

Note that the primal objective achieved at the end is precisely the algorithm's revenue. Thus, these invariants along with Theorem 6.8 immediately imply a $1 - 1/e$ competitive ratio:

$$\text{ALG} = \text{primal} \geq (1 - 1/e)\text{dual} \geq (1 - 1/e)\text{primal optimal} \geq (1 - 1/e)\text{OPT}.$$

It remains to define the updates which go hand-in-hand with the algorithm decisions. Define $\zeta := (1/1 - 1/e)$. If the algorithm allocates an incoming query j to an advertiser i then we set x_{ij} and β_j and increase α_i as follows:

$$x_{ij} = 1, \quad \beta_j = \zeta v_i b_{ij}, \quad \Delta\alpha_i = \frac{1}{B_i}\zeta(1 - v_i)b_{ij}. \tag{6.6}$$

We are ready to prove that the three invariants hold:

- Invariant 1 holds by the choice of algorithm: it does not allocate a query to any advertiser who does not have sufficient budget remaining.
- Invariant 3 holds because the value of the primal LP increases by b_{ij} while that of the dual LP increases by $\Delta\alpha_i B_i + \beta_j = \zeta(1 - v_i)b_{ij} + \zeta v_i b_{ij} = \zeta b_{ij}$.
- Invariant 2 can be shown to hold iteratively. Assuming that existing dual constraints are satisfied until the time when some query j^* arrives (and is allocated to some advertiser i^*), we can show that the update after query j^* keeps them feasible. Consider such a constraint for advertiser i and query j:

$$\alpha_i b_{ij} + \beta_j \geq b_{ij}.$$

For a constraint pertaining to a previously arrived query $j \neq j^*$ and some i, the value of β_j remains unchanged, while the update for query j^* can only potentially increase α_i (and only for $i = i^*$). This keeps the inequality satisfied.

Thus the only interesting constraints are those corresponding to the new query j^*. For this, we will compute (for any i) the value of α_i after j^* has been allocated. Using spend_i^j and v_i^j to denote the values of spend_i and v_i at the time j arrives, we get, using the update rule from (6.6) and the algorithm's choice of normalizer from (6.5):

$$\alpha_i = \sum_{j \leq j^*: \, x_{ij}=1} \frac{1}{B_i} \zeta (1 - v_i^j) b_{ij} = \sum_{j \leq j^*: \, x_{ij}=1} \frac{1}{B_i} \zeta e^{-\left(1 - \frac{\text{spend}_i^j}{B_i}\right)} b_{ij}.$$

With the small-bids assumption, we can approximate this by an integral, giving:

$$\alpha_i = \int_{x=0}^{\text{spend}_i^{j^*}} \frac{1}{B_i} \zeta e^{-\left(1 - \frac{x}{B_i}\right)} dx - \frac{e^{\frac{\text{spend}_i^{j^*}}{B_i}} - 1}{e - 1} = 1 - \zeta v_i. \tag{6.7}$$

Since i^* is the advertiser maximizing $v_i b_{ij}$, we also have, from (6.6),

$$\beta_{j^*} = \zeta v_{i^*} b_{i^* j^*} \geq \zeta v_i b_{ij^*}, \quad \forall i. \tag{6.8}$$

From (6.7) and (6.8), we get, $\forall i$, $\beta_{j^*} \geq (1 - \alpha_i) b_{ij^*}$, thus proving that the dual constraints corresponding to j^* are also satisfied after j^* is allocated. $\qquad \square$

Optimality. To prove that no other algorithm can achieve a better competitive ratio, we find a distribution over input instances and show that no deterministic algorithm can achieve a revenue better than a fraction $1 - 1/e$ of OPT in expectation over this distribution. We then use the minimax theorem to prove the desired optimality statement. While we leave the details out as they are beyond our scope, we mention that this is the same approach as that used in Chapter 2 to prove optimality in the basic online bipartite matching problem, and the distribution over instances also turns out to be very similar to the distribution used there.

Remark 6.10. As opposed to an offline algorithm, which has access to an optimal set of normalizers v^* (as in Section 6.3), MSVV has to update its normalizers as the query sequence unfolds. The function (6.5) computes the normalizer as a function of the spend, and can be considered to be an online approximation to the optimal v^* for every instance. Since we can only hope to find an approximate dual, it also turns out that the relation between the dual α_i and the normalizer v_i in (6.7) is a scaled version of the optimal relation (6.3).

6.5 Stochastic Models

The adversarial model requires that the algorithm should hedge against all possible inputs. As a result the MSVV algorithm can be suboptimal for the benign instances that are likely to occur in real applications. Real-world instances often follow repeated patterns; therefore an algorithm that uses historic data can get a better revenue. With simple stochastic assumptions about the arrival of queries, we can breach the $1 - 1/e$ upper bound on the competitive ratio in the adversarial model.

The most significant result here is that the competitive ratio approaches 1 as the bid to budget ratio tends to 0. In this section, we demonstrate one such algorithm for the following stochastic model, which is similar to the model for the "secretary problem" discussed in Chapter 30.

Definition 6.11. In the *Random permutation model*, we assume that an adversary still picks the *set* of queries, the advertiser bids, and the budgets, but the *order* of arrival is permuted uniformly at random. This does not change OPT, but we now measure the algorithm's performance in expectation over this random permutation.

While we are interested in algorithms which achieve a ratio approaching 1, we note here that even the algorithms that we have already met perform better in this model. The simple highest-bidder strategy now achieves a competitive ratio of $1 - 1/e$, and MSVV achieves a ratio of at least 0.76.

Compared with the adversarial model, we make two additional assumptions. The first is required for the results, while the second is for ease of exposition.

Additional assumptions.

- We assume that the number of queries m is known to the algorithm; without such an assumption, no algorithm can get a competitive ratio that approaches 1 as the bid-to-budget ratio tends to 0. We also assume that m is large enough, i.e., $m \geq 1/\rho$ (recall that ρ is the bid-to-budget ratio, defined in Section 6.2).
- For simplicity of exposition, we assume that we know OPT. In fact, it is sufficient to have an estimate $\widehat{\text{OPT}}$ such that $\text{OPT} \leq \widehat{\text{OPT}} \leq c\text{OPT}$ for some universal constant c. We will prove a competitive ratio of the form $1 - O(\epsilon)$, where the constant c appears inside the $O(\epsilon)$ term. We can get such an estimate from the first fraction ϵ of queries. Ignoring these queries decreases the competitive ratio by an additional factor ϵ.

A control mechanism. We use an auction-based algorithm. In contrast with update (6.6), the normalizers can increase as well as decrease. The update acts as a control mechanism, trying to maintain a constant rate of budget spend. If the budget of an advertiser is spent too quickly, it decreases the normalizer, resulting in fewer queries matched and a lower rate of spend; conversely, if the budget is not spent quickly enough, it increases the normalizer. To determine the precise update formula, we use the *multiplicative weight update* (MWU) algorithm for what is known as the *learning from experts* problem. We define these next.

Definition 6.12. *Learning from experts* is another online problem, where there are N experts and, in each round $t \in [T]$, each expert $i \in [N]$ gets a reward of $r_{i,t}$. The algorithm has to pick one expert in each round and gets the same reward as that expert, but it has to choose the expert before seeing the rewards. The goal is to maximize the total reward of the experts picked in all the rounds, in order to minimize the *regret*, which is the difference between the expected reward of the algorithm and the reward of the best single expert in hindsight.

The MWU algorithm. The MWU algorithm is *randomized*: it picks expert i in round t with probability $\theta_{i,t}$. The algorithm maintains a weight for each expert; the weights are all initialized to 1. After each round, the weights are updated multiplicatively with an exponent proportional to the rewards. The probabilities $\theta_{i,t}$ are normalized versions of the weights $w_{i,t}$, so that they sum up to 1. Let $\epsilon \in [0, 1/2]$ be a parameter of the algorithm. The update is

$$w_{i,t+1} = \begin{cases} w_{i,t}(1+\epsilon)^{r_{i,t}} & \text{if } r_{i,t} \geq 0, \\ w_{i,t}(1-\epsilon)^{-r_{i,t}} & \text{if } r_{i,t} < 0. \end{cases} \tag{6.9}$$

The MWU algorithm has the following regret guarantee.

Theorem 6.13. *Suppose that the rewards are all in* $[-1, 1]$. *For any expert* $i \in [N]$, *we have that*

$$\sum_{t \in [T], i \in [N]} \theta_{i,t} r_{i,t} \geq \sum_t r_{i,t} - \epsilon \sum_t |r_{i,t}| - \frac{\ln N}{\epsilon}. \tag{6.10}$$

The online dual learning (ODL) algorithm. We will abuse the notation and denote the query that appears at time step t as $j(t)$; here $j(\cdot)$ is a random permutation of $[m]$. We denote $x_{ij} = 1$ to indicate that the algorithm has matched query j to advertiser i, and set $x_{ij} = 0$ otherwise. We define an instance of the learning from experts problem, with one expert for each advertiser, and an additional expert that corresponds to not matching the query to anyone else, i.e., $N = n + 1$. We set the rewards for the experts as follows:

$$\forall i \in [n], r_{i,t} = \left(\frac{b_{i,j(t)} x_{i,j(t)}}{B_i} - \frac{1}{m} \right) \frac{1}{\rho}. \tag{6.11}$$

The scaling by $1/\rho$ makes the rewards as large as possible while still keeping them in $[-1, 1]$. The reward of the expert $n + 1$ is always 0. We can see that the cumulative reward at any time is proportional to the difference between the fraction of the budget spent and the fraction of the time elapsed.

The Lagrange multipliers in an auction-based algorithm capture the trade-off between the opportunity to increase the objective versus the risk of violating a constraint, but the $\theta_{i,t}$, being a probability distribution, do not have the right scale. We define $\alpha_{i,t}$ by multiplying $\theta_{i,t}$ by a factor OPT to scale it to the objective, and dividing by B_i to capture the scale of the constraint:

$$\alpha_{i,t} := \frac{\theta_{i,t} \text{OPT}}{B_i}. \tag{6.12}$$

As mentioned in Section 6.3, the normalizer is $v_{i,t} = 1 - \alpha_{i,t}$. When all the $\alpha_{i,t}$ are greater than 1, we cannot or have not match the query to any advertiser. The entire ODL algorithm is summarized in Algorithm 6.1.

Intuition. While it may seem counterintuitive that spending more results in higher rewards, notice that a higher probability $\theta_{i,t}$ of picking an expert i leads to a lower

---

Algorithm 6.1 ODL algorithm for the random permutation model.

Initialize parameter $\epsilon \in [0, \frac{1}{2}]$.
Initialize, for all $i \in [n+1]$, $\theta_{i,1}$ and $w_{i,1}$ as in the MWU algorithm.
for all $t = 1, \ldots, m$ **do**
    For all $i \in [n]$, set $\alpha_{i,t}$ as in (6.12).
    if $\forall i \in [n]$, $\alpha_{i,t} > 1$ **then**
        Set $x_{i,j(t)} = 0$ for all $i \in [n]$.
    else
        Let i^* be the highest normalized bidder, $\arg\max_{i \in [n]} b_{i,j(t)}(1 - \alpha_{i,t})$.
        if Matching $j(t)$ to i^* exceeds their budget **then**
            Exit.
        else
            Match $j(t)$ to i^*. Set $x_{i^*,j(t)} = 1$, and $x_{i,j(t)} = 0$ for all $i \neq i^*$.
        end if
    end if
    $\forall i \in [n]$, set rewards $r_{i,t}$ as in (6.11). Set $r_{n+1,t} = 0$.
    Update $w_{i,t+1}, \theta_{i,t+1}$ as in the MWU algorithm (6.9).
end for

---

normalizer $v_{i,t}$, which is the desired direction of change. The Lagrangian interpretation of this is that a higher spend results in a higher chance of violating the constraint, and therefore we should increase the *penalty* α_i. For advertisers that are budget constrained, the algorithm tries to keep the fraction of budget spent close to the fraction of time elapsed. For the rest of the advertisers we expect a negative reward on average, which drives the weight down to zero and the normalizer to one; clearly, there is no benefit from discounting their bids.

Let ALG denote the objective realized by the ODL algorithm. The following theorem shows that it achieves a competitive ratio of $1 - o(1)$.

Theorem 6.14. *In the random permutation model, for any $\epsilon \in [0, 1/2]$ such that $\epsilon^2 \geq \rho \ln(n+1)$, we have that $\mathbb{E}[\text{ALG}] \geq \text{OPT}(1 - O(\epsilon))$, i.e., there is a universal constant c such that $\mathbb{E}[\text{ALG}] \geq \text{OPT}(1 - c\epsilon)$.*

Proof For the sake of simplicity, we analyze the algorithm assuming that the queries are sampled *with replacement* instead of sampling without replacement, as in the random permutation model. In the rest of this proof, we assume that each query $j(t)$ is an i.i.d. sample from the set $[m]$ of all queries. Handling sampling without replacement results in additional terms that can also be bounded by $O(\epsilon)\text{OPT}$, but this is outside the scope of this chapter.

Let $x_{i,j}^*$ denote the offline optimal matching. Let T be the last query that was succesfully matched, i.e., matching query $j(T+1)$ would exceed the chosen advertiser's budget. If this never happens, then let $T = m$. The proof is broken down into three steps.

---

1. Auction: Since for each $t \in [T]$ the algorithm matches the query $j(t)$ to the advertiser with the highest normalized bid $(1 - \alpha_{i,t})b_{i,j(t)}$, the normalized bid of the advertiser matched to $j(t)$ in the offline optimal matching can only be lower:

$$\sum_{i \in [n]} b_{i,j(t)}(1 - \alpha_{i,t})x_{i,j(t)} \geq \sum_{i \in [n]} b_{i,j(t)}(1 - \alpha_{i,t})x^*_{i,j(t)}.$$

Summing up this inequality over all $t \in [T]$ and noting that

$$\text{ALG} = \sum_{t \in [T], i \in [n]} b_{i,j(t)}x_{i,j(t)},$$

we have that

$$\text{ALG} \geq \sum_{t \in [T], i \in [n]} \left(b_{i,j(t)}(1 - \alpha_{i,t})x^*_{i,j(t)} + b_{i,j(t)}\alpha_{i,t}x_{i,j(t)} \right). \tag{6.13}$$

2. Stochasticity: The assumption that queries will be sampled with replacement allows us to replace the terms corresponding to the offline optimal matching in (6.13) by their expectations.

For each i and t, conditioned on all the queries that appeared up to time $t-1$, the expectation of $b_{i,j(t)}x^*_{i,j(t)}$ is less than B_i/m. This is so because each new draw is independent of everything that came before, and $\sum_{j \in [m]} b_{ij}x^*_{i,j} \leq B_i$. Similarly, for each t, the expectation of $\sum_{i \in [n]} b_{i,j(t)}x^*_{i,j(t)}$ is $(1/m)\text{OPT}$. Taking expectations, and using these to replace the terms corresponding to the optimal allocation in (6.13), we have that

$$\mathbb{E}[\text{ALG}] \geq \mathbb{E}\left[\frac{T}{m}\text{OPT} + \sum_{t \in [T], i \in [n]} \alpha_{i,t}\left(b_{i,j(t)}x_{i,j(t)} - \frac{B_i}{m} \right) \right]. \tag{6.14}$$

3. The MWU guarantee: After proper scaling, the second term inside the expectation on the right-hand side of (6.14) is exactly the reward of the MWU algorithm, which we can bound using the regret guarantee in Theorem 6.13. In fact, we can bound these terms with probability 1, and not just in expectation, to show that the right-hand side of (6.14) is at least $(1 - O(\epsilon))\text{OPT}$. This bound is summarized in Lemma 6.15, which completes the proof. $\qquad\square$

Lemma 6.15. *It holds that*

$$\frac{T}{m}\text{OPT} + \sum_{t \in [T], i \in [n]} \alpha_{i,t}\left(b_{i,j(t)}x_{i,j(t)} - \frac{B_i}{m} \right) \geq (1 - O(\epsilon))\text{OPT}.$$

Proof The main idea behind this proof is to apply the regret guarantee for the MWU algorithm as stated in Theorem 6.13, by suitably choosing the expert with which to compare. The rewards for the experts problem have been defined so that the second term on the left-hand side of the lemma statement is proportional to the expected reward of the MWU algorithm. This follows from using the definitions of $\alpha_{i,t}$ and $r_{i,t}$:

$$
\sum_{t\in[T],i\in[n]} \alpha_{i,t}\left(b_{i,j(t)}x_{i,j(t)} - \frac{B_i}{m}\right) = \sum_{t\in[T],i\in[n]} B_i\alpha_{i,t}\left(\frac{b_{i,j(t)}x_{i,j(t)}}{B_i} - \frac{1}{m}\right)
$$
$$
= \rho\text{OPT} \sum_{t\in[T],i\in[n]} \theta_{i,t}r_{i,t}. \tag{6.15}
$$

Next, using Theorem 6.13, we can relate (6.15) to the reward of any one expert $i' \in [n+1]$:

$$
\rho\text{OPT} \sum_{t\in[T],i\in[n]} \theta_{i,t}r_{i,t} \geq \left(\sum_{t\in[T]}(r_{i',t} - \epsilon|r_{i',t}|) - \frac{\ln(n+1)}{\epsilon}\right)\rho\text{OPT}
$$
$$
\geq \left(\sum_{t\in[T]}(r_{i',t} - \epsilon|r_{i',t}|)\right)\rho\text{OPT} - \epsilon\text{OPT}. \tag{6.16}
$$

Inequality (6.16) follows from the fact that $\epsilon^2 \geq \rho \ln(n+1)$, as assumed in the hypothesis of Theorem 6.14. Now comes the main part, where we instantiate the choice of expert i' appropriately, so that the right-hand side of (6.16) is at least $(1 - O(\epsilon) - T/m)\text{OPT}$. We consider two cases, where we choose either the expert whose spend exceeds the budget or the $(n + 1)$th expert when no advertiser runs out of budget.

Case 1, no advertiser runs out of budget: $T = m$. In this case, we choose $i' = n + 1$, for whom the rewards are always zero. We therefore have that

$$
\sum_{t\in[T]}(r_{i',t} - \epsilon|r_{i',t}|) = 0 \geq 1 - \epsilon - \frac{T}{m},
$$

because $T = m$. Hence, the lemma follows.

Case 2, some advertiser runs out of budget: In this case, the algorithm stops because in time step $T+1$, matching $j(T+1)$ as per the algorithm would exceed the chosen advertiser's budget. Let this advertiser be i'. From the definition of ρ, we have that advertiser i' has spent at least a $1 - \rho$ fraction of its budget:

$$
\sum_{t\in[T]} b_{i',j(t)}x_{i',j(t)} \geq B_{i'} - b_{i',j(T+1)} \geq B_{i'}(1 - \rho). \tag{6.17}
$$

From the definition of the reward in (6.11), this implies that ρ times the total reward of expert i' up to time T is at least $1 - \rho - T/m \geq 1 - \epsilon - T/m$, because, as per the hypothesis in Theorem 6.14, we have $\rho \leq \epsilon^2/\log n < \epsilon$. If (6.16) only had the reward terms then we would be done, but we also need to bound the terms $\epsilon|r_{i',t}|$. Nonetheless, a similar argument works. From the definition of the reward in (6.11) and the triangle inequality, we have

$$
|r_{i',t}|\rho \leq \frac{b_{i',j(t)}x_{i',j(t)}}{B_{i'}} + \frac{1}{m}
$$
$$
\Rightarrow (r_{i',t} - \epsilon|r_{i',t}|)\rho \geq (1 - \epsilon)\frac{b_{i',j(t)}x_{i',j(t)}}{B_{i'}} - \frac{1+\epsilon}{m}.
$$

Summing this over all $t \in [T]$ and using (6.17), we obtain

$$\sum_{t \in [T]} (r_{i',t} - \epsilon |r_{i',t}|)\rho \geq \sum_{t \in [T]} \left((1 - \epsilon)\frac{b_{i',j(t)} x_{i',j(t)}}{B_{i'}} - \frac{1 + \epsilon}{m} \right)$$

$$\geq (1 - \epsilon)(1 - \rho) - (1 + \epsilon)\frac{T}{m} \geq 1 - 3\epsilon - \frac{T}{m},$$

where the last inequality holds since $\rho \leq \epsilon$ and $T \leq m$. This implies that the right-hand side of (6.16) is at least $(1 - 4\epsilon - T/m)\mathrm{OPT}$. The lemma follows. $\square$

6.6 Packing Mixed Integer Linear Programs

Besides the AdWords problem, there is a variety of problems that arise in the space of ad allocation, mostly because of different types of constraints and input models. In one variant, instead of a budget constraint we have a *capacity* constraint: a limit on the number of matches to an advertiser. Such constraints occur widely in *display advertising*, which refers to banner ads shown on web pages and apps. The capacity constraint gives rise to the problem of *online edge-weighted bipartite matching problem*. A $1 - \frac{1}{e}$ worst case competitive algorithm for this problem, with a *free disposal* assumption, is presented in Chapter 5. In this section we present a general class of problems that capture many such variants.

Packing mixed integer linear program (Packing MILPs). In this abstraction, each $j \in [m]$ corresponds to a request for ad allocation. We have *local* constraints (6.20) (see below) that specify all the different ways in which we may fulfill this request. We abstract these local constraints by saying that the vector $(x_{ij})_{i \in [n]}$ belongs to the set $\mathcal{A}_j$; this is typically modeled as a mixed integer-linear constraint. More generally, this set could be any discrete or continuous set, and we abstract out the details by requiring that we have a computationally efficient algorithm that maximizes a linear objective function over this set. We assume that not fulfilling a request is always an option, by requiring that the zero vector is always in $\mathcal{A}_j$. The equivalent of the small-bids assumption here is that $\mathcal{A}_j \subseteq [0, \rho]^n$. The *global* constraints (6.19) tie the different ad allocation requests together in the form of packing constraints. We consider a normalized version of these constraints, where the right-hand side values are all ones. Such a problem is captured by the following mathematical problem:

$$\text{maximize} \sum_{i \in [n], j \in [m]} v_{ij} x_{ij} \tag{6.18}$$

$$\text{s.t.} \ \forall i \in [n], \sum_{j \in [m]} x_{ij} \leq 1 \tag{6.19}$$

$$\forall j \in [m], \ (x_{ij})_{i \in [n]} \in \mathcal{A}_j \subseteq [0, \rho]^n. \tag{6.20}$$

Matching problems as special cases. In the AdWords problem, the global constraints are the budget constraints. The local constraint is that a query may be matched to at most one advertiser. This is modeled by defining $\mathcal{A}_j$ to be a set of $n + 1$ vectors in n dimensions, where the bid of the ith vector is a fraction of the budget for the ith advertiser in the ith dimension and equals 0 for all other dimensions. The $(n+1)$th vector is the zero vector. In the edge-weighted bipartite matching problem, the global constraints are capacity constraints and the local constraints are matching constraints. The set $\mathcal{A}_j$ is a set of $n+1$ vectors in n dimensions, where the ith vector equals the inverse of the capacity of the ith advertiser in the ith dimension and equals 0 for all other dimensions, the $(n+1)$th vector being the zero vector.

An algorithm for the stochastic model. For the class of packing MILPs, it is impossible to get *any* constant-factor approximation in the adversarial model without problem-specific assumptions such as in the edge-weighted matching with free disposal problem. In the stochastic model, we can generalize the ODL algorithm from Section 6.5 to achieve a $1 - O(\epsilon)$ competitive ratio. The algorithm follows an identical framework. As before, we assume that we know OPT. We again use the MWU algorithm as a subroutine, with $n+1$ experts, one for each constraint and one corresponding to the request not being fulfilled. At any time $t \in [m]$, we maintain Lagrange multipliers $\alpha_{i,t}$ for each $i \in [n]$, by scaling the probability $\theta_{i,t}$ of playing expert $i \in [n]$ as per the MWU algorithm, as follows: $\alpha_{i,t} := \text{OPT}\theta_{i,t}$. We choose the vector $(x_{ij})_{i \in [n]} \in \mathcal{A}_j$ by maximizing the Lagrangian function restricted to that request, $\sum_{i \in [n]}(v_{ij} - \alpha_{i,t})x_{ij}$. If at any time this choice causes a constraint to be violated then we skip fulfilling this and all subsequent requests. Otherwise, we set the reward of expert $i \in [n]$ as follows, and update the expert probabilities for the next step using the MWU algorithm. The reward of expert $n+1$ is always 0. We have

$$\forall i \in [n], \qquad r_{i,t} = \left(x_{i,j(t)} - \frac{1}{m} \right) \frac{1}{\rho}. \tag{6.21}$$

We can show that this algorithm is $1 - O(\epsilon)$ competitive for the random permutation model. The theorem statement and proof are very similar to that of Theorem 6.14; a detailed presentation is outside the scope of this chapter.

6.7 Autobidding: A Decentralized Approach to Matching

So far, we have framed ad allocation as a centralized matching problem in which the auctioneer factors advertiser budgets into the matching decisions. In this section, we take a different view of the problem: here, the auctioneer runs a simple auction for each query and does not even have knowledge of the budgets. Instead, the constraints are managed via *autobidding*. As opposed to manual bidding in which an advertiser specifies a per-keyword bid, an autobidding system allows advertisers to express their high-level goals and constraints and automatically translates those into per-auction bids.

We will first formalize this problem (Section 6.7.1) and will then present an optimal bidding algorithm from one advertiser's point of view (Section 6.7.2). We then connect this back to the matching problem and present analytical results on the quality of the matching derived in such a decentralized approach (Section 6.7.3).

6.7.1 Formulation of Autobidding under Constraints

We will present a very general formulation of the autobidding problem, but it is useful to keep in mind an important motivating example called target cost-per-acquisition (TCPA). Here the advertiser's goal is to maximize acquisitions (sales derived from the ad campaign, also known as conversions), subject to an upper bound on the average cost-per-acquisition (CPA). The upper bound (the target-CPA) will be denoted as T.

Fix an advertiser for whom we are designing a bidding agent. Let p_j be the price of an ad on query j for this advertiser; for simplicity, we will assume in this chapter that there is only a single ad-slot per query. Note that p_j depends on the bids of the other advertisers, who may themselves be solving such an optimization problem via a bidding agent; we will visit this interaction in Section 6.7.3. For now assume that the price p_j of each query j is fixed. We further assume for now that we know the entire query sequence in advance, as well as the values of the p_j. Then, we can formulate the following *selection problem*, i.e., which queries would the advertiser like to buy so as to maximize their objective while staying within their constraints.

Consider the following abstract LP (on the left, below) with a set of constraints indexed by $\mathcal{C}$ and non-negative constants v_j, B^c, and w_j^c, for queries j and constraints $c \in \mathcal{C}$. The x_j are decision variables for whether to buy query j at a cost p_j. The constant v_j stands for the value that the advertiser derives from the ad on query j, and the other constants are set to capture the various constraints. The LP on the right is the dual of the LP on the left and we will use it which we will use shortly. The LPs are as follows:

$$
\begin{array}{l|l}
\text{maximize } \sum_j v_j x_j \text{ s.t.} \quad (6.22) & \text{minimize } \sum_j \delta_j + \sum_c \alpha_c B^c \text{ s.t.} \quad (6.24) \\
\forall c \in \mathcal{C}: \sum_j p_j x_j \leq B^c + \sum_j w_j^c x_j, & \forall j: \delta_j \geq \sum_c \alpha_c (w_j^c - p_j) + v_j, \\
x_j \leq 1, & \forall j: \delta_j \geq 0, \\
x_j \geq 0, \quad (6.23) & \forall c \in \mathcal{C}: \alpha_c \geq 0. \quad (6.25)
\end{array}
$$

Note that this is a fractional version of the selection problem, not an integer version ($x_j \in \{0, 1\}$). We will disregard this difference since an optimal solution for an instance in general position has at most $|\mathcal{C}|$ non-integer x_j which can be set to 0 without much loss in objective value or constraint violation for large markets.

Examples. The above primal LP captures a wide range of autobidding strategies that are offered to advertisers. For example, TCPA is a special case. Let cvr_j denote the conversion rate, which is the probability that query j to the advertiser about an ad results in a conversion; this prediction is made by a machine learning system at the time when query j arrives. Then the objective is obtained by setting $v_j = \text{cvr}_j$ and the TCPA constraint is obtained by setting the corresponding $B^c = 0$ and $w_j^c = T \text{cvr}_j$. As a further example, we can add a budget constraint by setting the corresponding B^c as the budget and $w_j^c = 0$.

6.7.2 Optimal Bidding Algorithm

We now leverage the LP formulation to come up with a bidding formula which can achieve the same optimal choice of queries as in the selection problem. The dual constraint (6.25) can be rewritten as

$$\forall j : \frac{\delta_j}{\sum_c \alpha_c} \geq \left(\frac{v_j + \sum_c \alpha_c w_j^c}{\sum_c \alpha_c} - p_j \right). \tag{6.26}$$

We will use the right-hand side of (6.26) as our bidding formula, assuming we know an optimal dual solution. Set the bid for query j to be

$$\text{bid}(j) := \frac{v_j + \sum_c \alpha_c w_j^c}{\sum_c \alpha_c}. \tag{6.27}$$

Theorem 6.16. *Assuming that we have access to optimal values of the dual variables α_c, the bid formula (6.27) results in an auction outcome identical to an optimal primal solution x_j, if the underlying auction is truthful.*

Proof With this bid, if the advertiser wins the query j in the auction, this means that the right-hand side of (6.26) is positive (ignoring ties), and therefore $\delta_j > 0$ in the optimal solution to the LP. By the complementary slackness conditions, noting that δ_j is the dual variable for the primal constraint (6.23), the following holds in an optimal solution: $\delta_j > 0 \Rightarrow x_j = 1$. Thus, the bid wins only queries j which are in the optimal primal solution.

On the other hand, if the advertiser loses query j in the auction, this means that the right-hand side of (6.26) is negative, and, since $\delta_j \geq 0$, the constraint (6.26) cannot be tight. Again by the complementary slackness condition, noting that x_{ij} is the primal variable corresponding to this constraint, we find that $x_{ij} = 0$ in the optimal primal solution. Thus, the advertiser's bid does not lose any queries from the optimal selection.

In summary, since the underlying auction is truthful, the advertiser wins precisely the auctions in which the bid (6.27) is at least the price (the highest bid among other bidders), and the advertiser also wins precisely the queries chosen by the optimal primal solution. □

Remark 6.17. Note that while we have presented the simple case of one ad-slot per query, the proof holds more generally, e.g., in a position auction when the advertiser's ad can be placed in one of multiple ad-slots in a query. The optimal bid is the result of both selecting the highest-utility option (owing to the truthfulness of the auction) and making the same selection as the optimal primal solution (owing to the complementary slackness conditions).

Examples. For TCPA, with α_T as the dual for the TCPA constraint, we get

$$\text{bid}_{\text{TCPA}}(j) = \left(T + \frac{1}{\alpha_T} \right) \text{cvr}_j. \tag{6.28}$$

Adding a budget constraint to TCPA gives another dual variable α_B, yielding

$$\text{bid}(j) = \left(\frac{1 + T\alpha_T}{\alpha_T + \alpha_B}\right)\text{cvr}_j.$$

The bid formula depends on a knowledge of the optimal duals α_c. In practice, the duals can be estimated from past data logs and updated online in a control loop that depends on the state of the corresponding constraint. In fact LP (6.22) is a special case of the MILP (6.18) in Section 6.6; therefore we can use the algorithm from that section.

6.7.3 The Price of Anarchy: Suboptimality of the Decentralized Approach

We now ask what would happen if all advertisers use the optimal autobidding agents to make their bids. What would be the efficiency of the eventual matching? This is tricky to answer because each advertiser's bidding LP depends on all the other advertisers' LPs, as the price p_j is determined from all the bids in the auction for j. For ease of exposition, we restrict the analysis in this section to the special case of TCPA autobidding; a slightly more involved analysis works for the general autobidding LP (6.22).

First, it can be shown that under the assumption of a large market, an equilibrium does exist for any setting of advertiser target-CPA values. That is, if each advertiser uses the bidding formula (6.28) to convert their target-CPA value to auction bids then there is a stable outcome: a set of dual variables which are consistent with each other via the auction prices. The proof uses Brouwer's fixed point theorem, but we do not include it here. The question in which we are interested is, what is the loss in efficiency of the matching produced by this decentralized (bidding- and auction-based) system, compared with an optimal centralized matching solution? For this we need to define a metric for the efficiency of a matching in this setting.

Constrained welfare. Since each advertiser in TCPA autobidding aims to maximize the number of conversions, a natural efficiency metric would be the total number of conversions across all the advertisers. However, this turns out not to be a very useful metric. The reason is that matchings obtained via bidding and auction have to satisfy the advertisers' spend constraints, while an optimal matching can achieve a very high value by allocating queries free of charge. For example, if there is an advertiser with a high conversion rate for all queries but with very stringent constraints on spend then the optimal matching can achieve an unreasonably high objective by allocating all queries to this advertiser for free. To bring the comparison between an optimal matching and an auction-implemented matching to common ground, we introduce the constrained welfare of a matching, defined for the general bidding LP (6.22) as follows.

Definition 6.18.

$$\text{Constrained welfare} := \sum_{i \in [n]} \min_{c \in \mathcal{C}} \left(B_i^c + \sum_j w_{ij}^c x_{ij}\right).$$

Here, recall that $[n]$ is the set of advertisers and C is the set of constraints. The x_{ij} are the decision variables for whether query j gets matched to advertiser i, and the B_i^c and w_{ij}^c are the constants in the ith advertiser's LP. The definition of constrained welfare takes the smallest right-hand side of the constraints for each advertiser and adds them up. Noting that all the left-hand sides are the spends of the advertisers, we can see that this captures the *maximum willingness to spend* for any given matching. Note that for the special case of TCPA autobidding, this becomes

$$\text{Constrained welfare (TCPA)} = \sum_{i \in [n]} T(i) \sum_j x_{ij} \text{cvr}_{ij} \tag{6.29}$$

where $T(i)$ is the target-CPA bound for advertiser i and cvr_{ij} is the conversion rate for i's ad on query j. This is the total *target-CPA-weighted* conversion, which is intuitively the correct aggregation of conversions across advertisers.

Definition 6.19. With this definition of welfare, we can now define our suboptimality measure, the *constrained price of anarchy* as

$$\text{CPoA} := \max_{I \in \mathcal{I}} \min_{EQ(I)} \frac{\text{CW(OPT}(I))}{\text{CW(EQ}(I))}.$$

Here $\mathcal{I}$ is the set of all possible instances, CW denotes constrained welfare, $\text{OPT}(I)$ is the matching which maximizes CW for instance I, and $\text{EQ}(I)$ denotes the set of matchings achieved in any equilibrium of the decentralized approach. We can now bound the suboptimality of the equilibrium matching.

Theorem 6.20. *For the general autobidding setting (LP(6.22)), CPoA ≤ 2.*

Proof As mentioned earlier, for simplicity of exposition we will prove this statement only for the special case of TCPA. Fix an optimal matching OPT and any equilibrium matching EQ. Let Q_1 be the set of queries which EQ allocates to the same advertiser as OPT does, and let Q_2 be the rest of the queries. Denote the contribution to the CW (as defined in (6.29)) from a subset Q of queries in OPT and in EQ as $\text{CW(OPT} \mid Q)$ and $\text{CW(EQ} \mid Q)$ respectively. By definition, the contribution of Q_1 is identical for EQ and OPT. Thus

$$\text{CW(EQ)} \geq \text{CW(EQ} \mid Q_1) = \text{CW(OPT} \mid Q1). \tag{6.30}$$

Define $\text{spend}_{eq}(i)$ as the total spend of advertiser i in the equilibrium solution, and $\text{spend}_{eq}(j)$ as the spend on query j in the equilibrium solution. Let $\text{OPTB}(j)$ denote the advertiser to which OPT matches query j. For queries in Q_2, the following holds:

$$\begin{aligned}
\text{CW(EQ)} &\geq \sum_{i \in [n]} \text{spend}_{eq}(i) &&= \sum_{j \in Q} \text{spend}_{eq}(j) \geq \sum_{j \in Q_2} \text{spend}_{eq}(j) \\
&\geq \sum_{j \in Q_2} \text{bid}(\text{OPTB}(j), j) &&\geq \sum_{j \in Q_2} T(\text{OPTB}(j)) \text{cvr}(\text{OPTB}(j), j) \\
&= \text{CW(OPT} \mid Q_2).
\end{aligned} \tag{6.31}$$

The first inequality is from the general definition of CW (Definition 6.18) and the constraints in the LP. The third inequality holds because the advertiser

OPTB(j) is one of the price setters for j and we have a second price auction. The last inequality is from the bidding formula (6.28) for the advertiser OPTB(j). The last equality is from the definition of CW for TCPA, (6.29). Adding (6.30) and (6.31) completes the proof. □

6.8 The Design of Sponsored Search Auctions

We now take a deeper look at the auctions underlying these matching mechanisms. One may consider the auction for a query as a matching mechanism within the query, matching ads to slots on the webpage, and the matching mechanisms of the previous sections as a layer on top, matching aggregate advertiser demands and constraints to the query supply.

Preliminaries. Consider a webpage that can display a number $S > 1$ of *slots*. Suppose that there are $n > S$ bidders. Each slot s has a *click-through rate* (CTR) $x_s \in [0, 1]$. This is the probability that a visitor will click on an ad that is located in position s.[2] To simplify the notation, define $x_s = 0$ for $s > S$, and suppose that CTRs decrease according to the numbering of the slots, i.e., $x_1 > x_2 > \cdots > x_S$. Bidder i has a *value* $v_i > 0$ for a click on her ad. The expected value of bidder i for slot s is $v_i x_s$.

In a general auction setting, the bidders place their bids for the items being sold, and the auction decides the allocation (who wins what) and the prices for each winner. In our setting, the bid b_i of an advertiser i represents its value v_i. However, b_i may not equal to v_i, i.e., the value may be misreported. The goal of the auction is to maximize the *economic efficiency*, which is the total value allocated; an allocation which maximizes the efficiency is said to be *efficient*.[3] In our setting, if the auction allocates advertiser i_s to slot s then the total efficiency is $\sum_s v_{i_s} x_s$. The *utility* that an advertiser i gets in an allocation in which it is assigned slot s and pays a *per-click price* of p_s is taken to be $x_s(v_i - p_s)$.

Example 6.21. Suppose that there are $n = 3$ bidders, A, B and C, and that there are $S = 2$ slots. Let the values be $v_A = 10, v_B = 6, v_C = 2$ and the slot CTRs be $x = (0.3, 0.2)$. The efficient allocation is to allocate A to slot 1 and B to slot 2, yielding an efficiency of 4.2. If an auction makes this allocation and charges A a per-click price of $p_1 = 8$ and B a per-click price of $p_2 = 1$, then A's utility is $0.3 \times (10 - 8) = 0.6$ and B's utility is $0.2 \times (6 - 1) = 1.0$.

An auction is called *truthful* if, after knowing the rules of the auction, the utility-maximizing bid of every bidder equals its value (i.e., $b_i = v_i$). Truthful auctions have the advantage that bidders do not have to strategize in their bidding and the analysis of the auction outcome also becomes simpler.

We will look at the two most commonly used auctions in this setting. Before defining them, first consider the case when there is only one slot. This becomes a simple

---

[2] We use this notation for simplicity of exposition. In reality, the click-through rate of an ad in a certain position depends both on the ad-specific CTR and the position-specific CTR. For our purposes we can absorb the ad-specific CTR into the value of the bidder.

[3] There are also other goals in auction design, such as maximizing auctioneer revenue.

single-item auction setting, which is well studied. In this case, the *second-price auction* (SP) is well known to be both truthful and efficient. It allocates the item to the highest bidder and charges a price equal to the second highest bid. In the next two sections we will see two different generalizations of SP, and study the relationship between them.

6.8.1 The Vickrey–Clarke–Groves (VCG) Auction

The VCG auction is a truthful generalization of the SP auction. The idea is to make the efficient allocation and charge each bidder the *externality* it imposes on the other bidders, i.e., the loss in value to the other bidders in the efficient allocation, compared with their value in the efficient allocation without this bidder.[4] In our setting, VCG has a simple and elegant formulation: order the bidders by their bids, so that $b_1 \geq b_2 \geq \cdots \geq b_n$, and allocate bidder s to slot s (for $1 \leq s \leq S$). The cost for bidder s is obtained by considering the effect of removing it, in which case the bidders $s+1$ to $S+1$ move up one slot. Noting that $b_i = v_i$, $\forall i$ (since VCG is truthful), the expected payment for bidder s becomes

$$p_s x_s = \sum_{t=s+1}^{S+1} v_t(x_{t-1} - x_t) = \sum_{t=s}^{S} v_{t+1}(x_t - x_{t+1}). \tag{6.32}$$

Adding these up, we obtain that the expected VCG revenue is

$$\sum_{s=1}^{S} s v_{s+1}(x_s - x_{s+1}). \tag{6.33}$$

Example 6.21 (contd.). In our example, VCG matches bidder A to slot 1 and bidder B to slot 2. Bidder A pays $2 \times 0.2 + 6 \times (0.3 - 0.2) = 1.0$, which is a per-click price of $1.0/0.3$. Bidder A's utility is therefore $0.3 \times v_A - 1.0 = 2$; B pays $2 \times 0.2 = 0.4$, a per-click price of 2, and so B's utility is $0.2 \times v_B - 0.4 = 0.8$.

6.8.2 The Generalized Second-Price (GSP) Auction

Instead of VCG, some sponsored search auctions are based on a different generalization of SP, simply called the generalized second-price auction (GSP). Here again, reordering the bidders by their bids, GSP allocates bidder s to slot s, but charges bidder s a per-click price p_s equal to the bid of the next highest bidder b_{s+1}. GSP is not truthful, as shown by the following example.

Example 6.21 (contd.). In our example, suppose the bidders bid the following bids truthfully: $b_A = 10, b_B = 6, b_C = 2$. Then A's utility is $0.3 \times (v_A - 6) = 1.2$. Now suppose that A reduces its bid to 5; then it wins slot 2, and gets a price of $b_C = 2$. This increases its utility to $0.2 \times (v_A - 2) = 1.6$.

---

[4] Note how this becomes the second-highest bid in a single-item setting.

Equilibria in GSP auctions. We can analyze the GSP auction by characterizing its equilibria. A set of bids (b_s) is an *equilibrium* if the resulting prices (p_s) satisfy the following conditions:

$$(v_s - p_s)x_s \geq (v_s - p_t)x_t \qquad \text{if } t > s, \qquad (6.34)$$
$$(v_s - p_s)x_s \geq (v_s - p_{t-1})x_t \qquad \text{if } t < s. \qquad (6.35)$$

These two constraints indicate that the bidder who is winning slot s at a price of p_s would not benefit by changing its bid and obtaining slot t instead. Note how there is an asymmetry in the prices the bidder can obtain at slot t: for $t > s$, the price is p_t but for $t < s$ the price is p_{t-1}. The latter price occurs because the bidder displaces the bidders between slots t and s when it moves to slot t.

We will focus on a subset of the set of equilibrium prices by removing this asymmetry. We call an equilibrium *symmetric* if the prices satisfy

$$(v_s - p_s)x_s \geq (v_s - p_t)x_t$$

for all t. This is a subset because $p_t = b_{t+1} \leq b_t = p_{t-1}$.

Even though GSP is not truthful, we can show that its symmetric equilibria have good properties and hence we may expect good outcomes.

GSP is efficient at symmetric equilibria. The only allocation that supports any symmetric equilibrium is the allocation that ranks the ads by their value.

Theorem 6.22. *If a set of bids $b_i, i \in [S]$, is such that $b_1 \geq b_2 \geq \cdots \geq b_S$ is a symmetric equilibrium for the GSP auction then $v_1 \geq v_2 \geq \cdots \geq v_S$.*

Proof Consider the following symmetric equilibrium conditions for the pair of bidders s and $s + 1$, in which each prefers its own allocation and price to that of the other:

$$x_s(v_s - p_s) \geq x_{s+1}(v_s - p_{s+1}),$$
$$x_{s+1}(v_{s+1} - p_{s+1}) \geq x_s(v_{s+1} - p_s).$$

Adding these two inequalities and rearranging terms gives us

$$(x_s - x_{s+1})(v_s - v_{s+1}) \geq 0.$$

Since we have ordered the slots in the decreasing order of click-through rate, $x_s \geq x_{s+1}$ and therefore $v_s \geq v_{s+1}$. $\qquad \square$

Revenue dominance of GSP vs. VCG. The revenue of the GSP auction at any symmetric equilibrium is higher than the revenue of the VCG auction.

Assumption. The top losing bidder bids his value, i.e., $b_{S+1} = v_{S+1}$. For this bidder, the most reasonable strategy is to bid as high as possible in trying to win some slot.

Theorem 6.23. *If a set of bids $b_i, i \in [S]$, is such that $b_1 \geq b_2 \geq \cdots \geq b_S$ is a symmetric equilibrium for the GSP auction then the GSP revenue is at least the revenue of the VCG auction given in (6.33).*

Proof We will prove something stronger, that the GSP revenue from *each slot* is at least the VCG revenue from the same slot, given in (6.32). We will do this by reverse induction, starting from the last slot S. The price p_S for the last slot is b_{S+1}, which from the assumption stated above is equal to v_{S+1}. Hence, the GSP revenue from the last slot is $x_S p_S = x_S v_{S+1}$, which is the same as the VCG revenue.

For any slot $s \leq S - 1$, assume that the GSP revenue from slot $s + 1$ is at least the VCG revenue from it. We now prove the same for slot s. We consider the symmetric equilibrium condition that says bidder $s + 1$ does not prefer to be in slot s instead, which imposes a lower bound on the revenue from slot s:

$$x_{s+1}(v_{s+1} - p_{s+1}) \geq x_s(v_{s+1} - p_s)$$
$$\Rightarrow p_s x_s \geq v_{s+1}(x_s - x_{s+1}) + x_{s+1} p_{s+1}.$$

Using the induction hypothesis and the VCG revenue for slot $s + 1$ from (6.32), we have that

$$x_{s+1} p_{s+1} \geq \sum_{t=s+1}^{S} v_{t+1}(x_t - x_{t+1}).$$

Adding the two inequalities above gives the required bound. $\square$

6.9 Bibliographic Notes

The AdWords problem was introduced in [17], which also provided the optimal MSVV algorithm in the adversarial model. The proof was combinatorial, based on their notion of trade-off-revealing LPs. Subsequently the connection to online primal–dual algorithms was made in [6]. The hardness of the offline problem without the small-bids assumption was proved in [7]. The first online algorithm achieving a competitive ratio better than one half (0.5016) for the general problem without the small-bids assumption was provided in [15]. The stochastic random-order model for AdWords was introduced in [12], and showed that the greedy algorithm achieves a competitive ratio of $1 - 1/e$. The first asymptotically optimal algorithm for the random-order model was provided in [8]; it was also shown that we need to know the number of queries m to get such an algorithm. The display ads problem and the generalization to packing MILPs was introduced in [11] and [4]. The idea of using the experts problem to solve the packing of LPs online was introduced in [14]. The algorithm and analysis in Section 6.5 were adapted from [3], in which it was generalized to convex programming. Theorem 6.13 on the regret guarantee for MWU is from [5]. The formulation and results in Section 6.7 were provided in [2], For a more comprehensive survey of models and results for ad allocations, see [16]. An analysis of the VCG and GSP auctions was given in [18], [9], and [1].

The estimates of advertising spend in the introduction were taken from [10]. The section on auto-bidding algorithms was motivated by performance-based auto-bidding products and strategies provided by most internet advertising companies, e.g., [13].

References

[1] Agrawal, Shipra, and Devanur, Nikhil R. 2014. Fast algorithms for online stochastic convex programming. Pages 1405–1424 of: *Proc. 26th Annual ACM-SIAM Symposium on Discrete Algorithms*. SIAM.

[2] Aggarwal, Gagan, Badanidiyuru, Ashwinkumar, and Mehta, Aranyak. 2019. Autobidding with constraints. Pages 17–30 of: *Proc. International Conference on Web and Internet Economics*. Springer.

[3] Aggarwal, Gagan, Goel, Ashish, and Motwani, Rajeev. 2006. Truthful auctions for pricing search keywords. Pages 1–7 of: *Proc. 7th ACM Conference on Electronic Commerce*. ACM.

[4] Agrawal, Shipra, Wang, Zizhuo, and Ye, Yinyu. 2014. A dynamic near-optimal algorithm for online linear programming. *Operations Research*, **62**(4), 876–890.

[5] Arora, Sanjeev, Hazan, Elad, and Kale, Satyen. 2012. The multiplicative weights update method: A meta-algorithm and applications. *Theory of Computing*, **8**(1), 121–164.

[6] Buchbinder, Niv, Jain, Kamal, and Naor, Joseph Seffi. 2007. Online primal–dual algorithms for maximizing ad-auctions revenue. Pages 253–264 of: *Proc. European Symposium on Algorithms*. Springer.

[7] Chakrabarty, Deeparnab, and Goel, Gagan. 2010. On the approximability of budgeted allocations and improved lower bounds for submodular welfare maximization and GAP. *SIAM Journal on Computing*, **39**(6), 2189–2211.

[8] Devanur, Nikhil R, and Hayes, Thomas P. 2009. The AdWords problem: Online keyword matching with budgeted bidders under random permutations. Pages 71–78 of: *Proc. 10th ACM conference on Electronic commerce*. ACM.

[9] Edelman, Benjamin, Ostrovsky, Michael, and Schwarz, Michael. 2007. Internet advertising and the generalized second-price auction: Selling billions of dollars worth of keywords. *American Economic Review*, **97**(1), 242–259.

[10] eMarketer. 2020. Worldwide Digital Ad Spending. https://forecasts-na1.emarketer.com/5a4d1e53d8690c01349716b8/5a4d1bcfd8690c01349716b6. Accessed: 2021-03-27.

[11] Feldman, Jon, Henzinger, Monika, Korula, Nitish, Mirrokni, Vahab S., and Stein, Cliff. 2010. Online stochastic packing applied to display ad allocation. Pages 182–194 of: *Proc. European Symposium on Algorithms*. Springer.

[12] Goel, Gagan, and Mehta, Aranyak. 2008. Online budgeted matching in random input models with applications to AdWords. Pages 982–991 of: *Proc. Symposium on Discrete Algorithms*, vol. 8.

[13] Google. 2021. Auto-bidding products support page. https://support.google.com/google-ads/answer/2979071. Accessed: 2021-03-27.

[14] Gupta, Anupam, and Molinaro, Marco. 2014. How experts can solve LPs online. Pages 517–529 of: *Proc. European Symposium on Algorithms*. Springer.

[15] Huang, Zhiyi, Zhang, Qiankun, and Zhang, Yuhao. 2020. AdWords in a panorama. Pages 1416–1426 of: *Proc. 61st IEEE Annual Symposium on Foundations of Computer Science*. IEEE.

[16] Mehta, Aranyak. 2013. Online matching and ad allocation. *Foundations and Trends® in Theoretical Computer Science*, **8**(4), 265–368.
[17] Mehta, Aranyak, Saberi, Amin, Vazirani, Umesh, and Vazirani, Vijay. 2007. AdWords and generalized online matching. *Journal of the ACM*, **54**(5), 22–es.
[18] Varian, Hal R. 2007. Position auctions. *International Journal of Industrial Organization*, **25**(6), 1163–1178.

CHAPTER SEVEN

Spectrum Auctions from the Perspective of Matching

Paul Milgrom and Andrew Vogt

7.1 Introduction

In July 1994, the United States Federal Communications Commission (FCC) conducted the first economist-designed auction for radio spectrum licenses. In the years since, governments worldwide have come to rely on auction mechanisms to allocate – and reallocate – rights to use electromagnetic frequencies. Over the same period, novel uses for spectrum have increased both the demand for licenses and auction prices, which has generated greater interest in the nuances of spectrum markets and spurred the development of spectrum auction design. In August 2017, the FCC completed the Broadcast Incentive Auction, a two-sided repurposing of an endogenously determined quantity of spectrum. That reallocation ranks among the most complex feats of economic engineering ever undertaken. The next generations of wireless networks are poised to extend this growth and to demand further innovation in the markets and algorithms that are used to assign spectrum licenses.

What does all this have to do with matching theory? Radio spectrum, like most physical resources, is heterogeneous. This creates a matching element: efficient allocations must assign the right frequencies to the right users.

A radio spectrum license grants its holder the right to use a particular band of frequencies in a particular geographical area, subject to restrictions on signal power, interference with nearby users, and other regulations. Signals sent using different frequencies travel differently. Generally, lower frequencies can support communication over greater distances, passing through diverse obstructions such as raindrops, trees, and concrete walls. That reach is an advantage for serving large rural areas or for providing outdoor coverage among tall buildings. Higher frequencies are less useful for long-distance transmissions, but their short range is an advantage for supporting multiple users simultaneously, as when neighboring households share the same frequencies for their wi-fi applications. Sometimes even very small differences in frequencies can be important, because interference can be caused by harmonics between frequencies being used in the same device.

Efficient matching of frequencies to users is only part of the challenge for radio spectrum auctions: efficient spectrum allocations must also assign the right *quantities* (amounts of bandwidth) to different users. Within a given band the spectrum is often almost homogeneous, and then efficiency is mostly about allocating the right quantities to each user, so that the main role of prices is the usual one found in economics textbooks.

A further challenge for auctions lies in the way preferences must be reported. Although the matching literature includes models of matching with prices, it pays little attention to how participants might report those preferences or their corresponding demand functions. Multi-product demand functions embed much more information than simple rank-order lists and it is far from obvious how such demands should be reported for use in a direct mechanism.

Partly because of this demand-reporting problem, spectrum auctions usually eschew direct mechanisms in favor of multi-round mechanisms, in which bidders can respond in complicated ways to incrementally evolving prices. The advantage of dynamic auctions is that they allow bidders to adjust their purchases in ways that accommodate both values and budget constraints. A disadvantage is that they also alter bidding incentives, increasing strategic complexity and manipulability of the mechanism. The relative magnitudes of these advantages and disadvantages vary across applications, which helps to account for the historical successes and failures of multi-round spectrum auctions.

Most of the simple, elegant results of matching theory depend on the assumption that agents report preferences that satisfy a substitutes condition. Consequently, another important concern in auction design is the failure of the substitutes condition, which can also be described as the presence of complementarities (see Chapter 15). Bidders in spectrum auctions often view licenses as complements: buying one license increases the value of another. This can arise when a bidder prefers to hold licenses for adjacent frequencies or licenses that cover adjacent territories, when there are financial returns for larger operational scale and scope, or when budget constraints force a choice between one expensive license and several cheaper ones. The seriousness of the problems that result from the failure of the substitutes condition and the best practical remedies to address them vary depending on the source of the complementarities.

Another important difference between traditional matching theory and auction theory lies in the welfare analysis. In most countries, the spectrum regulator is less concerned about the profits of the telecommunications companies, or even about expected revenue, than about consumer welfare and how the auction outcome will affect competition in the consumer market. The regulator often prefers a market in which many companies compete to provide consumers with low-cost high-quality services that are widely available, even in small communities in rural or mountainous areas where the private cost of providing service may be high. It is not possible to understand the market design decisions made by spectrum regulators around the world without understanding the salience of their concerns about consumer welfare, retail competition, and universal service.

This chapter begins, in Section 7.2, by reviewing the deep connections between two-sided matching markets with and without money. The extension of the two-sided matching problem to incorporate prices subsumes, as special cases, not only models of matching without prices and of bilateral matching with prices but also certain auction problems. We then describe early spectrum auction designs and their properties under naive bidding. The first spectrum auction designs were adopted after theorists demonstrated that, under certain assumptions "about bidders' values (whether items are substitutes) and behaviors (whether strategies are naive".

those designs could lead to allocations and prices approximating a competitive equilibrium.

In Section 7.3, we turn to the issue of bidder incentives in spectrum auctions. Most often, buyers in these auctions seek to acquire multiple licenses, so matching theorems about dominant strategies for buyers of a single item do not apply. The most important competition issues for spectrum auction design are similar to those present in homogeneous goods markets, such as anti-competitive behavior, market concentration, and broader societal interests.

Section 7.4 focuses on complementarities. Although the licenses sold in spectrum auctions often include substitutes, it is also common for bidders to view some licenses as complements. This is at odds with the early matching and auction literature, which mostly assumed that the items to be allocated are substitutes or that the markets are large in ways that make failures of substitution unimportant. Radio spectrum auctions rarely have many competing participants, and complements in radio spectrum create meaningful complications that have led to the use of new designs and to interesting subtleties in auction bidding strategies.

Section 7.5 explores the theory of descending clock auctions for a wider range of problems than just those in which items are substitutes, with particular attention to the problem of designing the Broadcast Incentive Auction. Descending clock auctions are shown to be a new kind of deferred acceptance algorithm, and to share properties with DA algorithms in the substitutes case. We describe seven significant disadvantages of the classic Vickrey auction design, each of which can be avoided by this class of clock auctions.

7.2 Spectrum Auction Algorithms

7.2.1 Static Matching with Prices

Since the introduction of models for matching without prices (the Gale–Shapley college admissions or marriage problem) and one-to-one matching with prices (the Shapley–Shubik house assignment game), it has been clear that the two theories are closely connected. Those foundational matching models can be combined and generalized within the Kelso–Crawford model of matching between firms and workers: each worker can work for only one firm, but each firm can employ multiple workers, with wages selected from a finite set. Both firms and workers have preferences over their match partners and the contractual wage. With the important assumption that workers are substitutes, so that increasing the wage of one worker does not reduce a firm's demand for any other worker, a deferred-acceptance process with offers that include prices leads to a stable allocation.

When the set of wages is a singleton, the worker–firm model is logically equivalent to the college admissions model but with a more general substitutes preference structure. If each worker always prefers the firm offering her the highest wage, the deferred acceptance algorithm in this model amounts to a simultaneous auction in which workers offer their services to the highest bidders. If, instead of using a direct mechanism, this process is run dynamically with automated bidders that represent the firms, then the model anticipates many of the rules of the simultaneous multiple-round auction that was later used for selling radio spectrum licenses. If each firm has only a single opening, the matching problem can also be reduced to the model of one-to-one matching with prices. Thus, the worker–firm model nests the earlier models of matching with and without prices and allows the reinterpretation of the deferred acceptance algorithm as an auction mechanism with automated bidders.

The substitutes condition provides an important simplification in this matching model, because it is exactly the condition that ensures that during a labor-market auction with rising wages, a firm never chooses to reject a worker that it had wanted to hire when the wages of other workers were lower. Consequently, the demand for a given worker can only fall when that worker's own wage rises, which happens only when there is excess demand for that worker. Wages in the auction continue to rise until the demand for each worker is exactly one, which is known as the market-clearing situation.[1]

Connections between matching problems and spectrum auctions can also be found within the (further) generalized model of two-sided matching with contracts (see Chapter 27). The intuition is again that an auction is equivalent to a particular matching of buyers to sellers, with the restrictions that buyers are differentiated only by the price they are willing to pay and that sellers care only about those prices. If there is only one firm or seller – an auctioneer – then the model of matching with contracts can be reduced to a particular auction mechanism called the generalized clock-proxy algorithm. In a clock-proxy auction, as in other deferred-acceptance matching algorithms, the offering side must express its preferences using an exhaustive and static rank-order list. However, in practice many auctions designs that have been used to allocate spectrum rights instead employ a dynamic process in which the offering side can incrementally adjust its bids.

7.2.2 Simultaneous Multiple-Round Auction

The inaugural 1994 Federal Communications Commission (FCC) spectrum auction used the newly–invented simultaneous multiple-round (SMR) auction format. This design has since become common for government sales of spectrum licenses around the world. It uses a dynamic process that resembles the firm-proposing deferred acceptance algorithm with prices, in which the radio spectrum licenses to be sold correspond to workers who each prefer the highest money offer they receive.

In the SMR auction, multiple items are offered for sale by a single auctioneer. Participants bid in a series of rounds, in which each new bid for an item must be submitted at a higher price, subject to a minimum increment. Each round of bidding is conceptually similar to a round of tentative offers in the DA algorithm. The notion of a best proposal is replaced with that of the "standing high bid" (and its associated "standing high bidder"), which is the highest bid submitted for the item to that point in the auction (and the bidder that submitted it). Similar to the process in the DA algorithm, bidding continues until there is a round in which there are no new bids for any item. At that point, the standing high bids become winning, which determines both the allocation and the final prices.

---

[1] Although this intuition is nearly correct, there are some challenging technical details to be addressed because, at some wage vectors, firms may be indifferent among workers, so the firms' demands functions may not be well defined and the formal analysis must use demand correspondences. These details, however, can be managed to find an exact equilibrium. With the substitutes condition, ascending auctions with discrete increments will also find approximate market equilibria. When the substitutes condition fails, however, new issues can arise, as described in Section 7.4.

Mechanism 7.1 (Simultaneous multiple-round auction).

1. **Initialization**: The auctioneer sets a reserve price for each item. The initial standing high bidder for each item is the auctioneer, and the initial standing high bid is the reserve price.

Until there is a round in which no new bids are made, do:

2. **New bids**: Bidders submit new bids for any desired items, indicating the prices they are willing to pay. Each new bid for an item must be no less than its minimum allowable price.
3. For each item, the auctioneer tentatively accepts a standing high bid, equal to the maximum of the previous standing high bid and any new bids. Ties are broken randomly. The auctioneer reveals the standing high bid and standing high bidder for each item.
4. The minimum allowable price for each item is set equal to its standing high bid plus an additional increment.

Output the matching of items to bidders and the prices for each item.

There are clear similarities between the DA algorithm and the SMR auction, but there are also important differences. The DA algorithm is a direct mechanism, in which participants report what they would demand from any available set of items. With multiple items and prices, specifying a complete demand function can be a daunting task. The SMR auction, by contrast, is a dynamic mechanism in which bidders are never required to make exhaustive reports. Instead, they receive information about each round's results and can use that information to adjust their next bids. This eliminates some of the guesswork required under static formats (such as sealed-bid auctions) and lowers the risk of ex-post bidder regret. Another effect of this dynamic reporting regime is to allow bidders to express some demands that are incompatible with substitutes preferences; perhaps most importantly, bidders can ensure that their bids across all items respect overall budget constraints.

However, the rich set of bidding possibilities within a dynamic mechanism also enables strategies that may be harmful to the operation of the auction. One example arises when a bidder limits its participation early in the auction, because it prefers to wait to see how high the prices for one item may rise before it decides how much to bid for another. If many bidders refrain from bidding early in the auction, with each attempting to be the last to bid, then some bidders are sure to be disappointed and the number of auction rounds could grow impractically large. The FCC's original SMR auction design mitigated that problem by adopting the Milgrom–Wilson *activity rule*, which limited each bidder's bids in any round relative to its overall bidding activity in the previous round. All subsequent SMR auctions and related dynamic designs have incorporated some sort of activity rule.

The outcome of an SMR auction resembles that of the DA algorithm if participants bid as if items were substitutes. As in ordinary demand theory, a set of items are said to be *substitutes* if, whenever that set of items uniquely maximizes a bidder's profit at some prices, the same set remains a profit-maximizing choice at any new price vector with the same prices for the items that were being demanded and weakly higher prices for all other items. When each bidder in an SMR auction has preferences satisfying the substitutes condition and naively regards the prices it faces as fixed – equal to the current price for items for which it is the standing high bidder and equal to the current price plus one increment for all other items – the SMR auction exactly follows the rounds of the DA algorithm. In this case, the final prices and outcome form a competitive equilibrium of an economy that is "close" to the actual one, in which participants' values for each combination of items are reduced by one increment for each of the items in that combination that the bidder does not win in the auction. This implies that any inefficiency is at most proportional to the size of the auction bid increment.

7.2.3 Clock Auction with Assignment Round

In many recent spectrum auctions, licenses have been grouped into product categories within which the licenses are mostly interchangeable. In that case, the SMR auction can be closely approximated by a clock auction in which a single price applies to all licenses in the same category. For example, the regulator might offer licenses with slightly different frequencies that cover the same geographic area, and group these together in a single product category. Given the prices, each bidder specifies the *quantities* of each product that it wishes to buy. For each category in which licenses are overdemanded in the current round, the auctioneer raises the prices for the next round. Other prices remain unchanged. A bidder may increase but may not reduce its demand for a product with an unchanged price.[2] This auction process continues until there is no excess demand for any product category.[3]

A clock auction mechanism determines the quantities of each license category won by each bidder but not the assignment of specific licenses. In spectrum auctions, bidders do often care about the particular frequencies they will be allowed to use. Efficiency typically demands that all winning bidders should receive contiguous blocks of spectrum, to minimize interference issues at frequency boundaries with different licensees. Perhaps all bidders also wish to avoid a particular "impaired" frequency that conflicts with existing uses of the same or nearby frequencies. Perhaps one bidder wants to avoid a particular frequency because of harmonic interactions with another of its licensed frequencies.

To determine the final license assignment and address these issues, the clock auction is followed by a final bidding round called the "assignment round." In a typical assignment round, each bidder submits a set of bids that express its values for alternative assignments, given the quantities of licenses that it has won in each product category. The auctioneer selects the bids that maximize the total value, usually subject to the constraints that each winner is assigned a contiguous block of frequencies of the correct size and that no two assigned blocks intersect. These become the winning bids, and the additional payments to be made in the assignment round may be set by a first or second price payment rule.

---

[2] Notice that if the different products are substitutes for a bidder then it has no wish to reduce demand for licenses whose prices have not increased.

[3] Standard clock auctions do not use the notion of a standing high bidder, but this creates the possibility that, in some round, demand may start strictly above the available supply but fall strictly below during the round. Most clock auctions implement additional rules to prevent this, refusing to honor demand reductions that would result, for a product, in aggregate demand that is less than supply.

Mechanism 7.2 (Clock auction with assignment round).

1. **Initialization**: The auctioneer sets an initial clock price for each product category.

Until there is a round in which no new bids are made, do:

2. **New bids**: Bidders submit new bids for any desired products, indicating their quantity demand at the current clock prices.
3. The auctioneer reveals the aggregate demand for each product. The clock price for each product that is overdemanded is set equal to its previous price plus an additional increment.

As an intermediate step, output the matching of products to bidders and the prices for each product.

4. **Assignment round**: Accept additional bids to assign bidders to specific items, consistent with the matching of products to bidders.

Output the matching of items to bidders and the prices for each item.

Because clock auctions aggregate similar items into larger product categories, they simplify bidding and speed up auctions. For example, suppose there is a category of 10 nearly identical spectrum licenses, and 11 bidders that each want only one license. Bidders can (nearly) describe their preferences with just one bid price, rather than 10, which simplifies bidding. The auction process is also faster, because an SMR auction would require 10 rounds with different standing high bidders to raise the price for all items, with the price of only one license rising by one increment in each round. In contrast, a clock auction that categorized the licenses as identical would raise the single price associated with all 10 licenses in one round. In this way, this clock auction requires both fewer bids in each round and fewer rounds to reach completion.

7.3 Bidder Incentives and Regulator Objectives

Both matching theory and auction theory include results about truthful reporting being a dominant strategy when the bidder or offeror seeks a single item or a single match and preferences on the other side satisfy a substitutes condition. This connection has been analyzed in the literature and is not damaging to efficiency or competitive pricing. More serious problems arise when bidders seek to acquire multiple items and have the option of reducing the quantities they demand at any price to reduce the market-clearing price. Much as in textbook economics, the seriousness of this problem depends on the shares that the largest bidders are likely to hold.

Several spectrum auctions have failed after the major bidders all reduced demand in an early round, producing substantially lower spectrum prices relative to other similar auctions. A German auction in 1999 concluded after only two rounds, with two large bidders splitting the available spectrum 50–50. Similarly, Ofcom's 2021 auction of spectrum in the 700 MHz and 3.6 GHz frequencies ended at low prices with balanced divisions of spectrum among the winning bidders.

The role of dynamic multiple-round auctions in facilitating these low-price outcomes is theoretically a subtle one. Sealed-bid uniform-price Treasury bond auctions are, in principle, vulnerable to a similar kind of manipulation, in which sophisticated bidders could potentially reduce demand to manipulate prices.

Even setting aside the matching element, there are two things that distinguish spectrum auctions from their Treasury auction counterparts. One is the very small number of bidders and the absence of uncertainty created by other bidders. With two bidders and an even number of spectrum licenses, for example, there is a focal outcome in which each bidder bids for half the available spectrum. The second relates to how bidders settle on an expected final outcome. Although there is currently no theory of communication in dynamic auctions, bidders appear sometimes to be able to coordinate their expectations through a series of bids, settling on a market division in which the winners avoid competing against one another in ways that might drive up auction prices. In other cases, where the likely preferences of competing bidders are common knowledge, strong bidders may be able to unilaterally enforce particular settlements by threatening to raise prices on licenses that their opponents desire.

In contrast with labor, school, or medical matching, the regulator designing a spectrum auction is most often a government regulator that cares not only about revenues but also about reducing concentration in the retail market in which the spectrum buyers compete. Buyers calculate values in spectrum auctions by forecasting revenue and cost streams with and without the spectrum and then computing the difference, so part of the value of any license comes from denying that spectrum resource to a competitor, which typically leads to an increase in the bidder's market share. Since the value of this *market foreclosure* (limiting the opportunities available to competitors) is usually higher for dominant firms, allocations that maximize these values lead to too much foreclosure of weaker firms. In some cases new entrants have been reluctant to compete for licenses at all, given the high costs of auction preparation and the likelihood that established bidders will bid above the use value of the spectrum, as measured by cost avoidance, in order to maintain their larger market positions.

Regulators also generally care about promoting better service to rural and mountainous areas where service is costly to provide. A good rural phone service makes it easier to provide emergency services and to keep citizens informed and engaged, among other public benefits.

In practice, regulators advance these interests and others in multiple ways, some of which involve the auction rules. To block foreclosure, regulators may use the following: spectrum caps, which limit the quantity of spectrum that can be won by any single bidder; set-asides, which disqualify some incumbent firms from bidding on certain licenses; or discounts for new entrants, which require small bidders to pay only a fraction of the value of their winning bids in an auction. To promote rural phone services and to further limit foreclosure, licenses may come with build-out requirements, such that the winner is required to return the license if it fails to build supporting infrastructure to use the spectrum over a sufficiently large area, or over rural areas in particular. The efficiency of any individual auction is almost always desirable, but from a regulatory perspective it may be only one of several competing interests in the overall market.

7.4 Substitutes and Complements

The earliest models of matching theory and early auction models shared the common assumption that each participant – firm or worker, buyer or seller – is looking for only one partner or only one good. Goods cannot be complements in those one-to-one matching models.

When the model is expanded to allow one side to desire multiple matches – say a firm that wants to hire several workers – the simplest generalizations involve assuming that goods or people are substitutes. The Gale–Shapley DA algorithm finds a stable outcome for the college admissions problem when colleges regard students as substitutes, but not generally otherwise, and a similar finding applies to the Kelso–Crawford model when firms regard workers as substitutes. It is not just that the algorithms themselves fail: without substitutes, stable matches may not exist. One example arises when two doctors in a couple want jobs in the same city and so regard offers from hospitals in any one city as complements: offers are valuable as a pair but of little value individually. Similar results apply to equilibrium theory. When goods are substitutes, the SMR auction under straightforward bidding finds a near-equilibrium and the ascending clock auction finds an exact competitive equilibrium, but both can fail when goods are not substitutes. In an auction market with a single seller and many buyers, the Vickrey outcome is in the core of the market game if goods are substitutes and there are ascending auctions that mimic the Vickrey outcome. Without substitutes, the Vickrey outcome is not generally in the core and prices can be too low to be market clearing.

Just as the assumption of substitutes is inconsistent with a pair of doctors seeking residencies at hospitals in the same city, it is also at odds with observed bidder demand for spectrum licenses. Spectrum licenses can be complementary for a variety of reasons. Users of radio spectrum often have greater value for adjacent frequencies than for slightly separated frequencies, because adjacency reduces the number of boundary frequencies at which users need to coordinate with others to avoid interference. Similarly, there can be significant economies of scale and scope that make packages of licenses more valuable than the sum of individual values: licenses to use tiny amounts of frequency bandwidth or small geographic coverage areas may even have zero value because they must be combined with others to merit the infrastructure investments needed for a viable wireless system. Bidder budgets, too, can make licenses complements. For example, suppose that a buyer has values of $(30, 30, 40)$ for three items A, B, and C and that it values sets of licenses at the sum of the item values. With a budget exceeding \$100, the demand for each license would depend just on its own price. If the buyer's budget is just \$10, however, and the price vector is $(5, 5, 10)$, then the buyer maximizes its net value by demanding A and B, but if the price of A then rises by 1 then the buyer maximizes by dropping both A and B to demand C alone. That pattern, in which a price increase for A reduces the demand for B, is what it means for the two licenses to be complements in demand, at least over that range of prices.

It is no coincidence that the substitutes condition often fails in practice, because the condition is non-generic: substitutes valuations must satisfy a potentially large collection of linear equations. Given a set of items $S = \{A, B, C, \dots\}$, any three elements A, B, C, and any subset $T \subseteq S - \{A, B, C\}$, if v is a substitutes valuation then the two largest numbers from the set $\{v(AT) + v(BCT), v(BT) + v(ACT),$

$v(CT) + v(ABT)$} must be equal.[4] With many goods, this leads to a large set of equations that v must satisfy. If S is a large set then this implies many restrictions on v, so the class of substitutes valuations is of a much lower dimension than the unrestricted class of valuations.

An important way in which spectrum auction design falls outside the scope of matching market design is the way in which the spectrum products are defined. In standard matching theory and the markets to which it has most often been applied, the items to be matched (people, jobs, organs, online ad impressions) are defined *a priori*, but the same is not true for spectrum licenses. In a hypothetical world, one might imagine that regulators would prefer to sell "postage stamp" licenses with tiny geographic areas and paper-thin bands of spectrum, allowing bidders to assemble bespoke collections of these small licenses to meet their operating needs. But such licenses are hardly likely to be substitutes, and trying to sell them using either a matching-like mechanism or an SMR design has no good theoretical properties and risks dramatically inefficient outcomes. To mitigate this problem most effectively, the regulator must carefully define the bandwidth, geographic coverage, time period, technological restrictions, and regulatory restrictions that apply to the licenses.

In many countries, mobile providers operate nationwide networks, so there is little to be gained by offering spectrum licenses that serve smaller geographic areas. For this reason, many regulators commonly sell only nationwide licenses, which eliminates the geographic adjacency problem, fully addressing that kind of complementarity. For these same countries, if a new frontier of contiguous frequencies is offered for sale then an assignment round following a clock auction can also guarantee the licensing of contiguous frequencies to each of the winners. In more recent auctions, where old uses are being shut down to make room for new ones, frequencies may not be contiguous and other bidders may have already licensed some intervening frequency blocks. In those settings, to minimize the frequency-contiguity problem, design often involves offering incentives to existing licensees to include their old blocks in the auction.

7.4.1 Exposure Risk

Bidders often differ in their demands in ways that make it impossible to package license rights so as to reflect the interests of every buyer. In such cases, one approach is to tailor license definitions to serve the needs of a particular class of bidders. For example, a regulator might simultaneously allocate licenses that cover the same area at different geographic scales – smaller licenses to serve the needs of local service providers and larger licenses to suit the requirements of national operators.

The alternative is to allow bidders to assemble collections of smaller licenses that, taken together, meet their business objectives. This can work well for an SMR auction when licenses are substitutes, because if a bidder bids straightforwardly according to its true demand then a standing high bidder for a license after any auction round will still want to buy that license even if subsequent competition raises the prices of other licenses. Without the substitutes restriction, however, a straightforward bidder can come to regret its past bids. A buyer who wants and bids for the

---

[4] Suppose that, for given valuations, the first of these terms is larger than the other two. Then there exists some price evolution such that increasing the price of B can reduce demand for C, as the bidder switches from bidding for B and C to bidding just for A.

package AB may become the standing high bidder on the license A, but subsequent bidding may increase the price of license B. The substitutes condition asserts exactly that such a price increase does not reduce the bidder's demand for A, so it will never wish to withdraw its demand for A.

If valuations do not satisfy the substitutes condition, then if the bidder bids for A during the auction, it is exposed to the risk of winning that license when it wishes it had not. If it does not bid for A, it risks missing a profitable opportunity. This challenge to bidding well in an auction is called the *exposure problem*, and it has become a central concern in modern spectrum auction design.

A bidder in an SMR may be tempted to respond to the exposure problem by sitting out the early part of the auction, waiting to bid until late in the auction when it may have a better idea of what the prices for different items will be. For example, the bidder who wants package AB and is uncertain about whether B will be too expensive might choose to bid for B only and, upon learning that it can win B at a low price, might only then begin to bid for A. If many bidders behave in that way then the auction could stall – after all, it is not possible for every bidder to be the last to bid in an SMR auction. Such behaviors are limited by activity rules, but those rules cannot shield bidders from the risk of acquiring a less valuable subset of their desired licenses.

7.4.2 Managing Exposure Risk

The theoretical treatments of the exposure problem focus on the possibility that a bidder without substitutes preferences can be caught on the horns of a dilemma: the bidder must either curtail its participation or risk losing money. Closer analysis reveals, however, that the magnitude of the exposure problem depends on price uncertainty. In the example above, if the bidder could narrow its forecast for the price of license B, it would find that one of its two main options – bidding aggressively or dropping out early – would almost always lead to a near-optimal outcome. Generally, if a bidder expects that, even without its own participation, auction prices will likely be very high or very low then its exposure risk is easily managed.

Even when a simple high-versus-low characterization does not apply, bidders in spectrum auctions can sometimes adopt strategies that substantially mitigate the exposure problem. Doing so involves using information that emerges during the auction (especially about demands at different price levels) that is not revealed by any traditional direct mechanism. Still, the exposure problem remains a meaningful concern. This has inspired attempts to create mechanisms that avoid the exposure problem more generally, without the need for special adaptations by bidders.

It is possible, in principle, to design a spectrum auction to avoid the exposure problem completely. Bidders in such *combinatorial auctions* submit all-or-nothing *package bids* for collections of licenses. The best-known combinatorial auction design is the *Vickrey auction*, in which a bidder expresses its values for every desired combination of licenses. Given the bids, the auctioneer computes the assignment that maximizes the total value of the license allocation and then sets prices according to the famous Vickrey formula, in which each bidder pays the opportunity cost of the licenses it acquires – that is, the difference between the maximum value of all the licenses to the other bidders and the value ultimately assigned to the other bidders.

Vickrey auctions are challenged in several ways when licenses are not substitutes; problems include low prices and vulnerability to collusion, even by losing bidders. Corresponding first-price auctions avoid these problems in selected full information equilibria, but there are also inefficient equilibria in that setting and there are no general analyses of the incomplete-information case.

A serious concern about both Vickrey and first-price auction designs is that their good theoretical properties depend on bidders being able to express values for every combination of licenses that they might win. With n distinct licenses, there are $2^n - 1$ such combinations, which for many spectrum auctions is an impractically large number for bidders to evaluate. These sealed-bid designs are most valuable when the number of packages of licenses that a bidder can win is small.

7.5 Descending Clock Auctions

In the previous section we described failures of the substitutes condition arising from bidder valuations; those failures destroyed some of the good properties of the deferred acceptance algorithm, leading spectrum regulators to adopt entirely new designs. In a procurement auction context, the substitutes condition can also fail in another way, when the suppliers' offerings are not substitutes from the perspective of the auctioneer. This situation arose in the two-sided US Broadcast Incentive Auction of 2016–2017 and led to the development of a new class of deferred acceptance algorithms: (generalized) descending clock auctions.

The economic problem to be solved arose from two market trends. One was that over-the-air (OTA) TV broadcasting was declining in economic value, as more consumers used cable, satellite, and Internet-based services, rather than watching programs by radio broadcast. Another was that, since Apple's introduction of the iPhone, the use of spectrum for mobile broadband was increasing dramatically. Because of the intricate set of interference constraints governing each of these uses, the transition called for a coordinated change in which certain TV channels would be cleared from their use for TV broadcasts and made available for mobile broadband.

The market design needed to respect a constraint that each TV broadcaster had the right to continue to serve viewers in its broadcast area. Nearly every broadcaster, however, had different rights from any other. The viewers reached by each broadcast tower depended on its location, broadcast power, and orientation, so the number of channels that would be needed to allow a set of stations to continue OTA broadcasts depended on the precise combinations of these requirements. In short, from the perspective of the auctioneer that hoped to clear a uniform band by buying out a set of broadcasters, the substitutes condition failed badly.

To promote value-enhancing trades, the Broadcast Incentive Auction included several components: a voluntary *reverse auction* to identify a set of stations to be acquired and prices to pay them; a *forward auction* to sell the mobile broadband licenses created by the vacated spectrum; a *reassignment plan* to assign channels to stations that would continue to broadcast on-air; and an overarching *market clearing procedure* to determine how many channels would be cleared.[5]

---

[5] Note that the term "clear" is used here with two different meanings. *Market clearing*, used in the same sense as in previous sections, was satisfied for the overall Incentive Auction when the supply of spectrum sold in the reverse auction matched the demand for new spectrum licenses in the forward auction. Separately, the reverse auction *cleared* TV channels for new uses by paying winning stations to cease broadcasting.

When the auction finished in 2017, winning broadcasters were paid about $10 billion to relinquish their broadcast rights and mobile operators paid the government about $20 billion for the mobile broadband licenses. This auction was a central pillar of the National Broadband Plan, ultimately freeing 84 MHz of spectrum to be used for broadband and other services throughout much of the United States.

The process used by the auction had to solve several novel problems. First, it was unclear in the period before the auction exactly what rights broadcasters had to the already–licensed spectrum. Licenses could not be simply revoked; but if every broadcaster had the right to continue broadcasting on its historical channel then the need to clear a contiguous block of channels, and the same channels in every city, would lead to an intractable hold-out problem. The FCC and Congress ultimately decided that TV stations that chose not to sell their license rights could be reassigned to other channels, with the auction proceeds covering their retuning costs. With no TV station able to block the assignment of any particular channel, the hold-out problem was eliminated and the stage was set for price competition among stations that wished to sell their rights within the same broadcast area.

Second, the auction process needed to determine how many channels to clear from TV broadcast uses. Each TV broadcast channel occupies a 6 MHz spectrum frequency. For any given number of channels, the government would try to buy spectrum rights sufficient to clear that many channels. Then, it would create and sell new mobile broadband licenses using the same frequencies. The revenues from the sale were required to cover the cost of acquiring licenses plus certain other expenses, including the cost of retuning the TV stations that continued on-air.

To decide how many channels to clear, the FCC announced opening prices before bidding started and required each station to declare whether it would participate in the reverse auction, which included a commitment to sell its rights at the opening price. The prices offered to each participant could only fall in the subsequent rounds of the reverse auction, so the opening price represented the most that a station could possibly receive to cease broadcasting. Using those participation decisions, the FCC determined the maximum number of channels that could possibly be cleared and opened the auction using that quantity as both its demand in the reverse auction and the available supply in the forward auction. It then ran the two auctions. If the revenues from the forward auction were insufficient to cover the costs of the reverse auction plus the additional costs then the number of channels to be cleared would be decreased and the process would continue. Because the auction to buy broadcast rights used a certain descending clock auction and the sale of broadband licenses used an ascending clock auction, the prices in each auction were able to proceed monotonically as the clearing target was adjusted over time.

A third novelty of the Broadcast Incentive Auction was the design of its reverse auction. The FCC staff had initially proposed adapting the Vickrey auction to this context, on the basis of its status as the unique strategy-proof mechanism that always selects efficient outcomes. That advantage is important, but the Vickrey auction was nevertheless rejected in favor of a novel descending clock auction – an adaptation of a deferred-acceptance algorithm – which was expected to perform much better for this auction problem.

7.5.1 Seven Weaknesses of the Vickrey Auction

Why not use a Vickrey auction, given its celebrated theoretical properties? Offsetting the Vickrey auction's advantages are seven disadvantages – each of which can be overcome by an alternative auction design.

Computational feasibility. The first disadvantage is computational. If broadcast rights were to be purchased using a Vickrey auction, the first steps would be to collect bids and compute the set of stations with the lowest total bids, subject to the constraint that the set would be sufficient to clear the desired number of channels. For the Broadcast Incentive Auction, even checking just the *feasibility* of clearing a set of channels with certain station rights is an extremely challenging computational problem. To understand the reason, consider a simplification of the actual channel assignment problem.

Suppose that the TV interference constraints that need to be satisfied can be represented by a simple graph. Each node in the graph is a TV station that will continue to broadcast; each arc (edge) represents a pair of stations that cannot be assigned to the same channel without creating unacceptable interference. For the Broadcast Incentive Auction, before any clearing there were about 2,400 nodes (stations) and 137,000 arcs (interference overlaps) in that graph, and the auction ultimately cleared about 200 stations. To check whether a particular set of stations can continue to broadcast using a given set of channels, it is necessary either to find an assignment of nodes to channels such that no two connected nodes are assigned to the same channel or to show that no such assignment exists. Replacing the word "channel" by "color," this is a version of the famously hard *graph-coloring problem*. The graph-coloring problem is *NP-complete*, which implies that, for any algorithm, and under standard assumptions, there is a sequence of such problems of increasing size such that the solution time grows exponentially in the problem size. In practice, this means that some large problems can be intractable: there may be no algorithm by which a fast computer can solve all of them, even with years of computation.

In the actual setting of the Incentive Auction, the interference between two stations depends on the exact channels each is assigned, making the problem even more complex. There were also additional constraints to prevent any station near the US border from interfering with Mexican or Canadian broadcasters. In total, there were about 2.7 million detailed constraints, which made the scale of the feasibility-checking problem even larger. The FCC's computational experiments confirmed that this problem was sufficiently hard that a Vickrey auction, which is based on such a minimization of total bids, would not be viable.

Bidder trust. The second reason that a Vickrey auction was inappropriate for this application is that it requires bidders to place too much trust in the auctioneer. Each bidder would effectively be told: "Tell us your station value. We will tell you whether your bid was a winning one and, if so, how much you will be paid. Unfortunately, we cannot guarantee that our computations will be accurate, because the computations are too difficult. Also, the data on which they are based are, by law, confidential, so you will be unable to check our computations." Meeting the goal of clearing a large number of channels required the participation of as many broadcasters as possible, so if many bidders had been deterred by concerns of trust, it would have substantially undermined the success of the auction.

Winner privacy. A third concern is that the Vickrey auction does not "preserve winner privacy" – that is, all bidders in the auction would have been asked to report the lowest price that they would accept. In past second-price reverse auctions, commentators have often highlighted to the public that some winning bidders (those ultimately selected to sell an item or provide a service) had offered to accept a certain low price but were actually paid a much higher price. It is likely that a similar objection would apply to every winning bidder, making managing public reception of the auction a significant challenge.

Budget constraints. Fourth, the FCC had decided to clear as many channels as possible in the reverse auction, subject to a budget constraint determined by the revenues from the forward auction. This imposed a budget constraint on the reverse auction itself. If the reverse auction yields a cost for clearing a particular number of channels that exceeds the budget, then the auctioneer must reduce that number and continue the auction. The Vickrey auction is not consistent with any budget condition; it chooses its outcome based on maximizing an objective on some constraint set that depends on the allocation, not on the Vickrey prices themselves, which are determined in part by the values of certain losing bid combinations. If the FCC had tried to conduct a Vickrey auction and then to rerun it for a different channel target in the case where costs were too high, it would no longer have been a Vickrey auction – nor would it have possessed the Vickrey auction's desirable strategy-proofness and efficiency properties.

Group strategy-proofness. A fifth disadvantage is that the Vickrey auction is not group strategy-proof. Consider an example with only three stations, A, B, and C, with station values v_A, v_B, and v_C. Suppose that the coverage of stations A and C overlaps, as does the coverage of stations B and C. Before the auction, stations A and B broadcast simultaneously on channel 1, while station C uses channel 2.

If the auctioneer wants to clear one of the two channels for resale and leave the remaining OTA broadcaster(s) in the other channel, then it has two options: it can buy rights from both A and B to clear channel 1, which is efficient whenever $v_A + v_B < v_C$, or it can buy the rights of station C to clear channel 2. If A and B win, they are taken off the air and would be paid the Vickrey prices $p_A = v_C - v_B$ and $p_B = v_C - v_A$, while station C would receive $p_C = v_A + v_B$ if it wins. If stations A and B collude and both bid 0, they would win and each receive payment v_C. This is profitable for them whenever $\max\{v_A, v_B\} < v_C$, which can happen even if stations A and B would lose the auction under truthful bidding. Vickrey auctions are rare in their vulnerability to profitable collusion (even without compensating cash transfers) by losing bidders.

Price competitiveness. Sixth, the Vickrey auction is not generally price competitive: there can be a collection of *losing* bidders sufficient to clear the channels who would be willing to accept a lower total price than the Vickrey prices. In the example above, if A and B win then $p_A + p_B = 2v_C - v_A - v_B > v_C$, so that station C would have been willing to cease broadcasting at a price less than $p_A + p_B$. Vickrey prices are always competitive when the products are substitutes, so this may be regarded as a problem associated with complementarities.

——— **169** ———

Trading off efficiency and cost. Seventh, the Vickrey auction is a single, fixed design that aims only to maximize efficiency. Although it is easy to extend the Vickrey design to include maximum prices for each station, cost-minimizing designs require much more: they must replace the objective of maximizing the total value in each realization by the objective of maximizing the sum of the "virtual costs."

7.5.2 Avoiding the Seven Weaknesses

For the case in which each bidder has a single item to sell, the class of descending clock auctions avoids all seven weaknesses of the Vickrey auction. Like SMR auctions, descending clock auctions share some characteristics with the deferred acceptance algorithm, but with additional variations. The FCC design – used to procure broadcast rights from TV stations in the Broadcast Incentive Auction – is but one member of this class.

> **Mechanism 7.3** (Descending clock auction). A descending clock auction evolves over a sequence of rounds, numbered by $t = 1, 2, \ldots$ Let N denote the set of initial bidders. At the beginning of each round t, there is some set of bidders $A(t) \subseteq N$ that are the *active bidders*, which have not yet rejected any price offer and are eligible to become winners, while the other bidders $Z(t) \equiv A(t)^C$ have rejected a price offered before time t and have exited the auction. A *history* of the auction up to the start of round t is a collection $A^t = \{A(1), \ldots, A(t)\}$, where $A(t) \subseteq A(t-1) \subseteq \cdots \subseteq A(1) = N$; H is the set of all possible histories.
>
> Each descending clock auction is characterized by a pricing rule $p \colon H \to \mathbb{R}^N_+$, which maps each possible history A^t into a vector of prices for round t. In a *descending* auction, the prices in each round are no higher than in the previous round: $\forall (t \geq 2, A^t), p(A^t) \leq p(A^{t-1})$. If a bidder is active and its price changes then it may choose either to *remain*, in which case it will again be active in the next round, or to *exit*, becoming inactive. An active bidder whose price does not change is offered no choice and also remains active. Each bidder observes only its own price, so its strategy in the auction is a mapping from a sequence of prices into a decision to *remain* or *exit*.
>
> The auction is closed at the beginning of the first round T in which the specified prices do not change: $p(A^T) = p(A^{T-1})$. At this point, the winners of auction p are the bidders who are still active – that is, those in the set $A(T)$ – and they sell at the final prices $p(A^{T-1})$.
>
> The quoted prices are relevant only to active bidders, so restricting p to allow price reductions only for active bidders does not affect the economic or game-theoretic analysis of the auction outcome. Any pricing function p satisfying each of these restrictions is a descending clock auction, and any two different price functions p and p' satisfying the restrictions are different auctions, in the sense that, for some bidder strategies, they lead to different outcomes.

For the game-theoretic analysis, we assume that each seller in the reverse auction plans to sell only a single item and has only one option: to sell or not. The designers of the Broadcast Incentive Auction believed that this single-item description would apply to the vast majority of likely winners (successful sellers) in that auction, because the large station groups mainly included more valuable stations, which were less likely to ultimately be sold.[6] For this single-item case, the class of descending clock auctions allows the auctioneer to avoid each of the seven weaknesses of the Vickrey auction.

Computational feasibility. The computational challenges of any particular descending clock auction p arise from the complexity of computing its pricing function. For the Broadcast Incentive Auction, to ensure that the final outcomes would satisfy the non-interference constraints, the computations considered the stations one by one, as if at each time t the price were decreased for just one station. If the software determined that it would be feasible to "pack" the currently considered station – meaning to assign channels, without violating feasibility constraints, to a set of stations consisting of the current station and the other stations that either previously exited the auction or did not participate then the price offered to that station would be reduced. Otherwise, the station would be considered infeasible to pack and its price would remain forever unchanged.

During the auction, each active station might be checked many times as its price was reduced over time; there were expected to be roughly 10,000 feasibility checking operations required. To make the process fast enough for human bidders, the FCC limited the time allowed for feasibility checking by allotting a maximum time to each problem – typically about 60 seconds. Since feasibility checking is NP-complete, the checking software would sometimes report that the allotted time was not enough: it had run out of time and could not decide whether it was feasible to pack the station. Such a report was treated in the same way as if packing had been proved to be infeasible: the station's price would not be reduced and would remain frozen for the remainder of the auction. With these specifications, the auction was guaranteed to finish all its computations in a reasonable amount of time and to output a feasible set of stations to continue over-the-air broadcasting. Thus, *computational feasibility* was guaranteed.

Theorem 7.4. *Every descending clock auction accommodates computation time limits. That is, for every descending clock auction p, there exists another descending clock auction p_C such that $p_C(A^t) = p(A^t)$ whenever that pricing rule can be computed within the time limit and such that if p always leads to feasible solutions after every history of feasible solutions then p_C does so as well. A computationally feasible descending clock auction can be constructed by setting $p_C(A^t) = p(A^{t-1})$ when computation time expires.*

Thus, the descending clock auction design can tolerate small failures in computation. The Vickrey auction is not similarly robust: its desirable properties require the precise calculation of all winning prices.

One might nevertheless expect the NP-completeness of the packing problem to affect the quality of the final outcome. NP-completeness, however, is a worst-case criterion, meaning roughly that it is impossible to construct a feasibility checker that solves *all* the desired problems quickly. However, the Incentive Auction software

---

[6] The actual Incentive Auction also included other options for some station owners, allowing them to swap their UHF broadcast rights for VHF rights plus compensation, which are options that we do not discuss here.

team was able to build a customized feasibility checker that solved about 99% of the problems in the typical allotted time of about 60 seconds per problem.

How did the 1% of checking failures affect performance? When packing a station is feasible but the checker fails to discover that, then the auction price for that station could have been reduced but was not, so that the station remains active and may eventually become winning (by being paid to cease broadcasting). The consequence could be that the station is paid an unnecessarily high price or that it is purchased to clear a channel when it need not have been purchased at all. Most feasibility-checking failures, however, do not happen early in the auction when prices are high, because few stations have exited at that point and packing additional stations is easy. Instead, failures mostly happen late in the auction after many stations have exited, when packing becomes hard. Consequently, the expectation of the software team was that the 1% checking failures would have only a modest effect on overall efficiency and cost.

Bidder trust. Bidders in any descending clock auction face a simple decision each round: whether to agree to sell their item at the stated price. If a bidder chooses not to sell, it exits the auction; if it chooses to continue bidding, its price can only decrease. No matter what the other rules may be or how others may bid, the bidder's dominant strategy is *honest bidding*, which dictates that it continue if its clock price exceeds its value and exit otherwise.

In the language of [11], every descending clock auction is obviously strategy-proof (see Chapter 27). This means that at any information set reachable by honest bidding, the lowest payoff that the bidder can receive on any branch by continuing to bid honestly is at least as high as the highest payoff that it can get on any (possibly different) branch by some deviation.

Theorem 7.5. *Every descending clock auction is obviously strategy-proof. In an obviously dominant strategy σ, the bidder remains if the price exceeds its value and exits if the price is less than its value.*

Proof At every information set, following the strategy σ always leads to a non-negative payoff, while deviating leads to a non-positive payoff. $\square$

Obvious strategy-proofness eliminates much of the bidder's need to trust the auctioneer. While no bidder can verify whether the auctioneer is following the announced rules correctly, it can easily follow whether its prices decrease from round to round – and this alone determines its optimal strategy. The bidder's strategy does not depend on whether the auctioneer has erred or cheated in undetectable ways.

Winner privacy. Unlike a Vickrey auction, each winning bidder in a descending clock auction p reveals just enough information about its value during the auction to become a winner. All that an observer learns about a winning bidder from its bids in the auction is that the winner is willing to accept the final price, which is precisely the minimum information required to determine that the bidder should be part of the final allocation. This condition can be described as (*unconditional*) *winner privacy*.

Theorem 7.6. *Every descending clock auction satisfies unconditional winner privacy.*[7]

Group strategy-proofness. Descending clock auctions are weakly group-strategy-proof, which means that, in the absence of side payments among participants, there exists no coalition of bidders who can all do strictly better for themselves by deviating to play any other joint strategy. The proof of this follows from their obvious strategy-proofness. Consider the bidder who would first be called upon to deviate: the best outcome that bidder can achieve by deviating is no better than the worst it could get from continuing to bid honestly, so the deviation payoff cannot exceed the equilibrium payoff.[8]

Theorem 7.7. *Every descending clock auction is weakly group-strategy-proof.*

Budget constraints. Each descending clock auction that can achieve a desired allocation when a given budget constraint is not binding can be adapted to a new descending clock auction that does the same and accommodates the budget constraint. Suppose we are given a descending clock auction p and a budget B. Define p_B to be a *budget-respecting extension* of p for budget B if p_B is a descending clock auction for which the total cost can never exceed B, and, for any value profile v for which p realizes a total cost less than B, the allocations resulting from p_B and from p coincide.

The construction of one such p_B from p is easy and intuitive, so we can describe it in terms of the Broadcast Incentive Auction. In any round before the terminal round of p, p_B sets the same prices as p. If, in the terminal round for p, the total prices exceed the budget B then decrease all prices by \$1 and iterate until the total prices of active bidders are no more than B. Other budget-respecting extensions of p can be described similarly, but they use different rules for price reductions after what would have been the terminal round for p. All such extensions are still descending clock auctions, and thus the other theoretical properties continue to hold. This may be contrasted with the Vickrey auction, for which no similar construction is possible.

Theorem 7.8. *Given any descending clock auction p and any budget $B > 0$, there is a descending clock auction p_B that is a budget-respecting extension of p.*

Price competitiveness. A strategy-proof direct mechanism is *price competitive* if, for every value profile v, the set of winning bidders W and the prices they are paid coincide with those of some full-information Nash equilibrium of a first-price auction (with the same winner selection rule), in which every losing bidder bids its value. For any descending clock auction, there is a corresponding direct mechanism in which the bidders report their values and the mechanism plays the obviously dominant strategies on behalf of each bidder.

Theorem 7.9. *Every descending clock auction is price competitive.*

---

[7] Furthermore, if a strategy-proof mechanism satisfies unconditional winner privacy then the same allocation can be implemented by a descending clock auction.

[8] By a similar argument, every obviously strategy-proof mechanism is group strategy-proof.

Proof Unconditional winner privacy implies that the only information that the algorithm uses about winning bidders' values is that they are no higher than the final prices, so if the winning bidders were able to report values equal to their prices instead of reporting truthfully, the algorithm would output the same set of winners.

In a first-price auction, the prices are equal to the bids. Winner privacy in the clock auction implies that if any winning bidder were to raise its bid then it would become a loser, so such a bid would be an inferior response to the strategies of the others. If a winning bidder were to reduce its bid then its price would fall, so that, too, is an inferior response. Hence, winning bidders' bids in a first-price auction are the best responses to the other bidders' bid profile. By monotonicity, the losing bidders that increase their bids are still losers and losing bidders that reduce their bids cannot earn a positive payoff. So, the losing bidders, too, are playing their best responses. □

Cost minimization and other objectives. Next, we evaluate when and how descending clock auctions can be designed to achieve nearly maximum efficiency or minimum total procurement cost (or to approximately optimize other objectives) subject to incentive and participation constraints. Since all descending clock auctions are obviously strategy-proof and pay zero to losing bidders, the incentive and participation constraints are always satisfied.

In the Broadcast Incentive Auction, each TV station bidder becomes either a winner in set W or a loser in set L. After the auction, all the losers must be assigned to channels to continue OTA broadcasting, and the auction algorithm must ensure that such an assignment does not create unacceptable interference among those losers. The winners in the auction are paid to give up their broadcast rights.

Informally, this descending clock auction is an algorithm for a *packing problem*, in which losing bidders must be packed into a given set of broadcast channels. The steps of this algorithm are *greedy* – they select losing bidders irreversibly and without regard to the order of future exit decisions – and the full procedure is a *reverse* greedy algorithm because it iteratively selects *losers* rather than winners. In matching theory, algorithms that work by greedily rejecting individual offers are more commonly called *deferred acceptance algorithms*.

Formally, an instance of a packing problem $(v, s, \mathcal{F}, \omega)$ consists of a profile $v \in [0, \bar{v}]^N$ of station values, a profile $s \in \mathcal{S}^N$ of observed station characteristics (for example, s_n might encode station n's location, broadcast power, pre-auction channel, and population coverage, as well as the distribution from which v_n is drawn), a set $\mathcal{F} \subseteq \mathcal{P}(N)$ of feasible packings with the free-disposal property that $Z \subset Z' \in \mathcal{F} \Rightarrow Z \in \mathcal{F}$, and a value $\omega(v_n, s_n)$ of each station that is successfully packed. The problem is to solve

$$\max_{L \in \mathcal{F}} \sum_{n \in L} \omega(v_n, s_n).$$

This problem of maximizing the total value of the stations that will continue OTA broadcasting is a packing problem with $\omega(v_n, s_n) = v_n$. To minimize expected procurement costs, we adapt Myerson's optimal auction analysis to this problem. In outline, the first step is to determine the prior distribution of values for each station, which depends on its known characteristics s_n. The virtual value then depends on that distribution and on v_n, so it can be written as $\omega(v_n, s_n)$. Myerson showed that the expected total virtual cost of the winners is equal to the expected total payment to the winners. Consequently, the expected-cost-minimizing auction maximizes the total virtual values of the losers: it solves the problem given above.

Greedy algorithms can be applied to packing problems to approximate the optimal solution. To illustrate this, consider the classic *knapsack problem*, in which each item has a value v_n and a size s_n. The collection of feasible sets consists of those for which the total size of the items does not exceed the capacity C of the knapsack: $\mathcal{F} = \{Z \subseteq \mathcal{P}(N)| \sum_{n \in Z} s_n \leq C\}$. Finding the optimal packing for the knapsack problem is NP-hard, but a greedy algorithm for this problem is fast and often performs well. This greedy algorithm first ranks the items according to $\omega(v_n)/s_n$, from largest to smallest, and then adds the elements to the knapsack in that order, one at a time. If adding any particular element n would cause the knapsack constraint to be violated or would select an item with $\omega(v_n) < 0$, the algorithm skips that element and continues to the next. This procedure always leads to a feasible packing, with a total objective that is at least $1 - \max_n s_n/C$ of the optimum.

In the auction context, suppose that we adopt a direct mechanism and an algorithm that selects the losers Z using a reverse greedy algorithm. To do this, we specify a ranking function $r(v_n, s_n)$. Without loss of generality, we can limit the range of r to be $[0, 1]$. The algorithm is initialized by setting $Z = \emptyset$. It then applies the following steps iteratively:

1. Set $\hat{Z} = \{n \notin Z | Z \cup \{n\} \in \mathcal{F}, r(v_n, s_n) > 0\}$.
2. Terminate if $\hat{Z} = \emptyset$.
3. Set $\hat{n} \in \arg\max_{n \in \hat{Z}} r(v_n, s_n)$ (breaking any ties in favor of the station with the lower index n) and update Z to $Z \cup \{\hat{n}\}$.

For strategy-proof implementation, the winner selection rule must be "monotonic," so the greedy ranking function must be non-decreasing in v_n. Clock auctions as we have defined them have discrete price decrements, but, by using sufficiently small price increments, they can approximate any monotonic ranking function.

Theorem 7.10. *For every reverse greedy algorithm associated with a ranking function $r(v_n, s_n)$ that is non-decreasing in its first argument, there is a family $\{p^k\}$ of k-round descending clock auctions, such that, for every value profile v and all k sufficiently large, straightforward bidders exit auction p^k in the same order as the selection order of the reverse greedy algorithm.*

Proof The family of descending clock auctions is constructed as follows. For auction p^k, time is indexed by $t \in \{0, 1/k, 2/k, \ldots, (k-1)/k, 1\}$. The set of selected items before time t is denoted by $Z^k(t)$ and the price vector then by $p^k(t)$. The auction initializes with $Z^k(0) = \emptyset$ and all station prices are given by the high price $p_n^k(0) = \bar{v}$. Prices are set as follows:

$$p_n^k(t) = \begin{cases} q_n(t) \equiv \sup\{q \in [0, \bar{v}]|r(q, s_n) \leq 1 - t\} & \text{if } Z^k(t) \cup \{n\} \in \mathcal{F}, \\ p_n^k(t - 1/k) & \text{otherwise.} \end{cases}$$

Thus, the price offered to a station is reduced only if the station can be packed; and, if reduced, the price is set to control the effect of the station's characteristics s_n on its ranking relative to other stations. (To break ties, each round consists of N sub-rounds, in which the clock prices of stations $1, \ldots, N$ are adjusted sequentially, beginning with station $n = 1$. If any station n exits in a sub-round then $Z^k(t)$ is updated, the prices $p_m^k(t)$ for the stations $m > n$ are recomputed, and the processing continues with station $n + 1$.) By inspection, this pricing rule defines a descending clock auction p^k.

A straightforward bidder exits at time t if its price is then less than its value, so, if station n exits at time t then $v_n > p_n^k(t) = q_n(t)$. If there are no ties in the auction and station m can be feasibly packed but has not yet exited at t, then $v_m \leq p_m^k(t) = q_m(t)$. Hence, $r(v_n, s_n) \geq r(q_n(t), s_n) > r(p_m^k(t), s_m) \geq r(v_m, s_m)$. Thus, without ties, the clock auction packs feasible stations in the same order as the reverse greedy algorithm. If there are no ties in the reverse greedy algorithm then, for k sufficiently large, there are no ties in the clock auction. If, however, there are ties in the greedy algorithm then they are broken in the same way as in the clock auction and, inductively, the same applies to each subsequent choice. □

According to this theorem, every reverse greedy algorithm can be approximated by a descending clock auction that leads to exactly the same packing with arbitrarily high probability, but the full class of algorithms that can be implemented by clock auctions is much larger. As we have seen, the set of stations that is packed by a descending clock auction can depend on the prices that are paid to bidders, which is helpful for meeting budget constraints, and clock auctions remain computable even when the exact feasibility checking required by the greedy algorithm is impracticably difficult.

For minimizing expected total procurement costs, we adapt the famous formulation of Myerson's optimal auction design. Assume that the bidders' values v_n are independently distributed with known distributions F_n with strictly positive densities f_n on an interval $[0, \bar{v}]$. Adapting Myerson's analysis to a procurement problem, define the *virtual cost* for a bidder with value v_n to be $C_n(v_n) = v_n + F_n(v_n)/f_n(v_n)$. Myerson's lemma, rewritten for the procurement case, states that for any Bayesian incentive-compatible mechanism with zero payments to losing bidders, the expected total payment to winning bidders in W is $\mathbb{E}\left[\sum_{n \in W} C_n(v_n)\right]$. This lemma applies to all descending clock auctions. For brevity, we limit attention to the case in which each function $C_n(\cdot)$ is increasing and continuous. For this case, as Myerson showed, the optimal mechanism selects winners for each realization of the value profile v according to

$$x(v) \in \operatorname*{argmin}_{\{W \mid W^C \in \mathcal{F}\}} \sum_{n \in W} C_n(v_n).$$

Since $L = W^C$, an equivalent characterization of the allocation rule is

$$x(v)^C \in \operatorname*{arg\,max}_{L \in \mathcal{F}} \sum_{n \in L} C_n(v_n).$$

By Theorem 7.10, every greedy algorithm for this latter problem can be approximated arbitrarily closely by a descending clock auction.

In the actual Broadcast Incentive Auction, the station value distributions F_n were not known, the assumption of independent station values was tenuous, and the interference constraints were not knapsack constraints; however, the two preceding examples guided the choice of an auction pricing function. The observable station characteristics were taken to be $s_n = (Pops_n, Links_n)$, where $Pops_n$ is the population reached by the broadcast signal and $Links_n$ is the number of station links in the broadcast interference graph. By analogy with the knapsack problem, $Links_n$ was expected to be a size-like variable, measuring the difficulty of packing a station on-air. For the Myerson-like cost minimization, $Pops_n$ parameterized the station-value distribution. The price for going off-air in any round t offered to any still-feasible station n was

$$p_n^{FCC}(t) = Links_n^{0.5} Pops_n^{0.5} p_0^{FCC}(t),$$

where $p_0^{FCC}(t)$, called the "base clock price," would fall during the auction following a predetermined schedule. This particular pricing function was explained to participants by noting that $Links$ and $Pops$ were weighted equally and that multiplying both $Links$ and $Pops$ by the same constant multiplies the price by the same factor. The auction design team predicted that the $Links_n$-adjustment would improve the quality of packing, just as the size adjustment does in the greedy algorithm for the knapsack problem. Similarly, the $Pops_n$-adjustment would continue to offer a higher per-$Pops$ price to smaller stations, encouraging the smaller stations to be the ones to sell. Analysis of the Myerson-optimal auction with varied assumptions about the distributions of values suggested that this would be a robust characteristic of a cost-reducing auction.

7.6 Conclusion

Spectrum allocation problems occupy an intermediate space between commodities markets and discrete matching markets, often incorporating elements of both. Prices are important to allocate spectrum quantities efficiently, but the licenses are sufficiently specialized that matching the right combinations of frequencies to users is also critical, so matching analyses play a central role. Because spectrum allocation problems also encounter the traditional challenges of thin markets and complex regulator objectives, the theory is not subsumed by matching theory but remains deeply informed by it.

7.7 Bibliographic Notes

Much of the theory initially used to analyze spectrum auctions is the same as matching theory, including the seminal results in [6] on one-to-one matching without prices and [18] on one-to-one matching with prices, the unifying results of [9] within the many-to-one worker–firm model, and the extension to contracts in [8] and [5]. The algorithmic properties of auctions for the case of substitutes were further developed in [4], [12], and [7]. These papers, however, paid little attention to the incentive issues for dynamic auction mechanisms and the special problems associated with pervasive failures of the substitutes condition.

Section 7.3 emphasized broader market issues, as collected by [10]. In [17] a game-theoretic analysis of the ascending clock auction was provided; this highlighted a vulnerability to collusive-seeming outcomes that has been important in practice. An analysis of Treasury auctions and incentive challenges in uniform-price sealed-bid auctions was given in [2].

The paper [1] provided results about the virtues and weaknesses of Vickrey auctions, as described in Section 7.4, while in [3] an analysis of first-price auctions was offered.

Despite what appears to be a vast difference between the mathematical structure of matching theory and the problems of the Broadcast Incentive Auction, the auction design can be understood as a kind of deferred acceptance algorithm, in which bidders make a sequence of offers that are rejected and replaced until, finally, the bids that were never rejected become the winning ones. The auction design itself could not have succeeded without a careful design of the spectrum rights, developed by Evan Kwerel and John Williams and codified by legislation, and new algorithms for NP-hard packing problems, developed by a team headed by Kevin Leyton-Brown. The papers [13] and [14] formalize and analyze the class of clock auctions from which the FCC's reverse auction was derived. Variations of their results form the basis of Section 7.5. In [16] computational experiments were reported that examined the realized efficiency of the Incentive Auction. The paper [15] provided seminal results in the theory of optimal auctions, and [11] introduced the concept of obviously strategy-proof mechanisms.

References

[1] Ausubel, Lawrence M., and Milgrom, Paul. 2006. The lovely but lonely Vickrey auction. *Combinatorial Auctions*, **17**, 22–26.

[2] Back, Kerry, and Zender, Jaime F. 1993. Auctions of divisible goods: On the rationale for the treasury experiment. *Review of Financial Studies*, **6**(4), 733–764.

[3] Bernheim, B. Douglas, and Whinston, Michael D. 1986. Menu auctions, resource allocation, and economic influence. *Quarterly Journal of Economics*, **101**(1), 1–31.

[4] Demange, Gabrielle, Gale, David, and Sotomayor, Marilda. 1986. Multi-item auctions. *Journal of Political Economy*, **94**(4), 863–872.

[5] Fleiner, Tamás. 2003. A fixed-point approach to stable matchings and some applications. *Mathematics of Operations Research*, **28**(1), 103–126.

[6] Gale, D., and Shapley, L. S. 1962. College admissions and the stability of marriage. *American Mathematical Monthly*, **69**(1), 9.

[7] Gul, Faruk, and Stacchetti, Ennio. 2000. The English auction with differentiated commodities. *Journal of Economic Theory*, **92**(1), 66–95.

[8] Hatfield, John William, and Milgrom, Paul R. 2005. Matching with contracts. *American Economic Review*, **95**(4), 913–935.

[9] Kelso, Alexander S., and Crawford, Vincent P. 1982. Job matching, coalition formation, and gross substitutes. *Econometrica*, **50**(6), 1483.

[10] Klemperer, Paul. 2002. What really matters in auction design. *Journal of Economic Perspectives*, **16**(1), 169–189.

[11] Li, Shengwu. 2017. Obviously strategy-proof mechanisms. *American Economic Review*, **107**(11), 3257–87.

[12] Milgrom, Paul. 2000. Putting auction theory to work: The simultaneous ascending auction. *Journal of Political Economy*, **108**(2), 245–272.

[13] Milgrom, Paul, and Segal, Ilya. 2014. Deferred-acceptance auctions and radio spectrum reallocation. Pages 185–186 of: *Proc. 15th ACM Conference on Economics and Computation*. ACM.

[14] Milgrom, Paul, and Segal, Ilya. 2020. Clock auctions and radio spectrum reallocation. *Journal of Political Economy*, **128**(1), 1–31.

[15] Myerson, Roger B. 1981. Optimal auction design. *Mathematics of Operations Research*, **6**(1), 58–73.

[16] Newman, Neil, Leyton-Brown, Kevin, Milgrom, Paul, and Segal, Ilya. 2020. incentive auction design alternatives: A simulation study. Pages 603–604 of: *Proc. 21st ACM Conference on Economics and Computation*. ACM.

[17] Riedel, Frank, and Wolfstetter, Elmar. 2006. Immediate demand reduction in simultaneous ascending-bid auctions: A uniqueness result. *Economic Theory*, **29**(3), 721–726.

[18] Shapley, L. S., and Shubik, M. 1971. The assignment game I: The core. *International Journal of Game Theory*, **1**(1), 111–130.

CHAPTER EIGHT

School Choice

Atila Abdulkadiroğlu and Aram Grigoryan

8.1 Introduction

Parental choice in school assignment has become a major educational reform in recent decades. School districts in the USA and around the world have been increasingly adopting market design solutions for assignment of pupils to public schools, grounded in recent advances in the fields of matching theory, mechanism design, and computer science.

The roots of such changes in the USA can be traced back to educational inequality in urban districts. Traditional neighborhood-based assignments limit disadvantaged populations' access to good schools clustered in affluent neighborhoods. Such assignments also tend to segregate neighborhoods through housing markets and public-school financing regimes. In addition to these concerns, in the last few decades school districts have been moving away from one-size-fits-all models of schooling, by adopting alternative curricula and pedagogical approaches to serve student populations with varying needs. Furthermore, alternative school management models such as charter schools are being used to create competitive market forces on schools and teachers. Consequently, meeting the needs of highly heterogeneous student populations with highly heterogeneous schooling options via neighborhood-based assignments becomes infeasible. Parental choice and preference-based school assignment become an integral part of enrollment planning.

This chapter offers a brief overview of the school choice problem in three parts. Section 8.2 formulates the problem as a one-to-many two-sided matching problem, in which students rank schools in strict preference order and schools rank students in strict priority order. It focuses on trade offs among three common policy objectives: efficiency, stability, and incentive compatibility. Section 8.3 generalizes the model to incorporate ties or indifferences in schools' priority rankings, which are a prominent feature of public-school assignment. Section 8.4 addresses diversity concerns and distributional objectives in school choice. Those objectives are analyzed in an axiomatic framework and solutions based on reserves and quotas are discussed.

8.2 School Choice Problem

A school choice problem is a one-to-many matching problem with a finite set of applicants A, a finite set of schools S, a vector of school capacities $q = (q_s)_{s \in S}$, a preference profile $\succ_A = (\succ_a)_{a \in A}$, and a priority profile $\succ_S = (\succ_s)_{s \in S}$. The setup corresponds to Setting III in Chapter 1 of this book. The preference ranking of applicant a is a complete, transitive, and antisymmetric binary relation over the set $S \cup \{a\}$. For $s, s' \in S \cup \{a\}$, we use $s \succ_a s'$ to denote that a prefers s to s'. Also, we use $s \succeq_a s'$ to denote that either $s \succ_a s'$ or $s = s'$. We say that school s is acceptable for applicant a if $s \succ_a a$. Similarly, the priority ranking of school s is a complete, transitive, and antisymmetric binary relation over $A \cup \{s\}$. For $a, a' \in A$, we use $a \succ a'$ to denote that a has a higher priority at s than a'. We say that applicant a is eligible for school s if $a \succ_s s$. We fix $(A, S, q, \succ_S)$, and refer to a school choice problem by $\succ_A$.

A matching μ is a mapping $\mu : A \cup S \to 2^A \cup S$ such that, for all $a \in A$ and $s \in S$,

- $\mu(a) \in S \cup \{a\}$,
- $\mu(s) \subseteq A$, $|\mu(s)| \leq q_s$,
- $\mu(a) = s$ if and only if $a \in \mu(s)$,
- $\mu(a) \succeq_a a$, and
- $a \succ_s s$ for all $a \in \mu(s)$.

The last two requirements in the definition of matching are known in the literature as individual rationality constraints. We prefer to embed them directly in the definition of matching in order to simplify other definitions and our exposition. An algorithm is a rule that gives a matching for each problem $\succ_A$.

An applicant–school pair $(a, s) \in A \times S$ blocks matching μ if $s \succ_a \mu(a)$, a is eligible for s, and either $|\mu(s)| < q(s)$ or $a \succ_s a'$ for some $a' \in \mu(s)$. A matching is **stable** if it is not blocked by any applicant–school pair. As shown in Chapter 1, a stable matching always exists and can be found by the deferred acceptance (DA) algorithm.

The matching μ Pareto-dominates the matching μ' if $\mu(a) \succeq_a \mu'(a)$ for every applicant a and $\mu(a) \succ_a \mu'(a)$ for some applicant a. A matching is *(Pareto) efficient* if it is not Pareto dominated by any matching.

Stability and efficiency emerge as major policy objectives in school choice. Stability aims to eliminate blocking instances, i.e., a situation where an applicant has not been assigned to a more preferred school and the school either has an empty seat or a lower priority applicant is assigned there. In the literature, these are also called priority violations or justified-envy instances. Efficiency promotes applicant welfare by assigning applicants to their highest-ranked choices without harming other applicants' assignments. It is not always possible to meet both stability and efficiency.[1] The following example demonstrates incompatibility between these two objectives:

Example 8.1. Suppose there are three applicants $A = \{a_1, a_2, a_3\}$ and two schools $S = \{s_1, s_2\}$, each school with one seat. The preferences and priorities are as follows:

---

[1] Efficiency is defined only with respect to applicants' welfare: schools are viewed as objects to be consumed with no preferences of their own. If we interpret schools' priorities as their preferences, and redefine efficiency to also incorporate schools' preferences, any stable outcome would be efficient.

$$a_1 : s_1, s_2 \qquad s_1 : a_2, a_3, a_1$$
$$a_2 : s_2, s_1 \qquad s_2 : a_1, a_3, a_2$$
$$a_3 : s_2, s_1$$

where $a_1 : s_1, s_2$ means $s_1 \succ_{a_1} s_2$. Consider two matchings

$$\mu_1 = \begin{pmatrix} a_1 & a_2 & a_3 \\ s_2 & s_1 & a_3 \end{pmatrix}, \qquad \mu_2 = \begin{pmatrix} a_1 & a_2 & a_3 \\ s_1 & s_2 & a_3 \end{pmatrix}.$$

That is, μ_1 matches a_1 to s_2, a_2 to s_1 and a_3 to herself. It is easy to check that μ_1 is the unique stable matching. However, μ_1 is Pareto-dominated by μ_2. Thus, no matching is stable and efficient in this problem.

The following notion of constrained efficiency emerges naturally.

Definition 8.2. A matching is *applicant-optimal stable* if it is stable and is not Pareto dominated by any stable matching.

In this example, there is a unique stable matching that every applicant weakly prefers to any other stable matching. This matching constitutes the unique applicant-optimal stable matching. The deferred acceptance (DA) algorithm solves the trade-off between stability and efficiency by selecting the applicant-optimal stable matching. In other words, DA maximizes applicant welfare subject to the stability constraint. Consequently,

Observation 8.3. *When a stable and efficient matching exists, DA finds it.*

The notions of stability and efficiency extend to algorithms naturally. An algorithm is stable (efficient) if it produces a stable (efficient) matching for every problem. For an algorithm φ, let $\varphi(\succ_A)$ denote the matching it produces for preference profile $\succ_A$. Then $\varphi(\succ_A)(a)$ is applicant a's match. An algorithm φ Pareto-dominates another algorithm ψ if $\varphi(\succ_A)(a) \succeq_a \psi(\succ_A)(a), \forall a \in A$ for every problem $\succ_A$, and $\varphi(\succ_A)$ Pareto-dominates $\psi(\succ_A)$ for some problem $\succ_A$.

A third notion concerns eliciting applicant preferences truthfully. An algorithm φ is *dominant strategy incentive compatible (DSIC)* if submitting preference rankings truthfully is a dominant strategy for each applicant in the game induced by the algorithm, that is, if for every $\succ_A$, $a \in A$, and $\succ_a'$,

$$\varphi(\succ_A)(a) \succeq_a \varphi(\succ_a', \succ_{A-a})(a),$$

where $\succ_{A-a}$ denotes the preferences of all applicants except a in $\succ_A$. The definition of a DSIC algorithm takes into account only the applicants' incentives to misreport preferences: schools are viewed as non-strategic agents that truthfully reveal their priority rankings. The reader can refer to Chapter 2 for a general discussion on preference revelation incentives.

In Chapter 4 it was shown that DA is stable and DSIC. Applicant incentives have been integral in the decisions of several districts to adopt DA for school assignment in their choice programs. For example, before switching to DA, Boston Public Schools were using the Algorithm 8.1, which gives incentives for families to rank schools higher in their application forms in order to improve their odds of being assigned there.

Algorithm 8.1 Immediate acceptance (IA).

Set $k = 1$. Until no applicant is rejected, do:
1. Each remaining applicant applies to her kth most preferred acceptable school. Set $k = k + 1$.
2. Each school admits the highest-priority applicants up to its capacity. The school's capacity is reduced by the number of admitted applicants, who are removed from the problem.

We illustrate the IA algorithm through an example. Consider the school choice problem in Example 8.1. In the first step of IA, s_1 admits a_1; s_2 considers a_2 and a_3 and admits a_3. The assignments are finalized as no more seats are left. So IA yields

$$\mu = \begin{pmatrix} a_1 & a_2 & a_3 \\ s_1 & a_2 & s_2 \end{pmatrix}.$$

Unlike in DA, assignments in IA are immediate. In this example, a_2 is not assigned any of her choices despite the fact that she is ranked highest by s_1. The reason is that a_1 ranks s_1 as her first choice, and so is considered for and assigned to the single seat at s_1 before a_2. This proves that IA is not stable.[2] Moreover, if, instead of her true preferences, a_2 ranked s_1 as first choice, she would have been assigned to s_1. That is, IA is not DSIC.

The intuition behind this preference manipulation under IA is more apparent from the following alternative implementation of the algorithm. In every school's priority ranking, elevate applicants that rank the school higher in their choice list, otherwise keep the priority ranking unchanged. Then run DA with the adjusted priority rankings. Since an applicant that ranks the school as higher in her choice list has a higher priority than an applicants who rank it lower, the former will never be rejected by the school in later rounds of DA. That is, all assignments in DA become final immediately. Consequently, an applicant may claim a higher ranking at a school and improve her odds of assignment to the school by ranking it higher in her choice list.

The failure of DSIC with IA yields two contrasting results. First, when market participants have full information about others' preferences and priorities, and that information is common knowledge, every Nash equilibrium outcome of the preference revelation game induced by IA is stable under true preferences. Therefore, the dominant strategy equilibrium of DA weakly Pareto-dominates every Nash equilibrium outcome of IA. Second, applicants may communicate information about their cardinal valuations of schools under IA via preference manipulation. For example, if an applicant values her first and second choices almost equally, and if her first choice is in high demand, she may skip it and rank her second choice as first choice. In contrast, applicants that do not have viable second and third choices may rank their first choices truthfully. Consequently, it is likely that a highly demanded school will

---

[2] Some districts grant higher priorities based on the applicants' ranking of the schools. For examples, schools may give higher priorities to applicants that the rank the school higher in their applications. The IA algorithm becomes stable with respect to these adjusted priorities.

be assigned to applicants without viable alternatives. This improves the efficiency of the assignment in a cardinal sense, which we do not define here.

Another contrast is between efficient DSIC algorithms and DA. Unlike in Observation 8.3, no efficient and DSIC algorithm always finds an efficient and stable matching whenever one exists.

Theorem 8.4. *No efficient and DSIC algorithm finds a stable and efficient matching whenever one exists.*

Proof Suppose for the sake of contradiction that φ is an efficient and DSIC algorithm that finds a stable and efficient matching whenever one exists. Consider a problem with three applicants $A = \{a_1, a_2, a_3\}$ and three schools $S = \{s_1, s_2, s_3\}$, each with unit capacity. Let preferences $\succ_A$ and priorities $\succ_S$ be as follows:

$$
\begin{array}{ll}
a_1 : s_1, s_2, s_3 & s_1 : a_3, a_1, a_2 \\
a_2 : s_1, s_2, s_3 & s_2 : a_2, a_3, a_1 \\
a_3 : s_3, s_1, s_2 & s_3 : a_2, a_1, a_3
\end{array}
$$

Then we have

$$
\varphi(\succ_A) = \begin{pmatrix} a_1 & a_2 & a_3 \\ s_1 & s_2 & s_3 \end{pmatrix},
$$

since that is the unique stable and efficient matching. Now consider a problem that differs from the original one in that a_2's preferences are $a_2 : s_1, s_3, s_2$. Let us denote that problem by $\succ'_A$. There are three efficient matchings in this problem;

$$
\mu_1 = \begin{pmatrix} a_1 & a_2 & a_3 \\ s_2 & s_1 & s_3 \end{pmatrix}, \qquad \mu_2 = \begin{pmatrix} a_1 & a_2 & a_3 \\ s_1 & s_3 & s_2 \end{pmatrix}, \qquad \mu_3 = \begin{pmatrix} a_1 & a_2 & a_3 \\ s_1 & s_2 & s_3 \end{pmatrix}.
$$

To show that φ is not DSIC, we consider the following cases:

1. $\varphi(\succ'_A) = \mu_1$. Then, $\varphi(\succ'_A) \succ_{a_2} \varphi(\succ_A)$, contradicting that φ is DSIC.
2. $\varphi(\succ'_A) = \mu_2$. Consider the problem that differs from $\succ'_A$ in that a_3's preferences are $a_3 : s_1, s_2, s_3$. We denote this problem by $\succ''_A$. Then,

$$
\varphi(\succ''_A) = \begin{pmatrix} a_1 & a_2 & a_3 \\ s_2 & s_3 & s_1 \end{pmatrix},
$$

since that is the unique stable and efficient matching. Hence, $\varphi(\succ''_A)(a_3) \succ'_{a_3} \varphi(\succ'_A)(a_3)$, contradicting that φ is DSIC.
3. $\varphi(\succ'_A) = \mu_3$. Consider the problem that differs from $\succ'_A$ in that a_2's preferences are $a_2 : s_3, s_1, s_2$. We denote this problem by $\succ'''_A$. Then,

$$
\varphi(\succ'''_A) = \begin{pmatrix} a_1 & a_2 & a_3 \\ s_2 & s_3 & s_1 \end{pmatrix},
$$

since that is the unique stable and efficient matching. Hence, $\varphi(\succ'''_A)(a_2) \succ'_{a_2} \varphi(\succ'_A)(a_2)$, contradicting that φ is DSIC.

This completes the proof of Theorem 8.4. $\qquad\square$

Corollary 8.5. *No efficient and DSIC algorithm Pareto-dominates DA.*

Since DA is not efficient, several efficient algorithms have been proposed as its alternatives. We discuss two such algorithms: top trading cycles (TTC) and efficiency adjusted deferred acceptance (EADA). Top trading cycles was introduced in the context of one-sided matching in Chapter 2. Below we describe the adaptation of the TTC algorithm for the school choice problem.

Algorithm 8.2 Top trading cycles (TTC).

Until there are no remaining applicants or no available seats, do:
1. Each school with an available seat points to the highest-priority remaining applicant.
2. Each remaining applicant points to her most preferred acceptable school with available places. If there is no such school, the applicant is removed from the problem.
3. A trading cycle is a list of applicants $(a_1, a_2, \ldots, a_K, a_{K+1} = a_1)$ for some $K \in \mathbb{Z}_+$, such that a_k points to a school that points to a_{k+1} for all $k \in \{1, 2, \ldots, K\}$. Select a trading cycle and match each applicant to a school to which she is pointing in that trading cycle. The capacity of each school in the trading cycle is reduced by one.

We now describe the EADA algorithm.

Algorithm 8.3 Efficiency adjusted deferred acceptance (EADA).

Until there are no remaining applicants, do:
1. Run the DA algorithm with the remaining applicants and schools with available seats and obtain a tentative matching.
2. We say a school is underdemanded if it never rejects an applicant during the implementation of the DA algorithm. All tentative acceptances at an underdemanded school are finalized and the corresponding applicants are removed from the problem. The underdemanded schools and applicants who hold no tentative acceptances are also removed from the problem.

Top trading cycles is efficient and DSIC. The EADA algorithm is efficient and Pareto-dominates DA, therefore it is not DSIC. We now discuss additional properties of these two algorithms in terms of the minimal instability among some classes of algorithms.

Definition 8.6. An algorithm φ is minimally unstable in a class $\mathcal{C}$ of algorithms if $\varphi \in \mathcal{C}$ and there is no $\psi \in \mathcal{C}$ such that the set of blocking pairs at $\psi(\succ_A)$ is a subset of the set of blocking pairs of $\phi(\succ_A)$ for every problem $\succ_A$, and a proper subset for some problem.

Theorem 8.7. *The EADA algorithm is minimally unstable in the class of efficient algorithms.*

In contrast, TTC is not minimally unstable in the class of efficient algorithms. However, for one-to-one problems (i.e., when each school has a unit capacity) TTC is minimally unstable in the class of efficient and DSIC algorithms.

Theorem 8.8. *Suppose that $q_s = 1, \forall s \in S$. Then TTC is minimally unstable in the class of efficient and DSIC algorithms.*

For general school capacities, there are no known polynomial time algorithms that are minimally unstable in the class of efficient and DSIC algorithms.

8.3 School Choice Problem with Indifferences

In practice, schools sort applicants into a few priority classes. For example, a school may grant priorities to applicants on the basis of whether their siblings are enrolled at the school, whether they reside within walking distance of the school, or whether they are applying from a failing school. Consequently, many applicants may share the same priority at a school. Unlike in earlier applications of matching theory to entry-level labor markets, this introduces ties or indifferences in schools' priority rankings. We generalize the school choice model of the previous section to accommodate indifferences. Formally, we assume that the priority ranking of school s is a complete and transitive binary relation on $A \cup \{s\}$. For $a, a' \in A$, we use $a \succsim_s a'$ to denote that a has a weakly higher priority at s than a'. Also, we use $a \succ_s a'$ to denote that $a \succsim_s a'$ and $a' \not\succsim_s a$, and $a \sim_s a'$ to denote that $a \succsim_s a'$ and $a' \succsim_s a$. As before, applicant a is eligible for school s if $a \succ_s s$. In this section we describe a problem by a pair $(\succ_A, \succsim_S)$, where $\succ_A = (\succ_a)_{a \in A}$ and $\succsim_S = (\succsim_s)_{s \in S}$.

The stability of a matching $\mu : A \cup S \to 2^A \cup S$ is defined as in the previous section, i.e., an applicant–school pair $(a, s) \in A \times S$ blocks matching μ if $s \succ_a \mu(a)$, a is eligible for s, and either $|\mu(s)| < q(s)$ or $a \succ_s a'$ for some $a' \in \mu(s)$. A matching is **stable** if it is not blocked by any applicant–school pair.

Indifferences in schools' priorities complicate the problem by aggravating the conflict between stability, efficiency, and incentives. Example 8.1 illustrates that some problems admit no stable and efficient matchings. However, in the previous section the existence of such a matching can be verified by running the DA. In contrast, when there are indifferences in schools' priorities, verifying the existence of a stable and efficient matching, and therefore finding one, is an NP-hard problem. Consider the special case of our model where the matching is one-to-one, i.e., where $|A| = |S|$ and $q_s = 1, \forall s \in S$. Also, assume that all schools are acceptable for all applicants and all applicants are eligible for all schools. We first prove the following lemma.

Lemma 8.9. *Deciding whether a given applicant–school pair can be matched in an efficient matching is an NP-hard problem.*

Proof We prove the statement by constructing a polynomial time reduction from the NP-hard problem of finding minimum-cardinality maximal matching on a subdivision graph.

For a graph $G = (V = \{v_1, v_2, \ldots, v_n\}, E = \{e_1, e_2, \ldots, e_m\}), m \geq n$, let $G' = (V' := V \cup E, E')$ be its subdivision graph, where

$$E' := \{\{e, v\} : e \in E, v \in V, v \text{ is incident with } e \text{ in } G\}.$$

We use v_{x_i} and v_{y_i} to denote the two vertices satisfying $(e_i, v_{x_i}), (e_i, v_{y_i}) \in E'$ for each $i \in \{1, 2, \ldots, m\}$. Let $K \leq m$ be an integer. The decision version of the minimum-cardinality maximal matching problem asks whether there is a maximal matching M with $|M| \leq K$.

For the given subdivision graph (G', E') and integer K, we construct the corresponding school choice problem $(A, S, q, \succ_A, \succsim_S)$ as follows:

- $A = \{a, a_{11}, a_{12}, \ldots, a_{1m}, a_{21}, a_{22}, \ldots, a_{2m}, b_1, \ldots, b_m\}$,
- $S = \{v_1, v_2, \ldots, v_n, w_1, w_2, \ldots, w_m, s_1, s_2, \ldots, s_{m+1}, t_1, t_2, \ldots, t_{m-n}\}$.
- For all $s \in S$, $q_s = 1$.
- For all $i \in \{1, 2, \ldots, m\}$, preferences are

$$a : s_{m+1}, s_m, \ldots, s_1$$
$$a_{1i} : w_i, v_{x_i}, v_{y_i}, s_{m+1}, s_m, \ldots, s_1$$
$$a_{2i} : w_i, v_{y_i}, v_{x_i}, s_{m+1}, s_m, \ldots, s_1$$
$$b_i : s_1, s_2, \ldots, s_{m+1}.$$

The remaining schools are ranked arbitrarily.
- Priorities are arbitrary.

To prove Lemma 8.9, it is sufficient to show that there is a maximal matching $M \subseteq E'$ of G' satisfying $|M| \leq K$ if and only if there is an efficient matching μ of $(A, S, \succ_A, \succsim_S)$ such that $\mu(a) = s_K$.

We will prove the "only if" part. The "if" part is left as an exercise. Suppose there is a maximal matching $M \subseteq E'$ of G' satisfying $|M| \leq K$. It is sufficient to construct an ordering of applicants such that the *serial dictatorship* under that ordering matches a to s_{K+1}. By definition of the subdivision graph G', the vertex e_i is connected to vertices v_{x_i} and v_{y_i}. Thus, at most one of the edges (e_i, v_{x_i}) and (e_i, v_{y_i}) can be in M. Let $I_M := \{i \in \{1, 2, \ldots, M\} : (e_i, v_{x_i}) \in M \text{ or } (e_i, v_{y_i}) \in M\}$.

We construct the serial dictatorship ordering as follows:

- If (e_i, v_{x_i}) is in M, rank a_{1i} ahead of a_{2i} in the ordering.
- If (e_i, v_{y_i}) is in M, rank a_{2i} ahead of a_{1i}.
- For each $i \in I_M$ and $j \in \{1, 2, \ldots, m\} \setminus I_M$, rank a_{1i} and a_{2i} ahead of a_{1j} and a_{2j}.
- Let J be a subset of indices in $\{1, 2, \ldots, m\} \setminus I_M$ with $|J| = m - K$. For all $i \in J$, rank a_{1i} ahead of a_{2i}.
- For all $i \in I_M \cup J$, rank a_{1i} and a_{2i} ahead of a. Rank a ahead of every other applicant.
- Otherwise, the ordering is arbitrary.

To complete the proof, we show that under the constructed ordering a is matched to s_{K+1}. Consider $i \in I_M$. If $(e_i, v_{x_i}) \in M$, a_{1i} is matched to w_1 and a_{2i} to v_{y_i}. Similarly, if $(e_i, v_{y_i}) \in M$, a_{2i} is matched to w_i and a_{1i} to v_{x_i}. Since M is a maximal matching, all schools $\{v_1, v_2, \ldots, v_n\}$ are matched to applicants in $\cup_{i \in I_M} \{a_{1i}, a_{2i}\}$. Now consider $i \in J$. Since a_{1i} is ranked ahead of a_{2i} in the ordering, a_{1i} is matched to w_i. Also, since all schools $\{v_1, v_2, \ldots, v_n\}$ are matched to applicants $\cup_{j \in I_M} \{a_{1j}, a_{2j}\}$, applicant a_{2i} is matched to her most preferred unmatched school in $\{s_1, s_2, \ldots, s_{m+1}\}$. Since $|J| = m - K$, applicants in $\{a_{2i} : i \in J\}$ are matched to schools $\{s_{m+1}, s_m, \ldots, s_{K+1}\}$. Thus a is ahead of everyone else in the ordering and hence she is matched to s_K. This completes the proof. $\qquad\square$

We can use Lemma 8.9 to establish the NP-completeness of deciding on the existence of a stable and efficient matching.

Theorem 8.10. *When school priorities involve indifferences, deciding whether there is a stable and efficient matching is an NP-complete problem.*

Any algorithm that is minimally unstable in the class of efficient algorithms gives a stable and efficient matching, whenever one exists. Therefore, Theorem 8.10 implies that, unless P = NP, there are no polynomial time algorithms that are minimally unstable in the class of efficient algorithms. This contrasts with the positive result of Theorem 8.7 for the strict priorities model.

We now prove Theorem 8.10.

Proof Verifying that the problem belongs in the NP category is left to the reader. We prove its NP-hardness by constructing a polynomial-time reduction from the NP-hard decision problem in Lemma 8.9.

Consider a school choice problem $(A, S, q, \succ_A, \succsim_S)$, where $|A| = |S|$, $q_s = 1, \forall s \in S$, all schools are acceptable for all applicants, and all applicants are eligible for all schools. Fix an applicant–school pair (a, s). We construct a different school choice problem $(\bar{A}, \bar{O}, \succ_{\bar{A}}, \succsim_{\bar{S}})$ such that there is an efficient matching that matches a to s in the former problem if and only if there is a stable and efficient matching in the latter problem.

Let $(\bar{A}, \bar{S}, \succ_{\bar{A}}, \succsim_{\bar{S}})$ be as follows:

- $\bar{A} = A \cup \{\bar{a}\}$ and $\bar{S} = S \cup \{\bar{s}\}$ for some $\bar{a} \notin A$ and $\bar{s} \notin S$.
- The restriction of $\succ_{\bar{A}}$ on S is $\succ_A$.
- School $\bar{s}$ is acceptable and least preferred for all applicants in $\bar{A}$ and $\succ_{\bar{a}}$ is otherwise arbitrary.
- Applicant $\bar{a}$ is eligible for all schools, and priorities satisfy
  - $a \succsim_s a' \succsim_s \bar{a}$ for all $a' \in \bar{A} \setminus \{a, \bar{a}\}$,
  - $a' \succsim_{s'} \bar{a} \succsim_{s'} a$ for all $a' \in \bar{A} \setminus \{a, \bar{a}\}$ and $s' \in S \setminus \{s\}$,
  - $a' \sim_{s'} a''$ for all $a', a'' \in \bar{A} \setminus \{a, \bar{a}\}$ and $s' \in \bar{S}$.

We say that $\bar{\mu} : \bar{A} \cup \bar{S} \to 2^{\bar{A}} \cup \bar{S}$ is a perfect matching if $\mu(a') \in \bar{S}, \forall a' \in \bar{A}$.

Claim *A perfect matching $\bar{\mu} : \bar{A} \cup \bar{S} \to 2^{\bar{A}} \cup \bar{S}$ is stable if and only if $\bar{\mu}(a) = s$ and $\bar{\mu}(\bar{a}) = \bar{s}$.*

First suppose that μ is a perfect matching satisfying $\bar{\mu}(a) = s$ and $\bar{\mu}(\bar{a}) = \bar{s}$. School s does not block $\bar{\mu}$, as $\bar{\mu}(s) = a$ has the highest priority at s. Similarly, $s' \in \setminus \{s, \bar{s}\}$ does not block $\bar{\mu}$ as $\bar{\mu}(s')$ has highest priority at s'. Finally, $\bar{s}$ does not block $\bar{\mu}$ as it is the least preferred school for all applicants. Now suppose

$\bar{\mu} \colon \bar{A} \cup \bar{S} \to 2^{\bar{A}} \cup \bar{S}$ is perfect and stable. By the definition of stability, $\bar{\mu}(a) \succeq_a s$. In particular, $\bar{\mu}(a) \neq \bar{s}$. Therefore, $\bar{\mu}(\bar{s}) = \bar{a}$ since otherwise $\big(\bar{\mu}(\bar{s}), \bar{\mu}(\bar{a})\big)$ blocks $\bar{\mu}$. Finally, $\bar{\mu}(\bar{a}) = \bar{s}$ implies $\bar{\mu}(a) = s$, since otherwise $(\bar{a}, \bar{\mu}(a))$ blocks $\bar{\mu}$.

In the final step of the proof we need to show that there is an efficient matching $\mu \colon A \cup S \to 2^A \cup S$ such that $\mu(a) = s$ for the problem $(A, S, \succ_A, \succsim_S)$ if and only if there is a stable and efficient matching $\bar{\mu} \colon \bar{A} \cup \bar{S} \to 2^{\bar{A}} \times \bar{S}$ for the problem $(\bar{A}, \bar{S}, \succ_{\bar{A}}, \succsim_{\bar{S}})$.

Suppose that there is an efficient matching $\mu \colon A \cup S \to 2^A \cup S$ such that $\mu(a) = s$. Consider the matching $\bar{\mu} \colon \bar{A} \cup \bar{S} \to 2^{\bar{A}} \times \bar{S}$ such that $\bar{\mu}(a') = \mu(a'), \forall a' \in A$ and $\bar{\mu}(\bar{a}) = \bar{s}$. Since μ is efficient and $\bar{s}$ is the least preferred school for all applicants in $\bar{A}$, $\bar{\mu}$ is also efficient. Since $\bar{\mu}$ is efficient, all schools are acceptable for applicants, and all applicants are eligible for schools, $\bar{\mu}$ is a perfect matching. Therefore, by the Claim, $\bar{\mu}$ is stable. This completes one part of the proof. Now suppose that there is a stable and efficient matching $\bar{\mu} \colon \bar{A} \cup \bar{S} \to 2^{\bar{A}} \times \bar{S}$. Since $\bar{\mu}$ is efficient, it is also perfect. Therefore, by the Claim, $\bar{\mu}(a) = s$ and $\bar{\mu}(\bar{a}) = \bar{s}$. Let $\mu \colon A \cup S \to 2^A \cup S$ be the restriction of $\bar{\mu}$ to $A \cup S$. Then, μ is efficient and $\mu(a) = s$. This completes the proof of Theorem 8.10. $\qquad\qquad\square$

The algorithms in the previous section were defined for settings with strict priorities, i.e., without indifferences in the schools' priority rankings. Those algorithms can be naturally adapted to the current setting by applying a tie-breaker. Formally, a tie-breaker is a complete, transitive, and antisymmetric binary relation over A. Given a profile of tie-breakers $\tau = (\tau_s)_{s \in S}$, we construct a strict priority ranking $\succ_s^\tau$ of school s as follows: $a \succ_s^\tau a'$ if and only if either $a \succ_s a'$, or $a \sim_s a'$ and $a\, \tau_s\, a'$. For a fixed tie-breaker profile τ, we define DA^τ by $\mathrm{DA}^\tau(\succ_A, \succsim_S) = \mathrm{DA}(\succ_A, \succ_S^\tau)$, where $\succ_S^\tau = (\succ_s^\tau)_{s \in S}$. We define TTC^τ and EADA^τ similarly. Despite the complications caused by ties in priorities, the adapted versions of algorithms in previous sections preserve some of their desirable properties, as summarized in the following theorem.

Theorem 8.11. *Let τ be an arbitrary tie-breaker.*

- *DA^τ is stable and DSIC.*
- *TTC^τ is efficient and DSIC.*
- *EADA^τ is efficient and Pareto-dominates DA^τ.*

Several desirable properties of these algorithms do not extend to the setting with indifferences. In this setting, TTC^τ is no longer minimally unstable in the class of efficient and DSIC algorithms when each school has a single seat available. The algorithm EADA^τ is not minimally unstable in the class of efficient algorithms. Also, DA^τ does not find a stable and efficient matching whenever one exists, and it is not applicant-optimal stable. We provide two stronger negative results.

Theorem 8.12. *No DSIC algorithm finds a stable and efficient matching whenever one exists.*

We leave the proof of this theorem as an exercise.

Theorem 8.13. *No DSIC algorithm is applicant-optimal stable.*

Proof Suppose for the sake of contradiction that φ is an applicant-optimal stable and DSIC algorithm. Consider a problem with three applicants $A = \{a_1, a_2, a_3\}$ and three schools $S = \{s_1, s_2, s_3\}$, each with a unit capacity. Let preferences $\succ_A$ and priorities $\succsim_S$ be as follows:

$$
\begin{array}{ll}
a_1: s_2, s_3, s_1 & s_1: a_1, a_2, a_3 \\
a_2: s_2, s_3, s_1 & s_2: a_3, (a_1, a_2) \\
a_3: s_1, s_2, s_3 & s_3: a_3, a_2, a_1
\end{array}
$$

There are two applicant-optimal stable matchings in this problem:

$$
\mu_1 = \begin{pmatrix} a_1 & a_2 & a_3 \\ s_2 & s_3 & s_1 \end{pmatrix}, \qquad \mu_2 = \begin{pmatrix} a_1 & a_2 & a_3 \\ s_3 & s_2 & s_1 \end{pmatrix}.
$$

To show that φ is not DSIC, we consider the following cases:

1. $\varphi(\succ_A, \succsim_S) = \mu_1$. Consider the problem $(\succ'_A, \succsim_S)$ that differs from $(\succ_A, \succsim_S)$ in that a_2's preferences are $a_2: s_2, s_1, s_3$. Then we have

$$
\varphi(\succ'_A, \succsim_S) = \begin{pmatrix} a_1 & a_2 & a_3 \\ s_3 & s_2 & s_1 \end{pmatrix},
$$

   since that is the unique applicant-optimal stable matching. However, $\phi(\succ'_A, \succsim_S)(a_2) \succ_{a_2} \phi(\succ_A, \succsim_S)(a_2)$ contradicts that φ is DSIC.

2. $\varphi(\succ_A, \succsim_S) = \mu_2$. Consider the problem $(\succ''_A, \succsim_S)$ that differs from $(\succ_A, \succsim_S)$ in that a_1's preferences are $a_1: s_2, s_1, s_3$. Then we have

$$
\varphi(\succ''_A, \succsim_S) = \begin{pmatrix} a_1 & a_2 & a_3 \\ s_2 & s_3 & s_1 \end{pmatrix},
$$

   since that is the unique applicant-optimal stable matching. However, $\phi(\succ''_A, \succsim_S)(a_1) \succ_{a_1} \phi(\succ_A, \succsim_A)(a_1)$ contradicts that φ is DSIC.

This completes the proof of Theorem 8.13. $\qquad\square$

Theorems 8.12 and 8.13 highlight the tension between stability, (Pareto) optimality, and incentive compatibility. The next result shows that DA^τ is a constrained optimal compromise between these opposing objectives.

Theorem 8.14. *Let τ be an arbitrary tie-breaker profile. Then, no DSIC algorithm Pareto-dominates DA^τ.*

A common practical concern is whether all schools should use the same tie-breaker or different ones. If the tie-breaker profile is of the former type, i.e., $\tau_s = \tau_{s'}, \forall s, s' \in S$, we refer to it as a single tie-breaker profile. The following suggests that restricting attention to DA with single tie-breaker profiles does not sacrifice efficiency.

Theorem 8.15. *For any applicant-optimal stable matching μ for problem $(\succ_A, \succsim_S)$, there is a single tie-breaker profile τ such that $\mu = DA^\tau(\succ_A, \succsim_S)$.*

Tie-breakers are usually generated randomly. One common practice is drawing a random lottery number for each applicant that determines a single tie-breaker profile. One argument against single tie-breaking is that an applicant with a bad random lottery number will lose to other applicants at every school of her choice. If she had a new random number at every choice, that would give her a better chance of being assigned to some desirable school. We refer to this latter implementation as multiple tie-breaking.

The set of stable matchings that can be generated by DA with single tie-breaking is a subset of the set of stable matchings that can be generated by DA with multiple tie-breaking. So, Theorem 8.15 implies that any stable matching that can be generated by multiple tie-breaking but not single tie-breaking is necessarily Pareto-dominated by another stable matching. This result potentially suggests the desirability of implementing DA with single tie-breaking.

We complete this section by giving a polynomial time applicant-optimal stable algorithm. For a given stable matching μ, applicant a desires school s if $s \succ_a \mu(s)$. Let $D_s(\mu)$ be the set of applicants that have the highest $\succsim_s$ priority at school s among all the applicants who desire s. A *stable improvement cycle* of size $K \in \mathbb{Z}_+$ is a list of applicants $(a_1, \ldots, a_K, a_{K+1} = a_1)$, such that, for every $k \in \{1, 2, \ldots, K\}$,

- $\mu(a_k) \in S$,
- a_k desires $s = \mu(a_{k+1})$,
- $a_k \in D_s(\mu)$.

By the stability of μ, every school in the matching $\mu(a_{k+1})$ must fill the school's capacity, since otherwise $(a_k, \mu(a_{k+1}))$ would form a blocking pair. A new matching is obtained by reassigning every a_k to $\mu(a_{k+1})$. The new matching Pareto-dominates μ since each a_k is matched to a more preferred school and the matchings of applicants in $A \setminus \{a_1, \ldots, a_K\}$ are unchanged. Furthermore, since each a_k has the highest priority at $\mu(a_{k+1})$ among those who desire $\mu(a_{k+1})$, the resulting matching does not create any blocking pairs. So the new matching is also stable. This observation is summarized in the following lemma.

Lemma 8.16. *If μ is stable but not applicant-optimal stable, then there is a stable improvement cycle. Moreover, reassigning applicants by the stable improvement cycle gives a stable matching that Pareto-dominates μ.*

This yields the following polynomial time applicant-optimal stable algorithm:

Algorithm 8.4 Stable improvement cycles.

---
1. **Initialization:** Pick a random tie-breaker profile τ and set $\mu = \mathrm{DA}^\tau(\succ_A, \succ_S)$.
2. **Cycles:** As long as there is a stable improvement cycle, assign each applicant in the cycle to the school that the applicant desires in the cycle and set μ to the resulting matching.

Theorem 8.17. *The SIC algorithm is applicant-optimal stable.*

Proof Let $\mu_1 = \mathrm{DA}^\tau(\succ_A, \succ_S), \mu_2, \ldots, \mu_T = \mu$ be the sequence of matchings that emerge during the implementation of the SIC algorithm. By Lemma 8.16 and an induction argument, μ_t is a stable matching for each $t \in \{1, 2, \ldots, T\}$. In particular, μ is stable. By the description of the SIC algorithm, there is no stable improvement cycle at the matching μ. Therefore, again by Lemma 8.16, μ is applicant-optimal stable. This completes the proof of Theorem 8.17. $\quad\square$

8.4 Controlled School Choice Problem

Diversity among enrolled students at schools is a major policy objective for many school districts in the USA. Despite their appealing properties, none of the aforementioned algorithms achieve diversity without further restrictions in the problem. For example, data shows that applicants prefer schools closer to their home. Also, schools tend to grant neighborhood priority to applicants living within a certain distance from school. When neighborhoods are segregated along income lines, these algorithms assign a higher proportion of applicants from wealthy families at schools in affluent areas. Similarly, lower-income applicants are assigned in higher proportions to schools in poor neighborhoods.

In practice, diversity is usually controlled by giving priority to a certain type of applicants for a certain number of places or by limiting the number of applicants of a type that can be admitted at schools. We refer to the first type of control as reserves and the second type as quotas. Earlier applications of matching theory to school choice adopted intuitive modifications to the algorithms while preserving their appealing properties. Recent work has developed rigorous axiomatic foundations for diversity control in school choice. We summarize the latter approach in this section.

8.4.1 Preliminaries

Consider the school choice problem with strict priorities of Section 8.2 and extend it as follows. Assume that there is a finite set of applicant types T and a mapping $\tau : A \to T$ that determines each applicant's type. Applicants a and a' have the same type if $\tau(a) = \tau(a')$. For a set of applicants $A' \subseteq A$, let

$$A'_t = \{a \in A' : \tau(a) = t\}$$

be the set of type-t applicants in A'.

For example, when the goal is diversity in family income level, T may include income levels, $T = \{\text{low income}, \text{middle income}, \text{high income}\}$. Likewise, a district may use average achievement at pupils' current schools in order to achieve academic diversity. In that case, if schools are graded, the type space may be set as $T = \{A, B, C, D, \text{and below}\}$. However, our model does not cover the case where types are multidimensional, such as $T = \{\text{low income}, \text{middle income}, \text{high income}\} \times \{A, B, C, D, \text{and below}\}$, and the goal is to achieve diversity in both dimensions. Such generalizations bring in complications related to complementarities that are beyond the scope of this chapter.

In the previous sections, when a school considers a set of applicants, it selects applicants up to its capacity in priority order, and uses a tie-breaker in cases of indifferences. In a sense, each school deems applicants with higher priority as better and selects the best subset based on the priority ordering of applicants and its capacity. In the following, we allow general school preferences which are potentially based on applicant priorities or other criteria.

In general, the preferences of a school $s \in S$ over the subsets of applicants can be represented by a choice rule $C_s: 2^A \to 2^A$, where $C_s(A') \subseteq A'$ and $|C_s(A')| \le q_s$ for all $A' \subseteq A$. The choice rule indicates a subset of applicants that a school desires to admit from each considered set.

The choice rules in Section 8.2 are said to be *responsive* to $\succ_S$, i.e., they select highest priority applicants up to the capacity. Responsive choice rules may not achieve diversity objectives. Section 8.4.2 below focuses on axiomatic foundations for choice rules that balance the conflict between selecting higher-priority applicants and achieving diversity. Those rules are based on reserves and quotas, which impose soft lower bounds and hard upper bounds on the number of applicants of each type that a school can choose, respectively.

Before proceeding, we reintroduce notions related to matching with general choice rules, which will be discussed in Chapter 11 of this book.

Definition 8.18. A matching μ is blocked by applicant–school pair (a, s) if $s \succ_a \mu(a)$ and $a \in C_s(\mu(s) \cup \{a\})$. A matching is (pairwise) stable if it is not blocked by any applicant–school pair.

If C is responsive to $\succ_S$, this definition reduces to the one in Section 8.2.

Definition 8.19. A choice rule is *substitutable* if, for all $a \in A'' \subseteq A' \subseteq A$,

$$a \in C_s(A') \Rightarrow a \in C_s(A'').$$

Substitutability eliminates complementarity between applicants in school preferences. If applicant a is chosen from A' then a will also be chosen from a smaller set A'' on the basis of her own merits, not on complementarity with some applicant that is present in $C_s(A')$ but not in A''.

Definition 8.20. A choice rule satisfies the *irrelevance of rejected applicants*, if, for all $A' \subseteq A$,

$$a \notin C_s(A' \cup \{a\}) \text{ implies } C_s(A') = C_s(A' \cup \{a\}).$$

In other words, the irrelevance of rejected applicants says that when an applicant is not chosen from a set, removing the applicant from the set does not impact the selection of the remaining applicants.

Definition 8.21. A choice rule satisfies the *law of aggregate demand*, if, for all $A'' \subseteq A' \subseteq A$,

$$|C_s(A'')| \le |C_s(A')|.$$

In other words, a choice rule that satisfies the law of aggregate demand chooses weakly more applicants when additional applicants are considered. Substitutability and the irrelevance of rejected applicants guarantee that a deferred acceptance algorithm, which we define next, gives a stable matching. Substitutability and the law of aggregate demand guarantee that the algorithm is also DSIC.

For given choice rules $(\mathcal{C}_s)_{s \in S}$, deferred acceptance works as given in Algorithm:

Algorithm 8.5 Deferred acceptance for general choice rules (DA).

Until no applicant is rejected: do

1. Each applicant applies to the most preferred of her chosen schools that has not rejected her.
2. For each school $s \in S$, let $A^s \subseteq A$ denote the set of applicants that apply to s. School s rejects all applicants not in $\mathcal{C}_s(A^s)$.

Theorem 8.22. *Suppose that $(\mathcal{C}_s)_{s \in S}$ are substitutable choice rules.*

- *If the $(\mathcal{C}_s)_{s \in S}$ satisfy the irrelevance of rejected applicants, then DA is stable and Pareto-dominates any other stable algorithm.*
- *If the $(\mathcal{C}_s)_{s \in S}$ satisfy the law of aggregate demand, then DA is DSIC and stable and Pareto-dominates any other stable algorithm.*

In the following subsection, unless noted otherwise, we study a single school's choice rule and drop the school subscript in the notation.

8.4.2 Reserves and Quotas

Diversity is commonly achieved by guaranteeing a certain number of places at a school for applicants of a certain type. We refer to such places as type-specific reserves. To formalize this, let $R = (r_t)_{t \in T} \in \mathbb{Z}_0^{|T|}$ such that $\sum_{t \in T} r_t \leq q$ denote the vector of type-specific reserves. Then,

Definition 8.23. A choice rule is *reserves-respecting* for R if, for all $A' \subseteq A$ and $t \in T$,

$$|\mathcal{C}(A')_t| \geq \min\{|A'_t|, r_t\}.$$

Another tool for achieving diversity is the use of type-specific quotas. Quotas limit the number of applicants of a certain type at the school. Let $Q = (q_t)_{t \in T} \in \mathbb{Z}_0^{|T|}$ such that $\sum_{t \in T} q_t \geq q$ denote the vector of type-specific quotas. Then,

Definition 8.24. A choice rule is *quotas-respecting* for Q if, for all $A' \subseteq A$ and $t \in T$,

$$|\mathcal{C}(A')_t| \leq q_t.$$

In what follows we fix the vectors R and Q, in such a way that $r_t \leq q_t$ for all $t \in T$, and we will not refer to them when talking about reserves- and quotas-respecting choice rules.

The class of reserves- and quotas-respecting choice rules is large. Later in this section we show that a reasonable set of desirable properties or axioms reduces this class to a single reserves- and quotas-respecting choice rule given by the following algorithm.

Algorithm 8.6 Reserves-and-quotas rule

From a set of applicants $A' \subseteq A$,
1. For each $t \in T$, select up to r_t of type-t applicants in A' according to the ordering $\succ$.
2. For the remaining applicants, select the highest-priority applicants one-by-one without exceeding type-specific quotas.

Two special cases of the reserves-and-quotas rule are the *reserves rule* and the *quotas rule*. The former rule is obtained by setting $q_t = q$ for all $t \in T$. The latter is obtained by setting $r_t = 0$ for all $t \in T$. The reserves-and-quotas rule satisfies certain desirable properties as summarized in the next lemma.

Lemma 8.25. *Let C be the reserves-and-quotas rule. Then C is substitutable and satisfies the law of aggregate demand.*

Lemma 8.25 and Theorem 8.22 imply the following result.

Theorem 8.26. *Consider a controlled school choice problem where C_s is a reserves-and-quotas rule for every $s \in S$. Then, DA is stable and DSIC and it Pareto-dominates any other stable algorithm.*

In the remainder of this chapter we show that the reserves-and-quotas rule is the unique reserves-respecting and quotas-respecting choice rule satisfying some desirable properties or axioms. The first property says that an applicant is rejected only if the school is full or type-specific quotas are binding. Choice rules that do not satisfy this property may be considered inefficient or wasteful.

Definition 8.27. A choice rule C is *non-wasteful* if, for all $A' \subseteq A$ and $a \in A'$,

$$a \in A' \setminus C(A') \text{ and } |C(A')| < q \text{ imply } |C(A')_{\tau(a)}| = q_{\tau(a)}.$$

Reserves- and quotas-respecting choice rules cannot always choose the highest-priority applicants. This may lead to priority violations. We say a choice rule C violates the priority of applicant a at A' if there is an $a' \in A'$ such that

$$a \in A' \setminus C(A'), a' \in C(A'), \text{ and } a \succ a'.$$

The following property of a choice rule requires that priority violations only happen across different types.

Definition 8.28. A choice rule C is *within-type priority compatible* if, for all $A' \in A$,

$$a \in C(A'), d' \in A' \setminus C(A'), \text{ and } \tau(a) = \tau(a') \text{ imply } a \succ a'.$$

The next property of a choice rule prohibits priority violations between any two applicants whenever the chosen applicant's type is sufficiently represented and the non-chosen applicant's type is not.

Definition 8.29. A choice rule C is *across-type priority compatible* if, for all $A' \subseteq A, a \in C(A')$, and $d' \in A' \setminus C(A')$,

$$\left| C(A')_{\tau(a)} \right| > r_{\tau(a)} \text{ and } \left| C(A')_{\tau(a')} \right| < q_{\tau(a')} \text{ imply } a \succ a'.$$

Although priority violations cannot be eliminated completely, a reasonable objective is to minimize them in some class of choice rules.

Definition 8.30. A choice rule C is *priority-violations minimal* in the class of choice rules Γ if $C \in \Gamma$ and, for any $C' \in \Gamma$ and $A' \subseteq A$, the number of applicants whose priority is violated at $C(A')$ is smaller than that at $C'(A')$.

Finally, our last property requires that the choice rule selects the highest-priority applicants, subject to some other properties being satisfied.

Definition 8.31. A choice rule is *priority maximal* in a class of choice rules Γ if $C \in \Gamma$ and, for any $C' \in \Gamma$ and $a, d' \in A' \subseteq A$,

$$a \in C(A') \setminus C'(A') \text{ and } d' \in C'(A') \setminus C(A') \text{ imply } a \succ a'.$$

We now state the main result of this section.

Theorem 8.32. *The following are equivalent:*

1. *C is the reserves-and-quotas rule.*
2. *C is priority-violations minimal in the class of reserves-respecting, quotas-respecting, and non-wasteful choice rules.*
3. *C is priority maximal in the class of reserves-respecting, quotas-respecting, non-wasteful, and within-type priority-compatible choice rules.*
4. *C is a reserves-respecting, quotas-respecting, non-wasteful, within-type priority-compatible, and across-type priority-compatible choice rule.*

The proof of Theorem 8.32 is left as an exercise.

There are other well-studied reserves- and quotas-respecting choice rules that share some of the desirable properties of the above reserves-and-quotas rule. For example, suppose there are no type-specific quotas, i.e., $q_t = q$ for all $t \in T$, and consider a choice rule that in stage 1 selects up to $q - \sum_{t \in T} r_t$ highest-priority applicants, in stage 2 chooses r_t highest-priority remaining type-t applicants for each $t \in T$, and in stage 3 fills the remaining seats (if any) with highest-priority remaining applicants. It is easy to see that such a rule is reserves-respecting, non-wasteful, and within-type priority compatible. We demonstrate how this alternative choice rule compares with the reserves-and-quotas rule through an example.

Example 8.33. Suppose there are two types $T = \{L, H\}$, low-income and high-income, and three applicants $A = \{a_1, a_2, a_3\}$ with $L = \tau(a_1) = \tau(a_3) \neq \tau(a_2) = H$. Assume $r_L = 1$ and $r_H = 0$ i.e., one seat is reserved for a low-income applicant and no seat is reserved for a high-income applicant. There are no type-specific quotas, i.e., $q_L = q_H = q = 2$. Finally, suppose that $a_1 \succ a_2 \succ a_3$. When we apply the reserves-and-quotas rule, a_1 is chosen in stage 1 and a_2 is chosen in stage 2. The set of chosen applicants is $\{a_1, a_2\}$, which features one low-income and one high-income applicant. When we apply the alternative choice rule from the previous paragraph, a_1 is chosen in stage 1 and a_3 is chosen in stage 2. The set of chosen applicants $\{a_1, a_3\}$ consists entirely of low-income applicants.

Example 8.33 demonstrates that different reserves-respecting, quotas-respecting, non-wasteful, and within-type priority-compatible choice rules may have different distributional outcomes, such as different number of low- or high-income applicants. Thus, the resulting type distribution depends not only on the sizes of the reserves and quotas, but also on the choice rule used. Choosing the appropriate choice rule in the presence of reserves and quotas is of central practical importance and has gained widespread academic interest. Theorem 8.32 provides an axiomatic foundation for the reserves-and-quotas rules. More specifically, it implies that any other reserves-respecting, quotas-respecting, non-wasteful, and within-type priority-compatible choice rule fails to minimize priority violations, choose highest-priority applicants, or satisfy across-type priority compatibility. For example, in Example 8.33, the alternative rule violates the priority of applicant a_2. In contrast, there are no priority violations under the reserves-and-quotas rule.

Besides the differences in distributional outcomes, different reserves- and quotas-respecting choice rules may have different welfare implications for applicants. One practical question is whether applicants prefer diversity to be achieved through reserves or through quotas. One potential argument against using quotas is that they allow situations where applicants are rejected by the school even when it has available places. Another potential argument is that it may have the perverse effect of harming the intended beneficiaries. This is illustrated by the following example.

Example 8.34. There are three applicants $A = \{a_1, a_2, a_3\}$ and two schools $S = \{s_1, s_2\}$ with $q_{s_1} = 2$ and $q_{s_2} = 1$. Suppose $T = \{t_L, t_H\}$, $\tau(a_1) = \tau(a_2) = t_H$, and $\tau(a_3) = t_L$. The preferences and priorities are as follows:

$$a_1: s_1, s_2 \qquad s_1: a_1, a_2, a_3$$
$$a_2: s_1, s_2 \qquad s_2: a_2, a_3, a_1$$
$$a_3: s_2, s_1$$

Suppose that school s_i uses the reserve-and-quotas rule for vectors (R_i, Q_i) such that $r_{it_L} = r_{it_H} = 0$ and $q_{it_L} = q_{it_H} = q_{s_i}$ for $i \in \{1, 2\}$. That is, there are no reserves and quotas are non-binding for both types at both schools. The DA outcome for this problem is

$$\mu = \begin{pmatrix} a_1 & a_2 & a_3 \\ s_1 & s_1 & s_2 \end{pmatrix}.$$

Now suppose that s_1 uses the reserves-and-quotas rule for vectors (R'_1, Q'_1), which differ from (R_1, Q_1) in that $q'_{it_H} = 1$. The DA outcome for this problem is

$$\mu' = \begin{pmatrix} a_1 & a_2 & a_3 \\ s_1 & s_2 & s_1 \end{pmatrix}.$$

The only low-income applicant a_3 prefers $\mu(a_3)$ to $\mu'(a_3)$. Thus, imposing quotas for high-income applicants may harm low-income applicants.

Our final result concerns how reserves and quotas compare in terms of aggregate welfare. The result is that when there are two types, such as low- and high-income, all applicants are better off if diversity is achieved through reserves for low-income applicants, rather than quotas for high-income applicants, when the size of reserves in the first choice rule is q minus the size of the quotas in the second one.

Theorem 8.35. *Suppose $T = \{t_L, t_H\}$. Let (R, Q) be such that $r_{t_H} = 0$ and $q_{t_L} = q_{t_H} = q$, and let (R', Q') be such that $r'_{t_L} = r'_{t_H} = 0$, $q'_{t_L} = q$, and $q'_{t_H} = q - r_{t_L}$. Consider two problems: one where all schools use the reserves-and-quotas rule for (R, Q), and the other where all schools use the reserves-and-quotas rule for (R', Q'). Then, all applicants weakly prefer the DA outcome in the first problem to that in the second one.*

As Theorem 8.35 suggests, in some scenarios low-income reserves are more desirable than high-income quotas. However, in general either rule may perform better or worse in terms of either applicant welfare or distributional outcomes.

8.5 Exercises

Exercise 8.1 Consider the school choice problem of Section 8.2. We say that the priorities $\succ_S$ are *acyclic* if there are no applicants $\{a_1, a_2, a_3\}$ and schools $\{s_1, s_2\}$ such that

$$a_1 \succ_{s_1} a_2 \succ_{s_1} a_3 \succ_{s_2} a_1.$$

Prove that priorities $\succ_S$ are acyclic if and only if

$$\mathrm{DA}(\succ_A) = \mathrm{TTC}(\succ_A) \text{ for all preferences } \succ_A.$$

Exercise 8.2 Prove that TTC is not minimally unstable in the class of efficient algorithms (Hint: you should consider using Theorem 8.4).

Exercise 8.3 Consider the model in Section 8.3.
- Let μ be a stable matching for the problem $(\succ_A, \succsim_S)$. Show that there is a tie-breaker profile τ such that μ is a stable matching for the problem $(\succ_A, \succsim_S^\tau)$.
- Prove Theorem 8.15.

Exercise 8.4 Prove the missing steps in Lemma 8.9.

Exercise 8.5 Prove Theorem 8.12.

Exercise 8.6 Prove Theorem 8.32.

8.6 Bibliographic Notes

The modeling of school choice as a two-sided matching model is due to [4]. The existence of a stable matching and the applicant-optimal stability of DA for substitutable choice rules satisfying the irrelevance of rejected applicants or law-of-aggregate-demand applicants (Theorem 8.22) are based on [16] and [8]. The incompatibility of stability and efficiency (Example 8.1) was shown in [21]. The discussion about welfare comparisons of DA and IA was based on [14] and [6]. The result that no efficient and DSIC algorithm Pareto-dominates DA (Theorem 8.4 and Corollary 8.5) and the EADA algorithm are due to [18]. The description of EADA that we used in the text was based on [24]. The minimal instability of EADA (Theorem 8.7) and TTC (Theorem 8.8) were shown in [20] and [5], respectively. In [9] it was shown that the latter result is robust to other and/or stronger notions of minimal instability.

Lemma 8.9 was given in [22]. The NP-completeness of the problem of verifying the existence of a stable and efficient matching (Theorem 8.10) and that no DSIC mechanism finds a stable and efficient matching whenever one exists (Theorem 8.12) are from [2]. The result that no DSIC algorithm is applicant-optimal stable (Theorem 8.13) and the SIC algorithm are due to [13]. That no DSIC algorithm Pareto-dominates DA with any tie-breaker is form [7]. The result that every applicant-optimal stable matching can be achieved by DA with some single tie-breaker (Theorem 8.15) has been independently highlighted by [11], [12], and [7].

The controlled school choice model and the quotas rule were introduced in [4]. The DSIC property of the quotas rule is due to [1], and is also implied in [16]. The reserves rule and its DSIC property are due to [15]. Characterizations of the reserves rule and the quotas rule were given in [10]. The characterization of reserves-and-quotas rule as the unique reserves- and quotas-respecting, non-wasteful, within-type priority-compatible, and across-type priority-compatible reserve-and-quotas rule (Theorem 8.32, parts 1–4) is due to [17]. The characterizations of the reserves-and-quotas rule as the unique maximal-violations and maximal-priority rules in their respective classes (Theorem 8.32, parts 1–3) is by [3]. A related priority maximality result for the reserves rule was given in [23] for a setting with multidimensional types. Example 8.34 is from [19]. The superior welfare properties of the reserves rule over the quotas rule for two types (Theorem 8.35) are from [15].

References

[1] Abdulkadiroğlu, Atila. 2005. College admission with affirmative action. *International Journal of Game Theory*, **33**, 535–549.

[2] Abdulkadiroğlu, Atila, and Grigoryan, Aram. 2020. *Efficient and envy minimal matching*. Working Paper.

[3] Abdulkadiroğlu, Atila, and Grigoryan, Aram. 2021. *Priority-based assignment with reserves and quotas*. National Bureau of Economic Research, Working Paper w28689.

[4] Abdulkadiroğlu, Atila, and Sönmez, Tayfun. 2003. School choice: A mechanism design approach. *American Economic Review*, **93**(3), 729–747.

[5] Abdulkadiroğlu, Atila, Che, Yeon-Koo, Pathak, Parag, Roth, Alvin, and Tercieux, Olivier. 2020. Efficiency, justified envy, and incentives in priority-based matching. *American Economic Review: Insights*.

[6] Abdulkadiroğlu, Atila, Che, Yeon-Koo, and Yasuda, Yosuke. 2011. Resolving conflicting preferences in school choice: The "Boston" Mechanism reconsidered. *American Economic Review*, **101(1)**, 399–410.

[7] Abdulkadiroğlu, Atila, Pathak, Parag A., and Roth, Alvin E. 2009. Strategy-proofness versus efficiency in matching with indifferences: Redesigning the New York City High School match. *American Economic Review*, **99(5)**, 1954–1978.

[8] Aygün, Orhan, and Sönmez, Tayfun. 2013. Matching with contracts: Comment. *American Economic Review*, **103**(5), 2050–2051.

[9] Doğan, Battal, and Ehlers, Lars. 2020. *Robust minimal instability of the top trading cycles mechanism*. Working Paper.

[10] Echenique, Federico, and Yenmez, Bumin M. 2015. How to control controlled school choice. *American Economic Review*, **105**(8), 2679–2694.

[11] Ehlers, Lars. 2006. *Respecting priorities when assigning students to schools*. Working Paper.

[12] Erdil, Aytek. 2006. *Two-sided matching with ties*. PhD dissertation.

[13] Erdil, Aytek, and Ergin, Haluk. 2008. What's the matter with tie-breaking? Improving efficiency in school choice. *American Economic Review*, **98**, 669–689.

[14] Ergin, Haluk, and Sönmez, Tayfun. 2006. Games of school choice under the Boston Mechanism. *Journal of Public Economics*, **90**, 215–237.

[15] Hafalir, Isa E., Yenmez, M. Bumin, and Yildirim, Muhammed A. 2013. Effective affirmative action in school choice. *Theoretical Economics*, **8**(2), 325–363.

[16] Hatfield, John William, and Milgrom, Paul. 2005. Matching with contracts. *American Economic Review*, **95**, 913–935.

[17] Imamura, Kenzo. 2020. Meritocracy versus diversity. Working Paper.

[18] Kesten, Onur. 2010. School choice with consent. *Quarterly Journal of Economics*.

[19] Kojima, Fuhito. 2012. School choice: Impossibilities for Affirmative action. *Game and Economic Behavior*, **75**(2), 685–693.

[20] Kwon, Hyukjun, and Shorrer, Ran I. 2020. *Justified-envy-minimal efficient mechanisms for priority-based matching*. Working Paper.

[21] Roth, Alvin E. 1982. The economics of matching: Stability and incentives. *Mathematics of Operations Research*, **7**, 617–628.

[22] Saban, Daniela, and Sethuraman, Jay. 2015. The complexity of computing the random priority allocation matrix. *Mathematics of Operations Research*, **40**(4), 1005–1014.

[23] Sönmez, Tayfun, and Yenmez, Bumin M. 2021. *Affirmative action in India via vertical, horizontal, and overlapping reservations*. Working Paper.

[24] Tang, Qianfeng, and Yu, Jingsheng. 2014. A new perspective on Kesten's school choice with consent idea. *Journal of Economic Theory*, **154**, 543–561.

CHAPTER NINE

Kidney Exchange

Itai Ashlagi

9.1 Introduction

Transplantation is the treatment of choice for patients with end-stage renal disease (ESRD), which is a leading cause of death. No country has enough kidneys for transplants and the shortage around the world is only growing. At the beginning of 2020 there were about 100,000 ESRD patients on the deceased-donor waiting list in the USA and the waiting time was, on average more than 3.5 years. Other than improving health quality, transplantation also saves a few hundred thousand dollars over a patient's remaining on dialysis.

While efforts are under way to increase the availability of deceased-donor kidneys, another source of donation is living donors, since a healthy person who has two kidneys can remain healthy with one kidney. However, living donors are often either blood-type (ABO) or tissue-type incompatible with the person to whom they wish to donate. At the same time it is against the law almost everywhere in the world to pay a living donor to donate a kidney.[1] Kidney exchange (KE) arose as a barter economy for swapping kidneys between incompatible patient–donor pairs.

An example for an exchange between two incompatible pairs (R1, D1) and (R2, D2) is given in Figure 9.1. Thus D1 is ABO-incompatible with P1 and D2 is ABO-incompatible with P2. But there is a possibility of an exchange, as P1 is compatible with D1 and P2 is compatible with D2 (assuming they are also tissue-type compatible).

The first kidney exchange took place in Korea in 1991. Until 2003, few exchanges took place in the USA, but in 2020 the number of transplants from kidney exchanges

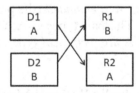

Figure 9.1 Two-way exchange between two incompatible pairs (R1, D1) and (R2, D2).

[1] The only exception is Iran, where there is a legal monetary market.

in the USA reached more than 1000, more than 15% of which were live donor transplants.

There are numerous kidney exchange programs around the world arranging exchanges between incompatible pairs. This chapter provides only a basic overview to the development, design, and frictions in kidney exchange. For detailed surveys and a variety of topics that have been omitted from this text see [7], [11], and [25].

9.2 Preliminaries: The Exchange Pool

In an *exchange pool* there is a set of incompatible patient–donor pairs and, possibly, some non-directed donors (NDDs), who have no intended recipient. Denote the set of pairs by V, which induces a *compatibility graph* $D_V = (V, E)$, with edge set E. In this graph, of which the set of nodes is V, there is a directed link from node v to node u if the donor at node v is compatible with the patient at node u (assuming u is in an incompatible pair).

There are two types of exchange. A *cyclic* exchange is a cycle that includes distinct nodes in the graph D_V (involving only incompatible pairs). We refer to such a cycle of length k as a k-way cycle. A *chain* is a path that begins with an NDD and involves distinct nodes. The length of the chain is the number of edges in the path. An allocation is a set of disjoint exchanges. We say that a node v is matched in a given allocation if there exists an exchange in the allocation that includes v. Each patient that belongs to an exchange in the allocation is said to be matched to the node that precedes it in that exchange.

Medical compatibilities. For a donor to be compatible with a patient it must be the case that they are (i) ABO compatible and (ii) tissue-type compatible. ABO compatibility means that the patient cannot receive a kidney from a donor who has a blood antigen (A or B) that the patient does not have. So, an O donor is ABO compatible with any patient whereas an O patient can receive a kidney only from an O donor but an AB patient can receive a kidney from any donor.

In addition to blood antigens, each donor has human leukocyte antigens (HLA). A patient is tissue-type compatible with the donor if she has no antibodies to the donor's antigens. This type of compatibility is verified using a *crossmatch* test.

Pair types. The compatibility structure naturally classifies pairs on the basis of their difficulty to match. It will be convenient to refer to pairs by their blood types. For example, an A–B patient–donor pair is one in which the patient has blood type A and the donor has blood type B. An exchange pool is likely to have fewer A-O pairs than O-A pairs because A-O pairs are often compatible (since they are ABO compatible) and choose to go through a direct live-donor transplant. So A-O, AB-O, B-O, AB-B, and AB-A types are *overdemanded* (the patient is ABO-compatible with the donor, but not vice versa). The pair types O-A, O-B, O-AB, A-AB, and B-AB are *underdemanded*, A-B and B-A are *reciprocal* types, and O-O, A-A, B-B, and A-A are *self-demanded* types.

9.3 Individually Rational Mechanisms

This section describes early proposals for mechanisms that account for pairs' preferences. In particular it is assumed a pair $v = (p, d)$ has a preference $\succeq_v$ over all other nodes in the pool for which their donor is compatible with p; this can be thought of as an ordering over the donor from which the pair prefers to receive a transplant. Throughout this section we will assume for simplicity that that the pool consists only of incompatible pairs. This section is based on [20] and [21].

9.3.1 General Preferences

An early proposal for organizing exchanges was to apply the Top Trading Cycles (TTC) algorithm [24], which was described originally to solve the following house-allocation problem. There are n agents each of which is initially endowed with one house. Every agent in the market has a strict preference ranking over acceptable houses, including their own, and monetary transfers are not allowed.[2]

In kidney exchange an incompatible patient–donor pair can be thought of an agent and her house. Suppose that the preference order $\succeq_v$ for each pair $v = (p, d)$ is strict. Applying TTC to a pool of incompatible patient–donor pairs works as follows.

Top trading cycles for incompatible pairs.

1. Each patient–donor pair indicates its most preferred pair in the pool (the one from which they would most like to receive a kidney).
2. A search is made for a cycle in the induced directed graph. If a cycle does not exist, terminate.
3. Otherwise, each patient in the cycle is matched with the donor to which she points and all pairs in the cycle are removed from the pool. Return to the first step.

The following lemma follows from the properties of the TTC mechanism.

Lemma 9.1 [20]. *The set of exchanges resulting from the TTC algorithm is Pareto efficient. Moreover, the mechanism that elicits pairs' preferences and runs the TTC algorithm is strategy-proof.*

Observe that the TTC algorithm may find an exchange that involves many incompatible pairs. This creates a real challenge from adopting this algorithm in practice, for the following reasons.

1. Cyclic exchanges are typically done *simultaneously* so that every incompatible pair donates a kidney no later than receiving a kidney. Consider for example a two-way exchange between two incompatible pairs, as in Figure 9.1 and suppose that P1 has already received a kidney from D2. However, D1 may renege or become too sick to donate, leaving P1 without an intended donor.
2. Arranging a large exchange simultaneously is logistically complicated. For example, an exchange with three pairs involves six surgical teams and and six operating rooms. So in practice exchanges are typically limited to at most two or three pairs.

---

[2] The TTC algorithm finds a Pareto efficient allocation that is also a Pareto improvement to the initial allocation.

9.3.2 Binary Preferences

Eliciting strict preference rankings is typically not practiced. Instead programs often often ask pairs (or their surgeons) to indicate which compatible donors they find acceptable. Let us consider such preferences and assume in this section that cycles are restricted to exactly two pairs.

Consider an exchange pool and let E_v be the set of directed links in the graph which point to v. So this set includes the nodes which have a donor who is compatible with v.

The mechanism described here requires a priority order over nodes. A priority order ρ is an indexing of the n nodes $1, 2, \ldots, n$ such that the smaller the index, the higher the priority.

Two-way priority mechanism.

1. Each pair v reports a subset $Q_v \subset E_v$ that she finds acceptable.
2. Construct the graph $G = (V, \cup_v Q_v)$. Let $\mathcal{M}$ be the set of allocations that consist of two-way cycles and that match the maximum number of nodes in G.
3. Select the allocations in $\mathcal{M}$ lexicographically with respect to the given priority order.

Observe that selecting an allocation of two-way cycles in G (step 2) is equivalent to selecting a matching in a non-directed graph in which there is a link between u and v, if and only if there is a link from u to v and a link from v to u. It is well known from graph theory that all maximal allocations (of two-way cycles) have the same number of cycles.

Selecting an arbitrary allocation in $\mathcal{M}$ after the second step may result in scenarios where some pairs may benefit from misreporting. Consistency with the priority order ensures incentive compatibility:

Lemma 9.2 [21]. *The two-way priority mechanism is strategy-proof and Pareto efficient.*

9.4 Market Thickness in Static Exchange Pools

The feasible types of exchanges are tightly related to the number of transplants that can be arranged. And conversely the thickness of the market also impacts the desired types of exchange. This section explores this relation in static pools.

One concern is that large cyclic exchanges are impractical especially when multiple hospitals are involved. We begin with exploring the loss that follows from limiting the cycle length in a large typical pool. Suppose that a patient p who is ABO compatible with the blood of a donor d has a probability q of being tissue-type compatible with that donor (in practice q may depend on the sensitivity of the patient, but this will not be important for our purposes).

We will apply the following classic result from random graph theory by Erdos and Renyi to study large pools.[3]

Lemma 9.3 (Erdos–Renyi). *Consider a bipartite graph with n nodes on one side and αn nodes on the other side, for some $\alpha \geq 1$. Moreover there is a non-directed*

---

[3] Versions of this lemma are also given in Chapters 16 and 18 on large-market and dynamic matching.

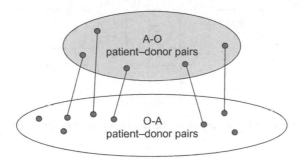

Figure 9.2 A-O and O-A patient–donor pairs. In a large pool all A-O pairs are matched in an efficient allocation with O-A pairs.

edge between every two nodes on opposite sides independently with probability at least $\log n/n$. Then the probability that there exist a perfect matching (a matching of n nodes on each side) converges to 1 as n grows large.

As a first exercise for applying the lemma suppose that the pool consists of n O–O patient–donor pairs. So every patient and every donor has blood type O. As n grows large, the Erdos–Renyi lemma implies that all but at most one pair can be matched with high probability using two-way cycles (simply having half the pairs on each side).

Consider next the set of A-O and O-A patient–donor pairs in the pool and assume that there are n O-A pairs and γn A-O pairs ($\gamma < 1$). Note that A-O pairs can potentially match in two ways with each other and with O-A pairs, while O-A pairs can potentially match only with other A-O pairs. Intuitively, when the graph is large, it is inefficient to match A-O pairs with each other. Indeed, the Erdos–Renyi lemma implies that for large n there is an allocation with n two-way cycles in which every A-O pair is matched with a different O-A pair (see Figure 9.2).

One can expand this analysis to large random exchange pools. To create such a random pool, first generate n incompatible pairs as follows: using the ABO blood-type distribution in the population create a patient–donor pair and add the pair to the pool if they are either ABO incompatible or tissue-type incompatible. Then generate directed links between every pairs if the patient of one pair and the donor of the other pair are ABO and tissue-type compatible with each other.

Lemma 9.4 [7, 22]. *Consider a large random exchange pool with n incompatible pairs. As n grows large, with high probability there exists an efficient allocation that requires cycles of no more than size 3 with the following properties:*

1. *Every self-demanded pair X-X is matched in a two-way or a three-way exchange with other self-demanded pairs (no more than one three-way exchange is needed, in the case of an odd number of X-X pairs).*
2. *Either every B-A pair is matched in a two-way exchange with an A-B pair or every A-B pair is matched in a two-way exchange with a B-A pair.*
3. *Let $X, Y \in \{A, B\}$ and $X \neq Y$. If there are more Y-X pairs than X-Y pairs then every Y-X pair that is not matched with an X-Y pair is matched in a three-way exchange with an O-Y pair and an X-O pair.*

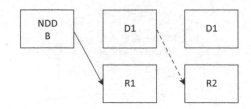

Figure 9.3 Two-way chain initiated by an non-directed donor.

4. *Every AB-O pair is matched in a three-way exchange with an O-A pair and an A-AB pair.*
5. *Every overdemanded pair X-Y that is not matched as above is matched with an an underdemanded Y-X pair.*

The lemma implies that, in large exchange pools, there is no harm from restricting the cycle length to be at most 3. This is directly connected to the ABO compatibility structure. When only two-way cycles are allowed there is still some loss. The reason stems from the likely imbalance between the number of A-B and B-A pairs in the pool. If A-B pairs are in larger supply, then each of the remaining pairs (that does not match a B-A pair in a two-way cycle) can match in a three-way cycle with an O-A pair and a B-O pair.

However, in practice pools are not sufficiently large and therefore tissue-type incompatibilities play an important role. Even at the US National Kidney Registry, the largest exchange program, for about 7% of the O transplanted organs the recipient is a non-O patient (despite the scarcity of O donors).

One strategy for increasing the size of pools is to bring in more easy-to-match pairs. One such type of pairs is compatible pairs. Such pairs, which can go through a direct living transplant, can benefit from kidney exchange by finding a a better kidney (such as one from a younger donor or one that has a better HLA match). Compatible pairs increase the supply of O donors and may also help to match highly sensitized patients. In Section 9.6 we discuss how to increase the market thickness that arises due to free-riding behavior by hospitals that match internally easy-to-match pairs.

Another strategy that is responsible for a large fraction of kidney exchange transplants in the USA uses chains. Each non-directed donor can initiate a chain and does not expect to receive a kidney in return. So one can organize chains sequentially and non-simultaneously, while enssuring that a pair does not donate a kidney before receiving a kidney. So, if a link is broken, the pair that was supposed to receive a kidney can still participate in a future match (Figure 9.3).

In a sparse pool, it is intuitive that two-way cycles between two O-O pairs with a highly sensitized patient may not be very common. We return in Section 9.7 to illustrate the advantage of chains in a dynamic evolving exchange pool.

9.5 Optimization

Kidney exchange programs usually adopt optimization algorithms to find matches using cycles and chains within their pool. The static optimization problem is to maximize the weighted number of transplants using disjoint feasible cycles and chains.

Weights capture the weak priorities of the program. This problem is NP-complete [1] even without chains.[4]

Consider the compatibility graph $G = (V, E)$. The set V can be partitioned into nodes P, consisting of patient–donor pairs, and nodes N, consisting of NDDs. Let w_e be the weight on the directed edge e and for each exchange (chain or cycle) C let w_C be the sum of the weights of the edges in that exchange. Let $\mathcal{C}_k$ be the set of cycles with at most k edges and $\mathcal{C}h_j$ the set of chains with at most j edges. (By adding a directed edge from each pair to each NDD, chains can be viewed as cycles that include an NDD.) Let $\mathcal{C}_k(v)$ and $\mathcal{C}h_j(v)$ be the subsets of cycles and chains that contain node v, respectively. A simple formulation that allows cycles of length at most k and chains of length at most j is:

$$\max \sum_{C \in \mathcal{C}_k \cup \mathcal{C}h_j} w_C z_C$$

$$\text{s.t.} \sum_{C \in \mathcal{C}_k(v)} z_C + \sum_{C \in \mathcal{C}h_j(v)} z_C \leq 1 \quad v \subset V,$$

$$z_C \in \{0, 1\} \quad C \in \mathcal{C}_k \cup \mathcal{C}h_j.$$

In small pools this formulation can usually be solved directly by an optimization solver. For larger pools, one may run into computational challenges, and researchers have developed several algorithms based on different formulations (such as flows) and optimization techniques (using column generation, constraint generation, etc.). See [7] for more details and references and [11] for a survey about optimization practices in European countries.

Typically, instances can be solved using simple algorithms, since pools in the steady state are usually sparse with many hard-to-match pairs. Moreover, we note that a pool that is large and dense probably indicates flaws in the matching process. However, optimization helps to ensure the prioritizing of highly sensitized patients and to avoid inefficient matches.

9.6 Collaboration and Free Riding

Multi-hospital (or national) exchange programs create another game. Hospitals may have the option of deciding whether to submit a pair to the program or to match it internally. This free riding behavior can harm efficiency and the chance of matching some more difficult pairs. Similar challenges arise between countries that attempt to establish collaborations.

9.6.1 Impossibility Results

Consider an exchange pool with with incompatible pairs and let k be the largest feasible cycle size. There is also a finite set of hospitals H. Assume that each pair is associated with a single hospital $h \in H$ and denote the set of pairs of each hospital h by V_h. An exchange that matches only pairs at hospital h is called an *internal* exchange.

---

[4] The problem can be solved in polynomial time in two cases: if all exchanges are limited to size 2 this becomes a maximum matching problem, or if the chains and cycles are of an unbounded size this becomes a maximum-flow problem.

Given an allocation (a set of disjoint exchanges) M and a set of nodes V', let $M(V')$ be the subset of nodes in V' matched by M. An allocation M in the graph induced by $V = \cup_h V_h$ is not *individually rational* if there exists a hospital h and an allocation M_h in the graph induced by V_h such that $|M(V_h)| < |M_h(V_h)|$.

A simple example illustrates the tension between individual rationality (IR) and efficiency when $k > 2$.

Example 9.5. Consider two hospitals h_1 and h_2. Hospital h_1 has two pairs a_1 and a_2 which it can match internally in a two-way cycle. Hospital h_2 has two pairs b_1 and b_2 that cannot be matched internally but can be part of a three-way cycle together with a_1. The three-way cycle is the only efficient allocation, but it is not individually rational since only one pair is matched for hospital 1.

The following shows that there is no trade off between individual rationality and efficiency when $k = 2$.

Claim 9.6. *If $k = 2$ there is an efficient allocation that is individually rational.*

The proof follows directly from using an alternating path algorithm for finding a maximum matching in the non-directed graph induced by all two-way cycles (beginning with an internal allocation at each hospital of maximum cardinality).

Consider next the following class of mechanisms. First the mechanism elicits from hospitals a subset of its pairs. Second, the mechanism selects an allocation in the graph induced by the set of reported pairs. The utility of the hospital is the number of its pairs matched by the mechanism plus the number of pairs it matches internally in the internal graph induced by the set of pairs that the hospital withholds.

Proposition 9.7 [23]. *Suppose $k = 2$. Then no IR mechanism is both efficient and strategy-proof.*

Proof Suppose the compatibility graph is the one given by Figure 9.4. There are two hospitals a and b. The white nodes are associated with hospital a and the black nodes with hospital b.

Observe that every efficient allocation leaves one node unmatched. There are two cases. First suppose that when both hospitals submit all their nodes only two of hospital b's nodes are matched. In this case hospital b is better off withholding pairs b_2 and b_3 and matching them internally; note that in this case b_1 is matched in the maximum allocation by the mechanism. In the other case, when both hospitals submit all their nodes, one of hospital a's nodes remains

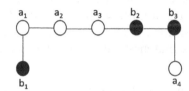

Figure 9.4

unmatched. A similar argument shows that in this case hospital a is better off withholding internally nodes a_1 and a_2. $\qquad\square$

The impossibility result uses a stylized example which may be representative (and hospitals may not be able to guess which pairs to withhold without the entire graph). However, the structure of kidney exchange pools is helpful to better understand this game and redesign it. Hospitals struggle to match their hard-to-match pairs (underdemanded pairs as well as pairs with very highly sensitized patients). In particular, they are more likely to match internally easy-to-match pairs. We use this intuition next as we approach the problem using classic economic theory to analyze an exchange program as producer of transplants. The following subsection is based on [2].

9.6.2 A Point System

Consider a a kidney exchange as a platform that elicits submission from hospitals and rewards hospitals with transplants. The are I types of submission, and let $\mathbf{q} = (q_i)_i = 1, \ldots, I$ be the quantities of each submitted type. The productivity of the platform, or how many transplants it can generate, is given by a production function $f(\mathbf{q})$.

The function f satisfies constant returns to scale at $\mathbf{q}$ if its elasticity with respect to scale $\mathbf{q}$ equals 1. This implies that $\nabla f(\mathbf{q}) \cdot \mathbf{q} = f(\mathbf{q})$.

Hospitals will re rewarded for these submissions by the platform with transplants. Rewards are assumed to be linear in submissions and anonymous, so there is a vector $\mathbf{p} = (p_i)_{i \in I}$ indicating the expected number of transplants awarded to the hospital per submission i. A hospital h that submits a vector of submissions $\mathbf{q}^h$ receives $\mathbf{pq}^h$ transplants. All generated transplants are allocated to hospitals.

Assume that every hospital h has some cost $C^h(\mathbf{q}^h)$ for submitting $\mathbf{q}^h$, which, for example, can be interpreted as the number of internal transplants that the hospital forgoes in order to submit $\mathbf{q}^h$. The utility of the hospital is the number of transplants it receives from the platform minus its cost. Hospital welfare is defined by

$$W(\mathbf{q}^1, \mathbf{q}^2, \ldots, \mathbf{q}^H) = f\left(\sum_h \mathbf{q}^h\right) - \sum_h C^h(\mathbf{q}^h). \tag{9.1}$$

Given a rewards vector $\mathbf{p}$, a hospital should be able to decide what to supply to the platform, that is

$$\mathbf{S}^h(\mathbf{p}) = \arg\max_{\mathbf{q}} \mathbf{pq}^h - C^h(\mathbf{q}^h). \tag{9.2}$$

The following result provides the optimal reward vectors.

Lemma 9.8 [2].   *Consider a vector of rewards p and an allocation $(q^h)_{h \in H}$ that maximizes hospital welfare subject to all hospitals supplying optimally $q^h \in S^h$ and subject to $f(q) = p \cdot q$. Then the platform rewards each type of submission with its marginal product minus some adjustment term that depends on the elasticity of supply:*

$$p = \nabla f(q) - A(q). \tag{9.3}$$

If in addition f has a constant return to scale at q, then $p = \nabla f(q)$ and the allocation maximizes hospital welfare.

The lemma states that hospitals should be rewarded approximately with their marginal contribution to the platform. The main challenge is the constraint that requires that the total reward that the platforms allocates equals the number of transplants. When f has a constant return to scale, the adjustment term is zero and the platform rewards marginal products exactly equally. But otherwise the platform must shade the rewards.

The lemma has several implications. A platform that simply attempts to find maximum matchings without accounting for the supply from each hospital creates opportunity for free riding. Consider an extreme example in which 1 hospital has only underdemanded pairs and another has both underdemanded and overdemanded pairs. If the platform does not account for the marginal contribution, the second hospital may end up not enrolling overdemanded pairs to the platform.

The lemma further states that, when exhibiting constant returns to scale, hospital welfare can then be maximized with linear rewards. One way to apply this result in practice is using a *point system*. So after each submission the hospital will be credited with points equal to the marginal product of that submission, a point is subtracted after each transplant.

The model analyzed here can be viewed as a steady-state or static model. An interesting open question is the dynamic marketplace induced by such a point system. Intuitively, the points of each hospital should not diverge much, and so a classic folk theorem suggest that the point system may prevent free riding and sustain cooperation between hospitals.

Another approach to handle free riding is using allocations that are based on the Shapley value [10], or mechanisms that use optimization with fairness constraints [18].

9.7 Dynamic Matching

Kidney exchange pools are dynamic with, pairs arriving and being matched over time. Matching pairs fast may reduce waiting times but also may reduce match opportunities by thinning the market. To illustrate this, consider an exchange pool that today has pairs a,b,c and feasible two-way cycles (a, b) and (b, c). Suppose that on the next day pair d arrives and cycle (c, d) becomes feasible. Waiting for d can result in matching all four pairs by the selection of cycles (a, b) and (c, d). However, a greedy policy that selects (b, d) today will leave a and d unmatched tomorrow.

An analysis for dynamic matching in kidney exchange pools when compatibility is based on blood types was given in [26]. The characterization is similar to that for the static large market model. This section focuses on dynamic matching policies when tissue types play an important role.

9.7.1 Matching in Sparse Pools

Consider an infinite-horizon model in which at every period $t = 0, 1, 2, \ldots$ a single pair arrives. Further assume that in the first period there is an altruistic donor in the pool. Assume that every donor in the pool can donate to any other patient independently with probability p and that patients are indifferent between donors with whom they are compatible. Patients and donors leave the pool only when they match. This model abstracts away from blood types and helps to illustrate the need for larger cycles of chains.

The *waiting time* of a patient is the time at which she is matched minus her arrival time. Matching policies will be evaluated by the average waiting time over patients. We compare policies in which agents can match through two-way cycles with policies that match agents through a chain.

By Little's law, since the arrival rate is one pair per period, the average waiting time corresponds to the average number of pairs in the pool, over a long horizon at the steady state. So, given the fixed arrival rate, fewer pairs in the system implies that pairs match faster.

A *greedy* policy matches a pair whenever it becomes possible. When only two-way cycles are feasible, the greedy policy forms a cycle immediately it becomes possible to do so, and the two pairs in the cycle are removed from the pool (so that after such a cycle is formed the pool has no other cycles). In the case of a chain, assume that the chain is initiated with the NDD donor, and once the last donor in the chain has a compatible unmatched patient, we randomly pick one of its neighboring compatible patients. Assume that matches that are formed occur instantaneously.

The following results analyze the performance of matching policies in the regime in which $p \to 0$.

Lemma 9.9 [5]. *Assume only two-way cycles are feasible. The greedy policy achieves a waiting time of $(\ln 2)/p^2$. Moreover, the average waiting time under any policy is at least $(\ln 2)/p^2$.*

Proof We sketch how to establish the lower bound. In the steady state, the arrival rate equals the departure rate. So any policy should remove, on average, a cycle every two periods. As a result, an arriving pair should form a two-way cycle with some existing node, with probability at least one half, on average. Therefore the probability of forming some two-way cycle is exactly $1 - (1 - p^2)^{|V(t)|}$ where $V(t)$ is the set of pairs in the pool at time t. This implies a lower bound of $(\ln 2)/p^2$ on the expected number of pairs in the system under any policy in the steady state.

We can provide some intuition for the waiting time under the greedy policy. The number of pairs in the pool under the greedy policy behaves as a random walk, with a downward step occurring exactly when the new pair forms a twoway cycle. So the random walk has a negative drift when the probability of the new pair forming a cycle with an existing pair exceeds one half even by just a little. This ensures that the number of pairs in the pool does not grow much beyond the minimum level needed to ensure that new arrivals form two-way cycles with probability of at least one half, and so the performance of the greedy policy closely matches the lower bound. $\square$

Lemma 9.10 [7, 12]. *Assume that matches are made through a (never-ending) chain. The greedy policy achieves an average waiting time of $O((1/p)\log(1/p))$.*

The idea behind this lemma is that when the number of pairs in the pool is large enough, and in particular of the order $O((1/p)\log(1/p))$ a new chain match will form and will match (at once) a large fraction of these pairs – this can be shown by using random walks on directed random graph. An elegant and very simple analysis of this theorem is given in [12].

Together Lemmas 9.9 and 9.10 illustrate that chains improve waiting times in sparse pools. The interested reader can find in the above-cited papers an analysis of settings with more altruistic donors or other matching policies.

Kidney exchange pools typically include both low and highly sensitized patients, who differ substantially in their chances to be tissue-type compatible with a random donor. A simple extension of the model above is to have two types of pairs with low (L) and highly sensitized (S) patients (still assuming no ABO incompatibility). The former have incoming match probability p_L and the latter an incoming match probability p. Assume further that each type arrives according to a Poisson process with a fixed positive arrival rate. The following states that two-way matching is sufficient only if the chain is sufficiently thick.

Lemma 9.11 [8]. *Assume p_L is constant and $p \to 0$. If L pairs arrive faster than S pairs, greedy two-way matching or greedy chain matching each yield an average waiting time of $O(1/p)$. Otherwise, the average waiting time under two-way matching is $O(1/p^2)$.*

Matching through a chain creates chain segments, each of which ends when the last pair in the chain cannot match anyone in the pool. A new segment begins when a new pair arrives to which the last pair in the previous segment can connect. When S pairs arrive more frequently than L pairs, S pairs accumulate in the pool and L pairs are those that trigger and initiate chain segments. Moreover, the larger the arrival rate of L pairs, the shorter the chain segments [8].

The models above assume that agents do not depart the pool without a match. In [3] this important assumption was considered and the value from knowing the departure times was studied. Suppose agent becomes *critical* after some time (independently drawn) after which she leaves the pool immediately. We say that the *loss ratio* of a policy is the chance that an agent is not matched under that policy.

Lemma 9.12 [3]. *Suppose there is a single agent type with match probability p and two-way cycles and assume that the critical times are observable. The loss ratio between matching agents when they become critical and matching greedily vanishes as $p \to 0$.*

For further optimization approaches based on dynamic programming see [14], [15].

9.7.2 Waiting and Matching in Unbalanced Pools

Consider an infinite-horizon model with two types of pairs (or agents), H and E and assume agents can match only via two-way cycles. Every H agent can form a match (a two-way cycle) with every E agent in the pool independently with probability p. Every E agent can also form a match with any other E agent independently with probability q.[5]

---

[5] This model can be thought of a pool with underdemanded and overdemanded pairs (say A–O and O–A pairs).

The E agents arrive at the pool according to a Poisson process with rate m, and the H agents arrive at the pool according to an independent Poisson process with rate $(1 + \lambda)m$, where $\lambda > 0$. An agent that arrives at the pool at time t becomes *critical* after Z units of time in the market, where Z is distributed exponentially with mean d, independently between agents. We refer to $1/d$ as the *criticality rate*. The latest time that an agent can match is the time she becomes critical, $t + Z$ (after which the agent leaves the pool unmatched).

A matching policy selects at any time t a matching (a set of disjoint two-way cycles) in the pool. A greedy policy is defined similar to the previous subsection. We evaluate a policy by measuring (i) the match rate for each type, which is the fraction of agents of that type that get matched, and (ii) the average waiting time of agents of each type.

In contrast with the previous section, we fix the matching probabilities, p and q, and study the pool as it grows large.

A policy is *asymptotically optimal* if for every $\epsilon > 0$ there exists m_ϵ such that, when $m \geq m_\epsilon$, *no* type of agent can improve its match rate $q_\Theta(m)$ or expected waiting time $w_\Theta(m)$ by more than ϵ when changing to any other policy. We now consider batching policies.

Lemma 9.13 [9]. *A batching policy with batch length T achieves match rates of*

$$(q_H^B, q_E^B) = \left(\frac{1 - e^{-T/d}}{(1 + \lambda)T/d}, \frac{1 - e^{-T/d}}{T/d} \right).$$

In particular a batching policy is not asymptotically optimal.

Many kidney exchange programs execute matching periodically; these programs differ in their period length. A *batching policy* executes a maximal match every T units of time. When there are multiple maximal matches, the policy selects randomly one that maximizes the number of matched H agents. The parameter T is called the batch length.

Lemma 9.14 [9]. *The greedy policy is asymptotically optimal. Moreover, as the arrival rate m grows large the match rates of hard- and easy-to-match pairs under the greedy policy are $(1/(1 + \lambda), 1)$, respectively, and their expected waiting times are $(w_H^G, w_E^G) = (\lambda d/(1 + \lambda), 0)$.*

With more H than E pairs, many H pairs will accumulate under any policy. So a greedy policy will match an E agent upon arrival with an H agent, with high probability. Under a batching policy an arriving agent has to wait until the next time a match is identified. So the average waiting time is at least half the batch length. Moreover, some agents, including E agents, become critical during this time, resulting in a suboptimal match rate.

A key assumption made in this section was that the planner attempts to maximize the number of transplants and minimize waiting times. But matches have heterogeneous values (e.g., life years from a transplant) and in such situations non-greedy algorithms may play an important role.

9.8 Bibliographic Notes

This chapter has offered a brief introduction to kidney exchange but has omitted several exciting challenges. One is match failures; the medical data only helps to verify virtual compatibility and a crossmatch test is still required to verify compatibility. Researchers have adopted numerous algorithmic approaches to address this challenge (e.g., [12, 16, 17, 29]). Another topic of growing interest is relaxing the requirement of simultaneity by allowing donors to donate before their intended patient receives a kidney [3, 27, 28]. Finally, still in its infancy is the innovation of global kidney exchange [19], which seeks to organize exchanges between wealthy countries and middle income countries with financial barriers to transplantation.

References

[1] Abraham, David J., Blum, Avrim, and Sandholm, Tuomas. 2007. Clearing algorithms for barter exchange markets: Enabling nationwide kidney exchanges. Pages 295–304 of: *Proc. 8th ACM Conference on Electronic Commerce*. ACM.

[2] Agarwal, Nikhil, Ashlagi, Itai, Azevedo, Eduardo, Featherstone, Clayton R., and Karaduman, Ömer. 2019. Market failure in kidney exchange. *American Economic Review*, **109**(11), 4026–70.

[3] Akbarpour, Mohammad, Combe, Julien, He, Yinghua, Hiller, Victor, Shimer, Robert, and Tercieux, Olivier. 2020. Unpaired kidney exchange: Overcoming double coincidence of wants without money. Pages 465–466 of: *Proc. 21st ACM Conference on Economics and Computation*. ACM.

[4] Akbarpour, Mohammad, Li, Shengwu, and Gharan, Shayan Oveis. 2020. Thickness and information in dynamic matching markets. *Journal of Political Economy*, **128**(3), 000–000.

[5] Anderson, Ross, Ashlagi, Itai, Gamarnik, David, and Kanoria, Yash. 2017. Efficient dynamic barter exchange. *Operations Research*, **65**(6), 1446–1459.

[6] Ashlagi, Itai, and Roth, Alvin E. 2014. Free riding and participation in large scale, multi-hospital kidney exchange. *Theoretical Economics*, **9**(3), 817–863.

[7] Ashlagi, Itai, and Roth, Alvin E. 2021. Kidney exchange: An operations perspective. *Management Science*. forthcoming.

[8] Ashlagi, Itai, Burq, Maximilien, Jaillet, Patrick, and Manshadi, Vahideh. 2019. On matching and thickness in heterogeneous dynamic markets. *Operations Research*, **67**(4), 927–949.

[9] Ashlagi, Itai, Nikzad, Afshin, and Strack, Philipp. 2019. Matching in dynamic imbalanced markets. Available at SSRN 3251632.

[10] Biró, Péter, Kern, Walter, Pálvölgyi, Dömötör, and Paulusma, Daniel. 2019. Generalized matching games for international kidney exchange. https://dl.acm.org/doi/10.5555/3306127.3331721.

[11] Biró, Péter, van de Klundert, Joris, Manlove, David, Pettersson, William, Andersson, Tommy, Burnapp, Lisa, Chromy, Pavel, Delgado, Pablo, Dworczak, Piotr, Haase, Bernadette, et al. 2019. Modelling and optimisation in European kidney exchange programmes. *European Journal of Operational Research*. www.sciencedirect.com/science/article/pii/S0377221719307441.

[12] Blum, Avrim, and Mansour, Yishay. 2020. Kidney exchange and endless paths: on the optimal use of an altruistic donor. Working Paper.

[13] Blum, Avrim, Gupta, Anupam, Procaccia, Ariel, and Sharma, Ankit. 2013. Harnessing the power of two crossmatches. Pages 123–140 of: *Proc. 14th ACM Conference on Electronic Commerce*. ACM.

[14] Dickerson, John P., Procaccia, Ariel D., and Sandholm, Tuomas. 2012. Dynamic matching via weighted myopia with application to kidney Exchange. In: *Proc. Association for the Advancement of Artificial Intelligence*. https://dl .acm.org/doi/10.5555/2900728.2900918.

[15] Dickerson, John P., Procaccia, Ariel D., and Sandholm, Tuomas. 2012. Optimizing kidney exchange with transplant chains: Theory and reality. Pages 711–718 of: *Proc. 11th International Conference on Autonomous Agents and Multiagent Systems*, vol. 2. International Foundation for Autonomous Agents and Multiagent Systems.

[16] Dickerson, John P., Procaccia, Ariel D., and Sandholm, Tuomas. 2019. Failure-aware kidney exchange. *Management Science*, **65**(4), 1768–1791.

[17] Klimentova, Xenia, Pedroso, João Pedro, and Viana, Ana. 2016. Maximising expectation of the number of transplants in kidney exchange programmes. *Computers & Operations Research*, **73**, 1–11.

[18] Klimentova, Xenia, Viana, Ana, Pedroso, Joao Pedro, and Santos, Nicolau. 2020. Fairness models for multi-agent kidney exchange programmes. *Omega*, **102**, 102333. www.sciencedirect.com/science/article/abs/pii /S0305048320306873.

[19] Rees, Michael A., Dunn, Ty B., Kuhr, Christian S., Marsh, Christopher L., Rogers, Jeffrey, Rees, Susan E., Cicero, Alejandra, Reece, Laurie J., Roth, Alvin E., Ekwenna, Obi, et al. 2017. Kidney exchange to overcome financial barriers to kidney transplantation. *American Journal of Transplantation*, **17**(3), 782–790.

[20] Roth, Alvin E., Sönmez, Tayfun, and Ünver, M. Utku. 2004. Kidney exchange. *Quarterly Journal of Economics*, **119**(2), 457–488.

[21] Roth, Alvin E., Sönmez, Tayfun, and Ünver, M. Utku. 2005. Pairwise kidney exchange. *Journal of Economic Theory*, **125**(2), 151–188.

[22] Roth, Alvin E., Sönmez, Tayfun, and Ünver, M. Utku. 2007. Efficient kidney exchange: Coincidence of wants in markets with compatibility-based preferences. *American Economic Review*, **97**(3), 828–851.

[23] Roth, Alvin E., Sönmez, Tayfun, and Ünver, M. Utku. 2007. Notes on forming large markets from small ones: Participation incentives in multi-center kidney exchange. Unpublished.

[24] Shapley, Lloyd, and Scarf, Herbert. 1974. On cores and indivisibility. *Journal of Mathematical Economics*, **1**(1), 23–37.

[25] Sönmez, Tayfun, and Ünver, M. Utku. 2013. Market design for kidney exchange. *Handbook of Market Design*, pp. 93–137.

[26] Ünver, M. Utku. 2010. Dynamic kidney exchange. *Review of Economic Studies*, **77**(1), 372–414.

[27] Veale, Jeffrey L., Nassiri, Nima, Capron, Alexander M., Danovitch, Gabriel M., Gritsch, H. Albin, Cooper, Matthew, Redfield, Robert R., Kennealey, Peter T., and Kapur, Sandip. 2021. Voucher-based kidney donation and redemption for future transplant. *Journal of the American Medical Association, Surgery*. https://pubmed.ncbi.nlm.nih.gov/34160572/

[28] Wall, Anji E., Veale, Jeffrey L., and Melcher, Marc L. 2017. Advanced donation programs and deceased donor-initiated chains – 2. Innovations in kidney paired donation. *Transplantation*, **101**(12), 2818–2824.

[29] Wang, Wen, Bray, Mathieu, Song, Peter X.-K., and Kalbfleisch, John D. 2017. A look-ahead strategy for non-directed donors in kidney paired donation. *Statistics in Biosciences*, **9**(2), 453–469.

PART THREE

Theory

Normative Properties for Object Allocation Problems: Characterizations and Trade-Offs

Lars Ehlers and Bettina Klaus

10.1 Introduction

We consider the allocation of indivisible objects among agents when monetary transfers are not allowed. Agents have strict preferences over the objects (possibly regarding not getting any object) and are assigned at most one object. We will also assume that each object comes with capacity one.

How should one allocate offices to faculty members at a university when a department moves into a new building or when the current office allocation is not considered optimal anymore? Ideally, an allocation rule would be (i) fair and equitable, (ii) efficient, and (iii) incentive robust (also see Chapter 4 on "Objectives"). Of course, as we will see in this chapter, our three objectives might find different formulations depending on the exact allocation situation. Unfortunately, often the most natural properties to reflect (i)–(iii) are not compatible and thus an ideal allocation method usually does not exist.

In the first part of the chapter (Section 10.3), each agent is endowed with one object, has strict preferences over the set of objects, and agents can trade objects. For these so-called Shapley–Scarf exchange problems, the strong core consists of a unique allocation that can be computed by the top trading cycles algorithm. We start with positive news for this model: the so-called *top trading cycles rule* is characterized by (i) voluntary participation (*individual rationality*), (ii) efficiency (*Pareto optimality*), and (iii) incentive robustness (*strategy-proofness*).

In the second part of the chapter (Sections 10.4 and 10.5), the set of objects is commonly owned by the agents and all objects are acceptable. Then, *serial dictatorship rules* are characterized by (i) *neutrality* and (iii) *group strategy-proofness* (or, alternatively, *strategy-proofness* and *non-bossiness*); serial dictatorship rules also satisfy (ii) *Pareto optimality*. One could interpret this result as positive news since again objectives (i)–(iii) are compatible, but serial dictatorship rules might be criticized as unfair owing to their hierarchical spirit (e.g., the agent with the highest priority will always receive his best object). If one does not require *neutrality* then a much larger class of rules emerges: instead of requiring the same order of agents for all objects (which determines the sequence of dictators on which the serial dictatorship rule is based), one could allow for a different order of agents for each object, which can be considered as improving fairness aspect (i). We present this class of rules, the so-called *endowment inheritance rules*, in Section 10.5 and just note without a proof that they are part of a much larger class of rules, the *hierarchical exchange rules*, that are characterized by (ii) *Pareto optimality* and (iii) *reallocation-proofness* and *group strategy-proofness* (or alternatively, *strategy-proofness* and *non-bossiness*).

In the third part of the chapter (Section 10.6), each object is (possibly) endowed with a priority ordering over agents, thus capturing the rights of agents to receive the object. For this setup, one of the most widely applied rules nowadays is the agent-proposing *deferred acceptance rule*, which reflects (i) fairness in the form of *stability* (or *absence of justified envy*). Deferred acceptance rules tick boxes (i) and (iii) but unfortunately not (ii) (see Exercise 10.6). For deferred acceptance rules we present a characterization where the priority orderings are derived from the normative properties (for the setup of the second part of the chapter): deferred acceptance rules are the only (variable population) rules satisfying (i) $\emptyset$-*individual rationality* and *population monotonicity*, (ii) *weak non-wastefulness*, and (iii) *strategy-proofness*.

Finally (Section 10.7), we discuss how top trading cycles rules, serial dictatorship rules, endowment inheritance rules, deferred acceptance rules, and their properties are related. We then conclude by briefly discussing the embedding of the presented results into the literature (Section 10.9).

10.2 The Basic Model

We present a common notation for all three parts of the chapter. Let $N = \{1, \ldots, n\}$ denote the finite set of *agents*. A non-empty subset $S \subseteq N$ is called a *coalition*. Let $O = \{o_1, \ldots, o_m\}$ denote the finite set of *(real) objects*, and by $\emptyset$ denote the *null object*. Each real object can be assigned to only one agent, whereas the null object can be assigned to an arbitrary number of agents. An *allocation (for N)* is a mapping $a: N \to O \cup \{\emptyset\}$ such that, for all $i \neq j$, $a(i) = a(j)$ implies $a(i) = a(j) = \emptyset$. We denote the set of *all allocations (for N)* by $\mathcal{A}_N$. For allocation a, *agent i's allotment* is denoted by a_i (rather than $a(i)$).

We assume that each agent has a *strict preference relation R_i* over all possible allotments. A strict preference relation R_i is a complete, antisymmetric, and transitive relation on $O \cup \{\emptyset\}$. Let $i \in N$. Then, for any two allotments a_i, b_i, a_i is *weakly better than b_i* if $a_i R_i b_i$, and a_i is *strictly better than b_i*, denoted by $a_i P_i b_i$, if $[a_i R_i b_i$ and not $b_i R_i a_i]$. Finally, since preferences are strict, a_i is *indifferent to b_i*, denoted by $a_i I_i b_i$, only if $a_i = b_i$. The set of *all (strict) preferences* is denoted by $\mathcal{R}$. Sometimes we write $R_i : o \, o' \cdots$ to denote strict preferences, where o is the most R_i-preferred object in $O \cup \{\emptyset\}$, o' is the most R_i-preferred object in $(O \cup \{\emptyset\}) \setminus \{o\}$, and the remaining preferences are arbitrary. For agent i with preferences R_i, we say that *object $o \in O \cup \{\emptyset\}$ is acceptable* if $o R_i \emptyset$ and is *unacceptable* if $\emptyset P_i o$. Let $A(R_i)$ denote the set of *acceptable objects under R_i*. Let $\underline{\mathcal{R}}$ be the subdomain of $\mathcal{R}$ where all real objects are acceptable; thus $\underline{\mathcal{R}}$ denotes the *set of all acceptable (strict) preferences*.

A *preference profile* is a list $R = (R_1, \ldots, R_n) \in \mathcal{R}^N$. We assume that agents only care about their own allotments. Hence, agents' preferences over allocations are determined by preferences over allotments, i.e., for each $i \in N$ and for any $a, b \in \mathcal{A}_N$, $a_i P_i b_i$ implies $a P_i b$ and $a_i = b_i$ implies $a I_i b$. Following standard notation, for any coalition $S \subseteq N$, (R'_S, R_{-S}) is the preference profile that is obtained from R when all agents $i \in S$ change their preferences from R_i to R'_i. In particular, $R_{-i} = R_{N \setminus \{i\}}$.

We next introduce a voluntary participation and two efficiency requirements for allocations. Let $R \in \mathcal{R}^N$ and $a \in \mathcal{A}_N$. Then:

1. a is *$\emptyset$-individually rational* if, for all $i \in N$, $a_i \, R_i \, \emptyset$;
2. a is *weakly non-wasteful* if, for all $i \in N$ and all $o \in O$, $[o \, P_i \, \emptyset$ and $a_i = \emptyset]$ implies that, for some $j \in N$, $a_j = o$;
3. a is *Pareto dominated* by $b \in \mathcal{A}_N$ if, for all $i \in N$, $b_i \, R_i \, a_i$ and, for some $j \in N$, $b_j \, P_j \, a_j$;
4. a is *Pareto optimal* if it is not Pareto dominated by another allocation.

An *(allocation) problem* is now fully described by a triplet (N, O, R), which we simply denote by R (only in Section 10.6 will we allow the set of agents to vary). A *rule* φ is a function that associates with each problem $R \in \mathcal{R}^N$ an allocation $\varphi(R)$; for each $i \in N$, $\varphi_i(R)$ denotes agent i's allotment under rule φ.

Let $\mathbb{P}$ denote a property of an allocation. Then, a rule satisfies property $\mathbb{P}$ if it only assigns allocations with property $\mathbb{P}$. Typically, (i) fairness or equitability properties and (ii) efficiency properties are modeled in this way, i.e., "locally" via properties of allocations. However, (iii) incentive robustness properties are typically modeled "globally" by considering and linking changes in problems due to changes in preference profiles.

Strategy-proofness requires that no agent can ever benefit from misrepresenting his preferences, i.e., rule φ is *strategy-proof* if, for each $R \in \mathcal{R}^N$, each $i \in N$, and each $R_i' \in \mathcal{R}$, $\varphi_i(R) \, R_i \, \varphi_i(R_i', R_{-i})$.

Group strategy-proofness requires that no coalition can ever benefit from jointly misrepresenting its preferences, i.e., rule φ is *group strategy-proof* if, for each $R \in \mathcal{R}^N$, there does not exist a coalition $S \subseteq N$ and preferences $R_S' \in \mathcal{R}^S$ such that, for all $i \in S$, $\varphi_i(R_S', R_{-S}) \, R_i \, \varphi_i(R)$ and, for at least one $j \in S$, $\varphi_j(R_S', R_{-S}) \, P_j \, \varphi_j(R)$.

Non-bossiness requires that no agent can ever change the allocation, without changing his allotment, by misrepresenting his preferences, i.e., rule φ is *non-bossy* if, for each $R \in \mathcal{R}^N$, each $i \in N$, and each $R_i' \in \mathcal{R}$, $\varphi_i(R) = \varphi_i(R_i', R_{-i})$ implies $\varphi(R) = \varphi(R_i', R_{-i})$.

In what follows, sometimes rules are defined on the subdomain of acceptable preferences, $\underline{\mathcal{R}}^N$, and *(group) strategy-proofness* and *non-bossiness* are then adjusted accordingly by requiring that agents can deviate only by reporting preferences belonging to $\underline{\mathcal{R}}$. The following can be proven in Exercise 10.1.

Proposition 10.1 [15]. *A rule $\varphi \colon \mathcal{R}^N \to \mathcal{A}_N$ ($\varphi \colon \underline{\mathcal{R}}^N \to \mathcal{A}_N$) satisfies strategy-proofness and non-bossiness if and only if it satisfies group strategy-proofness.*

10.3 Top Trading Cycles Rules

We first consider *Shapley–Scarf exchange problems* [19], i.e., we consider exchange markets formed by n agents and by the same number of indivisible objects: $N = \{1, \ldots, n\}$ and $O = \{o_1, \ldots, o_n\}$. Each agent $i \in N$ owns one object, say o_i, desires exactly one object, has the option to trade the initially owned object in order to get a better one, and ranks all objects as acceptable. Hence, the set of problems equals $\underline{\mathcal{R}}^N$ and a rule is given by $\varphi \colon \underline{\mathcal{R}}^N \to \mathcal{A}_N$.

A rule φ is *individually rational* if, for each $R \in \underline{\mathcal{R}}^N$ and each $i \in N$, $\varphi_i(R) \, R_i \, o_i$. This property reflects the fact that agent i owns object o_i and models voluntary participation. Furthermore, it implies that at any chosen allocation all real objects are assigned and no agent ever receives the null object.

A central solution concept is the *strong core solution* (the *weak core solution* is the topic of Exercise 10.2). For $R \in \underline{\mathcal{R}}^N$, coalition S *weakly blocks* allocation a if there exists an allocation $b \in \mathcal{A}_N$ such that (i) $\cup_{i \in S}\{b_i\} = \cup_{i \in S}\{o_i\}$ and (ii) for all $i \in S$, $b_i \, R_i \, a_i$ and, for some $j \in S$, $b_j \, P_j \, a_j$. Allocation a is a *strong core allocation* if it is not weakly blocked by any coalition. In [19] it was shown that a strong core allocation always exists. Furthermore, in [18] it was proved that, when preferences are strict, the set of strong core allocations equals a singleton. Using the so-called top trading cycles algorithm (due to David Gale, see [19]) one can easily calculate the unique strong core allocation.

Top trading cycles algorithm.

Input: a problem $R \in \underline{\mathcal{R}}^N$ (which implicitly includes the initial endowment allocation).

Step 1. Let $N_1 := N$ and $O_1 := O$. We construct a (directed) graph with the set of nodes $N_1 \cup O_1$. For each agent $i \in N_1$ we add a directed edge to his most preferred object in O_1. For each directed edge (i, o), we say that agent i *points to* object o. For each object $o \in O_1$ we add a directed edge to its owner.

A *trading cycle* is a directed cycle in the graph. Given the finite number of nodes, at least one trading cycle exists for this graph. We assign to each agent in a trading cycle the object to which he points and remove all other trading cycle agents and objects. We define N_2 to be the set of remaining agents and O_2 to be the set of remaining objects and, if $N_2 \neq \emptyset$ (equivalently, $O_2 \neq \emptyset$), we continue with Step 2. Otherwise we stop. In general, at Step t we have the following:

Step t. We construct a (directed) graph with the set of nodes $N_t \cup O_t$ where $N_t \subseteq N$ is the set of agents that remain after Step $t - 1$ and $O_t \subseteq O$ is the set of objects that remain after Step $t - 1$.

For each agent $i \in N_t$ we add a directed edge to his most preferred object in O_t. For each object $o \in O_t$ we add a directed edge to its owner.

At least one trading cycle exists for this graph and we assign to each agent in a trading cycle the object to which he points and remove all other trading cycle agents and objects. We define N_{t+1} to be the set of remaining agents and O_{t+1} to be the set of remaining objects and, if $N_{t+1} \neq \emptyset$ (equivalently, $O_{t+1} \neq \emptyset$), we continue with Step $t + 1$. Otherwise we stop.

Output. The top trading cycles algorithm terminates when each agent in N has been assigned an object in O (this takes at most $|N|$ steps). We denote the object in O that agent i obtained by $\mathrm{TTC}_i(R)$.

The top trading cycles rule chooses for each problem R the allocation $\mathrm{TTC}(R)$.

Theorem 10.2 [14]. *The top trading cycles rule is the only rule $\varphi \colon \underline{\mathcal{R}}^N \to \mathcal{A}_N$ satisfying individual rationality, Pareto optimality, and strategy-proofness.*

The proof that a rule φ that satisfies *individual rationality*, *Pareto optimality*, and *strategy-proofness* equals the *top trading cycles rule* essentially uses the following insights and steps.

At Step 1 of the top trading cycles algorithm, each agent trading receives his favorite object. We can now show that rule φ does the same, as follows.

Any agent whose favorite object is his own endowment, by *individual rationality*, trades with himself.

For any real trading cycle (with more than one agent), if trading agents all ranked their favorite object first and their endowment second, by *individual rationality* they would receive either their endowment or their favorite object. However, if one trading cycle agent receives his endowment, he would interrupt all possible trade and hence all agents in the cycle would also receive their endowments. But that would be Pareto dominated by trading cycle agents receiving their favorite objects, a contradiction to *Pareto optimality*. Hence, each trading cycle agent receives his favorite object.

Of course, we have just assumed that preferences for trading cycle agents have a specific form, which generally does not need to be the case. This is when *strategy-proofness* enters the picture. We can now show that, from the specific preference profile we assumed, one can go back to the original preference profile by changing trading cycle agents' preferences one by one. Each time, owing to *strategy-proofness*, an agent who changes his preferences still gets his favorite object (as do the others). Thus, at the end, the trading cycle agents in Step 1 trade in the same way under TTC and φ.

This proof step can now be repeated for each step of the top trading cycles algorithm and the proof that $\varphi = \text{TTC}$ is then complete.

Proof Exercise 10.3 is dedicated to showing that the top trading cycles rule satisfies all the properties in Theorem 10.2. Let a rule $\varphi: \underline{\mathcal{R}}^N \to \mathcal{A}_N$ satisfy *individual rationality*, *Pareto optimality*, and *strategy-proofness*. Let $R \in \underline{\mathcal{R}}^N$. We will show that $\text{TTC}(R) = \varphi(R)$. Note that it suffices to consider the first step of the top trading cycles algorithm: once we have shown that, for each first-step trading cycle that is formed for R, each agent in the cycle obtains the same allotment under TTC and φ, we can use the same arguments to show that for each second-step trading cycle formed for R, each agent in the cycle obtains the same allotment under TTC and φ, etc.

Thus, consider a trading cycle formed in the first step of the top trading cycles algorithm for R. Note that an agent who *points* at his own object will receive it due to *individual rationality*. Hence, consider a trading cycle consisting of agents $i_0, \ldots, i_K$, $K \geq 1$, and objects $o_{i_0}, \ldots, o_{i_K}$. Note that each agent $i_k \in \{i_0, \ldots, i_K\}$, according to his preferences R_{i_k}, prefers object $o_{i_{k+1}}$ most among the objects in O.

For every $i_k \in \{i_0, \ldots, i_K\}$ we define preferences $R'_{i_k} \in \underline{\mathcal{R}}^N$ such that $o_{i_{k+1}} o_{i_k} \cdots$ (modulo K), e.g., by moving o_{i_k} to a position just after $o_{i_{k+1}}$ (without changing the ordering of other objects). We omit the mention of "modulo K" in what follows.

Consider the preference profile $R^0 = (R'_{\{i_0, \ldots, i_K\}}, R_{-\{i_0, \ldots, i_K\}})$. For each $0 \leq k \leq K$, $\text{TTC}_{i_k}(R^0) = o_{i_{k+1}}$. Furthermore, by *individual rationality*, for each $0 \leq k \leq K$, $\varphi_{i_k}(R^0) \in \{o_{i_k}, o_{i_{k+1}}\}$. So, the set of objects allocated to agents in $\{i_0, \ldots, i_K\}$ at allocation $\varphi(R^0)$ equals $\{o_{i_0}, \ldots, o_{i_K}\}$. Hence, by *Pareto optimality*, for each $i_k \in \{i_0, \ldots, i_K\}$, $\varphi_{i_k}(R^0) = o_{i_{k+1}} = \text{TTC}_{i_k}(R^0)$.

Next, let $l_1 \in \{i_0, \ldots, i_K\}$ be such that $\text{TTC}_{l_1}(R^0) = o_{l_1+1}$. Consider the preference profile $R^1 = (R'_{\{i_0, \ldots, i_K\} \setminus \{l_1\}}, R_{-(\{i_0, \ldots, i_K\} \setminus \{l_1\})}) = (R_{l_1}, R^0_{-l_1})$. Assume that, starting from R^0, agent l_1 changes his preferences from R'_{l_1} to R_{l_1}. Then, since agent l_1's trading cycle has not changed, $\text{TTC}_{l_1}(R^0) = \text{TTC}_{l_1}(R^1) = o_{l_1+1}$. Considering the same preference change under rule φ, by *strategy-proofness* we have $\varphi_{l_1}(R^1) \, R_{l_1} \, \varphi_{l_1}(R^0)$. Recall that $\varphi_{l_1}(R^0) = o_{l_1+1}$ is agent l_1's favorite object. Hence, $\varphi_{l_1}(R^1) = o_{l_1+1}$. Next, by *individual rationality*, for each $i_k \in \{i_0, \ldots, i_K\} \setminus \{l_1\}$, $\varphi_{i_k}(R^1) \in \{o_{i_k}, o_{i_{k+1}}\}$. So, the set of objects allocated to agents in $\{i_0, \ldots, i_K\}$ at allocation $\varphi(R^1)$ equals $\{o_{i_0}, \ldots, o_{i_K}\}$. Then, by *Pareto optimality*, for each $i_k \in \{i_0, \ldots, i_K\}$, $\varphi_{i_k}(R^1) = o_{i_{k+1}} = \text{TTC}_{i_k}(R^1)$.

Now, let $l_2 \in \{i_0, \ldots, i_K\} \setminus \{l_1\}$ be such that $\text{TTC}_{l_2}(R^1) = o_{l_2+1}$. Consider the preference profile $R^2 = (R'_{\{i_0,\ldots,i_K\}\setminus\{l_1,l_2\}}, R_{-(\{i_0,\ldots,i_K\}\setminus\{l_1,l_2\})}) = (R_{l_2}, R^1_{-l_2})$. Assume that, starting from R^1, agent l_2 changes his preferences from R'_{l_2} to R_{l_2}. Then, since agent l_2's trading cycle has not changed, $\text{TTC}_{l_2}(R^1) = \text{TTC}_{l_2}(R^2) = o_{l_2+1}$. Considering the same preference change under rule φ, by *strategy-proofness* we have $\varphi_{l_2}(R^2) \, R_{l_2} \, \varphi_{l_2}(R^1)$. Recall that $\varphi_{l_2}(R^1) = o_{l_2+1}$ is agent l_2's favorite object. Hence, $\varphi_{l_2}(R^2) = o_{l_2+1}$. Since the choice of agents $\{l_1, l_2\} \subseteq \{i_0, \ldots, i_K\}$ was arbitrary, then, by the same argument, changing the roles of l_1 and l_2 we obtain that $\varphi_{l_1}(R^2) = o_{l_1+1}$. Next, by *individual rationality*, for each $i_k \in \{i_0, \ldots, i_K\} \setminus \{l_1, l_2\}$, $\varphi_{i_k}(R^1) \in \{o_{i_k}, o_{i_{k+1}}\}$. So, the set of objects allocated to agents in $\{i_0, \ldots, i_K\}$ at allocation $\varphi(R^2)$ equals $\{o_{i_0}, \ldots, o_{i_K}\}$. Then, by *Pareto optimality*, for each $i_k \in \{i_0, \ldots, i_K\}$, $\varphi_{i_k}(R^2) = o_{i_{k+1}} = \text{TTC}_{i_k}(R^2)$.

We continue to replace the preferences of agents in $\{i_0, \ldots, i_K\} \setminus \{l_1, l_2\}$ one at a time as above until we reach the preference profile R, with the conclusion that, for each $i_k \in \{i_0, \ldots, i_K\}$, $\varphi_{i_k}(R) = \text{TTC}_{i_k}(R)$. $\qquad \square$

10.4 Serial Dictatorship Rules

We now consider *(object allocation) problems*, i.e., we consider problems consisting of n agents and the same number of indivisible objects: $N = \{1, \ldots, n\}$ and $O = \{o_1, \ldots, o_n\}$. In contrast with the previous section, all objects are commonly owned. Each agent desires exactly one object and considers all objects to be acceptable. Again, the set of problems equals $\underline{\mathcal{R}}^N$ and the rule is given by $\varphi : \underline{\mathcal{R}}^N \to \mathcal{A}_N$.

We will consider rules satisfying *weak non-wastefulness*, which on $\underline{\mathcal{R}}^N$ implies that, for any chosen allocation, all real objects are assigned and no agent ever receives the null object.

In addition, we will also require that rules are immune to the renaming of objects: let $\sigma : O \to O$ be a bijection. Then, given $R_i \in \mathcal{R}$, we define $\sigma(R_i)$ by [for each pair $o, o' \in O$, $o \, R_i \, o'$ if and only if $\sigma(o) \, \sigma(R_i) \, \sigma(o')$]. Furthermore, given $R \in \underline{\mathcal{R}}^N$, let $\sigma(R) = (\sigma(R_i))_{i \in N}$ and, given allocation $a \in \mathcal{A}_N$, let $\sigma(a) \in \mathcal{A}_N$ be defined by [for each $i \in N$, if $a_i \in O$ then $(\sigma(a))_i = \sigma(a_i)$ and if $a_i = \emptyset$ then $(\sigma(a))_i = \emptyset$]. Now, a rule is *neutral* if, for each $R \in \underline{\mathcal{R}}^N$ and each bijection $\sigma : O \to O$, $\varphi(\sigma(R)) = \sigma(\varphi(R))$.

The following algorithm uses a permutation $\pi : N \to N$ of the agents that is used as an ordering of (serial) dictators.

Serial dictatorship algorithm.

Input: a problem $R \in \underline{R}^N$ and an ordering of the agents π.

Step 1. Let $\mathrm{SD}^{\pi}_{\pi(1)}(R)$ be agent $\pi(1)$'s most $R_{\pi(1)}$-preferred object in O.

Step $t \geq 2$ Let $\mathrm{SD}^{\pi}_{\pi(t)}(R)$ be agent $\pi(t)$'s most $R_{\pi(t)}$-preferred object in $O \setminus \{\mathrm{SD}^{\pi}_{\pi(1)}(R), \ldots, \mathrm{SD}^{\pi}_{\pi(t-1)}(R)\}$.

Output. After n steps, allocation $\mathrm{SD}^{\pi}(R)$ is determined.

A rule $\varphi \colon \underline{\mathcal{R}}^{N} \to \mathcal{A}_{N}$ is a *serial dictatorship rule* if there is an ordering of agents $\pi \colon N \to N$ such that, for each $R \in \underline{\mathcal{R}}^{N}$, $\varphi(R) = \mathrm{SD}^{\pi}(R)$.

Theorem 10.3 [21]. *Serial dictatorship rules are the only rules $\varphi \colon \underline{\mathcal{R}}^{N} \to \mathcal{A}_{N}$ satisfying weak non-wastefulness,[1] strategy-proofness, non-bossiness, and neutrality.*

The proof that a rule φ that satisfies *weak non-wastefulness, strategy-proofness, non-bossiness,* and *neutrality* is a serial dictatorship rule proceeds roughly as follows.

First, a "maximal conflict" preference profile where all agents rank all objects in the same order is assumed. Since by *weak non-wastefulness* all objects are assigned, the allocation for these maximal conflict preferences induces an order π on the set of agents. The aim of the proof now is to show that this order induces a serial dictatorship, with the agent who receives the most preferred object as first "dictator", the agent receiving the second most preferred object as second dictator, etc.

Thus, according to π, there is a candidate for first dictator, without loss of generality, agent 1. Now it is assumed by contradiction that agent 1 does not always receive his most preferred object. Then, by combining *neutrality, strategy-proofness,* and *non-bossiness,* a contradiction is reached. The proof then proceeds by induction to conclude that the rule is a serial dictatorship based on π.

Proof Exercise 10.4 is dedicated to showing that *serial dictatorship rules* satisfy all the properties in Theorem 10.3.

Let a rule $\varphi \colon \underline{\mathcal{R}}^{N} \to \mathcal{A}_{N}$ satisfy *weak non-wastefulness, strategy-proofness, non-bossiness,* and *neutrality.*

For each $i \in N$, let $\hat{R}_{i} \in \underline{\mathcal{R}}$ be such that $o_{1}\ o_{2}\ \cdots\ o_{n}\ \emptyset$. Let $\hat{R} = (\hat{R}_{i})_{i \in N}$. By *weak non-wastefulness,* all objects are assigned at allocation $\varphi(\hat{R})$. Without loss of generality, for each $i \in N$, let $\varphi_{i}(\hat{R}) = o_{i}$. We show by induction that φ is the serial dictatorship rule with respect to the order $\pi \colon 1\ 2\ \cdots\ n$, i.e., for each $i \in N$, $\pi(i) = i$. First, we show that agent 1 always receives his most preferred object.

Induction basis. For all $R \in \underline{\mathcal{R}}^{N}$, $\varphi_{1}(R) = \mathrm{SD}^{\pi}_{1}(R)$, which we prove by contradiction. Suppose that there exists $R \in \underline{\mathcal{R}}^{N}$ such that $\varphi_{1}(R)$ is not the most R_{1}-preferred object. By *neutrality* (Exercise 10.4), we may assume that o_{1} is the most R_{1}-preferred object. Because all objects are assigned, there exists an agent $j \in N \setminus \{1\}$ such that $\varphi_{j}(R) = o_{1}$. Now, again by *neutrality* (Exercise 10.4), we may assume that $\varphi_{1}(R) = o_{j}$. By another application of *neutrality* (Exercise 10.4), we may also assume that, for each $i \in N \setminus \{1, j\}$, $\varphi_{i}(R) = o_{i}$. Note that by the above renaming of objects and *neutrality,* we have $[\varphi_{1}(\hat{R}) = o_{1}$ and $\varphi_{j}(\hat{R}) = o_{j}]$, $[\varphi_{1}(R) = o_{j}$ and $\varphi_{j}(R) = o_{1}]$, and, for each $i \in N \setminus \{1, j\}$, $\varphi_{i}(R) = o_{i} = \varphi_{i}(\hat{R})$.

---

[1] Svensson [21] circumvented *weak non-wastefulness* by considering only allocations that do not assign the null object.

Now let $\bar{R} \in \mathcal{R}^N$ be such that $\bar{R}_1 : o_1\, o_j\, \cdots$, $\bar{R}_j : o_1\, o_j\, \cdots$, and, for each $i \in N\setminus\{1,j\}$, $\bar{R}_i : o_i\, \cdots$. Then, starting from $\hat{R}$ and applying *strategy-proofness* and *non-bossiness* successively, we obtain $\varphi_1(\bar{R}) = o_1$ (from $\varphi_1(\hat{R}) = o_1$) whereas starting from R and applying *strategy-proofness* and *non-bossiness* successively, we obtain $\varphi_1(\bar{R}) \neq o_1$ (from $\varphi_1(R) \neq o_1$), which is a contradiction.

Induction hypothesis. For all $R \in \mathcal{R}^N$ and each $i \in \{1,\ldots,k\}$, $\varphi_i(R) = \mathrm{SD}_i^\pi(R)$.

Induction step. We show that, for any $R \in \mathcal{R}^N$, agent $k + 1$ receives his most preferred object in $O \setminus \{\mathrm{SD}_1^\pi(R),\ldots,\mathrm{SD}_k^\pi(R)\}$. Suppose that this is not the case. Then there exists $R \in \mathcal{R}^N$ such that $\varphi_{k+1}(R) \neq \mathrm{SD}_{k+1}^\pi(R)$. By the induction hypothesis, for each $i \in \{1,\ldots,k\}$, $\varphi_i(R) = \mathrm{SD}_i^\pi(R)$. We distinguish four cases.

In the first case, suppose that $R_{\{1,\ldots,k\}} = \hat{R}_{\{1,\ldots,k\}}$. Then, by the induction hypothesis, for each $i \in \{1,\ldots,k\}$, $\varphi_i(R) = o_i = \mathrm{SD}_i^\pi(R)$. Using the same arguments as in the induction basis (by fixing $\hat{R}_{\{1,\ldots,k\}}$) and the fact that $\varphi_{k+1}(\hat{R}) = o_{k+1}$, it follows that agent $k + 1$ is assigned the most R_{k+1}-preferred object among $O \setminus \{o_1,\ldots,o_k\}$ at $\varphi(R)$, which is a contradiction.

In the second case, suppose that for each $i \in \{1,\ldots,k\}$, $\varphi_i(R) = o_i = \mathrm{SD}_i^\pi(R)$. Then o_1 is the most R_1-preferred object, and, for each $i \in \{2,\ldots,k\}$, o_i is the most R_i-preferred object in $O \setminus \{o_1,\ldots,o_{i-1}\}$. Let $R' = (\hat{R}_{\{1,\ldots,k\}}, R_{N\setminus\{1,\ldots,k\}})$. Applying *non-bossiness* and *strategy-proofness* successively to φ and SD^π, it follows that, for each $i \in \{1,\ldots,k\}$, $\varphi_i(R') = o_i = \mathrm{SD}_i^\pi(R')$ and $\varphi_{k+1}(R') = \varphi_{k+1}(R) \neq \mathrm{SD}_{k+1}^\pi(R) = \mathrm{SD}_{k+1}^\pi(R')$. Then R' belongs to the first case, which leads to a contradiction.

In the third case, suppose that the sets of allotted objects via φ and SD^π are the same, i.e., $\{\varphi_1(R),\ldots,\varphi_k(R)\} = \{o_1,\ldots,o_k\} = \{\mathrm{SD}_1^\pi(R),\ldots,\mathrm{SD}_k^\pi(R)\}$. Now let $\sigma : O \to O$ be such that, for each $i \in \{1,\ldots,k\}$, $\sigma(\varphi_i(R)) = o_i$, and, for each $o \in O\setminus\{o_1,\ldots,o_k\}$, $\sigma(o) = o$. Then by the *neutrality* of φ and SD^π, we have, for each $i \in \{1,\ldots,k\}$, $\varphi_i(\sigma(R)) = o_i = \mathrm{SD}_i^\pi(\sigma(R))$ and $\varphi_{k+1}(\sigma(R)) \neq \mathrm{SD}_{k+1}^\pi(\sigma(R))$. Then, $\sigma(R)$ belongs to the second case, which leads to a contradiction.

In the fourth case, suppose that the sets of allotted objects via φ and SD^π are not the same, i.e., $\{\varphi_1(R),\ldots,\varphi_k(R)\} \neq \{o_1,\ldots,o_k\}$. Then, similarly to the previous case, let $\sigma : O \to O$ be such that, for each $i \in \{1,\ldots,k\}$, $\sigma(\varphi_i(R)) = o_i$, and, for each $o \in O\setminus(\{o_1,\ldots,o_k\} \cup \{\varphi_1(R),\ldots,\varphi_k(R)\})$, $\sigma(o) = o$. Then by the *neutrality* of φ and SD^π, we have, for each $i \in \{1,\ldots,k\}$, $\varphi_i(\sigma(R)) = o_i = \mathrm{SD}_i^\pi(\sigma(R))$ and $\varphi_{k+1}(\sigma(R)) \neq \mathrm{SD}_{k+1}^\pi(\sigma(R))$. Thus, $\sigma(R)$ belongs to the second case again, which leads to a contradiction. $\square$

10.5 Endowment Inheritance Rules

We now consider *(object allocation) problems* formed by n agents and an arbitrary number of indivisible objects: $N = \{1,\ldots,n\}$ and $O = \{o_1,\ldots,o_m\}$. We combine aspects of the two previous sections in that property rights over objects (as present in Shapley–Scarf exchange problems and used by the top trading cycles rule) will be modeled via permutations of the agents (as used in the serial dictatorship rules).

Endowment inheritance rules allocate objects to agents using an iterative procedure that is similar to the top trading cycles algorithm except that, apart from agents possibly owning multiple objects, it also specifies an ordering of inheritance of the objects in an iterative hierarchical manner. Each object is the individual "endowment" of an agent and we apply a round of top trading cycles exchange to these endowments. Given that multiple endowments are allowed, after the agents in top trading cycles are removed from the problem with only their allotted objects, their unallocated endowments are re-assigned as endowments to agents who are still present. In other words, these objects that are left behind are "inherited" as new endowments by agents who have not received their allotments yet. Notice that then each remaining object is the endowment of some remaining agent and the top trading cycles algorithm is well defined at the second stage. We determine the allotments of agents who are in top trading cycles in this round, remove them with their allotted objects, and determine the endowments of the remaining agents for the next stage. And so on, until for each agent we have specified an allotment in this way.

The initial endowments and the hierarchical endowments at later rounds are determined using object-specific permutations of the agents that indicate the order of inheritance. Thus, each endowment inheritance rule is defined by an *endowment inheritance table* $\pi = (\pi_o)_{o \in O}$ such that, for each object $o \in O$, π_o is a permutation of N.

Endowment inheritance algorithm.

Input: a problem $R \in \mathcal{R}^N$ and an endowment inheritance table π.

For each Step $t \in \{1, \ldots, m\}$, we give recursive definitions of the associated hierarchical endowments $E_t(i, R)$, top choices $T_t(i, R)$, trading cycles $S_t(i, R)$, assigned individuals $W_t(R)$, and assigned real objects $F_t(R)$. For every problem $R \in \mathcal{R}^N$ and Step t, let $W^t(R) \equiv \cup_{z=1}^{t} W_z(R)$ and $F^t(R) \equiv \cup_{z=1}^{t} F_z(R)$. Let $W^0(R) = \emptyset$ and $F^0(R) = \emptyset$.

Step t. If agent $i \in N \setminus W^{t-1}(R)$ is ranked highest with respect to object $o \in O \setminus F^{t-1}(R)$ among all agents in $N \setminus W^{t-1}(R)$, then o belongs to his hierarchical endowment at Step t. The null object $\emptyset$ is part of each agent's endowment. The *hierarchical endowments* at Step t are as follows:

$$
E_t(i, R) = \left\{ o \in O \setminus F^{t-1}(R) \,\middle|\, i = \arg \min_{j \in N \setminus W^{t-1}(R)} \{\pi_o(j)\} \right\} \cup \{\emptyset\}.
$$

Next, each agent $i \in N \setminus W^{t-1}(R)$ identifies his *top choice* in $(O \cup \{\emptyset\}) \setminus F^{t-1}(R)$:

$$
T_t(i, R) = o \Leftrightarrow o \in (O \cup \{\emptyset\}) \setminus F^{t-1}(R) \quad \text{and} \quad \text{for all } o' \in (O \cup \{\emptyset\}) \setminus F^{t-1}(R), \, o \, R_i \, o'.
$$

A *trading cycle* consists of a set of agents in $N \setminus W^{t-1}(R)$ who would like to exchange objects from their hierarchical endowments in a "cyclical way" such that each of them receives his top choice. The trading cycles $S_t(i, R)$ are as follows:

Table 10.1 Endowment inheritance table π. The numbers refer to the agents in N.

π_a	π_b	π_c	π_d	π_e	π_f
2	1	2	1	2	2
1	2	1	2	1	1
3	3	3	3	3	3
4	4	4	5	5	4
5	5	5	4	4	5

$$
S_t(i, R) \equiv
\begin{cases}
\{j_1, \ldots, j_g\} & \text{if } \{j_1, \ldots, j_g\} \subseteq N \setminus W^{t-1}(R) \text{ such that} \\
& |\{j_1, \ldots, j_g\}| = g \text{ and, for all } v \in \{1, \ldots, g\}, \\
& T_t(j_v, R) \in E_t(j_{v+1}, R) \text{ where } i = j_1 = j_{g+1}, \\
\emptyset & \text{otherwise.}
\end{cases}
$$

The agents in a trading cycle are assigned their top choices from the set of objects that have not been assigned yet. The *assigned individuals* are

$$W_t(R) \equiv \{i \in N \mid S_t(i, R) \neq \emptyset\}.$$

The *assigned real objects* are

$$F_t(R) \equiv \{T_t(i, R) \in O \mid i \in W_t(R)\}.$$

Note that for all $R \in \mathcal{R}^N$ there exists a last stage $t^* \leq m$ such that either $W^{t^*}(R) = N$ or $F^{t^*}(R) = O$ and, for all $t < t^*$, $W^t(R) \neq N$ and $F^t(R) \neq O$.

Given an endowment inheritance table π, for all $R \in \mathcal{R}^N$ the allocation chosen by the *endowment inheritance rule* φ^π is defined as follows. For all $i \in N$,

$$
\varphi_i^\pi(R) \equiv
\begin{cases}
T_t(i, R) & \text{if for some } t \in \{1, \ldots, m\}, i \in W_t(R), \\
\emptyset & \text{otherwise.}
\end{cases}
$$

A rule φ is an *endowment inheritance rule* if there exists an endowment inheritance table π such that, for each $R \in \mathcal{R}^N$, $\varphi(R) = \varphi^\pi(R)$.

Example 10.4. Let $N = \{1, 2, 3, 4, 5\}$ and $O = \{a, b, c, d, e, f\}$. Consider the *endowment inheritance rule* defined by the endowment inheritance table π, Table 10.1. Associated with each object is a permutation of the agents (given by the column corresponding to the object).

For example, the first column of the endowment inheritance table π, Table 10.1, shows that object a is agent 2's initial endowment, and is (possibly) inherited by agents 1, 3, 4, and 5, in that order. We illustrate the use of this table for the preference profile $R \in \mathcal{R}^N$ given in Table 10.2, which shows the rankings of objects from the top down for each agent.

Step 1. The initial endowments are given by the first row of the endowment inheritance table, Table 10.1. The endowments are $E_1(1, R) = \{b, d\}$ for agent 1, $E_1(2, R) = \{a, c, e, f\}$ for agent 2, and $\emptyset$ for agents 3, 4, and 5. Then,

Table 10.2 Preference profile R. The letters refer to the objects in O.

R_1	R_2	R_3	R_4	R_5
a	b	b	d	a
f	f	e	a	b
d	a	c	b	f
e	c	a	c	c
c	d	d	e	d
b	e	f	f	e

$T_1(1, R) = a$, $T_1(2, R) = b$, $T_1(3, R) = b$, $T_1(4, R) = d$, and $T_1(5, R) = a$ are the top choices of the agents in $O \cup \{\emptyset\}$. Hence, $\{1, 2\}$ is the only cycle under which 1 receives a from 2 and 2 receives b from 1, i.e., $S_1(1, R) = S_1(2, R) = \{1, 2\}$, $W_1(R) = \{1, 2\}$, and $F_1(R) = \{a, b\}$.

Step 2. Since agents 1 and 2 have already received their allotments, objects c, d, e, and f are left behind from 1's and 2's endowments. These objects are inherited by agent 3, i.e., $E_2(3, R) = \{c, d, e, f\}$ and $E_2(4, R) = E_2(5, R) = \emptyset$. Then, 3 picks his top choice, object e, among the remaining objects. So $S_2(3, R) = \{3\}$, $W_2(R) = \{3\}$, and $F_2(R) = \{e\}$.

Step 3. Now only agents 4 and 5 remain. Agent 4 inherits $\{c, f\}$ and 5 inherits $\{d\}$, i.e., $E_3(4, R) = \{c, f\}$ and $E_3(5, R) = \{d\}$. Because $T_3(4, R) = d$ and $T_3(5, R) = f$, 4 and 5 form a trading cycle and receive their top choices in $\{c, d, f\}$, i.e., $S_3(4, R) = S_3(5, R) = \{4, 5\}$, $W_3(R) = \{4, 5\}$, and $F_3(R) = \{d, f\}$.

Thus $\varphi^\pi(R) = (a, b, e, d, f)$ are the allotments to $(1, 2, 3, 4, 5)$. $\qquad\square$

The class of endowment inheritance rules is a subclass of Pápai's [15] hierarchical exchange rules, which generalize the idea of endowment inheritance from endowment inheritance tables to more general endowment inheritance structures (for instance by allowing for endowment inheritance trees). The next property was introduced in [15] to exclude joint preference manipulations by two individuals who plan to swap objects ex-post under the condition that this collusion changes both their allotments and is self-enforcing in the sense that neither agent changes his allotment if he misreports while the other agent reports the truth.

A rule φ is *reallocation-proof* if, for each problem $R \in \mathcal{R}^N$ and each pair of agents $i, j \in N$, there exist no preferences $\tilde{R}_i, \tilde{R}_j \in \mathcal{R}$ such that

$$\varphi_j(\tilde{R}_i, \tilde{R}_j, R_{-\{i,j\}}) \, R_i \, \varphi_i(R),$$
$$\varphi_i(\tilde{R}_i, \tilde{R}_j, R_{-\{i,j\}}) \, P_j \, \varphi_j(R),$$

and, for $k = i, j$,

$$\varphi_k(R) = \varphi_k(\tilde{R}_k, R_{-k}) \neq \varphi_k(\tilde{R}_i, \tilde{R}_j, R_{-\{i,j\}}).$$

We state the following result without a proof.

Theorem 10.5 [15]. *Hierarchical exchange rules are the only rules $\varphi \colon \underline{\mathcal{R}}^N \to \mathcal{A}_N$ satisfying Pareto optimality, strategy-proofness, non-bossiness, and reallocation-proofness.*

10.6 Deferred Acceptance Rules

We now consider *variable-population (object allocation) problems*, i.e., object allocation problems consisting of coalitions $N' \subseteq N$ and a set of real objects O. In other words, not necessarily all agents belonging to N are present. Let $\mathcal{R}^{N'}$ denote the set of preference profiles for coalition N' and, similarly, $\mathcal{A}_{N'}$ the set of allocations for N'. Now a variable-population rule is a mapping

$$\varphi \colon \cup_{\emptyset \neq N' \subseteq N} \mathcal{R}^{N'} \to \cup_{\emptyset \neq N' \subseteq N} \mathcal{A}_{N'}$$

such that for each $\emptyset \neq N' \subseteq N$ and each $R \in \mathcal{R}^{N'}$ we have $\varphi(R) \in \mathcal{A}_{N'}$.

When the sets of agents vary, a natural property is *population monotonicity*, which is a so-called *solidarity property* requiring that those who are not responsible for a change in a problem (the initially present agents) are all affected in the same way by that change (the presence of additional agents). Since in this type of resource-allocation problem, more agents competing for the same resources is bad news, the natural requirement is that, as the set of agents becomes larger, the initially present agents all become (weakly) worse off. Formally, for any $\emptyset \neq N'' \subseteq N' \subseteq N$ and any $R \in \mathcal{R}^{N'}$, for each $i \in N''$, $\varphi_i(R_{N''}) \, R_i \, \varphi_i(R)$.

Given an object $o \in O$, let $\succ_o$ denote a *priority ordering on* N, e.g., $\succ_o \colon 1 \, 2 \, \cdots \, n$ means that agent 1 has a higher priority for object o than agent 2, who has a higher priority for object o than agent 3, etc. Let $\succ \equiv (\succ_o)_{o \in O}$ denote a *priority structure*. Then, given a priority structure $\succ$ and a problem $R \in \mathcal{R}^{N'}$, we can interpret $(R, \succ)$ as a *marriage market* [9] where the set of agents N', for instance, corresponds to the set of women, the set of objects O corresponds to the set of men, the preferences at R correspond to women's preferences over the available men, and the priority structure $(\succ_o)_{o \in O}$ specifies the men's preferences over the women.

Stability is an important requirement for many real-life matching markets and it turns out to be essential in our context of allocating indivisible objects to agents as well. Given a problem $R \in \mathcal{R}^{N'}$ and priority structure $\succ$, an allocation $a \in \mathcal{A}_{N'}$ is *stable under* $\succ$ if there exists no agent–object pair $(i, o) \in N' \times (O \cup \{\emptyset\})$ such that $o \, P_i \, a_i$ and (i) $o = \emptyset$ or (ii) there exists no $j \in N'$ such that $a_j = o$, or (iii) there exists $j \in N'$ such that $a_j = o$ and $i \succ_o j$.[2] Furthermore, rule φ is *stable* if there exists a priority structure $\succ$ such that, for each problem $R \in \mathcal{R}^{N'}$ (with $N' \subseteq N$), $\varphi(R)$ is *stable* under $\succ$. Note that *stability* implies $\emptyset$-*individual rationality* and *weak non-wastefulness*, but it does not imply *Pareto optimality* (see Exercise 10.6).

---

[2] A situation with an agent–object pair (i, o) such that (i) constitutes a violation of $\emptyset$-*individual rationality* while (ii) can be interpreted as the allocation being *wasteful*, and if (iii) is the case, then agent i has *justified envy* against agent j. Hence, *stability* is equivalent to the properties $\emptyset$-*individual rationality*, *non-wastefulness* and *no justified envy*.

For any marriage market $(R, \succ)$, we denote by $\text{DA}^{\succ}(R)$ the agent-optimal stable allocation that is obtained by using the agent-proposing deferred acceptance algorithm [9]. A rule $\varphi \colon \mathcal{R}^N \to \mathcal{A}$ is a *deferred acceptance rule* if there is a priority structure $\succ$ such that, for each $R \in \mathcal{R}^N$, $\varphi(R) = \text{DA}^{\succ}(R)$.

Theorem 10.6 [7]. *Deferred acceptance rules are the only variable-population rules satisfying Ø-individual rationality, weak non-wastefulness, strategy-proofness, and population monotonicity.*

The proof that a rule φ that satisfies *Ø-individual rationality*, *weak non-wastefulness*, *strategy-proofness*, and *population monotonicity* is a deferred acceptance rule proceeds roughly as follows.

First, for each real object $o \in O$, a "maximal conflict" preference profile, where all agents declare the object o as the only acceptable object, is considered. By *Ø-individual rationality* and *weak non-wastefulness*, the object is assigned to an agent. When this agent leaves with the object, the residual maximal conflict preference profile for the remaining agents is taken into account and the sequence of maximal-conflict preferences induces an order $\succ_o$ on the set of agents. Since this can be done for each real object, a priority structure $\succ$ is thus constructed.

The aim of the remainder of the proof is then to show that this priority ordering, together with the deferred acceptance algorithm, determines all outcomes of the rule.

Proof First, note that all deferred acceptance rules are *stable* and that *stability* implies *Ø-individual rationality* and *weak non-wastefulness*. In [4] and [17] the *strategy-proofness* of all deferred acceptance rules was proved. In [2], the comparative statics of deferred acceptance rules were studied, and from the results it follows that all deferred acceptance rules are population monotonic. Hence, deferred acceptance rules satisfy all the properties of Theorem 10.6.

Second, let φ be a rule satisfying *Ø-individual rationality*, *weak non-wastefulness*, and *population-monotonicity* (we will add *strategy-proofness* later on). We will construct a priority structure using maximal-conflict preference profiles.

Let $o \in O$ and $R^o \in \mathcal{R}$ be such that $A(R^o) = \{o\}$. We denote the set of all preference relations that have $o \in O$ as the unique acceptable object by $\mathcal{R}^o$. For any coalition $S \subseteq N$, let $R_S^o = (R_i^o)_{i \in S}$ be such that, for each $i \in S$, $R_i^o = R^o$.

Consider the problem R_N^o. By *Ø-individual rationality* and *weak non-wastefulness*, for some $j \in N$, $\varphi_j(R_N^o) = o$; say $j = 1$. Then, for all $i \in N \setminus \{1\}$, we set $1 \succ_o i$.

Next consider the problem $R_{N \setminus \{1\}}^o$. By *Ø-individual rationality* and *weak non-wastefulness*, for some $j \in N \setminus \{1\}$, $\varphi_j(R_{N \setminus \{1\}}^o) = o$; say $j = 2$. Then, for all $i \in N \setminus \{1, 2\}$, we set $2 \succ_o i$.

By induction, we obtain $\succ_o$ for any real object o and thus a priority structure $\succ = (\succ_o)_{o \in O}$ for N. It is easy to show that *Ø-individual rationality*, *weak non-wastefulness*, and *population-monotonicity* imply that, for any $o \in O$ and any $i, j \in N$ such that $i \succ_o j$, $\varphi_i(R^o, R^o) = o$ and $\varphi_j(R^o, R^o) = \emptyset$ (Exercise 10.6).

Let φ satisfy *strategy-proofness*. With the following step, Theorem 10.6 follows. Note that $\text{DA}^{\succ}$ satisfies all the properties of Theorem 10.6.

Let $S \subseteq N$, $R \in \mathcal{R}^S$, and denote by $Z(R) := |\{i \in S \mid |A(R_i)| \leq 1\}|$ the number of agents who find at most one object acceptable. Let $R \in \mathcal{R}^S$ be such that $\varphi(R) \neq \mathrm{DA}^\succ(R)$ and assume that $Z(R)$ is maximal, i.e., for all $R' \in \mathcal{R}^S$ such that $\varphi(R') \neq \mathrm{DA}^\succ(R')$, $Z(R) \geq Z(R')$.

We first show that, for each $i \in S$ such that $\varphi_i(R) \neq \mathrm{DA}_i^\succ(R)$, $|A(R_i)| = 1$. If $\varphi_i(R) \, P_i \, \mathrm{DA}_i^\succ(R)$, by $\emptyset$-*individual rationality*, $\varphi_i(R) = o \in O$. If $|A(R_i)| = 1$ then we are done. If $|A(R_i)| > 1$ then consider $(R^o, R_{-i}) \in \mathcal{R}^S$ where R^o is as in the construction of $\succ$. By the *strategy-proofness* and $\emptyset$-*individual rationality* of both φ and $\mathrm{DA}^\succ$, $\varphi_i(R^o, R_{-i}) = o$ and $\mathrm{DA}_i^\succ(R^o, R_{-i}) = \emptyset$. Hence, (R^o, R_{-i}) is such that $\varphi(R^o, R_{-i}) \neq \mathrm{DA}^\succ(R^o, R_{-i})$ and $Z(R^o, R_{-i}) > Z(R)$; contradicting our assumption that $Z(R)$ was maximal. If $\mathrm{DA}_i^\succ(R) \, P_i \, \varphi_i(R)$ then $\mathrm{DA}_i^\succ(R) := o \in O$ and the proof that $|A(R_i)| = 1$ proceeds as before (with $\mathrm{DA}^\succ$ in the role of φ and vice versa). Hence, for each $i \in S$ such that $\varphi_i(R) \neq \mathrm{DA}_i^\succ(R)$, $|A(R_i)| = 1$. By *strategy-proofness*, we can assume that, for each $i \in S$ such that $\varphi_i(R) \neq \mathrm{DA}_i^\succ(R)$, $R_i = R^o$ where R^o is as in the construction of $\succ$.

If $o = \mathrm{DA}_i^\succ(R) P_i \varphi_i(R) = \emptyset$ then by *weak non-wastefulness* there exists $j \in S \setminus \{i\}$ such that $\varphi_j(R) = o$. Hence, $\varphi_j(R) \neq \mathrm{DA}_j^\succ(R)$ and $R_j = R^o$ where R^o is as in the construction of $\succ$. Thus, $(R_i, R_j) = (R^o, R^o)$ and $o = \varphi_j(R) \, P_j \, \mathrm{DA}_j^\succ(R) = \emptyset$. Now $\mathrm{DA}_i^\succ(R) = o$, and *population monotonicity* (and $\emptyset$-*individual rationality*) for $\mathrm{DA}^\succ$ imply $\mathrm{DA}_i^\succ(R_i, R_j) = o$ and $\mathrm{DA}_j^\succ(R_i, R_j) = \emptyset$. Hence, $i \succ_o j$. Next, $\varphi_j(R) = o$ and *population monotonicity* (and $\emptyset$-*individual rationality*) for φ imply $\varphi_j(R_i, R_j) = o$ and $\varphi_i(R_i, R_j) = \emptyset$. Hence, $j \succ_o i$, a contradiction.

If $o = \varphi_i(R) \, P_i \, \mathrm{DA}_i^\succ(R) = \emptyset$ then by *weak non-wastefulness* there exists $j \in S \setminus \{i\}$ such that $\mathrm{DA}_j^\succ(R) = o$. We obtain a contradiction as above. $\qquad\square$

Theorem 10.6 implies the following additional result. We call a priority structure $\succ$ *acyclic* if there do not exist distinct $i, j, k \in N$ and distinct $o, o' \in O$ such that $i \succ_o j \succ_o k$ and $k \succ_{o'} i$. In [8] it was shown that acyclicity of the priority structure $\succ$ is necessary and sufficient for the deferred acceptance rule based on $\succ$ to be *Pareto optimal*.

Corollary 10.7 [7]. *Deferred acceptance rules with acyclic priority structures are the only (variable population) rules satisfying Pareto optimality, strategy-proofness, and population monotonicity.*

The above corollary follows immediately from Theorem 10.6 and [8], as *Pareto optimality* implies both $\emptyset$-*individual rationality* and *weak non-wastefulness*.

10.7 Relationships Between Classes of Rules

We have introduced four classes of rules in our chapter: the top trading cycles rule, serial dictatorship rules, endowment inheritance (hierarchical exchange) rules, and deferred acceptance rules. These classes of rules and their properties are very closely related.

First, endowment inheritance rules are a natural extension of the top trading cycles rule from the model of Section 10.3, where each agent is endowed with exactly one object, to the model considered in Sections 10.4 and 10.5, where the number of objects is arbitrary: instead of explicit endowments, an inheritance table administers property rights and inheritance of those property rights whenever necessary. Specifically, the top trading cycles rule is an endowment inheritance rule for the special situation where the number of objects equals the number of agents and where the endowment inheritance table lists each agent as top agent for exactly one object, which then essentially turns into his endowment.

Next, an endowment inheritance rule is specified by an endowment inheritance table π while a deferred acceptance rule is specified by a priority structure $\succ$. Note that while inheritance tables and priority structures come with different background stories (property rights versus priority rankings) both are mathematically identical concepts: for each object, a permutation of agents is specified. So the inputs for these rules can be chosen to be the same and the difference lies solely in how that input is used to compute the output. This gives rise to the following question:

> For which endowment inheritance tables/priority structures do endowment inheritance rules and deferred acceptance rules produce the same results?

Clearly, serial dictatorship rules form a class of rules in that intersection, but more rules qualify.

Theorem 10.8 [11]. *Endowment inheritance rules and deferred acceptance rules always produce the same outcomes if and only if the endowment inheritance tables/priority structures used are acyclic.*

Finally, Table 10.3 shows the trade-offs of some of the key properties we have discussed for the different classes of rules.

Table 10.3 Rules and their properties.

Rules	PO	IR	SP	NB	ST	PMON	NEU
Serial dictatorship	✓	✓	✓	✓	✓	✓	✓
acyclic deferred acceptance / acyclic endowment inheritance	✓	✓	✓	✓	✓	✓	
Deferred acceptance		✓	✓	✓	✓	✓	
endowment inheritance / hierarchical exchange	✓	✓	✓	✓			

Notation:

PO, *Pareto optimality*;

IR, *individual rationality*, respectively *∅-individual rationality*;

SP, *strategy-proofness*;

NB, *non-bossiness*;

ST, *stability*;

PMON, *population monotonicity*;

NEU, *neutrality*.

10.8 Exercises

Exercise 10.1 (*Strategy-proofness* and *non-bossiness* ⇔ *group strategy-proofness*). Prove Proposition 10.1.

Exercise 10.2 (Weak preferences and weak or strong cores). Consider a Shapley–Scarf exchange problem where agent $i \in N$ owns object o_i with weak preferences in $\underline{\mathcal{W}}$; any $R_i \in \underline{\mathcal{W}}$ is transitive and complete and all real objects are strictly preferred to the null object.

For $R \in \underline{\mathcal{W}}^N$, coalition S *strictly blocks* allocation a if there exists an allocation $b \in \mathcal{A}_N$ such that (a) $\cup_{i \in S}\{b_i\} = \cup_{i \in S}\{o_i\}$ and (b), for all $i \in S$, $b_i P_i a_i$. Allocation a is a *weak core allocation* if it is not strictly blocked by any coalition. Furthermore, an allocation a is *competitive under R* if there exist prices $p: O \to \mathbb{R}_+$ such that, for all $i \in N$, (i) $p(a_i) \le p(o_i)$ and (ii) $x P_i a_i$ implies $p(x) > p(o_i)$. Let SC(R) denote the set of strong core allocations of R, WC(R) denote the set of weak core allocations of R, and comp(R) denote the set of competitive allocations under R.

(a) Show that the strong core might be empty for certain $R \in \underline{\mathcal{W}}^N$. In addition, show that if SC(R) $\neq \emptyset$ then for all $a, b \in$ SC(R) we have that, for all $i \in N$, $a_i I_i b_i$.

(b) Let $R \in \underline{\mathcal{W}}^N$. Then, $\hat{R} \in \underline{\mathcal{R}}^N$ is a *strict resolution of R* if it breaks ties in R to obtain strict preferences, i.e., for all $x, y \in O \cup \{\emptyset\}$ and all $i \in N$, $x P_i y$ implies $x \hat{P}_i y$. Let ST(R) denote the set of all strict resolutions of R. Then, show that

$$\text{comp}(R) = \cup_{\hat{R} \in ST(R)}\{\text{TTC}(\hat{R})\}.$$

(c) Show the following inclusion relations and also establish that they might be strict for some problems:

$$\text{SC}(R) \subseteq \text{comp}(R) \subseteq \text{WC}(R).$$

Exercise 10.3 (*Top trading cycles rules*). Show that the top trading cycles rules satisfy *individual rationality*, *Pareto optimality*, and *strategy-proofness*. Also show that when $|N| \ge 3$, a top trading cycles rule may not be *stable*.

Exercise 10.4 (*Serial dictatorship rules*). Show that the serial dictatorship rules satisfy *Pareto optimality* (which implies *weak non-wastefulness*), *strategy-proofness*, *non-bossiness*, *neutrality*, and *population monotonicity*. Work out the use of *neutrality* in the proof of Theorem 10.3's induction basis; in particular, derive the required renaming of objects σ.

Exercise 10.5 (*Properties of endowment inheritance rules*). Which of the properties *∅-individual rationality*, *Pareto optimality*, *strategy-proofness*, *non-bossiness*, *neutrality*, *population monotonicity*, and *stability* do the endowment inheritance rules satisfy and which ones do they not satisfy? Explain (prove) your answers. Note that no characterization of endowment inheritance rules has been established until now.

Exercise 10.6 (*Deferred acceptance rules*). Prove the statement in the proof of Theorem 10.6 that, for any $o \in O$ and any $i, j \in N$ such that $i \succ_o j$, $\varphi_i(R^o, R^o) = o$ and $\varphi_j(R^o, R^o) = \emptyset$.

Let $\succ$ be a priority structure. Show that the deferred acceptance rule $DA^{\succ}$ is not *Pareto optimal* if $\succ$ violates acyclicity.

Exercise 10.7 (*Immediate acceptance rules*). Immediate acceptance algorithm:
Input: a problem $R \in \mathcal{R}^N$ and a priority structure $\succ$.

Step 1. Each agent applies to his favorite object in $O \cup \{\emptyset\}$. Each real object $o \in O$ accepts the applicant who has the highest priority and rejects all the other applicants. The null object $\emptyset$ accepts all applicants.

Step $t \geq 2$. Each applicant who was rejected at step $t - 1$ applies to his next favorite object in $O \cup \{\emptyset\}$. Each real object $o \in O$ that has not been assigned yet accepts the applicant who has the highest priority and rejects all the other applicants. Each real object that has been assigned already rejects all applicants and the null object $\emptyset$ accepts all applicants.

Output. The algorithm terminates when each agent is accepted by a real object or the null object. We denote the object in O that accepted agent i by $IA_i^{\succ}(R)$.

A rule $\varphi \colon \mathcal{R}^N \to \mathcal{A}$ is an *immediate acceptance rule* if there is a priority structure $\succ$ such that, for each $R \in \mathcal{R}^N$, $\varphi(R) = IA^{\succ}(R)$.

Which of the properties $\emptyset$-*individual rationality*, *Pareto optimality*, *strategy-proofness*, *non-bossiness*, *neutrality*, *population monotonicity*, and *stability* do immediate acceptance rules satisfy and which ones do they not satisfy? Explain (prove) your answers.

10.9 Bibliographic Notes

Theorem 10.3 ([21], Theorem 1) showed that a rule satisfies *neutrality*, *strategy-proofness*, and *non-bossiness* if and only if it is a serial dictatorship rule.[3] The following two research contributions showed what happens when *neutrality* is dropped.

In [15], hierarchical exchange rules were introduced. These form a class of rules that extend the way in which the top trading cycles rule works [9] by specifying ownership rights for the objects in an iterative hierarchical manner and by allowing for associated iterative top trading cycles. Theorem 10.5 ([15], Theorem) showed that a rule satisfies *Pareto optimality*, *group strategy-proofness*, and *reallocation-proofness* if and only if it is an hierarchical exchange rule. In [16, Theorem 1] this result was extended using a full characterization of the class of *Pareto optimal* and *group strategy-proof* rules, called trading cycles rules. The set of trading cycles rules extends the set of hierarchical exchange rules by allowing agents not only to own objects throughout the iterative trading cycles allocation procedure but to also have a different "control right" called "brokerage" (a broker cannot necessarily consume a brokered object directly himself but he can trade it for another object).

In [20] a model was considered with publicly as well as individually owned objects and the authors characterized an important extension of the class of endowment inheritance rules, the *YRMH-IGYT (you request my house – I get your turn)* rules,

---

[3] As mentioned in Section 10.4, in our model we need to add *weak non-wastefulness* to ensure that all objects are allocated, while Svensson incorporated this assumption into his model.

which were introduced by [1]: a rule satisfies *individual rationality*, *Pareto optimality*, *strategy-proofness*, *weak neutrality*,[4] and *consistency*[5] if and only if it is a YRMH-IGYT rule. Such rules are essentially serial dictatorship rules that adapt to individual ownership rights that agents have for objects. In [10, Theorems 2 and 3], it was shown that a rule is an endowment inheritance rule based on ownership-adapted acyclic priorities if and only if it satisfies *individual rationality*, *Pareto optimality*, *strategy-proofness*, *consistency*, and either *reallocation-proofness* or *non-bossiness*.

Note that we have simplified our object allocation models by assuming that only one copy of each object is available. Usually, a more general model of object allocation with quotas is studied: for each object type, more than one object can be assigned, up to a fixed quota; e.g., in school choice problems, school places at a specific school can be assigned until the school's specific capacity quota is reached. For object allocation with quotas, in both [8] and [10] allocation rules were studied, along with their properties in relation to acyclic inheritance tables/priority structures. In [8] and [10] different notions of acyclicity were used that coincide for our simplified model (see Section 10.6); we refer the interested reader to the original papers. In [8, Theorem 1] it was shown that for the deferred acceptance rule $DA^{\succ}$, the following are equivalent: $DA^{\succ}$ is *Pareto optimal*, $DA^{\succ}$ is *group strategy-proof*, $DA^{\succ}$ is *consistent*, and $\succ$ is Ergin acyclic. In [10, Theorems 1 and 2] Ergin's acyclicity condition was strengthened and it was shown that an endowment inheritance rule based on an inheritance table π equals a deferred acceptance rule based on a priority structure $\succ$ if and only if $\succ = \pi$ is Kesten acyclic.

Finally, we would also like to briefly mention that the presented characterizations of deferred acceptance rules have been established for object allocation with quotas. More generally, the authors of [12], [5], and [6] characterized so-called *choice-based* deferred acceptance rules, which use responsive and substitutable choice functions to define the associated deferred acceptance algorithm. For yet another widely used class of rules, immediate acceptance rules (see Exercise 10.7), characterization results based on responsive and substitutable choice functions were presented in [13] and [3].

Acknowledgements

Lars Ehlers acknowledges financial support from the SSHRC (Canada). Bettina Klaus acknowledges financial support from the SNSF (Switzerland) through project 100018_162606. We thank Somouaoga Bonkoungou, Di Feng, and Seckin Özbilen for their helpful feedback and comments.

References

[1] Abdulkadiroğlu, Atila, and Sönmez, Tayfun. 1999. House allocation with existing tenants. *Journal of Economic Theory*, **88**, 233–260.

[2] Crawford, Vincent P. 1991. Comparative statics in matching markets. *Journal of Economic Theory*, **54**, 389–400.

---

[4] A rule is *weakly neutral* if it is independent of the names of the publicly owned objects.

[5] A rule is *consistent* if the following holds: suppose that after objects are allocated according to the rule, some agents leave with their assigned objects but no object that was individually owned by a remaining agent was removed. Then, if the remaining agents were to allocate the remaining objects according to the rule, each of them would receive the same object.

[3] Doğan, Battal, and Klaus, Bettina. 2018. Object allocation via immediate-acceptance: Characterizations and an affirmative action application. *Journal of Mathematical Economics*, **79**, 140–156.

[4] Dubins, Lester E., and Freedman, David A. 1981. Machiavelli and the Gale–Shapley algorithm. *American Mathematical Monthly*, **88**, 485–494.

[5] Ehlers, Lars, and Klaus, Bettina. 2014. Strategy-proofness makes the difference: Deferred-acceptance with responsive priorities. *Mathematics of Operations Research*, **39**, 949–966.

[6] Ehlers, Lars, and Klaus, Bettina. 2016. Object allocation via deferred-acceptance: Strategy-proofness and comparative statics. *Games and Economic Behavior*, **97**, 128–146.

[7] Ehlers, Lars, Klaus, Bettina, and Pápai, Szilvia. 2002. Strategy-proofness and population-monotonicity for house allocation problems. *Journal of Mathematical Economics*, **38**, 329–339.

[8] Ergin, Haluk İ. 2002. Efficient resource allocation on the basis of priorities. *Econometrica*, **70**, 2489–2497.

[9] Gale, David, and Shapley, Lloyd S. 1962. College admissions and the stability of marriage. *American Mathematical Monthly*, **69**, 9–15.

[10] Karakaya, Mehmet, Klaus, Bettina, and Schlegel, Jan-Christoph. 2019. Top trading cycles, consistency, and acyclic priorities for house allocation with existing tenants. *Journal of Economic Theory*, **184**, 104948.

[11] Kesten, Onur. 2006. On two competing mechanisms for priority-based allocation problems. *Journal of Economic Theory*, **127**, 155–171.

[12] Kojima, Fuhito, and Manea, Mihai. 2010. Axioms for deferred acceptance. *Econometrica*, **78**, 633–653.

[13] Kojima, Fuhito, and Ünver, M. Utku. 2014. The "Boston" school choice mechanism: An axiomatic approach. *Economic Theory*, **55**, 515–544.

[14] Ma, Jinpeng. 1994. Strategy-proofness and the strict core in a market with indivisibilities. *International Journal of Game Theory*, **23**, 75–83.

[15] Pápai, Szilvia. 2000. Strategyproof assignment by hierarchical exchange. *Econometrica*, **68**, 1403–1433.

[16] Pycia, Marek, and Ünver, M. Utku. 2017. Incentive compatible allocation and exchange of discrete resources. *Theoretical Economics*, **12**, 287–329.

[17] Roth, Alvin E. 1982. The economics of matching: Stability and incentives. *Mathematics of Operations Research*, **7**, 617–628.

[18] Roth, Alvin E., and Postlewaite, Andrew. 1977. Weak versus strong domination in a market with indivisible goods. *Journal of Mathematical Economics*, **4**, 131–137.

[19] Shapley, Lloyd, and Scarf, Herbert. 1974. On cores and indivisibility. *Journal of Mathematical Economics*, **1**, 23–37.

[20] Sönmez, Tayfun, and Ünver, M. Utku. 2010. House allocation with existing tenants: A characterization. *Games and Economic Behavior*, **69**, 425–445.

[21] Svensson, Lars-Gunnar. 1999. Strategy-proof allocation of indivisible goods. *Social Choice and Welfare*, **16**, 557–567.

CHAPTER ELEVEN

Choice and Market Design

Samson Alva and Battal Doğan

11.1 Introduction

In this chapter we explore topics inspired by two peculiarities present in a number of matching markets and market design problems.

The first concerns the foundations of choice behavior in matching markets in the tradition of revealed preference. Agents in such markets face *combinatorial* choice problems. The hallmark of such problems is the agent's freedom to combine elementary things into a bundle that determines the outcome. For instance, in labor-matching markets, firms can freely choose any combination of potential employees who have applied (including none of them).

The second concerns the viability of designing a mechanism through a two-part factorization: the first part focuses on the particulars of how the planner and the agents (or their algorithmic proxies) interact in the mechanism, and the second part focuses on the planner's preferences and objectives. Recent developments in object allocation and matching demonstrate that the planner's choice-behavior in the mechanism can come from a rich set of possibilities without disturbing the strategic incentives of agents.

The salient example is public school choice through centralized assignment, which resembles a two-sided matching market but with an important distinction. Students are agents both in the sense of being able to determine their own choices and in the sense of having normative welfare weight for the planner. However, schools are typically considered a resource for consumption and so lack agency in the first sense. From Chapter 1, we know that the deferred acceptance algorithm with students as proposers yields the stable outcome most preferred by students. We also know that the direct mechanism that determines an outcome using it is strategy-proof for students.

But if schools lack agency, how can they make choices in the algorithm? The insight is that the planner can assume the role of agent for the schools in the operation of the deferred acceptance algorithm, making choices amongst the applicants at each step. These choices can vary according to the planner's preferences or objectives while preserving incentive compatibility if the choice rule is independent of preference reports and satisfies additional conditions.

So, how much can these choice rules vary? The important requirement is that rejections made in the course of the deferred acceptance algorithm are final in a certain sense. This property holds true if the choices are made according to the maximization of a fixed substitutable preference. What is relevant for design is that a growing list of interesting choice rules not based on preference maximization have been defined that also ensure the finality-of-rejections property.

What corresponds to stability if schools do not have preferences? A straightforward interpretation is that the stability of a matching is the absence of a school and a student (or group of students) who prefers that school to their assignment, where the school would take them given its current assignees when the choice is made according to the planner's choice rule. Unlike in truly two-sided markets, however, we cannot be assured of the Pareto efficiency of a stable matching since welfare is only relevant to students and the requirement of stability places constraints on the allocation. Any changes to a stable allocation according to the choice rule would also reduce the welfare of some students. If the choice rule is a complete expression of various aspects of planner objectives that are separate from student welfare then stable allocations necessarily exhibit trade-offs between the collective welfare of students and every aspect of planner objectives, whereas allocations that are "blocked" necessarily have an aspect that has no trade-off.

The upshot is that incentive-compatible market design for combinatorial or discrete goods may fruitfully be pursued through *choice function design*, especially when Pareto efficiency is not paramount but instead is subject to being traded off with other planner objectives. Our aim is to provide the foundation necessary to follow this recent design paradigm.

Section 11.2 defines the primary choice models of interest and discusses issues that pertain to modeling choice behavior, including a detailed discussion of combinatorial choice. Section 11.3 covers the minimum amount of revealed preference theory necessary to understand some of its implications for combinatorial choice. Section 11.4 is centered on the behavioral properties of combinatorial choice, while Section 11.5 describes the remarkable structure induced by the property of path independence. In Section 11.6 we study some combinatorial choice rules that have been featured in recent market design applications. Section 11.7 formalizes the above discussion and illustrates the relationship between choice behavior, stability, and deferred acceptance. For students seeking a deeper understanding, we offer some guidance in Section 11.9 and exercises in Section 10.9.

11.2 Modeling Choice Behavior

We will study the *choice behavior* of an *actor* in an *environment*. The essential description of any *instance* of the choice behavior of such an actor consists of a *choice* (or *chosen alternative*), the *budget set* of possible *alternatives* from which the choice was made, and the prevailing *conditions* in the environment.

A collection of instances of choice behavior may be factorable into a *choice setting* and a *choice function*, where the choice setting defines a *space of alternatives*, a *domain of states*, and a *budget map* identifying the budget set at each state,[1] and the choice function identifies the choice at each state.[2]

A *choice model* is a choice setting together with a *choice function space*, which describes the class of *admissible* choice behaviors.

11.2.1 General Model of Choice Behavior

A *general choice model* is a tuple $(\mathcal{X}, \Pi, B, \mathbb{C})$, where $\mathcal{X}$ is a space of alternatives, Π is a domain of states, B is a *budget map* taking each state π to a nonempty budget set $B(\pi) \subseteq \mathcal{X}$, and $\mathbb{C}$ is a space of choice functions, which are maps c from Π to $2^{\mathcal{X}}$ such that $c(\pi)$ is a non-empty subset of $B(\pi)$. An example of a problem that calls for a general choice model is the study of demand, where budget sets are defined as a function of prices and an expenditure limit.

When the environmental state is thought to affect choice behavior only through the budget set it defines, we can simplify to a *pure choice model*. This is a tuple $(\mathcal{X}, \mathcal{B}, \mathbb{C})$, where the budget set map is replaced by a budget set domain $\mathcal{B}$, which is a collection of subsets of $\mathcal{X}$, and the choice functions are maps c from $\mathcal{B}$ to $2^{\mathcal{X}}$ such that $c(B)$ is a non-empty subset of B.

We make a few important remarks on interpretation.

Remark 11.1 (Decisiveness). We interpret a choice behavior as *decisive* if and only if the chosen set from a budget set is a singleton. This is to say that alternatives are *mutually exclusive* of each other. There are a few different interpretations of non-singleton choice, simply called *partial* choice. Because formal axioms require interpretation, it is important to lay out the interpretation for any formal analysis. A common interpretation is the indifference of the chooser between alternatives in the chosen set. Another interpretation is that the chosen set is an intermediate stage in a multi-stage choice procedure, the ultimate alternative being determined at a later stage.[3]

The usefulness of these models for understanding positive or normative theories of choice depends upon whether there is more structure to the entities of the model, that is, the space of alternatives and the domain of states and budget sets. The assumptions made about structure help to classify a variety of settings and models of choice.

11.2.1.1 Structure on the Set of Alternatives

In an *abstract setting*, the space of alternatives $\mathcal{X}$ is simply a set with no structure assumed. It is the baseline model for social choice theory, examined in Chapter 4.

---

[1] In this framework, the state encodes the environmental conditions and the budget set, which is decoded using the budget map. No two instances could have the same state but different budget sets.

[2] If two instances have the same state but different choices, then the choice behavior is not deterministic with respect to the state. We can relax the requirement that the choice function must identify only one alternative as chosen. Why might there be two instances with the same state and different choices, given that the budget set is completely determined by the state? This suggests an incompleteness in the description of the state, arising from two sources, the environmental conditions or the actor's internal state.

[3] This interpretation might seem to contradict the mutual exclusivity interpretation of alternatives. But this can modeled as partial observed choice, where the final chosen alternative is known only to be in the partially observed chosen set.

Given the general applicability of results for the model, it is the setting for the standard theory of rationalizability and revealed preference.

In an *economic setting*, the nature of the goods to be chosen defines the structure of the space of alternatives, where goods are construed broadly to include immaterial things such as relationship matches or radio spectrum. Let K be the number of kinds of goods, each kind being homogeneous and measurable.[4] Then we can model $\mathcal{X}$ as a subset of the vector space $\mathbb{R}^K$, such as the positive orthant $\mathbb{R}^K_+$, with its usual order and algebraic structure. Each alternative is a *bundle* of the K kinds of goods, represented by a vector in $\mathcal{X}$. Discreteness of the kind $k \in K$ is represented when the kth component of each vector in $\mathcal{X}$ is an integer, whereas perfect divisibility is represented when the kth component varies in an interval of real numbers.[5] For example, if all K kinds of goods come in non-negative discrete quantities, we have a *discrete setting* whenever $\mathcal{X}$ is a rectangular subset of $\mathbb{Z}^K_+$.

The quintessential discrete setting is one with heterogeneous and perfectly indivisible goods. Take, for example, a firm aiming to hire workers from a labor market, where the market conditions affect the pool of workers available for hire. A resolution of the choice problem corresponds to a cohort of hired workers. Or consider, instead, an MBA student wanting to determine courses to take in a given semester. A resolution of that choice problem is a schedule of courses. Here, $\mathcal{X}$ is said to have a *combinatorial goods* structure, since alternatives in $\mathcal{X}$ involve combinations of the indivisible goods. Market design and matching is replete with combinatorial choice problems. If E is the set of indivisible goods, each alternative is a bundle that combines zero or one unit of each good, representable as a subset of E. The space of alternatives $\mathcal{X}$ is the set 2^E, which is the power set of E equipped with its canonical structure as a Boolean algebra.[6]

Remark 11.2. There is an important distinction between an element of E and the singleton set containing this element. Each element can be interpreted as a distinct "feature" or dimension of the space of alternatives, whereas the singleton set is the unique alternative that has as its only feature the element it contains.

Remark 11.3. The alternative with none of the elements of E present is represented by the empty set. In the matching market example above, it is the alternative of hiring no worker or of not enrolling in school for the semester.

---

[4] For our purposes, assuming homogeneity is without loss of generality, as long as the notion of indistinguishability defines an equivalence relation over goods. Heterogeneity within a kind of good can be dealt with by an appropriate homogeneous refinement.

[5] For $a \in \mathbb{R}$, $x = (x_k)_{k \in K}$, and $y = (y_k)_{k \in K}$ in $\mathbb{R}^K$, $x \le y$ if and only if $x_k \le y_k$ for each $k \in K$, $x + y$ is the tuple $(x_k + y_k)_{k \in K} \in \mathbb{R}^K$, and ax is the tuple $(ax_k)_{k \in K} \in \mathbb{R}^K$. So, the space of alternatives $\mathcal{X}$ is a subset of an ordered vector space. If $\mathbb{R}$ is replaced by $\mathbb{Z}$ throughout, then the background space for $\mathcal{X}$ is an ordered $\mathbb{Z}$-module.

[6] A collection of subsets of a given set is a Boolean algebra if arbitrary unions, as well as arbitrary intersections, of members of the collection are also members of the collection and complements of members of the collection are also members of the collection. In fact, $\mathcal{X}$ as defined has the structure of a power set algebra, which has a minor distinction as a type of Boolean algebra. By the representation theorem for Boolean algebras a finite Boolean algebra is isomorphic to some power set algebra, but there are infinite Boolean algebras that do not have a power set algebra representation. We will avoid the realm of the infinite in this chapter, so the distinction is immaterial.

11.2.1.2 Structure on the Domain of States and Budget Sets

In economic settings with goods having market prices, the state of the environment comprises a price vector quoted in terms of a unit of account called "money" and an endowment of money or of goods; a demand function describes the choice behavior of the agent. This is a setting with *price-based budget sets*.[7]

In some cases, money is a currency that has valuable uses outside of the context of the problem domain. Examples include the auction environments used to sell bands of electromagnetic spectrum (see Chapter 7) or advertisement slots on a webpage (see Chapter 6). However, in other cases money is solely a construct of a mechanism or setting, with no valuable use outside this context. Examples of this include the allocation of courses in some business schools through pseudomarket mechanisms (see Chapter 8). So, money with outside value is a good that directly affects the agent's utility whereas money with no outside value is artificial or *token* money, which only indirectly affects the agent's utility through its use as a unit of account for prices and expenditure limits in the budget constraint.

In an abstract setting of pure choice, the domain of states is identified with a domain of budget sets. Budget domains may yet have structure in a neutral setting, through conditions on cardinality. The budget domain is *complete* if it contains every finite subset of alternatives. It is *additive* if the union of two budget sets in the domain is also in the domain. It is *connected* if for every trio of alternatives (possibly indistinct) there is a budget set in the domain that contains exactly these alternatives.

With a structure on the space of alternatives, natural structures on budget sets and domains emerge. For example, in economic settings with goods in measurable quantities, *free disposal* allows an actor to reduce the quantity of one or more kinds of goods in a bundle without cost. In matching settings, where a good represents a particular relationship match, *voluntary participation* allows an actor to drop one or more relationships without dropping others. Since for these settings we represent alternatives as vectors in an ordered vector space with partial order $\leq$, free disposal or voluntary participation maps to the requirement that a budget set is *downward closed*, which means that it contains all vectors that are lesser in the partial order than some vector in it.[8] We say the budget domain is *comprehensive* if every budget set in it is downward closed. For example, the price-based budgets domain is comprehensive.

In many matching settings, in addition to budgets being downward closed, actors possess another liberty in constructing a bundle, that of unrestricted combination. Suppose a firm has applicant pools Y and Y' from two different recruiting channels. What are the bundles (that is, teams of workers) that the firm could consider hiring? Voluntary participation permits any team Z, drawn from one of the two pools. Unrestricted combination means that the firm could form a team from any combination of the applicants in pool Y and in pool Y'. Since bundles are subsets of E, combinations are defined by unions.

---

[7] A price-based budget set is defined by an inequality constraint that is linear in the prices ($\langle p, x \rangle \leq b$), the bound b being a given expenditure limit (a money endowment) or the market value $\langle p, x_0 \rangle$ of a given endowment of goods x_0.

[8] In formal notation, a budget set B is said to be downward closed if, for every $x, y \in \mathcal{X}$, $x \in B$, and $y \leq x$, it holds that $y \in B$.

Definition 11.4. A budget domain is a *combinatorial choice domain* if (1) the domain is *comprehensive*, (2) every budget set B in the domain is *join-closed*, that is, for every pair of bundles $x, y \in B$, $x \vee y \in B$, and (3) every bundle Y is *potentially budget constrained*, that is, Y is $\subseteq$-maximal for some budget in the domain.

If a bundle Y is potentially budget constrained, there is a price vector p and expenditure limit b such that Y is inclusion maximal in a price-based budget set.

11.2.2 Combinatorial Models of Choice Behavior

As our overview should have made clear, the combinatorial setting brings considerable structure with it. We define two models of choice that directly incorporate this structure.

A *combinatorial choice model* is a tuple $(E, \mathcal{D}, \mathbf{C})$, where E is a finite set of elements, $\mathcal{D} \subseteq 2^E$ is a non-empty domain of *option sets*, and $\mathbf{C}$ is a set of *combinatorial choice functions*, which are functions $C \colon \mathcal{D} \to 2^E$ such that $C(Y) \subseteq Y$ for each option set Y. We will generally assume that the domain of option sets is *complete*, that is $\mathcal{D} = 2^E$, in which case we can drop its notation in the tuple.

Remark 11.5. Each $C \in \mathbf{C}$ models *decisive* choice behavior even when, for some option set Y, $C(Y)$ is a set with more than one element. To reiterate Remark 11.2, elements are features or dimensions of the space of alternatives but not themselves alternatives. Instead, an alternative or bundle is a set of elements, hence a subset of E. To allow for partial choice, choice correspondences from $\mathcal{D}$ to 2^E would be needed. We do not pursue this more general approach here, however.

Remark 11.6. An option set is not a budget set, because it is not the set of all bundles available. Instead, it comprises the elements that may be combined into bundles. However, when the domain of budgets is infinite, as in the next model we discuss, correspondences are largely unavoidable when some sort of continuity is desirable.

A *combinatorial demand model* is a tuple $(E, \Omega, B, \mathbf{D})$, where E is a finite set of elements, Ω is a non-empty set, B is the budget map $B \colon \mathbb{R}^E_{++} \times \Omega \rightrightarrows 2^E$, and $\mathbf{D}$ is the set of *combinatorial demand correspondences*, which are correspondences $D \colon \mathbb{R}^E_{++} \times \Omega \rightrightarrows 2^E$ such that $D(p, \omega) \subseteq B(p, \omega)$ for each $(p, \omega) \in \mathbb{R}^E_{++} \times \Omega$.

As with the combinatorial choice model above, an alternative is a bundle of goods that is defined as a subset of elements from E. Identify each bundle $Z \in 2^E$ with the vector in $\mathbb{R}^E$, also denoted by Z, that has entry 1 at index $a \in E$ if $a \in Z$ and entry 0 otherwise. We are most interested in settings with a money endowment and linear prices, and so we will take Ω to be a subset of $\mathbb{R}_+$ and $B(p, \omega) = \{Z \in 2^E : \langle p, Z \rangle \leq \omega\}$. It should be clear that this is simply a general choice model $(\mathcal{X}, \Pi, B, \mathbf{C})$ with combinatorial goods (see p. 240) and price-based budget sets (see p. 242), where $\mathcal{X} = 2^E$ and Π has been factored into a price vector space $\mathbb{R}^E_{++}$ and an endowment space Ω.

11.2.3 Faithful Representations of Combinatorial Choice Models

It is natural to ask what is the relationship between combinatorial choice models and the pure choice models previously described. As we now describe, each combinatorial choice model is *behaviorally isomorphic* to some pure choice model with combinatorial goods and budget sets. This means that each combinatorial choice model is a *faithful* representation of a pure choice model.

Given a combinatorial choice model $(E, \mathcal{D}, \mathbf{C})$, define $\mathcal{X} = 2^E$, $\mathcal{B} = \{2^Y : Y \in \mathcal{D}\}$, and $\mathbb{C}$ to be the set of all $c : \mathcal{B} \to 2^{\mathcal{X}}$ such that $c(2^Y) = \{C(Y)\}$ for every $Y \in \mathcal{D}$. Then $(\mathcal{X}, \mathcal{B}, \mathbb{C})$ is a pure choice model where the space of alternatives $\mathcal{X}$ is structured as a power set algebra, the budget domain $\mathcal{B}$ is both comprehensive and join-closed, and the choice functions in $\mathbb{C}$ are decisive. Moreover, if the domain of option sets is complete ($\mathcal{D} = 2^E$) then $\mathcal{B}$ is a combinatorial choice domain. The mapping from combinatorial choice models to pure choice models so defined is denoted $\mathfrak{F}$.

Take a pure choice model $(\mathcal{X}, \mathcal{B}, \mathbb{C})$, where all choice functions in $\mathbb{C}$ are decisive, the space of alternatives is a finite Boolean lattice $(\mathcal{X}, \leq, \vee, \wedge)$, and $\mathcal{B}$ is a collection of subsets of $\mathcal{X}$ that is comprehensive with respect to $\leq$ and join-closed with respect to $\vee$. Denote the mapping, defined below, from pure choice models with this structure to combinatorial choice models by $\mathfrak{G}$. Let E be the set of *atoms* of the Boolean lattice $\mathcal{X}$; atoms are simply those members of the lattice with only the bottom of the lattice below them. These correspond naturally to the set of elements in a combinatorial model, because every member of the lattice is the join of the set of atoms below it. By the representation theorem for Boolean lattices, there is an isomorphism from $\mathcal{X}$ to the power set algebra 2^E of atoms, with the usual set operators and inclusion serving the lattice operators and order.[9] That is, $\mathfrak{G}$ maps each $x \in \mathcal{X}$ to $\{a \in E : a \leq x\}$. Each budget set $B \in \mathcal{B}$ is mapped to an option set $\mathfrak{G}(B) = \bigcup_{y \in B} \mathfrak{G}(y)$. Since B is comprehensive and join-closed, $\wedge B$ is the bundle $x \in B$ that is the greatest in terms of the underlying partial order on alternatives $\leq$. Then $\mathfrak{G}(x)$, the set of atoms below x, is equal to $\mathfrak{G}(B)$. So, define the domain of option sets $\mathcal{D} = \{\mathfrak{G}(B) : B \in \mathcal{B}\}$, which can be seen as a collection of subsets of E. Moreover, if $\mathcal{B}$ is a combinatorial choice domain then the domain of option sets is complete. Finally, each choice function $c \in \mathbb{C}$ is mapped to a function $\mathfrak{G}(c) = C : \mathcal{D} \to 2^E$ such that $C(\mathfrak{G}(B)) = \mathfrak{G}(c(B))$. It should be clear that each type of object is mapped bijectively from one model to the other.

11.3 Revealed Preference and Choice Behavior

A *theory of choice* describes how choice behavior is determined. It will posit the *existence* of theoretical entities (e.g. preferences, priorities, information) and rules or laws for how these entities produce choice behavior. When applied to a particular choice setting, it generates a model of choice with that setting. If the generated choice model describes the choice behavior being studied, we say the behavior (or model) is *rationalized* by the theory.

In this section we study rationalizability by the theory of preference-based (utility-based) choice, discussed in Chapter 4. Recall that the theory postulates that the agent

---

[9] The representability of $\mathcal{X}$ as a power set algebra is characterized by $\mathcal{X}$ being a complete and atomic Boolean lattice; these conditions are automatically satisfied if $\mathcal{X}$ is finite. The isomorphism between combinatorial and pure choice models can be extended to infinite spaces if we strengthen join-closed to complete-join-closed.

has a preference relation (utility function) and as a rule chooses any one of the most preferred (utility-maximizing) alternatives from a given budget set.

Fix a pure choice model $(\mathcal{X}, \Pi, B, \mathbb{C})$.

We model preferences by a binary relation R on $\mathcal{X}$, where $x\,R\,y$ denotes "x is at least as preferred as y". Let $\overline{\mathcal{R}}$ be the set of all preference relations on $\mathcal{X}$. Unlike the definition on pg. 84, we allow for intransitivity and incompleteness. The transitive closure of a binary relation R, denoted $\tau(R)$, is the inclusion-smallest transitive relation that contains R. It means that $x\,\tau(R)\,y$ if and only if there exists a finite sequence $x_0, \ldots, x_n$ such that $x_0 = x$, $x_n\,R\,y$ and, for every $m = 0, \ldots, n-1$, $x_m\,R\,x_{m+1}$.[10] The set of R-greatest alternatives in a subset B of $\mathcal{X}$, denoted top(B, R), is equal to $\{x \in B : \forall y \in B, xRy\}$. The *preference-maximization choice rule* Γ determines the choices to be the set of preference-greatest alternatives in the budget set. It maps each preference relation R to a choice function Γ^R, defined by $\Gamma^R(B(\pi)) = \text{top}(B(\pi), R)$ for every $\pi \in \Pi$. We say that Γ^R is the choice function induced by R.

A choice function $c \in \mathbb{C}$ is (transitively) *rationalized* by a (transitive) preference relation R, which is called a (transitive) *rationalization* of c, if c is induced by R under the preference-maximization choice rule, that is, if $c = \Gamma^R$.

11.3.1 Rationalizability and Revealed Preference

Questions for any theory intended as a positive analysis of observed choice include the following. Is the theory *falsifiable*, that is, are there observable choice patterns that are inconsistent with the theory? Is the theory *testable*, that is, given data on choice behavior, is there an effective test based solely on the data that will correctly falsify the theory or correctly provide a rationalization? We address both these questions through an analysis of revealed preference.

We say that alternative x is *revealed-preferred* to alternative y, denoted $x\,R_c\,y$, if there exists a problem $\pi \in \Pi$ such that x is chosen and y is in the budget set (i.e., $x \in c(\pi)$ and $y \in B(\pi)$). If for some problem x is chosen and y is in the budget set but not chosen, we say that x is *revealed-strictly-preferred* to y, denoted $x\,R_c^s\,y$. It is important to note that R_c^s might not be the asymmetric part of R_c. For example, there could be one budget set at which x and y are chosen (so that $x\,R_c\,y\,R_c\,x$) and another budget set at which x and y are available but only x is chosen (so x that $R_c^s\,y$).

We begin with a result that explains the central place of the revealed preference relation in the analysis of rational choice. From the point of view of testability, it implies that a potentially exhaustive search for a rationalization in the preference space is not required.

Proposition 11.7. *A choice function c is rationalizable if and only if it is rationalized by its revealed preference relation R_c.*

Proof The "if" direction is immediate. To prove the other direction, notice that $c(\pi) \subseteq \text{top}(B(\pi), R_c)$ follows directly from the definition of revealed preference. Moreover, any rationalization must extend the revealed preference

---

[10] The transitive closure of R is equivalently defined by $\tau(R) = \bigcap_{R' \in \mathcal{R}^\tau} R'$, where $\mathcal{R}^\tau$ is the set of all transitive relations R' such that $R' \supseteq R$.

relation. That is, for every pair of alternatives x and y and every rationalization R of c, $x \; R_c \; y$ implies $x \; R \; y$. Since x revealed-preferred to y implies that there is a $\pi \in \Pi$ such that $x \in c(\pi)$ and $y \in B(\pi)$, the definition of rationalization implies $c(\pi) = \text{top}(B(\pi), R)$, and so $x \; R \; y$. Finally, the set of greatest alternatives expands when the preference relation is extended; that is, $\text{top}(B(\pi), R_c) \subseteq \text{top}(B(\pi), R)$. $\qquad\qquad\square$

11.3.2 WARP and Rationalizability

A choice function c satisfies the *weak axiom of revealed preference* (WARP) if, for every pair of alternatives x and y, if x is revealed-preferred to y, then y is not revealed-strictly-preferred to x.

The weak axiom of revealed preference is the foundational axiom of revealed preference theory. We begin our exploration of its implications in the pure choice setting.

Theorem 11.8. *If c is a choice function that satisfies WARP then*

1. *it is rationalizable;*
2. *it is transitively rationalizable if the domain of budget sets $B(\Pi)$ is connected or additive.*

Proof From the proof of Proposition 11.7, we simply need to show that WARP implies, for every $\pi \in \Pi$, that $\text{top}(B(\pi), R_c) \subseteq c(\pi)$. The reader should verify that a choice function satisfies WARP if and only if the revealed strict preference relation is equal to the asymmetric component of the revealed preference relation.

As for rationalizability by a transitive preference relation, suppose first that the domain of budget sets is connected. Let $x \; R_c \; y$ and $y \; R_c \; z$. Take the set $\{x, y, z\}$, which connectedness assures us is a budget set in the domain. By WARP, we see that z chosen implies that y is chosen and thus that x is chosen. Indeed, this argument applies symmetrically to all members of $\{x, y, z\}$. Then, assuming the choice function is non-empty, all three are chosen, implying $x \; R_c \; z$ and so the transitivity of the revealed preference relation.

The case with an additive domain of budgets is left as Exercise 11.1. $\qquad\square$

We can understand the implication of WARP for combinatorial choice models by making use of the isomorphisms mapping between combinatorial and pure choice.

Theorem 11.9. *Suppose that a combinatorial choice model $(E, 2^E, \mathbf{C})$ and a pure choice model $(\mathcal{X}, \mathcal{B}, \mathbb{C})$ are isomorphic, i.e., $(E, 2^E, \mathbf{C})$ and $(\mathcal{X}, \mathcal{B}, \mathbb{C})$ are isomorphically mapped from the first to the second by $\mathfrak{F}$ and second to the first by $\mathfrak{G}$, the inverse of F. Then $C \in \mathbf{C}$ satisfies IRE (the irrelevance of rejected elements) if and only if $c = \mathfrak{F}(C)$ satisfies WARP.*

The behavioral implications for a combinatorial choice model of various conditions formalized in the pure choice model can be obtained through its faithful representation. See Section 11.9 for a reference.

We turn next to the combinatorial demand model. The utility maximization theory posits that an agent has a utility function u and his demand $D^u(p, m)$ is derived as the set of choices that maximize u subject to constraints placed by the prices p and money budget m. The appropriate analysis depends on whether money provides direct utility. We assume so. The agent gets utility $u(A, t)$ from consuming a pair consisting of a bundle of items and a quantity of money (A, t), where u is strictly monotonic in money.

Faced with $(p, m) \in \Pi$, where m could be interpreted as an endowment of money, the agent chooses (A, t) to maximize $u(A, t)$ subject to the budget constraint $\langle p, A \rangle + t \leq m$. The derived demand for bundles of items $D^u(p, m)$ consists of each bundle $A \in \mathcal{X}$ that for some $t \in \mathbb{R}$ maximizes u at (p, m). This is so because we can identify t from $A \in D^u(p, m)$ by $t = m - \langle p, A \rangle$, given monotonicity in money.

Consider a utility that is quasilinear in money, as introduced in Chapter 4, so that $u(A, t) = v(A) + t$ for some $v : 2^E \to \mathbb{R}$ called the valuation function. As long as any lower bound on money consumption is not binding, quasilinearity simplifies demand analysis by eliminating income effects. That is, for any two (p, m) and (p, m'), $D^u(p, m) = D^u(p, m')$.

Given this irrelevance of the money budget on the demand for items, we do not need to indicate its level. Can a given demand correspondence be explained by maximization of some objective function that is quasilinear in prices?

A positive answer to the question requires some intuitive restrictions on D. First, we say D satisfies the *law of demand* if, for every p, p', every $A \in D(p)$, and every $A' \in D(p')$, $\langle p - p', A - A' \rangle \leq 0$. To understand the meaning of this requirement, notice that it implies a version of the weak axiom of revealed preference adapted to this setting. This axiom states that, for any bundles A and A' and prices p and p', if bundles A and A' are demanded at prices p and p', respectively, and furthermore bundle A' is worth less at prices p, then bundle A is more expensive than A' at price p'. That is, if $A \in D(p)$, $A' \in D(p')$, and $\langle p, A' \rangle < \langle p, A \rangle$ then $\langle p', A \rangle > \langle p', A' \rangle$.

We also need a continuity property. Demand function D is *upper hemicontinuous* if, for every $p \in \mathbb{R}^E_{++}$, there exists an open neighborhood V of p such that $D(q) \subseteq D(p)$ for every $q \in V$.

Proposition 11.10. *For any quasilinear utility function u, the derived demand function D^u on domain Π satisfies the weak axiom of revealed preference and upper hemicontinuity.*

Proof To prove WARP, let $p \in \mathbb{R}^E_{++}$, $A \in D^u(p)$, $A' \in D^u(p')$, and $\langle p, A' \rangle < \langle p, A \rangle$. From utility maximization, $v(A) - \langle p, A \rangle \geq v(A') - \langle p, A' \rangle$ and $v(A') - \langle p', A' \rangle \geq v(A) - \langle p', A \rangle$. Thus these two inequalities yield $\langle p', A \rangle - \langle p', A' \rangle \geq v(A) - v(A') \geq \langle p, A \rangle - \langle p, A' \rangle$. But then $\langle p, A' \rangle < \langle p, A \rangle$ implies $\langle p', A \rangle - \langle p', A' \rangle \geq 0$ as desired.

Define $U(A, p) = v(A) - \langle p, A \rangle$ for each bundle A and price vector p. To prove upper hemicontinuity, notice that, for each bundle A, U is continuous in prices. Fix a price vector p. Let W be the maximum utility attained at p, i.e., $W = U(A, p)$ for some maximizing bundle $A \in D^u(p)$. Define V_A to be the preimage under $U(A, \cdot)$ of the open set (∞, W). Let $V = \cap_{A \in 2^E \setminus D^u(p)} V_A$. Note that, for every bundle A, $A \notin D^u(p)$ if and only if $U(A, p) < W$. Thus, $A \notin D^u(p)$ implies $p \in V_A$, and so $p \in V$. The continuity of a function means that the preimage of an open set is open, so V_A is an open set. Then V is open, since it is a finite intersection of open sets, given that 2^E is finite. Finally, for any $A \in 2^E \setminus D^u(p)$, we have $V \subseteq V_A$, so, for any $q \in V$, $U(A, q) \in (\infty, W)$. Thus $A \notin D^u(q)$, establishing upper hemicontinuity. □

The converse also holds.

Theorem 11.11 (Rationalizability). *For any combinatorial demand D on domain Π that satisfies the law of demand and upper hemicontinuity, there exists a quasilinear utility u that rationalizes it, that is, the derived demand function D^u equals D.*

Owing to its complexity, we omit the proof, a reference for which is given in Section 11.8.

11.4 Combinatorial Choice Behavior

In this section we describe some types of choice behavior that are particular to combinatorial choice settings. Fix a combinatorial choice model $(E, \mathbf{C})$ with a complete domain of option sets, and let C be a combinatorial choice function.

Substitutability turns out to be essential in market design applications in order to ensure convergence to a stable matching when the deferred acceptance algorithm takes the choice rules of institutions (such as schools) as input.

We say C satisfies *substitutability* if the elements chosen from a given option set that remain available in a given subset of this option set are amongst the chosen elements from that subset. That is, for each $S, T \in 2^E$,

$$\text{if } T \subseteq S \text{ then } C(S) \cap T \subseteq C(T).$$

We say C satisfies (combinatorial) *path independence* if the choice from a given option set is the same as the choice from the collection of elements chosen from each of two option sets whose union equals the given option set. That is, for each $S, T \in 2^E$,

$$C(S \cup T) = C(C(S) \cup C(T)).$$

In fact, path independence is equivalent to substitutability together with the following choice-invariance condition. We say that C satisfies the *irrelevance of rejected elements* if the removal of some rejected elements from the option set leaves the set of chosen elements unchanged. That is, for each $S, T \in 2^E$,

$$\text{if } C(S) \subseteq T \subseteq S \text{ then } C(S) = C(T).$$

Theorem 11.12. *A combinatorial choice function is path independent if and only if it satisfies substitutability and IRE.*

Proof Substitutability is equivalent to the following subadditivity condition: $C(S \cup T) \subseteq C(S) \cup C(T)$ for every $S, T \in 2^E$. We will make use of this result, whose proof is left as an exercise (see Exercise 11.3).

Suppose that C satisfies substitutability and IRE. Let $S_1, S_2 \in 2^E$. Then $C(S_1 \cup S_2) \subseteq C(S_1) \cup C(S_2) \subseteq S_1 \cup S_2$, where the first inclusion holds by substitutability and its equivalence to subadditivity, and the second inclusion holds by the definition of a choice function. Then $C(S_1 \cup S_2) = C(C(S_1) \cup C(S_2))$ follows from IRE, proving path independence.

Suppose that C satisfies path independence. By path independence, $C(S \cup T) = C(C(S) \cup C(T)) \subseteq C(S) \cup C(T)$, so subadditivity (and thus substitutability) is satisfied, where the second equality follows from the definition of a choice function. To show IRE, suppose that $C(S) \subseteq T \subseteq S$, so that $C(T) = C(C(S) \cup T) = C(C(S) \cup T \cup C(S))$. Then $C(C(S) \cup T \cup C(S)) = C(C(C(S) \cup T) \cup C(S)) = C(C(T) \cup C(S)) = C(T \cup S) = C(S)$, where the first and third equalities follow from path independence and the second from the previous line of equalities. Putting the chain of equalities together yields $C(T) = C(S)$. $\qquad\square$

We say C satisfies *size monotonicity* if the number of chosen elements does not decrease when the the option set is expanded. That is, for each $S, T \in 2^E$,

$$\text{if } T \subseteq S \text{ then } |C(T)| \leq |C(S)|.$$

Proposition 11.13. *If C satisfies substitutability and size monotonicity then it also satisfies path independence.*

Proof We first show that IRE is satisfied. Let $C(S) \subseteq T \subseteq S$. By substitutability, $C(S) \cap T \subseteq C(T)$. Then $C(S) \subseteq C(T)$. By size monotonicity, $|C(T)| \leq |C(S)|$. But then $C(S) = C(T)$. So IRE is satisfied. Then from Theorem 11.12, we obtain path independence. $\qquad\square$

11.5 Path-Independent Choice

As we will see in Section 11.7, path independence is crucial to arriving at a stable outcome via a deferred acceptance algorithm, so it is worth understanding the structure that it entails. We describe two results regarding the structure of path-independent choice functions that offer insight into the previously studied lattice structure of stable matchings.

Fix a finite combinatorial choice model $(E, \mathbf{C})$ with a complete domain of option sets, and fix a path-independent combinatorial choice function C. To simplify the discussion, assume that *no element is irrelevant to C*, that is, for every $a \in E$, there exists $S \in 2^E$ such that $a \in C(S)$. All the results in this section have a simple adaptation for functions C that do not satisfy this condition.

11.5.1 The Lattice of Maximal Option Sets of a Path-Independent Choice Function

We will now show how a path-independent choice function can be represented by a particular lattice of sets.

Two option sets $S, T \in 2^E$ are *choice-equivalent* if $C(S) = C(T)$.

Lemma 11.14. *For each $S \in 2^E$, there exists a unique set $S^\sharp \in 2^E$ such that, for every $T \in 2^E$, T is choice-equivalent to S if and only if $C(S) \subseteq T \subseteq S^\sharp$.*

Proof Let $\mathbf{pre}_C(Y)$ be the preimage of $Y \in 2^E$ under C, defined by $\mathbf{pre}_C(Y) = \{T \in 2^E : C(T) = Y\}$. Then the collection of all option sets that are choice-equivalent to S is simply $\mathbf{pre}_C(C(S))$.

Define $S^\sharp = \bigcup \mathbf{pre}_C(C(S))$. First, note that C is *idempotent* since it is path independent (see Exercise 11.2 for the definition). Second, if $T_1, T_2 \in \mathbf{pre}_C(C(S))$ then $C(T_1 \cup T_2) = C(C(T_1) \cup C(T_2)) = C(C(S) \cup C(S)) = C(C(S))$, where the first equality is from path independence and the third from idempotence. This shows that the preimage is closed under finite unions. Since E is finite, it means that $\bigcup \mathbf{pre}_C(C(S)) \in \mathbf{pre}_C(C(S))$ and so $S^\sharp$ is the unique maximal member of the preimage of $C(S)$. Next, if $C(T) = C(S)$ then $C(S) \subseteq T$, since $C(T) \subseteq T$ by definition. Finally, if T satisfies $C(S) \subseteq T \subseteq S^\sharp$ then $C(T) = C(S)$, since $C(S^\sharp) = C(S)$ and since C satisfies IRE, given Theorem 11.12. □

We say an option set S is *maximal* if there is no larger option set from which the same set of elements can be chosen. So S is maximal if and only if $T \supseteq S$ implies $C(T) = C(S)$. From the previous lemma we know that option set S is maximal if and only if $S = S^\sharp$, with $S^\sharp$ as defined in the lemma's statement.

Let $\mathcal{M}$ denote the set of maximal option sets for C, ordered by set inclusion. The following characterizes the predecessors in $\mathcal{M}$ of a maximal option set S.

Lemma 11.15. *For each $S \in \mathcal{M}$ and each $a \in C(S)$, $S \setminus \{a\} \in \mathcal{M}$.*

Proof To obtain a contradiction, suppose there exist $S \in \mathcal{M}$ and $a \in C(S)$ such that $S \setminus \{a\} \notin \mathcal{M}$. Let $S' \in \mathcal{M}$ such that $C(S') = C(S \setminus \{a\})$. Since $S \setminus \{a\} \notin \mathcal{M}$, $S \setminus \{a\} \subsetneq S'$. Now, consider the option set $S' \cup \{a\}$. Note that $S \subsetneq S' \cup \{a\}$. Moreover, since C is path independent, $C(S' \cup \{a\}) = C(C(S') \cup \{a\})$. Since $C(S') = C(S \setminus \{a\})$, we get $C(S' \cup \{a\}) = C(C(S \setminus \{a\}) \cup \{a\})$. Again by path independence, $C(C(S \setminus \{a\}) \cup \{a\}) = C(S)$. Thus, we get $C(S' \cup \{a\}) = C(S)$. Since $S \subsetneq S' \cup \{a\}$, this contradicts that $S \in \mathcal{M}$. □

We now prove that the intersection of maximal option sets is a maximal option set.

Lemma 11.16. *The family of maximal sets $\mathcal{M}$ is intersection-closed, that is, $S_1, S_2 \in \mathcal{M}$ implies $S_1 \cap S_2 \in \mathcal{M}$.*

Proof Let $S_1, S_2 \in \mathcal{M}$ and define $T = S_1 \cap S_2$. To show $T \in \mathcal{M}$, it is sufficient to show that $T^\sharp = T$. Notice that $C(S_1 \cup T^\sharp) = C(C(S_1) \cup C(T^\sharp)) = C(C(S_1) \cup C(T)) = C(S_1 \cup T) = C(S_1)$, where the first and third equalities are from path independence and the second is from the definition of choice-equivalence. Then $S_1 \cup T^\sharp$ is choice-equivalent to S_1. By the same argument, $S_2 \cup T^\sharp$ is choice-equivalent to S_2. Since S_1 and S_2 are maximal, $T^\sharp$ is a subset of S_1 and S_2, but, by Lemma 11.14, $T^\sharp \supseteq T = S_1 \cap S_2$, proving $T^\sharp = T \in \mathcal{M}$. □

Since E is a clearly a maximal set, $\mathcal{M}$ has a top, that is, a greatest member E (under $\subseteq$). A useful fact about any finite and intersection-closed family of sets with a

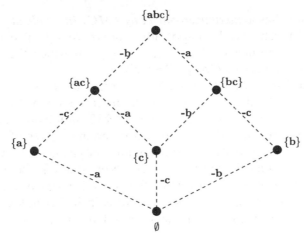

Figure 11.1 Hasse diagram of the lattice of maximal option sets of Example 11.18, with elements that are chosen in boldface.

top is that set inclusion is a complete lattice order, with the meet operator coinciding with set intersection.[11]

Theorem 11.17. *The family of maximal sets $\mathcal{M}$ ordered by set inclusion is a complete lattice of sets, with E at the top and $\emptyset$ at the bottom.*

Also observe that all maximal sets and the entire choice lattice can be constructed starting from E and subtracting a chosen element at each step.

Example 11.18. Suppose $E = \{a, b, c\}$ and suppose C satisfies $C(\{a, b, c\}) = \{a, b\}$ and $C(S) = S$ for each S with $|S| \leq 2$. It is easy to verify that C satisfies path independence. Figure 11.1 displays the Hasse diagram of the lattice of $\mathcal{M}$ defined by C. To see how it is obtained, first imagine drawing the top of the lattice, $E = \{a, b, c\}$. Then, by removing each of the chosen elements b and a, we obtain the predecessors of E at the level below: $\{a, c\}$ and $\{a, c\}$. The remainder of the diagram is obtained in a similar fashion.

11.5.2 Maximizer-Collecting Rationalization

Recall that, for any set S and binary relation $\succeq$, $\text{top}(S, \succeq)$ denotes the set of $\succeq$-greatest elements in S, that is, $\text{top}(S, \succeq) = \{a \in S : \forall b \in S, a \succeq b\}$.

The *maximizer-collecting* choice rule AM corresponding to a finite sequence of linear orderings $(\succeq)_1^m = (\succeq_1, \ldots, \succeq_m)$ is defined for each $S \in 2^E$ by collecting the maximizers in S of each linear ordering in the sequence, that is,

$$\text{AM}[(\succeq)_1^m](S) = \bigcup_{i \in \{1, \ldots, m\}} \text{top}(S, \succeq_i).$$

---

[11] The join operator is equal to the set union only if the family is also closed under set unions. Otherwise, the join of two sets is given by the intersection of all upper bounds in the family of the two sets.

A choice function C has a *maximizer-collecting (MC) rationalization* – also known as an Aizerman–Malishevski decomposition – of size $m \in \mathbb{N}$ if there exists a finite sequence of linear orderings $(\succeq)_1^m = (\succeq_1, \ldots, \succeq_m)$ for which the choice function defined by the MC choice rule $\mathsf{AM}[(\succeq)_1^m]$ equals C.

To illustrate an MC rationalization, let us return to the choice function C in Example 11.18. Let $\succeq_1$ and $\succeq_2$ be the linear orderings defined as $a \succeq_1 c \succeq_1 b$ and $b \succeq_2 c \succeq_2 a$. We observe that C has an MC rationalization via $\{\succeq_1, \succeq_2\}$. Consider the option set $\{a, b, c\}$. Note that a is the maximizer of $\succeq_1$ and b is the maximizer of $\succeq_2$. That is, collecting the maximizers yields $\{a, b\}$, which coincides with $C(\{a, b, c\})$. Consider the option set $\{b, c\}$. Note that c is the maximizer of $\succeq_1$ and b is the maximizer of $\succeq_2$. So, collecting the maximizers yields $\{b, c\}$, which again coincides with $C(\{b, c\})$. It can be verified that the coincidence holds for every option set. In fact, the next result shows that any path-independent choice function has an MC rationalization.

Theorem 11.19. *A choice function is path independent if and only if it has an MC rationalization.*

Proof Let C be a path-independent choice function. That any MC rationalizable choice function is path independent is to be shown in Exercise 11.5.

Define a binary relation $\rightarrow$ on $\mathcal{M}$ as follows: for each $S, T \in \mathcal{M}$, $S \rightarrow T$ if $S = T$ or $T = S \setminus \{a\}$ for some $a \in C(S)$. From Lemma 11.15, we see that $\rightarrow$ is the predecessor relation in the partially ordered set $(\mathcal{M}, \subseteq)$. So naturally $\supseteq$ is the transitive closure of $\rightarrow$.

We will construct a sequence of linear orderings and verify that C has an MC rationalization via that sequence. Remember that E and $\emptyset$ are the top and bottom members of $\mathcal{M}$, respectively. Take any path in $\rightarrow$ that connects E to $\emptyset$, say $E \rightarrow S_1 \rightarrow \cdots \rightarrow S_k \rightarrow \emptyset$. By the definition of $\rightarrow$, note that $k = n - 1$ and there exists an ordering of elements $(a_1, \ldots, a_n)$ such that $\{a_1\} = E \setminus S_1$, $\{a_i\} = S_{i-1} \setminus S_i$ for each $i \in \{2, \ldots, n-1\}$, and $\{a_n\} = S_{n-1}$. This defines a linear ordering $\succeq$ by $a_1 \succeq \cdots \succeq a_n$. Let O be the set of all orderings obtainable in this manner, which must have finite cardinality m. We show that C has an MC rationalization by any sequence $(\succeq)_1^m = (\succeq_1, \ldots, \succeq_m)$ of linear orders drawn from O without replacement.

First, we show that $C(S) \subseteq \mathsf{AM}[(\succeq)_1^m](S)$. Take any $S \in 2^E$. Take any $a \in C(S)$. Invoking Lemma 11.14, let $T = S^\sharp$. Note that $S \subseteq T$. Consider any path in $\rightarrow$ that connects E to $\emptyset$ and includes T and $T \setminus \{a\}$, recognizing that at least one must exist. Consider the linear ordering constructed for this path, say $\succeq \in (\succeq)_1^m$. Note that $T \setminus \{a\}$ constitutes the set of elements that are ranked below a at $\succeq$, that is, $T \setminus \{a\} = \{b \in E \setminus \{a\} : a \succeq b\}$. Since $S \subseteq T$, a is the maximizer of $\succeq$ in S.

Next, we show that $\mathsf{AM}[(\succeq)_1^m](S) \subseteq C(S)$. Each $a \in \mathsf{AM}[(\succeq)_1^m](S)$ is the maximizer of $\succeq_j$ in S for some $\succeq_j \in (\succeq)_1^m$. Define $T = E \setminus \{b : b \succ_j a\}$. Since a is the maximizer of $\succeq_j$ in S, it must hold that $S \subseteq T$. By the construction of $\succeq_j$, $T \in \mathcal{M}$ and $a \in C(T)$. By Theorem 11.12, C satisfies substitutability and so $a \in C(S)$. $\square$

Let us illustrate, using the choice function C in Example 11.18, how the MC rationalization is constructed from the lattice of maximal option sets $\mathcal{M}$, as explained in the proof of Theorem 11.19. Observe that in the choice lattice in Figure 11.1, there are three different paths that connect $E = \{1, 2, 3\}$ to $\emptyset$: (P1) $\{a, b, c\} \rightarrow \{b, c\} \rightarrow \{c\} \rightarrow \emptyset$, (P2) $\{a, b, c\} \rightarrow \{a, c\} \rightarrow \{a\} \rightarrow \emptyset$, and (P3) $\{a, b, c\} \rightarrow \{a, c\} \rightarrow \{c\} \rightarrow \emptyset$. Listing the subtracted chosen elements while we follow each path yields three priority orderings: $a \succeq_1 b \succeq_1 c$, $b \succeq_2 c \succeq_2 a$, and $b \succeq_3 a \succeq_3 c$. In fact, $(\succeq_1, \succeq_2, \succeq_3)$ provides an MC rationalization of C. Remember that we have already discovered that C is MC rationalized by just the first two priority orderings $(\succeq_1, \succeq_2)$. That is, the MC rationalization constructed in the proof of Theorem 11.19 is not necessarily a *minimum-size* MC rationalization. In fact, it is the maximum-size MC rationalization in the sense that it includes every linear ordering that can appear in any MC rationalization.

11.6 Combinatorial Choice from Priorities and Capacities

Choice rules that make use of priorities to ration a scarce discrete resource, such as admissions to a school, have been attractive to market designers. In this section, we study a few different classes of rules that make use of priorities.

Fix a finite combinatorial choice model $(E, \mathbf{C})$ with a complete domain of option sets. A *priority ordering* $\succeq$ is a complete, transitive, and anti-symmetric binary relation over E, where $a \succ b$ denotes that a is of higher priority than b. The *capacity q* is a non-negative integer.

The *priority maximization* choice rule defines for each pair $(q, \succeq)$ a choice function $C^{q, \succeq} \in \mathbf{C}$ as follows. For each $S \in 2^E$, if $|S| \leq q$ then $C^{q, \succeq}(S) = S$; otherwise, $C^{q, \succeq} \in \mathbf{C} = \{s_1, \ldots, s_q\} \subseteq S$, where $m < q$ implies $s_m \succ s_q$ and $s \in S \setminus \{s_1, \ldots, s_q\}$ implies $s_q \succ s$. Let $\mathbf{C}^{prio}$ be the set of all choice functions defined by the priority maximization choice rule from $(q, \succeq)$ pairs.

A choice function $C \in \mathbf{C}$ is *capacity-filling for capacity q* if $|C(S)| = \min\{|S|, q\}$ for every $S \in 2^E$. It is *capacity-filling* if there exists a capacity q for which it is capacity-filling.

A choice function $C \in \mathbf{C}$ *respects priorities $\succeq$* if, for every $S \in 2^E$ and every $a, b \in S$, if $a \in C(S)$ and $b \notin C(S)$ then $a \succ b$. Respecting priority simply means that every chosen element has higher priority than every element available but not chosen.

It is not hard to see that each $C^{q, \succeq}$ is capacity-filling for capacity q and respects priority $\succeq$. Left as Exercise 11.6 is the straightforward proof that, for any $(q, \succeq)$, if $C \in \mathbf{C}$ is capacity-filling for capacity q and respects priorities $\succeq$ then $C = C^{q, \succeq}$.

Theorem 11.20. *A choice function is capacity-filling for capacity q and respects priorities $\succeq$ if and only if it is defined by the priority-maximization choice rule from $(q, \succeq)$.*

A linear order R on 2^E is a *responsive preference over bundles* if, for every $S \in 2^E$, (1) for every $a \in E$, $S \cup \{a\} \, R \, S$, (2) for every $a, b \in E \setminus S$, $S \cup \{a\} \, R \, S \cup \{b\}$ if and only if $a \, R \, b$.

A choice function is *q-responsively rationalized* if there exists a responsive preference R over bundles 2^E and a capacity limit $q \in \mathbb{Z}_+$ such that, for every $S \in 2^E$, $C(S) = \text{top}(\beta(S, q), R)$, where $\beta(S, q) = \{T \subseteq S : |T| \leq q\}$.

Theorem 11.21. *A choice function is q-responsively rationalized if and only if it is capacity-filling for capacity q and respects priorities for some priority ordering* $\succeq$.

Given a choice function $C \in \mathbf{C}$, the *revealed-strict-priority relation* of C, denoted $\succ^*$, is defined by $a \succ^* b$ if and only if there exists $S \in 2^E$ such that $a, b \in S$, $a \in C(S)$, and $b \notin C(S)$. We say C satisfies the *weak axiom of revealed strict priority (WARSPrio)* if, for every $a, b \in E$, if a is revealed-strictly-prioritized by choice function C to b then b is not revealed-strictly-prioritized by C to a. This axiom is equivalent to the requirement of asymmetry of revealed strict priority.

Theorem 11.22. *A choice function is q-responsively rationalized if and only if it satisfies WARSPrio and is capacity-filling.*

Proof The necessity of capacity-filling (and hence size monotonicity) and WARSPrio is left to the reader; see Exercise 11.7. For the sufficiency part, suppose that C satisfies size monotonicity and WARSPrio.

We show that $\succ^*$, the revealed strict priority of X, is transitive. Take $a_1, a_2, a_3 \in E$ such that $a_1 \succ^* a_2 \succ^* a_3$. These are necessarily distinct elements. Let $S \subseteq E \setminus \{a_1, a_2\}$ be such that $a_1 \in C(S \cup \{a_1, a_2\})$ and $a_2 \in S \setminus C(S \cup \{a_1, a_2\})$, which is well defined given $a_1 \succ^* a_2$. Let $T = S \setminus C(S)$. So we have $a_1 \in C(S)$ and $a_2 \in T$, and, for every $b \in C(S)$ and $b' \in T$, we have $b \succ^* b'$. Also, WARSPrio implies $a_3 \notin C(S)$, since $a_2 \in T$ and $a_2 \succ^* a_3$. If $a_3 \in S$ then we immediately have $a_1 \succ^* a_3$.

So, suppose $a_3 \notin S$. If there exists $b \in S$ such that $b \in C(S)$ and $b \notin C(S \cup \{a_3\})$ then WARSPrio implies that, for every $b' \in T$, $b' \notin C(S \cup \{a_3\})$. This in turn implies $a_3 \notin C(S \cup \{a_3\})$, since we are given $a_2 \succ^* a_3$. But then $C(S \cup \{a_3\}) \subseteq S \setminus T = C(S)$. Since size monotonicity (and so capacity-filling) implies $|C(S)| \leq |C(S \cup \{a_3\})|$, $C(S \cup \{a_3\}) = C(S)$. This yields $a_1 \succ^* a_3$.

By the Szpilrajn extension theorem, there exists a linear ordering $\succeq$ such that, for each $a, b \in E$ with $a \neq b$, $a \succ^* b$ implies $a \succ b$. Let $q = \text{top}\{|C(S)| : S \in 2^E\}$. Necessarily, capacity-filling implies capacity-filling for capacity q as defined. We now show that, for each $S \in 2^E$, $C(S)$ is obtained by choosing the highest priority elements according to $\succeq$ until the capacity q is reached or no element is left. If $|S| \leq q$, by capacity-filling $C(S) = S$ and the claim trivially holds. Suppose that $|S| > q$ and suppose the claim does not hold. By capacity-filling, this means that there exist $a, b \in S$ such that $a \in C(S)$, $b \notin C(S)$, and $a \succeq b$. The facts $a \in C(S)$ and $b \notin C(S)$ imply $a \succ^* b$, which contradicts $a \succeq b$ by the construction of $\succeq$. $\square$

The WARSPrio axiom does not necessarily imply substitutability when capacity-filling is not true. Exercise 11.8 asks for an example of this. When capacity filling holds true, substitutability is a weaker property than WARSPrio.

Remark 11.23. Given the discussion in Section 11.2.2, a priority ordering over E is not a preference over alternatives, which would have to be a relation over 2^E. In particular, WARP speaks to preferences and WARSPrior to priorities, and their relationship to each other for the combinatorial setting is not immediate. However, if $|C(S)| = 1$ for all $S \in 2^E$ then we might identify elements of E with alternatives and recognize they have equivalent implications for such C. Note that Theorem 11.22 connects the question of rationalizability by preferences over alternatives to an axiom (WARSPrio) defined in the language of combinatorial choice. Since in the present setting WARP is equivalent to IRE by Theorem 11.9, WARSPrio is a stronger requirement than WARP, for a capacity-filling choice function C.

A *priority sequence* is a sequence of priority orderings on E. In Section 11.5.2 we saw that priority sequences define path-independent choice functions under the MC choice rule, where each priority in the sequence identifies its maximizer in the given option set and the chosen set is just the collection of these maximizers. An interpretation of this rule is that there is no rivalry between the priorities in the sequence, which takes mathematical expression in the fact that the choice defined by the rule is invariant under permutations in the sequencing of a given priority sequence.

A natural cousin to the MC choice rule is *sequenced priority maximization with rivalry*. It defines, for each pair $(q, (\succeq_m)_{m=1}^{m=q})$ of a capacity and a sequence of q priority orderings, a choice function $C^{q,(\succeq_m)_1^q} \in \mathbf{C}$ as follows. If $|S| \leq q$ then $C^{q,(\succeq_m)_1^q}(S) = S$; otherwise $C^{q,(\succeq_m)_1^q}(S) = \{s_1, \ldots, s_q\}$ where $s_1 = \mathrm{top}(S, \succeq_1)$ and, for each $m \in \{2, \ldots, q\}$,

$$s_m = \mathrm{top}(S \setminus \{s_1, \ldots, s_{m-1}\}, \succeq_m).$$

Let $\mathbf{C}^{seq\text{-}prio\text{-}riv}$ be the set of all choice functions defined through the sequenced priority maximization with rivalry choice rule.

Theorem 11.24. *Every $C \in \mathbf{C}^{seq\text{-}prio\text{-}riv}$ is capacity-filling and satisfies substitutability.*

Proof Capacity-filling directly follows from the definition of $\mathbf{C}^{seq\text{-}prio\text{-}riv}$. To see substitutability, take any $S, T \in 2^E$ and $a \in E$ such that $a \in T \subseteq S$. Suppose that $a \in C(S)$. If $|T| < q$ then trivially $a \in C(T)$. Suppose that $|T| \geq q$. Then there exists $k \in \{1, \ldots, q\}$ such that a is the maximizer of $\succeq_k$ when the maximizers of the priority orderings are computed sequentially at S, as in the definition of the sequenced priority maximization with rivalry choice rule. Observe that when the maximizers of the priority orderings are computed sequentially at $T \subseteq S$, a is either the maximizer of $\succeq_k$ or the maximizer of $\succeq_{k'}$ for some $k' < k$. Hence, $a \in C(T)$. $\square$

In some applications, the set of elements E comes with the structure (L, λ), where λ is a map from E *onto* a set L. This structure induces the partition $\{E_l\}_{l \in L}$, where $E_l = \{a \in E : \lambda(a) = l\}$.

Consider again the problem with a capacity q and a single priority ordering $\succeq$ on E. A *reserves profile* for the partition structure (L, λ) is an indexed set $\{r_l : l \in L\}$ of non-negative integers that respects capacity, that is, $\sum_{l \in L} r_l \leq q$. The interpretation we pursue here is that r_l is a reserve of capacity for the elements in E_l.

The *reserves-based priority maximization* choice rule defines, for each triple $(q, (r_t)_{t \in T}, \succeq)$ based on capacity q, a reserves profile and a priority ordering, that is, a choice function $C^{q,(r_t)_{t \in T},\succeq}$ such that the chosen set from options S is determined by the following two-stage procedure:

First stage: For each $l \in L$, the r_l-highest priority elements that are in both E_l and S are chosen, with all of them being chosen if they number no more than r_l.

Second stage: The residual capacity q' is the original q less the number of elements chosen in the first stage. From amongst the elements of S not chosen in the first stage, the q'-highest priority ones are chosen (or all of them if they number no more than q').

Let $\mathbf{C}^{res}$ be the set of all choice functions definable by the reserves-based priority maximization choice rule.

Theorem 11.25. *Each $C \in \mathbf{C}^{res}$ is capacity-filling and satisfies substitutability.*

Proof Capacity-filling follows straightforwardly from the definition of $\mathbf{C}^{res}$. To prove substitutability, take any $S, T \in 2^E$ and $a \in E$ such that $a \in T \subseteq S$ and suppose that $a \in C(S)$. Let $l = \lambda(a)$. If $|T| < q$ then trivially $a \in C(T)$, so suppose that $|T| \geq q$.

First suppose that a is chosen in the first stage of the procedure from S. Then a is one of the top r_l elements from $E_l \cap S$ with respect to $\succeq$. Since $T \subseteq S$, a is one of the top r_l elements also from $E_l \cap T$ with respect to $\succeq$ and chosen in the first stage of the procedure from T. Hence, $a \in C(T)$.

What we have just proved is that the choice function defined by the choices from only the first stage of the procedure satisfies substitutability. Since at the second stage the elements under consideration for choice are exactly those present at the start of the first stage but not chosen, substitutability of the first stage implies that no element in T that is chosen in the first stage from the option set S will be present at the start of the second stage when the procedure is applied to T. That is, the set of elements that could be chosen at the start of the second stage is a monotonic function of the option set at the start of the first stage. Then $a \in C(T)$ for the reason given in Theorem 11.24, which states that choice functions defined by the priority maximization rule satisfy substitutability. $\square$

Let us illustrate the two classes of choice functions above with an example.

Example 11.26. Let $E = \{1, 2, 3, 4, 5\}$ be a set of students. Let $L = \{l, m, h\}$ denote a partition of the students into low, medium, and high socioeconomic status, such that $\lambda(5) = l$, $\lambda(1) = \lambda(4) = m$, and $\lambda(2) = \lambda(3) = h$. Let $\succeq$ be defined as $1 \succ 2 \succ 3 \succ 4 \succ 5$. Let $q = 3$.

Let C_1 be the choice function in $\mathbf{C}^{seq\text{-}prio\text{-}riv}$ defined by the sequenced priority maximization with rivalry rule using $(\succeq, \succeq^l, \succeq^m)$, where $\succeq^l$ and $\succeq^m$ are obtained from $\succeq$ by moving the low- and medium-socioeconomic-status students to the top of the priority ordering, respectively. That is, $3 \succ^l 5 \succ^l 1 \succ^l$

$2 \succ^l 4$ and $4 \succ^m 1 \succ^m 2 \succ^m 3 \succ^m 5$. So $C_1(E)$ is obtained by first choosing the highest-priority student, who is student 1, then from the remaining set choosing the highest-priority l-student, who is student 5, and finally, from the remaining set, again choosing the highest-priority-l-student, who is student 4. That is, $C_1(E) = \{1, 4, 5\}$. Note that the way in which C_1 operates features a preference for diversity along with a preference for respecting $\succeq$.

Let C_2 be the choice function in $\mathbf{C}^{res}$ defined by the reserves-based priority maximization rule $r_l = r_m = 1$ and $r_h = 0$. Note that, for example, $C_2(E)$ is obtained by first choosing one highest-priority-l student, who is 5, and one highest-priority-m student, who is 1, and then from the remaining set, choosing the highest-priority student, who is 2. That is, $C_2(E) = \{1, 2, 5\}$. Note that the way in which C_2 operates also features a preference for diversity along with a preference for respecting $\succeq$.

This example illustrates how choice rules incorporating diversity considerations into choice behavior can differ in the choices made even in a simple case. In the context of school choice, Chapter 8 studies this kind of issue.

We close this section by addressing the pattern of results in the choice function design approach that we have explored in this section. From examining the proof of Theorem 11.25, it can be seen that a more general result could be shown by adapting the arguments made.

The *two-stage selection with rivalry choice rule* $\mathcal{H}$ is defined for each pair of choice functions (C_1, C_2) by the following choice procedure applied to each option set S:

First stage: Choose those elements in S that C_1 would choose.
Second stage: From amongst the elements of S not chosen in the first stage, choose those elements that C_2 would choose.

For each pair of choice functions (C_1, C_2), let $\mathcal{H}[C_1 \rightarrowtail C_2]$ be the choice function defined by this rule.

Theorem 11.27. *If C_1 and C_2 are capacity-filling choice functions that satisfy substitutability then $\mathcal{H}[C_1 \rightarrowtail C_2]$ is capacity-filling and satisfies substitutability.*

The proof is left as Exercise 11.9.

11.7 Choice and Deferred Acceptance

In one-to-many matching applications where agents are matched with objects, the combinatorial choice rules associated with objects to determine matchings are intimately tied with (i) the relationships between different stability notions, (ii) the relationships between different formulations of the deferred acceptance algorithm, and (iii) the stability properties of the algorithm's outcomes. We will illustrate this in a simple one-to-many matching model. Many of these results hold for general models of matching with contracts, covered in Chapter 3.

There is a set of agents A and a set of objects O. Each agent $i \in A$ has a preference relation R_i over $O \cup \{\emptyset\}$ that is complete, transitive, and antisymmetric, where $\emptyset$ denotes being unmatched (or the outside option). We also write $a \ P_i \ b$ if $a \ R_i \ b$

and $a \neq b$. An object $a \in O$ is *acceptable* for i if $a \; R_i \; \emptyset$. Each object $a \in O$ has a choice rule $C_a : 2^A \rightarrow 2^A$ which associates with each set of applicants $S \subseteq A$ a non-empty set of chosen agents $C_a(S) \subseteq S$, with the interpretation that each chosen agent receives a copy of the object.

A matching μ is an assignment of objects to agents such that each agent receives at most one object. When agent $i \in A$ is matched with object $a \in O$, we write $\mu(i) = a$ and $i \in \mu(a)$. An agent $i \in A$ might also be unmatched at μ, which we denote by $\mu(i) = \emptyset$.

11.7.1 Stability

A central property for matchings is *stability*, which roughly means that the matching is robust to agents possibly acting to circumvent the match. Even in the context of centralized resource allocation, where the objects are not agents in the usual sense, stability has normative foundations, as discussed in the introduction to this chapter. Below are some alternative formulations of stability.

A matching μ is *individually stable* if it is acceptable to every agent $i \in A$ and, for every object $a \in O$, $C_a(\mu(a)) = \mu(a)$. A matching μ is *α-stable* if it is individually stable and there does not exist an agent $i \in A$ and an object $a \in O$ such that $a \; P_i \; \mu(i)$ and $i \in C_a(\mu(a) \cup \{i\})$. A matching μ is *β-stable* if it is individually stable and there does not exist an agent $i \in A$ and an object $a \in O$ such that $a \; P_i \; \mu(i)$ and $C_a(\mu(a) \cup \{i\}) \neq \mu(a)$.

Note the difference between the above two versions of stability: in the α-version the agent i who approaches a must be chosen by a in order to successfully circumvent the matching, while in the β-version it is sufficient if the initial matching of a is disrupted. Under IRE, these two versions are equivalent.

Lemma 11.28. *Without any assumptions on objects' choice rules, β-stability implies α-stability but not vice versa. If objects' choice rules satisfy IRE then α-stability is equivalent to β-stability.*

Proof We can simply assume that individual stability holds. On one hand, if μ is not α-stable then there exist $i \in A$ and $a \in O$ such that $a \; P_i \; \mu(i)$ and $i \in C_a(\mu(a) \cup \{i\})$, which implies that $C_a(\mu(a) \cup \{i\}) \neq \mu(a)$. Hence, μ is not β-stable. On the other hand, if μ is not β-stable then there exist $i \in A$ and $a \in O$ such that $a \; P_i \; \mu(i)$ and $C_a(\mu(a) \cup \{i\}) \neq \mu(a)$. If C_a satisfies IRE then $i \in C_a(\mu(a) \cup \{i\})$ and so μ is not α-stable.

An example with two agents and one object can be constructed to show that the equivalence fails without IRE, even with substitutability satisfied. $\square$

A matching μ is *group stable* if it is individually stable and there does not exist a non-empty set of agents $S \subseteq A$ and an object $a \in O$ such that $a \; P_i \; \mu(i)$ for each $i \in S$, and $S \subseteq C_a(\mu(a) \cup S)$.

Lemma 11.29. *If objects' choice rules satisfy substitutability, α-stability is equivalent to group stability.*

Proof Again, we can simply assume that individual stability holds. If μ is not group stable then there exist a non-empty set of agents $S \subseteq A$ and an object a such that $a \; P_i \; \mu(i)$ for each $i \in S$, and $S \subseteq C_a(\mu(a) \cup S)$. Take any $i \in S$. By substitutability, $i \in C_a(\mu(a) \cup \{i\})$, so μ is not α-stable. The reverse direction is immediate. $\square$

Thus, substitutability and IRE give us a single natural theory of stability.

Corollary 11.30. *If objects' choice rules satisfy substitutability and IRE then α-stability, β-stability, and group stability are equivalent.*

11.7.2 Deferred Acceptance

Below are two versions of the deferred acceptance algorithm. There is only one difference between the two algorithms: the choice-keeping deferred acceptance (CK-DA) algorithm keeps only the proposals of the set of chosen applicants from the previous step, while the applicant-keeping version (AK-DA) keeps all proposals received. The AK-DA algorithm is often called the cumulative offer algorithm (with simultaneous proposals).

Algorithm 11.1 Deferred acceptance algorithms, CK-DA and AK-DA, differing only at line numbers 1 and 2

---

1   initialize: every agent i is **Active** and every object is `AvailableTo`(i),
2   **while** *some agent is* **Active do**
3   Each **Active** agent i proposes to **Top** object `AvailableTo`(i)
4   **for** *each object o* **do**
5   **Chosen** = $\texttt{ChoiceFunction}_o$ (**Proposers** $\cup$ `KeptProposals`(o))
6   Agents not **Chosen** are **Rejected** if they are **Proposers** or `Held`(o)
7   Each **Rejected** agent i no longer has o `AvailableTo`(i)
8   Each **Rejected** agent i with one or more objects `AvailableTo`(i) is set as **Active**; every other agent is no longer **Active**
9   `Held`(o) $\leftarrow$ **Chosen**
10   **if** *Choice-Keeping DA* **then**
11            $\mid$ `KeptProposals`(o) $\leftarrow$ **Chosen**
12   **end**
13   **if** *Applicant-Keeping DA* **then**
14            $\mid$ `KeptProposals`(o) $\leftarrow$ **Proposers** $\cup$ `KeptProposals`(o)
15   **end**
16   **end**
17   **end**
18   return: a copy of each object is assigned to each agent meaning

---

Lemma 11.31. *Both the CK-DA and AK-DA algorithms stop in finitely many steps without any assumptions on objects' choice rules.*

This lemma holds since both algorithms terminate when there are no active agents and, in each iteration of the proposal phase, either the set of active agents shrinks or an agent's proposal is rejected, shrinking his set of available objects. With finite sets of agents and objects, the algorithms terminate.

Do CK-DA and AK-DA algorithms necessarily produce a feasible outcome, that is, a matching?

Lemma 11.32. *The CK-DA algorithm produces a matching (a feasible outcome) without any assumptions on objects' choice rules. The AK-DA algorithm produces a matching if objects' choice rules are substitutable; otherwise, the AK-DA algorithm might not produce a matching.*

We omit the relatively simple proof. However, it is worth understanding the role of substitutability in ensuring a feasible outcome for the AK-DA algorithm. Without substitutability, it is possible that a proposal by agent i is rejected by an object a but, at a later step, because of other proposals to a following i's rejection, i is chosen from the necessarily expanded set of proposals. In the interim, i may have proposed to another object and be held by it. If this situation continues to hold at algorithm termination, the outcome is not a matching because it is infeasible for i. With substitutability, the choice functions have the monotonic rejection property (see Exercise 11.3) on expanding sets, thereby ensuring a feasible outcome as the set of proposals to each object expands in the running of the AK-DA algorithm.

What conditions on objects' choice rules imply that the CK-DA and AK-DA algorithms are outcome-equivalent? Substitutability is not sufficient for this equivalence; see Exercise 11.10. For such an equivalence, we need IRE in addition to substitutability.

Lemma 11.33. *If objects' choice rules satisfy IRE and substitutability then the CK-DA and AK-DA algorithms are outcome-equivalent; in fact, after each round of agents proposing and objects choosing, the tentatively accepted (i.e., held) proposals coincide.*

If objects' choice rules fail substitutability or IRE then the outcomes of the CK-DA and AK-DA algorithms might differ.

We next investigate the stability properties of the two deferred acceptance algorithms.

Lemma 11.34. *If objects' choice rules satisfy IRE and substitutability then the outcome of the CK-DA algorithm is a stable matching. If objects' choice rules satisfy IRE then the outcome of the AK-DA algorithm is a stable matching.*

If objects' choice rules fail substitutability or IRE then the outcome of the CK-DA might be an unstable matching; see Exercise 11.10. Also, if objects' choice rules just fail IRE then the outcome of the AK-DA might still be an unstable matching. The following table summarizes the conditions required on objects' choice rules to guarantee the feasibility and stability of the CK-DA and AK-DA algorithms.

11.8 Exercises

Exercise 11.1 Complete the proof of Theorem 11.8, by showing that WARP implies transitive rationalizability when the domain B is additive.

Table 11.1 Choice conditions required for various properties of deferred acceptance outcomes. The heading of the last column means that the outcome will be the same as in AK-DA.

	Feasible	Stable	= AK-DA
CK-DA	none	path independence	path independence
AK-DA	substitutability	IRE	none

Exercise 11.2 A function f mapping a space to itself is *idempotent* if f composed with f is equal to f (i.e. $f \circ f = f$). Show that a combinatorial choice function C is idempotent if it satisfies substitutability or IRE.

Exercise 11.3 For a combinatorial choice function C on E, show that each of the following properties is equivalent to substitutability:

(a) *Subadditivity:* $\forall S, T, C(S \cup T) \subseteq C(S) \cup C(T)$.
(b) *Monotone rejection:* $\forall S, T$, if $S \subseteq T$ then $S \setminus C(S) \subseteq T \setminus C(T)$.
(c) *Antitone non-rejection:* $\forall S, T$, if $S \subseteq T$ then $C(S) \cup (E \setminus S) \supseteq C(T) \cup (E \setminus T)$.

Exercise 11.4 For a contraction mapping f on the powerset $\mathcal{S}$ of a set S, i.e., a mapping f satisfying $\forall S_1 \in \mathcal{S}, f(S_1) \subseteq S_1$, show that each of the following statements is equivalent to path independence:

(a) f satisfies the equation $f(S_1 \cup S_2) = f(f(S_1) \cup S_2)$.
(b) f is idempotent and *additive-in-the-image*: $f(f(S_1 \cup S_2)) = f(f(S_1) \cup f(S_2))$.

Exercise 11.5 Show that MC rationalizability implies path independence.

Exercise 11.6 Complete the proof of Theorem 11.20.

Exercise 11.7 Complete the necessity part of the proof for Theorem 11.22, that if a choice function does not satisfy capacity-filling or WARSPrio then it is not capacity-constrained responsive.

Exercise 11.8 Construct an example of a combinatorial choice function that satisfies the WARSPrio but violates substitutability.

Exercise 11.9 Adapt the proof of Theorem 11.25 to prove Theorem 11.27.

Exercise 11.10 For both the following, find an example of a one-to-many matching problem with the information provided:

(a) The CK-DA and AK-DA algorithms produce different outcomes and the objects' choice functions satisfy substitutability.
(b) The CK-DA algorithm produces an unstable outcome and the objects' choice functions satisfy IRE.

11.9 Bibliographic Notes

The article [15] is a very useful survey containing some results we have presented here, and many worthwhile results we have not. The book [3] gives a lucid treatment of revealed preference theory with a focus on the partial observability of choice behavior and questions of falsifiability and testability.

In [8] the term combinatorial choice was introduced and the number of substitutable choice functions counted. Theorem 11.9 and other behavioral implications for combinatorial choice of some classic requirements such as WARP, Sen's α, and Plott's path independence [17] are studied in [2], by means of the behavioral isomorphism between combinatorial and pure choice models. Theorem 11.11 is due to [4].

The characterization of path-independent choice functions by lattices of sets has appeared in various different forms in the literature since at least [11]. The lattice structure we described in Section 11.5.1 and Theorem 11.17 are due to [14]. MC rationalizability and Theorem 11.19 are due to [1]. In [7] and [13] the minimum size of an MC rationalization was investigated.

Theorem 11.22 on responsive rationalizations of combinatorial choice functions is from [5]. The sequenced priority maximization with rivalry choice rules were first considered in [12] in a matching-with-contracts model (see Chapter 3 for the definition of this model). Reserve-based priority maximization choice rules are axiomatically characterized in [9].

There are two topics omitted in the chapter that we encourage the serious student to explore. First, the space of path-independent choice functions on a given ground set has a remarkable lattice structure of its own [6] and many choice rules defined in the choice function design literature, including those examined in Section 11.6, can be understood as operators on the space of choice functions. Second, there is a body of work falling under discrete convexity theory that has found increasing success in the study of discrete goods settings with money. One salient result pertains to combinatorial demand: the combinatorial demand function derived from a valuation function satisfies substitutability (as defined for the matching with salaries model of Chapter 3) if and only if the valuation function is $M^\natural$-concave, which is an adaptation of concavity for discrete spaces [10]. In [16] a comprehensive survey is offered of discrete convex analysis with extensive references to applications in economics.

References

[1] Aizerman, Mark A., and Malishevski, Andrey V. 1981. General theory of best variants choice: Some aspects. *IEEE Transactions on Automatic Control*, **26**(5), 1030–1040.

[2] Alva, Samson. 2018. WARP and combinatorial choice. *Journal of Economic Theory*, **173**(1), 320–333.

[3] Chambers, Christopher P., and Echenique, Federico. 2016. *Revealed Preference Theory*. Econometric Society Monographs. Cambridge University Press.

[4] Chambers, Christopher P., and Echenique, Federico. 2018. A characterization of combinatorial demand. *Mathematics of Operations Research*, **43**(1), 222–227.

[5] Chambers, Christopher P., and Yenmez, M. Bumin. 2018. A simple characterization of responsive choice. *Games and Economic Behavior*, **111**, 217–221.

[6] Danilov, Vladimir, and Koshevoy, Gleb. 2005. Mathematics of Plott choice functions. *Mathematical Social Sciences*, **49**(3), 245–272.

[7] Doğan, Battal, Doğan, Serhat, and Yildiz, Kemal. 2021. On capacity-filling and substitutable choice rules. *Mathematics of Operations Research*, https://doi.org/10.1287/moor.2021.1128.

[8] Echenique, Federico. 2007. Counting combinatorial choice rules. *Games and Economic Behavior*, **58**(2), 231–245.

[9] Echenique, Federico, and Yenmez, M. Bumin. 2015. How to control controlled school choice. *American Economic Review*, **105**(8), 2679–2694.

[10] Fujishige, Satoru, and Yang, Zaifu. 2003. A note on Kelso and Crawford's gross substitutes condition. *Mathematics of Operations Research*, **28**(3), 463–469.

[11] Johnson, Mark R., and Dean, Richard A. 2001. Locally complete path independent choice functions and their lattices. *Mathematical Social Sciences*, **42**(1), 53–87.

[12] Kominers, Scott Duke, and Sönmez, Tayfun. 2016. Matching with slot-specific priorities: Theory. *Theoretical Economics*, **11**(2), 683–710.

[13] Kopylov, Igor. 2022. Minimal rationalizations. *Economic Theory*, **73**(4), 859–879.

[14] Koshevoy, Gleb A. 1999. Choice functions and abstract convex geometries. *Mathematical Social Sciences*, **38**(1), 35–44.

[15] Moulin, Hervé. 1985. Choice functions over a finite set: A summary. *Social Choice and Welfare*, **2**(2), 147–160.

[16] Murota, Kazuo. 2016. Discrete convex analysis: A tool for economics and game theory. *Journal of Mechanism and Institution Design*, **1**(1), 151–273.

[17] Plott, Charles R. 1973. Path independence, rationality, and social choice. *Econometrica*, **41**(6), 1075–1091.

CHAPTER TWELVE

Combinatorics of Stable Matchings

Tamás Fleiner

12.1 Introduction

The goal of this chapter is to illustrate a combinatorial approach to various stable matching related models and to convince the reader that this may lead to fascinating results. In particular, with the help of the terminology and the proof technique of graph theory, we shall study topics that have already been covered in Chapter 1 in connection with aspects 1 and 3 listed there. Our secret goal is to popularize this unconventional approach among those who are interested in stable matchings.

There are two main messages of this present chapter. The first message is this: in the study of stable-matching-related topics, graph theory is more useful than many would think. The second message is that here the standard method of a mathematician often works very well: insightful observations may become paving blocks on the way towards interesting new results. For example, instead of proving results from scratch, we may reduce one problem to another. In this way, as well as sparing extra effort we can see connections between various problems. Let us consider the details!

In Section 12.2, we introduce the notion of stable b-matchings, which allow a unified framework for one-to-one, many-to-one, and many-to-many stable matchings, and we also introduce the edge removal lemma, a tool that provides a straightforward proof of many basic results on stable matchings. This section also contains further useful results for bipartite and non-bipartite stable matching instances (that is, both for one- and two-sided markets). Using the edge removal lemma in Section 12.3 for bipartite graphs, we illustrate how well-known results such as the lattice, median, and splitting properties of stable matchings in two-sided markets follow in our approach.

Section 12.4 is devoted to applications of stable matchings on graph paths and list-edge colorings. In Section 12.5, we present two tricks that allow us to reduce stable b-matching problems to stable matchings. Such kinds of construction can reduce so-called stable flow problems to bipartite stable b-matching problems or extend certain properties of bipartite stable matchings to non-bipartite instances.

Each section ends with a reference to a couple of exercises. Some can be solved easily with the results listed in the particular section; others (denoted by asterisks) are tougher and meant for experts in combinatorics. Finally, Section 12.7 contains a brief survey on the related literature and hints for the exercises are provided at the end of the chapter.

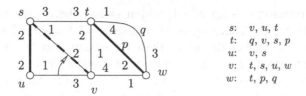

Figure 12.1 A graph with preferences at the vertices, showing a matching.

In this chapter we assume that the reader is familiar with the notion of partially ordered sets (i.e., posets), lattices, and lattice operations. However, we will finish this introduction with a crash course on graphs. Figure 12.1 shows a graph $G = (V, E)$ with vertex set $V = \{s, t, u, v, w\}$ and edge set E of eight edges represented by thin, thick, or dashed lines connecting two vertices. Vertices s, v, and w are the neighbors of t and the set $E(t) = \{ts, tv, p, q\}$ is the set of edges incident to vertex t. (Note that edges and vertices are both named by lower case letters, and if there is no ambiguity then an edge can be denoted by listing its two vertices.) The degree of t is the number of its edges: $d(t) = |E(t)| = 4$. Edges p and q are two "parallel" edges that connect vertices t and w; the latter vertex has degree $d(w) = 3$. Unlike in Chapter 1, here a matching is a set of edges rather than an involution $\mu \colon V \to V$. Hence, the set $\{su, p\}$ of thick edges is a matching, as no two edges in this set share a vertex (i.e., they are disjoint). We may remove edges and vertices from graphs. For example, $G-p$ denotes the graph we get from G after the removal of edge p from the edge set of G and $G-w$ is the graph with four vertices and five edges that we get after we remove vertex w and all the edges incident to w.

A *stable matching instance* consists of a graph G and a linear preference order $\prec_v$ on $E(v)$ for each vertex v of G. In Figure 12.1 the numbers on edges near the vertices show the rank of the particular edge according to the corresponding vertex. Hence $sv \succ_s su \succ_s st$, that is, sv is the most preferred edge of vertex s and st is the least preferred one[1]. The arrow from edge vu to edge vs indicates that v prefers vs to vu. In a traditional terminology, the vertices of a graph are often called agents and a contract is a synonym for an edge. The preference lists on the right-hand side of Figure 12.1 represent a traditional notation for the stable matching instance on the left. (Due to the multiple contract possibilities between two agents, we have slightly extended this notation: if there are parallel copies of the same edge, we list the name of the edge.)

12.2 The Edge Removal Lemma

Our first goal is to formulate the edge removal lemma, a robust and powerful tool that enables us to simplify stable matching problems. Beforehand, we define the necessary notions.

Definition 12.1. For a graph $G = (V, E)$ and degree bound $b \colon V \to \mathbb{Z}_+$, a subset F of E is a *b-matching* if $|F(v)| \leq b(v)$ holds for each vertex v of G.

---

[1] In the literature, the preference order $\prec_v$ often comes from the rank, that is, edge e is preferred to f by v if $e \prec_v f$ holds. Here we abandon this terminology and adopt the one defined in Chapter 1.

That is, a b-matching is a set of edges that satisfy the degree bounds given by the function b. Hence the edges su, sv, tw in Figure 12.1 form a 2-matching (i.e., a b-matching with $b = 2$), but the set of these edges can also be considered as a b-matching for other degree bounds, for example, for $b(s) = b(t) = 2$, $b(u) = b(w) = 1$ and $b(v) = 3$. Note that a 1-matching is just a set of disjoint edges of G, that is, a 1-matching is synonym to a matching or, in yet other words, the notion of a b-matching generalizes that of a matching.

Definition 12.2. Let $G = (V, E)$ be a graph and $\prec_v$ be a linear preference order on $E(v)$ for each $v \in V$. An edge f *dominates* edge e of G if $f \succ_v e$ holds for some vertex v of G. A subset F of E *dominates* edge e if there is some edge f of F that dominates e. A subset S of E is a *stable matching* if the set of edges that are dominated by S is exactly $E \setminus S$.

If $b \colon V \to \mathbb{Z}_+$ is a degree bound then subset F of E b-dominates edge e if there is a vertex v of G and there are different edges $f_1, f_2, \ldots, f_{b(v)}$ of F such that $f_i \succ_v e$ holds for $1 \le i \le b(v)$. A set S of edges is a *stable b-matching* if the set of edges that are dominated by S is $E \setminus S$. A *stable b-matching instance* is given by a graph G, linear preference orders $\prec_v$ on $E(v)$ for each vertex v of G, and a degree bound $b \colon V \to \mathbb{Z}_+$.

So, if some vertex prefers edge f to e then f dominates e. A set F of edges b-dominates e if there is a vertex v of e such that F contains $b(v)$ different edges that v prefers to e. For example, in Figure 12.1, p and q dominate one another while edges tv, vw, q 2-dominate p. Clearly, a set S of edges is a $(b\text{-})$matching if and only if S does not $(b\text{-})$dominate any edge in S. Consequently, any stable $(b\text{-})$matching must be a $(b\text{-})$matching, and a $(b\text{-})$matching is stable if and only if it $(b\text{-})$dominates every other edge of G.

Note that stability does not depend only on the graph G but also on the linear preference orders. Therefore when we talk about a stable $(b\text{-})$matching in a graph G we assume that there is an underlying system of linear preferences that is clear from the context. Note also that the traditional definition of stability is based on blocking, which we define as follows. (See page 27 for the definition of a blocking pair.)

Definition 12.3. Edge e *(b-)blocks* a set F of edges (or, in other words, F is *(b-)blocked* by edge e) if $e \notin F$ and F does not $(b\text{-})$dominate e.

It is easy to see that a matching M is stable if and only if M is not blocked by any edge. A similar statement is true for b-matchings.

Now we return to ordinary matchings and describe the tool that is the key of the deferred acceptance algorithm due to Gale and Shapley. (See page 22.) It says that whenever the situation in Figure 12.2 occurs, the removal of the dominated edge does not change the set of stable matchings.

Lemma 12.4 (Edge removal lemma). *Assume that a graph $G = (V, E)$ and a liner preference order $\prec_v$ on $E(v)$ for each $v \in V$ comprise a stable matching instance. If uw is the most preferred edge of u and $uw \succ_w vw$ then S is a stable matching of G if and only if S is a stable matching of $G - vw$.*

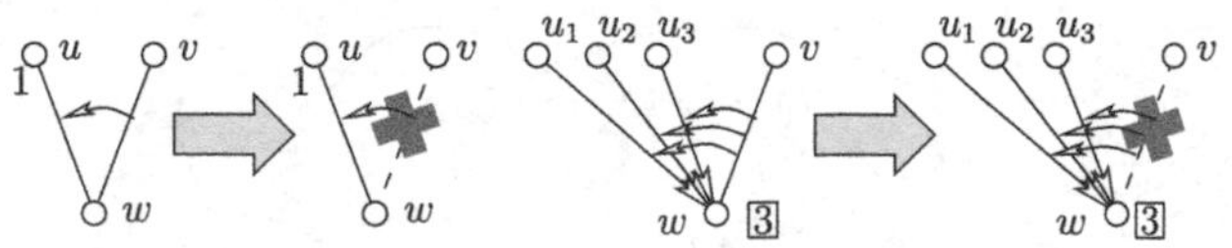

Figure 12.2 Safe removal of an edge in the cases of a stable matching and a b-matching. The boxed numbers are degree bounds.

The edge removal lemma is our number one tool to find a stable matching. It says that we can safely remove certain edges from the underlying graph without creating or killing a single stable matching. In this way we can reduce the problem of finding a stable matching in the original graph to finding a stable matching in a graph with (possibly many) fewer edges.

Proof Assume that S is a stable matching in G and assume for contradiction that $vw \in S$. Then $uw \notin S$ because S is a matching. As uw is the first choice of u, S cannot dominate uw, contradicting the stability of S. Consequently, no stable matching of G contains vw, and hence any stable matching of G is a stable matching of $G - vw$.

Assume now that S is a stable matching of $G - vw$. If $uw \in S$ then S dominates vw at vertex w. Otherwise, if $uw \notin S$ then S must dominate uw at w as uw is the first choice of u. This yields that S dominates vw at w and consequently, S is a stable matching of G. $\square$

The right-hand side of Figure 12.2 gives an illustration of our next result, a generalization of the edge removal lemma to b-matchings. Assume that a graph $G = (V, E)$, degree bound $b \colon V \to \mathbb{Z}_+$, and linear preference order $\prec_u$ on $E(u)$ are given. An edge e is a $\prec_u$-*best edge of u* (or a *best edge of u*, if $\prec_u$ is clear from the context) if no set of edges can b-dominate e at u, that is, if u is one of the best $b(u)$-edges of u. In Figure 12.2, arcs (arrows) leaving the vertices u_i denote the best edges of the u_i. We can generalize Lemma 12.4 as follows.

Theorem 12.5. *Let $G = (V, E)$ be a graph, $b \colon V \to \mathbb{Z}_+$ a degree bound, and $\prec_v$ be a linear preference order on $E(v)$ for each $v \in V$. If edges $u_1 w, u_2 w, \ldots, u_{b(u)} w$ are best edges of $u_1, u_2, \ldots, u_{b(w)}$, respectively, and $u_i w \succ_w vw$ holds for $1 \le i \le b(w)$ then S is a stable b-matching of G if and only if S is a stable b-matching of $G - vw$.*

We encourage the interested reader to extend the proof of Lemma 12.4 to a proof of Theorem 12.5.

Let us explore the structure of stable (b-)matching instances after all possible edge removals of Theorem 12.5 have been performed. Assume first that $b \equiv 1$ and we cannot remove any edge of graph G according to Lemma 12.4. Now if uv is the most preferred edge of u then uv must be the least preferred edge of v. Let us orient the most preferred edge of u away from u for every non-isolated vertex u of G. In this way, every non-isolated vertex of G has exactly one outgoing arc[2] and at most one incoming arc. So, after these edge orientations, the number of arcs in the graph is the

[2] In graph terminology, an oriented edge is called an arc.

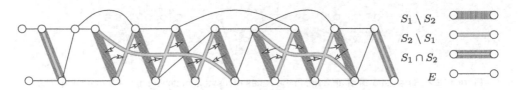

Figure 12.3 Two stable matchings.

number of (non-isolated) vertices. Hence each such vertex must receive exactly one arc; that is, the least preferred edge of each vertex of G must be the most preferred edge of another vertex. The following definition formulates this property.

Definition 12.6. A stable matching instance G with preference orders $\prec_v$ has the *first–last property* if the least preferred edge of each vertex is a best edge of another vertex.

Apparently, Definition 12.6 can be interpreted also for graphs with a degree bound b, and a more or less straightforward change of the argument directly above Definition 12.6 justifies the following result.

Observation 12.7. *If no edge removal is possible according to Theorem 12.5 then the underlying stable b-matching instance has the first–last property.*

Observation 12.7 is particularly useful in the design of an efficient algorithm that finds a stable b-matching in a not necessarily biparitite graph. The details are beyond the scope of this chapter.

12.2.1 The Structure of Non-Bipartite Stable b-Matchings

Our next goal is to explore the structure of stable matchings. It turns out that the old trick of combinatorists (namely, taking the symmetric difference[3] whenever one sees two matchings) works here as well.

Lemma 12.8. *Assume that S_1 and S_2 are both stable matchings of a graph G. Then the symmetric difference $S_1 \triangle S_2$ consists of cycles with cyclic preferences along the edges. Consequently, S_1 and S_2 cover the same set of vertices: $V(S_1) = V(S_2)$.*

Figure 12.3 illustrates the two stable matchings in Lemma 12.8. There might be vertices uncovered by both stable matchings S_1 and S_2, common edges of S_1 and S_2, and preference cycles along which edges of S_1 and S_2 alternate. (To emphasize that graph G might not be bipartite, we have indicated graph edges that belong to neither of th matchings S_1 and S_2.) We leave the proof of Lemma 12.8 to the reader with the remark that the following argument may provide a hint.

Our next goal is to study the behavior of stable b-matchings. Assume that a graph $G = (V, E)$ is given with linear preferences $\prec_v$ and degree bound $b \colon V \to \mathbb{Z}_+$ and

---

[3] The symmetric difference of sets A and B is $A \triangle B = (A \setminus B) \cup (B \setminus A)$.

let S_1 and S_2 be two stable b-matchings. Pick an edge from the symmetric difference $S_1 \triangle S_2$, say $e \in S_1 \setminus S_2$. As $e \notin S_2$, e must be dominated by S_2 at some vertex v of e. Let us orient e towards v and do the same for each edge in $S_2 \triangle S_1$.

Observe that if edge $e_1 \in S_1 \setminus S_2$ is oriented towards v then there must be $b(v)$ different edges of S_2 that all succeed e_1 in $\prec_v$. Hence $|S_2(v)| = b(v) \geq |S_1(v)|$, and all edges in $S_2(v) \setminus S_1(v)$ must be oriented away from v. This yields that, after the above orientation of $S_1 \triangle S_2$, every vertex has at least as many outgoing arcs as the number of incoming arcs, that is, no vertex has an outdegree that is less than its indegree. As both the total indegree and the total outdegree equal $|S_1 \triangle S_2|$, each inequality between the in- and outdegrees must in fact be an equality. Hence $|S_1(v) \setminus S_2(v)| = |S_2(v) \setminus S_1(v)|$ follows for every vertex v of G, and if $S_1(v) \neq S_2(v)$ then $|S_1(v)| = |S_2(v)| = b(v)$ must hold. These observations generalize previous results of Roth to the non-bipartite setting as follows.

Corollary 12.9. *Assume that S_1 and S_2 are stable b-matchings in G.*

1. $V(S_1) = V(S_2)$, *that is, any two stable b-matchings cover the same vertices.*
2. *(Rural hospitals theorem) If $|S_1(v)| < b(v)$ then $S_1(v) = S_2(v)$.*
3. *(Comparability theorem) If $S_1(v) \neq S_2(v)$ then the $\prec_v$-best $b(v)$ edge of $S_1(v) \cup S_2(v)$ is either $S_1(v)$ or $S_2(v)$.*

The rural hospitals theorem states that if vertex v is not saturated in some stable b-matching then any stable b-matching uses the same edges from $E(v)$, i.e., any two stable b-matchings look the same for vertex v. To see part 3 of the corollary, imagine how the $\prec_v$-best arc pointing to v can be dominated by the "other" matching. The above comparability theorem has a less well-known consequence that turns out to be particularly useful in the linear description of stable b-matching polyhedra.

Theorem 12.10 (Splitting property of stable b-matchings). *In any stable b-matching instance determined by a graph $G = (V, E)$, preferences $\prec_v$, and degree bound $b \colon V \to \mathbb{Z}_+$, for every vertex $v \in V$ there is a partition of $E(v)$ into $b(v)$ (possibly empty) parts $E_1(v), E_2(v), \ldots, E_{b(v)}(v)$ such that $|E_i(v) \cap S| \leq 1$ holds for any stable b-matching S.*

A consequence of Theorem 12.10 is that, for any stable b-matching instance, we can define a stable matching instance in such a way that any stable b-matching in the original instance corresponds to a stable matching in the new instance. The construction goes as follows. Split up every vertex v of the original instance into $b(v)$ vertices $v_1, v_2, \ldots, v_{b(v)}$ and replace each edge uv by an edge $u_i v_j$ if $e \in E_i(u) \cap E_j(v)$, where $E_i(u)$ is part of the partition defined in Theorem 12.10. The preference orders $\prec_{v_i}$ in the new instance are inherited from $\prec_v$ of the original instance.

Proof of Theorem 12.10 Let $e_1 \succ_v e_2 \succ_v \cdots$ be the preference order on $E(v)$. We assign each of these edges to one of the parts $E_1(v), E_2(v), \ldots, E_{b(v)}(v)$: first we assign e_1, then e_2, and so on. Assume for the sake of contradiction that some edge e_k cannot be assigned to any of these parts. The reason for this must be that there are stable b-matchings $S^1, S^2, \ldots, S^{b(v)}$ such that S^i contains edges e_k and e^i with $e^i \succ_v e_k$ and e^i is already assigned to $E_i(v)$ for $1 \leq i \leq b(v)$. Let S denote the $b(v)$ $\prec_v$-best edges of $\bigcup_{i=1}^{b(v)} S^i(v)$. As $e^i \succ e_k$ holds for $1 \leq i \leq b(v)$, we have $e_k \notin S$. By the generalized comparability theorem (part 3 of Corollary 12.9), S must coincide with one of the sets $S^1(v), S^2(v), \ldots, S^{b(v)}(v)$ and hence S must contain e_k, a contradiction. This proves that the above greedy method does indeed split $E(v)$ into $b(v)$ parts.

See Exercises 12.1–12.8 for this subsection. □

12.3 Bipartite Stable Matchings

In this section we consider so-called two-sided markets that correspond to the case where the underlying graph in the stable-matching instance is a bipartite one. Graph G is bipartite if its vertices can be split into two sides (it is customary to call the vertices men on one side and women on the other side) such that every edge of G connects two vertices on different sides, that is a man and a woman. We shall study the structural and algorithmic aspects of bipartite stable matchings.

How can we find a stable matching in a bipartite graph? A most natural approach is an application of the edge removal lemma (Lemma 12.4). We have seen before that when no more edge removal is possible then the instance has the first–last property: if edge $e = uv$ is the worst choice of u then e is the best choice of v and vice versa. This means that the first choices of men are the the worst choices of (different) women, so these first choices form a stable matching $\overline{S}$ in the reduced instance after all the possible edge removals have taken place. As no edge removal changes the set of stable matchings, stable matching $\overline{S}$ assigns each man with his best possible stable partner while each women receives her worst possible stable partner in the matching $\overline{S}$. This proves the following result.

Theorem 12.11. *If a graph $G = (V, E)$ in a stable matching instance is bipartite with parts $V = M \cup W$ then there exists a stable matching in G. If the parts of G are formed by men and women then there is a stable matching $\overline{S}$ in which $\overline{S}(m)$ is $\prec_m$-best among those edges of $E(v)$ that can belong to a stable matching for every man $m \in M$ and $\overline{S}(w)$ is $\prec_w$-worst among those edges of $E(w)$ that can belong to a stable matching for every woman $w \in W$.*

An exchange of the roles of men and women provides another stable matching $\underline{S}$ (that eventually may coincide with $\overline{S}$) in which women receive their best possible and men receive their worst possible stable partners.

Definition 12.12. The stable matchings $\overline{S}$ and $\underline{S}$ in Theorem 12.11 are called *man-optimal* and *woman-optimal*, respectively.

We have seen how to find the man- or woman-optimal stable matchings, by removing edges from the underlying graph according to the edge removal lemma. Note, however, that the deferred acceptance algorithm of Gale and Shapley works somewhat differently: it does not perform all possible edge removals but only specific ones. Namely, both vertices u and v in Lemma 12.4 must be men (and vertex w must be a woman); moreover the removed edge vw must be $\prec_v$-best (see Figure 12.2). That is, in the deferred acceptance algorithm only best edges get deleted while the edge removal lemma enables us to get rid of other edges as well. An advantage of the deferred acceptance algorithm is that it is easier to implement, partly because it uses fewer edge removals. But if we are not concerned with algorithmic issues then our profit from the edge removal lemma may manifest itself in structural results like the first–last property. This is useful for example in generalizing Irving's algorithm to find a generalized stable b-matching in a non-bipartite graph. The details are beyond the scope of this chapter.

Similar results hold for bipartite stable b-matchings. If no edge removal is possible by Theorem 12.5 in some bipartite stable b-matching instance then the best edges from the men define a stable b-matching (the man-optimal one) and, likewise, the best edges from the women also define a stable b-matching (the woman-optimal b-matching). Again, the deferred acceptance algorithm removes an edge vw if vw is a best edge of v on the right of Figure 12.2. (After such an edge removal, the degree of v might drop below $b(v)$.) Just as in the case of stable matchings, in the man-optimal stable b-matching $\overline{S}$, every man m receives the $b(m)$ $\prec_m$-best edges that can be assigned to him in a stable b-matching. However, it is not true in general that every woman w receives the worst $b(w)$ edges that can be assigned to her in a stable b-matching. This latter fact has to do with the comparability theorem, and we encourage the reader to work out the details.

12.3.1 The Lattice of Stable Matchings

The existence of man- and woman-optimal stable (b-)matchings follows also from an important structural result, namely, the lattice property of stable (b-)matchings. To describe it, we define a partial order on stable b-matchings.

Definition 12.13. We say that $S_2 \preceq_M S_1$ for stable b-matchings S_1 and S_2 if men unanimously prefer S_1 to S_2, that is, if the $b(m)$ $\prec_m$-best edge in $S_1(m) \cup S_2(m)$ is $S_1(m)$ for every man m. A partial order $\prec_W$ is defined similarly for women.

Clearly, both relations $\prec_M$ and $\prec_W$ are partial orders. However, they have a closer relation described by the following lemma. Roth calls it the "opposition of common interest" between the two-sides of a two sided matching market.

Lemma 12.14. *In any bipartite stable b-matching instance, the partial orders $\prec_M$ and $\prec_W$ are opposite to one another: $S_1 \prec_M S_2$ holds for stable matchings S_1 and S_2 if and only if $S_2 \prec_W S_1$.*

We leave the proof of Lemma 12.14 to the reader but remark that the proof below can be extended to a proof of of Lemma 12.14. The following theorem justifies that the partial order $\prec_M$ is a lattice order. This is done by exhibiting the lattice operations themselves.

Theorem 12.15. *Let S_1 and S_2 be two stable b-matchings of the same instance on a bipartite graph G. Define $S_1 \vee S_2$ by choosing the $b(m)$ $\prec_m$-best edges for each man m out of $S_1(m) \cup S_2(m)$. (If for some m there are fewer than $b(m)$ edges from which to pick from then pick all of them.) Then $S_1 \vee S_2$ is a stable b-matching. Let $S_1 \wedge S_2$ denote the stable b-matching thus constructed when the roles of men and women are exchanged. Then, for every edge e of G, e is contained in the same number of sets from S_1 and S_2 and from $S_1 \vee S_2$ and $S_1 \wedge S_2$, that* *is, modular equality* $\chi(S_1) + \chi(S_2) = \chi(S_1 \vee S_2) + \chi(S_1 \wedge S_2)$ *holds for the characteristic vectors* χ.

The following proof of Theorem 12.15 leans heavily on basic properties of graphs. Those readers who are unfamiliar with graph theory may want to skip it whilst keeping the message that standard graph arguments easily imply the result. Note that graph G is *connected* if for any two vertices of G there is a path connecting them in G. It is easy to see that the vertex set of any graph G can uniquely be decomposed into connected components: no edge of G connects two different components and the edges of each component form a connected graph.

Proof First we prove that $S_1 \vee S_2$ is a b-matching. Just as in the proof of Corollary 12.9, orient each edge e in $S_1 \triangle S_2$ towards the vertex where the other b-matching dominates e. As we have seen before, for each vertex v the number of arcs that enter v is the same as the number of arcs that leave v. Moreover, if some arc entering v belongs to S_i then all arcs that leave v must belong to S_j (where $i \neq j$) and all arcs that enter v must belong to S_i.

So, in each connected component of the graph defined by the edges in $S_1 \triangle S_2$ either all edges of $S_1 \setminus S_2$ are oriented from a man to a woman and all edges of $S_2 \setminus S_1$ are oriented from a woman to a man, or vice versa: edges of $S_1 \setminus S_2$ are oriented from a woman to a man and all edges of $S_2 \setminus S_1$ are oriented from a man to a woman. Consequently, for each vertex v of G, $(S_1 \vee S_2)(v)$ is either $S_1(v)$ or $S_2(v)$. It follows that $S_1 \vee S_2$ is indeed a b-matching.

To prove the stability of $S_1 \vee S_2$, let $e = mw \notin S_1 \vee S_2$ be any edge. Without limiting generality, we may assume that $(S_1 \vee S_2)(m) = S_1(m)$. As $e \notin S_1$, S_1 must b-dominate e. If S_1 b-dominates e at vertex m then $S_1 \vee S_2$ also b-dominates e at m. Otherwise, e is not b-dominated by S_1 at vertex m and hence (by the definition of $S_1 \vee S_2$) e is not b-dominated by S_2 at m either. It follows that both matchings S_1 and S_2 must b-dominate e at vertex w. As $(S_1 \vee S_2)(w)$ coincides either with $S_1(w)$ or with $S_2(w)$, $S_1 \vee S_2$ also b-dominates e at w.

This proves that every edge e outside $S_1 \vee S_2$ is b-dominated by $S_1 \vee S_2$. As $S_1 \vee S_2$ itself is a b-matching, $S_1 \vee S_2$ is a stable b-matching. A similar proof (with an exchange of the roles of men and women) shows that $S_1 \wedge S_2$ is also a stable b-matching.

It is clear from the definition that if edge e belongs to neither S_1 nor S_2 then e belongs to neither $S_1 \vee S_2$ nor $S_1 \wedge S_2$. If e belongs to exactly one of these matchings then, depending on its orientation, e belongs to exactly one of $S_1 \vee S_2$ and $S_1 \wedge S_2$. Finally, if $e \in S_1 \cap S_2$ then the comparability theorem (part 3 of Corollary 12.9) yields that e belongs to both $S_1 \vee S_2$ and $S_1 \wedge S_2$. This justifies the modularity property and finishes the proof of Theorem 12.15. $\square$

12.3.2 Median Stable b-Matchings

Note that Theorem 12.15 directly implies the existence of man- and woman-optimal stable matchings: the join ($\vee$ operation) of all stable b-matchings is a stable b-matching that is $\prec_M$-best for the men, and similarly the meet ($\wedge$) of all stable b-matchings is the woman-optimal one.

Theorem 12.15 has an interesting generalization. This has to do with the so-called median property of stable b-matchings. Let $S_1, S_2, \ldots, S_n$ be (not necessarily different) stable b-matchings in a bipartite instance. From the comparability theorem (part 2 of Corollary 12.9) it follows that subsets $S_1(v), S_2(v), \ldots, S_n(v)$ are pairwise comparable in the sense that the set of $b(v) \prec_v$-best edges of $S_i(v) \cup S_j(v)$ is either $S_i(v)$ or $S_j(v)$. Hence these b-matchings can be rearranged as $S_v^1, S_v^2, \ldots, S_v^n$ such that, for any $1 \leq i \leq j \leq n$, the $b(v) \prec_v$-best edge in $S_v^i(v) \cup S_v^j(v)$ is $S_v^i(v)$. From the lattice property of stable b-matchings, it follows that $S = S_1 \vee S_2 \vee \cdots \vee S_n$ is a stable b-matching and in this matching, m is incident to edges of $S(m) = S_m^1(m)$ for each man m and w is incident to edges $S(w) = S_w^n(w)$ for each woman w. But more is true, and this is the main content of the following result.

Theorem 12.16. *If $S_1, S_2, \ldots, S_n$ are (not necessarily different) stable b-matchings in a bipartite instance where sets M of men and W of women form the bipartition then $S^k = \bigcup_{m \in M} S_m^k(m)$ is a stable matching for any $1 \leq k \leq n$. Moreover, $S^k = \bigcup_{w \in W} S_w^{n-k+1}(w)$.*

That is, if each man picks his kth best assignment out of n given stable b-matchings then these choices do not only form a stable b-matching but also assign each women to her $(n - k + 1)$th best assignment.

Proof Define $(S')_m^k := \bigwedge_{i=1}^k S_m^i$ for each man m. Clearly, $(S')_m^k$ is a stable b-matching that assigns $S_m^k(m)$ to man m. Any other man m' gets assigned to his worst assignment out of the k assignments $S_m^1(m), S_m^2(m), \ldots, S_m^k(m)$. Hence, in $(S')_m^k$, m' is assigned to $S_{m'}^\ell(m')$ for some $k \leq \ell$.

Define a stable b-matching $S^k := \bigvee_{m \in M}(S')_m^k$. In this b-matching every man m is matched to his best assignment out of the b-matchings $(S')_{m'}^k$. So every man m will be assigned to $S_m^k(m)$ by the above observation. The proof of the second part of the theorem is left to the interested reader. □

For example, if every agent picks her kth=best assignment out of $2k - 1$ stable b-matchings then these choices determine a median stable b-matching that is "equally fair" to everybody.

See Exercises 12.9–12.11 for this subsection.

12.4 Applications

In this section we illustrate the application of results on stable matchings by proving various interesting theoretical results.

12.4.1 A Poset Generalization

The first application we present here has to do with so-called kernels in directed graphs.

Theorem 12.17. *Let $D = (V, A_1 \cup A_2)$ be a directed graph on the vertex set V such that its arc set is decomposed into disjoint sets A_1 of red arcs and A_2 of green arcs with the property that there is no monochromatic directed cycle in D. Then there exists a subset K of V such that no monochromatic directed path connects* *two different vertices of K and there is a monochromatic directed path from any vertex outside K to some vertex of K.*

Note that the above requirement on the disjointness of A_1 and A_2 is not a crucial condition: any two-colored arc can be replaced by two parallel arcs, one red and one green. To prove Theorem 12.17, we show the following equivalent form in terms of partially ordered sets. An antichain in a poset is a set of pairwise-incomparable elements.

Theorem 12.18. *If $\leq_1$ and $\leq_2$ are two partial orders on a finite ground set V then there is a common antichain K of $\leq_1$ and $\leq_2$ with the property that K dominates any other element, that is, for any element v of $V \setminus K$ there exists some element $k \in K$ such that $k >_1 v$ or $k >_2 v$ holds.*

The equivalence of Theorems 12.17 and 12.18 follows from the well-known connection between posets and acyclic directed graphs. Any partial order $\leq$ determines an acyclic directed graph on the ground set of $\leq$ by taking arcs uv where $u < v$. Conversely, if D is an acyclic directed graph then it determines a partial order on its vertices by defining $u \leq v$ if there is a directed path from u to v in D.

The common antichain in Theorem 12.18 is called a stable antichain of $\leq_1$ and $\leq_2$. Note that the stable marriage theorem of Gale and Shapley (the part of Theorem 12.11 on the existence of stable matchings) is a direct consequence of Theorem 12.18. Namely, define two partial orders $\leq_M$ and $\leq_W$ on the edge set of the underlying bipartite graph G of the given stable matching instance such that $e \leq_M f$ for edges e and f if $e \leq_m f$ for some man m and $e \leq_W f$ if $e \leq_w f$ for some woman w. An antichain of $\leq_M$ is a set of the edges of G that do not share a man-vertex, and similarly for $\leq_W$. Consequently, a subset M of edges of G is a common antichain of $\leq_M$ and $\leq_W$ if and only if M is a matching. The domination property of a common antichain in Theorem 12.18 translates exactly to the stability of M.

Proof of Theorem 12.18 First, we prove the following extension of the edge removal lemma (Lemma 12.4). If v is a $\leq_1$-maximal element of V with $v \geq_2 u$ then the set of stable antichains of V coincides with the set of stable antichains of $V - u$. Indeed, if u belongs to a common antichain then v is not dominated, hence no stable antichain of V contains u. That is, any stable antichain of V is a stable antichain of $V - u$ as well. Assume now that K is a stable antichain of $V - u$. Then either $v \in K$ or v is dominated by some other element w with $w \geq_2 v$. Consequently, u is dominated either by v or by w, hence K is a common antichain of V.

Remove elements from V as long as it is possible according to the above observation. When no more removal is possible then the remaining set V' has the property that the set K of $\leq_1$-maximal elements of V' forms an antichain in $\leq_2$. As K is an antichain for the partial order $\leq_1$, K forms a stable antichain of V'. Hence, by the above observation, K is a stable antichain of V as well. $\square$

Note that the extension of the edge removal lemma in the above proof allows us to extend the deferred acceptance algorithm of Gale and Shapley to find a stable antichain for two posets. Note also that Theorem 12.17 is a special case of a well-known result by Sands, Sauer, and Woodrow [13]. The difference is that the latter result has the same conclusion without the acyclicity assumption. However, it

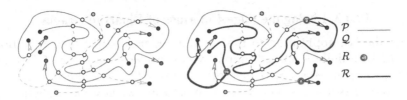

Figure 12.4 Disjoint paths in Pym's theorem; R denotes the set of switching vertices.

is not very difficult to prove the more general result from Theorem 12.17 with the help of so-called graph condensation. We do not discuss this latter notion here but encourage the interested reader to discover the proof from this hint.

12.4.2 The Linking Property of Directed Paths

There is another interesting result on directed paths that has to do with bipartite stable matchings.

Theorem 12.19 (Pym's theorem). *If D is a directed graph and each of P and Q is a collection of vertex-disjoint directed paths of D then there exists a collection R of vertex-disjoint paths of D such that*

1. *each starting vertex of a path of P is a starting vertex of some path of R and each starting vertex of a path of R is a starting vertex of some path of P or of Q,*
2. *each terminal vertex of a path of Q is a terminal vertex of some path of R and each terminal vertex of a path of R is a terminal vertex of some path of P or of Q, and*
3. *any path of R consists of a (possibly empty) initial segment of a path of P and a (possibly empty) end segment of some path of Q.*

Figure 12.4 illustrates Theorem 12.19.

Sketch of the proof. Define a bipartite stable matching instance as follows. The vertices of a bipartite graph G correspond to the paths in P and Q of G. Each common vertex v of a path P of P and a path Q of Q yields an edge e_v between vertices P and Q. For a path P of P, we have $e_v <_P e_u$ if v succeeds u on P. Similarly, for path Q of Q, we have $e_v <_Q e_u$ if u succceeds v on Q. Let S be a stable matching in the bipartite stable matching instance thus defined and let R be the vertices of D that correspond to the edges in S. Now merge initial segments of P-paths to end segments of Q-paths along the vertices of R. (Hence, if some path in $P \cup Q$ does not contain a vertex in R then this entire path belongs to R.) These merges result in a collection R of paths with the desired property: an intersection of two paths in R would correspond to a blocking edge in the above stable matching instance. $\square$

12.4.3 Listing the Edge-Colorings of Bipartite Graphs

To present the last application in this section, we need some further notions. Let $G = (V, E)$ be a finite loopless[4] graph. A *proper edge-coloring* of G is an assignment of colors to the edges of G such that no two edges that share a vertex receive the same color. (As it is customary in combinatorics, when we talk about colors we mean natural numbers.) For each edge $e \in E$, let $L(e) \subset \mathbb{N}$ be a set of colors available for e. We say that G is *L-edge-choosable* if G has an *L-edge-coloring*, that is, a proper edge-coloring $c : E \to \mathbb{N}$ such that $c(e) \in L(e)$ holds for each edge e of E. A graph G is called *k-edge-choosable* if G is *L-edge-choosable* whenever $|L(e)| \geq k$ holds for any edge e of G. The famous list coloring conjecture states that any finite loopless graph G is $\chi'(G)$-edge-choosable, where the chromatic index $\chi'(G)$ denotes the minimum number of colors needed to properly color the edges of G. By generalizing the famous Dinitz conjecture, Galvin proved the list coloring conjecture for bipartite multigraphs. To present Galvin's result, we need a construction of a bipartite preference system. This shows that it is possible to define preferences on the edges of a bipartite graph such that no edge of the graph is dominated by too many other edges.

Lemma 12.20. *If $c : E \to \{1, 2, \ldots, k\}$ is a proper edge-coloring of a bipartite graph $G = (A \cup B, E)$ with parts A and B then there are linear preferences $\prec_v$ for each vertex v on $E(v)$ such that for every edge $e = uv$ of G we have*

$$\varphi(e) := |\{f \in E(u) : f \succ_u e\}| + |\{f \in E(v) : f \succ_v e\}| \leq k - 1 . \tag{12.1}$$

Proof For each vertex a of A and edges $e, f \in E(a)$ let $e \succ_a f$ if $c(e) < c(f)$. For each vertex b of B and edges $e, f \in E(b)$ let $e \succ_b f$ if $c(e) > c(f)$. Assume $ab \in E$ is an edge of G that has color $c(ab) = i$. Then $|\{f \in E(u) : f \succ_a e\}| \leq i - 1$ and $|\{f \in E(v) : f \succ_b e\}| \leq k - i$, and hence $\varphi(e) \leq i - 1 + k - i = k - 1$. □

Theorem 12.21 (Galvin). *Any k-edge-colorable bipartite graph G is k-edge-choosable.*

Proof Assume that $L(e) \subset \mathbb{Z}_+$ is a list of at least k colors for each edge e of G. We need to show that G is *L-edge-choosable*. Define preference orders for k-edge-colorable graph G as in Lemma 12.20. In what follows, we pick those edges of G that receive color i for each color $i = 1, 2, \ldots$ one after the other.

Define $E^i := \{e \in E : i \in L(e)\}$ as the set of i-colorable edges and let $G^i := (V, E^i)$. As G is bipartite, each G^i is also bipartite. For $i = 0, 1, 2, \ldots$ define S^i as a stable matching of the graph $G^i \setminus (S^0 \cup \cdots \cup S^{i-1})$ for restricted preference orders $\prec_v$. Such a matching S^i exists by the stable marriage theorem of Gale and Shapley (the first part of Theorem 12.11).

To show that G is *L-edge-choosable*, give a color i to the edges of the S^i. As all the S^i are matchings, no two edges of the same color share a vertex. Moreover, each colored edge e receives its color $c(e)$ from its list $L(e)$. The only thing left is to show that each edge of G does belong to some S^i, that is, each edge receives some color.

---

[4] Loopless means that the graph does not have an edge with two coinciding verticies.

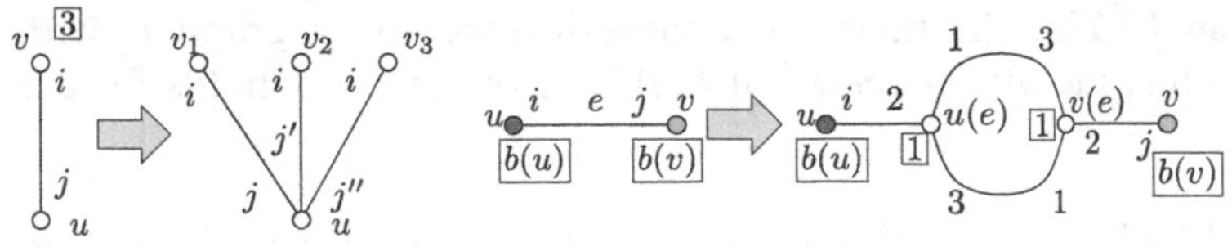

Figure 12.5 Node splitting of v (left) and cycle-insertion for edge $e = uv$ (right). The boxed numbers are the degree bounds and $j < j' < j'' < j + 1$ holds for the preference order $\prec_u$.

Observe that if $e = uv \notin S^i$ then either $e \in S^j$ for some $j < i$ (hence e received color j before S^i was defined) or S^i contains an edge f such that $f \succ_u e$ or $f \succ_v e$. So, if e does not receive any color, that is, if $e \notin \bigcup \{S^j : j \in L(e)\}$ then there is an $f^j \in S^j$ for each $j \in L(e)$ with $f^j \succ_u e$ or $f^j \succ_v e$. This is impossible as $|L(e)| \geq k$ and $\varphi(e) \leq k - 1$. This contradiction proves that the above algorithm finds a proper L-edge coloring of G.

See Exercises 12.12–12.14 for this subsection. $\qquad \square$

12.5 Stable b-Matchings

In this section we illustrate how it is possible to prove new results by a reduction to known results. We shall concentrate on the direct consequences of these reductions on the existence of stable structures rather than elaborating on algorithmic or other aspects. Our example for this scenario shows how to reduce stable b-matching problems to stable matchings. Assume that a stable b-matching instance is given by a graph $G = (V, E)$, preferences $\prec_v$ on $E(v)$ for each vertex v of G, and a degree bound $b \colon V \to \mathbb{Z}_+$. Our goal is to construct a graph $G' = (V', E')$ and preferences $\prec'_u$ on $E'(u)$ for each $u \in V'$ such that there is a strict correspondence between stable b-matchings of the former instance and stable matchings of the latter. If we manage to do so then any algorithm that finds a stable matching in the latter instance can be used to find a stable b-matching of the former. Or, we can prove various properties of stable b-matchings from the corresponding property of stable matchings.

So how does this reduction work? Here is an appealing idea: perform node-splitting. That is, one after another replace every vertex v by $b(v)$ copies $v_1, v_2, \ldots, v_{b(v)}$ with $b(v_1) = b(v_2) = \cdots = b(v_{b(v)}) = 1$ and introduce new edges $uv_1, uv_2, \ldots, uv_{b(v)}$ for every edge uv of G. Each preference order $\prec'_{v_i}$ is inherited from $\prec_v$. Moreover, also change the preference orders of the neighbors of v in such a way that $uv_1 \succ'_u uv_2 \succ'_u \cdots \succ'_u uv_{b(v)}$ and $uv_i \prec'_u e$ if $uv \prec_u e$. (This is illustrated in Figure 12.5.) Let G^b denote the graph and $\prec^b_{v_i}$ the preference orders that we get after all these replacements.

Unfortunately, this construction does not provide the sort of instance G' that we need. The reason is that edge uv of G has $b(u)b(v)$ copies in G^b, and several of them might be disjoint. This means that a stable matching in G^b might use edge uv several times. However, this would happen only if there were disjoint edges among the $b(u)b(v)$ copies. If $b(u) = 1$ or $b(v) = 1$ the then edge uv does not cause such a problem. This useful property is formulated below.

Definition 12.22. A stable b-matching instance on a graph G with degree bound b has the *mto property*[5] if $b(u) = 1$ or $b(v) = 1$ holds for every edge uv of G.

Lemma 12.23. *Assume that a stable b-matching instance on G has the mto property. Then, for any stable matching M^b of the stable matching instance G^b defined above, $\varphi(M^b) = \{uv : u_i v_j \in M^b\}$ is a stable b-matching of G. Moreover, for any stable b-matching M of G, there exists a stable matching M^b of G^b such that $M = \varphi(M^b)$ holds.*

The proof of Lemma 12.23 is rather straightforward and we leave it to the reader. Lemma 12.23 achieves our goal but only for instances with the mto property. Is there some way to reduce any stable b-matching instance to one with this mto property? The answer is yes, and it can be achieved with the following cycle insertion trick.

Assume that $b(u) > 1$ and $b(v) > 1$ holds for edge uv in some stable b-matching instance on graph G. By a cycle insertion along edge $e = uv$ we mean the removal of edge uv from G and the introduction of two new vertices, four new edges, degree bounds, and preferences, as in Figure 12.5. It turns out that any stable b-matching of the inserted instance corresponds to a unique stable b-matching of the original instance and any stable b-matching of the original instance can be represented this way in the inserted instance.

Lemma 12.24. *Assume G^* is the stable b-matching instance we get from G by a cycle insertion along edge $e = uv$. Then, for any stable b-matching M of G^*, $uu(e) \in M$ if and only if $vv(e) \in M$. Moreover, for any stable b-matching M of G, there exists a stable b-matching M^* of G^* such that M and M^* agree on $G - e$ and $e \in M$ if and only if $uu(e) \in M^*$. Finally, for any stable b-matching M^* of G^*, there exists a stable b-matching M of G such that M^* has the property described in the previous sentence.*

We leave the proof of Lemma 12.24 to the reader. Now Lemmas 12.23 and 12.24 allow us to construct an algorithm to find a stable b-matching based on an algorithm that finds a stable matching or to deduce properties of stable b-matchings (from known properties of stable matchings). We can do this in two steps. First, insert a cycle along those edges of G that have no vertex with degree bound 1, and hence transform the problem into one with the mto property. Then, in this problem we may apply node splitting to each vertex with degree bound greater than 1. Each stable matching of the instance thus generated induces a stable b-matching of the original instance, and any stable b-matching in the original instance is induced by a stable matching of the reduced instance. Observe that the useful feature of the above reduction is that it preserves the bipartiteness of the underlying graph. A somewhat inconvenient feature is that the size of the graph may grow quite a bit. So, to find a stable b-matching, the stable matching algorithm when applied to the reduced graph must work on a larger input. This remark may be valid also for other similar reductions. Sometimes it is possible to speed up the algorithm significantly

---

[5] mto stands for many to one.

on the reduced instance and in other cases the fact that a reduction exists may help to find an efficient algorithm.

See Exercises 12.15-12.18 for this subsection.

12.6 Exercises

Exercise 12.1 Determine all stable matchings of the graph in Figure 12.1.

Exercise 12.2 Prove Theorem 12.5 and Lemma 12.8.

Exercise 12.3 Assume that, by repeated applications of the edge removal lemma, edge e in G gets deleted. Is it true that a matching M is stable in G if and only if M is stable in $G - e$?

Exercise 12.4 Assume that every edge e of G is contained in some stable matching of G. Prove that every stable matching of G remains stable if we reverse the preference order of each vertex of G.

Exercise 12.5 Assume that edge $e = uv$ is the worst in both preference orders $\prec_u$ and $\prec_v$. Prove that if some stable matching contains e then e belongs to every stable matching of the same instance.

Exercise 12.6 (Kürschák problem from 2016[6]) Let $1 \leq k \leq n$ be integers. How many subsets of set $\{1, 2, \ldots, n\}$ can be chosen such that out of any two of these subsets, one of them consists of the k smallest elements of the union of the two subsets?

Exercise 12.7 Prove that $|\{S(v) : S$ is a stable b-matching$\}| \leq \max\left(1, d(v) - b(v) + 1\right)$ holds for any vertex in any stable b-matching instance. That is, no vertex v can be matched in $d(v) - b(v)$ different ways in a stable b-matching of the same instance.

Exercise 12.8 Is it true that any stable matching in the stable matching instance defined directly after Theorem 12.10 corresponds to a stable b-matching of the original instance?

Exercise 12.9 Is it possible that some edge e of bipartite graph G is not contained in any stable matching but the sets of stable matchings of G and of $G - e$ are different?

Exercise 12.10 (*) Assume that for any two edges $f_1, f_2 \in F$ there is a stable matching of bipartite graph G that contain both f_1 and f_2. Prove that there is a stable matching of G that contains all edges of F.

Exercise 12.11 (Kürschák problem from 2007) Prove that any finite subset H of the planar grid has a subset K with the properties that
  - any line parallel with one of the axes (i.e., either the vertical or horizontal axis) intersects K in at most two points,

---

[6] The Kürschák Competition is the oldest modern mathematical competition, not only in Hungary but also in the world. It was founded in 1894 and consists of three problems every year. The problems often have a neat but highly non-trivial solution. Competitors are students up to and including the first year of university.

- any point of $H \setminus K$ is on a segment with endpoints in K and parallel with one of the axes.

Exercise 12.12 (Kürschák problem from 2016) Prove that any finite subset A of the positive integers has a subset B with the properties below.
- If b_1 and b_2 are different elements of B then neither b_1 and b_2 nor $b_1 + 1$ and $b_2 + 1$ are multiples of one another, and
- for any element a of set A there exists some element b of B such that either a divides b or $b + 1$ divides $a + 1$.

Exercise 12.13 (*) Assume that the edges of a bipartite graph G can be colored by k colors and $L(e)$ is a list of available colors for each edge e of G. Prove that it is possible to find a subset $C(e)$ of $L(e)$, for each edge e of G, such that $|C(e)| \geq \lfloor |L(e)|/k \rfloor$ and $C(e)$ and $C(f)$ are disjoint whenever edges e and f share a vertex.

Exercise 12.14 (*) Generalize Theorem 12.21 by proving the following special case of the famous list coloring conjecture. Assume that the edges of a graph G can be properly colored by k colors and $L(e)$ is a list of at least k colors for each edge e of G. Prove that if the edges of no odd cycle of G contain a common color in their lists then G is L-edge-choosable.

Exercise 12.15 Let $G = (V, E)$, preferences $\prec_v$, and degree bound $b : V \to \mathbb{Z}_+$ determine a (non-bipartite) stable b-matching instance. Define $G' = (V', E')$, where $V' = \{v_1, v_2 : v \in V\}$ contains two copies of each vertex of G and $E' = \{u_1 v_2, u_2 v_1 : uv \in E\}$ has two edges for each edge of G. The preference $\prec'_{u_i}$ is inherited from $\prec_u$, and $b'(v_1) = b'(v_2) = b(v)$ for every vertex v of G. Prove that G' with preferences $\prec'_v$ and degree bound b' defines a bipartite stable b-matching instance in such a way that M is a stable b-matching of G if and only if $M' = \{u_1 v_2, u_2 v_1 : uv \in M\}$ is a stable b'-matching of G'.

Exercise 12.16 Prove the following median property for non-bipartite stable b-matchings. Assume that $S_1, S_2, \ldots, S_{2k-1}$ are stable b-matchings of graph G. Prove that there is a stable b-matching S of G such that $S(v)$ coincides with the kth $\prec_v$-best among $S_1(v), S_2(v), \ldots, S_{2k-1}(v)$ for every vertex v of G.

Exercise 12.17 Prove the statement in Exercise 12.10 for non-bipartite graphs.

Exercise 12.18 (*) Prove that if the edges of a cycle C of length $2k$ in a non-bipartite graph G are colored alternatingly red and green and each red edge is blocking the matching of the green edges then one of the green edges is not contained in any stable matching of G. (This exercise is based on an idea of András Frank.)

12.7 Bibiographic Notes

In this chapter we illustrated that the use of the edge removal lemma (Lemma 12.4) leads to elegant proofs of various results on stable matchings. It seems that the result itself has been observed by many. For example, the so-called extended Gale–Shapley algorithm described in the book [10] performs all possible edge removals according to the edge removal lemma. Also, the generalization of the edge removal lemma

(Theorem 12.5) is implicitely proved in [1] (see Lemma 4.2 and Observation 4.3 in that article). However, the approach itself originates from a collaboration with Ron Aharoni and for some time has been used on certain courses that cover this topic at the Budapest University of Technology and Economics and at the Aquincum Institute of Technology. The present chapter is probably the first official publication presenting this approach.

The splitting property of stable b-matchings (Theorem 12.10) is a key to the linear description of the stable b-matching polyhedron in [4]. The theorem on median stable b-matchings (Theorem 12.16) was proved first for stable matchings in [14] using linear programming tools. The general theorem comes from [2] and the one-to-many special case was rediscovered in [11].

Theorem 12.17 is a special case of a result in [13] and the stable-matching-related proof of Pym's theorem (Theorem 12.19) comes from [3]. It is interesting to see, regarding Theorem 12.21, that in [9], the author explains that his approach is not motivated by stable matchings. these are just special cases of his result. Formal generalizations of Theorem 12.21 were proved in [7] and [6]. The reduction in Section 12.5 is described in [1]. Further stable-matching-related problems that can be solved by reducing one problem to another can be found in [5] and [8].

Finally, a remark on the change of the motivating example for stable-matching-related models. While in 1962 the description of a marriage market on a set of men and women was a perfectly acceptable choice, nowadays more and more people express loudly how offensive they find it when marriages in such models have to involve exactly one man and one woman. To help these individuals to concentrate on the scientific part, in this work we have not talked about marriages. Instead, we have just assumed that men and women can become *partners* of one another. We sincerely hope that this approach remains a fine motivating example as long as there are sports events for mixed doubles.

Hints for the Exercises

12.1 Use Lemma 12.4.

12.2 Theorem 12.5: try to follow the proof of Lemma 12.4. Lemma 12.8: every edge of $S_i \setminus S_j$ is dominated by some edge in $S_j \setminus S_i$.

12.3 No, it is not true. M may be stable in $G - e$ but not stable in G.

12.4 Prove that if $e \notin S$ then S dominates e at exactly one vertex (according to the original preferences).

12.5 No cycle with cyclic preferences may contain edge uv.

12.6 The smallest elements of these subsets are pairwise different.

12.7 Use the previous exercise and Corollary 12.9.

12.8 No. Take $b \equiv 2$ on four parallel edges with opposite preference orders.

12.9 Yes. Take two disjoint 4-cycles with cyclic preferences and an edge e connecting them. The connecting edge is the middle choice for both of its vertices.

12.10 Use Theorem 12.16 and apply induction on $|F|$.

12.11 Generalize the deferred acceptance algorithm.

12.12 Apply Theorem 12.18.

12.13 Introduce parallel edges, extend preferences, and follow Galvin's method.

12.14 Find appropriate preferences and follow Galvin's method.

12.15 M' is clearly a b'-matching. If $uv \notin M$ is dominated at u by M then $u_i v_j$ is dominated at u_i by M'.

12.16 Use Exercise 12.15 and the corresponding property of bipartite instances.

12.17 Use Exercise 12.16 and apply induction on $|F|$ as in Exercise 12.10.

12.18 Indirectly, for each green edge e, pick some stable matching S_e containing e, and let S be the multiset consisting of these S_e. Each green edge is weakly dominated k times by S and each the red edge is weakly dominated at least k times by S. However, the red edges altogether are weakly dominated by S at least k times fewer than the green edges, a contradiction.

References

[1] Cechlárová, Katarína, and Fleiner, Tamás. 2005. On a generalization of the stable roommates problem. *ACM Transactions on Algorithms*, **1**(1), 143–156.

[2] Fleiner, Tamás. 2002. Some results on stable matchings and fixed points. Technical report, EGRES report TR-2002-8, ISSN 1587-4451. `www.cs.elte.hu/egres`.

[3] Fleiner, Tamás. 2003a. A fixed-point approach to stable matchings and some applications. *Mathematics of Operations Research*, **28**(1), 103–126.

[4] Fleiner, Tamás. 2003b. On the stable b-matching polytope. *Mathematical Social Sciences*, **46**(2), 149–158.

[5] Fleiner, Tamás. 2014. On stable matchings and flows. *Algorithms*, **7**(1), 1–14.

[6] Fleiner, Tamás. 2018. A note on restricted list edge-colourings. *Combinatorica*, **38**(04).

[7] Fleiner, Tamás, and Frank, András. 2010. Balanced list edge-colourings of bipartite graphs. *Electronic Notes in Discrete Mathematics*, **36**, 837–842.

[8] Fleiner, Tamás, and Kamiyama, Naoyuki. 2016. A matroid approach to stable matchings with lower quotas. *Mathematics of Operations Research*, **41**(2), 734–744.

[9] Galvin, Fred. 1995. The list chromatic index of a bipartite multigraph. *Journal of Combinatorial Theory Series B*, **63**(1), 153–158.

[10] Gusfield, Dan, and Irving, Robert W. 1989. *The stable marriage problem: structure and algorithms*. MIT Press.

[11] Klaus, Bettina, and Klijn, Flip. 2006. Median stable matching for college admissions. *International Journal of Game Theory*, **34**(1), 1–11.

[12] Pym, J. S. 1969. A proof of the linkage theorem. *Journal of Mathematical Analysis and Applications*, **27**, 636–638.

[13] Sands, B., Sauer, N., and Woodrow, R. 1982. On monochromatic paths in edge-coloured digraphs. *Journal of Combinatorial Theory Series B*, **33**(3), 271–275.

[14] Teo, Chung-Piaw, and Sethuraman, Jay. 1998. The geometry of fractional stable matchings and its applications. *Mathematics of Operations Research*, **23**(4), 874–891.

CHAPTER THIRTEEN

Algorithmics of Matching Markets

Jiehua Chen and David Manlove

13.1 Introduction

Chapter 1 described classical results for two-sided matching markets involving the assignment of workers to firms based on their preferences over one another. The underlying matching problem is known in the literature as the Stable Marriage problem, and in its canonical form it corresponds to Setting I from Chapter 1. The objective is to find a *stable matching*, a one-to-one assignment of workers to firms such that no worker and firm prefer one another to their assigned partners.

The Stable Marriage problem has been the focus of a great deal of attention in the literature, and one reason for this is that the classical problem and its variants feature in many practical applications. These include entry-level labor markets, school choice, and higher education admission. For example, a many-to-one extension of Stable Marriage known as the Hospitals/Residents problem (captured by Setting III in Chapter 1) models the assignment of graduating medical students to hospital posts. The National Resident Matching Program (NRMP) administers this process in the USA, which involves applications from over 40,000 aspiring junior doctors per year. At the heart of the NRMP is an algorithm for the Hospitals/Residents problem.

Centralized matching schemes (also known as clearinghouses) such as the NRMP typically involve large numbers of participants, and thus it is imperative that they incorporate efficient algorithms. Chapter 1 described an efficient algorithm for the Stable Marriage problem and showed how to extend it to the Hospitals/Residents problem. In practice, however, there are often additional features of a matching market that have to be taken into consideration, which lead to generalizations of the Stable Marriage problem that have thus far not been considered in this book from an algorithmic point of view.

For example, it is very likely that a large hospital participating in the NRMP, having many applicants, may not have enough information to rank them objectively in strict order of preference. It may prefer to rank several applicants equally, in tied batches, indicating that it is indifferent between them. This is especially likely if hospitals' preference lists are derived from scores (e.g., originating from academic assessments); several applicants may have equal scores, making them essentially indistinguishable.

Another direction involves computing "fair" stable matchings. Chapter 1 described the lattice structure that holds for the set of stable matchings in an instance of the Stable Marriage problem (see Definition 1.37). The Gale–Shapley deferred acceptance algorithm (see Page 6) computes a stable matching μ that is either at the top or at the bottom end of this lattice. That is, matching μ is either worker-optimal or firm-optimal – but in each case, optimality for the workers or the firms comes at the expense of the other set of agents, since these matchings are the worst possible for the firms and workers, respectively. One may instead wish to find a stable matching that is fair to both sides of the market; one example of such a matching is an *egalitarian stable matching*, where the overall dissatisfaction of the agents, the so-called egalitarian cost, is minimized.

A further extension concerns the case in which the agents involved in the market form a single set, rather than two disjoint sets as before. In this case we obtain the non-bipartite version of Stable Marriage called the Stable Roommates problem. This problem has applications in P2P networking, as well as in dormitory allocation and in pairing players for chess or tennis tournaments.

In many of these variants, computing certain types of stable matchings becomes an NP-hard problem. Given the practical significance of these matching problems, the importance of finding ways to cope with this complexity should be clear. The purpose of this chapter is to focus on two examples where finding types of "optimal" stable matchings is NP-hard, and to illustrate the algorithmic techniques that typically have been applied in order to find optimal or approximate solutions.

The first problem that we focus on concerns finding a stable matching that maximizes the number of workers that are matched, given an instance of a variant of Stable Marriage in which preference lists may include ties and need not involve every member of the other side of the market. We first give a reduction to demonstrate the NP-hardness of this problem. Then we give an exposition of Király's approximation algorithm, which achieves a performance guarantee of $\frac{3}{2}$ using a technique that subsequently has been widely applied in various matching problem scenarios.

The second problem involves finding an egalitarian stable matching in a given instance of the Stable Roommates problem. This is an NP-hard problem, and for this we show how techniques from parameterized algorithmics give rise to fixed-parameter algorithms when the parameter is the egalitarian cost of the solution. Specifically, these methods involve kernelization and the use of bounded search trees, which are used extensively in designing fixed-parameter algorithms.

The remainder of this chapter is organized as follows. In Section 13.2, we define preliminary notation and terminology, and give formal definitions of the key problems that will be considered in this chapter. Section 13.3 focuses on the variant of Stable Marriage with ties and incomplete lists where we seek a maximum cardinality stable matching. The fixed-parameter algorithms for finding an egalitarian stable matching in an instance of the Stable Roommates problem are described in Section 13.4. We list some open problems in Section 13.5 that are related to the problems tackled in Sections 13.3 and 13.4. Finally Section 13.6 gives some chapter notes, including references for the key existing results on which we have relied.

13.2 Preliminaries

13.2.1 Definitions of Key Notation and Terminology

We begin by defining notation and terminology that will be used throughout this chapter. First, for each natural number t, we denote the set $\{1, 2, \ldots, t\}$ by $[t]$.

Let $V = [n]$ be a set of n agents. Each agent $i \in V$ has a subset $V_i \subseteq V$ of agents that it finds *acceptable* as a partner and has a *preference list* $\succeq_i$ on V_i (i.e., a transitive and complete binary relation on V_i). Here, $x \succeq_i y$ means that i *weakly prefers* x over y. We use $\succ_i$ to denote the asymmetric part (i.e., $x \succeq_i y$ and $\neg(y \succeq_i x)$) and $\sim_i$ to denote the symmetric part (i.e., $x \succeq_i y$ and $y \succeq_i x$) so that $x \succ_i y$ means that i *strictly prefers* x to y while $x \sim_i y$ means that i regards x as tied with y. We may omit the subscript in the $\succ_i$, $\succeq_i$, and $\sim_i$ notation if it is clear from the context. For two agents x and y, we call x *most acceptable* to y if x is a maximal element in the preference list of y. Note that an agent can have more than one most acceptable agent.

A *preference profile* $\mathcal{P}$ for V is a collection $(\succeq_i)_{i \in V}$ of preference lists for each agent $i \in V$. To a preference profile $\mathcal{P} = (V, (\succeq_i)_{i \in V})$ we assign an *acceptability graph* G, which has V as its vertex set, and an edge between each pair of agents that find each other acceptable. Without loss of generality, we assume that G does not contain isolated vertices, meaning that each agent has at least one agent that it finds acceptable. A preference profile $\mathcal{P}$ may have the following properties: it is *complete* if the underlying acceptability graph is complete (i.e., it contains an edge between each pair of agents); otherwise, it is *incomplete*. The profile $\mathcal{P}$ has *ties* if there is an agent $i \in V$ for which there are two agents $x, y \in V_i$ such that $x \sim_i y$; we say that x and y are *tied* by i; otherwise, if $\mathcal{P}$ has no ties, it is said to be *strict*.

When illustrating a preference profile, in a given agent's preference list and for a given indexed set S of agents, the notation $[S]$ refers to all agents in S listed in an arbitrary but fixed strict order, whilst the notation (S) indicates a tie containing all agents in S, in both cases in the position where the symbol occurs.

The *rank* of an agent i in the preference list of some agent j, denoted $\mathsf{rank}_j^{\mathcal{P}}(i)$, is the number of agents x that j strictly prefers over i:

$$\mathsf{rank}_j^{\mathcal{P}}(i) := |\{x \in V \mid x \succ_j i\}|.$$

We will omit the superscript from $\mathsf{rank}_j^{\mathcal{P}}(i)$ if the instance is clear from the context.

Given a preference profile $\mathcal{P}$ for a set V of agents, recall that a *matching* $\mu \subseteq E(G)$ is a set of disjoint pairs $\{i, j\}$ of agents. For a pair $\{i, j\}$ of agents, if $\{i, j\} \in \mu$ then the *partner* of i, denoted by $\mu(i)$ is defined to be j; otherwise we call this pair *unmatched*. If agent i has *no partner*; i.e., i is not involved in any pair in μ, we say that i is *unmatched* by μ. If no agent is unmatched by μ then μ is *perfect*.

Given a matching μ of $\mathcal{P}$, an unmatched pair $\{i, j\} \in E(G) \setminus \mu$ *is blocking* μ if each of i and j is either unmatched or prefers the other to her assigned partner, i.e., it holds that (i) i is unmatched by μ or $j \succ_i \mu(i)$, and (ii) j is unmatched by μ or $i \succ_j \mu(j)$. We call a matching μ *stable* if no unmatched pair is blocking μ.

13.2.2 Central Computational Problems

We now define formally the main computational problems that we will be studying in the remainder of this chapter. We begin with the Stable Roommates problem, which is defined as follows:

STABLE ROOMMATES (SRTI)
Input: A preference profile $\mathcal{P} = (V, (\succeq_i)_{i \in V})$ for a set V of n agents.
Question: Does $\mathcal{P}$ admit a stable matching?

The SRTI acronym denotes the fact that preference lists may contain ties and the preference profile may be incomplete. We use SRI to refer to the special case of SRTI in which preference lists are strictly ordered (but the preference profile may be incomplete).

The bipartite restriction of Stable Roommates, called Stable Marriage, has as input two disjoint sets W and F of agents (referred to as the *workers* and *firms* respectively in Chapter 1), where $|W| + |F| = n$, such that each agent from one set has a preference list that ranks a subset of the agents from the other set. In other words, the acceptability graph of a Stable Marriage instance is a bipartite graph on W and F. We call the corresponding preference profile a *bipartite preference profile*. The notions that we have introduced for Stable Roommates can be restricted intuitively to also work for Stable Marriage. For instance, the preference profile of a Stable Marriage instance is *complete* if the underlying acceptability graph is a complete bipartite graph.

STABLE MARRIAGE (SMTI)
Input: A bipartite preference profile $\mathcal{P} = (W, F, (\succeq_i)_{i \in W \cup F})$ for two disjoint sets W and F of agents, where $|W| + |F| = n$.
Question: Does $\mathcal{P}$ admit a stable matching?

Analogously, we use SMI to refer to the restriction of SMTI where each preference list is strictly ordered (but the preference profile may be incomplete).

When ties are not present, determining whether an instance of SRI (and thus SMI) admits a stable matching, and finding one if it does, can be done in $O(n^2)$ time. Moreover, every instance of SMI is a "yes" instance since it always admits a stable matching. However, when preferences have ties, the problem of deciding whether a stable matching exists, given an instance of SRTI, becomes NP-complete even if the preferences are complete.

The situation for SMTI is more positive: SMTI still admits a stable matching, even if the preferences may be incomplete. But there may be stable matchings with different cardinalities. By breaking the ties arbitrarily, one can find a stable matching in $O(n^2)$ time. However, finding one with maximum cardinality becomes NP-hard. The corresponding optimization problem, called Max-Card Stable Marriage, is defined as follows:

MAX-CARD STABLE MARRIAGE (MAX-SMTI)
Input: A bipartite preference profile $\mathcal{P} = (W, F, (\succeq_i)_{i \in W \cup F})$ for two disjoint sets W and F of agents, where $|W| + |F| = n$.
Output: A stable matching for $\mathcal{P}$ with the largest cardinality.

$1: 3 \succ 6 \succ 2,$ $2: 4 \succ 1 \succ 6 \succ 3,$

$3: 6 \succ 1 \succ 2 \succ 5,$ $4: 5 \succ 2 \succ 8,$

$5: 3 \succ 4 \succ 7 \succ 8,$ $6: 2 \succ 3 \succ 1,$

$7: 5,$ $8: 4 \succ 5.$

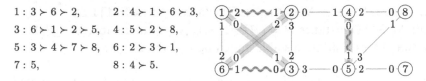

Figure 13.1 Left: An SRI instance with eight agents; it admits two stable matchings in which agents 7 and 8 are never matched. Right: The corresponding acceptability graph, with edges labeled with ranks. The stable matching marked in pale gray and solid lines has egalitarian cost 7 while the stable matching marked in darker gray with wavy lines has egalitarian cost 8; recall that each unmatched agent induces a cost that equals the length of her preference list.

Stable matchings in an instance $\mathcal{P}$ of SRTI may not be unique. To find an "optimal" stable matching in $\mathcal{P}$, one can take agents' satisfaction towards a matching μ into account. This is formally captured by the *egalitarian cost* of μ, denoted by $\gamma(\mu)$, and defined as follows:

$$\gamma(\mu) := \sum_{i \in V(\mu)} \mathsf{rank}_i^{\mathcal{P}}(\mu(i)) + \sum_{k \in V \setminus V(\mu)} |V_k|,$$

where $V(\mu) := \{i, j \in V \mid \{i, j\} \in \mu\}$ denotes the set of matched agents in μ. A stable matching μ is *egalitarian* if $\gamma(\mu)$ is a minimum, taken over all stable matchings in $\mathcal{P}$. We now define a decision problem that is associated with finding an egalitarian stable matching:

EGALITARIAN STABLE ROOMMATES DECISION (EGAL-SRTI-DEC)
Input: A preference profile $\mathcal{P} = (V, (\succeq_i)_{i \in V})$ for a set V of n agents, and a non-negative integer γ.
Question: Does $\mathcal{P}$ admit a stable matching with $\gamma(\mu) \leq \gamma$?

See Figure 13.1 for an example. We let EGAL-SRI-DEC denote the special case of EGAL-SRTI-DEC in which preference lists are strictly ordered (but may be incomplete). The bipartite restriction of EGAL-SRI-DEC is denoted by EGAL-SMI-DEC. EGAL-SMI-DEC is solvable in polynomial time, but the variant in which preferences are complete and may contain ties is NP-complete. On the other hand EGAL-SRI-DEC is NP-complete even for complete lists.

In Section 13.3 we study MAX-SMTI and give a reduction to show that this problem is NP-hard even if the ties occur on one side only. We also present a simple and elegant approximation algorithm due to Király for this special case of MAX-SMTI, proving that it has a performance guarantee of $\frac{3}{2}$. In Section 13.4 we investigate the parameterized complexity of EGAL-SRI-DEC. We show that EGAL-SRI-DEC is fixed-parameter tractable with respect to the parameter "egalitarian cost" via two efficient algorithms.

13.3 Stable Marriage with Ties and Incomplete Lists

13.3.1 NP-hardness of MAX-SMTI

In this section we show that MAX-SMTI is NP-hard. In particular, we show that this result holds even if the ties occur in the preference lists on one side only. The result is established by proving that the following decision problem is NP-complete for this restriction on the placement of ties:

MAX-CARD STABLE MARRIAGE DECISION (MAX-SMTI-DEC)
Input: An SMTI instance $\mathcal{P} = (W, F, (\succeq_i)_{i \in W \cup F})$ and an integer $s \geq 0$.
Question: Does $\mathcal{P}$ admit a stable matching μ with $|\mu| \geq s$?

Theorem 13.1. MAX-SMTI-DEC *is NP-complete, even if the ties occur in the preference lists on one side only.*

Proof Clearly MAX-SMTI-DEC is in NP, since checking whether a given matching is stable and has cardinality at least s can be done in polynomial time. To show NP-hardness, we give a reduction from the NP-complete problem INDEPENDENT SET, as follows. An instance of INDEPENDENT SET comprises a graph $G = (V, E)$ and an integer $h \geq 0$, and the problem is to decide whether G has an *independent set* (i.e., a subset of vertices that are pairwise non-adjacent to each other) of size h.

The general idea behind the reduction is as follows: introduce vertex and edge agents, corresponding to the vertices and edges of the graph, and h pairs of selector agents which must be matched with the vertex agents in any maximum-size stable matching. The preferences of the vertex and edge agents will ensure that the vertex agents that are matched to the selector agents induce an independent set.

Let $I = ((G = (V, E), h)$ be an instance of Independent Set, where $V = \{v_1, v_2, \ldots, v_{n'}\}$ and $E = \{e_1, e_2, \ldots, e_{m'}\}$. Construct a MAX-SMTI-DEC instance I' as follows. Firstl, let $W' = W \cup S \cup E^U$ be the set of workers in I', where $W = \{w_1, w_2, \ldots, w_{n'}\}$, $S = \{s_1, s_2, \ldots, s_h\}$, and $E^U = \{e_j^{u_i}, e_j^{u_{i'}} \mid e_j = \{u_i, u_{i'}\} \in E\}$. Next, let $F' = U \cup T \cup E \cup F$ be the set of firms in I', where $U = \{u_1, u_2, \ldots, u_{n'}\}$, $T = \{t_1, t_2, \ldots, t_h\}$, $E = \{e_1, e_2, \ldots, e_{m'}\}$, and $F = \{f_1, f_2, \ldots, f_{m'}\}$.

Intuitively, for $v_i \in V$, agents u_i and w_i correspond to vertex v_i in G. For each edge $e_j = \{u_i, u_{i'}\} \in E$, agents e_j, f_j, $e_j^{u_i}$, and $e_j^{u_{i'}}$ correspond to edge e_j in G. Although the notation for the agent e_j in I' is the same as that for the edge e_j in G, the precise meaning should be clear from the context. Finally, the agents in $S \cup T$ are intended to receive partners that correspond to h vertices that have been selected in an independent set in G.

The preference profile $\mathcal{P}$ in I' is described in Figure 13.2. Also see Figure 13.3 for an illustration of the reduction. We observe that the preference lists of the firms in $T \cup E$ contain ties, while the preference lists of the firms in $U \cup F$ and those of the workers are strictly ordered. To complete the construction of $I' = (\mathcal{P}, s)$, we let the target size of stable matching be $s = n' + 2m' + h$.

Clearly I' can be constructed from I in linear time, and the number of agents on each side of I' is s. We claim that I has an independent set of size h if and only if I' has a stable matching of size s. Before proving the claim, we give some further intuition for the reduction as follows. The vertices $v_i \in V$ of an independent set in G correspond to firms $u_i \in U$ that are matched to a worker in S. Since each such firm u_i prefers all workers $e_j^{u_i} \in E^U$, where v_i is an endpoint of edge $e_j = \{v_i, v_{i'}\}$, by stability each such worker $e_j^{u_i}$ must be matched to her first choice e_j, meaning that $e_j^{u_{i'}}$ must be matched to her third choice f_j. In turn, $e_j^{u_{i'}}$ prefers $u_{i'}$ to her partner, and hence, by stability, $u_{i'}$ cannot be

Workers' preference lists:

$$
\begin{array}{lll}
w_i: & [T] \succ u_i & \forall i \in [n'] \\
s_j: & u_1 \succ u_2 \succ \cdots \succ u_{n'} & \forall j \in [h] \\
e_j^{u_i}: & e_j \succ u_i \succ f_j & \forall e_j \in E \text{ with } e_j = \{v_i, v_{i'}\} \\
e_j^{u_{i'}}: & e_j \succ u_{i'} \succ f_j & \forall e_j \in E \text{ with } e_j = \{v_i, v_{i'}\}.
\end{array}
$$

Firms' preference lists:

$$
\begin{array}{lll}
u_i: & w_i \succ [\{e_j^{u_i} \mid v_i \in e_j \text{ for some edge } e_j \in E\}] \succ s_1 \succ s_2 \succ \cdots \succ s_h & \forall i \in [n'] \\
t_j: & (W) & \forall j \in [h] \\
e_j: & (\{e_j^{u_i}, e_j^{u_{i'}}\}) & \forall e_j \in E \text{ with } e_j = \{v_i, v_{i'}\} \\
f_j: & [\{e_j^{u_i}, e_j^{u_{i'}}\}] & \forall e_j \in E \text{ with } e_j = \{v_i, v_{i'}\}.
\end{array}
$$

Figure 13.2 Preference lists in the instance I' of MAX-SMTI-DEC constructed in the proof of Theorem 13.1. Given a set of agents A, recall that $[A]$ denotes all agents in A listed in an arbitrary but fixed strict order, whilst (A) indicates a tie containing all agents in A.

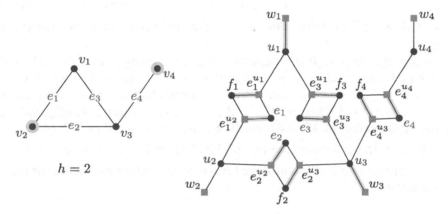

Figure 13.3 Illustration of the NP-hardness reduction for the proof of Theorem 13.1. Left: An instance of INDEPENDENT SET. The independent set solutions containing $V' = \{v_2, v_4\}$ are highlighted with pale gray outer rings. Right: The acceptability graph of the constructed instance; for the sake of readability, the agents from $S \cup T$ are omitted. The crucial edges of the stable matching which correspond to the independent set V' are marked in pale gray.

matched to a worker in S. We thus obtain that at most one endpoint of e_j corresponds to a firm matched to a worker in S, which establishes the independence property.

To prove the "only if" direction, assume that $V' := \{v_{i_1}, v_{i_2}, \ldots, v_{i_h}\}$ is an independent set in G, where $i_1 < i_2 < \cdots < i_h$. We form a matching μ of size s in I' as follows.

1. For each $z \in [h]$, add to μ the two pairs $\{w_{i_z}, t_z\}$ and $\{s_z, u_{i_z}\}$.
2. For each $v_i \in V \setminus V'$, add to μ the pair $\{w_i, u_i\}$.
3. For each edge $e_j \in E$ with $e_j = \{v_i, v_{i'}\}$, where $i < i'$, if $v_i \in V'$ then add to μ the two pairs $\{e_j^{u_i}, e_j\}$ and $\{e_j^{u_{i'}}, f_j\}$; otherwise add to μ the two pairs $\{e_j^{u_{i'}}, e_j\}$ and $\{e_j^{u_i}, f_j\}$.

Please notice that in Step (3), if neither v_i nor $v_{i'}$ belong to V', adding $\{e_j^{u_i}, e_j\}$ and $\{e_j^{u_{i'}}, f_j\}$ instead of $\{e_j^{u_{i'}}, e_j\}$ and $\{e_j^{u_i}, f_j\}$ to the matching μ also preserves stability. Clearly $|\mu| = 2h + (n' - h) + 2m' = s$, and μ matches all agents in I'. We claim that μ is stable in I'.

Clearly no firm in $T \cup E$ can be involved in a blocking pair of μ in I'. Neither can any firm in F, since no worker prefers a firm in F to her partner. Neither can an unmatched pair $\{w_{i'}, u_{i'}\}$, for some $i' \in [n']$, block μ, since $w_{i'}$ does not prefer $u_{i'}$ to her partner in μ. Suppose that an unmatched pair $\{s_j, u_{i'}\}$ blocks μ, for some $i' \in [n']$ and $j \in [h]$. Then, $u_{i'} = u_{i_z}$ and $\{s_z, u_{i_z}\} \in \mu$ for some $z \in [h]$, by construction of μ. As $u_{i'}$ prefers s_j to $\mu(u_{i'})$, it follows that $j < z$. By construction of μ, $\{s_j, u_{i_j}\} \in \mu$, and as $i_j < i_z$ it follows that s_j does not prefer $u_{i'}$ to $\mu(s_j)$, a contradiction.

Finally suppose that $\{e_j^{u_{i'}}, u_{i'}\}$ blocks μ, where $e_j \in E$ and $u_{i'} \in e_j$. Then, $\mu(u_{i'}) \in S$, which implies that $v_{i'} \in V'$. Thus, by the construction of μ, it follows that $\{e_j^{u_{i'}}, e_j\} \in \mu$. This implies that $e_j^{u_{i'}}$ has her most-preferred partner in μ, and thus $\{e_j^{u_{i'}}, u_{i'}\}$ does not block μ after all, a contradiction. Hence, μ is stable in I'.

Conversely, suppose that I' admits a stable matching μ of size s. Then all agents in I' are matched in μ. Define the set $V' := \{v_i \in V \mid \mu(u_i) \in S\}$. Clearly $|V'| = h$. We claim that V' is an independent set in G. For, suppose that $e_j = \{v_i, v_{i'}\} \in E$ where $u_i \in V'$ and $u_{i'} \in V'$. Then $\mu(u_i) \in S$ and $\mu(u_{i'}) \in S$ by the construction of V'. As f_j must be matched in μ, either $\{e_j^{u_i}, f_j\} \in \mu$ or $\{e_j^{u_{i'}}, f_j\} \in \mu$. In the former case $\{e_j^{u_i}, u_i\}$ blocks μ in I', whilst in the latter case $\{e_j^{u_{i'}}, u_{i'}\}$ blocks μ in I'. Both of these form a contradiction and hence the claim is established. $\qquad\square$

13.3.2 Király's Approximation Algorithm for MAX-SMTI with One-Sided Ties

In this section we describe Király's $\frac{3}{2}$-approximation algorithm for the special case of MAX-SMTI in which the ties occur in the preference lists on one side only. We also show how to prove that the algorithm is correct and has performance guarantee $\frac{3}{2}$. In what follows, we assume without loss of generality that we are given an instance $\mathcal{P} = (W, F, (\succeq_i)_{i \in W \cup F})$ of MAX-SMTI in which the ties occur in the firms' lists only, and workers' lists do not contain ties. Henceforth we refer to this special case of MAX-SMTI as MAX-SMTI-TF.

Király's algorithm for MAX-SMTI-TF is similar to the classical Gale–Shapley algorithm for Stable Marriage in that it involves a series of applications from workers to firms, and possible rejections of workers by firms. A key distinction is that Király's algorithm allows a worker w_i who has been rejected by every firm on her preference list to have a "second chance" and to apply to them again in a second pass through her list. During this second pass, w_i is said to be *promoted*, which means that, for any firm f_j on her list, w_i has a higher priority according to f_j than any unpromoted worker with which she is tied on f_j's list. To formalize this, we define the notion of *favors* as follows.

Definition 13.2. A firm f_j is said to *favor* a worker w_i over another worker w_k if either (i) or (ii) holds, as follows:

(i) f_j strictly prefers w_i to w_k (i.e., $w_i \succ_{f_j} w_k$), or
(ii) w_i and w_k are tied in f_j's list, and w_i is promoted whilst w_k is not.

A worker can only be promoted once: after a second pass through her list, if w_i has again been rejected by every firm on her list then w_i will not be able to apply to any firm again and will be unmatched in the final matching. We say that w_i is *exhausted* if w_i has been rejected from every firm in her preference list (either during a first pass or a second pass through her list).

Algorithm 13.1 Király's approximation algorithm for MAX-SMTI-TF.

Input: An MAX-SMTI-TF instance $\mathcal{P} = (W, F, (\succeq_i)_{i \in W \cup F})$

1   $\mu := \emptyset$
2   **foreach** $w_i \in W$ **do**
3      $promoted(w_i) := $ false
4      $exhausted(w_i) := $ false
5   **while** some $w_i \in W$ is unmatched **and** *(!promoted(w_i) or !exhausted(w_i))* **do**
6   **if** *exhausted(w_i)* **then**
7          $promoted(w_i) := $ true
8          $exhausted(w_i) := $ false
9   reactivate w_i `// i.e., set `w_i` to have been rejected`
             `by no firms`
10      $f_j := $ most-preferred firm on w_i's list that has not yet rejected her
       `// `w_i` applies to `f_j
11   **if** f_j is unmatched **then** $\mu := \mu \cup \{\{w_i, f_j\}\}$
12   **else**
13   **if** f_j favors w_i over $\mu(f_j)$ **then**   `// recall Definition 13.2`
14   f_j rejects $\mu(f_j)$
15              $\mu := (\mu \cup \{\{w_i, f_j\}\}) \setminus \{\{\mu(f_j), f_j\}\}$
16   **else** f_j rejects w_i
17   **if** w_i *is rejected by every firm on her list* **then** $exhausted(w_i) := $ true
18 **return** μ

A pseudocode description of Király's algorithm is given in Algorithm 13.1. We now give an explanation of the algorithm. Initially the matching μ is empty, and booleans for each worker w_i are set to indicate that w_i has not been promoted yet and w_i is not exhausted yet. The main loop iterates as long as there is some worker w_i who is unmatched, and additionally w_i has not been promoted yet or w_i is not yet exhausted. If w_i is exhausted then, as we know that w_i has not been promoted by line 5, w_i has completed only one pass through her preference list. In preparation for a second pass through her list, we then set w_i as promoted and not exhausted, and "reactivate" w_i, meaning that we now assume that no firms have rejected w_i.

Lines 10–16 of the algorithm are similar to the Gale–Shapley algorithm for STABLE MARRIAGE. That is, w_i applies to the most-preferred firm f_j on her list that has not yet rejected her. If f_j is unmatched then it accepts the application and becomes assigned to w_i. Otherwise f_j is already matched to some worker w_k in μ. If f_j favors w_i over w_k (see Definition 13.2) then f_j rejects w_k and becomes assigned to w_i instead;

otherwise f_j rejects w_i and remains assigned to w_k. Notice here that if w_i is promoted, she can displace an unpromoted worker w_k assigned to f_j even if w_i and w_k are tied in f_j's list. Finally line 17 ensures that a worker is set to be exhausted if she has been rejected by every firm on her list.

The following series of lemmas establish the correctness of the algorithm.

Lemma 13.3. *Given an instance $\mathcal{P}$ of MAX-SMTI-TF, all possible executions of Király's algorithm as applied to $\mathcal{P}$ produce a stable matching μ in $\mathcal{P}$.*

Proof Let μ be the matching returned by the algorithm and suppose that $\{w, f\}$ blocks μ. Then either w is unmatched in μ and finds f acceptable or else w is matched in μ and strictly prefers f to $\mu(f)$. In either case w applied to f and it rejected her because either (i) it was already assigned to a worker w' and it did not favor w over w' or (ii) it subsequently received an application from a worker w' whom it favored over w. In either case, either w' and w are tied in f's list or f strictly prefers w' to w. Hence f weakly prefers w' to w. Moreover, any subsequent change of partner for f cannot cause it to become strictly worse off, so f weakly prefers $\mu(f)$ to w. Hence $\{w, f\}$ does not block w after all, a contradiction. □

Lemma 13.4. *Given an instance $\mathcal{P}$ of MAX-SMTI-TF, any execution of Király's algorithm as applied to $\mathcal{P}$ produces a stable matching μ in $\mathcal{P}$ such that $|\mu| \geq \frac{2}{3}|\mu'|$, where μ' is any stable matching in $\mathcal{P}$.*

Proof By Lemma 13.3, Király's algorithm produces a stable matching μ. Let μ' be a maximum cardinality stable matching and let $G' = (V, E')$ be a subgraph of the acceptability graph of $\mathcal{P}$ where $V = W \cup F$ and $E' = \mu \oplus \mu'$ (here $\oplus$ denotes the symmetric difference of μ and μ'). Then the connected components of G' are paths and cycles whose edges alternate between μ and μ' (we refer to these components as alternating paths and alternating cycles, respectively). We first claim that G' has no alternating path of length three whose end edges belong to μ'.

For, suppose for a contradiction that $\{w', f\}$, $\{f, w\}$, $\{w, f'\}$ is an alternating path of length three, where $\{w', f\} \in \mu'$, $\{f, w\} \in \mu$, and $\{w, f'\} \in \mu'$. Then each of w' and f' is unmatched in μ. This means that w' applied to (and was rejected by) every firm on her preference list as an unpromoted and promoted worker, and f' did not receive an application from any worker. We deduce that w was never promoted, and moreover that w strictly prefers f to f', otherwise she would have applied to f' (recall that workers do not have ties in their lists).

After w' was promoted, w' applied to f. As in the proof of Lemma 13.3, since $\mu(f) = w$, f rejected w' because either (i) it was already assigned to a worker w'' and it did not favor w' over w'' or (ii) it subsequently received an application from a worker w'' whom it favored over w'. Moreover, any subsequent change of partner for f cannot cause it to become strictly worse off, so f weakly prefers $\mu(f) = w$ to w'.

Suppose that w and w' are tied in f's list. Then the same is true for w' and w'' (possibly $w'' = w$). Moreover w'' must be promoted, for otherwise f would have favored w' over w'' (recall that w' has been promoted). But f would ultimately exchange its partner for an unpromoted worker in μ, namely w, which is impossible. Hence f strictly prefers w to w'. It follows that $\{w,f\}$ blocks μ', a contradiction. Hence the claim is established.

Now let C be any connected component of G'. If C is an alternating path whose end edges belong to μ', it follows from our preceding argument that $|C| \neq 3$, and it follows from the stability of μ that $|C| \neq 1$. Hence $|C| \geq 5$, and $|\mu \cap C| \geq \frac{2}{3}|\mu' \cap C|$. If C is an alternating cycle, an alternating path of even length, or an alternating path of odd length whose end edges belong to μ, clearly $|\mu \cap C| \geq |\mu' \cap C|$. The lemma thus follows. $\qquad\square$

Lemma 13.5. *Given an instance $\mathcal{P}$ of* MAX-SMTI-TF, *Király's algorithm as applied to $\mathcal{P}$ runs in $O(L)$ time, where L is the total length of the workers' preference lists.*

Proof Each worker applies at most twice to the same firm (once as an unpromoted worker and once as a promoted worker) so the number of iterations of the main **while** loop is $O(L)$. Each worker is reactivated at most once, and hence the total time taken for reactivation is $O(L)$. Using an array to store the ranks of workers in the firms' preference lists (allowing a firm to decide whether it favors one worker to another in $O(1)$ time), and using a stack to keep track of unmatched workers, Király's algorithm can be implemented to run in $O(L)$ time. $\qquad\square$

Together, Lemmas 13.3 to 13.5 lead to the following conclusion.

Theorem 13.6. *Király's algorithm is a $\frac{3}{2}$-approximation algorithm for* MAX-SMTI-TF.

We now give an example to illustrate the execution of Király's algorithm; the example also shows that the bound of $\frac{3}{2}$ is tight.

Example 13.7. Consider the following instance $\mathcal{P}$ of MAX-SMTI-TF:

$$
\begin{array}{ll}
w_1: \quad f_2 \succ f_1 & f_1: \quad w_1 \\
w_2: \quad f_2 \succ f_3 & f_2: \quad w_1 \sim w_2 \\
w_3: \quad f_3 & f_3: \quad w_2 \succ w_3
\end{array}
$$

The following execution trace results in a matching μ_1 of cardinality two:

- w_1 applies to f_2, $\{w_1,f_2\}$ is added to μ_1;
- w_2 applies to f_2, f_2 rejects w_2;
- w_2 applies to f_3, $\{w_2,f_3\}$ is added to μ_1;
- w_3 applies to f_3, f_3 rejects w_3, w_3 is exhausted;
- w_3 is promoted and reactivated;
- w_3 applies to f_3, f_3 rejects w_3, w_3 is exhausted.

On the other hand, $\mathcal{P}$ admits a stable matching μ_2 of cardinality three, comprising pairs $\{w_1,f_1\}$, $\{w_2,f_2\}$, $\{w_3,f_3\}$. Note that if w_2 applies first in the above execution trace then the matching μ_2 will ultimately be returned. $\qquad\square$

13.4 Stable Roommates without Ties: Two Parameterized Algorithms

13.4.1 Introduction

In this section, we focus on EGAL-SRI-DEC. Since this problem is NP-hard, exact algorithms presumably need superpolynomial time when measured only in the input length. A way out, without resorting to randomness or approximation, is given by the framework of *parameterized algorithmics* in which we aim to exploit structural properties of the input, measured by so-called integer-valued *parameters*. In this way, we can design more refined exact algorithms by viewing their running time as a function of both the input size and the parameter. One central goal of parameterized algorithmics is to design *fixed-parameter algorithms*, which solve any instance I of a given a problem Q with respect to a parameter k in $f(k)|I|^{O(1)}$ time, where f is some computable function (usually exponential) of the parameter k and $|I|$ denotes the size of (an arbitrary encoding of) I.

In the EGAL-SRI-DEC problem the parameter could be the upper bound γ on the egalitarian cost of a matching for which wer are aiming. In this section, we provide two fixed-parameter algorithms for EGAL-SRI-DEC with respect to the parameter "egalitarian cost γ," which run in $O(n^2 + (\gamma + 1)^\gamma \gamma^2)$ time and $O(2^\gamma n^2)$ time, respectively.

When the preferences do not have ties, there are various structures that can be utilized for designing efficient algorithms. For instance, whenever there are two agents x and y who are each other's most acceptable agents (i.e., $\mathsf{rank}_x(y) = \mathsf{rank}_y(x) = 0$), every stable matching must contain the pair $\{x, y\}$, which has zero cost. Hence, we can safely add such pairs to an egalitarian solution matching without disturbing the egalitarian cost. After we have matched all pairs of agents with zero cost, all remaining unmatched agents induce cost at least 1 when they are matched. Thus, to obtain a matching with egalitarian cost at most γ, there can remain at most 2γ agents and moreover no agent can be matched to an agent with rank higher than γ.

Indeed, we can go one step further and consider an even smaller parameter than the overall egalitarian cost, namely one where we subtract both the cost induced by the unmatched agents and by pairs that appear in every stable matching (called *fixed pairs*) from the cost for which we are aiming. Note that fixed pairs and unmatched agents are unique and can be found in polynomial time by the following structural results.

Theorem 13.8. *For each instance $\mathcal{P} = (V, (\succ_i)_{i \in V})$ of SRI with n agents, one can in $O(n^2)$ time (i) compute the set of all pairs of agents which appear in every stable matching, and (ii) partition the agent set V into two disjoint subsets V^m and V^u such that every stable matching matches every agent from V^m and none of the agents from V^u.*

To apply Theorem 13.8, we introduce six additional notions.

Definition 13.9. For an instance $(\mathcal{P}, \gamma)$ of EGAL-SRI-DEC, let $\mathsf{F}(\mathcal{P})$ denote the set consisting of all fixed pairs of $\mathcal{P}$. Further, let $\mathsf{V}(\mathsf{F}(\mathcal{P})) := \{x, y \in V \mid \{x, y\} \in \mathsf{F}(\mathcal{P})\}$ and $\gamma(\mathsf{F}(\mathcal{P}))$ denote the set of agents in $\mathsf{F}(\mathcal{P})$ and the egalitarian cost induced by the fixed pairs in $\mathsf{F}(\mathcal{P})$, respectively. Let $\mathsf{V}^u(\mathcal{P})$ denote the set consisting of all agents that are unmatched in all stable matchings. Let $\mathsf{V}^r(\mathcal{P})$

denote the set of remaining agents *not* from $V(F(\mathcal{P})) \cup V^u(\mathcal{P})$. Define $\hat{\gamma} :=$
$\gamma - \gamma(F(\mathcal{P})) - \sum_{z \in V^u(\mathcal{P})} |V_z|$.

By Theorem 13.8 and by Definition 13.9, the sets $V_F(\mathcal{P})$, $V^u(\mathcal{P})$, and $V^r(\mathcal{P})$ partition the whole agent set V. Note that, since each agent in $V^r(\mathcal{P})$ must be matched by each stable matching so that the cost, together with her partner, is at least one, each stable matching has an egalitarian cost bounded as follows.

Observation 13.10. *Every stable matching μ of an* SRI *instance $\mathcal{P}$ satisfies*
$$\gamma(\mu) \geq \frac{|V^r(\mathcal{P})|}{2} + \gamma(F(\mathcal{P})) + \sum_{z \in V^u(\mathcal{P})} |V_z|.$$

In the remainder of this section, we apply two well-established parameterized techniques: *kernelization* and *bounded search tree algorithms* and obtain two fixed-parameter algorithms for EGAL-SRI-DEC with respect to the "reduced" parameter $\hat{\gamma}$ (see Definition 13.9).

13.4.2 Kernelization for EGAL-SRI-DEC

A *kernelization* is a *polynomial time* preprocessing algorithm that transforms an instance I of a problem Q with parameter value k into an *equivalent* instance I' of Q with parameter value k' with $|I'| + k' \leq g(k)$, where g is a computable function. The resulting instance I' together with k' is called a *kernel* and g is referred to as the *size* of the kernel. Typically, kernelization is based on several polynomial time executable *data-reduction rules* which translate an instance to an equivalent one while ultimately shrinking the instance size.

We show that EGAL-SRI-DEC admits a kernel of quadratic size for the parameter $\hat{\gamma}$.

Theorem 13.11. EGAL-SRI-DEC *admits a size-$O(\hat{\gamma}^2)$ kernel with at most $4\hat{\gamma} + 2$ agents and with each preference list of size at most $\hat{\gamma} + 1$. The kernel can be computed in $O(n^2)$ time. Hence,* EGAL-SRI-DEC *can be solved in $O(n^2 + (\hat{\gamma} + 1)^{\hat{\gamma}} \hat{\gamma}^2)$ time.*

Proof We show that given an instance $I = (\mathcal{P}, \gamma)$ of EGAL-SRI-DEC with $\mathcal{P} = (V, (\succ_i)_{i \in V})$, Algorithm 13.2 produces a kernel with at most $4\hat{\gamma} + 2$ agents with preference list length at most $\hat{\gamma} + 1$ each; we note that each of the following blocks of lines in the algorithm can be considered as a reduction rule: line 2, lines 3–5, and lines 6–10. Briefly put, our kernelization algorithm will delete all agents in $V(F(\mathcal{P})) \cup V^u(\mathcal{P})$, i.e., keep all agents in $V^r(\mathcal{P})$, and replace the deleted agents by a small number of dummy agents to maintain the egalitarian-cost structure. In the following when saying that some lines in the algorithm are *correct* we mean that the instances before and after conducting those lines are equivalent.

First, the correctness of line 2 is given by Observation 13.10 and the definition of $\hat{\gamma}$. Second, the introduction of $2\hat{\gamma} + 2$ dummy agents in lines 3–5 does not contribute any egalitarian cost to any stable matching; hence, these lines are correct.

Third, in lines 6–10, we update the preference lists of all original agents that will stay in the kernel. These are those agents that belong to $V^r(\mathcal{P})$ (see line 6). To see why the inner loop in lines 7–9 is correct, let us consider an arbitrary agent x with $x \in V^r(\mathcal{P})$ and one of her acceptable agents from V_x, say y. In order to obtain a stable matching with egalitarian cost at most γ, agent x cannot be assigned to y if the sum of their respective ranks exceeds $\hat{\gamma}$ (see the first condition in line 8), owing to Observation 13.10. Moreover, by Theorem 13.8, no stable matching will match x with y if $y \in V(F(\mathcal{P})) \cup V^u(\mathcal{P})$. Hence, we can safely replace y with some dummy agent in line 9 if y satisfies one of the two conditions given in line 8.

Finally, by the same reasoning as above, it is also correct in line 10 to remove from the preference list of $x \in V^r(\mathcal{P})$ all agents y' that have $\mathsf{rank}_x^{\mathcal{P}}(y')$ higher than $\hat{\gamma}$. It remains to show that the updated preference lists are symmetric, meaning that an agent x remains in the preference list of another agent y if and only if y remains in the preference list of x. Towards a contradiction, suppose that x and y are two agents with $x, y \in V^r(\mathcal{P})$ such that y remains in the preference list of x, while x does not remain in the preference list of y. Then, by lines 8 and 10 it follows that $\mathsf{rank}_x^{\mathcal{P}}(y) + \mathsf{rank}_y^{\mathcal{P}}(x) \leq \hat{\gamma}$. This further implies that $\mathsf{rank}_y^{\mathcal{P}}(x) \leq \hat{\gamma}$, and hence x must also remain in the preference list of y, a contradiction.

Altogether, for each agent $x \in V^r(\mathcal{P})$, her updated preference list has at most $\hat{\gamma} + 1$ agents, each of which is from $D \cup V^r(\mathcal{P})$.

It remains to bound the size of the kernel. The kernel has $|V^r(\mathcal{P})|$ original agents and $2\hat{\gamma} + 2$ dummy agents. By line 2 we know that $|V^r(\mathcal{P})| \leq 2\hat{\gamma}$. Thus, the kernel has at most $4\hat{\gamma} + 2$ agents. As for the lengths of the preference lists, by line 10 each remaining original agent has at most $\hat{\gamma} + 1$ agents in her list. This means that the total length of the preference lists of the remaining original agents is at most $2\hat{\gamma}(\hat{\gamma}+1)$. Since we have introduced $2\hat{\gamma}+2$ dummy agents, each ranking some unique dummy agent in the first place, there remain $2\hat{\gamma}(\gamma + 1)$ entries in the preference lists of all dummy agents to be filled up with original agents. By line 9, we ensure that each dummy agent has at most $\hat{\gamma} + 1$ agents in her preference list.

As for the running time of Algorithm 13.2, note that $|V| = n$. By Theorem 13.8, computing $F(\mathcal{P})$, $V^u(\mathcal{P})$, and $V^r(\mathcal{P})$ takes $O(n^2)$ time. Line 2 can be conducted in $O(n)$ time. Constructing the dummy agents in lines 3–5 takes $O(\hat{\gamma})$ time. The number of iterations in the two loops in lines 6–7 and in line 10 is $O(n\hat{\gamma})$. Using an array to store the ranks of the agents in the preference list of each agent and an array to mark whether an agent is in $V(F(\mathcal{P}))$, $V^u(\mathcal{P})$, or $V^r(\mathcal{P})$, we can test the condition in line 8 in $O(1)$ time. Using an array to store the preference list of $\succ_x$ and a counter to mark a dummy agent d_i whose preference list has length less than $\hat{\gamma}+1$, we can perform the replacement in line 9 in $O(1)$ time.

Thus, in total, Algorithm 13.2 takes $O(n^2)$ time. The claimed running time in the third statement can be shown for instance via an exhaustive brute-force search of all $(\hat{\gamma} + 1)^{\hat{\gamma}}$ possible matchings on the remaining agents from $V^r(\mathcal{P})$ to check whether one of them is stable in $O(\hat{\gamma}^2)$ time. Note that the depth of the search tree is bounded by $\hat{\gamma}$ since we are building at most $\hat{\gamma}$ pairs. □

Algorithm 13.2 Kernelization for EGAL-SRI-DEC.

Input: An instance $I = (\mathcal{P} = (V = [n], (\succ_i)_{i \in V}), \gamma)$ of EGAL-SRI-DEC

1 $\hat{\gamma} := \gamma - \gamma(\mathsf{F}(\mathcal{P})) - \sum_{x \in \mathsf{V}^u(\mathcal{P})} |V_x|$

2 **if** $|\mathsf{V}^r(\mathcal{P})| > 2\hat{\gamma}$ **then return** a trivial no-instance

3 $D := \{d_i \mid 1 \le i \le 2(\hat{\gamma} + 1)\}$ // Create dummy agents

4 **foreach** $i \in [\hat{\gamma} + 1]$ **do**

5 $\quad$ Construct the preference lists $\succ_{d_{2i-1}}$ and $\succ_{d_{2i}}$ of d_{2i-1} and d_{2i} such that $\mathrm{rank}_{d_{2i-1}}(d_{2i}) = \mathrm{rank}_{d_{2i}}(d_{2i-1}) = 0$

$\quad$ // Update the preference lists of the agents in $\mathsf{V}^r(\mathcal{P})$

6 **foreach** *agent* $x \in \mathsf{V}^r(\mathcal{P})$ **do**

7 $\quad$ **foreach** *agent* $y \in V_x$ *with* $\mathrm{rank}_x^{\mathcal{P}}(y) \le \hat{\gamma}$ **do**

8 $\quad\quad$ **if** $\mathrm{rank}_x^{\mathcal{P}}(y) + \mathrm{rank}_y^{\mathcal{P}}(x) > \hat{\gamma}$ *or* $y \in \mathsf{V}(\mathsf{F}(\mathcal{P})) \cup \mathsf{V}^u(\mathcal{P})$ **then**

9 $\quad\quad\quad$ In list $\succ_x$, replace y with a dummy $d \in D$, using a different dummy d for each such y to ensure that d's list length is at most $\hat{\gamma} + 1$, and append x to $\succ_d$

10 $\quad$ Remove all agents y' from $\succ_x$ with $\mathrm{rank}_x^{\mathcal{P}}(y') > \hat{\gamma}$

11 **return** $(\mathsf{V}^r(\mathcal{P}) \cup D, (\succ_i)_{i \in \mathsf{V}^r(\mathcal{P})} + (\succ_d)_{d \in D}, \hat{\gamma})$

Example 13.12. To illustrate Algorithm 13.2, consider the instance I given in Figure 13.1. One can verify that it has exactly two stable matchings, $\mu_1 = \{\{1, 3\}, \{2, 6\}, \{4, 5\}\}$ and $\mu_2 = \{\{1, 2\}, \{3, 6\}, \{4, 5\}\}$. Observe that $\mathsf{F}(\mathcal{P}) = \{\{4, 5\}\}$. According to Theorem 13.8, the agent set can be partitioned into $\mathsf{V}(\mathsf{F}(\mathcal{P})) = \{4, 5\}$, $\mathsf{V}^u(\mathcal{P}) = \{7, 8\}$, $\mathsf{V}^r(\mathcal{P}) = \{1, 2, 3, 6\}$. The egalitarian costs of μ_1 and μ_2 are $\gamma(\mu_1) = 7$ and $\gamma(\mu_2) = 8$, respectively.

Let $\gamma = 7$. Then, by Definition 13.9, we obtain that $\hat{\gamma} = 3$. The preference lists returned by the algorithm could look as follows, where $D = \{d_1, d_2, \ldots, d_8\}$:

$1: 3 \succ 6 \succ 2, \qquad 2: d_1 \succ 1 \succ 6 \succ d_2, \qquad 3: 6 \succ 1 \succ d_1 \succ d_2, \qquad 6: 2 \succ 3 \succ 1,$

$d_1: d_2 \succ 2 \succ 3, \qquad d_2: d_1 \succ 2 \succ 3, \qquad \forall i \in \{2, 3, 4\}: d_{2i-1}: d_{2i}, \qquad d_{2i}: d_{2i-1}.$

13.4.3 Bounded Search Tree Algorithms for EGAL-SRI-DEC

Besides kernelization, another simple but useful parameterized technique is the use of *bounded search tree algorithms*. They are a restricted variant of exhaustive search algorithms which use the parameter to cut the branches in the search tree. Roughly speaking, they recursively apply the following branching steps until an equivalent and "easy-to-solve" instance is found. In each branching step on an input instance I,

(i) we identify a small set of elements such that at least one element in the set belongs to a solution,

(ii) and then branch into considering all possible "smaller" instances, each of which is obtained by fixing one element of the subset as part of the solution.

If in each branching step the size of the identified subset is bounded by $f(k)$, and the depth of the branching is bounded by $g(k)$, where f and g are two computable functions depending only the parameter k, then the execution of such an algorithm results in a search tree with $f(k)^{g(k)}$ nodes. If the identification of each subset in the branching runs in polynomial time, i.e., $|I|^{O(1)}$ time, then we obtain a fixed-parameter algorithm.

Now, we show that EGAL-SRI-DEC can be solved by a simple *bounded search tree* algorithm to obtain the following result.

Theorem 13.13. EGAL-SRI-DEC *can be solved in $O(2^{\hat{\gamma}} n^2)$ time.*

Proof Let $I = (\mathcal{P} = (V, (\succ_i)_{i \in V}), \gamma)$ be an instance of EGAL-SRI-DEC. Let $\mathsf{F}(\mathcal{P})$, $\mathsf{V}^u(\mathcal{P})$, $\mathsf{V}^r(\mathcal{P})$, and $\hat{\gamma}$ be as defined in Definition 13.9. By Observation 13.10, we assume that $\hat{\gamma} \geq 0$, otherwise we halt, reporting that I is a no-instance.

First, we set $\mu := \mathsf{F}(\mathcal{P})$ because all stable matchings must contain all fixed pairs from $\mathsf{F}(\mathcal{P})$. Our branching algorithm will extend the matching μ to find a stable one with egalitarian cost at most γ (or report that no such matching exists) and works as follows.

As long as $\hat{\gamma} > 0$ and there remains a not-yet-matched agent u from $\mathsf{V}^r(\mathcal{P})$ with $|V_u^*| \geq 1$, where $V_u^* := \{v \in V_u \cap \mathsf{V}^r(\mathcal{P}) \mid \mathsf{rank}_u(v) + \mathsf{rank}_v(u) \leq \hat{\gamma}\}$, pick an arbitrary such agent. Further, let $\mathsf{best}(u)$ denote the unique agent $v \in V_u^*$ with $\mathsf{rank}_v(u) = 0$ (if she exists) such that $\mathsf{rank}_u(v)$ is the smallest, i.e.,

$$\mathsf{best}(u) := \begin{cases} \operatorname{argmin}_{v \in V_u^*} \{\mathsf{rank}_u(v) \mid \mathsf{rank}_v(u) = 0\} & \text{if some } v \text{ has } \mathsf{rank}_v(u) = 0, \\ \bot & \text{otherwise.} \end{cases}$$

Branch into all possible ways of matching u as follows, distinguishing between two cases:

- If $\mathsf{best}(u) \neq \bot$ then, for each $v \in V_u^*$ with $\mathsf{rank}_u(v) \leq \mathsf{rank}_u(\mathsf{best}(u))$, branch into adding $\{u, v\}$ to μ; note that, by definition, u cannot be matched with an agent with rank higher than $\mathsf{rank}_u(\mathsf{best}(u))$ as otherwise $\{u, \mathsf{best}(u)\}$ would form a blocking pair.
- Otherwise, for each $v \in V_u^*$, branch into adding $\{u, v\}$ to μ.

For each of the branches, update $\mathsf{V}^r(\mathcal{P}) := \mathsf{V}^r(\mathcal{P}) \setminus \{u, v\}$, decrease the remaining budget $\hat{\gamma} := \hat{\gamma} - \mathsf{rank}_u(v) - \mathsf{rank}_v(u)$, and continue as follows:

(i) If $\hat{\gamma} < 0$ or there exists an agent $u' \in \mathsf{V}^r(\mathcal{P})$ with $|V_{u'}^*| = 0$ then stop and reject the current μ.
(ii) If $\hat{\gamma} > 0$ and $\mathsf{V}^r(\mathcal{P}) \neq \emptyset$ then recurse with an arbitrary agent $u' \in \mathsf{V}^r(\mathcal{P})$.
(iii) If $\hat{\gamma} = 0$ then check whether the matching μ is stable for $\mathcal{P}$. Accept μ if it is stable, otherwise reject it.

Correctness. It is straightforward to see that $\mathcal{P}$ has a stable matching of egalitarian cost at most γ if and only if one of the leaves (Case (iii)) in the produced search tree accepts.

Running time. The running time of the algorithm is bounded by the number of nodes in the search tree multiplied by the time used for each node. The time used for each node is bounded by the time required for computing $\mathsf{F}(\mathcal{P})$, $\mathsf{V}^u(\mathcal{P})$, $\mathsf{V}^r(\mathcal{P})$, $\mathsf{best}(u)$, and V_u^* for all $u \in \mathsf{V}^r(\mathcal{P})$, which is $O(n^2)$ (see also Theorem 13.8).

In order to bound the number of nodes in the search tree, we first bound the number of leaves in the tree. To this end, let $N(k)$ and $L(k)$ denote the upper bounds on the number of nodes and leaves, respectively, in a search tree in relation to its height k. Clearly, if a search tree algorithm solves a problem instance with parameter value k and calls itself recursively on problem instances with parameter values at most $k - d_1, k - d_2, \ldots, k - d_q$ with $1 \leq d_1 \leq d_2 \leq \cdots \leq d_q \leq k$ then an upper bound on the number of leaves in the built search tree is given by the following linear recurrence : $L(k) \leq L(k - d_1) + L(k - d_2) + \cdots + L(k - d_q)$. Assuming that $L(k) = \lambda^k$ (where λ is a positive constant), the recurrence is satisfied if the following holds:

$$\lambda^{d_q} - \lambda^{d_q - d_1} - \lambda^{d_q - d_2} - \cdots - \lambda^{d_q - d_q} = 0. \tag{13.1}$$

Using standard analysis, we know that the left-hand side of (13.1), called the *characteristic polynomial* of the recurrence, has a unique positive root λ_0 such that $L(k) = \lambda_0^k$.

To find the unique positive root λ_0, we analyze the decrease of the budget (the parameter) in each call of our algorithm, distinguishing between two cases:

- If $\mathsf{best}(u) \neq \perp$ then $\mathsf{rank}_u(\mathsf{best}(u)) \leq \hat{\gamma}$ and the recursive procedure makes at most $\mathsf{rank}_u(\mathsf{best}(u)) + 1$ recursive calls. Accordingly, the budget in these calls is decreased by at least $1, 2, \ldots, \mathsf{rank}_u(\mathsf{best}(u)), \mathsf{rank}_u(\mathsf{best}(u))$, respectively; note that $\mathsf{best}(u) \in V_u^*$. To see why the budgets in the first $\mathsf{rank}_u(\mathsf{best}(u))$ calls are updated in this way, we observe that, for each agent $u \in V^r(\mathcal{P})$ and each acceptable agent $v' \in V_u^*$ with $\mathsf{rank}_u(v') < \mathsf{rank}_u(\mathsf{best}(u))$, the definition of $\mathsf{best}(u)$ implies that $\mathsf{rank}_{v'}(u) \geq 1$.
- If $\mathsf{best}(u) = \perp$ then $|V_u^*| \leq \hat{\gamma}$ and the recursive procedure makes $|V_u^*|$ recursive calls. The budget in these calls is decreased by at least $1, 2, \ldots, |V_u^*|$, respectively. To see why the budgets are updated in this way, we observe that $\mathsf{best}(u)$ does not exist, so each acceptable agent $v' \in V_u^*$ has $\mathsf{rank}_{v'}(u) \geq 1$.

The characteristic polynomials of the recurrence (13.1) in the two cases are thus

$$\lambda^{\hat{\gamma}} - \lambda^{\hat{\gamma}-1} - \lambda^{\hat{\gamma}-2} - \cdots - \lambda^{\hat{\gamma}-\hat{\gamma}} - \lambda^{\hat{\gamma}-\hat{\gamma}} \text{ and}$$

$$\lambda^{\hat{\gamma}} - \lambda^{\hat{\gamma}-1} - \cdots - \lambda^{\hat{\gamma}-\hat{\gamma}}, \text{ respectively.}$$

Since the unique positive root of the first polynomial is 2, while the unique positive root of the second polynomial is less than 2, our search tree has $L(\hat{\gamma}) \leq 2^{\hat{\gamma}}$ leaves since its height is bounded by $\hat{\gamma}$.

Now, to bound the number of nodes in the tree, observe that $N(1) = 1$ and $N(\hat{\gamma}) = N(\hat{\gamma} - 1) + L(\hat{\gamma})$. This implies that $N(\hat{\gamma}) \leq 2 \times 2^{\hat{\gamma}} - 1$ since $L(\hat{\gamma}) \leq 2^{\hat{\gamma}}$. Altogether, our algorithm runs in $O(2^{\hat{\gamma}} n^2)$ time. $\qquad\square$

13.5 Selected Open Questions

In Section 13.3 we presented a simple yet elegant $\frac{3}{2}$-approximation algorithm for MAX-SMTI-TF. In fact, a stronger, but more complex, approximation algorithm for this problem is known, with performance guarantee $(1 + 1/e) \approx 1.3679$, and this is the best current upper bound at the time of writing. The best current lower bound for this problem is $\frac{5}{4} - \varepsilon$, for any $\varepsilon > 0$, assuming the unique games conjecture (UGC) holds. For the general MAX-SMTI problem (where ties can be on both sides), the best current approximation algorithm has performance guarantee $\frac{3}{2}$, whilst the best current lower bound is $\frac{4}{3} - \varepsilon$, for any $\varepsilon > 0$, assuming UGC. It remains open to close these gaps for both MAX-SMTI and MAX-SMTI-TF by providing improved approximation algorithms or stronger inapproximability results, leading to tighter upper and lower bounds.

In Section 13.4, we saw that EGAL-SRI-DEC admits a polynomial kernel, and hence is fixed-parameter tractable with respect to the egalitarian cost γ. When the preferences may have ties, EGAL-SRTI-DEC still admits a fixed-parameter algorithm with running time $2^{O(\gamma \log \gamma)}(n \log n)^3$. It would be interesting to know whether EGAL-SRTI-DEC also admits a polynomial kernel when ties are present. The running time given in Theorem 13.13 is tight in the sense that there exists no $2^{o(\gamma)}n^{O(1)}$-time algorithm for EGAL-SRI-DEC for the case without ties, unless the *exponential time hypothesis* fails. Another question is whether the $2^{O(\gamma \log \gamma)}(n \log n)^3$-time algorithm for the case with ties is tight.

13.6 Bibliographic Notes

We note that our definition of a blocking pair is consistent with that of Gusfield and Irving [10], but the definition given in Chapter 1 for Setting II is slightly different. Nevertheless, both versions lead to the same notion of a stable matching. In the presence of ties, our stability definition is also referred to as *weak stability* in the literature; we note here that two stronger stability definitions (so-called *strong stability* and *super-stability*) have been considered also, but the set of matchings satisfying either of these criteria may be empty (see [17], Chapter 3).

Gale and Shapley [7] gave an $O(n^2)$ algorithm to find a stable matching in an instance of SMI, whilst Irving [12] found a stable matching or reports that none exists, given an instance I of SRI. We note that all stable matchings in I have the same size, and match the same set of agents ([10], Section 4.5.2) Ronn [20] proved that deciding whether a stable matching exists, given an instance of SRTI, is NP-complete even for complete preference lists.

Irving [13] showed that a stable matching in an instance I of SMTI can be found in $O(n^2)$ time, Manlove et al. [18] observed that stable matchings in I can have different cardinalities. The NP-hardness of MAX-SMTI for the special case in which the ties occur on one side only was first established in [18]. However, the proof of Theorem 13.1 incorporates a new reduction from Indepedent Set that has not appeared previously in the literature.

Approximation algorithms for MAX-SMTI were surveyed by Cechlárová et al. [1]. The approximation algorithm for MAX-SMTI-TF, described in Section 13.3.2, is due to Király [16]. The correctness and efficiency of the algorithm (i.e., it always returns a stable matching, it has a performance guarantee of $\frac{3}{2}$ and it can be implemented to run in linear time), and the example showing that the performance guarantee is tight, were all given in [16]. Further details regarding the data structures required for efficient implementation of Király's algorithm can be found in [10, Section 1.2.3].

Theorem 13.8(i) was observed by Gusfield [9, Lemma 7.1]. Theorem 13.8(ii) was established by Gusfield and Irving [10, Theorem 4.5.2]. The running time in Theorem 13.8 was obtained using Irving's algorithm [12] to solve SRI.

The NP-hardness of EGAL-SRI-DEC for complete preference lists was established by Feder [6], where a two-approximation algorithm was given for minimizing the egalitarian cost. Cseh et al. [4] provided a dichotomy result regarding the maximum length ℓ of the preference lists, and showed that it is polynomial time solvable if $\ell = 2$, and is NP-hard for $\ell \geq 3$. The polynomial time algorithm for EGAL-SMI-DEC was given by Irving et al. [14], whilst the NP-completeness result for the extension of EGAL-SMI-DEC to the case where preference lists are complete but can include ties is due to Manlove et al. [18].

Notice from the definition of egalitarian cost that an unmatched agent contributes the length of her preference list to this measure. In the absence of ties, the value of this contribution is irrelevant since the set of unmatched agents is the same across all stable matchings in $\mathcal{P}$. For the case with ties, the situation changes, and we could for example have defined the contribution of an unmatched agent to the egalitarian cost to be n. However, since finding an egalitarian stable matching is NP-hard even for instances of SRI with complete preference lists, any contribution to the egalitarian cost for an unmatched agent results in the same hardness result. The choice of value has significance only when reasoning about parameterized complexity in SRTI: giving unmatched agents an egalitarian cost n only makes devising an FPT algorithm easier. Chen et al. [3] also investigated the parameterized complexity for the cases when the egalitarian cost of an unmatched agent is a constant value or zero.

The polynomial kernel and the fixed-parameter tractability result for EGAL-SRI-DEC parameterized by the egalitarian cost γ were given in [3], where it was also shown that EGAL-SRTI-DEC is fixed-parameter tractable with respect to the parameter γ. Discussion on the exponential time hypothesis can be found in [11]. For more information about the UGC, mentioned in Section 13.5, see [15].

Further algorithmic results for matching markets can be found in [17]. More specifically, parameterized algorithms and complexity results for other matching problems under preferences can be found in [3] and [8]. More techniques from parameterized algorithmics can be found in the following textbooks: [5] and [19].

Acknowledgements

The authors would like to thank Tamás Fleiner and Zhiyi Huang for valuable comments on an earlier version of this chapter that helped to improve the presentation. Jiehua Chen was supported by the WWTF research project (VRG18-012). David Manlove was supported by grant EP/P028306/1 from the Engineering and Physical Sciences Research Council.

References

[1] Cechlárová, Katarína, Cseh, Ágnes, and Manlove, David. 2019. Selected open problems in matching under preferences. *Bulletin of the European Association for Theoretical Computer Science*, **128**, 14–38.

[2] Chen, Jiehua. 2019. Computational complexity of stable marriage and stable roommates and their variants. Techical Report. *arXiv:1904.08196 [cs.GT]*.

[3] Chen, Jiehua, Hermelin, Danny, Sorge, Manuel, and Yedidsion, Harel. 2018. How hard is it to satisfy (almost) all roommates? Pages 35:1–35:15 of: *Proc. 45th International Colloquium on Automata, Languages, and Programming*.

[4] Cseh, Ágnes, Irving, Robert W., and Manlove, David F. 2019. The stable roommates problem with short lists. *Theory of Computing Systems*, **63**(1), 128–149.

[5] Cygan, Marek, Fomin, Fedor V., Kowalik, Lukasz, Lokshtanov, Daniel, Marx, Dániel, Pilipczuk, Marcin, Pilipczuk, Michal, and Saurabh, Saket. 2015. *Parameterized Algorithms*. Springer.

[6] Feder, Tomás. 1992. A new fixed point approach for stable networks and stable marriages. *Journal of Computer and System Sciences*, **45**(2), 233–284.

[7] Gale, David, and Shapley, Lloyd S. 1962. College admissions and the stability of marriage. *American Mathematical Monthly*, **69**, 9–15.

[8] Gupta, Sushmita, Roy, Sanjukta, Saurabh, Saket, and Zehavi, Meirav. 2018. Some Hard Stable Marriage Problems: a Survey on Multivariate Analysis. Pages 141–157 of: Neogy, S. K., Bapat, Ravindra B., and Dubey, Dipti (eds.), *Mathematical Programming and Game Theory*. Indian Statistical Institute Series. Springer Singapore.

[9] Gusfield, Dan. 1988. The structure of the stable roommate problem: efficient representation and enumeration of all stable assignments. *SIAM Journal on Computing*, **17**(4), 742–769.

[10] Gusfield, Dan, and Irving, Robert W. 1989. *The Stable Marriage Problem – Structure and Algorithms*. Foundations of Computing Series. MIT Press.

[11] Impagliazzo, Russell, Paturi, Ramamohan, and Zane, Francis. 2001. Which problems have strongly exponential complexity? *Journal of Computer and System Sciences*, **63**(4), 512–530.

[12] Irving, Robert W. 1985. An efficient algorithm for the "stable roommates" problem. *Journal of Algorithms*, **6**(4), 577–595.

[13] Irving, Robert W. 1994. Stable marriage and indifference. *Discrete Applied Mathematics*, **48**(3), 261–272.

[14] Irving, Robert W., Leather, Paul, and Gusfield, Dan. 1987. An efficient algorithm for the "optimal" stable marriage. *Journal of the ACM*, **34**(3), 532–543.

[15] Khot, Subhash. 2002. On the Power of Unique 2-Prover 1-Round Games. Pages 767–775 of: *Proc. 34th Annual ACM Symposium on Theory of Computing*. Association for Computing Machinery.

[16] Király, Zoltán. 2011. Better and simpler approximation algorithms for the stable marriage problem. *Algorithmica*, **60**, 3–20.

[17] Manlove, David F. 2013. *Algorithmics of Matching Under Preferences*. Series on Theoretical Computer Science, vol. 2. World Scientific.

[18] Manlove, David F., Irving, Robert W., Iwama, Kazuo, Miyazaki, Shuichi, and Morita, Yasufumi. 2002. Hard variants of stable marriage. *Theoretical Computer Science*, **276** (1-2), 261–279.

[19] Niedermeier, Rolf. 2006. *Invitation to Fixed-Parameter Algorithms*. Oxford University Press.

[20] Ronn, Eytan. 1990. NP-complete stable matching problems. *Journal of Algorithms*, **11**(2), 285–304.

CHAPTER FOURTEEN

Generalized Matching: Contracts and Networks

John William Hatfield, Ravi Jagadeesan, Scott Duke Kominers,
Alexandru Nichifor, Michael Ostrovsky, Alexander Teytelboym, and
Alexander Westkamp

14.1 Introduction

Many real-world settings incorporate features that go beyond the standard matching setting described in Chapter 1. In particular, whether a given partner is acceptable may depend on the terms of the relationship, such as wages, hours, specific job responsibilities, and the like. In [4] and [33] it was shown that it is possible to extend classical matching frameworks to determine not only who matches with whom but also additional terms – such as wages – that specify the full "contractual" terms of exchange.

Moreover, in many settings, one side of the market has a multi-unit demand which cannot always be represented by a simple ranking of contracts and a capacity constraint. For instance, a hospital may have both a research position and a clinical position (as specified in the contract), and rank candidates differently for each position. A firm may have two positions and one ranking of candidates but may also desire that, if possible, at least one hire have a particular feature, such as fluency in a foreign language. And a baseball team may prefer different catchers depending on the pitchers it has available.

In [10], [19], [24], [33], and [40] it was shown that, when buyers have multi-unit demand, some form of *substitutability* in buyers' preferences is key to ensuring the existence of stable outcomes. Substitutability requires that no two contracts are complements, in the sense that if a contract is rejected given some opportunity set, that contract will still be rejected as more opportunities become available. Thus, both our hospital and our firm above have substitutable preferences, while our baseball team does not. That said, certain types of complementarities can be accommodated under many-to-one matching with contracts. The many-to-one matching with contracts framework unified matching and auctions, and has led to a number of high-profile real-world applications such as the reorganization of the US Army's cadet-branch matching system [14], [41], [42], and the Israeli Psychology Master's Match [18].

The theory of matching with contracts extends to cover two-sided settings in which agents on both sides may have multi-unit demand [9], [10], [22], [34]. For instance, buyers in an auction may demand multiple goods when the auctioneer has many items for sale. Most results from many-to-one matching with contracts extend naturally to this setting.

The theory can also be extended to more complex market environments. In [39] supply-chain settings were considered in which intermediaries may both buy from upstream firms and sell to downstream firms, so the firm is no longer exclusively just a buyer or just a seller; see also [21] and [45]. The appropriate definition of substitutability for such settings is somewhat subtle: it requires that an intermediary treats contracts in which he is a buyer as substitutes, and treats contracts in which he is a seller as substitutes, but treats contracts in which he is a buyer as complementary with contracts in which he is a seller.[1] Indeed, the theory extends beyond supply chains to arbitrarily complex trading networks, in which agents may buy from and sell to any other agent. However, the existence of stable outcomes is not immediate in such settings. In [25] it was shown that stable outcomes do exist when transfers are encoded into the contracts, agents' preferences are quasilinear in the transfers, and agents' preferences are substitutable. Meanwhile it was shown in [11], [12], [13] that stable outcomes exist even without transferable utility, as long as payments are not affected by distortionary frictions.

Section 14.2 introduces a general matching with contracts framework. Section 14.3 then considers two-sided matching settings and gives a characterization of when stable outcomes can be found in such settings. Section 14.4 examines the supply chain and trading network settings, generalizing many results of Section 14.3. Finally, Section 14.5 extends the matching with contracts framework to allow for transfers.

14.2 The Framework

Consider a finite set of *agents* I, a finite set of contractual *terms* T, and a set of bilateral *contracts* $X \subseteq I \times I \times T$. A contract $x = (s, b, t) \in X$ represents a relationship between two agents, a "seller" $s \in I$ and a "buyer" $b \in I \setminus \{s\}$, under terms $t \in T$. For example, in an exchange economy with indivisible goods and no monetary transfers, a contract $x = (s, b, t)$ would represent the transfer of some (unit of) good t from seller s to buyer b; alternatively, the terms t could represent any combination of goods transferred, services provided, and a price or wage. For any given contract $x = (s, b, t) \in X$, we denote by $s(x)$ the associated seller s, by $b(x)$ the associated buyer b, and by $t(x)$ the associated contract terms t. Given any set of contracts $Y \subseteq X$, we denote by $Y_{i \to} \equiv \{y \in Y : s(y) = i\}$ the set of contracts for which i is a seller, by $Y_{\to i} \equiv \{y \in Y : b(y) = i\}$ the set of contracts in which i is a buyer, and by $Y_i \equiv Y_{i \to} \cup Y_{\to i}$ the set of all contracts for which agent i is involved.

Each agent $i \in I$ is endowed with a *choice correspondence* C^i that specifies which sets of contracts agent i would choose to sign from any fixed set of available contracts, and so $C^i(Y) \subseteq \wp(Y_i)$ for all $Y \subseteq X$, where $\wp$ denotes the power set of Y_i. We say that agent i has *unit demand* if for all $Y \subseteq X$ we have that $|Z| \leq 1$ for all $Z \in C^i(Y)$. Whenever the choice correspondence is single-valued on all inputs, i.e., $C^i(Y) = \{Z\}$ for all $Y \subseteq X$, we call C^i a *choice function* and write $C^i(Y) = Z$.

In our examples it will often be helpful to describe choice correspondences as arising from preference rankings over sets of contracts. A weak preference relation $\succeq_i$ for agent i over subsets of X_i *induces* a choice correspondence C^i for i, under which

---

[1] If each contract specifies the transfer of an underlying object, then this definition of substitutability is natural; it requires that an agent treat the underlying objects as substitutes [27].

$$C^i(Y) = \max_{\succeq_i}\{Z \subseteq X_i : Z \subseteq Y\},$$

where by $\max_{\succeq_i}$ we mean the maxima with respect to the ordering $\succeq_i$; that is, $C^i(Y)$ contains all subsets of Y that are most preferred with respect to $\succeq_i$. When an agent has a single-valued unit-demand choice correspondence (i.e., a unit-demand choice function), this can be induced by a preference relation over contracts involving that agent.

14.3 Two-Sided Matching with Contracts

In this section we focus on two-sided matching markets, that is, we assume that the set of agents I can be partitioned into a set of *buyers* B and *sellers* S such that, for every contract $x \in X$, we have $\mathsf{s}(x) \in S$ and $\mathsf{b}(x) \in B$. We also assume throughout this section that choice correspondences are single-valued on all inputs. We may thus define the aggregate choice functions of buyers and sellers: for each $Y \subseteq X$, let $C^S(Y) = \cup_{s \in S} C^s(Y)$ and $C^B(Y) = \cup_{b \in B} C^b(Y)$, respectively. Finally, we also assume throughout this section that every choice function satisfies the *irrelevance of rejected contracts condition*, i.e., that i considers rejected contracts to be irrelevant in the sense that, for all $Y \subseteq X$ and all $x \in Y \setminus C^i(Y)$, we have that $C^i(Y \setminus \{x\}) = C^i(Y)$.[2]

14.3.1 Many-to-Many Matching with Contracts

One important condition on preferences that guarantees the existence of stable outcomes is *(gross) substitutability*.

> **Definition 14.1.** The choice function of agent $i \in I$ is *(gross) substitutable* if for all $Y \subseteq X$ and all contracts $x, z \in X$, we have that $z \in C^i(Y \cup \{x, z\})$ implies $z \in C^i(Y \cup \{z\})$.

Substitutability may equivalently be defined by considering how the set of contracts that an agent rejects (i.e., does not choose) varies across different inputs. Formally, for an agent $i \in I$ and a set of contracts $Y \subseteq X$, let $R^i(Y) \equiv Y \setminus C^i(Y)$ be the *rejected set*. The condition in Definition 14.1 is then equivalent to requiring that, for all $Y, Z \subseteq X$ such that $Y \subseteq Z$, we have $R^i(Y) \subseteq R^i(Z)$. Note that if the choice function of every buyer (seller) is substitutable then the aggregate choice function C^B (C^S) is substitutable.

Next, we introduce the standard notion of *pairwise stability*, which parallels the definition of stability from Chapter 1.

> **Definition 14.2.** An outcome $A \subseteq X$ is *pairwise stable* if it is:
>
> 1. *Individually rational*: For all $i \in I$, $C^i(A) = A_i$.
> 2. *Pairwise unblocked*: There does not exist a buyer–seller pair $(b, s) \in B \times S$ and a contract $z \in (X_b \cap X_s) \setminus A$ such that $z \in C^b(A \cup \{z\}) \cap C^s(A \cup \{z\})$.

---

[2] See [2].

The first main result of this section shows that pairwise stable outcomes are guaranteed to exist when all agents' choice functions are (gross) substitutable. Moreover, the set of pairwise stable outcomes is a lattice with respect to the order $\sqsupseteq_B$, where $Y \sqsupseteq_B Z$ if $Y_b = C^b(Y \cup Z)$ for all $b \in B$, and with respect to the order $\sqsupseteq_S$, where $Z \sqsupseteq_S Y$ if $Z_s = C^s(Y \cup Z)$ for all $s \in S$. And, as in Chapter 1, among pairwise stable outcomes these two orders are "opposed," in the sense that if both Y and Z are stable and $Y \sqsupseteq_B Z$ then $Z \sqsupseteq_S Y$.

Theorem 14.3 [22]. *Assume that the choice functions of all agents are substitutable. Then the set of pairwise stable outcomes is a non-empty lattice with respect to $\sqsupseteq_B$ and $\sqsupseteq_S$; in particular, there exists a buyer-optimal/seller-pessimal (as well as a seller-optimal/buyer-pessimal) pairwise stable outcome.*

Theorem 14.3 generalizes the existence results of Chapters 1 and 3. Moreover, incorporating contractual terms substantially extends the domain of applications we can consider, including such settings as matching with wages [33] and multi-unit demand auctions [36].

Proof of Theorem 14.3 To prove Theorem 14.3, we introduce a *generalized deferred acceptance* (DA) operator, show that the set of pairwise stable outcomes corresponds to the set of fixed points of this operator, and then use Tarski's fixed-point theorem to establish that the set of fixed points of the generalized DA operator is a non-empty lattice.

Given two sets of contracts $X^S, X^B \subseteq X$, we define the generalized DA operator as follows:

$$\Phi(X^S, X^B) = (\Phi^S(X^B), \Phi^B(X^S)),$$
$$\Phi^S(X^B) = \{x \in X : x \in C^B(X^B \cup \{x\})\}, \qquad (14.1)$$
$$\Phi^B(X^S) = \{x \in X : x \in C^S(X^S \cup \{x\})\}.$$

Here, we can think of X^S (at each iteration of the operator) as the set of contracts available to sellers (and X^B as the set of contracts available to buyers). To determine whether a contract x is available to sellers (in the next iteration) given X^B, we ask whether x would be chosen by buyers if $X^B \cup \{x\}$ were available to buyers; analogously, to determine whether a contract x is available to buyers (in the next iteration) given X^S, we ask whether x would be chosen by sellers if $X^S \cup \{x\}$ were available to sellers.

Lemma 14.4. *If (X^S, X^B) is a fixed point of Φ then $A = X^S \cap X^B$ is pairwise stable, $C^B(X^B) = A$, and $C^S(X^S) = A$. Furthermore, if all agents have substitutable preferences and A is pairwise stable then $\Phi(A, A)$ is a fixed point of Φ.*

Proof We start by assuming that (X^S, X^B) is a fixed point of Φ and, letting $A = X^S \cap X^B$, we show that $C^B(X^B) = A$, that $C^S(X^S) = A$, and that A is pairwise stable.

- $C^B(X^B) = A$: *Let $x \in A$ be arbitrary. Since $x \in X^S$ and $X^S = \Phi^S(X^B)$, we have $x \in C^B(X^B \cup \{x\})$. Since $x \in X^B$, we obtain $x \in C^B(X^B)$. Thus, since x was arbitrary, we have $A \subseteq C^B(X^B)$.*

Next, consider some $x \in X^B \setminus X^S$. If $x \in C^B(X^B)$, then we have $x \in C^B(X^B \cup \{x\})$ and therefore $x \in \Phi^S(X^B)$. Since $x \notin X^S$, we obtain a contradiction to our assumption that $X^S = \Phi^S(X^B)$.

- $C^S(X^S) = A$: *An argument analogous to the preceding argument shows that* $C^S(X^S) = A$.
- *A is pairwise stable: Individual rationality of A for buyers follows since $C^B(X^B) = A$ (from our preceding argument) and thus – since agents' choice functions satisfy the irrelevance of rejected contracts condition – we have that $C^B(A) = A$. We now show that A is pairwise unblocked. Let $z \in X \setminus A$ be arbitrary and assume that $z \notin X^S$; the case where $z \notin X^B$ is analogous. We will argue that $z \notin C^B(A \cup \{z\})$; if so, then $\{z\}$ does not block A. Since $X^S = \Phi^S(X^B)$, we have that $z \notin C^B(X^B \cup \{z\})$; thus, since $C^B(X^B) = A$, by the irrelevance of rejected contracts condition, $z \notin C^B(A \cup \{z\})$. Next, we assume that A is pairwise stable, we let $(X^S, X^B) = \Phi(A, A)$, and we show that $A = X^S \cap X^B$ and (X^S, X^B) is a fixed point of Φ.*
- *$A = X^S \cap X^B$: If $A \nsubseteq X^S \cap X^B$, the definition of Φ immediately implies that A is not individually rational. If there were a contract $z \in (X^S \cap X^B) \setminus A$, we would have $z \in C^B(A \cup \{z\})$ (as $z \in X^S$) and $z \in C^S(A \cup \{z\})$ (as $z \in X^B$) so that A would be blocked by $\mathsf{b}(z)$ and $\mathsf{s}(z)$.*
- *(X^S, X^B) is a fixed point of Φ: We show that $\Phi^S(X^B) = X^S$; the fact that $\Phi^B(X^S) = X^B$ follows by an analogous argument. We show first that $\Phi^S(X^B) \subseteq X^S$. Let $y \in \Phi^S(X^B)$ be arbitrary. By the definition of Φ, we have that $y \in C^B(X^B \cup \{y\})$. By substitutability, we obtain that $y \in C^B(A \cup \{y\})$ and therefore $y \in \Phi^S(A) = X^S$. Now, we argue that $X^S \subseteq \Phi^S(X^B)$. Let $y \in X^S$ be arbitrary. Since $X^S = \Phi^S(A)$, we obtain that $y \in C^B(A \cup \{y\})$. If $y \notin \Phi^S(X^B)$, we would have $y \notin C^B(X^B \cup \{y\})$ and, by the irrelevance of rejected contracts condition, there is some $z \in X^B \setminus A$ such that $z \in C^B(X^B \cup \{y\})$. By substitutability, we have that $z \in C^B(A \cup \{z\})$ and thus $z \in X^S$. Hence, $z \in X^S \cap X^B$ and this contradicts $X^S \cap X^B = A$.* $\square$

For the remainder of the proof of Theorem 14.3, we introduce the following order on $X \times X$: $(X^S, X^B) \vdash (\tilde{X}^S, \tilde{X}^B)$ if and only if $X^S \subseteq \tilde{X}^S$ and $X^B \supseteq \tilde{X}^B$.

We show first that Φ is isotone with respect to $\vdash$. For that purpose, take any pair $(X^S, X^B), (\tilde{X}^S, \tilde{X}^B) \in X \times X$ such that $(X^S, X^B) \vdash (\tilde{X}^S, \tilde{X}^B)$. We need to show that $\Phi(X^S, X^B) \vdash \Phi(\tilde{X}^S, \tilde{X}^B)$, or $\Phi^S(X^B) \subseteq \Phi^S(\tilde{X}^B)$ and $\Phi^B(X^S) \supseteq \Phi^B(\tilde{X}^S)$. To show that $\Phi^S(X^B) \subseteq \Phi^S(\tilde{X}^B)$, take some $y \in X$ such that $y \in C^B(X^B \cup \{y\})$. By substitutability and the fact that $X^B \supseteq \tilde{X}^B$, we immediately obtain $y \in C^B(\tilde{X}^B \cup \{y\})$ and thus $y \in \Phi^S(\tilde{X}^B)$. The argument to show that $\Phi^B(X^S) \supseteq \Phi^B(\tilde{X}^S)$ is completely symmetric.

Since Φ is isotone with respect to $\vdash$, Tarski's fixed-point theorem implies that the set of fixed points is a non-empty lattice with respect to $\vdash$.

To complete the proof, we now show that the set of pairwise stable outcomes is a lattice with respect to the order $\sqsupseteq_S$. Take any two fixed points $(X^S, X^B), (\tilde{X}^S, \tilde{X}^B) \in X \times X$ of Φ such that $(X^S, X^B) \vdash (\tilde{X}^S, \tilde{X}^B)$. Let $A = X^S \cap X^B$ and $\tilde{A} = \tilde{X}^B \cap \tilde{X}^S$. We claim that $\tilde{A} \sqsupseteq_S A$. By the first part of Lemma 14.4, we have that $C^B(X^B) = A$ and $C^B(\tilde{X}^B) = \tilde{A}$. Since $X^B \supseteq \tilde{X}^B$, we obtain that $C^B(A \cup \tilde{A}) = A$. A similar argument establishes that $C^S(A \cup \tilde{A}) = \tilde{A}$.

Hence, the lattice property of the set of stable outcomes follows from the lattice property of the set of fixed points of Φ. $\qquad\square$

Next, we define a concept of stability that allows arbitrary groups of agents to coordinate in order to block some outcome.

Definition 14.5. An outcome $A \subseteq X$ is *stable* if it is:

1. *Individually rational*: For all $i \in I$, $C^i(A) = A_i$.
2. *Unblocked*: There does not exist a non-empty set of contracts $Z \subseteq X \setminus A$ such that $Z \subseteq C^B(A \cup Z) \cap C^S(A \cup Z)$.

Note that while pairwise stability requires only the absence of blocks consisting of a single contract, stability requires the absence of blocking sets of contracts; hence, by definition, stability is more stringent than pairwise stability.

Our next result shows that under substitutability, pairwise stability and stability are equivalent.

Theorem 14.6 [22]. *If all choice functions are substitutable, then any pairwise stable outcome is stable.*

It turns out that substitutability is necessary in a maximal domain sense for the guaranteed existence of stable outcomes.[3] Consider markets in which the contract set is *exhaustive* in the sense that, for each pair $(b, s) \in B \times S$, there exists a contract $x \in X$ such that $\mathsf{b}(x) = b$ and $\mathsf{s}(x) = s$.

Theorem 14.7 [22]. *Suppose that there are at least two sellers and the contract set is exhaustive. If the choice function of agent $s \in S$ is not substitutable then there exist substitutable choice functions for the other agents such that no stable outcome exists.*

The following example shows how to construct an economy without a stable outcome given an agent with non-substitutable preferences; the proof of Theorem 14.7 generalizes the structure of this example.

Example 14.8 [22]. Consider a seller s with the choice function C^s induced by the preference ordering

$$\succ_s: \{x, y\} \succ \varnothing,$$

where $\mathsf{b}(x) \neq \mathsf{b}(y)$. Note that C^s is not substitutable, as $C^s(\{x, y\}) = \{x, y\}$ while $C^s(\{y\}) = \varnothing$. Now, suppose that there exists another seller s' and two contracts x' and y' with s' such that $\mathsf{b}(x') = \mathsf{b}(x)$ and $\mathsf{b}(y') = \mathsf{b}(y)$, and suppose that the choice function of s' is induced by the preference relation

$$\succ_{s'}: \{y'\} \succ \{x'\} \succ \varnothing.$$

---

[3] The existence of stable outcomes in the presence of non-substitutability can sometimes be obtained in large market frameworks like those of Chapter 16.

Finally, suppose that $b(x)$ has choice function $C^{b(x)}$ induced by the preference ordering

$$\succ_{b(x)}: \{x'\} \succ \{x\} \succ \varnothing$$

and $b(y)$ has choice function $C^{b(y)}$ induced by the preference ordering

$$\succ_{b(y)}: \{y\} \succ \{y'\} \succ \varnothing.$$

The outcome $\{x, y\}$ is not stable, as $\{x'\}$ is a blocking set. However, for any other individually rational allocation A, we must have that $A_s = \varnothing$; but then, either $\{x, y\}$ is a blocking set (if $x' \notin A$) or $\{y'\}$ is a blocking set (if $x' \in A$).

We now introduce a second restriction on agents' choice functions which requires that the *number* of chosen contracts weakly increases when the set of available contracts increases (in a superset sense).

Definition 14.9. The choice function of a buyer $i \in B$ (seller $i \in S$) satisfies the *law of aggregate demand (supply)* if for any pair of contracts $Y, Z \subseteq X$ such that $Y \subseteq Z$, we have that $|C^i(Y)| \leq |C^i(Z)|$.

When combined with substitutability, the laws of aggregate supply and demand allow us to generalize the *rural hospitals theorem* of Chapter 1 to our many-to-many setting.

Theorem 14.10 [22]. *If the choice functions of all agents are substitutable and satisfy the laws of aggregate supply and demand, then for each agent $i \in I$, the number of contracts that i signs is invariant across all stable outcomes.*

One can use the preceding theorem to show that a mechanism that picks the buyer-optimal or seller-optimal stable outcome is dominant-strategy incentive compatible, or *strategy-proof*, for all unit-demand buyers or sellers, respectively.

Theorem 14.11 [22]. *If the choice functions of all agents are substitutable and satisfy the laws of aggregate supply and demand then the buyer-optimal stable mechanism is strategy-proof for all unit-demand buyers and the seller-optimal stable mechanism is strategy-proof for all unit-demand sellers.*

Theorem 14.11 generalizes the strategy-proofness result of Chapter 1 to allow for substitutable preferences for the other side of the market. However, the next example shows that the incentive-compatibility results do not extend beyond the unit-demand case.

Example 14.12 [24]. Consider a seller s with the choice function C^s induced by the preference ordering

$$\succ_s: \{x, y\} \succ \{x, z\} \succ \{y, z\} \succ \{x\} \succ \{y\} \succ \{z\} \succ \varnothing;$$

that is, s prefers $b(x)$ to $b(y)$ to $b(z)$ and desires at most two contracts. Additionally, there is a seller s' with the unit-supply choice function $C^{s'}$ induced by the preference ordering

$$\succ_{s'}: \{y'\} \succ \{x'\} \succ \{z'\} \succ \varnothing,$$

where $b(x) = b(x') \neq b(y) = b(y') \neq b(z) = b(z') \neq b(x)$.

The choice functions of the buyers are induced by the preferences

$$\succ_{b(x)}: \{x'\} \succ \{x\} \succ \varnothing$$
$$\succ_{b(y)}: \{y\} \succ \{y'\} \succ \varnothing$$
$$\succ_{b(z)}: \{z\} \succ \{z'\} \succ \varnothing.$$

The only stable outcome is $\{x', y, z\}$. However, if s were to report

$$\hat{\succ}_s: \{x, z\} \succ \{x\} \succ \{z\} \succ \varnothing,$$

then the only stable outcome under the reported preferences would be $\{x, y', z\}$; this outcome is preferred by s even under the preferences $\succ_s$.

14.3.2 Many-to-One Matching with Contracts

A case of special interest is the many-to-one matching with contracts setting, introduced and developed by [10], [24], and [33]; see also [40]. In this setting, buyers have unit demand. It is immediate that stable outcomes exist in this setting when sellers' choice functions are substitutable (Theorem 14.3) and, when sellers' choice functions satisfy the law of aggregate supply, the buyer-optimal stable mechanism is strategy-proof for buyers (Theorem 14.11).

However, it is no longer the case that substitutability is necessary (even in the maximal domain sense of Theorem 14.7) for the existence of stable outcomes.

Example 14.13 [19]. Consider a seller s with the choice function C^s induced by the preference ordering

$$\succ_s: \{x, y\} \succ \{\tilde{x}\} \succ \{x\} \succ \{y\} \succ \varnothing,$$

where $b(x) = b(\tilde{x}) \neq b(y)$. Note that C^s is not substitutable, as $C^s(\{\tilde{x}, x\}) = \{\tilde{x}\}$ while $C^s(\{\tilde{x}, x, y\}) = \{x, y\}$.

However, a stable outcome always exists as long as other sellers have substitutable choice functions. To see this, note that $b(x)$ must either prefer $\{x\}$ to $\{x'\}$ or prefer $\{x'\}$ to $\{x\}$. In the former case we can treat the choice function of s *as if* it were induced by

$$\succ_s: \{x, y\} \succ \{x\} \succ \{y\} \succ \varnothing,$$

and these preferences induce a substitutable choice function; moreover, the outcome of a *buyer-proposing deferred acceptance mechanism* (under the new preferences) will be stable (with respect to the original preferences), as x will never be rejected, and so $b(x)$ must obtain a contract at least as good as x. In the latter case, we can treat the choice function of s *as if* it were induced by[4]

$$\succ_s: \{\tilde{x}\} \succ \{y\} \succ \varnothing,$$

---

[4] Here, by the buyer-proposing mechanism, we mean the fixed point of the generalized DA operator (14.1) obtained by starting at $(\varnothing, X)$ and iterating.

and these preferences also induce a substitutable choice function. Moreover, the outcome of a buyer-proposing deferred acceptance mechanism (under the new preferences) will be stable (with respect to the original preferences), as $\tilde{x}$ will never be rejected, and so $b(x)$ must obtain a contract at least as good as $\tilde{x}$.

14.3.2.1 Weakened Substitutability Conditions

Examples like that in Example 14.13 have motivated the search for conditions on seller preferences that ensure the existence of stable outcomes. A number of weakened substitutability conditions that guarantee the existence of stable outcomes have been found. Moreover, many of these conditions guarantee the existence of a stable and strategy-proof (for unit demand buyers) mechanism. In [20], for example, the authors identified the following condition, called *unilateral substitutability*.

Definition 14.14. The choice function of a seller s is *unilaterally substitutable* if, for all x, z such that $b(x) \neq b(z)$ and all $Y \subseteq X \setminus (X_{b(x)} \cup X_{b(z)})$, we have that

$$z \notin C^s(\{x\} \cup Y \cup \{z\}) \setminus C^b(Y \cup \{z\}).$$

In [20] it was shown that when the choice function of each seller is unilaterally substitutable, a stable outcome always exists; moreover, a stable outcome can be found by any *cumulative offer mechanism* (and, in fact, the outcome of the cumulative offer mechanism does not depend on the ordering used by the mechanism).[5] Moreover, when the choice function of each seller also satisfies the law of aggregate supply, any cumulative offer mechanism is strategy-proof.

Later, a more general condition under which stable outcomes are guaranteed to exist – *substitutable completability* – was introduced by [23]. Substitutable completion interprets certain non-substitutable choice functions in many-to-one matching with contracts as substitutable choice functions in the setting of many-to-many matching with contracts. In the setting of Example 14.13, for instance, we can think of "completing" the choice function of buyer b as allowing b to choose the

---

[5] For any ordering $\vdash$ over the set of contracts and preferences $\succ$ for the (unit-demand) buyers, the outcome of the *cumulative offer mechanism* is determined by the following algorithm:

Step 0: The set of contracts *available* to the sellers is $A^0 \equiv \varnothing$.
Step $t \geq 1$: Construct the set

$$U^t \equiv \{x \in X \setminus A^{t-1} : b(x) \notin b(C^S(A^{t-1})), \ C^{b(x)}(\{x\}) = x,$$
$$\text{and } \nexists z \in (X_{b(x)} \setminus A^{t-1}) \text{ such that } C^{b(x)}(\{x, z\}) = z\}.$$

If U^t is empty then the algorithm terminates and the outcome is $C^S(A^{t-1})$; otherwise, $A^t \equiv A^{t-1} \cup \{y\}$, where y is the highest-ranked contract in U^t according to $\vdash$.

Here, the set U^t is composed of contracts x such that:

1. the contract x has not yet been offered;
2. the buyer of x does not have any contract chosen by the sellers from A^{t-1};
3. the buyer of x finds x acceptable; and
4. the buyer of x does not have any other not-yet-offered contract z that they prefer to x.

(infeasible) set of contracts $\{x, \tilde{x}\}$ whenever it is available, i.e., to have a choice function $\hat{C}^s$ induced by

$$\hat{\succ}_s\colon \{x, \tilde{x}\} \succ \{x, y\} \succ \{\tilde{x}\} \succ \{x\} \succ \{y\} \succ \varnothing. \tag{14.2}$$

Note that $\hat{C}^s$ is substitutable; thus, by Theorem 14.3, there must exist a stable outcome A with respect to the completed choice function. However, since $\mathsf{b}(x)$ has unit demand, A cannot involve both x and $\tilde{x}$; hence, A must also be stable with respect to C^s.

More generally, when all the buyers' choice functions satisfy a condition called substitutable completability, there exists a lattice of stable outcomes that correspond to fixed points of (14.1) under a substitutable completion.[6]

Definition 14.15 [23]. A choice function C^s for seller s is *substitutably completable* if there exists a choice function $\hat{C}^s$ such that:

1. For all $Y \subseteq X$, we have that either $\hat{C}^s(Y) = C^s(Y)$ or there exists a buyer b such that $|[\hat{C}^s(Y)]_{\to b}| \geq 2$.
2. The choice function $\hat{C}^s$ is substitutable.

It turns out that substitutable completability is sufficient for the existence of a stable outcome.

Theorem 14.16 [23]. *Assume that the choice functions of all sellers are substitutably completable and buyers have unit demand. Then a stable outcome exists.*

Moreover, when the profile of choice functions is substitutably completable in such a way that each completion satisfies the law of aggregate demand, any cumulative offer mechanism is strategy-proof for buyers.

Theorem 14.17 [23]. *If every seller's choice function has a substitutable completion that also satisfies the law of aggregate demand, and buyers have unit demand, then any cumulative offer mechanism is strategy-proof for buyers.*

All unilaterally substitutable choice functions are substitutably completable [29], [46].

In fact, considerably weaker conditions are necessary and sufficient to guarantee that there is a stable mechanism that is strategy-proof for buyers; moreover, whenever a stable and strategy-proof mechanism exists, the cumulative offer mechanism is the unique stable and strategy-proof mechanism [28].[7]

---

[6] However, there may also exist other stable outcomes: for instance, when we use the substitutable completion (14.2), and the choice functions of the buyers are induced by

$$\succ_{\mathsf{b}(x)}\colon \{\tilde{x}\} \succ \{x\} \succ \varnothing$$

$$\succ_{\mathsf{b}(y)}\colon \{y\} \succ \varnothing,$$

the only fixed point of (14.1) corresponds to $\{\tilde{x}\}$, even though both $\{\tilde{x}\}$ and $\{x, y\}$ are stable. Note also that the full set of stable outcomes does not form a lattice in the usual way, as $\mathsf{b}(x)$ strictly prefers a different stable outcome than $\mathsf{b}(y)$.

[7] In particular, [27] showed that any when a stable and strategy-proof mechanism is guaranteed to exist, then that mechanism is equivalent to a *cumulative offer mechanism*, and in fact all cumulative offer mechanisms produce the same outcome. (The cumulative offer mechanism was defined in footnote 5.)

However, the existence of a stable outcome can be guaranteed under still weaker conditions; [20] introduced *bilateral substitutability*, which is enough to ensure that the cumulative offer mechanism produces a stable outcome. Subsequently, [28] introduced *observable substitutability across doctors*, which is necessary and sufficient to guarantee that the cumulative offer mechanism produces a stable outcome. However, observable substitutability across doctors is not the maximal domain of choice functions for which stable outcomes can be guaranteed; finding precise conditions on choice functions that ensure the existence of stable outcomes is an open problem.

14.3.2.2 Applications

The weakened substitutability conditions just discussed have been useful in real-world settings. In particular, in many-to-one matching with contracts settings, agents on the side with multiunit demand frequently have choice functions that are not substitutable and yet still allow for stable and strategy-proof matching. For instance, the US Military Academy (West Point) assigns graduating cadets to branches of service via a centralized system in which contracts encode not only the cadet and branch of service but also potential additional guaranteed years of service. Branches rank cadets according to a strict order-of-merit list but also prioritize contracts with additional guaranteed years for a fixed number of positions. As it turns out, this preference structure introduces non-substitutabilities since the offer of a contract with additional years may induce a service branch to choose a previously rejected contract; nevertheless, the choice functions of the branches are substitutably completable (and, in fact, unilaterally substitutable) and thus admit stable and strategy-proof matching [42]. This observation has led to a redesign of not only the mechanism used to assign West Point cadets but also the mechanism used to assign ROTC cadets to branches of service [5], [14]. Additionally, [35] developed a generalization of the cadet–branch matching framework, called *slot-specific priorities*, which allowed for the types of non-substitutabilities seen in the cadet-branch matching setting; this framework has proven useful in a number of real-world contexts, including school choice programs in Boston [8] and Chicago [7].

Weakened substitutability conditions were also key in the redesign of the Israeli Psychology Masters Match [18]. They have also proven fruitful in the analysis of entry-level labor markets with regional caps, such as the Japanese medical-residency matching program [30], [31], [32], the assignment of legal traineeships in Germany [6], the allocation of students to the Indian Institutes of Technology [3], and interdistrict school choice programs [17].

14.4 Supply Chains and Trading Networks

While early work on matching with contracts focused on two-sided settings, most of the key insights can be extended to a more general framework in which an agent can act as both a buyer and a seller. In [39] the two-sided setting was generalized to multi-layered supply chains, in which agents buy from agents "upstream" and sell to agents "downstream." In [12], [13], and [25] an even more general trading network setting was considered in which no *a priori* restrictions are placed on the set of possible contractual relationships.

In this section, we first consider the supply chain setting and then the more general case of trading networks. We maintain the assumptions that choice correspondences are single-valued and satisfy the irrelevance-of-rejected-contracts condition.

In supply chains and trading networks, an *intermediary* (i.e., an agent i such that there exist contracts x and y such that $\mathsf{s}(x) = i = \mathsf{b}(y)$) often sees contracts of which he is the seller and contracts of which he is the buyer as complements. The *full substitutability* condition extends (gross) substitutability to intermediaries by requiring that an intermediary consider contracts for which he is a buyer to be (gross) substitutes, contracts for which he is a seller to be (gross) substitutes, and a contract in which he is a buyer to be a (gross) complement to contracts in which he is a seller.

Definition 14.18. The choice function of agent i is *fully substitutable*, if for all $Y \subseteq X$ and all $x, z \in X$, both of the following conditions hold:

- *Same-side substitutability:* If $x, z \in X_{i \to}$ and $z \in C^i(Y \cup \{x, z\})$ then $z \in C^i(Y \cup \{z\})$. Similarly, if $x, z \in X_{\to i}$ and $z \in C^i(Y \cup \{x, z\})$ then $z \in C^i(Y \cup \{z\})$.
- *Cross-side complementarity:* If $x \in X_{i \to}$, $z \in X_{\to i}$, and $z \notin C^i(Y \cup \{x, z\})$ then $z \notin C^i(Y \cup \{z\})$. Similarly, if $x \in X_{\to i}$, $z \in X_{i \to}$, and $z \notin C^i(Y \cup \{x, z\})$ then $z \notin C^i(Y \cup \{z\})$.

Intuitively, full substitutability requires that the agents see the goods that flow through the network as gross substitutes.

14.4.1 Supply Chains

One important special case is that of networks that are (directed) acyclic. Such networks allow for "vertical" supply chain structures in which some agents intermediate-trade between agents who only buy and agents who only sell, but these networks rule out "horizontal" trade among intermediaries. Formally, we say that the economy is a *supply chain* if there do not exist contracts $x_1, \ldots, x_n$ such that $\mathsf{b}(x_\ell) = \mathsf{s}(x_{\ell+1})$ for all $1 \le \ell \le n - 1$ and $\mathsf{b}(x_n) = \mathsf{s}(x_1)$.

We next extend the concept of pairwise stability to trading networks. Instead of considering blocking contracts, we consider blocks of the form of chains in the network.

Definition 14.19. An outcome $A \subseteq X$ is *chain-stable* if it is:

1. *Individually rational*: For all $i \in I$, $C^i(A) = A_i$.
2. *Chain unblocked*: There does not exist an ordered set $Z = \{z_1, \ldots, z_n\} \subseteq X \setminus A$ such that $\mathsf{s}(z_\ell) = \mathsf{b}(z_{\ell+1})$ for all $1 \le \ell \le n - 1$ and such that $Z_i \subseteq C^i(Z \cup A)$ for all $i \in I$.

We now extend Theorem 14.3 to supply chains.

Theorem 14.20 [39]. *In supply chains, if the choice functions of all agents are fully substitutable then chain-stable outcomes exist.*

$$\underline{\qquad}\quad 314 \quad \underline{\qquad}$$

The proof of Theorem 14.20 is similar to the proof of Theorem 14.3. We first define aggregate choice functions C^S and C^B as follows:

$$C^S(Y, Y') \equiv \bigcup_{i \in I} C^i(Y_{i \rightarrow} \cup Y'_{\rightarrow i})_{i \rightarrow},$$

$$C^B(Y, Y') \equiv \bigcup_{i \in I} C^i(Y_{\rightarrow i} \cup Y'_{i \rightarrow})_{\rightarrow i}.$$

Here, $C^S(Y, Y')$ is the set of contracts that are chosen by their sellers when given access to the sale contracts in Y and the purchase contracts in Y'; $C^B(Y, Y')$ is defined analogously. For each $X^B, X^S \subseteq X$, we then define a generalized DA operator by

$$\Phi(X^S, X^B) = (\Phi^S(X^B, X^S), \Phi^B(X^S, X^B)),$$

$$\Phi^S(X^B, X^S) = \{x \in X : x \in C^S(X^B \cup \{x\}, X^S)\},$$

$$\Phi^B(X^S, X^B) = \{x \in X : x \in C^B(X^S \cup \{x\}, X^B)\}.$$

Proof of Theorem 14.20. The key to the proof is the following version of Lemma 14.4.

Lemma 14.21. *In supply chains, if (X^S, X^B) is a fixed point of Φ, then $A = X^S \cap X^B$ is chain-stable and $C^B(X^B, X^S) = C^S(X^S, X^B) = A$. Conversely, in supply chains in which the choice functions of all agents are fully substitutable, if A is a chain-stable outcome, then $\Phi^N(A, A)$ is a fixed point of Φ for sufficiently large N.*

Proof sketch. The proof of Lemma 14.21 is similar to the proof of Lemma 14.4, but is more subtle due to the presence of the intermediaries.

Assume first that (X^S, X^B) is a fixed point of Φ and let $A = X^S \cap X^B$. A similar argument to the proof of Lemma 14.4 shows that $C^B(X^B, X^S) = C^S(X^S, X^B) = A$, and, as in the proof of Lemma 14.4, it follows that A is individually rational. To show that A is chain-unblocked, one can inductively apply the argument from the proof of Lemma 14.4 to show that fixed points give rise to pairwise unblocked outcomes. We leave the details of this inductive argument as an exercise for the reader.

Next, let A be a chain-stable outcome and let $(X^S(n), X^B(n)) = \Phi^n(A, A)$ for positive integers n. A similar argument to the proof of Lemma 14.4 shows that $X^S(1) \cap X^B(1) = A$. One then shows inductively that $X^S(n) \cap X^B(n) = A$, that $X^S(n) \supseteq X^S(n-1)$, and that $X^B(n) \supseteq X^B(n-1)$; again we leave the details of this argument as an exercise for the reader. As X is finite, it follows that $\Phi^{|X|}(A, A)$ is a fixed point of Φ. □

Considering the ordering $\vdash$ on $X \times X$ introduced in the proof of Theorem 14.3, full substitutability implies that Φ is isotone with respect to $\vdash$. As a result, Tarski's fixed point theorem guarantees that Φ has a fixed point (X^S, X^B). By Lemma 14.21, $C^B(X^S, X^B) = C^S(X^B, X^S)$ is a stable outcome. □

We next extend the concept of stability to supply chain settings and compare it to chain stability.

Definition 14.22. An outcome $A \subseteq X$ is *stable* if it is:

1. *Individually rational*: For all $i \in I$, $C^i(A) = A_i$.
2. *Unblocked*: There does not exist a set $Z = \{z_1, \ldots, z_n\} \subseteq X \setminus A$ such that $Z_i \subseteq C^i(Z \cup A)$ for all $i \in I$.

The following straightforward extension of Theorem 14.6 shows that in supply chains in which agents have fully substitutable choice functions, if an outcome is not blocked by a chain of contracts then it is also not blocked by more general sets of contracts.

Theorem 14.23 [21]. *In supply chains, if the choice functions of all agents are fully substitutable then every chain-stable outcome is stable.*

As in the case of two-sided many-to-many markets, full substitutability comprises a maximal domain for the guaranteed existence of stable outcomes.

Theorem 14.24 [21]. *In supply chains, if the choice function of an agent i is not fully substitutable and for all distinct $j, k \in I$ there exists $(i, j, t) \in X$ for some $t \in T$, then there exist substitutable choice functions for the other agents such that no stable outcome exists.*

14.4.2 Trading Networks

To understand the role of the acyclicity assumption in Theorem 14.20, we show via example that (chain-)stable outcomes may not exist in general trading networks, even under full substitutability.

Example 14.25. There are two intermediaries i_1, i_2 and one buyer b. The set of contracts is $X = \{x, y, z\}$ and we have that $\mathsf{s}(x) = \mathsf{s}(z) = \mathsf{b}(y) = i_1$, that $\mathsf{s}(y) = \mathsf{b}(x) = i_2$, and that $\mathsf{b}(z) = b$. Note that the contracts x and y comprise a cycle. The agents' choice functions are induced by the preferences

$$\succ_{i_1} : \{y, z\} \succ_{i_1} \{x, y\} \succ_{i_1} \varnothing$$
$$\succ_{i_2} : \{x, y\} \succ_{i_2} \varnothing$$
$$\succ_b : \{z\} \succ_b \varnothing;$$

these choice functions are fully substitutable.

However, there is no chain-stable outcome. To see why, note that the only individually rational outcomes are $\{x, y\}$ and $\varnothing$. But $\{x, y\}$ blocks the outcome $\varnothing$, while $\{z\}$ blocks the outcome $\{x, y\}$.

In fact, in trading networks, it is NP-complete to determine whether a stable outcome exists as well as whether a given outcome is stable – even if all agents' choice functions are fully substitutable [11]. To analyze trading networks with cycles, we therefore consider a different extension of pairwise stability to trading networks. Under this concept, which we call trail stability, blocking contracts occur in a sequence and agents evaluate pairs of consecutive contracts in isolation rather than in reference to the entire set of blocking contracts.

Definition 14.26. An outcome $A \subseteq X$ is *trail-stable* if it is:

1. *Individually rational*: For all $i \in I$, $C^i(A) = A_i$.
2. *Trail unblocked*: There does not exist a sequence $z_1, \ldots, z_n \in X \setminus A$ of contracts such that $\mathsf{s}(z_\ell) = \mathsf{b}(z_{\ell+1})$ and $\{z_\ell, z_{\ell+1}\} \subseteq C^{\mathsf{s}(z_\ell)}(\{z_\ell, z_{\ell+1}\} \cup A)$ for all $1 \le \ell \le n-1$, $z_1 \in C^{\mathsf{s}(i_1)}(\{z_1\} \cup A)$, and $z_n \in C^{\mathsf{b}(z_n)}(\{z_n\} \cup A)$.

In supply chains, trail stability coincides with chain stability. To understand the difference between the two concepts in general trading networks, note that in Example 14.25, the outcome $\varnothing$ is a trail-stable outcome but is not chain-stable. Trail-stable outcomes turn out to exist in general trading networks under full substitutability.

Theorem 14.27 [12]. *If the choice functions of all agents are fully substitutable then trail-stable outcomes exist.*

To prove Theorem 14.27, we apply the fixed-point argument from the proof of Theorem 14.20 but use the following extension of Lemma 14.21 to trading networks.

Lemma 14.28 [1]. *If (X^S, X^B) is a fixed point of Φ. then $A = X^S \cap X^B$ is trail-stable and $C^B(X^B, X^S) = C^S(X^S, X^B) = A$. Conversely, if the choice functions of all agents are fully substitutable and A is a trail-stable outcome then $\Phi^N(A, A)$ is a fixed point of Φ for sufficiently large N.*

The proof of Lemma 14.28 is similar to the proof of Lemma 14.21, and is left as an exercise for the reader.

14.5 Transfers

Finally, we consider a setting with continuous transfers. A *contract* x is now a pair $(\omega, p_\omega) \in \Omega \times \mathbb{R}$ that specifies a bilateral trade $\omega \in \Omega$ between a *buyer* $\mathsf{b}(\omega) \in I$ and a *seller* $\mathsf{s}(\omega) \in I \setminus \{\mathsf{b}(\omega)\}$ in exchange for a monetary transfer p_ω (to be paid to the seller from the buyer). The set of possible contracts is $X \equiv \Omega \times \mathbb{R}$. A set of contracts $Y \subseteq X$ is *feasible* if it does not contain two or more contracts for the same trade: formally, Y is feasible if $(\omega, p_\omega), (\omega, \hat{p}_\omega) \in Y$ implies that $p_\omega = \hat{p}_\omega$. We call a feasible set of contracts an *outcome*. An outcome specifies a set of trades along with associated prices but does not specify prices for trades that are not in that set. We let $\tau(Y)$ be the set of trades that are associated with some contract in Y, i.e.,

$$\tau(Y) \equiv \{\psi \in \Psi : (\psi, p_\psi) \in Y \text{ for some } p_\psi \in \mathbb{R}\}.$$

An *arrangement* is a pair $[\Psi; p]$ with $\Psi \subseteq \Omega$ and $p \in \mathbb{R}^\Omega$. Note that an arrangement specifies prices for *all* the trades in the economy.

Each agent i has a *valuation* (or *preferences*) $u_i \colon \wp(\Omega_i) \to \mathbb{R} \cup \{-\infty\}$ over the sets of trades in which they are involved, with $u_i(\varnothing) \in \mathbb{R}$; we use $u^i(\psi) = -\infty$ to denote that ψ is infeasible for i. The valuation u_i over bundles of trades gives rise to a quasilinear utility function U_i over bundles of trades and associated transfers. Specifically, for any feasible set of contracts $Y \subseteq X$, we define

$$U_i(Y) \equiv u_i(\tau(Y)) + \sum_{(\omega, p_\omega) \in Y_{i \to}} p_\omega - \sum_{(\omega, p_\omega) \in Y_{\to i}} p_\omega,$$

and, slightly abusing the notation, for any arrangement $[\Psi; p]$ we define

$$U_i([\Psi; p]) \equiv u_i(\Psi) + \sum_{\psi \in \Psi_{i\rightarrow}} p_\psi - \sum_{\psi \in \Psi_{\rightarrow i}} p_\psi.$$

The *demand correspondence* of agent i, given a price vector $p \in \mathbb{R}^\Omega$, is defined by

$$D_i(p) \equiv \arg\max_{\Psi \subseteq \Omega_i} \{U_i([\Psi; p])\}.$$

There is a natural analogue of the full substitutability condition for demand correspondences: whenever the price of an input (i.e., a trade in $\Omega_{\rightarrow i}$) increases, then i's demand for other inputs weakly increases (in the superset sense) and her supply of outputs (i.e., trades in $\Omega_{i\rightarrow}$) weakly decreases (in the subset sense); an analogous condition is required for the case where the price of an output decreases. As shown by [27], full substitutability for demand correspondences is equivalent to full substitutability for choice correspondences (as well as several other conditions). Hence, from now on we will simply say that agents' preferences are fully substitutable. We now formally define competitive equilibria for our setting.

Definition 14.29. An arrangement $[\Psi; p]$ is a *competitive equilibrium* if, for all $i \in I$,

$$\Psi_i \in D_i(p).$$

The theorem below shows that competitive equilibria exist, and are essentially equivalent to stable outcomes, when agents' preferences are fully substitutable.[8]

Theorem 14.30 [25]. *If agents' preferences are fully substitutable then competitive equilibria exist and are stable. Furthermore, for any stable outcome A, there exist prices $p_{\Omega \setminus \tau(A)}$ for the non-realized trades in $\Omega \setminus \tau(A)$ such that $[\tau(A), (p_{\tau(A)}, p_{\Omega \setminus \tau(A)})]$ is a competitive equilibrium.*

Finally, we relax the assumption that utility is perfectly transferable between agents. We suppose that instead of depending quasilinearly on net payments, utility can depend arbitrarily on the entire vector of payments. That is, we suppose that each agent i has a utility function $U_i: \wp(\Omega_i) \times \mathbb{R}^{\Omega_i} \rightarrow \mathbb{R} \cup \{-\infty\}$, and define utility over feasible sets Y of contracts by

$$U_i(Y) \equiv U_i(\tau(Y), t(Y)),$$

where

$$t(Y) = \begin{cases} p_\omega & \text{if } \omega \in \tau(Y)_{i\rightarrow}, \text{ where } (\omega, p_\omega) \in Y, \\ -p_\omega & \text{if } \omega \in \tau(Y)_{\rightarrow i}, \text{ where } (\omega, p_\omega) \in Y, \\ 0 & \text{otherwise.} \end{cases}$$

This framework allows us to incorporate the possibility of frictions, such as distortionary taxes on payments on different trades. As with the quasilinear case, the full substitutability condition extends to this setting with continuous prices. In this

---

[8] The existence of competitive equilibria has also been shown in related exchange economy settings (see, e.g., [15], [43], [44]) in which each agent can only be a buyer or a seller.

setting, under full substitutability and regularity conditions on agents' utility functions, competitive equilibria exist and essentially coincide with trail-stable outcomes. Nevertheless, stable outcomes do not generally exist when distortionary frictions are present. Intuitively, distortions do not preclude the existence of equilibrium but they can cause equilibrium to be inefficient; however, trail-stable outcomes can often be blocked by agents who can coordinate transfers in ways that reduce the impact of the frictions.

14.5.1 Applications

One possible market design application of the trading network framework is peer-to-peer energy trading. Many energy markets around the world are shifting from large-scale centralized power generation towards inflexible, small-scale, renewable energy resources. In these energy markets, there are not only traditional suppliers (which we model as sellers) and traditional consumers (which we model as buyers), but also many "prosumers" (consumers who also generate power, e.g., using residential solar panels; we model these as intermediaries). Contracts specify a discrete quantity of energy offered by one agent to another at a given time and price. It turns out that full substitutability is a reasonable approximation of preferences of agents in such an energy market [37], [38] if, for example, economies of scale in generation are absent. Trail-stable outcomes can be computed second-by-second, thereby maintaining overall system balance without any recourse to a centralized system operator.

14.6 Exercises

Exercise 14.1 Explain why the last statement of Example 14.13 is true.

Exercise 14.2 Assume one seller has the non-substitutable preferences given in Example 14.13. Construct (multi-unit) preferences for other buyers and sellers in such a way that no stable outcome exists. (At least one buyer will have to have multi-unit demand – why?)

Exercise 14.3 Prove that if one seller has preferences given by (with $b(x) \neq b(y) = b(y') \neq b(z) \neq b(x)$)

$$\{x, y, z\} \succ \{y'\} \succ \{x, z\} \succ \{x, y\} \succ \{y, z\} \succ \{x\} \succ \{z\} \succ \{y\} \succ \varnothing,$$

and if the preferences of the other sellers are substitutable, and buyers have unit-demand preferences, then a stable outcome must exist.

Exercise 14.4 Complete the proof of Lemma 14.21 or Lemma 14.28.

References

[1] Adachi, Hiroyuki. 2017. Stable matchings and fixed points in trading networks: A note. *Economics Letters*, **156**, 65–67.

[2] Aygün, Orhan, and Sönmez, Tayfun. 2013. Matching with Contracts: Comment. *American Economic Review*, **103**, 2050–2051.

[3] Aygün, Orhan, and Turhan, Bertan. 2017. Large-scale affirmative action in school choice: Admissions to IITs in India. *American Economic Review Papers & Proceedings*, **107**, 210–213.

[4] Crawford, Vincent P., and Knoer, Elsie Marie. 1981. Job matching with heterogeneous firms and workers. *Econometrica*, **49**, 437–450.

[5] Defense Visual Information Distribution Service. 2020. New innovations improve branching process for cadets, branches. www.dvidshub.net/news/ 379351/new-innovations-improve-branching-process-cadets-branches.

[6] Dimakopoulos, Philipp D., and Heller, C.-Philipp. 2019. Matching with waiting times: The German entry-level labor market for lawyers. *Games and Economic Behavior*, **115**, 289–313.

[7] Dur, Umut, Pathak, Parag A., and Sönmez Tayfun. 2020. Explicit vs. statistical targeting in affirmative action: Theory and evidence from Chicago's exam schools. *Journal of Economic Theory*, **187**, 104–996.

[8] Dur, Umut, Kominers, Scott Duke, Pathak, Parag A., and Sönmez, Tayfun. 2018. Reserve design: Unintended consequences and the demise of Boston's Walk Zones. *Journal of Political Economy*, **126**, 2457–2479.

[9] Echenique, Federico, and Oviedo, Jorge. 2006. A theory of stability in many-to-many matching markets. *Theoretical Economics*, **1**, 233–273.

[10] Fleiner, Tamás. 2003. A fixed-point approach to stable matchings and some applications. *Mathematics of Operations Research*, **28**, 103–126.

[11] Fleiner, Tamás, Jankó, Zsuzsanna, Schlotter, Ildikó, and Teytelboym, Alexander. Forthcoming. Complexity of stability in trading networks. *International Journal of Game Theory*.

[12] Fleiner, Tamás, Jankó, Zsuzsanna, Tamura, Akihisa, and Teytelboym, Alexander. 2018. Trading networks with bilateral contracts. Oxford University Working Paper.

[13] Fleiner, Tamás, Jagadeesan, Ravi, Jankó, Zsuzsanna, and Teytelboym, Alexander. 2019. Trading networks with frictions. *Econometrica*, **87**, 1633–1661.

[14] Greenberg, Kyle, Pathak, Parag A., and Sönmez, Tayfun. 2021. Mechanism design meets priority design: Redesigning the US Army's Branching Process. Technical Report of the National Bureau of Economic Research.

[15] Gul, Frank, and Stacchetti, Ennio. 1999. Walrasian equilibrium with gross substitutes. *Journal of Economic Theory*, **87**, 95–124.

[16] Gul, Frank, and Stacchetti, Ennio. 2000. The english auction with differentiated commodities. *Journal of Economic Theory*, **92**, 66–95.

[17] Hafalir, Isa Emin., Kojima, Fuhito., and Yenmez, M. Bumin. 2022. Interdistrict school choice: A theory of student assignment. *Journal of Economic Theory*, **201**, 105–441.

[18] Hassidim, Avinatan, Romm, Assaf, and Shorrer, Ran I. 2017. Redesigning the Israeli Psychology Master's Match. *American Economic Review Papers & Proceedings*, **107**, 205–209.

[19] Hatfield, John William, and Kojima, Fuhito. 2008. Matching with contracts: Comment. *American Economic Review*, **98**, 1189–1194.

[20] Hatfield, John William, and Kojima, Fuhito. 2010. Substitutes and stability for matching with contracts. *Journal of Economic Theory*, **145**, 1704–1723.

[21] Hatfield, John William, and Kominers, Scott Duke. 2012. Matching in networks with bilateral contracts. *American Economic Journal: Microeconomics*, **4**, 176–208.

[22] Hatfield, John William, and Kominers, Scott Duke. 2017. Contract design and stability in many-to-many matching. *Games and Economic Behavior*, **101**, 78–97.

[23] Hatfield, John William, and Kominers, Scott Duke. 2019. Hidden substitutes. Harvard University Working Paper.

[24] Hatfield, John William, and Milgrom, Paul. 2005. Matching with contracts. *American Economic Review*, **95**, 913–935.

[25] Hatfield, John William, Kominers, Scott Duke, Nichifor, Alexandru, Ostrovsky, Michael, and Westkamp, Alexander. 2013. Stability and competitive equilibrium in trading networks. *Journal of Political Economy*, **121**, 966–1005.

[26] Hatfield, John William, Kominers, Scott Duke, and Westkamp, Alexander. 2017. Stable and strategy-proof matching with flexible allotments. *American Economic Review Papers & Proceedings*, **107**, 214–219.

[27] Hatfield, John William, Kominers, Scott Duke, Nichifor, Alexandru, Ostrovsky, Michael, and Westkamp, Alexander. 2019. Full substitutability. *Theoretical Economics*, **14**, 1535–1590.

[28] Hatfield, John William, Kominers, Scott Duke, and Westkamp, Alexander. 2021. Stability, strategy-proofness, and cumulative offer mechanisms. *Review of Economic Studies*, **88**, 1457–1502.

[29] Kadam, Sangram Vilasrao. 2017. Unilateral substitutability implies substitutable completability in many-to-one matching with contracts. *Games and Economic Behavior*, **102**, 56–68.

[30] Kamada, Yuichiro, and Kojima, Fuhito. 2012. Stability and strategy-proofness for matching with constraints: A problem in the Japanese medical match and its solution. *American Economic Review*, **102**, 366–370.

[31] Kamada, Yuichiro, and Kojima, Fuhito. 2015. Efficient matching under distributional constraints: Theory and applications. *American Economic Review*, **105**, 67–99.

[32] Kamada, Yuichiro, and Fuhito Kojima. 2018. Stability and strategy-proofness for matching with constraints: A necessary and sufficient condition. *Theoretical Economics*, **13**, 761–793.

[33] Kelso, Jr., Alexander S., and Crawford, Vincent P. 1982. Job matching, coalition formation, and gross substitutes. *Econometrica*, **50**, 1483–1504.

[34] Klaus, Bettina, and Walzl, Markus. 2009. Stable many-to-many matchings with contracts. *Journal of Mathematical Economics*, **45**, 422–434.

[35] Kominers, Scott Duke, and Sönmez, Tayfun. 2016. Matching with slot-specific priorities: Theory. *Theoretical Economics*, **11**, 683–710.

[36] Milgrom, Paul. 2004. *Putting Auction Theory to Work*. Cambridge University Press.

[37] Morstyn, Thomas, Teytelboym, Alexander, and McCulloch, Malcolm D. 2018a. Bilateral contract networks for peer-to-peer energy trading. *IEEE Transactions on Smart Grid*, **10**, 2026–2035.

[38] Morstyn, Thomas, Teytelboym, Alexander, and McCulloch, Malcolm D. 2018b. Designing decentralized markets for distribution system flexibility. *IEEE Transactions on Power Systems*, **34**, 2128–2139.

[39] Ostrovsky, Michael. 2008. Stability in supply chain networks. *American Economic Review*, **98**, 897–923.

[40] Roth, Alvin E. 1984. Stability and polarization of interests in job matching. *Econometrica*, **52**, 47–57.

[41] Sönmez, Tayfun. 2013. Bidding for army career specialties: Improving the ROTC Branching Mechanism. *Journal of Political Economy*, **121**, 186–219.

[42] Sönmez, Tayfun, and Switzer, Tobias B. 2013. Matching with (branch-of-choice) contracts at United States Military Academy. *Econometrica*, **81**, 451–488.

[43] Sun, Ning, and Yang, Zaifu. 2006. Equilibria and indivisibilities: Gross substitutes and complements. *Econometrica*, **74**, 1385–1402.

[44] Sun, Ning, and Yang, Zaifu. 2009. A double-track adjustment process for discrete markets with substitutes and complements. *Econometrica*, **77**, 933–952.

[45] Westkamp, Alexander. 2010. Market structure and matching with contracts. *Journal of Economic Theory*, **145**, 1724–1738.

[46] Zhang, Jun. 2016. On sufficient conditions for the existence of stable matchings with contracts. *Economics Letters*, **145**, 230–234.

CHAPTER FIFTEEN

Complementarities and Externalities

Thành Nguyen and Rakesh Vohra

15.1 Introduction

David Gale and Lloyd Shapley formulated the problem of finding a stable matching and identified a setting where such matchings always exist via the deferred acceptance algorithm (DA) (see Chapter 1). The algorithm is a thing of beauty and no one exposed to it is immune to its charms. It has inspired others to enlarge the domains in which it is applicable.

However, in the presence of preference complementarity, stable matchings are not guaranteed to exist (see Section 15.3 for an example). This is a problem because there are many settings of practical importance in which agents' preferences exhibit complementarities. In school choice, for example, this can arise in two ways. First, parents with multiple children have preferences over *subsets* of schools their children are assigned to rather than individual schools. Second, schools themselves may have preferences over the distribution of characteristics of the students they admit.

Furthermore, even if a stable matching does exist, the DA algorithm is not guaranteed to find it. The reason is that at each iteration of the algorithm when a "proposing" agent is rejected, the decision is irrevocable. This excludes the possibility of accommodating complementarities in preferences on the accepting side. A proposing agent by him- or herself may be ranked individually below other agents but in concert with another agent may be ranked high.

To overcome this problem, we present Scarf's lemma, which yields an alternative proof for the existence of stable matchings. While Scarf's proof lacks some of the desirable features of the DA, it is much more powerful in an entirely different way: it gives us the tools to incorporate complementarities and externalities while preserving the guaranteed existence of a stable solution.

The question of the existence of a stable matching is closely related to that of non-emptiness of the core of a non-transferable utility cooperative game. A key tool in the study of non-transferable utility cooperative games is Scarf's lemma. It provides a sufficient condition for the non-emptiness of the core of an NTU co-operative game. The lemma makes three important contributions. The first is to frame the problem of finding a matching as a special case of a more general problem about coalition formation. The second is an extension of the notion of stability to "fractional" assignments of agents to coalitions, called domination. The third is establishing the existence of "stable" fractional assignments. The connection to stability has been neglected, perhaps, because the study of non-transferable utility (NTU) co-operative games fell out of fashion. This is unfortunate. To paraphrase Scarf from another context:

> Our message boils down to a simple straightforward piece of advice; if economists are to study stability, the first step is to take our trusty DA algorithm, pack it up carefully in mothballs, and put it away respectfully; it has served us well for many a year. In the presence of complementarities, it simply doesn't do the job it was meant to do.

When complementarities are present, stable matching need not exist (see Section 15.3). Further, pairwise stability does not always imply group stability as discussed in Chapter 10. Pairwise stable matchings need not be Pareto optimal, but group stable matchings are Pareto optimal.

This chapter will survey proposals to surmount the problem of non-existence as well as identifying group stable matchings. It emphasizes the role of Scarf's lemma. So as to strike a balance between the perspective of the parachutist and that of the truffle hunter, we restrict our discussion to two-sided many-to-one matching problems.

15.2 Existence of Stable Matching, Revisited

15.2.1 Scarf's Lemma

In this section we state a version of Scarf's lemma that is adapted to the matching context. We show how it implies the existence of a stable matching in the setting originally considered by Gale and Shapley.

Let $\mathcal{A}$ be an $n \times m$ non-negative matrix with at least one non-zero entry in each row and $q \in \mathbb{R}^n_+$. Associated with each row $i \in \{1, \ldots, n\}$ of $\mathcal{A}$ is a strict order $\succ_i$ over the set of columns j for which $\mathcal{A}_{i,j} > 0$.

To interpret, suppose for a moment that $\mathcal{A}$ is a 0–1 matrix. Associate each row of $\mathcal{A}$ with an agent and interpret each column to be the characteristic vector of a coalition of agents. Hence, $\mathcal{A}_{ij} = 1$ means that agent i is in the jth coalition. Then $\succ_i$ can be interpreted as agent i's preference ordering over all the columns, or coalitions, of $\mathcal{A}$ of which i is a member. No restrictions on $\succ_i$ are imposed.

Consider the system $\{x \in \mathbb{R}^m_+ : \mathcal{A}x \leq q\}$. The positive elements of a feasible x can be interpreted as corresponding to the feasible coalitions that can be formed. We illustrate with an example.

Example 15.1.   Consider an instance of the stable matching problem that consists of two hospitals (h_1, h_2), each with capacity 1, and two unmarried doctors (d_1, d_2). This is the setting of [21]. The preferences are as follows: $d_1 \succ_{h_1} d_2; d_1 \succ_{h_2} d_2; h_2 \succ_{d_1} h_1; h_2 \succ_{d_2} h_1$.

We describe the set of feasible matchings as the solution to a system of inequalities. The constraint matrix of this system will be the matrix $\mathcal{A}$ that is used when invoking Scarf's lemma.

Introduce variables $x_{(d_i, h_j)} \in \{0, 1\}$ for $i \in \{1, 2\}$ and $j \in \{1, 2\}$ where $x_{(d_i, h_j)} = 1$ if and only if d_i is assigned to h_j and is zero otherwise. In the 4×4 matrix, $\mathcal{A}$ given below, each row corresponds to an agent (a hospital or a doctor), and each column corresponds to a doctor–hospital pair. An entry $\mathcal{A}_{ij}$ of the matrix $\mathcal{A}$ is 1 if and only if the agent corresponding to row i is a member of the coalition corresponding to column j. Otherwise, $\mathcal{A}_{ij} = 0$. The inequality $\mathcal{A}x \leq q$ models the capacity constraints of the hospital and the constraint that each doctor can be assigned to at most one hospital. In this example $q = \mathbf{1}$. For each row i of $\mathcal{A}$, the strict order on the set of columns j for which $\mathcal{A}_{ij} \neq 0$ is the same as the preference ordering of agent i. Specifically, we have the following system:

$$
\begin{pmatrix}
 & (d_1,h_1) & (d_1,h_2) & (d_2,h_1) & (d_2,h_2) \\
h_1 & 1 & 0 & 1 & 0 \\
h_2 & 0 & 1 & 0 & 1 \\
d_1 & 1 & 1 & 0 & 0 \\
d_2 & 0 & 0 & 1 & 1
\end{pmatrix} \cdot x \leq
\begin{pmatrix} 1 \\ 1 \\ 1 \\ 1 \end{pmatrix}; \quad \text{order:} \quad
\begin{array}{l}
col_1 \succ_{h_1} col_3 \\
col_2 \succ_{h_2} col_4 \\
col_2 \succ_{d_1} col_1 \\
col_3 \succ_{d_2} col_4.
\end{array}
$$

We now define the notion of domination.

Definition 15.2. A vector $x \geq 0$ satisfying $\mathcal{A}x \leq q$ *dominates* column k of $\mathcal{A}$ if there exists a row i such that $\sum_{j=1}^{n} \mathcal{A}_{ij}x_j = q_i$ and, for all columns $l \in \{1, \ldots, m\}$ such that $\mathcal{A}_{i,l} > 0$ and $x_l > 0$, we have $l \succeq_i k$.

The next example will illustrate that when a dominating vector x is integer-valued this is precisely the notion of stability.

Example 15.3. Recall Example 15.1. Every integer solution to $\mathcal{A}x \leq \mathbf{1}$ corresponds to a matching and vice versa. Notice that $x = (1,0,0,1)^T$ corresponds to the matching $(d_1,h_1); (d_2,h_2)$. It is not stable because it is blocked by (d_1,h_2). In the language of Scarf's lemma, $x = (1,0,0,1)^T$ is not a dominating solution because x does not dominate the column corresponding to (d_1,h_2). The solution $x = (0,1,1,0)^T$ is, however, a dominating solution and corresponds to a stable matching.

Lemma 15.4 [46]. *Let $\mathcal{A}$ be an $n \times m$ non-negative matrix and $q \in \mathbb{R}^n_+$. Then there exists an extreme point of $\{x \in \mathbb{R}^m_+ : \mathcal{A}x \leq q\}$ that dominates every column of $\mathcal{A}$.*

Proof The proof is by reduction to the existence of a Nash equilibrium in a two-person game. By scaling we can assume that q is the vector containing all 1's, denoted $\mathbf{1}$. Let $\mathcal{C}$ be a matrix defined as follows:

- If $\mathcal{A}_{ij} = 0$ then $\mathcal{C}_{ij} = 0$.
- If $\mathcal{A}_{ij} > 0$ and j is ranked at t in the preference list of i then $\mathcal{C}_{ij} = -N^t$, for $N \geq n$.

The jth columns of $\mathcal{A}$ and $\mathcal{C}$ will be denoted $\mathcal{A}^j$ and $\mathcal{C}^j$ respectively.

We now associate a two-person game with the pair $(\mathcal{A}, \mathcal{C})$. The payoff matrix for ROW, the row player, will be $\mathcal{A}$. The payoff matrix for COLUMN, the column player, will be $\mathcal{C}$. Let (x^*, y^*) be an equilibrium pair of mixed strategies for this game, where x^* is a mixed strategy for the ROW player (payoff matrix $\mathcal{A}$) and y^* is the mixed strategy for COLUMN (payoff matrix $\mathcal{C}$).

Let R^* be ROW's expected payoff and C^* be the expected payoff to COLUMN. Clearly $\mathcal{A}x^* \leq R^*\mathbf{1}$. We will show that x^*/R^* is a dominating solution.

Suppose the columns of $\mathcal{A}$ are sorted in such a way that $x_i^* > 0$ for $1 \leq i \leq k$ and $x_i^* = 0$ for $k+1 \leq i \leq n$. COLUMN's expected payoff when playing each column $1, \ldots, k$ is exactly C^*, and when playing any other column is at most C^*. If COLUMN plays one of the first k columns uniformly at random, her expected payoff is also C^*, i.e.,

$$\frac{1}{k}y^*(\mathcal{C}^1 + \cdots + \mathcal{C}^k) = \sum_i y_i^* \frac{(\mathcal{C}_{i1} + \mathcal{C}_{i2} + \cdots + \mathcal{C}_{ik})}{k} = C^*.$$

Choose any column j. We will show that x^* dominates j. As x^* is a best response to y^* it must hold that

$$\sum_i y_i^* \mathcal{C}_{ij} \leq C^* = \sum_i y_i^* \frac{(\mathcal{C}_{i1} + \mathcal{C}_{i2} + \cdots + \mathcal{C}_{ik})}{k}.$$

$$\Rightarrow \exists y_r^* > 0 \text{ s.t. } \mathcal{C}_{rj} \leq \frac{(\mathcal{C}_{r1} + \mathcal{C}_{r2} + \cdots + \mathcal{C}_{rk})}{k}.$$

Hence,

$$y_r^* > 0 \Rightarrow \mathcal{A}_{r1}x_1^* + \cdots + \mathcal{A}_{rk}x_k^* = R^* > 0.$$

Therefore, at least one of $\mathcal{A}_{r1}, \ldots, \mathcal{A}_{rk}$ is non-zero. Hence, at least one of $\mathcal{C}_{r1}, \ldots, \mathcal{C}_{rk}$ is non-zero and $\mathcal{C}_{ij} \neq 0 \Rightarrow \mathcal{A}_{ij} \neq 0$.

Assume that, among the columns $1, \ldots, k$, $\mathcal{A}_{r1} \neq 0$ and column 1 is the least preferred. Let ℓ be the rank of column 1 in that preference ordering. Recall that $\mathcal{C}_{r1} = -N^\ell$. Hence,

$$\frac{\mathcal{C}_{r1} + \mathcal{C}_{r2} + \cdots + \mathcal{C}_{rk}}{k} \leq \frac{\mathcal{C}_{r1}}{k} = \frac{-N^l}{k} < -N^{l-1}.$$

By definition, $N > n \geq k$. Therefore, $\mathcal{C}_{rj} < -N^{\ell-1}$. This shows, first, that $\mathcal{C}_{rj} < 0$ and thus $\mathcal{A}_{rj} \neq 0$, and so j is in the preference list of row i; second, the ranking of j is below column 1. In other words, row i does not prefer j to any of the columns 1 to k. $\square$

Scarf himself gave a finite-time algorithm for finding a dominating extreme point, however, the problem of finding a dominating solution is PPAD complete. Thus, it has a worst-case complexity equivalent to that of computing a fixed point, but this is not a barrier to implementation. For example, building on [7], a course allocation scheme that relies on a fixed-point computation has been proposed and implemented at the Wharton School.

Example 15.5. Continuing with Example 15.3, we see by the Birkhoff–von Neumann theorem that every non-negative extreme point of the system $\mathcal{A}x \leq \mathbf{1}$ is integral. Therefore, it follows by Scarf's lemma that a stable matching exists. The same theorem shows that the conclusion generalizes to more than two single doctors and more than two unit-capacity hospitals.

We draw the reader's attention to three features of Scarf's lemma. First, it does not distinguish between two-sided versus multilateral settings. Any family of feasible coalitions of agents that can be expressed using linear inequalities with non-negative coefficients is acceptable. Second, the notion of domination adjusts to the set of coalitions encoded in the columns of the $\mathcal{A}$. In this way, one encodes *multilateral* stability and not just pairwise stability (see Chapter 14). Third, it assumes that preferences can be represented as a strict ordering over coalitions. Allowing for indifference simply raises familiar issues about what constitutes a blocking coalition. Must every member be strictly better off or does it suffice for no one to be worse off and at least one member to be strictly better off (see [43])? The simplest resolution is to allow for indifferences. To see this suppose that in Definition 15.2, column j is such that $x_j = 0$. Then, the corresponding row i may be indifferent between column j and all columns k such that $A_k x_k > 0$. It would be natural in this case to call x a weakly dominating solution. This is the definition used in Section 15.4.2. One can also handle indifferences via a lexicographic tie-breaking rule. That is, if a row is indifferent between two columns, then it breaks ties using the preferences of another row. See Section 15.3.1 for an example.

In many matching settings, it is more common to represent the preferences of at least one side via choice functions rather than a preference ordering. Section 15.3.1 gives one example of how this can be handled by Scarf's lemma. Section 15.4.2 gives another.

In the subsequent sections, we discuss applications of Scarf's lemma to matching settings with complementarities. We begin with the problem of matching with couples. It is the simplest and most well-known instance of preference complementarity in two-sided matching. It will illustrate two things. First, how the lemma may be deployed even when the underlying preferences are not described by orderings. Second, how the lemma can be used even in a setting where a stable matching is not guaranteed to exist.

15.2.2 Rounding

There is no guarantee that a dominating solution will be integral. When a dominating solution is fractional, it is natural to "round" it into an integer solution while preserving domination. There is a price to be paid because the rounded solution may be infeasible. For the moment, set this aside. The following result shows that if we round the fractional dominating solution in the right way then domination is maintained.

Theorem 15.6. *Suppose that we are given a dominating solution x of $\{\mathcal{A}x \leq q, x \geq 0\}$. Let $\bar{x} \geq 0$ be an integral solution such that if $x_i = 0$ then $\bar{x}_i = 0$. Let $\bar{q} := \mathcal{A}\bar{x}$; then $\bar{x}$ is an integral dominating solution of $\{\mathcal{A}x \leq \bar{q}, x \geq 0\}$.*

In the applications discussed below, the system $\{\mathcal{A}x \leq q, x \geq 0\}$ can be expressed as the intersection of two systems of linear inequalities:

$$Ax \leq b, \tag{15.1}$$
$$Cx \leq d, \tag{15.2}$$
$$0 \leq x \leq e. \tag{15.3}$$

Here e is the vector containing all 1's.

The constraints in (15.1) are "hard" in that they cannot be violated. They correspond to the constraints of the unit-demand side. The constraints in (15.2) are "soft", i.e., we allow them to be violated but not by too much.

By adding slack variables, we can always assume that (15.1) and (15.2) hold at equality, i.e., $Ax = b$ and $Cx = d$. Given a fractional extreme-point solution, x^*, to (15.1)–(15.3) we can use the iterative rounding technique to round it into a 0–1 vector $\bar{x}$ such that $\{A\bar{x} = b, C\bar{x} = d+\delta d\}$, where $\|\delta d\|_\infty$ is bounded. Here $\|\cdot\|_\infty$ refers to the ℓ- infinity norm. The precise value of $\|\delta d\|_\infty$ will depend on the proportion of non-zero entries in the matrix C (its sparsity).[1]

We will describe one iteration of the technique. Let $\mathcal{Q} = \begin{bmatrix} A \\ C \end{bmatrix}$ and $q = \begin{bmatrix} b \\ d \end{bmatrix}$. Let J be the index set of the *non-integral* components of x^* and J^c its complement. The vector x^* restricted to these components is denoted x^*_J. Hence, every component of x^*_J is positive. The components corresponding to J^c are already integer-valued and so we leave these untouched. Our focus is on rounding up the components in J.

Denote by $\mathcal{Q}|_J$ the submatrix of $\mathcal{Q}$ consisting of the columns indexed by J. As x^* is an extreme point, the number of non-integral components of x^*, $|J|$, is equal to the maximum number of *linearly independent* rows of $\mathcal{Q}|_J$.

Now let A^*, C^* be the submatrices of A and C that correspond to the constraints that bind at x^*, i.e. $\mathcal{Q}|_J = \begin{bmatrix} A^* \\ C^* \end{bmatrix}$. Similarly define b^* and d^*. Hence, x^*_J satisfies

$$\mathcal{Q}|_J x^*_J = \begin{bmatrix} b^* \\ d^* \end{bmatrix} - \mathcal{Q}|_{J^c} x^*_{J^c} = q^*. \tag{15.4}$$

Notice that the components corresponding to J^c have been taken over to the right-hand side, which is consistent with the idea that we are leaving them untouched.

By the extreme-point property of x^*, the matrix $\mathcal{Q}|_J$ is invertible and so of full rank. Suppose we delete a row, say row i, from the matrix C. Call the reduced matrix $\mathcal{Q}|_J[-i]$ and denote the corresponding right-hand side by $q^*[-i]$. Notice that $\mathcal{Q}|_J[-i]x^*_J = q^*[-i]$. The null space of $\mathcal{Q}|_J[-i]$ is one-dimensional. Let $z \neq 0$ be a vector in the null space and consider $x^*_J + \epsilon z$ for some $\epsilon \neq 0$. Then, $\mathcal{Q}|_J[-i](x^*_J+\epsilon z) = q^*[-i]$. Hence, the vector z represents a direction in which we can move x^*_J so as to satisfy all constraints except the one that was removed.

For a suitable choice of ϵ we can ensure that $e \geq x^*_J + \epsilon z \geq 0$. In fact, by making $|\epsilon|$ sufficiently large we can maintain this property and ensure that $x^*_J + \epsilon z$ has at least one more integral component than x^*_J has. By executing these steps iteratively, we will arrive eventually at a vector with all integral components.

Now, $x^*_J + \epsilon z$ will violate exactly one constraint, the one corresponding to the ith row of C, which was deleted. If C_i denotes this row, the magnitude of this violation will scale with $C_i \epsilon z$, a quantity bounded by the number of non-zero entries in C_i. Hence, when choosing a row to delete, we look for one with a small number of non-zero entries. The existence of such a row will follow from the sparsity of C. A matrix possessing a small proportion of non-zero entries yet having a large number of non-zero entries in each row is clearly impossible.

---

[1] Statements of this kind can be viewed as a refinement of the Shapley–Folkman–Starr lemma [48].

15.3 Couples Matching

We describe a version of the problem that is studied, for example, in [42]. Let H be the set of hospitals, D^1 the set of single (unpaired) doctors, and D^2 the set of doctor couples. Each couple $c \in D^2$ is denoted by $c = (f, m)$. For each couple $c \in D^2$ we denote by f_c and m_c the first and second member of c. The set of all doctors D is given by $D^1 \cup \{m_c | c \in D^2\} \cup \{f_c | c \in D^2\}$.

Each single doctor $s \in D^1$ has a strict preference relation $\succ_s$ over $H \cup \{\emptyset\}$, where $\emptyset$ denotes the outside option for each doctor. Each couple $c \in D^2$ has a strict preference relation $\succ_c$ over $H \cup \{\emptyset\} \times H \cup \{\emptyset\}$, i.e., over pairs of hospitals including the outside option. The need for ordered pairs arises because couples will have preferences over which member is assigned to which hospital. While a couple consists of two agents they should be thought of as a single agent with preferences over ordered pairs of slots. This is the source of complementarities.

A hospital or an ordered pair of hospitals is acceptable to a single doctor or a couple if they are ranked above the outside option in the doctor's and couple's preferences, respectively.

Each hospital $h \in H$ has a fixed capacity $k_h > 0$. Unlike the doctors, a hospital's preferences are not characterized by an ordering over subsets of D but by a choice function $Ch_h(.): 2^D \to 2^D$. While a choice function can be associated with every strict preference ordering over subsets of D, the converse is not true. The information contained in a choice function is sufficient to recover only a partial order over the subsets of D.

Representing the preferences of one side using a choice function, while popular, is a *modeling choice*. Sometimes it is motivated by a desire to adapt the DA algorithm to a many-to-one setting. In other cases, it can be justified on the grounds that the relevant side is unable to articulate a preference ordering over all subsets but can provide a rule for selection instead. We will return to this matter later in the chapter.

We assume, as is standard in the literature, that $Ch_h(.)$ is responsive (see Chapter 3), which means that h has a strict priority ordering $\succ_h$ over the elements of $D \cup \{\emptyset\}$. If $\emptyset \succ_h d$, we say d is not acceptable to h. For any set $D^* \subset D$, hospital h's choice from that subset, $Ch_h(D^*)$, consists of the (up to) k_h highest-priority doctors among the acceptable doctors in D^*. Formally, $d \in Ch_h(D^*)$ if and only if $d \in D^*$; $d \succ_h \emptyset$ and there exists no set $D' \subset D^* \setminus \{d\}$ such that $|D'| = k_h$ and $d' \succ_h d$ for all $d' \in D'$. Notice that responsiveness rules out preference complementarity on the hospital side.

A matching μ is an assignment of every single doctor to a hospital or his or her outside option and an assignment of couples to at most two positions (in the same or different hospitals) or their outside option, such that the total number of doctors assigned to any hospital h does not exceed its capacity k_h. A matching satisfies individual rationality if all hospitals receive only acceptable doctors, and all doctors and couples are assigned to acceptable choices.

A matching μ can be "blocked" in three different ways: first, by a pair (d, h) such that $d \in D^1$ prefers h to $\mu(d)$ and h would select d possibly over a doctor currently assigned to it; second, by a couple $c \in D^2$ and a hospital h such that the couple prefers to be assigned to h over their current assignments and h would accept them, possibly over some of its current assignments; third, by a couple and two distinct hospitals. In this case, the couple would prefer to be assigned to the two hospitals (one to each) over their current assignment and each hospitals would accept a member of the couple over at least one of their current assignment. A matching μ is *stable with respect to a capacity vector k* if μ is individually rational and cannot be blocked in any of the three ways just described.

The example below, due to [30], shows that in the presence of couples a stable matching need not exist.

Example 15.7. Suppose there are two hospitals h_1 and h_2 and three doctors $\{d_1, d_2, d_3\}$. Doctors $\{d_1, d_2\}$ are a couple while d_3 is a single doctor. The capacity of each hospital is 1 and the priority ordering of h_1 is

$$d_1 \succ_{h_1} d_3 \succ_{h_1} \emptyset \succ_{h_1} d_2.$$

The priority ordering for hospital h_2 is

$$d_3 \succ_{h_2} d_2 \succ_{h_2} \emptyset \succ_{h_2} d_1.$$

The preference ordering of the couple is $(h_1, h_2) \succ_{(d_1,d_2)} \emptyset$, while that of doctor d_3 is $h_1 \succ h_2 \succ \emptyset$.

15.3.1 Choice Functions versus Orderings

Examples 15.1, 15.3 and 15.5 suggest how one might approach the couples matching problem. For each single doctor d and hospital h that are mutually acceptable, let $x_{(d,h)} = 1$ if d is assigned to h and 0 otherwise. Similarly, for each couple $c \in D^2$ and distinct $h, h' \in H$ such that (h, h') is acceptable to c and the first and second member of c are acceptable to h and h', respectively, let $x_{(c,h,h')} = 1$ if the first member of c is assigned to h and the second is assigned to h'. Let $x_{(c,h,h')} = 0$ otherwise.[2] Finally, for a couple c and a hospital h that are mutually acceptable, let $x_{(c,h,h)} = 1$ if both members of the couple are assigned to hospital $h \in H$ and 0 otherwise. Every 0–1 solution to the following system is a feasible matching and vice versa:

$$\sum_{d \in D^1} x_{(d,h)} + \sum_{c \in D^2} \sum_{h' \neq h} x_{(c,h,h')} + \sum_{c \in D^2} \sum_{h' \neq h} x_{(c,h',h)} + \sum_{c \in D^2} 2x_{(c,h,h)} \leq k_h \ \forall h \in H, \quad (15.5)$$

$$\sum_{h \in H} x_{(d,h)} \leq 1 \ \forall d \in D^1, \quad (15.6)$$

$$\sum_{h,h' \in H} x_{(c,h,h')} \leq 1 \ \forall c \in D^2, \quad (15.7)$$

Unfortunately, the extreme points of this system are not guaranteed to be integer–valued.

Let $\mathcal{A}$ be the matrix whose entries are the coefficients of the system (15.5)–(15.7). In (15.5)–(15.7), each agent (single doctor, couple, and hospital) is represented by a single row. Each column or variable corresponds to a coalition of agents (an assignment of a single doctor to a hospital or a couple to a pair of hospital slots that are mutually acceptable).

---

[2] Note that $x_{(c,h,h')}$ does not represent the same thing as $x_{(c,h',h)}$.

To apply Scarf's lemma we need each of the rows in (15.5)–(15.7) to have an ordering over the columns that is in the support of that row. For the rows associated with a single doctor and a couple, we can use their preference ordering over the hospitals (or pairs of hospitals in the case of couples).

For the rows associated with hospitals, this will depend on how the preferences of hospitals are modeled. If they are characterized by an ordering over subsets of doctors then its induces an ordering over the columns associated with coalitions involving either a single doctor or a couple and the hospital h. Notice that this ordering incorporates preference complementarity on the hospital side. If we are content to model hospital preferences in this way, we can immediately invoke Scarf's lemma to deduce the existence of a *fractional* stable matching.

However, as noted earlier, hospital preferences are more commonly encoded using responsive choice functions rather than preference orderings. We will outline how to use each hospital's choice function to induce an ordering over the columns associated with coalitions involving either a single doctor or a couple and that hospital. Formally, we use hospital h's priority ordering, $\succ_h$, to generate an *artificial* ordering $\succ_h^*$ over single doctors and couples with the property that domination with respect $\succ_h^*$ corresponds to stability with respect to the underlying choice function.

Hospital h will order these columns on the basis of its ranking of the corresponding doctors assigned to h. If the column corresponds to an assignment of both members of a couple to h then h's ranking of this column depends on the ranking of the "worse" member of the couple, as determined by $\succ_h$. Under this ordering, there can be ties between columns that correspond to the different ways in which a couple is assigned. For example suppose that one member is assigned to h, while the other is assigned elsewhere. To break the ties between these columns, h uses the preference ordering of the couple. We denote by $\succ_h^*$ this new ordering. We illustrate the construction of $\succ_h^*$ in the following example.

Example 15.8. There are two hospitals h, h', one couple $c = (d_1, d_2)$, and a single doctor, d_3. Hospital h's priority ordering is $d_1 \succ_h d_3 \succ_h d_2$. We use to $\succ_h$ to induce an ordering $\succ_h^*$ over $x_{(c,h,h')}$, $x_{(c,h',h)}$, $x_{(c,h,h)}$, and $x_{(d_3,h)}$. In $x_{(c,h,h')}$, d_1 is assigned to h; in $x(c, h', h)$, d_2 is assigned to h; in $x_{(d_3,h)}$, d_3 is assigned to h; and in $x_{(c,h,h)}$ both d_1 and d_2 are assigned to h. In the induced ordering, hospital h will rank $x_{(c,h,h)}$ on the basis of the member of c who is lower in h's priority order, which is d_2. Thus, $x_{(c,h,h')} \succ_h^* x_{(d_3,h)} \succ_h^* x_{(c,h',h)} \sim x_{(c,h,h)}$. The tie between $x_{(c,h',h)}$ and $x_{(c,h,h)}$ has been broken using the preference ordering of c. Namely, $x_{(c,h',h)} \succ_h^* x_{(c,h,h)}$ if and only if $x_{(c,h,h')} \succ_c x_{(c,h,h)}$.

15.3.2 Soft Capacity Constraints

If a stable matching does not exist and we are not prepared to yield on stability, something else must be sacrificed. [36] propose relaxing the hospital capacity constraints. While not a universal panacea, there are settings where capacity constraints are "soft"; see, for example, [10].

How does the softness of the hospital capacity constraints help? Scarf's lemma gives us a fractional dominating solution to the system (15.5)–(15.7). We then apply the iterative rounding procedure to obtain an integer dominating solution. The rounded solution will violate (15.5) only. For this to be useful the amount by which the constraints (15.5) are violated should be modest. Informally, for any instance of the stable matching problem with couples, find a stable matching with respect to a "nearby" instance, which is obtained by altering the initial capacities of the hospitals. The next result shows this to be possible. Subsequently, we outline why such a result is possible.

A matching with respect to a capacity vector k is a 0–1 solution to (15.5)–(15.7). It is stable with respect to a capacity vector k if it is dominating.

Theorem 15.9. *For any capacity vector k, there is a capacity vector k^* and a stable matching with respect to k^*, such that $\max_{h \in H} |k_h - k_h^*| \leq 2$. Furthermore, $\sum_{h \in H} k_h \leq \sum_{h \in H} k_h^* \leq \sum_{h \in H} k_h + 4$.*

Theorem 15.9 shows that by judiciously *redistributing* capacities between hospitals only a small injection of additional capacity occurs needed to ensure the existence of a stable matching.

If one imposes restrictions on a couple's preferences one can improve these bounds. One such restriction occurs when couples prefer to be together, rather than apart, and a hospital must accept either both members of the couple or none. In [14] a real-world instance was reported where such a restriction was imposed by the designer. While this restriction relaxes the problem because each blocking coalition involves only the preferences of a single hospital, a stable matching is still not guaranteed to exist. One might expect that under the above restriction some modification of the DA algorithm could be useful. Indeed, in [11] the DA algorithm was adapted to this instance. It yields the first bound in Theorem 15.9, i.e., $\max_{h \in H} |k_h - k_h^*| \leq 2$. However, it can give no bound to the aggregate increase in capacity. In contrast, the technique outlined here improves the bound on individual hospitals to $\max_{h \in H} |k_h - k_h^*| \leq 1$, while preserving the bound on the aggregate increase in capacity.

15.4 Complementarity via Constraints

When preference complementarity is present on the hospital side, it is convenient to incorporate this via distributional constraints on the set of feasible matchings. In residency matching, the planner may wish to limit the number of residents assigned to a particular geographical *region*. In the context of school admissions, the planner wishes to ensure some level of representation of disadvantaged groups within each school. The introduction of additional constraints necessitates revisiting the definition of stability. Specifically, is a blocking coalition allowed to violate the additional constraints?

15.4.1 Regional Capacity Constraints

We examine a stable matching problem with regional capacity constraints proposed in [26]. It involves single doctors only and hospitals that are assigned to one or more sets called "regions." Let $R^1, R^2, \ldots, R^t$ be the set of regions. Interpreted literally, regions would correspond to sets that partition the set of hospitals, but we do not insist on such a restriction. In addition to the capacity constraint of each hospital, each region R^s has a cap K_s on the number of residents that can be assigned to it, which may be less than the total capacity of all the hospitals within it.

Using the same notation as before we can describe the set of feasible matchings as the 0–1 solutions of the following:

$$\sum_{d \in D^1} x_{(d,h)} \leq k_h \; \forall h \in H, \tag{15.8}$$

$$\sum_{h \in H} x_{(d,h)} \leq 1 \; \forall d \in D^1, \tag{15.9}$$

$$\sum_{h \in R^s} \sum_{d \in D^1} x_{(d,h)} \leq K_s \; \forall s = 1, \ldots, t. \tag{15.10}$$

As before, each single doctor has a strict preference ordering over the hospitals in H. Each hospital has responsive preferences. As there are no couples we can interpret hospital h's priority ordering $\succ_h$ as a preference ordering over the doctors in D^1.

In [33] the issue of stability was dealt with by endowing each region with a preference ordering over single doctors. This was essential to make the problem well defined. To see why, suppose two hospitals in the same region each have capacity 1. The regional capacity constraint is 1 as well. Hence, at most one of these hospitals can be matched to a doctor. Suppose two doctors have a preference for being matched to the hospitals in this region. One doctor prefers the first hospital and the other the second. Each hospital's preference ordering alone cannot determine which one of these doctors will be matched to the region. Thus, there is a need for a regional ordering over doctors. Hence, each constraint of (15.8)–(15.10) has an ordering over the columns or variables that "intersect" it. In this way all the conditions needed to invoke Scarf's lemma are present.[3]

If the collection of regions forms a laminar family, then for any pair R^s and R^p either one is contained in the other or they are disjoint. A standard result (e.g. [16]) says that if the regions form a laminar family then every extreme point of (15.8)–(15.10) is integral. Hence, this system admits an integral dominating solution, i.e., a pairwise stable matching exists. In [33] and [20] the same result was derived using the DA algorithm. However, if one drops the laminarity restriction on the regions, the DA algorithm fails. As will be shown next, Scarf's lemma can still be deployed and generate a matching that satisfies the stronger condition of group stability.

15.4.2 Multiple-Dimensional Knapsack Constraints

In this section only, we depart from the doctor–hospital metaphor, as it will not bear the strain of the variations we now consider. The setting is that of assigning families who happen to be refugees to localities within their country of refuge (see [13, 38]). It will generalize the problem of couples matching in two ways. First, on one side is a set F of families of varying sizes. Couples matching corresponds to families of size at most 2. The hospital side corresponds to localities. However, unlike hospitals, the preferences of the localities cannot simply be described by a responsive

---

[3] In [26], hospitals have choice functions rather than preference orderings. See Section 15.3.1 for a discussion of how one can adapt Scarf's lemma to the case of choice functions.

choice function because families consume *multiple* resources, not just space, and do so at different intensities. For example, the educational resources consumed will depend on the number of school-age children. The senior care resources consumed will depend upon the number of elderly. Each locality is also interested in the likelihood of family members finding employment. This setting will also be used to show how one can ensure group stability rather than just pairwise stability.

Let L be the set of localities l and for each $\ell \in L$ and family $f \in F$ let $v_{1,f}$ be a cardinal value $v_{\ell,f}$ that increases with the probability of member of f finding employment in ℓ.

For each $f \in F$, let a_f^1, a_f^2, a_f^3 be the number of children, adults, and elderly in the family f. For each $l \in L$ let $c_\ell^1, c_\ell^2, c_\ell^3$ be the limits on the number of children, adults, and elderly that locality ℓ can absorb.

Given a subset of families K, denote by $ch_\ell(K)$ the choice function (the correspondence) of locality ℓ. Locality ℓ will select a subset of families in K that satisfies its capacity constraints on children, adults, and the elderly and maximizes the sum of the chosen $v_{\ell,f}$. If we set $z_{\ell f} = 1$ when family f is selected by locality ℓ and zero otherwise, $ch_\ell(K)$ can be expressed as a solution of the following integer program:

$$\max \sum_{f \in K} v_{\ell f} z_{\ell f} \tag{15.11}$$

$$\text{s.t.} \sum_{f \in K} a_f^s z_{\ell f} \leq c_\ell^s, \text{ for } s \in \{1, 2, 3\}, \tag{15.12}$$

$$z_{\ell f} \in \{0, 1\}. \tag{15.13}$$

Now, $ch_\ell(K)$ does not satisfy the substitutes property. In fact, the preferences here can exhibit both substitutes and complementarity. A pairwise stable matching need not exist and even if it did, it need not be Pareto optimal; see [38] for an example.

If one follows the approach taken thus far, each column of the matrix $\mathcal{A}$ corresponds to a family and location pair. Therefore, domination would only capture pairwise stability. To capture group stability, we need the columns to correspond to all potential blocking coalitions. The resulting $\mathcal{A}$ matrix is dense, which means that the rounding step cannot guarantee small violations of the soft capacity constraints.

In [38] this problem was overcome by introducing contracts that specified both a family–locality match as well as a "price" for each of the scarce resources that are consumed by the family at that locality. A *contract* between family f and locality ℓ is represented by a variable $x_{f,\ell,p} \in [0, 1]$, where p is a three-dimensional price vector specifying one price $p_{f,\ell}^s$ for each constraint or resource s at ℓ. Interpret $v_{f,\ell}$ as the total value of the match between family f and locality ℓ. The prices must be chosen so as to apportion the value between the family and the locality by the resources consumed, i.e.,

$$\sum_{s=1}^3 a_{f,\ell}^s \times p_{f,\ell}^s \leq v_{f,\ell}. \tag{15.14}$$

Let $P_{f,\ell}$ be the set of all feasible price vectors p satisfying equation (15.14).

The following infinite-dimensional linear system describes the set of all feasible fractional matchings:

$$\sum_{\ell \in L} \sum_{p \in P_{f,\ell}} x_{f,\ell,p} \leq 1 \qquad \text{for every family } f, \tag{15.15}$$

$$\sum_{f \in F} \sum_{p \in P_{f,\ell}} \frac{a_{f,\ell}^s}{c_\ell^s} \times x_{f,\ell,p} \leq 1 \qquad \text{for every locality } \ell \text{ and } s \in \{1, 2, 3\}. \tag{15.16}$$

If we discretize the sets $P_{f,\ell}$, this will ensure that the system (15.15), (15.16) is finite-dimensional. In fact, in [38] it is shown that there is a sufficiently small but positive discretization such that a dominating solution with respect to the discretized system is dominating with respect to the original system.

It remains to specify the ordering of each row over the columns that are in the support of that row.

- *Consider the constraint (15.15). Its associated ordering is based on the preference list $\succ_f$ of family f over localities. The row corresponding to a family f is indifferent between any two columns $x_{f,\ell,p}$ and $x_{f,\ell,p'}$ for any $p \neq p'$.*
- *Consider the constraint (15.16), which corresponds to the locality–service pair (ℓ, s). The corresponding ordering is based on the decreasing order of the price $p_{f,\ell}^s$. Therefore, the (ℓ, s)-row prefers $x_{f,\ell,p}$ to $x_{f',\ell,p'}$ if $p_{f,\ell}^s > p_{f',\ell}^{\prime s}$. Hence, the column corresponding to the (ℓ, s)-row prefers the contract that "pays" a higher price for s. The (ℓ, s)-row is indifferent between the other columns.*

It is not obvious that these orderings capture any information about the preferences of localities, but in fact they do, as shown in [38]. The key is that the prices of the contracts in a dominating solution correspond to the dual variables associated with (15.16).

Let x^* be a dominating solution to the system (15.15), (15.16). For each pair (f, ℓ), there is at most one $p \in P_{f,\ell}$ such that $x_{f,\ell,p}^* > 0$. By setting

$$z_{f\ell}^* = \sum_{p \in P_{f,\ell}} x_{f,\ell,p}^*,$$

we obtain a fractional matching. Furthermore, for each locality ℓ, define the set of families K to be the families that are assigned with positive probability to a less desirable locality compared with ℓ. One can show that $z_{f\ell}^*$ is an optimal fractional solution to (15.11)–(15.13); this can be verified by using the price vector p for which $x_{f,\ell,p}^* > 0$ to generate dual variables that complement the chosen primal solution. This shows that $z_{f\ell}^*$ is a fractional (weakly) group–stable matching.

Using the iterative rounding technique discussed in Section 15.2.2, we can round the fractional group-stable matching z^* to an integer $\bar{z}$, which satisfies (15.15) and a relaxed (15.16), whose right-hand side is replaced by $1 + \Delta$ where $\Delta :=$ $\max_{f,\ell} \{\sum_{s=1}^3 a_{f,\ell}^s / c_\ell^s\}$. Thus, the rounding technique yields an integral matching $\bar{z}$ that corresponds to a group-stable matching with respect to new capacities $\bar{c}_\ell^s$, where $\bar{c}_\ell^s \leq (1 + \Delta)c_\ell^s$.

15.4.3 Proportionality Constraints

The application of Scarf's lemma requires a constraint matrix $\mathcal{A}$ that describes all feasible assignments of agents to coalitions and must be non-negative. When distributional concerns are expressed in terms of proportions, i.e., the fraction of students of a particular type must be within some specified percentage of all students, this condition is not met.

One can replace proportionality constraints with capacity constraints. Suppose, for example, the constraint states that at most 20% of the students in a 100-seat school can be of a particular type. Replace this with the requirement that at most 20 students in the school must be of the relevant type. This switch is not benign because it assumes that the school will be at full capacity. Whether this is true depends on student preferences and the algorithm used to assign them to schools. Hence, we insist on the proportionality constraints but we will treat them as being "soft", which is consistent with the way in which rules are written in some school choice settings. We now show how to describe the set of feasible matchings using linear inequalities.

As before, let D^1 be the set of single doctors. For each hospital h, let $D^h := \{d : d \succ_h \emptyset, h \succ_d \emptyset\}$ be the set of single doctors acceptable to h and who find h acceptable. Each D^h is partitioned into T_h sets: $D^h = D_1^h \cup D_2^h \cup \cdots \cup D_{T_h}^h$. A doctor $d \in D_t^h$ is said to be of type t for hospital h. No two hospitals need have the same partition. Thus, one hospital may choose to partition doctors by race and another by socioeconomic status.

The proportionality constraint is that at each hospital h, the proportion of doctors of type t, for each t, must be at least α_t^h of the total number of doctors assigned to hospital h. The set of feasible matchings corresponds to all feasible 0–1 solutions to the following:

$$\sum_{h \in H} x_{dh} \leq 1 \ \forall d \in D^1, \tag{15.17}$$

$$\sum_{d \in D^1} x_{dh} \leq k_h \ \forall h \in H, \tag{15.18}$$

$$\alpha_t^h \left[\sum_{d \in D^1} x_{dh} \right] - \sum_{d \in D_h^t} x_{dh} \leq 0 \ \forall t = 1, \ldots, t_h \ \forall h \in H. \tag{15.19}$$

Here $0 \leq \alpha_t^h \leq 1, \sum_t \alpha_t^h \leq 1$. Notice that setting all variables to zero is a feasible solution.

In the presence of (15.19), one needs to modify the usual notion of blocking to rule out blocking pairs that violate (15.19). One might define (h, d) to be a blocking pair if d prefers h to her current match and either (i) h can accept d without violating its capacity and proportionality constraints, or (ii) h can replace a lower-ranked doctor (according to $\succ_h$) with d so that h's capacity and proportionality constraints are not violated. This is a weak notion of stability that can lead to a matching that is "wasteful". The empty matching, for example, would be stable! Even if one excluded empty matchings as candidates for being considered stable, we would have a problem, as shown in the next example.

Example 15.10. Consider a single hospital h with capacity 100 and 100 doctors $d_1, \ldots, d_{100}$. All doctors strictly prefer to be matched to h than remain unmatched, while the priority order of the hospital is $d_1 \succ_h d_2 \succ_h \cdots \succ_h d_{100}$. The set of doctors is divided into two subgroups, $D_1^h = \{d_1, d_3, \ldots, d_{99}\}$ and $D_2^h = \{d_2, d_4, \ldots, d_{100}\}$. The proportionality constraint is that at least 50% of the doctors in each subgroup are accepted.

Under the naive stability definition above, the matching that assigns d_1, d_2 to h is stable because no *single* doctor can form a blocking coalition with h owing to the proportionality constraints. This matching is undesirable compared with the one that assigns all doctors to h.

To overcome the waste of 98 positions in Example 15.10, one must allow each hospital to accept subsets of doctors who demand this without violating the constraints. Therefore, stability in this context cannot be restricted just to pairwise stability. One must allow for "coalitional" blocks that contain multiple doctors. We refer the reader to [27, 37] for further details.

Once one settles on an appropriate definition of stability, the second difficulty is how to apply Scarf's lemma. Some of the coefficients in inequality (15.19) are negative. Thus a direct application of Scarf's lemma is impossible. However, in [37] a way around this was proposed. Denote the constraints (15.17), (15.18) by $\mathcal{A}x \leq b$. Denote (15.19) by $\mathcal{M}x \geq 0$. Now, $\{x \in \mathbb{R}_+^n | \mathcal{M}x \geq 0\}$ is a polyhedral cone and can be rewritten as $\{\mathcal{V}z | z \geq 0\}$, where $\mathcal{V}$ is a finite non-negative matrix. The columns of $\mathcal{V}$ correspond to the **generators** of the cone $\{x \in \mathbb{R}_+^n | \mathcal{M}x \geq 0\}$. The "trick" is to apply Scarf's lemma to $\mathcal{P}' = \{z \geq 0 : \mathcal{A}\mathcal{V}z \leq b\}$ and use rounding to yield an integer x^* that is stable and such that

$$\sum_{h \in H} x_{dh}^* \leq 1 \ \forall d \in D^1,$$

$$\sum_{d \in D^1} x_{dh}^* \leq k_h \ \forall h \in H,$$

$$\bar{\alpha}_t^h \left[\sum_{d \in D} x_{dh}^* \right] \leq \sum_{d \in D_h^t} x_{dh}^* \ \forall t \ h \in H,$$

where

$$|\alpha_t^h - \bar{\alpha}_t^h| \leq \frac{2}{\sum_{d \in D} x_{dh}^*}.$$

Notice that the violation of proportionality constraints at hospital h is bounded by

$$\frac{2}{\# \text{ assigned students at } h}.$$

If a hospital accepts more than 100 students, the matching violates the diversity constraints by at most 2%. However, the violation increases as the number of accepted students decreases, which can be interpreted as smaller schools having "softer" diversity constraints. What determines whether a school receives a small or large number of acceptable students are the student preferences. The set of "small" schools cannot be determined *a priori* from capacity information alone. A large-capacity school that is unpopular could end up with a student number that is well below its capacity. Thus, relaxing its proportionality constraints allows it to recruit more students.

15.5 Other Methods

In this section, we briefly discuss other methods for dealing with complementarities and externalities in matching.

15.5.1 Restricting Preferences

In the matching with couples problem, we can guarantee the existence of a stable matching by restricting the preferences of couples in such a way as to limit the degree of complementarity exhibited. In [30], for example, a restriction (called weakly responsive) was proposed based on interpreting a couple's preference ordering over ordered pairs as being a particular aggregation of the individual preferences of each member of the couple.

Under this restriction, It was shown in [30] that a stable matching exists via the DA algorithm. However, the DA algorithm must have access to the preference orderings of each member of the couple as well as the couple's ordering. Hence, whether one can use the DA algorithm in practice will depend on how couples are asked to communicate their preferences.

Other examples of restrictions are found in [8], [40], and [47]. As in [30], certain complementarities in preferences are ruled out. Interestingly, it was shown in [49] that under some of these preference restrictions, all dominating extreme points are integers. This is surprising given that not all the extreme points of (15.5)–(15.7) are integers.[4]

On the flip side, by allowing for "extreme" kinds of complementarities such as "all or nothing", one can guarantee the existence of stable matchings. See [41] for an example.

When the hospital side has distributional preferences, it is common to modify its choice function so as to favor various groups. If the modified choice function is specified in the right way, the DA algorithm (or some variant) will find a stable matching. However, there is no ex-post guarantee on the realized distribution.[5] Examples of this approach can be found in [17]. In lieu of an ex-post guarantee, some authors focus on priorities that will produce distributions that are closest to a target distribution; see [18] and [15].

15.5.2 Large Markets

In other settings (see [3]) it is well known that one can wash away the problems caused by complementarities by making the underlying economy large. The same is true in the matching context as well. See Chapter 16 for more details.

It is shown in [32] and [2], for example, that, in a setting where applicant preferences are drawn independently from a distribution, as the size of the market increases

---

[4] In the case of weakly responsive preferences, the algorithm for finding a dominating extreme point only requires access to the couple's ordering and not the individual ones.

[5] If one is not careful, there is also a "circularity" problem, in that stability is defined with respect to the modified choice function.

and the proportion of couples in the total number of applicants approaches 0 a stable matching exists and can be found with high probability using a modification of the DA algorithm. However, it was demonstrated in [2] that when the proportion of couples is positive, the probability that no stable matching exists is bounded away from 0 even when the market's size increases.

Beyond the large but finite setting is the continuum. In [22] a nice summary was provided of the measure-theoretic issues associated with defining both what constitutes a matching as well as stability with a continuum of agents on both sides. It was proposed in [22] that matchings be interpreted as joint distributions over the characteristics of the populations to be matched and a novel stability notion was introduced for pairwise matchings based on sampling. It was shown that stable matchings exist and, importantly, correspond precisely to the limits of stable matchings for finite-agent models.

Previous work has assumed a continuum of agents on one side only or that there are a finite number of distinct types of agents. This has the advantage of side-stepping some of the measure-theoretic issues present in [22] as well as providing an "interpretable" characterizations of stability. In [5], [4] and [9], for example, the existence was guaranteed of a stable matching and it was characterized in terms of thresholds, which are the analog of prices.

Even in these cases, Scarf's lemma may be useful. In [50], for example, a convexity condition for matching problems was introduced that via Scarf's lemma implies that the core is non-empty. It allows for arbitrary contracting networks, multilateral contracts, and complementary preferences. The condition is not related to preferences but to the space of feasible matchings. It requires that the set of feasible allocation is convex and that for each potential block, the set of unblocked allocations is also convex. This convexity condition is present in [4], which allowed the author to extend that paper to doctors having continuous preferences over a continuum of alternatives.

15.5.3 Relax the Stability Requirement

A third approach is to relax the stability requirement. In [35], for example, it was proposed that one should find a matching that admits the minimum number of blocking pairs. However, it was shown that this problem is also NP-hard and difficult to approximate. Even were this not the case, this relaxation of stability is problematic. Consider a stable matching with a single blocking coalition. It is possible that if this block were to form, it would trigger an entire chain of blocks that were not initially present. Others modify the notion of stability so that some modification of the DA algorithm will succeed. See for example, [31] and [14]. Depending on the context, these modifications may not capture the original spirit of the notion of stability.

15.6 Open Questions

An attractive feature of the DA algorithm is that it is strategy-proof for the proposing side but that is not a property enjoyed by all dominating solutions. A natural question is whether it is possible to identify a dominating solution in a strategy-proof way.

Just as the DA algorithm can be modified to find a stable matching that favors one side or the other, one may ask whether the same is true for dominating solutions. In two-sided settings how does one find a dominating solution that favors one side over the other?

Finally, it would be interesting to identify other instances where determining a dominating solution can be executed in polynomial time.

15.7 Bibliographic Notes

The stable matching problem was introduced in [21]. Examples of extensions of [21] can be found in [19], [23], [24], and [39].

Complementarities and side constraints are studied in many applications of matching markets. For examples of complementarities in school choice see [12] and [10]. [1], [25], and [6] deal with proportionality constraints by converting them into constraints on absolute numbers.

The Scarf quote that was paraphrased appears in [44]. The published version of Scarf's lemma is in [46]. The version of the lemma we state appears in [45]. A modernized version can be found in [29]. The proof given follows [45] with a simplification that avoids a double limit argument. The first finite-time algorithm for finding a dominating extreme point was given in [46]. The proof that the problem of finding a dominating extreme point is PPAD complete is in [28]. The iterative rounding technique is described in [34].

Acknowledgements

We thank two anonymous referees for their valuable suggestions.

References

[1] Abdulkadiroglŭ, A., and Sönmez, T. 2003. School choice: A mechanism design approach. *American Economic Review*, **93**(3), 729–747.

[2] Ashlagi, I., Braverman, M., and Hassidim, A. 2014. Stability in large matching markets with complementarities. *Operations Research*, **62**(4), 713–732.

[3] Aumann, R. J. 1964. Markets with a continuum of traders. *Econometrica*, **32**(1–2), 39–50.

[4] Azevedo, E., and Hatfield, J. W. 2015. Existence of equilibrium in large matching markets with complementarities.

[5] Azevedo, E. M., and Leshno, J. D. 2021. A supply and demand framework for two-sided matching markets. *Journal of Political Economy*, **124**(5), 1235–1268.

[6] Biró, P., Fleiner, T., Irving, R. W., and Manlove, D. F. 2010. The college admissions problem with lower and common quotas. *Theoretical Computer Science*, **411**(34), 3136–3153.

[7] Budish, E. 2011. The combinatorial assignment problem: Approximate competitive equilibrium from equal incomes. *Journal of Political Economy*, **119**(6), 1061–1103.

[8] Cantala, D. 2004. Matching markets: The particular case of couples. *Economics Bulletin*, **3**(45), 1–11.

[9] Che, Y.-K., Kim, J., and Kojima, F. 2015. Stable matching in large economies.

[10] Correa, J., Epstein, R., Escobar, J., Rios, I., Bahamondes, B., Bonet, C. et al. 2019. School choice in Chile. In *Proc. 2019 ACM Conference on Economics and Computation*, pp. 325–343.

[11] Dean, B. C., Goemans, M. X., and Immorlica, N. 2006. The unsplittable stable marriage problem. In: *Proc. 4th IFIP International Conference on Theoretical Computer Science, TCS 2006*, pp. 65–75. Springer.

[12] Delacrétaz, D. 2019. Stability in matching markets with sizes. Working Paper.

[13] Delacrétaz, D., Kominers, S. D., Teytelboym, A. 2019. Matching mechanisms for refugee resettlement. Technical Report Working Paper.

[14] Dur, U., Morrill, T., and Phan, W. 2018. Family ties: School assignment with siblings. Technical report, mimeo.

[15] Echenique, F., and Yenmez, M. B. 2015. How to control controlled school choice. *American Economic Review*, **105**(8), 2679–94.

[16] Edmonds, J., and Giles, R. 1997. A min-max relation for submodular functions on graphs. In: *Annals of Discrete Mathematics*, vol. 1, pp. 185–204. Elsevier.

[17] Ehlers, L., Hafalir, I. E., Yenmez, M. B., and Yildirim, M. A. 2014. School choice with controlled choice constraints: Hard bounds versus soft bounds. *Journal of Economic Theory*, **153**, 648–683.

[18] Erdil, A., and Kumano, T. 2012. Prioritizing diversity in school choice. Working Paper, Washington University.

[19] Fleiner, T. 2003. A fixed-point approach to stable matchings and some applications. *Mathematics of Operations Research*, **28**(1), 103–126.

[20] Fleiner, T., and Kamiyama, N. 20212. A matroid approach to stable matchings with lower quotas. In: *Proc. 23rd Annual ACM-SIAM Symposium on Discrete Algorithms*, pp. 135–142. SIAM.

[21] Gale, D., and Shapley, L. S. 1962. College admissions and the stability of marriage. *American Mathematical Monthly*, **69**(1), 9–15.

[22] Greinecker, M., and Kah, C. 2020. Pairwise stable matchings in large economies. https://onlinelibrary.wiley.com/doi/full/10.3982/ECTA16228.

[23] Hatfield, J. W., and Kojima, F. 2010. Substitutes and stability for matching with contracts. *Journal of Economic Theory*, **145**(5), 1704–1723.

[24] Hatfield, J. W., and Milgrom, P. R. 2005. Matching with contracts. *American Economic Review*, **95**(4), 913–935.

[25] Huang, C.-C. 2010. Classified stable matching. In: *Proc. 21st Annual ACM-SIAM Symposium on Discrete Algorithms*, pp. 1235–1253. Society for Industrial and Applied Mathematics.

[26] Kamada, Y., and Kojima, F. 2015. Efficient matching under distributional constraints: Theory and applications. *American Economic Review*, **105**(1),67–99.

[27] Kamada, Y., and Kojima, F. 2017. Stability concepts in matching under distributional constraints. *Journal of Economic theory*, **168**, 107–142.

[28] Kintali, S. 2008. Scarf is PPAD-complete. *CoRR*, abs/0812.1601.

[29] Király, T., and Pap, J. 2008. Kernels, stable matchings, and Scarf's lemma. Working Paper, Egerváry Research Group, TR-2008-13.

[30] Klaus, B., and Klijn, F. 2005. Stable matchings and preferences of couples. *Journal of Economic Theory*, **121**(1), 75–106.

[31] Klijn, F., and Masso, J. 2003. Weak stability and a bargaining set for the marriage model. *Games and Economic Behavior*, **42**, 91–100.

[32] Kojima, F., Pathak, P. A., and Roth, A. E. 2013. Matching with couples: Stability and incentives in large markets. *Quarterly Journal of Economics*, **128**(4), 1585–1632.

[33] Kojima, F., Tamura, A., and Yokoo, M. 2018. Designing matching mechanisms under constraints: An approach from discrete convex analysis. *Journal of Economic Theory*, **176**, 803–833.

[34] Lau, L. C., Ravi, R., and Singh, M. 2011. *Iterative Methods in Combinatorial Optimization*, vol. 46. Cambridge University Press.

[35] Manlove, D. F., McBride, I., and Trimble, J. 2017. "Almost-stable"matchings in the hospitals/residents problem with couples. *Constraints*, **22**(1), 50–72.

[36] Nguyen, T., and Vohra, R. 2018. Near-feasible stable matchings with couples. *American Economic Review*, **108**(11), 3154–69.

[37] Nguyen, T., and Vohra, R. 2019. Stable matching with proportionality constraints. *Operations Research*, **67**(6), 1503–1519.

[38] Nguyen, H., Nguyen, T., and Teytelboym, A. 2019. Stability in matching markets with complex constraints. In: *Proc. Conference on Economics and Computation*, p. 61.

[39] Ostrovsky, M. 2008. Stability in supply chain networks. *American Economic Review*, **98**(3), 897–923.

[40] Pycia, M. 2012. Stability and preference alignment in matching and coalition formation. *Econometrica*, **80**(1), 323–362.

[41] Rostek, M., and Yoder, N. 2020. Matching with complementary contracts. *Econometrica*, **88**(5), 1793–1827.

[42] Roth, A. E. 1984. The evolution of the labor market for medical interns and residents: A case study in game theory. *Journal of Political Economy*, **92**(6), pp. 991–1016.

[43] Roth, A. E., and Postlewaite, A. 1977. Weak versus strong domination in a market with indivisible goods. *Journal of Mathematical Economics*, **4**(2), 131–137.

[44] Scarf, H. 1994. The allocation of resources in the presence of indivisibilities. *Journal of Economic Perspectives*, **8**(4), 111–128.

[45] Scarf, H. E. 1965. An elementary proof of a theorem on the core of an *n* person game. Cowles Foundation Working Paper.

[46] Scarf, H. E. 1967. The core of an *n*-person game. *Econometrica*, **35**(1), pp. 50–69.

[47] Sethuraman, J., Teo, C.-P., and Qian, L. 2006. Many-to-one stable matching: Geometry and fairness. *Mathematics of Operations Research*, **31**(3), 581–596.

[48] Starr, R. M. 1969. Quasi-equilibria in markets with non-convex preferences. *Econometrica*, pages 25–38.

[49] Tang, D., Nguyen, T., Subramanian, V., and Vohra, R. 2018. Computational testing of scarf's algorithm for near feasible stable matching with couples. Technical Report, University of Michigan, Ann Arbor.

[50] Wu, X. 2018. Core of convex matching games: A Scarf's lemma approach. Working Paper, Columbia University, Department of Economics.

CHAPTER SIXTEEN

Large Matching Markets

Jacob D. Leshno

Large matching models allow for a simpler description of matching markets. In physics, models of a handful of molecules are complicated, but it is simple to characterize the behavior of a gas consisting of great numbers of molecules moving in all directions. Likewise, by considering continuum models or the limit of increasingly large markets we are able to tractably characterize the main features of the market and to abstract away from discreteness constraints or pathological situations.

The analytic tractability of large matching models allows us to ask a richer set of questions. To motivate the discussion, this chapter focuses on one such vein of questions: does the choice of the proposing side in the DA algorithm matter? If it does, how much does it matter? These questions pose a long-standing puzzle. In [17] it was shown that men receive their optimal matching in the men-proposing DA but their pessimal matching under the women-proposing DA. However, this theoretical result does little to inform us about the magnitude of the difference, and simple examples show that it is possible that the difference is very large and it is also possible that there is no difference at all. Given a real market, should we expect this difference to be large or small? In this chapter, we will show that large matching models can allow us to answer this practical question.

Further, to reap the benefits that large markets offer, we need to develop a language. A lay person may not find it natural to consider eating an infinitesimally larger apple. Indeed, most students are somewhat perplexed when they first learn about derivatives. On the other hand, a trained economist may be surprised that a grocer will not sell $\sqrt{2}$ apples, being so used to thinking of goods as infinitely divisible. By abstracting away from discreteness constraints, economists have gained a great deal of intuition, employing the tools of calculus to analyze problems and gaining important intuition in the form of marginal effects.

The models we review in this chapter develop a language that provides us with a strong set of tools to better understand matching markets. Models of random matching markets allow us to give the more nuanced and useful answer of what is likely to happen, ignoring possible but highly unlikely pathological cases. The analysis will allow us to quantify the magnitude of effects and find which market features are important to consider. Continuum matching markets allow us to use the tools of calculus and answer questions such as the following. How will the market respond to a change? Where should the planner direct investment in order to improve welfare?

In addition, these models also provide a foundation for the econometric tools that allow estimation of parameters that are necessary inputs to answer these questions.

The remainder of the chapter is organized as follows. Section 16.1 discusses models of one-to-one matching in which preferences are randomly drawn, focusing on using such models to understand the effect of the choice of proposing side in DA. Section 16.2 discusses a many-to-one model in which a continuum of students is matched to a finite number of schools. Either section can be read independently of the other.

16.1 Random Matching Markets and the Puzzle for the Proposing Side

When Roth and Peranson [33] were tasked with redesigning the National Resident Matching Program (NRMP), both students and hospitals lobbied to have their side propose. As we have proved in previous chapters, all men are weakly better off under the men-proposing DA (MPDA) than under any other stable matching. A simple example with two men and and two women illustrates this:

Example 16.1 (Two-by-two economy). Consider a market with two women w_1, w_2 and two men m_1, m_2 with preferences as follows:

$$m_1 : w_1 \succ w_2 \qquad\qquad w_1 : m_2 \succ m_1$$
$$m_2 : w_2 \succ w_1 \qquad\qquad w_2 : m_1 \succ m_2$$

Under MPDA both men are matched to their top choice, and under woman-proposing DA (WPDA) both men are matched to their bottom choice.

However, the choice of proposing side ended up being almost irrelevant in practice. Roth and Peranson simulated both the student and hospital-proposing algorithms on real past data and found that the choice of proposing side made very little difference. Although some students did benefit from having their side propose, less than one in a thousand medical students were affected. And even those who were affected mostly received a similarly ranked match.

This finding posed a theoretical challenge. While the theory correctly predicted that men did weakly benefit from having their side propose, it failed to inform us that the choice of proposing side is immaterial. In Example 16.1 choice of proposing side affects all agents, and determines whether an agent receives their top choice or least preferred choice. What explains this difference? Does this imply there is something special about the preferences submitted to the NRMP? What should we expect in other markets?

16.1.1 Saying the Market is "Large" is Not Enough

One conjecture (motivated by the title of this chapter) might be that the NRMP matches over 20,000 doctors every year, while Example 16.1 includes only two men and two women. What if we restrict attention to markets that have many agents?

Example 16.2 (Large market with opposite preferences). Consider a market with n women $\{w_1, \ldots, w_n\}$ and n men $\{m_1, \ldots, m_n\}$ with preferences

$$m_i \colon w_i \succ w_{i+1} \succ \cdots \succ w_n \succ w_1 \succ \cdots \succ w_{i-1}$$
$$w_i \colon m_i \prec m_{i+1} \prec \cdots \prec m_n \prec m_1 \prec \cdots \prec m_{i-1}$$

Under MPDA all men are matched to their top choice, and under WPDA all men are matched to their bottom choice.

Example 16.2 shows that the choice of proposing side can have a large effect in a market of any size. The following example goes further, showing that in the absence of some additional structure the number of agents in the market is, in a sense, irrelevant.

Example 16.3 (Island replication) Consider a market with $2n$ women $\{w_1^k, w_2^k\}_{k \leq n}$ and $2n$ men $\{m_1^k, m_2^k\}_{k \leq n}$ with preferences

$$m_1^k \colon w_1^k \succ w_2^k \succ \emptyset \qquad\qquad w_1^k \colon m_2^k \succ m_1^k \succ \emptyset$$
$$m_2^k \colon w_2^k \succ w_1^k \succ \emptyset \qquad\qquad w_2^k \colon m_1^k \succ m_2^k \succ \emptyset$$

This market is equivalent to n copies of the market from Example 16.1, as men m_1^k, m_2^k can only match to women w_1^k, w_2^k.

16.1.2 Random Matching Markets

From these examples and the NRMP simulations we learn that the choice of proposing side can matter considerably for some economies but makes little difference for others.

Therefore, our next step is to explore a range of economies. A natural starting point is to explore economies drawn uniformly at random.[1] A *random matching market* is composed of a set of men $\mathcal{M}$ and a set of women $\mathcal{W}$ in which preferences are generated by drawing a complete preference list for each man and each woman independently and uniformly at random. Thus, for each man m, we draw a complete ranking $\succ_m$ from a uniform distribution over the $|\mathcal{W}|!$ possible rankings.

We introduce two metrics to assess the benefit to the proposing side.

Definition 16.4. Given a matching μ, the *men's average rank of wives* is given by

$$R_{\text{MEN}}(\mu) = \frac{1}{|\mathcal{M} \setminus \bar{\mathcal{M}}|} \sum_{m \in \mathcal{M} \setminus \bar{\mathcal{M}}} \text{Rank}_m(\mu(m)),$$

where $\bar{\mathcal{M}}$ is the set of men who are unmatched under μ.[2]

---

[1] For tractability, the model assumes preferences are uncorrelated. We will allow arbitrary correlations in Section 16.2.

[2] $\bar{\mathcal{M}}$ does not depend on μ because an agent who is unmatched in some stable matching is unmatched in any stable matching.

Similarly, the *women's average rank of husbands* is given by

$$R_{\text{WOMEN}}(\mu) = \frac{1}{|\mathcal{W}\setminus\bar{\mathcal{W}}|} \sum_{w\in\mathcal{W}\setminus\bar{\mathcal{W}}} \text{Rank}_w(\mu(w)),$$

where $\bar{\mathcal{W}}$ is the set of women who are unmatched under μ.

The men-proposing DA (MPDA) produces the men optimal stable matching (MOSM), and the woman-proposing DA (WPDA) produces the women optimal stable matching (WOSM). Recall that these are the extreme points in the lattice of stable matchings. In particular, each man is matched to his most preferred spouse under the MOSM and to his least preferred spouse under the WOSM (out of all the women he is matched to in some stable matching). If a man is matched to the same woman under both the MOSM and WOSM then he has a unique stable partner. In [31] and [22] the MOSM and WOSM were characterized for a random matching market with $|\mathcal{W}| = |\mathcal{M}| = n$ as n grows large.

Theorem 16.5 [31]. *In a random matching market with n men and n women, the fraction of agents who have multiple stable partners converges to 1 as $n \to \infty$. Furthermore,*

$$\frac{R_{\text{MEN}}(\text{MOSM})}{\log n} \xrightarrow{p} 1,$$

$$\frac{R_{\text{MEN}}(\text{WOSM})}{n/\log n} \xrightarrow{p} 1.$$

In words, there is a substantial benefit to the proposing side in a typical random matching market with n men and n women. The benefits are widespread; most men strictly prefer their spouse in the MOSM over their spouse in the WOSM. The benefits are also large; under the MOSM a man is matched to his $\log(n)$th-most-preferred wife (on average), while under the WOSM a man is matched to his $(n/\log(n))$th-most-preferred wife (on average). For example, if we randomly draw a market with $n = 1,000$ man and women, then each man expects to be matched to his $\log(1000)$th $\approx$ 7th most-preferred wife under the MOSM, but to his $1000/\log(1000)$th $\approx$ 145th most-preferred wife under the WOSM. Since the core of the economy is the set of stable matchings, we can unequivocally say that the core is large.

While we may not necessarily be interested in the behavior of large random matching markets, it is useful to consider $n \to \infty$ for two reasons. First, it is much easier to prove and characterize the asymptotic behavior. Second, by taking limits we can gain an intuition for the "first-order effect" in the market, abstracting away from secondary issues. As a result, proofs can be more elegant and provide more intuition.

16.1.3 Random Matching Markets with Short Preference Lists

Theorem 16.5 poses a puzzle. In [33] had data for multiple years were used and a dramatically smaller effect in the NRMP data was observed. What makes the NRMP so different from random matching markets? It was conjectured in [33] that the difference was due to a different distribution of preference lists. Most students' preference lists included a few dozen hospitals at most, and omit the vast majority of hospitals.

A *random matching market with short preference lists* is composed of a set of men $\mathcal{M}$ and a set of women $\mathcal{W}$ in which women have arbitrary complete preference lists, and the preferences of each man are generated by drawing k women uniformly and independently. The size of the market is $n = |\mathcal{W}| = |\mathcal{M}|$. We consider the case where $k \ll n$, that is, markets where the number of participants is large relative to the length of randomly drawn preference lists.

Theorem 16.6 [20]. *In a random matching market with short preference lists with n men and n women, for any fixed length of preference list k the expected fraction of agents who have multiple stable partners converges to 0 as $n \to \infty$.*

In other words, large economies in which one side has constant-length randomly drawn preference lists have a small set of stable matchings, in the sense that most agents have the same partner under all stable matchings. This type of result is often referred to in the literature as a *core convergence* result.

Note that this result only holds for *randomly* drawn short preference lists. Example 16.3 illustrates a large economy with short preference list that has many stable matchings.

To prove the result, it is sufficient to determine the probability that a given man m_0 is matched to the same woman under the MOSM and the WOSM. While we can easily calculate both using DA with either side proposing, it is not *a priori* clear how we can tractably obtain the probability that both matchings assign m_0 to the same partner. Therefore, the proof leverages the structure of stable matchings, and it uses *rejection chains* and algorithm given in [29] to determine whether m_0 has multiple stable partners.

Consider the man m_0 in a randomly drawn market such that the MOSM μ matches m_0 to $\mu(m_0) = w_0 \in \mathcal{W}$. If there is another stable matching μ' such that $\mu'(m_0) = w' \neq w_0$ then the matching μ' remains stable even if we change the preferences of woman w_0 so that she finds m_0 unacceptable. This change will make woman w_0 reject man m_0 if he proposes to her in MPDA. Because the order in which the men propose in men-proposing DA does not affect the resulting match, we can first run MPDA until we reach the MOSM, and only then reject man m_0 and track the following steps of the algorithm.

The sequence of proposals following the rejection of m_0 by $\mu(m_0) = w_0$ is called a *rejection chain*. The algorithm continues with a proposal from man m_0 to his next most preferred potential wife. If m_0 proposed to a woman who is already matched to a more preferred husband, m_0's proposal will be rejected and m_0 will keep proposing. If m_0 proposed to a woman who prefers m_0 over her current match m_1, m_0's proposal will be temporarily accepted and m_1 will start proposing. This generates a chain of proposals, where at any time at most one man is making a proposal, and a new man starts proposing when displaced by the previous man.

The chain can terminate in one of three ways: (i) a proposing man has exhausted his preference list, (ii) a man proposed to an unmatched woman $w \neq w_0$ and the proposal was accepted, or (iii) a man proposed to woman w_0, who is unmatched after rejecting m_0, and the proposal was accepted. If (i) or (ii) happened, the algorithm will output a matching in which the set of agents that are matched is different from the set of agents matched under μ, and therefore the outputted matching cannot be stable under the original economy (since by the rural hospital theorem any stable matching leaves the same agents unmatched). It is a good exercise to show this implies that there are no stable matchings in which man m_0 is matched to a woman w such that $\mu(m_0) \succ m_0 w$. If (iii) happened, then the algorithm will output a matching μ' in which the set of agents that are matched is the same as the set of agents matched under μ, and it is also a good exercise to show that this is a new stable matching in which m_0 is matched to a different wife such that $\mu'(m_0) \prec_{m_0} \mu(m_0)$.

It remains to determine the probability that a rejection chain terminates in (iii), and not in (i) or (ii). To do so, we first calculate the expected number of women that are unmatched in any stable matching. Let X be the (random) number of women that do not appear in any man's preference list (i.e., all men find them unacceptable). Clearly, X is a lower bound for the number of unmatched women.

By the previous arguments, the probability that man m_0 has an additional stable partner is at most the probability that the rejection chain terminates with a proposal to woman w_0 (his original partner) and not with a proposal to an unmatched woman. By the principle of deferred decision, we can dynamically draw the men's preferences only as the algorithm asks the men to propose. The next proposal by a men will be drawn uniformly at random among all women to whom the man did not previously propose, and therefore is at least as likely to go to an unmatched woman (who was not previously proposed to) as it is to go to w_0. Thus, the probability that w_0 receives a proposal before all of the unmatched women is at most $1/(1 + X)$.

A probabilistic calculation (using a variant of the occupancy problem) shows that for any fixed length of preferences list k and market size n, we have that the expectation of this probability is

$$E\left[\frac{1}{1+X}\right] \leq \frac{e^{k+1} + k^2}{n}.$$

By the linearity of expectation, this bounds the expected fraction of men who have more than one possibility of a stable partner, completing the argument.

16.1.4 Unbalanced Random Matching Markets

While Theorem 16.6 provides us with an answer to the puzzle presented by the NRMP data, it leaves some open questions as well. The contrast with Theorem 16.5 shows that the assumption that in fact they are short is essential, and preference lists need to be so short (and random) that many agents remain unmatched. However, this does not correspond to the economies we see in the NRMP; preferences lists may be short, but agents choose a preference list that is likely to get them matched.

Another remaining challenge is giving a prediction for general markets that do not have the particular features of the model, namely markets that are not necessarily large or with short preference lists. Should we expect a substantial benefit to the proposing side in most matching markets?

As it turns out, in any documented matching market the benefit to the proposing side is negligible, and the choice of the proposing side in DA is immaterial. In other words, the data suggest that the small core documented in the NRMP is the typical case. If a matching market asks you to predict whether the choice of proposing side will make a difference, the empirical data suggest that this choice will have a negligible effect.

In [7] an explanation was provided for why general matching markets will have a small core. A key observation is that Theorem 16.5 considers markets in which the number of women is exactly equal to the number of men. To gain intuition, consider standard markets with payments. In standard markets an exact balance between buyers and sellers can generate a large core, but this is eliminated by any imbalance. For example, consider a market with 100 buyers with unit demand who are willing to pay 1 for an item, and 100 sellers each offering one unit of the item with reservation value of 0. The core of this market is large, and any price between 0 and 1 will generate a core allocation. In contrast, in a market with 100 buyers and 101 sellers there is a unique market clearing price equal to 0, because one seller must be unmatched and willing to sell for any positive price. This provides motivation to consider what happens in *unbalanced matching markets* in which there are different numbers of men and women (see Figure 16.1).

Theorem 16.7 [7]. *In a random matching market with n men and n + 1 women the fraction of agents who have multiple stable partners converges to 0 as n → ∞. Moreover, for any ε > 0 and sufficiently large n, in every stable matching μ we have*

$$R_{\text{MEN}}(\mu) \leq (1 + \varepsilon) \log n,$$

$$R_{\text{WOMEN}}(\mu) \geq \frac{n}{(1 + \varepsilon) \log n}.$$

In other words, even the slightest imbalance eliminates the benefit to proposing side and, while there may be multiple stable matchings, the choice of proposing side makes little difference. That is, balanced random matching markets (which have exactly the same number of men and women) are special and atypical (see also Theorem 16.12 below). This suggests that in practice we should see a small core in any matching market, as exactly balanced markets are unlikely.[3]

Theorem 16.7 also shows the benefit to the short side, regardless of the proposing side. If there are n men and n women, the proposing side receives their $\log(n)$th most preferred partner, and the other side receives their $n/\log(n)$th most preferred partner. If we add an additional woman to the market, men will be better off and the existing women will be worse off. Therefore, we should expect the men to receive their $\log(n)$th partner if the men propose and we add another woman. More surprising is that in an unbalanced market, men receive their $\log(n)$th most preferred partner in every stable matching. For example, in a market with 1000 men and 1001 women, a man is matched to his 7th-most-preferred partner (on average), and a woman is matched to her 145th-most-preferred partner in *any* stable matching.

When the imbalance is greater, the benefit to the shorter side is greater, and the choice of proposing side is insignificant.

---

[3] Balanced random matching markets impose a particular distribution of preferences and assume that agents find every possible partner acceptable. In practice, we might expect agents' preferences to be more highly correlated, and that some agents will generally be found unacceptable. Since both tend to shrink the set of stable matchings, we should expect a small core.

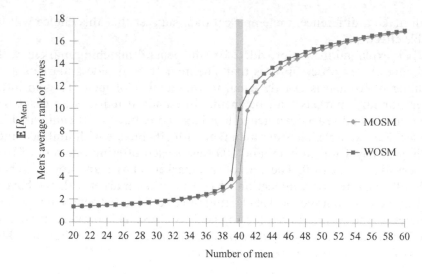

Figure 16.1 Average rank of men, for various numbers of men and $|\mathcal{W}| = 40$ women.

Theorem 16.8 [7]. *Fix $\lambda > 0$. In a random matching market with n men and $(1+\lambda)n$ women the fraction of agents who have multiple stable partners converges to 0 as $n \to \infty$. Moreover, for sufficiently large n, in every stable matching μ the men's average rank of wives is at most κ, and the women's average rank of husbands is at least $n/(1 + \kappa)$ where $\kappa = (1 + \lambda)\log(1 + 1/\lambda)$ is a constant that depends only on λ.*

In other words, substantial imbalance leads to an allocation that is very beneficial to the short side. For example, if $\lambda = 0.05$, that is, a market with 5% extra women, then men will be matched, on average, with roughly their 3rd-most-preferred woman. The women's average rank of husbands (even if women propose) is only a factor of $(1 + \kappa)/2 = 2.1$ better than if they are matched with a random man.

The proof of Theorems 16.7 and 16.8 again relies on an analysis of rejection chains. As in the proof of Theorem 16.6, it is sufficient to evaluate the result of MPDA and WPDA; MPDA is tractable, since each man proposes to a small number of women (roughly $\log(n)$), and the next woman to whom any man will propose is, approximately, drawn uniformly at random. But WPDA is not as tractable – since a woman makes many proposals, the next proposal of a woman substantially depends on the set of men to whom she has already proposed. Therefore, instead of evaluating WPDA we evaluate MPDA and analyze rejection chains to show that MPDA and WPDA will be very close.

The proof of Theorem 16.8 is similar to that of Theorem 16.6. Consider a man m_0 who is matched under MPDA to woman w_0. If there are n men and $(1+\lambda)n$ women, λn women will remain unmatched. Since there is a large fraction of unmatched women, the rejection chain that starts with w_0 rejecting m_0 is much more likely to reach one of the λn unmatched women than w_0.

The proof of Theorem 16.7 requires a more delicate analysis of rejection chains. If there are n men and $n+1$ women in the market, there will be only a single unmatched woman in the market, and a proposal is almost equally likely to go to w_0 as it is likely to go to an unmatched woman. To prove the result, we need to consider all rejection chains jointly. To do so tractably, the proof follows the calculation of the WOSM through a sequence of rejection chains and keeps tracks of the set of women S that have already obtained their WOSM partner. The key observation that simplifies the analysis is that if the run of a rejection chain includes a woman from S accepting a proposal, it must be that the rejection chain terminates without finding a new stable matching (that is, in (i) or (ii); see the discussion at the end of Section 16.1.3); otherwise the chain also finds a more preferred partner for a woman in S and we have a contradiction. Using this observation, the proof follows from two steps. First, S grows quickly because once we find a rejection chain that ends in an unmatched woman, all the women that were part of the chain must have been matched to their WOSM partner. Second, once S is large, it is likely that any proposal will reach a woman in S and we can terminate the chain knowing that it cannot lead to a new stable matching.

16.1.5 Small Random Markets

All the theorems we consider in this section are stated for $n \to \infty$, which greatly simplifies the proofs. Obtaining results for finite random markets is considerably more challenging, but simulations can help us evaluate when we should expect the asymptotic results to be relevant. Simulations of unbalanced markets show that the asymptotic characterization accurately describes markets even with 40 agents (see Figure 16.1).

16.2 Continuum Matching Markets

The previous section used a sequence of increasingly large matching markets. A natural question is whether we can directly capture the limit object, as this limit object may allow us to simplify the analysis. As it turns out, the answer is positive for a different class of matching problems: many-to-one matching markets where one side is large.[4] For example, colleges and schools match to a large number of students. The continuum formulation gives a tractable characterization of stable matchings in the form of cutoffs, an admission threshold for each college. This means that we can describe stable matchings by a low-dimensional object, and find stable matchings by solving simple demand equations.

16.2.1 Formal Model

Consider a matching market where there is a finite set of colleges and each college can match with a large number of students. We start by describing the limit economy in which each college is matched with a continuum of students (as introduced in [10]). The description of such an economy needs to capture (i) the preferences

---

[4] One can also define a limit economy for large one-to-one economies in which the number of agents on both sides grows large, but in such a limit markets each agent has a preference over the infinite agents on the other side of the the the market (see Section 16.4.2).

of colleges over students and their capacity limits, and (ii) the preferences of students over colleges. The standard approach to describe (i) is to assume responsive preferences [32] and represent the college's preferences by a preference ordering over all students and a capacity. Because the set of students is infinite, we instead represent the preferences of a college by assigning a *score* to each student, where a student with a higher score is more preferred by the college. This allows us to describe how colleges rank a given student by a vector of scores, one score for each college.

Formally, a continuum matching market is described as follows. There is a finite set of colleges $\mathcal{C} = \{1, \ldots, C\}$ that is to be matched to a continuum of students. A student is described by type $i = (\succ^i, r^i)$. Student i's preferences over colleges are given by $\succ^i$. The vector $r^i \in [0, 1]^{\mathcal{C}}$ describes the colleges' preferences over student i, where college c prefers student i over student j if $r^i_c > r^j_c$. We refer to r^i_c as the rank or the score of student i at college c. Given that scores represent ordinal information, we can rescale the scores so that a student i's score at college c is the percentile of i in c's ranking over students.[5] We use $\Theta = \mathcal{L}(\mathcal{C}) \times [0, 1]^{\mathcal{C}}$ to denote the set of all possible student types, where $\mathcal{L}(\mathcal{C})$ is the set of all strict orderings over $\mathcal{C}$. Note that different colleges can have different rankings over students. To simplify the notation, we assume in this chapter that all students and colleges are acceptable.[6]

A continuum market is given by $E = [\mathcal{C}, \eta, q]$ where η is a measure over the set of students Θ and $q = (q_1, \ldots, q_C)$ is the capacity of each college. We can use this representation to describe a standard discrete many-to-one matching market with a finite number of students by taking η to be a measure with finitely many equally sized atoms, with each atom corresponding to a single discrete student. While we will later consider discrete economies, this representation is particularly useful in allowing us to think of economies in which each student is infinitesimal.

Assumption 16.9. *Students and colleges have strict preferences. That is, every college's indifference curves are of η-measure 0. Thus, for any $x \in [0, 1]$ we have that* $\eta\left(\{j \in \Theta : r^j_c = x\}\right) = 0.$

Assumption 16.9 ensures that $\eta(i) = 0$ for any $i \in \Theta$. The following example illustrates a continuum economy for school choice.

Example 16.10 (The line city). Consider a matching market consisting of two schools $\mathcal{C} = \{1, 2\}$ with capacities q_1, q_2. Students live on the segment $[0, 1]$ connecting school 1 and school 2, and are uniformly distributed on this line. A student in location $x \in [0, 1]$ prefers school 1 over school 2 with probability $pr(x) = 1 - x$ and prefers school 2 with probability $1 - pr(x) = x$. Both schools give higher priority to students who live closer to the school. That is, the score of a student in location x is $(1 - x, x)$.

---

[5] That is, without loss of generality we can take $r^i_c = \eta\left(\{j \in \Theta : r^i_c > r^j_c\}\right) / \eta(\Theta)$.

[6] This is without loss of generality, as we can introduce an additional college and additional student to represent being unassigned. (Recall that being unassigned is equivalent to matching with a partner that is always willing to form a blocking pair).

This economy is captured by $\mathcal{C} = \{1, 2\}$ and the measure η given by

$$\eta\left(\{i : 2 \succ^i 1, r_2^i \in [a, b], r_1^i = 1 - r_2^i\}\right) = \int_a^b (1 - pr(x))dx$$
$$= \frac{b^2 - a^2}{2}$$

for $a < b \in [0, 1]$ and $\eta\left(\{i : 1 - r_1^i \neq r_2^i\}\right) = 0$.

As the example shows, a continuum market allows arbitrary correlations between the preferences of students over colleges and the preferences of colleges over students. This model can also describe markets in which college priorities are distributed independently of student preferences (e.g., for school choice [1]) as a particularly tractable case.

A matching for a continuum economy is given by a mapping $\mu : \Theta \to \mathcal{C} \cup \{\emptyset\}$. Each student i is assigned to a college $\mu(i)$, with $\mu(i) = \emptyset$ denoting that the student is unassigned. With slight abuse of notation we write $\mu(c)$ for the set $\mu^{-1}(c)$ of students assigned to c. To avoid measure-theoretic issues, we also require that for each $c \in \mathcal{C} \cup \{\emptyset\}$ we have that the set $\mu(c)$ is measurable and that the set $\{i : \mu(i) \prec^i c\}$ is open.

As in the discrete model, a student–college pair (i, c) blocks a matching μ if they can both benefit from matching to each other. A formal definition for the continuum setting is that (i, c) blocks the matching μ if $c \succ^i \mu(i)$ and either (i) c did not fill its capacity, that is, $\eta(\mu(c)) < q_c$, or (ii) there exists $j \in \mu(c)$ such that $r_c^i > r_c^{j}$.[7] A matching μ is stable if it is not blocked by any student college pair and $\eta(\mu(c)) \leq q_c$ for all $c \in \mathcal{C}$.

16.2.2 Cutoffs and Demand

To obtain a tractable representation of stable matchings, we introduce some additional notation. A cutoff for college c is a minimal score $p_c \in [0, 1]$ required for admission to c. Given a vector of cutoffs $p = (p_c)_{c \in \mathcal{C}}$, we define the budget set of student i to be the set of colleges to which student i can be admitted, denoted by $B^i(p) = \{c \in \mathcal{C} : r_c^i \geq p_c\}$. The demand of student i given cutoffs p is i's most preferred college from his budget set,

$$D^i(p) = \max_{\succ^i} B^i(p)$$

where $D^i(p) = \emptyset$ if $B^i(p) = \emptyset$. Finally, the aggregate demand for college c given cutoffs p is given by

$$D_c(p|\eta) = \eta\left(\{i : D^i(p) = c\}\right).$$

We write $D_c(p)$ when η is clear from the context, and denote the overall demand by $D(p) = (D_c(p))_{c \in \mathcal{C}}$.

Consider a decentralized admission mechanism which posts cutoffs p and assigns each student to their most preferred college out of their budget set, that is, $\mu(i) =$

---

[7] Because we are working with a continuous mass of students, a college can technically always match to an additional infinitesimal student. However, a model that allows a college always to admit an additional student would not match the real markets that we are interested in analyzing. Using a strict inequality in the definition makes capacity constraints in the continuum model match the applications in which we are interested.

$D^i(p)$. The resulting matching μ will be envy-free; if student i prefers college c over her assigned college $\mu(i)$ it must be that $c \notin B^i(p)$, and therefore for any student $j \in \mu(c)$ we have that $r_c^j \geq p_c > r_c^i$. The resulting matching may not be stable because a college c can be assigned more students than its capacity, or because a college is assigned strictly fewer students than its capacity and some other students would like to be assigned to that college.

We say that the cutoffs p are market clearing cutoffs if for all $c \in C$ we have that $D(p) \leq q$, and if $D_c(p) < q_c$ then $p_c = 0$. That is, no college is assigned more students than its capacity, and a college that does not fill its capacity has a cutoff equal to 0.[8]

By the previous arguments, market clearing cutoffs p induce a stable matching given by $\mu(i) = D^i(p)$. The following lemma from [10] shows the reverse is also true; stable matchings are equivalent to market clearing cutoffs.

Lemma 16.11. *Stable matchings are equivalent to market clearing cutoffs. That is, every stable matching μ corresponds to market clearing cutoffs p defined by $p_c = \inf\{r_c^i : i \in \mu(c)\}$. Every market clearing cutoff p corresponds to a stable matching μ defined by $\mu(i) = D^i(p)$.*

The correspondence also preserves the lattice structure. If p, p' are both market clearing cutoffs, we can define cutoffs $p^+ = \max(p, p')$ and $p^- = \min(p, p')$ (the min and max are taken coordinate by coordinate). The cutoffs p^+, p^- are also market clearing cutoffs. Moreover, if μ, μ' are the stable matchings corresponding to p, p' then p^+ corresponds to $\mu \wedge \mu'$, which matches each student i to $\min_{\succ i}\{\mu(i), \mu'(i)\}$, and p^- corresponds to $\mu \vee \mu'$, which matches each student i to $\max_{\succ i}\{\mu(i), \mu'(i)\}$.

The equivalence of stable matchings and market clearing cutoffs is more general, and there are many related characterizations in the literature (e.g., [11], [4], [1], [16]). It is particularly useful in continuum economies where the cutoff characterization offers a tractable way to solve for stable matchings.

16.2.3 Calculating a Stable Matching

Let us revisit the market from Example 16.10. Consider cutoffs p_1, p_2. College 1 is in the budget set of a student if $r_1^i \geq p_1$; this corresponds to the students whose location is $x \in [0, 1 - p_1]$. College 2 is in the budget set of students whose location is $x \in [p_2, 1]$. A student remains unassigned if her location is in $[1 - p_1, p_2]$ and her budget set is empty. If $q_1 + q_2 < 1$ then some students must remain unassigned; therefore $1 - p_1 < p_2$, all students are assigned to the single college in their budget set, and $1 - p_1 = q_1, 1 - p_2 = q_2$. If $q_1 + q_2 \geq 1$, all students can be assigned and we have that $1 - p_1 \geq p_2$. In this case, the demand for college 1 is from all the students whose location is in $[0, p_2]$ (who have the budget set $\{1\}$) plus the students whose location is in $[p_2, 1 - p_1]$ (who have the budget set $\{1, 2\}$) who prefer college 1:

$$D_1(p) = p_2 + \int_{p_2}^{1-p_1} pr(x)dx = \frac{1 - p_1^2 + p_2^2}{2}.$$

Likewise, the demand for college 2 is $D_2(p) = (1 + p_1^2 - p_2^2)/2$.

---

[8] If $\sum_c q_c < \eta(\Theta)$, that is, there are more students than college seats, then it is sufficient to require that $D(p) = q$. This is because in such a case it is impossible to have market clearing cutoffs such that $D_c(p) < q_c$ for some c.

Suppose $q_1 + q_2 > 1$, and that, without loss of generality, $q_1 > 1/2$. Because it is impossible for both colleges to fill their capacity, one of the cutoffs must be equal to 0, and it is easy to verify that it must be p_1 that equals 0. If $q_2 < 1/2$ there is a unique solution to $D_2(p) = q_2$, which is $p_2 = \sqrt{1 - 2q_2}$. If $q_2 \geq 1/2$ we have a unique solution $p_2 = p_1 = 0$.

If $q_1 + q_2 = 1$ there are multiple market clearing cutoffs and multiple stable matchings. For example, if $q_1 = q_2 = 1/2$ then any $p_1 = p_2 \in [0, 1]$ are market clearing cutoffs.

16.2.4 Generic Uniqueness of Stable Matchings

The calculation of market clearing cutoffs shows that it is possible for a continuum economy to have multiple market clearing cutoffs and, correspondingly, the multiple stable matchings. But this calculation also shows that a multiplicity of stable matchings happens only for particular knife-edge parameters. when the school capacity is exactly equal to the number of students. This aligns with the intuition from random matching markets – a multiplicity of stable matchings arises only when the market is balanced. The continuum model allows us to formalize that this is a knife-edge situation, and to show that generically a matching market has a unique stable matching.

The following theorem requires a technical condition, namely that η is regular. The distribution of student types η is regular if the image under $D(\cdot|\eta)$ of the closure of the set

$$\{P \in [0, 1]^C : D(\cdot|\eta) \text{ is not continuously differentiable at } P\}$$

has Lebesgue measure 0. This technical condition is satisfied if, for example, $D(\cdot|\eta)$ is continuously differentiable or if η admits a continuous density.

Theorem 16.12 [10]. *Suppose η is regular. Then for almost any vector of capacities q the market (η, q) has a unique stable matching.*

In other words, we can ensure a unique stable matching by slightly perturbing the college capacities q.

16.2.5 Calculating and Optimizing for Welfare

Let us revisit the market from Example 16.10 again. The market clearing conditions allowed us to solve for the stable matching for any q_1, q_2. This allows us to treat the capacities q_1, q_2 as decision variables. For example, it is natural to ask what are the optimal capacities q_1, q_2 that maximize the sum of student utilities subject to some constraints or costs.

To define welfare, we need to specify a cardinal utility. A simple specification that is consistent with the distribution of ordinal preferences in Example 16.10 is that a student in location $x \in [0, 1]$ has utility $1 - x/2$ if assigned to school 1 and utility $1 - (1 - x)/2 + \varepsilon$ if assigned to school 2, where $\varepsilon \sim U[-1/2, 1/2]$ is an independent random taste shock. Unassigned students receive utility of 0.

We can obtain tractable expressions for welfare by conditioning on a student's location and budget set. The expected utility of a student in location x who has the budget set $\{1\}, \{2\}$ is $u_{\{1\}}(x) = 1 - x/2$ and $u_{\{2\}}(x) = x/2$, respectively. The expected utility of the student in location x who has the budget set $\{1, 2\}$ is given by

$$u_{\{1,2\}}(x) = \int_{-\frac{1}{2}}^{\frac{1}{2}} \max\left[1 - x/2, x/2 + \varepsilon\right] d\varepsilon$$

$$= \int_{-\frac{1}{2}}^{x} \max\left[1 - x/2\right] d\varepsilon + \int_{x}^{\frac{1}{2}} \max\left[x/2 + \varepsilon\right] d\varepsilon$$

$$= \frac{1}{2}\left(x^2 - x + 2\right).$$

Combining these expressions with the previously derived expressions for the cutoffs, we obtain the following expressions for the welfare. If $q_1 + q_2 < 1$ then $p_1 = 1 - q_1, p_2 = 1 - q_2$, and the welfare is

$$\int_0^{q_1} u_{\{1\}} dx + \int_{1-q_2}^1 u_{\{2\}} dx = q_1 - q_1^2/4 + q_2 - q_2^2/4 .$$

If $q_1 + q_2 > 1$ with $q_1 > 1/2 > q_2$ we have that $p_1 = 0$ and $p_2 = \sqrt{1 - 2q_2}$ and the welfare is

$$\int_0^{p_2} u_{\{1\}} dx + \int_{p_2}^1 u_{\{1,2\}} dx = \frac{11}{12} - \frac{1}{6}(1 - 2q_2)^{3/2} .$$

16.2.6 Random Sampling and Relation to Discrete Economies

One important interpretation of the continuum matching model is that the measure η represents the distribution from which finite economies are sampled. Understanding the properties of finitely drawn economies is crucial for empirical work (e.g., [17]). This interpretation is also useful for understanding the continuum model and its relation to the finite matching model. The results below show that indeed we can think of continuum models as an approximation for finite models in which each student is small relative to the capacity of schools.

As an illustration, consider Israeli college admission. As in many countries (the USA being an exception), college admission is determined by a student's grade in standardized national exams. Each program in each university ranks students according to a score that is calculated on the basis of the subjects the student took and the grades the student received. Different programs use different weights and can have different rankings over students.

Each year, there will be a different cohort of students applying. But assuming that exams are consistent from one year to the next, we expect that the overall distribution of students is similar from one year to the next. A standard statistical approach is to consider each year as a draw from the same population.

Formally, we model college admission in a given year as a finite sample $F^k = [\eta^k, q^k]$ of size k from a continuum economy $E = [\eta, q]$. We normalize the total mass of students to be $\eta(\Theta) = 1$. The continuum economy represents the potential population of students, and η captures the joint distribution over student preferences and student scores (generated by the distribution of student grades). A finite sample

$F^k = [\eta^k, q^k]$ is generated by randomly drawing k students from η and scaling the capacity vector $q^k = \lfloor kq \rfloor$.

It was shown in [10] that if E has a unique stable matching (which generically holds) then that stable matching of F^k will converge to the stable matching of E as $k \to \infty$. Moreover, a characterization was given of the distribution of market clearing cutoffs P^k for the randomly drawn economy F^k.

Theorem 16.13 [10]. *Let P^* be the unique market clearing cutoff for the continuum economy $E = [\eta, q]$. Assume that, for $\sum_c q_c < 1$, $D(\cdot | \eta)$ is differentiably continuous, and that $\partial D(P^*)$ is non-singular. Then the asymptotic distribution of the difference between P^k and P^* satisfies*

$$\sqrt{k}(P^k - P^*) \xrightarrow{d} \mathcal{N}(0, \partial D(P^*)^{-1} \Sigma^D (\partial D(P^*)^{-1})'),$$

where $\mathcal{N}(\cdot, \cdot)$ denotes a C-dimensional normal distribution with given mean and covariance matrix. The matrix Σ^D is given by

$$\left(\Sigma^D \right)_{cd} = \begin{cases} q_c(1 - q_d) & \text{if } c = d, \\ -q_c q_d & \text{if } c \neq d. \end{cases}$$

16.3 Exercises

Exercise 16.1 Show that if (i) or (ii) occurs in the algorithm given in Section 16.1.3, then there are no stable matchings in which a man m_0 is matched to a woman w such that $\mu(m_0) \succ_m w$.

Exercise 16.2 Show that if (iii) occurs in the algorithm given in Section 16.1.3, the resulting matching is a new stable matching in which m_0 is matched to a different wife such that $\mu'(m_0) \prec_{m_0} \mu(m_0)$.

Exercise 16.3 Write down an economy that captures the following and calculate its stable matching and market clearing cutoffs. There are n colleges with identical capacities $q_1 = q_2 = \cdots = q_n = q$. Student preferences are independent of any college's rankings, and a college's ranking over students is independent of other college's ranking. Student preferences are drawn uniformly at random.

Exercise 16.4 Write down an economy that captures the following and calculate its stable matching and market clearing cutoffs. There are n colleges with identical capacities $q_1 = q_2 = \cdots = q_n = q$. Student preferences are independent of any college's rankings, and a college's ranking over students is independent of other college's ranking. All student have the preference ordering $1 \succ 2 \succ 3 \ldots \succ n$.

Exercise 16.5 Give an example with two colleges and a continuum of students where there are multiple stable matchings. (Hint: Think of the opposite preferences economy.) Find a slight perturbation to this economy that leads to an economy with a unique stable matching.

16.4 Bibliographic Notes

16.4.1 Other Applications of Random Matching Markets and Rejection Chains

Random matching markets and the analysis of rejection chains can be applied to answer other questions as well. It was shown in [23] that a school can benefit from misreporting its preferences if there is a rejection chain that brings a more preferred student to apply to the school. In a random many-to-one economy with short lists, in which a school can be matched to a constant number of students and the number of both schools and students is sufficiently large, schools will not be able to benefit by misreporting their preferences. In [12] a large matching market was analyzed in which colleges offer two kinds of positions, with and without a scholarship, as considered in Chapter 14. In that model preferences are random, but a student who is rejected from a position with a scholarship is likely to apply to the same college without a scholarship. As a result, rejection chains were used are likely to return to the college, and colleges can benefit from misreporting their preference.

In [24] and [6], rejection chains were used to analyze a matching market with couples. While it is possible that a market with couples will have no stable matching, the NRMP has succeeded in finding a stable matching with couples since its redesign. These papers provide a theoretical explanation, showing that the market is likely to have a stable matching as long as there are not too many couples in the market.

A random matching market was estimated in [30]. Stable matching was formulated as a discrete choice problem, in which each agent chooses his match from the budget of an agent from the other side who is willing to form a blocking pair. Analysis of rejection chains was used to show that this choice problem is well formulated because the agent's budget set is almost independently of the agent's stated preferences. As the market grows large, each agent's budget set includes more options. It is well known that agent utility in discrete choice models is inflated with the number of options, and [30] provides proper scaling that ensures the market maintains its key properties as it grows. In [25], markets with idiosyncratic and common taste shocks with bounded support were analyzed and it was shown that as the market grows large all stable matchings become assortative on the common taste shocks and that they match agents to spouses who give almost the maximal possible idiosyncratic taste shock.

The publications [14] and [35] use markets with randomly drawn preferences to evaluate the welfare of different mechanisms and preference distributions. In [28] it was shown that many mechanisms coincide as the market grows large.

16.4.2 Additional Applications of Continuum Models

The article [2] introduced a matching model for school choice with random tie breaking. In [8] a continuum model was used to tractably study the market power of large firms in a matching markets, and it was shown that a large firm can benefit from reducing its capacity. The intuition is that the firm rejects marginal matches of low value and receives instead infra-marginal matches of high value. In [13] a continuum model was used to study decentralized college admission when a college faces a risk of being over or under capacity.

In [5] and [34] a continuum model was used to optimize over different school choice mechanisms. The article [27] provides a cutoff characterization for the top trading cycles mechanism for school choice. A tractable continuum model allows for optimization of investment in school quality.

Continuum models are also used to analyze markets with complementarities [9], [14] and to show the existence of stable matchings under more general preferences. In [26] the continuum model was used to give a simple cutoff characterization of stable matchings when students have peer-dependent preferences.

In [21] a more general matching model was developed that allows for multi-sided matchings. The authors of [19] generalize the notion of stability to a one-to-one matching between arbitrary sets of men and women. In [18] logical compactness was used to characterize matching markets with infinitely many agents.

References

[1] Abdulkadiroglu, Atila, Che, Yeon-Koo, and Yasuda, Yosuke. 2011. Resolving conflicting preferences in school choice: The "Boston mechanism" reconsidered. *American Economic Review*, **101**(1), 399–410.

[2] Abdulkadiroğlu, Atila, Che, Yeon-Koo, and Yasuda, Yosuke. 2015. Expanding "choice" in school choice. *American Economic Journal: Microeconomics*, **7**(1), 1–42.

[3] Abdulkadiroğlu, Atila, Angrist, Joshua D., Narita, Yusuke, and Pathak, Parag A. 2017. Research design meets market design: Using centralized assignment for impact evaluation. *Econometrica*, **85**(5), 1373–1432.

[4] Adachi, Hiroyuki. 2003. A search model of two-sided matching under non-transferable utility. *Journal of Economic Theory*, **113**(2), 182–198.

[5] Ashlagi, Itai, and Shi, Peng. 2016. Optimal allocation without money: An engineering approach. *Management Science*, **62**(4), 1078–1097.

[6] Ashlagi, Itai, Braverman, Mark, and Hassidim, Avinatan. 2014. Stability in large matching markets with complementarities. *Operations Research*, **62**(4), 713–732.

[7] Ashlagi, Itai, Kanoria, Yash, and Leshno, Jacob D. 2017. Unbalanced random matching markets: The stark effect of competition. *Journal of Political Economy*, **125**(1), 69–98.

[8] Azevedo, Eduardo M. 2014. Imperfect competition in two-sided matching markets. *Games and Economic Behavior*, **83**, 207–223.

[9] Azevedo, Eduardo M, and Hatfield, John William. 2012. Complementarity and multidimensional heterogeneity in matching markets. Unpublished mimeo.

[10] Azevedo, Eduardo M, and Leshno, Jacob D. 2016. A supply and demand framework for two-sided matching markets. *Journal of Political Economy*, **124**(5), 1235–1268.

[11] Balinski, Michel, and Sönmez, Tayfun. 1999. A tale of two mechanisms: Student placement. *Journal of Economic theory*, **84**(1), 73–94.

[12] Biró, Péter, Hassidim, Avinatan, Romm, Assaf, Shorrer, Ran I., and Sóvágó, Sándor. 2020. Need versus merit: The large core of college admissions markets. *arXiv preprint arXiv:2010.08631*.

[13] Che, Yeon-Koo, and Koh, Youngwoo. 2016. Decentralized college admissions. *Journal of Political Economy*, **124**(5), 1295–1338.

[14] Che, Yeon-Koo, and Tercieux, Olivier. 2019. Efficiency and stability in large matching markets. *Journal of Political Economy*, **127**(5), 2301–2342.

[15] Che, Yeon-Koo, Kim, Jinwoo, and Kojima, Fuhito. 2019. Stable matching in large economies. *Econometrica*, **87**(1), 65–110.

[16] Fleiner, Tamás, and Jankó, Zsuzsanna. 2014. Choice function-based two-sided markets: Stability, lattice property, path independence and algorithms. *Algorithms*, **7**(1), 32–59.

[17] Gale, D., and Shapley, L. L. 1962. College admissions and the stability of marriage. *American Mathematical Monthly*, **69**, 9–15.

[18] Gonczarowski, Yannai A., Kominers, Scott Duke, and Shorrer, Ran I. 2019. To infinity and beyond: Scaling economic theories via logical compactness.

[19] Greinecker, Michael, and Kah, Christopher. 2018. Pairwise stable matching in large economies. https://onlinelibrary.wiley.com/doi/full/10.3982/ECTA16228.

[20] Immorlica, N., and Mahdian, M. 2005. Marriage, honesty, and stability. Pages 53–62 of: *Proc. 16th Annual ACM-SIAM Symposium on Discrete Algorithms*.

[21] Jagadeesan, Ravi. 2017. Complementary inputs and the existence of stable outcomes in large trading networks. Page 265 of: Was published in *ECMA*: https://onlinelibrary.wiley.com/doi/full/10.3982/ECTA16228.

[22] Knuth, D. E., Motwani, R., and Pittel, B. 1990. Stable husbands. In *Proc. 1st Annual ACM-SIAM Symposium on Discrete Algorithms*, volume 1, pp. 1–14.

[23] Kojima, F., and Pathak, P. A. 2009. Incentives and Stability in Large Two-Sided Matching Markets. *American Economic Review*, **99**, 608–627.

[24] Kojima, Fuhito, Pathak, Parag A., and Roth, Alvin E. 2013. Matching with couples: Stability and incentives in large markets. *Quarterly Journal of Economics*, **128**(4), 1585–1632.

[25] Lee, SangMok. 2017. Incentive compatibility of large centralized matching markets. *Review of Economic Studies*, **84**(1), 444–463.

[26] Leshno, Jacob D. 2020. Stable matching with peer effects in large markets – Existence and cutoff characterization. Unpublished mimeo.

[27] Leshno, Jacob, and Lo, Irene. 2020. The cutoff structure of top trading cycles in school choice. *Review of Economic Studies*, **88**(4), 1582–1623.

[28] Liu, Qingmin, and Pycia, Marek. 2016. Ordinal efficiency, fairness, and incentives in large markets. Working Paper.

[29] McVitie, D. G., and Wilson, L.B. 1971. The stable marriage problem. *Communications of the ACM*, **14(7)**, 486–490.

[30] Menzel, Konrad. 2015. Large matching markets as two-sided demand systems. *Econometrica*, **83**(3), 897–941.

[31] Pittel, B. 1989. The average number of stable matchings. *SIAM Journal on Discrete Mathematics*, **2(4)**, 530–549.

[32] Roth, A. E. 1985. The college admissions problem is not equivalent to the marriage problem. *Journal of Economic Theory*, **36**(2), 277–288.

[33] Roth, Alvin E., and Peranson, Elliott. 1999. The redesign of the matching market for American physicians: Some engineering aspects of economic design. *American Economic Review*, **89**(4), 748–780.

[34] Shi, Peng. 2019. Optimal priority-based allocation mechanisms. Available at SSRN 3425348.

[35] Yariv, L., and Lee, S. 2014. On the efficiency of stable matchings in large markets. https://pubsonline.informs.org/doi/abs/10.1287/mnsc.2020.3925.

CHAPTER SEVENTEEN

Pseudomarkets

Marek Pycia

17.1 Introduction

Pseudomarkets are allocation mechanisms for one-sided matching markets, an environment introduced in Chapter 2.[1] Participants of pseudomarkets provide the mechanism with a representation of their cardinal utilities, and the resulting allocation is calculated as part of a Walrasian equilibrium of an auxiliary market, whose participants pay for their allocations with fictitious (token) money that has no value outside the allocation mechanism. Pseudomarkets differ from the majority of no-transfer allocation mechanisms – e.g., serial dictatorships, top trading cycles, trading cycles, probabilistic serial dictatorships, and deferred acceptance (see Chapter 10) – in that they elicit from participants not only an ordinal ranking of the objects being allocated but also the cardinal aspects, or intensity, of the agents' preferences. Eliciting intensities is made possible by the potentially random nature of allocations. A reliance on intensities allows pseudomarkets to allocate objects more efficiently than the ordinal mechanisms but this advantage comes at the cost of increased complexity and potentially more opportunities for gaming the mechanism (weaker incentive compatibility).

This chapter defines pseudomarket mechanisms and examines their incentive and efficiency properties. Its primary focus is on theory, particularly in single-unit demand settings such as school choice. The chapter also discusses selected experimental and empirical results and extends the analysis to multi-unit demand settings such as course allocation.

17.2 Preliminaries: Walrasian Equilibria in Discrete Settings

We study a finite one-sided matching market with agents $i, j, k \in I = \{1, \dots, |I|\}$ and indivisible objects or goods $x, y, z \in X = \{1, \dots, |X|\}$. Each object x is represented by a number of identical copies $|x| \in \mathbb{N}$. If agents have outside options, we treat them as objects in X; in particular, this implies that $\sum_{x \in X} |x| \geq |I|$.

---

[1] Pseudomarket mechanisms were proposed in [12]. The name reflects the idea of replicating a Walrasian market inside an allocation mechanism. These mechanisms are also known as Hylland–Zeckhauser mechanisms or token-money mechanisms.

We assume that agents demand a probability distribution over objects. This assumption is known as *single-unit demand*; we discuss its relaxation in Section 17.5. We denote by $q_i^x \in [0, 1]$ the probability that agent i obtains a copy of object x. Agent i's random *assignment* $q_i = (q_i^1, \ldots, q_i^{|X|})$ is a probability distribution on X; we denote the set of such probability distributions by $\Delta(X)$ and we also refer to them as individual assignments. Agents are expected-utility maximizers: agent i's utility from random assignment q_i is $u_i(q_i) = v_i q_i = \sum_{x \in X} v_i^x q_i^x$ where $v_i = (v_i^x)_{x \in X} \in [0, \infty)^{|X|}$ is the vector of agent i's von Neumann–Morgenstein valuations for object $x \in X$.[2]

The set of economy-wide random assignments is $\Delta(X)^I$. An economy-wide assignment $q = (q_i^x)_{i \in I, x \in X}$ is *feasible* if $\sum_{i \in I} q_i^x \le |x|$ for every object x. An individual assignment is deterministic if it puts a mass unit 1 on one of the objects; an economy-wide assignment is deterministic if all individual assignments are deterministic. A mathematical result known as the Birkhoff–von Neumann theorem states that a feasible random assignment can be expressed as a lottery over feasible deterministic assignments.

We say that a feasible economy-wide assignment q^* and a vector $p^* \in \mathbb{R}_+^X$ constitute an *equilibrium* for a constraint vector $w^* \in \mathbb{R}_+^I$ if $q^* = (q_i^*)_{i \in I}$ satisfies $p^* \cdot q_i^* \le w_i^*$ for all $i \in I$ and $u_i(q_i) > u_i(q_i^*) \implies p^* \cdot q_i > w_i^*$ for all $(q_i)_{i \in I} \in \Delta(X)^I$. This definition formally resembles the standard definition of Walrasian equilibrium.[3] The vector p^* is usually interpreted as a *price vector* and the constraint vector w^* is interpreted as a *budget vector*, an interpretation we adopt. In this interpretation, agents' budgets consist of fictitious token money that allows the agents to buy probabilities but is otherwise worthless: unspent token money does not enter agents' utility. Referring to the subset of $\Delta(X)$ satisfying $p^* \cdot q_i^* \le w_i^*$ as agent i's budget set, we can restate the first inequality above as meaning that q_i^* is in the budget set, and we can restate the second inequality as meaning that no individual assignment that is preferred to q_i^* is in the budget set. As an illustration consider the following.

Example 17.1. Suppose that there are two objects x and y such that $|x| = 1$ and $|y| = 2$, and three agents $1, 2$, and 3 such that agents 1 and 2 prefer x to y and agent 3 prefers y to x. While with three or more objects we would need to further specify cardinal utilities to fully describe the environment; with just two objects all specifications of cardinal utilities are equivalent. The reason is that our analysis is invariant under adding a constant to all utilities and under multiplying them by a positive constant. With budgets $w_1 = w_2 = w_3 = 1$ and

---

[2] The single-unit demand assumption that we impose implies that the restriction to non-negative utilities is immaterial; cf. the discussion of Example 17.1.

[3] When $\sum_{x \in X} |x| = |I|$, this definition implies that all object copies are allocated. Beyond this special case, market clearing is more subtle and is discussed later. The key differences from the standard theory of Walrasian equilibrium are as follows: (i) we study discrete objects while the objects in the standard theory are divisible, and (ii) the unspent balances of the of w_i^* have no value in our setting while the unspent balances are valuable in the standard theory. These two differences further imply that a key property of the standard Walrasian theory – local non-satiation – fails in our setting. While this chapter includes comparisons with the standard Walrasian theory, the chapter's substantive analysis is self-contained and presumes no background in Walrasian theory. A reader interested in such background might wish to consult e.g., [9] or [3] for classical developments, and [14] or [13] for contemporary treatments.

prices $p_1 = 2$ and $p_2 = 0$, the equilibrium assignment is $q_1 = q_2 = \begin{pmatrix} 0.5 \\ 0.5 \end{pmatrix}$ and $q_3 = \begin{pmatrix} 0 \\ 1 \end{pmatrix}$.

In this example the equilibrium happens to be unique, but in general in our model there might be multiple equilibria, just as in the standard Walrasian theory.

17.2.1 Market Clearing and the Existence of Equilibrium

For any budget vector w and sufficiently high prices p, the existence of an equilibrium implementing some distribution vector q follows from the standard properties of agents' demands. For any agent i, we define this agent's demand correspondence as

$$d_i(p) = \arg \max_{q_i \in \Delta(X), pq_i \leq w_i} u_i(q_i).$$

For each p, the budget set of agent i is non-empty and compact. Thus, the continuity of the objective u_i in q_i implies that the demand $d_i(p)$ is non-empty and compact. The linearity of u_i and the convexity of the maximization domain imply that $d_i(p)$ is convex. As the mapping from p to the budget set is both upper and lower hemicontinuous, Berge's maximum theorem implies that d_i is upper hemicontinuous. By definition of the demand correspondence, for any non-negative price vector p this price vector and any distribution vector q, such that $q_i \in d_i(p)$ for each $i \in I$, satisfy individual agents' equilibrium conditions: for each agent i the distribution q_i is in the budget set, and no assignment preferred to q_i is in the budget set. Furthermore, by setting the prices sufficiently high we can ensure that q is feasible.

More interestingly there always exists an equilibrium in which the *market clears* in the following complementary-slackness sense: for each $x \in X$, if $p_x^* > 0$ then $\sum_{i \in I} q_i^{*x} = |x|$.

Theorem 17.2 (Existence). *For any budget vector $w^* \in \mathbb{R}_+^I$, there is an equilibrium (q^*, p^*) satisfying market clearing.*

The complementary slackness form of market clearing is necessary and caused by the possibility that agents may be satiated: an agent assigned probability 1 for their most favorite object cannot raise their utility further. In particular, if the most favorite object is relatively inexpensive, such an agent might not spend all their budget. As an illustration of the market-clearing property, consider an *outside option* defined as an object o with many copies, $|o| \geq |I|$.[4] If the supply inequality is strict, $|o| > |I|$, then complementary slackness implies that the price of the outside option is 0.

Like its analogue in the standard Walrasian analysis, the proof of the existence theorem relies on the Kakutani fixed-point theorem.

Proof In the proof, we refer to vectors $p \in \mathbb{R}^X$ as price vectors even though such vectors allow negative prices; the price vector $p^* \in \mathbb{R}_+^X$ that we construct

---

[4] With slightly more involved but substantially the same analysis we could introduce agent-specific outside options in a similar manner.

has only non-negative prices, however. Let $w = \max\{w_1, \ldots, w_{|I|}\}$ and let $t(p) = (\max\{0, p_x\})_{x \in X}$ be a projection of the vector $p \in \mathbb{R}^X$ onto $\mathbb{R}^X_+$. For sufficiently large $M > 0$, the price vector adjustment function

$$f(p) = t(p) + \left(\sum_{i \in I} d_i(t(p)) - (|x|)_{x \in X} \right)$$

maps the compact Cartesian–product space $\times_{x \in X}[-|x|, M]$ into itself because, if the price p_x of good x is higher than $w|I|$ then the sum $\sum_{i \in I} d_i(t(p))_x$ of agents' demands for x is lower than $|x|$ and thus $f(p)_x \leq p_x$.

The properties of demand correspondences d_i established above imply that f is upper hemicontinuous and takes values that are non-empty, convex, and compact. Thus, by the Kakutani fixed-point theorem, there exists a fixed point $\hat{p} \in f(\hat{p})$. The fixed point property of $\hat{p}$ implies that for each x

$$(|x| + (\hat{p}_x - t_x(\hat{p})))_{x \in X} \in \sum_{i \in I} d_i(t(\hat{p})),$$

and hence there is a $q^* \in \times_{i \in I} d_i(p^*)$ for which

$$(|x| + (\hat{p}_x - t_x(\hat{p})))_{x \in X} = \sum_{i \in I} q_i^*.$$

By construction, q^* and $p^* = t(\hat{p})$ are in equilibrium provided q^* is feasible, that is, that $0 \leq \sum_{i \in I} q_i^{*x} \leq |x|$ for each $x \in X$. The first inequality obtains because $q_i^* \in d_i(p^*)$, and the second inequality obtains because $t_x(\hat{p}) \geq \hat{p}_x$. The market-clearing property is satisfied because, for positive p_x^*, we have $\hat{p}_x - t_x(\hat{p}) = 0$ and hence $\sum_{i \in I} q_i^{*x} = |x| + (\hat{p}_x - t_x(\hat{p})) = |x|$. □

17.2.2 Cheapest Distribution Selection

In our analysis of incentives and efficiency, a special role is played by equilibria satisfying the following property: an equilibrium (q^*, p^*) satisfies the *cheapest purchase property* if, for all $i \in I$ and $q_i \in \Delta(X)$, the utility ranking $u_i(q_i) \geq u_i(q_i^*)$ implies $p^* \cdot q_i \geq p^* q_i^*$.[5] Because an agent demand $d_i(p)$ is non-empty and compact, for any price vector p^* there exists a distribution q_i satisfying the above implication. More interestingly, these distributions can be selected in a way that preserves the equilibrium construction.

Remark 17.3 (Existence of cheapest purchase pseudomarkets). For any budgets $w_i^* \geq 0, i \in I$, there is an equilibrium (q^*, p^*) satisfying the market-clearing property and the cheapest-purchase property. The proof follows the same steps as the proof of Theorem 17.2 except that we restrict individual demands $d_i(p)$ to distributions satisfying the cheapest-purchase property.

The cheapest-purchase property is satisfied by all pseudomarket equilibria when each agent has a unique favorite object, as then either the agent can purchase with

---

[5] The property of purchasing the cheapest distribution is also known as the *least-expensive lottery property* in single-unit demand settings and as the *cheapest bundle property* in multi-unit demand settings.

probability 1 the most favorite object (and then this agent's demand is a singleton at equilibrium prices) or else the agent spends as little as possible on other objects in order to spend more token money on the purchase of the most favorite object. Unlike in the standard Walrasian analysis, however, the cheapest-purchase property might fail for some utility profiles. Example 17.5 below illustrates such a possibility.

17.2.3 Token Money versus Trade in Endowments

Could we replace the token money with endowments of the probabilities being traded? In standard Walrasian equilibrium we could, but the failure of local non-satiation in the discrete allocation context that we are studying breaks this possibility. We can see this by revisiting Example 17.1. Suppose that in this example we endow each agent with probability $\frac{1}{3}$ of object x and probability $\frac{2}{3}$ of object y. Does there exist a feasible economy-wide assignment q^* and a price vector $p^* \in \mathbb{R}_+^X$ such that

$$p^* \cdot q_i^* \leq p^* \begin{pmatrix} 1/3 \\ 2/3 \end{pmatrix} \text{ for all } i \in \{1, 2, 3\} \text{ and } u_i(q_i) > u_i(q_i^*) \implies p^* \cdot q_i > p^* \begin{pmatrix} 1/3 \\ 2/3 \end{pmatrix}$$

for all $(q_i)_{i \in \{1,2,3\}} \in \Delta(\{x, y\})^{\{1,2,3\}}$? Exercise 17.1 asks the reader to verify that such an assignment and price vector do not exist.

17.3 Eliciting Agents' Utilities

So far, we have assumed that agents' utilities are known. In applications this information needs to be elicited. A mechanism elicits agents' information and this information determines the mechanism's outcome. In our setting, each agent's information is the agent's utility and the mechanism's outcome is the economy-wide assignment.

A *pseudomarket mechanism* maps a profile of utilities $(u_i)_{i \in I}$ to an equilibrium assignment for some budget vector w^*. We allow the budget vector to depend on the profile of utilities. Even when budgets do not depend on the reported utilities, there are many budget vectors and the uniqueness of equilibrium is not assured; thus, there might be many pseudomarket mechanisms. Of particular importance are pseudomarket mechanisms in which budgets are equal, as in Example 17.1.[6]

Can we expect agents to report their utilities truthfully? The question is usually conceptualized in terms of incentives to do so, and the usual goal – known as incentive compatibility – is to ensure that by providing us with truthful reports the agents maximize (or nearly maximize) their payoffs. Agents' incentives in general depend on what they know or believe, including what they know or believe about other agents. A gold standard of incentive compatibility is strategy-proofness because it imposes no assumptions on agents' beliefs. A mechanism is *strategy-proof* if reporting the true utility is a dominant strategy for each agent, that is, if the agent's expected utility after reporting their true utility is weakly higher than after any other report irrespective of the reports of other agents (see Chapter 4).

---

[6] If $\lambda > 0$ and an assignment q^* and prices p^* are in equilibrium for budgets w^*, then the same assignment q^* and prices λp^* are in equilibrium for budgets w^*/λ. In particular, the set of equilibrium allocations is the same for any $w_1^* = \cdots = w_{|I|}^* > 0$.

17.3.1 Fixed-Price Pseudomarkets

Pseudomarkets can be strategy-proof. Suppose that there is an outside option, and fix a profile of agents' budgets. Then we have

Theorem 17.4 (Strategy proofness). *Any pseudomarket mechanism with fixed prices and budgets is strategy-proof.*

This result follows because, with fixed prices, a truthful revelation of an agent's utility implies that the mechanism assigns the agent a probability distribution that maximizes the agent's reported utility. Recall that the feasibility of assignments is assumed in any pseudomarket mechanism. This assumption implies that the prices of some objects may need to be sufficiently high to ensure that the demand for these objects does not exceed supply. As a consequence of the high prices, the assignments generated by strategy-proof pseudomarkets might be suboptimal and the market-clearing condition from Theorem 17.2 might fail.

17.3.2 Asymptotic Incentive Compatibility

Can we still preserve agents' incentives to truthfully reveal their utilities if we endogenize the prices in a way that guarantees market clearing? The answer turns out to resemble that in the standard Walrasian analysis: in general, market-clearing pseudomarkets are not strategy-proof but they are asymptotically incentive compatible in large markets; the intuitive reason for the latter result is that, in large markets, agents become unable to substantially influence prices.[7]

We model a large market as a sequence of replica economies. In an n-fold replica of the base economy from Section 17.2, the set of objects is still X but there are $n|x|$ copies of each object, and each agent i with utility u_i from the base economy is replaced by n agents with utility u_i; the set of agents is then denoted I_n.[8] To simplify the exposition, we further assume that the space $U \subseteq \mathbb{R}_+^X$ of possible utilities of an agent is finite and that the space of utility profiles is U^{I_n}. We fix a sequence of budget vectors w^n in which each agent replacing the same agent in the base economy has the same budget. Each utility profile $u_{I_n} \in U^{I_n}$ is associated with a distribution over U, in which the probability mass put on each $u \in U$ is equal to the fraction of agents in I_n whose utility function is u.

As in standard Walrasian analysis, we establish asymptotic incentive compatibility only for regular economies. To define them, we use the metric $\rho(\mu, \nu) = \max_{u \in U^{I_n}} |\mu(u) - \nu(u)|$ to measure the distance between two distributions μ and ν on U^{I_n}. A distribution of utilities μ^* is *regular* if there exists a neighborhood B of μ^* in the metric space just defined and a non-empty finite set of continuous mappings $p(\cdot)$ from distributions $\mu \in B$ to market-clearing pseudomarket price vectors

---

[7] More is known: if there are three or more agents and three or more objects, and each agent's domain of possible utility functions equals the entire $\mathbb{R}_+^{|X|}$, then no mechanism that satisfies strategy-proofness and Pareto efficiency can give the same utility to any two agents with same utility functions. A pseudomarket mechanism with equal budgets satisfies this symmetry condition, and we will see that some such mechanisms are Pareto efficient; hence they cannot be strategy-proof.

[8] Notice that if prices p^* and assignments $q_1^*, \ldots, q_{|I|}^*$ are in equilibrium for budgets $w_1, \ldots, w_{|I|}$ then the same prices and assignments in which each agent replacing i receives q_i^* are in equilibrium for budgets such that each agent replacing i has budget w_i.

$p(\mu)$ satisfying the cheapest-purchase property such that, for every $\mu \in B$, (i) every market-clearing pseudomarket price vector satisfying the cheapest-purchase property equals one of the $p(\mu)$ and (ii) no two price vectors $p(\mu)$ are the same. We say that an economy is regular when the associated distribution of utilities is regular. Replica economies based on Example 17.1 give us an example of regular utility distributions.

Example 17.5. In an n-fold replica of the economy from Example 17.1, there are two objects x and y such that $|x| = n$ and $|y| = 2n$, and $3n$ agents such that $2n$ agents prefer x to y and the remaining agents prefer y to x. Let $U = \{1, 2, \ldots, 10\}^{\{x,y\}}$ be the space of possible utilities, and suppose that agents of the first type have utility $u(x) = 7 > u(y) = 3$ while agents of the second type have utility $u(x) = 2 < u(y) = 8$. Each agent's budget is $w_i = 1$. For each such replica economy and prices $p_1 = 2$ and $p_2 = 0$, the assignment that gives

the first type of agents $\begin{pmatrix} 0.5 \\ 0.5 \end{pmatrix}$ and the second type of agents $\begin{pmatrix} 0 \\ 1 \end{pmatrix}$ are in

equilibrium.

For a fixed $\varepsilon > 0$, an ε-ball around the distribution putting mass $\frac{2}{3}$ on utility function $(7, 3)$ and mass $\frac{1}{3}$ on $(2, 8)$ consists of distributions putting mass in $\left(\frac{2}{3} - \varepsilon, \frac{2}{3} + \varepsilon \right)$ on utility function $(7, 3)$, mass in $\left(\frac{1}{3} - \varepsilon, \frac{1}{3} + \varepsilon \right)$ on $(2, 8)$, and mass ε or lower on other utility functions. For reasons discussed in Example 17.1, the equilibrium prices depend only on the mass $\mu(x \succ y)$ of agents preferring x to y, the mass $\mu(x \prec y)$ of agents preferring y to x, and the mass $\mu(x \sim y)$ of agents who are indifferent. Suppose the ε-ball we look at is sufficiently small that object x is scarce, $\mu(x \succ y) > \frac{1}{3}$, while object y is abundant, $\mu(x \prec y) + \mu(x \sim y) < \frac{2}{3}$. Then, for any distribution in this ball, the equilibrium price vectors satisfy $p_y = 0$ and $p_x = 3(\mu(x \succ y) + \lambda\mu(x \sim y))$ for some $\lambda \in [0, 1]$; note that the price $p_x > 1$ reflects the scarcity of object x. The equilibrium assignments at those prices depend on λ in the following way: agents

preferring y and a fraction λ of indifferent agents obtain probabilities $\begin{pmatrix} 0 \\ 1 \end{pmatrix}$

while the remaining agents obtain probabilities $\begin{pmatrix} 1/p_x \\ 1 - 1/p_x \end{pmatrix}$. The cheapest

purchase property is satisfied only by equilibria with a price vector in which $\lambda = 0$.

In the analysis of agents' incentives in large markets we focus on pseudomarket mechanisms that select equilibria with prices that depend only on the distribution of utility functions, as in the example above, and not on which agent has which utility function. In equilibrium, the prices and an agent's budget determine the agent's resulting utility, and hence – with prices and budgets determined – the equilibrium assignment selected by the pseudomarket mechanism does not impact agents' incentives. When talking about a mapping of the utility distributions to equilibrium prices, this focus allows us to talk about one mapping instead of a sequence of pseudomarket mechanisms.

A sequence of pseudomarket mechanisms – and the corresponding mapping from the utility distribution to prices – is *asymptotically incentive compatible* on a sequence of replica economies if the maximum utility gain of an agent from submitting a utility profile different from the truth vanishes along the sequence. That is, for every $\varepsilon > 0$, there exists n^* such that $n > n^*$ implies that the utility gain from unilateral misreporting for every agent in the n-fold replica is bounded by ε when everyone else is truth-telling. Notice that the utility gain from unilateral misreporting is uniformly bounded for all agents but the bound might depend on the utility distribution.

The pseudomarket mechanisms constructed in Example 17.5 are asymptotically incentive compatible. Exercise 17.2 asks the reader to extend the price construction beyond the ball discussed in Example 17.5 in such a way that these pseudomarkets are strategy-proof.[9]

Theorem 17.6 (Asymptotic incentive compatibility). *For every fixed budget vector on the base economy, there exists a pseudomarket mechanism that is asymptotically incentive compatible on any sequence of economies that are replicas of the regular base economy. Furthermore, we may require the pseudomarket mechanism to clear the market and satisfy the cheapest-purchase property for regular economies.*

Proof In view of the discussion above, to prove Theorem 17.6 it is sufficient to construct a mapping from utility distributions to market-clearing equilibrium prices. Take any regular distribution μ^* and notice that its regularity implies that there is an open neighborhood B of μ^* and a finite set of distinct continuous mappings $p(\cdot)$ from distributions $\mu \in B$ to market-clearing pseudomarket price vectors $p(\mu)$ satisfying the cheapest-purchase property, and that every market-clearing pseudomarket price vector satisfying the cheapest-purchase property lies on one of these price mappings. Let $B(\mu^*)$ be the union of all open sets containing μ^* for which this regularity property holds. The regularity property extends to the entire $B(\mu^*)$. Because any regular distribution has an open neighborhood of regular distributions, any distribution from the topological boundary of $B(\mu^*)$ is not regular. The sets $B(\mu^*)$ thus constitute an open partition of the set of regular distributions. On each $B(\mu^*)$ we can thus separately pick a continuous mapping $p(\cdot)$ from distributions $\mu \in B(\mu)$ to market-clearing pseudomarket price vectors $p(\mu)$ satisfying the cheapest-purchase property. The union of these mappings maps all regular distributions to such equilibrium prices and is continuous at any regular distribution. For non-regular distributions we can set any market-clearing equilibrium prices, whose existence is guaranteed by Theorem 17.2 and Remark 17.3.

To conclude the proof, consider the n-fold replica of an economy with regular utility distribution μ. Let $\mu_{(i,u)}$ be the utility distribution if some agent i submits a report u instead of u_i while other agents report truthfully. The ρ-distance between μ and $\mu_{(i,u)}$ is $1/n\,|I|$. By taking sufficiently large n we can

---

[9] The strategy-proofness is not a general property but is a by-product of there being just two objects in this example.

ensure that this distance is arbitrarily small. As the price function p^* is continuous at μ we can further infer that for large n the impact of agent i's deviation on prices is arbitrarily small. Because agents' utilities are continuous in prices, the theorem follows. □

Note that the constructed pseudomarket mechanism satisfies market clearing and the cheapest-purchase property on all economies, not only on regular ones.[10] Some of the assumptions that we have made simplified the setting but played no substantive role in the argument. For instance, instead of studying replica economies at any sequence of economies such that the utility distribution converges to a regular distribution, we can also allow the budget vector to depend continuously on the distribution of utilities and relax the assumption that U is finite. For general U, we would use the Prohorov metric to measure the distance between two distributions μ and ν.

17.3.3 Preference Reporting

In the analysis so far we have assumed that agents are able to report their preferences, a standard assumption in mechanism design. In the context of no-transfer allocation, the competing mechanisms, mentioned at the beginning of the chapter, require only the reporting of ordinal preferences, which is *prima facie* easier than reporting cardinal utilities. Not only do cardinal utilities contain more information – and hence may require more effort to be learn by mechanism participants – but they might be harder to conceptualize and communicate than ordinal ranking. How is a market participant to conceptualize their value of an object such as a medical transplant or a school assignment in the context in which these objects are not usually evaluated in terms of money? Utilities in our model reflect comparisons among lotteries, and the mechanism might elicit these comparisons directly. The list of all lotteries is however much longer than the list of all sure outcomes.

The issue was experimentally evaluated in the context of course assignment at the Wharton School at the University of Pennsylvania. The conclusion of the experiment was that reporting cardinal preferences entails more errors than reporting ordinal ones, but that despite these errors pseudomarkets performed better than the status quo mechanism then used by Wharton.[11] In effect, the course assignment at Wharton is now run via a pseudomarket mechanism.

17.4 Efficiency

Pseudomarkets have good efficiency properties and their efficiency is the key reason why one might want to use them to assign objects. A feasible assignment q is ex-ante Pareto efficient – or, simply, *efficient* – if no other feasible assignment is weakly preferred by all agents and strictly preferred by some agents. Note that when an efficient assignment is represented as a lottery over feasible deterministic assignments, all deterministic assignments in the support of the lottery are efficient as well.

[10] The restriction to regular economies plays a role in the extensions of Theorem 17.6 discussed later.

[11] The preferences over course assignments are harder to report than preferences over schools because the course preferences are over bundles of objects (courses) as opposed to single objects (schools). Hence we should be careful in making inferences for single-unit demand problems, such as school choice, from a multiunit demand problem such as course assignment. See also the discussion of multi-unit demand pseudomarkets in Section 17.5.2).

17.4.1 Efficiency of Pseudomarkets

Not all pseudomarkets are efficient. The high-price pseudomarkets from Theorem 2 do not need to be. However, by selecting equilibria satisfying market clearing and the cheapest-purchase property, we can ensure that a pseudomarket is efficient, obtaining an analogue of the first welfare theorem familiar from Walrasian analysis.

Theorem 17.7 (Efficiency of pseudomarkets). *Let (q^*, p^*) be an equilibrium for some budgets $w^* \in \mathbb{R}_+^{|I|}$ and suppose that the market-clearing and cheapest-purchase properties hold. Then q^* is efficient.*

The proof follows the steps of the standard Walrasian analysis with the cheapest-purchase property replacing the assumption that agents prefer to have more money rather than less money.

Proof By way of contradiction, suppose $q^* \in \Delta(X)^I$ is not efficient. Then there is an allocation $q \in \Delta(X)^I$ such that $\sum_{i \in I} q_i^x \leq |x|$ and $u_i(q_i) \geq u_i(q_i^*)$ for all $i \in I$, with at least one inequality strict. If agent i is satiated under q_i^*—that is the agent receives probability 1 of her most preferred object—then the cheapest purchase property implies that $p^* \cdot q_i \geq p^* \cdot q_i^*$. If an agent i is not satiated then $p^* \cdot q_i \geq p^* \cdot q_i^*$ by the same argument that works in standard competitive equilibrium theory with non-satiated agents. Indeed, suppose $p^* \cdot q_i < p^* \cdot q_i^*$ and let $r_i \in \Delta(X)^I$ put probability 1 on a most preferred object of agent i. We can then find a small weight $\alpha > 0$ such that $u_i(\alpha r_i + (1 - \alpha) q_i) > u_i(q_i^*)$ and $p^* \cdot (\alpha r_i + (1 - \alpha) q_i) \leq p^* \cdot q_i^* \leq w_i^*$, contradicting that q_i^* was an optimal choice in i's budget set. Agents i for whom the inequality $u_i(q_i) \geq u_i(q_i^*)$ is strict are not satiated and the strict-preference analogue of the above argument gives us $p^* \cdot q_i > p^* \cdot q_i^*$.

Summing up the inequalities we derived above, we conclude that $\sum_{i \in I} p^* \cdot q_i > \sum_{i \in I} p^* \cdot q_i^*$. There is thus an object x with positive price $p_x^* > 0$ and such that $\sum_{i \in I} q_i^x > \sum_{i \in I} q_i^{*x}$; for this object, market clearing implies that $\sum_{i \in I} q_i^{*x} = |x|$. Thus $\sum_{i \in I} q_i^x > |x|$ contradicting the assumption that $\sum_{i \in I} q_i \leq |x|$. $\square$

Market clearing and the cheapest purchase property are both needed to guarantee the efficiency of a pseudomarket assignment. Without market clearing, assigning some of the unassigned supply might raise an agent's utility and hence lead to a Pareto dominant assignment. Without the cheapest purchase property, an indifferent agent buying an unnecessarily expensive distribution might impose a negative externality on other agents.[12]

---

[12] Consider, for instance, an economy with one unit of object x, one unit of object y, and two agents: one agent strictly prefers x to y, while the other agent is indifferent between the two. There is then an inefficient equilibrium, which violates the cheapest purchase property, in which each agent has a budget of 1, the price of good x is 2, the price of good y is 0, and both agents buy with probability 0.5 good x and with probability 0.5 good y. See also Example 17.5, where the pseudomarket equilibria with index $\lambda > 0$ violate the cheapest-purchase property and are inefficient.

17.4.2 Pseudomarkets' Efficiency Edge over Ordinal Mechanisms

Efficiency is the main advantage of pseudomarkets over ordinal mechanisms. Consider the following comparison between pseudomarkets and random priority, a standard ordinal mechanism also known as random serial dictatorship (see Chapters 2, 4, 8 and 10).

Example 17.8. Consider three agents $1, 2, 3$ and three objects with one copy for each agent. Take $\epsilon \in \left(0, \frac{1}{4}\right)$ and suppose that agent 2's valuations for the objects are $v_2^3 = 1$, $v_2^2 = 1 - \epsilon$, and $v_2^1 = \epsilon$ while, the valuations of agents $i = 1, 3$ are $v_i^3 = 1$, $v_i^2 = 2\epsilon$, and $v_i^1 = \epsilon$. We may think of these objects as schools: school 3 is the most popular and agent 2 lives in the neighborhood of school 2 while the other agents do not.

Random priority assigns to each agent a probability $\frac{1}{3}$ for each school. This assignment is not efficient. Indeed, each agent would strictly prefer the following assignment: agent 2 receives with probability 1 school 2 and each of the remaining two agents receives probability $\frac{1}{2}$ of school 1 and probability $\frac{1}{2}$ school 3.

The latter – Pareto dominant – assignment can be implemented as the outcome of a pseudomarket mechanism with prices $p_1 = 2$, $p_2 = 1$, and $p_3 = 0$ and budgets $w_1 = w_2 = w_3 = 1$.

The efficiency advantage illustrated in this example remains true for ordinal mechanisms other than random priority. For ordinal mechanisms that treat agents symmetrically, the advantage is easy to see in the setting of the example, but the per-capita advantage hinges neither on the symmetry of random priority nor on the other particulars of the environment. Similar examples can be constructed for assignment markets of any size and schools with arbitrary number of places. Indeed, the average utility gain of pseudomarket mechanisms over ordinal ones – even the per-capita utility gains – can be arbitrarily large in sufficiently large markets.

What are the measures of the utility gains? We could measure these gains by looking at differences in willingness to pay. The school assignment problem gives us also other measures of utility gain: a difference in an agent's utility from being assigned to one school versus another can be evaluated in terms of, for example, how much longer the travel time, or distance, to the preferred school would need to be in order to make an agent indifferent between the two schools.

In terms of the distance measure, the per-capita efficiency advantage of eliciting cardinal information in the data from the New York City school district was estimated to be 3.11 miles; that is, the improvement in moving from assignments based on only ordinal rankings to assignments based on cardinal information is equivalent to shrinking the distances so that each school is on average 3.11 miles closer to each student attending it.

17.4.3 Pseudomarket Representation of Efficient Assignments

Can we implement all efficient assignments through pseudomarkets? The positive answer resembles the second welfare theorem of Walrasian analysis and it facilitates discrete mechanism design.

Theorem 17.9 (Pseudomarket representation of efficient assignments). *If feasible assignment q^* is efficient then there exists a budget vector $w^* \in \mathbb{R}_+^{|I|}$ and a price vector $p^* \in \mathbb{R}_+^{|X|}$ such that q^* and p^* constitute an equilibrium with budgets w^*.*

The standard Walrasian argument breaks down in the discrete setting we are studying. Referring to the sum of individual assignments as the corresponding *aggregate assignment*, we can recapitulate the standard proof as follows. Let Y be the set of aggregate feasible assignments and Z be the set of aggregate assignments that Pareto-dominate a fixed efficient assignment $q^* = (q_i^*)_{i \in I}$ that we want to implement in equilibrium; these sets are disjoint, the concavity of utility ensures that Z is convex while the feasibility condition enssures that Y is convex. If now some agent $i \in I$ strictly prefers some q_i to q_i^* then $q = (q_i, q_{-i}^*)$ Pareto-dominates q^* and partial separation gives us $p^* \cdot \left(q_i + \sum_{j \in I \setminus \{i\}} q_j^* \right) \geq w \geq p^* \cdot \sum_{j \in I} q_j^*$. The second inequality can be shown to be an equality, allowing us to set $w_i^* = p^* \cdot q_i^*$.

The next step of the argument relies on the separating hyperplane theorem: for any two disjoint convex sets $Y, Z \subseteq \mathbb{R}^n$ there exists a price vector $p^* \in \mathbb{R}^n$ and budget $w \in \mathbb{R}$ such that $p^* \cdot z \geq w \geq p^* \cdot y$ for each $z \in Z$ and $y \in Y$. We interpret these inequalities as a *partial separation* of Y and Z; the *separation is full* if one of the inequalities can be assumed to be strict. The separating hyperplane theorem tells us that

$$u_i(q_i) > u_i(q_i^*) \implies p^* \cdot q_i \geq w_i^*.$$

This implication is weaker than required in equilibrium, and it needs to be strengthened to

$$u_i(q_i) > u_i(q_i^*) \implies p^* \cdot q_i > w_i^*$$

for all $i \in I$ and for all $(q_i)_{i \in I} \in \Delta(X)^I$. The last step of the standard proof is by contradiction: we take an assignment $q = (q_i)_{i \in I}$ that Pareto-dominates q^* while there is an agent i for whom q_i costs the same as q_i^*; in a small open neighborhood of q we then find an assignment that still Pareto-dominates q^* while being cheaper than it, contrary to the weak implication above.[13]

In our setting, the standard separating hyperplane theorem partially separates the Pareto dominating aggregate assignments from the feasible ones, and so we obtain the weak implication above, but the last step of the above proof fails. The reason is that this last step relies on the local non-satiation of standard Walrasian agents: for each assignment there is a nearby assignment that they strictly prefer. In effect, the set of aggregate assignments that strictly Pareto-dominate an assignment is an open set. Both of these properties fail in our setting. Local non-satiation fails when agents obtain their most preferred object. The failure of openness is illustrated by the following.

Example 17.10. There are three objects: object 1 with three copies, and objects 2 and 3 with one copy each. We are assigning these objects to four

---

[13] The prices p^*, distributions q^*, and budgets w^* satisfying the system of weak implications are called a quasi-equilibrium.

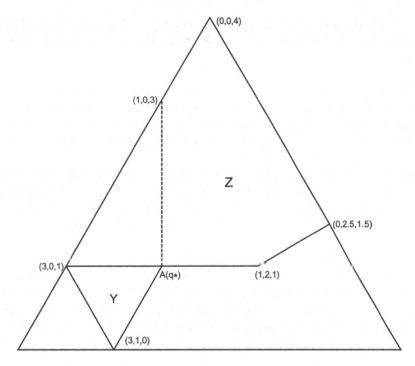

Figure 17.1 The simplex of (potentially infeasible) aggregate assignments in Example 17.10. The aggregate assignment $A(q^*)$ is on the intersection of the boundaries of sets Y and Z.

agents: the odd-numbered agents 1 and 3 have von Neumann–Morgenstern utility vector $v = (1, 0, 2)$, and the even-numbered agents 2 and 4 have utility vector $v' = (0, 2, 1)$. Assigning the odd-numbered agents the distribution $q_1^* = q_3^* = (\frac{1}{2}, 0, \frac{1}{2})$ and the even-numbered agents the distribution $q_2^* = q_4^* = (\frac{1}{2}, \frac{1}{2}, 0)$ is efficient. In particular, the aggregate assignment of q^* is $A(q^*) = \sum_i q_i^* = (2, 1, 1)$. Figure 17.1 places this point in the barycentric simplex of aggregate assignments. Set Y represents feasible aggregate assignments in the simplex; it is the triangle spanned by $A(q^*)$, $(3, 0, 1)$, and $(3, 1, 0)$. Set Z represents aggregate assignments corresponding to some assignment q in which all agents are weakly better off than under q^* and at least one agent is strictly better off (because q^* is efficient, these assignments q are not feasible). Set Z is a pentagon spanned by five points:

- $(2, 1, 1)$, the aggregate assignment corresponding to q^*,
- $(1, 2, 1)$, the aggregate assignment when the odd-numbered agents obtain q^* and the even-numbered agents obtain $(0, 1, 0)$,
- $(0, 2\frac{1}{2}, 1\frac{1}{2})$, the aggregate assignment when the odd-numbered agents obtain $\left(0, \frac{1}{4}, \frac{3}{4}\right)$ and the even-numbered agents obtain $(0, 1, 0)$,
- $(0, 0, 4)$, the aggregate assignment when each agent obtains good 3,
- $(1, 0, 3)$, the aggregate assignment when the odd-numbered agents obtain q^* and the even-numbered agents obtain $(0, 0, 1)$.

Only the middle three of these five points belong to Z, and one of the borders of Z, the dashed line, is disjoint with Z. Thus, the set Z is neither open nor closed.

The failure of openness of the set of Pareto dominant assignments breaks the standard proof. In particular, in the above example there is a horizontal hyperplane that partially, but not fully, separates Y and Z, a hyperplane that could not exist in a standard Walrasian analysis. At the same time, in this example there are many hyperplanes fully separating Y and Z.

It turns out that in the discrete settings that are considering, fully separating hyperplanes always exist even though the equivalence of full and partial separation fails. We now provide a proof that relies on the following mathematical lemma. In this lemma, a polyhedron is any intersection of closed half-spaces.

Lemma 17.11 (Full separation lemma). *Let $Y \subset \mathbb{R}^n$ be a closed and convex polyhedron. Let $Z \subset \mathbb{R}^n$ be convex, non-empty, and such that its closure $\bar{Z} \subset \mathbb{R}^n$ is a closed and convex polyhedron. Suppose that $Z \cap Y = \emptyset$ and that, for all $y \in Y \cap \bar{Z}$, $\delta \in \mathbb{R}^n$, and $\varepsilon > 0$, if $y + \delta \in Z$ then $y - \varepsilon\delta \notin \bar{Z}$. Then, there exists a price vector $p^* \in \mathbb{R}_+^n$ and a budget $w \in \mathbb{R}$ such that, for any $z \in Z$ and $y \in Y$, we have $p^* \cdot z > w \geq p^* \cdot y$ and, for any $\bar{z} \in \bar{Z}$ and $y \in Y$, we have $p^* \cdot \bar{z} \geq w \geq p^* \cdot y$.*

In the above example both sets Y and Z are polyhedra, and other conditions of the lemma are satisfied as well. Given the lemma, the proof of the second welfare theorem hinges on showing that the assumptions of the lemma are satisfied.

Proof of Theorem 17.9 We denote by $A(q)$ the aggregate assignment $A(q)$ associated with q, that is $A(q) = \sum_{i \in I} q_i$. We write $q \succ q^*$ when q Pareto-dominates q^*, that is, when $u_i(q_i) \geq u_i(q_i^*)$ for every $i \in I$ with at least one strict inequality. Let $Z = \{A(q) : q \succ q^*, q \in \Delta(X)^I\}$. If Z is empty then we can support q^* as equilibrium assignment by setting all prices to zero and giving agents arbitrary budgets. Suppose thus that Z is non-empty and notice that Z is convex. Let $\bar{Z}$ be the topological closure of Z, and notice that $\bar{Z}$ is a non-empty convex polytope. Let Y be the set of aggregate assignments $A(q)$ corresponding to feasible assignments q. This set is a closed and convex poly-tope, and the efficiency of q^* implies that the intersection of Z and Y is empty. To use the full separation lemma, we need the following $\qquad\qquad \square$

Claim. For any $y \in Y \cap \bar{Z}$, $\delta \in \mathbb{R}^{|X|}$, and $\varepsilon > 0$, if $y + \delta \in Z$ then $y - \varepsilon\delta \notin \bar{Z}$.

Proof of the claim. If $y + \delta \in Z$ then there is a $q \succ q^*$ such that $A(q) = y + \delta$. By way of contradiction, assume $y - \varepsilon\delta \in \bar{Z}$. Thus, there is a $\tilde{q} = (\tilde{q}_i)_{i \in I}$ such that $u_i(\tilde{q}_i) \geq u_i(q_i^*)$ for every $i \in I$ and $A(\tilde{q}) = y - \varepsilon\delta$. Then, the random assignment

$$\bar{q} = \frac{\varepsilon}{1+\varepsilon} q + \frac{1}{1+\varepsilon} \tilde{q}$$

is feasible, and the linearity of utilities in probabilities implies that $\bar{q} \succ q^*$. But this contradicts efficiency of q^*, proving the claim.

This claim and the full separation lemma imply that there exists a price vector $p^* \in \mathbb{R}_+^{|X|}$ and a budget $w \in \mathbb{R}$ such that $p^* \cdot z > w \geq p^* \cdot y$, for any $z \in Z$ and $y \in Y$. Since q^* is feasible, $\sum_{i \in I} q_i^* \in Y$ and thus $p^* \cdot \sum_{i \in I} q_i^* \leq w$. Furthermore, $p^* \cdot \sum_{i \in I} q_i^* \geq w$ because $q^* \in \bar{Z}$. We conclude that $p^* \cdot \sum_{i \in I} q_i^* = w$. Now, if we take some q_i that some agent $i \in I$ strictly prefers to q_i^* then $q_i + \sum_{j \in I \setminus \{i\}} q_j^* \in Z$, and we have $p^* \cdot \left(q_i + \sum_{j \in I \setminus \{i\}} q_j^* \right) > w = p^* \cdot \left(q_i^* + \sum_{j \in I \setminus \{i\}} q_j^* \right)$. Consequently we have $p^* \cdot q_i > p^* \cdot q_i^*$, proving that p^* and q^* constitute an equilibrium for budgets $w_i^* = p \cdot q_i^*$. $\square$

17.5 Fairness, Multiple-Unit Demand, Priorities, and Constraints

17.5.1 Fairness

In addition to efficiency, a key objective in mechanism design is fairness. A frequently invoked fairness objective is envy-freeness. A mechanism is *envy-free* if no participant strictly prefers the distribution of another participant to their own. Envy-freeness implies that if two agents have the same utility function then they are indifferent between their respective distributions.

Pseudomarkets can achieve envy-freeness:

Theorem 17.12 (Envy-freeness). *The pseudomarket mechanism in which all agents are endowed with equal budgets is envy-free.*

Indeed, if an agent strictly preferred another agent's distribution, then the outcome would not be in equilibrium because the cost of the preferred distribution would be within the first agent's budget.

Exercise 17.4 asks the reader to verify that the converse statement is not true: there are envy-free efficient assignments that cannot be implemented via equal-budget pseudomarkets, even though, as we have seen in Theorem 17.9, they can be implemented by other pseudomarkets.

17.5.2 Multi-Unit Demand

So far we have focused on the single-unit demand environment in which agents demand a probability distribution over objects. With two important exceptions – equilibrium existence and the implementability of random assignments as lotteries over deterministic ones – our analysis can be easily extended to the multi-unit demand environments.

In *multi-unit demand* environments, we continue to have a set of agents I and a set of objects X, with each object x represented by a finite number of copies $|x|$. Agents now demand probability distributions over bundles: a *bundle* might contain multiple copies of multiple objects. By $B_i \subseteq \times_{x \in X} \{0, 1, \ldots, |x|\}$ we denote the finite set of admissible individual bundles for agent i. For instance, setting $B_i = \{ b \in \times_{x \in X} \{0, 1, \ldots, |x|\} \mid \sum_{x \in X} b^x = 1 \}$ we can embed the single-unit demand environment as a special case of the multi-unit demand environment. A deterministic assignment of bundles $(b_i)_{i \in I} \in \times_{i \in I} B_i$ is feasible if $\sum_{i \in I} b_i^x \leq |x|$. A (random) assignment is feasible if it can be represented as a lottery over feasible deterministic assignments. The definition of pseudomarket equilibrium is the same as before except that distributions over bundles play the role of distributions over objects.

In this multi-unit demand setting we encounter two subtleties. First, in the single-unit demand setting, the Birkhoff–von Neumman theorem guaranteed the feasibility of every assignment such that the expectation of the number of copies of each object x assigned is weakly lower than the supply of this object, $|x|$. This key property is not guaranteed in the general multi-unit assignment setting.

Example 17.13. There are three agents 1, 2, 3 and four objects $x_1, \ldots, x_4$ such that $|x_1| = |x_2| = |x_3| = 1$ and $|x_4| = 2$. Consider the assignment in which agent i receives with probability $\frac{1}{2}$ bundle $\{x_i, x_{i+1 \mod 3}\}$ and with probability $\frac{1}{2}$ bundle $\{x_4\}$.[14] In expectation, one and a half copies of object x_4 and one copy of each of the objects $x_1, \ldots, x_3$ are assigned. However, we can verify that this assignment cannot be expressed as a lottery over feasible deterministic assignments.

In the special case in which agents' utilities over bundles are additively separable in terms of the utilities of objects in the bundle, the non-implementability of Example 17.13 can be overcome by assigning to agents distributions over copies of individual objects instead of distributions over bundles; the sum of an agent's probabilities then does not need to equal 1 and hence we refer to them as quantities. Breaking the bundles in this way leads in the above example to each agent i receiving a quantity $\frac{1}{2}$ of object x_i, a quantity $\frac{1}{2}$ of object $x_{i+1 \mod 3}$, a quantity $\frac{1}{4}$ of object x_4, and a quantity $\frac{1}{4}$ of object x_5. This broken-up assignment can be implemented as a lottery that places a probability $\frac{1}{2}$ on giving each agent i half of object x_i and half of object x_4 and places a probability $\frac{1}{2}$ on giving each agent i half of object $x_{i+1 \mod 3}$ and half of object x_4.

Second, for some budget vectors – including the equal-budget one – the equilibrium existence is not guaranteed.

Example 17.14. There are four agents 1, 2, 3, 4 and four objects $x_1, \ldots, x_4$, each with two copies. Agent i's most preferred bundle consists of the three objects different from x_i and their second most preferred bundle is $\{x_i\}$. We may check that if agents have equal budgets then no pseudomarket equilibrium satisfies market clearing even if we require the assignments to be feasible only in expectation.

The non-existence of market-clearing equilibria can be addressed by adjusting the budgets and allowing for limited failures of market clearing.

The rest of our analysis transfers more easily to the multi-unit setting. The analogues of the incentive Theorems 17.4 and 17.6, and the fairness Theorem 17.12 hold true. The conclusion of the efficiency Theorem 17.7 can be strengthened: equilibrium assignments are not only efficient but they are also not dominated by assignments

---

[14] The term $i + 1 \mod 3$ equals $i + 1$ for $i = 1, 2$, and it equals 1 for $i = 3$.

that are merely feasible in expectation; in turn, for such assignments, the efficiency Theorem 17.9 also holds true.[15]

17.5.3 Priorities and Constraints

Assignments may be subject to constraints. A popular type of constraint in single-unit demand assignment is based on endowing objects (e.g., schools) with priorities over agents (cf. Chapter 8) and requiring the underlying deterministic assignments to *honor* these *priorities* in the following sense: any object that an agent i prefers to the object assigned to him has all its copies assigned to agents whose priority regarding the object is at least as high as that of i. This constraint is known as stability.

Pseudomarkets have been adapted to guarantee that priorities are honored. The adaptation allows for the prices of objects to differ across agents in such a way that an agent with weakly higher-priority faces a weakly lower price. In equilibrium, there is at most one priority level at which the price can belong to $(0, \infty)$; for higher priority levels the price is 0 and for lower ones the price is prohibitively high, e.g., infinite. The existence and incentive-compatibility results continue to hold for such priority-adjusted pseudomarkets.

Multi-unit demand environments allow for a wide variety of constraints. By allowing for individualized sets of feasible deterministic assignments, the model introduced above already allows for many constraints. For example, it allows for some places at a school to be reserved for some types of applicants, while allowing all applicants to compete for the remaining seats. To model such a constraint we create an auxiliary object "reserved seats", which are feasible only for selected applicants.

In addition, the conjunctions of *linear constraints* – requiring that a weighted sum of probabilities that agents receive specific bundles is weakly lower or higher than some baseline – are particularly tractable. Under linear constraints, the above incentive and efficiency results continue to hold true. Existence is more subtle: it has been established for some linear constraints and it may require allowing different prices for agents differently impacted by the constraints, just as in the case of priority-based constraints above.

17.6 Exercises

Exercise 17.1 Consider the modification of Example 17.1 discussed in Section 17.2.3 and show that no assignment q^* and price vector $p^* \in \mathbb{R}_+^X$ satisfies $p^* \cdot q_i^* \leq p^* \begin{pmatrix} 1/3 \\ 2/3 \end{pmatrix}$ for all $i \in \{1, 2, 3\}$ and that $u_i(q_i) > u_i(q_i^*) \implies p^* \cdot q_i > p^* \begin{pmatrix} 1/3 \\ 2/3 \end{pmatrix}$ for all $(q_i)_{i \in \{1,2,3\}} \in \Delta(\{x, y\})^{\{1,2,3\}}$.

---

[15] The multi-unit versions of these results formally hold true irrespective of whether market-clearing equilibria exist. However, Theorems 17.6, 17.12, and 17.7 are only useful when the relevant equilibria exist.

Exercise 17.2 In the environment of Example 17.5, find a strategy-proof pseudo-market mechanism such that for the equilibrium price vectors we have $p_y = 0$ and $p_x = 3\mu$ $(x \succ y)$ for any distribution in the small ball studied therein.

Exercise 17.3 Verify the construction of sets Y and Z in Example 17.10.

Exercise 17.4 (a) Construct a single-unit demand environment and an efficient and envy-free assignment that cannot be implemented via an equal-budget pseudo-market. (b) Construct a non-equal-budget pseudomarket that implements the assignment from part (a).

Exercise 17.5 Verify that the assignment constructed in Example 17.13 is not feasible.

Exercise 17.6 Verify that there does not exist a pseudomarket equilibrium in which all agents have equal budgets in the environment of Example 17.14 even if we require the assignments to be feasible only in expectation.

Exercise 17.7 Extend Theorem 17.7 to the multi-unit demand environment.

17.7 Bibliographic Notes

Section 17.2 is based on [12]. Section 17.3.1 is based on [18]. Section 17.3.2 is based on [11], except for the impossibility result in footnote [7], which comes from [20]. For an alternative take on large-market incentives, the reader may also want to consult [4]. Section 17.3.3 is based on [7]. Section 17.4.1 is based on [12]. The example in Section 17.4.2 is based on [2] and [18], and the gain discussion that follows draws additionally on [19]. The discussion of utility measurement draws on [8], but primarily on [1], in which the gain potential in New York City was estimated. Section 17.4.3 is based on [16]; the proof of Lemma 17.11 can be found in this paper. The theorem of Section 17.5.1 comes from [12] while the discussion of the converse comes from [15]. This section focuses on ex-ante envy-freeness (before the realization of lotteries), and for a discussion of ex-post envy-freeness the reader might want to consult [5]. In Section 17.5.2, the model comes from [5], the pseudomarket definition and the efficiency results come from [16], and the incentive-compatibility results come from the present author's notes. The discussion of the implementability counterexample is based on [6] and [17]; the resolution for additively separable utilities is from [12] and [6]. The non-existence example comes from [5] as does its approximation-based resolution. In Section 17.5.3, the discussion of priorities follows [11]. The discussion of efficiency under linear constraints follows [16], the discussion of incentives is based on the present author's notes, and the discussion of existence follows [10].

Acknowledgements

Federico Echenique, Tuomas Kari, Julian Teichgrłaber, and Alexander Teytelboym gave me detailed and careful comments on this chapter, and I would also like to thank Yinghua He, Nicole Immorlica, Antonio Miralles, Vijay Vazirani, Jianye Yan, and, particularly, William Zame for conversations that shaped my thinking on pseudomarkets.

References

[1] Abdulkadiroglu, Atila, Agarwal, Nikhil, and Pathak, Parag A. 2017. The welfare effects of coordinated assignment: Evidence from the New York City High School Match. *American Economic Review*, **107**(12), 3635–3689.

[2] Abdulkadiroglu, Atila, Che, Yeon-Koo, and Yasuda, Yasuke. 2011. Resolving conflicting preferences in school choice: The Boston mechanism reconsidered. *American Economic Review*, **101**(1), 399–410.

[3] Arrow, Kenneth J., and Hahn, Frank H. 1971. *General Competitive Analysis*. Holden-Day.

[4] Azevedo, Eduardo M., and Budish, Eric. 2019. Strategyproofness in the large. *Review of Economic Studies*, **86**, 81–116.

[5] Budish, Eric. 2011. The combinatorial assignment problem: Approximate competitive equilibrium from equal incomes. *Journal of Political Economy*, **119**, 1061–1103.

[6] Budish, Eric, Che, Yeon-Koo, Kojima, Fuhito, and Milgrom, Paul. 2013. Designing random allocation mechanisms: Theory and applications. *American Economic Review*, **103**, 585–623.

[7] Budish, Eric, and Kessler, Judd B. 2020. Can market participants report their preferences accurately (enough)? Working paper.

[8] Calsamiglia, Caterina, Martínez-Mora, Francisco, and Miralles, Antonio. 2019. Cardinal assignment mechanisms: Money matters more than it should. Working Paper.

[9] Debreu, Gerard. 1959. *Theory of Value. An Axiomatic Analysis of Economic Equilibrium*. Yale University Press.

[10] Echenique, Federico, Miralles, Antonio, and Zhang, Jun. 2021. Constrained pseudo-market equilibrium. *American Economic Review* (Forthcoming).

[11] He, Yinghua, Miralles, Antonio, Pycia, Marek, and Yan, Jianye. 2018. A pseudo-market approach to assignment with priorities. *American Economic Journal: Microeconomics*, **10**(3), 272–314.

[12] Hylland, Aanund, and Zeckhauser, Richard. 1979. The efficient allocation of individuals to positions. *Journal of Political Economy*, **87**, 293–314.

[13] Kreps, David M. 2013. *Microeconomic Foundations I: Choice and Competitive Markets*. Princeton University Press.

[14] Mas-Colell, Andreu, Whinston, Michael D., and Green, Jerry R. 1995. *Microeconomic Theory*. Oxford University Press.

[15] Miralles, Antonio, and Pycia, Marek. 2015. Large vs. continuum assignment economies. Working Paper.

[16] Miralles, Antonio, and Pycia, Marek. 2021. Foundations of pseudomarkets: Walrasian equilibria for discrete resources. *Journal of Economic Theory*, **196**(105303), 1–24.

[17] Nguyen, Thành, Peivandi, Ahmad, and Vohra, Rakesh. 2016. Assignment problems with complementarities. *Journal of Economic Theory*, **165**, 209–241.

[18] Pycia, Marek. (2014). The cost of ordinality. Working Paper.
[19] Pycia Marek. 2019. Evaluating with statistics: Which outcome measures differentiate among matching mechanisms? Working Paper.
[20] Zhou, Lin 1990. On a conjecture by Gale on one-sided matching problems. *Journal of Economic Theory*, **52**, 123–135.

CHAPTER EIGHTEEN

Dynamic Matching

Mariagiovanna Baccara and Leeat Yariv

18.1 Introduction

Many matching environments are inherently dynamic – participants arrive at the market over time, or interact dynamically before forming matches. For example, in a child-adoption process, children become available progressively and often wait for a match while being cared for by social services, incurring wait costs in terms of well-being and long-term outcomes. Similarly, potential families pay attorney and agency fees while waiting to be matched to a child. For kidney donations, the US Department of Health and Human Services reports that a new patient is added to the kidney transplant list every 14 minutes and about 3000 patients are added each month. Since health conditions of potential recipients can potentially deteriorate as time passes, the timing of matches is crucial for minimizing the loss of lives: in 2014, 4761 patients died while waiting for a kidney transplant and another 3668 people became too sick to receive one. In the realm of public housing, families are often placed on waitlists before obtaining housing units, which become available stochastically. And so on and so forth.

To set the stage for our analysis, consider a simple setting in which squares S and rounds R arrive over time. For simplicity, suppose that any square and round are compatible, or agreeable, to one another with some probability p.[1] Consider then a bipartite graph connecting k squares with k rounds, where a link appears only when the corresponding pair is compatible; see Figure 18.1. This is a random graph, each link occurring with probability p.

A bipartite graph as such induces a *perfect matching* if there exists a matching $\mu: S \longrightarrow R$ that is injective and surjective, where $\mu(s) = r$ implies that s and r are linked in the graph (but not necessarily the converse: only some links are implemented when the induced matching is constructed). The following is a well-known result.

Proposition 18.1 [10]. *As long as the graph is sufficiently connected, namely as long as p approaches* 0 *more slowly than* $\log k / k$, *there is a perfect matching with probability approaching* 1 *as k grows large.*

[1] In principle, we could allow for heterogeneity among squares and rounds and allow the compatibility probability to depend on agents' types. Indeed, in the organ-donation context, some blood types are more common than others. The probability p we consider here could be thought of as the minimal compatibility probability across types.

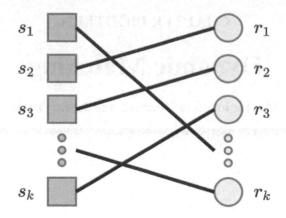

Figure 18.1 Compatability-based random preferences.

Thus, even if compatibility rates are very low, a large enough population of market participants would allow us to nearly guarantee a perfect match for everyone. Similar results hold when agents are heterogeneous and some matches generate greater surplus than others: in a very large population, it is almost always possible to create the maximal number of efficient matches and to minimize the loss due to less desirable matches.

In reality, when a market populates over time or when interactions between agents occur dynamically, waiting for a match is costly. Thus, in general, we cannot rely on the desirable asymptotic features of such markets. At the heart of work on the optimal design of clearinghouses in such settings is then the trade-off between market thickness, which yields high-quality matches, and costly waiting.

In this chapter, we illustrate how this trade-off affects the optimal design of matching mechanisms in different settings, from one-sided matching or allocation environments, in which one side of the market has preferences over items constituting the other market side, to two-sided markets, in which both sides of the market have preferences over matched partners.

18.2 Dynamic One-Sided Allocations

We start with a description of one-sided allocation problems in which scarce items – public housing, daycare slots, organs from deceased donors, etc. – arrive over time and are allocated to waiting agents. Importantly, there is heterogeneity in agents' valuations of items. In the following analysis, we consider two potential impediments to the socially optimal allocation: first, the social planner may be unable to impose item assignments on unwilling agents, who would rather wait for more preferable options; second, agents' preferences over items may not be transparent to the social planner.

18.2.1 Priority Protocols in Discretionary Settings

In this subsection we compare alternative priority protocols that a planner can implement when agents maintain discretion over the acceptance of an item offered to them. We study this problem in a setting in which the number of agents allowed to wait in line is fixed, and a new participant can join the line as soon as a waiting agent is assigned an item and leaves the market.

Consider a waitlist that, for simplicity, consists of only two agents, who are ranked according to their order of arrival: $\rho = 1, 2$. In every time period, one item becomes available and is offered to the agents according to an independently determined priority order. Specifically, the item is offered to the agents according to their order of arrival ρ with probability $r \in [\frac{1}{2}, 1]$, and according to the reverse order with probability $1 - r$. Hence, $r = 1$ represents the first-in–first-out (FIFO) protocol, while $r = \frac{1}{2}$ represents an equal-weight lottery. If the first agent to whom the item is offered declines it, the item is offered to the other agent. If the second agent also passes, the item goes to waste. If the $\rho = 1$ agent accepts the item, she leaves the market and the other agent gets her slot; namely, it is labeled with $\rho = 1$, while a new agent joins the waitlist with a $\rho = 2$ label. If the second, $\rho = 2$, agent is assigned the item, he leaves the market and a new agent replaces him as $\rho = 2$. Each period, agents incur a waiting cost $c > 0$. Assume that the reservation utility is sufficiently low that agents entering the waitlist never leave without being assigned an item.

We start with the *private value case* in which each agent's valuation for each item is independent, equals 1 with probability $p \in (0, 1)$, and 0 otherwise. Any agent i always accepts an item that she values at 1. Let $q(i)$ denote agent i's probability of acceptance of an item that she values at 0. For $i = 1, 2$, agent i's continuation value, the difference between her expected value and her expected cost is:

$$V(i) = \frac{A(i)}{B(i)} - \frac{ic}{B(i)},$$

where

$$A(1) = p\left[r + (1 - r)(1 - p)(1 - q(2))\right],$$
$$A(2) = p\left[2 - p - (1 - p)(rq(1) + (1 - r)q(2))\right],$$
$$B(1) = \left[p + (1 - p)q(1)\right]\left[r + (1 - r)(1 - q(2))(1 - p)\right],$$
$$B(2) = \left[p + (1 - p)q(1)\right]\left[r + (1 - r)(1 - p)(1 - q(2))\right]$$
$$\quad + \left[p + (1 - p)q(2)\right]\left[1 - r + r(1 - p)(1 - q(1))\right].$$

For example, $A(1)$ represents the expected value of the item picked by agent 1. The item is valued at 1 for agent 1 with probability p, in which case agent 1 accepts it whenever it is offered. The agent is offered the item first with probability r. The item is offered to agent 1 after being rejected by agent 2 with probability $(1 - r)(1 - p)(1 - q(2))$.

The probabilities of misallocation and waste are

$$\mu = p(1 - p)\left[rq(1) + (1 - r)q(2)\right]$$

and

$$v = (1 - p)^2(1 - q(1))(1 - q(2)),$$

respectively. Unsurprisingly, the probability of waste v is independent of the queuing protocol r. It is easy to check that there are three equilibria comprising pure Markov strategies, $\{q^j(1), q^j(2)\}_{j=1}^3$, where $q^1(1) = q^1(2) = 0$, $q^2(1) = 0$, $q^2(2) = 1$, and $q^3(1) = q^3(2) = 1$.

In all three equilibria, an increase in r leads to an increase in $V(1)$. We now focus on the effect of an increase in r on $V(2)$. Intuitively, there are two effects at work. An increase in r decreases the probability with which agent 2 is offered the item first, and therefore decreases agent 2's continuation value. However, an increase in r also increases the continuation value of agent 1, and therefore makes agent 1 more selective. This latter effect benefits agent 2, since every item rejected by agent 1 is offered to agent 2 next, potentially generating a strictly positive value for him. As it turns out, the two effects cancel one another and, in all three equilibria, any increase in r leaves $V(2)$ unchanged. We can conclude that an increase in r weakly increases the equilibrium values of both agents and leaves the probability of waste unchanged. Finally, the probability of misallocation is negatively correlated with agents' equilibrium values, and it is weakly decreasing in r.

Next, consider the *common value case* in which the values of the two agents are perfectly correlated. We can express the continuation value as in the private value case, where now

$$A(1) = rp,$$
$$A(2) = p,$$
$$B(1) = r\left[p + (1 - p)q(1)\right] + (1 - r)(1 - p)\,q(1)(1 - q(2)),$$
$$B(2) = 1 - (1 - p)(1 - q(1))(1 - q(2)).$$

For example, as before, $A(1)$ represents the expected value of the item picked by agent 1. Since values are correlated, the only case in which agent 1 is offered an item of value 1 is when she is first in line. The expected value is then rp.

Since the two agents value all items in the same way, there is never misallocation. The probability of waste is

$$v = (1 - p)(1 - q(1))(1 - q(2)),$$

which is again independent of r. As in the private value case, it is easy to check that there are three pure-strategy Markov equilibria $\{\tilde{q}^j(1), \tilde{q}^j(2)\}$, where $\tilde{q}^1(1) = \tilde{q}^1(2) = 0$, $\tilde{q}^2(1) = 0$, $\tilde{q}^2(2) = 1$, and $\tilde{q}^3(1) = \tilde{q}^3(2) = 1$. An increase in r always increases $V(1)$ and does not affect $V(2)$. The reasoning behind the effect on $V(2)$ is slightly different from that pertaining to the private value case. Specifically, in the common value case the only scenario in which an agent can make a positive payoff is by being offered the item first. An increase in r lowers the probability with which agent 2 is approached first. However, it also increases the rate at which agent 1 accepts an item and leaves the market, freeing her spot on the waitlist for agent 2. Again, the two effects balance one another, leaving $V(2)$ unaffected by changes in r.

To summarize, this analysis illustrates two settings in which the FIFO queuing protocol dominates a lottery, from both the participants' and the social planner's perspectives.

18.2.2 Buffer-Queues Mechanism with Private Preferences

Consider now a setting in which a large set of agents is present at time $t = 0$ and, at each period, a new item arrives at the market. The items can be of two sorts: an A-item with probability p_A, and a B-item with probability $p_B \equiv 1 - p_A$. Agents can also be of two types. Agents of type α prefer A-items, while agents of type β prefer B-items. Each agent is of type α with probability p_α and of type β with probability $p_\beta \equiv 1 - p_\alpha$. For simplicity, assume that the system is *balanced*; that is, $p_A = p_\alpha \equiv p$. Each agent gets utility $v > 0$ from being assigned her preferred item, and 0 from being assigned a different item. As before, the waiting costs that agents incur before being matched are linear, and the per-period cost is $c > 0$. For example, this setup fits the allocation process of public housing units to families that vary in their preferences over housing units' attributes: location, the unit's floor in the building, etc.

Without observing agents' types, the social planner needs to select a mechanism μ to allocate each arriving item to an agent, and we allow the social planner to impose assignments on agents if needed. Since the system is assumed to be overloaded, an item is assigned at every period – i.e., there is no waste. Therefore, the total wait cost is constant across allocations, and the social planner's goal is to minimize the welfare loss due to items' misallocation. Given an assignment μ, if ξ_t is an indicator equal to 1 if the arriving item at t is misallocated, the long-run misallocation rate is $\xi = \limsup_{T \to \infty} \sum_{t=0}^{T} \xi_t$. Therefore, the welfare loss from misallocation is

$$WFL = v\xi.$$

As a convenient benchmark, consider a sequential assignment mechanism that assigns the arriving item to an arbitrary agent without agents having any discretion on whether to accept or decline any item. It is easy to see that such a mechanism generates a misallocation rate of $\xi^{SA} = 2p(1-p)$. Can we do better than this mechanism by inducing agents to report their types truthfully?

It is possible to induce agents to reveal their type by allowing them discretion over whether to accept an item offered immediately or a different item at some future time. Such a mechanism yields an endogenous separation of the agents into two sets: those who have not yet been approached, and those who have been approached in the past and have decided to wait for their preferred item. Those agents who are waiting after having been approached form the *buffer queue* (*BQ*). Agents in the buffer queue are divided into those who are waiting for an A-item, in the A-buffer queue (*A-BQ*), and those who are waiting for a B-item, in the B-buffer queue (*B-BQ*). Since items' arrival is stochastic, agents in the buffer queue face uncertainty regarding the time at which they will receive their desired item. As buffered agents accumulate, the mechanism needs to take their presence into consideration as new offers are made to subsequent agents. For $x = A, B$, a *buffer-queue policy* for x-items governs the maximal number of agents that are allowed in the x-BQ and how each new x-item is allocated to the agents waiting in the x-BQ.

Definition 18.2 (Buffer-queue policy). For $x = A, B$, a $\langle \overline{k}^x, \varphi^x \rangle$ buffer-queue policy for x consists of a threshold $\overline{k}^x$ of the number of agents in the x-BQ and, for any length $k \leq \overline{k}^x$ of the x-BQ, a probability $\varphi_k^x(i)$ with which an agent in position $1 \leq i \leq k$ of the x-BQ is assigned the item x. Therefore, $\varphi_k^x(i) \geq 0$ for any $1 \leq i \leq k \leq \overline{k}^x$, and $\sum_{i=1}^{k} \varphi_k(i) = 1$ for any $1 \leq k \leq \overline{k}^x$.

Definition 18.3 (Buffer-queue mechanism). A buffer-queue mechanism $\mathcal{M} = \langle \overline{k}^A, \varphi^A, \overline{k}^B, \varphi^B \rangle$ specifies a buffer-queue policy for each item and, for $x = A, B$, if an x-item arrives, it implements the following steps:

1. If the x-BQ is not empty, the x-item is assigned to an agent in the x-BQ according to φ^x.
2. If the x-BQ is empty, the mechanism sequentially approaches new agents until the x-item is assigned. Let $y \neq x$. For each newly approached agent:
   (a) If the y-BQ currently has $k - 1 < \overline{k}^y$, the mechanism offers the agent the choice of (i) taking the x-item immediately, or (ii) declining the x-item and joining the y-BQ in the kth position to receive a y-item in the future according to φ^y. If the agent chooses (i), the period ends, and if the agent chooses (ii), the mechanism approaches another new agent.
   (b) If the y-BQ currently has $\overline{k}^y$ agents, then the new agent is assigned the x-item and the period ends.

A buffer-queue mechanism is incentive compatible if, whenever the buffer queue is not full, any agent chooses to join that buffer queue rather than accept a less desirable item; that is, agents are *truthful*. For example, consider an unapproached agent of type α who is offered a B-item. The agent has the choice of either taking that item or revealing that she is mismatched and being placed in the A-BQ in position k. In that case, suppose w_k^A is the expected number of periods that the agent will have to wait until receiving an A-item. Given w_k^A, the agent prefers to join the A-BQ if $v - cw_k^A \geq 0$, or $w_k^A \leq v/c \equiv \overline{w}$. If the agent believes that other agents are truthful, the expected wait w_k^A depends only on $\left\langle \overline{k}^A, \varphi^A \right\rangle$. Therefore, $\mathcal{M}$ is referred to as *incentive compatible* if $w_k^x \leq \overline{w}$ for all $k \leq \overline{k}^x$ and $x = A, B$; put differently, if an equilibrium occurs when all agents are truthful.

The dynamics of a buffer-queue mechanism when agents are truthful are captured by an ergodic Markov chain with state space $\{-\overline{k}^B, \ldots, \overline{k}^A\}$, where the state $k \geq 0$ indicates that k agents are waiting in the A-BQ, and $k \leq 0$ indicates that $|k|$ agents are waiting in the B-BQ. Note that at most one of the queues can be non-empty at any given time.

Buffer queues can be used to study the performance of a single waitlist governed by a FIFO priority order. All agents wait in an ordered line and know their position. Each arriving item is offered to the first agent in the queue. If that agent declines, the item is offered to the second agent in line, and so on. All agents who decline an item keep their positions in the queue. The following result allows us to quantify the equilibrium welfare loss associated with this protocol.

Proposition 18.4 (Equilibrium of a FIFO waitlist). *The single FIFO waitlist has a unique equilibrium in which the outcome is identical to a buffer-queue mechanism $\mathcal{M} = \langle \overline{k}^A, \varphi^A, \overline{k}^B, \varphi^B \rangle$ when agents are truthful, φ^A and φ^B follow a FIFO order, and $\overline{k}^A = \overline{k}^B = \lfloor p\overline{w} \rfloor$. The welfare loss is given by*

$$WFL^{FIFO} = \frac{2vp(1 - p)}{(1 - p) \lfloor p\overline{w} \rfloor + p \lfloor (1 - p)\overline{w} \rfloor + 1}.$$

The intuition behind Proposition 18.4 is simple. Consider an agent of type α in position k of a single waitlist. If the agent is offered an A-item, she will accept. If she is offered a B-item, it must be the case that $k - 1$ agents before her declined the same item, since they are waiting for A. Therefore, the agent is expected to wait k/p periods before being offered an A-item. This implies that the agent prefers to wait if and only if $v - kc/p \geq 0$, or $k \leq p\overline{w}$. The Markov-chain structure of the buffer queues allows an easy computation of the welfare loss. As the wait cost approaches zero, the welfare loss of the single FIFO waitlist in the balanced case vanishes.

Finally, we can characterize a welfare-maximizing incentive-compatible buffer-queue mechanism. To do so, we first define a *load independent expected wait (LIEW)* policy for item $x = A, B$. This is a buffer-queue policy $\langle \overline{k}^x, \varphi^x \rangle$ in which, when agents are truthful, the expected wait w for agents in the queue does not depend on their position in the queue or on the number of other agents in the queue. A mechanism $\mathcal{M} = \langle \overline{k}^A, \varphi^A, \overline{k}^B, \varphi^B \rangle$ is a LIEW mechanism if $\langle \overline{k}^x, \varphi^x \rangle$ is *LIEW* for $x = A, B$. We have

Proposition 18.5 (Optimal buffer queue). *Let* $\mathcal{M}^* = \langle \overline{k}^A, \varphi^A, \overline{k}^B, \varphi^B \rangle$ *be a LIEW mechanism such that* $\overline{k}^A = \overline{k}^B = \overline{k}^{LIEW}$, *where*

$$\overline{k}^{LIEW} = \lfloor 2p\overline{w} \rfloor - 1.$$

Then $\mathcal{M}^*$ *is incentive compatible and achieves weakly higher welfare when agents are truthful than any other incentive-compatible buffer-queue mechanism.*

To understand the ideas underlying Proposition 18.5, observe that, since misallocations decrease as $\overline{k}^A$ and $\overline{k}^B$, welfare maximization requires the maximization of $\overline{k}^A$ and $\overline{k}^B$ subject to the incentive-compatibility constraint. Now, we can establish that any buffer-queue policy with $\overline{k} > \overline{k}^{LIEW}$ is not incentive compatible. To see this, notice that for a policy to be incentive compatible, for any $k \leq \overline{k}$, any agent who joins the buffer queue at position k must expect a wait w_k such that $w_k \leq \overline{w}$, so that $E[w] \leq \overline{w}$. In the balanced case, the average number of people in the buffer queue is $L = \frac{\overline{k}+1}{2}$. Little's law implies that $E[w] = \frac{L}{p} = \frac{\overline{k}+1}{2p} \leq \overline{w}$, or $\overline{k} \leq \lfloor 2p\overline{w} \rfloor - 1$. Therefore, if $\overline{k} > \overline{k}^{LIEW}$, there must be at least one position k' such that $w_{k'} > \overline{w}$, thereby violating incentive compatibility.

It is possible to show that $\mathcal{M}^*$ reduces the welfare loss to almost half that of the FIFO mechanism. Intuitively, any buffer-queue mechanism compensates agents that reject a mismatch by promising them a better match in the future, albeit at the cost of additional wait time. In a FIFO mechanism, agents who join the buffer queue when it is relatively short obtain larger net payoffs than those joining the buffer queue later on, for whom the incentive-compatibility constraint is binding. A LIEW mechanism induces the same expected wait time for all agents. It is then able to accommodate more agents in the buffer queue while maintaining incentive compatibility.

18.3 Dynamic Two-Sided Matching

18.3.1 Dynamic Matching with Fixed Participants

Many real markets have a fixed set of participants interacting in a dynamic fashion. For instance, every year, new economics graduate students enter the job market for academic positions. The set of candidates and the available positions are, by and large, set at the start of each year and interactions between market participants occur dynamically: universities often invite candidates to interviews sequentially and the generation of offers often spans several months. Many other markets share those features: the market for new law clerks, freshly minted rabbis, etc. Even the medical match, while famously governed by a centralized clearinghouse, is preceded by interactions – namely, interviews – that occur over time and are by and large decentralized. How do such decentralized markets work? What matches can they achieve? Will they be stable?

One natural way to answer these questions is to describe precisely a two-sided *decentralized matching market game* in which participants interact over time. The main ingredients of such a game are naturally the underlying preference distribution of participants and the information available to them.

Consider the following simple setup. A market corresponds to a triplet $(\mathcal{S}, \mathcal{R}, U)$, where $\mathcal{S} = \{1, \ldots, S\}$ is a finite set of squares – say, hiring firms – and $\mathcal{R} = \{1, \ldots, R\}$ is a finite set of rounds – say, potential employees. Match utilities can then be described as follows:

$$U = \left\{ \underbrace{\left\{ u_{ij}^s \right\}}_{\text{\textbf{square } } i\text{'s utility from matching with } j}, \quad \underbrace{\left\{ u_{ij}^r \right\}}_{\text{\textbf{round } } j\text{'s utility from matching with } i} \right\}.$$

For simplicity, we can assume that, for any participant, remaining unmatched generates a utility of 0 and that all match utilities are strictly positive.

Certainly, if a market has multiple stable matchings, any dynamic interaction would conceivably suffer from coordination problems: even if participants aimed at establishing a stable outcome, they would need to agree on which one. Consider then the simple case in which utilities are such that there is a unique stable matching, which we denote by μ_M.

One way to model market interactions is via a dynamic version of the deferred acceptance (DA) algorithm. At every period $t = 1, 2, \ldots$ there are two stages. First, the squares simultaneously decide whether and to whom to make an offer, where an unmatched square can have at most one offer out. Then, each round j who has received an offer from square i can accept, reject, or hold the offer. If such an offer is accepted at period t, square i is matched to round j irreversibly. Square i then receives a payoff of $\delta^t u_{ij}^r$ and round j receives a payoff of $\delta^t u_{ij}^w$, where $\delta \leq 1$ is the market discount factor. Unmatched agents receive 0 throughout the game. Importantly, in contrast with the way in which a direct-revelation version of DA operates, squares need not make offers in order of their preference lists and rounds need not hold only offers that are their favorites. In particular, squares can approach rounds multiple times, much as in labor-market applications, where some individuals may receive repeat offers from particular employers.

Regarding market monitoring, assume that squares and rounds observe receipt, rejection, and deferral only of offers in which they are involved. However, whenever an offer is accepted, the whole market is informed of the union. Similarly, whenever there is market exit, all participants are informed. We make these assumptions because of their realism. While individuals or firms are privy to details of offers they engage with, they are unlikely to know the ins and outs of all offers made in the market. Nonetheless, theoretically, one could consider various alternatives to this monitoring structure.

We now consider the Nash equilibria of such a market game. As it turns out, we can always implement the unique stable outcome μ_M through equilibrium:

Proposition 18.6 (Equilibrium with fixed participants). *There exists a Nash equilibrium in strategies that are not weakly dominated that generates the unique stable matching.*

The intuition of this proposition is straightforward. Indeed, consider the following profile. At $t = 1$, each square i makes an offer to round $\mu_M(i)$. Each round j accepts the highest-ranked square that is at least as good as $\mu_M(j)$, breaking any ties in favor of $\mu_M(j)$. The round leaves immediately if she receives no offers and all squares are matched or have exited. Otherwise, off the equilibrium path, squares and rounds revert to strategies that emulate the DA algorithm.

Nonetheless, there can be other (unstable) equilibrium outcomes, as the following example illustrates.

Example 18.7 (Multiplicity). Suppose that $\mathcal{S} = \{s_1, s_2, s_3\}$, $\mathcal{R} = \{r_1, r_2, r_3\}$, and that utilities induce the following ordinal preferences:

$$
\begin{array}{ll}
s_1: \quad r_2 \succ r_1 \succ r_3 & \qquad r_1: \quad s_1 \succ s_3 \succ s_2 \\
s_2: \quad r_1 \succ r_2 \succ r_3 & \qquad r_2: \quad s_2 \succ s_1 \succ s_3 \\
s_3: \quad r_1 \succ r_2 \succ r_3 & \qquad r_3: \quad s_1 \succ s_3 \succ s_2
\end{array}
$$

We continue assuming that all participants are acceptable.

These preferences induce a unique stable matching μ_M such that $\mu_M(s_i) = r_i$ for all i.

As it turns out, we can induce another matching μ, where s_1 and s_2 swap their partners and match with their favorite rounds, as long as the discount factor δ is high enough. Namely, we can implement in equilibrium $\mu(s_1) = r_2$, $\mu(s_2) = r_1$, and $\mu(s_3) = r_3$.

How can that be done in equilibrium? Consider the following profile of strategies. In period 1, s_3 makes an offer to r_3, who accepts any offer from a square ranked at least as high as r_3. Squares s_1 and s_2 make no offers, while rounds r_1 and r_2 accept offers only from their favorite squares. In period 2, each square s_i, with $i = 1, 2$, makes an offer to $\mu(s_i)$. Rounds r_1 and r_2 accept any offer. Upon any observable deviation, all remaining agents revert to emulating (square-proposing) DA strategies.

Why is this profile an equilibrium? Notice that s_3 and r_3 are bound to match with one another. They therefore respond best by doing so in the first period. In fact, they have a strict preference for doing so with any discount factor smaller than 1. With s_3 and r_3 out of the way, the resulting "sub-market" exhibits the following restricted preferences:

$$
\begin{array}{ll}
s_1: \quad r_2 \succ r_1 & \qquad r_1: \quad s_1 \succ s_2 \\
s_2: \quad r_1 \succ r_2 & \qquad r_2: \quad s_2 \succ s_1
\end{array}
$$

In particular, this sub-market entails two stable matchings: one matching s_i with r_i for $i = 1, 2$ and one matching s_i with r_{3-i} for $i = 1, 2$. What transpires from period 2 onwards is essentially the profile we used to prove Proposition 18.1: each square makes an offer to their most-preferred stable partner. Notice that the rounds are not using weakly dominated strategies in this example. In particular, if square s_i makes an offer to r_i in period 1, for $i = 1, 2$, that offer would be accepted immediately. Nonetheless, for high enough discount factors, these squares would prefer to wait for one period to get their most preferred partner.

This example hinges on the dynamic nature of interactions. Agents are making *contingent* offers: conditional on s_3 and r_3 leaving the market, s_1 and s_2 target their most favored stable partners. For example, in the job-market context, this suggests that certain participants could be placed in a "waitlist" and approached with an offer only after other participants have been matched. Clearly, what allows this example to occur is the fact that, despite the overall market having a unique stable matching, one sub-market has multiple stable matchings. Ruling out the possibility that sub-markets exhibit multiple stable matchings eliminates such examples when combined with appropriate refinements.[2]

18.3.2 Dynamic Matching with Evolving Participants

In many two-sided matching processes, such as child adoption and kidney exchanges, participants arrive over time. Likewise, many labor markets entail unemployed workers and job openings that become available at different periods. Such settings open the door to new questions regarding the operations of both decentralized and centralized interactions.

18.3.2.1 Dynamic Stability

When market participants arrive over time, certain matches might be created along the way – patients get transplants, parents adopt children, individuals get public housing, etc. In such settings, attempts to block a market matching are constrained by the fact that only a subset of individuals is available at any point in time. We start by modifying the standard notion of stability for such settings.

For illustration purposes, we consider a particularly simple setting. Suppose that there are only two periods, $t = 1, 2$. A finite set of squares $\mathcal{S}$ all arrive at $t = 1$. A finite set of rounds $\mathcal{R}$ arrive in two installments: a subset of rounds $\mathcal{R}_1 \subset \mathcal{R}$ arrives at $t = 1$ and a subset $\mathcal{R}_2 \subset \mathcal{R}$ arrives at $t = 2$, where

$$\mathcal{R}_1 \cap \mathcal{R}_2 = \varnothing \text{ and } \mathcal{R}_1 \cup \mathcal{R}_2 = \mathcal{R}.$$

Thus, only one side of the market appears in increments. Furthermore, there is certainty on future arrivals.

---

[2] One can show that, with *aligned* preferences, where there is no "preference cycle" in the matrix of match surpluses, the iterated elimination of weakly dominated strategies generates a unique equilibrium prediction, which is stable. As a note about refinements, owing to our assumptions on the structure of monitoring, subgame perfection has little bite. Public monitoring occurs only through market exits, which limit the set of proper subgames.

We assume that squares are discounted-utility maximizers. That is, for each $s \in S$, there is a utility $u(s, \cdot): \mathcal{R} \to \mathbb{R}$ and a discount factor $\delta_s \in [0, 1]$, such that s's utility from matching with round r at time t is given by $\delta_s^t u(s, r)$. We also assume that remaining unmatched generates zero utility: $u(s, s) = 0$. We make similar assumptions when it comes to rounds, but distinguish between rounds arriving at period 1 and rounds arriving at period 2. Namely, each round $r \in \mathcal{R}$ is associated with a utility $v(\cdot, r): S \to \mathbb{R}$, where we assume that $v(r, r) = 0$. Furthermore, each round r in $\mathcal{R}_1$ uses a discount factor $\delta_r \in [0, 1]$. Agents in $\mathcal{R}_2$ experience no discounting as they exist for only one period in the market. At any time t, only available agents can match with one another. Consequently, we can define a *period-t matching* as an injective map $m_t: S \cup \bigcup_{\tau=1}^{t} \mathcal{R}_\tau \to S \cup \bigcup_{\tau=1}^{t} \mathcal{R}_\tau$ such that (i) for all $s \in S$, $m_t(s) \in \{s\} \cup \bigcup_{\tau=1}^{t} \mathcal{R}_\tau$, and (ii) for all $r \in \bigcup_{\tau=1}^{t} \mathcal{R}_\tau$, $m_t(r) \in S \cup \{r\}$. Let M_t denote the set of all period-t matchings.

Naturally, period-1 matchings impose constraints on period-2 matchings. Namely, if an agent is matched in period 1, she cannot be rematched in period 2. Formally, a pair $(m_1, m_2) \in M_1 \times M_2$ is *feasible* if for all $s \in S$, if $m_1(s) \neq s$ then $m_2(s) = m_1(s)$ (and since m_2 is injective, $m_2(m_1(s)) = s$). Let M denote the set of all feasible matchings.

Even when the set of participants is fixed, we have seen already that the dynamics allow for matchings to be *contingent* on prior market interactions. The same occurs when market participation evolves: period-2 matchings can depend on the matchings implemented in period 1. Our object of analysis is therefore a *contingent* matching. Such a matching specifies the selection of a period-1 matching and, for each matching in period 1, the selection of a period-2 matching. Formally, a *contingent matching* μ is a map

$$\mu: \{\varnothing\} \cup M_1 \to M_1 \cup M_2$$

such that $\mu(\varnothing) \in M_1$ and, for all $m_1 \in M_1$, $\mu(m_1) \in M_2$ and $(m_1, \mu(m_1))$ is feasible.

We are now ready to define the dynamic stability of a contingent matching. It entails two conditions. First, once a matching is formed in period 1, the matching in period 2 must be stable among the remaining agents and the new entrants, for much the same reasons as those described in Chapter 1 on static markets. The period-2 matching should then be individually rational and entail no blocking pairs. Second, taking the outcomes of period 2 as given, no group of agents in period 1 can beneficially deviate from the prescribed matching.

Definition 18.8 (Dynamic stability). A contingent matching μ is dynamically stable if:

1. For each $m_1 \in M_1$, the resulting period-2 matching $\mu(m_1)$ is stable, entailing no blocking individuals or pairs;
2. There is no set $A \subseteq S \cup R_1$ that can implement m_1 in such a way that all agents in A prefer $(m_1, \mu(m_1))$ to $(\mu(\varnothing), \mu(\mu(\varnothing)))$. Namely, there is no group of agents in $t = 1$ that can improve their outcomes by changing who they are matched with at $t = 1$, or who they are waiting to match with at $t = 2$, or both.

Suppose a contingent matching μ is individually rational but not dynamically stable. Then, either there exists a pair of contemporary agents that prefer matching to one another over their prescribed partners under μ, or there exists a group of $t = 1$ agents who can block by waiting to be matched.

We can also define the *core* analogously to the way in which it is defined for static matching markets. Namely, a contingent matching μ is in the core if there is no agent who would rather remain single than match according to μ and there is no pair that would prefer to generate a (feasible) match at some point over their prescribed matches under μ. Formally, that there is no blocking pair means that there is no $s \in \mathcal{S}$ and $r \in \mathcal{R}_t$ such that

$$\delta_s^{1(r \in \mathcal{R}_2)} u(s, r) > U(s, m_\mu) \quad \text{and} \quad v(s, r) > V_t(r, m_\mu),$$

where U is the discounted utility for the squares and V_t is the utility for rounds arriving at time t.

What is the difference between the core and dynamically stable contingent matchings? There are two main differences. First, in the core, even if $b \in \mathcal{R}_2$, a and b can form a blocking coalition at the outset. Essentially, there is no concern for the arrival time of different agents. Second, blocking coalitions in the core compare the payoffs they obtain by blocking with the payoffs they obtain from the matching prescribed by μ. In contrast, dynamic stability requires that a coalition that blocks by waiting in period 1 compares its payoff under μ to the payoffs generated in the *continuation matching* originated by the block.

Unfortunately, dynamically stable matchings do not always exist, as the following example illustrates.

Example 18.9. Suppose $\mathcal{S} = \{$Erdős, Kuhn, Gale$\}$, $\mathcal{R}_1 = \{$Renyi, Tucker$\}$, and $\mathcal{R}_2 = \{$Shapley, Nash$\}$.

In what follows, we consider rankings of any square s over elements of the form (r, t), where if s ranks (r, t) over (r', t'), then $\delta_s^t u(s, r) > \delta_s^{t'} u(s, r')$. We further assume that all agents prefer to match with specified agents over remaining unmatched.[3] The rankings and specified agents are as follows, where alternatives are ranked from left to right:

Erdős:	(Shapley, 0)	(Shapley, 1)	(Renyi, 0)	(Renyi, 1)
Kuhn:	(Shapley, 1)	(Nash, 0)	(Tucker, 0)	(Nash, 1)
Gale:	(Tucker, 0)	(Tucker, 1)	(Shapley, 0)	(Shapley, 1)

and

Renyi:	Erdős		
Tucker:	Kuhn	Gale	
Shapley:	Gale	Erdős	Kuhn
Nash:	Kuhn		

Assume that, for all r, the discount δ_r is sufficiently high that $v(s, r) > v(s', r)$ implies that $\delta_r v(s, r) > v(s', r)$.

---

[3] In addition, we assume non-trivial discounting, so that $(r, 0)$ is always preferable to $(r, 1)$ for any r.

If μ is dynamically stable, then Gale has to be matched under μ. Otherwise, he would be unmatched at $t = 2$ and could block with Shapley. Thus, Gale has to be matched, either with Tucker at $t = 1$ or with Shapley at $t = 2$.

Let $m_1 = \mu(\varnothing)$. Suppose Gale is matched with Shapley. It has to be that $m_1(\text{Kuhn}) = \text{Tucker}$ and $m_1(\text{Erdős}) = \text{Renyi}$. Indeed,

1. Kuhn cannot be unmatched because he would block with Nash at $t = 2$, and
2. Kuhn blocks a match with Nash by matching early with Tucker since, importantly, he does not like to wait for Nash.

However, the unique stable matching at $t = 2$, when only Erdős is matched with Renyi at $t = 1$, matches Kuhn with Shapley, whom Kuhn prefers to Tucker. Hence, Kuhn blocks any such contingent matching μ by waiting.

Similar reasoning rules out the case in which Gale is matched with Tucker at $t = 1$.

What drives non-existence in the example? It is discounting: Kuhn prefers Nash to Tucker but does not want to wait for him. That is why Kuhn cannot be matched to Tucker in period 2.

Consider then a market with *trivial discounting*, so that if $u(s, r) > u(s, r')$ then $\delta_s u(s, r) > u(s, r')$, for any square s and rounds r, r'.

Proposition 18.10 (Existence). *If preferences satisfy trivial discounting, the set of dynamically stable contingent matchings is non-empty.*

At the root of the impact of discounting are cycles. In the example above, Kuhn prefers Shapley at $t = 2$, Shapley prefers Gale, Gale prefers Tucker immediately, who prefers Kuhn. So, if Kuhn were matched to Tucker and Gale were matched to Shapley, both Kuhn and Shapley would want to swap their partners. As we have seen, this allows for deviations such as those in which Kuhn beneficially waits for period 2 to match.

In general, a *simultaneous preference cycle* is an alternating sequence of squares and rounds, $r_1, s_1, r_2, s_2, \ldots, r_N$, where $r_1 = r_N$, such that, when considering period-1 preferences,

1. Each square s_i prefers $r_{(i+1)\bmod N}$ to r_i, but both of these rounds are acceptable to s_i;
2. Each round r_i prefers s_i to s_{i-1}, but both of these squares are acceptable to r_i.[4]

We can now summarize the impacts of such cycles on the structure and existence of dynamically stable matchings.

Proposition 18.11 (Preference cycles). *If a core matching is not part of a dynamically stable contingent matching then there is a preference cycle. If there are no preference cycles, the set of dynamically stable contingent matchings coincides with the core.*

---

[4] We interpret $s_0 = s_N$ so that, for r_1, this implies that s_1 is preferable to s_N.

18.3.2.2 A Simple Model of Dynamic Centralized Design

The notion of dynamic stability offers a decentralized benchmark for considering markets in which agents arrive in sequence. It is also natural to consider the optimal design of clearinghouses in such settings. We now analyze a simple model in which the optimal centralized clearinghouse can be characterized. As we have already seen, one hurdle that an evolving market presents is that agents may prefer partners that arrive later than they do. Waiting for them comes at a cost.

Suppose that, in each period, one square and one round arrive at the market. Assume that each square is of a desirable, or high, type H with probability p and of a less desirable, or low, type L with probability $1 - p$. Similarly, suppose that each round is of a desirable type h with probability p and of a less desirable type l with probability $1 - p$. Let U_{xy} denote the surplus that any type x of square and any type y of round generates when matched with each other, for $x = H, L, y = h, l$.[5]

For simplicity, assume supermodular preferences, so that

$$U \equiv U_{Hh} + U_{Ll} - U_{Hl} - U_{Lh} > 0.$$

In particular, an efficient matching entails the maximal number of (H, h) and (L, l) pairs.

We assume $p \in (0, 1)$ so that, conceivably, a social planner might want market participants to wait in order to generate more efficient matchings. This assumption guarantees that thicker markets generate greater overall match surplus.

Assume that all agents suffer a cost $c > 0$ for each period on the market without a match. In particular, any pair that is held in the market for a period generates a loss of $2c$ to the planner.

Suppose agents depart the market only upon matching. As long as remaining unmatched generates sufficiently low utilities, this restriction is consistent with individual rationality.[6]

Consider general dynamic mechanisms, where the social planner can create matches between available agents at every period. Formally, at any time t, before a new square–round pair arrives, a queue is represented by (k_H, k_h, k_L, k_l), where the lengths of the queues of squares are given by k_H and k_L for H-squares and L-squares, respectively. Similarly, the lengths of the queues of rounds are given by k_h and k_l for h-rounds and l-rounds, respectively.

We focus on stationary and deterministic mechanisms. At time t, *after* a new square–round pair enters the market, there is a queue $\mathbf{n}^t = (n_H^t, n_h^t, n_L^t, n_l^t)$, where the indices correspond to types as before. A mechanism is characterized by a mapping $\mu : \mathbb{Z}_+^4 \to \mathbb{Z}_+^4$ such that for every $\mathbf{n} \in \mathbb{Z}^4$, $\mu(\mathbf{n}) = \mathbf{m} = (m_{Hh}, m_{Hl}, m_{Lh}, m_{Ll})$ is a feasible profile of matches, with m_{xy} corresponding to the number of matches generated between any type x of square and any type y of round.[7] Once matches are created, a new queue $\mathbf{k} = (k_H, k_h, k_L, k_l)$ contains the remaining agents:

---

[5] These surpluses can be generated naturally by individual agents' utilities from matching with agents of different types.

[6] Individual rationality can be defined once individual utilities from matches are specified. The idea that remaining unmatched yields extremely low payoffs is relevant for many of the applications to which such a model speaks. For instance, parents seeking to adopt a child may suffer greatly by not finding a match. Similarly, patients seeking an organ donor may suffer dire consequences from not being matched.

[7] Naturally, the social planner cannot match more agents than are available, so we must have that $m_{xh} + m_{xl} \leq n_x$ for $x \in \{H, L\}$ and, similarly, $m_{Hy} + m_{Ly} \leq n_y$ for $y \in \{h, l\}$.

$$k_x = n_x - (m_{xh} + m_{xl}) \text{ for } x \in \{H, L\},$$
$$k_y = n_y - (m_{Hy} + m_{Ly}) \text{ for } y \in \{h, l\}.$$

The surplus generated by matches $\mathbf{m}$ is

$$S(\mathbf{m}) \equiv \sum_{(x,y)\in\{H,L\}\times\{h,l\}} m_{xy} U_{xy}.$$

The waiting costs incurred by retaining the agents $\mathbf{k}$ are

$$C(\mathbf{n}, \mathbf{m}) \equiv c \left(\sum_{x\in\{H,h,L,l\}} k_x \right).$$

The welfare generated at time t is then

$$w(\mathbf{n}^t, \mathbf{m}^t) \equiv S(\mathbf{m}^t) - C(\mathbf{n}^t, \mathbf{m}^t).$$

The social planner assesses the performance of a mechanism using the *average welfare*, defined as:

$$W(\mu) \equiv \lim_{T\to\infty} \frac{1}{T} \mathbb{E} \left[\sum_{t=1}^{T} w(\mathbf{n}_t, \mu(\mathbf{n}_t)) \right].$$

The average welfare is well defined in that it can be shown that the above limit exists for every mechanism μ.

An *optimal mechanism* is a mechanism achieving the maximal average welfare. An optimal mechanism exists since there is only a finite number of stationary and deterministic mechanisms leading to a bounded stock of agents in each period.

Lemma 18.12 (Congruent matches). *Any optimal mechanism requires (H, h) and (L, l) pairs to be matched as soon as they become available.*

The intuition for this lemma is the following. If the social planner holds on to an (H, h) pair, it is only for the hope of matching the relevant agents with a future L-square and an l-round. However, our supermodularity assumption implies that this would entail an efficiency loss. Hence, the planner may as well match the (H, h) pair immediately. Symmetric logic follows for any available (L, l) pair.

Thus, the optimal mechanism potentially holds on to agents only when they form incongruent pairs. Intuitively, the optimal mechanism cannot hold an exceedingly large number of agents since the waiting costs would be prohibitive. In fact, the following holds:

Proposition 18.13 (Optimal mechanism). *An optimal dynamic mechanism is identified by a pair of thresholds $(\bar{k}_H, \bar{k}_h) \in Z_+$ such that*

1. *whenever more than $\bar{k}_H$ H-squares are present, $n_H - \bar{k}_H$ pairs of the type (H, l) are matched immediately, and*
2. *whenever more than $\bar{k}_h$ h-rounds are present, $n_h - \bar{k}_h$ pairs of the type (L, h) are matched immediately.*

Since the environment here is fully symmetric, we can assume, without substantial loss of generality, that $\bar{k}_H = \bar{k}_h = \bar{k}$.[8]

Write $k_{Hh} = k_H - k_h$. The value of k_{Hh} captures both the number of agents onto which the social planner holds on to and their type: when $k_{Hh} > 0$, there are H-squares and l-rounds waiting, while when $k_{Hh} < 0$, there are L-squares and h-rounds waiting. The quantity k_{Hh} follows a Markov process, where states correspond to values $-\bar{k} \leq k_{Hh} \leq \bar{k}$.

Notice that, for any $-\bar{k} < k_{Hh} < \bar{k}$, the stock of agents held by the planner does not change if an (H, h) or an (L, l) pair arrives, which occurs with probability $p^2 + (1 - p)^2$. The stock changes, up or down, if an (H, l) or an (L, h) pair arrives, each occurring with a probability of $p(1 - p)$.

We can therefore characterize the Markov chain associated with k_{Hh} through the transition formula $\mathbf{x}^{t+1} = \mathbf{T}_{\bar{k}}\mathbf{x}^t$, where $\mathbf{x}^t$ is a $(2\bar{k} + 1)$-dimensional vector such that its kth entry equals 1 whenever, at time t, $k_{Hh} = k$, and equals 0 otherwise:

$$
\mathbf{T}_{\bar{k}} = \begin{bmatrix} 1 - p(1 - p) & p(1 - p) & 0 & & & 0 \\ p(1 - p) & p^2 + (1 - p)^2 & & & & \\ 0 & & \cdots & & & \\ & & & p^2 + (1 - p)^2 & p(1 - p) \\ 0 & & & p(1 - p) & 1 - p(1 - p) \end{bmatrix}.
$$

The resulting process is ergodic, implying a unique steady-state distribution, which is the uniform distribution over states. That is, in the steady state, k_{Hh} takes each of its possible $2\bar{k} + 1$ values with probability $1/(2\bar{k} + 1)$.

We now use the characterization of the steady-state distribution to identify the costs and benefits for any $\bar{k}$. In state j, $2|j|$ participants are present on the market. The expected total waiting costs are therefore:

$$
C(\bar{k}) = \frac{1}{2\bar{k} + 1} \left(\sum_{j=-\bar{k}}^{\bar{k}} 2|j| \right) c = \frac{\bar{k}(\bar{k} + 1)c}{2\bar{k} + 1}.
$$

To calculate the expected benefits, suppose an (H, l) pair (similarly for an (L, h) pair) arrives at the market when the state is j. If $-\bar{k} \leq j < 0$, the optimal mechanism creates one (H, h) match and one (L, l) match, generating a surplus of $U_{Hh} + U_{Ll}$. If $0 \leq j < \bar{k}$, the mechanism creates no matches, generating no match surplus. If $j = \bar{k}$, the mechanism creates an (H, l) match, generating a surplus of U_{Hl}. Any congruent pair arriving at the market is matched immediately and generates its corresponding match surplus. Thus, after algebraic manipulations, the expected per-period total match surplus is

$$
B(\bar{k}) = pU_{Hh} + (1 - p)U_{Ll} - \frac{p(1 - p)U}{2\bar{k} + 1}.
$$

The optimal $\bar{k}$ maximizes $B(\bar{k}) - C(\bar{k})$. We can therefore fully characterize the optimal mechanism in this setting.

---

[8] For almost all parameters of this environment, there is a unique optimal mechanism with such identical thresholds. However, for a negligible set of parameters, as will soon become apparent, additional asymmetric thresholds generate the same level of average welfare.

Proposition 18.14 (Optimal threshold). *The threshold*

$$\overline{k}^* = \left\lfloor \sqrt{\frac{p(1-p)U}{2c}} \right\rfloor$$

identifies an optimal dynamic mechanism, and it is generically unique.

The optimal threshold $\overline{k}^*$ balances market thickness and waiting costs. It decreases in c and is positive only when costs are sufficiently low, namely when $c \leq p(1-p)U/2$. The optimal threshold increases as $p(1-p)$, the probability of an incongruent pair's arrival, and is maximized at $p = 1/2$.[9]

When the optimal threshold is implemented, the resulting welfare can then be calculated as follows:

$$W^*(c) = pU_{Hh} + (1-p)U_{Ll} - \frac{p(1-p)U}{2\overline{k}^* + 1} - \frac{\overline{k}^*(\overline{k}^* + 1)c}{2\overline{k}^* + 1}.$$

From supermodularity, the maximal conceivable welfare, when there are no waiting costs and an infinitely thick market, is given by

$$S_\infty = pU_{Hh} + (1-p)U_{Ll}.$$

Naturally, $W^*(c) \leq S_\infty$. In fact, this inequality is strict for any $c > 0$. We can now consider the comparative statics of $W^*(c)$ with respect to costs. First, the optimal welfare decreases in c. Indeed, for $c_1 > c_2$, the social planner can emulate the mechanism designed for c_1 when waiting cost c_2 is in place. That would generate the same matching surplus under both costs but a lower average waiting cost under c_2. Second, the welfare loss is concave in c. To see this, we utilize the fact that the optimal threshold $\overline{k}^*$ decreases in c. Therefore, as c increases, fewer individuals wait and the effect of a marginal cost increase is smaller. We therefore have the following:

Corollary 18.15 (Optimal welfare). *The welfare under the optimal mechanism is given by $W^*(c) = S_\infty - \Theta(c)$, where $\Theta(c)$ is continuous, increasing, and concave in c, $\lim_{c \to 0} \Theta(c) = 0$, and $\Theta(c) = p(1-p)U$ for all $c \geq p(1-p)U/2$.*

As a direct consequence, for vanishingly small waiting costs, the optimal mechanism achieves approximately the maximal conceivable welfare.

18.3.2.3 Other Considerations

Organ donation is a natural environment in which participants – patients seeking an organ and donors willing to give an organ – arrive over time and need to be paired. Furthermore, waiting for a transplant is costly for patients. A substantial fraction of organ donation is from cadavers. The allocation then is in many ways simpler. Preferences of patients are by and large observable: their blood and tissue type, their urgency, demographics, etc. The system can then generate (Pareto) efficient allocations without much concern for incentive-compatibility constraints.[10]

---

[9] Uniqueness of the optimal threshold breaks down only when $\sqrt{p(1-p)U/2c}$ is an integer, which occurs for a zero-measure set of parameters.

[10] See Section 30.7 of Chapter 30 for a related discussion.

In kidney exchanges, patients arrive with a live donor – a family member, a friend, etc. – who is not necessarily a compatible match. Can there be beneficial swaps between patients and their donors that would induce agents to enter the system to begin with? The timing of such swaps is also important. Matching all compatible pairs reduces waiting costs. However, keeping some desirable donors in the pool – say, those with O blood type, who are blood-type compatible with any patient – can have future benefits, in terms of facilitating other exchanges or finding immediate matches for future patients in particularly critical health conditions.

In the first analysis of this issue, it was shown in [14] that if only two-way exchanges are allowed, every optimal mechanism matches all compatible pairs immediately. Nonetheless, when multi-way exchanges are allowed, the efficient mechanism may require holding some available matches to keep relatively scarce donors available for future use.

Along similar lines, one can consider environments in which agents can at some point become critical and drop out of the system if not matched immediately. Consider random compatibility between pairs, which can be formulated in graph-theoretic terms.[11] Participating (incompatible) patient–donor pairs constitute the graph's nodes and arrive at a Poisson rate of $m \geq 1$ in an interval of time $[0, T]$. Any two such pairs are compatible with probability $p = d/m$, with $d > 0$. Moreover, pairs become critical at a Poisson rate normalized to 1. If they are not matched immediately, critical pairs perish. Otherwise, there is no waiting cost. Given a matching policy, the resulting expected number of pairs that perish can be thought of as the *loss* of the policy. A planner, observing the set of pairs that become critical, seeks to minimize loss. While characterizing the optimal matching algorithm of this model is computationally difficult, it is easy to see that it has to satisfy the following two conditions: (i) since there are no waiting costs, two connected pairs are matched only if at least one is critical, and (ii) if a critical pair is connected to someone else, it is always matched immediately.

Furthermore, it is possible to obtain quantitative insights on the performance of the optimal algorithm by considering the following two simple algorithms:

Definition 18.16 (Greedy algorithm). If any new pair enters the market at time t, match it randomly with any existing compatible pair, if such a pair exists.

Definition 18.17 (Patient algorithm). If a pair becomes critical, match it randomly with any compatible pair. Otherwise, hold onto pairs.

Both these algorithms are obviously suboptimal since they do not use any information regarding the underlying graph. Denote by $L(G)$ and $L(P)$ the loss associated with the Greedy and Patient algorithms, respectively, over the horizon $[0, T]$.

Proposition 18.18 (Loss bounds). *For $d \geq 2$, as $T, m \to \infty$, we have:*

$$L(G) \geq \frac{1}{2d + 1} \quad and \quad L(P) \leq \frac{1}{2}e^{-d/2}.$$

---

[11] Two patient–donor pairs are compatible if a swap of donors and patients yields compatibility in terms of blood type, tissue type, etc.

Proposition 18.18 suggests that the Patient algorithm's loss is exponentially small, while the Greedy algorithm's loss is not. That is, the option value of waiting before matching pairs is large. To see why, suppose there are z pairs in the market. If a new pair enters the market under the Greedy algorithm, or becomes critical under the Patient algorithm, the probability that no pair on the market is compatible is $(1 - d/m)^z$. However, the number of pairs in the market depends on the algorithm under consideration. As more pairs wait under the Patient algorithm, the market is thicker, which reduces the probability of any critical pair being unmatched. To estimate the performance of the Patient algorithm, it is useful to establish a lower bound on the loss achieved by the optimal algorithm, which we denote by L^*.

Proposition 18.19 (Efficiency of the Patient algorithm). *Let A be any algorithm that observes the set of critical pairs with associated loss $L(A)$. Then, for $d \geq 2$, as $T, m \to \infty$,*

$$L^* \geq \frac{e^{-d(1+L(A))/2}}{d+1}.$$

Substituting the Patient algorithm for A, we obtain

$$L^* \geq \frac{e^{-(d/2)(1+(e^{-d/2})/2)}}{d+1}$$

or, as $T, m \to \infty$,

$$L(P) - L^* \leq e^{-d/2} \left[\frac{1}{2} - \frac{e^{-(d/4)e^{-d/2}}}{d+1} \right],$$

indicating that the performance of the optimal algorithm is close to that of the Patient algorithm. This suggests that the benefit of allowing the market to thicken before the matching of pairs is substantial, even if the implemented mechanism does not fully exploit all the information contained in the network structure.

18.4 Bibliographic Notes

The model described in Section 18.2.1 relies on [6]. The model described in Section 18.2.2 is analyzed in [12]. While that model assumes agents are heterogenous in the items they prefer, say public-housing units, recent work considers settings in which agents agree on the ranking of the items but differ in their preference intensities; see [13]. In addition, when the items are thought of as services – e.g., medical services by junior or senior physicians, legal aid from rookie or experienced lawyers, etc. – the distribution of these services can be endogenized. Namely, junior service providers become senior providers after attending to a sufficient number of tasks. In such settings, the balance between service quality and wait times needs to account for the training possibilities that affect the future distribution of available services. See [3] for details.

Our discussion of decentralized market games in Section 18.3.1 relies on a model offered by [11], while the main example in that section relates to an example appearing in [9]. In [11], decentralized market games were also studied in settings in which agents have incomplete information about others' preferences. It was shown that incomplete information introduces another hurdle for (complete-information) stability, even when market participants are very patient and interactions offer ample opportunities for learning. Dynamic decentralized interactions have been studied using laboratory experiments as well; see [1] and [8]. While stability has strong drawing power with complete information, the introduction of transfers or incomplete information impedes stability.

The notion of dynamic stability described in Section 18.3.2.1, as well as the example in that subsection, were suggested in [7]. This work offers a definition of stability for far more general dynamic settings than those sketched here, allowing for multiple periods and uncertainty about agents' arrival over time.

Our discussion in Section 18.3.2.2 of optimal clearinghouses in environments in which agents on two market sides arrive over time relies on [4]. In that article a discretionary counterpart was also analyzed in which participants *choose* whether to wait for a more desirable partner.[12] It was shown that agents wait excessively, not internalizing the externalities on other agents who arrive after them.

The literature on dynamic matching arguably started from the consideration of organ donation; see Part III of this book. In [14], the value of multi-way swaps was shown. The results described in Section 18.3.2.3 appear in [2].[13]

The discussion in this chapter illustrates the different ways by which waiting costs are modeled: as flow costs, discounted match values, or through the likelihood of urgently needing a match. Which modeling method is used naturally depends on the application. In decentralized interactions, costs can take either form. From a market-design perspective, however, discounting introduces several challenges. First, the market designer may need to keep track of the *arrival time* of participants, placing a heavy computational and potentially logistical burden. Second, agents who have waited for a long time exhibit low discounted match values and would then receive lower weight in the market designer's considerations. In contrast, in many applications, seniority lends an advantage – for example, patients waiting for a long time for an organ or families queuing for public housing are prioritized.

There are many natural directions in which the models described in this chapter could be extended. While transfers are banned or limited in many applications such as organ donation, child adoption, and public housing, they are present in many others, particularly when considering dynamic labor markets. Their consideration could enrich our models substantially. The effects of incomplete information regarding the underlying preferences in the market would also be an interesting direction to pursue further in this area.

References

[1] Agranov, M., Dianat, A., Samuelson, L., and Yariv, L. 2022. Paying to match: Decentralized markets with information frictions. Mimeo.

[12] Individual utilities are assumed to be such that all squares prefer *h*-rounds and all rounds prefer *H*-squares.

[13] The decentralized settings considered here and in the context of organ donation differ from those of the search and matching literature presented in Chapter 22. Those models commonly assume a stationary type distribution. Stationarity might be reasonable in very large markets, but is harder to square with smaller markets in the applications to which this chapter speaks. For example, data from one US child adoption facilitator who links adoptive parents and birth mothers indicates a rate of about 11 new potential adoptive parents and 13 new birth mothers entering the facilitator's operation each month, see [3].

[2] Akbarpour, M., Li, S., and Gharan, S. O. 2020. Thickness and information in dynamic matching markets. *Journal of Political Economy*, **128**, 783–815.

[3] Baccara, M., Collard-Wexler, A., Felli, L., and Yariv, L. 2014. Child-adoption matching: Preferences for gender and race. *American Economic Journal: Applied Economics*, **6**, 133–58.

[4] Baccara, M., Lee, S., and Yariv, L. 2020. Optimal dynamic matching. *Theoretical Economics*, **15**, 1221–1278.

[5] Baccara, M., Lee, S., and Yariv, L. 2022. Task allocation and on-the-job training. Mimeo.

[6] Bloch, F. and Cantala, D. 2017. Dynamic assignment of objects to queuing agents. *American Economic Journal: Microeconomics*, **9**, 88–122.

[7] Doval, L. 2021. Dynamically stable matching. Mimeo.

[8] Echenique, F., Robinson-Cortés, A., and Yariv, L. 2022. An experimental study of decentralized matching. Mimeo.

[9] Echenique, F., Wilson, A. J., and Yariv, L. 2016. Clearinghouses for two-sided matching: An experimental study. *Quantitative Economics*, **7**, 449–482.

[10] Erdős, P. and Rényi, A. 1964. On random matrices. *Publications of the Mathematical Institute of the Hungarian Academy of Sciences*, **3**, 455–460.

[11] Ferdowsian, A., Niederle, M., and Yariv, L. 2022. Strategic decentralized matching: The effects of information frictions. Mimeo.

[12] Leshno, J. 2019. Dynamic matching in overloaded waiting lists. Mimeo.

[13] Ortoleva, P., Safonov, E., and Yariv, L. 2022. Who cares more? Allocation with diverse preference intensities. Mimeo.

[14] Ünver, M. U. 2010. Dynamic kidney exchange. *Review of Economic Studies*, **77**, 372–414.

CHAPTER NINETEEN

Matching with Search Frictions

Hector Chade and Philipp Kircher

19.1 Introduction

The frictionless matching literature, started by the seminal and beautiful papers by [25] and [43], has long acknowledged that agents in the market might be linked to only a small number of agents on the other side (see [42] and the literature building on it). In this chapter we investigate search processes that bring agents from both sides together but prevent them from interacting with the whole market. Although search frictions are pervasive in labor, marriage, and housing markets, we will cast the models in this chapter in terms of a labor market where workers and firms match. We will study how search frictions affect sorting patterns among matched partners (workers and firms), transfers (wages), and the probabilities of forming a match (hiring probabilities).

We explore this topic both through the lens of random search and through recent theories of directed search where agents can target their search to attributes of their partners on the other side. By going over several models of matching with search frictions, our hope is that the reader will learn how to introduce search frictions in matching settings, the main pitfalls that one needs to tackle, and some insights that have received attention in this relatively recent but growing literature with many open problems. Broader surveys are referenced in the final section.

19.2 Benchmark: Frictionless Case

We will begin by considering a well-known and useful benchmark that builds on [6]. Since this is an assignment game, whose properties are analyzed in detailed in Chapter 4 of this book, we will just focus on the large-market case and derive some basic equilibrium properties that we will contrast with the case with search frictions.

Assume a market with an equal unit-mass continuum of heterogeneous workers and firms. Each worker has an attribute (skill) $x \in [0, 1]$, with cumulative distribution function (cdf) G and strictly positive density g. Each firm has an attribute (productivity) $y \in [0, 1]$, with cdf H and strictly positive density h. If a worker with attribute x matches with a firm with attribute y then the pair produces an output $f(x, y)$ that is freely divided between the two parties (they both have quasilinear preferences), so there is *perfectly transferable utility*. The function f is C^2, positive, and such that $f(0,0) = 0$. Unmatched agents obtain a payoff equal to zero.

Matching in this market is one-to-one, and for our purposes it will suffice to define a matching as a function $\mu : [0, 1] \to [0, 1]$ that is *measure preserving*. Furthermore, and as is standard in the literature that applies this setup to labor and marriage markets, we will focus on monotone matching: *positive sorting*, given by $H(\mu(x)) = G(x)$ for all x, so that $\mu(x) = H^{-1}(G(x))$ for all x; and *negative sorting*, given by $H(\mu(x)) = 1 - G(x)$ for all x, so that $\mu(x) = H^{-1}(1 - G(x))$ for all x. In particular, if $G = H$ then we have $\mu(x) = x$ for all x under positive sorting.

Consider the planner's problem in this setting. Since preferences are quasilinear, the planner maximizes aggregate output (see 4.2.1). It follows by a standard rearrangement inequality that if f is supermodular, that is, $f_{xy} \geq 0$, then positive sorting is efficient, while negative sorting is optimal if f is submodular. The same turns out to be true under a competitive equilibrium. Before turning to the details, let us provide some intuition. Assume that f is supermodular and consider two workers with attributes x_ℓ and x_h, $x_\ell < x_h$, and two firms with attributes y_ℓ and y_h, $y_\ell < y_h$. By supermodularity, $f(x_h, y_h) - f(x_\ell, y_h) \geq f(x_h, y_\ell) - f(x_\ell, y_\ell)$, which, in words, says that the firm with attribute y_h, when competing with y_ℓ for x_h versus x_ℓ, can outbid y_ℓ since the increase in output from matching x_h instead of x_ℓ is larger for y_h than for y_ℓ. In a competitive market, this force will turn out to be enough to construct an equilibrium with positive sorting.

A competitive equilibrium is a triple (μ, w, π), where $w : [0, 1] \to \mathbb{R}$ is a wage function such that, for each x, $w(x)$ is the wage of a worker with attribute x and $\pi : [0, 1] \to$ is a profit function such that, for each y, $\pi(y)$ is the profit of a firm with attribute y. Let us assume that f is supermodular and derive a competitive equilibrium with positive sorting (a similar argument can be used in the case of f submodular and negative sorting).

Consider a firm with attribute y facing a wage function w. The firm solves $\max_{x \in [0,1]}(f(x, y) - w(x))$, and the first-order condition is $f_x(x, y) = w'(x)$. To turn this into an equilibrium condition we insert $y = \mu(x) = H^{-1}(G(x))$ to obtain $f_x(x, \mu(x)) = w'(x)$ for all x. Integrating and using that $f(0, 0) = 0$ implies $w(0) = 0$, we obtain that the candidate for the equilibrium w is

$$w(x) = \int_0^x f_x(s, \mu(s))ds.$$

Moreover, choosing x such that $y = \mu(x)$ (or $x = \mu^{-1}(y)$) gives a global optimum for a firm with attribute y. To see this, assume $x' < x$, and note that

$$f(x, y) - w(x) \geq f(x', y) - w(x') \Leftrightarrow f(x, y) - f(x', y) \geq w(x) - w(x') = \int_{x'}^x f_x(s, \mu(s))ds$$

$$\Leftrightarrow \int_{x'}^x f_x(s, \mu(x))ds \geq \int_{x'}^x f_x(s, \mu(s))ds,$$

where the first equality holds by the definition of w, and the last expression by the fundamental theorem of calculus and $y = \mu(x)$. But, since f is supermodular, $f_x(s, \mu(x)) \geq f_x(s, \mu(s))$ for all $s \in [x', x]$. Similarly if $x' > x$, thus showing the asserted global optimality.

We can also solve the problem in which each worker with attribute x faces a profit function π, and we obtain an expression for π, similar to the one above, which satisfies that, for each (x, y) such that $y = \mu(x)$, the pair exhausts the match output: $f(x, \mu(x)) = w(x) + \pi(\mu(x))$. Hence, the triple (μ, w, π) is a competitive equilibrium with positive sorting.[1] Finally, one can show that, for those (x, y) not matched with each other, $w(x) + \pi(y) > f(x, y)$, thereby showing that the competitive equilibrium delivers a stable matching.[2]

The tractable expressions (μ, w, π) provide a lot of information about equilibrium properties. For example, note that

$$w''(x) = f_{xx}(x, \mu(x)) + f_{xy}(x, \mu(x))\mu'(x),$$

and thus w is convex in x if $f_{xx} \geq 0$, both under positive sorting (where $\mu' > 0$ and $f_{xy} \geq 0$) and negative sorting (where $\mu' < 0$ and $f_{xy} \leq 0$). For another example, suppose that we index G by a parameter τ and H by t, so that higher τ or t increases G or H in a first-order stochastic dominance sense. Then it is easy to verify that $\mu_t(x) = -H_t(\mu(x)|t)/h(\mu(x)|t) \geq 0$ and $\mu_\tau(x) = G_\tau(x|\tau)/h(\mu(x)|\tau) \leq 0$, where the subscripts denote partial derivatives with respect to the parameter indexing the type distributions. This is intuitive: an improvement in the distribution of firm productivity makes better firms less scarce and increases the competition for better workers, thus increasing the attribute of the firm matched to each worker. The opposite is true if there is an improvement in the distribution of skills. It follows that $w_t(x) \geq 0$ and $w_\tau(x) \leq 0$.

As an illustration, let $f(x, y) = xy$, $G(x) = x^\alpha$, $\alpha > 0$, and $H(y) = y^\beta$, $\beta > 0$. Since $f_{xy} = 1 > 0$, equilibrium matching exhibits positive sorting: $\mu(x) = x^{\alpha/\beta}$. Also, since $f_x(x, y) = y$ and thus $f_x(x, \mu(x)) = \mu(x) = x^{\alpha/\beta}$ for all x, the wage function w is $w(x) = \int_0^x s^{\alpha/\beta} ds = (\beta/(\alpha + \beta))x^{(\alpha+\beta/\beta)}$ for all x, and the profit function π is $\pi(y) = (\alpha/(\alpha + \beta))y^{(\alpha+\beta/\alpha)}$ for all y. Note that w is strictly convex in x, and that the above comparative statics hold if we interpret α and β as τ and t.

If instead of having flexible transfers we assume the extreme case of *strictly non transferable utility* (e.g., either there are no transfers at all or the division of f is exogenously set as, say, equal division), then positive sorting obtains if f is increasing in each argument. To see this, note that if a high-attribute worker is matched with a low-attribute firm whereas a low-attribute worker is matched with a high-attribute firm then the matching would be unstable since the high-attribute agents could form a blocking pair.

Note that both the supermodularity of f that yields positive sorting under perfectly transferable utility and the monotonicity in the partner's attribute of f that yields positive sorting under strictly non-transferable utility are *distribution-free* conditions: they hold for any cdfs G and H. We will pursue this goal below when obtaining conditions for positive sorting under search frictions.

---

[1] If f is strictly supermodular then any competitive equilibrium exhibits positive sorting.

[2] The assumptions of equal-size populations and zero unmatched payoff can be relaxed; the only difference is that a positive measure of agents remains unmatched. Similarly, the results above obtain under weaker differentiability assumptions, and the smoothness properties of w and π can be formally justified. Finally, uniqueness follows from $w(0) = 0$; if not then equilibrium is parameterized by the wage of the lowest-attribute agent.

19.3 Search Frictions: Some Modeling Choices

Many economic situations do not fit the frictionless world analyzed above. Indeed, in labor, marriage, and housing markets, and in some product markets, to name a few, it takes time and resources to find a suitable partner for production or consumption purposes, be it an appropriate firm for a worker's skill, a marriage partner, a seller with a house that suits a buyer's tastes, or a seller with some quality product that a buyer values more than others.

To model these markets, the literature has enriched the standard competitive setting by introducing search frictions. There are two standard choices on how to model these frictions: directed search and random search. In directed search, at least in its standard formulation, the main issue is not that the process of finding a partner is time consuming but that there are coordination frictions, so some agents may remain unmatched due to the stochastic nature of the matching process. Most of the important insights of directed search models can be gathered from a one-period version thereof. In random search, agents meet potential partners over time according to some stochastic process and this task takes time and resources, which makes it costly to delay accepting a match. These models are dynamic by construction, since agents solve an optimal stopping problem in their search for partners. Since non-stationary search can seriously complicate the analysis of these markets, the usual focus has been on the steady state.

Another important modeling choice is whether utility is transferable or not. Two polar cases have been analyzed: perfectly transferable and strictly non-transferable. Under the latter case, the problem on the one hand simplifies since there is no need to specify how transfers are set, but on the other hand it is more complex since partners may disagree in their decision of whether to form a match. Under the former, one needs to specify how the terms of trade are set since there is no Walrasian auctioneer to clear the market. In directed search, posted transfers are commonly used, while in random search the Nash bargaining solution (NBS) is the standard protocol used.

There is also a choice regarding how to model heterogeneity. A natural choice, on which we will focus, assumes as in the frictionless model that agents have an attribute that is fixed and observable by potential partners. This affords a rich but much more complex analysis of matching under search frictions. Another choice, which is more tractable and has been used in the literature on search and matching since some early contributions in the 1970s, is to assume that agents are ex-ante identical but ex-post heterogeneous (that is, in each meeting, each potential partner considers an idiosyncratic and payoff-relevant attribute of her partner before accepting an offer). We will go over a relatively recent contribution that models heterogeneity in this ex-post way.

A key feature in modeling search frictions is how to determine the stochastic process that generates the meetings among agents. A common modeling device is to assume that there is a matching function that yields the total number of meetings as a function of the number of unmatched agents on each side of the market.[3] From it one can derive the meeting probabilities that each agent faces. Two common specifications in the literature are the so-called linear and quadratic search technologies. In the linear case the total number of meetings is linear in the number of unmatched

---

[3] In some cases the existence of such a function can be justified by an appropriate stochastic process and an appeal to the law of large numbers with a continuum of random variables.

agents, and thus the probability of an agent meeting any given partner is independent of how many searchers are in the market. In the quadratic case, the total number of meetings is quadratic in the number of searchers, and thus the probability of an agent meeting a partner is linear in the number of unmatched partners.

Finally, a choice that is just a matter of convenience under random search is whether to set up a model in discrete or continuous time. The latter simplifies the analytical derivations while the former makes the setup more amenable to empirical or quantitative work.

19.4 Directed Search

19.4.1 One-to-One Matching

Consider a market where workers with heterogeneous attributes $x \in [0, 1]$ supply a unit of labor, firms with attributes $y \in [0, 1]$ want to hire a unit labor to produce non-negative output $f(x, y)$, where f is C^2 and is strictly increasing in attributes, and output is perfectly transferable. The simplest way of introducing search frictions is to assume that workers with attribute x and firms with attribute y meet in submarkets indexed by three objects: the attributes x and y and the transfer w. For each triple (x, y, w), there is an endogenous measure n and r of workers and firms in this market, which is their choice variable. The number of matches in a market is given by a positive matching function m, so that $m(n, r)$ is the number of matches in this market with measures n and r. This implies that markets with different agents' attributes and wages are separated. The classical frictionless assignment is the limit where $m(n, r) = \min\{n, r\}$, i.e., the short side certainly trades in each market. With search frictions it is usually assumed that m is strictly increasing and strictly concave in each argument, and exhibits constant returns to scale. Hence, the matching probabilities of workers and firms are $\alpha(\theta) = m(\theta, 1)$ and $\gamma(\theta) = m(\theta, 1)/\theta$, where the ratio $\theta = n/r$ is called the queue length. Clearly α is decreasing in the queue length, as this means more competition by other workers in the queue length for the same job, while γ is increasing for analogous reasons.

Since knowledge of the queue length is sufficient for all parties to make optimal choices, a market is characterized by the combination of (x, y, w) and its queue length θ. The queue length is determined by the number of agents that want to trade in the market. Let R be the cdf of firms over markets, so that $R(x, y, w)$ is the measure of firms with attributes below y that want to trade in markets with worker attributes below x and wages below w. Let N be the cdf for workers, with $N(x, y, w)$ interpreted similarly. For any x and any $x' > x$ as well as for any y and $y' > y$, it has to hold that no more workers or firms attempt to trade than exist in the population, which requires that

$$N(x', \infty, \infty) - N(x, \infty, \infty) \leq G(x') - G(x) \quad \text{and} \tag{19.1}$$

$$R(\infty, y', \infty) - R(\infty, y', \infty) \leq H(y') - H(y), \tag{19.2}$$

If agents can make at least zero profits, they will all trade and these conditions will hold with equality. If workers can only attempt to trade in markets where some firms are present, this is equivalent to N being absolutely continuous with respect to G.

Then the queue length function satisfies

$$\theta = \frac{dN}{dG},\qquad(19.3)$$

so it indeed just reflects the ratio of workers to firms (which formally means it is the Radon–Nikodym derivative of N with respect to G).

Take a market (x, y, w) and its queue length function $\theta(x, y, w)$. A worker x who attempts to trade in this market in equilibrium (i.e., where the market is in the support of N) obtains utility

$$U(x) = \alpha(\theta(x, y, w))w \geq \max_{(x,y',w')} \alpha(\theta(x, y', w'))w',\qquad(19.4)$$

while a firm y which attempts to trade in this market (i.e., where the market is in the support of R) obtains utility

$$J(y) = \gamma(\theta(x, y, w))[f(x, y) - w] > \max_{(x',y,w')} \gamma(\theta(x', y, w'))[f(x', y) - w'].\qquad(19.5)$$

A worker's utility is simply the trading probability times the wage while a firm obtains the trading probability multiplied by output $f(x, y)$, but it has to pay the wage. Importantly, what agents obtain by trading in a market in equilibrium has to be at least as good as what they could obtain in any other market. Note that this means *any* other market including those that are not offered in equilibrium. If one takes an equilibrium allocation for which it is not possible to find off-equilibrium queue lengths that satisfy these inequalities, it is easy to show that this means that there is at least one firm type and one worker type that would prefer to deviate and create a new market (with a new wage and queue length) and each be strictly better off. So the inequalities capture the standard *no-blocking market condition*.

Note that in a blocking market there would still be search frictions, and the fact that the blocking market has a queue length entails that the deviation would be by many agents. A more suitable explanation for the off-equilibrium queue length comes from finite games, where firms move first and post a wage and workers move second after observing all wages. In the symmetric subgame, after the wage announcements workers probabilistically choose where to trade, which generates queues at the various firms. If a single firm wants to deviate it can do so, and some workers will react and put a positive probability on going to the new wage. One can easily show that (19.5) and (19.4) are satisfied if and only if

$$J(y) = \max_{(x,w,\theta)} \gamma(\theta)[f(x, y) - w]\qquad(19.6)$$

s.t. $\alpha(\theta)w = U(x),$

where $U(x)$ and $J(y)$ are the equilibrium utilities given by (19.5) and (19.4), So, it is as if the firm chooses the worker, the wage, and the tightness, as long as it offers at least the utility that the worker could get elsewhere in the market.

An equilibrium in this market is simply a combination of trading strategies (N, R) and associated queue-length function θ such that (19.1)–(19.5) hold. Agents (x, y) match if there exists a market (x, y, w) that is in the support of their trading strategies N and R. With some abuse of notation, call $\mu(x)$ the correspondence of all $y's$ that are matched to x. Matching is pure if μ is a function, that is, $\mu(x)$ is a singleton for all x.

We will follow [21] and derive conditions for positive sorting. Assume that a strictly increasing matching μ exists. The optimality condition (19.6) can be rewritten as

$$\max_{(x,w,\theta)} \gamma(\theta) f(x,y) - \theta U(x). \tag{19.7}$$

Problem (19.7) resembles the problem of a firm that has frictionless production function $\gamma(\theta) f(x,y)$ that combines the labor from the workers that queue, and the firm has to pay each worker in the queue his/her market value. These models are often called "competitive search models" because they capture an aspect of a competitive market. Condition (19.7) reduces to the condition in the frictionless case above, with the queue length and the matching probability equal to 1 and with worker's utility interpreted as his wage.

Fix $\hat{x}$ as matched to $\hat{y} = \mu\left(\hat{x}\right)$. They have to satisfy (19.7) for some $\hat{\theta}$ (which is itself dependent on $\hat{x}$). In particular they have to satisfy the first-order conditions[4]

$$\gamma(\hat{\theta}(\hat{x})) f_x(\hat{x}, \mu(\hat{x})) - \hat{\theta}(\hat{x}) U_x(\hat{x}) = 0, \tag{19.8}$$

$$\gamma'(\hat{\theta}(\hat{x})) f(\hat{x}, \mu(\hat{x})) - U(\hat{x}) = 0. \tag{19.9}$$

The first condition, with respect to the worker type is analogous to the condition in the frictionless case. Since the utility of workers is the product of the matching probability and the wage as in the constraint of (19.6), this reduces to a wage that equals the marginal product (since $\gamma(\theta) = \theta\alpha(\theta)$). This is identical to the setting without search frictions in Section 19.2, except that now the identity of the matched firm might be different. Workers are no longer matched to the firm that has the same rank in the type distribution. More or fewer workers might queue for any given firm type. How many workers queue for a given firm type is characterized by the second first-order condition (19.9). This is the novel condition in this search setup. These first-order conditions can combined with (19.3) to characterize this economy via a differential equation system that can be easily solved numerically. More relevant for the sorting question, optimality requires that the second-order conditions hold. In particular, the determinant of

$$\begin{pmatrix} \gamma(\hat{\theta}(\hat{x})) f_{xx}(\hat{x}, \mu(\hat{x})) - \hat{\theta}(\hat{x}) U(\hat{x}) & \gamma'(\hat{\theta}(\hat{x})) f_x(\hat{x}, \mu(\hat{x})) - U'(\hat{x}) \\ \gamma'(\hat{\theta}(\hat{x})) f_x(\hat{x}, \mu(\hat{x})) - U'(\hat{x}) & \gamma''(\hat{\theta}(\hat{x})) f(\hat{x}, \mu(\hat{x})) - U(\hat{x}) \end{pmatrix}$$

has to be positive. Differentiating (19.8) and (19.9) along the equilibrium path gives conditions including $\mu'(\hat{x})$ (they also include $\hat{\theta}'(\hat{x})$ but this drops out after rearranging). Substituting this into the determinant reveals that $\mu'(\hat{x})$ is positive if and only if, for all x,

$$EC(f)EC(m) \geq 1, \tag{19.10}$$

where $EC(f) \equiv (f_{xy}f)/(f_x f_y)$ and $EC(m) \equiv (m_{rs}m)/(m_r m_s)$, and where we have suppressed the arguments (x, y) and (n, r), respectively. If these functions have constant returns, these definitions capture the elasticity of complementarity of the production and matching functions; the elasticity of complementarity is simply the inverse of the more familiar elasticity of substitution. The condition has to hold along the equilibrium path, but if one wants to ensure positive sorting for any type distributions then one needs $EC(f) \geq 1/\underline{EC(m)}$ for all (x, y), where $\underline{EC(m)}$ is the infimum of

---

[4] Note that $U(x)$ is continuous and increasing in equilibrium, so it is differentiable almost everywhere.

the elasticity of complementarity of the matching function $m(\cdot, \cdot)$ over its arguments (n, r).

Condition (19.10) becomes the relevant sorting condition under directed search. This condition may be understood by noting that production in this economy is given by the product mf, i.e., by the product of the number of matches and the output. So sorting depends on the product of their elasticities of complementarity.

Is this stronger or weaker than the standard supermodularity condition that ensures sorting in frictionless matching markets? It is indeed stronger. This is evident since it requires cross-partial derivative f_{xy} to be bounded from zero as all other terms are strictly positive in condition (19.10). Another way to see this is to note that for most matching functions the elasticity of complementarity lies in a closed subset of $(1, \infty)$, and so the transformation $\kappa = EC/(EC - 1)$ lies in $(1, \infty)$. Then (19.10) requires that $\sqrt[\kappa]{f}$ is supermodular. This can be verified by taking its cross-partial derivative and noting that this is positive if and only if $EC(f) \geq 1 - \kappa^{-1}$, so that (19.10) holds. So, for x and $x' \searrow r$ and y and $y' > v$, the supermodularity of $\sqrt[\kappa]{f}$ amounts to

$$\sqrt[\kappa]{f(x', y')} + \sqrt[\kappa]{f(x, y)} \geq \sqrt[\kappa]{f(x, y')} + \sqrt[\kappa]{f(x', y)}. \tag{19.11}$$

Since output is increasing in types, $f(x, y')$ and $f(x', y)$ are closer together than $f(x', y')$ and $f(x, y)$. By Jensen's inequality a concave transformation makes it harder to satisfy this condition, and the higher κ is, the more difficult this becomes. This root-supermodularity condition has as its limit log-supermodularity for $\kappa \to \infty$, which captures the case of a Cobb–Douglas matching function.[5] An intermediate case is $\kappa = 2$, which is the most stringent requirement on the popular urn-ball matching function, where workers apply to firms within a market at random. At the other extreme, for $\kappa \to 1$ this recovers the classical supermodularity condition, which arises as the matching function becomes Leontief, meaning that the short sides of each market match perfectly.

The root-supermodularity of f turns out to be a tight distribution-free condition for positive sorting (there is an analogous result for negative sorting).

Proposition 19.1 (Positive sorting under directed search). *For any distributions of worker and firm attributes, the equilibrium exhibits positive sorting if and only if*

$$\frac{f_{xy}(x, y)f(x, y)}{f_x(x, y)f_y(x, y)} \geq \underline{EC(m)}^{-1}$$

for all (x, y). For most matching functions this is equivalently to requiring the supermodularity of $(f)^{1/\kappa}$, where $\kappa = \underline{EC(m)}/(\underline{EC(m)} - 1) \in (1, \infty)$.

The proof of sufficiency follows the logic explained above, while necessity obtains by considering the failure of the condition on a set of positive measure and then constructing distributions of attributes that put most measure on this set.

Why is this condition stronger than supermodularity? In a frictionless market, sorting is governed by advantages in output: if [19.11] holds for $k = 1$ then more output is produced when high types match with high types and low types match with low types than when they cross-match. This output is transferred to the two sides

---

[5] A function $f : \mathbb{R}^n \to \mathbb{R}_+$ is log-supermodular if $\log f$ is supermodular.

to ensure that matching arises. With frictions, even if output is higher for extreme matches (high with high, low with low), this is not the only driving force that governs output. Output also depends on the probability of matching, and the cost of not matching is higher for high types. To the extent that it is cheaper to add low types to a market, this can offset sorting in production. In the extreme case where output is additively separable in types, matching is negatively assortative. Here it does not matter who matches with whom. What matters is that high types are able to trade. For that, they need to be in a market with many agents from the other side, but that leads to low matching probabilities for the other side. So it is best to have low types on the other side, for whom the loss from not matching is less severe. Condition (19.10) trades off these forces succinctly. It can be shown that it captures the optimal assignment given the frictions. The driving forces are similar in other models such as those relying on random search, though the mixing of types makes this harder to discern.

What can this model capture? It captures *both* the complementarities in producing value as well as the difficulties in finding a partner. Waiting times are substantial in labor markets, where unemployment and open vacancies are the consequences. But similar concerns also arise in marriage and housing markets, where it takes time to find a partner. This theory highlights that the waiting times of different types, transfers, and the matching of types are interrelated. Higher types might not necessarily get higher wages if their matching probabilities improve very quickly. They might also not necessarily match more quickly if better workers are matched with even better firms for whom the matching probabilities are even more important. The matching probabilities can be recovered from (19.8) and (19.9), which, together with (19.3), give a differential equation system for μ', θ', and w' along the equilibrium path.

19.4.2 Many-to-One Matching

The literature in matching theory and also in macroeconomics has considered settings where firms can hire multiple workers. To illustrate the connection, consider a particularly simple and tractable version: we still assume a continuum of workers and firms, but now also assume that firms can hire a measure η of workers. A firm's output is produced according to a function $f(x, y, \eta)$, so it depends on worker and firm attributes and the number of such workers. The firm can post a measure v of vacancies at convex cost $c(v)$. Assuming the law of large numbers, it then hires $v\gamma(\theta)$ workers when it has attracted a queue length θ. Otherwise the same structure as in the previous section applies: agents take the queue lengths as given and choose optimally; queue lengths have to be correct on the equilibrium path; and off the equilibrium path the market utility assumption holds. In analogy with the previous section, the firms maximization problem is now

$$\max_{(x,w,v,\theta)} f(x, y, \eta) - w\eta - c(v)$$

$$\text{s.t. } \alpha(\theta)w = U(x) \quad \text{and} \quad \eta = v\gamma(\theta). \tag{19.12}$$

Consider three particularly relevant cases.

Case 1: Frictionless matching. This arises when $\gamma(\theta) = \min\{1, \theta\}$ and $c(v) = 0$, so that matching frictions have no bite.

Case 2: Linear vacancy creation costs. This is captured by $c(v) = cv$ and has been a popular special case in the literature.

Case 3: One-to-one matching. This arises when $c(v) = 0$ for $v \leq 1$ and $c(v) = \infty$ otherwise, and $f(x, y, \eta) = \eta \tilde{f}(x, y)$. Obviously in this case firms post their unit of vacancies, and substitution implies that their output is $\gamma(\theta)\tilde{f}(x, y)$, as in objective function [19.6].

To understand the sorting implications in the following proposition, it is useful to define $F(x, y, N, R) \equiv Rf(x, y, N/R)$, which represents the output of R firms if they split N workers optimally between them. We obtain

Proposition 19.2 (Positive sorting with large firms). *Consider the model with large firms just defined. In the frictionless case (Case 1) positive assortative matching requires that along the equilibrium path we have*

$$F_{xy}F \geq F_{yN}F_{xR}. \tag{19.13}$$

The same condition applies in the case of linear vacancy costs (Case 2). In the case of one-to-one matching (Case 3) the sorting condition remains as $EC(\tilde{f})EC(m) \geq 1$.

Sketch of the proof: In Case 1 the firm's problem can be written as $\max_{(x,w,\eta)}$ $f(x, y, \eta) - \eta U(x)$. This is very close to problem (19.7) in the previous section, but with n replacing θ and with the first part not being multiplicatively separable. Following similar steps leads to $f_{xy} - f_{y\eta}[f_{x\eta} - f_x/\eta]/f_{\eta\eta} \geq 0$. Replacing f by F and noting that F gives constant returns in (N, R) allows us to rewrite this as (19.13). To see heuristically why the matching frictions in Case 2 do not alter the sorting condition, note that distortions usually arise because a firm changes its worker type to improve the chances of hiring. But here it can do this at constant marginal cost simply by creating more vacancies, which does not distort the production efficiency. This is not so in Case 3, where the firm cannot expand vacancies. So it has to rely on changing he type of worker that it hires. The matching frictions appear in the sorting condition, because the mathematics are not changed relative to the previous section. □

The sorting condition (19.13) trades off complementarities between the types on the left with the variation in efficiency of the better types with the number of workers on the right. This section shows not only how firm size, sorting, and search frictions can be combined in a tractable framework. It also highlights that the extent to which the matching frictions appear in the sorting condition depends on the other means that firms have to improve matching prospects. Search frictions do not appear when firms can mitigate them by simply creating more vacancies. But if this is not possible, they become an important determinant. We note that the large-firms model without frictions but with production function $f(x, y, \eta) = \tilde{f}(x, y)\gamma(\eta)$ leads via (19.13) to exactly the sorting condition (19.10) for one-to-one matching. Here one can see the "competitive" nature of competitive search, though the search version allows for different interpretations: not everyone gets matched and therefore the probabilities of being idle and the waiting times can be analyzed. Also, expected pay to workers is not the same as actual pay since those with low hiring chances get paid more even if their expected utility (pay) is the same.

19.4.3 Miscellaneous

The frictionless-matching literature has long recognized that not all market participants are connected. Most of the research done so far assumes that the few links are
random. These theories shed some light on where workers apply for jobs, but they
focus on an extreme case where workers approach only one market/firm at a time.

A small amount of the literature analyzes the case where workers apply to more
than one firm or market. This makes the analysis more realistic but magnifies the
difficulties in analyzing the resulting network between workers and firms, and in
particular working out who ends up working for whom: now if a worker is offered a
job, he might prefer it over unemployment but he might prefer other jobs even more.

A promising alternative is to consider a stable matching amongst those agents that
are matched in the application process. This corresponds to a deferred acceptance
idea of wage setting: firms offer their preferred worker the job, workers receive multiple offers and tentatively accept one, and rejected firms continue to make offers.
A worker who tentatively accepts a job can change his mind if a better job comes
along later. The matching is non-transferable at this stage as the wages are fixed at
this point. This setup is reminiscent of the matching in the market for medical interns, where job conditions apparently are set in advance, workers apply to a subset
of positions, and the final matching is the worker-optimal stable matching.

This has so far been explored only for homogeneous workers. In this case, consider
workers who send two applications (though the number can be endogeneized via a
cost function). Now, these workers have two market utilities: the first one is

$$U_1 = \max_{y,w} \alpha(\tilde{\theta}(y,w))w$$

for their low-wage application. They will accept this if they fail with their high-wage
application. For the high-wage application their utility is given by

$$U_2 = \max_{y,w} \alpha(\tilde{\theta}(y,w))w + (1 - \alpha(\tilde{\theta}(y,w)))U_1,$$

which takes into account both the probability and wage of the current job as well
as the option of accepting the low-wage job should they fail. Note that $\tilde{\theta}$ is not the
raw queue length; now it is the *effective queue length* of applicants who end up not
accepting better wages. Only these workers are in competition for the current job.

From the firm's perspective only effective applicants matter, as those who take
better jobs are not relevant. One can show that a firm then solves, in analogy to
(19.6), the following problem:

$$\max_{w,\theta} \ \gamma(\theta)[f(y) - w]$$

$$\text{s.t. } \alpha(\theta)w = U_1, \tag{19.14}$$

$$\text{or } \alpha(\theta)w + (1 - \alpha(\theta))U_1 = U_2. \tag{19.15}$$

That is, its effective queue length has to deliver either the high or the low market
utility, whichever is best. Even when firms are homogeneous, as analyzed in [28],
this leads to wage dispersion as some firms cater to low wage applications at low-
matching probabilities, while other firms cater to high-wage applications but trade
more quickly.

With firm heterogeneity there is a single-crossing condition that ensures that the high-wage firms sort into the higher-wage segment so that (19.15) binds, while low-productivity firms sort into the low-wage segment, where (19.14) binds. In a large market this is efficient, in a constrained sense that takes matching frictions as given.

We are not aware of any work yet that introduces two-sided heterogeneity into this setting. This is clearly a route for future research.

19.5 Random Search

Under random search, agents meet partners in a probabilistic fashion and search is costly, which is usually modeled as a time cost (discounting) or as a fixed search cost.[6] It is common to assume an infinite horizon and that the market is in steady state, with some form of replenishment of the populations. Potential partners arrive over time according to some stochastic process. If the model is in continuous time, the standard assumption is a Poisson process with constant arrival rate. However, not all meetings end up in a match, since agents are selective in their choice of partners. And since search is costly and time consuming, agents do not wait for their "ideal partner" and are willing to accept partners with attributes within an acceptable range.

For pedagogical reasons, we will proceed in two steps. First, in order to zero-in on some of the issues involved in modeling random search and matching, we will analyze a setting in which workers and firms are all ex-ante identical but, upon meeting a potential partner, each observes a payoff-relevant random attribute of the partner and then decides whether to form a match. Both the equilibrium with perfectly transferable utility and the equilibrium with strictly nontransferable utility can be easily analyzed. Second, we will embellish the setting by allowing agents to be ex-ante heterogeneous, as in the frictionless case, and then we will shed light on equilibrium sorting patterns.

In each model, there is a trivial equilibrium where agents accept nobody. To avoid this annoyance, henceforth we will assume that agents, if indifferent, do accept a partner.

19.5.1 Ex-Ante Identical Agents

Consider a unit measure of workers and the same measure of firms. Both firms and workers are ex-ante identical. Time is continuous and the horizon is infinite. Over time, agents meet according to a Poisson process with rate $\rho > 0$. The meeting technology is linear in the fraction ξ of the agents that are unmatched (there are constant returns to scale). When a worker and a firm meet, each draws a realization of the partner's attribute. That is, the worker draws an attribute $y \in [0, 1]$ from a cdf H with density h and the firm draws an attribute $x \in [0, 1]$ from a cdf G with density g. After observing these ex-post attributes, they accept or reject the match. If both accept, then the match forms and each agent receives a constant payoff (to be specified below) over the duration of the match. Matches are destroyed according to another (independent) Poisson process with rate $\delta > 0$, in which case both agents go

---

[6] For other dynamic models of matching, see also Chapter 18.

back to the market as unmatched individuals.[7] Agents discount the future at a rate $r > 0$, and there is also a fixed search cost c for sampling partners over time.

Let us consider first the case with perfectly transferable utility. Assume that if the attributes drawn in a meeting between a worker and a firm are x and y then the pair can produce a flow output $f(x, y)$ while the match lasts, where f is continuous and strictly increasing in each argument. That is, at each instant there is a flow output $z = f(x, y)$ to distribute. Given H and G, we can derive the cdf Q of z and focus on distributing z.[8] We want to derive the flow payoffs $w(z)$ for the worker and $\pi(z)$ for the firm that they obtain while matched. A standard assumption in the literature is that these are derived using the Nash bargaining solution (NBS), which splits the surplus of the relationship. What is the surplus? The outside option of the worker is the value U of being unmatched, while for the firm that value is denoted by J. That is, in flow terms the surplus to divide at each instant is $z - rU - rJ$, and thus the NBS yields $w(z) = rU + 0.5(z - rU - rJ)$ and $\pi(z) = rJ + 0.5(z - rU - rJ)$. Crucially, note that both the worker and the firm will accept being matched if and only if $z \geq rU + rJ$, since for each party the flow payoff of being matched in this case is higher than the flow payoff of being unmatched. Hence, both parties *agree* on what matches to form. We will see that in fact this is not true without transfers.

Consider a worker. The recursive equation that describes U over a small time interval dt is

$$U = \frac{1}{1 + rdt} \left(-cdt + \rho dt \int_{\underline{z}}^{\overline{z}} \max\{V(z), U\} \, dQ(z) + (1 - \rho dt)U \right),$$

where $V(z)$ is the worker's value of being matched with a partner with whom the total output is z, that is

$$V(z) = \frac{1}{1 + rdt} \left(w(z)dt + \delta dt U + (1 - \delta dt)V(z) \right).$$

Intuitively, over a small interval of time dt, an unmatched worker pays cdt, samples a firm with probability ρdt, in which case the worker decides whether to accept or reject the match, and with probability $1 - \rho dt$ continues the search, which has value U. Over the same interval dt, if a worker is matched with a firm that generates output z, the worker enjoys a payoff of $w(z)dt$ but faces a return to being unmatched that occurs with probability δdt and yields U from that point onwards, while with the complementary probability the worker obtains $V(z)$ from that point onwards.

Multiplying both sides of each equation by $1 + rdt$, simplifying, and letting dt go to zero yields

$$rU = -c + \rho \int_{\underline{z}}^{\overline{z}} \max\{V(z) - U, 0\} \, dQ(z)$$

$$= -c + \frac{\rho}{2(r + \delta)} \int_{\underline{z}}^{\overline{z}} \max\{z - rU - rJ, 0\} \, dQ(z)$$

$$= -c + \frac{\rho}{2(r + \delta)} \int_{a_w}^{\overline{z}} (z - a_w) dQ(z),$$

---

[7] The same qualitative results obtain if instead of exogenous match destruction we assume that matched agents leave the market and there is a measure δ of new agents of each side entering the market at each instant.

[8] Since z is a function of the random variables x and y, the cdf of z, Q, is given by $Q(z) = \int_{\underline{z}}^{\overline{z}} G(\varphi(y, z)) dH(y)$, where φ is the inverse of f with respect to its first coordinate.

where for the second equality we used $(r+\delta)V(z) = w(z)+\delta U$ and the expression for $w(z)$ to obtain $V(z) - U$, and where the third equality follows from $z - rU - rJ \geq 0$ if and only if $z \geq rU + rJ \equiv a_w$.

Following exactly the same steps for the firm's problem, we obtain

$$rJ = -c + \frac{\rho}{2(r+\delta)} \int_{a_f}^{\bar{z}} (z - a_f)dQ(z),$$

and, as explained above, $a_w = a_f = rU + rJ$ and we denote the common threshold by a. Adding the expressions for rU and rJ, and using that $\int_a^{\bar{z}}(z-a)dQ(z) = \int_a^{\bar{z}}(1 - Q(z))dz$, we obtain

$$a + 2c = \frac{\rho}{(r+\delta)} \int_a^{\bar{z}} (1 - Q(z))dz. \tag{19.16}$$

Given a, the steady-state fraction of unmatched agents on each side is calculated as follows: The flow into the fraction ξ of unmatched agents consists of $\delta(1-\xi)$, the fraction of matched agents whose matches were destroyed, while the flow out of ξ consists of those unmatched agents who form a match, whose measure is $\xi(1-Q(a))$. In equilibrium both are equal, and thus

$$\xi = \frac{\delta}{\delta + (1 - Q(a))}. \tag{19.17}$$

An equilibrium is a pair (a, ξ) that satisfies equations (19.16) and (19.17). It is easy to show that (19.16) has a unique solution, which is interior if c is not too large. And since the meeting technology is linear, ξ does not enter (19.16), and thus once we obtain a we automatically obtain ξ via (19.17). Multiplicity can arise if the meeting technology exhibits increasing returns to scale, as in the quadratic case (then one would need to solve (19.16) and (19.17) simultaneously, as u would enter (19.16)).

Proposition 19.3 (Ex-ante identical agents, transferable utility). *In the transferable utility case, there exists a unique equilibrium (a, ξ).*

Note the effects of search frictions: since search is costly, agents do not sample partners until finding a match with $z = \bar{z}$, but instead accept a range of matches. And since agents have the option value of continuing the search, they only accept matches above a threshold.

Consider now the strictly non-transferable utility case, and assume for simplicity that the flow payoff to each agent in a match is the ex-post attribute of the partner (nothing is gained by more generality). Intuitively, agents will optimally choose a threshold for the partner's attribute above which they accept the partner and below which they continue the search. But, unlike the perfectly transferable utility case, the two potential partners to a match may disagree in their decision.

The recursive equation that describes the value of being unmatched for a worker is now

$$U =$$

$$\frac{1}{1 + rdt} \left(-cdt + \rho(1 - G(a_f))dt \int_0^1 \max\{V(y), U\} dH(y) + (1 - \rho(1 - G(a_f))dt)U \right),$$

where $V(y)$ is the value of being matched with a partner with attribute y, that is,

$$V(y) = \frac{1}{1 + rdt}\left(ydt + \delta dt U + (1 - \delta dt)V(y)\right).$$

The intuitive meanings of U and $V(y)$ are the same as before, except that (i) only firms that are sampled and that observe a worker's attribute above a_f accept the match, which occurs with probability $\rho(1 - G(a_f))dt$, and (ii) the flow payoff if a worker is matched with a firm with attribute y is ydt. Following the same steps as above we obtain an equation that determines the threshold a_w:

$$a_w + c = \frac{\rho(1 - G(a_f))}{r + \delta}\int_{a_w}^{1}(1 - H(y))dy. \tag{19.18}$$

A similar derivation holds for firms, whose threshold a_f solves

$$a_f + c = \frac{\rho(1 - H(a_w))}{r + \delta}\int_{a_f}^{1}(1 - G(x))dx. \tag{19.19}$$

Given (a_w, a_f), the steady-state fraction of unmatched agents is calculated as follows. The flow into ξ is $\delta(1 - \xi)$, while the flow out of ξ consists of those unmatched agents who form a match, whose measure is $\xi(1 - H(a_w))(1 - G(a_f))$. In equilibrium both are equal, and thus

$$\xi = \frac{\delta}{\delta + (1 - H(a_w))(1 - G(a_f))}. \tag{19.20}$$

An equilibrium is a triple (a_w, a_f, ξ) that satisfies equations (19.18)–(19.20).[9] Since ξ does not appear in (19.18) and (19.19), once we solve for (a_w, a_f) we automatically obtain the equilibrium value of ξ. To solve for the equilibrium thresholds, note that (19.18) defines a_w as a continuous and decreasing function of a_f, and (19.19) defines a_f as a continuous and decreasing function of a_w. A simple application of the intermediate value theorem yields that, if c is not too large, there exists an equilibrium with interior thresholds. A bit more work reveals that if the densities g and h are log-concave then the equilibrium is unique.[10]

> **Proposition 19.4** (Ex-ante identical agents, non-transferable utility). *Under strict non-transferable utility, there exists an equilibrium (a_w, a_f, ξ), which is unique if g and h are log-concave.*

An interesting contrast with the transferable utility case is that, in the absence of log-concavity, there can be multiple equilibria. To see how they may emerge, suppose that workers are very selective (high a_w). Then they accept with small probability, which induces firms to be less selective (low a_f). But then workers face a high

---

[9] Note that if the two populations were symmetric, that is, if H and G were the same, or what is qualitatively equivalent, if there were a single population, then $a_w = a_f$, and a single equation would determine the equilibrium threshold. Note also that if, instead of the rate of match destruction, δ is the measure of new agents who enter the market then (19.20) is the same and the only difference in the value functions is that $V(y)$ would simply be y/r.

[10] A function $z: \mathbb{R} \to \mathbb{R}_+$ is log-concave if $\log z$ is concave. If z is twice differentiable then z is log-concave if and only if $zz'' - z'^2 \leq 0$. Actually, uniqueness obtains under the weaker condition that the indefinite integrals of $1 - G$ and $1 - H$ are log-concave.

probability of being accepted and this rationalizes their selectivity. The opposite can happen if workers accepts with high probability, and multiplicity can ensue.

This tractable model is amenable to extensions and also to comparative statics exercises with changes in c, δ, ρ, H, and G, which we leave to the reader.

19.5.2 Heterogeneous Agents

We now turn to the richer case in which agents are heterogeneous at the outset. This will provide us with a clear analog with random search of the frictionless case of Section 19.2. Although there are several relevant papers, we will describe the model and results in [47] for the transferable utility case, [49] for the strictly nontransferable utility case, and [4] for the transferable case with fixed search costs. As in these papers, we will assume that there is only one population (the "partnership model"), with attributes distributed with cdf G having continuous density $g > 0$. Clearly, the model can be reinterpreted as one with two populations, workers and firms, with the same distributions of attributes. We will follow these papers and assume a quadratic search technology (partners with a given attribute arrive at a rate proportional to their presence in the unmatched pool), but will comment on how the model extends.

All the work done for the ex-ante identical case will pay off now when we are deriving the unmatched and matched values in the heterogeneous agents case, as the steps followed are analogous.

Consider first the perfectly transferable utility case. An unmatched agent meets agents with attributes $y \in Y$ at a rate $\rho \int_Y \xi(y)dy$, where $\rho > 0$ and, with some abuse of notation, ξ is the unmatched density function, satisfying $0 \leq \xi(x) \leq g(x)$ for all x. In a meeting, each agent accepts or rejects the potential partner, and a match forms if and only if both accept. Formally, each agent with attribute x chooses a (measurable) set $A(x) \subseteq [0, 1]$ containing the agents' attributes that he accepts. In turn, agents with x are accepted by agents with attributes in $\Omega(x) = \{y|x \in A(y)\}$. Hence, an agent with attribute x has a matching set given by $\mathcal{M}(x) = A(x) \cap \Omega(x)$. Once formed, a match lasts until it exogenously dissolves, an event that occurs with Poisson rate $\delta > 0$.[11]

Unmatched agents obtain zero flow payoff. If an agent with attribute x matches with one with y, then the pair can produce and distribute between them a flow output $f(x, y)$ while the match lasts, with f positive, symmetric, and $\mathcal{C}^2$. The match surplus is $f(x, y) - rU(x) - rU(y)$, where U describes the value of being unmatched for each agent as a function of her attribute. As before, we will assume NBS, so x obtains a flow payoff $rU(x) + 0.5(f(x, y) - rU(x) - rU(y))$ and y obtains $rU(y) + 0.5(f(x, y) - rU(x) - rU(y))$, and thus both accept if and only if $f(x, y) \geq rU(x) + rU(y)$.

The recursive equation that determines the unmatched value for x is:

$$U(x) = \frac{1}{1 + rdt} \left(-cdt + \rho dt \left(\int_{\Omega(x)} \xi(y)dy \right) \mathbb{E}[\max\{V(y, x), U(x)\}|y \in \Omega(y)] \right.$$
$$\left. + \left(1 - \rho dt \int_{\Omega(x)} \xi(y)dy \right) U(x) \right),$$

---

[11] Alternatively, one can assume an inflow of agents of each attribute that enters the market at each instant.

where

$$V(y, x) = \frac{1}{1 + rdt} \left((rU(x) + 0.5(f(x, y) - rU(x) - rU(y)))dt \right.$$
$$\left. + \delta dt U(x) + (1 - \delta dt) V(y, x) \right).$$

By the standard limiting argument used above, after some algebra (which uses $V(y, x) - U(x) = 0.5(f(x, y) - rU(x) - rU(y))/(r + \delta)$), we obtain

$$rU(x) = -c + \frac{\rho}{2(r + \delta)} \int_{M(x)} (f(x, y) - rU(x) - rU(y)) \xi(y) dy, \qquad (19.21)$$

where $M(x) = \{y | f(x, y) - rU(x) - rU(y) \geq 0\}$, since a match forms between x and y if and only if there is a positive match surplus.

An equilibrium is a triple (M, U, ξ) such that, given ξ, $M(x)$ is optimal for each x and yields unmatched value $rU(x)$ (that is, satisfies (19.21) for each x), and, given M, the unmatched density ξ satisfies, for each x, the balanced flow condition

$$\delta (g(x) - \xi(x)) = \rho \xi(x) \int_{M(x)} \xi(y) dy.$$

Under the assumptions made on f, an equilibrium exists.

The strict non-transferable utility version of the model requires the following modifications. When unmatched, an agent obtains zero payoff, while if an agent with attribute x matches with one with attribute y then x enjoys $f(x, y) > 0$, where f is symmetric, continuously differentiable, and strictly increasing in the partner's attribute, that is, $f_y > 0$. As before, each agent with x chooses $A(x) \subseteq [0, 1]$, and is accepted by agents with attributes in $\Omega(x)$.

The recursive equation that determines the unmatched value for x is the same as above, except that $V(y, x)$ is given by

$$V(y, x) = \frac{1}{1 + rdt} \left(f(x, y) dt + \delta dt U(x) + (1 - \delta dt) V(y, x) \right).$$

By the usual limiting and simplifying argument we obtain

$$rU(x) = -c + \frac{\rho}{r + \delta} \int_{\Omega(x)} \max\{f(x, y) - rU(x), 0\} \xi(y) dy.$$

It is clear that x will accept y as a partner if and only if $y \geq a(x)$, and thus $A(x) = [a(x), 1]$, where $a(x)$ satisfies $f(x, a(x)) = rU(x)$, and, since all agents will use a threshold strategy, we have that $\Omega(x) = \{y | x \geq a(y)\}$. Using $a(x)$ in the recursion for $rU(x)$ we obtain, after simple algebra,

$$rU(x) = -c + \frac{\rho}{r + \delta} \int_{\Omega(x) \cap [a(x), 1]} (f(x, y) - rU(x)) \xi(y) dy.$$

Using $f(x, a(x)) = rU(x)$ and manipulating yields

$$f(x, a(x)) + c = \frac{\rho}{r + \delta} \int_{\Omega(x) \cap [a(x), 1]} (f(x, y) - f(x, a(x))) \xi(y) dy. \qquad (19.22)$$

Note that this is very similar to the expressions we derived in the ex-ante identical-agents case, except that now a is a function of the attribute x.

An equilibrium is a pair (a, ξ), such that $a(x)$ is optimal for each x given ξ (that is, it satisfies (19.22) for each x), and the unmatched density ξ satisfies, for each x, the balanced flow condition

$$\delta\left(g(x) - \xi(x)\right) = \rho\xi(x) \int_{\Omega(x) \cap [a(x), 1]} \xi(y) dy.$$

Under the assumption made on f, an equilibrium exists.[12]

Unlike the case with ex-ante identical agents, little is known about uniqueness or multiplicity in these models. In a setting with two attribute levels, multiplicity can ensue. Consider a strictly non-transferable utility case, with high- and low-attribute firms and workers. Under the assumption that an agent's flow payoff is the partner's attribute, there can be two equilibria that coexist: in one equilibrium high-attribute agents accept only high-attribute agents and low-attribute agents match only with low-attribute agents, and in the other equilibrium everyone accepts everyone. How are these equilibria supported? If high only accept high, then their presence in the unmatched pool is larger, and this rationalizes their behavior and hence the first equilibrium. If high-attribute agents are not selective at all, then their presence in the unmatched pool is more scarce, which justifies their lack of selectivity. Understanding these composition effects further is an interesting open problem. Also, nothing is known about the equilibrium comparative statics of these models with heterogeneous agents.

19.5.3 Sorting

A property that has been fleshed out is monotone sorting in these models. Clearly, not everyone matching with someone of the same attribute can emerge in equilibrium, owing to the presence of search frictions. Intuitively, one would surmise that complementarities in f would lead to at least some form of positive dependence between matched partners' attributes so that, roughly, on average high-attribute agents match with high-attribute agents. Similarly for negative sorting.

In [47] this intuition was formalized with the following useful definition: there is *positive sorting* if the correspondence M is increasing in the strong-set order. That is, if, for all $x' > x$, $y \in M(x)$ and $y' \in M(x')$ then $\min\{y, y'\} \in M(x)$ and $\max\{y, y'\} \in M(x')$. Similarly, there is *negative sorting* if $\max\{y, y'\} \in M(x)$ and $\min\{y, y'\} \in M(x')$. Note that this definition trivially subsumes the frictionless case, where matching sets are singletons.

It will prove more useful for us to use the following definition of sorting, which is equivalent to the one given when $M(x)$ is closed and non-empty for all x. We will say that there is positive sorting (negative sorting) if $M(x) = [a(x), b(x)]$ for all x, with a and b increasing (decreasing).

Consider the transferable utility case. Assume that there is a fixed search cost but no discounting or exogenous match destruction, and that, once a pair matches, they divide the output and leave the market. If one retraces the steps above when deriving U, we now obtain that, for each x, U satisfies

---

[12] In [49] an equilibrium is a triple (M, U, ξ), where $M(x) = \Omega(x) \cap A(x)$ is the matching set of x; this is more convenient when proving the continuity properties of a suitable operator that has a fixed point.

$$0 = -c + \frac{\rho}{2} \int_{\mathcal{M}(x)} (f(x,y) - U(x) - U(y))\xi(y)dy, \qquad (19.23)$$

which is called the constant surplus condition since $\rho \int_{\mathcal{M}(x)} (f(x,y) - U(x) - U(y))\xi(y)dy = 2c$ for all x, so every agent has the same expected surplus in equilibrium.

It was shown in [4] that if f is supermodular, then positive sorting obtains. The proof strategy was first to show that $\mathcal{M}(x)$ is non-empty and closed for each x (and hence is compact-valued). It was then shown that the bounding functions a and b are increasing in x and that $x \in \mathcal{M}(x)$ for all x (everyone is willing to match with someone of the same attribute). Finally, these two properties were used to show that $\mathcal{M}(x)$ is convex for each x, that is, $\mathcal{M}(x) = [a(x), b(x)]$.

Since the proof is rather long, we will content ourselves with an intuitive argument that sheds light on the result. Assume that $\mathcal{M}(x) = [a(x), b(x)]$. We will show that if f is supermodular then a and b are increasing in x. To see this, note that we can rewrite (19.23) as follows:

$$U(x) = \frac{-2c + \rho \int_{a(x)}^{b(x)} (f(x,y) - U(y))\xi(y)dy}{\rho \int_{a(x)}^{b(x)} \xi(y)dy}$$

$$= \max_{a,b \in [0,1]} \frac{-2c + \rho \int_a^b (f(x,y) - U(y))\xi(y)dy}{\rho \int_a^b \xi(y)dy},$$

where the second equality follows since $\mathcal{M}(x)$ is optimal for each x. Note that the presence of search frictions implies that $a(x) < b(x)$ for all x. Also, the first-order conditions are found to be, after some algebra, $f(x, a(x)) - U(a(x)) - U(x) = 0$ and $f(x, b(x)) - U(b(x)) - U(x) = 0$ for each x, and the envelope theorem yields $U'(x) = \int_{a(x)}^{b(x)} f_x(x,y)\xi(y)dy / \int_{a(x)}^{b(x)} \xi(y)dy$. Totally differentiating the first-order conditions and using the expression for U' yields

$$a'(x) = \frac{\int_{a(x)}^{b(x)} (f_x(x,y) - f_x(x, a(x)))\xi(y)dy}{f_y(x, a(x)) - U'(a(x))},$$

$$b'(x) = -\frac{\int_{a(x)}^{b(x)} (f_x(x, b(x)) - f_x(x, y))\xi(y)dy}{f_y(x, b(x)) - U'(b(x))}.$$

The numerator in both expressions is positive if f is supermodular. And since all $y \in [a(x), b(x)]$ yield a positive surplus for x, it must be the case that $f_y(x, a(x)) - U'(a(x)) \geq 0$ and $f_y(x, b(x)) - U'(b(x)) \leq 0$. Hence, $a' \geq 0$ and $b' \geq 0$, and positive sorting ensues under the premise that $\mathcal{M}(x)$ is convex for each x. But, as mentioned, the supermodularity of f also suffices for the matching sets to be convex, which justifies the premise.

A similar argument in the discounted case without fixed search costs reveals that a and b are increasing under the convexity of matching sets if f is supermodular and $f_y(0, y) \leq 0$ (see [50], Section 5.2). Convexity of matching sets, however, is much harder to ensure, and in [47] it was shown that it holds if, in addition, f_x and f_{xy} are log-supermodular.

————— 420 —————

All told, we have the following result:

Proposition 19.5 (Positive sorting with perfectly transferable utility). *Assume that $f \geq 0$ and f is C^2. Then the following conditions are sufficient for any equilibrium to exhibit positive sorting. (i) Discounting and no fixed search cost: f supermodular, f_x and f_{xy} log-supermodular, and $f_y(0, y) \leq 0 \leq f_y(1, y)$; (ii) fixed search cost and no discounting: f supermodular.*

There are symmetric results for negative sorting as well. For some intuition of the difference between (i) and (ii), note that under fixed search costs the constant-surplus condition holds, and hence the cost of waiting (the difference between the unmatched value today and the unmatched value after an interval dt) is independent of the agent's attribute since it is just c. So they all react identically to search frictions, and only the properties of the output function matter for sorting. The cost of waiting is attribute-dependent in the discounted case, because higher types lose more from waiting. They are more willing to accept lower-attribute partners if this helps to speed up their time until matching. This is similar to the argument above that positive sorting requires higher complementarities under directed search frictions than in the frictionless case when firms have a single vacancy (Section 19.4.1), yet under random search the conditions that discipline matching sets are more complex.

Let us now derive conditions for positive sorting in the strictly non-transferable utility case. Positive sorting requires that a is increasing in x, in which case $\Omega(x) = [0, b(x)]$, where b also increases in x (it is the inverse of a), and hence the matching sets are $[a(x), b(x)]$ for all x.

We will provide conditions on f that ensure positive sorting. We will first show that if $\Omega(x) = [0, b(x)]$ for all x and b is increasing *then* a is increasing under suitable conditions on f, and hence there is positive sorting. Then we will discuss how to justify the premises.

Since $\Omega = [0, b(x)]$, (19.22) becomes

$$f(x, a(x)) + c = \frac{\rho}{r + \delta} \int_{a(x)}^{b(x)} (f(x, y) - f(x, a(x))) \xi(y) dy. \tag{19.24}$$

Since b is increasing and f is C^1, we can differentiate (almost everywhere) with respect to x. Using that $f_y > 0$, we obtain after manipulation that the sign of $a'(x)$ is the same as the sign of

$$\frac{\rho}{r + \delta} \left(\int_{a(x)}^{b(x)} (f_x(x, y) - f_x(x, a(x))) \xi(y) dy \right.$$

$$\left. + (f(x, b(x)) - f(x, a(x))) \xi(b(x)) b'(x) \right) - f_x(x, a(x)).$$

Note that the last term can be rewritten as follows:

$$f_x(x, a(x)) = \frac{f_x(x, a(x))}{f(x, a(x))} f(x, a(x))$$

$$= \frac{f_x(x, a(x))}{f(x, a(x))} \left(-c + \frac{\rho}{r + \delta} \int_{a(x)}^{b(x)} (f(x, y) - f(x, a(x))) \xi(y) dy \right),$$

where the last equality uses (19.24). Inserting this into the above expression and simplifying reveals that $a'(x) \geq 0$ if and only if the following expression is positive:

$$\frac{\rho}{r+\delta} \left(\int_{a(x)}^{b(x)} \left(f_x(x,y) - f(x,y) \frac{f_x(x,a(x))}{f(x,a(x))} \right) \xi(y) dy \right.$$

$$\left. + (f(x,b(x)) - f(x,a(x))) \xi(b(x)) b'(x) \right) + c \frac{f_x(x,a(x))}{f(x,a(x))}.$$

The second term inside the largest parentheses is positive since $f_y > 0$ and $b' \geq 0$, and the first term is positive if f is log-supermodular since $f_x(x,\cdot)/f(x,\cdot)$ is increasing in y. Hence, if $c = 0$ then $a' \geq 0$ if f is log-supermodular, and positive sorting is obtained. And if $c > 0$ *and* we add the assumption that $f_x \geq 0$, then positive sorting obtains with *both* discounting and a fixed search cost. Finally, if in the recursive equations that define $U(x)$ and $V(x,y)$ we assume that $c > 0$, $r = \delta = 0$, and $V(x,y) = f(x,y)$ (an agent with x obtains $f(x,y)$ when matched with y and exits the market), then redoing the steps above we obtain that positive sorting ensues if f is supermodular.

These insights so far assume that $\Omega(x) = [0, b(x)]$ for each x and b is increasing in x. But this must be the case: by the presence of search frictions, there is a neighborhood of $x = 1$ such that agents with attributes in that interval are accepted by everyone, so $b(x) = 1$ for those agents. In this case we have just shown that a is increasing in that neighborhood. And since a and b are the inverse of each other, we can construct the next lower tier of attributes and pin down a again for them. Continuing in this fashion shows that a and b are increasing and $\Omega(x) = [0, b(x)]$ for all x.

Summarizing, we have the following positive sorting result:

Proposition 19.6 (Positive sorting with strictly nontransferable utility). *Assume that $f_y > 0$. Then the following conditions are sufficient for any equilibrium to exhibit positive sorting. (i) Discounting and no fixed search cost: f log-supermodular; (ii) fixed search cost and no discounting: f supermodular; (iii) discounting and fixed search cost: f log-supermodular and $f_x \geq 0$.*

In all these cases, it is clear that $f_y > 0$ is not sufficient for positive sorting, and further properties of f are called for. For some intuition, consider (i). We saw that $a(x)$ satisfies $f(x, a(x)) = rU(x)$ and thus $a'(x) \geq 0$ if and only if $rU'(x) \geq f_x(x, a(x))$, which does not involve f_y. That is, for each x, the unmatched value must rise faster than the marginal flow payoff of matching with $a(x)$. Log-supermodularity ensures that this holds for all x.

19.5.4 Identification in Search and Matching Environments

For several years, the literature described above stayed within the realm of theory. But in recent years there is an emerging literature that focuses on empirical questions that can be answered through the lens of these sorting models: how much of the rise in wage inequality has been due to changes in worker and firm attributes, and the sorting between them? Search models offer the possibility of the separate identification of worker and firm types: since not always the same worker and firm are matched because of frictions, one can possibly disentangle the different contributions to the production of final output. Modern matched employer–employee data provide an identifier for a worker and a firm that are matched at each point in time, and the wages paid. While usually the worker's output is not observed, this potentially allows some insight into the value created by the worker and the firm.

A popular econometric technique to study such data relies on two-sided fixed effects, both for workers and firms. It requires a particular separability property of wages, so that a firm that pays more needs to do so for all workers. One can ask whether this is a sensible specification in light of the model just discussed. Even in a simple random search framework with transferable utility, as in the previous section leading to Proposition 19.6, this turns out always to be violated, posing a challenge to such simple specifications.

Consider such a setting, and let x be the worker attribute and y the firm attribute. It holds that wages might not rise in y. To see this, recall that the flow payoff for a worker with x when matched with a firm with y is given by $w(x, y) = rU(x) + 0.5(f(x, y) - rU(x) - rU(y))$. This is the wage in a labor market setting. But as explained in the previous section the matching set is given by $\mathcal{M}(x) = \{y | f(x, y) - rU(x) - rU(y) \geq 0\}$. Note that at the lowest and the highest attribute of firms that want to match with x, the surplus (the second term in $w(x, y)$) is zero, and thus the wage equals the continuation value of x, which is the lowest possible outcome. At intermediate partner types the wage is strictly higher. So the wage rises at the low end but falls for the highest partner types, as summed up in the first paragraph of the following proposition:

Proposition 19.7 (Wages are non-monotone in partner type). *Assume that $f_y > 0$ and that there is sufficient complementarity for positive sorting. For a worker with attribute x and with strictly interior matching set $\mathcal{M}(x)$, wages are rising in the partner's attribute at the low end of the matching set but are falling in the partner's attribute at the upper end of the matching set.*

Given these worker and firm attributes, the production function can be identified up to a constant.

The reason why the proposition holds is that high-attribute partners prefer to wait for those with even better attributes with whom they have complementarities, and only if a partner with attribute x is willing to accept a low wage can a match form. Clearly, this violates a specification with fixed effects where a rise in the firm's attribute means a rise in wages for all workers. Here, this will occur for the high-attribute workers but not for the low-attribute workers in its matching set. While such non-monotonicities have turned out to be pervasive in search and sorting models, empirically this remains under discussion.

While two-sided fixed effects are clearly not appropriate in a model of this kind, there still exists the possibility of identifying important aspects of the production function, as the last paragraph of Proposition 19.7 states. Intuitively, how quickly wages change across workers in a firm, and across firms for a given worker, can identify the production function. While the literature has provided empirically more tractable strategies, a simple way to highlight this possibility is to note that after one has identified the worker and firm attributes, one can in principle observe the wage $w(x, y)$ with enough data. Then the cross partial differential of the wages

$w_{xy}(x, y) = f_{xy}(x, y)/2$ identifies the cross partial differential of the production function. And since $f(x, y) = f(0, 0) + \int_0^x \int_0^y f_{xy}(x', y') dy' dx'$, this identifies the production function up to a constant.

Finally, it might be worth noting that worker and firm attributes can indeed be identified under discounting but not otherwise, though the full argument would exceed this survey. The main point here is to highlight that these models have clear empirical predictions that can be exploited to shed light on important phenomena such as the drivers of wage inequality, though care has to be given regarding the exact empirical approach.

19.6 Bibliographical Notes

Section 19.1. For a survey on sorting in search and matching models, see [16], and for directed search models, see [52].

Section 19.2. There are numerous extensions and applications of the frictionless framework both with and without transfers. A partial list of articles is [33] for the case of imperfectly transferable utility, [31] and [34] for matching with task assignments, [35] for multidimensional attributes, [14] for matching with externalities, [30] for a development economics application, [24] for CEO and firms assignment, and [18], [7], and [15] for pre-match investments.

Section 19.3. In [19] linear and quadratic search technologies were introduced, [39] provides a micro-foundation based on birth–death stochastic processes.

Section 19.4. The model of the one-to-one matching case is based on [44] and [21]. One particular feature of the model in Sections 19.4.1 is that it assumes bilateral meetings: in a given market there is only one type of agent from the other side, and a meeting with any one of them leads to a match. This is relaxed in other works that make more structural assumptions. In [45] and [46] it was assumed that firms post a wage schedule that lists for each worker attribute a wage and also a priority rule in the event that multiple workers apply to the job. Section 19.4.2 is based on [23]. For an example with many-to-one matching and no transfers, in a college admissions context, see [17] (the article [16] provides a simple overview of that paper). In this model, there are two ranked colleges and a continuum of heterogeneous students. Students apply to colleges by solving a portfolio problem. In turn colleges observe only a signal of the caliber of each student in the applicant pool and then set admission thresholds, accepting all calibers above the cutoff. So matching is many-to-one, and students face search frictions akin to the directed one in this section. Among other things, it is shown that in a world with imperfect information, sorting is positive in a first-order stochastic dominance sense. The model in Section 19.4.3 is from [28]. Other papers with multiple applications are [3], [29], [51], and [26].

Section 19.5. The analysis in Section 19.5.1 is based on [11]. The analysis in Section 19.5.2 borrows heavily from the seminal frameworks in [47] (for perfectly transferable utility) and [49] (for strictly non-transferable utility), and the case with perfectly transferable utility and a fixed search cost is based on [4]. In [32] existence proofs were extended in both the perfectly transferable and strictly nontransferable utility cases to cover (i) a larger class of meeting technologies that subsumes the quadratic and linear classed, (ii) exogenous entry flows in each period instead of match destruction, and (iii) allowing for two different populations. Proposition 19.5 combines the main sorting result in [47] and [4], while, for Proposition 19.6, part (i) is in [49], part (ii) is in [38], and part (iii) is new. In [10] it is shown that there can be multiple equilibria, and our description of the two-attribute example follows the one in that paper. Other papers on search with heterogeneous agents and with an emphasis on sorting are [37], [48], [38], [10], [12], [20], and [8]. Except in [38], where the case without transfers and fixed search costs under supermodular f was analyzed, the other papers focus on special match output functions f. All the papers cited assume that an agent's attribute is perfectly observable. However, in [13] it is assumed that a noisy signal of a partner is observed at each meeting, which introduces an acceptance-curse effect due to adverse selection. Under the monotone likelihood-ratio property of the signal, in [13] it is shown that an equilibrium in threshold strategies that are increasing in attributes exists. And although each agent has a positive probability of being accepted by any other agent, the equilibrium exhibits positive sorting in the sense that the cdf over attributes with which an agent of attribute x matches with is increasing in x in the first-order stochastic dominance sense. One limitation of all the models we have described with random search is that matching is one-to-one. A different avenue of research, started by [41], assumes that firms do not have capacity constraints and allows for on-the-job search, thus providing a rich set of transitions over time. Unfortunately, when attributes are one-dimensional, the standard model exhibits no sorting. However, there is sorting if they are multi-dimensional, as shown by [40]. A promising avenue for future research is to combine the two literatures by allowing for capacity-constrained firms and many-to-one matching. Section 19.5.4 builds mostly on [22]. Non-monotonicities of the wage in the firm type have also been observed in on-the-job search models with sorting [36] and [5] and in directed search models with multilateral matching [2]. The identification of worker types and firm type is developed in [27]. The two-sided fixed-effect method, which is challenged, was developed in [1]. Whether this holds true in the data is not without challenge; see, e.g., [9].

References

[1] Abowd, J. M., Kramarz, F., and Margolis, D. N. 1999. High wage workers and high wage firms. *Econometrica*, **67**(2), 251–333.

[2] Abowd, John M., Perez-Duarte, S., and Schmutte, I. 2018. Sorting between and within industries: A testable model of assortative matching. *Annals of Economics and Statistics*, **129**, 1–32.

[3] Albrecht, J., Gautier, P., and Vroman, S. 2006. Equilibrium directed search with multiple applications. *Review of Economic Studies*, **73**, 869–901.

[4] Atakan, A. 2006. Assortative matching with explicit search costs. *Econometrica*, **74**, 667–680.

[5] Bagger, J., and Lentz, R. 2020. An equilibrium model of wage dispersion with sorting. *Review of Economic Studies*. https://academic.oup.com/restud/article-abstract/86/1/153/4995193.

[6] Becker, G. 1973. A theory of marriage I. *Journal of Political Economy*, **81**, 813–846.

[7] Bhaskar, V., and Hopkins, E. 2016. Marriage as a rat race: Noisy premarital investments with assortative matching. *Journal of Political Economy*, **124**, 992–1045.

[8] Bloch, F., and Ryder, H. 1999. Two-sided search, marriages, and matchmakers. *International Economic Review*, **41**, 93–115.

[9] Bonhomme, S., Lamadon, T., and Manresa, E. 2020. A distributional framework for matched employer employee data. *Econometrica*. https://onlinelibrary .wiley.com/doi/abs/10.3982/ECTA15722.

[10] Burdett, K., and Coles, M. 1997. Marriage and Class. *Quarterly Journal of Economics*, **112**, 141–168.

[11] Burdett, K., and Wright, R. 1998. Two-sided search with nontransferable utility. *Review of Economic Dynamics*, **1**, 220–245.

[12] Chade, H. 2001. Two-sided search and perfect segregation with fixed search costs. *Mathematical Social Sciences*, **42**, 31–51.

[13] Chade, H. 2006. Matching with noise and the acceptance curse. *Journal of Economic Theory*, **129**(1), 81–113.

[14] Chade, H. and Eeckhout, J. 2020. Competing teams. *Review of Economic Studies*, **87**, 1134–1173.

[15] Chade, H., and Lindenlaub, I. 2021. Risky matching. *Review of Economic Studies*. https://academic.oup.com/restud/article-abstract/89/2/626/6295890.

[16] Chade, H., Eeckhout, J., and Smith, L. 2017. Sorting through search and matching models in economics. *Journal of Economic Literature*, **55**, 493–544.

[17] Chade, H., Lewis, G., and Smith, L. 2014. Student portfolios and the college admissions problem. *Review of Economic Studies*, **81**, 971–1002.

[18] Cole, H., Mailath, G., and Postlewaite, A. 2001. Efficient non-contractible investments in large economies. *Journal of Economic Theory*, **101**(2), 333–373.

[19] Diamond, P., and Maskin, E. 1979. An equilibrium analysis of search and breach of contract I: Steady states. *Bell Journal of Economics*, **10**, 282–316.

[20] Eeckhout, J. 1999. Bilateral search and vertical heterogeneity. *International Economic Review*, **40**, 869–887.

[21] Eeckhout, J., and Kircher, P. 2010. Sorting and decentralized price competition. *Econometrica*, **78**, 539–574.

[22] Eeckhout, J., and Kircher, P. 2011. Identifying sorting – in theory. *Review of Economic Studies*, **78**(3), 872–906.

[23] Eeckhout, J., and Kircher, P. 2018. Assortative matching with large firms. *Econometrica*, **86**, 85–132.

[24] Gabaix, X., and Landier, A. 2008. Why has CEO pay increased so much?. *Quarterly Journal of Economics*, **123**, 49–100.

[25] Gale, D., and Shapley, L. 1962. College admissions and the stability of marriage. *American Mathematical Monthly*, **69**, 9–15.

[26] Gautier, P., and Holzner, C. 2017. Simultaneous search and efficiency of entry and search intensity. *American Economic Journal: Microeconomics*, **9**, 245–282.

[27] Hagedorn, M., Law, T. H., and Manovskii, I. 2017. Identifying equilibrium models of labor market sorting. https://onlinelibrary.wiley.com/doi/abs/10.39 82/ECTA11301.

[28] Kircher, P. 2009. Efficiency of simultaneous search. *Journal of Political Economy*, **117**, 861–913.

[29] Kircher, P., and Galenianos, M. 2009. Directed search with multiple job applications. *Journal of Economic Theory*, **114**, 445–471.

[30] Kremer, M. 1993. The O-ring theory of economic development. *Quarterly Journal of Economics*, **108**(3), 551–75.

[31] Kremer, M., and Maskin, E. 1996. Wage inequality and segregation by skill. Working Paper.

[32] Lauermann, S., Noldeke, G., and Troger, T. 2020. The balance condition in search-and-matching models. *Econometrica*, **88**, 595–618.

[33] Legros, P., and Newman, A. 2007. Beauty is a beast, Frog is a prince: Assortative matching with nontransferabilities. *Econometrica*, **75**, 1073–1102.

[34] Legros, P., and Newman, A. 2010. Co-ranking mates: Assortative matching in marriage markets. *Economics Letters*, **106**, 177–179.

[35] Lindenlaub, I. 2017. Sorting multidimensional types: Theory and application. *Review of Economic Studies*, **84**, 718–789.

[36] Lise, J., Meghir, C., and Robin, J.-M. 2016. Matching, sorting and wages. *Review of Economic Dynamics*, **19**, 63–87.

[37] McNamara, J., and Collins, E. 1990. The job-search problem as an employer–candidate game. *Journal of Applied Probability*, **28**, 815–827.

[38] Morgan, P. 1996. Two-sided search and matching. SUNY-Buffalo working paper.

[39] Mortensen, D. 1982. *The Matching Process as a Noncooperative Bargaining Game. The Economics of Information and Uncertainty*, pp. 233–258. University of Chicago Press.

[40] Postel-Vinay, F. and Lindenlaub, I. 2020. Multidimensional sorting under random search. Working Paper.

[41] Postel-Vinay, F., and Robin, J. M. 2002. Equilibrium wage dispersion with worker and employer heterogeneity. *Econometrica*, **70**(6), 2295–2350.

[42] Roth, A., and Peranson, E. 1999. The redesign of the matching market for american physicians: Some engineering aspects of economic design. *American Economic Review*, **89**, 748–780.

[43] Shapley, L., and Shubik, M. 1972. The assignment game I: The core. *International Journal of Game Theory*. https://link.springer.com/article/10.1007/BF01753437.

[44] Shi, S. 2001. Frictional assignment I. efficiency. *Journal of Economic Theory*, **98**, 232–260.

[45] Shi, S. 2002. A directed search model of inequality with heterogeneous skills and skill-biased technology. *Review of Economic Studies*, **69**(2), 467–491.

[46] Shimer, R. 2005. The assignment of workers to jobs in an economy with coordination frictions. *Journal of Political Economy*, **113**, 996–1025.

[47] Shimer, R., and Smith, L. 2000. Assortative matching and search. *Econometrica*, **68**(2), 343–369.

[48] Smith, L. 1992. Cross-sectional dynamics in a two-sided matching model. mimeo.

[49] Smith, L. 2006. The marriage model with search frictions. *Journal of Political Economy*, **114**(6), 1124–1146.

[50] Smith, L. 2011. Frictional matching models. *Annual Review of Economics*, **3**, 319–338.

[51] Wolthoff, R. 2018. Applications and interviews: Firms' recruiting decisions in a frictional labor market. *Review of Economic Studies*, **85**, 1314–1351.

[52] Wright, R., Guerrieri, V., Kircher, P., and Julien, B. 2020. Directed search: A guided tour. *Journal of Economic Literature*. www.aeaweb.org/articles?id=10.1257/jel.20191505.

CHAPTER TWENTY

Unraveling

Guillaume Haeringer and Hanna Halaburda

20.1 Introduction

Matching markets are often coordinated, meaning that participants meet at a specific venue and date (e.g., a conference for the academic job market). This is so whether markets are *centralized* or *decentralized*.[1] There are often some "technical" reasons for such coordination. For instance, in many matching markets participants are required to hold some certification, degree, or permit. Students going to college need first to graduate from high school and thus apply when in 12th grade. The same holds for candidates on the academic job market who need to have gained a PhD (or to be near completion of a PhD), and for medical interns who need to have graduated (or to be near graduation) from medical school. Coordinating on a specific date has another benefit: it increases market thickness.

These markets have in common that there is a time structure, with a precise date or period at which the matching process is supposed to take place. *Unraveling* is a phenomenon which has been observed in many real-life markets and which consists of agents deciding who is matched with whom, *well in advance* before those matches start working for one another, and/or before the market participants have fulfilled the requirements for being on the market. There is ample evidence of unraveling in entry-level labor markets, and a famous example is the US market for medical interns until 1945, where hospitals were making offers to students as early as two years before their graduation (i.e., well before actual employment would start). Unraveling was nearly eliminated after the various American medical associations agreed to switch to a centralized matching mechanism using an algorithm (which turned out to be equivalent to Gale's and Shapley's deferred acceptance algorithm).

Unraveling becomes a problem when the resulting matching is not "optimal." For instance, in order to avoid the risk of ending up unmatched, a worker w may accept an early offer from a firm ranking low in her preferences (and similarly for the firm), thereby forgoing the possibility of accepting an offer from a more preferred firm f at

---

[1] The distinction between centralized and decentralized markets lies in who makes the matching decisions. In a centralized market agents delegate to a clearing house the matching decisions (possibly following some recommendation, such as by submitting a preference list over potential matches). Coordination is a distinct concept, roughly meaning that market participants "agree" or "coordinate" to go to the market at the same period and location and/or with a common culture (e.g., allowing agents to renege an offer after having accepted it, or not).

a later date. Such a firm f may then have no other option than hiring a worker less preferred than w, and thus (w, f) would form a blocking pair in the final matching. That is, unraveling may yield unstable and/or inefficient matchings. Instability and/or inefficiency of the matching may prevail under unraveling.

The successful implementation of a stable matching mechanism for the USA medical match suggests that stability is a key factor to curbing unraveling. The intuition is relatively simple. Agents will agree to match early if their matching prospects when doing so are preferred to the outcome they would obtain by matching later. Clearly, such pre-arranged matches can occur only if some agents on both sides of the market agree. Unraveling is thus not dissimilar to a coalition of workers and firms (or hospitals and doctors) "blocking" the market mechanism, and therefore the presence of unraveling would signal that the market mechanism does not produce stable matchings. Consequently, market institutions prone to unraveling would eventually fail, while markets that output stable matchings should not be subject to unraveling and would persist over time.

This intuition has been supported by observing the evolution of the various medical markets in the United Kingdom, where, as in the USA, recent medical graduates need to find a position in a hospital for their residencies. However, unlike the US market, the British market consists of several regional markets, each with its own procedure. Cities such as Edinburgh or Cardiff that used a stable algorithm in the 1970s or 1980s were still using the same algorithm in the 1990s. In contrast, cities such as Birmingham, Newcastle, or Sheffield that were not using a stable matching algorithm abandoned, over time, the use of those algorithms.

That stability can prevent unraveling was also observed in the laboratory by John Kagel and Alvin Roth within a setting that mimics the conditions observed in the US or British medical markets (and in many of the models we will study in this chapter). In this experiment subjects played the role of workers and firms, and both sides were divided into low- and high-productivity agents. Payoffs were designed such that high-productivity workers and firms would prefer to be matched to each other. One of the most interesting treatments that was studied consisted of first running a decentralized market over two periods, and then a centralized market in the third period for the subjects who were unmatched at the end of the second period. Two types of centralized markets were considered: one using the deferred acceptance algorithm and one using an unstable matching algorithm. Subjects who matched early (i.e., in the first or second period) would have to pay an extra cost (higher for period 1 than for period 2), a clear incentive not to match early. Subjects had to first play the matching game, without using a centralized mechanism in the last period, 10 times and then the hybrid matching game (decentralized for two periods then centralized) 5 times.[2] The experimental results confirmed the intuition we just formulated: early matching is pervasive but drops only when the deferred acceptance is used.

We will see in this chapter that unraveling is a more complex issue. To begin with, additional experimental and theoretical results show that using a stable matching mechanism does not always prevent unraveling. There is thus a need to understand which features can incentivize agents to cause unraveling: the matching process, the information agents have about each other, the extent of competition between agents

---

[2] For 10 repetitions without a centralized matching the decentralized game lasted three periods.

(often related to how similar agents' preferences are), etc. Most models adopt a similar structure, consisting of a two-period matching problem where unraveling manifests as agents matching in the first period, although some models stick to the initial interpretation of unraveling (i.e., a one-period matching mechanism with some agents blocking the mechanism). Almost all models have a two common features (albeit not necessarily modeled in the same way). First, the markets studied in these models are generally decentralized markets. This is so because unraveling is usually a phenomenon observed in such markets; unraveling with centralized markets (that use a stable mechanism) is rare. Also, it is often easier to perform some comparative statics in a decentralized model. Second, uncertainty or asymmetric information plays a central role. Incentives to match early are particularly pronounced when agents face some risk in their decision. Uncertainty can enter the picture in different ways: agents might not know the preferences of the other participants (and thus how competitive the market is), or whether there is an oversupply or undersupply of positions, or the "values" of their potential partners. All these aspects show that unraveling is a complex phenomenon that can have many different causes.

20.2 Stable Mechanisms Are Not Enough to Prevent Unraveling

The empirical and experimental evidence that we have just outlined strongly suggests that the use of a stable matching mechanism can prevent unraveling. The problem turns out to be more complex, though. The analysis of the British medical market suggests that unstable matching mechanisms are prone to fail, but what about the other way around? That is, can a stable matching mechanism prevent unraveling from occurring? A famous case study is the market for gastroenterologists in the USA. Until 1985 this market was decentralized and suffered from unraveling. In 1986 a centralized stable matching mechanism was implemented, but it broke down and was abandoned after 1996. The triggering event was a sharp decrease in the number of positions offered (which was anticipated), and an even larger decrease of candidates. This imbalance set in motion unraveling. Another factor that played a major role was asymmetric information regarding market thickness. While all participants (hospitals and doctors) knew the number of offered positions, doctors had little knowledge about the number of candidates they were competing against (and how those candidates were ranked by the hospitals). This information was known by hospitals by simply looking at the applications they received.

From a theoretical perspective it can also be shown that stability does not eliminate unraveling. To see this, consider a model with a set W of workers and a set F of firms (both finite), and let $c: F \to \mathbb{Z}$ denote a firm's capacities. That is, we are considering here a many-to-one matching problem. Each worker $w \in W$ has a strict preference relation $\succ_w$ over $F \cup \{w\}$ and each firm has a strict preference $\succ_f$ relation over 2^W. We denote by $\succ_{-S}$ the profile $(\succ_v)_{v \notin S}$ and by $\succ^S$ the restriction of $\succ = (\succ_v)_{v \in W \cup F}$ to S. Similarly c_{-f} is the vector of capacities of the firms in $F \backslash \{f\}$. A mechanism is a mapping φ that depends on the set of workers and firms, the preference profile, and the firms' capacities.

Our objective here is to show that unraveling can occur even when a stable matching mechanism is used. Unraveling here will be simply captured by the situation where firms and workers engage in *pre-arranged* matches before the mechanism is run.

When a firm f and a worker w agree on a pre-arranged match, then the worker will end up being matched to that firm. For the firm the final matching is slightly more complex if the firm has still some extra capacity. In this case the firm f will participate in the matching mechanism in a reduced problem where the worker w is no longer present and f's capacity has been decreased by one unit.

Definition 20.1. A matching mechanism φ is *manipulable via pre-arranged matches* if there is a worker w and a firm f such that

$$f \succeq_w \varphi_w (W \cup F, \succ, c) \tag{20.1}$$

$$\{w\} \cup \varphi_f(W \setminus \{w\} \cup F, \succ_{-w}^{N \setminus \{w\}}, (c_{-f}, c_f - 1)) \succeq_f \varphi_f(W \cup F, \succ, c). \tag{20.2}$$

Theorem 20.2. *There is no matching mechanism that is both stable and non-manipulable via pre-arranged matches.*

Proof Let $W = \{w_1, w_2, w_3, w_4, w_5\}$, $F = \{f_1, f_2\}$, and $c(f_1) = c(f_2) = 2$. The preferences are

$P_{w_1}: h_2, h_1$ $\qquad P_{f_1}: \{w_1, w_2\}, \{w_1, w_3\}, \{w_1, w_4\}, \{w_2, w_3\},$

$\qquad\qquad\qquad\qquad\qquad w_1, w_2, w_3, w_4$

$P_{w_2}: h_1, h_2$ $\qquad P_{f_2}: \{w_2, w_3\}, \{w_2, w_5\}, \{w_1, w_3\}, \{w_2, w_5\}, \{w_1, w_3\}, \{w_1, w_4\},$

$P_{w_3}: h_1, h_2$ $\qquad\qquad\qquad w_2, w_3, w_1, w_4, w_5$

$P_{w_4}: h_1, h_2$

$P_{w_5}: h_2, h_1$

Under these preferences there is a unique stable matching, which will be selected by any stable stable mechanism:

$$\mu^* = \begin{pmatrix} f_1 & f_2 \\ \{w_2, w_3\} & \{w_1, w_4\} \end{pmatrix}.$$

Consider a pre-arranged match between w_4 and f_1. In the problem without w_1 and with f_1's capacity reduced to 1 there are two stable matchings,

$$\mu_1 = \begin{pmatrix} f_1 & f_2 \\ \{w_1\} & \{w_2, w_3\} \end{pmatrix}, \qquad \mu_2 = \begin{pmatrix} f_1 & f_2 \\ \{w_2\} & \{w_1, w_3\} \end{pmatrix}.$$

If the stable mechanism selects μ_1 then f_1 ends up being matched to w_4 (pre-arranged) and $w_1 = \mu_1(f_1)$, which is preferred to $\mu^*(f_1)$. If instead μ_2 is selected then f_2 can also benefit by pre-arranging a match with w_5. Indeed, in the new reduced market (with w_4 and w_5 with pre-arranged matches to f_1 and f_2, respectively) there is a unique stable matching, μ_3, where $\mu_3(f_1) = w_1$ and $\mu_3(f_2) = w_2$. This is a profitable move for f_2, and thus f_1's pre-arrangement with w_4 always pays off, whether the mechanism selects μ_1 or μ_2. $\square$

Unraveling usually pertains to decentralized markets, i.e., markets that do not use a clearinghouse with participants asked to submit preference lists over potential matches.

20.3 Market Timing and the Nature of Offers

One of the most salient features of unraveling relates to the nature of the offers that firms make to workers, which can either be *exploding* or *open*. The former describes an offer that workers must accept or reject immediately (i.e., in the same period, in a model with discrete time). In contrast, a worker receiving an open offer can hold it for several periods and decide later whether to reject it. Exploding offers are particularly stringent for workers when they cannot renege on the offer after having accepted it. Whether firms can make exploding offers and whether workers can reject an offer they previously accepted is stipulated informally by the market culture, although in some cases it can be explicitly stated. For instance, most graduate schools in the USA subscribe to a resolution which states that students do not need to respond to offers before April 15, and if an exploding offer is made prior to that date students have the option to renege on it afterwards.[3]

Intuitively, unraveling is less likely when firms make open offers, or when workers can reject an exploding offer that they accepted at an earlier date. But this does not imply that unraveling necessarily occurs if firms make exploding offers where acceptance is binding; one needs some degree of uncertainty for unraveling to occur.

We consider a one-to-one matching problem with a set $W = \{w_1, \ldots, w_W\}$ of workers and a set $F = \{f_1, \ldots, f_F\}$ of firms. There are two periods. All workers have the same preferences $\succ_W$ over firms, with firm F being the most preferred, then firm $F - 1, \ldots$, and firm 1 being the least preferred. The payoff to a worker is equal to the index of his match. So, a worker matched to firm h obtains a payoff equal to $F - h + 1$. We add "+1" so that workers strictly prefer being matched to remaining unmatched; the same will hold for firms. Firms also have identical preferences over workers, denoted $\succ_F$, but those preferences are revealed only in period 2. In period 1 a public signal $\widehat{\succ}$ is observed by all agents; this indicates workers' qualities (captured by a ranking of workers). With probability α we have $\succ_F = \widehat{\succ}$ and, with probability $1 - \alpha$, $\succ_F$ is taken randomly from the set of all $F!$ possible orderings. As for workers, a firm's payoff depends on the worker's rank: a firm matched to the worker ranked kth under $\succ_F$ obtains a payoff equal to $W - h + 1$.

At each period all firms make simultaneously at most one offer, and all workers simultaneously accept or reject their offer. Acceptance of an offer is binding and a worker leaves the market together with his firm after accepting an offer. All actions are publicly observed. We first check that the second-period matching is uniquely identified in equilibrium.

Lemma 20.3. *Suppose that firms are not allowed to make exploding offers. For any workers' decisions about first-period offers there is always a unique stable matching in the market restricted to period 2.*

Proof Note that firms whose offers have been held by a worker from the first period cannot make new offers in the second period. Let $\widehat{F}$ be the set of firms that have not made an offer in the first period or had their first-period offer rejected in period 2. Consider the highest-ranked worker in period 2, say, w_m, and let $v_m \in F \cup \{\emptyset\}$ be the offer that w_m holds from period 1. At any stable matching, that worker will be matched to $f_m := \max_{\succ_W} \widehat{F} \cup \{v_m\}$. If not, then

---

[3] Council of Grammar Schools (CGS) resolution at www.cgsnet.org.

w_m and f_m will block the matching. Consider now the second-highest-ranked worker, say, w_{m-1}, and let $v_{m-1} \in F \cup \{\emptyset\}$ be the offer that w_{m-1} holds from period 1. Note that if $v_m \in F$ then v_m is not available to w_{m-1}, whether w_m rejects it or not. So, at any stable matching, w_{m-1} will be matched to $f_{m-1} := \max_{>_W} \widehat{F} \cup \{v_{m-1}\} \setminus \{f_m\}$. If not then w_{m-1} and f_{m-1} would block the matching. Continuing this way with $w_{m-2}, w_{m-3}, \ldots$, we get a unique stable matching. $\qquad \square$

Proposition 20.4. *When firms are not allowed to make exploding offers, the stable matching is the unique equilibrium and there is no unraveling.*

Proof Notice first that holding a first-period offer is a weakly dominating strategy. We use the notation from the proof of Lemma 20.3. To see this, suppose that a worker, say, w_k, receives an offer from, say, f, in period 1. If he holds that offer, let f_k be the best offer in period 2 and let f_h be the best offer he receives if in period 1 he rejects f's offer (possibly $f_k = f$). So $f_h \neq f$ and $f_h \in \widehat{F}$. Suppose that w_k is better off rejecting f's offer in period 1. That is, $f_h \succ_W f_k$ and thus $h < k$. If w_k rejects f's offer then there must be a worker $i < k$ such that, at the new (unique) stable matching, w_i is matched to f. So we have $f \succ_W f_i$ (i.e., in period 2, f, now being available, makes an offer to w_i, which is accepted). For simplicity, assume that w_i is the only worker among $\{w_1, \ldots, w_{k-1}\}$ having a different match because w_k rejected f's offer.[4] Since w_i is the only worker with a different stable match (for workers $w_1, \ldots, w_{k-1}$), $f_h = f_i$. But then $f \succ_W f_h$, so w_k cannot be better off rejecting f's offer.

Since all workers hold their period-1 offers, it is a dominant strategy for the top firm to wait for the second period to make an offer (when the top worker's identity is known with certainty). Consequently, the second firm is also better off waiting for the second period, and so on until the lowest-ranked firm. $\qquad \square$

Proposition 20.5. *When firms are allowed to make exploding offers, an equilibrium with full unraveling exists if and only if $W \leq F$ and $\alpha \geq (W - 2)/W$ (i.e., the signal is sufficiently accurate).*

Proof Suppose that $W > F$ and there is an equilibrium where all firms make an exploding offer in period 1. It is not difficult to show that, for each $h = 1, \ldots, F$, firm f_h makes an offer to the worker ranked hth according to the signal $\widehat{\succ}$.[5] But then the lowest-ranked firm is better off deviating and making an offer in period 2 to the best available worker according to the realized ranking (in the worst case the worker ranked Fth according to $\widehat{\succ}$).[6] So, there must be an excess demand, i.e., $W \leq F$.

With all firms making exploding offers in period 1, the firm ranked h in $\succ_W$ makes an offer to the worker ranked h in $\widehat{\succ}_F$. In this case the lowest-ranked worker's payoff is $F - W + 1$. Denote that worker by w. The largest possible gain

---

[4] The proof goes through if there are more such workers but it becomes more cumbersome.

[5] Implicitly we have assumed that the belief about the expected rank of a worker under $\succ_F$ being conditional on his rank in $\widehat{\succ}_F$, is the same for all firms. Offers made in this equilibrium are necessarily assortative according to $\widehat{\succ}_F$ and $\succ_W$.

[6] Note that for a fully fledged proof we would need to take into account possible rejections by workers after that firm's deviation. The firm's incentives would not be affected.

from deviation occurs when the highest-ranked firm deviates and the lowest-ranked worker rejects his first-period offer. Under this deviation there would be two workers left in period 2, the worker w' ranked highest under $\hat{\succ}_F$ (who was supposed to have an offer from the top-ranked firm), and the lowest-ranked worker. The firm ranked $F - W + 1$ is no longer available. Using Lemma 20.3 the lowest-ranked worker (under $\hat{\succ}_W$) can be matched to the highest-ranked firm (if $w \succ_F w'$) or the firm ranked $F - W$ (if $w' \succ_F w$). The former case occurs with probability

$$\frac{1-\alpha}{W!} \times \frac{W!}{2} = \frac{1-\alpha}{2}.$$

So w's highest expected payoff is

$$\frac{1-\alpha}{2}F + \frac{1+\alpha}{2}(F - W).$$

For w not to deviate we thus require that his expected payoff, obtained by accepting the offer from the firm ranked $F - W + 1$, is larger than the payoff obtained under a deviation by the top-ranked firm:

$$F - W + 1 > \frac{1-\alpha}{2}F + \frac{1+\alpha}{2}(F - W).$$

Using $W \leq F$ this yields $\alpha > \overline{\alpha} := (W - 2)/W$. Hence, if the signal is sufficiently precise, i.e., $\alpha > \overline{\alpha}$, worker w will not reject the offer made to him after the top firm deviates in period 1.

Using similar calculations it can be shown that the top firm will prefer the expected payoff from being matched to the top worker (according to $\hat{\succ}$) than being matched in period 2 to the top worker among the bottom $W - F$ workers (according to $\hat{\succ}$). □

20.4 Uncertainty as a Source of Unraveling

One of the most common sources of unraveling is agents' risk aversion: matching early is a form of insurance. The basic intuition is that, by matching early, agents can reduce the uncertainty attached to their payoff if they match later. A standard approach to capture this uncertainty is through the presence of incomplete information. In a matching setting this is done by assuming that in the first period agents are uncertain about the value of their match, and this uncertainty is resolved in the second period.

20.4.1 Insurance

To this end, here we will consider again a two-period matching model between workers and firms where agents have some *ability* level and the value of a match between a worker and a firm will depend on their abilities. Incomplete information enters the picture because the ability is only realized in the second period. In the first period firms and workers have a *type*, which is a signal about each other's ability. Hence, a type gives a probability distribution of ex-post ability. Agent's types are commonly observed. For a worker we denote by x his type and X his ability. Similarly, y denotes a firm's type and Y its ability.

We do not model the matching process *per se*. That is, we assume that the matching is decentralized (i.e., there is no clearinghouse that matches agents) and thus our analysis will consider competitive equilibria.

All agents enjoy the proceeds of their match in the second period, once the ability levels are realized. For a firm of ability Y matched to a worker of ability X the production function is $F(X, Y)$, which we assume to be twice continuously differentiable. Higher ability yields higher output (so $F_1, F_2 > 0$) and, more importantly, we assume that there is complementarity in ability, i.e., $F_{12} > 0$.[7]

In this model firms and workers have the choice between matching in the first period (i.e., interim matching) or in the second period (i.e., ex-post matching). The complementarity assumptions ensures that the matching between agents not matched in the first period is always assortative.

20.4.1.1 Matching Early versus Matching Later

We start our analysis by documenting the trade-off between matching early and matching in the second period. To this end, we will simply compare the payoffs and their variance when all agents match in the second period with the case when they all match in the first period.

For simplicity, assume that the distributions of abilities X and Y are identical. Assuming a continuum of agents on both sides, a worker of ability X matched in period 2 will be matched to a firm of ability $Y = X$. Thus, conditional on the worker being of type x, we can calculate the expected production using a Taylor expansion and get

$$\mathbb{E}\left[F(X, X) \mid x\right] \approx F(x, x) + \sigma^2 \frac{F_{11} + 2F_{12} + F_{22}}{2}. \tag{20.3}$$

In contrast, if workers and firms match in period one, i.e., before ability is revealed, and assuming that workers of type x will be matched to a firm of type $y = x$, then the expected output is now conditional on both agents being of the same type. So the expected output is (again using a Taylor expansion)

$$\mathbb{E}\left[F(X, X) \mid x, x\right] \approx F(x, x) + \sigma^2 \frac{F_{11} + F_{22}}{2}, \tag{20.4}$$

One can immediately see that with complementarities, i.e., $F_{12} > 0$, matching in period 2 is efficient. However, the payoff from matching early can be less volatile. To see this, suppose the workers' payoff is half of (20.3) or (20.4) for matching in period 2 or period 1, respectively. Then the variance of the payoff for matching in period 2 is

$$\mathrm{Var}[F(X, X) \mid x] \approx \frac{\sigma^2}{4} \left(F_1^2 + 2F_1 F_2 + F_2^2\right), \tag{20.5}$$

and for matching in period 1 it is

$$\mathrm{Var}[F(X, X) \mid x, x] \approx \frac{\sigma^2}{4} \left(F_1^2 + F_2^2\right). \tag{20.6}$$

---

[7] Where F_1, F_2, F_{12} denote the derivatives $\frac{\partial F}{\partial X}, \frac{\partial F}{\partial Y}, \frac{\partial^2 F}{\partial X \partial Y}$, respectively.

Therefore, if agents are sufficiently risk-averse then matching early may be preferred by them.

20.4.1.2 Early-Contracting Equilibrium

The main question is then whether there exists an equilibrium where some agents (or all) match in the first period. This model may admit many different type of equilibria. We focus here on equilibria where high types (workers and firms) match in the first period while low types wait for the second period.

To this end we will denote by $u_*(x)$ and $U_*(x)$ the payoff to a worker of type x who is matched in the first or second period, respectively. Similarly, $v_*(y)$ and $V_*(y)$ denote the payoff of a firm of type y from matching in the first or second period, respectively.

We consider here an *early contracting equilibrium*, which is given first by a matching and second by payoff functions $u_*(x)$ and $v_*(y)$, for all types x and y, respectively. The equilibrium payoff functions have the following four properties:

(i) For a worker of type x who matches early, $u_*(x) \geq U_*(x)$ for all types x; for a firm of type y that matches early, $v_*(y) \geq V_*(y)$ for all types y.

(ii) For all workers of type x who match in the second period, $u_*(x) = U_*(x)$ for all types x; for all firms of type y that match in the second period, $v_*(y) = V_*(y)$.

(iii) For all worker–firm pairs of types x and y, respectively, that match early, there exists an income-sharing contract that yields $u_*(x)$ to the worker and $v_*(y)$ to the firm.

(iv) For a firm of type y (whether matching in the first or second period) and for a worker of type x, there is no worker of type x and a contract that yields $u_*(x)$ to the worker and a payoff strictly greater than $v_*(y)$ to the firm, for all types y.

Condition (i) simply says that workers and firms who match early have no incentive to deviate and wait for the second period. Condition (ii) relates to the agents waiting for the second period and just states that their overall equilibrium payoff $U_*(x)$ should indeed be equal to their second period payoff, $U_*(x)$ and $V_*(y)$, respectively. Condition (iii) is a payoff feasibility constraint, and condition (iv) implies that no worker–firm pair can benefit by signing a different contract.

In this definition of equilibrium we can view workers' equilibrium payoffs $u_*(x)$ as the price for an early match with type x. Firms matching early will then match to the worker type that gives the highest payoff subject to the constraint that the worker's payoff is $u_*(x)$ and that the firm's payoff is greater than if the firm waits (that payoff would be equal to $V_*(y)$). On the other hand, for all firms opting to wait, their payoff from matching early, $v_*(y)$, is lower than their payoff from waiting, $V_*(y)$.

Under this definition of equilibrium we can identify under which conditions early matching is *assortative*. To see this, denote by $w(x, y)$ the sum of the payoffs of a type-x worker and type-y firm that are matched together in the first period.

Proposition 20.6. *If $w(x, y)$ has positive cross partial derivatives for all x and y then, for any early contracting equilibrium, there do not exist types $x_1 < x_2$ and types $y_1 < y_2$ such that a type-x_1 worker contracts with a type-y_2 firm and a type x_2-worker contracts with a type-y_1 firm.*

Proof Take such an equilibrium (non-assortative), with payoffs $u_*(x_1)$ and $u_*(x_2)$. Type y_2 is better off with x_1 than with x_2 if

$$w(x_1, y_2) - u_*(x_1) \geq w(x_2, y_2) - u_*(x_2).$$

Similarly, type y_1 is better off with x_2 than with x_1 if

$$w(x_2, y_1) - u_*(x_2) \geq w(x_1, y_1) - u_*(x_1).$$

Adding these two inequalities we get

$$w(x_1, y_2) + w(x_2, y_1) \geq w(x_1, y_1) + w(x_2, y_2),$$

which can be written as

$$\int_{x_1}^{x_2} \frac{\partial w(x, y_1)}{\partial x} dx \geq \int_{x_1}^{x_2} \frac{\partial w(x, y_2)}{\partial x} dx.$$

This contradicts the assumption that $w(x, y)$ has positive cross partial derivatives. $\qquad \square$

For the remainder of this section we will assume that the utility derived by a worker and a firm for a contract C (i.e., which specifies a matching and a division of the production's revenue) are respectively

$$U(C) = E[C] - r_1 \text{Var}(C), \qquad V(C) = E[C] - r_2 \text{Var}(C), \qquad (20.7)$$

where r_1 and r_2 indicate the degrees of the workers' and firms' risk aversion, respectively.

We can check whether these payoff functions can ensure a first-period assortative matching, i.e., whether the condition of Proposition 20.6 is satisfied. When workers and firms match early, an optimal sharing rule allocates $\lambda F(X, Y) + c$ to the worker and $(1 - \lambda)F(X, Y) - c$ to the firm, with c a transfer payment. The expected utility for a type-x worker is then

$$u(x, y) = \frac{r_2}{r_1 + r_2} E[F(X, Y) \mid x, y] + c - r_1 \left(\frac{r_2}{r_1 + r_2} \right)^2 \text{Var}\left[F(X, Y) \mid x, y\right],$$

and, for a firm of type y, the expected utility is

$$v(x, y) = \frac{r_1}{r_1 + r_2} E[F(X, Y) \mid x, y] - c - r_2 \left(\frac{r_1}{r_1 + r_2} \right)^2 \text{Var}\left[F(X, Y) \mid x, y\right].$$

So in this case we have

$$w(x, y) = E[F(X, Y) \mid x, y] - \left(\frac{r_1 r_2}{r_1 + r_2} \right) \text{Var}[F(X, Y) \mid x, y]. \qquad (20.8)$$

The cross partial derivative of $w(x, y)$ is then

$$\mathbb{E}\left[F_{12}(X, Y) | x, y\right] - \left(\frac{2r_1 r_2}{r_1 + r_2} \right) \times \left(\text{Cov}(F, F_{12} | x, y) + \text{Cov}(F_1, F_2 | x, y) \right). \qquad (20.9)$$

This condition is readily satisfied if, for instance, firms are risk neutral and workers risk averse. Indeed, in this case $r_1 > 0$ and $r_2 = 0$, and thus the derivative is equal to $\mathbb{E}\left[F_{12}(X, Y) | x, y\right]$, which is positive since $F_{12} > 0$. The intuition is relatively straightforward. Since types are observable and firms are risk neutral, workers will be fully "insured." More interesting is that the complementarity in the production function implies that high-type firms can outbid low-type firms when competing for high-type workers, thus yielding an assortative matching.

In order to show that we can have an early contracting equilibrium it is useful to be more specific about the payoffs. For the rest of our analysis we will assume that the production has the form $F(X, Y) = XY$. The ability distribution X conditional on type x is $N(x, \sigma^2)$ and, similarly, for firms' ability Y conditional on type y the distribution is $N(y, \sigma^2)$. Types are distributed over $[\underline{t}, \overline{t}]$, with $\underline{t}$ large enough that $x > 0$. Finally, the income-sharing rule is such that an ability-X worker's payoff is $X^2/2$ and an ability-Y firm's payoff is $Y^2/2$.

Using (20.7) a type-x worker's expected utility from waiting is

$$U_*(x) = E\left[\frac{X^2}{2} \mid x\right] - r_1 \operatorname{Var}\left[\frac{X^2}{2} \mid x\right] = \frac{1}{2}(x^2 + \sigma^2) - \frac{r_1}{4}(4x^2\sigma^2 + 2\sigma^4), \quad (20.10)$$

and for a firm of type y the payoff from waiting is

$$V_*(y) = \frac{1}{2}(y^2 + \sigma^2) - \frac{r_2}{4}(4y^2\sigma^2 + 2\sigma^4). \quad (20.11)$$

Consider now a worker of type x matching early, receiving a payoff equal to $u_*(x)$, and matched to a type-y firm. From (20.8), that firm's payoff is

$$v(x, y) = xy - \frac{r_1 r_2}{r_1 + r_2}(x^2\sigma^2 + y^2\sigma^2 + \sigma^4) - u_*(x). \quad (20.12)$$

In the equilibrium we are constructing the early match is assortative, i.e., firms and workers of equal types match together in the first period. So we should have $v(y, y) = \operatorname{argmax}_x v(x, y)$. Using the first-order condition for (20.12) we obtain

$$u_*(x) = \left(\frac{1}{2} - \frac{r_1 r_2 \sigma^2}{r_1 + r_2}\right) + u_0. \quad (20.13)$$

Recall that our objective is to show that we can have an early contracting equilibrium where high-type workers and high-type firms match in the first period. To this end we now show that there is a threshold z such that workers of type $x \geq z$ and firms of type $y \geq z$ match early, while the other agents wait for the second period. So workers and firms of type z are indifferent between matching early and waiting, and we thus have

$$U_*(z) = u_*(z) \qquad \text{and} \qquad V_*(z) = v_*(z).$$

Since the early match is assortative, a firm of type z is matched to a worker of type z and thus, using (20.12),

$$v(z, z) = z^2 - \frac{r_1 r_2}{r_1 + r_2}(2z^2\sigma^2 + \sigma^4) - u_*(z),$$

with $u_*(z)$ given by (20.13). Using (20.10) and (20.11), we can solve for u_0 and z and obtain

$$u_0 = \frac{\sigma^2(r_2^2 - r_1^2)}{2(r_1^2 + r_2^2)} - \frac{r_1 r_2 \sigma^4}{2(r_1 + r_2)}, \quad (20.14)$$

$$z = \left(\frac{r_1 + r_2}{r_1^2 + r_2^2} - \frac{\sigma^2}{2} \right)^{1/2}.$$ (20.15)

We can now check that we have an early contracting equilibrium. We first need to verify that agents of type higher than z are matched in the first period to agents of the same type. From (20.10) and (20.13) we have $u_*'(x) > U_*'(x)$. Since $u_*(z) = U_*(z)$, we have $u_*(x) > U_*(x)$ if and only if $x > z$. Similarly, (20.11) and

$$v_*(y) = y^2 + \frac{r_1 r_2}{r_1 + r_2}(2y^2\sigma^2 + \sigma^4) - u_*(y)$$

imply that $v_*'(y) \geq V_*'(y)$ and thus $v_*(y) > U_*(y)$ if and only if $y > z$. Hence, workers and firms of type higher than the cutoff z match early, and thus from Proposition 20.6 agents of equal type match together.

Second, we need to verify that no firm of type $y \geq z$ can be better off by matching with a worker of type $x < z$ (and similarly, no worker of type $x \geq z$ can be better off by matching with a firm of type $y < z$). Since a type-y firm that matches early is better off matching with a type-y worker than a type-x worker we have $v_*(y) = w(y, y) - u_*(y) \geq w(y, x) - u_*(x)$. Since for $x < z$ we have $u_*(x) < U_*(x)$, the type-y firm can be matched with a type-$x < z$ worker only if that worker gets at least $U_*(x)$. Hence, the firm would get a payoff strictly lower than $v_*(y)$. The case for a worker of type $x \geq z$ matching with a firm of type $y < z$ is symmetric.

Finally, we need to check that agents of type lower than z cannot gain by matching early. To this end, it suffices to show that the gain from matching early is less than the sum of their period-2 payoff, i.e., $(w, x) \leq U_*(x) + V_*(y)$.

Using the previous equations we have

$$U_*(x) + V_*(y) - w(x, y) = \frac{1}{2}(x - y)^2 + \frac{(r_1^2 + r_2^2)\sigma^2}{r_1 + r_2}\left(z^2 - \frac{r_1^2}{r_1^2 + r_2^2}x^2 - \frac{r_2^2}{r_1^2 + r_2^2}y^2 \right).$$

Since $z > x, y$, the right-hand side is positive, the desired result.

We can use (20.15) to derive some comparative statics results and understand how risk aversion is the main driver behind early contracting. First, note that z decreases whenever r_1 and r_2 increase (with the difference between r_1 and r_2 constant). That is, as agents become more risk averse, more agents match early in equilibrium. Also, as the uncertainty increases (i.e., σ^2 increases), the cutoff z again decreases.

20.4.2 Beyond Insurance

From the above analysis we may conclude that insurance, because of agents' risk aversion, stands out as a key explanation for unraveling and that agents' risk aversion is a key motive to explain why workers' and firms' decisions are driven by the insurance motive. However, unraveling holds only under certain payoffs configurations: agents need to be "sufficiently risk averse" – see the comments after (20.6).

It turns out that, even without any insurance motive, unraveling may occur. That is, even if agents prefer higher (and more risky) outcomes to less preferred (and less risky) ones we may still observe agents preferring to match early. Also, the point can be made without requiring specific payoff configurations such as a sufficiently high risk aversion, as in the previous model or in the example in the proof of Theorem 20.2.[8]

To this end we consider a finite one-to-one matching model similar to the one used for Theorem 20.2. Unraveling will be captured in this model with a slightly more general approach to pre-arranged matches, namely agents' blocking a matching mechanism with another matching mechanism.[9] We depart, however, from that model, first by assuming that the matching mechanism can be a *random mechanism*, meaning that the mechanism may output a probability distribution over matchings. In order to study whether some agents want to block a mechanism we thus need a preference relation over the probability distribution of matchings. The most robust way to do this is to use a stochastic dominance relation. An agent prefers a mechanism φ to another mechanism φ' if the probability distribution over the partners under φ *first-order stochastically dominates* the probability distribution over the partners under φ'.[10]

A second departure is that we will assume that there is incomplete information regarding agents' preferences. To deal with that we have to make the distinction, as in any Bayesian game, between the ex-ante, interim, and ex-post stages. We are interested here in *interim stability*, which is defined as follows. Given a prior β over preference profiles, a coalition V of workers and firms *blocks in the interim* the mechanism ϕ if there is another mechanism ϕ' that matches agents in V with probability 1 and a set of preference profiles for the coalition V, $\succ_V$, such that, for any preference profile that has a positive probability under the beliefs β, all agents in V prefer their match under ϕ' to that under ϕ. A mechanism is *interim stable* at a prior β if no coalition of agents blocks in the interim at β.

When all uncertainty is resolved we talk about *ex-post stability*. A coalition V of workers and firms *block ex-post* a mechanism if there exists a mechanism ϕ' that matches agents in V with probability 1 and all agents in V prefer the matching under ϕ' to the matching under ϕ.

Before going further two remarks are in order. First, as we have intuited above, the mechanisms ϕ and ϕ' in the above definition need not be deterministic mechanisms, i.e., they might be random mechanisms.

Second, note that the definitions of blocking (interim or ex-post) are reminiscent of the core.

Lemma 20.7. *If a mechanism ϕ is interim stable then ϕ is ex-post stable.*

Proof Suppose that ϕ is not ex-post stable. So, for some profile $\succ$ there is a coalition A and a mechanism ϕ' such that all agents in A prefer ϕ' to ϕ at $\succ$. Consider a prior that puts probability 1 on $\succ$. So A also blocks ϕ, and thus ϕ is not interim stable. $\qquad\square$

Theorem 20.8. *No mechanism is interim stable.*

[8] In that example f_1 prefers $\{w_1, w_4\}$ to $\{w_2, w_3\}$. If it were the opposite then f_1 would not benefit from a pre-arranged match with w_4. Note that if f_1 prefers w_h to w_{h+1} (for $h = 1, 2, 3$) both $\{w_1, w_4\} \succ_{f_1} \{w_2, w_3\}$ and $\{w_2, w_3\} \succ_{f_1} \{w_1, w_4\}$ are possible under a simple assumption such as responsive preferences.

[9] In the model of Theorem 20.2 we can say for instance that firm f_1 and worker w_4 prefer the mechanism that matches f_1 and w_4 (and matches f_1 and w_1, too) to the mechanism that outputs the matching μ^*.

[10] A random matching μ first-order stochastically dominates a random matching μ' if, for all agents v, $\mathbb{P}[\mu(v) \succeq v'] \geq \mathbb{P}[\mu'(v) \succeq v']$ for each v'.

Proof Suppose that each agent's preferences are i.i.d. uniform over the agents on the other side. Consider the following profile,

$$P_{m_1}: w_1, w_2, w_3 \qquad\qquad P_{w_1}: m_1, m_2, m_3$$
$$P_{m_2}: w_1, w_3, w_2 \qquad\qquad P_{w_2}: m_1, m_3, m_2$$
$$P_{m_3}: w_3, w_1, w_2 \qquad\qquad P_{w_3}: m_3, m_1, m_2$$

and let ϕ be an interim stable mechanism. So ϕ is also ex-post stable. If an ex-post stable mechanism matches w_1 and m_1 with probability less than 1 then m_1 and w_1 can deviate by becoming matched. The same holds for m_3 and w_3. Hence, those two pairs are always matched under $\phi(P)$ and thus m_2 and w_2 are matched to each other.

Let σ be any permutation of workers and the firms, such that $\sigma(M) = M$ and $\sigma(W) = W$, and we denote by $\sigma(\succ)$ the profile such that $\sigma(\succ)_{\sigma(v)}(\sigma(v')) = \succ_v (v')$, where $\succ_v (v')$ is the rank of v' in $\succ_v$. Consider the mechanism ϕ' such that if P' is obtained from P with a permutation σ then $\phi'(P')$ gives the matching $\{\sigma(m_1)\sigma(w_2), \sigma(m_2)\sigma(w_1), \sigma(m_3)\sigma(w_3)\}$, and $\phi'(P') = \phi(P')$ otherwise.

For the profile $\succ$, ϕ' gives four agents their first choices and two agents their second choices, while ϕ gives four agents their first choices and two agents their *third* choices. Since preferences are i.i.d. uniform, that is the case for any permutation of P, too. So, under ϕ', the interim expected matches have probabilities 2/3 and 1/3 of getting the first and second choices, respectively, and for ϕ to get the first and third choices. For profiles that are not a permutation of $\succ$, all agents are indifferent between ϕ and ϕ'. Hence, for all agents, ϕ' stochastically dominates ϕ, so ϕ is preferred. $\qquad\Box$

20.5 Structural Conditions

In the models analyzed in the previous sections it was made made clear that uncertainty or asymmetric information is a key component that may cause the market to unravel. However, most of these results also rely, to some extent, on having agents on each side of the market with similar preferences. Intuitively, when preferences over potential matches are very dissimilar, agents do not compete with each other and thus the incentive to match early is reduced.[11] One crucial question is what role do "similar preferences" play in unraveling? In this section we present and analyze a model that aims to address this question.

We consider a model with W workers and F firms, with $W > F$. All workers have the same strict preferences $\succ_W$ over firms, with $f_F \succ f_{F-1} \succ \cdots \succ f_1$. All firms are *acceptable* to workers, i.e., a worker prefers to be matched to any firm than remaining unmatched. As with the models in the other sections, there are two periods. Workers' preferences over firms are commonly known from the beginning of the game. Firms' preferences over workers are revealed only in the second period. In the first period, for all firms, all workers are ex-ante identical.

We assume that in the first period firms know whether their preferences will be similar in the second period. To formalize this we first consider two polar cases. The first case occurs when firms' preferences are drawn from a distribution G_1, a

---

[11] This is a rough intuition; we also need the uncertainty to be sufficiently low that in expectation preferences still remain sufficiently similar.

joint distribution such that all firms' preferences over workers are identical, and each preference ordering has the same probability, $\frac{1}{W!}$, of being realized. The other case is when firms' preferences are drawn from a distribution G_0 which corresponds to each firm's preferences being drawn randomly and independently from all possible rankings (and with probability $\frac{1}{W!}$ each).

Between these two polar cases there is a continuum of joint distributions G_ρ, with $\rho \in [0, 1]$ and $G_\rho = \rho G_1 + (1 - \rho)G_0$. The parameter ρ is the measure of similarity of preferences. The preferences are more similar for larger ρ. Note that the marginal distributions (i.e., for individual firms) are uniform under G_ρ, as they are under G_1 and G_0. Hence, all workers are ex ante identical to any firm. Yet, the firms' expectations over matching in $t = 2$ depend on ρ (and the matching mechanism).

It will prove useful to use cardinal representations of agents' preferences. To this end, let u_i be the utility to a worker from being matched to firm f_i, with $u_F > u_{F-1} > \cdots > u_1 > 0$, and let v_i be the utility accruing to a firm from being matched to its ith most preferred worker, with $v_W > v_{W-1} > \cdots > v_1 > 0$.

Finally, we assume that in the first period firms can make (exploding) offers to workers who can either accept their offer (at most one) or reject it. Acceptance is binding so that a firm and a worker matched in the first period are no longer present in period 2. In period 2 there is a matching mechanism $\mathcal{M}$ that matches the remaining agents. That mechanism can be centralized or decentralized.

Proposition 20.9. *A stable mechanism may not be successful in preventing unraveling, for sufficiently high ρ.*

Proof Suppose the matching mechanism in $t = 2$ is the stable matching mechanism (since the workers have identical preferences, there is a unique stable matching for any preferences of the firms). Let $E\pi_f(o_S \mid \rho)$ denote firm f's expected payoff from the ex-post stable outcome under G_ρ.

If the firms' preferences are identical, f_i will be matched with its ith preferred worker (when restricting firms' preferences to the workers who are still present in period 2). However, if the firms' preferences are independent, f_i can be matched with any of the workers that it ranks from 1 to i with equal probability. Hence, the expected value of waiting for the stable match is lower under identical preferences than under independent preferences. And by the structure of G_ρ, it holds more generally: for any $\rho \in [0, 1]$, the expected value of waiting for the stable match, $E\pi_f(o_S \mid \rho)$, decreases as ρ increases. Moreover, for any ρ, $E\pi_f(o_S \mid \rho)$ increases with f.

The expected payoff from early matching in $t = 1$, π^0, is the same for any similarity of preferences and any firm (it is a random match):

$$\pi^0 \equiv \frac{1}{W} \sum_{k=1}^{W} v_k .$$

Firm f would prefer to contract early when $\pi^0 > E\pi_f(o_S \mid \rho)$. Note that it is the lower-ranked firms that prefer to contract early. This follows directly from the fact that, for any ρ, the expected value of the stable match increases with f.

So there will be a threshold, H_ρ^0, such that firms $f < H_\rho^0$ prefer to contract early:

$$H_\rho^0 \equiv \max \left\{ f \mid \pi^0 > E\pi_f(o_S \mid \rho) \right\} .$$

Note that since $E\pi_f(o_S \mid \rho)$ decreases as ρ increases, preferences that are more similar induce more firms to match early, i.e., H_ρ^0 increases with ρ.

For early contracting to occur, a worker also needs to want to contract early. A worker who has an early offer from f at hand accepts this offer if it is better than the value of random match, that is, if $u_f > \frac{1}{W} \sum_{i=1}^{F} u_i$. This implies that there is also some threshold, L^0, such that an early offer made by $f > L^0$ is accepted:

$$L^0 \equiv \min \left\{ f \mid u_f > \frac{1}{W} \sum_{i=1}^{F} u_i \right\} .$$

Unraveling will thus occur whenever these two thresholds offer a non-empty set, $L^0 \leq H_\rho^0$. Hence, unraveling may occur in equilibrium even though in the second period the matching mechanism is stable; and it is more likely to occur as ρ increases. $\qquad\square$

For any market (i.e, sets W and F and payoff functions u and v for workers and firms, respectively), increasing ρ increases the probability that the interval between the two thresholds will be non-empty, and thus the probability that unraveling will occur increases too.

Interestingly, this model exhibits some complementarities in unraveling. As the number of firms making offers in the first period increases, the expected payoff for workers staying until the second period decreases. A first and immediate effect is that it will induce workers to accept first-period offers they would initially not accept. In turn, this may increase the number of firms making early offers. Whether all firms do unravel will depend on the parameters, though.

20.6 Information Disclosure and Unraveling

In almost all the approaches we have presented to explain unraveling, uncertainty plays a crucial role. However, in all those models the level of uncertainty is not a strategic variable that the agents could alter, and often those models do not expose the extent to which the level of uncertainty can lead agents to match early (or not). This section aims to address this question, by considering a model where an agent can decide how much information to disclose and to see whether this can mitigate or exacerbate unraveling.[12]

The model is substantially different from the previous models that we have considered in that there are *three* types of agents: students (or future workers), schools, and firms. As for the other models, the objective is to match students or workers to firms;

[12] The models analyzed in Section 20.3 and 20.4.1 also allowed for some comparative statics by varying the level of uncertainty (through α and σ^2, respectively). The model here differs substantially because we allow a change in uncertainty level for some agents only, whereas in the previous sections that change would hold for all agents.

we suppose that students have an ability that is unknown to the firms. However, that ability is known by the schools (i.e., through students' transcripts), who can choose how much information regarding students' abilities they want to disclose.

For each school there is a continuous, exogenous distribution of ability levels with support $a \in [a_L, a_H]$ that is commonly known. However, the exact ability of a student is only observed by the school in which the student is enrolled. Positions offered by a firm have a *desirability* $q \in [q_L, q_H]$. The distribution of position desirability is common knowledge.[13] We assume that there is an equal mass of positions offered by firms and students.

For each ability level (of one of its students), a school reveals to the positions offered by firms an *expected ability* $\widehat{a} \in [a_L, a_H]$. We make the following assumption: the average ability of students who are told that they have an expected ability of $\widehat{a}$ is equal to $\widehat{a}$. In other words, the information disclosed must be statistically correct.

Students care about position desirability and those offering positions care about students' abilities. Hence, students have identical preferences and so do those offering positions. Therefore the resulting matching will be *assortative*.

Finally, schools care about the average desirability of the positions its students achieve in the matching. We denote by $Q(\widehat{a})$ the mapping from expected ability to desirability. That is, given an expected ability disclosed by the school of $\widehat{a}$, $Q(\widehat{a})$ indicates the percentile of the desirability of the position to which the student will be matched.

The following example shows that it is not always in the interest of schools to reveal full information.

Example 20.10. There are two schools, each with a proportion 0.5 of the available students. At schools 1 and 2 students' qualities are distributed uniformly over [0, 50] and [0, 100], respectively. If both schools reveal abilities truthfully, then the mapping from expected ability to desirability is

$$Q(\widehat{a}) = \begin{cases} \frac{3\widehat{a}}{2} & \text{if } \widehat{a} \leq 50, \\ \frac{\widehat{a}}{2} + 50 & \text{if } \widehat{a} \geq 50. \end{cases}$$

For instance, a student with ability 20 (resp. 60) gets a job in the 30th (resp. 80th) desirability percentile. For school 2, the average job placement is $\frac{1}{2}\left(\frac{3 \times 25}{2} + (\frac{75}{2} + 50)\right) = 62.5$.

If, however, school 2 does not reveal students' abilities then the expected ability of each student is 50, yielding an average job placement of 75, a profitable deviation. Hence, full disclosure does not necessarily lead to an equilibrium in this model.

In this model, schools are the main players; once schools have chosen a disclosure policy the matching between students and job positions is uniquely defined (and thus schools' payoffs). An important preliminary result is the following.

---

[13] The distribution of desirabilities is positive on $[q_L, q_H]$, continuous, and given.

Proposition 20.11. *In equilibrium, any two students of the same expected ability obtain equally desirable positions.*

Proof Suppose that in equilibrium there is a positive proportion of students with expected ability $\hat{a}$ that obtain positions in an interval $[q_1, q_2]$. Since there is a positive proportion of such students, there must be at least one school that has a proportion m of students with some students with an ability lower than $\hat{a}$ and others with an ability higher than $\hat{a}$. We claim that the school can deviate with the following strategy: suppose that a proportion ε having an expected ability equal to $\hat{a} - \delta$, and thus the rest having an expected ability a bit higher than $\hat{a}$. For sufficiently small ε and δ, the net change in average desirability is positive. So such an equilibrium does not exist. $\square$

Suppose a school reveals information such that students' expected abilities are b or c. Allowing for this differentiation is only optimal for the school if by mixing students of these abilities it could not raise its payoff, i.e., if $\alpha Q(b) + (1 - \alpha)Q(c) \geq Q(\alpha b + (1-\alpha)c)$ for any $\alpha \in [0, 1]$. Since this reasoning can be applied to every pair of ability values, and assuming the equilibrium is *connected* (i.e., for any expected level $\hat{a}$ there is a school that produces students of all expected abilities in an ε-neighborhood of $\hat{a}$), $Q(\hat{a})$ has to be convex.

An important implication of the convexity of $Q(\cdot)$ is the following. If a school does mix students of different abilities, the desirability cannot be strictly convex, so $Q(\cdot)$ must be linear.[14] Therefore, if $Q(\hat{a})$ is strictly convex at a certain expected ability level a, it is fully informative at $Q(a)$, i.e., students with ability above a get positions better than $Q(a)$, and students with ability below a get positions worse than $Q(a)$, and thus $Q(a) = Q_T(a)$ where Q_T denotes the desirability mapping that ensues if all students' abilities are revealed truthfully.

Now, if Q_T is convex, the schools cannot do better by withholding the information; then $Q(\hat{a})$ is also convex. If, however, Q_T is concave, at least one school can do better if it withdraws all types for which Q_T is concave, and thus $Q(\hat{a})$ must be linear. It can be shown that the desirability mapping in equilibrium does not depend on how students are assigned to schools as long as the aggregate distribution is kept constant. Hence, given a distribution of student's abilities across schools the same amount of information is disclosed in all equilibria.[15] This amount of information is called a *balanced amount of information*.

We thus have some understanding of how schools' strategic disclosures can affect the matching between students and positions. To see how this is related to unraveling consider a two-period model, where in the first period there is no information about students' abilities (only the distribution of abilities for each school), and in the second period schools disclose to the firms' positions some information about students' abilities (under the assumption that this information is statistically correct).

The next result shows how information disclosure can help prevent unraveling.

---

[14] This is an argument similar to the difference between a lottery and a certainty-equivalent lottery in choice theory with a risk-lover decision maker.

[15] The proof of that result is somewhat involved; see Section 20.7.

Theorem 20.12. *If, in period 2, schools reveal a balanced amount of information, then no position can increase the expected ability of its match by making an early offer.*

Proof In period 1 since no information is revealed to the job positions, all students in a school, say, i, have the same expected ability, $\widehat{a}_i$.

Take any student from school i, with expected ability equal to $\widehat{a}_i$, and let $\widehat{a}$ be the student's ability (revealed in period 2). Therefore, if he waits until period 2 to accept some offer of a job position, he will be assigned to a position with desirability $Q(\widehat{a})$. By the law of iterated expectations, $\mathbb{E}\left[\widehat{a}\right] = \widehat{a}_i$. Since $Q(\widehat{a})$ is convex, $\mathbb{E}\left[Q(\widehat{a})\right] \geq Q(\widehat{a}_i)$, which implies that the student will only accept an early offer of a position that is at least as desirable as $Q(\widehat{a}_i)$. But positions with desirability $Q(\widehat{a}_i)$ and higher get a student of expected ability at least $\widehat{a}$ if they wait until period 2, and so they cannot benefit from moving early. □

20.7 Bibliographic Notes

Unraveling for the hospital-intern market is documented in [8] and the experiment in the introduction is from [3]. The failure of the gastroenterology market is documented in [5]. Theorem 20.2 is from [9]. Proposition 20.4 and 20.5 are from [7]. The early contracting equilibrium presented in Section 20.4.1 is from [4]. Lemma 20.7 and Theorem 20.8 are from [1]. This analysis provides a result similar to Theorem 20.8 but for ex-ante stability (i.e., when agents' do not know their own preferences). The model and results of Sections 20.5 and 20.6 are from [2] and [6], respectively.

References

[1] Arnosti, Nick, Immorlica, Nicole, and Lucier, Brendan. 2015. The (non)-existence of stable mechanisms in incomplete information environments. Pages 46–59 of: *Proc. International Conference on Web and Internet Economics.* Springer.

[2] Halaburda, Hanna. 2010. Unravelling in two-sided matching markets and similarity of preferences. *Games and Economic Behavior*, **69**(2), 365–393.

[3] Kagel, John H., and Roth, Alvin E. 2000. The dynamics of reorganization in matching markets: A laboratory experiment motivated by a natural experiment. *Quarterly Journal of Economics*, **115**(1), 201–235.

[4] Li, Hao, and Suen, Wing. 2000. Risk sharing, sorting, and early contracting. *Journal of Political Economy*, **108**(5), 1058–1091.

[5] McKinney, C. Nicholas, Niederle, Muriel, and Roth, Alvin E. 2005. The collapse of a medical labor clearinghouse (and why such failures are rare). *American Economic Review*, **95**(3), 878–889.

[6] Ostrovsky, Michael, and Schwarz, Michael. 2010. Information disclosure and unraveling in matching markets. *American Economic Journal: Microeconomics*, **2**(2), 34–63.

[7] Pan, Siqi. 2018. Exploding offers and unraveling in two-sided matching markets. *International Journal of Game Theory*, **47**(1), 351–373.

[8] Roth, Alvin E. 1984. The evolution of the labor market for medical interns and residents: A case study in game theory. *Journal of Political Economy*, **92**(6), 991–1016.

[9] Sönmez, Tayfun. 1999. Can pre-arranged matches be avoided in two-sided matching markets? *Journal of Economic Theory*, **86**(1), 148–156.

CHAPTER TWENTY-ONE

Investment in Matching Markets

Matthew Elliott and Eduard Talamàs

21.1 Introduction

Non-contractible investments are often made before a matching market is entered. Firms create vacancies before hiring workers, while workers acquire human capital before looking for a job; manufacturers and suppliers form specific relationships with each other; entrepreneurs invest in their businesses before securing support from venture capitalists; and so on.

The hold-up problem can be a significant barrier to efficient investments in these settings. Investments are often sunk by the time people bargain over how to share the returns of these investments. Since bargaining need not give each agent the full surplus generated by her investment, private and social investment incentives need not be aligned.

In this chapter, we analyze investments made prior to participation in a matching market—paying particular attention to the hold-up problem. We focus on finite one-to-one matching markets with transfers. Our objective is to highlight some key forces that shape investment decisions in matching markets, rather than to survey the literature. The outline is as follows.

Section 21.2 illustrates the main questions on which we will focus in the context of a market that matches designers with design studios. Section 21.3 describes our benchmark model, which treats investment decisions as a non-cooperative game and the matching or bargaining process as a cooperative game. Section 21.4 discusses the conditions that need to hold in order for the private and social investment incentives for a given person to be aligned.

Building on the analysis in Section 21.4, Section 21.5 presents and discusses the main result of this chapter: everyone on one side of the market simultaneously obtains their full marginal product—and hence has good investment incentives—if the bargaining process in the matching stage ends up selecting this side's optimal core outcome. Section 21.6 provides a new proof of this classic result. Section 21.7 indicates the core work that we draw on and briefly discusses some closely related questions and areas of active research.

21.2 Motivating Example

Consider a market that matches designers with design studios. Before entering this market, each designer and each design studio can make non-contractible investments—ranging from very specific to very general—that shape the gains from trade in the matching stage.

In the case of designers, general investments might include learning skills that are valuable in any design studio and specific investments might include learning how to use a particular type of software that is only used by a particular design studio.

In the case of studios, general investments might include commercial efforts to strengthen connections with potential clients and financiers, and more specific investments might include acquiring hardware, software, and office space that facilitate certain kinds of design processes.

We are interested in understanding the extent to which designers and design studios have incentives to invest efficiently. Focusing on transferable utility, this is simply the extent to which the private incentives to make non-contractible investments in such markets are consistent with the maximization of the gains from trade.

The answer to this question hinges on the designers' and studios' expectations of the returns that each kind of investment will generate. This depends, in turn, on their expectations of the investments that others will make as well as how their investment choices will affect those to whom they will match and on what terms.

This chapter focuses on the following questions. First, how do the bargaining outcomes reached in the matching stage affect the extent to which designers and studios appropriate the marginal returns of their different investments? Second, are there bargaining outcomes or norms which guarantee that all designers and studios have incentives to make efficient investments? Finally, are designers and studios more likely to have good incentives to make general investments rather than specific investments?

21.3 Model

Suppose that the set of agents is $N := I \cup J$, where I is a finite set of workers and J is a finite set of firms. There are two stages. In stage 1, agents make non-contractible investments that shape their matching surpluses. In stage 2, they bargain over which matches to form and how to share the resulting surplus.

21.3.1 Stage 1: Investments

Each agent k in N simultaneously chooses an attribute a_k in A_k at cost $c_k(a_k)$. These choices represent non-contractible investments. For instance, in the example above, the possible investments include specific and general investments available to both designers and studios.

The matching surplus generated when worker i matches to firm j depends on their attribute choices, and is given by the function $s: A_i \times A_j \to \mathbb{R}_+$. If an agent does not match with any other agent, we think of her as being matched to herself, and we set $s(a_k, a_k) = 0$ for all a_k in A_k.

For each agent k, there is a null attribute $0 \in A_k$ such that $c_k(0) = 0$, and the surplus that agent k with this null attribute generates with any other agent is 0. Choosing attribute 0 can be interpreted as staying out of the market.

21.3.2 Stage 2: Pairwise Stable Outcome

Once the attribute choices have been made, each worker can match with at most one firm and vice versa. We model this matching process as a cooperative game.

Given the agents' choices of attributes, the matching game in stage 2 is an *assignment game*: there are two populations of agents (workers and firms), and each pair of agents (one from each population) is able to generate a weakly positive surplus if they match.

An *outcome* in the assignment game is a matching (each worker matching with no more than one firm and each firm matching to no more than one worker) and a payoff profile. We denote worker i's payoff by $w_i \geq 0$ and firm j's payoff by $v_j \geq 0$.

Definition 21.1. A *matching* is a function $\mu: N \to N$ such that (i) each worker is mapped either to a firm or to herself, (ii) each firm is mapped either to a worker or to itself, and (iii) worker i is mapped to firm j if and only if firm j is mapped to worker i.

Definition 21.2. A payoff profile $(w, v) \in \mathbb{R}_+^I \times \mathbb{R}_+^J$ is *feasible for the matching* μ if $w_i = 0$ whenever $\mu(i) = i$, $v_j = 0$ whenever $\mu(j) = j$, and $w_i + v_{\mu(i)} \leq s(a_i, a_{\mu(i)})$ otherwise. A payoff profile is *feasible* if it is feasible for some matching.

Definition 21.3. A payoff profile (w, v) is *stable* if it is feasible and, for all workers i and all firms j, $w_i + v_j \geq s(a_i, a_j)$. A matching associated with a stable payoff profile is a *stable matching*.

21.3.3 Stable Matchings

Fix an attribute profile $a \in A := \bigtimes_{k \in N} A_k$. For brevity, for every worker–firm pair (i, j), we denote the matching surplus $s(a_i, a_j)$ by $s(i, j)$. A payoff profile is stable if and only if it is in the core of the assignment game – where the value $V(S)$ of any coalition $S \subseteq N$ is the maximum surplus that can be generated by matching pairs of agents in S. We sometimes write $V(a)$ for $V(N)$.

An immediate and useful implication of stable payoffs', being in the core is that in all stable outcomes a surplus-maximizing match must be selected (otherwise, the grand coalition would have a profitable deviation). Generically there is a unique such match, so stability uniquely pins down who matches with whom – but not the resulting payoffs. When there are multiple surplus-maximizing matches, any one of them can support any stable payoff profile. For simplicity, we often assume that there is a unique surplus-maximizing match.

A considerable amount is known about the structure of stable payoffs. For example, the set of stable payoff profiles forms a complete lattice both for the partial ordering of workers' payoffs and for the partial ordering of firms' payoffs. In particular, there is a worker-optimal stable payoff profile $(\overline{w}, \underline{v})$ in which all workers simultaneously receive their maximum possible stable payoffs and all firms simultaneously receive their minimum possible stable payoffs. Similarly, there is a firm-optimal stable payoff profile $(\underline{w}, \bar{v})$ in which all firms simultaneously receive their maximum possible stable payoffs and all workers simultaneously receive their minimum possible stable payoffs.

21.3.4 Equilibrium

There are usually many stable outcomes associated with any given attribute profile a. Hence, in order to understand agents' investment incentives in stage 1, we need to specify which stable outcome in stage 2 is associated with each attribute profile chosen in stage 1. We describe this selection via a bargaining function $g \colon A \to \mathbb{R}_+^N$ that selects a stable payoff profile for each attribute profile a. For any attribute profile a and any agent k, we denote by (a_{-k}, a_k') the profile a but with a_k swapped for a_k'.

Definition 21.4. An *equilibrium* is a pair (g, a) such that

1. $g \colon A \to \mathbb{R}_+^N$ where, for any attribute profile a, we have that $g(a) = (w(a), v(a))$ is a stable payoff profile in the assignment game with attribute profile a;
2. for each worker i and each of her potential attributes a_i' in A_i,

$$w_i(a_{-i}, a_i) - c_i(a_i) \geq w_i(a_{-i}, a_i') - c_i(a_i');$$

3. for each firm j and each of its potential attributes a_j' in A_j,

$$v_j(a_{-j}, a_j) - c_j(a_j) \geq v_j(a_{-j}, a_j') - c_j(a_j').$$

21.4 Private Investment Incentives

As our focus is on private investment incentives in decentralized markets, we model bargaining over the terms of trade in reduced form through a bargaining function g which is exogenously given (e.g., determined by exogenous institutions and social norms). For example, the sharing of a surplus between designers and studios might be determined by historical factors, their different degrees of experience and familiarity with the matching and bargaining process, etc. We will sometimes consider specific bargaining functions.

Example 21.5. Given an attribute profile a, the *midpoint bargaining function g* is such that, if i and j are matched in the surplus-maximizing match, the surplus they generate is split as follows:

$$\left(\underline{w}_i(a) + \frac{s(a_i, a_j) - \underline{w}_i(a) - \underline{v}_j(a)}{2}, \; \underline{v}_j(a) + \frac{s(a_i, a_j) - \underline{w}_i(a) - \underline{v}_j(a)}{2} \right),$$

where $\underline{w}_i(a)$ and $\underline{v}_j(a)$ are the minimum core payoffs of i and j when the attribute profile is a. In other words, each agent receives her minimum core payoff, and then any remaining surplus in each stable match is split equally.

Since the maximum core payoffs of a worker i and firm j that match under the optimal match are $\overline{w}_i = s(a_i, a_j) - \underline{v}_j$ and $\overline{v}_j = s(a_i, a_j) - \underline{w}_i$, respectively, this payoff profile can be rewritten as

$$\left(\frac{\underline{w}_i + \overline{w}_i}{2}, \frac{\underline{v}_j + \overline{v}_j}{2} \right).$$

In other words, each agent receives the midpoint between her minimum core payoff and her maximum core payoff. As the core is convex, these payoffs are in the core and hence stable.

Given a bargaining function g, we are interested in understanding the extent to which efficient attribute choices can arise in equilibrium regardless of the investment opportunities available on either side.

For concreteness, in this section we focus on the investment incentives of an arbitrary firm j. Given the symmetry between workers and firms, the analysis also holds, *mutatis mutandis*, for an arbitrary worker.

As we are in a transferable-utility environment, an attribute profile a is Pareto efficient, henceforth *efficient*, if and only if it maximizes the surplus net of investment costs $V(a) - \sum_{k \in N} c_k(a_k)$. An efficient attribute profile a is also *constrained efficient*, in the sense that each agent k's choice of attribute a_k maximizes $V(a_{-k}, a_k) - c_k(a_k)$ in a way that is conditional on the others' attributes a_{-k}.

Definition 21.6. Given an attribute profile a, firm j's investment is *constrained efficient* if, for all a'_j in A_j, $V(a_{-j}, a_j) - c_j(a_j) \geq V(a_{-j}, a'_j) - c_j(a'_j)$.

Efficient attribute profiles are constrained efficient, but constrained-efficient attribute profiles need not be efficient. Even when everyone makes constrained-efficient investments, coordination problems can lead to inefficient investments.

For example, if designers do not expect studios to make substantial investments, they might not have any incentive to make substantial investments, and vice versa, so neither designers nor studios investing much before entering the market might be constrained efficient. Although we will touch on coordination problems at various junctures, in the main we will focus on constrained efficiency, abstracting away from coordination problems.

Because stable outcomes need not give anyone the full social return of her attribute choices, constrained-efficient attribute choices need not be compatible with private investment incentives. The following result identifies a condition on the bargaining function g that is both necessary and sufficient to guarantee that a given agent makes constrained efficient investments in equilibrium.

Definition 21.7. Given an attribute profile a, firm j's *ex-post marginal product* is $V(a) - V(a, -j)$, where $V(a, -j)$ denotes the maximum total surplus achievable subject to the constraint that firm j matches to itself.

Proposition 21.8. *Consider an arbitrary bargaining function g and an arbitrary firm j with a non-trivial attribute choice (i.e., $|A_j| \geq 2$).*

1. *If, for every attribute profile a, $g_j(a)$ is j's ex-post marginal product, then j's investment is constrained efficient in all equilibria.*
2. *If there exists an attribute profile a such that $g_j(a)$ is not j's ex-post marginal product, then there exist cost functions $\{c_k\}_{k \in N}$ such that j's investment is not constrained efficient in any equilibrium.*

Proof of part 1 Suppose that the bargaining function g gives firm j its ex-post marginal product; that is,

$$v_j(a') = V(a') - V(a', -j) \text{ for every attribute profile } a'. \tag{21.1}$$

Consider an arbitrary equilibrium attribute profile a. Since j's equilibrium attribute choice is a best response to the others' choices, we have that, for every a'_j in A_j, $v_j(a) - c_j(a_j) \geq v_j(a_{-j}, a'_j) - c_j(a'_j)$ or, using (21.1),

$$V(a) - V(a, -j) - c_j(a_j) > V(a_{-j}, a'_j) - V(a_{-j}, a'_j, -j) - c_j(a'_j).$$

Since $V(a, -j) = V(a_{-j}, a'_j, -j)$, it follows that

$$V(a) - c_j(a_j) \geq V(a_{-j}, a'_j) - c_j(a'_j) \text{ for all } a'_j \text{ in } A_j.$$

That is, j's attribute choice a_j is constrained efficient. $\square$

Proof of part 2 Consider an attribute profile a such that $g_j(a)$ is not j's ex-post marginal product. In particular, suppose that $g_j(a) = V(a) - V(a, -j) - \epsilon$, where $\epsilon \neq 0$. Note that $a_j \neq 0$, since a firm choosing the null attribute 0 necessarily obtains its marginal product 0. Note also that ϵ must be positive, otherwise firm j would receive more than its marginal contribution to the total surplus, and the coalition of all agents other than j would have a profitable deviation. In other words, such a payoff profile would not be in the core and hence it would not be stable.

Suppose that, for every attribute $\widehat{a}_j$ in $A_j - \{a_j, 0\}$, $c_j(\widehat{a}_j)$ is sufficiently high that choosing $\widehat{a}_j$ is a dominated strategy in stage 1. Suppose also that, for every agent $k \neq j$, $c_k(a_k)$ is sufficiently low that she will choose a_k in equilibrium.[1] Finally, suppose that $c_j(a_j)$ satisfies

$$0 < V(a) - V(a, -j) - c_j(a_j) < \epsilon.$$

In this case, $(a_{-j}, 0)$ is not constrained efficient because, given the others' attributes a_{-j}, the null attribute 0 generates zero social surplus while the attribute a_j generates strictly positive social surplus. But $(a_{-j}, 0)$ is the only attribute profile that can be implemented in equilibrium. Indeed, choosing a_j gives worker j a strictly negative net payoff when the others choose a_{-j}, while her net payoff from choosing 0 is 0. $\square$

The following example illustrates the role that our assumption that firm j has access to the null attribute 0 plays in part 2 of Proposition 21.8: without this assumption, firm j's equilibrium investment might be constrained efficient for all cost functions even if it never receives its marginal product.

---

[1] This construction might require setting $c_k(a_k) < 0$, which is a legitimate possibility in our framework. Similar statements can be proved if we were to allow only for non-negative investment costs.

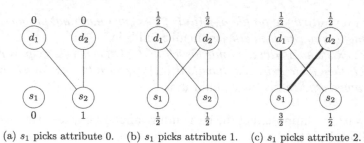

(a) s_1 picks attribute 0.   (b) s_1 picks attribute 1.   (c) s_1 picks attribute 2.

Figure 21.1 Thin and thick links between nodes indicate pairs of agents that generate 1 and 2 units of surplus by matching, respectively. The number labels in each panel represent the stable payoffs chosen by the midpoint bargaining function.

Example 21.9. Consider a simple version of the example described in Section 21.2 in which there are only two designers, d_1 and d_2, two design studios, s_1 and s_2, and only general-purpose investments available. Suppose that the bargaining function is the midpoint function described in Example 21.5. Every agent can choose between attributes 0, 1, and 2, with costs 0, c_1, and c_2, respectively, and the surplus of each match is the product of its members' attributes; that is, $s(a_i, a_j) = a_i a_j$.

Now fix the attributes of every agent but studio s_1 to be 1, and focus on this studio's private investment incentives. The three possible payoff profiles (corresponding to s_1's three possible attributes) are illustrated in Figure 21.1.

If studio s_1 chooses attribute 0, its ex-post marginal product is 0 and it obtains a gross payoff of 0. If it chooses attribute 1, its ex-post marginal product is 1 and it obtains a gross payoff of $1/2$. If it chooses attribute 2, its ex-post marginal product is 2 and it obtains a gross payoff of $3/2$.

Note that, even though s_1 receives its ex-post marginal product only when it chooses attribute 0, it receives the full social value of its investment deviation from attribute 1 to attribute 2. As a result, *if it had no access to attribute 0*, it would choose attribute 1 if $c_2 - c_1 > 1$ and attribute 2 if $c_2 - c_1 < 1$. These choices are surplus maximizing. In particular, in this case its investment would necessarily be constrained efficient regardless of the investment costs c_1 and c_2.

However, since s_1 does have access to the null investment 0, its optimal investment need not be constrained efficient. For example, if $3/2 < c_2 < 2$ and $1/2 < c_1 < 1$ then s_1's privately optimal investment is the null attribute 0, even though both alternative attribute choices 1 and 2 generate a strictly greater overall surplus net of investment costs.

One interpretation of the availability of the null investment choice is that it introduces an individual rationality (or participation) constraint. Under this interpretation, this example illustrates how satisfying the incentive-compatibility constraints between the different investment alternatives available to those participating in the market does not guarantee constrained-efficient investments once the participation constraints are taken into account.

Another potential source of inefficiencies is miscoordination. For instance, in this example, inefficient equilibria in which everyone chooses attribute 0 can coexist with equilibria in which everyone obtains strictly positive net payoffs.

21.5 Efficient Investments

Proposition 21.8 above highlights the fact that giving an agent her ex-post marginal product is crucial to guaranteeing that she makes constrained-efficient investments in equilibrium. Before discussing the extent to which this property can simultaneously hold for all agents, we provide a useful interpretation of an agent's ex-post marginal product in terms of the value of rematching when she leaves the market.

21.5.1 Marginal Product and the Value of Rematching

For each subset $S \subseteq N$ of agents, consider an efficient matching $\eta^S : S \to S$. Such a matching η^S must maximize the surplus $V(S)$ obtainable by the coalition S. For brevity, for every agent k in S we denote $\eta^S(k)$ by η_k^S. Note that, for any firm j,

$$V(N) - V(N - j) = \sum_{j' \in J} s(\eta_{j'}^N, j') - \sum_{j' \in J-j} s(\eta_{j'}^{N-j}, j')$$

$$= s(\eta_j^N, j) - \Phi(j), \tag{21.2}$$

where $\Phi(j)$ denotes *the value of rematching* (i.e., of implementing the new optimal matching η^{N-j}) *after j has been removed from the market*.[2] That is,

$$\Phi(j) := \sum_{j' \in J-j} \left[s(\eta_{j'}^{N-j}, j') - s(\eta_{j'}^N, j') \right].$$

An analogous expression holds for any worker i.

21.5.2 Main Result

The following result highlights that there is always a stable payoff profile that gives all the agents on one side of the market their ex-post marginal products.

Theorem 21.10. *The ex-post marginal product $V(N) - V(N - j)$ of each firm j is its payoff $\bar{v}_j$ in the firm-optimal stable profile.*

The combination of Proposition 21.8 and Theorem 21.10 implies that there exists a bargaining function g that ensures that all firms simultaneously have appropriate investment incentives (i.e., the bargaining function g that, for any given attribute profile a, selects the firm-optimal stable payoff profile). An analogous result holds for the worker-optimal stable payoff profile, so there also exists a bargaining function that ensures that all workers have appropriate investment incentives.

Unfortunately, however, the bargaining function that ensures that all firms simultaneously have appropriate investment incentives is different from the bargaining function that ensures that all workers simultaneously have appropriate investment incentives – except in the special case in which the core is a singleton for every possible attribute profile a. Hence, except in this special case, the bargaining function g cannot simultaneously give everyone her marginal product.

---

[2] For any set S, we often write $S - j$ (rather than $S \setminus \{j\}$) to mean S excluding j.

Corollary 21.11. *Unless the core uniquely pins down payoffs for every attribute profile, no bargaining function g can guarantee that private incentives to invest are aligned with the maximization of the gains from trade.*

Given a constrained-efficient attribute profile, the requirement to guarantee that it can be implemented in equilibrium is that its associated assignment game has a singleton core. Indeed, in this case, this attribute profile can be implemented in equilibrium regardless of the investment technology. Unfortunately, however, there is no reason to expect this to necessarily be the case in applications – even as markets become thick.

In the case of exogenous attributes, an active area of study investigates the conditions on the matching surpluses under which the core shrinks to a point when the market becomes large. In the presence of investment decisions, however, the matching surpluses are endogenous and there is no reason to expect the endogenous attribute choices to lead to a small core – even as the market gets large.

For any given attribute profile, Proposition 21.12 below provides three ways to express workers' minimum stable payoffs as relatively simple functions of the surpluses that are available. These expressions are helpful for understanding investment incentives in the typical scenario in which the core does not pin down outcomes uniquely.

Proposition 21.12. *In the firm-optimal stable payoff profile, worker i's payoff is equal to all of the following:*

1. *the value $\Phi(\eta_i^N)$ of rematching after her partner η_i^N leaves the market,*
2. *her ex-post marginal product $V(N - \eta_i^N) - V(N - \eta_i^N - i)$ when the set of agents is everyone but her partner η_i^N, and*
3. *her ex-post marginal product when an identical agent enters the market.*

An immediate implication of Proposition 21.12 is that a worker i receives her ex-post marginal product at the firm-optimal stable payoff profile if and only if her ex-post marginal product is the same before and after her partner η_i^N in the optimal matching leaves the market.

We defer the proofs of Theorem 21.10 and Proposition 21.12 to Section 21.6. We now discuss some of the main implications of these results for investment incentives.

21.5.3 Generality of the Investment Technology

It is worth noting that we have placed very little structure on the investment technology. This makes the results widely applicable. For instance, as in Example 21.9, the framework can capture investments on the extensive margin (e.g., costly participation decisions by designers to be active in the labor market and by studios to create vacancies) as well as on the intensive margin (e.g., how many years of education a designer pursues and how much hardware and software a studio acquires). In addition, there can be investments that are completely specific and only increase the surplus of a particular match, other investments that are general and increase the surplus of every match, and the whole spectrum of possibilities in between.

21.5.4 One-Sided Investments

A special case of interest occurs when only one side of the market has non-contractible investment choices before entering the market. This would be the case if, for example, studios had opportunities to invest prior to matching but designers did not. Then, an immediate implication of Proposition 21.8 and Theorem 21.10 would be that if g selects the studio-optimal core payoff profile then the investments in stage 1 will necessarily be constrained efficient in equilibrium.

On the one hand, this is a simple and sharp result that holds for any investment technology to which the agents on the investing side of the market might have access. On the other hand, the practical relevance of this result depends on the extent to which we expect the process of bargaining and matching to result in this particular extreme point of the core.

We might hope that social norms and institutions have a tendency to evolve to enhance efficiency. This hope gains credence once we note that there are simple natural mechanisms that lead to the required bargaining function. For example, if a social norm implies that workers can only increase their wages using outside offers then a corresponding dynamic adjustment process that starts with very low wages will bid up wages only until the firm-optimal stable payoffs are obtained.

21.5.5 Two-sided Under- and Over-Investment

When both sides of the market have access to investments, it is typically impossible to provide appropriate investment incentives to everyone at the same time. Proposition 21.12 can help us understand the inefficiencies that are likely to be present in this case.

For the sake of illustration, suppose that the bargaining function implements the firm-optimal payoffs, but that both workers and firms have investments to make before entering the market. We have already seen that workers are then likely to have poor incentives to make investments that increase the value of their match. Indeed, worker i's payoff is equal to the value of rematching when her partner η_i^N leaves the market; this need not be related to $s(i, \eta_i^N)$. Hence worker i will, at the margin, not have any incentive to make an investment that only increases the surplus $s(i, \eta_i^N)$ that she generates with the person with whom she matches in equilibrium.

This case is a particularly acute example of the hold-up problem in matching markets. But the trouble does not only come from potential under-investment: the fact that, in the firm-optimal stable payoff profile, worker i's payoff is equal to the value $\Phi(\eta_i^N)$ of rematching implies that worker i has incentives to pursue only investments that increase the surplus of matches that do not occur in equilibrium.

In particular, worker i might not only have incentives to under-invest in the match of which she will be part in equilibrium, but also *to over-invest in alternative matches of which she will not be part in equilibrium.*

Investments that only increase the surplus of unrealized matches are pure over-investments—in the sense that they generate no new surplus and serve only to redistribute existing surplus. Moreover, while these problems can be ameliorated by moving away from the extreme point of the core, unfortunately this merely shifts these problems to the other side of the market.

21.5.6 General-Purpose Investments

Investment inefficiencies are particularly acute when investments are purely relationship specific. When instead worker i's investments are of a more general-purpose nature, they might increase the value $\Phi(\eta_i^N)$ of rematching at a similar rate to that of the surplus $s(i, \eta_i^N)$ of her equilibrium match. If worker i's available investments change the value $\Phi(\eta_i^N)$ by the same amount as the surplus $s(i, \eta_i^N)$ of her equilibrium match, then Proposition 21.12 implies that worker i fully appropriates the social rewards of her marginal investment deviations. Hence, even if the firm-optimal payoffs are selected, when the relevant investments are general purpose, workers can have appropriate investment incentives as well.

21.6 Proofs of the Main Results

To prove Theorem 21.10 and Proposition 21.12 above, it is helpful first to put some structure on how an agent's marginal product depends on the available matching opportunities. Let I_j and J_j be the sets of workers and firms that rematch when an arbitrary firm j is removed from the market; that is,

$$I_j := \{i \in I : \eta_i^N \neq \eta_i^{N-j}\} \text{ and } J_j := \{j' \in J : \eta_{j'}^N \neq \eta_{j'}^{N-j}\}.$$

Also let $N_j := I_j \cup J_j$, and denote the cardinality of this set by n_j. The following lemma describes useful properties of the optimal rematchings that occur when an arbitrary firm j is removed from the market.

Lemma 21.13. *For every firm j, consider the sequence $\mathcal{S}_j = \mathcal{S}_j(1), \ldots, \mathcal{S}_j(n_j)$ with $\mathcal{S}_j(1) = j$ and, for every $1 \leq q < n_j$,*

1. *if $\mathcal{S}_j(q)$ is in J then $\mathcal{S}_j(q+1) = \eta_{\mathcal{S}_j(q)}^N$;*
2. *if $\mathcal{S}_j(q)$ is in I then $\mathcal{S}_j(q+1) = \eta_{\mathcal{S}_j(q)}^{N-j}$.*

The sequence $\mathcal{S}_j$ contains every agent in N_j. Moreover, for any $1 \leq q \leq n_j$, if $\mathcal{S}_j(q)$ is in J then $\mathcal{S}_{\mathcal{S}_j(q)} = (\mathcal{S}_j(q'))_{q'=q}^{n_j}$.

In other words, the optimal sequence of rematchings after the removal of a firm j has a chain-like structure which is such that, if we cut it at any firm $\mathcal{S}(q)$, the remaining sequence $\mathcal{S}(q), \mathcal{S}(q+1), \ldots, \mathcal{S}(n_i)$ determines the optimal rematching when this firm $\mathcal{S}(q)$ is removed from the market instead of j. We leave the proof of Lemma 21.13 as an exercise and illustrate it here with a simple example.

Example 21.14. Suppose that the matchings illustrated in Figures 21.2(a), (b) are the only optimal ones given that the sets of agents are $\{w_1, w_2, w_3, f_1, f_2, f_3\}$ and $\{w_1, w_2, w_3, f_2, f_3\}$, respectively.

Note that all the remaining workers and firms are involved in the optimal rematching after firm f_1 is removed from the market, and the sequence $\mathcal{S}_{f_1}$ defined by Lemma 21.13 is $(f_1, w_1, f_2, w_2, f_3, w_3)$. Consider the case in which firm f_2 is removed instead of firm f_1. Lemma 21.13 implies that the optimal rematching sequence $\mathcal{S}_{f_2}$ in this case is (f_2, w_2, f_3, w_3).

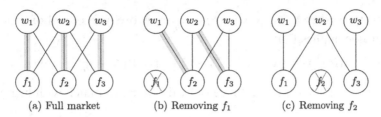

Figure 21.2 Thin links between nodes indicate pairs of agents that generate a strictly positive surplus by matching. In panels (a) and (b), the shaded links between nodes identify the surplus-maximizing matches. In panel (c), the surplus-maximizing matches are not shown.

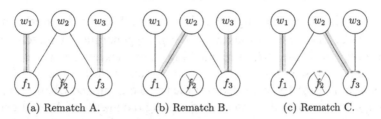

Figure 21.3 Thin links between nodes indicate pairs of agents that generate a strictly positive surplus by matching. The shaded links between nodes identify candidate surplus-maximizing matchings.

Consider an optimal matching when the agent set is $\{w_1, w_2, w_3, f_1, f_3\}$ (see Figure 21.2(c)). Clearly, this must be one of the three rematchings illustrated in Figure 21.3. Lemma 21.13 implies that the surplus-maximizing matching is the one shown in Figure 21.3(c). To see that this is indeed the surplus-maximizing matching, note that

$$s(w_1, f_1) + s(w_2, f_3) > \max\left[s(w_1, f_1) + s(w_3, f_3), s(w_2, f_1) + s(w_3, f_3)\right].$$

That $s(w_1, f_1) + s(w_2, f_3) > s(w_1, f_1) + s(w_3, f_3)$ follows directly from the fact that the surplus-maximizing matching depicted in Figure 21.2(b) is optimal. That $s(w_1, f_1) + s(w_2, f_3) > s(w_2, f_1) + s(w_3, f_3)$ follows from the fact that, since the matching depicted in Figure 21.2(a) is optimal, $s(w_1, f_1) + s(w_2, f_2) > s(w_1, f_2) + s(w_2, f_1)$ and, since the matching depicted in Figure 21.2(b) is optimal, $s(w_1, f_2) + s(w_2, f_3) > s(w_2, f_2) + s(w_3, f_3)$.

Proof of Theorem 21.10 We will show by construction that there are stable payoffs in which $v_j = V(N) - V(N - j)$ for all firms j. These are the firms' optimal stable payoffs because if $v_j > V(N) - V(N - j)$ then the coalition $N - j$ would have a profitable deviation.

Let $v_j = V(N) - V(N - j)$ for all firms j. If worker i matches with a firm j in the efficient match η^N, set $w_i = s(i, j) - v_j$; otherwise set $w_i = 0$. It is enough to show that these payoffs (w, v) are stable.

For every worker i, $w_i = s(i, \eta_i^N) - v_{\eta_i^N}$.[3] Moreover, our choice of stable payoff profile implies that

$$w_i = s(i, \eta_i^N) - v_{\eta_i^N} = s(i, \eta_i^N) - (V(N) - V(N - \eta_i^N)) = \Phi(\eta_i^N).$$

Hence, the most worker i could receive by deviating to match with firm $j \neq \eta_i^N$ is

$$s(i,j) - v_j = s(i,j) - \left[s(\eta_j^N, j) - \Phi(j) \right].$$

It is enough to show that

$$\Phi(\eta_i^N) \geq s(i,j) - s(\eta_j^N, j) + \Phi(j) \text{ for all firms } j. \tag{21.3}$$

That is, the value of rematching when i's partner η_i^N leaves the market must be at least as large as the net surplus $s(i,j) - s(\eta_j^N, j)$ generated by matching i with any firm j plus the value $\Phi(j)$ of rematching when j leaves the market.

This is easiest to see in the case in which worker i is not in the set of workers that must rematch for the gains from trade to be maximized when j is removed (i.e., $i \notin I_j$). In this case, the rematching among the agents in N_j that generates rematching value $\Phi(j)$ when firm j is removed is feasible after worker i deviates to match to j. Hence, when η_i^N is removed from the market, this rematching along with the matching of i to j is feasible. As $\Phi(\eta_i^N)$ is the value of rematching when η_i^N is removed from the market, inequality (21.3) must hold in this case.

To derive inequality (21.3) in the alternative case in which worker i is in I_j, we rely on Lemma 21.13: the agents in N_j can be arranged into a sequence S_j with $S_j(q) = \eta_i^N$ for some $1 \leq q \leq n_j$, and $(S_j(q'))_{q'=q}^n = S_{\eta_i^N}$. Letting $\widehat{J}_j := J_j \cap \{S_j(1), \ldots, S_j(q)\}$, we have that

$$\Phi(j) = \sum_{j' \in J_j - j} \left[s(\eta_{j'}^{N-j}, j') - s(\eta_{j'}^N, j') \right]$$

$$= \underbrace{\sum_{j' \in \widehat{J}_j - j} \left[s(\eta_{j'}^{N-j}, j') - s(\eta_{j'}^N, j') \right]}_{\Psi(\eta_i^N, j)} + \Phi(\eta_i^N).$$

Hence, (21.3) follows from the fact that $\Psi(\eta_i^N, j)$ is bounded above by $s(\eta_j^N, j) - s(i,j)$. Indeed, otherwise it would be possible to match the firms in $\widehat{J}_j - j$ according to η^{N-j} and worker i to firm j while matching all other workers according to η^N, and this would generate more surplus than matching all workers according to η^N, contradicting the optimality of the match η^N. □

Proof of Proposition 21.12 For worker i, as argued in the above proof of Theorem 21.10, we must have $w_i = s(i, \eta_i^N) - v_j$ in any stable outcome with all agents present. Thus, we must have that

$$\underline{w}_i = s(i, \eta_i^N) - \overline{v}_{\eta_i^N} = s(i, \eta_i^N) - \left(V(N) - V(N - \eta_i^N) \right) = \Phi(\eta_i^N),$$

---

[3] To prevent i and η_i^N having a jointly profitable deviation, we need $w_i + v_{\eta_i^N} \geq s(i, \eta_i^N)$; and to prevent the other agents having a profitable coalitional deviation, we need $w_i + v_{\eta_i^N} \leq s(i, \eta_i^N)$.

where the second equality follows from Theorem 21.10 and the final equality follows from equation (21.2).

For part 2, we need to show that

$$\underline{w}_i = V(N - \eta_i^N) - V(N - \eta_i^N - i). \tag{21.4}$$

First note that

$$\underline{w}_i = s(i, \eta_i^N) - \overline{v}_{\eta_i^N} = s(i, \eta_i^N) - V(N) + V(N - \eta_i^N)$$

for all workers i. Equation (21.4) then holds because when an efficiently matched pair of agents (in this case i and η_i^N) are both removed, the surplus-maximizing match leaves all other agents matched as they were before, so $V(N) = s(i, \eta_i^N) + V(N - i - \eta_i^N)$.

We leave part (iii) of the proposition as an exercise.

$\square$

21.7 Discussion

21.7.1 Investment Efficiency and Strategy-Proofness

The main result of this chapter, Theorem 21.10, is from [15] (see also [5]). The seminal paper [15] considers a mechanism designer who wants to achieve efficiency while eliciting workers' preferences. It is shown that the worker-optimal core allocation gives every worker her marginal product, so the mechanism designer can elicit workers' preferences and obtain efficiency by selecting this point in the core.

For a very nice and well-known application of the key ideas in this chapter in the context of one-sided investments (in this case, to form relationships that facilitate trade), see [13]. Our analysis of two-sided over- and under-investment in finite assignment games is based on [7]. The differences between agents' incentives to make general versus specific investments were pointed out in [2] and the main insights that we discuss regarding these differences were already anticipated there.

Our claim that the firm-optimal stable outcome arises when workers rely on outside offers to bid up their wages is broadly based on the dynamic adjustment process described in [4]. This process is generalized in [12] and [6].[4]

The connection between strategy-proofness and investment efficiency goes back at least to [20], where it was shown that that the Vickrey–Clarke–Groves mechanisms induce efficient investments because they force each agent to internalize the social gains or losses from changes in his or her valuation over outcomes.

The connection between giving workers good incentives to truthfully report their type and implementing the worker-optimal core outcome also holds in non-transferable utility (NTU) environments. In such environments, when workers submit preference lists and the deferred acceptance algorithm allocates them to firms, the deferred acceptance algorithm is dominant-strategy incentive compatible and implements the worker-optimal match. However, in NTU environments there is no equivalence between creating good incentives for truthfully revealing types and creating efficient investment incentives.

To see this, consider a version of our environment in which the surplus of each match is always split equally between the corresponding worker and firm. This turns

---

[4] The famous Hungarian method developed by [14] also yields this outcome.

our model into an NTU environment. Now suppose that, in the worker-optimal match, worker 1 is matched to firm 1, worker 1 receives wage x, and hence firm 1 receives a payoff x as well. Suppose also that worker 1 has access to an investment that would increase these payoffs by y (to $x + y$), while leaving the payoffs obtained in other matches unaffected. After making such an investment, the worker-optimal match must still match worker 1 to firm 1. Thus, worker 1's payoff will increase by $y/2$. However, if the cost of the investment is $c \in (y/2, y)$ then worker 1 will not make the investment despite the fact that it increases the joint surplus of firm 1 and worker 1.

The key difference between the non-transferable and transferable utility environments is of course the margin on which outcomes can adjust. Whereas in a transferable-utility world wages are free to adjust, in an NTU world adjustments can occur only on the extensive margin of who matches to whom. In general, then, it is unsurprising that the coarse instrument of adjusting the match is insufficient to provide good investment incentives for investments that operate on the intensive margin.[5]

21.7.2 Perfect Competition

In [11] a rigorous formulation of perfect competition in the assignment model is provided. It is shown that imperfect competition is generic in finite assignment economies and perfect competition is generic in a natural family of continuum assignment economies. Elegant but less constructive proofs of Theorem 21.10 and Proposition 21.12 were given that use the subdifferential of the total surplus function (see their Proposition 1). Throughout we have focused on finite settings. There is a rich literature on investment in competitive matching settings with a continuum of buyers and sellers. See, for example, [16]–[18].

21.7.3 Alternative Approach: Bargaining Function Can Depend on Investment Costs

Taking the bargaining function g as an exogenous object determined by social norms and institutions, we investigated the extent to which this function gives agents incentives to invest efficiently. In particular, we have focused on the question of when efficiency can be achieved for a given bargaining function g independently of the investment costs. Assuming that the investment choice of agent i includes the option of not entering the market (which imposes a natural individual rationality constraint), we have argued that this requires agent i to obtain her ex-post marginal product in the matching stage.

As illustrated in Example 21.9, when no individual rationality constraints are present, guaranteeing that agent i's equilibrium investments are constrained efficient requires the weaker condition that she obtains the full change in social surplus created by any of her possible investment deviations. [3] discuss richer examples under

---

[5] Interestingly, in large markets adjustments on the extensive margin become richer, and it is sometimes possible to provide good investment incentives in non-transferable utility (NTU) environments (see, for example, [19]).

which this is the case, and describe conditions that ensure that this weaker property is satisfied in finite markets.

An alternative approach is to ask a related but substantially different question: Given the investment costs, is there a bargaining outcome that ensures that efficient investments can be implemented in equilibrium? This approach does not take the bargaining function as given, but instead asks whether efficient investments are consistent with equilibrium. In [3] it was shown that the answer is yes.

For some intuition, consider the case in which agents can contract on their investments. The resulting investment and bargaining game can be seen as an assignment game, so efficiency (including in this case investment efficiency) can be achieved without any transfers at the investment stage. In particular, if a matching is efficient then it is stable in this assignment game with complete contracts. Given that the ability to write contracts expands only the set of potential deviations that agents can entertain, this efficient outcome is also an equilibrium when agents cannot write such contracts.[6]

21.8 Final Remarks

In this chapter we have emphasized that social norms and institutions that shape how surplus is shared in finite matching markets are unlikely to prevent hold-up problems. We conclude by briefly discussing the sensitivity of this message to the following two important assumptions that we have made throughout: (i) the bargaining function selects a stable payoff profile, and (ii) the market is static—in the sense that there is no entry of new agents over time.

Regarding stability, it seems intuitive that two agents with a profitable pairwise deviation should be able to realize these gains. However, extending standard non-cooperative bargaining models to a market setting yields outcomes that need not be stable even when the non-cooperative bargaining frictions vanish, and this has the potential to further distort agents' investment incentives (see, for example, [10], [1], and [8]).

Regarding entry, in the context of a general non-cooperative bargaining game with dynamic entry, it was shown in [9] that the hold-up problem necessarily disappears as bargaining frictions vanish if and only if there is a minimal amount of competition always present in the market. This suggests that taking into account the dynamic nature of many matching markets of interest can overturn some of the negative implications of the results highlighted in this chapter.

21.9 Exercises

Exercise 21.1 Suppose that there are two workers and two firms. Each agent can choose either to *invest* or to *not invest*. The matching surplus of each worker–firm pair is

2	units of surplus	if *both* members of the pair have invested,
1	unit of surplus	if *only one of them* has invested, and
0	units of surplus	if *neither of them* has invested.

[6] See [18] for a detailed exposition of this argument.

Not investing costs zero, and investing costs c.

(a) Show that, for any investment profile, if a matching does not match any agent to herself then it generates weakly more surplus than any other matching.

(b) Let $x_i \in \{0, 1\}$ represent agent i's investment choice. Find a function $\hat{g}: \{0, 1\} \to \mathbb{R}_+$ such that if each agent i that has invested x_i receives payoff $\hat{g}(x_i)$ then these payoffs are feasible (they sum to weakly less than the overall surplus obtained) and agents' private investment incentives are aligned with social investment incentives—i.e., for every agent i and any investments of the other agents, agent i finds it optimal to invest if and only if this increases the total net surplus generated by an efficient match.

(c) Show that for any investment profile there is a stable outcome in which each agent i's payoff is $\hat{g}(x_i)$.

(d) Let $S \in \{0, 1, 2\}^4$ be a tuple describing the surplus that can be obtained by any worker–firm pair. Show that there *does not* exist any function $f: \{0, 1, 2\}^4 \to \mathbb{R}_+^4$ such that (i) the payoffs $f(S)$ are feasible and (ii) each agent always receives a payoff equal to her marginal contribution to the total surplus.

Exercise 21.2 Consider n workers and $m < n$ firms. Each worker i has a different type $\alpha_i \in [0, 1]$, and each firm j also has a different type $\beta_j \in [0, 1]$. We label workers 1 to n and firms 1 to m so that $\alpha_1 > \alpha_2 > \cdots > \alpha_n$ and $\beta_1 > \beta_2 > \cdots > \beta_m$. The matching surplus of worker i and firm j is $\alpha_i \beta_j$. The bargaining function selects the firms' optimal stable payoffs. We say that a matching is *assortative* if, for $k = 1, \ldots, m$, firm k matches to worker k.

(a) Show that there is a unique stable matching and it is assortative.

(b) Derive the firms' optimal stable payoffs.

(c) Suppose that, prior to matching, an arbitrary firm k can make an investment that increases its matching surplus with worker i to $\alpha_i \beta_k + r$, where $r > 0$, while leaving the other surpluses unaffected. The cost of such an investment is $c > 0$. When should this firm invest?

(d) Now suppose instead that, prior to matching, every worker i has access to an investment $x_i \in [0, 1]$ that improves her type while firms have no investment opportunities. Specifically, each worker i can increases her type to $\theta_i + r(x_i)$, where r is a strictly increasing, twice differentiable, and concave function with $r(0) = 0$. The cost of worker i making an investment x_i is $c(x_i)$, where c is an increasing, twice differentiable, and strictly convex function with $c(0) = 0$, $c'(0) = 0$, and $\lim_{x \to 1} = \infty$.

    (i) Assuming worker i matches to firm i for $i = 1, \ldots, m$ find the payoff-maximizing investment for worker m.

    (ii) Assuming worker i matches to firm i for $i = 1, \ldots, m$, find the payoff-maximizing investment for each worker.

    (iii) Show that there is an equilibrium in which worker i matches to firm i for $i = 1, \ldots, m$.

    (iv) Show that the investments in this equilibrium are inefficient.

    (v) Let S and S^* be the total net surplus generated by efficient investments and equilibrium investments, respectively. Letting $\Delta = \beta_1 - \beta_m$, is $\lim_{\Delta \to 0}(S - S^*) > 0$?

———   **464**   ———

(vi) Suppose now instead that there are more firms than workers ($m > n$), and each worker k makes an investment satisfying $r'(x_k)\beta_{k+1} = c'(x_k)$. Is $\lim_{\Delta \to 0}(S - S^\star) > 0$?

Exercise 21.3 (Challenging). In this exercise you are asked to extend the logic of Example 21.14 to prove Lemma 21.13.

(a) Show that Lemma 21.13 holds trivially if $\eta_i^N = i$.

(b) Show that a weak subset of the agents in N_i can be arranged into a sequence, starting with agent η_i^N, satisfying

(1) if $\mathcal{S}_i(q)$ is in I then $\mathcal{S}_i(q + 1) = \eta_{\mathcal{S}_i(q)}^N$;

(2) if $\mathcal{S}_i(q)$ is in J then $\mathcal{S}_i(q + 1) = \eta_{\mathcal{S}_i(q)}^{N-i}$,

such that (i) the sequence ends when it reaches either a firm $j \in J_i$ such that $\eta_k^{N-i} = j$, or (ii) the sequence ends when it reaches a worker $k \in I_i$ such that $\eta_{l_\theta}^N = k$, or (iii) the sequence does not end.

(c) Show that the above sequence must end.

(d) Show that all agents in N_i can be arranged into a sequence like that described in part (b).

(e) Show that if $\mathcal{S}_i(q') = k \in I$ then $N_k = \{\mathcal{S}_i(q) : q \geq q'\}$.

Exercise 21.4 (Challenging). This exercise guides you through the proof of part (iii) of Proposition 21.12.

(a) Let i' be an identical copy of i. Show that if $\eta_i^{N+i'} = \eta_i^N$ or $\eta_{i'}^{N+i'} = \eta_i^N$ then, in the firm-optimal stable payoff profile (when the set of agents is N), worker i's payoff is its ex-post marginal product after i' has been added to the market.

(b) Show that either $\eta_i^{N+i'} = \eta_i^N$ or $\eta_{i'}^{N+i'} = \eta_i^N$.

Acknowledgements

We gratefully acknowledge financial support from the European Research Council under the grant EMBED #757229 (Elliott) and the Cambridge Institute for New Economic Thinking (Talamàs). Felix Mylius and Alastair Langtry provided excellent research assistance.

References

[1] Abreu, Dilip, and Manea, Mihai. 2012. Markov equilibria in a model of bargaining in networks. *Games and Economic Behavior*, **75**(1), 1–16.

[2] Becker, Gary S. 1962. Investment in human capital: A theoretical analysis. *Journal of Political Economy*, **70**(5, Part 2), 9–49.

[3] Cole, Harold Linh, Mailath, George, and Postlewaite, Andrew. 2001. Efficient non-contractible investments in finite economies. *BE Journal of Theoretical Economics*, **1**(1), 1–34.

[4] Crawford, Vincent P., and Knoer, Elsie Marie. 1981. Job matching with heterogeneous firms and workers. *Econometrica*, **49**(2) 437–450.

[5] Demange, Gabrielle. 1982. Strategyproofness in the assignment market game. Laboratorie d' Econométrie de V. Ecole Polytechnique.

[6] Demange, Gabrielle, Gale, David, and Sotomayor, Marilda. 1986. Multi-item auctions. *Journal of Political Economy*, **94**(4), 863–872.

[7] Elliott, Matthew. 2015. Inefficiencies in networked markets. *American Economic Journal: Microeconomics*, **7**(4), 43–82.

[8] Elliott, Matt, and Nava, Francesco. 2019. Decentralized bargaining in matching markets: Efficient stationary equilibria and the core. *Theoretical Economics*, **14**, 211–251.

[9] Elliott, Matthew, and Talamàs, Eduard. 2021. Bargaining foundations for price taking in matching markets. Mimeo. Available at SSRN: https://ssrn.com/abstract=3218411

[10] Gale, Douglas, and Sabourian, Hamid. 2006. Markov equilibria in dynamic matching and bargaining games. *Games and Economic Behavior*, **54**(2), 336–352.

[11] Gretsky, Neil E., Ostroy, Joseph M., and Zame, William R. 1999. Perfect competition in the continuous assignment model. *Journal of Economic Theory*, **88**(1), 60–118.

[12] Kelso, Alexander S., and Crawford, Vincent P. 1982. Job matching, coalition formation, and gross substitutes. *Econometrica*, **50**(6)1 483–1504.

[13] Kranton, Rachel E., and Minehart, Deborah F. 2001. A theory of buyer–seller networks. *American Economic Review*, **91**(3), 485–508.

[14] Kuhn, Harold W. 1955. The Hungarian method for the assignment problem. *Naval Research Logistics Quarterly*, **2**(1-2), 83–97.

[15] Leonard, Herman B. 1983. Elicitation of honest preferences for the assignment of individuals to positions. *Journal of Political Economy*, **91**(3), 461–479.

[16] Mailath, George J., Postlewaite, Andrew, and Samuelson, Larry. 2013. Pricing and investments in matching markets. *Theoretical Economics*, **8**(2), 535–590.

[17] Mailath, George J., Postlewaite, Andrew, and Samuelson, Larry. 2017. Premuneration values and investments in matching markets. *Economic Journal*, **127**(604), 2041–2065.

[18] Nöldeke, Georg, and Samuelson, Larry. 2015. Investment and competitive matching. *Econometrica*, **83**(3), 835–896.

[19] Peters, Michael, and Siow, Aloysius. 2002. Competing premarital investments. *Journal of Political Economy*, **110**(3), 592–608.

[20] Rogerson, William P. 1992. Contractual solutions to the hold-up problem. *Review of Economic Studies*, **59**(4), 777–793.

CHAPTER TWENTY-TWO

Signaling in Two-Sided Matching Markets

Soohyung Lee

22.1 Introduction

In a two-sided matching market, participants' welfare crucially depends on four aspects: the likelihood of forming a match, the time and monetary costs associated with forming a match, the quality of the match, and its duration. As a result, an institutional change or a new technology affecting any of the four aspects has an impact on the outcomes in the market. For example, technological advancements (e.g., online platforms) may increase the number and types of candidates a person may encounter compared with the status quo, ultimately changing matching patterns. In a related way, changes in legal systems (e.g., divorce laws) may affect the benefits from being matched (i.e., match quality), thus changing who is matched with whom and the duration of a match compared with the case without those changes.

Economists have developed several branches of literature examining the extent to which a policy of interest may affect matching markets. Furthermore, a group of researchers, namely market designers, pays special attention to the challenges that participants in a matching market experience and proposes alternative systems to alleviate these challenges through theoretical, empirical, and experimental studies. This chapter examines the challenges raised by information asymmetry in a two-sided matching market and the use of *signaling* as a means of alleviating those challenges. In Section 22.2, we lay out a simple theoretical setting to illustrate the challenges and examine two types of signaling: preference signaling and quality signaling. In Sections 22.3 and 22.4, we briefly summarize the lessons from theoretical analyses and empirical examinations, respectively. Section 22.5 concludes our discussion.

22.2 Setting

We lay out a setup consisting of a two-sided matching market with one-to-one matching, in order to place our discussions in a concrete format. For simplicity, we refer to agents as men and women in a marriage market, but these labels can be changed to firms and workers, schools and students, buyers and sellers, and so on.

22.2.1 Preferences and Information Revelation

22.2.1.1 Value of a Match

If man m and woman w form a match, the match provides values $V_{m,w}$ for the man and a value $W_{m,w}$ for the woman. The benefits from the match are defined as

$$V_{m,w} = M(X_m, X_w) + \epsilon_{m,w} \quad \text{and} \quad W_{m,w} = F(X_m, X_w) + u_{m,w},$$

where X_m and X_w refer to man m's and woman w's characteristics (e.g., age, years of education); M and F are functions that map characteristics into a scalar; and $\epsilon_{m,w}$ and $u_{m,w}$ are random shocks, i.i.d. with mean zero. We denote the values of remaining single by $V_{m,\emptyset} = 0$ and $W_{\emptyset,w} = 0$.

22.2.1.2 Transferability

There are two modeling approaches regarding the utilities from a match: the use of transferable versus non-transferable utilities. In a transferable utility model, men and women (positively or negatively) compensate their match partners according to the net values they bring to the match when they get married (e.g., a dowry or bride price). Thus, individuals decide to accept or reject a match on the basis of the utility they will receive from the marriage (e.g., $V_{m,w}$, $W_{m,w}$) and the transfer they pay or receive. In contrast, in a non-transferable utility model, men and women cannot compensate their match partners.

Transferable utility models have been popular in economics studies examining marriage markets. This strand of the literature studies the underlying mechanisms generating assortative matching, or homogamy, commonly observed around the world. People of similar age, education, and socioeconomic background tend to marry one another. Specifically, suppose that X_m and X_w are one-dimensional, $\epsilon_{m,w} = u_{m,w} = 0$, $\partial^2 M(X_m, X_w)/\partial X_m \partial X_w > 0$ and $\partial^2 W(X_m, X_w)/\partial X_m \partial X_w > 0$. That is, a person's type can be aggregated to a one-dimensional index, and there exists complementarity between men and women. Under this setting, if there are no frictions then the marriage market equilibrium matches the best man with the best woman, the second best man with the second best woman and so on. Thus, marriages under this equilibrium exhibit positive assortative matching.

An important limitation of transferable utility models is that they cannot account for the possibility that individuals from the two sides may disagree on whether to form a match (e.g., unilateral divorce). Furthermore, in reality, many matching markets do not have tools for agents to transfer their utilities, especially when they do not involve monetary transactions (e.g., public school assignment). Even if they do, there may be limited scope for transfers (e.g., due to limited commitment devices), which may generate disagreement among agents.[1] As we are interested in agents' behaviors, not assortative matching *per se*, we focus only on the case of non-transferable utilities for the remainder of this chapter.

---

[1] Consider the following marriage market example. Suppose that Wendy considers Michael suitable for marriage only if he would do *all* the household chores, while Michael finds Wendy attractive no matter what. Suppose that divorce is costly and that doing household chores would not bring joy to Michael. Then, once married to Wendy, Michael might do some of, but not all, the household chores, just enough for Wendy not to file for divorce. Furthermore, it would be realistically impossible for a third party to force Michael to do all the household chores. Therefore, anticipating this situation, Wendy may not accept a marriage offer from Michael.

22.2.1.3 Correlation in Preferences

The preference rankings of an agent can be correlated with those of another. For example, suppose that $\epsilon_{m,w} = u_{m,w} = 0$. Then, two individuals from the same side with the same characteristics (e.g., m and m' with $X_m = X'_m$) have the same preference rankings across individuals from the opposite side. Alternatively, individuals have idiosyncratic (or uncorrelated) preferences when $M(X_m, X_w) = W(X_m, X_w)$ for all m and w, and when $\epsilon_{m,w}$ and $u_{m,w}$ are independent across all m and w.

In a realistic setting, both deterministic and random components may play important roles in shaping individuals' preference rankings. For example, men and women may have idiosyncratic tastes in selecting their partners, but, to a certain degree, they may agree on what types of men and women are attractive. This situation can be accounted for by a class of preferences called *block-correlated* preferences, proposed by [17]. Under block-correlated preferences, individual are classified into blocks. All men agree about the preference ranking of blocks but, within a block, men have idiosyncratic preferences regarding women. Likewise all women agree about the ranking of male blocks but have idiosyncratic preferences regarding men within a block.

22.2.2 Matching Technologies

There are two theoretical approaches to modeling how market participants may find potential partners. In the first approach, agents observe other market participants and compare multiple candidates simultaneously (i.e., simultaneous matching). In this simultaneous setting, an agent makes his/her decision on the basis of not only the value of remaining single, but also what candidates are available for a potential match. This setting is commonly studied in the market design literature. Examples include student–school matching, in which students compare multiple schools at once and submit applications, and junior economist markets in which new economics PhDs and universities search for matches.

In the second approach, each agent encounters agents from the opposite side one at a time (i.e., sequential or dynamic matching). The agent accepts or rejects the match in comparison with the value of remaining single and of continuing to search for a partner in the next period. If both agents agree, a match is formed. This setting is commonly used to analyze the dynamics of marriage and labor markets. An aggregate "matching function" randomly draws one agent from each side among available market participants. The likelihood of a market participant being paired with a potential mate (i.e., the arrival rate) may depend on the number of market participants and the intensity of the search. An agent's reservation utility depends on the arrival rate, discount rate, and expected match quality. If the current match quality exceeds the reservation utility of both parties, then a match is formed.

A real-world matching market is likely to have features from both settings. In fact, recent studies analyze a dynamic matching market in which agents encounter multiple potential mates at a given time.

22.2.3 Information Revelation and Signaling

Market participants may not observe all the relevant deterministic and random components when making their decisions. To alleviate the lack of information, participants may employ methods to acquire further information (e.g., a date for marriage or an interview for a job search) and/or to provide further information to others by signaling. We classify signals into two categories: preference signaling and quality signaling. Both types are discussed below.

22.2.3.1 Preference Signaling

With *preference signaling*, a user can deliver information to other market participants about how likely he/she is to form a match with them, but not what matching quality he/she can bring to the match if he/she forms a match with any of them.

Assuming that the utility from a match is non-transferable and that idiosyncratic components are independent, a person's idiosyncratic component of match quality does not affect the match quality that the match partner can receive. Nonetheless, market participants may still want to know about others' idiosyncratic components through preference signaling because they can predict the likelihood of a potential partner forming a match with them. This prediction can be critical in a matching market where market participants have limited ability to explore possible matches owing to limitations of time and money. In reality, people and firms have a limited capacity to schedule meetings (e.g., interviews and dates) to gather further information. Thus it is extremely important for an agent to screen out the candidates who do not think highly of them, and to allocate the capacity to those who are acceptable to them and also willing to accept matches with them.

Simultaneous matching market. First, consider a marriage market with a simultaneous matching technology. That is, men and women observe all other market participants. For simplicity, suppose that, first, men request dates with multiple women; then, women accept or reject dating requests; and finally, men and women choose their marriage partners among those they dated. Men have limited slots for dating requests, and women have limited slots for dates. Thus, men cannot send dating requests to all women. Likewise, women cannot accept all dating requests from men.

Man m and woman w may form a marriage not only if the marriage provides sufficient benefits to them, but also if there is no other participant who is willing to form a match and who provides more benefits to either m or w. Thus, man m's chance of getting married to w depends on the set of agents that m and w contacted for dates and the likelihood of getting married for each agent in the set.

Owing to the limited slots for dating requests, man m needs to allocate his slots to those women who will probably like him enough that he has a reasonable chance of marrying them. For this reason, preference signaling can be useful for individuals to make their decisions. As an example, consider man m whose observable characteristics generate a low match quality for women whose observable characteristics are the same as those of woman w. In this case, man m expects that woman w is out of reach, so he may not send her a dating request to avoid wasting his time. However, suppose that woman w thought highly of him because of the high value of the random component $u_{m,w}$. If w can signal her preference to m (i.e., via preference signaling) then m may send her a dating request.

Despite the potential benefit of improving efficiency, preference signaling has a critical weakness when adopted in a real market. That is, it is difficult to establish the credibility of such signaling because the cost is low, unlike the quality signaling to be described in the next subsection. However, it can still be credible if there is a mechanism that limits the extent to which a participant can use preference signaling. A well-known example is signaling in the market for hiring new economics PhDs. We discuss this and other real-world examples in Section 22.4.

Sequential matching market. Second, consider a marriage market with a sequential matching technology. In this theoretical setting, there is little use of preference signaling. Unlike a simultaneous matching market, an agent does not directly compete with other agents from the same side. Rather, he/she needs only to compare the match quality of the partner set up by the technology with the present discounted value of remaining single and of waiting for another match in the subsequent period (i.e., his/her reservation utility).

For example, if man m encounters woman w thanks to the matching technology, man m will accept w as a partner if the match quality that w can provide exceeds his reservation utility, independently of whether woman w finds him attractive or not. For this reason, the information about w's preference does not affect man m's decision.

In reality, agents may still value preference signaling in a market resembling the sequential matching market described above. For example, people may want to avoid rejection and thus preference signaling can be useful for them to make their decisions. In fact, ample studies from the psychology literature document the pain of rejection. Recent research from economics formalizes this possibility in analyzing two-sided matching markets.

22.2.3.2 Quality Signaling

With *quality signaling*, a user can deliver the information to other market participants about what matching quality he/she can bring to matches if he/she forms a match with any of them.

Consider our model presented in Section 22.2.1. Suppose that some characteristics of an agent (i.e., X_m and X_w) are not observable to other market participants. Then, agents may want to use signaling mechanisms to inform others about their characteristics that directly affect matching quality. For example, match quality can depend on a person's intellectual capacity (e.g., intelligence quotient (IQ)). Although IQ is hard to observe, one's IQ can be inferred by one's educational attainment or test scores. Woman w may decide to inform other participants about her high IQ by obtaining a high test score. Suppose that obtaining high test scores costs less to those individuals with high cognitive skills compared with their counterparts with low cognitive skills. If the difference in cost is sufficiently large, all high-type individuals will obtain high test scores, while all low-type individuals will obtain low test scores or will not even take a test. Thus, test scores can signal a person's cognitive skills to other participants.

Quality signaling can credibly deliver information to other participants if using it is costly in terms of time and money, and the cost depends on the underlying trait to be signaled. For this reason, quality signaling is sometimes referred to as *costly signaling*. Furthermore, quality signaling can be generated by third parties (e.g., customer reviews in online marketplaces). If receiving good customer reviews is less costly for high-quality sellers than for low-quality sellers, consumers may infer the quality of services and products they can get from a particular seller on the basis of reviews by past customers.

22.3 Lessons from Theoretical Analyses
22.3.1 Preference Signaling

A growing number of studies examine the question of whether (and, if so, the extent to which) introducing a preference signaling mechanism improves a matching market, in terms of the number of matches and the welfare of agents. The answers to these questions depend on market structures and agents' preferences. This subsection examines two examples illustrating the effect of preference signaling.

22.3.1.1 Example 1: Decentralized Setting

Here we present an example based on [17] to illustrate the effect of introducing preference signaling under a decentralized market. Consider a market with two men $\{m_1, m_2\}$ and two women $\{w_1, w_2\}$. The payoffs are 1 if each individual is matched with his/her most preferred person, x if he/she is matched with the second most preferred person, and 0 if he/she is unmatched. These assumptions depict the situation in which $V_{m,w}, W_{m,w} \in \{x, 1\}$ and $V_{m,\emptyset} = W_{\emptyset,w} = 0$ in our model from Section 22.2.

Suppose that, ex ante, individuals' preferences are random, uniform, and independent. Then, the probability of each man preferring w_1 to w_2 is one half. Likewise, the probability of each woman preferring m_1 to m_2 is one half. Before joining the matching market, individuals learn their own preferences, but they do not know the preferences of others.

Without preference signaling. Consider the case in which, once preferences are realized, each of the two men first makes a marriage offer to only the woman of his choice, and then each woman either accepts one out of the available offers or remains unmatched. Then, there is a unique sequential equilibrium in which the men send their offers to their most preferred women, and then women accept the most preferred available men. The intuition is that, at the acceptance stage, women will choose the best candidate based on their preferences. As each man does not know the preferences of the other individuals, his best response is to send an offer to his most preferred woman. In this equilibrium, on average, there are 1.5 matches, and the expected payoff is 0.75 for each man and $(2 + x)/4$ for each woman.

With preference signaling. Now, we consider a setting in which each woman may send a signal to a man. The signal does not transmit any other information. In this setting, there are two types of equilibria: babbling and non-babbling equilibria. Under a babbling equilibrium, the men ignore signals from the women and thus the setting generates the same outcomes as the setting without signals in terms of the number of matches and payoffs for each individual. Alternatively, under a non-babbling equilibrium, the men interpret a signal as a sign of being the man more preferred by that the woman and the women send a signal to their top male candidate (i.e., their more preferred man).

Under a non-babbling equilibrium, a man who receives a signal from his top woman will make her an offer since she will definitely accept his offer. If one of the two men receives no signal, it means that both women sent their signals to the other man. Then, one of the two women should be rejected by the other man, with one half probability. Therefore, the best response is to send an offer to his top candidate woman even if she did not send him a signal. Lastly, if he receives a signal only from his second best candidate then he may make an offer to that woman (i.e., responding to the signal), or to his top candidate (i.e., ignoring the signal). If the gap between the top and the second best candidates is sufficiently small (i.e., $x > 0.5$) then the first man is better off sending an offer to the woman who sent the signal. By doing so, he can eliminate the chance of being unmatched. In this case, the expected number of matches is 1.75, and the expected payoff is $(5 + 2x)/8$ for each man and $(6 + x)/8$ for each woman.

Alternatively, if the gap between the top and the second best candidates is large $(x < 0.5)$, then there are two equilibria in pure strategies. One is the case in which both men ignore signals. This setting generates the same outcomes as the setting without signaling. The other is the case in which both men respond to signals. If both men respond to signals, the expected number of matches is 1.75, and the expected payoff is $(5 + 2x)/8$ for each man and $(6 + x)/8$ for each woman.

Effect of introducing a preference signaling mechanism. Comparing the two settings with and without preference signaling shows that the number of matches is weakly larger in the setting with preference signaling than in the setting without signaling. It also shows that the introduction of a preference signaling mechanism may increase the welfare of the agents who can send signals, while its effect on the agents who receive signals is ambiguous.

22.3.1.2 Example 2: Centralized Setting

Now we adapt an example from [1] that examines the role of preference signaling in a centralized matching market. Consider a case in which three men $\{m_1, m_2, m_3\}$ and three women $\{w_1, w_2, w_3\}$ search for partners by submitting their preference rankings to a centralized intermediary. The centralized intermediary uses a deferred acceptance (DA) algorithm to determine who is to be matched with whom. If there are ties in preference rankings, the intermediary randomly breaks them.

The women have no preferences among the three men (i.e., $W_{1,w} = W_{2,w} = W_{3,w}$ for $w \in \{1, 2, 3\}$), while the men's preferences are represented by the following table:

$V_{1,1} = 4$	$V_{1,2} = 1$	$V_{1,3} = 0$
$V_{2,1} = 4$	$V_{2,2} = 1$	$V_{2,3} = 0$
$V_{3,1} = 3$	$V_{3,2} = 2$	$V_{3,3} = 0$

Without preference signaling. By strategy-proofness, all the men submit truthful rankings of the women. As a result, men are assigned each woman with a probability of $1/3$, and the expected payoff is $5/3$ for all men.

With preference signaling. Next consider a modified version of the DA, called the choice-augmented deferred acceptance (CADA) algorithm, as proposed by [1]. Under the CADA algorithm, the intermediary requires each man to submit his preference ranking for the women as well as the name of a "target" woman of his choice (i.e., a preference signal). Then, it runs the DA algorithm to assign men to women, but it uses the preference signals to breaks ties in favor of those who sent preference signals.

Suppose that m_1 and m_2 send their preference signals to w_1 while m_3 sends his signal to w_3. Then, the intermediary will assign $m_i, i \in \{1, 2\}$, to $w_j, j \in \{1, 3\}$, with probability one half and m_3 to w_2, resulting in an expected payoff of 2 for all men.

Effect of introducing a preference signaling mechanism. The outcomes with and without preference signaling show that men are better off with preference signaling. The benefit arises because, with preference signaling, men can express the intensity of their preference for certain women in addition to preference rankings. By incorporating these intensities to break ties, the centralized intermediary can increase the payoffs for market participants.

22.3.2 Quality Signaling

As discussed in Section 22.3.2, quality signaling, particularly in terms of education, has been heavily studied in labor economics. However, most of those studies are in general empirical, not theoretical, and regard education decisions as a one-sided optimization problem. Thus, they do not directly incorporate the matching problem with firms or partners.

In contrast, market designers have been examining options to create an environment with more accurate quality signals. For example, new entrants into an online marketplace, by definition, have few customers providing feedback. With a lack of feedback, consumers will be hesitant to buy products and services from them, generating a vicious cycle of low sales and little feedback. Another strand of research examines the possibility of using monetary compensation to incentivize people to provide feedback; this research is based on field experiments and case studies. None of these studies examines one-to-one matching settings. For that reason, we examine the following example, deviating from the one-to-one matching settings we have examined so far.

22.3.2.1 Example 3: Recommender System

Here we present an example from [14] to illustrate one possibility of what a market designer may devise. Consider a situation in which a market designer devises a system to recommend a new product to customers to generate a sufficient number of reviews. The reviews generated by consumers are shared by other consumers to learn about the quality of the new product in the next period. Specifically, suppose that a movie is released at time $t = 0$ and a unit mass of agents arrives at each time $t = 1, 2$. The quality of the movie (ω) is either good ($\omega = 1$) or bad ($\omega = 0$). If the movie is good (bad), the consumer gets a surplus of 1 (0). The quality of the movie is unknown at the time of its release, with prior $p^0 = \Pr(\omega = 1) \in [0, 1]$. Watching the movie costs each agent $c \in (p^0, 1)$.

Unlike the consumers, the market designer receives a signal $\sigma \in \{g, n\}$ about the quality of the movie, with probabilities

$$\Pr[\sigma = g | \omega] = \begin{cases} p_0 & \text{if } \omega = 1; \\ 0 & \text{if } \omega = 0, \end{cases}$$

and $\Pr[\sigma = n|\omega] = 1 - \Pr[\sigma = g|\omega]$. That is, the market designer receives good news only when the movie is good, but on the other hand she may not receive any news about the new movie.

Without quality signaling. If a consumer at $t = 1$ watches the new movie without a signal, her expected payoff is $p^0 - c$, which is negative. Therefore, no consumers at $t = 1$ will watch the movie, and the same is true for the consumers at $t = 2$.

With quality signaling. Consider a signaling mechanism in which the designer sends a positive signal (i.e., "good" news) to all consumers if the designer receives a "good" signal, and α fraction of consumers if she receives no signal about the movie. Then, the consumers who receive the good signal will predict the likelihood of the movie being good as

$$P_1(\alpha) = \frac{\rho_0 p^0 + \alpha p^0 (1 - \rho_0)}{\rho_0 p^0 + (1 - \rho_0 p^0)\alpha}.$$

If α is 1 then the consumers will find the recommendation uninformative, and, thus, they will not watch the movie. However, if α is 0 then the consumers who receive positive signals from the market designer will watch the movie.

Therefore, by choosing an appropriate value of α, the market designer can incentivize some consumers to watch the movie, find out its quality, and share that information with other consumers, even when the designer does not receive a good signal.

Suppose that the objective of the market designer is to maximize the social welfare, as measured by the sum of consumers' surplus at $t = 1$ and that at $t = 2$ discounted by a factor $\delta \in (0, 1)$. If the prior p^0 is sufficiently high (i.e., $p^0 \geq \hat{p}^0 = c/\{(1-\rho_0)(1+\delta)(1-c)+c\}$), then it is optimal to set α as $\hat{\alpha}$, where

$$\hat{\alpha} = \frac{(1 - c)\rho_0 p^0}{c(1 - \rho_0 p^0) - p^0(1 - \rho_0)}.$$

The resulting social welfare is

$$W(\alpha) = p^0(\rho_0 + (1 - \rho_0)\alpha)(1 - c)(1 + \delta) - \alpha(1 - p^0)c.$$

Effect of introducing a quality signaling mechanism. The potential benefit from introducing a quality signaling mechanism arises because the market designer observes information, namely signals, that is unavailable to consumers. By passing that information to consumers, the designer can increase social welfare. However, the quality signaling mechanism may not increase payoffs for all consumers. Specifically, with the introduction of quality signals, all consumers at $t = 2$ are better off because they obtain more accurate information about the quality of the movie. Those consumers at $t = 1$ who do not receive signals from the designer have the same payoffs in both cases (i.e., with or without quality signaling). Lastly, owing to the signaling system, the consumers at $t = 1$ who receive signals from the designer can be better or worse off. For example, if $\rho_0 < \delta/(1 + \delta)$ and $p^0 \in (\hat{p}^0, c)$ then consumers at $t = 1$ who receive good signals from the designer are worse off because their expected payoffs are negative. In other words, the market designer sacrifices some consumers at $t = 1$ for a "greater" good, namely social learning.

22.4 Signaling in Practice
22.4.1 Preference Signaling

In many markets subject to *congestion*, agents express their special interest in some participants, formally or informally. This subsection examines several real-world examples of preference signaling and studies examining the impact of this signaling on matching outcomes.

22.4.1.1 AEA's Economists' Job Market

The junior economics PhD market is coordinated through the American Economic Association (AEA). During the annual meeting of the Allied Social Science Association (ASSA) in January, employers interview candidates, typically over a single weekend, invite selected interviewees for campus visits, and make offers to some of the candidates who visited the campus and gave job seminars. Since a typical employer interviews approximately 20 candidates out of hundreds of applicants, he/she must strategically choose interviewees based not only on their quality but also on their willingness to accept an offer if the employer makes one. For this reason, preference signaling can be useful to employers when selecting interviewees.

Prior to 2006, graduate students on the market could convey their interest informally through advisors and their connections with employers. Since 2006, the AEA has offered a formal signaling service to junior economics PhDs. Using the service, job applicants can send signals to up to two employers to indicate their interest in receiving an interview during the ASSA meeting. Once the job applicants send their signals to the AEA, the AEA collects the information and sends each employer a list of job applicants before the ASSA meeting. The credibility of the signaling comes from the scarcity of signals relative to the total number of employers.

In [17] 785 individuals who participated in the 2007-2008 AEA job market were surveyed and whether their job applications yielded interview requests from employers was examined. In this sample, job applications combined with AEA signaling were 27.5% more likely to yield interviews compared to those without signaling. This finding should not be considered to show the causal impact of signaling, because of data limitations: the sample is not representative and includes only a limited amount of information about jobs and applicants. As a result, we cannot rule out the possibility that the omitted variables associated with preference signaling may have driven the finding. However, it is still an important and promising finding for researchers, particularly market designers, because it suggests the possibility that by designing a proper signaling system we can address real-world challenges, namely market congestion and the resulting inefficiency.

22.4.1.2 College Admission

In the USA, many universities use early admission programs, where high school seniors apply to exactly one college before the general application period. By limiting the number of applications to one college, applicants can credibly signal their special interest to colleges. This single-application system is helpful for lower-ranked colleges to identify candidates who are interested in them. As a result, colleges may be willing to admit applicants whose academic qualifications may not be strong enough to gain admission through the regular application process.

Researchers present supporting empirical evidence. For example, it was found in [6] that, by using early application, average applicants to 14 selective colleges could double their chances of getting an offer. It was also shown that the benefit of using early application was not large for applicants with high scholastic aptitude test (SAT) scores (e.g., in the 1600s in SAT-1) because their chances of receiving an offer were high even in the regular admission process, whereas the benefit is large for applicants whose expected acceptance rate is around or slightly less than 50% in regular admission. In line with this finding, advising services for US college applicants recommend that students use early application, especially early decision, because it shows a college that they consider it a top choice.[2]

Besides this formal system, students can express their interest in colleges informally. For example, collegedata.com, an online service providing college application advice, claims that "demonstrated interest" is a factor of considerable importance to colleges. The service advises students to demonstrate interest by visiting a college, scheduling an interview even if it is not required, attending a campus event, and following the college admission office on social media.[3] A recent study [19] examines applications outcomes of a US college and finds that on-site contacts through campus visits can increase the acceptance probability by as much as 40 percentage points for students in the highest quartile of the SAT score distribution.

Colleges outside the USA also appear to be concerned about students' preferences. Similarly to early application in the USA, colleges in South Korea infer students' preferences by forcing students to choose between them and other competing institutions at the application stage. Specifically, at the beginning of each academic cycle, the Korean Ministry of Education designates a few dates for colleges to interview their applicants or conduct college-specific tests. As the interviews and tests require the physical presence of applicants, students are allowed to apply to only one college from those that conduct interviews on the same date. Thus, by strategically selecting its assessment date to be the same as that of a competing institute, a college can filter out students who prefer the competing institute.

In Chile, a group of colleges formed a centralized admission system in which students submit preference lists with up to 12 options, defined by college and by major study, and the DA algorithm assigns students to colleges. Although this centralized setting does not raise the concern that congestion will occur, some colleges still solicit student preferences. Specifically, the University of Chile and the Catholic University, the two most prominent universities in Chile, impose a restriction that they will not review applicants who rank them below a certain threshold.

22.4.1.3 Online Dating

Online dating platforms are another setting that uses preference signaling. For example, Plentyoffish.com sells "Serious Member" badges and Cupid.com allows members to attach a rose icon to a limited number of messages to potential dating partners. However, it is rather rare to find studies examining the extent to which preference signaling affects the matching outcomes.

---

[2] See www.collegedata.com/en/prepare-and-apply/apply-yourself/be-an-outstanding-applicant/how-to-demonstrate-your-interest-to-colleges/

[3] See www.collegedata.com/en/prepare-and-apply/apply-yourself/until-college-admissions-decisions-arrive/demonstrate-interest-after-applying/

An exception is [28]. A field experiment was conducted using a dating event through a Korean online dating service. Participants were randomly endowed with two or eight "virtual roses" that a participant could use for free to signal special interest when asking for a date. All else being equal, a dating request accompanied by a virtual rose had a 20% greater chance of being accepted, and the positive effect was even larger if the most desirable suitors used them for average participants who might not take a dating offer without a rose seriously. Not surprisingly, the participants endowed with eight roses had more dates than their counterparts with two roses.

22.4.1.4 Other Labor Markets

Job markets for US medical residency programs are known for congestion, and there have been active discussions of how to address this problem; one suggestion involves preference signaling. For example, for the American Orthopedic Surgery Residency, [9] documents that the electronic application system lowers the costs for applicants to submit numerous applications, and, as a result, programs receive too many applications and have difficulty discerning which candidates have a special interest in them. In this paper, the idea of introducing a signaling system in residency matching was put forward. Likewise, [35] proposes a signaling mechanism in which applicants indicate their special interests in several programs for the specialty of otolaryngology – head and neck surgery (OTO-HNS).

Compared with specialized labor markets (e.g., economists' job market or medical residency), a generic labor market includes a large number of heterogeneous participants, and participants are not limited to conducting their search and hiring within a fixed time span. Even in such a labor market, which is less concerned about congestion, preference signaling is used (e.g., sending a thank you note after interviews), and recruiters appear to respond to it.

Owing to data limitation, it is difficult to establish clean empirical evidences of the need for preference signaling and its causal effects. However, there are a growing number of studies aiming to do so. For example, in [25] hiring managers were recruited as subjects and an experiment was conducted. It was shown that managers penalize highly capable candidates relative to less capable but adequate candidates. The reason is that managers expect that highly capable candidates may not be as interested in their firms as the less capable candidates, so they expect that the highly capable ones may leave the firms quickly or may not invest much in firm-specific human capital once they are hired. Although they do not explicitly examine preference signaling *per se*, the authors' findings nicely show that preference signaling can be useful in communicating a candidate's interest to a firm, allowing the firm to hire a highly capable candidate whom it may have otherwise rejected for fear that the candidate would leave the firm quickly.

22.4.2 Quality Signaling

There are many real-world examples consistent with the theoretical predictions regarding quality signaling. Quality signaling can account for people's incentives to obtain a diploma or to buy luxury goods (i.e., to indulge in conspicuous consumption) to show off their talents and socioeconomic status. In biology, researchers regard the extravagance of the peacock's tail as a way to indicate its biological superiority. The signaling value of education, sometimes referred to as the *sheepskin effect*, has been intensively examined by labor economists. It is, however, generally difficult to prove empirically that an agent's use of quality signals sways the decisions of other agents.

In online two-sided markets (e.g., Airbnb, Amazon, and eBay), service providers often employ a "reputation based feedback system." In these markets, participants can signal their quality to other participants through reputation and feedback mechanisms available in online services (e.g., consumer reviews). As feedback information is a public good, economists would predict low participation rates. Yet, among those who used eBay in 2007, about 70% provided feedback, a surprisingly high rate.

Despite a high rate of feedback, there are other practical concerns. Consumers may be subject to biases, and sellers may manipulate feedback by soliciting favorable feedback or even creating fake reviews.[4] To improve the quality of customer feedback, some marketplaces filter out suspicious reviews and/or provide an objective measure based on their rich internal information.

A related point is that in some online two-sided markets, participants have the option to post more information about themselves (e.g., an option to post photos at Prosper.com, a P2P lending service). By providing more information, they may signal their characteristics to other participants. However, in reality, the extent to which the information voluntarily provided is relevant to quality and is, therefore, useful for other participants to make their decisions is not obvious. For example, in [23] Prosper.com was examined and it was found that individual lenders incorrectly interpreted the information given to them, leading them to systematically make poor choices.

22.5 Concluding Remarks

This chapter has examined the extent to which signaling – of preference and quality – affects outcomes in a two-sided market and the possibility of using a signaling system to address marketplace failure. We conclude this chapter by presenting possible instruments to address the underlying causes generating the need for signaling in the first place.

Market designers, including service providers and policy makers, may set application or search costs sufficiently high to deter unnecessary applications. By doing so, they may possibly be addressing congestion, alleviating the need for preference signaling. Regarding quality signaling, market designers may provide additional information based on their rich internal data to participants, thus reducing information asymmetry and alleviating the need for signaling. For example, for a particular agent, a market designer can filter out participants that do not have a reasonable chance of forming a match with him/her. Such filtering can be achieved if market

---

[4] It is worth noting that biased consumer reviews are not unique to online two-sided markets. For example, student evaluations have been found to systematically favor male teachers [10], and the gender bias persists in a randomized experimental setting in which the gender of teachers is independent of teaching quality [33].

designers render those who are not likely to form a match invisible, or if they recommend a smaller set of candidates for review.

22.6 Bibliographic Notes

Marriage models with transferability utility assumptions include the seminal work [8]. See [11] for an overview of the literature, and [36] for a detailed discussion of the pros and cons of transferable and non-transferable utility assumptions.

Recent studies analyzing hybrid search models include [4], and [2]. These papers examine the possibility of balancing an agent's desire to settle the transaction quickly and maintaining the thickness of the market.

The paper [24] gives an example of the study of the fear of rejection in two-sided matching markets.

In Section 22.3.1.1, Example 1 is based on [18], which presents a generalized framework and conducts welfare analyses for the situation where a signaling mechanism is introduced into a two-sided matching market without transfers. Example 2 is based on [1] which studies the relative benefit from adapting the CADA algorithm to the DA algorithm in a centralized matching market. Example 3 is based on [14] which examines a generalized setting in which a market designer aims to facilitate collective learning among consumers by introducing a quality signaling mechanism. There are several other studies in the market design literature examining quality signaling. They include [29], which gives a case study on Alibaba, [13] for field experiments on eBay, and [12] for field experiments on Amazon's Mechanical Turk and a Chinese online retailer.

For college admissions in South Korea, see [7] for an overview of college admission systems, and [15] for how Korean colleges devise their admission criteria to reduce the risk of under- or over-enrollment. For the Chilean setting, see [20] and [21] for a detailed description of the college admission system.

The article [22] provides a summary of using preference signaling in dating markets.

Examples of recent studies estimating the sheepskin effect include [37], [27], and [31].

We have relied heavily on [16] for our discussion of feedback systems. Regarding how to improve feedback systems, see [30] on Yelp's filtering algorithm, and [32] on designing an objective measure based on internal information.

There have been several recent studies analyzing how to address information asymmetry and congestion in two-sided markets. For example, [3], [4] and [26] examine instruments for narrowing down down possible choices in two-sided matching markets. Regarding information disclosure, [34] studied a dynamic (sequential) two-sided matching market and it was found that full information disclosure may lead to excessive rejections by sellers, damaging the likelihood of forming a match within a given time frame.

Acknowledgements

Associate Professor, Graduate School of International Studies, Seoul National University, and IZA. contact: soohlee@snu.ac.kr, www.soohyunglee.com. I greatly benefitted from the thorough and constructive comments by Matthew Elliott, Aram Grigoryan, and Eduard Talamàs.

References

[1] Abdulkadiroglu, A., Che, Y.-K., and Yasuda, Y. 2015. Expanding "choice" in school choice. *American Economic Journal: Microeconomics*, **7**(1), 1–42.

[2] Akbarpour, A., Li, S., and Gharan, S. O. 2020. Thickness and information in dynamic matching markets. *Journal of Political Economy*, **128**(3), 783–815.

[3] Arnosti, N., Johari, R., and Kanoria, Y. forthcoming. Managing congestion in matching markets. *Manufacturing and Service Operations Management, special issue on Sharing Economy and Innovative Marketplaces.*

[4] Ashlagi, I., Jaillet, P., and Manshadi, V. H. 2013. Kidney exchange in dynamic sparse heterogenous pools. Working Paper, available at web.stanford.edu/iashlagi/papers/KE-AJM.pdf.

[5] Ashlagi, I., Braverman, M., Kanoria, Y., and Shi, P. 2020. Clearing matching markets efficiently: Informative signals and match recommendations. *Management Science*, **66**(5), 1873–2290.

[6] Avery, C., Fairbanks, A., and Zeckhauser, R. 2003. *The Early Admissions Game: Joining the Elite.* Harvard University Press.

[7] Avery, C., Lee, S., and Roth, A. E. 2014. College admissions as non-price competition: The Case of south korea. NBER Working Paper, No. 20774.

[8] Becker, G. S. 1973. A theory of marriage: Part i. *Journal of Political Economy*, **81**(4), 813–46.

[9] Bernstein, J. 2017. Not the last word: Want to match in an orthopaedic surgery residency? Send a Rose to the Program Director. *Clinical Orthopaedics and Related Research*, **475**, 2845–2949.

[10] Boring, A. 2017. Gender biases in student evaluations of teaching. *Journal of Public Economics*, **145**, 27–41.

[11] Browning, M., Chiappori, P.-A., and Weiss, Y. 2014. *Economics of the Family.* Cambridge University Press.

[12] Burtch, G., Hong, Y., Bapna, R., and Griskevicius, V. 2018. Stimulating online reviews by combining financial incentives and social norms. *Management Science*, **64**(5), 2065–2082.

[13] Cabral, L., and Li, L. 2015. A dollar for your thoughts: Feedback-conditional rebates on ebay. *Management Science*, **61**(9), 2052–2063.

[14] Che, Y.-K., and Hörner, J. 2018. Recommender systems as mechanisms for social learning. *Quarterly Journal of Economics*, **133**(2), 871–925.

[15] Che, Y.-K., and Koh, Y. 2016. Decentralized college admissions. *Journal of Political Economy*, **124**(5), 1295–1338.

[16] Chen, Y., Cramton, P., List, J. A., and Ockenfels, A. 2020. Market design, human behavior and management. NBER Working Paper, No. 26873.

[17] Coles, P., Cawley, J., Levine, P. B., Niederle, M., Roth, A. E., and Siegfried, J. J. 2010. The job market for new economists: A market design perspective. *Journal of Economic Perspectives*, **24**(4), 187–206.

[18] Coles, P., Kushnir, A., and Niederle, M. 2013. Signaling in matching markets. *American Economic Journal: Microeconomics*, **5**(2), 99–134.

[19] Dearden, J., Li, S., Meyerhoeffer, C., and Yang, M. 2017. Demonstrated interest: Signaling behavior in college admissions. *Contemporary Economic Policy*, **35**(4), 630–657.

[20] Espinoza, R., Lee, S., and Lopez, H. 2017. Endogenous market formation: theory and evidence from chilean college admissions. Working Paper.

[21] Figueroa, N., Lafortune, J., and Saenz, A. 2018. Do you like me enough? The impact of restricting preferences ranking in a university matching process. Working Paper.

[22] Fisman, R. 2012. Will you accept this digital rose? *Slate*, February 13, available at https://slate.com/business/2012/02/internet-dating-how-digital-roses-can-make-it-a-better-experience.html.

[23] Freedman, S., and Jin, G. 2017. The information value of online social networks: Lessons from peer-to-peer lending. *International Journal of Industrial Organization*, **51**, 185–222.

[24] Gall, T., and Reinstein, D. 2019. Losing face. *Oxford Economic Papers*, **72**(1), 164–190.

[25] Galperin, R. V., Hahl, O., Sterling, A. D., and Guo, J. 2020. Too good to hire? Capability and inference about commitment in labor markets. *Administrative Science Quarterly*, **65**(2), 275–313.

[26] He, Y., and Magnac, T. 2019. Application costs and congestion in matching markets. TSE Working Paper, No. 7-870.

[27] Jepsen, C., Mueser, P. R., and Troske, K. 2016. Labor market returns to the GED using regression discontinuity analysis. *Journal of Political Economy*, **124**(3), 621–649.

[28] Lee, S., and Niederle, M. 2015. Propose with a rose? Signaling in Internet dating markets. *Experimental Economics*, **18**, 731–755.

[29] Li, L., Tadelis, S., and Zhou, X. forthcoming. Buying reputation as a signal of quality: Evidence from an online marketplace. *Rand Journal of Economics*. https://onlinelibrary.wiley.com/doi/abs/10.1111/1756-2171.12346.

[30] Luca, M., and Zervas, G. 2016. Fake it till you make it: Reputation, competition, and Yelp review fraud. *Management Science*, **62**(12), 3412–3427.

[31] Martorell, P., and Clark, D. 2014. The signaling value of a high school diploma. *Journal of Political Economy*, **122**(2), 282–318.

[32] Masterov, Dimitriy V., Mayer, Uwe F., and Tadelis, Steven. 2015. Canary in the e-commerce coal mine: Detecting and predicting poor experiences using buyer-to-seller messages. Pages 81–93 of: *Proc. 16th ACM Conference on Economics and Computation*.

[33] Peterson, D. A., Biederman, L. A., Andersen, D., Ditonto, T. M., and Roe, K. 2019. Mitigating gender bias in student evaluations of teaching. *PLoS One*, **14**(5), e0216241.

[34] Romanyuk, G., and Smolin, A. 2019. Cream skimming and information design in matching markets. *American Economic Journal: Microeconomics*, **11**(2), 250–276.

[35] Salehi, Parsa P., Benito, Daniel, and Michaelides, Elias. 2018. A novel approach to the National Resident Matching Program – The star system. *JAMA Otolaryngology – Head & Neck Surgery*, **144**(5), 397–398.

[36] Smith, L. 2006. The marriage model with search frictions. *Journal of Political Economy*, **114**(6), 1124–1144.

[37] Tyler, J. H., Murnane, R. J., and Willett, J. B. 2000. Estimating the labor market signaling value of the GED. *Quarterly Journal of Economics*, **115**(2), 431–468.

CHAPTER TWENTY-THREE

Two-Sided Markets and Matching Design

Renato Gomes and Alessandro Pavan

23.1 Introduction

Two-sided markets are markets in which agents match through a platform, which designs and prices matching opportunities. Typical examples include: ad-exchanges matching advertisers with publishers; media outlets matching readers or viewers with content providers and advertisers; video-game consoles matching gamers with game developers; operating systems matching end-users with software developers; e-commerce websites matching buyers with sellers; business-to-business platforms matching procurers with service providers; and employment agencies matching employers with job seekers.

In the last few years, platform markets have gained a prominent role in the organization of business activities. As a result, a conspicuous literature has flourished examining various aspects of such markets, ranging from pricing to platform design. In this chapter, we focus on monopolistic pricing and its connection with matching design. Section 23.2 contains a flexible model of platform-mediated matching with transfers. Section 23.3 reviews some of the classical results on monopolistic pricing in two-sided markets. Section 23.4 extends some of these results to markets in which both the platform and the agents face uncertainty over the distribution of preferences over the two sides of the market and hence over the eventual participation decisions. Section 23.5 considers markets in which the platform engages in discriminatory practices matching different agents to different subsets of the participating agents from the other side of the market. It first addresses the case of one-to-one matching and then the case of many-to-many matching. Throughout the entire chapter, special attention is given to the distortions in the provision of matching services that emerge in two-sided markets when the platform enjoys significant market power.

23.2 General Setup

Consider a "large" two-sided market in which the impact of each individual agent in isolation on the platform's profits is small. We capture such a situation by assuming that each side is populated by a *unit-mass* continuum of agents. This is a point of departure with respect to what has been assumed in other chapters of this book (see, however, Chapter 16 for other benefits of assuming a large market). The assumption of a continuum of agents permits us to illustrate in the simplest possible way the distortions that arise when agents are privately informed and the platform has market power. It also permits us to bridge the analysis of matching design in this chapter with the literature on two-sided markets in industrial organizations, where demands are smooth.

To capture the platform's market power in the starkest possible terms, we consider a situation where a single platform matches agents from the two sides of the market.

Each agent from each side $k = a, b$ has a type ω_k drawn from a distribution F_k with support Ω_k, independently across agents (from either side of the market). Agents privately know their types.

A matching mechanism consists of a *matching rule* and a *payment rule* for each side of the market. By the revelation principle, without loss of generality we can focus on direct-revelation mechanisms. Accordingly, we define a matching mechanism as $M := \{\mathbf{s}_k(\cdot), \mathbf{p}_k(\cdot)\}_{k=a,b}$, where, for each $k = a, b$ and each $\omega_k \in \Omega_k$, $\mathbf{s}_k(\omega_k) \subset \Omega_{-k}$ is the set of types from side $-k$ (that is, from the opposite side of the market) to which type ω_k is matched, whereas $\mathbf{p}_k(\omega_k)$ is the payment asked from or given to the agent. Formally, $\mathbf{p}_k : \Omega_k \to \mathbb{R}$ (both positive and negative payments are allowed), while $\mathbf{s}_k : \Omega_k \to \mathcal{C}(\Omega_{-k})$, where $\mathcal{C}(\Omega_{-k})$ is a subset of the power set of Ω_{-k} describing the collection of *admissible matching sets*. This set captures technological or institutional constraints on the shapes of the matching sets. For instance, in the case of one-to-one matching, $\mathcal{C}(\Omega_{-k})$ is the collection of singleton sets $\{\omega_{-k}\}$.

A matching rule $\{\mathbf{s}_k(\cdot)\}_{k=a,b}$ is *feasible* if and only if the following reciprocity condition holds for all $\omega_k \in \Omega_k, k = a, b$:

$$\omega_{-k} \in \mathbf{s}_k(\omega_k) \Rightarrow \omega_k \in \mathbf{s}_{-k}(\omega_{-k}). \tag{23.1}$$

We assume that agents' preferences are quasilinear. Namely, the utility that a side-k agent of type ω_k derives from the matching set $\tilde{s}_k \in \mathcal{C}(\Omega_{-k})$ when making a payment $\tilde{p}_k \in \mathbb{R}$ to the platform is equal to $u_k(\tilde{s}_k | \omega_k) - \tilde{p}_k$, where the real-valued function $u_k(s_k | \omega_k)$ describes the agent's gross payoff. Therefore, the payoff that type ω_k obtains when reporting type ω_k' under the mechanism M is given by

$$\hat{U}_k(\omega_k, \omega_k'; M) := u_k(\mathbf{s}_k(\omega_k') | \omega_k) - \mathbf{p}_k(\omega_k'),$$

whereas the payoff from truthful reporting of his type is equal to $U_k(\omega_k; M) := \hat{U}_k(\omega_k, \omega_k; M)$. A mechanism M is *individually rational* (IR) if $U_k(\omega_k; M) \geq 0$ for all $\omega_k \in \Omega_k, k = a, b$, and is *incentive compatible* (IC) if $U_k(\omega_k; M) \geq \hat{U}_k(\omega_k, \omega_k'; M)$ for all $\omega_k, \omega_k' \in \Omega_k, k = a, b$. The definition of incentive compatibility is the same as in the mechanism design literature; it is de facto equivalent to the notion of *strategy-proofness* in Chapter 4 and used in most of the matching literature.

A feasible matching rule is *implementable* if there exists a payment rule $\{\mathbf{p}_k(\cdot)\}_{k=a,b}$ such that the mechanism $M = \{\mathbf{s}_k(\cdot), \mathbf{p}_k(\cdot)\}_{k=a,b}$ is individually rational and incentive compatible.

Example 23.1. Let $\Omega_k = [\underline{\omega}_k, \bar{\omega}_k] \subset \mathbb{R}_+$ and $u_k(s_k | \omega_k) = \omega_k |s_k|$, $k = a, b$, with $|s_k| := \int_{s_k} dF_{-k}(\omega_{-k})$ denoting the measure of the set s_k. A feasible matching rule $\{\mathbf{s}_k(\cdot)\}_{k=a,b}$ is implementable if and only if $|\mathbf{s}_k(\cdot)|$ is non-decreasing,

$k = a, b$. To see this, note that $u_k(s_k|\omega_k)$ is supermodular. Hence, if type ω_k weakly prefers the pair $(\mathbf{s}_k(\omega_k), \mathbf{p}_k(\omega_k))$ to the pair $(\mathbf{s}_k(\tilde{\omega}_k), \mathbf{p}_k(\tilde{\omega}_k))$ and $|\mathbf{s}_k(\omega_k)| > |\mathbf{s}_k(\tilde{\omega}_k)|$, then any type $\omega'_k > \omega_k$ strictly prefers the pair $(\mathbf{s}_k(\omega_k), \mathbf{p}_k(\omega_k))$ to the pair $(\mathbf{s}_k(\tilde{\omega}_k), \mathbf{p}_k(\tilde{\omega}_k))$, which implies that the mechanism $M = \{\mathbf{s}_k(\cdot), \mathbf{p}_k(\cdot)\}_{k=a,b}$ is incentive compatible only if $|\mathbf{s}_k(\cdot)|$ is non-decreasing, $k = a, b$. Lastly, to see that any feasible rule $\{\mathbf{s}_k(\cdot)\}_{k=a,b}$ such that $|\mathbf{s}_k(\cdot)|$ is non-decreasing, $k = a, b$, is implementable, consider a mechanism M in which the payment rule is given by $\mathbf{p}_k(\omega_k) = \omega_k \mathbf{s}_k(\omega_k) - \int_{\underline{\omega}_k}^{\omega_k} |\mathbf{s}_k(\tilde{\omega}_k)| d\tilde{\omega}_k$, for all $\omega_k \in \Omega_k$, $k = a, b$. It is then easy to see that, because $|\mathbf{s}_k(\cdot)|$ is non-decreasing,

$$
\begin{aligned}
U_k(\omega_k; M) &= \int_{\underline{\omega}_k}^{\omega_k} |\mathbf{s}_k(\tilde{\omega}_k)| d\tilde{\omega}_k \\
&\geq \int_{\underline{\omega}_k}^{\omega'_k} |\mathbf{s}_k(\tilde{\omega}_k)| d\tilde{\omega}_k + (\omega_k - \omega'_k)|\mathbf{s}_k(\omega'_k)| \\
&= \hat{U}_k(\omega_k, \omega'_k; M),
\end{aligned}
$$

which implies that the mechanism M is incentive compatible. That the same mechanism is also individually rational follows from the fact that $U_k(\omega_k; M) = \int_{\underline{\omega}_k}^{\omega_k} |\mathbf{s}_k(\tilde{\omega}_k)| d\tilde{\omega}_k \geq 0$ for all ω_k, $k = a, b$. Hence the monotonic rule $\mathbf{s}_k(\cdot)\}_{k=a,b}$ is implementable. $\quad\square$

In what follows, we specialize the above formulation to capture specific aspects of pricing and matching design in two-sided markets.

23.3 Pricing in Two-Sided Markets

The study of pricing in two-sided markets originally focused on environments characterized by the absence of discrimination (across agents from the same side), and the presence of cross-side network effects.

The first property implies that all side-k agents that join the platform are assigned the same matching set. This restriction is motivated by the inability of many two-sided platforms to customize matching opportunities.[1] Accordingly, for $k = a, b$, there are sets $\{\hat{\Omega}_k\}_{k=a,b}$, with $\hat{\Omega}_k \in \mathcal{C}(\Omega_{-k}) \neq \emptyset$, such that, for any $\omega_k \in \Omega_k$, either $\mathbf{s}_k(\omega_k) = \emptyset$, meaning that type ω_k is excluded, or $\mathbf{s}_k(\omega_k) = \hat{\Omega}_{-k}$, where $\hat{\Omega}_{-k}$ is the set of participating types from the side $-k$. Feasibility obviously requires that $\mathbf{s}_k(\omega_k) = \hat{\Omega}_{-k}$ if and only if $\omega_k \in \hat{\Omega}_k$ for $k = a, b$. We say that such a matching rule induces the *single network* of participating agents $(\hat{\Omega}_a, \hat{\Omega}_b)$.

The presence of cross-side network effects is captured by the following assumptions on the agents' types and preferences. The type of each agent is a two-dimensional vector $\omega_k = (\omega_k^s, \omega_k^i) \in \mathbb{R}^2$, where ω_k^s denotes the agent's *stand-alone value*, that is, the benefit the agent derives from all products and services that the platform provides in addition to matching agents from the two sides of the market, whereas ω_k^i is the agent's *interaction benefit*, that is, the value the agent derives from interacting with agents from the other side of the market. The gross utility of a

---

[1] For instance, in a shopping mall or fair, it is impossible or impractical to prevent all participating buyers and sellers from freely interacting.

type-ω_k agent from being matched to a set $s_k \subseteq \Omega_{-k}$ of types from the other side of the market takes the form

$$u_k(s_k|\omega_k) := \omega_k^s + \omega_k^i |s_k|, \tag{23.2}$$

where $|s_k| := \int_{s_k} dF_{-k}(\omega_{-k})$ is the measure of the set s_k. Accordingly, the presence of more agents from the opposite side enhances the utility of a side-k agent of type ω_k if and only if $\omega_k^i > 0$. In advertising markets, for instance, it is typically assumed that advertisers (on side a) have positive interaction benefits, $\omega_a^i > 0$, whereas consumers (on side b) have negative interaction benefits $\omega_b^i < 0$ (that is, they dislike advertising). In this example, a consumer's (positive) stand-alone value is the utility she derives from the content provided by the platform (e.g., news or services), whereas an advertiser's (negative) stand-alone value is the cost of producing the advertisement.

The next lemma relates the matching rules inducing a single network to the transfer rules that implement them. The proof is straightforward and hence omitted. To simplify, assume that, whenever *indifferent*, agents join the platform.

Lemma 23.2. *A matching rule $\{s_k(\cdot)\}_{k=a,b}$ inducing a single network $(\hat{\Omega}_a, \hat{\Omega}_b)$ is implementable if and only if there exist access prices P_a and P_b such that, for all $k = a, b$,*

$$\hat{\Omega}_k = \left\{ \omega_k \in \Omega_k : \omega_k^s + \omega_k^i |\hat{\Omega}_{-k}| \geq P_k \right\}. \tag{23.3}$$

In light of Lemma 23.2, consider a game in which the side-k agents receive an offer to join the platform at a price P_k, and in which the agents' participation decisions are simultaneous. There exists an equilibrium of this game in which each side-k agent joins the platform if and only if $\omega_k \in \hat{\Omega}_k$. However, the equilibrium need not be unique. For example, when the agents' stand-alone values are identically equal to zero, that is, $\omega_k^s = 0$, and the interaction benefits are homogenous within and across sides, that is, $\omega_k^i = 1$ for $k = a, b$, any price vector (P_a, P_b) with $0 \leq P_a, P_b \leq 1$ implements the single complete network $\hat{\Omega}_k = \Omega_k$, $k = a, b$. The implementation is, however, partial, in that the game also admits a continuation equilibrium in which none of the agents participates.

In the rest of this section, consistently with the mechanism design literature, we shall disregard the multiplicity issue and describe the platform's problem as choosing a pair of participation values (N_a, N_b), with $N_k = |\hat{\Omega}_k|$ denoting the mass of agents from side k joining the platform. By virtue of Lemma 23.2, such a pair of participation values can be supported in equilibrium if and only if there exist sets $(\hat{\Omega}_a, \hat{\Omega}_b)$ and prices (P_a, P_b) satisfying (23.3) and $N_k = |\hat{\Omega}_k|$, $k = a, b$.

23.3.1 Profit-Maximizing Prices

We consider three scenarios, corresponding to different specifications of the agents' preferences. To this end, denote by F_k^s and F_k^i the marginal distributions of the joint cdf F_k, and by f_k (alternatively, f_k^s, f_k^i) the density of F_k (alternatively, of F_k^s, F_k^i) if it exists. We let $\mathbf{1}\{A\}$ be the indicator function, taking the value 1 if statement A is true and zero otherwise.

Scenario 1. Agents are heterogeneous in their stand-alone values but homogenous in their interaction benefits, with the latter equal to $\omega_k^i > 0$. In this case, $F_k(\omega_k) = \mathbf{1}\left\{\omega_k^i \geq \omega_k^i\right\} F_k^s(\omega_k^s)$, with the marginal distribution F_k^s absolutely continuous over $\mathbb{R}$.

Scenario 2. Agents are heterogeneous in their interaction benefits but homogenous in their stand-alone values, which we normalize to zero with no loss of generality: $\omega_k^s = 0$. In this case, $F_k(\omega_k) = \mathbf{1}\left\{\omega_k^s \geq 0\right\} F_k^i(\omega_k^i)$, with the marginal distribution F_k^i absolutely continuous over $\mathbb{R}$.

Scenario 3. Agents are heterogeneous in both their stand-alone values and their interaction benefits. In this case, F_k is absolutely continuous over $\mathbb{R}^2$.

In light of Lemma 23.2, we can formulate the platform's problem in terms of the measure of agents that join from each side of the market. To do so, fix $(N_a, N_b) \in (0, 1]^2$ and, for each $k \in \{a, b\}$, define $P_k(N_a, N_b)$ as the unique solution to the system of equations given by

$$N_k = \int_{\left\{\omega_k \in \Omega_k : \omega_k^s + \omega_k^i N_{-k} \geq P_k\right\}} dF_k(\omega_k), \qquad k = a, b. \tag{23.4}$$

Intuitively, the two equations in (23.4) identify the access prices that implement a single network in which the measure of the participating agents from each side $k = a, b$ is equal to $N_k > 0$. In any of the three scenarios considered above, the inverse demand functions $P_k(N_a, N_b)$, $k = a, b$, are differentiable. We then define the *own-price demand elasticity on side k* as

$$\varepsilon_k(N_a, N_b) := -\frac{P_k(N_a, N_b)}{N_k} \left(\frac{\partial P_k}{\partial N_k}(N_a, N_b)\right)^{-1}.$$

Fixing the measure N_{-k} of participating agents from side $-k$, $1/\varepsilon_k$ captures the sensitivity of the side-k inverse demand with respect to variations in the side-k participation N_k. Equivalently, given the prices $(P_a, P_b) = \{P_k(N_a, N_b)\}_{k=a,b}$ implementing the participation vector (N_a, N_b), $\varepsilon_k(N_a, N_b)$ is the elasticity of the side-k direct demand with respect to variations in the side-k price, for fixed participation on side $-k$.

Next, assume that the platform incurs a participation cost c_k^s for each side-k agent it brings on board, and an interaction cost c^i for every interaction between the two sides that it induces. For any (N_a, N_b), its profit is then equal to

$$\Pi(N_a, N_b) := \sum_{k=a,b} N_k \left(P_k(N_a, N_b) - c_k^s\right) - c^i N_a N_b.$$

Proposition 23.3. *Consider a profit-maximizing platform designing a single network, and let the agents' preferences be given by (23.2). The profit-maximizing prices (P_a^*, P_b^*), along with the participation profile (N_a^*, N_b^*) that they induce, solve*

$$\frac{P_k^* - \left[c_k^s + N_{-k}^* \left(c^i - \tilde{\omega}_{-k}^i(N_a^*, N_b^*)\right)\right]}{P_k^*} = \frac{1}{\varepsilon_k(N_a^*, N_b^*)} \tag{23.5}$$

for $k = a, b$, where $P_k^* = P_k(N_a^*, N_b^*)$, with $P_k(N_a, N_b)$ given by (23.4), and where

——— **488** ———

$$\tilde{\omega}^i_{-k}(N^*_a, N^*_b) := \mathbb{E}\left[\omega^i_{-k}|\omega^s_{-k} + \omega^i_{-k}N^*_k = P^*_{-k}\right]$$

is the average interaction benefit of those agents from side $-k$ who are indifferent between participating and not participating, under the profile (N^*_a, N^*_b).

Proof The result is obtained by differentiating the objective function $\Pi(N_a, N_b)$ with respect to N_k, $k = a, b$, and then noting that

$$\frac{\partial P_k(N_a, N_b)}{\partial N_k}\frac{N_k}{P_k(N_a, N_b)} = -\frac{1}{\varepsilon_k(N_a, N_b)}$$

and that

$$\frac{\partial P_{-k}(N_a, N_b)}{\partial N_k} = \tilde{\omega}^i_{-k}(N_a, N_b),$$

where the last property follows from the implicit function theorem applied to (23.4). □

Condition (23.5) is instrumental to understanding how pricing in two-sided markets differs from pricing in more traditional one-sided environments. Relative to the classic Lerner formula for monopoly pricing, two differences stand out. The first is that, when choosing its side-k price, the platform must account for the fact that its effective side-k marginal cost is endogenous and depends on the set of participating agents on the side $-k$. Indeed, when it increases the participation on side k, to hold constant the participation on side $-k$ the platform must adjust its price on side $-k$ by $\tilde{\omega}^i_{-k}(N_a, N_b)$, which is the average interaction benefit among all agents on side $-k$ who are indifferent between joining the platform and staying out. When this term is positive, this effect contributes to a reduction in the side-k marginal cost, whereas the opposite is true when $\tilde{\omega}^i_{-k}(N_a, N_b) < 0$.

The second difference is that the demand elasticities are a function of the entire profile (N_a, N_b) of participating agents. Because of cross-side network effects, the participation of side $-k$ affects the willingness to pay off the participating agents on side k, and hence the elasticity of the side-k demand with respect to the side-k price.

The "two-sided" Lerner formula in (23.5) highlights that price skewness is a fundamental feature of markets with cross-side network effects. If, for instance, the demand elasticity is low on side a, but high on side b, the platform tends to set high prices on the former side, and low (potentially negative) prices on the latter side. In light of such considerations, the prices on each side should not be taken *in vacuo* for competition policy purposes: neither is a low price on side b a sign of predation (below-cost pricing) or is a high price on side a a sign of abuse of market power (a high markup). Rather, the welfare effects of monopolistic pricing should be evaluated by comparing prices on each side to their efficient counterparts, as we show next.

23.3.2 Welfare-Maximizing Pricing

Let the social welfare function include all agents' utilities and the platform's profit. Accordingly, the welfare induced by a single network with participation profile (N_a, N_b) is given by

$$W(N_a, N_b) := \sum_{k \in \{a,b\}} \int_{\{\omega_k:\omega^s_k+\omega^i_k N_{-k} \geq P_k(N_a,N_b)\}} \left(\omega^s_k + \omega^i_k N_{-k} - c^s_k\right) dF_k(\omega_k)$$

$$- c^i N_a N_b.$$

The term inside the integral is the total gross surplus of the matches enabled by the platform (the sum of the agents' utilities net of all participation costs), while the last term is the platform's total interaction cost. The next proposition derives the welfare–maximizing participation profile, which we hereafter refer to as the *efficient participation profile*.

Proposition 23.4. *Consider a welfare-maximizing platform designing a single network, and let the agents' preferences be given by (23.2). The welfare-maximizing prices (P_a^e, P_b^e) along with the efficient participation profile (N_a^e, N_b^e) that they induce solve*

$$P_k^e = c_k^s + N_{-k}^e \left(c^i - \bar{\omega}_{-k}^i(N_a^e, N_b^e) \right) \tag{23.6}$$

for $k = a, b$, where $P_k^e = P_k\left(N_a^e, N_b^e\right)$, with $P_k(N_a, N_b)$ given by (23.4) and where

$$\bar{\omega}_{-k}^i(N_a^e, N_b^e) := \mathbb{E}\left[\omega_{-k}^i | \omega_{-k}^s + \omega_{-k}^i N_k^e \geq P_{-k}^e \right]$$

is the average interaction benefit of the participating agents from side $-k$.

Proof The result is obtained by differentiating the objective function $W(N_a, N_b)$ with respect to N_k, $k = a, b$, and then applying the implicit function theorem to (23.4) to obtain the formula for $\partial P_k(N_a, N_b)/\partial N_k$. $\square$

Condition (23.6) is the two-sided incarnation of the Pigouvian precept, according to which, to achieve efficiency, agents should be charged (or remunerated) for the externalities they impose on other market participants (as in the Vickrey–Clark–Groves mechanism). The price on each side is equal to the total marginal cost that the platform incurs to bring a marginal agent on board, adjusted by the network externality that the marginal agent exerts on the participating agents from the other side of the market. This externality equals the measure of the agents on side $-k$ multiplied by the average interaction benefit among *all the participating agents* on side $-k$. Note the contrast with the pricing practiced by a profit-maximizing monopolist, whereby only the externality imposed on the *marginal* agents from the opposite side is taken into account.

23.3.3 Distortions

To understand how the profit-maximizing price profile compares with its efficient counterpart, let us take the difference between (23.5) and (23.6). This leads to the following decomposition:

$$P_k^* - P_k^e = \underbrace{\frac{P_k^*}{\varepsilon_k(P_a^*, P_b^*)}}_{\text{markup}} + \underbrace{N_{-k}^e \left(\bar{\omega}_{-k}^i(N_a^e, N_b^e) - \tilde{\omega}_{-k}^i(N_a^e, N_b^e) \right)}_{\text{Spence distortion}}$$

$$+ \underbrace{N_{-k}^e \left(\tilde{\omega}_{-k}^i(N_a^e, N_b^e) - \tilde{\omega}_{-k}^i(N_a^*, N_b^*) \right)}_{\text{displacement distortion}} + \underbrace{\left(N_{-k}^e - N_{-k}^* \right) \left(\tilde{\omega}_{-k}^i(N_a^*, N_b^*) - c^i \right)}_{\text{scale distortion}}.$$

$$\tag{23.7}$$

The usual markup distortion reflects the market power enjoyed by the monopolistic platform. The Spence distortion captures the fact that a profit-maximizing monopolist, when setting the price on side k, internalizes the effect of expanding the side-k participation on the marginal agent from side $-k$, rather than on all participating agents from side $-k$. The displacement distortion accounts for the difference between the benefits that the marginal agents on the side $-k$ derive from the expansion of the side-k participation under profit-maximizing and efficient allocation, respectively. In turn, the scale distortion reflects the difference between the participation on side $-k$ induced by the profit-maximizing monopolist and a welfare-maximizing platform: the net average benefit $\tilde{\omega}^i_{-k} - c^i$ that the marginal agents on the side $-k$ derive from the expansion of the side-k participation (net of the platform's interaction cost) applies to a measure of agents equal to N^*_{-k} under profit maximization, whereas it applies to N^e_{-k} agents under welfare maximization.

In general, it is not possible to sign the net effect of these four distortions. As a result, the profit-maximizing prices can be either higher or lower than their efficient counterparts in either one or both sides of the market. To obtain further insights, it is useful to express prices on a *per-unit* basis, that is, by normalizing the side-k price by the size of the participation on side $-k$. Further, assume that the participation costs are equal to zero on each side so that $c^s_a = c^s_b = 0$. Letting $p^*_k := P^*_k/N^*_{-k}$ and $p^e_k = P^e_k/N^e_{-k}$ denote the side-k per-unit price under profit maximization and welfare maximization, respectively, we then have that

$$
p^*_k - p^e_k = \underbrace{\frac{p^*_k}{\varepsilon_k(N^*_a, N^*_b)}}_{\text{markup}} + \underbrace{\left(\bar{\omega}^i_{-k}(N^e_a, N^e_b) - \tilde{\omega}^i_{-k}(N^e_a, N^e_b)\right)}_{\text{Spence distortion}}
$$

$$
+ \underbrace{\left(\tilde{\omega}^i_{-k}(N^e_a, N^e_b) - \tilde{\omega}^i_{-k}(N^*_a, N^*_b)\right)}_{\text{displacement distortion}}, \tag{23.8}
$$

Corollary 23.5. *Consider a monopolistic platform designing a single network, and let the agents' preferences be given by (23.2).*

1. *Under Scenario 1, the displacement and Spence distortions are nil. The per-unit price on each side is higher under profit maximization than under welfare maximization: $p^*_k > p^e_k$, $k = a, b$.*
2. *Under Scenario 2, the Spence distortion is always positive on both sides, whereas the displacement distortion is negative on at least one side. Moreover, the sum of the per-unit prices is higher under profit maximization than under welfare maximization: $p^*_a + p^*_b > p^e_a + p^e_b$.*

Proof Part 1 follows directly from (23.8). For part 2, note that $\bar{\omega}^i_{-k}(N^e_a, N^e_b) - \tilde{\omega}^i_{-k}(N^e_a, N^e_b) > 0$ because, by definition, $\tilde{\omega}^i_{-k}(N^e_a, N^e_b) = p^e_{-k}$ whereas $\bar{\omega}^i_{-k}(N^e_a, N^e_b)$ is the expectation over all ω^i_{-k} satisfying $\omega^i_{-k} \geq p^e_{-k}$. Hence, the Spence distortion is always positive. Because, $\tilde{\omega}^i_{-k}(N^e_a, N^e_b) = p^e_{-k}$ and $\tilde{\omega}^i_{-k}(N^*_a, N^*_b) = p^*_{-k}$, condition (23.8) can be rewritten as

$$
p^*_a + p^*_b = p^e_a + p^e_b + \underbrace{\frac{p^*_k}{\varepsilon_k(N^*_a, N^*_b)}}_{\text{markup}} + \underbrace{\left(\bar{\omega}^i_{-k}(N^e_a, N^e_b) - \tilde{\omega}^i_{-k}(N^e_a, N^e_b)\right)}_{\text{Spence distortion}}
$$

for $k = a, b$. Because the markup and the Spence distortion are both positive, we have that $p_a^* + p_b^* > p_a^e + p_b^e$. Therefore, for some k, $p_k^* > p_k^e$. Because the displacement distortion is equal to $-(p_{-k}^* - p_{-k}^e)$, it follows that the displacement distortion is negative on at least one side of the market. □

Corollary 23.5 shows that, under Scenarios 1 or 2, total per-unit prices are excessively high when set by a profit-maximizing monopolist. Interestingly, in Scenario 2, this does not rule out the possibility that the profit-maximizing price on one side of the market is lower than its efficient counterpart. As we shall see in Section 23.5, this possibility stems from the platform's inability to discriminate among agents from the same side of the market. When discrimination is possible, all agents from both sides face higher prices under profit maximization than under welfare maximization.

23.4 Unknown Preference Distribution

We now consider markets in which the joint distribution of preferences in the population is *unknown*, both to the platforms and to each agent from either side of the market. This dimension is important because it introduces uncertainty over the size of the network externalities.

Specifically, suppose that preferences are consistent with the specification in Scenario 1. The uncertain "aggregate state" of the world is thus given by the pair of distributions $F^s = (F_a^s, F_b^s)$ from which the agents' stand-alone valuations are drawn. As in the previous section, each ω_k^s is drawn from F_k^s independently across all agents. To keep things simple, further assume that each agent's stand-alone valuation ω_k^s parameterizes both the agent's preferences and the agent's beliefs over the aggregate state. For simplicity, the platforms are assumed not to possess any private information.

For any $\omega_k^s \in \mathbb{R}$, $k = 1, 2$, denote by $Q_k^s(\omega_k^s)$ the measure of agents from side k that the platform believes to have stand-alone valuations no smaller than ω_k^s.

Next, consider the agents. For any $k = a, b$, and any $(\omega_k^s, \omega_{-k}^s) \in \mathbb{R}^2$, let $M_{-k}^s(\omega_{-k}^s | \omega_k^s)$ denote the measure of agents from side $-k$ with stand-alone valuation no smaller than ω_{-k}^s, as expected by any agent from side k with stand-alone valuation equal to ω_k^s. These functions thus reflect the agents' beliefs over the cross-sectional distribution of preferences on the other side of the market. They may capture, for example, how consumers use their own appreciation of the features of a new platform's product (e.g., its operating system, interface, and the like) to form beliefs over the number of applications that will be developed for the new product. Importantly, such beliefs need not coincide with the platforms' beliefs.

For any ω_k^s, we assume that $M_{-k}^s(\omega_{-k}^s | \omega_k^s)$ is strictly decreasing in ω_{-k}^s, and differentiable in each argument.

Definition 23.6. Preferences are *aligned* if, for all ω_{-k}^s, $M_{-k}^s(\omega_{-k}^s | \omega_k^s)$ is increasing in ω_k^s, $k = a, b$. They are *misaligned* if, for all ω_{-k}^s, $M_{-k}^s(\omega_{-k}^s | \omega_k^s)$ is decreasing in ω_k^s, $k = a, b$.

When preferences are aligned, agents with a higher appreciation for a platform's product also expect a higher such appreciation by agents from the opposite side, whereas the opposite occurs when preferences are misaligned. Importantly, the definition does not presume that stand-alone valuations are drawn from a common prior. It simply establishes a monotonic relationship between beliefs and stand-alone valuations.

The special case of a common prior corresponds to the case in which all players commonly believe that $F^s = (F_a^s, F_b^s)$ is drawn from a set of distributions $\mathscr{F}$ according to a distribution $\mathbf{F}$. In this case, the platforms' and the agents' beliefs are given by

$$Q_k^s(\omega_k^s) = \mathbb{E}_{\mathbf{F}}[1 - F_k^s(\omega_k^s)] \text{ and } M_{-k}^s\left(\omega_{-k}^s|\omega_k^s\right) = \frac{\mathbb{E}_{\mathbf{F}}\left[\left(1 - F_{-k}^s(\omega_{-k}^s)\right)f_k^s\left(\omega_k^s\right)\right]}{\mathbb{E}_{\mathbf{F}}\left[f_k^s\left(\omega_k^s\right)\right]},$$

where, as in the baseline model, f_k^s denotes the density of F_k^s and all expectations are computed by integrating over $\mathscr{F}$ under the common prior $\mathbf{F}$.

A strategy profile for the agents then constitutes a *continuation (Bayes–Nash) equilibrium*, in the game that starts after the platform announces its access prices $P = (P_a, P_b)$, if each agent's participation decision is a best response to all other agents' equilibrium strategies.

Each agent from side k with stand-alone valuation ω_k^s then joins the platform if and only if

$$\omega_k^s + \omega_k^i \mathbb{E}\left[N_{-k}|\omega_k^s\right] \geq P_k, \tag{23.9}$$

where $\mathbb{E}\left[N_{-k}|\omega_k^s\right]$ is the participation on side $-k$ expected by the agent. Provided that the interaction benefits (ω_a^i, ω_b^i) are not too large, we then have that, for any vector of prices (P_a, P_b), the demand expected by the platform on each side $k = a, b$ is given by $Q_k^s(\hat{\omega}_k^s)$, where $(\hat{\omega}_a^s, \hat{\omega}_b^s)$ is the unique solution to the system of equations given by

$$\hat{\omega}_k^s + \omega_k^i M_{-k}^s\left(\hat{\omega}_{-k}^s|\hat{\omega}_k^s\right) = P_k, \quad k = a, b. \tag{23.10}$$

Now, suppose the platform aims at getting on board N_a agents from side a and N_b agents from side b. Because the platform does not know the exact distribution of preferences, N_a and N_b must be interpreted as the participation expected by the platform, where the expectation is taken over all possible distributions F^s using the platform's own beliefs. Given (23.10), the platform should set prices (P_a, P_b) such that the thresholds $(\hat{\omega}_a^s, \hat{\omega}_b^s)$ satisfy $Q_k(\hat{\omega}_k^s) = N_k$, $k = a, b$. The key difference with respect to the case of complete information is the following. When the platform adjusts its prices so as to change the participation it expects from side k, while keeping constant the participation it expects from side $-k$, it does not need to keep constant the side-k's marginal agent's beliefs over the participation of side $-k$. This is so because uncertainty over the distribution of preferences in the population introduces de facto statistical dependence between the agents' beliefs over the other side's participation and their own preferences, reflected in the fact that

$$\frac{\partial \mathbb{E}[N_{-k}|\hat{\omega}_k^s]}{\partial \hat{\omega}_k^s} = \frac{\partial M_{-k}^s\left(\hat{\omega}_{-k}^s|\hat{\omega}_k^s\right)}{\partial \hat{\omega}_k^s} \neq 0. \tag{23.11}$$

In particular, when preferences are aligned between the two sides, $\mathbb{E}[N_{-k}|\hat{\omega}_k^s]$ is increasing in $\hat{\omega}_k^s$ whereas the opposite is true when preferences are misaligned. In the first case, this novel effect contributes to *steeper* inverse-demand curves, whereas in the second case it contributes to *flatter* inverse demands. When preferences are aligned, the new marginal agent that the platform attracts by lowering its price on side k is more pessimistic about the participation of the other side than any of the infra-marginal agents who are already on board (those with a higher stand-alone valuation). To bring the new marginal agent on board, the platform must thus cut its side-k price more than it would have done under complete information. Importantly, this novel effect is present even if the platform adjusts its price on side $-k$ so as to maintain its expectation of that side's participation constant (which amounts to maintaining $\hat{\omega}^s_{-k}$ constant).

The above novel effects play an important role in how platforms price access to their network on each side of the market. Using (23.10), we can reformulate the platform's objective in terms of the participation thresholds $(\hat{\omega}^s_a, \hat{\omega}^s_b)$ rather than the prices (P_a, P_b) that induce these thresholds. Accordingly, the platform chooses $(\hat{\omega}^s_a, \hat{\omega}^s_b)$ to maximize

$$\sum_{k=a,b} \left\{ \hat{\omega}^s_k + \omega^i_k M^s_{-k}\left(\hat{\omega}^p_{-k} | \hat{\omega}^s_k\right) - c^s_k \right\} Q^s_k(\hat{\omega}^s_k) - c^i Q^s_a(\hat{\omega}^s_a) Q^s_b(\hat{\omega}^s_b). \tag{23.12}$$

We then have the following result:

Proposition 23.7. *Suppose that preferences are as in Scenario 1 and that the distribution of preferences over the two sides is unknown to the agents and the platform. The profit-maximizing prices (P^*_a, P^*_b), along with the stand-alone thresholds $\left(\hat{\omega}^{s*}_a, \hat{\omega}^{s*}_b\right)$ they induce, satisfy the following optimality conditions:*

$$P^*_k = c^s_k + c^i Q^s_{-k}(\hat{\omega}^{s*}_{-k}) + \left[1 + \omega^i_k \frac{\partial M^s_{-k}\left(\hat{\omega}^{s*}_{-k} \mid \hat{\omega}^{s*}_k\right)}{\partial \hat{\omega}^s_k} \right] \frac{Q^s_k(\hat{\omega}^{s*}_k)}{|dQ^s_k(\hat{\omega}^{s*}_k)/d\hat{\omega}^s_k|}$$

$$+ \omega^i_{-k} \frac{\partial M^s_k\left(\hat{\omega}^{s*}_k \mid \hat{\omega}^{s*}_{-k}\right)}{\partial \hat{\omega}^s_k} \frac{Q^s_{-k}(\hat{\omega}^{s*}_{-k})}{|dQ^s_k(\hat{\omega}^{s*}_k)/d\hat{\omega}^s_k|}, \tag{23.13}$$

with $P^*_k = \hat{\omega}^{s*}_k + \omega^i_k M^s_{-k}\left(\hat{\omega}^{s*}_{-k} | \hat{\omega}^{s*}_k\right),\ k = a, b.$

Proof The result follows directly from differentiating the profit function in (23.12) and then using (23.10). □

Note that the price formula in (23.13) is the incomplete-information analogue of the corresponding complete-information formula

$$P^*_k = c^s_k + c^i N^*_{-k} - \frac{\partial P_k(N^*_a, N^*_b)}{\partial N_k} N^*_k - \frac{\partial P_{-k}(N^*_a, N^*_b)}{\partial N_k} N^*_{-k}, \tag{23.14}$$

derived above. It requires that profit does not change when the platform increases the participation it expects from side k (given its own beliefs), while adjusting the price on side $-k$ to maintain the participation it expects from keeping side $-k$ constant.

In particular, the last term on the right-hand side of (23.13) is the benefit of cutting the price on side k due to the possibility of raising the price on side $-k$, typical of two-sided markets (see (23.5)).[2] Note, however, an important difference with respect to the case of complete information. The *measure* of additional agents from side

---

[2] Observe that $\partial M_k\left(\hat{\omega}^{s*}_k \big| \hat{\omega}^{s*}_{-k}\right)/\partial \hat{\omega}^s_k < 0$, irrespective of whether preferences are aligned or misaligned.

k that the platform expects to bring on board by cutting its price on side k now differs from the *measure* of agents expected by the marginal agent on side $-k$ (the agent with signal $\hat{\omega}^{s*}_{-k}$ who is indifferent between joining and not joining). This novel effect is captured by the term

$$\frac{\partial \mathbb{E}[N_k \mid \hat{\omega}^{s*}_{-k}]}{\partial N_k}\bigg|_{\hat{\omega}^{s*}_{-k}=\text{const}} = -\frac{\partial M^s_k\left(\hat{\omega}^{s*}_k \mid \hat{\omega}^{s*}_{-k}\right)}{\partial \hat{\omega}^s_k}\frac{1}{|dQ^s_k(\hat{\omega}^{s*}_k)/d\hat{\omega}^s_k|}$$

in (23.13).[3] Irrespective of whether preferences are aligned or misaligned between the two sides, this term is always positive, thus contributing to a lower price on side k.

The term in square brackets on the right-hand side of (23.13) captures the adjustment in the side-k price necessary to expand the side-k demand. Interestingly, this term accounts for how a variation in the participation from side k comes with a variation in the beliefs of the side-k's marginal agent about the participation from side $-k$ (the second term in the square bracket). Such a variation occurs even when the platform adjusts its price on side $-k$ to maintain unchanged the identity of the marginal agent on that side (thus maintaining constant the participation expected by the platform from that side). As indicated above, when preferences are aligned across sides this effect contributes to a steeper inverse demand on each side and hence, other things being equal, to higher prices. The opposite is true in markets in which preferences are misaligned. The latter effect has no counterpart under complete information.

We conclude this section by comparing the profit-maximizing prices with their efficient counterparts. To this purpose, consider the problem of a planner who shares the same beliefs as the platform (which is always the case when stand-alone values are drawn from a common prior). The planner's problem then consists in choosing $\left(\hat{\omega}^s_a, \hat{\omega}^s_b\right)$ so as to maximize

$$\hat{W}\left(\hat{\omega}^s_a, \hat{\omega}^s_b\right) := \sum_{k=a,b}\int_{\{\omega^s_k \geq \hat{\omega}^s_k\}}\left(\omega^s_k + \omega^i_k M^s_{-k}\left(\hat{\omega}^s_{-k} \mid \omega^s_k\right) - c^s_k\right)d[1 - Q^s_k(\omega_k)]$$
$$- c^i Q^s_a(\hat{\omega}^s_a)Q^s_b(\hat{\omega}^s_b).$$

Proposition 23.8. *Consider a welfare-maximizing platform designing a single network, and let the agents' preferences be as in Scenario 1. The welfare-maximizing prices (P^e_a, P^e_b), along with the efficient stand-alone thresholds $\left(\hat{\omega}^{se}_a, \hat{\omega}^{se}_b\right)$ that they induce solve*

$$P^e_k = c^s_k + c^i Q^s_{-k}(\hat{\omega}^{se}_{-k}) + \omega^i_{-k}\frac{\int_{\{\omega^s_{-k}\geq\hat{\omega}^{se}_{-k}\}}\left(\frac{\partial M^s_k\left(\hat{\omega}^{se}_k \mid \omega^s_{-k}\right)}{\partial \hat{\omega}^s_k}\right)d[1 - Q^s_{-k}(\omega^s_{-k})]}{|dQ^s_k(\hat{\omega}^{se}_k)/d\hat{\omega}^{se}_k|},$$

(23.15)

where $P^e_k = \hat{\omega}^{se}_k + \omega^i_k M^s_{-k}\left(\hat{\omega}^{se}_{-k} \mid \hat{\omega}^{se}_k\right)$, for $k = a, b$.

---

[3] Under complete information, $\frac{\partial M^s_k\left(\hat{\omega}^s_k \mid \hat{\omega}^p_{-k}\right)}{\partial \hat{\omega}^s_k} = \frac{1}{|dQ^s_k(\hat{\omega}^s_k)/d\hat{\omega}^s_k|}$, in which case the second term in (23.13) reduces to $\omega^i_{-k}N_{-k}$, as discussed above.

Proof The result follows directly from differentiating the welfare function in (23.12) and then using (23.10) to relate the stand-alone thresholds to the prices that induce them. □

When combined with Proposition 23.7, the result in the previous proposition identifies the distortions due to market power. First, as is the case under complete information, a profit-maximizing platform accounts for the effect that a reduction in the side-k price has on the profit collected from all infra-marginal agents from the same side. This effect is captured by the third term on the right-hand side of (23.13). This is the same markup distortion as that discussed above. The novelty relative to complete information is that the adjustment in the side-k price must account for the difference between the platform's beliefs and those of side-k's marginal agents. Other things being equal, such a difference contributes to larger distortion when preferences are aligned and to a smaller one when they are misaligned. Second, a profit-maximizing platform internalizes the effect of expanding the side-k participation by looking at the externality exerted on the marginal agent from side $-k$ instead of all participating agents from side $-k$. This effect is the analogue of the sum of the Spence and displacement distortions discussed above and is captured by the difference between the last term in (23.13) and the last term in (23.15). Other things being equal, whether such distortions are amplified or mitigated by dispersed information depends to a large extent on the modularity of the beliefs, that is, on whether $|\partial M_k^s \left(\hat{\omega}_k^{se} \mid \omega_{-k}^s \right) /\partial \hat{\omega}_k^s|$ is increasing or decreasing in ω_{-k}^s. The last factor contributing to a discrepancy between the profit-maximizing and the welfare-maximizing prices is a scale distortion analogous to that under complete information but again adjusted for the difference in beliefs between the marginal and the infra-marginal agents.

23.5 Matching Design

Matching design relaxes one of the the key restrictions in the analysis of pricing in two-sided markets, namely, the absence of discrimination (within agents from the same side). This opens the door to customized matching rules, where the matching set of each participating agent depends on his type.

23.5.1 One-to-One Matching

We first consider markets in which matching is one-to-one, capturing situations of rivalry or of severe capacity constraints on the part of agents. Recall that, in this case, the set $C(\Omega_{-k})$ is the collection of all singletons $\{\omega_{-k}\}$, with $\omega_{-k} \in \Omega_{-k}$.

We identify the type of each agent with a *vertical* characteristic which we refer to as *quality*. We let $\Omega_k = [\underline{\omega}_k, \bar{\omega}_k] \subset \mathbb{R}_{++}$ denote the set of types from side k, and assume that the type of each side-k agent is an independent draw from the distribution F_k.

Agents' preferences take the following form: for each $\omega_k \in \Omega_k$, the gross utility that each side-k agent with type ω_k derives from the matching set $s_k = \{\omega_{-k}\}$ is given by

$$u_k(s_k|\omega_k) := \phi_k(\omega_k, \omega_{-k}), \tag{23.16}$$

where the function ϕ_k is differentiable, equi-Lipschitz continuous, strictly increasing in both arguments, and supermodular. Accordingly, the surplus of each match increases with each involved agents' quality, and the gain from a better-quality partner is higher for agents of higher quality. A simple example satisfying these assumptions is the multiplicative surplus function $\phi_a(\omega_a, \omega_b) = \omega_a \omega_b$, often assumed in applications.

The cost that the platform incurs for each match it induces is $c \in \mathbb{R}_+$. To make things simple (but interesting), assume that $\sum_k \phi_k(\underline{\omega}_a, \underline{\omega}_b) \le c \le \sum_k \phi_k(\bar{\omega}_k, \bar{\omega}_k)$.

To properly describe the platform's matching design problem, we first need to amend the definition of matching rules introduced in Section 23.2. Namely, it is necessary to allow for stochastic matching rules that assign to each type a distribution over the type of the matching partner from the opposite side.

To do so formally, let $\hat{\Omega}_k$ be the (Lebesgue-measurable) set of participating types from side k. For any $\omega_k \in \Omega_k \setminus \hat{\Omega}_k$, $\mathbf{s}_k(\omega_k) = \emptyset$. For $\omega_k \in \hat{\Omega}_k$, however, $\mathbf{s}_k(\omega_k) \in \Delta(\hat{\Omega}_{-k})$ is a probability measure over $\hat{\Omega}_{-k}$ describing the likelihood that each side-k agent of type ω_k is matched with any of the participating types from the other side of the market. We denote by $G_{\mathbf{s}_k}(\cdot|\omega_k)$ the cdf associated with the measure $\mathbf{s}_k(\omega_k)$.

Feasibility then dictates that the sets of participating agents from the two sides have the same measure, $|\hat{\Omega}_a| = |\hat{\Omega}_b|$, where, as before, $|\hat{\Omega}_k|$ is the F_k-measure of the set $\hat{\Omega}_k$. This requirement is self-explanatory, as no one-to-one matching rule can be constructed when the measure of participating agents is unequal across sides. In addition, feasibility also requires that the measure of types from side $-k$ matched with any subset $\tilde{\Omega}_k \subseteq \hat{\Omega}_k$ of participating types from side k have the same measure as $\tilde{\Omega}_k$. That is, for any $\tilde{\Omega}_k \subseteq \hat{\Omega}_k$,

$$|\tilde{\Omega}_k| := \int_{\tilde{\Omega}_k} dF_k(\omega_k) = \int_{\hat{\Omega}_{-k}} \int_{\tilde{\Omega}_k} dG_{\mathbf{s}_{-k}}(\omega_k|\omega_{-k}) dF_{-k}(\omega_{-k}),$$

where the double integral on the right-hand side is the total measure of agents from side $-k$ that are matched to those agents from side k whose type is in $\tilde{\Omega}_k$. Because the equality above has to hold for any measurable set $\tilde{\Omega}_k$, we can define the joint distribution $\mathbf{F}$ according to $d\mathbf{F}(\omega_k, \omega_{-k}) := dG_{\mathbf{s}_{-k}}(\omega_k|\omega_{-k}) dF_{-k}(\omega_{-k})$. Note that, by construction, this joint distribution couples the marginals $|\hat{\Omega}_a|^{-1} F_a$ and $|\hat{\Omega}_b|^{-1} F_b$.

Accordingly, feasibility requires that *there exists* a joint distribution $\mathbf{F}$, with support $\hat{\Omega}_a \times \hat{\Omega}_b$ and marginals $|\hat{\Omega}_a|^{-1} F_a$ and $|\hat{\Omega}_b|^{-1} F_b$, such that, for each $\omega_k \in \hat{\Omega}_k$, $G_{\mathbf{s}_k}(\cdot|\omega_k)$ is the conditional distribution of ω_{-k} given ω_k, as induced by the joint cdf $\mathbf{F}$. Intuitively, this requirement guarantees that *any* profile of *realized* matches satisfies the reciprocity condition (23.1). Heuristically, the function $\mathbf{F}$ describes the distribution of matched pairs under the rule $\{\mathbf{s}_k(\cdot)\}_{k=a,b}$.

For instance, *random matching* (with full participation, that is, with $\hat{\Omega}_k = \Omega_k$, $k = a, b$) corresponds to the joint cdf $\mathbf{F}$ defined by $\mathbf{F}(\omega_a, \omega_b) = F_a(\omega_a) F_b(\omega_b)$, for all $(\omega_a, \omega_b) \in \Omega$, and the associated stochastic matching rule has cdfs $G_{\mathbf{s}_a}(\cdot|\omega_a) = F_b$ and $G_{\mathbf{s}_b}(\cdot|\omega_b) = F_a$, for all $(\omega_a, \omega_b) \in \Omega$. In this example, the partner of each side-k agent is drawn (independently across agents) from the marginal distribution F_{-k}, irrespectively of the agent's own type.

The case of a *deterministic* matching rule corresponds to the case where each type from each side $k = a, b$ is assigned a single type from the opposite side. We shall abuse notation and write the corresponding matching rule as $\mathbf{s}_k(\omega_k) = \omega_{-k}$, with the understanding that, in this case, $G_{s_k}(\cdot|\omega_k)$ is a degenerate Dirac delta assigning probability 1 to type $\{\omega_{-k}\}$. Formally, this corresponds to an endogenous joint distribution $\mathbf{F}$ whose conditional distribution $\mathbf{F}_{-k|k}$ specifies a collection of Dirac deltas, one for each ω_k from sides $k = a, b$.

A deterministic matching rule of special interest is the (truncated) *positive assortative* rule. In order to define it formally, we first need to introduce the following:

Definition 23.9. A pair of absolutely continuous random variables (X, Y), with cdfs F_X and F_Y, respectively, is co-monotonic if there is a random variable U uniformly distributed over $[0, 1]$ such that $X = F_X^{-1}(U)$ and $Y = F_Y^{-1}(U)$, where $F_k^{-1}(U) := \inf\{\omega_k \in \Omega_k : F_k(\omega_k) \geq U\}$.

As it is well known, any random variable can be represented as being generated from a draw from a uniform distribution (according to the probability integral transform theorem). The definition imposes that the draw be the same across the two random variables, implying that the two variables are related by the identity $Y = F_Y^{-1}(F_X(X))$. Co-monotonic random variables are intimately related to positive assortative matching:

Definition 23.10. A matching rule $\{s_k(\cdot)\}_{k=a,b}$ is truncated positive assortative if, for each $k \in \{a, b\}$, there exists a participation threshold $\hat{\omega}_k \in \Omega_k$ such that

$$s_k(\omega_k) = \begin{cases} (F_{-k})^{-1}(F_k(\omega_k)) & \text{if} \quad \omega_k \geq \hat{\omega}_k, \\ \varnothing & \text{if} \quad \omega_k < \hat{\omega}_k. \end{cases}$$

Therefore, a positive assortative matching rule renders the types of matched agents as co-monotonic random variables (also note that, by feasibility, $F_a(\hat{\omega}_a) = F_b(\hat{\omega}_b)$).

23.5.1.1 Efficient Matching Design

Using the notation introduced above, a platform's welfare-maximization problem consists of choosing a pair of sets $(\hat{\Omega}_a, \hat{\Omega}_b)$ and a joint distribution $\mathbf{F}$ over $\hat{\Omega}_a \times \hat{\Omega}_b$ that couples the marginals $|\hat{\Omega}_a|^{-1}F_a$ and $|\hat{\Omega}_b|^{-1}F_b$ to maximize[4]

$$\hat{W}(\mathbf{F}; \hat{\Omega}_a, \hat{\Omega}_b) := |\hat{\Omega}_a| \int_{\hat{\Omega}_a \times \hat{\Omega}_b} (\phi_a(\omega_a, \omega_b) + \phi_b(\omega_b, \omega_a) - c) \, d\mathbf{F}(\omega_a, \omega_b).$$

Proposition 23.11. *Consider a welfare-maximizing platform designing one-to-one matches, and let the agents' preferences be given by (23.16). The efficient matching rule is truncated positive assortative with participation thresholds $(\hat{\omega}_a^e, \hat{\omega}_b^e)$ satisfying $\hat{\omega}_b^e = F_b^{-1}(F_a(\hat{\omega}_a^e))$ and*

$$\phi_a(\hat{\omega}_a^e, \hat{\omega}_b^e) + \phi_b(\hat{\omega}_a^e, \hat{\omega}_b^e) = c. \tag{23.17}$$

Proof First, consider the case for which $c = 0$. It is evident that, in this case, it is never optimal to exclude any type, implying that $(\hat{\Omega}_a, \hat{\Omega}_b) = (\Omega_a, \Omega_b)$.

---

[4] Because of one-to-one matching, the measure of matches induced by the platform is $|\hat{\Omega}_a| = |\hat{\Omega}_b|$.

Next, let the the match surplus function be a step function with coefficients $(\alpha, \beta) \in \mathbb{R}^2$:

$$\phi_k(\omega_a, \omega_b) = \phi^{\alpha,\beta}(\omega_a, \omega_b) := \mathbf{1}\{\omega_a \geq \alpha\}\,\mathbf{1}\{\omega_b \geq \beta\}.$$

Observe that, in this case, the welfare-maximizing matching rule is untruncated positive assortative (in that $\hat{\omega}_k = \underline{\omega}_k$ for each k).

For general match surplus functions, let $\phi(\omega_a, \omega_b) := \sum_{k=a,b} \phi_k(\omega_k, \omega_{-k})$, and consider the function $\Phi(\omega_a, \omega_b)$ defined by

$$\Phi(\omega_a, \omega_b) := \frac{\phi(\omega_a, \omega_b) - \phi(\underline{\omega}_a, \omega_b) - \phi(\omega_a, \underline{\omega}_b) + \phi(\underline{\omega}_a, \underline{\omega}_b)}{\phi(\bar{\omega}_a, \bar{\omega}_b) - \phi(\underline{\omega}_a, \bar{\omega}_b) - \phi(\bar{\omega}_a, \underline{\omega}_b) + \phi(\underline{\omega}_a, \underline{\omega}_b)}$$

for all $(\omega_a, \omega_b) \in \Omega$. Because ϕ is supermodular, Φ is a cdf with support Ω. Obviously,

$$\Phi(\omega_a, \omega_b) = \int_\Omega \phi^{\alpha,\beta}(\omega_a, \omega_b) d\Phi(\alpha, \beta).$$

Now consider the objective function

$$\tilde{W}(\mathbf{F}) := \int_\Omega \Phi(\omega_a, \omega_b) d\mathbf{F}(\omega_a, \omega_b) = \int_\Omega \int_\Omega \phi^{\alpha,\beta}(\omega_a, \omega_b) d\mathbf{F}(\omega_a, \omega_b) d\Phi(\alpha, \beta),$$

where the equality follows from Fubini's theorem. From the arguments above, among all joint cdfs that couple F_a and F_b, the one that maximizes the integral $\int_\Omega \phi^{\alpha,\beta}(\omega_a, \omega_b) d\mathbf{F}(\omega_a, \omega_b)$ is the cdf $\mathbf{F}^*$ that renders ω_a and ω_b co-monotonic random variables. Because this is true for all $(\alpha, \beta) \in \Omega$, we conclude that $\tilde{W}(\mathbf{F})$ is maximized by $\mathbf{F}^*$. Because Φ has the form $\Phi(\omega_a, \omega_b) = \delta\phi(\omega_a, \omega_b) + \sum_k \gamma_k \varphi_k(\omega_k) + K$, where δ, γ_a, γ_b, and K are constants, and where each function $\varphi_k(\omega_k)$ is invariant in ω_{-k}, it is then easy to see that, when $c = 0$, $\mathbf{F}^*$ also maximizes $\hat{W}(\mathbf{F}; \Omega_a, \Omega_b)$ over all joint cdfs $\mathbf{F}$ that couple the marginals F_a and F_b. We conclude that the untruncated positive assortative matching rule is optimal when $c = 0$.

Next consider the case for which $c > 0$. Because each $\phi_k(\omega_a, \omega_b)$ is strictly increasing in both arguments, it is easy to see that the welfare-maximizing participation sets $\hat{\Omega}_k^e$ have the form $\hat{\Omega}_k^e = [\hat{\omega}_k^e, \bar{\omega}_k]$ for some $\hat{\omega}_k^e \geq \underline{\omega}_k$, $k = a, b$. Because it is never efficient to match any pair of types $(\omega_a, \omega_b) \in \Omega$ for which $\sum_k \phi_k(\omega_a, \omega_b) - c < 0$, we then conclude that the welfare-maximizing participation thresholds $\hat{\omega}_a^e$ and $\hat{\omega}_b^e$ satisfy (23.17). Applying the arguments above to the truncated marginals $|\hat{\Omega}_a^e|^{-1} F_a$ and $|\hat{\Omega}_b^e|^{-1} F_b$ then yields the result that the function $\hat{W}(\mathbf{F}; \hat{\Omega}_a, \hat{\Omega}_b)$ is maximized by the truncated positive assortative rule with participation sets $(\hat{\Omega}_a^e, \hat{\Omega}_b^e)$.

The next lemma establishes the implementability of truncated positive assortative rules.

Lemma 23.12. *Let $\{s_k(\cdot)\}_{k=a,b}$ be a truncated positive assortative matching rule. Then $\{s_k(\cdot)\}_{k=a,b}$ can be implemented by the following payment rule:*

$$p_k(\omega_k) = \phi_k(\omega_k, s_k(\omega_k)) - \int_{\hat{\omega}_k}^{\omega_k} \frac{\partial \phi_k}{\partial \omega_k}(\tilde{\omega}_k, s_k(\tilde{\omega}_k)) d\tilde{\omega}_k,$$

for all $\omega_k \in \Omega_k$, $k = a, b$.

Proof. Consider the mechanism defined by the matching rule $\{s_k(\cdot)\}_{k=a,b}$ along with the payment rule $\{\mathbf{p}_k(\cdot)\}_{k=a,b}$ in the lemma. Each agent with type ω_k then chooses a report ω'_k to maximize

$$\phi_k(\omega_k, s_k(\omega'_k)) - \phi_k(\omega'_k, s_k(\omega'_k)) + \int_{\hat{\omega}_k}^{\omega'_k} \frac{\partial \phi_k}{\partial \omega_k}(\tilde{\omega}_k, s_k(\tilde{\omega}_k)) d\tilde{\omega}_k.$$

Because $s_k(\cdot)$ is monotone and ϕ_k is supermodular, it is then easy to see that truthful reporting uniquely maximizes the agent's payoff. $\quad\square$

The result in the proposition then follows from the arguments above along with Lemma 23.12. $\quad\square$

It is easy to verify that the efficient rule in Proposition 23.11 is essentially unique (that is, up to zero-measure perturbations). This implies that random matching is never optimal if the total match surplus ϕ is supermodular.

23.5.1.2 Profit-Maximizing Matching Design

Having derived the efficient one-to-one matching rule (Proposition 23.11), we now turn to its profit-maximizing counterpart. The platform's profit under any incentive compatible mechanism $\{s_k(\cdot), \mathbf{p}_k(\cdot)\}_{k=a,b}$ is equal to

$$\Pi := \sum_{k=a,b} \int_{\hat{\Omega}_k} \mathbf{p}_k(\omega_k) dF_k(\omega_k) - c|\hat{\Omega}_a|.$$

The next lemma expresses the platform's profit solely in terms of the endogenous joint distribution $\mathbf{F}$ induced by the matching rule $\{s_k(\cdot)\}_{k=a,b}$.

Lemma 23.13. *Suppose that $\{s_k(\cdot)\}_{k=a,b}$ is an implementable matching rule with participation sets $\hat{\Omega}_k = [\hat{\omega}_k, \overline{\omega}_k]$, $\hat{\omega}_k \in \Omega_k$, $k = a, b$, and let $\mathbf{F}$ be the endogenous joint distribution over $\hat{\Omega}_a \times \hat{\Omega}_b$ induced by $\{s_k(\cdot)\}_{k=a,b}$. The platform's maximal profit under such a rule is given by*

$$\Pi(\mathbf{F}; \hat{\Omega}_a, \hat{\Omega}_b) = |\hat{\Omega}_a| \int_{\hat{\Omega}_a \times \hat{\Omega}_b} \left(\widehat{\phi}_a(\omega_a, \omega_b) + \widehat{\phi}_b(\omega_b, \omega_a) - c \right) d\mathbf{F}(\omega_a, \omega_b),$$

where

$$\widehat{\phi}_k(\omega_k, \omega_{-k}) := \phi_k(\omega_k, \omega_{-k}) - \left(\frac{1 - F_k(\omega_k)}{f_k(\omega_k)} \right) \frac{\partial \phi_k}{\partial \omega_k}(\omega_k, \omega_{-k})$$

is the side-k virtual match surplus, $k = a, b$.

Proof Let $\{\mathbf{p}_k(\cdot)\}_{k=a,b}$ be any payment rule implementing $\{s_k(\cdot)\}_{k=a,b}$ and let $M = \{s_k(\cdot), \mathbf{p}_k(\cdot)\}_{k=a,b}$ be the mechanism defined by $\{s_k(\cdot)\}_{k=a,b}$ and $\{\mathbf{p}_k(\cdot)\}_{k=a,b}$. For any participating type $\omega_k \in \hat{\Omega}_k$, the equilibrium payoff (that is, the payoff under truth-telling) is equal to

$$U_k(\omega_k; M) = \int_{\hat{\Omega}_{-k}} \phi_k(\omega_k, \omega_{-k}) dG_{s_k}(\omega_{-k}|\omega_k) - \mathbf{p}_k(\omega_k).$$

The envelope theorem implies that

$$U_k(\omega_k; M) = U_k(\hat{\omega}_k; M) + \int_{\hat{\omega}_k}^{\omega_k} \int_{\hat{\Omega}_{-k}} \frac{\partial \phi_k}{\partial \omega_k}(\tilde{\omega}_k, \omega_{-k}) dG_{s_k}(\omega_{-k}|\omega_k) d\tilde{\omega}_k.$$

Hence,

$$
\mathbf{p}_k(\omega_k) = \int_{\hat{\Omega}_{-k}} \phi_k(\omega_k, \omega_{-k}) dG_{\mathbf{s}_k}(\omega_{-k}|\omega_k)
$$
$$
- \int_{\hat{\omega}_k}^{\omega_k} \int_{\hat{\Omega}_{-k}} \frac{\partial \phi_k}{\partial \omega_k}(\tilde{\omega}_k, \omega_{-k}) dG_{\mathbf{s}_k}(\omega_{-k}|\omega_k) d\tilde{\omega}_k - U_k(\hat{\omega}_k; M).
$$

Substituting the above expression into the profit function Π and integrating by parts we have that

$$
\Pi = \sum_k \int_{\hat{\Omega}_k} \int_{\hat{\Omega}_{-k}} \left(\phi_k(\omega_k, \omega_{-k}) - \left(\frac{1 - F_k(\omega_k)}{f_k(\omega_k)} \right) \frac{\partial \phi_k}{\partial \omega_k}(\omega_k, \omega_{-k}) \right)
$$
$$
\times \, dG_{\mathbf{s}_k}(\omega_{-k}|\omega_k) dF_k(\omega_k) - \sum_k |\hat{\Omega}_k| U_k(\hat{\omega}_k; M) - c|\hat{\Omega}_a|. \tag{23.18}
$$

Clearly, any profit-maximizing transfer scheme implementing the matching rule $\{\mathbf{s}_k(\cdot)\}_{k=a,b}$ must satisfy $U_k(\hat{\omega}_k; M) = 0$, $k = a, b$. Feasibility requires that $dG_{\mathbf{s}_k}(\omega_{-k}|\omega_k) dF_k(\omega_k) = |\hat{\Omega}_k| d\mathbf{F}(\omega_k, \omega_{-k})$. Combining the above properties then yields the result. $\qquad\square$

Next, observe that, in any incentive compatible mechanism M, if $\mathbf{s}_k(\omega_k) \neq \emptyset$ then necessarily $\mathbf{s}_k(\omega_k') \neq \emptyset$ for all $\omega_k' > \omega_k$, $k = a, b$. Hence, under any profit-maximizing mechanism, the participating set on each side has the interval structure $\hat{\Omega}_k = [\hat{\omega}_k, \overline{\omega}_k]$, for some $\hat{\omega}_k \in \Omega_k$. In light of this observation and the result in Lemma 23.13, we have that the problem of a profit-maximizing platform is identical to that of a welfare-maximizing platform, after one replaces the match surplus function by its virtual counterpart. Accordingly, the next result follows from Proposition 23.11.

Proposition 23.14. *Consider a profit-maximizing platform designing one-to-one matches, and let the agents' preferences be given by (23.16). Suppose that, for each $k \in \{a, b\}$, the virtual match surplus function $\widehat{\phi}_k(\omega_k, \omega_{-k})$ is supermodular. Then, the profit-maximizing matching rule is a truncated positive assortative rule with participation thresholds $(\hat{\omega}_a^*, \hat{\omega}_b^*)$ satisfying $\hat{\omega}_b^* = F_b^{-1}(F_a(\hat{\omega}_a^*))$ and*

$$
\widehat{\phi}_a(\hat{\omega}_a^*, \hat{\omega}_b^*) + \widehat{\phi}_b(\hat{\omega}_a^*, \hat{\omega}_b^*) = c.
$$

Hence, when the virtual match surplus functions $\widehat{\phi}_k$ satisfy the same properties as their primitive counterparts ϕ_k, $k = a, b$, the matching partner of any participating agent is the same as under welfare maximization. Profit maximization, however, introduces extensive-margin distortions, in that it excludes an inefficiently large set of agents from both sides.

How strong is the requirement that virtual match surpluses are supermodular? For an illustration, suppose that $\phi_k(\omega_k, \omega_{-k}) = \omega_k \omega_{-k}$. Then $\widehat{\phi}_k(\omega_k, \omega_{-k})$ being supermodular is equivalent to the usual regularity condition from mechanism design requiring that the virtual values

$$
\omega_k - \left(\frac{1 - F_k(\omega_k)}{f_k(\omega_k)} \right)
$$

are strictly increasing. For other match value functions, this supermodularity condition is harder to satisfy. When the condition is not satisfied, profit-maximization, in addition to excluding too many agents, leads to inefficient matching of the participating agents.[5]

23.5.2 Many-to-Many Matching Design

Now suppose that the platform can engage in many-to-many matching, therefore customizing the matching set that each agent receives. Formally, $\mathcal{C}(\Omega_{-k})$ is now the collection of all (measurable) subsets of Ω_{-k}. As in the previous subsection, continue to denote each agent's type by the unidimensional characteristics $\omega_k \in \Omega_k := [\underline{\omega}_k, \overline{\omega}_k] \subseteq \mathbb{R}$ but now allow the latter to take on negative values. An agent's type continues to parameterize both the agent's preferences and the utility she brings to agents from the other side. In particular, let $\sigma_k(\omega_k) \in \mathbb{R}_+$ denote the "salience" (prominence) of each agent from side k with type ω_k. Such salience contributes positively to the utility of those agents from side $-k$ who like interacting with the side-k agents and negatively to those who dislike it. To make things simple, assume that the absolutely continuous distribution F_k (with density f_k) from which each ω_k is drawn is "regular," meaning that the function $\omega_k - [1 - F_k(\omega_k)]/f_k(\omega_k)$ is non-decreasing.

Next, assume that the gross payoff $u_k(\mathbf{s}|\omega_k)$ that an agent from side k obtains by interacting with a set of types $\mathbf{s} \in \mathcal{C}(\Omega_{-k})$ from the opposite side takes the form

$$u_k(\mathbf{s}|\omega_k) = \omega_k g_k\left(|\mathbf{s}|_{-k}\right), \tag{23.19}$$

where $g_k(\cdot)$ is a positive, strictly increasing, and continuously differentiable function satisfying $g_k(0) = 0$, and where

$$|\mathbf{s}|_{-k} := \int_{\omega_{-k} \in \mathbf{s}} \sigma_{-k}(\omega_{-k}) dF_{-k}(\omega_{-k}) \tag{23.20}$$

is the aggregate *salience* of the set $\mathbf{s}$.

An agent from side k with a negative ω_k is thus one who dislikes interacting with agents from the opposite side. To avoid trivial cases, assume that $\overline{\omega}_k > 0$ for some $k \in \{a, b\}$. The functions $g_k(\cdot)$, $k = a, b$, capture increasing (alternatively, decreasing) marginal utility (alternatively, disutility) for the matching intensity.

Finally, assume that all costs are equal to zero, so as to simplify the analysis. Following standard arguments from mechanism design, it is easy to verify that a mechanism M is individually rational and incentive compatible *if and only if* the following conditions jointly hold for each side $k = a, b$:[6]

(i) the matching intensity of the set $\mathbf{s}_k(\omega_k)$ is non-decreasing;
(ii) the payoff $U_k(\omega_k; M)$ of those agents with the lowest type is non-negative;
(iii) the pricing rule satisfies the envelope formula

$$\mathbf{p}_k(\omega_k) = \omega_k g_k\left(|\mathbf{s}_k(\omega_k)|_l\right) - \int_{\underline{\omega}_k}^{\omega_k} g_k\left(|\mathbf{s}_k(x)|_{-k}\right) dx - U_k(\underline{\omega}_k; M). \tag{23.21}$$

---

[5] Indeed, it can be easily shown that the converse to Proposition 23.14 is true; namely, that positive assortative matching is optimal only if the total virtual match surplus is supermodular.

[6] See also Example 23.1.

It is also easy to see that, in any mechanism that maximizes the platform's profit, the IR constraints of those agents with the lowest types bind, that is, $U_k(\underline{v}_k; M) = 0$, $k = a, b$. As already shown above, the problem of maximizing the platform's profit is then analogous to that of maximizing welfare in a fictitious environment in which the agents' types are equal to their virtual analogues. To economize on notation, for any $k = a, b$ and for any $\omega_k \in \Omega_k$, let $\varphi_k^W(\omega_k) := \omega_k$ and $\varphi_k^P(\omega_k) := \omega_k - [1 - F_k(\omega_k)]/f_k(\omega_k)$. The platform's problem thus consists in finding a pair of matching rules $\{s_k(\cdot)\}_{k=a,b}$ that maximize

$$\sum_{k=a,a} \int_{\Omega_k} \varphi_k^h(\omega_k) g_k \left(|s_k(\omega_k)|_l\right) dF_k(\omega_k) \tag{23.22}$$

among all rules that satisfy the above monotonicity constraint (i) and the reciprocity condition (23.1). Hereafter, we will say that a matching rule $\{s_k^h(\cdot)\}_{k=a,b}$ is h-optimal if it solves the above h-problem, with the understanding that when $h = W$ this means that the rule is efficient, that is, welfare-maximizing, whereas when $h = P$ the rule is profit-maximizing.

For future reference, for $h = W, P$, we also define the *reservation value* $r_k^h :=$ $\inf\{\omega_k \in \Omega_k : \varphi_k^h(\omega_k) \geq 0\}$ when $\{\omega_k \in \Omega_k : \varphi_k^h(\omega_k) \geq 0\} \neq \emptyset$.

23.5.2.1 Threshold Rules

Definition 23.15. A matching rule is a *threshold rule* if there exists a pair of weakly decreasing functions $t_k: \Omega_k \to \Omega_{-k} \cup \{\emptyset\}$ along with threshold types $\hat{\omega}_k \in \Omega_k$ such that, for any $\omega_k \in \Omega_k$, $k = a, b$,

$$s_k(w_k) = \begin{cases} [t_k(\omega_k), \overline{\omega}_{-k}] & \text{if } \omega_k \geq \hat{\omega}_k, \\ \emptyset & \text{otherwise,} \end{cases}$$

and, for any $\omega_k \in [\hat{\omega}_k, \overline{\omega}_k]$,

$$t_k(\omega_k) = \min\{\omega_{-k} : t_{-k}(\omega_{-k}) \leq \omega_k\}. \tag{23.23}$$

The interpretation is that any type below $\hat{\omega}_k$ is excluded, while a type $\omega_k > \hat{\omega}_k$ is matched to any agent from the other side whose type is above the threshold $t_k(\omega_k)$. To satisfy the reciprocity condition (23.1), the threshold functions $\{t_k(\cdot)\}_{k=a,b}$ have to satisfy the property (23.23).

Note that threshold rules are always implementable because the matching intensity is non-decreasing under such rules. However, many other implementable matching rules do not have a threshold structure.

Proposition 23.16. *Assume that one of the following two sets of conditions holds:*

1. *the functions $g_k(\cdot)$ are weakly concave, and the functions $\sigma_k(\cdot)$ are weakly increasing, for both $k = a, b$;*
2. *the functions $g_k(\cdot)$ are weakly convex, and the functions $\sigma_k(\cdot)$ are weakly decreasing, for both $k = a, b$.*

Then both the profit-maximizing and the welfare-maximizing matching rules are threshold rules.

Proof sketch. Consider an agent for whom $\varphi_k^h(\omega_k) \geq 0$. Ignoring the monotonicity constraints, it is easy to see that it is always optimal to assign to this agent a matching set that includes all agents from the other side whose φ_l^h-value is non-negative. The reason is that these latter agents (i) contribute positively to type ω_k's payoff and (ii) have non-negative φ_l^h-values, which implies that adding type ω_k to the latter agents' matching sets (as required by reciprocity) never reduces the platform's payoff.

Next, consider an agent for whom $\varphi_k^h(\omega_k) < 0$. It is also easy to see that it is never optimal to assign to this agent a matching set that contains agents from the opposite side whose φ_{-k}^h-values are also negative. This is so because matching two agents with negative h-valuations decreases the platform's payoff.

Now suppose that $g_k(\cdot)$ is weakly concave and $\sigma_k(\cdot)$ is weakly increasing, on both sides. Pick an agent from side k with $\varphi_k^h(\omega_k) > 0$ and suppose that the platform wants to assign to this agent a matching set whose intensity

$$q = |\mathbf{s}|_{-k} > \int_{[r_{-k}^h, \bar{\omega}_{-k}]} \sigma_{-k}(\omega_{-k}) dF_{-k}(\omega_{-k})$$

exceeds the aggregate matching intensity of those agents from side $-k$ with non-negative φ_l^h-values (that is, for whom $\omega_l \geq r_l^h$). That $g_k(\cdot)$ is weakly concave and $\sigma_k(\cdot)$ is weakly increasing, along with the fact that types are private information, implies that the *least costly* way to deliver such a matching intensity is to match the agent to all agents from the opposite side whose $\varphi_{-k}^h(\omega_{-k})$ value is the least negative. The reason is that (i) these latter agents are the most attractive ones, and (ii) by virtue of g_{-k} being concave, using the same agents from side $-k$ with negative φ_{-k}^h-valuations *intensively* is less costly than using different agents with negative φ_l^h-valuations. Threshold rules thus *minimize the costs of cross-subsidization* by delivering to those agents who play the role of consumers (that is, whose φ_k^h-valuation is non-negative) matching sets of high quality in the most economical way.

Next, suppose that the $g_k(\cdot)$ are weakly convex, and the $\sigma_k(\cdot)$ are weakly decreasing, on both sides. The combination of the above properties with the fact that types are private information implies that the most profitable way of using any agent with type ω_k for whom $\varphi_k^h(\omega_k) < 0$ is to match him to those agents from side $-k$ with the highest positive φ_{-k}^h-valuations, the reason being that (i) these latter types are the ones that benefit the most from interacting with type[7] ω_k and (ii) they are the least salient and hence exert the lowest negative externalities on type ω_k. A threshold structure is thus optimal in this case as well. $\square$

The matching allocations induced by threshold rules are consistent with the practice followed by many media platforms (e.g., newspapers) of exposing all readers to premium ads (displayed in all versions of the newspaper) but only those readers with a high tolerance to advertising to discount ads (displayed only in the tabloid or printed version).

---

[7] Indeed such types have matching sets with the highest matching intensity – as required by incentive compatibility – and, because of the convexity of $g_{-k}(\cdot)$, the highest marginal utility for meeting additional agents.

23.5.2.2 *Distortions*

We conclude by discussing the distortions in the provision of matching services due to market power.

Proposition 23.17. *Assume that the conditions for the optimality of the threshold rules in Proposition 23.16 hold and that, in addition, the functions $\psi_k^h \colon \Omega_k \to \mathbb{R}$ defined by*

$$\psi_k^h(\omega_k) := \frac{\varphi_k^h(\omega_k)}{g'_{-k}\left(\|[\omega_k, \bar{\omega}_k]\|_k\right) \cdot \sigma_k(\omega_k)}$$

are strictly increasing, $k = a, b$, $h = W, P$. Then, relative to the welfare-maximizing rule, the profit-maximizing rule (i) completely excludes a larger group of agents, that is, $\hat{\omega}_k^P \geq \hat{\omega}_k^W$, $k = a, b$, and (ii) matches each agent who is not excluded to a subset of his efficient matching set, that is, $\mathbf{s}_k^P(\omega_k) \subseteq \mathbf{s}_k^W(\omega_k)$, for all $\omega_k \geq \hat{\omega}_k^P$, $k = a, b$.

Proof sketch. Let $\hat{g}_k \colon \Omega_{-k} \to \mathbb{R}_+$ be the function defined by

$$\hat{g}_k(\omega_{-k}) := g_k\left(\left\|[\omega_{-k}, \bar{\omega}_{-k}]\right\|_{-k}\right) = g_k\left(\int_{\omega_{-k}}^{\overline{\omega}_{-k}} \sigma_{-k}(x)dF_{-k}(x)\right),$$

$k = a, b$. The utility that an agent with type ω_k obtains under a threshold rule from the matching set $[t_k(\omega_k), \overline{\omega}_{-k}]$ is then equal to $\omega_k \hat{g}_k\left(t_k(\omega_k)\right)$. Then let $\triangle_k^h \colon \Omega_k \times \Omega_{-k} \to \mathbb{R}$ be the function defined by

$$\triangle_k^h(\omega_k, \omega_{-k}) := -\hat{g}'_k(\omega_{-k})\varphi_k^h(\omega_k)f_k(\omega_k) - \hat{g}'_{-l}(\omega_k)\varphi_{-k}^h(\omega_{-k})f_{-k}(\omega_{-k}), \qquad (23.24)$$

for $k = a, b$. Note that $\triangle_a^h(\omega_a, \omega_b) = \triangle_b^h(\omega_b, \omega_a)$ represents the marginal effect on the platform's h-objective of decreasing the threshold $t_k^h(\omega_k)$ below ω_{-k} while also reducing the threshold $t_{-k}^h(\omega_{-k})$ below ω_k by reciprocity. One can then show that, under the conditions in the proposition, when $\triangle_k^h(\underline{\omega}_k, \underline{\omega}_{-k}) \geq 0$, the h-optimal matching rule is such that $\mathbf{s}_k^h(\omega_k) = \Omega_l$ for all $\omega_k \in \Omega_k$, $k = a, b$.[8] In this case, the platform induces all agents to get on board from either side of the market. When, instead, $\triangle_k^h(\underline{\omega}_k, \underline{\omega}_{-k}) < 0$, the h-optimal matching rule has the following structure: (a) If $\triangle_k^h(\bar{\omega}_k, \underline{\omega}_{-k}) > 0$, the optimal rule induces bunching at the top on side k and no exclusion at the bottom on side $-k$ (that is, $\hat{\omega}_{-k} = \underline{\omega}_{-k}$, with $t_{-k}^h(\underline{\omega}_{-k})$ given by the unique solution to $\triangle_k^h(t_{-k}^h(\underline{\omega}_{-k}), \underline{\omega}_{-k}) = 0$); (b) If $\triangle_k^h(\bar{\omega}_k, \underline{\omega}_{-k}) < 0$, the optimal policy induces exclusion at the bottom on side $-k$ and no bunching at the top of side k ($\hat{\omega}_{-k} = t_k^h(\bar{\omega}_k)$, with $t_k^h(\bar{\omega}_k)$ given by the unique solution to $\triangle_k^h(\bar{\omega}_k, t_k^h(\bar{\omega}_k)) = 0$). Intuitively, wherever possible, the platform balances the marginal gains of expanding the matching set of each agent with the corresponding marginal cost, taking into

---

[8] Equivalently, $t_k^h(\omega_k) = \underline{\omega}_{-k}$, for all $\omega_k \in \Omega_k$, $k = a, b$.

account the constraint imposed by reciprocity and the optimality of using a threshold structure.[9] The results in the proposition then follow from the above properties along with the fact that $\varphi_k^P(\omega_k) \leq \varphi_k^W(\omega_k)$ for all $\omega_k \in \Omega_k$, $k = a, b$. ☐

The role of the extra condition in the proposition is to guarantee that, under the h-optimal rule, bunching occurs only at the bottom of the distribution, where it takes the form of exclusion ($\mathbf{s}_k^h(\omega_k) = \emptyset$ for all $\omega_k < \hat{\omega}_k^h$), or at the very top of the distribution, where agents are matched to all agents on board from the other side of the market (that is, $\mathbf{s}_k^h(\omega_k) = [\hat{\omega}_{-k}^h, \bar{\omega}_k]$ for all $\omega_k > t_{-k}(\hat{\omega}_{-k}^h)$).[10] To interpret the condition, take the case of profit maximization, $h = P$. The numerator in $\psi_k^h(\omega_k)$ is the agent's "virtual type". This term captures the effect on the platform's profit of expanding the intensity of the matching set of each side-k individual with type ω_k, taking into account that this expansion requires increasing the rents of all side-k agents with higher types. In other words, it captures the marginal value of a type-ω_k agent as a *consumer*. The denominator, however, captures the effect on the platform's profit of adding such an agent to the matching set of any agent from the opposite side whose matching set is $[\omega_k, \bar{\omega}_k]$ (that is, whose threshold $t_{-k}^h(\omega_{-k}) = \omega_k$). In other words, it captures the marginal value of a type-ω_k agent as an *input*, under a threshold rule. The condition then requires that the contribution of an agent as a consumer increases faster than his contribution as an input.

The intuition for the result in the proposition is the following. Under profit maximization, the platform internalizes only the effects of cross-subsidization on marginal revenues (which are proportional to the virtual valuations), rather than their effects on welfare (which are proportional to the true valuations). Contrary to other mechanism design problems, inefficiencies do not necessarily vanish as agents' types approach the "top" of the distribution (that is, the highest valuation of the matching intensity). The reason is that, although virtual valuations converge to the true valuations as agents' types approach the top of the distribution, the cost of cross-subsidizing these types remains strictly higher under profit maximization than under welfare maximization, owing to the infra-marginal losses implied by reciprocity on the opposite side.

23.6 Conclusions

The organization of the chapter reflects, to a large extent, the evolution of many platform markets from a format where all agents on board are matched to all participating agents from the opposite side of the market (the case considered in most of the earlier literature) to one where platforms engage in more sophisticated design, matching participating agents in a customized manner. Strong market power in such

---

[9] The formal proof is tedious and requires adapting some calculus-of-variation results to the non-standard reciprocity constraint given by (23.23). However, the intuition is fairly straight-forward and is well captured by the property of the marginal net benefit function Δ_k^h above.

[10] Note that the condition is equivalent to the property that the marginal benefit function Δ_k^h satisfies the following single-crossing property: whenever $\Delta_k^h(\omega_k, \omega_{-k}) \geq 0$, then $\Delta_k^h(\omega_k, \omega'_{-k}) > 0$ for all $\omega'_{-k} > \omega_{-k}$ and $\Delta_k^h(\omega'_k, \omega_{-k}) > 0$ for all $\omega'_k > \omega_k$. This single-crossing property guarantees that, whenever the Euler condition $\Delta_k^h(\omega_k, t_k^h(\omega_k)) = 0$ admits an interior solution $\underline{\omega}_{-k} < t_k^h(\omega_k) < \bar{\omega}_{-k}$, the threshold $t_k^h(\omega_k)$ is strictly decreasing. The condition in the proposition is the "weakest" regularity condition that rules out non-monotonicities (or bunching) in the matching rule.

markets may result in the complete exclusion of many agents from either side of the market, and/or to inefficient matching whereby those agents on board are either matched to the wrong partners (in the case of one-to-one matching) or to a subset of their efficient matching set (in the case of many-to-many matching). Such distortions call for regulation and government interventions, an area that is receiving growing attention in recent years.

The analysis in this chapter has confined attention to markets dominated by a single platform. An important part of the literature studies competition between platforms in multi-sided markets, both in the case in which agents can multi-home (that is, join multiple platforms) and in the case where they single-home (that is, join at most one platform). Another area that has started receiving attention recently is that of dynamics, whereby agents strategically time their joining of the platform, experience shocks to their preferences over time, and learn the attractiveness of potential partners by interacting with them. The literature is also now considering richer specifications of the agents' preferences by allowing for different combinations of *vertical and horizontal* differentiation that permit one to investigate the effects of targeting, a form of third-degree price discrimination often encountered in mediated matching markets. Finally, in recent work, matching markets have been studied where agents are asked to submit match-specific bids and where the selection of the matches is done through auctions that use match-specific scores to control for the agents' prominence in the market, a practice employed by many ad-exchanges and sponsored-search engines.

23.7 Bibliographical Notes

Section 23.3 is based on [18], [1], [19], [22], and [20]. In particular, we considered three scenarios regarding agents' preferences: Scenario 1 is was studied in [1], Scenario 2 was studied in [18], and Scenario 3 was studied in [19] and [22]. Section 23.4 is based on [16]. Section 19.5 is based on [8], [15], [11], and [12].

The literature on competing platforms mentioned in Section 23.6 is very broad. See [6], [7], [1], [19], and [2] for earlier contributions and [21] for recent developments. See also [4] and [17] for overviews of this literature.

The literature on platform pricing in dynamic settings mentioned in Section 23.6 includes [14] and [5]. The case where agents learn about the attractiveness of potential partners over time and submit bids for specific interactions, mentioned in Section 23.6 was examined in [9] and [10]. The case where platforms practice a combination of second- and third-degree price discrimination, also mentioned in Section 23.6, is examined in [3] and [13].

References

[1] Armstrong, M. 2006. Competition in two-sided markets. *Rand Journal of Economics*, **37**(3), 668–691.

[2] Armstrong, M., and Wright, J. 2007. Two-sided markets, competitive bottlenecks and exclusive contracts. *Economic Theory*, **32**(2), 353–380.

[3] Belleflamme, P., and Peitz, M. 2020. Network goods, price discrimination, and two-sided platforms. Mimeo, University of Bonn and University of Mannheim.

[4] Belleflamme, P., and Peitz M., 2021. *The Economics of Platforms: Concepts and Strategy*. Cambridge University Press.

[5] Biglaiser, G., and Crémer J., 2020. The value of incumbency in heterogeneous platforms. *American Economic Journal: Micro*, **12**(4), 229–269.

[6] Caillaud, B., and Jullien B., 2001. Competing cybermediaries. *European Economic Review*, **45**(4–6), 797–808.

[7] Caillaud, B., and Jullien B., 2003. Chicken & egg: Competition among intermediation service providers. *Rand Journal of Economics*, **34**(2), 309–328.

[8] Damiano, E. and Li H., 2007. Price discrimination and efficient matching. *Economic Theory*, **30**, 243–263.

[9] Fershtman, D., and Pavan A., 2017. Pandora's auctions: Dynamic matching with unknown preferences. *American Economic Review*, **107**(5) 186–190.

[10] Fershtman, D., and Pavan A., 2020. Matching auctions. *Rand Journal of Economics*, **53**(1), 32–62.

[11] Galichon, A., 2016. *Optimal Transport Methods in Economics*. Princeton University Press.

[12] Gomes, R., and Pavan A., 2016. Many-to-many matching and price discrimination. *Theoretical Economics*, **11**, 1005–1052.

[13] Gomes, R., and Pavan A., 2020. Price customization and targeting in matching markets. *Rand Journal of Economics*, forthcoming.

[14] Halaburda, H., Jullien, B., and Yehezkel Y., 2020. Dynamic competition with network effects: Why history matters. *Rand Journal of Economics*, **51**(1), 3–31.

[15] Johnson, T., 2013. Matching through position auctions. *Journal of Economic Theory*, **148**, 1700–1713.

[16] Jullien, B., and Pavan A., 2019. Information management and pricing in platform markets. *Review of Economic Studies*, **86**(4), 1666–1703.

[17] Jullien, B., Pavan, A., and Rysman M., 2021. Two-sided markets and network effects. *Handbook of Industrial Organization*, forthcoming.

[18] Rochet, J. C., and Tirole J., 2003. Platform competition in two-sided markets. *Journal of the European Economic Association*, **33**(4), 549–570.

[19] Rochet, J. C., and Tirole J., 2006. Two-sided markets: A progress report. *Rand Journal of Economics*, **37**(3), 645–667.

[20] Tan, H., and Wright J., 2018. A price theory of multi-sided platforms: Comment. *American Economic Review*, **108**(9), 2761–2762.

[21] Tan, G., and Zhou J., 2021. Price competition in multi-sided markets. *Review of Economic Studies*, **88**(2), 1002–1030.

[22] Weyl, G., 2010. A price theory of two-sided markets. *American Economic Review*, **100**(4), 1642–1672.

PART FOUR

Empirics

CHAPTER TWENTY-FOUR

Matching Market Experiments

Yan Chen

24.1 Introduction

Since the 1990s, economic research has played an increasingly important role in the practical organization and design of markets. In many of the successful cases of market design, such as labor market clearinghouses, formal procedures for student assignment to public schools, centralized systems for the allocation of courses, theoretical and experimental research have complemented each other and influenced the design of market institutions. In this chapter, I will survey a number of experimental methods used in matching market experiments, starting with laboratory experiments, where the experimenter has the most control over the environment, followed by lab-in-the-field experiments, and ending with field experiments. Before separately examining each of the three types of experiments, I briefly mention some common features of these experiments and experimental research.

Common to all three types of experiments is the *random assignment* of individuals or groups of individuals to the treatment and control conditions. Random assignment generates statistically equivalent samples and ensures that "treatment" status (concerning the aspect of an experiment that the researcher wants to understand causally) is not correlated with any unobservable factor that can affect the outcomes of interest.

After researchers finalize their experiment design, they should *pre-register* their experiment design, sample size calculation, hypotheses, and data analysis plan before data collection starts. Pre-registration increases the credibility of the results and improves the transparency of the research process. Furthermore, it helps a researcher to clearly report the study and helps others who may wish to build on it. Note that pre-registration does not preclude researchers from exploratory analysis. Rather, a researcher can report pre-registered and exploratory analysis in separate sections of their paper.

Lastly, an increasing number of top journals in economics and management require authors to deposit data, analysis code, and experimental instructions with a community-recognized or general repository; this facilitates both exact replications and robustness checks.[1] For the purpose of replication, I encourage authors to keep a meticulous record of their data, metadata, and analysis code.

---

[1] For example, the American Economic Association journals require authors to deposit data and materials with the AEA Data and Code Repository at Open ICPSR: www.openicpsr.org/openicpsr/aea.

24.2 Laboratory Experiments

A *laboratory experiment* is an investigation of a set of hypotheses in a laboratory, where the system under study is under the *control* of the experimenter. This means that the subject pool, the nature of the experimental treatments under study, the randomization method, and the measurement procedures used are all determined by the experimenter. A typical laboratory experiment employs a standard subject pool of students, an abstract framing, and an imposed set of rules. An increasing number of laboratory experiments are conducted online, using online labor market participants, on platforms designed for behavioral experimentation, such as Amazon's Mechanical Turk, Dynata (formerly known as Research Now), LabintheWild, Prolific, and YouGov. I consider experiments conducted on these platforms as laboratory experiments.

Economists use laboratory experiments for three purposes: to test theory, to influence policymakers, and to discover robust behavioral regularities about which existing theory has little to say. In the process of bringing a theoretical idea or result to practice, the research strategy is often to observe the performance of the new market design in the context of the simple environments that can be created in a laboratory and to assess its performance relative to what it is intended to do and relative to the theory upon which its creation rests. For this reason, laboratory experiments are often compared to wind tunnel aerodynamic testing. Another advantage of laboratory experiments is that they can provide behavioral data at a level of detail unavailable in the field.

24.2.1 Induced-Value Method

Since the economic theories under test rely heavily on individual maximization of utility, experimental economists use the technique of *induced preferences* to design laboratory experiments, which is based on the induced-value theory formalized by Vernon Smith.

We define a microeconomic system $S = (e, I)$, consisting of an environment, e, and an institution, I. The environment is characterized by a collection of vectors $e = (e^1, \ldots, e^N)$, where $e^i = (u^i, T^i, \omega^i)$ represents an agent's privately known utility function u^i, technology endowment T^i, and commodity endowment ω^i. The institution, $I^i = (M^i, h^i(m), c^i(m), g^i(t_0, t, T))$, is a collection of the set of messages that the agent can send (M^i), the allocation rules ($h^i(m)$), cost imputation rules ($c^i(m)$), and, potentially, adjustment process rules ($g^i(t_0, t, T)$) for the agent. Within the microeconomic system, agents choose messages (or actions) based on a function of their characteristics, and the institutions determine the allocations for each agent based on those messages.

The purpose of laboratory experiments in economics is to control the elements of the microeconomic system defined above, while observing agents' messages (or actions) and the resulting outcomes. The key idea in induced-value theory is that the proper use of a reward medium allows an experimenter to induce pre-specified characteristics in experimental subjects, and the subjects' innate characteristics become less relevant.

Definition 24.1 (Induced-value method). To induce subjects' pre-specified characteristics in a laboratory using a reward medium, the induced-value method specifies that three sufficient conditions must be met:

1. *Monotonicity:* participants should prefer more reward medium to less, and not become satiated. Domestic currency satisfies monotonicity, and is the most frequently used reward medium in lab experiments.
2. *Salience:* a participant receives rewards based on her actions (and those of other participants), defined by institutional rules in the experiment. For example, converting each subject's profit earned in the experiment to the domestic currency at a pre-announced rate satisfies salience, whereas a fixed payment does not, as it does not depend on the participant's actions in the lab.

   It is important that participants are informed of how their actions will be translated into outcomes by the institution and understand the process. This is specified in the experimental instructions.
3. *Dominance:* changes in participants' utility from the experiment come predominantly from the reward medium, and other influences are negligible. Experimenters can strive to satisfy dominance by neutralizing other factors. For example, participants often care about how they perform relative to others. If each subject is paid in private, it becomes difficult or impossible to know others' rewards.

In addition to satisfying these three conditions, the experimenter must make sure subjects understand the rules and how their earnings in the experiment are derived. Without this understanding, there is no reason to believe that preferences have been successfully induced. Consequently, the experimenter uses several techniques to help subjects understand the experimental environment and the institutions, including working through practice examples, answering questions in public, and using quizzes to verify comprehension. All of these communications from the experimenter to the subjects are documented in the *experimental instructions*, which should be included in the appendix of any experimental paper, and are often published on the journal website as part of the supplemental material. The experimental instructions should contain sufficient details about the experiment to enable its replication by other experimenters.

In what follows, I use a laboratory experiment on school choice as an example to demonstrate the application of the induced-value method to a matching market experiment. The experiment is designed to evaluate the performance of three school choice mechanisms, the student-proposing DA and top trading cycles (TTC), as well as the popular Boston immediate acceptance mechanism (IA). Chapter 8 formally defines and characterizes the theoretical properties of these mechanisms. Until 2005, neither of these two theoretically appealing mechanisms had been in use at any school district in the USA. By contrast, IA has been influential in practice. School districts which have used IA and its variants include Boston, Cambridge, Denver, Minneapolis, Seattle, and St. Petersburg-Tampa. Given that IA is not strategy-proof, field data that rely on stated preferences cannot adequately assess the performance of IA. Researchers turn to controlled laboratory experiments to compare the performance of these three mechanisms.

Example 24.2 (A laboratory experiment on school choice).   In [10], experimental environments were designed to capture the key aspects of the school choice problem and to simulate the complexity inherent in potential applications of the mechanisms. A 3×2 complete factorial design was implemented. Along the first dimension, the mechanisms (IA, DA and TTC) were varied; along the second dimension, the environments were varied. There was a designed environment as well as a random environment to test for robustness.

To simulate the complexity inherent in real-world applications, relatively large sessions were used. For all treatments, in each session, there are 36 students and 36 school slots (available places) across seven schools. These schools differ in size, geographic location, specialty, and quality of instruction in each specialty. Each school slot is allocated to one participant. Schools vary in their quality, specialty, and capacity, whereas students live in different school districts and thus have different priorities at various schools. Students are randomly assigned to live in the school district of one of the seven schools, in accordance with the number of slots available at each school. Two schools have three school slots, and five schools have six school slots. Students living in a school's district are given priority at that school.

In this *designed environment*, a "realistic" environment was constructed by correlating student preferences with both school proximity and quality. In this environment, two schools (A and B) are higher-quality schools, while the remaining ones are lower-quality schools. Among the two high-quality schools, A is stronger in arts and B is stronger in sciences. Similarly, there are two types of students: odd-labeled students are gifted in sciences, while even-labeled students are gifted in arts.

Each student's ranking of the schools is generated by a utility function, which depends on the school's quality, the proximity of the school, and a random factor. The utility function of each student has three components:

$$u^i(S) = u_p^i(S) + u_q^i(S) + u_r^i(S),$$

where

- $u_p^i(S)$ represents the proximity utility for student i at school S. This utility is 10 if student i lives within the walk zone of school S and zero otherwise.
- $u_q^i(S)$ represents the quality utility for student i at school S. For odd-labeled students (i.e., for students who are gifted in sciences), $u_q^i(A) = 20$, $u_q^i(B) = 40$, and $u_q^i(S) = 10$ for $S \in \{C, D, E, F, G\}$. For even-labeled students (i.e., for students who are gifted in arts), $u_q^i(A) = 40$, $u_q^i(B) = 20$, and $u_q^i(S) = 10$ for $S \in \{C, D, E, F, G\}$.
- $u_r^i(S)$ represents a random utility (uniform in the range 0–40) which captures diversity in tastes.

Based on the resulting ranking, the monetary payoff to each student is $16 for her first choice, $13 for her second choice, $11 for her third choice, $9 for her fourth choice, $7 for her fifth choice, $5 for her sixth choice, and $2 for her last choice. The payoffs between different outcomes are sufficiently dispersed that there is a monetarily salient difference ($14) between getting one's top choice and getting one's last choice.

Table 24.1 Payoff table in the designed environment [10]

Student ID	Schools						
	A	B	C	D	E	F	G
1	**13**	16	9	2	5	11	7
2	**16**	13	11	7	2	5	9
3	**11**	13	7	16	2	9	5
⋮	⋮	⋮	⋮	⋮	⋮	⋮	⋮
⋮	⋮	⋮	⋮	⋮	⋮	⋮	⋮
34	16	11	2	7	5	13	**9**
35	7	16	2	5	11	13	**9**
36	16	13	5	7	9	2	**11**

Note: Each row represents the induced preference for each type of participants (out of 36).

Table 24.1 presents the monetary payoff, i.e., the induced preferences over schools, for each participant as a result of the type of school she holds at the end of the experiment. Boldfaced numbers indicate that the participant lives within the school district of that school. For example, participant 1 lives within the school district of school A. She will be paid $13 if she holds a slot at school A at the end of the experiment, $16 if she holds a slot at school B, $9 if she holds a slot at school C, etc. Therefore, participant 1's induced preference ranking over the seven schools is $B \succ_1 A \succ_1 F \succ_1 C \succ_1 G \succ_1 E \succ_1 D$.

To check the robustness of the results with respect to changes in the environment, a *random environment* was implemented, where, for each participant, the payoff for attending each school is a distinct integer in the range 1–16, chosen without replacement. In the case where the district school has the highest payoff, the entire row is discarded for the student and a new payoff vector is constructed. Otherwise, the decision for the participant would be trivial under all three mechanisms. As participants' induced preferences are less correlated in the random environment compared with those in the designed environment, the authors of [10] characterized them by a first-choice accommodation index.

The main advantage of using two different environments is that it enables the authors to interpolate and extrapolate the experimental results to environments characterized by different levels of competitiveness, operationalized as the first-choice accommodation index.

This experiment consisted of 12 experimental sessions, two for each of the six treatments. A *between-subject design* was used, which means that each subject only participates in one of the six treatments. In each session, participants are given a payoff schedule which states how much money they would receive if they are matched with each school, based on the school's priority ranking for the individual. Participants are informed how the mechanism would determine the matches, and are asked to rank the schools.

Results show that, in both environments, the proportion of truthful preference revelation under IA is significantly lower than that under either DA or TTC, as theory predicts. This experiment also identified a pattern of preference manipulation under IA called *district school bias*, where a participant puts her district school (or safe school) into a higher position than that in the true preference order. At the aggregate level, in the designed environment it was found that DA is most efficient, followed by TTC and then IA, and in the random environment DA and IA have approximately the same efficiency, while TTC is less efficient, despite the prediction of the theory that TTC would be the most efficient.

Robustness of experimental results. Several school choice experiments have been conducted using either the same environments as [10] or different environments, testing different aspects of the same set of mechanisms. Collectively, researchers have found that:

1. Truthful preference-revelation comparisons across mechanisms (IA < {DA, TTC}) and the prevalent manipulation pattern (district school bias) have been found in subsequent studies using either identical environments [5], [15] or different environments [28].
2. The efficiency ranking across mechanisms is not robust. In [10], recombinant estimation was used to compute efficiency, with 200 recombinations per subject. When the number of recombinations per subject increases to 100,000, however, all mechanisms lead to similar efficiency levels [6].
3. The comparison between DA and TTC is sensitive to the amount of information given to the subjects, even though both mechanisms are strategy-proof. When subjects only know their own preference, DA performs better than TTC in terms of truthful preference revelation and efficiency [10]. By contrast, when subjects have complete information about others' preferences, TTC performs better than DA in both truthful preference revelation and efficiency [28], [15].
4. Regardless of the environment or information condition, DA remains the mechanism that achieves the highest proportion of stable or envy-free allocations [5], [10], [15], [22].

Impact on practice. In 2005, the Boston Public School Committee voted to replace IA with a version of DA after IA was shown to be vulnerable to strategic manipulation both theoretically and experimentally. In this case, experimental data had helped to make the case for DA in Boston's decision to switch from IA in 2005.

24.2.2 Inducing and Eliciting Beliefs

In market design experiments, the experimenter can induce beliefs in the same way that she can induce preferences, i.e., by writing the probability distribution of types into the experimental instructions. For example, in an experiment designed to study information acquisition in school choice, suppose that each market has three students, $i \in \{1, 2, 3\}$, and three schools, $s \in \{A, B, C\}$. Each school has one available slot and ranks students by a lottery. Student cardinal preferences are i.i.d. draws from the distribution in Table 24.2.

In addition to writing it down in the experimental instructions, the experimenter should ensure that subjects know that everyone in the lab shares a common prior. More fundamentally, the experimenter should strive to approach *common knowledge*

Table 24.2 Payoff table for the experiment [9]

Students	$s = A$	$s = B$	$s = C$
$i \in \{1,2,3\}$	100	10 with probability 4/5; 110 with probability 1/5	0

of the game form and rationality, which is assumed for various solution concepts in game theory. For example, in a matching market with multiple Nash equilibria, subjects need to coordinate their actions to achieve a mutually desirable outcome. Successful coordination depends crucially on their mutual understanding about each others' behavior. The necessary condition for this mutual understanding is the presence of common knowledge regarding the nature of the game. While common knowledge can affect fundamental game theory concepts, it is difficult to achieve common knowledge in the laboratory or the field. In what follows, I discuss the methods that experimentalists have used to approach common knowledge in the laboratory.

24.2.2.1 Approaching Common Knowledge: Common Information

The most commonly used method to approach common knowledge in the lab is to read common instructions publicly out loud in front of all participants, which enables subjects to infer common knowledge using the presence of *common information*. Subjects are sure that others have received the same information. This method has been advocated by the pioneers of experimental economics and adopted in the early laboratories in Arizona, Bonn, Caltech, and Pittsburgh.

The read-aloud method is sometimes adapted for specific constraints. For example, when interacting subjects are not in the same room (or the same city), the experimenter can read the instructions out loud and specifically add the following sentence in the instructions, "The other group receives the same information as you do and knows that you also get this information." Thus, the experimenter publicly announces that every subject receives identical instructions. In another method of approaching common knowledge, the subjects read their instructions in private first. Once everyone has finished reading, the experimenter then reads aloud a summary of the key points in public to create common information.

A particularly interesting variation of the read-aloud method uses video instructions, which would potentially have the benefit of being able to use the same instructions, via audio played out loud during one treatment and via headphones in another treatment to vary the presence of common information. In addition to using video instructions with audio played out loud in public, experimenters can implement an incentivized quiz and group students on the basis of whether they have passed the incentivized quiz. In one treatment, after the quiz, subjects received a screen that said "There are 10 subjects in your group. Every subject in your group correctly answered all the questions on the quiz." This is a step further towards achieving common knowledge.

In sum, when theory requires common knowledge, experimentalists use different methods to create common information, which reduces the strategic uncertainty faced by the subjects. For market design experiments where the solution concepts require common knowledge, the common information condition should be preserved in the experiment.

24.2.2.2 Eliciting Beliefs: Scoring Rules

In market design experiments, it is often desirable to elicit agents' beliefs in order to test theories or make policy recommendations. For example, eliciting beliefs in an incentive-compatible way is often useful for market design experiments on information acquisition and provision. From the large literature on belief elicitation in experimental economics, I discuss several practical techniques to elicit beliefs in an incentive-compatible manner and the problems involved in their use.

To start with, we are interested in eliciting the beliefs of an agent about a binary random variable consisting of an event and its complements, $\{A, A^c\}$. Let $p \in [0, 1]$ be a subject's true belief about the likelihood of event A, and $r \in [0, 1]$ be her reported probability. A *scoring rule*, $S_A(r)$, is a function that maps the beliefs that a subject reports about a random variable and the ex post realization of that random variable into a payoff for the subject. We now define a proper scoring rule.

Definition 24.3 (Proper scoring rule). A scoring rule for a risk-neutral decision maker is proper if and only if

$$p = \arg \max_{r \in [0,1]} pS_A(r) + (1 - p)S_{A^c}(r).$$

More generally, when there are n possible events, $i = 1, 2, \ldots, n$, and a subject reports vectors $r = (r_1, r_2, \ldots, r_n)$, the scoring rule defines a collection of scoring functions, $S = (S_1, S_2, \ldots, S_n)$, where $S_i(r)$ specifies a score when event i occurs, as a function of the forecast r. We now define two commonly used scoring rules.

The quadratic scoring rule (QSR) is defined as follows:

$$S_i(r) = \alpha - \beta \sum_{k=1}^{n} (I_k - r_k)^2,$$

where $\alpha, \beta > 0$ are constants and I_k is an indicator function that equals 1 if the kth event is realized and zero otherwise. It can be shown that the quadratic scoring rule is proper when a decision maker is risk neutral and maximizes expected utility. When one or both of these assumptions break down, researchers have either resorted to using calibration experiments to transform subjects' reports or to new classes of scoring rules. I discuss one such scoring rule below.

The binarized scoring rule (BSR) is a flexible method that elicits truthful beliefs independently not only of a subject's risk attitudes but also of whether she is an expected utility maximizer. The BSR works as follows. A subject reports a belief r to the experimenter. The random variable of interest, X, is observed. The experimenter draws a random number, R, uniformly from $[0, U]$, where U is often taken as an upper bound for the empirical distribution of losses, e.g., from the pilot sessions. The agent receives a big prize if the value of the loss function $l(X, r) \leq R$ and a small prize otherwise. The loss function used depends on what information the experimenter is interested in eliciting. For example, to elicit beliefs about the mean, one can use $l(X, r) = (x - m)^2$, where m is the expected reported value; if one wants to elicit beliefs about the median, one can use $l(X, r) = |x - md|$, where md is the median. If one wants to elicit an entire distribution, discretized into n values or intervals, then one can use $l(X, r) = \sum_{i=1}^{n} (I_i - p_i)^2$, where I_i is an indicator function.

Evidence from a large number of laboratory experiments indicates that beliefs elicited in the laboratory are meaningful, i.e., they are generally used as the basis for behavior. Furthermore, the process of eliciting beliefs seems not to be too intrusive on subjects' behavior.

24.2.3 Using Robots: Better Control and Larger Scale

Researchers can design an experiment in which both human participants and computerized agents (robots) are subjects. Robots have been used in laboratory experiments in market design for various reasons. There are three advantages associated with the human–robot design in a laboratory setting. The first advantage is to simplify the strategic environment faced by human subjects when they play robots with well-defined strategies. This allows the experimenter to study whether participant responses change depending on their opponent's level of strategic sophistication. The second advantage is related to statistical independence. Since there is no interaction among human subjects in a human–robot session, each human subject can be treated as an independent observation. The third advantage is the experimenter's ability to conduct an experiment on a large scale. In an all-human experiment the number of subjects in a group is limited by the capacity of the lab, whereas in a human–robot design the scale is limited only by the processing power of the computers. In what follows, I discuss two types of robots for market design experiments.

24.2.3.1 *Truthful Robots*

Truthful robots are programmed to report their preferences truthfully. For example, in a school choice experiment, truthful robots always rank schools truthfully, regardless of their priority. This represents a dominant strategy under DA or TTC, but a naive one under IA. In a typical human–robot treatment with truthful robots, human subjects know the truthful robots' strategies precisely. In such scenarios, human subjects do not face strategic uncertainty as they know the realization of truthful robots' strategies with certainty.[2]

The use of truthful robots in the experimental matching literature dates back to the previous century [24].[3] More recently, in [21], the ability to control robots' strategies was employed to compare how different strategies used by other players impact the human subjects' strategies under TTC. The human subjects play the role of a student, with three additional student roles played by robots in competition for slots at four schools, each with one slot available. Subjects simultaneously provide preference rankings for two treatments, the baseline treatment and one of four experimental treatments, where what they are told about the robot players' strategies differs in each treatment.

In the baseline treatment, participants are told the robots' preferences and that robots will submit their true preference rankings. The four experimental treatments vary the robots' strategies and whether the human subjects know these strategies. Results show that participants are more likely to reveal their true preferences in the baseline treatment than in any of the experimental treatments. This indicates that

---

[2] Strategic uncertainty refers to the uncertainty about the actions of other players.

[3] In many auction experiments, human subjects interact with robots who are randomly assigned valuations for the object(s) and bid their dominant strategies. I will not be reviewing this literature here, however.

experiments with complete information are likely to classify more participants as understanding the strategy-proofness property of TTC than is actually the case.

These papers took advantage of the ability to manipulate strategies of competing players by using robots in their design. This allowed the researchers to provide evidence that when human subjects know their competitors' strategies, they are more likely to use the same strategy. In the case when the other players are best-responding, this leads the human subjects to also best-respond.

24.2.3.2 Empirical Robots

Empirical robots use strategies previously used by human subjects under a similar experimental condition, i.e., human subjects of the same type, in the same period, with a corresponding priority lottery number. These human strategies might come from existing studies or existing sessions of the current study.

In [14], how market size in the school choice model impacts students' strategies under the IA and DA mechanisms was studied. Due to monetary and physical constraints, it is difficult to perform large-scale laboratory experiments. Therefore, using robots in place of human agents is a useful alternative. The laboratory experiment in [18] included small (four-student), medium (40 student), and large (4,000-student) settings. In each setting, there are four schools with an equal number of slots at each, so that there is a slot available for every student in each treatment. There are four types of student preferences, with equal proportions of students having each type in each treatment. The preferences are designed so that all students' priority school is neither their best nor worst option. Participants are told the entire payoff table, schools' capacities and priorities, and their own lottery number.

Robots were used in some of the medium-sized trials and all of the large ones. The robots were programmed to either replicate the strategies chosen by human subjects in the medium-size setting (*empirical robots*), or to reveal their preferences truthfully (*truthful robots*). In the empirical-robot setting, human subjects were aware of the potential strategies that the robots could use, but not what their actual strategies would be. For example, in the medium-size sessions, a robot of type 2 with priority lottery number 15 in period 12 will randomly pick one of the n choices made by the human subjects of type 2 with priority lottery number 15 at period 12 in the corresponding all-human medium scale sessions. In comparison, in the truthful robot setting, human subjects knew exactly how the robots would submit their preferences.

It was found that market size had no effect on the strategies human subjects chose when playing against truthful robots, but larger markets led to increased best response behavior when the human subjects were playing against empirical robots, under both mechanisms.

Using empirical robots in laboratory experiments can also lead to potential generalizability issues. If human subjects act differently when they interact with robots rather than other human subjects, the results might not be valid for real life applications. By using both all-human and human–robot subjects in the medium sized treatments, it could be established in [14] that when the robots are playing strategies drawn from those of humans, the human subjects treat them the same as when they are playing against other humans.

With the increasing importance of AI in our work and lives, researchers should study how humans interact with robots to design more effective markets and institutions.

24.3 Lab-in-the-Field Experiments

While most conventional laboratory experiments employs a standard subject pool of students, an abstract framing, and an imposed set of rules, *lab-in-the-field experiments* use non-standard subject pools, with either induced preferences or real-world preferences.[4] In market design experiments, lab-in-the-field experiments use real market participants who have experience with an existing institution and who would be the natural participants for any new market design. I use two examples in the context of course allocation to demonstrate the power of lab-in-the-field experiments.

Allocating course seats (places to students is a daunting task faced by universities every semester. It is a technically difficult problem in market design, as it involves assigning each student a package of indivisible goods from a large number of classes where some are substitutes and others are complements. To achieve the goals of efficiency and equity, some business schools use preference-ranking mechanisms (revealed ordinal preferences) while others use variants of bidding systems (revealed cardinal preferences) in which students are given a fixed budget of tokens to bid on courses. In such bidding systems, bids serve the dual roles of inferring student preferences over courses and determining student priorities for courses.

In [35], a theoretical analysis of course bidding was presented, where it was shown that these dual roles may easily conflict. That is, preferences inferred from the bids might differ significantly from students' true preferences. Furthermore, the Gale–Shapley student-optimal stable mechanism (GS) was proposed; this can be implemented by asking students for their preferences in addition to their bids over courses. The GS mechanism operates as follows:

Step 1: Each student is tentatively placed in her top three choices from her preference list. If a course has more students than its capacity, the lowest-bidding students for that course are dropped, so that each course tentatively holds no more students than its capacity.

Step k, $k \geq 2$: Each student rejected from a course at step $k - 1$ is tentatively placed in her next-choice course. Each course then tentatively retains those who have the highest bidding points among the new students as well as those tentatively retained at an earlier step. If a course holds more students than its capacity, the lowest-bidding students for that course are dropped, so that each course tentatively holds no more students than its capacity.

The algorithm terminates when no student is dropped from a course or all options on the students' preference list have been exhausted. The tentative assignments become final.

Example 24.4 (A lab-in-the-field experiment with induced values). To compare the new mechanism with the existing bidding system, a field survey was reported in [26], which was complemented by a lab-in-the-field experiment at the Ross School of Business at the University of Michigan, which uses a course-bidding system. In this system, each student is endowed with a fixed

---

[4] In the classification given in [23], laboratory experiments with non-standard subject pools are called *artefactual field experiments*, whereas those with both non-standard subject pools and field contexts are called *framed field experiments*.

budget of bidding points, which they can allocate among courses in which they are interested. Students are then sorted in decreasing order by the points they place on a course, which generates a priority list. A serial dictatorship mechanism is then executed in priority order, subject to course quota and feasibility constraints. After the students submitted the bids but *before* course allocations were made, an Associate Dean at the Ross School sent a personalized email to each student within a few hours of the official closure of course bidding. The email contained a list of all courses on which the student had placed bids in descending order of bid points and asked the students to rank the courses, generating a rank-ordered list (ROL). The ROLs were then used in their counterfactual analysis using GS, leading to the conclusion that a potential transition to GS is likely to lead to significant efficiency improvement: among the 489 students who submitted a rank-ordered list, 101 of them unambiguously preferred the GS mechanism while two strictly preferred the status quo. The others were indifferent.

While the counterfactual analysis is informative, three factors are out of the researchers' control. First, as the researchers could not observe students' true preferences, they could not measure whether students revealed their true preferences in the ROLs. Second, they did not have any control over students' beliefs about other students' preferences over the set of courses. Lastly, they did not know whether the two bidding mechanisms would result in similar bid distributions from students if they were run separately.

In comparison, a lab-in-the-field experiment enabled the researchers to control or measure these three factors. In a complementary lab-in-the-field experiment using real market participants, namely MBA students, and the induced value method, the authors again found an improvement in efficiency under GS. Depending on the metric used, truthful preference revelation under GS is between 67% and 83%.

Another lab-in-the-field experiment with induced values uses medical students immediately after their participation in the National Resident Matching Program, which uses a modified version of DA [30]. Researchers find that 23% of participants misrepresent their preferences and explore factors that predict preference misrepresentation. The results are striking as the participants are highly trained and incentivized.

A second example of course-bidding system is used by Harvard Business School. The previous system encouraged strategic behavior and often failed to produce efficient outcomes [3]. To address these deficiencies, a new allocation mechanism was proposed in [2] that elicits from students their preferences over bundles of courses and uses these preferences to compute a price for each course that would form an approximate competitive equilibrium from equal income (A-CEEI). At these prices, each student receives the most preferred bundle of courses that she could afford. As the number of participants grows large, the amount of approximation as well as the incentives to misrepresent preferences would become small. The main advance of [2] compared with [35] was to allow student to express preferences over bundles of courses rather than over individual courses, thus capturing potential substitutability or complementarity among various courses.

To implement A-CEEI in practice, market designers need to deal with the issue of preference reporting over bundles of courses, which would be prohibitively large. A practical mechanism will necessarily use a simplified preference reporting language, which in turn raises the empirical question of how well the restricted preferences would approximate true preferences. The Wharton Business School at the University of Pennsylvania used to have an old course-bidding system, called the Wharton Auction. This will be discussed in the next Example.

Example 24.5 (A lab-in-the-field experiment with real-world preferences). In [4], a novel lab-in-the-field experiment was reported that compared the performance of A-CEEI with the existing Wharton Auction. There are several interesting features in the experiment's design. For example, the subjects are Wharton MBA students who have experience with the Wharton Auction, and who would be the future users of A-CEEI if it were adopted. Instead of endowing these subjects with induced values, they bring their real preferences into the lab. Specifically, subjects report preferences over a subset of courses to be offered the following semester, making it a realistic task. An innovation in the preference reporting language is the use of binary comparisons, in the form of "Do you prefer Schedule A or Schedule B?" which is cognitively simple compared with ranking over all possible schedules. It was found that A-CEEI outperformed the incumbent Wharton Auction on measures of efficiency and fairness.

Impact on practice. The experimental results helped persuade the Wharton committee to adopt a simple version of A-CEEI, called *Course Match*, which replaced its old course-bidding system in 2013. Survey data suggest that A-CEEI has increased student satisfaction with their assigned schedule.

24.4 Field Experiments

A *field experiment* is a randomized study conducted in real-world settings, where the environment is the one in which participants undertake these tasks naturally without knowing that they are in an experiment. While field experiments have the advantage of generating exactly the variation researchers want in their data, they are often challenging to implement. They might be too expensive, or ethically infeasible. Successful implementations of field experiments often involve partnering with government agencies, online platforms, firms, or NGOs.

When designing a field experiment, researchers might consider three aspects of programs that can be randomly assigned to create treatment and control groups:

1. Access: researchers can choose which participants will be offered access to a treatment;
2. Timing: researchers can choose when to provide access; or
3. Encouragement: researchers can choose which participants will be given encouragement to participate in a treatment.

I will discuss each of these aspects and demonstrate their efficacy through examples.

24.4.1 Access

Suppose researchers can offer a random subset of participants access to a treatment. Let N be the number of subjects, and let m be the number of subjects who are assigned to the treatment group. Assume that N and m are integers such that $0 < m < N$. The most basic forms of random assignment allocate treatments such that every subject has the same probability of being treated. A *simple random assignment* refers to a procedure whereby each subject is allocated to the treatment group with probability m/N. In comparison, a *complete random assignment* refers to a procedure that allocates exactly m units to treatment. While simple and complete random assignments are frequently used in field experiments, augmenting them with blocking has practical advantages.

Definition 24.6 (Block random assignment). A block random assignment is a procedure whereby subjects are partitioned into subgroups, called blocks or strata, and complete or simple random assignment occurs within each block.

Blocking has several practical advantages. On the statistical front, block random assignment helps reduce sampling variability. Furthermore, blocking facilitates subgroup analysis by ensuring that (blocked) subgroups are available for study. Lastly, under blocking, covariate adjustment (using the variables that formed the blocks) will tend to have a negligible effect on the estimates, reducing the chance that researchers will be confronted with substantively different estimates of the average treatment effects. On the administrative front, blocking can easily accommodate administrative requirements, which sometimes specify how many subjects of a given profile must be in the treatment group.

To illustrate how blocking works, I will discuss a field experiment implemented at an online dating website, where researchers use blocking in an intuitive way. They first partition the participants into male and female blocks, and then use a simple random assignment to vary participants' signal endowments within each block. See Chapter 16 for an overview of signaling in matching markets.

Example 24.7 (An online dating field experiment). In [27] a field experiment was used in an online dating setting to examine whether a signaling method increases the probability of a match and how the signaling method is utilized.

The experiment took place at an online dating site in South Korea, with participants aged in their 20s or 30s seeking partners of the opposite sex. In the first stage, participants could browse each other's profiles and ask up to 10 participants out on dates. They could attach at most one rose to their proposal, which was meant to signal a high level of interest. Next, participants responded to the proposals they received, and could accept up to 10 proposals. Then the company sent participants their matches' contact information so that they could arrange a date.

Most participants were given two roses that they could attach to proposals, but 20% randomly chosen participants of each sex were given 8 roses. Participants were unaware that some subjects had more roses than others. Since there could be unknown factors that lead to proposals with roses being more likely to be accepted, the authors used whether participants were given 2 or 8 roses as an instrumental variable to determine whether participants were more likely to accept a proposal with a rose attached, since participants who were given 8 roses were significantly more likely to have a rose attached to their proposal.

It was found that sending a rose leads to a 20% increase in the probability of the proposal being accepted, holding all else equal. Participants who were given 8 roses instead of 2 ended up with more dates. The authors also found that participants did not use their roses in an optimal way: 32% of men and 69% of women did not use all their roses, and participants often used their roses on people from the top desirability group who did not accept their proposals. These results suggest that there is a potentially large gain from introducing preference signaling as well as educating market participants in how to strategically use signaling.

Note that a *within-subject design* is an example of blocking where each subject experiences every experimental condition in an random order. An example of such a design is provided in [25], where the effects were examined of application costs on congestion in matching students to the master's programs at the Toulouse School of Economics. Since congestion is costly, it could be more efficient if some applicants were deterred from applying through application costs. However, if application costs are too high, it could lead to lower match quality.

To analyze the effects of application costs on congestion, the authors of [25] used a field experiment where first-year master's students apply to seven second-year programs under three variants of the DA algorithm and the IA algorithm. The three variants of DA are the traditional DA, truncated DA where students can only rank four programs, and DA with costs where students have to write motivation letters for all choices ranked after the top three. Students participated in all four *treatments* in a random order, and were told that one would be used to actually match students, so that they had an incentive to try their best.

The results showed that truncated DA and costly DA successfully reduce congestion, and do not harm match quality when costs are low. The authors advocate for costly DA on the basis that students have the option of applying to more programs if they believe it is worth the costs, and that it is more flexible.

24.4.2 Timing: Phase-In design

When everyone must receive the treatment eventually, researchers can randomly select who is phased into the program first and who receives it later. The group not yet phased in forms the control group. This is called the *phase-in design*.

In situations when logistical or financial constraints mean that coverage must be expanded slowly, randomization may be the fairest way to choose who receives the treatment first.

In other situations, especially for researchers working with technology companies, the phase-in design is often deployed as part of the product-testing phase (*beta testing*). For example, prior to June 2017, Uber did not have in-app tipping on its platform, whereas Lyft did. Uber announced its introduction of the tipping feature and implemented the feature using a phase-in design. Researchers randomized three cities to receive tipping on June 20, 2017 (the alpha launch), followed by a randomly chosen half of the cities in the USA and Canada on July 6, 2017 (the beta launch). The remaining cities launched the tipping feature on July 17, 2017 (the full roll-out), serving as the control group.

Example 24.8 (A labor market field experiment). In collaboration with Teach For America (TFA) in Chicago, the paper [11] examined the impact of changing the labor market matching algorithm from the first offer mechanism (FO) to the school-*position* proposing deferred acceptance algorithm (DA). The author of [11] worked with the organization to stagger the roll-out of DA. In the first year, the matching mechanism for high school teachers changed to the DA, while FO remained as the matching mechanism for elementary school teachers. In the second year, both markets used DA. Results show that matching teachers with DA increased teacher retention through their two-year commitment to TFA by between 6 and 12 %.

In addition to conducting field experiments, researchers can take advantage of policy makers' decision to stagger the roll-out of a new market design. For example, in the context of college admissions in China, Sichuan province implemented the new parallel mechanism in its tier-1 admissions, while keeping the IA mechanism in other tiers. Since the year in which students participate in the college admissions process is primarily determined by their year of birth, well before the change in the mechanism that was used, students in the study do not self-select into the different mechanisms. Using a difference-in-differences approach, researchers have found that when the province moved to the parallel mechanism, students applied to more colleges and listed more prestigious colleges as their top choices. They further found that the student–college matching outcome became more stable [13].

24.4.3 Encouragement Design

An *encouragement design* is used when researchers are unable to randomly assign access to a program, but can randomly assign encouragement to take up the program. This approach is useful when we want to evaluate a program that is already open to all eligible people but the take-up is low. In an encouragement design, the program continues to be open to all eligible people, but only a random subset (the treatment group) will receive extra encouragement to take up the program. The idea is to increase the probability of take-up by the encouraged. Therefore, the encouragement acts as an instrument in predicting take-up.

Example 24.9 (A college application field experiment).   In collaboration with the University of Michigan Undergraduate Admissions Office, an investigation was made in [17] of how the HAIL (High Achieving Involved Leader) scholarship affects the application, admission, enrollment, and persistence of high-achieving low-income students. The scholarship does not increase financial aid; instead, financially qualified high school seniors were informed they were guaranteed the same grant aid that they would qualify for in expectation if admitted. Using an encouragement design, the researchers sent out personalized mailings to high-achieving low-income seniors in Michigan public high schools. Half of the 500 public high schools were randomized into the *treatment*, while the remaining schools constituted the control group. Clustered random assignment was used to minimize *spillovers*.

Results showed that HAIL substantially increased college application (68% versus 26%) and enrollment rates (27% versus 12%). Furthermore, students offered the

HAIL scholarship persisted in college at substantially higher rates than students in the control group.

Impact on practice. HAIL is now a permanent program at the University of Michigan Undergraduate Admissions, operating in all high schools in the state of Michigan.

24.5 Bibliographic Notes

The induced-value method is from [34] and Chapter 2 of [18]. Approaching common knowledge is based on [11]. Eliciting beliefs is based on [33].

The categorization, definitions, and characterizations of lab-in-the-field experiments and field experiments come from [23]. The course allocation examples are an adjusted version of Section 4.3 in [12]. The organization of field experiments is based on [20]. The Uber tipping example is based on [7] and [8]. The definitions and characterizations of simple, complete, and block random assignment come from [19].

Recent surveys on market design experiments include [32] on auction and two-sided matching experiments, [29] on auction and matching experiments, and [22] on school choice and college admissions experiments.

Acknowledgements

I thank YingHua He, Soohyung Lee, and Muriel Niederle for their helpful comments and discussions and Kenna Garrison and Chang Ge for excellent research assistance.

References

[1] Abdulkadiroğlu, A., and Sönmez, T. 2003. School choice: A mechanism design approach. *American Economic Review*, **93**(3), 729–747.

[2] Budish, E. 2011. The combinatorial assignment problem: Approximate competitive equilibrium from equal incomes. *Journal of Political Economy*, **119**(6), 1061–1103.

[3] Budish, E., and Cantillon, E. 2012. The multi-unit assignment problem: Theory and evidence from course allocation at Harvard. *American Economic Review*, **102**(5), 2237–71.

[4] Budish, E., and Kessler, J. B. 2022. Can market participants report their preferences accurately (enough)? *Management Science*, **68**(2), 1107–1130.

[5] Calsamiglia, C., Haeringer, G., and Klijn, F. 2010. Constrained school choice: An experimental study. *American Economic Review*, **100**(4), 1860–74.

[6] Calsamiglia, C., Haeringer, G., and Klijn, F. 2011. A comment on "School choice: An experimental study". *Journal of Economic Theory*, **146**(1), 392–396.

[7] Chandar, B., Gneezy, U., List, J. A., and Muir, I. 2019a. The drivers of social preferences: Evidence from a nationwide tipping field experiment. Working Paper 26380, National Bureau of Economic Research.

[8] Chandar, B. K., Hortacsu, A., List, J. A., Muir, I., and Wooldridge, J. M. 2019b. Design and analysis of cluster-randomized field experiments in panel data settings. Working Paper 26389, National Bureau of Economic Research.

[9] Chen, Y., and He, Y., 2021. Information acquisition and provision in school choice: An experimental study. *Journal of Economic Theory*, **197**, 105345.

[10] Chen, Y., and Sönmez, T. 2006. School choice: An experimental study. *Journal of Economic Theory*, **127**, 202–231.

[11] Chen, R., Chen, Y., and Riyanto, Y. E. 2020. Best practices in replication: A case study of common information in coordination games. *Experimental Economics*, **24**:2–30.

[12] Chen, Y., Cramton, P., List, J. A., and Ockenfels, A. 2021. Market design, human behavior and management. *Management Science*, **67**(9), 5317–5348.

[13] Chen, Y., Jiang, M., and Kesten, O. 2020. An empirical evaluation of Chinese college admissions reforms through a natural experiment. *Proceedings of the National Academy of Sciences*, **117**(50), 31696–31705.

[14] Chen, Y., Jiang, M., Kesten, O., Robin, S., and Zhu, M. 2018. Matching in the large: An experimental study. *Games and Economic Behavior*, **110**:295 – 317.

[15] Chen, Y., Liang, Y., and Sönmez, T. 2016. School choice under complete information: An experimental study. *Journal of Mechanism and Institution Design*, **1**(1), 45.

[16] Davis, J. M. 2021. Labor market design can improve match outcomes: Evidence from matching Teach For America teachers to schools. University of Oregon Working Paper.

[17] Dynarski, S., Libassi, C., Michelmore, K., and Owen, S. 2021. Closing the gap: The effect of reducing complexity and uncertainty in college pricing on the choices of low-income students. *American Economic Review*, **111**(6), 1721–56.

[18] Friedman, D., and Sunder, S. 1994. *Experimental Methods: A Primer for Economists*. Cambridge University Press.

[19] Gerber, A. S., and Green, D. P. 2012. *Field experiments: Design, Analysis, and Interpretation*. W. W. Norton.

[20] Glennerster, R., and Takavarasha, K. 2013. *Running Randomized Evaluations: A Practical Guide*. Princeton University Press.

[21] Guillen, P., and Hakimov, R. 2017. Not quite the best response: Truth-telling, strategy-proof matching, and the manipulation of others. *Experimental Economics*, **20**(3), 670–686.

[22] Hakimov, R., and Kübler, D. 2021. Experiments on centralized school choice and college admissions: A survey. *Experimental Economics*, **24**, 434–488.

[23] Harrison, G. W. and List, J. A. 2004. Field experiments. *Journal of Economic Literature*, **42**(4), 1009–1055.

[24] Harrison, G. W., and McCabe, K. A. 1996. Stability and preference distortion in resource matching: An experimental study of the marriage problem. In: Smith, V., D., *Research in Experimental Economics*, vol. 6. JAI Press.

[25] He, Y., and Magnac, T. 2021. Application costs and congestion in matching markets. *Economic Journal*, **132**(648), 2918–2950.

[26] Krishna, A., and Ünver, M. U. 2008. Improving the efficiency of course bidding at business schools: Field and laboratory studies. *Marketing Science*, **27**(2), 262–282.

[27] Lee, S., and Niederle, M. 2015. Propose with a rose? Signaling in internet dating markets. *Experimental Economics*, **18**(4), 731–755.

[28] Pais, J., and Pintér, Á. 2008. School choice and information: An experimental study on matching mechanisms. *Games and Economic Behavior*, **64**(1), 303–328.

[29] Pan, S. 2021. Experiments in market design. In Capra, C. M., Croson, R., Rigdon, M., and Rosenblat, T., eds., *Handbook of Experimental Game Theory*. Edward Elgar Publishing.

[30] Rees-Jones, A., and Skowronek, S. 2018. An experimental investigation of preference misrepresentation in the residency match. *Proceedings of the National Academy of Sciences*, **115**(45), 11471–11476.

[31] Romero, J., and Rosokha, Y. 2019. The evolution of cooperation: The role of costly strategy adjustments. *American Economic Journal: Microeconomics*, **11**(1), 299–328.

[32] Roth, A. E. 2015. Experiments in market design. In Kagel, J. H. and Roth, A. E., eds., *The Handbook of Experimental Economics*, vol. 2. Princeton University Press.

[33] Schotter, A., and Trevino, I. 2014. Belief elicitation in the laboratory. *Annual Review of Economics*, **6**(1), 103–128.

[34] Smith, V. L. 1982. Microeconomic systems as an experimental science. *American Economic Review*, **72**: 923–955.

[35] Sönmez, T., and Ünver, M. U. 2010. Course bidding at business schools. *International Economic Review*, **51**(1), 99–123.

CHAPTER TWENTY-FIVE

Empirical Models of Non-Transferable Utility Matching

Nikhil Agarwal and Paulo Somaini

25.1 Introduction

Empirical models play a distinctive role in the study of matching markets. They provide a quantitative framework for measuring heterogeneity in preferences for schools [25], comparing school assignment mechanisms [1], [4], [15], understanding preferences in the marriage market [16], and measuring the effects of market power in the medical residency match [3]. The approach taken in these papers is based on first estimating the preferences of the agents in these markets and then using those estimates to make economic conclusions. This chapter provides a unified framework for analyzing agents' preferences in empirical matching models with non-transferable utility. Our objective is to provide a roadmap of the existing literature and highlight avenues for future research.

Unlike in the textbook model of consumer choice, in a matching market agents cannot choose with whom to match with at posted prices. As examples, marriages are formed by mutual consent; schools do not admit all students willing to pay their tuition; public housing is allocated via waiting lists that use priorities; and employers and job applicants must compete with others in a labor market. Moreover, agents on both sides of the market have preferences over whom to transact with, whereas firms rarely care about the identity of a potential consumer. Importantly, prices do not serve as the sole rationing device that equilibrates demand and supply.

Models of two-sided matching with non-transferable utility have three main features. First, the market has two sides – workers and firms, or schools and students – with agents on at least one side having preferences over the range of agents on the other. This excludes one-sided matching problems, such as the matching of patients and living donors in kidney exchange markets. Second, agents form partnerships by mutual consent. And third, the terms of matching are fixed in advance. That is, either an agent on one side of the market cannot compensate an agent on the other side to enter into a partnership or such compensation, if any, is determined exogenously. This excludes models with transferable utility, which are discussed in Chapter 26 of this book.

Estimating preferences in matching markets depends crucially on the data that is available and on institutional details about how the market is organized. We will consider two common data environments with the goal of identifying and estimating a random utility model, further described in Section 25.2. In the first environment, the researcher has access only to data on realized matches. The second environment occurs when the researcher has data from a centralized assignment mechanism that elicits preferences in the form of rank-order lists of options. The appropriate approach to learning about the preferences of agents differs in these two environments, and the discussion in this chapter is split along these lines.

Learning about preferences when only data on final matches is available requires assuming a notion of equilibrium that results in these matches. The predominant concept used for this purpose is known as pairwise stability (see Chapter 1 of this book and [43]). If a match is stable, then one cannot find a pair of agents, one from each side, that would strictly prefer to match with each other relative to their current assignment. This concept is motivated by the idea that agents would have an incentive to break a match that is not stable. The challenge with using stability is that preferences on either side of the market could determine the final matches. Section 25.3 outlines various approaches for estimating preferences with such data.

In some cases, it is also possible to obtain more direct information on preferences when a centralized assignment mechanism is used to determine allocations. These mechanisms have had a big impact in numerous real-world contexts [41], including in school districts and residency programs around the world. The mechanisms require agents to indicate their preferences over being matched with agents on the other side of the market, which are then used as inputs in an algorithm that determines a final assignment. A researcher who knows the algorithm and has access to data on reported preferences has strictly more information than one with access only to data on realized allocations. A recent literature has developed methods for utilizing these reported preferences in a wide range of mechanisms. Estimating preferences is straightforward if participants report their true ordinal preferences but it depends on the properties of the mechanism and behavioral assumptions in other cases. Section 25.4 provides a brief overview of these approaches.

A theme in this chapter is that the flexibility of the preference model that can be identified depends crucially on the available data. As we will discuss below, only data on final matches typically require stronger independence assumptions than data on reported preferences. Similarly, our ability to estimate preferences in a one-to-one matching market will be more limited than in a many-to-one market, and estimating preferences of agents on both sides of the market is more demanding than only for one side. Our hope is to provide a guide to these trade-offs on the current research frontier in a unified framework.

25.2 Empirical Model

We consider a two-sided matching market in which agents on one side, indexed by $i \in \mathcal{I} = \{1, \ldots, I\}$, are assigned to agents on the other side, indexed by $j \in \mathcal{J} = \{1, \ldots, J\}$. Agents $i \in \mathcal{I}$ may be matched with at most one agent in $\mathcal{J}$, but agents $j \in \mathcal{J}$ may be matched with $q_j \geq 1$ agents in $\mathcal{I}$. Agents on both sides may also remain unmatched.

Agents on each side of the market have preferences over the agents with whom they match. We will represent these preferences using a random utility model. Specifically, the utility of i from being matched with j is denoted by u_{ij}, and the utility of j from being matched with i is denoted by v_{ji}. In non-transferable utility models, these utilities cannot be changed by the agents in the market.[1] Moreover, the formulation implicitly assumes that the utility that an agent receives from a given match does not depend on the other matches in the market. In particular, in the many-to-one context, the utility j receives from being matched with i does not depend on the other agents with whom j is matched.[2]

Our goal will be to identify and estimate the joint distributions of the vectors of random utilities $\boldsymbol{u}_i = (u_{i1}, \ldots, u_{iJ})$ and $\boldsymbol{v}_i = (v_{1i}, \ldots, v_{Ji})$ conditional on observable characteristics.[3] Let u_{i0} and v_{j0} denote the utility of remaining unmatched.

We start by considering one side of the market. The most general form of the utility of i being matched with j that we will employ is given by

$$u_{ij} = u(x_j, z_i, \xi_j, \epsilon_i) - d_{ij}, \tag{25.1}$$

where z_i and x_j are vectors of observed characteristics for i and j, respectively, and d_{ij} is a scalar observable that potentially varies with both i and j.[4] The quantity ϵ_i captures unobserved determinants of agent i's preferences. It may be multidimensional and include j-specific taste shocks. The quantity ξ_j includes unobserved characteristics of j. The quantity d_{ij} is an observable, match-specific characteristic (e.g., a measure of the distance between i and j) that we will use as a numeraire, i.e., it represents a metric for utility.

A random utility model requires scale and location normalizations because choices (under uncertainty) are invariant under a positive affine transformation of utilities. Accordingly, we will normalize the value of the outside option to zero, i.e., $u_{i0} = 0$. Observe that the unit coefficient on d_{ij} represents a scale normalization.[5]

The identification and estimation of this model are usually studied in an environment in which the random variables for each i and each j are independent and identically distributed draws from some population distribution. Moreover, we will typically assume a conditional independence condition:

$$\epsilon_i \perp \boldsymbol{d}_i \mid z_i, x, \left(\xi_j\right)_{j=1}^{J}, \tag{25.2}$$

where $\boldsymbol{d}_i = (d_{i1}, \ldots, d_{iJ})$ and $x = (x_1, \ldots, x_J)$. The independence condition (25.2) assumes that agent i's unobserved taste shocks are independent of the vector of numeraire match-specific characteristics $\boldsymbol{d}_i$, conditional on the other observed characteristics of i, z_i, and the vectors of observed and unobserved characteristics of agents on the other side of the market, $x, \left(\xi_j\right)_{j=1}^{J}$, respectively. This assumption must be evaluated within each empirical application, and it is typically reasonable if x is a sufficiently rich control.[6]

---

[1] Theoretical models of non-transferable utility are also closely related to settings that involve matching with contracts (see [26], [27]). We are not aware of empirical work that directly works with such models. The most closely related work is on models with imperfectly transferable utility by [23].

[2] This assumption is sometimes referred to as "responsive preferences" (see [43], Chapter 5).

[3] We refer the reader to [34] for the formal definition of identification that we employ in this chapter.

[4] Recent results in [8] suggest that it may be possible to generalize this specification to allow utility to be non-linear but still separable in d_{ij}.

[5] The above specification also assumes that all agents dislike increases in d_{ij}. This restriction is not essential in many cases, as discussed below, and the sign of this coefficient can be estimated.

[6] Relaxing this assumption is a fruitful avenue for future research. It probably requires augmenting the model to incorporate other sources of exogenous variation and specifying how it affects the data-generating process.

Example (School choice), In this canonical example, let i denote a student and j denote a school. The term u_{ij} is the utility that student i, or her parents, derive from being matched with school j. If we let d_{ij} be the distance from i's residence to j's location (as in [2], for example), then the student's or her parents' preferences can be summarized in terms of their "willingness to travel." In this example, the conditional independence assumption requires that the distance to a school be independent of other unobserved determinants of preferences for schools. This assumption may be a good approximation if z_i includes sufficiently rich data about a student's achievement, demographics, and socioeconomic characteristics. Relaxing this assumption would be likely to require a model of residential choice and sorting based on unobserved factors that influence preferences for schools.

While the analysis of identification can often allow for general functional forms, empirical methods will typically use additional parametric assumptions to ease the computational burden and to get statistically precise estimates with finite sample sizes. The most convenient functional forms depend on the available data and the mechanism or setting being analyzed.

A commonly used parametric form encompassed by the above model assumes that

$$u_{ij} = x_j'\beta + x_j'\bar{\gamma}z_i + \xi_j + x_j'\gamma_i + \varepsilon_{ij} - d_{ij}, \tag{25.3}$$

where γ_i and ε_{ij} are mean-zero normally distributed random variables with variances to be estimated, and $\bar{\gamma}$ is a matrix conformable with x_j' and z_i. We denote by θ the vector of unknown parameters of the model, namely, $\beta, \bar{\gamma}, \xi_1, \ldots, \xi_J$ and the parameters governing the distribution of ε_{ij} and γ_i. These functional-form assumptions may be varied depending on the application.

This formulation is both tractable and flexible. It can capture many determinants of preferences and can be used to measure various aspects of preferences including quality differences across j due to observable and unobservable characteristics, preference heterogeneity across i due to observed and unobserved taste shifters, and also idiosyncratic preferences via ε_{ij}.

In some applications, the preferences on the other side of the market, v_{ji}, may be known from administrative data or institutional knowledge. For example, many schools and colleges use exam scores to rank students (e.g., [7], [21]). In these cases, v_{ji} does not need to be estimated.

When v_{ji} is unknown, one can specify an analogous model for the preferences of agents on the other side of the market. Specifically, the utility of agent $j \in \mathcal{J}$ for matching with agent $i \in \mathcal{I}$ is given by

$$v_{ji} = v(x_j, z_i, \eta_i) - w_{ji}, \tag{25.4}$$

where η_i is unobserved and w_{ji} has an interpretation analogous to d_{ij}. In this case, we would also normalize v_{i0} to zero and strengthen the independence assumption (25.2) to

$$(\eta_i, \epsilon_i) \perp (d_i, w_i) \mid z_i, x, (\xi_j)_{j=1}^J, \tag{25.5}$$

where $w_i = (w_{1i}, \ldots, w_{Ji})$.

A few assumptions in the preference model are worth pointing out. First, there are no externalities. An agent's utility depends only on her own matches. This rules out preferences for attending a school with specific peers or working in a firm with specific colleagues, for example. The current approach to capturing such preferences is to include characteristics of the student body from prior years, but capturing such peer effects is an important avenue for future research; see Section 25.5 for a more detailed discussion.[7] Second, the model abstracts away from the costs of acquiring information about the other side of the market by assuming that preferences are well formed. An exception is found in [36], which considers the possibility that preferences evolve after agents receive an initial assignment was considered.

Third, the model assumes that unobservable characteristics are independent of the observed characteristics. This assumption may be violated for several reasons, including if certain observed characteristics are chosen endogenously by agents in the market. For example, schools may invest in quality by hiring teachers in order to obtain a better set of students. Such endogenously selected characteristics pose empirical challenges, because we cannot directly interpret the measured relationship between the observed characteristics and the preferences as causal. Additionally, counterfactual situations that change the allocation mechanism or the market's competition level may alter the incentives to invest in the characteristic. Methods that account for these sources of endogeneity when analyzing counterfactuals deserve further research.

In this chapter, we will analyze preferences in two different data environments. In the first environment, we will assume that there is access only to information on final matches, and we will observe the identities of the agents in the market and their characteristics. We will use the assumption of stability defined in Chapter 1 in our empirical approach. In the second environment, we will assume access to information on the preferences of each agent as reported to an assignment mechanism. These reports need not be truthful. Chapters 1, 8, and 14 describe some commonly used mechanisms that we will study.

25.3 Analysis Using Final Matches and Stability

This section reviews different approaches when we observe only data on the realized matches from a single large matching market. Throughout, we will assume that these matches are stable (see Chapter 1) . We distinguish between the following three types of markets. The first type is one-to-one matching with a large number of agents on each side. A canonical example is the market for marriages between women and men.[8] The second type is few-to-one matching. Each agent in $\mathcal{J}$ can match with only a few agents in $\mathcal{I}$. Again, we assume that both I and J are large. The market for medical residencies is the canonical example of this type of matching market. Other entry-level labor markets with no salary bargaining can also fit this category if stability is a reasonable assumption. The third type is many-to-one matching. In this type, each agent in $\mathcal{J}$ can match with many agents in $\mathcal{I}$. We assume that I is large but J is small. The leading example of this type of setting is the assignment of students to schools.

---

[7] Two notable exceptions are [20] and [9].

[8] In other types of marriages, the matches cannot be described using a bipartite graph and are therefore not two-sided.

25.3.1 One-to-One Matching

Consider a market in which each agent in $\mathcal{J}$ can match with at most one agent in $\mathcal{I}$. Assume that both I and J are large. The analysis of this model has been split into two types. The first is based on the canonical single-index model (e.g., [12]) in which each side of the market is differentiated only by a vertical quality index. The second is the case where preferences are heterogeneous, so that two agents may have differing preferences over agents on the other side of the market. We discuss each of the two cases below.

25.3.1.1 Double-Vertical Model

In this model, all agents on each side of the market share the same preferences over all agents on the other side. In our notation, the utility of agent i from matching with j is

$$u_{ij} = u_j = u(x_j) + \xi_j,$$

where we replace the assumption in (25.2) by $\xi_j \perp x_j$. This model omits both observed and unobserved sources of quality heterogeneity, resulting in a desirability index for each agent j, denoted by u_j. The term $u(x_j)$ is the component explained by observables x_j, and ξ_j is the unobserved component. The preferences on the other side of the market are analogous:

$$v_{ji} = v_i = v(z_i) + \eta_i,$$

where $\eta_i \perp z_i$. The location for utilities is normalized by either setting the value of the outside option to 0 or picking an arbitrary value $\bar{x}_j$ and seting $u(\cdot)$ to zero at that value. Because the model does not have a quasilinear term d_{ij} for normalizing the scale, we also set the slope of $u(\bar{x}_j)$ with respect to one of its components to 1. The normalization on the other side of the market is analogous.

Assume that we have access to data on the observable characteristics of the agents in a matching market. Therefore, we can identify and estimate the joint distribution $F_{X,Z}$ of the observable characteristics of matched agents. Since we are studying the marriage market between men and women, we follow convention in referring to side $\mathcal{I}$ as men and to side $\mathcal{J}$ as women.

In this model, a match is stable if and only if it exhibits perfect assortative matching on u_j and v_i. In such a set of matches, the tth most desirable man matches with the tth most desirable woman. Therefore, if F_U and F_V are the cumulative distribution functions of u_j and v_i, respectively, then an agent with characteristics (x_j, ξ_j) is matched with an agent with characteristics (z_i, η_i) only if

$$u(x_j) = F_U^{-1}\left(F_V(v(z_i) + \eta_i)\right) - \xi_j. \tag{25.6}$$

Now, consider two men i and i' with identical values of the observed index: $v(z_i) = v(z_{i'})$. These two men could have different values of η, and therefore their mates may differ. However, if we consider two populations of men, one with observed characteristics z_i and the other with observed characteristics $z_{i'}$, then the distribution of their desirability to women including the η terms will be identical. Thus, the two populations of men will have the same marriage prospects and the women with whom they match will have the same distribution of observed characteristics.

In the terminology employed [16], this reasoning allows us to identify "iso-attractiveness profiles" for men by looking at types that end up matching with women with the same distributions of observable characteristics. The same reasoning allows us to identify iso-attractiveness profiles for women.[9] In [16] v_i was allowed to depend on two observable characteristics: body-mass index (BMI) and wages.

To formalize the intuition, suppose that for any function ϕ_x of observables x_j there exists a function ϕ_v of the index v such that $\mathbb{E}[\phi_x(x_j)|z_i] = \phi_v(v(z_i))$, where $\mathbb{E}[\cdot]$ is the expectation operator. The left-hand side is observable, and the right-hand side is a composition of two unknown functions. By differentiating both sides with respect to two components of z_i, we can measure the marginal rate of substitution:

$$\frac{\partial v(z_i)/\partial z_{i,k}}{\partial v(z_i)/\partial z_{i,l}} = \frac{\partial \mathbb{E}\left[\phi_x(x_j)|z_i\right]/\partial z_{i,k}}{\partial \mathbb{E}\left[\phi_x(x_j)|z_i\right]/\partial z_{i,l}}$$

because the right-hand side is observed. Since the above argument provides only the ratio of derivatives, there is no *a priori* way to know whether desirability is increasing in any specific component. It is therefore necessary to assume that there is a characteristic that is known to be monotonically valued and is desirable.

A limitation of one-to-one matching data is that we are able to assess only the relative importance of two different components of the observables. In other words, the marginal rate of substitution between $x_{j,k}$ and $x_{j,k'}$ can be determined for any k and k', but we cannot determine the marginal rate of substitution between $x_{j,k}$ and ξ_j. More broadly, it is not possible to determine the contribution of the observables on either side to the overall variation in preferences.[10] We will discuss how to identify the relative contribution of observables and unobservables when we discuss few-to-one matches below.

25.3.1.2 Heterogeneous Preferences

A strong restriction in the above model is that all agents have the same preferences over the agents on the other side of the market. To make progress on relaxing this assumption, in [35] the model in [18] was revisited; in this model the utilities are parameterized as follows:

$$u_{ij} = u(x_j, z_i) + \varepsilon_{ij},$$
$$v_{ji} = v(x_j, z_i) + \eta_{ji},$$

where $u_{i0} = 0 + \max_{k=1,...,J}\{\varepsilon_{i0,k}\}$ and $v_{j0} = 0 + \max_{k=1,...,J}\{\eta_{j0,k}\}$. The error terms ε_{ij}, $\varepsilon_{i0,k}$, η_{ji}, and $\eta_{j0,k}$ are independent and identically distributed with an upper tail that is standard Gumbel, or logit for short. The paper [35] considered the limit of a sequence of economies indexed by J with an equal number of agents on each side and J growing large. Notice that the outside option also becomes more attractive as J increases. This choice is made in order to ensure that a fixed fraction of agents prefer to remain unmatched in a large market with many draws of ε_{ij} and η_{ji}.

---

[9] While in [16] more general preferences were considered, the main results in this paper, hold for the double-vertical model. More specific assumptions are required in the general case [17].

[10] Observe, however, that the polar cases where η_i and ξ_j are both identically equal to zero for all i and j can be ruled out. This is so because (25.6) reduces to $u(x_j) = F_U^{-1}(F_V(v(z_i)))$. In this case, men with a given set of characteristics z_i match with women whose observables lie exactly on an iso-attractiveness curve.

Under these assumptions, it was shown in [35] that the limiting probability density function of the types of agents that are matched with each other, denoted by $f(x, z)$, has a very tractable functional form. Specifically, we get that

$$\frac{f(x, z)}{f(*, z)f(x, *)} = \exp(u(x, z) + v(x, z)),$$

where $f(x, *)$ is the density of agents on side $\mathcal{I}$ remaining unmatched, and analogously, $f(*, z)$ is the density of agents on side $\mathcal{J}$ remaining unmatched. This convenient functional form is derived from the core insight that if some set $\mathcal{J}_i$ is willing to match with agent i then the probability that i gets matched with j is the probability that j is i's most preferred option in the set $\mathcal{J}_i$. And, similarly, i must be j's most preferred option. Each of these probabilities is given by a logit-like formula in a large market, and they are therefore proportional to $\exp(u(x, z))$ and $\exp(v(x, z))$ for sides $\mathcal{I}$ and $\mathcal{J}$, respectively. Hence, $f(x, z)$ is proportional to the product $\exp(u(x, z) + v(x, z))$. The probability of remaining unmatched provides the right normalizing constant.[11]

Another approach, due to [44], is to assume that matches depend only on the joint surplus $S(x_j, z_i) + \eta_{ij}$, but that the partners split this surplus via Nash bargaining after the match is formed. That is, side $\mathcal{I}$ receives $\lambda S(x_j, z_i) + \lambda \eta_{ij}$ from a realized match and side $\mathcal{J}$ receives $(1 - \lambda)S(x_j, z_i) + (1 - \lambda)\eta_{ij}$ for some $\lambda \in [0, 1]$. This model implies a constant ratio u_{ij}/v_{ji} for every pair of agents. Using the terminology in [37], this model exhibits aligned preferences, resulting in a unique pairwise stable match. A Bayesian approach was used in [44] to estimate the joint surplus in the market for venture capital, targeting the joint surplus function $S(x_j, z_i)$ directly.

These results stress the limitation of data from one-to-one matches, this time in a model with heterogeneous preferences. Namely, only some aggregate notion of joint surplus has been shown to be identified.[12] As in the double-vertical model, the difficulty still lies in trying to determine whether the preferences on side $\mathcal{I}$ or on side $\mathcal{J}$ are driving the observed matches.

25.3.2 Few-to-One Matching

The above discussion demonstrates that only some features of preferences – either the portion of utility determined by observables or the sum of the surpluses – can be identified given only data on final matches in a one-to-one matching market. However, answers to certain questions may require that the distribution of preferences on both sides be separately identified. For example, it is not sufficient to know only $u(\cdot)$ if we are interested in assessing the probability that a type x is preferred to x'. This probability depends on the full distribution of preferences.

One conjecture is that it is not possible to identify preferences on both sides of the market in a one-to-one matching market. In [19] this result was proved for the case of double-vertical preferences. As was argued in Section 25.3.1.1, it is possible to learn the functions $u(\cdot)$ and $v(\cdot)$ under mild restrictions. However, if there are unobserved

---

[11] This formula is remarkably similar to the formula of Choo and Siow for transferable utility models (see Chapter 26). In both cases, the relative frequencies of matches between types x, z depends monotonically on $u(x, z) + v(x, z)$.

[12] In an early work [33], a Bayesian approach was used to estimate heterogeneous preferences of both men and women over their partners. However, we are not aware of results that show identification in this model.

determinants of preferences on either side of the market then the matching will not be perfectly assortative in these indices. The reason is that the match is assortative on $u_j = u(x_j) + \xi_j$ and $v_i = v(z_i) + \eta_i$, not only on the components $u(x_j)$ and $v(z_i)$ that can be predicted by observables. However, the data can be rationalized by either setting $\xi_j \equiv 0$ for all j or $\eta_i \equiv 0$ for all i. This result follows because the double-vertical model places only a single restriction on the behavior expressed in (25.6), but there are two unobservables in the model, ξ_j and η_i. In other words, the matches are determined by unobserved determinants of preferences on both sides of the market, making them hard to disentangle.

In [19] it was also shown that this problem can be solved in many-to-one matching markets for the case of double-vertical preferences,[13] since a setting in which each agent j can match with multiple agents i on the other side has significantly more information than a market with one-to-one matching. Examples of many-to-one markets include labor markets such as the icononic medical residency match [42] as well as education markets such as college or school admissions.

As before, if preferences on both sides are vertical, matches are stable if and only if they exhibit perfect sorting. Formally, in such a market, consider a pair of students i and i' matched with the same college j. Equation (25.6) generalizes to

$$
\begin{aligned}
u(z_i) &= F_U^{-1}\left(F_V\left(v(x_j) + \xi_j\right)\right) - \eta_i, \\
u(z_{i'}) &= F_U^{-1}\left(F_V\left(v(x_j) + \xi_j\right)\right) - \eta_{i'}.
\end{aligned}
\tag{25.7}
$$

As in the marriage market problem, the lack of perfect sorting based on observables indicates the presence of the errors η_i and ξ_j. Now, however, the composition of the incoming class in each program provides additional information about the contribution of each of the error terms. The expressions (25.7) suggest that dispersion in the η terms, the unobserved shocks affecting residents' desirabilities, will cause a program to admit residents with heterogeneous observable determinants of human capital. Thus, the unobservables η_i contribute to the variance in the observable characteristics of residents within each program.

This model can be estimated using a simulated minimum distance estimator [3], [19]. The method consists of the following steps. First, define a set of moments of the data m that we will try to match with our model. Second, fix a vector of parameters $\theta = \{\beta, \gamma, \sigma_\eta, \sigma_\xi\}$ for the model and use them to simulate stable matches and obtain a simulated set of moments $m(\theta)$ as a function of the parameters. Third, compute the distance between the simulated moments and the moments observed in the data, e.g., $\|m - m(\theta)\|_W = \sqrt{(m - m(\theta))' W (m - m(\theta))}$. Fourth, search over θ to minimize the distance.[14]

In [3], three sets of moments for estimation were used. The first set of moments summarizes the general sorting patterns of residents across programs. Recall that x_j and z_i are column vectors; thus, $x_j z_i'$ is a matrix. Averaging this matrix over all matches yields, for I matches,

$$
\frac{1}{I} \sum_{i \in \mathcal{I}} \sum_{j \in \mathcal{J}} 1\left\{\mu(i) = j\right\} x_j z_i'.
$$

---

[13] The analysis of models with heterogeneous preferences and few-to-one matches remains open for further research.

[14] The text [45] provides an overview of best practices.

The second set of moments computes the within-program variances of resident observables for each component $z_{i,\ell}$ of z_i:

$$\frac{1}{I} \sum_{i \in \mathcal{I}} \left(z_{i,\ell} - \bar{z}_{i,\ell} \right)^2,$$

where $\bar{z}_i$ is the vector of average characteristic values of i's peers, that is, of residents allocated to the same program. The third set of moments computes the correlation between residents' characteristics and the average characteristics of the residents' peers for each set of components $z_{i,\ell}$ and $z_{i,k}$, for $k \neq \ell$:

$$\frac{1}{I} \sum_{i \in \mathcal{I}} z_{i,\ell} \hat{z}_{i,k},$$

where $\hat{z}_i$ is the average characteristics of i's peers excluding i.

The first set of moments summarizes aggregate sorting patterns based on observable characteristics, similar to the information used in [16]. The second and third sets of moments include the additional information that is required to identify the contribution of each error term.[15]

Estimates of this model using data on matches from the market for family medicine residencies show that several non-salary observables and unobservables make significant contributions to the programs' desirability indices, implying that residents are willing to forego higher salaries for training in more desirable programs. This preference gives desirable programs market power, allowing them to levy an implicit tuition of over \$23,000 through a markdown in salaries.

25.3.3 Many-to-One Matching

We now consider settings in which agents on side $\mathcal{J}$ can match with a large number of agents on side $\mathcal{I}$, when the number of agents on side $\mathcal{J}$ is small. The canonical examples of such settings are school and college admissions. We will therefore refer to agents on side $\mathcal{I}$ as students and to agents on side $\mathcal{J}$ as schools.

There are two relevant types of data in these settings. The first occurs when the preferences or priorities used by schools to admit students are known. That is, the researcher can directly ascertain how two students will be ranked, possibly up to a random tie-breaker. For example, many school districts grant priority to students in their walk zone and to students who have siblings already enrolled, and many college systems prioritize students using only high school grades or entrance exam scores. In this case, the researcher needs to estimate the preferences of the students for the schools.

The second case is more challenging because we need to estimate preferences on both sides of the market. This case is relevant to college admissions systems and entry-level job settings in which the rules used by agents on side $\mathcal{J}$ are unknown.

[15] Sorting patterns and simulation-based estimation methods were also used in [13] to estimate the preferences of teachers for working at various schools. Although the authors of that paper had access to data from many-to-one matches, they did not use this information to construct the latter two sets of moments. As a result, their approach may be susceptible to the non-identification issues discussed above.

In both cases, we consider the problem where only data on final matches is available, assuming that pairwise stability is satisfied. As before, this assumption requires justifications based on theory and institutional details on the process used in the market to assign students to schools. The main implication of the assumption is that stable matches can be characterized by a cutoff rule. It was shown by [10] that in a stable match, each student i is assigned to her most preferred school in the set

$$S(v_i; p) = \{j : v_{ji} \geq p_j\},$$

where $v_i = (v_{1i}, \ldots, v_{Ji})$. The vector of cutoffs $p = (p_1, \ldots, p_J)$ is set so that the total number of students i with school j as their preferred option within the set $S(v_i; p)$ does not exceed the capacity q_j at the school if $p_j > 0$. Moreover, in a market with an infinite number of students and a fixed number of schools, the stable match and the corresponding cutoffs p_j are unique.

25.3.3.1 Known Priorities: School Choice

Suppose we know each student's eligibility score for each school, denoted by v_{ji}, up to a tie-breaker, and the final assignment is stable. That is, $v_{ji} = v_j(z_i, \eta_i)$, where the function $v_j(\cdot)$ and the distribution of the tie-breaker η_i are known. The cutoff score p_j can be computed as the lowest eligibility score v_{ji} of a student that was matched to school j if the school does not have spare capacity. Otherwise, the cutoff p_j is equal to 0. The goal is then to estimate and identify the specification of preferences defined in (25.1).

This model was used in [21] to study high school admissions in Paris, which are determined by a deferred acceptance mechanism, and in [7] to study Turkish high schools that use an entrance exam to make admission decisions. This assumption can also be used to study higher education settings that use an entrance exam. For example, [14] uses stability to estimate preferences for colleges in Chile.

To see what can be learned from this information and the final assignments, consider the case with only two schools, 1 and 2, and an outside option 0. Figure, 25.1 shows five regions of utilities denoted by Roman numerals. Each region implies different ordinal preferences, except for region V, which pools the cases of $u_{i0} > u_{i1} > u_{i2}$ and $u_{i0} > u_{i2} > u_{i1}$. A student who is eligible for both schools will be assigned to school 1 if her utilities belong to either region I or II. Therefore, the share of students assigned to school 1 out of those eligible for both schools is an estimate of the total probability mass of the distribution of utilities in regions I and II. Similarly, the share assigned to school 2 is an estimate of the total probability mass in regions III and IV.

A student eligible only for school 1 can either be assigned to that school or remain unassigned. In the former case, we can infer that $u_{i0} < u_{i1}$, which is the darker shaded region in Figure 25.2. In the latter case, we can infer that $u_{i1} < u_{i0}$, which is lightly shaded. The share of students assigned to school 1 out of these students is an estimate of the total probability in regions I, II and, III of Figure 25.1.

These arguments are similar to those for standard consumer choice models but differ crucially in that not all students are assigned to their most preferred school. In this context, a student's choice set is constrained by her eligibility. Thus, observed assignments provide no information about preferences for schools that are not in a student's choice set. Learning about the full distribution of ordinal preferences for students with a vector of eligibility scores v_i requires extrapolation using data

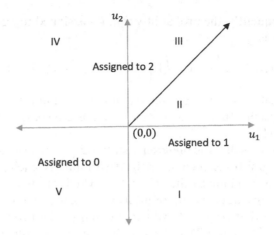

Figure 25.1 Stability – both schools are feasible.

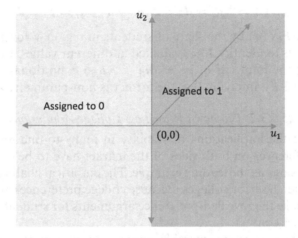

Figure 25.2 Stability – only one school is feasible.

from students with larger choice sets. In [21] this extrapolation was performed by assuming that the unobserved determinants of preferences in (25.1) are conditionally independent of eligibility given the observables included in the model. Formally, it is required that

$$\epsilon_i \perp v_i \mid z_i, d_i, \left\{x_j, \xi_j\right\}_{j=1}^{J}. \tag{25.8}$$

This assumption may be a reasonable approximation if z_i contains a rich set of student characteristics but can be violated, for example, if eligibility scores can be correlated with both unobserved student ability and unobserved preference parameters.

Under this assumption, the probability of each observed assignment can be used to construct a likelihood function given a parameterization of utilities. Specifically, let F_{U^*} denote the joint cdf of the random vector u_i^* with jth element equal to $u(x_j, z_i, \xi_j, \epsilon_i)$. We will drop the conditioning on $z_i, \left\{x_j, \xi_j\right\}_{j=1}^{J}$ for notational simplicity. The independence assumptions in (25.2) and (25.8) obviate the need to condition on d_i and v_i. Consequently, the probability that i is assigned to j given the parameter F_{U^*} can be written as

$$\mathbb{P}(\mu(i) = j | \, v_i = v, p, d_i = d; F_{U^*}) = \int 1 \left\{ u_j^* - d_j \geq u_{j'}^* - d_{j'} \text{ for all } j' \in S(v; p) \right\} dF_{U^*}.$$

This expression enables estimation via maximum likelihood or other likelihood-based methods. Specific functional forms that are convenient for estimation are further discussed in [5].

This expression shows that the preference shifter d plays a crucial role in identification. Under our assumptions, d changes the desirability of each school exogenously and, as a consequence, changes the schools to which students are assigned. This source of variation provides a wealth of information about agents' preferences. Consider the probability that $\mu(i) = 0$, which is equal to the probability that $u_i^* - d_i$ belongs to region V in Figure 25.1. This probability is identified in the two-school case if both schools are in the choice set or the assumption (25.8) holds. It is equal to

$$\mathbb{P}(\mu(i) = 0 | \, d_i = d) = \mathbb{P}(u_i^* - d \leq 0) = F_{U^*}(d).$$

Thus, we identify $F_{U^*}(d)$ by the share of students in region V for $d_i = d$. The variation in d allows us to identify F_{U^*} evaluated at different values. Finally, (25.1) and (25.2) imply that the joint cdf of $u_i = (u_{i1}, \ldots, u_{iJ})$ conditional on d is given by $F_{U|d}(u) = F_{U^*}(u + d)$, implying that the former is non-parametrically identified.[16]

25.3.3.2 Unknown Priorities: College Admissions

We now consider the implications of stability in many-to-one matching environments where preferences on both sides of the market have to be estimated. We will use college admissions as the leading example. The empirical challenge is not limited to estimating preferences for colleges. Because college preferences are unknown, it is not possible to make the revealed-preference arguments for students that we derived in the school choice context.

Nonetheless, there is a considerable amount of information available in the matches. Consider the simple case with $J = 2$. If student i is observed to be attending college $j = 1$, then we can make the following claims:

- Student i prefers college 1 to remaining unassigned: $u_{i1} \geq 0$.
- Student i clears the threshold for college 1: $v_{1i} \geq p_1$.
- Either student i prefers college 1 to college 2 or student i does not clear the threshold for college 2: $u_{i1} \geq u_{i2}$ or $v_{2i} < p_2$.

These restrictions define a set in a four-dimensional space that rationalizes the allocation of i to college 1.

A work in progress by Agarwal and Somaini shows how to learn about preferences on both sides of the market simultaneously for the model described by (25.1) and (25.4). In the model discussed in Section 25.3.3.1, the variation in d_i is used to identify the joint distribution of the J-dimensional vector of students' preferences $(u_{i1}, \ldots, u_{iJ})$. Similarly, the exogenous variations in d_i and w_i can be used to non-parametrically identify the joint distribution of the $2J$-dimensional vector

---

[16] It is also possible to develop the same identification argument using any other region in Figure 25.1. We choose region V because it is the negative orthant, which results in simpler expressions. Therefore, this model is over-identified.

$(u_{i1}, ..., u_{iJ}, v_{1i}, ..., v_{Ji})$, which is conditional on all observables, up to appropriate scale and location normalizations. A closely related prior argument in [29] yields a similar result under more stringent restrictions on (25.1).[17]

A detail about the location normalization in this model is worth noting. As before, it is possible to normalize u_{i0} to zero for all i and v_{j0} to zero for all j. Unfortunately, the location of v_{ji} is not identified when capacity is not known or when capacity limits are binding. The reason is that, for students who strongly prefer college j but were not admitted, we can only deduce that $v_{ji} < p_j$. Hence, only the distribution of the difference $v_{ji} - p_j$ is identified.

Methods for estimating this model are still a subject of ongoing research. We refer the interested reader to [3] and [29].

25.4 Analysis Using Reported Preferences

Many centralized matching algorithms ask participants to submit a report that is used as an input to determine a match. Correspondingly, a well-developed literature has taken advantage of the additional information contained in these reports and derived methods to estimate agents' preferences based on these reports. Methods for analyzing preferences in this richer data environment allow for more general preference models than the methods described in the previous section.

As in the many-to-one matching case, we call agents on side $\mathcal{I}$ students and agents on side $\mathcal{J}$ schools, since most of the applications studying rank-order data have been in the context of school choice. This focus corresponds to the widespread use of centralized mechanisms to assign students to schools. However, the methods discussed below are generally applicable to other settings where a researcher can obtain data on preferences.[18]

The discussion below is brief and focuses on the main differences from the previous section. We refer the reader to [5] for a more thorough review, including a more in-depth discussion of various parametric models and methods for estimating preferences.

25.4.1 Truthful Reports

An important goal when designing assignment mechanisms is strategy-proofness [1], [40]. In such a mechanism, no student can benefit from submitting a list that does not rank schools in order of her true preferences. Strategy-proofness of a school choice mechanism can also enable an empirical strategy if agents understand it and follow this recommendation. Specifically, if agent i ranks j above j' then we can infer that

$$u_{ij} > u_{ij'}.$$

[17] Specifically, it is assumed in [29] that $u_{ij} = u(x_j, z_i, \xi_j) - d_{ij} + \epsilon_{ij}$ and $v_{ji} = v(x_j, z_i, \xi_j) - w_{ji} + \eta_{ij}$, whereas Agarwal and Somaini (in progress) can work with the general case in which $u_{ij} = u(x_j, z_i, \xi_j, \varepsilon_i) - g(d_{ij})$ and $v_{ji} = v(x_j, z_i, \xi_j, \eta_i) - w_{ji}$ for a general function $g(\cdot)$.

[18] For example, in [30] preferences were estimated in an online dating context by analyzing the decision to contact a potential date. The decision to contact a potential date was interpreted as indicative of high utility. This approach allows the estimation of flexible preferences for men and women. A similar analysis was performed in [11] using a dataset of individuals, placing and responding to matrimonial advertisements in a newspaper. They asked ad-placers to rank the letters they received and list the letters which they are planning to follow up.

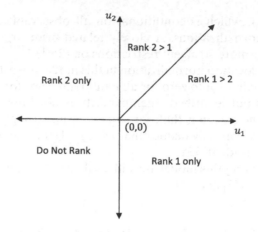

Figure 25.3 Revealed preferences – truthful reports.

It is less clear how to treat schools that are not ranked on the list. One approach is to assume that students rank all schools that are acceptable, i.e., preferable to the outside option. In this case, if j is the lowest-ranked school then $u_{ij} > u_{i0} > u_{ij'}$ if j' is not ranked. In this model, the various rank-order lists partition the space of utilities, as shown in Figure 25.3 for $J = 2$. The five regions in the figure correspond to the various ways in which two schools can be ranked, including the possibility that only one school or an empty list is submitted.

Observe that the rank-order lists provide richer information about preferences than in standard discrete choice models in which a consumer picks only her favorite product. Specifically, if a consumer picks option 1 in a standard discrete choice setting then we can deduce only that the consumer's utilities are in either the region labeled "Rank 1" or "Rank 1 > 2" in Figure 25.3, but we cannot distinguish between these two regions. The richer information in ordered lists can help identify heterogeneity in preferences. In the school choice context, students often rank many more schools, allowing for very rich specifications for the distribution of utilities (see [2] for examples). Allowing for such heterogeneity is important for accurately estimating the value of improving assignments.

As in Section 25.3.3.1, our goal is to identify the cdf F_{U^*}, i.e., the joint cdf of the random vector u_i^* with jth element equal to $u(x_j, z_i, \xi_j, \epsilon_i)$. We will drop the explicit conditioning on $z_i, \{x_j, \xi_j\}_{j=1}^{J}$ for notational simplicity and assume that the condition in (25.2) holds. Under this assumption, the probability that i submits the rank-order list $R = (j_1, j_2, \ldots, j_J)$ can be written as

$$\mathbb{P}\left(R| \, d_i = d; F_{U^*}\right) = \int 1 \left\{ u_{j_k}^* - d_{j_k} \geq u_{j_{k+1}}^* - d_{j_{k+1}} \text{ for all } k \in \{1, \ldots, J-1\} \right\} dF_{U^*}.$$

An important point to note is that we can do away with the independence assumption in (25.8) that is required in Section 25.3.3.1. This advantage is due to our ability to deduce whether the relation $u_{ij} > u_{ij'}$ depends on the endogenous choice set of the agent, as it did in Section 25.3.3.1. This is the case because the model assumes that agents report preferences truthfully irrespective of the preferences of agents on the other side of the market.

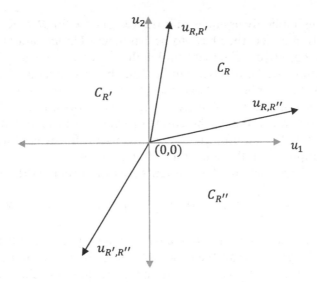

Figure 25.4 Manipulable mechanisms.

25.4.2 Manipulable Mechanisms

There are many school districts that use non-strategy-proof mechanisms. The widely criticized but still commonly used immediate acceptance mechanism, for example, prioritizes students who rank a school higher, generating strategic incentives. To understand what can be learned from reports in manipulable mechanisms, it is useful to think of reports as actions in a game. Each action is associated with an expected payoff. If agents maximize expected utility, we can infer that the observed report yields the highest expected payoff. This approach assumes a considerable degree of sophistication as it requires agents to perform two cognitively demanding tasks. First, they have to be able to calculate the expected payoff for each possible report. Second, they have to maximize over all possible reports. We focus on the case where agents have rational expectations and can optimize, and we conclude the section by discussing extensions.

Let $L_R \in \Delta^J$ be a probability vector representing an agent's beliefs about the probabilities with which she will be assigned to each of the J schools if she submits the report $R \in \mathcal{R}_\mathcal{I}$. The expected utility of this report is $u_i \cdot L_R$. If we observe the report R_i from student i, then optimality implies that $u_i \cdot L_{R_i} \geq u_i \cdot L_R$ for all $R \in \mathcal{R}_\mathcal{I}$. Let C_{R_i} be the set of utilities u_i such that the report R_i maximizes expected utility. This set is a convex cone in the space of utilities that contains the origin. Moreover, the collection of sets C_R for $R \in \mathcal{R}_\mathcal{I}$ partitions the space.[19] Figure 25.4 illustrates these sets for our simplified case with two schools. In this example, $u_{R,R'}$ represents utilities for which the student is indifferent between submitting R and R'. Similarly, a student with utilities given by $u_{R,R''}$ is indifferent between R and R''. The students with utility vectors in the set C_R (weakly) prefer R to the other reports.

---

[19] More precisely, every $u \in \mathbb{R}^J$ belongs to the interior of at most one of the sets in the collection and it belongs to at least one set C_R. There is one exception. If two reports R_i and R_i' result in the same vector of probabilities then the sets C_{R_i} and $C_{R_i'}$ will be identical to each other.

The discussion implicitly assumes that the vectors L_R for $R \in \mathcal{R}_\mathcal{I}$ are known to the researcher. In practice, they have to be estimated. Under rational expectations, these beliefs are objective assignment probabilities. It was shown in [4] that almost all the mechanisms used in practice can be described using a cutoff structure analogous to the one that applies to stable allocations. The distribution of these cutoffs in equilibrium determines the objective assignment probabilities. Thus, instead of estimating L_R, one can estimate the cutoff distribution instead, which is a lower-dimensional object. The cutoff structure is also useful for estimating beliefs under alternative assumptions on the belief formation process.

In this model, the probability that i submits the rank-order list R_i can be written as

$$\mathbb{P}\left(R_i \middle| \, \boldsymbol{d}_i = \boldsymbol{d}; F_{U^*} \right) = \int 1 \left\{ \left(\boldsymbol{u}^* - \boldsymbol{d} \right) \cdot L_{R_i} \geq \left(\boldsymbol{u}^* - \boldsymbol{d} \right) \cdot L_R \text{ for all } R \in \mathcal{R}_\mathcal{I} \right\} dF_{U^*}.$$

This expression follows because $(\boldsymbol{u}^* - \boldsymbol{d}) \cdot L_{R_i}$ is the expected utility from reporting R_i, which must be greater than the expected utility from any alternative report R. This expression forms the basis of estimation via maximum likelihood.

Several extensions have been based on this approach, but under alternative behavioral assumptions. Estimating L_R by surveying agents was proposed in [32]. The authors surveyed families participating in the school choice mechanism in New Haven and found significant differences between elicited and objective assignment probabilities. In [28] and [31] not all the conditions imposed by optimality were required. Instead, a few intuitive conditions that reports have to satisfy were derived and the implied revealed preference relations were used to estimate preferences. These approaches result in incomplete models of behavior that do not admit maximum-likelihood methods. In [4] and [15] mixture models were estimated in which some agents behave optimally while others behave naively, i.e., the latter report their true ordinal preferences even if it is in their interest to report something else. A more detailed survey of methods for incomplete and mixture models is provided in [5].

25.5 Applications, Extensions, and Open Questions

The empirical analysis of matching markets and related markets is still in a relatively early stage of development. This section highlights topics and areas of research that are ripe for study or have become active recently.

25.5.1 Applications

Comparing mechanisms. The theory on matching mechanisms has informed the implementation of coordinated mechanisms in various settings. Quantifying the benefits of centralization requires credible estimates of agents' preferences, using the methods proposed in this chapter. For example, in [2] an implementation of the New York City High School assignment system based on the deferred acceptance algorithm was used to quantify the welfare effects of coordinated school assignment. It was found that, following the reform that centralized the assignment process, students were placed in more desirable schools and were more likely to enroll in their assigned school. The analysis also compared the new DA-based system with the old system and with alternatives using a distance-metric utility function. On a scale ranging from a no-choice neighborhood assignment to the utilitarian optimal, the new system realized 80% of the potential gains, whereas the old system achieved one third at most. Other ordinal mechanisms studied in the theoretical literature were within a few percentage points of the DA-based system, suggesting that the primary gains arise from coordinating assignments.

The methods developed here have also been used to compare various coordinated mechanisms. A number of papers have compared the deferred acceptance mechanism with alternatives. Most of the work has compared this celebrated mechanism with the immediate acceptance mechanism (also known as the Boston mechanism). The common finding in this literature is that the immediate acceptance mechanism yields higher utility to students in the best case [4], [15], but that this conclusion is not robust if students make mistakes [4], [32]. We point the reader to [5] for a more detailed review of this literature.

Rationing and redistribution. Regulated prices and capacity constraints can result in rationing and redistribution. Distributional concerns are particularly important in education [25], [32], health care [6], and social assistance [48]. The design of real-world allocation mechanisms needs to consider ethical and political constraints alongside traditional issues pertaining to efficiency and incentives. For example, school districts often implement quotas to equalize access to high-quality education, and publicly provided health care may need to ensure that all citizens receive adequate treatment. Preference estimates are a key tool for understanding the performance and distributional consequences of various mechanisms.

The tools described above are also useful when centralized assignment mechanisms are not employed. For example, rationing occurs if providers can choose who to treat on the basis of their preferences. As in other matching markets, preferences on both sides of the market determine the final allocation.[20] This view is taken in [24] in the context of the market for nursing homes in California. The paper finds that providers tend to discriminate against Medicaid-eligible patients who require lengthy anticipated stays because they are not profitable.

25.5.2 Extensions

There are several directions in which the methods discussed in this chapter can be extended. We discuss a few below.

Dynamics. The models described in this chapter are static, in the sense that all agents arrive at the market simultaneously and match once and for all. However, there are environments such as the markets for child care, public housing, and organ transplants in which agents or units on one side of the market arrive over time, while agents on the other side can wait. These allocation systems often use waitlists to prioritize agents on the waiting side. These agents have to decide whether to match with a unit that has just arrived. This decision is informative about agents' preferences in

---

[20] The key feature is that, unlike standard consumers, patients cannot choose their most preferred healthcare provider at posted prices. Instead, the provider can exercise discretion on who to treat. Therefore, insurance contracts may also result in rationing.

the same way that reports are informative for static allocation systems. Leveraging this insight, in [6] the system that allocates deceased donor kidneys in the US was studied, in [48] public housing allocation was considered, and in [39] the allocation of bear-hunting permits was investigated.

Externalities: peer effects and competition. A central assumption in the framework described above is that each agent has preferences only over the agents with whom they match. There is relatively little work on externalities, whereby the matches of others also affect an agent's payoffs. There are at least two important reasons why the matches of others may be important.

The first reason can be classified as peer effects. For example, students may derive utility from their classmates, and workers may have preferences over their co-workers. In this case, i's preferences over j can depend on the set $\mu^{-1}(j)$. There is limited work on education markets that have addressed these issues (e.g., [9] and [20]). The typical approach here is to assume preferences for aggregate statistics of the composition of the student body in equilibrium.

The second reason is due to competitive effects. These are particularly important in industrial organization settings. For example, in [46] an entry game in the banking industry was modeled using the tools of two-sided matching games, in which a bank can enter a market by merging with an incumbent. In this entry game, payoffs are affected by the competitor banks that match in the market. Similarly, the paper [47] models the market for oil drilling leases as a matching game between oil companies and landlords that hold mineral rights. In this model, the terms that an oil company can negotiate depend on their overall market presence. A challenge in these settings is to find an appropriate notion of stability that allows for externalities to be present.[21]

25.6 Conclusion

Estimating preferences is a crucial first step toward understanding the effects of policy interventions in a matching market. Preference estimates enable both positive and normative analyses. Specifically, they can be used to predict how agents will behave after an intervention is implemented and how the allocation will change. They are also central to evaluating the welfare and distributional effects of such interventions.

However, standard tools for estimating consumer demand are not directly applicable in matching markets since prices do not clear the market. Instead, agents choose among an individualized set of options determined by the agents on the other side of the market that are willing to match with them. This choice set depends on an agent's desirability to the other side of the market. These features require the development of a new analytical toolset.

The appropriate toolset depends on whether the researcher has access to data only on final matches or also to data on preferences submitted to an allocation mechanism. In this chapter we discussed methods for both cases, outlining the assumptions required in order to make progress in each environment.

---

[21] Conditions for the existence of stable matchings with externalities is an active area of theoretical research. We refer the reader to [22] and [38], and the references therein, for some recent results.

A message of the chapter is that the data and institutional environment dictate whether a flexible preference model can be estimated. One-to-one matching markets require the most severe restrictions on preferences. The current set of results only justifies estimating either homogeneous vertical preferences or some notion of aggregate surplus in models that allow some heterogeneity. More flexible models of preferences can be learned from markets with many-to-one matches. However, data on rank-order lists enable the estimation of the most flexible models of preferences.

While the methods discussed in this chapter have focused on two-sided matching, they also apply to many related environments. For example, they apply to environments where rationing occurs owing to capacity constraints, which includes many education and healthcare markets, ranging from college admissions to the assignment of patients to nursing homes. Extensions of the two-sided matching models discussed here have also been used to describe the market for oil drilling leases and the allocation of organs to patients on a waiting list. We believe that there are many other applications and settings where insights from this rapidly growing literature can be applied in future research.

Acknowledgements

With permission of the respective publishers, this chapter reuses portions from [5] and adapts certain figures from [4].

References

[1] Abdulkadiroglu, Atila, and Sonmez, Tayfun. 2003. School choice: A mechanism design approach. *American Economic Review*, **93**(3), 729–747.

[2] Abdulkadiroglu, Atila, Nikhil Agarwal, and Pathak, Parag A. 2017. The welfare effects of coordinated school assignment: Evidence from the NYC high school match. *American Economic Review*, **107**(12), 3635–3689.

[3] Agarwal, Nikhil. 2015. An empirical model of the medical match. *American Economic Review*, **105**(7), 1939–1978.

[4] Agarwal, Nikhil, and Somaini, Paulo. 2018. Demand analysis using strategic reports: An application to a school choice mechanism. *Econometrica*, **86**(2), 391–444.

[5] Agarwal, Nikhil, and Somaini, Paulo. 2020. Revealed preference analysis of school choice models. *Annual Review of Economics*, **12**(1), 471–501.

[6] Agarwal, Nikhil, Ashlagi, Itai, Rees, Michael A., Somaini, Paulo, and Waldinger, Daniel. 2021. Equilibrium allocations under alternative waitlist designs: Evidence from deceased donor kidneys. *Econometrica*, **89**(1), 37–76.

[7] Akyol, Pelin, and Krishna, Kala. 2017. Preferences, selection, and value added: A structural approach. *European Economic Review*, **91**, 89–117.

[8] Allen, Roy, and Rehbeck, John. 2019. Identification with additively separable heterogeneity. *Econometrica*, **87**(3), 1021–1054.

[9] Allende, Claudia. 2019. Competition under social interactions and the design of education policies.

[10] Azevedo, Eduardo M., and Leshno, Jacob. 2016. A supply and demand framework for two-sided matching markets. *Journal of Political Economy*, **124**(5), 1235–1268.

[11] Banerjee, Abhijit, Duflo, Esther, Ghatak, Maitreesh, and Lafortune, Jeanne. 2013. Marry for what? Caste and mate selection in modern India. *American Economic Journal: Microeconomics*, **5**(2), 33–72.

[12] Becker, Gary S. 1973. A theory of marriage: Part I. *Journal of Political Economy*, **81**(4), 813–846.

[13] Boyd, Donald, Lankford, Hamilton, Loeb, Susanna, and Wyckoff, James. 2013. Analyzing the determinants of the matching of public school teachers to jobs: Disentangling the preferences of teachers and employers. *Journal of Labor Economics*, **31**(1), 83–117.

[14] Bucarey, Alonso. 2018. Who pays for free College? Crowding out on campus.

[15] Calsamiglia, Caterina, Fu, Chao, and Güell, Maia. 2020. Structural estimation of a model of school choices: The boston mechanism vs. its alternatives. *Journal of Political Economy*, **128**(2), 642–680.

[16] Chiappori, Pierre André, Oreffice, Sonia, and Quintana-Domeque, Climent. 2012. Fatter attraction: Anthropometric and socioeconomic matching on the marriage market. *Journal of Political Economy*, **120**(4), 659–695.

[17] Chiappori, Pierre André, Oreffice, Sonia, and Quintana-Domeque, Climent. 2020. Erratum: Fatter attraction: Anthropometric and socioeconomic matching on the marriage market.

[18] Dagsvik, John K. 2000. Aggregation in matching markets. *International Economic Review*, **41**(1), 27–58.

[19] Diamond, W., and Agarwal, N. 2017. Latent indices in assortative matching models. *Quantitative Economics*, **8**(3), 685–728.

[20] Epple, Dennis, Jha, Akshaya, and Sieg, Holger. 2018. The superintendent's dilemma: Managing school district capacity as parents vote with their feet. *Quantitative Economics*, **9**(1), 483–520.

[21] Fack, Gabrielle, Grenet, Julien, and He, Yinghua. 2019. Beyond truth-telling: Preference estimation with centralized school choice and college admissions. *American Economic Review*, **109**(4), 1486–1529.

[22] Fisher, James C. D., and Hafalir, Isa E. 2016. Matching with aggregate externalities. *Mathematical Social Sciences*, **81**, 1–7.

[23] Galichon, Alfred, Kominers, Scott Duke, and Weber, Simon. 2019. Costly concessions: An empirical framework for matching with imperfectly transferable utility. *Journal of Political Economy*, **127**(6), 2875–2925.

[24] Gandhi, Ashvin. 2022. Picking your patients: Selective admissions in the nursing home industry.

[25] Hastings, Justine S., Kane, Thomas, J. and Staiger, Douglas O. 2009. Heterogeneous preferences and the efficacy of public school choice.

[26] Hatfield, John William, and Milgrom, Paul R.. 2005. Matching with contracts. *American Economic Review*, **95**(4), 913–935.

[27] Hatfield, John William, Kominers, Scott Duke, Nichifor, Alexandru, Ostrovsky, Michael, and Westkamp, Alexander. 2013. Stability and competitive equilibrium in trading networks. *Journal of Political Economy*, **121**(5), 966–1005.

[28] He, Yinghua. 2017. Gaming the Boston school choice mechanism in Beijing.

[29] He, Yinghua, Sinha, Shruti, and Sun, Xiaoting. 2022. Identification and estimation in many-to-one two-sided matching without transfers.

[30] Hitsch, Gunter J., Hortacsu, Ali, and Ariely, Dan. 2010. Matching and sorting in online dating. *American Economic Review*, **100**(1), 130–163.

[31] Hwang, Sam Il Myong. 2017. How does heterogeneity In beliefs affect students In the Boston mechanism?

[32] Kapor, Adam, Neilson, Christopher, and Zimmerman, Seth. 2020. Heterogeneous beliefs and school choice mechanisms. *American Economic Review*, **110**(5), 1274–1315.

[33] Logan, John Allen, Hoff, Peter D., and Newton, Michael A., 2008. Two-sided estimation of mate preferences for similarities in age, education, and religion. *Journal of the American Statistical Association*, **103**(482), 559–569.

[34] Matzkin, Rosa L. 2007. Nonparametric identification. In Heckman, J., and Learner, E., eds., *Handbook of Econometrics*, vol. 6B. Elsevier.

[35] Menzel, Konrad. 2015. Large matching markets as two-sided demand systems. *Econometrica*, **83**(3), 897–941.

[36] Narita, Yusuke. 2018. Match or mismatch? Learning and inertia in school choice.

[37] Niederle, Muriel, and Yariv, Leeat. 2009. Decentralized matching with aligned preferences.

[38] Pycia, Marek, and Yenmez, M. Bumin. 2022. Matching with externalities.

[39] Reeling, Carlson J., and Verdier, Valentin, 2020. Welfare effects of dynamic matching: an empirical analysis.

[40] Roth, Alvin E. 1982. The economics of matching: Stability and incentives. *Mathematics of Operations Research*, **7**(4), 617–628.

[41] Roth, Alvin E. 2018. Marketplaces, Markets, and Market Design. *American Economic Review*, **108**(7), 1609–1658.

[42] Roth, Alvin E., and Peranson, Elliott. 1999. The redesign of the matching market for american physicians: Some engineering aspects of economic design. *American Economic Review*, **89**(4), 748–780.

[43] Roth, Alvin E., and Sotomayor, Marilda A. Oliveira. 1992. *Two-Sided Matching*. Cambridge University Press.

[44] Sorensen, Morten. 2007. How smart is smart money? A two-sided matching model of venture capital. *Journal of Finance*, **62**(6), 2725–2762.

[45] Train, Kenneth E. 2009. *Discrete Choice Methods with Simulation*, Cambridge University Press.

[46] Uetake, Kosuke, and Watanabe, Yasutora. 2020. Entry by merger: Estimates from a two-sided matching model with externalities.

[47] Vissing, Ashley. 2018. One-to-many matching with complementary preferences: An empirical study of market concentration in natural gas leasing.

[48] Waldinger, Daniel. 2021. Targeting in-kind transfers through market design: A revealed preference analysis of public housing allocation. *American Economic Review*, **111**(8), 2660–2696.

CHAPTER TWENTY-SIX

Structural Estimation of Matching Markets with Transferable Utility

Alfred Galichon and Bernard Salanié

In matching models with transferable utility, the partners in a match agree to transact in the exchange of a transfer of numéraire (utility or money) from one side of the match to the other. While transfers may be non-zero-sum (if for instance there is diminishing marginal utility, frictions, or other costs) or constrained, we focus in this chapter on the simplest case of *perfectly transferable utility*, in which the transfers are unlimited and zero-sum: the transfer that has been agreed to by one partner is fully appropriated by the other side.[1] For simplicity, we also limit our discussion to the one-to-one bipartite model: each match consists of two partners, drawn from two separate subpopulations. The paradigmatic example is the *heterosexual marriage market*, in which the two subpopulations are men and women. We will use these terms for concreteness.

With perfectly transferable utility, the main object of interest is the *joint surplus function*. It maps the characteristics of a man and a woman into the surplus utility created by their match, relative to the sum of the utilities they would achieve by staying single. Knowing the joint surplus function is informative about the preferences of the partners and about their interaction within the match. It also opens the door to counterfactual analysis, for instance of the impact of policy changes.

We assume that the analyst observes a discrete set of characteristics for each individual: their education, their age, their income category, etc. Each combination of the values of these characteristics defines a *type*. In any real-world application, men and women of a given observed type will also vary in their preferences and more generally in their ability to create joint surplus in any match. We will assume that all market participants observe this additional variation, so that it contributes in determining the observed matching. On the other hand, by definition it constitutes *unobserved heterogeneity* for the analyst. The main challenge in this field is to recover the parameters of the joint surplus function without restricting too much this two-sided unobserved heterogeneity.

Matching with transferable utility solves a linear programming problem. In recent years it has been analyzed with the methods of *optimal transport*. Under an additional *separability* assumption, most functions of interest are convex; then *convex duality* gives a simple and transparent path to *identification* of the parameters of

---

[1] See Chapter 3 in the present volume.

these models.[2] The empirical implementation is especially straightforward when the unobserved heterogeneity has a *logit* form and the joint surplus is linear in the parameters. Then the parameters can be estimated by minimizing a globally convex objective function.

Section 26.1 introduces separable matching models. Section 26.2 presents assumptions under which the data on "who matches whom" (the *matching patterns*) identify the parameters of the joint surplus function, and possibly also of the distributions of unobserved heterogeneity. We will also show how these parameters can be estimated (Section 26.3), and how to compute the stable matchings for given parameter values (Section 26.4).

Notation. We use bold letters for vectors and matrices. For any doubly indexed variable $z = (z_{ab})$, we use the notation $z_{a.}$ to denote the vector of values of z_{ab} when b varies; and when a varies we use a similar notation, $z_{.b}$.

26.1 Matching with Unobserved Heterogeneity

26.1.1 Population and Preferences

We consider a population of men indexed by i and a population of women indexed by j. Each match must consist of one man and one woman; and individuals may remain single. If a man i and a woman j match, the assumption of *perfectly transferable utility* implies that their respective utilities can be written as

$$\alpha_{ij} + t_{ij},$$
$$\gamma_{ij} - t_{ij},$$

where t_{ij} is the (possibly negative) transfer from j to i.[3] Transfers can take all values on the real line, and are costless. We assume that each individual knows the equilibrium values of the transfers for all matches that he/she may take part in, as well as his/her pre-transfer utility $\alpha_{i.}$ or $\gamma_{.j}$.

One key feature of markets with perfectly transferable utility is that matching patterns do not depend on $\boldsymbol{\alpha}$ and $\boldsymbol{\gamma}$ separately, but only on their sums, which we call the joint surplus.[4]

Definition 26.1 (Joint surplus). The joint surplus of a match is the sum of (pre- or post-transfers) utilities:

$$\tilde{\Phi}_{ij} = (\alpha_{ij} + t_{ij}) + (\gamma_{ij} - t_{ij}) = \alpha_{ij} + \gamma_{ij}.$$

We extend the definition to singles with $\tilde{\Phi}_{i0} = \alpha_{i0}$ and $\tilde{\Phi}_{0j} = \gamma_{0j}$.

To see this, note that any change

$$(\alpha_{ij}, \gamma_{ij}) \rightarrow (\alpha_{ij} - \delta, \gamma_{ij} + \delta)$$

---

[2] We have collected the elements of convex analysis that we have used in Appendix A at the end of the chapter.

[3] If t_{ij} is negative, it should be interpreted as a transfer of $-t_{ij}$ from i to j. Also, $t_{i0} = t_{0j} = 0$.

[4] Strictly speaking, it only is a "surplus" when all α_{i0} and γ_{0j} are zero. We follow common usage here.

can be neutralized by adding δ to the transfer t_{ij}. This combined change leaves post-transfer utilities unchanged; therefore it does not affect the decisions of the market participants.

A *matching* is simply a set d of 0–1 variables d_{ij} such that $d_{ij} = 1$ if and only if i and j are matched, along with 0–1 variables d_{i0} (resp. d_{0j}) that equal 1 if and only if man i (resp. woman j) is unmatched (single). It is *feasible* if no partner is matched more than once: thus,

for all i, $\sum_j d_{ij} + d_{i0} = 1$ and, for all j, $\sum_i d_{ij} + d_{0j} = 1$.

26.1.2 Stability

Our notion of equilibrium is *stability*. Its definition in the context of models with perfectly transferable utility is as follows.[5]

Definition 26.2 (Stability – primal definition). A feasible matching is stable if and only if

- no match has a partner who would rather be single
- no pair of currently unmatched partners would rather be matched.

The first requirement translates into $\alpha_{ij} - \alpha_{i0} \leq t_{ij} \leq \gamma_{ij} - \gamma_{0j}$ for all matched pairs (i,j), that is if $d_{ij} = 1$. The second requirement is easier to spell out if we define u_i (resp. v_j) to be the post-transfer utility of man i (resp. woman j) at the stable matching. Then we require that if $d_{ij} = 0$, we cannot find a value of the transfer t_{ij} that satisfies both $\alpha_{ij} + t_{ij} > u_i$ and $\gamma_{ij} - t_{ij} > v_j$. Obviously, this is equivalent to requiring that $\tilde{\Phi}_{ij} \leq u_i + v_j$. Note that if $d_{ij} = 1$ then this inequality is binding since the joint surplus must be the sum of the post-transfer utilities. Moreover, the first requirement can be rewritten as $u_i \geq \alpha_{i0}$ for all men and $v_j \geq \gamma_{0j}$, with equality if man i or woman j is single.

We summarize this in an equivalent definition of *stability*.

Definition 26.3 (Stability – dual definition). A feasible matching d is stable if and only if the post-transfer utilities u_i and v_j satisfy

- for all i, $u_i \geq \tilde{\Phi}_{i0}$, with equality if i is unmatched; and for all j, $v_j \geq \tilde{\Phi}_{0j}$, with equality if j is unmatched
- for all i and j, $u_i + v_j \geq \tilde{\Phi}_{ij}$, with equality if i and j are matched.

The conditions in Definition 26.3 are exactly the *Karush–Kuhn–Tucker optimality conditions* of the following maximization program:

$$\max_{d \geq 0} \sum_{i,j} d_{ij} \tilde{\Phi}_{ij} + \sum_i d_{i0} \tilde{\Phi}_{i0} + \sum_j d_{0j} \tilde{\Phi}_{0j}$$

$$\text{s.t.} \quad \sum_j d_{ij} + d_{i0} = 1 \quad \forall i, \tag{26.1}$$

$$\sum_i d_{ij} + d_{0j} = 1 \quad \forall j, \tag{26.2}$$

---

[5] It can be seen as a special case of the more general definition of stability in Chapter 13. See Definition 13.2.1.

where u_i and v_j are the multipliers of the feasibility conditions. Thus the stable matchings maximize the total *joint surplus* under the feasibility constraints. Program 26.2 above is called the primal program. Since both the objective function and the constraints are linear, its *dual* has the same value. It minimizes the sum of the post-transfer utilities under the stability constraints:

$$\min_{(u_i),(v_j)} \sum_i u_i + \sum_j v_j$$

$$\text{s.t.} \quad u_i \geq \tilde{\Phi}_{i0} \ \forall i,$$

$$v_j \geq \tilde{\Phi}_{0j} \ \forall j,$$

$$u_i + v_j \geq \tilde{\Phi}_{ij} \ \forall i,j, \tag{26.3}$$

and the multipliers of the constraints equal the d_{i0}, d_{0j}, d_{ij} of the associated stable matching.

From an economic point of view, the linearity of these programs implies that, since the feasibility set is never empty (one can always leave all men and women unmatched), there exists a stable matching that is generically unique, and in particular there always exists a stable matching d whose elements are all integers (zero or one). This paints a very different picture from matching with non-transferable utility, described in Chapter 1 of the present volume (see also Section 13.2.2 of Chapter 13).

26.1.3 Separability

A proper econometric setting requires that we distinguish carefully what the analyst can observe from unobserved heterogeneity, which only the market participants observe. Most crucially, the analyst cannot observe all the determinants of the pre-transfer utilities α_{ij} and γ_{ij} generated by a hypothetical match between a man i and a woman j. *A priori*, these pre-transfer utilities could depend on interactions between characteristics that the analyst observes, between these characteristics and the unobserved heterogeneity, and between the unobserved heterogeneities of both partners.

We now define observed characteristics as *types* $x \in \mathcal{X}$ for men and $y \in \mathcal{Y}$ for women. These types are observed by all market participants as well as the analyst. There are n_x men of type x and m_y women of type y. The set of marital options that are offered to men and women is the set of types of partners on the other side of the market, plus singlehood. We continue to use the notation 0 for singlehood and we define $\mathcal{X}_0 = \mathcal{X} \cup \{0\}$ and $\mathcal{Y}_0 = \mathcal{Y} \cup \{0\}$ as the set of options that are available to respectively women and men.

Men and women of a given type also have other characteristics which are not observed by the analyst. A man i who has an observed type x, or a woman j who has an observed type y, may be a more or less appealing partner in any number of ways. In so far as these characteristics are payoff-relevant, they contribute to determining who matches whom. We will assume in this chapter that, contrary to the analyst, all participants observe these additional characteristics. To the analyst, they constitute *unobserved heterogeneity*. It is important to note that this distinction is data-driven: richer data converts *unobserved heterogeneity* into types.

Much of the literature has settled on excluding interactions between unobserved characteristics, and this is the path we take here. We impose:

Assumption 26.4 (Separability). *The joint surplus generated by a match between man i with type x and woman j with type y is*

$$\tilde{\Phi}_{ij} = \Phi_{xy} + \varepsilon_{iy} + \eta_{jx}. \tag{26.4}$$

The utilities of man i and woman j if unmatched are ε_{i0} and η_{j0} respectively.

In the language of analysis-of-variance models, the *separability* assumption rules out two-way interactions between unobserved characteristics that are conditional on observed *types*. While this is restrictive, it still allows for rich patterns of matching in equilibrium. For instance, all women may like educated men, but those women who give a higher value to education are more likely (everything being equal) to marry a more educated man, provided that they in turn have observed or unobserved characteristics that more educated men value more than less educated men.

Since the analyst can only observe types, we now redefine a matching as a collection μ of non-negative numbers: μ_{xy} denotes the number of matches between men of type x and women of type y, which is determined in equilibrium and observed by the analyst. All men of type x, and all women of type y, must be single or matched. This generates the feasibility constraints

$$N_x(\mu) := \sum_{y \in \mathcal{Y}} \mu_{xy} + \mu_{x0} = n_x \quad \forall x \in \mathcal{X},$$

$$M_y(\mu) := \sum_{x \in \mathcal{X}} \mu_{xy} + \mu_{0y} = m_y \quad \forall y \in \mathcal{Y}.$$

In the following, we denote $x_i = x$ if man i is of type x, and $y_j = y$ if woman j is of type y.

26.1.4 Equilibrium

Convex duality will be the key to our approach to *identification*. We start by rewriting the dual characterization of the stable matching in (26.3) as

$$\min_{\substack{u_i \geq \varepsilon_{i0} \\ v_j \geq \eta_{j0}}} \left(\sum_i u_i + \sum_j v_j \right)$$
$$\text{s.t.} \quad u_i + v_j \geq \tilde{\Phi}_{ij} \quad \forall i, j. \tag{26.5}$$

Given Assumption 26.4, the constraint in (26.5) can be rewritten as

$$(u_i - \varepsilon_{iy}) + (v_j - \eta_{jx}) \geq \Phi_{x_i y_j} \quad \forall i, j. \tag{26.6}$$

Define $U_{xy} = \min_{i:x_i=x} \{u_i - \varepsilon_{iy}\}$ and $V_{xy} = \min_{j:y_j=y} \{v_j - \eta_{jx}\}$ for $x, y \neq 0$; and, without loss of generality, set $U_{x0} = V_{0y} = 0$ for $x, y > 0$. The constraint becomes

$$U_{xy} + V_{xy} \geq \Phi_{xy} \quad \forall x, y.$$

Moreover, by definition $u_i = \max_{y \in \mathcal{Y}_0}(U_{x_i y} + \varepsilon_{iy})$ and $v_j = \max_{x \in \mathcal{X}_0}(V_{xy_j} + \eta_{jx})$, so that we can rewrite the *dual program* as

$$\min_{U,V} \left(\sum_i \max_{y \in \mathcal{Y}_0}(U_{x_i y} + \varepsilon_{iy}) + \sum_j \max_{x \in \mathcal{X}_0}(V_{xy_j} + \eta_{jx}) \right)$$
$$\text{s.t.} \quad U_{xy} + V_{xy} \geq \Phi_{xy} \quad \forall x, y.$$

Inspection of the objective function shows that the inequality constraint $U_{xy} + V_{xy} \geq \Phi_{xy}$ can be replaced by an equality; indeed, if it were strict, one could weakly improve the objective function while satisfying the constraint. Since this implies that $U_{xy} + V_{xy} = \Phi_{xy}$, we can replace V_{xy} with $\Phi_{xy} - U_{xy}$ to obtain a simple formula for the total *joint surplus*:

$$\mathcal{W} = \min_{U} \left(\sum_{i} \max_{y \in \mathcal{Y}_0}(U_{x_i y} + \varepsilon_{iy}) + \sum_{j} \max_{x \in \mathcal{X}_0}(\Phi_{xy_j} - U_{xy_j} + \eta_{jx}) \right). \tag{26.7}$$

We have just reduced the dimensionality of the problem from the number of individuals in the market to the product of the numbers of their observed types. Since the latter is typically orders of magnitude smaller than the former, this is a drastic simplification. Assumption 26.4 was the key ingredient: without it, we would have an unobserved term $\tilde{\xi}_{ij}$ interacting with the unobservables in the joint surplus $\tilde{\Phi}_{ij}$ and (26.6) would lose its nice separable structure.

Moreover, the nested min-max in (26.7) is not as complex as it seems. Consider the expression

$$G_x(U_{x\cdot}) := \frac{1}{n_x} \sum_{x_i = x} \max_{y \in \mathcal{Y}_0}(U_{xy} + \varepsilon_{iy}).$$

When the number of individuals n_x tends to infinity, G_x converges to the $\mathbb{E}$max operator, namely

$$G_x(U_{x\cdot}) := \mathbb{E}[\max_{y \in \mathcal{Y}_0}(U_{xy} + \varepsilon_{iy})].$$

We shall assume from now on that this *large-market limit* is a good approximation.[6]

Since the maximum is taken over a collection of linear functions $U_{x\cdot}$, its value is a convex function, and so is G_x. Defining $H_y(V_{\cdot y})$ similarly, we obtain

$$\mathcal{W} = \min_{U} \left(G(U) + H(\Phi - U) \right), \tag{26.8}$$

where

$$G(U) := \sum_{x \in \mathcal{X}} n_x G_x(U_{x\cdot}),$$

$$H(V) := \sum_{y \in \mathcal{Y}} m_y H_y(V_{\cdot y}).$$

These functions play a special role in our analysis. Since G is convex, it has a subgradient everywhere which is a singleton almost everywhere. It is easy to see that the derivative of $\max_{y \in \mathcal{Y}_0}(U_{xy} + \varepsilon_{iy})$ with respect to U_{xy} equals 1 if y achieves a strict maximum and 0 if it is not a strict maximum. As a consequence, the subgradient of G_x with respect to U_{xy} is[7] the proportion of men of type x whose match is of type y. We denote this proportion by $\mu^M_{y|x}$. Finally, we note that the subgradient of G with respect to U_{xy} is n_x times the subgradient of G_x, that is the number μ^M_{xy}. To conclude (and using similar definitions for H):

---

[6] See also Chapter 16 for matching in large markets.

[7] Neglecting the measure-zero cases where the subgradient is not a singleton.

$$\boldsymbol{\mu}^M = \partial G(U),$$
$$\boldsymbol{\mu}^W = \partial H(V).$$

In equilibrium we must have $\mu_{xy}^M = \mu_{xy}^W$ for all x, y. This should not come as a surprise as it translates the first-order conditions in (26.8):

$$\partial G(U) \cap \partial H(\boldsymbol{\Phi} - U) \neq \emptyset.$$

26.2 Identification

Now let us denote G^* the *Legendre–Fenchel transform* of the convex function G:

$$G^*(\mu) = \sup_a \left(\sum_{\substack{x \in \mathcal{X} \\ y \in \mathcal{Y}}} \mu_{xy} a_{xy} - G(a) \right).$$

It is another convex function; and by the theory of *convex duality* we know that since

$$\boldsymbol{\mu}^M = \partial G(U),$$

we also have $U = G^*(\boldsymbol{\mu}^M)$, that is,

$$U_{xy} = \frac{\partial G^*}{\partial \mu_{xy}}(\boldsymbol{\mu}^M). \tag{26.9}$$

Similarly,

$$V_{xy} = \frac{\partial H^*}{\partial \mu_{xy}}(\boldsymbol{\mu}^W). \tag{26.10}$$

26.2.1 Identifying the Joint Surplus

In equilibrium, $\boldsymbol{\mu}^M = \boldsymbol{\mu}^W := \mu$ and $U + V = \boldsymbol{\Phi}$; therefore we obtain

$$\Phi_{xy} = \frac{\partial G^*}{\partial \mu_{xy}}(\mu) + \frac{\partial H^*}{\partial \mu_{xy}}(\mu). \tag{26.11}$$

Observing the matching patterns thus identifies all values of U_{xy}, V_{xy}, and Φ_{xy}, provided that we have enough information to evaluate the function G. Since the shape of the function G depends only on the distribution of the *unobserved heterogeneity* terms, this is the piece of information we need.

Assumption 26.5 (Distribution of the unobserved heterogeneity). *For any man i of type x, the random vector $\boldsymbol{\varepsilon}_{i\cdot} = (\varepsilon_{iy})_{y \in \mathcal{Y}_0}$ is distributed according to $\mathbb{P}_x$.*

Similarly, for any woman j of type y, the random vector $\boldsymbol{\eta}_{j\cdot} = (\eta_{jx})_{x \in \mathcal{X}_0}$ is distributed according to $\mathbb{Q}_y$.

Note that (26.11) is a system of $|\mathcal{X}| \times |\mathcal{Y}|$ equations. To repeat, it identifies the $\boldsymbol{\Phi}$ matrix in the joint surplus as a function of the observed matching patterns (μ) and the shape of the functions G^* and H^*. The latter in turn depend only on the distributions $\mathbb{P}_x$ and $\mathbb{Q}_y$. It is important to stress that the joint surplus is uniquely identified given any choice of these distributions. Identifying the distributions themselves requires more restrictions and/or more data.

26.2.2 Generalized Entropy

We already know from Section 26.1.2 that the stable matching maximizes the total joint surplus. The corresponding *primal program* is

$$W(\Phi, n, m) = \max_{\mu \geq 0} \left(\sum_{\substack{x \in \mathcal{X} \\ y \in \mathcal{Y}}} \mu_{xy} \Phi_{xy} - \mathcal{E}(\mu; n, m) \right) \tag{26.12}$$

where

$$\mathcal{E}(\mu; n, m) = G^*(\mu; n) + \Pi^*(\mu, m)$$

is the *generalized entropy* of the matching μ. It is easy to check that the first-order conditions in (26.12) (which is globally concave) coincide with the *identification* formula (26.11).

The two parts of the objective function in (26.12) have a natural interpretation. The sum $\sum_{x,y} \mu_{xy} \Phi_{xy}$ reflects the value of matching on observed *types* only. The generalized entropy term $-\mathcal{E}(\mu; n, m)$ is the sum of the values that are generated by matching unobserved heterogeneities with observed types: e.g., men of type x with a high value of ε_{iy} being more likely to match with women of type y.

We have skipped over an important technical issue: the Legendre–Fenchel transform of G_x is equal to $+\infty$ unless $\sum_{y \in \mathcal{Y}} \mu_{xy} = N_x(\mu) - \mu_{x0} \leq n_x$. Therefore the objective function in (26.12) becomes minus infinity when any of these feasibility constraints is violated. There are two approaches to making the problem well behaved. We can simply add the constraints to the program. As it turns out, however, extending the generalized entropy beyond its domain is sometimes a much better approach, as we will show in Section 26.3.

26.2.3 The Logit Model

Following a long tradition in discrete choice models, much of the literature has focused on the case when the distributions $\mathbb{P}_x$ and $\mathbb{Q}_y$ are *standard type-I extreme value (Gumbel)* distributions. Under this distributional assumption, the G_x functions take a very simple and familiar form:

$$G_x(U_{x\cdot}) = \log \left(1 + \sum_{t \in \mathcal{Y}} \exp(U_{xt}) \right),$$

and the generalized entropy function $\mathcal{E}$ is just the usual *entropy*:

$$\mathcal{E}(\mu; n, m) = 2 \sum_{\substack{x \in \mathcal{X} \\ y \in \mathcal{Y}}} \mu_{xy} \log \mu_{xy} + \sum_{x \in \mathcal{X}} \mu_{x0} \log \mu_{x0} + \sum_{y \in \mathcal{Y}} \mu_{0y} \log \mu_{0y}. \tag{26.13}$$

Equation (26.11) can be rewritten to yield the following *matching function*, which links the numbers of singles, the joint surplus, and the numbers of matches:

$$\mu_{xy} = \sqrt{\mu_{x0}\mu_{0y}} \exp\left(\frac{\Phi_{xy}}{2}\right).$$

(26.14)

In the *logit* model, the distributions $\mathbb{P}_x$ and $\mathbb{Q}_y$ have no free parameter: the only unknown parameters in the model are those that determine the joint surplus matrix Φ. Using (26.14) gives the formula of *Choo and Siow*:

$$\Phi_{xy} = \log\frac{\mu_{xy}^2}{\mu_{x0}\mu_{0y}}$$

(26.15)

26.3 Estimation

In matching markets, the sample may be drawn from the population at the individual level or at the match level. Take the marriage market as an example. With individual sampling, each man or woman in the population would be a sampling unit. In fact, household-based sampling is more common in population surveys: when a household is sampled, data is collected on all its members. Some of these households consist of a single man or woman, and others consist of a married couple. We assume here that sampling is at the household level.

Recall that $\hat{\mu}_{xy}$, $\hat{\mu}_{x0}$ and $\hat{\mu}_{0y}$ are the number of matches of type (x, y), $(x, 0)$, and $(0, y)$, respectively in our sample. Denote by

$$N_h = \sum_{x\in\mathcal{X}} \hat{\mu}_{x0} + \sum_{y\in\mathcal{Y}} \hat{\mu}_{0y} + \sum_{\substack{x\in\mathcal{X}\\y\in\mathcal{Y}}} \hat{\mu}_{xy}$$

the number of households in our sample, and let

$$\hat{\pi}_{xy} = \frac{\hat{\mu}_{xy}}{N_h}, \quad \hat{\pi}_{x0} = \frac{\hat{\mu}_{x0}}{N_h}, \quad \text{and} \quad \hat{\pi}_{0y} = \frac{\hat{\mu}_{0y}}{N_h}$$

be the empirical sample frequencies of matches of types (x, y), $(x, 0)$, and $(0, y)$, respectively. Let π be the population analogue of $\hat{\pi}$. The estimators of the matching probabilities have the asymptotic distribution

$$\hat{\pi} \sim \mathcal{N}\left(0, \frac{V_\pi}{N_h}\right).$$

(26.16)

We seek to estimate a *parametric model* of the matching market. This involves specifying a functional form for the matrix Φ and choosing families of distributions for the *unobserved heterogeneities* $\mathbb{P}_x$ and $\mathbb{Q}_y$. We denote by λ the parameters of Φ and by β the parameters of the distributions, and our aim is to estimate $\theta = (\lambda, \beta)$. Depending on the context, the analyst may choose to allocate more parameters to the matrix Φ or to the distributions $\mathbb{P}_x$ and $\mathbb{Q}_y$. We assume that the model is well specified in that the data were generated by a matching market with true parameters θ_0.

We will assume in this section that the analyst is able to compute the stable matching μ^θ for any value of the parameters θ. We will provide several ways to do so efficiently in Section 26.4.

26.3.1 The Maximum Likelihood Estimator

In this setting, the log-likelihood function of the sample is simply the sum over all households of the log-probabilities of the observed matches. Let us fix the value of the parameters of the model at θ. We denote by μ^θ the equilibrium matching patterns for these values of the parameters and the observed margins n and m.

A household may consist of a match between a man of type x and a woman of type y, of a single man of type x, or of a single woman of type y. The corresponding probabilities are respectively $\mu^\theta_{xy}/N^\theta_h$, $\mu^\theta_{x0}/N^\theta_h$, and $\mu^\theta_{0y}/N^\theta_h$, where

$$N^\theta_h := \sum_{x,y \in \mathcal{X} \times \mathcal{Y}} \mu^\theta_{xy} + \sum_{x \in \mathcal{X}} \mu^\theta_{x0} + \sum_{y \in \mathcal{Y}} \mu^\theta_{0y}$$

is the number of households in the stable matching for θ, which in general differs from N_h. The log-likelihood becomes

$$\log L(\theta) := \sum_{x,y \in \mathcal{X} \times \mathcal{Y}} \hat{\mu}_{xy} \log \frac{\mu^\theta_{xy}}{N^\theta_h} + \sum_{x \in \mathcal{X}} \hat{\mu}_{x0} \log \frac{\mu^\theta_{x0}}{N^\theta_h} + \sum_{y \in \mathcal{Y}} \hat{\mu}_{0y} \log \frac{\mu^\theta_{0y}}{N^\theta_h}.$$

Maximizing this expression gives a *maximum likelihood estimator* that has the usual asymptotic properties: it is consistent, asymptotically normal, and asymptotically efficient. The maximization process may not be easy, however. In particular, the function $\log L$ is unlikely to be globally concave, and it may have several local extrema. This may make other approaches more attractive.

26.3.2 The Moment-Matching Estimator

A natural choice of parameterization for Φ^λ is the linear expansion

$$\Phi^\lambda_{xy} = \sum_{k=1}^{K} \lambda_k \phi^k_{xy}$$

where the basis functions ϕ^k_{xy} are given and the λ_k coefficients are to be estimated.

The *moment-matching estimator* uses the K equalities

$$\sum_{x,y} \mu^\theta_{xy} \phi^k_{xy} = \sum_{x,y} \hat{\mu}_{xy} \phi^k_{xy}$$

as its estimating equations. Both sides of these equalities can be interpreted as expected values of the basis function ϕ^k; in this sense, the estimator matches the observed and simulated (first) moments of the basis functions. By construction, it can only identify K parameters. We assume from now on that the values of the parameters of the distribution are fixed at β, and we seek to estimate λ.

Applying the envelope theorem to (26.12) shows that the derivative of the total joint surplus with respect to Φ_{xy} is the value of μ_{xy} for the corresponding stable matching. Using the chain rule, we obtain

$$\frac{\partial \mathcal{W}^\beta}{\partial \lambda_k}(\mu^\theta, \hat{n}, \hat{m}) = \sum_{x,y} \mu^\theta_{xy} \phi^k_{xy};$$

this allows us to rewrite the moment-matching estimating equations as the first-order conditions

$$\max_{\lambda} \left(\sum_{x,y} \hat{\mu}_{xy} \Phi_{xy}^{\lambda} - \mathcal{W}^{\beta}(\mu^{\theta}, \hat{n}, \hat{m}) \right). \tag{26.17}$$

Note that the function $\mathcal{W}$ is convex in Φ. Since Φ^{λ} is linear in λ, the objective function of (26.17) is globally convex. This is of course a very appealing property in a maximization problem.

We still have to evaluate $\mathcal{W}^{\beta}(\mu^{\theta}, \hat{n}, \hat{m}) = \sum_{x,y} \mu_{xy}^{\theta} \Phi_{xy}^{\lambda} - \mathcal{E}^{\beta}(\mu^{\theta}; \hat{n}, \hat{m})$. It is often possible to circumvent that step, however. To see this, remember that the *generalized entropy* is defined only when $N(\mu) = \hat{n}$ and $M(\mu) = \hat{m}$. Now take any real-valued functions f and g such that $f(0) = g(0) = 0$, and consider the *extended entropy* function

$$E^{\beta}(\mu; \hat{n}, \hat{m}) = \mathcal{E}^{\beta}(\mu; N(\mu), M(\mu)) + f(N(\mu) - \hat{n}) + g(M(\mu) - \hat{m}).$$

By construction, this function is well defined for any μ, and it coincides with $\mathcal{E}^{\beta}$ when $N(\mu) = \hat{n}$ and $M(\mu) = \hat{m}$. Therefore we can rewrite (26.12) as

$$\mathcal{W}^{\beta}(\Phi, n, m) = \max_{\mu \geq 0} \left(\sum_{\substack{x \in \mathcal{X} \\ y \in \mathcal{Y}}} \mu_{xy} \Phi_{xy} - E^{\beta}(\mu; n, m) \right)$$

$$\text{s.t } N(\mu) = \hat{n} \text{ and } M(\mu) = \hat{m}.$$

If moreover we choose f and g to be convex functions, this new program is also convex. As such, it has a dual formulation that can be written in terms of the Legendre–Fenchel transform $(E^{\beta})^*$ of E^{β}. Simple calculations show that the dual is

$$\mathcal{W}^{\beta}(\Phi, \hat{n}, \hat{m}) = \min_{u,v \geq 0} \left(\langle \hat{n}, u \rangle + \langle \hat{m}, v \rangle + (E^{\beta})^* (\Phi - u - v, -u, -v) \right)$$

where we denote $\Phi - u - v = (\Phi_{xy} - u_x - v_y)_{x,y}$.

Returning to (26.17), the program that defines the moment-matching estimator can now be rewritten as follows:

$$\max_{\lambda, u \geq 0, v \geq 0} \left(\sum_{x,y} \hat{\mu}_{xy} \Phi_{xy}^{\lambda} - \langle \hat{n}, u \rangle - \langle \hat{m}, v \rangle - (E^{\beta})^* (\Phi - u - v, -u, -v) \right). \tag{26.18}$$

This is still a globally convex program; and if we can choose f and g such that the extended entropy $(E^{\beta})^*$ has a simple Legendre–Fenchel transform, it will serve as a computationally attractive estimation procedure. In addition to estimating the parameters λ of the *joint surplus*, it directly yields estimates of the expected utilities u and v of each type. Moreover, after estimation the matching patterns can be obtained from

$$\begin{cases} \mu_{xy}^{\theta} = \dfrac{\partial (E^{\beta})^*}{\partial z_{xy}} (\Phi - u - v, -u, -v), \\[2mm] \mu_{x0}^{\theta} = \dfrac{\partial (E^{\beta})^*}{\partial z_{x0}} (\Phi - u - v, -u, -v), \\[2mm] \mu_{0y}^{\theta} = \dfrac{\partial (E^{\beta})^*}{\partial z_{0y}} (\Phi - u - v, -u, -v) \end{cases} \tag{26.19}$$

The logit model of Section 26.2.3 provides an illustration of this approach.

26.3.3 Estimating the Logit Model

Substituting estimates $\hat{\mu}$ of the matching patterns into formula (26.15) gives a closed-form estimator $\hat{\Phi}$ of the *joint surplus* matrix in the *logit model*. On the other hand, determining the equilibrium matching patterns μ for given primitive parameters Φ, n, m is more involved; and it is necessary in order to evaluate counterfactuals that modify these primitives of the model. We will show how to do this in Section 26.4.1 below. In addition, the analyst may want to assume that the joint surplus matrix Φ belongs in a parametric family Φ^λ. While this could be achieved by finding the value of λ that minimizes the distance between Φ^λ and the $\hat{\Phi}$ obtained from (26.15), the approach sketched in Section 26.3.2 is more appealing.

To construct an *extended entropy* function E in the logit model, we rely on the primitive of the logarithm $\mathcal{L}(t) = t \log t - t$; we define $f(T) = \sum_x \mathcal{L}(T_x)$, and similarly for g. They are clearly convex functions. The reason for this *a priori* non-obvious choice of strictly convex functions is that many of the terms in the derivatives of the resulting extended entropy cancel out. In fact, simple calculations give

$$E^*(z) = 2 \sum_{\substack{x \in \mathcal{X} \\ y \in \mathcal{Y}}} \exp\left(\frac{z_{xy}}{2}\right) + \sum_{x \in \mathcal{X}} \exp(z_{x0}) + \sum_{y \in \mathcal{Y}} \exp(z_{0y}). \tag{26.20}$$

Substituting into (26.18), the moment-matching estimator and associated utilities solve

$$\min_{\lambda, u \geq 0, v \geq 0} F(\lambda, u, v)$$

where

$$F(\lambda, u, v) = \sum_{x \in \mathcal{X}} \exp(-u_x) + \sum_{y \in \mathcal{Y}} \exp(-v_y) + 2 \sum_{\substack{x \in \mathcal{X} \\ y \in \mathcal{Y}}} \exp\left(\frac{\Phi^\lambda_{xy} - u_x - v_y}{2}\right)$$

$$- \sum_{\substack{x \in \mathcal{X} \\ y \in \mathcal{Y}}} \hat{\pi}_{xy}\left(\Phi^\lambda_{xy} - u_x - v_y\right) + \sum_{x \in \mathcal{X}} \hat{\pi}_{x0} u_x + \sum_{y \in \mathcal{Y}} \hat{\pi}_{0y} v_y.$$

This is the objective function of a *Poisson regression* with two-way fixed effects. Minimizing F is a very easy task; we give some specialized algorithms in Section 26.4, but problems of moderate size can also be treated using statistical packages handling generalized linear models. Denote by $\alpha = (\lambda, u, v)$ the set of arguments of F. The asymptotic distribution of the estimator of α is given in Appendix B at the end of this chapter.

26.3.4 The Maximum-Score Method

In most one-sided random utility models of discrete choice, the probability that a given alternative is chosen increases with its mean utility. Assume that alternative k has utility $U(x_{kl}, \theta_0) + u_{kl}$ for individual l. Let $K(l)$ be the choice of individual l and, for any given θ, denote by

$$R_l(\theta) \equiv \sum_{k \neq K(l)} \mathbf{1}\left(U(x_{l,K(l)}, \theta) > U(x_{kl}, \theta)\right)$$

the rank (from the bottom) of the chosen alternative $K(l)$ among the mean utilities. Choose any increasing function F. If (for simplicity) the u_{kl} are i.i.d. across k and l, maximizing the score function

$$\sum_l F(R_l(\theta))$$

over θ yields a consistent estimator of θ_0. The underlying intuition is simply that the probability that k is chosen is an increasing function of the differences of mean utilities $U(x_{kl}, \theta) - U(x_{k'l}, \theta)$ for all $k' \neq k$.

It seems natural to ask whether a similar property also holds in two-sided matching with transferable utility: is there a sense in which (under appropriate assumptions) the probability of a match increases with the surplus it generates?

If transfers are observed, then each individual's choices is just a one-sided choice model and the maximum score estimator can be used essentially as it is. Without data on transfers, the answer is not straightforward. In a two-sided model, the very choice of a single ranking is not self-evident. Insofar as the *optimal matching* is partly driven by unobservables, it is generally not true that the optimal matching maximizes the joint total non-stochastic surplus for instance.

One can give a positive answer for one of the models we have already discussed: the *logit* specification of Section 26.2.3. Formula (26.14) implies that, for any (x, x', y, y'), the double log-odds ratio $2 \log((\mu_{xy}\mu_{x'y'})/(\mu_{x,y'}\mu_{x'y}))$ equals the double difference

$$D_\Phi(x, x', y, y') \equiv \Phi_{xy} + \Phi_{x'y'} - \Phi_{x'y} - \Phi_{xy'}.$$

This direct link between the observed matching patterns and the unknown surplus function justifies a *maximum-score estimator*

$$\max_\Phi \sum_{(x,x',y,y')\in C} \mathbf{1}\left(D_\Phi(x, x', y, y') > 0\right)$$

where C is a subset of the pairs that can be formed from the data.

More generally, one can prove the following result.

Theorem 26.6 (Co-monotonicity of double-differences). *Assume that the surplus is separable and that the distribution of the unobservable heterogeneity vectors is exchangeable. Then, for all (x, y, x', y'), the log-odds ratio $D_\Phi(x, x', y, y')$ and the double difference $\log((\mu_{xy}\mu_{x'y'})/(\mu_{x,y'}\mu_{x'y}))$ have the same sign.*

While this is clearly a weaker result than in the logit model, it is enough to allow one to apply the same maximum-score estimator.

One of the main advantages of the maximum-score method is that it extends to more complex matching markets. It also allows the analyst to select the tuples of trades in C in such a way as to emphasize those that are more relevant in a given application. The price to pay is double, however. First, the maximum-score estimator maximizes a discontinuous function and converges slowly.[8] Second, the underlying monotonicity property only holds for distributions of unobserved heterogeneity, which excludes nested logit models and random coefficients, for instance.

[8] The maximum-score estimator converges at a cubic-root rate.

26.4 Computation

We now turn to efficient evaluation of the stable matching and the associated utilities for given values of the parameters. In this section, we consider any distributional parameters β as fixed, and we omit them from the notation.

26.4.1 Solving for Equilibrium with Coordinate Descent

First consider the determination of the equilibrium matching patterns for a given matrix Φ. In several important models, this can be done by adapting formula (26.18). A slight modification of the arguments that led to this formula shows that, for a given Φ, maximizing the following function yields the equilibrium utilities of all types:

$$\bar{F}(u, v) := \sum_{x,y} \hat{\mu}_{xy} \Phi_{xy} - \langle \hat{n}, u \rangle - \langle \hat{m}, v \rangle - E^* \left(\Phi - u - v, -u, -v \right).$$

Coordinate descent consists of maximizing $\bar{F}$ iteratively with respect to the two-argument vectors: with respect to u keeping v fixed, then with respect to v keeping u fixed at its new value, etc.

Let $v^{(t)}$ be the current value of v. Minimizing $\bar{F}$ with respect to u for $v = v^{(t)}$ yields a set of $|\mathcal{X}|$ equations in $|\mathcal{X}|$ unknowns: $u_x^{(t+1)}$ is the value of u_x that solves

$$\hat{n}_x = \sum_{y \in \mathcal{Y}} \frac{\partial E^*}{\partial z_{xy}} \left(\Phi - u - v^{(t)}, -u, -v^{(t)} \right)$$

$$+ \frac{\partial E^*}{\partial z_{x0}} \left(\Phi - u - v^{(t)}, -u, -v^{(t)} \right).$$

These equations can in turn be solved coordinate by coordinate: we start with $x = 1$ and solve the $x = 1$ equation for $u_1^{(t+1)}$ fixing $(u_2, \ldots, u_{|\mathcal{X}|}) = (u_2^{(t)}, \ldots, u_{|\mathcal{X}|}^{(t)})$; then we solve the $x = 2$ equation for $u_2^{(t+1)}$ fixing $(u_1, u_3, \ldots, u_{|\mathcal{X}|}) = (u_1^{(t+1)}, u_3^{(t)}, \ldots, u_{|\mathcal{X}|}^{(t)})$, etc. The convexity of the function E^* implies that the right-hand side of each equation is strictly decreasing in its scalar unknown, which makes it easy to solve.

The logit model constitutes an important special case for which these equations can be solved with elementary calculations, for any joint surplus matrix Φ. Define $S_{xy} := \exp(\Phi_{xy}/2) a_x := \exp(-u_x)$, and $b_y := \exp(-v_y)$. It is easy to see that the system of equations that determines $u^{(t+1)}$ becomes

$$a_x^2 + a_x \sum_{y \in \mathcal{Y}} b_y^{(t)} S_{xy} = n_x \quad \forall x \in \mathcal{X}.$$

These are $|\mathcal{X}|$ functionally independent quadratic equations, which can be solved in closed form and in parallel. Once this is done, a similar system of independent quadratic equations gives $b^{(t+1)}$ from $a^{(t+1)}$. Note that $a_x^{(0)} = \sqrt{\hat{\mu}_{x0}}$ and $b_y^{(0)} = \sqrt{\hat{\mu}_{0y}}$ are obvious good choices for initial values.

This procedure generalizes the *iterative proportional fitting procedure* (IPFP), also known as *Sinkhorn's algorithm*. It converges globally and very fast. Once the solutions a and b are obtained, the equilibrium matching patterns for this Φ are given by $\mu_{x0} = a_x^2$, $\mu_{0y} = b_y^2$, and $\mu_{xy} = a_x b_y S_{xy}$.

26.4.2 Gradient Descent

Suppose that the analyst has chosen to use (26.18) for estimation. The simplest approach to maximizing the objective function is through *gradient descent*. Denoting $\alpha = (\lambda, u, v)$, we start from a reasonable[9] $\alpha^{(0)}$ and iterate:

$$\alpha^{(t+1)} = \alpha^{(t)} - \epsilon^{(t)} \nabla F\left(\alpha^{(t)}\right)$$

where $\epsilon^{(t)} > 0$ is a small enough parameter. This gives

$$u_x^{(t+1)} = u_x^{(t)} + \epsilon^{(t)}\left(n_x - N_x(\mu^{(t)})\right),$$
$$v_y^{(t+1)} = v_y^{(t)} + \epsilon^{(t)}\left(m_y - M_y(\mu^{(t)})\right),$$
$$\lambda_k^{(t+1)} = \lambda_k^{(t)} + \epsilon^{(t)} \sum_{\substack{x \in \mathcal{X} \\ y \in \mathcal{Y}}} \left(\mu_{xy}^{(t)} - \hat{\mu}_{xy}\right) \phi_{xy}^k,$$

denoting by $\mu^{(t)}$ the result of substituting $(u^{(t)}, v^{(t)}, \lambda^{(t)})$ into (26.19).

This algorithm has a simple intuition: we adjust u_x in proportion to the excess of x types, v_y in proportion to the excess of y types, and λ in proportion to the mismatch between the kth moment predicted by α and the observed kth moment.

26.4.3 Hybrid Algorithms

The approaches in the previous two subsections can also be combined. In [5], alternating between coordinate descent steps on u and v and gradient descent steps on λ has been suggested. In the logit model, this would combine the updates

$$\begin{cases} \left(a_x^{(t+1)}\right)^2 + a_x^{(t+1)} \sum_{y \in \mathcal{Y}} b_y^{(t)} S_{xy}^{(t)} = n_x, \\ \left(b_y^{(t+1)}\right)^2 + b_y^{(t+1)} \sum_{x \in \mathcal{X}} a_y^{(t+1)} S_{xy}^{(t)} = m_y, \\ \lambda_k^{(t+1)} = \lambda_k^{(t)} + \epsilon^{(t)} \sum_{\substack{x \in \mathcal{X} \\ y \in \mathcal{Y}}} \left(a_x^{(t+1)} b_y^{(t+1)} S_{xy}^{(t)} - \hat{\mu}_{xy}\right) \phi_{xy}^k \end{cases}$$

where $S_{xy}^{(t)} = \exp(\sum_{k=1}^{K} \phi_{xy}^k \lambda_k^{(t)}/2)$.

A proof of the convergence of hybrid algorithms is given in [5], in a more general setting that allows for model selection based on penalty functions.

26.5 Other Implementation Issues

Let us now very briefly discuss three issues that often crop up in applications.

26.5.1 Continuous Types

While we have modeled types as discrete-valued in this chapter, there are applications where this is not appropriate. It is possible to incorporate continuous types into a separable model that feels very similar to the logit model of Section 26.2.3.

---

[9] In the logit model, $u_x^{(0)} = -\log(\hat{\mu}_{x0}/\hat{n}_x)$ and $v_y^{(0)} = -\log(\hat{\mu}_{0y}/\hat{m}_y)$ are excellent choices of initial values.

The idea is to model the choice of possible partners as generated by the points of a specific *Poisson process*. An interesting special case has a bilinear *joint surplus function* $\Phi(x, y) = x^\top A y$. It is easy to see that, at the optimum, the Hessian of the logarithm of the matching patterns equals A everywhere: for all $x \in \mathbb{R}^{d_x}$ and $y \in \mathbb{R}^{d_y}$,

$$\frac{\partial^2 \ln \mu}{\partial x \partial y}(x, y) = \frac{A}{2}.$$

As a consequence, the model is over-identified and therefore testable. Among other things, it makes it possible to test for the rank of the matrix A. If it is some $r < \min(d_x, d_y)$, then one can identify the "salient" combination of types that generate the joint surplus.

If moreover the distribution P of x and the distribution Q of y are Gaussians, then the *optimal matching* (X, Y) is a Gaussian vector whose distribution can be obtained in closed form. Suppose for instance that $d_x = d_y = 1$, $P = \mathcal{N}(0, \sigma_x^2)$, $Q - \mathcal{N}(0, \sigma_y^2)$, and $\Phi(x, y) = axy$, Then, at the optimum, $VX - \sigma_x^2$, $VY = \sigma_y^2$, and corr $(X, Y) = \rho$, where ρ is related to a by

$$a\sigma_x\sigma_y = \frac{\rho}{1 - \rho^2}.$$

26.5.2 Using Several Markets

We have focused on the case when the analyst has data on one market. If data on several markets are available matches do not cross market boundaries and some of the primitives of the model coincide across markets, then this can be used to relax the conditions necessary for *identification*.

As an example, in [6] census data on 30 cohorts in the USA were pooled in order to study the changes in the marriage returns in relation to education. To do this, they assumed that the supermodularity module of the function Φ changed at a constant rate over the period.

In [10] it was shown how, given a sufficient number of markets, one can identify the distribution of the *unobserved heterogeneity* if it is constant across the markets.

26.5.3 Using Additional Data

In applications to the labor market, for instance, the analyst often has some information on transfers – wages in this case. This information can be used in estimating the underlying matching model. It is especially useful if it is available at the level of each individual match. Aggregate data on transfers has more limited value [19].

26.6 Bibliographic Notes

Matching with perfectly transferable utility was introduced in [17] and its theoretical properties were elucidated in [20]. In [2, 3] it was made the cornerstone of an analysis of marriage. Sections 26.2 and 26.3 of this chapter are based on the approach developed in [13]. The extension of the logit model to continuous types was proposed in [8], following [7]. The authors of [8] applied it to study how the joint surplus from marriage depends on the Big Five psychological traits of the partners. In [16], continuous and discrete types were combined to model mergers between European firms. The results for the bilinear Gaussian models appeared in [4].

The maximum-score method for matching models was proposed in [9], taking inspiration from the classic paper [18]'s on one-sided discrete choice models. This estimator was used in [1] to study the Federal Communications Commission (FCC) spectrum auctions. Theorem 26.6 was proved in [14] and [15] for independent and identically distributed variables and in [10] it was extended to exchangeable variables.

Acknowledgements

We thank Nikhil Agarwal and Paulo Somaini for their comments and Gabriele Buontempo for superb research assistance. Support from ERC grant EQUIPRICE No. 866274 is acknowledged.

Appendix A: Reminders on Convex Analysis

We focus here on the results on which our chapter relies. For an economic interpretation in terms of matching, see Chapter 6 of [12].

In what follows, we consider a convex function $\varphi \mathbb{R}^n \to \mathbb{R} \cup \{+\infty\}$ which is not identically $+\infty$. If φ is differentiable at x, we denote its *gradient* at x as the vector of partial derivatives, that is, $\nabla \varphi(x) = (\partial \varphi(x) / \partial x_1, \ldots, \partial \varphi(x) / \partial x_n)$. In that case, one has for all x and $\tilde{x}$ in $\mathbb{R}^n$

$$\varphi(\tilde{x}) \geq \varphi(x) + \nabla \varphi(x)^\top (\tilde{x} - x).$$

Note that if $\nabla \varphi(x)$ exists then it is the only vector $y \in \mathbb{R}^n$ such that

$$\varphi(\tilde{x}) \geq \varphi(x) + y^\top (\tilde{x} - x) \quad \forall \tilde{x} \in \mathbb{R}^n; \tag{26.21}$$

indeed, setting $\tilde{x} = x + t e_i$ where e_i is the ith vector of the canonical basis of $\mathbb{R}^n$, and letting $t \to 0^+$, yields $y_i \leq \partial \varphi(x) / \partial x_i$, while letting $t \to 0^-$ yields $y_i \geq \partial \varphi(x) / \partial x_i$. This motivates the definition of the *subdifferential* $\partial \varphi(x)$ of φ at x as the set of vectors $y \in \mathbb{R}^n$ such that relation (26.21) holds. Equivalently, $y \in \partial \varphi(x)$ holds if and only if

$$y^\top x - \varphi(x) \geq \max_{\tilde{x}} \left\{ y^\top \tilde{x} - \varphi(\tilde{x}) \right\};$$

that is, if and only if

$$y^\top x - \varphi(x) = \max_{\tilde{x}} \left\{ y^\top \tilde{x} - \varphi(\tilde{x}) \right\}.$$

The above development highlights a special role for the function φ^* appearing in the expression above:

$$\varphi^*(y) = \max_{\tilde{x}} \left\{ y^\top \tilde{x} - \varphi(\tilde{x}) \right\},$$

which is called the *Legendre–Fenchel transform* of φ. By construction,

$$\varphi(x) + \varphi^*(y) \geq y^\top x.$$

This is called Fenchel's inequality; as we have just seen, it is an equality if and only if $y \in \partial\varphi(x)$. In fact, the subdifferential can also be defined as

$$\partial\varphi(x) = \arg\max_{y} \left\{ y^\top x - \varphi^*(y) \right\}.$$

Finally, the double Legendre–Fenchel transform of a convex function φ (the transform of the transform) is simply φ itself. As a consequence, the subgradients of φ and φ^* are inverses of each other. In particular, if φ and φ^* are both differentiable then

$$(\nabla\varphi)^{-1} = \nabla\varphi^*.$$

To see this, remember that $y \in \partial\varphi(x)$ if and only if $\varphi(x) + \varphi^*(y) = y^\top x$; but, since $\varphi^{**} = \varphi$, this is equivalent to $\varphi^{**}(x) + \varphi^*(y) = y^\top x$, and hence to $x \in \partial\varphi^*(y)$. As a result, the following statements are equivalent:

(i) $\varphi(x) + \varphi^*(y) = x^\top y$;

(ii) $y \in \partial\varphi(x)$;

(iii) $x \in \partial\varphi^*(y)$.

Appendix B: Asymptotic Distribution of the Logit Moment-Matching Estimator

In this appendix, we provide explicit formulas for the asymptotic distribution of the estimator of the matching surplus in the logit model of Section 26.3.3. The asymptotic distribution of the estimator $\hat{\alpha}$ is easy to derive by totally differentiating the first-order conditions $F_\alpha(\hat{\alpha}, \hat{\pi}) = 0$. This yields

$$\alpha \sim \mathcal{N}\left(0, \frac{V_\alpha}{N_h}\right)$$

where

$$V_\alpha = (F_{\alpha\alpha})^{-1} F_{\alpha\pi} V_\pi F_{\alpha\pi}^\top (F_{\alpha\alpha})^{-1}.$$

In this formula, V_π is as in (26.16) and the F_{ab} represent the blocks of the Hessian of F at $(\hat{\alpha}, \hat{\pi})$. Easy calculations show that $F_{\alpha\alpha}$ in turn decomposes into

$$\begin{pmatrix} F_{uu} & F_{uv} = \left(\frac{\pi_{xy}^\lambda}{2}\right)_{xy} & F_{u\lambda} = -\frac{1}{2}\left(\sum_y \pi_{xy}^\lambda \phi_{xy}^k\right)_{xk} \\ \cdot & F_{vv} & F_{v\lambda} = -\frac{1}{2}\left(\sum_x \pi_{xy}^\lambda \phi_{xy}^k\right)_{yk} \\ \cdot & \cdot & F_{\lambda\lambda} = \frac{1}{2}\left(\sum_{x,y} \hat{\pi}_{xy}\phi_{xy}^k\phi_{xy}^l\right)_{kl} \end{pmatrix}$$

where

$$F_{uu} = \mathrm{diag}\left(\left(\frac{1}{2}\sum_y \pi_{xy}^\lambda + \pi_{x0}^\lambda\right)_x\right) \text{ and } F_{vv} = \mathrm{diag}\left(\left(\frac{1}{2}\sum_x \pi_{xy}^\lambda + \pi_{0y}^\lambda\right)_y\right).$$

Moreover,

$$F_{\theta\pi} = \begin{pmatrix} (1_y^\top \otimes I_x) & I_x & 0 \\ (I_y \otimes 1_x^\top) & 0 & I_Y \\ (-\phi_{xy}^k)_{k,xy} & 0 & 0 \end{pmatrix}.$$

Once the estimates $\hat{\alpha}$ are obtained, we can apply (26.19) to compute the estimated matching patterns,

$$
\begin{cases}
\mu_{xy'}^{\hat{\alpha}} = \exp\left(\Phi_{xy}^{\hat{\lambda}} - \hat{u}_x - \hat{v}_y\right)/2), \\
\mu_{x0}^{\hat{\alpha}} = \exp\left(-\hat{u}_x\right), \\
\mu_{0y'}^{\alpha} = \exp\left(-\hat{v}_y\right).
\end{cases}
$$

References

[1] Bajari, P., and Fox, J. 2013. Measuring the efficiency of an FCC spectrum auction. *American Economic Journal: Microeconomics*, **5**, 100–146.

[2] Becker, G. 1973. A theory of marriage, part I. *Journal of Political Economy*, **81**, 813–846.

[3] Becker, G. 1974. A theory of marriage, part II. *Journal of Political Economy*, **82**, S11–S26.

[4] Bojilov, R., and Galichon, A. 2016. Matching in closed-form: Equilibrium, identification, and comparative statics. *Economic Theory*, **61**, 587–609.

[5] Carlier, Guillaume, Dupuy, Arnaud, Galichon, Alfred, and Sun, Yifei. Forthcoming. SISTA: Learning optimal transport costs under sparsity constraints. *Communications on Pure and Applied Mathematics*. https://doi.org/10.1002/cpa.22047.

[6] Chiappori, P.-A., Salanié, B., and Weiss, Y. 2017. Partner choice, investment in children, and the marital college premium. *American Economic Review*, **107**, 2109–67.

[7] Dagsvik, J. 2000. Aggregation in matching markets. *International Economic Review*, **41**, 27–58.

[8] Dupuy, A., and Galichon, A. 2014. Personality traits and the marriage market. *Journal of Political Economy*, **122**, 1271–1319.

[9] Fox, J. 2010. Identification in matching games. *Quantitative Economics*, **1**, 203–254.

[10] Fox, J. 2018. Estimating matching games with transfers. *Quantitative Economics*, **8**, 1–38.

[11] Fox, J., Yang, C., and Hsu, D. 2018. Unobserved heterogeneity in matching games with an appplication to venture capital. *Journal of Political Economy*, **126**, 1339–1373.

[12] Galichon, A. 2016. *Optimal Transport Methods in Economics*. Princeton University Press.

[13] Galichon, A., and Salanié, B. 2022. Cupid's invisible hand: Social surplus and identification in matching models. *Review of Economic Studies*, **89**, 2600–2629.

[14] Graham, B. 2011. Econometric methods for the analysis of Assignment Problems in the presence of complementarity and social spillovers. In Benhabib, J., Bisin, A., and Jackson, M. eds., *Handbook of Social Economics*. Elsevier.

[15] Graham, B. 2014. Errata on "Econometric methods for the analysis of assignment problems in the presence of complementarity and social spillovers." Berkeley mimeo.

[16] Guadalupe, M., Rappoport, V., Salanié, B., and Thomas, C. 2020. The perfect match. Columbia University mimeo.

[17] Koopmans, Tjalling C., and Beckmann, Martin. 1957. Assignment problems and the location of economic activities. *Econometrica*, **25**, 53–76.

[18] Manski, C. F. 1975. Maximum score estimation of the stochastic utility model of choice. *Journal of Econometrics*, **3**, 205–228.

[19] Salanié, Bernard. 2015. Identification in separable matching with observed transfers. Columbia University mimeo.

[20] Shapley, L., and Shubik, M. 1972. The assignment game I: The core. *International Journal of Game Theory*, **1**, 111–130.

PART FIVE

Related Topics

CHAPTER TWENTY-SEVEN

New Solution Concepts

Shengwu Li and Irene Lo

27.1 Introduction

In classical game theory, solution concepts are standardly interpreted as a prediction of behavior. That is, they assert how players will act, given a fully specified strategic environment.

> ... inherited from von Neumann and Morgenstern was that the goal of game theory should be to find the "solution" to each class of games, that would "solve" each kind of theory. They attached great importance to the idea that a solution, when found, would apply to all games in (at least) a very broad class, and therefore that an important property of prospective solutions should be that they should exist for all games [20].

By contrast, in the study of market design, the game is (at least partially) under the control of the designer. Hence, our problem is not to make a prediction for every game, but to pick a game that achieves our goals. This creates new roles for solution concepts, as this chapter will illustrate.

One new role for solution concepts is to select games in which incentives for the desired behavior are particularly strong or reliable. For instance, second-price auctions and ascending auctions are both strategy-proof (SP); truthful play is a best response to any opponent strategies. Nonetheless, human beings often deviate substantially from truthful play in second-price auctions but not in ascending auctions, even though these mechanisms are essentially equivalent. One way to account for this is to have a solution concept that formalizes our intuition that some games are easier to play than others. Section 27.2 introduces a solution concept, obvious strategy-proofness, that picks out some strategy-proof mechanisms as being especially easy to play.

Another new role for solution concepts is to implicitly model parts of the game that are not under the designer's control. For instance, a solution concept such as stability can be interpreted classically as predicting which matchings will occur. However, it can also be interpreted as predicting which matching mechanisms are vulnerable to players circumventing the mechanism. New solution concepts can augment our understanding and analysis of formal matching mechanisms, by providing a shorthand for moves in a larger game – one that is outside the designer's control and too complicated to model explicitly. Section 27.3 introduces several solution concepts capturing incomplete-information stability that together illustrate considerations in designing matching markets that are typically beyond the scope of the specified game but important for market outcomes.

27.2 Obvious Strategy-Proofness

Even in strategy-proof mechanisms, human beings do not always play optimally. Deviations from dominant-strategy play have been documented in the laboratory and in high-stakes mechanisms in the field. In particular, laboratory subjects make frequent mistakes in second-price auctions but rapidly identify the dominant strategy in ascending auctions. Thus, while the revelation principle ordinarily permits us to restrict attention to static mechanisms, understanding human behavior requires us to study mechanisms in the extensive form.

We have a finite set N of agents and a set X of outcomes. For each agent $n \in N$, we have a set of types T_n and a utility function $u_n \colon X \times T_n \to \mathbb{R}$. We denote $T \equiv \prod_n T_n$, with representative element t_n, and $T_{-n} \equiv \prod_{m \neq n} T_m$, with representative element t_{-n}. A *social choice rule* is a function $c \colon T \to X$.

Social choice rule c is *strategy-proof* (SP), if for all n, t_n, t_n', and t_{-n}, we have

$$u_n(c(t_n, t_{-n}), t_n) \geq u_n(c(t_n', t_{-n}), t_n). \tag{27.1}$$

27.2.1 Definition of Mechanisms in Extensive Form

A *mechanism for c* specifies a directed rooted tree with vertex set V and edge set E. Essentially, we start play from the root vertex, and at each step ask one agent a question about his type. Thus, each vertex $v \in V$ is associated with a non-empty set of type profiles for each agent $n \in N$, which we denote as $T_n^v \subseteq T_n$, and similarly $T^v \equiv \prod_n T_n^v$. For the root vertex $\bar{v}$, $T^{\bar{v}} = T$. Vertex v is *terminal* if it has no child; Z denotes the set of terminal vertices.

For each non-terminal vertex v, some agent whom we denote $P(v)$, is called to play; $\mathrm{out}(v)$ denotes the set of out-edges from v. Each edge $e \in \mathrm{out}(v)$ corresponds to a set of $P(v)$'s types, that is, $e \subseteq T_{P(v)}^v$. We require that $\mathrm{out}(v)$ forms a partition of $T_{P(v)}^v$; hence, we interpret the out-edges as answers to a question to $P(v)$ about his type.

Correspondingly, we interpret T_n^v as the types of player n that are consistent with the answers given so far. Hence, we require that if v' is an child of v reached by $e \in \mathrm{out}(v)$ then $T_{P(v)}^{v'} = e$, and, for all $n \neq P(v)$, $T_n^{v'} = T_n^v$.

We require that the social choice rule c is measurable with respect to the terminal vertices Z. To be precise,

1. the family of sets $\{T^v\}_{v \in Z}$ forms a partition of T, and
2. for any $v \in Z$ and any $t, t' \in T^v$, $c(t) = c(t')$.

Additionally, a mechanism specifies information sets for each agent n. Formally, $\mathcal{I}$ is a partition of the non-terminal vertices, with the property that, for any cell $I \in \mathcal{I}$ and any $v, v' \in I$, we have that

1. $P(v) = P(v')$, which we denote $P(I)$,
2. $T^v_{P(I)} = T^{v'}_{P(I)}$,
3. out(v) and out(v') specify the same partition, which we denote $\mathcal{A}(I)$.[1]

We use T^I_n to denote the types of n that are consistent with I, that is $\cup_{v \in I} T^v_n$. We use T^I_{-n} to denote the opponent type profiles consistent with I, that is, $\cup_{v \in I} T^v_{-n}$. For $t_n \in T^I_n$, we use $A(t_n, I)$ to denote the cell of $\mathcal{A}(I)$ that contains t_n.

27.2.2 Definition of Obvious Strategy-Proofness

Now we define a stronger incentive criterion that captures the idea that the agent may have difficulty reasoning about unobserved contingencies. That is, at each information set the agent knows the possible outcomes from each continuation strategy but cannot make a state-by-state comparison that conditions on the opponent type profile t_{-n}.

Since we are assuming that the agent cannot make state-by-state comparisons, we require that, for any information set that can be reached under the "truth-telling" strategy and for any deviation that starts at that information set, every possible outcome from truth-telling is at least as good as every possible outcome from deviating from the truth.

A mechanism for c is *obviously strategy-proof* (OSP) if for any agent n, for any information set I such that $n = P(I)$, for any $t_n, t'_n \in T^I_n$ and for any $t_{-n}, t'_{-n} \in T^I_{-n}$, if $A(t_n, I) \neq A(t'_n, I)$ then

$$u_n(c(t_n, t_{-n}), t_n) \geq u_n(c(t'_n, t'_{-n}), t_n). \tag{27.2}$$

Proposition 27.1. *If there exists an OSP mechanism for c, then c is SP.*

Proof We prove the contrapositive. Suppose c is not SP; then we can find n, t_n, t'_n, and t_{-n} such that

$$u_n(c(t_n, t_{-n}), t_n) < u_n(c(t'_n, t_{-n}), t_n), \tag{27.3}$$

which implies that $c(t_n, t_{-n}) \neq c(t'_n, t_{-n})$.

Given any extensive-form mechanism for c, c is measurable with respect to the terminal vertices. Hence, there exists an information set I such that $P(I) = n$, $t_n, t'_n \in T^I_n$, $t_{-n} \in T^I_{-n}$, and $A(t_n, I) \neq A(t'_n, I)$. For this information set (27.2) does not hold, so the mechanism is not OSP. $\qquad\square$

27.2.3 Auction Environment

Even when c is SP, not every extensive-form mechanism for c is OSP. We now illustrate this for auctions with a single object.

We impose additional structure on the primitives. Each outcome x consists of an allocation $y \in \{0, 1\}^N$ and payments $p \in \mathbb{R}^N$; y_n denotes the nth component of y and p_n the nth component of p. The set of feasible allocations is $Y \equiv \{y : \sum_n y_n \leq 1\}$,

---

[1] It would be natural to place more structure on an agent's information sets, for instance, by requiring that the agent has perfect recall. However, we do not require this for our present purposes.

Table 27.1 Social choice rule c^* for types $T_1 = T_2 = \{0, 1, 2\}$.

	$t_2 = 0$	$t_2 = 1$	$t_2 = 2$
$t_1 = 0$	1 wins at \$0	2 wins at \$1	2 wins at \$1
$t_1 = 1$	1 wins at \$0	1 wins at \$1	2 wins at \$2
$t_1 = 2$	1 wins at \$0	1 wins at \$1	1 wins at \$2

and the set of outcomes is $X \equiv Y \times \mathbb{R}^N$. The quantity t_n is agent n's value for the object; we assume $T_n \subseteq \mathbb{R}_0^+$. Each agent has quasilinear utility

$$u_n((y, p), t_n) = t_n y_n - p_n. \tag{27.4}$$

With an abuse of notation we decompose a social choice rule $c \colon T \to X$ into an allocation rule $\tilde{y} \colon T \to Y$ and a payment rule $\tilde{p} \colon T \to \mathbb{R}^N$. To ease our exposition, we will assume there are two agents, $|N| = 2$.

We now study a strategy-proof social choice rule that awards the object to the agent with the highest type, breaking ties in favor of agent 1. The rule $c^* = (y^*, p^*)$ is defined as follows:

$$y^*(t) = \begin{cases} (1, 0) & \text{if } t_1 \geq t_2, \\ (0, 1) & \text{otherwise,} \end{cases} \tag{27.5}$$

$$p_n^*(t) = \begin{cases} \inf\{t_n' \in T_n : \tilde{y}_n(t_n', t_{-n}) = 1\} & \text{if } \tilde{y}_n(t) = 1, \\ 0 & \text{otherwise.} \end{cases} \tag{27.6}$$

If $T_1 = T_2 = [\underline{t}, \overline{t}]$ for some $0 \leq \underline{t} < \overline{t}$, then the social choice rule c^* corresponds to a second-price auction. With integer type sets, the tie-breaking rule affects payments – agent 1 pays t_2 when he wins and agent 2 pays $t_1 + 1$ when he wins. Table 27.1 displays c^* for integer type sets; within the table "1" stands for agent 1 and "2" stands for agent 2.

One extensive-form mechanism for c^* is the revelation mechanism. At the root vertex $\overline{v}$, agent 1 fully reports his type, so out($\overline{v}$) is the finest partition on T_1. Next, agent 2 fully reports his type, and then the mechanism concludes. To represent "simultaneity," we specify that agent 2 does observe agent 1's report when making his own report.[2] We denote this mechanism $\mathcal{M}^{\text{rev}}$; it is depicted in Figure 27.1.

Our next proposition states that, under a mild condition, the revelation mechanism for c^* is not OSP. This illustrates that some standard mechanisms for strategy-proof social choice rules are not obviously strategy-proof.

Proposition 27.2. *If $T_1 \cap T_2$ has at least two distinct elements, then $\mathcal{M}^{\text{rev}}$ is not OSP.*

Proof Let us denote these elements with as $t_1 = t_2 < t_1' = t_2'$. Consider the information set I with which agent 1 is called to play. We have $t_1, t_1' \in T_1^I$ and $t_2, t_2' \in T_2^I$. By construction, $A(t_1, I) \neq A(t_1', I)$. Moreover,

---

[2] That is, the partition $\mathcal{I}$ of non-terminal vertices $V \setminus Z$ consists of $\{\overline{v}\}$ and its complement.

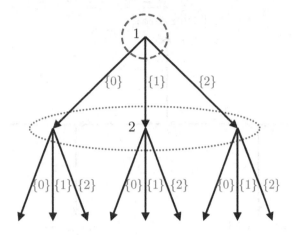

Figure 27.1 The mechanism $\mathcal{M}^{\text{rev}}$ for $T_1 = T_2 = \{0, 1, 2\}$.

$$u_1(c^*(t_1', t_2'), t_1') = 0 < t_1' - t_1 = u_1(c^*(t_1, t_2), t_1'), \qquad (27.7)$$

so $\mathcal{M}^{\text{rev}}$ is not OSP.[3] $\qquad\qquad\qquad\qquad\qquad\qquad\qquad\qquad\qquad\qquad$ $\square$

We have just established that even when a social choice rule is strategy-proof, not every extensive-form mechanism for the rule is obviously strategy-proof. Next we show that obvious strategy-proofness selects the ascending auction; it is the unique OSP extensive form for c^*.

27.2.3.1 OSP Characterizes the Ascending Auction

Because extensive-form mechanisms proceed in discrete steps, it is convenient to restrict T so that we can work out c^* with finitely many binary queries. Henceforth, we assume that $T_1 = T_2 = \{0, 1, 2, \dots, K\}$, for some integer K. We denote $\bar{t}_n = \max T_n$.

We now define an OSP mechanism for c^* – the ascending auction. Intuitively, the mechanism iteratively asks whether the agent's type is above some cutoff ("the going price"), alternating between the agents and raising the price when needed. Figure 27.2 depicts an ascending auction for the case $T_1 = T_2 = \{0, 1, 2\}$.

Definition 27.3. A mechanism for c^* is an *ascending auction* if it has perfect information (i.e. $\mathcal{I}$ is the finest partition) and there exists a pricing function $\rho: V \setminus Z \to \{0, 1, 2, \dots, K\}$ such that, for any non-terminal vertex v, where we denote $n = P(v)$:

1. The partition $\text{out}(v)$ consists of $\{t_n \in T_n^v : t_n \geq \rho(v)\}$ ("accepting the price") and $\{t_n \in T_n^v : t_n < \rho(v)\}$ ("quitting").
2. If v' is the child of v reached by the accepting edge then, for all $t \in T^{v'}$, if $y^*(t) = n$ then $p_n^*(t) \geq \rho(v)$.

---

[3] Even if we change $\mathcal{M}^{\text{rev}}$ by swapping the agent that goes first, the same argument still holds for agent 1's information set.

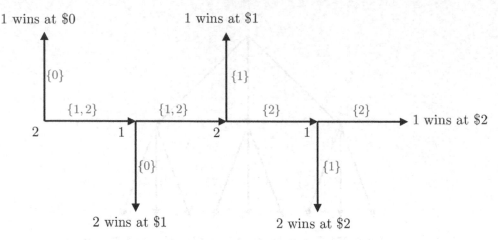

Figure 27.2 Ascending auction for $T_1 = T_2 = \{0, 1, 2\}$. All information sets are singletons. The black labels refer to agents 1 and 2.

3. If v' is the child of v reached by the quitting edge then, for all $t \in T^{v'}$, $y^*(t) \neq n$ and $p_n^*(t) = 0$.
4. For any v' that is a descendant of v, we have $\rho(v') \geq \rho(v)$.

Proposition 27.4. *A mechanism for c^* is obviously strategy-proof if it is an ascending auction.*

Proof Take any information set I and denote $P(I) = n$. Since $\mathcal{I}$ is the finest partition, we have $I = \{v\}$ for some non-terminal vertex v. Take any $t_n, t_n' \in T_n^I = T_n^v$ and any $t_{-n}, t_{-n}' \in T_{-n}^I = T_{-n}^v$. Suppose that $A(t_n, I) \neq A(t_n', I)$. Either $t_n \geq \rho(v)$ or $t_n < \rho(v)$. If $t_n \geq \rho(v)$ then $t_n' < \rho(v)$, and we have

$$u_n(c^*(t_n, t_{-n}), t_n) \geq 0 = u_n(c^*(t_n', t_{-n}'), t_n). \tag{27.8}$$

If $t_n < \rho(v)$ then $t_n' \geq \rho(v)$. Hence, either $y^*(t_n', t_{-n}') = n$ and $p_n^*(t_n', t_{-n}') \geq \rho(v)$, or $y^*(t_n', t_{-n}') \neq n$ and $p_n^*(t_n', t_{-n}') = 0$. This implies

$$u_n(c^*(t_n, t_{-n}), t_n) = 0 \geq u_n(c^*(t_n', t_{-n}'), t_n). \tag{27.9}$$

Thus, inequality (27.2) is satisfied, and the ascending auction for c^* is OSP. $\square$

Next we state the converse of Proposition 27.4. To ease exposition, we will restrict attention to mechanisms that are *terse*, meaning that, for any non-terminal vertex v,

1. v has at least two children, and
2. there exist $t, t' \in T^v$ such that $c(t) \neq c(t')$.

This restriction is without loss of generality, in the sense that, given any OSP mechanism for c, we can produce a terse OSP mechanism for c by "skipping" any vertices that violate the above requirements.

Proposition 27.5. *A mechanism for c^* is obviously strategy-proof and terse only if it is an ascending auction.*

We say that vertex v is *upward-closed* if, for $n = 1, 2$, $t_n \in T_n^v$ implies that, for all $t_n' > t_n$, $t_n' \in T_n^v$.

Lemma 27.6. *For any OSP mechanism for c^* and any non-terminal v, let us denote $n = P(v)$ and let I be the information set such that $v \in I$. If v is upward-closed then, for all $t_n \in T_n^v$ such that $y_n^*(t_n, \min T_{-n}^v) = 1$, we have that $A(t_n, I) = A(\bar{t}_n, I)$.*

Proof Suppose that we have v and $t_n \in T_n^v$ that constitute a counterexample to the lemma, so that $y_n^*(t_n, \min T_{-n}^v) = 1$, $A(t_n, I) \neq A(\bar{t}_n, I)$. (Since v is upward-closed, we have $\bar{t}_n \in T_n^v$ and $\bar{t}_{-n} \in T_{-n}^v$.) Then

$$u_n(c^*(\bar{t}_n, \bar{t}_{-n}), \bar{t}_n) = 0 < \bar{t}_n - t_n \leq u_n(c^*(t_n, \min T_{-n}^v), \bar{t}_n) \qquad (27.10)$$

so the mechanism is not OSP. $\qquad\qquad\square$

Lemma 27.7. *For any terse OSP mechanism for c^* and any non-terminal vertex v of the mechanism, v is upward-closed and either $\min T_1^v = \min T_2^v$ or $\min T_1^v + 1 = \min T_2^v$.*

Proof Observe that the root vertex $\bar{v}$ is upward-closed, and $\min T_1^{\bar{v}} = \min T_2^{\bar{v}}$. We now prove that if the statement holds for some arbitrary vertex v then it holds for any non-terminal child v'. Since T is finite and the mechanism is terse there are finitely many vertices, so this suffices to prove Theorem 27.7.

Suppose the statement holds for v. If v is terminal, then we are done. Otherwise, we have that v is upward-closed and either $\min T_1^v = \min T_2^v$ or $\min T_1^v + 1 = \min T_2^v$.

Case 1: $\min T_1^v = \min T_2^v$. In this case, Theorem 27.6 and terseness then imply that $P(v) = 2$. By Theorem 27.6, the partition specified by $\text{out}(v)$ consists of $\{\min T_2^v\}$ and its complement $T_2^v \setminus \{\min T_2^v\}$. If v' is the child reached by $\{\min T_2^v\}$, then $c^*(t) = c^*(\min T_1^{v'}, \min T_2^{v'})$ for all $t \in T_2^{v'}$. By terseness, v' is terminal. If v' is the child reached by $T_2^v \setminus \{\min T_2^v\}$ then v' is upward-closed, and $\min T_1^{v'} + 1 = \min T_2^{v'}$. Thus, Theorem 27.7 is satisfied at v'.

Case 2: $\min T_1^v + 1 = \min T_2^v$. Now, Theorem 27.6 and terseness imply that $P(v) = 1$. By Theorem 27.6, the partition specified by $\text{out}(v)$ consists of $\{\min T_1^v\}$ and its complement $T_1^v \setminus \{\min T_1^v\}$. The argument proceeds symmetrically. If v' is the child reached by $\{\min T_1^v\}$ then v' is terminal. If v' is the child reached by $T_1^v \setminus \{\min T_1^v\}$ then v' is upward-closed and $\min T_1^{v'} = \min T_2^{v'}$, so Theorem 27.7 is satisfied at v'. $\qquad\square$

Proof of Proposition 27.5 Now we combine Theorem 27.6 and Theorem 27.7 to prove Proposition 27.5. Take any non-terminal vertex v of an OSP mechanism for c^*. By Theorem 27.7, v is upward-closed and either $\min T_1^v = \min T_2^v$ or $\min T_1^v + 1 = \min T_2^v$.

Since the mechanism is terse, by Theorem 27.6, we have that

$$P(v) = \begin{cases} 2 & \text{if } \min T_1^v = \min T_2^v, \\ 1 & \text{otherwise.} \end{cases} \qquad (27.11)$$

Now let $\rho(v) = \min T_{P(v)}^v + 1$. Observe that by Theorem 27.6 and terseness, this choice of $\rho(v)$ satisfies clause 1 and clause 4 of Theorem 27.3. Let us denote $n = P(v)$.

If v' is the child of v reached by the accepting edge $\{t_n \in T_n^v : t_n \geq \rho(v)\}$, then, by the definitions of y^* and p^*, we have that, for all $t \in T^{v'}$, if $y^*(t) = n$ then $p_n^*(t) \geq p_n^*(\min T_n^v + 1, \min T_{-n}^v) = \rho(v)$. This proves clause 2.

If v' is the child of v reached by the quitting edge $\{t_n \in T_n^V : t_n < \rho(v)\}$, then we have that, for all $t \in T^{v'}$, $y^*(t) \neq n$ and $p_n^*(t) = 0$. This proves clause 3.

Observe that, for any distinct non-terminal vertices v and v' such that $P(v) = P(v')$, we have $T_{P(v)}^v \neq T_{P(v)}^{v'}$. Hence v and v' are not in the same information set, so the mechanism has perfect information. $\qquad\square$

27.2.4 Discussion

Obvious strategy-proofness captures one aspect of what it means for a mechanism to be simple. It formalizes the folk wisdom that dynamic auctions are easier to play than static auctions. There is a growing literature that seeks to understand the implications of simplicity for mechanism design.

27.3 Stability under Incomplete Information

Classical models for stable matching typically assume that agents have complete information about the *characteristics* and *preferences* of all agents in the market. However, in matching markets such as worker employment and college admissions, agents frequently have incomplete information about their options. We introduce some definitions of incomplete-information stability, and discuss how these definitions broaden our understanding of what outcomes may be reached by formal matching mechanisms and what informational elements should be considered when designing matching markets.

27.3.1 A Setting for Matching with Incomplete Information

We consider the matching of workers and firms in a non-transferable utility setting. Let W be a set of n workers and F a set of m firms. Let $\Omega \subseteq \mathbb{R}$ denote the set of possible worker types, and let $\omega: W \to \Omega$ be a function mapping each worker w to his type. There is one-sided incomplete information: the type $\omega(w)$ of worker w determines his preferences over firms as well as his position in each firm's preferences. The worker type function ω is drawn from a known distribution T, and each worker's type is his private information.

Each worker of type $\omega \in \Omega$ has a strict preference list $l(\omega)$ over the set $N(\omega) \subseteq F$ of firms that he prefers to being unmatched, and each firm $f \in F$ has a strict preference list $l(f)$ over the set $N(f) \subseteq \Omega$ of worker types that it prefers to being unmatched. If firm f is ahead of f' in a worker type ω's preference list, we write $f \succ_\omega f'$; similarly if worker type ω is ahead of ω' in f's preference list we write $\omega \succ_f \omega'$. We let $\emptyset$ denote being unmatched.

A *matching* is a function $\mu: W \to F \cup \{\emptyset\}$ matching workers to firms that is one-to-one on $\mu^{-1}(F)$. (In this chapter, for notational simplicity, we will write $\mu(f)$ instead

Figure 27.3 A matching that is unstable under complete information.

of $\mu^{-1}(f)$ for $f \in F$.) Notice that preferences are defined for worker types, but the matching is defined for workers. An *outcome* of the matching game (μ, ω) specifies a realized type assignment ω and a matching μ.

Example 27.8. Let I be an instance of the stable matching with incomplete information problem for three workers and three firms with the following types and preference lists:

$$\omega(w_1) = \omega_1, \ \omega(w_2) = \omega_2, \ \omega(w_3) = \omega_3,$$
$$l(\omega_1) = l(\omega_2) = l(\omega_3) = (f_1, f_2, f_3),$$
$$l(f_1) = l(f_2) = l(f_3) = (\omega_1, \omega_2, \omega_3).$$

In other words, all workers have the same preferences over firms, and all firms have the same preferences over worker types. Consider the perfect matching in instance I shown in Figure 27.3. If firms had complete information about workers' types, this matching would be unstable, as (w_1, f_1) would form a blocking pair. However, with incomplete information, f_1 may not be sure of whether it wishes to block with w_1. We explore this in the next section.

27.3.2 Inference and Stability

In a setting with incomplete information, the firms do not know worker types. We consider now the inferences that firms can make about worker types, and how to define stability given these inferences.

Recall that each worker knows his type, and, prior to the match no other agent knows the worker type of any other agent. We assume that, after matching, each firm f observes the matching of firms to workers, the distribution of worker types, and the type $\omega(\mu^{-1}(f))$ of their matched worker. We consider a notion of stability that captures the notion that *firms have common knowledge that the matching cannot be blocked*. This formulation resembles the game-theoretic notion of rationalizability, obtained via iterated elimination of strategies that are never best responses. Another analogy is the deductive iterations that arise in the classic "colored hats" problem, often used to illustrate common knowledge.

For some intuition, in Example 27.8 consider the pair (w_1, f_1). Suppose that f_1 has incomplete information and knows only that there is one of each worker type ω_1, ω_2, or ω_3 in the market. As f_1 is currently matched with a worker of type ω_2, it can infer that w_1 is either type ω_1 or type ω_3. Notice that matching with w_1 is advantageous for f_1 if $\omega(w_1) = \omega_1$ but disadvantageous if $\omega(w_1) = \omega_3$.

Is f_1 able to infer the type of w_1? One source of information is whether w_1 is willing to participate in the block. In the present instance all workers have the same preferences, so this does not help f_1 distinguish between the workers. Another source of information is whether other firms are willing to block. Firm f_1 can take the following line of reasoning. Suppose w_1 is the disadvantageous type, $\omega(w_1) = \omega_3$. Then firm f_1 knows that firm f_2 knows that it is matched to the lowest possible type and hence would be willing to block with w_3; similarly firm f_1 knows that w_3 is matched to the lowest possible firm and is willing to block with f_2. In other words, if $\omega(w_1) = \omega_3$ then (w_3, f_2) would be a blocking pair. Since the true type is $\omega(w_1) = \omega_1$, firm f_2 is not willing to block, from which f_1 can deduce that $\omega(w_1) = \omega_1$ and would be willing to block with w_1.

This line of iterated reasoning allows us to identify that f_1 will block this match, and so the match is not stable. In what follows, we will define stability by formalizing this iterated reasoning. We will also show that, in this incomplete-information setting, if all firms have the same ranking over worker types and all workers have the same ranking over firms then every stable matching is positive assortative.

Definition 27.9. A matching μ is *individually rational* if each matched agent prefers their match to being unmatched, i.e.,

$$\mu(w) \succ_{\omega(w)} \emptyset \ \forall w \in W, \text{ and}$$
$$\omega(\mu(f)) \succ_f \emptyset \ \forall f \in F.$$

Definition 27.10. Let Σ be a set of individually rational matching outcomes. For every firm f and outcome (μ, ω), let $\Sigma(f, \mu, \omega)$ be the set of outcomes in Σ that is consistent with firm f's information after outcome (μ, ω):

$$\Sigma(f, \mu, \omega) := \{(\mu, \omega') \in \Sigma \text{ s.t. } \omega'(\mu(f)) = \omega(\mu(f))\}.$$

A matching outcome (μ, ω) is Σ-*blocked* if there is a worker–firm pair (w, f) such that:

1. *Worker w is willing to block with f*, i.e., *worker w strictly prefers firm f to his match*:

$$f \succ_{\omega(w)} \mu(w).$$

2. *Firm f is willing to block with w*, i.e., firm f strictly prefers worker w to its match for every outcome consistent with its information where w would be willing to block with f:

$$\omega'(w) \succ_f \omega'\left(\mu^{-1}(f)\right)$$

for all $(\mu, \omega') \in \Sigma(f, \mu, \omega)$ such that $f \succ_{\omega'(w)} \mu(w)$.

A matching outcome $(\mu, \omega) \in \Sigma$ is Σ-*stable* if it is not Σ-blocked.

In other words, a matching outcome (μ, ω) is Σ-blocked if some worker-firm pair is willing to block μ for any outcome in Σ consistent with the firm's information given (μ, ω).

To define the set of stable outcomes, we start with the set of individually rational outcomes and iteratively remove blocked outcomes.

Definition 27.11. Let Σ^0 be the set of all individually rational outcomes. For $k \geq 1$, let

$$\Sigma^k := \{(\mu, \omega) \in \Sigma^{k-1} \mid (\mu, \omega) \text{ is } \Sigma^{k-1}\text{-stable}\}$$

be the set of outcomes in Σ^{k-1} that are not Σ^{k-1}-blocked. The set of *incomplete-information stable outcomes* is given by

$$\Sigma^\infty := \bigcap_{k=1}^{\infty} \Sigma^k.$$

If (μ, ω) is an incomplete-information stable outcome, the matching μ is an *incomplete-information stable matching* at ω.

Our first result is that incomplete-information stable matchings exist, i.e., the limit of the above sequence, Σ^∞, is non-empty.

Proposition 27.12. *Given workers W, firms F and worker types ω, there is an incomplete-information stable outcome (μ, ω), and so the set of incomplete-information stable matchings is non-empty.*

Proof If μ is a complete-information stable matching given worker types ω, then by definition μ is not blocked by any worker–firm pair given ω, and so $(\mu, \omega) \in \Sigma^k$ for each $k \geq 0$. $\qquad\square$

27.3.3 Assortativity of Stable Outcomes

The notion of incomplete-information stability defined in Definition 27.11 is relatively permissive, as a firm in a blocking pair (w, f) must strictly gain from matching with w for *all* possible worker types ω consistent with the firm's rationalizable beliefs. In this section, we show that despite this permissiveness, when agent preferences are aligned the only stable outcome is assortative matching.

Proposition 27.13. *Let I be an instance of the stable matching with incomplete information problem for n workers and $m = n$ firms. Suppose the distribution T is such that there is exactly one worker of each type $\omega_1, \ldots, \omega_n$, and there is an ordering of worker types $\omega_1, \omega_2, \ldots, \omega_n$ and firms $f_1, f_2, \ldots, f_n$ such that*

$$l(\omega_1) = l(\omega_2) = \cdots = l(\omega_n) = (f_1, f_2, \ldots, f_n),$$
$$l(f_1) = l(f_2) = \cdots = l(f_n) = (\omega_1, \omega_2, \ldots, \omega_n).$$

Then the only incomplete-information stable outcomes are of the form (μ, ω) where

$$\mu(\omega^{-1}(\omega_i)) = f_i \ \forall i.$$

The uniqueness of the stable outcome may seem evident given the strong assumption that all workers have the same preferences over firms; for example, firm f_1 knows that it can have its pick of workers. However, the firms have very little information about workers and the notion of blocking is very strict: even though f_1 knows it can have its pick of workers, it does not know which workers it prefers to its current match and it can block with a worker only if it is sure that, given the worker's willingness to block, the realized blocking pair will be advantageous. In what follows, we formalize the intuition that firms' *common knowledge* is sufficient for f_1 to block outcomes where it is not matched with the worker with type ω_1.

Remark 27.14. Stronger results about assortativity can be provided in a transferable utility setting. For example, with transferable utility, when agent valuations are supermodular and monotonic, stable matchings are *positive assortative* and maximize the total surplus. In addition, when agent valuations are submodular and monotonic, stable matchings are *negative assortative* and maximize the total surplus. Moreover, both results hold for any type distribution and any number of firms and workers. Intuitively, in a setting with transfers, firms are able to ascertain the relative ordering of workers both through *which firms* the workers are currently matched with, as well as *at which prices* the firms are willing to block.

27.3.3.1 Proof of Proposition 27.13

We now prove by induction on k that if $(\mu, \omega) \in \Sigma^k$ then, for all $i \le k$, the ith-lowest firm is matched to the ith-lowest-type worker, $\omega(\mu(f_{n-i+1})) = \omega_{n-i+1}$.

Base Case: $k = 1$. We show that if $(\mu, \omega') \in \Sigma^1$ then the lowest firm is matched to the lowest-type worker, $\omega'(\mu(f_n)) = \omega_n$.

Let (μ, ω') be such that $\omega'(\mu(f)) = \omega_n$ for some $f \ne f_n$. We will show that (μ, ω') is Σ^0-blocked by showing that the firm matched to the worst worker type and the worker matched to the worst firm type will be willing to block. Formally, we show that $(w = \mu(f_n), f)$ is willing to block, as follows:

1. Worker w strictly prefers firm f to his match f_n, since f_n is the firm least preferred by workers. Thus worker w is willing to block with f.
2. Firm f is matched to the worst type $\omega'(\mu(f)) = \omega_n$. Hence, for any outcome $(\mu, \omega'') \in \Sigma^0(f, \mu, \omega')$, firm f strictly prefers a worker of type $\omega''(w) \ne \omega_n$ to its match, i.e., $\omega''(w) \succ_f \omega_n = \omega''(\mu^{-1}(f))$. Thus firm f is willing to block with w.

Hence (μ, ω') is Σ^0-blocked. It follows that if $(\mu, \omega') \in \Sigma^1$ then $\omega'(\mu(f_n)) = \omega_n$.

Inductive Step. We show that if $(\mu, \omega) \in \Sigma^k$ then, for all $i \le k$, the ith-lowest firm is matched to the ith-lowest-type worker, $\omega(\mu(f_{n-i+1})) = \omega_{n-i+1}$.

If $i < k$ then the inductive hypothesis follows from the fact that $\Sigma^k \subseteq \Sigma^i$ and by strong induction on k.

If $i = k$, i.e., for Σ^k, we can prove the inductive hypothesis by showing that the firm matched to the kth-lowest worker type and the worker matched to the kth-lowest firm will be willing to block. Let (μ, ω') be such that $\omega'(\mu(f_i)) = \omega_i$ for all $i > n - k + 1$ and $\omega'(\mu(f)) = \omega_{n-k+1}$ for some $f \ne f_{n-k+1}$. We will show that (μ, ω') is Σ^{k-1}-blocked by showing that $(w = \mu(f_{n-k+1}), f)$ is willing to block, as follows:

1. Worker w strictly prefers firm f to his match f_{n-k+1}, since f_{n-k+1} is the least preferred firm of all workers within $F' = \{f_1, \ldots, f_{n-k+1}\}$, and $\omega'(\mu(f)) = \omega_{n-k+1} \notin \{\omega_i\}_{i>n-k+1}$ implies that $f \in F'$. Thus worker w is willing to block with f.

2. Consider any outcome $(\mu, \omega'') \in \Sigma^{k-1}(f, \mu, \omega')$. By strong induction the workers matched with the lowest firm types satisfy $\omega''(\mu(f_{n-i+1})) = \omega_{n-i+1}$ for all $i < k$. Consistency with (μ, ω') for f implies that $\omega''(\mu(f)) = \omega_{n-k+1}$. Since $w = \mu(f_{n-k+1})$ is matched with a different firm, it follows that $\omega''(w) \notin \{\omega_{n-i+1}\}_{i \leq k}$ and so $\omega''(w) \in \{\omega_1, \ldots, \omega_{n-k}\}$.

It follows that, for any outcome $(\mu, \omega'') \in \Sigma^{k-1}(f, \mu, \omega')$, firm f strictly prefers a worker of type $\omega''(w)$ to its match, i.e., $\omega''(w) = \omega_l$ for some $i \leq n - k$, $\omega''(\mu(f)) = \omega'(\mu(f)) = \omega_{n-k+1}$, and so $\omega''(w) \succ_f \omega''(\mu(f))$. Thus firm f is willing to block with w.

Hence (μ, ω') is Σ^{k-1}-blocked. It follows that if $(\mu, \omega') \in \Sigma^k$ then $\omega'(\mu(f_{n-k+1})) = \omega_{n-k+1}$.

To complete the proof of Proposition 27.13, it suffices to show that the outcome (μ, ω) given by $\mu(w_i) = f_i$ $\forall i$ is incomplete-information stable. This follows from the fact that μ is complete-information stable.

27.3.4 Beliefs

The preceding definition and discussion of incomplete-information stability illustrates the central role of *beliefs* in matching with incomplete information. Whether an outcome is stable depends on the firms' beliefs about the types of workers in potential blocking pairs, as ascertained from the non-existence of other blocking pairs.

Recall that we have assumed that, after matching, each firm f observes the distribution of worker types. This may seem a strange assumption, and we may instead prefer that the firm observes only the type ω' of its matched worker and makes inferences on other workers' types based only on T and ω'. However, such a relaxation of beliefs can be too permissive and allow many matchings to be stable, reducing its usefulness in characterizing mechanisms and predicting outcomes.

Proposition 27.15. *Let I be an instance of the stable matching with incomplete information problem for n workers and $m = n$ firms. Suppose that $\Omega = [0, 1]$, the distribution T is such that $\omega(w_i) \sim U[0, 1]$ and is independent across workers, and*

$$I(\omega) = (f_1, f_2, \ldots, f_m) \quad \forall \omega \in [0, 1],$$
$$I(f_i) \text{ satisfies } \omega \succ_{f_i} \omega' \; \forall \omega > \omega', \; i \in [n].$$

Then for any $\omega(\cdot)$ such that $\omega(w_i) > 0$ for all i, outcome (μ, ω) is incomplete-information stable if and only if the matching μ is maximal.

Note that the instance in Proposition 27.15 differs from the instance in Proposition 27.13 only in the distribution T of worker type functions. In both instances the only complete-information stable matching is the assortative matching, and in Proposition 27.13 we see that the only incomplete-information stable matching is the assortative matching. However, in the instance in Proposition 27.15 almost all matchings are incomplete-information stable (if $\omega(w_i) > 0 \; \forall i$); no firm will be willing to block with any worker since there is always a possibility that the worker has a lower type than that of their current match.

A number of other specifications of beliefs have been proposed, which require firms to be Bayesian in evaluating potential blocking. In a *Bayesian stable-matching outcome*, firms evaluate the value of a potential blocking partner by performing a Bayesian update with respect to the prior belief on the set of admissible types. Another approach is to specify beliefs both *on-path* in the realized outcome and *off-path* in potential coalitional deviations. Such definitions of incomplete-information stability have helped to shed light on the desired structure for mechanisms implementing stable outcomes.

An alternative approach is to consider the stability of the mechanisms. In a many-to-one college admissions setting, where students have *interdependent* types, a *stable mechanism* is defined in terms of Bayesian updates and potential blocking pairs are formed after the running of a specified mechanism. This formulation of beliefs highlights that *stability depends on the amount of information about the matching available to colleges*, and stable matchings are more likely to exist when the mechanism provides colleges with limited information outside their own matched students.

Finally, one may want to consider a belief-free notion of stability. One such definition has been provided in a many-to-one college admissions setting where student types are known but students do not know their preferences and can learn their value at each college for a cost. In this setting, *regret-free stable outcomes* refine the set of stable outcomes by ruling out blocking pairs and also by requiring students to have acquired information optimally. Regret-free stable outcomes can be characterized by cutoffs and *two-stage mechanisms* which (i) use partial student preferences to estimate these cutoffs and (ii) after the cutoffs can facilitate efficient student information acquisition and implement approximately regret-free stable outcomes.

27.4 Exercises

Exercise 27.1 Consider the instance of stable matching with incomplete information in Example 27.8, and the perfect matching μ in Figure 27.3:

$$\mu(f_1) = w_2, \ \mu(f_2) = w_1, \ \mu(f_3) = w_3.$$

In this exercise, we formalize the intuition at the beginning of Section 27.3.2 that (μ, ω) is not an incomplete-information stable outcome (where ω is defined in Example 27.8 as $\omega(w_i) = \omega_i \ \forall i$).

(a) Let μ' be an arbitrary perfect matching of workers to firms. Show that $(\mu', \omega') \in \Sigma^0$.

(b) Let ω' be defined by $\omega'(w_1) = \omega_3, \ \omega'(w_2) = \omega_2, \ \omega'(w_3) = \omega_1$. Show that (μ, ω') is Σ^0-blocked.

(c) Recall that ω is defined by $\omega(w_1) = \omega_1, \ \omega(w_2) = \omega_2, \ \omega(w_3) = \omega_3$. Show that (μ, ω) is Σ^1-blocked by demonstrating that (w_1, f_1) is willing to block. It follows that $(\mu, \omega) \notin \Sigma^2$ is not an incomplete-information stable outcome.

Exercise 27.2 In this exercise, we consider whether assortative matching (Proposition 27.13) continues to hold for unbalanced markets. In the following we will assume that $\omega(w_i) = \omega_i$ for all i, T is such that each permutation of types occurs with equal probability, and there is an ordering of worker types $\omega_1, \omega_2, \ldots, \omega_n$ and firms $f_1, f_2, \ldots, f_m$ such that

$$l(\omega_1) = l(\omega_2) = \cdots = l(\omega_n) = (f_1, f_2, \ldots, f_m),$$
$$l(f_1) = l(f_2) = \cdots = l(f_m) = (\omega_1, \omega_2, \ldots, \omega_n).$$

(a) Suppose there are more firms than workers, $m \geq n$. Show that there is a unique incomplete-information stable outcome (μ, ω), and that it is assortative, i.e., $\mu(w_i) = f_i \; \forall i \leq n$.

(b) Provide an example of a setting where there are more workers than firms, $n > m$, and there is an incomplete-information stable outcome (μ, ω) that is not assortative, i.e., $\mu(w_i) \neq f_i$ for some $i \leq m$.

27.5 Bibliographic Notes

Evidence of deviations from dominant-strategy play can be found in [8], [19], and [10]. In [12], the play in second-price auctions was compared with the to play in ascending auctions.

The result presented in Section 27.2 is due to [13]. In the paper [16] it is proved that, in designing OSP mechanisms, it is without loss of generality to restrict attention to games of perfect information. For further work on obvious strategy-proofness, see [3], [4], [18], and [1].

The definitions and results presented in Sections 27.3.1–27.3.3 are based on those in [15], which defines incomplete-information stability in a setting where a matched (firm, worker) pair can transfer utility through payments. More details on rationalizability can be found in [5] and [17]. The "colored hats" problem is due to [9].

Proposition 27.15 is due to [6], in which Bayesian stable-matching outcomes are also defined. The on-path and off-path approach to beliefs is due to [14]. Stable mechanisms were defined in [7], and regret-free stability was introduced in [11].

References

[1] Arribillaga, R. P., Massó, J., and Neme A., 2019. All sequential allotment rules are obviously strategy-proof. *Working Paper*.

[2] Arribillaga, R. P., Massó, J., and Neme A., 2020. On obvious strategy-proofness and single-peakedness. *Journal of Economic Theory*, **186**, 104992.

[3] Ashlagi, I. and Gonczarowski, Y. A. 2018. Stable matching mechanisms are not obviously strategy-proof. *Journal of Economic Theory*, **177**, 405–425.

[4] Bade, S. and Gonczarowski, Y. A. 2017. Gibbard–Satterthwaite success stories and obvious strategyproofness. In *Proc. 2017 ACM Conference on Economics and Computation*.

[5] Bernheim, B. D. 1984. Rationalizable strategic behavior. *Econometrica: Journal of the Econometric Society*. www.jstor.org/stable/1911196.

[6] Bikhchandani, S. 2017. Stability with one-sided incomplete information. *Journal of Economic Theory*, **168**, 372–399.

[7] Chakraborty, A., Citanna, A., and Ostrovsky, M. 2010. Two-sided matching with interdependent values. *Journal of Economic Theory*, **145**, 85–105.

[8] Chen, Y. and Sönmez, T. 2006. School choice: an experimental study. *Journal of Economic theory*, **127**, 202–231.

[9] Geanakoplos, J. 1994. Common knowledge. *Handbook of Game Theory with Economic Applications*, **2**, 1437–1496.

[10] Hassidim, A., Romm, A., and Shorrer, R. I. 2020. The limits of incentives in economic matching procedures. *Management Science*. https://pubsonline .informs.org/doi/abs/10.1287/mnsc.2020.3591.

[11] Immorlica, N., Leshno, J., Lo, I., and Lucier, B. 2020. Information acquisition in matching markets: The role of price discovery. *Available at SSRN*.

[12] Kagel, J. H., Harstad, R. M., and Levin, D. 1987. Information impact and allocation rules in auctions with affiliated private values: A laboratory study. *Econometrica*, **55**, 1275–1304.

[13] Li, S. (2017). Obviously strategy-proof mechanisms. *American Economic Review*, **107**, 3257–3287.

[14] Liu, Q. (2020). Stability and Bayesian consistency in two-sided markets. Available at SSRN 3577399.

[15] Liu, Q., Mailath, G. J., Postlewaite, A., and Samuelson, L. 2014. Stable matching with incomplete information. *Econometrica*, **82**, 541–587.

[16] Mackenzie, A. (2020). A revelation principle for obviously strategy-proof implementation. *Games and Economic Behavior*. www.sciencedirect.com/science/ article/pii/S0899825620301408.

[17] Pearce, D. G. (1984). Rationalizable strategic behavior and the problem of perfection. *Econometrica: Journal of the Econometric Society*. www.jstor.org/ stable/1911197

[18] Pycia, M. and Troyan, P. 2019. A theory of simplicity in games and mechanism design. Working Paper.

[19] Rees-Jones, A. 2018. Suboptimal behavior in strategy-proof mechanisms: Evidence from the residency match. *Games and Economic Behavior*, **108**, 317–330.

[20] Roth, A. E. and Wilson, R. B. 2019. How market design emerged from game theory: A mutual interview. *Journal of Economic Perspectives*, **33**, 118–43.

CHAPTER TWENTY-EIGHT

Machine Learning for Matching Markets

Zhe Feng, David C. Parkes, and Sai Srivatsa Ravindranath

28.1 Introduction

In this chapter we demonstrate the use of machine learning for the automated design of matching markets. This extends the reach of optimal design to problems that are challenging to solve analytically and provides new directions for economic theory, identifying gaps in current understanding.

This is a data-driven approach and assumes access to samples of agent values or preferences and makes use of differentiable representations of the rules of matching markets in enabling gradient-based optimization. We refer to this research agenda as that of *differentiable economics*. The framework involves the following four steps:

1. Design an *artificial neural network architecture* that provides a differentiable representation of a mapping from inputs such as preference reports to outcomes such as a distribution on matchings.
2. Formulate a *loss function* and define other quantities of interest, for example, the degree to which incentive compatibility is violated.
3. Adopt a suitable *training procedure* to minimize expected loss while incorporating constraints such as incentive compatibility.
4. Evaluate performance against baselines and interpret the learned mechanisms.

We first provide a primer on artificial neural networks in Section 28.2. Section 28.3 applies the framework to one-sided matching, and in particular to the design of revenue-optimal multi-item auctions. Section 28.4 applies the framework to a two-sided matching, and in particular to understand the design frontier between stability and strategy-proofness. In Section 28.5 we outline a number of open problems and interesting future directions.

28.2 Artificial Neural Networks

An *artificial neural network* (ANN) is a non-linear model of computation inspired by the brain that is commonly used in machine learning. Each unit in an ANN consists of a non-linear *activation function* applied to a weighted sum of inputs. See Figure 28.1, left, where the linear sum $\ell = w_0 + \sum_{i=1}^{J} w_i q_i$, for inputs $q_1, \ldots, q_J$, with weights $w_1, \ldots, w_J$, and *bias term* w_0. The quantity $\sigma : \mathbb{R} \to \mathbb{R}$ denotes the *activation*

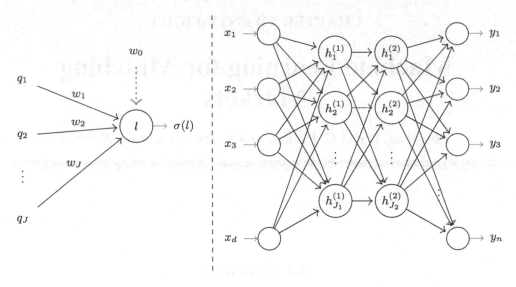

Figure 28.1 Left: A single unit in an artificial neural network. Right: A two-hidden-layer, fully connected, feed-forward artificial neural network.

function and the output is $\sigma(\ell)$. Some commonly used activation functions are the *sigmoid*, *tanh*, and *ReLU* or *LeakyReLU* activation functions (see Figure 28.2).

In a fully connected feed-forward ANN, several such units are stacked together and organized in layers, in such a way that the outputs of some units become inputs to others (see Figure 28.2, right).

Let $x \in \mathbb{R}^d$ denote the *input* to an ANN and $y \in \mathbb{R}^n$ the *output*. Let $w^{(1)}, w^{(2)}, \ldots, w^{(R)}$ denote the weights corresponding to each of $R \geq 1$ hidden layers, with J_r units in layer r; $w^{(R+1)}$ denotes the weights in the output layer. The weights $w = \{w^{(1)}, w^{(2)}, \ldots, w^{(R+1)}\}$ are the *parameters* for the ANN to learn, with the network defining the non-linear function $y = f^w(x)$.

Let $w_{ij}^{(r)}$ be the weight associated with the input from unit i in layer $r - 1$ (or from input x_i if $r = 1$) to unit j in layer r (or to output unit y_j if $r = R + 1$), and let $w_{0j}^{(r)}$ denote the associated bias term. The output $y \in \mathbb{R}^n$ is computed as follows:

$$h_j^{(1)} = \sigma\left(w_{0j}^{(1)} + \sum_{i=1}^{d} w_{ij}^{(1)} x_i\right) \qquad \forall j \in \{1, \ldots, J_1\}, \tag{28.1}$$

$$h_j^{(r)} = \sigma\left(w_{0j}^{(r)} + \sum_{i=1}^{J_{r-1}} w_{ij}^{(r)} h_i^{(r-1)}\right) \qquad \forall j \in \{1, \ldots, J_r\} \; \forall r \in \{2, \ldots, R\}, \tag{28.2}$$

$$y_j = \sigma\left(w_{0j}^{(R+1)} + \sum_{i=1}^{J_R} w_{ij}^{(R+1)} h_i^{(R)}\right) \qquad \forall j \in \{1, \ldots, n\}. \tag{28.3}$$

Learning is formulated as finding parameters w that minimize a *loss function* with respect to a distribution F on inputs x. A common approach is *supervised learning*, where there is a *target function* f^* and the loss function is

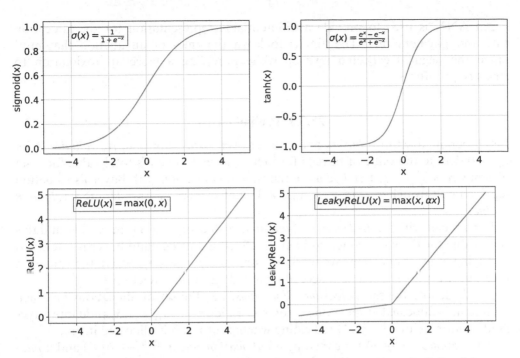

Figure 28.2 Top-Left: The *sigmoid* function maps a real number to the range [0, 1]. Top right: The tanh function is a scaled *sigmoid* function and is zero-centered and maps real numbers to the range [−1, 1]. **Bottom**: *ReLU* and *LeakyReLU* are piece wise linear functions that map reals to reals.

$$\mathcal{L}(w) = \mathbb{E}_{x \sim F}\left[loss(f^w(x), f^*(x))\right], \tag{28.4}$$

where *loss* is a differentiable function that quantifies how well f^w approximates f^*. As applied to economic design, the loss function will not come from supervision but directly captures the economic concept of interest.

Artificial neural networks are trained by updating parameters w to minimize loss on *training data* through a gradient descent procedure. A typical approach is to repeatedly sample a set of examples (a *mini-batch*) from the training data, with the parameters updated on mini-batch τ through a single iteration of stochastic gradient descent (SGD):

$$w_{ij}^r := w_{ij}^r - \alpha \times \nabla_{w_{ij}^r} \mathcal{L}^{(\tau)}(w), \quad \text{for each } i, j, \text{ and } r \in \{1, \ldots, R+1\}. \tag{28.5}$$

Here, $\alpha > 0$ is the *learning rate* and $\mathcal{L}^{(\tau)}(w)$ denotes the average loss on the examples in the τth mini-batch. Open-source software frameworks such as *PyTorch* and *TensorFlow* can be used to define and train ANNs.

28.3 Optimal Auction Design

We first illustrate the framework of differentiable economics for one-sided matching and *revenue-optimal auctions*. This is a suitable problem to study because the optimal auction for the sale of two items is not fully understood from an analytical viewpoint.

An ANN is used to provide a differentiable representation for the allocation rule and payment rule. The aim is to learn the rules of an auction that minimize the negated expected revenue while providing a close approximation to strategy-proofness.

28.3.1 Preliminaries

Let B denote a set of n *buyers* and G a set of m *items*. For *additive valuations*, let $v_{ij} \geq 0$ denote the value of buyer i for item j, so that buyer i's total value for a set of items S is $\sum_{j \in S} v_{ij}$. Let V denote the *valuation domain*, with buyer i's valuation represented through $v_i = (v_{i1}, \ldots, v_{im}) \in V$. Let $v = (v_1, \ldots, v_n)$ denote a *valuation profile*.

For a buyer with a *unit-demand valuation*, its value for a set S is $\max_{j \in S} v_{ij}$ and this is its value for the most preferred item. In effect, a unit-demand buyer is interested in buying at most one item. We work in a probabilistic setting, where the valuation v_i of buyer i is distributed i.i.d. according to a distribution function F_V.

Let X denote the set of *feasible allocations*, i.e., the set of allocations in which each item is allocated at most once. For $x \in X$, let $x_i = (x_{i1}, \ldots, x_{im})$ denote buyer i's allocation, with $x_{ij} \in \{0, 1\}$ indicating whether or not it is allocated item j.

An *auction* $A = (g, p)$ is defined by an *allocation rule* $g \colon V^n \to \Delta(X)$ and a *payment rule* $p \colon V^n \to \mathbb{R}^n$; $\Delta(X)$ is the probability simplex on feasible allocations, and g maps a reported valuation profile $\hat{v}$ to a possibly randomized allocation $g(\hat{v})$. The payment rule defines, for each buyer i, an expected payment $t_i = p(\hat{v})$.

We assume *quasilinear utility*, so that a buyer's utility is equal to the expected value minus payment. The following quantity plays an important role in learning approximately strategy-proof auctions.

Definition 28.1. (Regret). Buyer i's *regret* for truthful bidding on valuation profile v in auction $A = (g, p)$, when all the other buyers are truthful, is

$$\text{regret}_i(v) = \max_{v_i' \in V} \left[\left(v_i(g(v_i', v_{-i})) - p_i(v_i', v_{-i}) \right) - \left(v_i(g(v)) - p_i(v) \right) \right], \quad (28.6)$$

where $v_{-i} = (v_1, \ldots, v_{i-1}, v_{i+1}, \ldots, v_n)$.

A buyer's regret is the maximum amount by which it could increase its utility relative to truthful reporting by reporting a non-truthful valuation. This connects with the notion of strategy-proofness (see Chapter 4). An auction is *strategy-proof* if and only if every buyer has zero regret on every valuation profile.

28.3.2 Methodology

28.3.2.1 Step 1: Design an Artificial Neural Network

We consider a single neural network with two feed-forward components, namely the *allocation component* g^w and the *payment component* p^w (see Figure 28.3). Each component consist of multiple hidden layers ($h^{(r)}$ and $c^{(r)}$ in the figure) and an output layer. The components communicate through the value of the allocation.

This is the *RegretNet* architecture. The input is $n \times m$ reals, corresponding to bids. We write $b = (b_1, \ldots, b_n)$, where $b_i = (b_{i1}, \ldots, b_{im})$ and b_{ij} denotes the reported value

Allocation component

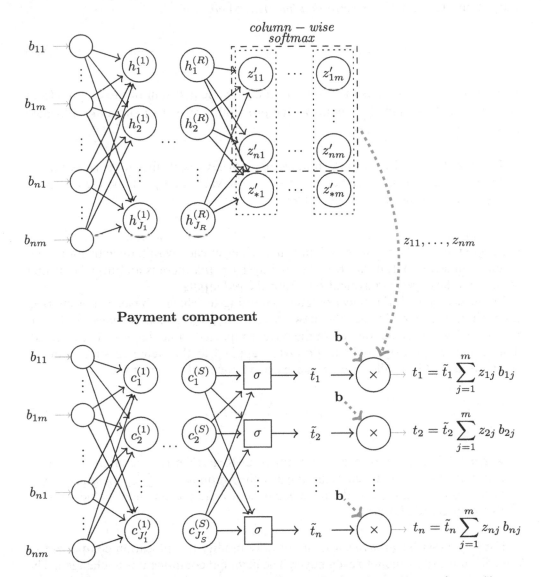

Figure 28.3 The allocation and payment component of the RegretNet architecture for a multi-item auction with n additive buyers and m items. The allocation component is a feed-forward network with $R(= 2)$ layers and softmax activation functions to determine the randomized allocation z. The payment component is a feed-forward network with $S(= 2)$ layers and sigmoid functions to determine the payment of each buyer as a fraction of the buyer's expected value (making use of the randomized allocation z).

(i.e., bid) of buyer i for item j. The network provides a differentiable representation of the auction rules. Let w_g and w_p denote the parameters in the allocation and payment component, respectively, with $w = (w_g, w_p) \in \mathbb{R}^d$, for d parameters.

The allocation component is function $g^w \colon V^n \to \triangle(X)$ and consists of two fully connected hidden layers, with 100 units in each layer, each with tanh activations, and a fully connected output layer. For each item $j \in G$, this outputs a vector $z_{1j}, \dots, z_{nj}$

with $\sum_{i=1}^{n} z_{ij} \leq 1$; z_{ij} is the probability that item j will be allocated to buyer i. Each output unit uses a *softmax activation function*, where

$$z_{ij} = softmax_i(z'_{1j}, \ldots, z'_{nj}, z'_{n+1,j}) = \frac{e^{z'_{ij}}}{\sum_{k=1}^{n+1} e^{z'_{kj}}}; \qquad (28.7)$$

here z'_{ij}, for each $i \in [n]$, is the result of taking a weighted sum of the outputs from the previous layer and $z'_{n+1,j}$ controls the probability that the item is not allocated ($e \approx 2.72$ is Euler's number).

Remark 28.2. The network architecture can represent allocation rules that tend to bundle items together, for example the value of z_{1j} may be high when z_{1k} is high, for items $j \neq k$ and buyer 1.

The payment component is a function $p^w : V^n \to \mathbb{R}^n$ and consists of two fully connected hidden layers, with 100 units in each layer each with tanh activations and a fully connected output layer. For each buyer $i \in [n]$, there is an output unit that represents the expected payment $t_i \in \mathbb{R}$ for the bid inputs.

To ensure *individual rationality* (IR), according to which a buyer is not charged more than its reported value, the network computes a *fractional payment*, $\tilde{t}_i \in [0, 1]$ for buyer i, which is the fraction of the buyer's reported value that it will be charged. This comes from a sigmoid function $\sigma(\ell_i)$ applied to the weighted sum from the previous layer. Given allocation z, the expected payment by buyer i is

$$t_i = \tilde{t}_i \times \sum_{j=1}^{m} z_{ij} \, b_{ij}. \qquad (28.8)$$

Remark 28.3. The expected payment from RegretNet can be interpreted as a lottery on payments, charging buyer i the amount $\tilde{t}_i \times \sum_{j=1}^{m} x_{ij} b_{ij}$ for 0–1 allocation x. In this way, the buyer's payment is no greater than its bid value for the realized allocation.

For buyers with *unit-demand valuations*, we modify the allocation component to allocate at most one item to each buyer. The payment component is unchanged. The modified allocation component outputs two scores, $s \in \mathbb{R}^{(n+1) \times m}$ and $s' \in \mathbb{R}^{n \times (m+1)}$, and computes the row-wise softmax and column-wise softmax of s and s', respectively. The probability z_{ij} is given by the minimum of the corresponding normalized scores:

$$z_{ij} = \min \left\{ \frac{e^{s_{ij}}}{\sum_{k=1}^{n+1} e^{s_{kj}}}, \frac{e^{s'_{ij}}}{\sum_{k=1}^{m+1} e^{s'_{ik}}} \right\}. \qquad (28.9)$$

28.3.2.2 Step 2: Formulate a Loss Function and Quantify the Violation of Strategy-Proofness

The loss function is the expected negated revenue, and minimizing loss is equivalent to maximizing revenue. For training data $\mathcal{D} = \{v^{(1)}, \ldots, v^{(L)}\}$ consisting of

L valuation profiles sampled i.i.d. from the valuation distribution, the empirical loss is

$$\mathcal{L}(w) = -\frac{1}{L} \sum_{\ell=1}^{L} \sum_{i=1}^{n} p_i^w(v^{(\ell)}). \tag{28.10}$$

Let $\text{regret}_i(v; w)$ denote the regret to buyer i at valuation profile v given an auction with parameters w. Given that regret is non-negative, the auction is strategy-proof up to zero-measure events if and only if, for all buyers $i \in [n]$, we have

$$\mathbb{E}_{v \sim F^V \times \cdots \times F^V} [\text{regret}_i(v; w)] = 0. \tag{28.11}$$

We quantity the *violation of strategy-proofness* to buyer i as

$$rgt_i(w) = \frac{1}{L} \sum_{\ell=1}^{L} \text{regret}_i(v^{(\ell)}; w). \tag{28.12}$$

The training problem is

$$\min_{w} \mathcal{L}(w) \tag{28.13}$$

$$\text{s.t.} \quad rgt_i(w) = 0, \quad \forall i \in [n].$$

28.3.2.3 Step 3: Adopt a Training Procedure

The training procedure uses gradient descent and *augmented Lagrangian optimization*. This solves a sequence of unconstrained optimization problems, for each of steps $k \in 0, 1, \ldots$, where the constraints on regret are incorporated within the objective. The kth step seeks parameters $w^{(k)}$ to minimize

$$C(w; \lambda_{rgt}^{(k)}, \rho) = \mathcal{L}(w) + \sum_{i \in [n]} \lambda_{rgt,i}^{(k)} \times rgt_i(w) + \frac{\rho}{2} \times \sum_{i \in [n]} rgt_i(w)^2, \tag{28.14}$$

where $\lambda_{rgt,i}^{(k)} \in \mathbb{R}$ is the *Lagrangian multiplier* for buyer i and $C(w; \lambda_{rgt}^{(k)}, \rho)$ augments a Lagrangian function with a quadratic penalty term, with parameter $\rho > 0$. This modified objective penalizes revenue by a quantity that depends on the degree of violation of strategy-proofness.

We initialize $\lambda_{rgt,i}^{(0)} = 0$. Given solution $w^{(k)}$ in step k, the Lagrangian multipliers are updated according to the rule

$$\lambda_{rgt,i}^{(k+1)} := \lambda_{rgt,i}^{(k)} + \rho \times rgt_i(w^{(k)}). \tag{28.15}$$

For each step k, the training procedure uses multiple stochastic gradient descent (SGD) mini-batch iterations to approximately solve

$$w^{(k+1)} \in \arg\min_w C(w; \lambda_{rgt}^{(k)}, \rho). \tag{28.16}$$

The gradient of revenue with respect to w is straightforward to calculate. For regret, the gradient is complicated by the nested maximization (28.6). To handle this, we first find a *defeating valuation*, $\hat{v}_i^{(\ell)}$, for buyer i at valuation profile $v^{(\ell)}$ (or just $v_i^{(\ell)}$ if there is no such mis-report). This is a valuation that provides better utility than that obtained by reporting truthfully. Given this, we approximate the gradient of regret as the gradient of the difference in utility to the buyer at report $\hat{v}_i^{(\ell)}$ compared with its true report:

$$\nabla_w\left[(v_i^{(\ell)}(g^w(\hat{v}_i^{(\ell)}, v_{-i}^{(\ell)})) - p_i^w(\hat{v}_i^{(\ell)}, v_{-i}^{(\ell)})) - (v_i^{(\ell)}(g^w(v^{(\ell)})) - p_i^w(v^{(\ell)}))\right]. \quad (28.17)$$

For a given valuation profile $v^{(\ell)}$ we search for a defeating valuation for buyer i by following gradient ascent in the input space, considering the buyer's utility with respect to its reported value (with the network parameters fixed). This is in the style of adversarial machine learning. For each buyer, we use multiple random starting valuations and take the best mis-report as the defeating valuation.

Although the training problem is non-convex, we have found that Lagrangian optimization with SGD, together with gradient ascent on inputs to find defeating valuations, can reliably learn auctions with near-optimal revenue and a very small violation of strategy-proofness.

28.3.3 Illustrative Experimental Results

We first present results for single-buyer two-item environments, for which there exist optimal designs from auction theory:

- 2 items, a single additive buyer, with item values $x_1, x_2 \sim U[0, 1]$ on item 1 and item 2, respectively. See Figure 28.4(a).
- 2 items, a single additive buyer, with item 1 value $x_1 \sim U[4, 16]$ and item 2 value $x_2 \sim U[4, 7]$. See Figure 28.4(b).
- 2 items, a single unit-demand buyer, with item values $x_1, x_2 \sim U[0, 1]$ on item 1 and item 2, respectively. See Figure 28.4(c).
- 2 items, a single unit-demand buyer, with item values $x_1, x_2 \sim U[2, 3]$ on item 1 and item 2, respectively. See Figure 28.4(d).

Table 28.1 summarizes the revenue and per-agent regret for the learned auctions, as evaluated on test data. For all four environments, the revenue is very close to the optimal revenue. For the additive $U[0, 1]$ environment, the revenue in RegretNet is slightly higher than optimal, reflecting that it is not quite strategy-proof (while assuming truthful reports for evaluating revenue).

Figures 28.4(a)–(d) give a comparison of the learned allocation rules with the optimal designs from economic theory. On the density plots for RegretNet we have superimposed the optimal allocation rule, with different regions delineated by dashed lines and the number in a region giving the probability that the item is allocated by the optimal rule. Not only is the revenue very close to optimal (Table 28.1), the allocation rules also capture the structure of the optimal designs.

Figure 28.5 gives results for a setting with two items and two additive buyers where the item values are i.i.d. uniform on the interval $[0, 1]$. This is so complicated that there is no known theoretically optimal design. As a baseline for comparison we use the previous best results from automated mechanism design (AM), which searches for the best auction in a parameterized family of strategy-proof auctions. The revenue falls during training, reflecting an improvement in strategy-proofness. The network learns an auction with essentially zero regret and expected revenue 0.878, which may be compared with the revenue 0.867 from the AMD baseline.

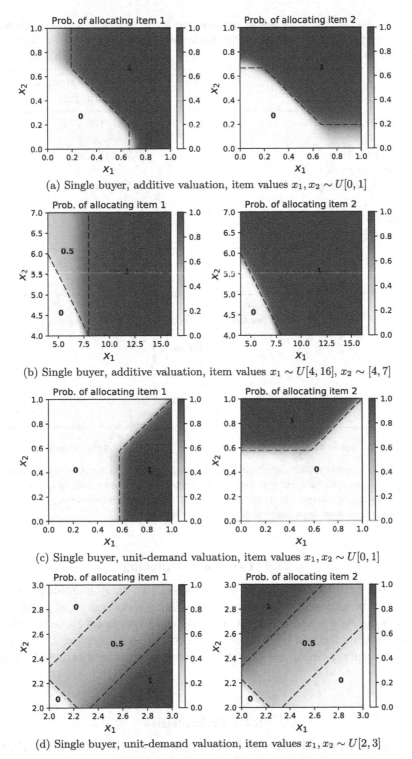

(a) Single buyer, additive valuation, item values $x_1, x_2 \sim U[0, 1]$

(b) Single buyer, additive valuation, item values $x_1 \sim U[4, 16]$, $x_2 \sim [4, 7]$

(c) Single buyer, unit-demand valuation, item values $x_1, x_2 \sim U[0, 1]$

(d) Single buyer, unit-demand valuation, item values $x_1, x_2 \sim U[2, 3]$

Figure 28.4 The allocation rule of a learned RegretNet auction for four different settings. We plot the probabilities of allocating item 1 (left) and item 2 (right), as functions of the buyer's value. The theoretically optimal allocation rule is superimposed, with different allocation regions in the optimal rule delineated by dashed lines (the number in a region gives the probability that the item is allocated according to the optimal rule).

Table 28.1 Expected revenue and expected, per-agent regret from RegretNet in single-buyer auction settings, comparing with the theoretically-optimal revenue (and also giving the normalized revenue, as a fraction of the optimal revenue).

Economic environment	Optimal revenue	RegretNet revenue (norm)	regret
2 item, 1 additive buyer, $x_1, x_2 \sim U[0, 1]$	0.550	0.554 (100.7%)	< 0.001
2 item, 1 additive buyer, $x_1 \sim U[4, 16]$, $x_2 \sim U[4, 7]$	9.781	9.734 (99.5%)	< 0.001
2 item, 1 unit-demand buyer, $x_1, x_2 \sim U[0, 1]$	0.384	0.384 (100.0%)	< 0.001
2 item, 1 unit-demand buyer, $x_1, x_2 \sim U[2, 3]$	2.137	2.137 (100.0%)	< 0.001

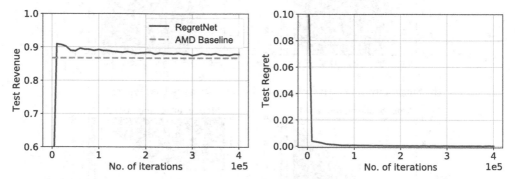

Figure 28.5 The test revenue and test regret from RegretNet as a function of the number of training iterations (i.e., the number of mini-batch updates) for an auction with two items and two additive buyers, with values $U[0, 1]$ for each item. The baseline represents the performance of the previous best result from automated mechanism design.

28.4 Two-Sided Matching

In this section, we turn to the automated design of two-sided matching markets. It is well known to be impossible to achieve both strategy-proofness and stability in two-sided matching. And yet little is known about how to trade off these two properties. Here, we illustrate the use of differentiable economics to explore the design frontier between strategy-proofness and stability and suggest new targets for economic theory.

28.4.1 Preliminaries

Let W denote a set of *n workers* and F denote a set of *m firms*. Each worker can be matched to at most one firm and each firm to at most one worker.

A *matching* μ is a set of (worker, firm) pairs, with each worker and firm participating in at most one match. Let $\mathcal{B}$ denote the set of all matchings. If a worker or firm remains unmatched, we will say that it is matched to $\perp$. If $(w, f) \in \mu$ then μ matches

w to f, and we write $\mu(w) = f$ and $\mu(f) = w$. We write $(w, \perp) \in \mu$ (resp. $(\perp, f) \in \mu$) to denote that w (resp. f) is unmatched.

Each worker has a *strict preference order* $\succ_w$ over the set $\overline{F} = F \cup \{\perp\}$. Each firm has a *strict preference order* $\succ_f$ over the set $\overline{W} = W \cup \{\perp\}$. An agent prefers to be unmatched than to be matched to agents ranked below $\perp$ (these are *unacceptable*, while other agents are *acceptable*). If worker w prefers firm f to f' then we represent this as $f \succ_w f'$, and similarly for firms. Let P denote the domain of preference profiles, with profile $\succ = (\succ_1, \ldots, \succ_n, \succ_{n+1}, \ldots, \succ_{n+m}) \in P$.

A pair (w, f) forms a *blocking pair* for a matching μ if w and f prefer each other to their partners in μ (or $\perp$ in the case that either or both are unmatched). A matching μ is *stable* if and only if there are no blocking pairs. A matching μ satisfies *individual rationality* (IR) if it is not blocked by any single agent, i.e., no worker or firm finds its partner unacceptable.

Remark 28.4. Stability is not satisfied by an empty matching. For example, if a matching μ leaves a worker w and a firm f unmatched, where w finds f acceptable and f finds w acceptable, then (w, f) is a blocking pair to μ.

28.4.2 Randomized matchings

A *randomized matching mechanism* g takes a reported preference profile $\succ$ and maps this to a distribution $g(\succ) \in \Delta(\mathcal{B})$ on matchings; $\Delta(\mathcal{B})$ denotes the probability simplex on the matchings, and $r \in [0, 1]^{(n+1) \times (m+1)}$ denotes the *marginal probability* $r_{wf} \geq 0$ with which worker w is matched with firm f, for $w \in W$ and firm $f \in F$. We require $\sum_{f' \in \overline{F}} r_{wf'} = 1$ for all $w \in W$ and $\sum_{w' \in \overline{W}} r_{w'f} = 1$ for all $f \in F$.

Theorem 28.5 (Birkhoff–von Neumann). *Given a randomized matching r, there exists a distribution on matchings with marginal probabilities equal to r.*

We also write $g_{wf}(\succ)$ to denote the marginal probability of matching worker w (or $\perp$) and firm f (or $\perp$) at a reported preference profile $\succ$. The following definition generalizes the concept of stability to randomized matchings.

Definition 28.6 (Ex ante justified envy). A randomized matching r causes *ex ante justified envy* if:

1. either some worker w prefers f over some (fractionally) matched firm f' (including $f' = \perp$) and firm f prefers w over some (fractionally) matched worker w', including $w' = \perp$ ("w has envy towards w'" and "f has envy towards f'"), or

2. some worker w finds a (fractionally) matched $f' \in F$ unacceptable, i.e., $r_{wf'} > 0$ and $\perp \succ_w f'$ or some firm f finds a (fractionally) matched $w' \in W$ unacceptable, i.e., $r_{w'f} > 0$ and $\perp \succ_f w'$.

A randomized matching r is *ex ante stable* if and only if it does not cause any ex ante justified envy. Ex ante stability reduces to the standard concept of stability for a deterministic matching. Part 2 of the definition requires that a randomized matching r should satisfy IR; i.e., for any worker w with $\perp \succ_w f'$ for firm f', $r_{wf'} = 0$ and, for any firm f with $\perp \succ_f w'$ for worker w', $r_{w'f} = 0$.

To define strategy-proofness, we say that $u_w : \overline{F} \to \mathbb{R}$ is a $\succ_w$-*utility* for worker w when $u_w(f) > u_w(f')$ if and only if $f \succ_w f'$, for all $f, f' \in \overline{F}$. We similarly define a $\succ_f$-*utility* for firm f. The following concept of ordinal strategy-proofness provides a strong version of incentive compatibility for randomized matching markets.

Definition 28.7 (Ordinal strategy-proofness.). A randomized matching mechanism g satisfies *ordinal strategy-proofness* if and only if, for all agents $i \in W \cup F$, for any preference profile $\succ$, for any $\succ_i$-utility u_i for agents i, and for all reports $\succ_i'$, we have

$$\mathbb{E}_{\mu \sim g(\succ_i, \succ_{-i})}[u_i(\mu(i))] \geq \mathbb{E}_{\mu \sim g(\succ_i', \succ_{-i})}[u_i(\mu(i))]. \tag{28.18}$$

By this definition, no worker or firm can improve its expected utility by misreporting its preferences whatever the utility function consistent with its preferences. For a deterministic mechanism, ordinal strategy-proofness reduces to strategy-proofness and the requirement that no agent benefits from a mis-report. In Section 28.4.4 we introduce a weaker notion of strategy-proofness that we use for learning trade-offs between strategy-proofness and stability.

28.4.3 Deferred Acceptance and RSD

Deferred acceptance (DA) algorithms provide stable mechanisms and are strategy-proof for the proposing side of the market.

Theorem 28.8. *Worker- or firm-proposing DA is stable but not ordinal strategy-proof.*

See Chapter 1. We also define the following simple mechanism (see also the section on random priority in Chapter 2).

Definition 28.9 (Random serial dictatorship (RSD)). For RSD we sample a *priority order* π on the set $W \cup F$ uniformly at random, such that $\pi_1, \pi_2, \ldots, \pi_{m+n}$ is a permutation on $W \cup F$ in decreasing order of priority. Proceed as follows:

- *Initialize matching μ to the empty matching.*
- *In the round $k = 1, \ldots, m + n$: if participant $\pi_k \in W \cup F$ is not yet matched in μ then add to the matching μ the match between π_k and its most preferred unmatched agent, or add $(\pi_k, \perp)$ if all remaining possibilities are unacceptable.*

Theorem 28.10. *Random serial dictatorship is ordinal strategy-proof but not stable.*

Proof For ordinal strategy-proofness, observe that an agent's own report has no effect on the choices of higher-priority agents. Truthful reporting ensures that the agent obtains its most preferred match of those available when it is its turn. Random serial dictatorship is not stable because an agent (say f) could select as its match an agent on the other side of the market for whom f is unacceptable. $\square$

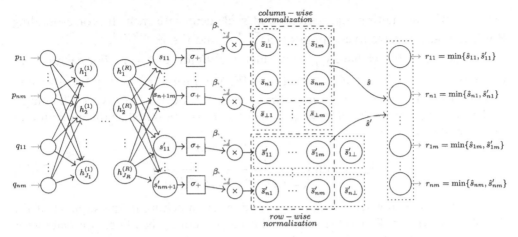

Figure 28.6 Matching network g for a set of n workers and m firms. Given inputs $p, q \in \mathbb{R}^{n \times m}$ the matching network is a feed-forward neural network with R hidden layers that uses softplus activation to generate non-negative scores and normalization to compute the marginal probabilities in the randomized matching. We additionally generated a Boolean mask matrix, β, and multiplied it with the score matrix before normalization, to ensure IR by making the probability of matches that are unacceptable zero.

28.4.4 Methodology

28.4.4.1 Step 1: Design an Artificial Neural Network

We use a neural network with parameters $\theta \in \mathbb{R}^d$ to represent a matching mechanism $g^\theta : P \to \triangle(\mathcal{B})$. We use a fully connected feed-forward neural network with four hidden layers, 256 units in each layer, leaky ReLU activations, and a fully connected output layer. See Figure 28.6.

We represent the preference orders at the input by adopting the *equi-spaced utility function*, which is an evenly spaced valid utility. For preference profile $\succ$, the equi-spaced utilities for worker $w \in W$ and firm $f \in F$ are denoted as $p_w^\succ = (p_{w1}^\succ, \ldots, p_{wm}^\succ)$ and $q_f^\succ = (q_{1f}^\succ, \ldots, q_{nf}^\succ)$, respectively. We also define $p_{w\perp}^\succ = 0$ and $q_{\perp f}^\succ = 0$. For example, we could have:

- For a preference order $\succ$ with $w_1 : f_1, f_2, \perp, f_3$, $p_{w_1}^\succ = (\frac{2}{3}, \frac{1}{3}, -\frac{1}{3})$.
- For a preference order $\succ$ with $w_1 : f_1, f_2, \perp, f_3, f_4$, $p_{w_1}^\succ = (\frac{2}{4}, \frac{1}{4}, -\frac{1}{4}, -\frac{2}{4})$.
- For a preference order $\succ$ with $f_1 : w_2, w_1, w_3, \perp$, $q_{f_1}^\succ = (\frac{2}{3}, 1, \frac{1}{3})$.

In this way, the vector $(p_{11}^\succ, \ldots, p_{nm}^\succ, q_{11}^\succ, \ldots, q_{nm}^\succ)$ constitutes the input to the network ($2 \times n \times m$ numbers). The output of the network is a vector $r \in [0, 1]^{n \times m}$ with $\sum_{j=1}^m r_{wj} \le 1$ and $\sum_{i=1}^n r_{if} \le 1$ for every every $w \in [n]$ and $f \in [m]$. This describes the marginal probabilities in a randomized matching for this input profile.

The network first outputs two sets of scores $s \in \mathbb{R}^{(n+1) \times m}$ and $s' \in \mathbb{R}^{n \times (m+1)}$. We apply the *softplus function* (denoted by σ_+) element-wise to these scores, where $\sigma_+(x) = \ln(1 + e^x)$. To ensure IR, we first construct a Boolean mask variable β_{wf}, which is zero only when the match is unacceptable to one of or both the worker and firm, i.e., when $\perp \succ_w f$ or $\perp \succ_f w$. We set $\beta_{n+1,f} = 1$ for $f \in F$ and $\beta_{w,m+1} = 1$

for $w \in W$. We multiply the scores s and s' element-wise with the corresponding Boolean mask variable to compute $\bar{s} \in \mathbb{R}_{\geq 0}^{(n+1) \times m}$ and $\bar{s}' \in \mathbb{R}_{\geq 0}^{n \times (m+1)}$.

For each $w \in \overline{W}$, we have $\bar{s}_{wf} = \beta_{wf} \ln(1 + e^{s_{wf}})$ for all $f \in F$. For each $f \in \overline{F}$, we have $\bar{s}'_{wf} = \beta_{wf} \ln(1 + e^{s'_{wf}})$ for all $w \in W$. We normalize $\bar{s}$ along the rows and $\bar{s}'$ along the columns to obtain *normalized scores*, $\hat{s}$ and $\hat{s}'$ respectively. The match probability r_{wf}, for worker $w \in W$ and firm $f \in F$, is computed as the minimum of the normalized scores:

$$r_{wf} = \min\left(\frac{\bar{s}_{wf}}{\sum_{f' \in \overline{F}} \bar{s}_{wf'}}, \frac{\bar{s}'_{wf}}{\sum_{w' \in \overline{W}} \bar{s}'_{w'f}} \right). \tag{28.19}$$

We have $r_{wf} = 0$ whenever $\beta_{wf} = 0$, and every matching in the support of the distribution will be IR. On the basis of this construction, the allocation matrix r is always weakly doubly stochastic (allowing for workers and firms to go unmatched) and can be decomposed to a convex combination of 0–1 weakly doubly stochastic matrices.

28.4.4.2 Step 2: Formulate a Loss Function and Quantify the Violation of Strategy-Proofness and Stability

To train the neural network we formulate a loss function $\mathcal{L}$ on training data $D = \{\succ^{(1)}, \ldots, \succ^{(L)}\}$, with each preference profile sampled i.i.d. from a distribution on profiles. The loss function is designed to represent the trade-off between strategy-proofness and stability.

Recall that $g^\theta(\succ) \in [0, 1]^{n \times m}$ denotes the randomized matching. We will write $g^\theta_{w\perp}(\succ) = 1 - \sum_{f=1}^{m} g^\theta_{wf}(\succ)$ and $g^\theta_{\perp f}(\succ) = 1 - \sum_{w=1}^{n} g^\theta_{wf}(\succ)$ to denote the probabilities of worker w and firm f being unmatched, respectively. For worker w and firm f, we define the *stability violation* at profile $\succ$ as

$$
stv_{wf}(g^\theta, \succ) = \left(\sum_{w'=1}^{n} g^\theta_{w'f}(\succ) \cdot \max\{q^\succ_{wf} - q^\succ_{w'f}, 0\} + g^\theta_{\perp f}(\succ) \cdot \max\{q^\succ_{wf}, 0\} \right)
$$
$$
\times \left(\sum_{f'=1}^{m} g^\theta_{wf'}(\succ) \cdot \max\{p^\succ_{wf} - p^\succ_{wf'}, 0\} + g^\theta_{w\perp}(\succ) \cdot \max\{p^\succ_{wf}, 0\} \right). \tag{28.20}
$$

This captures the first kind of ex ante justified envy in Definition 28.6, which is with regard to fractionally matched partners. We ignore the second kind of ex ante justified envy in defining the loss function because the learned mechanisms satisfy IR through the use of the Boolean mask matrix.

The overall *stability violation* of mechanism g^θ on profile $\succ$ is defined as

$$stv(g^\theta, \succ) = \frac{1}{2}\left(\frac{1}{m} + \frac{1}{n} \right) \sum_{w=1}^{n} \sum_{f=1}^{m} stv_{wf}(g^\theta, \succ). \tag{28.21}$$

The *expected stability violation* is $STV(g^\theta) = \mathbb{E}_\succ\left[stv(g^\theta, \succ) \right]$. We write $stv(g^\theta)$ to denote the average stability violation across multiple profiles.

Theorem 28.11. *A randomized matching mechanism g^θ is ex ante stable up to zero-measure events if and only if $STV(g^\theta) = 0$.*

Proof Since $stv(g^\theta, \succ) \geq 0$, we have that $STV(g^\theta) = \mathbb{E}_\succ\left[stv(g^\theta, \succ)\right] = 0$ if and only if $stv(g^\theta, \succ) = 0$ except on zero-measure events. Moreover, $stv(g^\theta, \succ) = 0$ implies $stv_{wf}(g^\theta, \succ) = 0$ for all $w \in W$, for all $f \in F$. This is equivalent to no ex ante justified envy. For firm f, this means, $\forall w' \neq w$, $q^\succ_{wf} \leq q^\succ_{w'f}$ if $g^\theta_{w'f} > 0$ and $q \succ_{wf} \leq 0$ if $g^\theta_{\perp f} > 0$. Then there is no ex ante justified envy for firm f. Analogously, there is no ex ante justified envy for worker w. If g^θ is ex ante stable, it trivially implies $STV(g^\theta) = 0$ by definition. $\square$

Example 28.12. Consider a market with three workers and three firms, and the following preference profile $(\succ)$:

$$
\begin{aligned}
w_1 &: f_2, f_3, f_1, \perp & f_1 &: w_1, w_2, w_3, \perp \\
w_2 &: f_2, f_1, f_3, \perp & f_2 &: w_2, w_3, w_1, \perp \\
w_3 &: f_1, f_3, f_2, \perp & f_3 &: w_3, w_1, w_2, \perp
\end{aligned}
$$

The matching found by a worker-proposing DA is $(w_1, f_3), (w_2, f_2), (w_3, f_1)$. This is a stable matching. Now consider the matching under RSD. We generate all possible priority orders and calculate the marginal matching probabilities as

$$
r = \begin{pmatrix} \frac{11}{24} & \frac{1}{4} & \frac{7}{24} \\ \frac{1}{6} & \frac{3}{4} & \frac{1}{12} \\ \frac{3}{8} & 0 & \frac{5}{8} \end{pmatrix}.
$$

Here, f_2 and w_2 are the most preferred options for w_2 and f_2, respectively, and they would always prefer to be matched with each other rather than being fractionally matched. Thus (w_2, f_2) has ex ante justified envy and RSD is not stable.

The stability violations are, from (28.20),

$$
stv_{wf}(g^{RSD}, \succ) = \begin{pmatrix} 0 & 0 & \frac{11}{2592} \\ \frac{1}{288} & \frac{1}{54} & 0 \\ 0 & 0 & 0 \end{pmatrix}.
$$

By (28.21), the overall stability violation is $stv(g^{RSD}, \succ) = \frac{17}{1944}$.

We turn now to the strategy-proofness. For this, we relax the requirement of ordinal strategy-proofness and consider incentive alignment for the equi-spaced utility function, denoted $u_i^{(eq)}$ for agent i. We say that a randomized mechanism is *strategy-proof for the equi-spaced utility* (SP) if and only if, for all agents $i \in W \cup F$, for any preference profile $\succ$, and for all reports $\succ'_i$, we have

$$
\mathbb{E}_{\mu \sim g^\theta(\succ_i, \succ_{-i})}\left[u_i^{(eq)}(\mu(i))\right] \geq \mathbb{E}_{\mu \sim g^\theta(\succ'_i, \succ_{-i})}\left[u_i^{(eq)}(\mu(i))\right]. \tag{28.22}
$$

Let $u_i^{(eq)}(r; \succ_i) = \mathbb{E}_{\mu \sim r}\left[u_i^{(eq)}(\mu(i))\right]$ denote the expected utility for randomized matching r. We define the *regret* of agent i at preference order $\succ$ as

$$regret_i(g^\theta, \succ) = \max_{\succ_i' \in P}\left[u_i^{(eq)}(g^\theta(\succ_i', \succ_{-i}); \succ_i) - u_i^{(eq)}(g^\theta(\succ); \succ_i)\right], \qquad (28.23)$$

where $\succ_{-i} = (\succ_1, \ldots, \succ_{i-1}, \succ_{i+1}, \ldots, \succ_{n+m})$. The per-agent regret on profile $\succ$ is

$$regret(g^\theta, \succ) = \frac{1}{2}\left(\frac{1}{n}\sum_{w \in W} regret_w(g^\theta, \succ) + \frac{1}{m}\sum_{f \in F} regret_f(g^\theta, \succ)\right). \qquad (28.24)$$

We define the *expected regret* as $RGT(g^\theta) = \mathbb{E}_{\succ}\left[regret(g^\theta, \succ)\right]$, and write $rgt(g^\theta)$ to denote the average per-agent regret across multiple profiles. We also refer to this as the *strategy-proof violation*.

Theorem 28.13. *A randomized matching mechanism g^θ is strategy-proof for equi-spaced utility up to zero-measure events if and only if $RGT(g^\theta) = 0$.*

The proof is similar to that for Theorem 28.11. Also, if the mechanism is deterministic then zero expected regret implies that no agent can improve its preference ranking for any mis-report (again up to measure-zero events).

The training problem for trading off stability and strategy-proofness, with $\lambda \in [0, 1]$ to control the trade-off, is

$$\min_\theta \lambda \, stv(g^\theta) + (1 - \lambda) \, rgt(g^\theta). \qquad (28.25)$$

28.4.4.3 Step 3: Adopt a Training Procedure

As with RegretNet, we make use of stochastic gradient descent for training. The gradient of the violation of stability with respect to parameters θ is straightforward to calculate. For the regret, the gradient is again made complicated by the nested maximization.

Given that two-sided matching has discrete types, for small problems we can compute the best mis-report by enumeration. For agent i, this is

$$\hat{\succ}_i^{(\ell)} \in \text{argmax}_{\succ_i'}\left[u_i^{(eq)}(g^\theta(\succ_i', \succ_{-i}^{(\ell)}); \succ_i^{(\ell)}) - u_i^{(eq)}(g^\theta(\succ^{(\ell)}); \succ_i^{(\ell)})\right]. \qquad (28.26)$$

We find the gradient of the regret of agent i with respect to parameters θ by fixing its mis-report accordingly and adopting truthful reports for other agents.

In addition, we define the *per-agent IR violation* at input profile $\succ$ as

$$irv(g^\theta, \succ) = \sum_{w=1}^{n}\sum_{f=1}^{m} g_{wf}^\theta(\succ)\left(\max\{-q_{wf}, 0\} + \max\{-p_{wf}, 0\}\right). \qquad (28.27)$$

We write $irv(g^\theta)$ to denote the average per-agent IR violation of a mechanism across multiple profiles. This *degree of IR violation* captures the second kind of ex ante justified envy in Definition 28.6 and is zero for the learned mechanisms and DA but non-zero for random serial dictatorship.

———— **606** ————

28.4.5 Illustrative Experimental Results

We studied both uncorrelated and correlated preferences.

- *Uncorrelated preference orders.* For each worker or firm, first sample uniformly at random from all preference orders. Then, with probability $p_{\text{trunc}} \geq 0$ (the *truncation probability*), choose at random a position at which to truncate this agent's preference order such that all subsequent positions are unacceptable.
- *Correlated preference orders.* First sample a preference order for each agent as in the uncorrelated case. Also sample, uniformly at random and independently and with the same truncation probability, a special worker preference order $\succ_{w*}$ and a special firm preference order $\succ_{f*}$. Each agent adopts the special preference order with probability $p_{\text{corr}} > 0$, i.e., $\succ_{w*}$ or $\succ_{f*}$ as appropriate to its side of the market.

We considered the following environments:

- $n = 4$ workers and $m = 4$ firms with uncorrelated preferences and $p_{\text{trunc}} = 0.5$.
- $n = 4$ workers and $m = 4$ firms with correlated preferences and varying $p_{\text{corr}} = \{0.25, 0.5, 0.75\}$ and $p_{\text{trunc}} = 0.5$.
- $n = 4$ workers and $m = 4$ firms with uncorrelated preferences and $p_{\text{trunc}} = 0$.

We varied the parameter λ between 0 and 1 in exploring the design frontier. In addition to stability and strategy-proofness, we also calculates the expected per-agent welfare for the equi-spaced utility function. We compared the learned mechanisms with RSD and DA. Because RSD does not guarantee IR, we include its IR violation as part of the reported stability violation. The DA algorithm and the learned mechanisms satisfy IR.

We also calculate the similarity with DA. For preference profile $\succ$, the similarity to the worker-proposing DA (with matching $g^{w\text{-DA}}$) is the fraction of the matching of the DA mechanism that is retained in the learned mechanism g^{θ}, and

$$sim(g^{\theta}, \succ) = \frac{\sum_{(w,f):g_{wf}^{w\text{-DA}}(\succ)=1} g_{wf}^{\theta}(\succ)}{\sum_{(w,f):g_{wf}^{w\text{-DA}}(\succ)=1} 1}. \tag{28.28}$$

We defined this analogously for firm-proposing DA, averaged the similarity across multiple profiles for each of the worker- and firm-proposing DAs, and defined the similarity $sim(g^{\theta})$ as the maximum of these two quantities.

We also quantified the amount of randomization by computing the *expected normalized per-agent entropy*. For the preference profile $\succ$, we calculated the normalized per-agent entropy (zero for a deterministic mechanism) as

$$H(g^{\theta}, \succ) = -\frac{1}{2n} \sum_{w \in W} \sum_{f \in \overline{F}} \frac{g_{wf}^{\theta}(\succ) \log_2 g_{wf}^{\theta}(\succ)}{\log_2 m} - \frac{1}{2m} \sum_{f \in F} \sum_{w \in \overline{W}} \frac{g_{wf}^{\theta}(\succ) \log_2 g_{wf}^{\theta}(\succ)}{\log_2 n}. \tag{28.29}$$

See Figures 28.7 and 28.8 for the results in environments with truncation. For Figure 28.7, we adopted as the DA baseline whichever of the worker- and firm-proposing DAs was better in terms of average SP-violation on test data. The learned design frontier dominates the convex combination of DA and RSD.

For Figure 28.8, we adopted as the DA baseline whichever of the worker- and firm- proposing DA was better in terms of per-agent welfare on test data. Figure 28.9

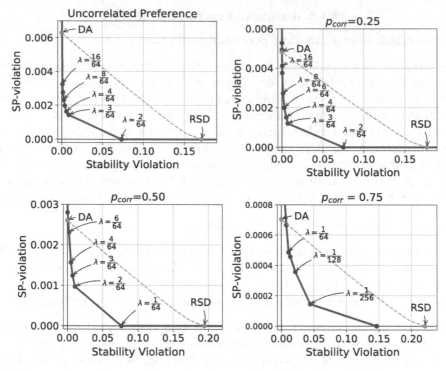

Figure 28.7 Truncated preference orders. The design frontier for the learned mechanisms for different choices of λ (red dots), and also showing the random serial dictatorship and the best worker- and firm-proposing DA for SP-violation. The sub-figures vary in the assumed correlation on preferences. The stability violation includes IR-violation for RSD.

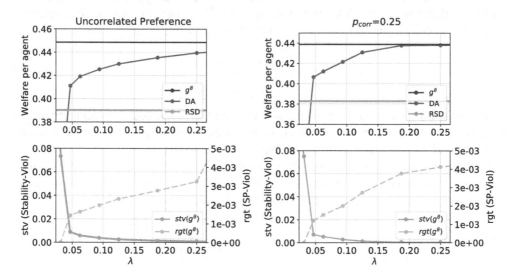

Figure 28.8 Truncated preference orders. Top: Per-agent welfare compared with RSD and the best of firm- and worker-proposing DA for welfare. Bottom: Stability violation and SP-violation. For DA this takes into account the best of firm- and worker-proposing DA for SP violation. The stability violations for RSD are 0.171 and 0.176 for uncorrelated and correlated preferences, respectively. The SP-violations for DA are 6e-03 and 5e-03 for uncorrelated and correlated preferences, respectively. The stability violation includes IR-violation for RSD.

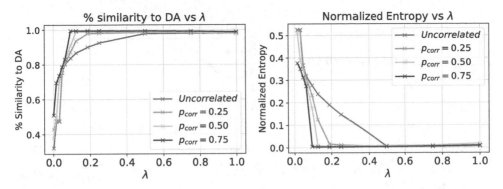

Figure 28.9 Truncated preferences. Left: Similarity of the learned mechanisms with DA. Right: Expected normalized per-agent entropy of the learned mechanisms.

shows that for larger values of λ ($\geq$ 0.2) the artificial neural network tends to learn a mechanism that is deterministic and equivalent to a DA mechanism.

Considering again Figures 28.7 and 28.8, we see that for very small λ values (emphasizing strategy-proofness) the learned mechanisms have welfare similar to that of RSD and with very small SP-violations but better stability than RSD. For slightly larger values of λ, say around 3/64, for small correlations between preferences, we learn mechanisms that are almost as stable as DA ($stv \leq 0.01$) but with much lower SP-violation ($rgt \leq 0.001$). These mechanisms have a welfare that is intermediate between RSD and DA. Comparing the scale of the y-axes in Figure 28.7, we see that a higher correlation between preferences has little effect on stability but tends to remove opportunities for strategic behavior and improve strategy-proofness.

Figure 28.10 presents results for the environment without truncation (we still allow truncation for mis-reports). Compared with the results in Figure 28.7, the SP-violation of DA is worse while the stability violation of RSD is better (because there can be no violation of IR). It is interesting that the learned mechanisms are able to achieve similar performance to the settings with truncation: very low stability violation ($stv \leq 0.005$) and very low SP-violation ($rgt \leq 0.001$). Whereas DA is stable on all inputs, including truncated inputs, the learned mechanisms can adopt different behaviors on profiles with truncations, recognizing that this does not affect in-distribution stability. To illustrate this, suppose firm f_1 has a preference order $w_2, w_1, w_3, w_4, \perp$ and suppose DA assigns the firm to w_4, its least preferred worker. Now, f_1 may truncate to $w_2, w_1, \perp, w_3, w_4$, in which case a DA might match the firm to w_1, its second preferred worker. In comparison, the ANN can learn not to match the firm to any worker after this truncation, improving SP without compromising stability.

Taken as a whole, these results suggest new directions for economic theory. For example, are there mechanisms that for some distributions are provably almost as stable as DA and yet considerably more strategy-proof, and can these mechanisms and distributions be characterized? Are there mechanisms that for some distributions are provably almost as strategy-proof as RSD and yet considerably more stable, and can these mechanisms and distributions be characterized?

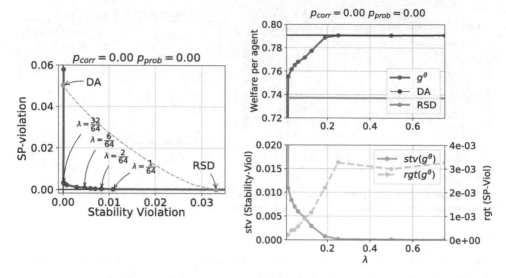

Figure 28.10 Non-truncated and uncorrelated preferences. Left: The design frontier for the learned mechanisms for different choices of λ (red dots) in an environment without preference truncation, and also showing RSD and the best of worker- and firm-proposing DA for SP-violation. Right: Per-agent welfare, stability violation, and SP-violation. For welfare, this *considers* the better of the worker- and firm-proposing DA for welfare. For SP-violation, this *considers* the better of the worker- and firm-proposing DA for SP-violation. The stability violation for RSD is 0.033 and the SP-violation for DA is 0.05.

28.5 Discussion

We have seen that ANNs are a flexible tool with which to design and study matching markets. In addition to the matching problems described in this chapter, ANNs have been applied to the following settings.

- Small combinatorial auctions, which are auctions in which a buyer's value for a package of items can be super-additive in its value for individual items.
- Bayesian incentive-compatible auctions for buyers with budget constraints.
- Incentive-aligned social choice mechanisms such as multi-facility location.
- Auctions that allocate items efficiently while also minimizing the total expected payment collected from buyers.

Differentiable economics has also led to the discovery of provably optimal auctions by making use of an architecture (RochetNet) that provides exact strategy-proofness for single-buyer settings. Methodological developments include the use of methods from robust machine learning to certify the worst-case violation of strategy-proofness by a learned mechanism as well as ANN architectures that impose symmetry on auction rules.

There are a number of interesting future directions, including new applications, to, for example, contract design, double auctions, and collusion-proof auctions. We need architectural innovations that incorporate characterization results from economic theory, and methods that provide robustness to adversarial inputs and that transform learned mechanisms with approximate properties of interest to mechanisms with exact properties. Scaling to larger combinatorial auction problems will require the use of succinct representations of inputs and outputs. The communication of results back to economic theory will be aided through methods of interpreting learned mechanisms, as well as lower- and upper-bounds on performance that serve to confirm opportunities for new theoretical developments.

28.6 Bibliographic Notes

The agenda of automated mechanism design (AMD) was introduced in [3] and early work made use of integer programming and linear programming. Later, work was done on optimizing within parameterized classes of mechanisms, leading for example to the AMD baseline in Figure 28.5 [12, 17].

The network architecture discussed in Section 28.3 is the RegretNet architecture from [7], which also provides generalization bounds for regret and revenue and experimental results for small combinatorial auctions; see also [8] for the single-buyer *RochetNet* architecture, which is exactly strategy-proof and has been used to support conjectures and discover new, provably optimal, auctions. The authors of [18] also derive theoretically optimal designs using a variation on RochetNet. Earlier, in [2] the study of the sample complexity was introduced for optimal auction design. In [9] expected *ex post* regret was used to quantify approximate strategy-proofness in studying the application of support-vector machines to AMD.

Differentiable economics has been applied to budget-constrained auction design [10], multi-facility location [11], and payment-minimizing mechanism design [19]. The paper [12] demonstrate how to develop certificates for approximate strategy-proofness. In [15], introduce permutation-equivariance was introduced into ANN architectures as a way to impose symmetry on learned auctions. Working with Bayesian incentive compatibility rather than dominant-strategy incentive compatibility, the papers [6] and [4] provide transforms of ϵ-IC mechanisms into IC mechanisms.

The development in this chapter of the application to two-sided matching design follows [16]; the authors adopted *ordinal SP* and quantified the violation of first-order stochastic dominance rather than adopting ex post regret and equi-utility as in the present chapter. The results are qualitatively similar to those presented here, and [1] provides a general result that applies when some agents are unmatched. The concept of ex ante justified envy is due to [13]. In [14] support-vector machines were applied to the design of stable matching mechanisms, and rules on the stable matching polytope were found (see Chapter 1).

The results presented here use the *PyTorch* deep learning library and the Adam optimizer with a learning rate of $\alpha = 0.001$. For the auction results, we used an augmented Lagrangian solver across 80 steps (with $\rho = 1$), where each step involve 5,000 mini-batch SGD iterations, each mini-batch consisting of 128 valuation profiles. For each profile, 25 iterations of gradient ascent were used to find a defeating valuation for each buyer. For the matching results, we trained for 50,000 mini-batch based SGD iterations, with each mini-batch consisting of 1,024 preference profiles.

Acknowledgements

We would like to thank the reviewers for their useful comments as well as our wonderful collaborators, Paul Dütting, Harikrishna Narasimhan, Scott Kominers, Shira Li, Jonathan Ma, and Noah Golowich. This work was supported in part by the Harvard Data Science Initiative and an award from Amazon Web Services.

References

[1] Budish, Eric, Che, Yeon-Koo, Kojima, Fuhito, and Milgrom, Paul. 2013. Designing random allocation mechanisms: Theory and applications. *American Economic Review*, **103**(2), 585–623.

[2] Cole, Richard, and Roughgarden, Tim. 2014. The sample complexity of revenue maximization. Pages 243–252 of: *Proc. 46th ACM Symposium on Theory of Computing*.

[3] Conitzer, Vincent, and Sandholm, Tuomas. 2002. Complexity of mechanism design. Pages 103–110 of: *Proc. 18th Conference on Uncertainty in Artificial Intelligence*.

[4] Conitzer, Vincent, Feng, Zhe, Parkes, David C., and Sodomka, Eric. 2020. Welfare-preserving ε-BIC to BIC transformation with negligible revenue loss. *CoRR*, abs/2007.09579.

[5] Curry, Michael, Chiang, Ping-yeh, Goldstein, Tom, and Dickerson, John. 2020. Certifying strategyproof auction networks. Pages 4987–4998 of: *Advances in Neural Information Processing Systems*, vol. 33.

[6] Daskalakis, Constantinos, and Weinberg, Seth Matthew. 2012. Symmetries and optimal multi-dimensional mechanism design. Pages 370–387 of: *Proc. 13th ACM Conference on Electronic Commerce*.

[7] Dütting, Paul, Feng, Zhe, Narasimhan, Harikrishna, Parkes, David C., and Ravindranath, Sai Srivatsa. 2019. Optimal auctions through deep learning. Pages 1706–1715 of: *Proc. 36th International Conference on Machine Learning*.

[8] Dütting, Paul, Feng, Zhe, Narasimhan, Harikrishna, and Parkes, David C. 2020. Optimal auctions through deep learning. *CoRR*, abs/1706.03459.

[9] Dütting, Paul, Fischer, Felix, Jirapinyo, Pichayut, Lai, John K., Lubin, Benjamin, and Parkes, David C. 2015. Payment rules through discriminant-based classifiers. *ACM Transactions on Economics and Computation*, **3**(1), 1–41.

[10] Feng, Zhe, Narasimhan, Harikrishna, and Parkes, David C. 2018. Deep Learning for revenue-optimal auctions with budgets. Pages 354–362 of: *Proc. 17th Conference on Autonomous Agents and Multi-Agent Systems*.

[11] Golowich, Noah, Narasimhan, Harikrishna, and Parkes, David C. 2018. Deep learning for multi-facility location mechanism design. Pages 261–267 of: *Proc. 27th International Joint Conference on Artificial Intelligence*.

[12] Guo, M., and Conitzer, V. 2010. Computationally feasible automated mechanism design: General approach and case studies. In: *Proc. 24th AAAI Conference on Artificial Intelligence*.

[13] Kesten, Onur, and Ünver, M. Utku. 2015. A theory of school-choice lotteries. *Theoretical Economics*, **10**(2), 543–595.

[14] Narasimhan, Harikrishna, Agarwal, Shivani, and Parkes, David C. 2016. Automated mechanism design without money via machine learning. In: *Proc. 25th International Joint Conference on Artificial Intelligence*.

[15] Rahme, Jad, Jelassi, Samy, Bruna, Joan, and Weinberg, S. Matthew. 2021. A permutation-equivariant neural network Architecture for auction fesign. Pages 5664–5672 of: *Proc. 35th AAAI Conference on Artificial Intelligence*.

[16] Ravindranath, Sai Srivatsa, Feng, Zhe, Li, Shira, Ma, Jonathan, Kominers, Scott D., and Parkes, David C. 2021. Deep learning for two-sided matching. *CoRR*, abs/2107.03427.

[17] Sandholm, Tuomas, and Likhodedov, Anton. 2015. Automated design of revenue-maximizing combinatorial auctions. *Operations Research*, **63**(5), 1000–1025.

[18] Shen, Weiran, Tang, Pingzhong, and Zuo, Song. 2019. Automated mechanism design via neural networks. In: *Proc. 18th International Conference on Autonomous Agents and Multiagent Systems*.

[19] Tacchetti, Andrea, Strouse, D. J., Garnelo, Marta, Graepel, Thore, and Bachrach, Yoram. 2019. A neural architecture for designing Truthful and efficient auctions. *CoRR*, abs/1907.05181.

CHAPTER TWENTY-NINE

Contract Theory

Gabriel Carroll

29.1 Introduction

In many matching markets, the matching itself is not the end of the story; participants make decisions or take actions that in turn affect how valuable the match is. Workers in online labor markets decide how carefully to work or how fast to get the job done. Buyers matched with sellers of goods may be able to choose from among multiple versions of a product and multiple methods of delivery. These parties' behavior depends on the incentives they face, such as rewards to the worker for good performance or the prices on different options offered to the buyer.

The traditional branch of economic theory dealing with the design of incentives is known as *contract theory*, and its elements will be presented in this chapter. As usual, incentive issues are tightly linked with asymmetries of information; essentially, if all parties were perfectly informed, there would be no incentive problems to solve. These asymmetries are often divided into two kinds: *hidden actions*, where one party does something that is not perfectly observed by the other, and *hidden information*, where one party knows something that affects preferences (as in most mechanism design problems). Both kinds of issues are studied through the *principal-agent framework*, a modeling approach that focuses on interactions between two participants, the *principal* (who designs the incentives) and the *agent* (who has the superior information and responds strategically).

A few words about modeling philosophy. Like most models in economics – and unlike most models in computer science and operations research – those in this chapter are "toy" models; that is, they are gross oversimplifications whose purpose is to develop concepts. Specialized algorithms to calculate optimal incentive schemes are typically of limited interest, because in practical situations one usually cannot describe the environment in enough detail to provide accurate input to the algorithm anyway. Given that the purpose is conceptual, we may as well formulate the models to be simple enough that solutions can be found by hand and their salient properties examined.

29.2 Hidden-Action Models

In hidden-action models, as the name implies, the agent can choose among several actions. For such models to be interesting, it should be the case that the action the agent would choose in the absence of incentives is different from the action that the principal would like chosen; such a situation is also referred to as one of *moral hazard*.

We will first offer a simple version of such a model that illustrates the essential elements. As we shall see, this model also has a simple solution – but arguably too simple for many purposes. We will then explore a couple of variants that address some shortcomings of the basic model and thereby highlight various considerations in incentive design.

It is common to introduce hidden-action models with the interpretation that the agent is a worker, and the principal is the boss, who has to motivate the agent to work. Although we follow this framing here, it is worth keeping in mind that these models have many other applications; Section 29.2.4 discusses some of them.

29.2.1 A Simple Benchmark Model

The agent can take various possible *actions* that create revenue, or *output*, for the principal, but these actions may be costly for himself. We take as given a finite set $Y \subseteq \mathbb{R}_+$ of possible *output levels*. The output produced is random, but its distribution depends on the action taken. We are not concerned with the physical description of the actions the agent can take, but only with their consequences for payoffs; we thus model them as follows:

Definition 29.1. An *action* is a pair $a = (F, c)$, where $F \in \Delta(Y)$ and $c \in \mathbb{R}_+$.

The interpretation is that the action generates output drawn from the distribution F, and it costs c to the agent. As a convention, we write $F(y)$ for the probability of drawing an output level y or less, and $f(y)$ for the probability of drawing exactly y.

Remark 29.2. Depending on the application, the cost c might be interpreted as money the agent has to spend, or simply as the monetary equivalent of the displeasure the agent experiences from exerting effort to perform the action.

Definition 29.3. A *technology* is a non-empty finite set of actions.

An instance of the model is given by a triple $(Y, \mathcal{A}, \underline{u})$, where Y is the set of possible output levels, $\mathcal{A}$ is the technology available to the agent, and $\underline{u} \in \mathbb{R}$ is the agent's *outside option*, the payoff he would receive by declining to transact with the principal.

The principal can give incentives via a *contract*, which specifies a recommended action and a payment for each level of output that might be produced.

Definition 29.4. A *contract* (a, w) consists of $a \in \mathcal{A}$ and a function $w \colon Y \to \mathbb{R}$.

The interaction between the parties is envisioned to proceed as follows:

- The principal proposes a contract.
- The agent can either reject the contract and earn his outside option $\underline{u}$ or accept the contract.

- If the agent accepts the contract, he chooses an action (F, c) from his technology. The principal does not observe the action directly, but she does observe the level of output it produces, $y \sim F$.
- The agent is then paid as promised by the contract, $w(y)$, and the principal keeps the rest, $y - w(y)$.

Here, and throughout this chapter, we assume the parties have quasilinear utility and evaluate random outcomes by their expected utility. So the agent's overall payoff from taking action (F, c), taking the cost into account, is $\mathbb{E}_{y \sim F}[w(y)] - c$, and the principal's corresponding payoff is $\mathbb{E}_{y \sim F}[y - w(y)]$.

Definition 29.5. We say the contract $((F, c), w)$ is *valid* if it satisfies the following two conditions:

- *(Incentive compatibility)* $\mathbb{E}_{y \sim F}[w(y)] - c \geq \mathbb{E}_{y \sim F'}[w(y)] - c'$ for all $(F', c') \in \mathcal{A}$.
- *(Individual rationality)* $\mathbb{E}_{y \sim F}[w(y)] - c \geq \underline{u}$.

The incentive-compatibility condition is also sometimes referred to by saying that w *implements* the action (F, c). Individual rationality expresses that the agent should be willing to accept the contract.

Remark 29.6. Why do we require contracts to include an action recommendation (and write incentive compatibility explicitly)? We could instead just say that w itself is the contract, and the agent chooses whichever action he prefers. But the above approach ensures there is no ambiguity about what the agent does if he has multiple optimal actions.

The principal's problem is to find a valid contract that maximizes her payoff. In this benchmark model, there is an easy solution. Define the *surplus* from an action (F, c) as $s(F, c) = \mathbb{E}_{y \sim F}[y] - c$. Let s^* be the maximum surplus among all actions in $\mathcal{A}$, and $(F^*, c^*) \in \mathcal{A}$ an action attaining it. Then:

Observation 29.7. *Offering payment* $w(y) = y - s^* + \underline{u}$, *together with recommending action* (F^*, c^*), *constitutes an optimal valid contract.*

Proof To see that the contract is valid: for any action (F, c) the agent takes, his payoff is $s(F, c)$ plus the constant $-s^* + \underline{u}$, so taking the surplus-maximizing action (F^*, c^*) is incentive compatible. The agent's resulting payoff is $\underline{u}$, so individual rationality is satisfied too.

To see that the contract is optimal, notice that it gives the principal a payoff of $s^* - \underline{u}$. There is no way for the principal to do better because, for any contract, whatever action (F, c) the agent takes, the sum of the two parties' payoffs equals the surplus $s(F, c) \leq s^*$. Since the agent's payoff needs to be at least $\underline{u}$, the principal gets at most $s^* - \underline{u}$. $\qquad \square$

Remark 29.8. The contract above is sometimes referred to as "selling the firm to the agent" for the price $s^* - \underline{u}$, i.e., it can be interpreted as asking the agent to pay $s^* - \underline{u}$ to the principal, then giving the agent ownership of the output.

In the above analysis, the principal does well by simply making the agent the beneficiary of the fruits of his labor, thus giving him incentives to choose his action efficiently.

Although this idea is intuitive, the resulting contract is often unrealistic. If the range of possible output levels is large (for example, the agent is responsible for a big project), this contract may end up specifying huge positive or negative payments depending on the realized output level y. There are various reasons why this might not be appropriate; here are two main ones.

- First, the agent might be *risk averse*: he might prefer a less-variable payment, even if its expected value is lower. This is modeled by assuming that the agent maximizes an expression such as $\mathbb{E}_{y \sim F}[u(w(y))] - c$, where $u \colon \mathbb{R} \to \mathbb{R}$ is some concave function, rather than simply maximizing $\mathbb{E}_{y \sim F}[w(y)] - c$. In this case, the principal can do better by offering the agent some insurance against the uncertainty in output.
- Second, there might be *limited liability*: large negative payments might just be impossible (there's no way to take away more money than the agent owns) or might be possible but illegal.

Risk aversion is widespread in many economic applications. However, we will turn our focus next to limited liability, as it allows us to stay within the quasilinear-utility framework.

Remark 29.9. We have made a rather stark assumption about how the parties interact: the principal proposes a contract, and the agent has to take it or leave it. In reality, we might imagine that there is some bargaining over the terms of the contract. Although we cannot predict the outcome without assuming more specifics on the bargaining process, it might be reasonable to assume they choose a contract w that is Pareto optimal (see Chapter 4). In this case, notice that if w gives the agent an expected payoff u then w must be an optimal contract for the principal in the model when the agent's outside option $\underline{u}$ is replaced by u. In other words, for a given $(Y, \mathcal{A})$, we can find all the Pareto optimal contracts by varying $\underline{u}$ and solving for the principal's optimal contract for each $\underline{u}$. In the model above this doesn't do much because the contract will always be of the form $w(y) = y - \text{constant}$, but the same observation can be applied to more complex models, such as the one in the next section.

29.2.2 A Model with Limited Liability

We can change the model to incorporate limited liability by adding a constraint that contracts should never pay less than some minimum amount. It is without loss of generality to assume this minimum is 0 (otherwise, we can renormalize it to 0 by simply translating the payments in all contracts, and the agent's outside option, by a constant).

Thus, for this section, we define valid contracts as follows.

Definition 29.10. The contract $((F, c), w)$ is *valid* if it satisfies the incentive compatibility and individual rationality constraints from Definition 29.5 and, further, also satisfies

- *(Limited liability)* $w(y) \geq 0$ for all y.

Remark 29.11. If $\underline{u} \leq -(\min_{(F,c)\in\mathcal{A}} c)$ then the individual rationality condition is redundant. In the previous section, individual rationality was needed to make the principal's problem interesting (otherwise the principal could make arbitrarily large profits by setting all values $w(y)$ to large negative numbers). With limited liability this is no longer the case, so sometimes we just assume that $\underline{u}$ is low enough that individual rationality can be ignored.

The interaction between the parties, and the goal of maximizing the principal's payoff, remain as before.

An optimal contract for this model can be found as follows. For any fixed action $(F, c) \in \mathcal{A}$, we can consider the payment functions w for which $((F, c), w)$ is valid (if any such w exists). Note that optimizing the principal's payoff among all such w is equivalent to minimizing $\mathbb{E}_{y \sim F}[w(y)]$ over such w. Moreover, given the choice of (F, c), the constraints in the definition of a valid contract are linear inequalities on w. Thus we have the following algorithm:

Algorithm 29.12

---

1. For each $(F, c) \in \mathcal{A}$, solve the LP to determine a payment function w that minimizes $\mathbb{E}_{y \sim F}[w(y)]$ subject to the validity of $((F, c), w)$. Record the payoff $v^*(F, c) = \mathbb{E}_{y \sim F}[y - w(y)]$ accordingly. (If the LP is infeasible, set $v^*(F, c) = -\infty$.)
2. Identify the action (F, c) for which $v^*(F, c)$ is maximized, and choose the corresponding optimal payment function w.

At this point, not much can be said about optimal contracts. For example, they may not be *monotone*: the agent may sometimes be paid less for higher levels of output. (See Exercise 29.1.) And, in general, an optimal contract will no longer implement the surplus-maximizing action. To make progress in describing properties of optimal contracts, we need to first make more specific assumptions about the structure of the problem.

One common way of imposing such structure is to assume that the agent's actions are ordered; higher actions may be interpreted as higher levels of effort, and we might assume that higher effort makes higher levels of output relatively more likely. Together with a convexity assumption on output distributions (see Remark 29.15), this leads to the following definition.

Definition 29.13. We say that the instance $(Y, \mathcal{A}, \underline{u})$ is *monotone convex* if the elements of Y can be labeled $\{y_1, \ldots, y_K\}$, with $y_1 < \cdots < y_K$, and the actions can be labeled $\{(F_1, c_1), \ldots, (F_J, c_J)\}$, with $c_1 < \cdots < c_J$, such that:

- *(Full support)* $f_j(y_k) > 0$ for all j and k;
- *(Monotone likelihood ratio property)*

$$\frac{f_j(y_k)}{f_j(y_{k-1})} > \frac{f_{j-1}(y_k)}{f_{j-1}(y_{k-1})} \quad \text{for all } 1 < j \leq J, 1 < k \leq K;$$

- *(Convexity)* for each $1 < j < J$, and each $1 \leq k < K$,

$$\frac{F_{j-1}(y_k) - F_j(y_k)}{c_j - c_{j-1}} \geq \frac{F_j(y_k) - F_{j+1}(y_k)}{c_{j+1} - c_j}.$$

Remark 29.14. In the simple case $K = 2$, we can think of the outcomes as "success" or "failure"; thus, higher effort makes success more likely.

Remark 29.15. The convexity assumption implies that the the probability of output above y_k (namely $1 - F_j(y_k)$) is a concave function of the effort c_j. It can be understood as saying that an intermediate effort level generates at least as good an output distribution as an equally costly randomization between high and low effort levels.

Proposition 29.16. *Suppose that $(Y, \mathcal{A}, \underline{u})$ is monotone convex, and assume $\underline{u}$ is low enough that the individual rationality constraint is redundant.*

There exists an optimal contract $((F, c), w)$ such that $w(y) = 0$ for all $y \neq y_K$.

Moreover, let (F_{j^*}, c_{j^*}) be the surplus-maximizing action (if there is more than one maximizer, let j^* be the highest). Then, any optimal contract implements an action (F_j, c_j) with $j \leq j^*$.

Proof First, a preliminary observation: we must have $f_{j-1}(y_K) < f_j(y_K)$ for each $j > 1$. This is so because iterated application of the monotone likelihood-ratio property implies

$$\frac{f_{j-1}(y_k)}{f_j(y_k)} > \frac{f_{j-1}(y_K)}{f_j(y_K)} \tag{29.1}$$

for each $k < K$, and so if $f_{j-1}(y_K) \geq f_j(y_K)$ then $f_{j-1}(y_k) > f_j(y_k)$ for each other k, and then we could not have $\sum_k f_{j-1}(y_k) = 1 = \sum_k f_j(y_k)$.

Now on to the contracting problem. It is evident that an action (F_1, c_1) can be implemented by paying 0 for every output level. We claim that, for each $j > 1$, the action (F_j, c_j) can be implemented by the payment function

$$w(y_K) = \frac{c_j - c_{j-1}}{f_j(y_K) - f_{j-1}(y_K)}, \qquad w(y_k) = 0 \text{ for } k < K,$$

leading to an expected payment

$$\mathbb{E}_{y \sim F_j}[w(y)] = f_j(y_K) \frac{c_j - c_{j-1}}{f_j(y_K) - f_{j-1}(y_K)}, \tag{29.2}$$

and that there is no cheaper way to implement (F_j, c_j).

First, let us show that action j cannot be implemented more cheaply than claimed. Consider any payment function w. We have

$$\mathbb{E}_{y \sim F_{j-1}}[w(y)] = \sum_{k=1}^K f_{j-1}(y_k) w(y_k)$$

$$\geq \sum_{k=1}^K \frac{f_{j-1}(y_K)}{f_j(y_K)} f_j(y_k) w(y_k)$$

$$= \frac{f_{j-1}(y_K)}{f_j(y_K)} \mathbb{E}_{y \sim F_j}[w(y)].$$

(In the inequality step, we have used (29.1) together with $w(y_k) \geq 0$.) So, if w implements (F_j, c_j) then

$$\mathbb{E}_{y \sim F_j}[w(y)] - c_j \geq \mathbb{E}_{y \sim F_{j-1}}[w(y)] - c_{j-1} \geq \frac{f_{j-1}(y_K)}{f_j(y_K)} \mathbb{E}_{y \sim F_j}[w(y)] - c_{j-1},$$

hence

$$\mathbb{E}_{y \sim F_j}[w(y)] \geq \frac{c_j - c_{j-1}}{1 - f_{j-1}(y_K)/f_j(y_K)},$$

which is the asserted lower bound. (The last step uses $f_{j-1}(y_K) < f_j(y_K)$ to ensure the denominator is positive.)

Now let us show that the claimed contract implements action j. That is, writing $r = (c_j - c_{j-1})/(f_j(y_K) - f_{j-1}(y_K))$, we need to show that

$$f_j(y_K)r - c_j \geq f_{j'}(y_K)r - c_{j'} \tag{29.3}$$

for each j'. Consider the convexity assumption for $k = K-1$ and any $1 < \tilde{j} < J$. Since $f_{\tilde{j}}(y_K) = 1 - F_{\tilde{j}}(y_{K-1})$, we can rewrite the assumption as

$$\frac{f_{\tilde{j}}(y_K) - f_{\tilde{j}-1}(y_K)}{c_{\tilde{j}} - c_{\tilde{j}-1}} \geq \frac{f_{\tilde{j}+1}(y_K) - f_{\tilde{j}}(y_K)}{c_{\tilde{j}+1} - c_{\tilde{j}}}. \tag{29.4}$$

In particular, for $\tilde{j} \leq j$, we have $f_{\tilde{j}}(y_K) - f_{\tilde{j}-1}(y_K) \geq r^{-1}(c_{\tilde{j}} - c_{\tilde{j}-1})$, and so, for any $j' < j$, by summing over $\tilde{j} = j' + 1, \ldots, j$ we conclude that $f_j(y_K) - f_{j'}(y_K) \geq \frac{1}{r}(c_j - c_{j'})$. This implies (29.3) for $j' < j$. Likewise, (29.4) gives us $f_{\tilde{j}}(y_K) - f_{\tilde{j}-1}(y_K) \leq \frac{1}{r}(c_{\tilde{j}} - c_{\tilde{j}-1})$ for $\tilde{j} > j$ and therefore, for any $j' > j$, summing over $\tilde{j} = j+1, \ldots, j'$ gives $f_{j'}(y_K) - f_j(y_K) \leq \frac{1}{r}(c_{j'} - c_j)$. This implies (29.3) for $j' > j$. Thus, the contract implements action j.

We have now shown that, for every action j, the cheapest way to implement it involves paying 0 for every $y \neq y_K$, which proves the first assertion of the proposition.

It remains to prove that any optimal contract implements an action $j \leq j^*$. For $j > 1$, let z_j denote the expected payment given in (29.2), and put $z_1 = 0$. We claim that $z_j + (c_{j+1} - c_j) \leq z_{j+1}$ for each $j < J$. If $j > 1$, we have

$$\begin{aligned}
z_j + (c_{j+1} - c_j) &= f_j(y_K)\frac{c_j - c_{j-1}}{f_j(y_K) - f_{j-1}(y_K)} + (c_{j+1} - c_j) \\
&\leq f_j(y_K)\frac{c_{j+1} - c_j}{f_{j+1}(y_K) - f_j(y_K)} + (c_{j+1} - c_j) \\
&= f_{j+1}(y_K)\frac{c_{j+1} - c_j}{f_{j+1}(y_K) - f_j(y_K)} \\
&= z_{j+1},
\end{aligned}$$

where we have used (29.4). If $j = 1$, the claim is immediate from the definition of z_j, so it holds in this case too. Thus, $z_j - c_j$ is increasing in j, or equivalently, $c_j - z_j$ is decreasing. Figure 29.1 may be helpful in visualizing the situation: if we take the segment between two successive points on the $(c_j, f_j(y_K))$ curve and extend it leftwards, it meets the horizontal axis at point $c_j - z_j$, and the figure shows how the concavity of the curve implies $c_j - z_j \geq c_{j+1} - z_{j+1}$.

——— **620** ———

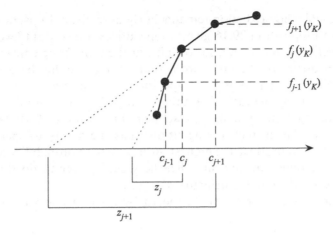

Figure 29.1 Costs to implement successive actions.

The principal's payoff from implementing the action (F_j, c_j) is $\mathbb{E}_{y \sim F_j}[y] - z_j$. We know that, for any $j > j^*$, we have

$$\mathbb{E}_{y \sim F_j}[y] - c_j < \mathbb{E}_{y \sim F_{j^*}}[y] - c_{j^*}$$

by the definition of j^*. Adding to this $c_j - z_j \le c_{j^*} - z_{j^*}$, we have

$$\mathbb{E}_{y \sim F_j}[y] - z_j < \mathbb{E}_{y \sim F_{j^*}}[y] - z_{j^*},$$

so that it is not optimal for the principal to implement (F_j, c_j). □

Remark 29.17. The optimal contract identified in Proposition 29.16 pays only for the highest output level and no other. An intuition is that, owing to the monotone likelihood-ratio assumption, this output level is the one whose probability is most reduced if the agent deviates to a lower action, and so loading all the payment onto this outcome is the most efficient way to discourage such deviations.

Remark 29.18. One of the basic lessons from this model is that, in general, the agent's action is "distorted downward" relative to the socially optimal action. Owing to limited liability, the principal cannot extract the full surplus of whatever action she induces, as she could in the previous section; some of the surplus is left to the agent, and more so for higher actions. Consequently, the principal's preference for inducing high actions is less strong than in the setting without limited liability. Note, however, that this lesson depends on the monotone convex structure we have imposed; see Exercise 29.3.

Remark 29.19. Notice that, under the optimal contract specified, the agent gets the same payoff from the targeted actions (F_j, c_j) and (F_{j-1}, c_{j-1}) (if $j > 1$). This confirms the importance, noted in Remark 29.6, of specifying how such indifference should be broken.

Although the analysis here leads to some useful insights – the idea of placing payment where it can efficiently discourage deviations, and the downward distortion–arguably the prediction remains fairly unrealistic. In particular, the optimal contract in Proposition 29.16 gives no incentives over output levels other than the highest level. This relies on a lot of faith in the monotone convex structure. If this structure is assumed when it is not actually correct (either because the principal oversimplifies in order to apply Proposition 29.16 or because her belief about the technology is simply wrong), then things can go haywire. Suppose, say, that the principal has adopted the optimal contract from Proposition 29.16, targeting some action (F_j, c_j), but that in fact, the agent also has the ability to spend a cost just slightly less than c_j, to produce the highest output y_K with probability equal to $f_j(y_K)$ or otherwise to produce no output. Then he would prefer to do this, potentially resulting in a severe drop in the principal's payoff.

Our next model incorporates this concern by assuming less knowledge of the technology.

29.2.3 A Robust Model

Let us keep the limited liability assumption, but now assume that the principal does not fully know the agent's technology. Instead, she only knows some actions that are available to the agent but envisions that there may be other actions available. Thus, an instance of the model is now given by $(Y, \mathcal{A}_0, \underline{u})$, where $\mathcal{A}_0$ is a technology representing the actions known to the principal.

For this section, let us make four assumptions that will simplify the analysis:

- Assume that $\underline{u} < -\min_{(F,c)\in\mathcal{A}_0} c$, so that individual rationality will not be a concern.
- Assume that $\min(Y) = 0$. (This is an innocuous normalization; it can be achieved by adding a constant to every element of Y without changing the principal's optimization problem.)
- Also assume that, for every $(F, c) \in \mathcal{A}_0$, $c > 0$. (This gets rid of some messy edge cases.)
- Assume there exists $(F, c) \in \mathcal{A}_0$ whose surplus $s(F, c)$ is positive.

We redefine contracts for this section as follows.

Definition 29.20. A *contract* is a function $w : Y \to \mathbb{R}_+$.

Thus, limited liability is incorporated, but a contract no longer prescribes what action the agent should take since this cannot be specified without knowing what actions are available.

Definition 29.21. Contract w *guarantees* a payoff level v to the principal if, for every technology $\mathcal{A}$ such that $\mathcal{A}_0 \subseteq \mathcal{A}$, there exists an action $(F, c) \in \mathcal{A}$ such that

- $\mathbb{E}_{y\sim F}[w(y)] - c \geq \mathbb{E}_{y\sim F'}[w(y)] - c'$ for every $(F', c') \in \mathcal{A}$, and
- $\mathbb{E}_{y\sim F}[y - w(y)] \geq v$.

Evidently, if a contract guarantees v, it also guarantees any $v' \leq v$. We may refer to the supremum of all v guaranteed by a given contract as *the guarantee* of the contract.

Thus, for any contract, we are interested in understanding the payoff that it guarantees to the principal in spite of her uncertainty about the true technology $\mathcal{A}$.

To illustrate how one can show that a contract guarantees a certain payoff, we now consider a particularly simple class of contracts.

Definition 29.22. Contract w is *linear* if there exists a fraction $\alpha \in (0, 1)$ such that $w(y) = \alpha y$ for all $y \in Y$.

Linear contracts are widely seen in practice: for example, think of sales agents who are paid a fixed percentage of each sale they make.

Observation 29.23. *Suppose that the principal uses a linear contract $w(y) = \alpha y$. Write $u_0(\alpha) = \max_{(F,c) \in \mathcal{A}_0} (\alpha \mathbb{E}_{y \sim F}[y] - c)$. Then, the contract guarantees a payoff $\frac{1-\alpha}{\alpha} u_0(\alpha)$.*

(In particular, note that the guarantee is positive if α is close to 1, because we assumed that a positive-surplus action exists.)

Proof Note that, for any technology $\mathcal{A}$ containing $\mathcal{A}_0$, and any action $(F, c) \in \mathcal{A}$ that is optimal for the agent, we have

$$\alpha \mathbb{E}_{y \sim F}[y] \geq \alpha \mathbb{E}_{y \sim F}[y] - c \geq u_0(\alpha),$$

since any action in $\mathcal{A}_0$ is also in $\mathcal{A}$. Therefore

$$\mathbb{E}_{y \sim F}[y - w(y)] = (1 - \alpha)\mathbb{E}_{y \sim F}[y] \geq \frac{1 - \alpha}{\alpha} u_0(\alpha). \qquad \square$$

After considering this argument, one might next ask: is there any theoretical reason to focus on linear contracts here? The next result shows that there is such a reason: given the goal of maximizing the guarantee, without loss of generality we can restrict attention to linear contracts.

Theorem 29.24. *If any contract w guarantees a payoff level $v > 0$, then there exists a linear contract that also guarantees v.*

The proof proceeds roughly as follows. First, we write down a linear program that identifies the "worst-case" action that the agent might choose if offered w. We then use a geometric separation argument to find a linear contract that matches w for this worst-case action, and show that, because the linear contract better aligns the agent's interests with the principal's, its guarantee can only be better than the worse-case action of the original contract.

Proof Denote $u_0(w) = \max_{(F,c) \in \mathcal{A}_0} (\mathbb{E}_{y \sim F}[w(y)] - c)$. We note that $u_0(w) < \max_y w(y)$, by our assumption that $c > 0$ for all $(F, c) \in \mathcal{A}_0$.

Consider the problem of minimizing $\mathbb{E}_{y \sim F}[y - w(y)]$ over all $F \in \Delta(Y)$ such that $\mathbb{E}_{y \sim F}[w(y)] \geq u_0(w)$. This is a linear program for F, and we claim that this problem has a solution where the constraint is satisfied with equality. If not then the constraint can be dropped, which would imply that the function $y - w(y)$ attains its minimum over Y at a point $\underline{y}$ with $w(\underline{y}) > u_0(w)$. Then

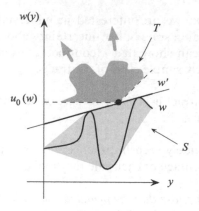

Figure 29.2 Separation argument and improvement to a linear contract.

consider the distribution F' that simply places probability 1 on this $\underline{y}$; if the technology is $\mathcal{A} = \mathcal{A}_0 \cup \{(F', 0)\}$ then the unique optimal action for the agent is $(F', 0)$. Since the principal then receives $\underline{y} - w(\underline{y}) \leq 0 - w(0) \leq 0$ (since $0 \in Y$), the contract cannot guarantee any payoff level above 0, a contradiction.

Now let $\widetilde{F}$ be a solution to the minimization problem above, and let $\widetilde{v}$ be the resulting objective value. We claim that $\widetilde{v}$ is exactly the guarantee of w, so that $\widetilde{v} \geq v$. Indeed, for any possible technology $\mathcal{A}$, an optimal action $(F, c) \in \mathcal{A}$ necessarily satisfies $\mathbb{E}_{y \sim F}[w(y)] \geq \mathbb{E}_{y \sim F}[w(y)] - c \geq u_0(w)$, i.e., F is feasible in the minimization problem, so $\mathbb{E}_{y \sim F}[y - w(y)] \geq \widetilde{v}$ and w guarantees at least $\widetilde{v}$. Conversely, for any $\varepsilon > 0$, by perturbing $\widetilde{F}$ we can find $F' \in \Delta(Y)$ such that $\mathbb{E}_{y \sim F'}[y - w(y)] < \widetilde{v} + \varepsilon$ and $\mathbb{E}_{y \sim F'}[w(y)] > u_0(w)$ (here we have used the fact that $u_0(w) < \max(w)$), so if we consider the technology $\mathcal{A} = \mathcal{A}_0 \cup \{(F', 0)\}$ then the agent's unique optimal action is $(F', 0)$, showing that w does not guarantee $\widetilde{v} + \varepsilon$.

Now we proceed to the separation argument. Define two convex subsets S and T of $\mathbb{R}^2$ as follows: S is the convex hull of all points $(y, w(y))$ for $y \in Y$, while T consists of all points (p, q) such that $q > u_0(w)$ and $p - q < \widetilde{v}$. These sets are disjoint: any point in their intersection would correspond to a feasible point in the minimization problem having objective value $p - q < \widetilde{v}$, which cannot exist. Therefore, there exists some line in $\mathbb{R}^2$ separating S and T. Expressing this statement algebraically, there exist values $\kappa, \lambda, \mu \in \mathbb{R}$, with κ, λ not both zero, such that

$$\kappa p + \lambda q \leq \mu \quad \text{for all } (p, q) \in S; \tag{29.5}$$

$$\kappa p + \lambda q \geq \mu \quad \text{for all } (p, q) \in T. \tag{29.6}$$

The argument is illustrated in Figure 29.2. Sets S and T are the two shaded regions. (Although we have assumed Y is finite, w is shown as a curve for visual clarity.)

Note that, for large M, the points $(-M, u_0(w) + 1/M)$ and $(\widetilde{v} + M, M + 1/M)$ are both in T. Hence, we must have $\kappa \leq 0$ and $\kappa + \lambda \geq 0$, since otherwise one or the other of these points would violate (29.6) for large enough M. Together with $(\kappa, \lambda) \neq (0, 0)$, these relations imply $\lambda > 0$. Also, note that the point

$(u_0(w)+\widetilde{v}, u_0(w)) = (\mathbb{E}_{y\sim\widetilde{F}}[y], \mathbb{E}_{y\sim\widetilde{F}}[w(y)])$ lies in S, and it also lies in the closure of T, so it must lie on the line:

$$\kappa(u_0(w) + \widetilde{v}) + \lambda u_0(w) = \mu. \tag{29.7}$$

The latter implies in turn that $\kappa < 0$ since if $\kappa = 0$, then (29.5) would imply $w(y) \le \mu/\lambda = u_0(w)$ for all y, contradicting $u_0(w) < \max(w)$.

Now we can define our new contract. Condition (29.5) implies that $w(y) \le (\mu - \kappa y)/\lambda$ for all $y \in Y$. Accordingly, define w' by $w'(y) = (\mu - \kappa y)/\lambda$. Then $w'(y) \ge w(y) \ge 0$ for all y, so w' is indeed a contract. (It is shown by the bold straight line in Figure 29.2.)

We claim that w' again guarantees at least $\widetilde{v}$. The calculation is a variant of that in Observation 29.23. Write $\alpha = -\kappa/\lambda > 0$ and $\beta = \mu/\lambda$, so $w'(y) = \alpha y + \beta$. Equation (29.7) can be rewritten as $(1-\alpha)u_0(w) - \alpha\widetilde{v} = \beta$. Now consider any technology $\mathcal{A}$ containing $\mathcal{A}_0$, and any $(F', c') \in \mathcal{A}$ optimal for the agent:

$$\mathbb{E}_{y\sim F'}[w'(y)] - c' \ge \max_{(F,c)\in\mathcal{A}_0} \left(\mathbb{E}_{y\sim F}[w'(y)] - c\right)$$

$$\ge \max_{(F,c)\in\mathcal{A}_0} \left(\mathbb{E}_{y\sim F}[w(y)] - c\right) = u_0(w),$$

where the second inequality follows from $w'(y) \ge w(y)$. Hence,

$$\alpha\mathbb{E}_{y\sim F'}[y] + \beta = \mathbb{E}_{y\sim F'}[w'(y)] \ge u_0(w),$$

and so

$$\mathbb{E}_{y\sim F'}[y - w'(y)] = (1 - \alpha)\mathbb{E}_{y\sim F'}[y] - \beta \ge (1 - \alpha)\left(\frac{u_0(w) - \beta}{\alpha}\right) - \beta = \widetilde{v}.$$

This shows that w' guarantees $\widetilde{v}$ as claimed.

At this point, we have shown that there exists an "affine" contract, i.e., one of the form $w'(y) = \alpha y + \beta$ with α, β constants, that guarantees $\widetilde{v} \ge v$. We have noted that $\alpha > 0$ and that $\beta = w'(0) \ge 0$. Note also that $\alpha < 1$, because otherwise $w'(y) \ge y$ for all y, contradicting the fact that w' has a positive guarantee. Finally, if $\beta > 0$ strictly, then replacing $w'(y)$ with just αy can only improve the guarantee (since, for any technology $\mathcal{A}$, the agent's optimal action is the same as before, and now the principal's payoff increases by β). After this change, our definition of a linear contract is met. $\square$

This theorem shows that, if contracts are evaluated by their worst-case guarantee, then a linear contract is optimal. (To be precise, we have not yet shown that the optimum is attained; for this, see Exercise 29.4.)

29.2.4 Applications of Hidden-Action Models

While we have focused on the employment application for hidden-action models, it is worth emphasizing that such models have many other applications. The concepts are relevant any time one party designs incentives that influence the action taken by another, by promising material rewards (which may be money, or something else, e.g. social status) contingent on a noisy signal of the action chosen. Here are just a few more examples to illustrate the breadth of applications.

- *Financial contracting:* An investor writes a contract with a startup founder, specifying how profits are shared between the parties; the investor needs to be offered an adequate return, while the founder needs to be given incentives to invest the money productively.
- *Health insurance:* A classic application featuring moral hazard and risk aversion. The company wants to design the insurance contract to protect the consumer against risks without incentivizing the consumer to spend too much on unnecessary procedures.
- *Reputation systems:* The design of the system by which ratings (for sellers on eBay, drivers on Lyft, etc.) translate into future business affects their incentives for performance.
- *Political accountability:* Voters can reelect politicians or not, depending how well they (appear to) have governed; some theorists have studied the extent to which these reelection incentives can induce good performance.

29.3 Hidden-Information Models

In hidden-information models, the agent holds private information about his preferences, and an allocation is chosen as a function of this information. Like hidden-action models, there is a wide variety of applications. Here, for concreteness, we will envision the principal as a seller of a product and the agent as a buyer. The product can be offered in different quality levels (think of a hotel offering various room types, or a cellphone provider offering multiple service plans), from which the buyer will choose depending on his preferences. Section 29.3.2 will list some other applications.

Here, we will present a classic version of such a model. We will adopt a formulation with continuous types, as this makes the mathematics particularly clean (and, if the reader has seen the theory of optimal auctions, much of the analysis will look familiar); but discrete formulations are also possible.

Models of this sort are also often called *screening* models: the seller "screens" the different types of buyer by offering multiple options that are chosen by the different types.

Remark 29.25. Some authors also call these models *adverse selection* models. There is some confusion in the literature about this term. It comes from the world of insurance, where different buyers may choose different products in a way that makes the products more costly for the seller to provide. For example, a health insurance contract that is sold at a high price but covers a large percentage of costs is especially likely to attract very sick people, and these are precisely the people that the insurance company would prefer *not* to attract. In the model presented below, there is nothing "adverse": the cost of providing a given quality q does not depend on who buys it. Nonetheless, the term is sometimes applied to such a model.

29.3.1 A Price-Discrimination Model

The agent can be given a product of *quality q*, which can be chosen from some interval $[\underline{q}, \overline{q}] \subseteq \mathbb{R}$. The agent's preference over qualities is determined by his *type θ*, drawn from a given interval $[\underline{\theta}, \overline{\theta}] \subseteq \mathbb{R}$. It is important that both the possible qualities and the types are "ordered," with higher types both overall valuing the product more and also having a stronger preference for high quality; we shall formalize this shortly.

If the agent of type θ purchases a good of quality q and pays a transfer t for it, his overall payoff is $u(q, \theta) - t$. We normalize the agent's outside option to 0. Here u is a function satisfying the following conditions:

- u is twice continuously differentiable. (We will denote its derivatives with respect to particular arguments using subscripts, thus writing u_θ, $u_{q\theta}$, etc.)
- u is weakly increasing in θ, for each $q \in [\underline{q}, \overline{q}]$. (It is common to interpret the minimum quality $\underline{q}$ as corresponding to not receiving a product, in which case one often sets $\underline{q} = 0$ and assumes $u(0, \theta) = 0$ for all θ.)
- u is *strictly supermodular*: for qualities $q' > q$, $u(q', \theta) - u(q, \theta)$ is strictly increasing in θ. (Given the differentiability assumption, this is equivalent to $u_{q\theta} \geq 0$, with strict inequality on a dense set.)

Producing (or acquiring) a product of quality q costs $c(q)$ to the principal. Thus, if the agent receives q and pays t, the principal's payoff is $t - c(q)$. Assume that c is continuous.

From the principal's point of view, the agent's type is unknown; it is drawn from a distribution F, assumed to have a density f on $[\underline{\theta}, \overline{\theta}]$, which is continuous and strictly positive throughout the interval. As before, we write $F(\theta)$ for the probability of drawing a type $\leq \theta$.

An instance of the model is then given by the tuple $(\underline{q}, \overline{q}, \underline{\theta}, \overline{\theta}, u, c, f)$.

We can envision the principal offering a price for each quality q (or perhaps a subset of the possible qualities), and letting the agent choose his favorite from the offered (quality, price) pairs. However, by the revelation principle (see Chapter 4), the outcome of such an interaction can equivalently be described by a (direct) *mechanism* that specifies the quality and price chosen by each type:

Definition 29.26. A *mechanism* (q, t) consists of two measurable functions $q: [\underline{\theta}, \overline{\theta}] \to [\underline{q}, \overline{q}]$ and $t: [\underline{\theta}, \overline{\theta}] \to \mathbb{R}$. Sometimes q is called the *allocation function* (or *allocation rule*) and t is the *payment function*.

Although we use the same notation q both for a typical quality level and for an allocation function (and t likewise), the meaning should be clear from the context.

Definition 29.27. The mechanism (q, t) is *valid* if it satisfies the following conditions:

- (Incentive compatibility) $u(q(\theta), \theta) - t(\theta) \geq u(q(\widehat{\theta}), \theta) - t(\widehat{\theta})$ for all $\theta, \widehat{\theta} \in [\underline{\theta}, \overline{\theta}]$.
- (Individual rationality) $u(q(\theta), \theta) - t(\theta) \geq 0$ for all $\theta \in [\underline{\theta}, \overline{\theta}]$.

The principal's expected payoff from the mechanism (q, t) is $\mathbb{E}_{\theta \sim F}[t(\theta) - c(q(\theta))]$. The problem is to find a valid mechanism that maximizes this payoff.

The allocation function q is *implementable* if there is some payment function t such that (q, t) is a valid mechanism (and we say that t *implements* q). A first question is what allocation functions are implementable – and what payments implement them.

Proposition 29.28. *If (q, t) is a valid mechanism then the function q is weakly increasing.*

Conversely, any weakly increasing q is implementable, and it is implemented by t if and only if there is some constant $C \geq 0$ such that

$$t(\theta) = u(q(\theta), \theta) - \int_{\underline{\theta}}^{\theta} u_\theta(q(\widetilde{\theta}), \widetilde{\theta}) \, d\widetilde{\theta} - C \tag{29.8}$$

for all θ.

Proof First, suppose that (q, t) is valid, and suppose for contradiction that $\theta < \theta'$ are two distinct types with $q(\theta) > q(\theta')$. By incentive compatibility,

$$u(q(\theta), \theta) - t(\theta) \geq u(q(\theta'), \theta) - t(\theta')$$

from which

$$u(q(\theta), \theta) - u(q(\theta'), \theta) \geq t(\theta) - t(\theta').$$

Similarly, $u(q(\theta'), \theta') - u(q(\theta), \theta') \geq t(\theta') - t(\theta)$. Combining the relations we obtain

$$u(q(\theta), \theta) - u(q(\theta'), \theta) \geq t(\theta) - t(\theta') \geq u(q(\theta), \theta') - u(q(\theta'), \theta').$$

This contradicts the strict supermodularity assumption, which tells us that $u(q(\theta), \cdot) - u(q(\theta'), \cdot)$ is strictly increasing. This shows that q must be weakly increasing.

Henceforth, fix any q that is weakly increasing. We first show that every function t implementing q has the form in (29.8). For such a t, let

$$U(\theta) = u(q(\theta), \theta) - t(\theta) \tag{29.9}$$

be the payoff earned by an agent of type θ in the mechanism. We claim that U is Lipschitz continuous. To see this, let λ be an upper bound for $|u_\theta|$ (which exists since u_θ is continuous); then, for any θ, θ', incentive compatibility implies

$$U(\theta') \geq u(q(\theta), \theta') - t(\theta) \geq \left(u(q(\theta), \theta) - \lambda|\theta' - \theta| \right) - t(\theta) = U(\theta) - \lambda|\theta' - \theta|.$$

Writing the corresponding inequality with θ and θ' reversed, and combining the two inequalities, we obtain $|U(\theta') - U(\theta)| \leq \lambda|\theta' - \theta|$, so U is Lipschitz continuous as claimed. This in turn implies that U is absolutely continuous, i.e., it is differentiable almost everywhere and is given by the integral of its derivative.

However, if we fix any $\theta \in (\underline{\theta}, \overline{\theta})$ at which U is differentiable, incentive compatibility says that $U(\theta') \geq u(q(\theta), \theta') - t(\theta)$ for all θ', with equality when $\theta' = \theta$. Both sides of this inequality are differentiable in θ' at the equality point $\theta' = \theta$, so their derivatives there must coincide, i.e.,

$$\frac{dU}{d\theta} = u_\theta(q(\theta), \theta).$$

Thus we have, for each θ,

$$U(\theta) - U(\underline{\theta}) = \int_{\underline{\theta}}^{\theta} u_\theta(q(\tilde{\theta}), \tilde{\theta}) \, d\tilde{\theta}.$$

Substituting into (29.9) and solving for $t(\theta)$ shows that $t(\theta)$ has the form given in (29.8), with $C = U(\underline{\theta})$. Finally, $C \geq 0$ follows from individual rationality.

Let us conversely show that any payment function as in (29.8) implements q. First, we verify incentive compatibility. Consider any θ and $\hat{\theta}$. Define U as in (29.9), and note that $U(\theta) = \int_{\underline{\theta}}^{\theta} u_\theta(q(\tilde{\theta}), \tilde{\theta}) \, d\tilde{\theta} + C$.

Now,

$$u(q(\hat{\theta}), \theta) - t(\hat{\theta}) = U(\hat{\theta}) + (u(q(\hat{\theta}), \theta) - u(q(\hat{\theta}), \hat{\theta})).$$

Checking incentive compatibility is thus equivalent to checking that

$$U(\theta) - U(\hat{\theta}) \geq u(q(\hat{\theta}), \theta) - u(q(\hat{\theta}), \hat{\theta}),$$

or equivalently

$$\int_{\hat{\theta}}^{\theta} u_\theta(q(\tilde{\theta}), \tilde{\theta}) \, d\tilde{\theta} \geq \int_{\hat{\theta}}^{\theta} u_\theta(q(\hat{\theta}), \tilde{\theta}) \, d\tilde{\theta}. \tag{29.10}$$

For $\hat{\theta} < \theta$, this is true because the monotonicity of q and supermodularity of u imply that $u_\theta(q(\tilde{\theta}), \tilde{\theta}) \geq u_\theta(q(\hat{\theta}), \tilde{\theta})$ for each $\tilde{\theta} > \hat{\theta}$. For $\hat{\theta} > \theta$, (29.10) has the integration ranges "reversed," with the lower endpoint above the upper endpoint, so it may be easier to understand in the equivalent form

$$\int_{\theta}^{\hat{\theta}} u_\theta(q(\tilde{\theta}), \tilde{\theta}) \, d\tilde{\theta} \leq \int_{\theta}^{\hat{\theta}} u_\theta(q(\hat{\theta}), \tilde{\theta}) \, d\tilde{\theta}.$$

Again, this is true because monotonicity and supermodularity ensure that $u_\theta(q(\tilde{\theta}), \tilde{\theta}) \leq u_\theta(q(\hat{\theta}), \tilde{\theta})$ on the relevant range of $\tilde{\theta}$.

Finally, $U(\underline{\theta}) = C \geq 0$, so individual rationality is satisfied for the type $\underline{\theta}$. For any other type θ, individual rationality then follows from incentive compatibility and the monotonicity of u in the type, as

$$u(q(\theta), \theta) - t(\theta) \geq u(q(\underline{\theta}), \theta) - t(\underline{\theta}) \geq u(q(\underline{\theta}), \underline{\theta}) - t(\underline{\theta}) \geq 0. \qquad \square$$

Given Proposition 29.28, we can rewrite the principal's problem as follows: choose a weakly increasing function $q \colon [\underline{\theta}, \overline{\theta}] \to [\underline{q}, \overline{q}]$ and a constant $C \geq 0$ to maximize

$$\int_{\underline{\theta}}^{\overline{\theta}} \left(u(q(\theta), \theta) - \int_{\underline{\theta}}^{\theta} u_\theta(q(\tilde{\theta}), \tilde{\theta}) \, d\tilde{\theta} - C - c(q(\theta)) \right) f(\theta) \, d\theta.$$

Clearly it is optimal to set $C = 0$. For the inner integral, we can swap the order of integration between θ and $\tilde{\theta}$ and then relabel $\tilde{\theta}$ as θ; with these steps, we can rewrite the principal's objective as

$$\int_{\underline{\theta}}^{\overline{\theta}} \left(u(q(\theta), \theta) - \frac{1 - F(\theta)}{f(\theta)} u_\theta(q(\theta), \theta) - c(q(\theta)) \right) f(\theta) \, d\theta. \tag{29.11}$$

The nice thing about this expression is that, for each value of θ, the integrand depends on $q(\theta)$ but not on the values of q at any other points. Thus, we can hope to optimize $q(\theta)$ for each θ separately.

With this in mind, we define the following objects:

Definition 29.29. The quantity $\bar{u}(q,\theta) = u(q,\theta) - \frac{1-F(\theta)}{f(\theta)}u_\theta(q,\theta)$ is the *virtual value* of type θ for quality q. The quantity $\bar{s}(q,\theta) = \bar{u}(q,\theta) - c(q)$ is the *virtual surplus* with type θ and quality q.

For each θ, let $q^\circ(\theta)$ be the quality that maximizes the virtual surplus $\bar{s}(q,\theta)$ (or the highest maximizer, if there is more than one). With a few further assumptions, we can characterize an optimal solution to the principal's problem.

Theorem 29.30. *Suppose that the utility function u is three times continuously differentiable, with $u_{q\theta\theta} \leq 0$ everywhere, and that the function $h(\theta) = f(\theta)/(1 - F(\theta))$ is differentiable and increasing in θ.*
Then, taking $q(\theta) = q^\circ(\theta)$, and taking payments $t(\theta)$ given by (29.8) with $C = 0$, gives a valid mechanism that maximizes the principal's payoff.

Proof It is immediate that the suggested allocation function maximizes (29.11) as long as it is indeed weakly increasing. To check this, we need to show that the virtual surplus $\bar{s}(q,\theta)$ is weakly supermodular (i.e., for $q' > q$, $\bar{s}(q',\theta) - \bar{s}(q,\theta)$ is weakly increasing in θ). This will imply the result, since if $\theta < \theta'$ but $q^\circ(\theta) > q^\circ(\theta')$, we would have $\bar{s}(q^\circ(\theta),\theta') - \bar{s}(q^\circ(\theta'),\theta') < 0 \leq \bar{s}(q^\circ(\theta),\theta) - \bar{s}(q^\circ(\theta'),\theta)$, contradicting supermodularity.

Writing $\bar{s}(q,\theta) = u(q,\theta) - u_\theta(q,\theta)/h(\theta) - c(q)$, we take the cross-partial derivative and find

$$\bar{s}_{q\theta} = u_{q\theta} - \frac{u_{q\theta\theta}}{h} + \frac{u_{q\theta}h_\theta}{h^2}.$$

Every term is non-negative, so $\bar{s}_{q\theta} \geq 0$, and $\bar{s}$ is supermodular. $\square$

Remark 29.31. The technical condition that h be increasing, or equivalently that $1 - F(\theta)$ be log-concave, is satisfied by many standard probability distributions, such as the uniform, truncated normal, or truncated exponential distributions.

It is common to compare the qualities in the principal's optimal mechanism with socially optimal qualities. For each type θ, let $q^*(\theta)$ be the quality that maximizes the surplus $s(q,\theta) = u(q,\theta) - c(q)$ (or the highest such quality, if there is more than one). Note that q^* is weakly increasing in θ, by an argument similar to the proof of Theorem 29.30, because the surplus is supermodular.

Observation 29.32. *For each θ, we have $q^\circ(\theta) \leq q^*(\theta)$, with equality at $\theta = \bar{\theta}$.*

Proof If $q^\circ(\theta) > q^*(\theta)$, we would have $s(q^\circ(\theta),\theta) < s(q^*(\theta),\theta)$ and $\bar{s}(q^*(\theta),\theta) \leq \bar{s}(q^\circ(\theta),\theta)$, implying $s(q^\circ(\theta),\theta) - \bar{s}(q^\circ(\theta),\theta) < s(q^*(\theta),\theta) - \bar{s}(q^*(\theta),\theta)$. But $s(q,\theta) - \bar{s}(q,\theta) = u_\theta(q,\theta)/h(\theta)$, which is weakly increasing in q, so we get a contradiction.

Also, to see the equality statement, just note that $\bar{s}(q,\theta) = s(q,\theta)$ when $\theta = \bar{\theta}$. $\square$

Observation 29.32 is often summarized by saying there is "no distortion at the top, downward distortion elsewhere." (Compare with Remark 29.18 concerning the hidden-action model.)

An intuition is that giving a less-than-efficient quality level to type θ reduces the total surplus, but it also increases the amount of money that the principal can extract from types above θ, because they are willing to pay an especially large amount to avoid getting stuck with a low quality. The optimal choice of quality trades off these two effects. For the highest type $\bar{\theta}$, there are no higher types, so the second effect disappears, which is why no distortion arises.

Remark 29.33. The idea behind the distortion is sometimes credited to the nineteenth-century civil engineer Jules Dupuit, who wrote the following about third-class train cars: "It is not because of the few thousand francs which would have to be spent to put a roof over the third-class carriages or to upholster the third-class seats that some company or other has open carriages with wooden benches ... What the company is trying to do is prevent the passengers who can pay the second-class fare from traveling third class; it hits the poor, not because it wants to hurt them, but to frighten the rich."

However, Dupuit went on to assert that first-class carriages were made excessively luxurious for the same reason. In the model here, this would mean that high types receive above-efficient quality levels. But the model does not predict this. One might think that giving a high type θ an excessive quality allows the seller to extract more payments from lower types, but this is incorrect: prices are limited by the high types' incentive to imitate lower types, not vice versa. (This depends on our assumption about outside options; see Exercise 29.6.)

Remark 29.34. As already mentioned, if the reader is familiar with the theory of optimal auctions, it will be noticed that many of the steps here are similar. This is more than coincidence; indeed, the one-buyer optimal "auction" is just a special case of this model, where q is interpreted as the probability of receiving the object rather than a quality, $u(q, \theta) = q\theta$ and $c(q) = 0$.

Remark 29.35. What happens if the extra assumptions of Theorem 29.30 do not hold? In this case, the allocation function q obtained by maximizing the virtual surplus may not be increasing, and therefore may not be implementable. Instead, a process called "ironing" must be applied to account for the monotonicity constraint on q, resulting in type intervals that all receive the same quality. Regardless, it remains true that an optimal mechanism only distorts downwards: if we consider any weakly increasing $q(\theta)$ that sometimes distorts upwards, the alternative allocation function $\min\{q(\theta), q^*(\theta)\}$ is also weakly increasing and yields a higher profit than q, by logic similar to Observation 29.32.

Remark 29.36. We could also imagine giving the seller more power by allowing randomized mechanisms that specify a probability distribution over qualities and payments for each type.

Randomizing the payment is not relevant, since our agent has quasilinear utility and so paying a random amount is equivalent to just paying the expected value. However, randomizing the allocation function can be useful in improved screening of the different types of agents. One can repeat the analysis above, allowing for randomized mechanisms, and show that the expected profit still equals the expected virtual surplus. For each type θ, the virtual surplus can be maximized over all randomized qualities by just putting probability 1 on $q^\circ(\theta)$. So if $q^\circ(\theta)$ is increasing, as it is under the assumptions of Theorem 29.30, then it remains optimal even among randomized mechanisms. However, when the assumptions do not hold, one can give instances in which randomized mechanisms do strictly better than deterministic ones.

29.3.2 Applications of Hidden-Information Models

As with hidden-action models, hidden-information models have many applications. For example, they can apply to sales of a product or service, not only when the allocation variable is quality but also when it is some other dimension, such as quantity or speed of service, that some buyer types value more than others. Here are some other domains of application, with suitable reinterpretations of the variables:

- *Seller-side information:* These models can also apply to trades where the seller, rather than the buyer, holds private information. For example, perhaps a firm is buying some input from a supplier and negotiating over the terms of sale, and the firm has uncertainty about the cost for the supplier to produce a given quality or quantity of the input.
- *Taxation:* Models based on the framework here are widely applied to study tax systems. Here, individuals have private information about their income-earning ability, and the tax schedule shapes their preferences for choosing one job (or level of work intensity) over another.

Many of the applications from Section 29.2 can also be approached through hidden-information models; one or the other approach may be more relevant depending on the situation. For example, suppose an employer hires a worker to produce output, and the worker's effort maps *deterministically* to output; however, the worker has private information about his ability, which determines how hard it is for him to produce any given level of output. This is naturally described by a hidden-information model, where θ is the worker's ability and q is the level of output he produces; the employer offers wages for each possible output level, and the different types of worker self-select. This is sometimes called a "false moral hazard" model.

29.4 Exercises

Exercise 29.1 Consider the hidden-action model with limited liability as in Section 29.2.2. Suppose that there are just two actions. Assume that $\underline{u}$ is low enough that individual rationality is not relevant.
  (a) Show that there is an optimal contract that pays a positive amount for at most one output level. Identify this contract explicitly.
  (b) Give an example of an instance where any optimal contract fails to be monotone: that is, there exist output levels $y < y'$ such that $w(y) > w(y')$.

Exercise 29.2 Consider the hidden-action model with limited liability as in Section 29.2.2. Assume that $\underline{u} > 0$. Let (F^*, c^*) be the surplus-maximizing action, with surplus s^*, and suppose there exists some output level y that receives positive probability under F^* but zero probability under F for any other $(F, c) \in \mathcal{A}$. Prove that the principal can achieve a payoff of $s^* - \underline{u}$.

Exercise 29.3 Consider the hidden-action model with limited liability as in Section 29.2.2. Give an instance where there is a unique surplus-maximizing action and where an optimal contract induces an action that has *higher* cost than the surplus-maximizing one.

Exercise 29.4 Consider the robust contracting model with limited liability as in Section 29.2.3. Consider a linear contract $w(y) = \alpha y$ with $\alpha \in (0, 1)$.

(a) Suppose that $u_0(\alpha) > 0$. Show that the guarantee of this contract is exactly $\frac{1-\alpha}{\alpha} u_0(\alpha)$.

(b) In terms of $\mathcal{A}_0$, characterize explicitly the value α for which this guarantee is maximized.

Exercise 29.5 Consider the robust contracting model, but now without limited liability. Thus, a contract is defined as a function $w : Y \to \mathbb{R}$, such that $\max_{(F,c)\in\mathcal{A}_0} \left(\mathbb{E}_{y\sim F}[w(y)] - c \right) \geq \underline{u}$ (to ensure individual rationality). A guaranteed payoff (for the principal) is defined as before. Identify the highest possible guaranteed payoff, and a contract that achieves it.

Exercise 29.6 Consider the hidden-information model in Section 29.3.1, but now suppose that higher types of agent have much higher outside options: the individual rationality constraint is replaced by requiring $u(q(\theta), \theta) - t(\theta) \geq \underline{u}(\theta)$ for each θ, where $\underline{u}$ is a function such that, for each q, $\underline{u}(\theta) - u(q, \theta)$ is increasing in θ. Repeat the analysis. What changes? (Note: To give a characterization of the optimal mechanism that is analogous to Theorem 29.30, you may need to modify the extra regularity assumptions made in that theorem.)

Exercise 29.7 Consider the hidden-information model, but now drop the differentiability assumptions on u: instead, assume only that u is continuous, weakly increasing in θ, and strictly supermodular. Show by example that there can be two different payment functions $t, t' : [\underline{\theta}, \overline{\theta}] \to \mathbb{R}$ that both implement the same allocation function q and such that $t' - t$ is not constant.

Exercise 29.8 Consider the hidden-information model, but now suppose that the agent learns his type *after* agreeing to transact with the principal. That is:

- first the principal offers a mechanism, specifying qualities and prices (q, t);
- the agent decides whether to accept the mechanism or reject it and receive his outside option payoff of 0;
- if the agent has accepted the mechanism, his type is drawn, $\theta \sim F$; and then
- he selects a (quality, price) pair from among those offered by the principal (he cannot exit the mechanism at this point, even if his best option gives him negative payoff).

Show how to formulate the incentive-compatibility and individual rationality constraints in this model. Identify an optimal mechanism. What is the principal's payoff?

29.5 Bibliographic Notes

A careful treatment of a hidden-action model with risk aversion (which we have not covered here) can be found in [3]. (The conditions in the "monotone convex" formulation here also appear in that paper.) A canonical reference for a formulation without risk aversion, and with limited liability, is [4]. The robust contracting model of Section 29.2.3 draws heavily on [1].

Classic references for the basic hidden-information model are [6] and [5]. The remark on randomized mechanisms draws on [8]. For the theory of optimal auctions, which uses much of the same machinery, see [7]. The passage from Jules Dupuit is as quoted in [2].

Acknowledgments

This writing was supported by an NSF CAREER grant. Ellen Muir provided valuable research assistance.

References

[1] Carroll, Gabriel. 2015. Robustness and linear contracts. *American Economic Review*, **105**(2), 536–63.

[2] Ekelund, Jr., Robert B. 1970. Price discrimination and product differentiation in economic theory: An early analysis. *Quarterly Journal of Economics*, **84**(2), 268–278.

[3] Grossman, Sanford J., and Hart, Oliver D. 1983. An analysis of the principal-agent problem. *Econometrica*, **51**(1), 7–46.

[4] Innes, Robert D. 1990. Limited liability and incentive contracting with ex-ante action choices. *Journal of Economic Theory*, **52**(1), 45–67.

[5] Maskin, Eric, and Riley, John. 1984. Monopoly with incomplete information. *RAND Journal of Economics*, **15**(2), 171–196.

[6] Mussa, Michael, and Rosen, Sherwin. 1978. Monopoly and product quality. *Journal of Economic Theory*, **18**(2), 301–317.

[7] Myerson, Roger B. 1981. Optimal auction design. *Mathematics of Operations Research*, **6**(1), 58–73.

[8] Strausz, Roland. 2006. Deterministic versus stochastic mechanisms in principal–agent models. *Journal of Economic Theory*, **128**(1), 306–314.

CHAPTER THIRTY

Secretaries, Prophets, and Applications to Matching

Michal Feldman and Brendan Lucier

30.1 Introduction to Sequential Online Decision-Making

A common theme in the study of markets is the tension that comes with making a decision. Should you accept the job offer you just received, or keep on going to interviews? Should you sell your car to this buyer who is driving a hard bargain, or keep it on the market a little longer? Should you book your flight now, or wait to see whether the price goes down? Over and over again we are faced with such choices in life: take a sure thing now, or push your luck to see what opportunities come later.

Such "push-your-luck" scenarios have been studied extensively in mathematics and economics. In their purest form they are referred to as stopping problems.[1] These come in finite, infinite, and continuous variants, but in this chapter we will focus on the finite version. In a finite stopping problem there are $n \geq 1$ rounds and a sequence of n values $v_1, v_2, \ldots, v_n$ that are initially unknown. The values are revealed online, one per round. In round 1 the value v_1 is revealed and the decision-maker must make an irrevocable choice: she can STOP, in which case the process ends and she obtains value v_1, or she can CONTINUE, in which case the value v_1 is lost and she moves on to round 2. The process continues until either a value is chosen or the final value is revealed in round n. The decision-maker's goal is to maximize the value she obtains.

A (possibly randomized) stopping policy decides, given a prefix of values $v_1, \ldots, v_k$, whether to stop and accept v_k or continue onward. Given such a policy ALG and a sequence of values $\mathbf{v} = (v_1, \ldots, v_n)$, we will write ALG($\mathbf{v}$) for the expected value accepted by the policy. Since we are fixing the sequence of rewards, the expectation here is over any randomization in the policy itself. Such a policy is an online algorithm so we can discuss its competitive ratio. Notice that the offline version of this optimization problem is trivial: the best policy in hindsight simply selects the largest value, obtaining a reward $\max_t\{v_t\}$. We will write OPT($\mathbf{v}$) $= \max_t\{v_t\}$ to denote this optimal offline reward.

In the setup described so far, the value sequence $\mathbf{v}$ is arbitrary and the competitive ratio of ALG is simply $\max_{\mathbf{v}} \text{OPT}(\mathbf{v})/\text{ALG}(\mathbf{v})$, the worst-case ratio between the maximum value and the (expected) value chosen by ALG. A simple first observation is that no non-trivial competitive ratio is possible in this fully adversarial

---

[1] We consider generalizations in later sections.

setting. The intuition for this is clear: starting from any point in time, there is one future sequence in which all subsequent values are 0, and another future sequence where the very next value is much larger than the one currently being offered. As the decision-maker has no hint about the relative likelihood of these options, it is impossible to make an informed decision. The following proposition makes this precise.

Claim 30.1. *In the fully adversarial model no algorithm can achieve a competitive ratio better than n. This is the competitive ratio of an algorithm that pre-selects an index $t \in [n]$ uniformly at random and always accepts element t.*

Proof We start by showing the (easy) upper bound. Fix $\mathbf{v}$ and take $t \in \arg\max\{v_t\}$. The algorithm will stop on round t with probability $1/n$, so even if we ignore the contribution of any other elements we have $\mathsf{ALG}(\mathbf{v}) \geq v_t/n = \mathsf{OPT}(\mathbf{v})/n$.

For the lower bound, let ALG be some arbitrary algorithm and choose some arbitrarily large $X > 0$. Consider the sequence $\mathbf{v} = (X, X^2, \ldots, X^n)$. On the input $\mathbf{v}$ there must be some round t such that ALG stops on round t with probability at most $1/n$. But now consider the sequence $\mathbf{v}' = (X, X^2, \ldots, X^t, 0, 0, \ldots, 0)$. Since $\mathbf{v}$ and $\mathbf{v}'$ are identical up to round t, ALG accepts on round t with probability at most $1/n$ on input $\mathbf{v}'$. Since the next-highest value in $\mathbf{v}'$ is X^{t-1} (or 0 if $t = 1$), and since $\mathsf{OPT}(\mathbf{v}') = X^t$, we have

$$\mathsf{ALG}(\mathbf{v}') \leq \frac{1}{n} X^t + \frac{n-1}{n} X^{t-1} \leq \left(\frac{1}{n} + \frac{1}{X}\right) \mathsf{OPT}(\mathbf{v}'). \qquad \square$$

Claim 30.1 suggests that in order to enable reasonable policies, we must weaken the adversary by providing additional information to the decision-maker. This is most commonly done by introducing some amount of randomness into the selection of the value sequence and evaluating the performance of the decision-maker in expectation over that stochasticity. In the next two sections we will introduce two different ways of doing exactly that.

30.2 The Secretary Problem

In the classic secretary problem, the set of values is arbitrary but they are assumed to arrive in a uniformly random order. It will be convenient to use separate notation for the sequence of values and the order in which they arrive. We write $\mathbf{w} = (w_1, \ldots, w_n)$ for the set of n values, assuming without loss of generality that $w_1 \geq \cdots \geq w_n$, and σ for a permutation over the indices 1 through n that determines the order in which the values arrive. Using this notation, the value observed in round t is $v_t = w_{\sigma(t)}$, and the time at which the jth highest value (w_j) arrives can be written as $\sigma^{-1}(j)$. For notational convenience we assume $w_t \neq w_{t'}$ for all $t \neq t'$ and hence "the jth highest value" is unambiguous, but all results in this section would hold even without this assumption. The objective is to maximize the probability of selecting the highest value. We say that an algorithm ALG *wins* if it selects the highest value and that ALG

is ρ-competitive if, for all weight profiles $\mathbf{w}$, ALG wins with probability at least $1/\rho$.[2] Here the probability is over the arrival order σ and any randomness in ALG.

Claim 30.1 shows that any meaningful result must take advantage of the random arrival order. A natural approach is to explore the arriving values for a while to get a sense of what a "good" value looks like and then to use these observations to assess the relative quality of the newly arriving values. Algorithm 30.3 presents a family of algorithms that we term *threshold-by-exploration*. An algorithm in this family explores the arriving values up to some round k, sets a threshold τ equal to the maximum value observed so far, and then selects the first value that exceeds τ thereafter.

Algorithm 30.3 Threshold-by-exploration algorithm for secretary.

1: Let $v_1, \ldots, v_n$ be the values in arrival order
2: Explore the first k elements, and let $\tau = \max_{t=1,\ldots,k} v_t$
3: **for** $t \in \{k+1, \ldots, n\}$ **do**
4:     **if** $v_t \geq \tau$ **then**
5:         Select v_t
6:     **end if**
7: **end for**

What is the best choice of k? As a warm-up, we show an instantiation of Algorithm 30.3 that is 4-competitive.

Theorem 30.2. *Algorithm 30.3 with $k = n/2$ is 4-competitive.*

Proof Whenever the highest value arrives at time $t > n/2$ and the second highest value arrives at time $t \leq n/2$, the threshold is set to be the second highest value, and the highest value is selected. This event happens with probability $(n/2)/n \cdot (n/2)/(n-1)$, which is greater than $\frac{1}{4}$ for every n. $\square$

The following theorem shows that the same algorithm with a slightly shorter exploration phase gives a better competitive ratio of e.

Theorem 30.3. *Algorithm 30.3 with $k = \lfloor \frac{n}{e} \rfloor$ is e-competitive (up to low-order terms).*

The key lemma in the proof of Theorem 30.3 is the following:

Lemma 30.4. *For any choice of k, Algorithm 30.3 selects the highest value with probability $\sum_{t=k+1}^{n} \frac{1}{n} \frac{k}{t-1}$.*

---

[2] Note the connection with the objective of maximizing value: if ALG wins with probability at least $1/\rho$ then $\mathbb{E}[\text{ALG}(\mathbf{v})] \geq (1/\rho) \text{OPT}(\mathbf{v})$.

Proof Fix k and denote Algorithm 30.3 by ALG; ALG selects the highest value if and only if the highest value arrives after round k and no other value is selected before the highest value arrives. That is,

$$\Pr[\text{ALG wins}] = \sum_{t=k+1}^{n} \Pr\left[\sigma^{-1}(1) = t, \text{ and no value is selected before round } t\right].$$

Let V_{t-1} be the set of values that arrive up to round $t-1$. Notice that ALG reaches round t if and only if the highest value in V_{t-1} arrives before or at round k. Let us denote this event by A_t. Then

$$\Pr[\text{ALG wins}] = \sum_{t=k+1}^{n} \Pr\left[\sigma^{-1}(1) = t\right] \Pr\left[A_t \mid \sigma^{-1}(1) = t\right].$$

Clearly we have $\Pr[\sigma^{-1}(1) = t] = \frac{1}{n}$ owing to the random arrival order. The term $\Pr[A_t \mid \sigma^{-1}(1) = t]$ is more subtle. Since we are conditioning on $\sigma^{-1}(1) = t$, the set V_{t-1} is a uniformly random set of size $t-1$ drawn from $n-1$ possible values. Therefore, the highest value in V_{t-1} arrives before or at round k with probability $(\frac{k}{t-1})$. $\qquad\square$

With Lemma 30.4 in hand, it is easy to prove Theorem 30.3.

Proof Approximating the sum by an integral, we get

$$\sum_{t=k+1}^{n} \frac{1}{n}\frac{k}{t-1} \geq \frac{k}{n}\int_{k}^{n} \frac{1}{x}\,dx = \frac{k}{n}\ln\left(\frac{n}{k}\right).$$

Differentiating the last expression and setting the derivative to 0, this term attains its maximum at $k = \lfloor\frac{n}{e}\rfloor$. Substituting $k = \lfloor\frac{n}{e}\rfloor$, we get $\frac{k}{n}\ln(\frac{n}{k}) \geq \frac{1}{e} - \frac{1}{n}$. $\qquad\square$

To summarize up to here, we have introduced the family of *threshold-by-exploration* algorithms, parameterized by the size of the exploration phase, and found that the best algorithm within this family sets an exploration phase of size $k = \lfloor\frac{n}{e}\rfloor$, and achieves a competitive ratio of e. However, the family of *threshold-by-exploration* algorithms is only one way to play this game. The next question any algorithm designer should ask herself is: can I do better?

The following theorem shows that when we are restricting attention to ranking-based algorithms – algorithms that make use of pairwise comparisons between values but are otherwise independent of the values themselves – no algorithm can achieve a better competitive ratio than e. In other words, *threshold-by-exploration* is best among all ranking-based algorithms. In Exercise 30.1 we prove that the same lower bound carries over to any type of algorithm.

Theorem 30.5. *No ranking-based algorithm can obtain a better competitive ratio than e.*

Proof Our strategy is to show that there is an optimal ranking-based algorithm ALG that is a *threshold-by-exploration* algorithm.

Let R_t denote the ranking of the value arriving in round t relative to all values that have arrived up to round t. For example, suppose $v_1 = 10$, $v_2 = 3$, and $v_3 = 5$. Then $R_1 = 1, R_2 = 2$, and $R_3 = 2$. Clearly $R_t \in [t]$ for all t. Since σ is drawn uniformly at random, all the R_t are independent and are drawn uniformly from $[t]$. In round t, ALG knows $R_1, \ldots, R_t$, but not $R_{t+1}, \ldots, R_n$. Using this terminology, ALG wins precisely if it stops in the latest round t for which $R_t = 1$.

An easy observation is that ALG should *reject* the element presented in any round t where $R_t > 1$. We can therefore describe ALG by a sequence $\mathbf{z} = (z_1, \ldots, z_n)$, where z_t is the probability that ALG accepts if it reaches round t and $R_t = 1$. For example, a *threshold-by-exploration* algorithm has $z_t = 0$ for all $t \leq k$ and $z_t = 1$ for all $t > k$.

Let B_t denote the event that $R_j > 1$ for all $j \geq t + 1$. This event means that the highest value arrives on or before round t. Since arrival is uniform, it holds that

$$\Pr[B_t] = \frac{t}{n}. \tag{30.1}$$

Let p_t be the probability that ALG wins, given that it reaches round t. For the final round $t = n$, this probability is easy to work out: ALG wins precisely if $R_n = 1$, which occurs with probability $1/n$, so $p_n = 1/n$. For $t < n$, we can work out the optimal behavior of ALG (and the value of p_t) by backward induction. If ALG rejects in round t (either because $R_t > 1$ or because $R_t = 1$ but ALG rejects anyway) then ALG moves on to round $t + 1$ and wins with probability p_{t+1}. If $R_t = 1$ and ALG accepts, then ALG wins if and only if event B_t occurs, which happens with probability $\frac{t}{n}$. We conclude that if ALG reaches round t and $R_t = 1$, it should accept if $p_{t+1} < \frac{t}{n}$ and reject if $p_{t+1} > \frac{t}{n}$. If $p_{t+1} = \frac{t}{n}$ then either choice is optimal; it is without loss to assume that ALG always accepts in this case. In particular, there is an optimal algorithm ALG with $z_t \in \{0, 1\}$ for all t.

All that remains is to show that there is some k such that $z_t = 0$ for all $t \leq k$ and $z_t = 1$ for all $t > k$. If $z_t = 1$ for all $t > 1$ then we are done, so suppose that $z_t = 0$ for some $t > 1$. That is, ALG always rejects in round t. This implies that (a) $p_{t+1} > \frac{t}{n}$, by optimality, and (b) $p_t = p_{t+1}$, since ALG will always reach round $t + 1$ if it reaches round t. This means that $p_t = p_{t+1} \geq \frac{t}{n} > \frac{t-1}{n}$, which implies $z_{t-1} = 0$ as well. We conclude that $\mathbf{z}$ is monotone, so the optimal ranking-based algorithm ALG is a *threshold-by-exploration* algorithm. $\square$

Discussion In this section we restricted attention to ranking-based algorithms. However, *threshold-by-exploration* algorithms are known to be best also among all algorithms, including those that can base decisions on the observed values. In addition, we restricted our attention to the objective of maximizing the probability of selecting the highest value. An equally interesting objective is maximizing the expected value of the selected element, and Exercise 30.3 asks the reader to show that the same tight guarantee of e applies.

30.3 The Prophet Inequality

For the secretary problem we allowed the set of values to be arbitrary and assumed the arrival order is uniformly permuted. In the prophet inequality we relax the fully adversarial problem in the opposite way: the arrival order is arbitrary, but we assume each value is drawn at random from a known distribution. We write $F = F_1 \times F_2 \times \cdots \times F_n$ for the distribution over value sequences, meaning each v_i is drawn independently from distribution F_i and $\mathbf{v}$ is drawn from F.

We want to design a stopping policy ALG that selects a high value in expectation over the randomness in $\mathbf{v}$. In this setting, ALG is ρ-competitive if $\mathbb{E}_{\mathbf{v} \sim F}[\mathsf{ALG}(\mathbf{v})] \geq \mathbb{E}_{\mathbf{v} \sim F}[\mathsf{OPT}(\mathbf{v})]/\rho$. Importantly, the policy we choose can depend on F. (After all, the distribution is known.) But, even armed with this knowledge, there is a lower bound of 2 on the competitive ratio of any stopping policy.

Theorem 30.6. *No policy achieves a competitive ratio better than* 2.

Proof Pick some arbitrarily small $\epsilon > 0$ and consider the following two-round instance. The first value v_1 is deterministically equal to 1. The second value v_2 is either $1/\epsilon$ with probability ϵ, or 0 otherwise. For this problem instance, $\mathbb{E}[\mathsf{OPT}(\mathbf{v})] = \epsilon/\epsilon + (1 - \epsilon) \cdot 1 = 2 - \epsilon$. On the other hand, no online algorithm can achieve an expected value greater than 1. Indeed, if it accepts on the first round then its value is certainly 1, and if it rejects on the first round then it obtains an expected value of 1 on the second round. So the competitive ratio of any algorithm is at least $2 - \epsilon$, for every $\epsilon > 0$. $\qquad\square$

It turns out that this lower bound is tight and a 2-competitive policy exists. In other words: there is an online policy that obtains at least half the expected reward attainable by someone who can see all the prizes in advance. This bound is what is commonly referred to as the "prophet inequality," since we can think of the offline benchmark as a prophet who knows in advance what prizes are coming.

What's more, the optimal competitive ratio of 2 can be achieved with an extremely simple policy. A *fixed-threshold* policy pre-calculates a single threshold τ that depends on the product distribution F, and then simply accepts the first value greater than τ. Such a policy is not necessarily optimal for every distribution F; indeed, it might not even accept any reward at all! Nevertheless, as we will show, there is always a fixed-threshold policy with competitive ratio 2.

Algorithm 30.4 *Fixed-threshold* algorithm for the prophet inequality

---

1: Let τ be a fixed threshold provided as a parameter
2: Let $v_1, \ldots, v_n$ be the values in arrival order
3: **for** $t \in \{1, ..., n\}$ **do**
4:    **if** $v_t > \tau$ **then**
5:       Select v_t
6:    **end if**
7: **end for**

One choice of τ that achieves this competitive ratio is half the expected maximum value. That is, $\tau = \frac{1}{2}\mathbb{E}_{\mathbf{v}\sim F}[\mathsf{OPT}(\mathbf{v})]$. Note that, in an interesting coincidence, 2-competitiveness means that the expected value of the algorithm is at least $\frac{1}{2}\mathbb{E}_{\mathbf{v}\sim F}[\mathsf{OPT}(\mathbf{v})]$ – which is exactly the threshold itself!

Example 30.7. Suppose that there are three rounds. Each of the three values is equally likely to be one of two options. The first value is either 1 or 6, the second is either 0 or 8, and the last is either 2 or 10. The expected maximum value is $\frac{1}{2}10 + \frac{1}{4}8 + \frac{1}{8}6 + \frac{1}{8}2 = 8$.

The proposed threshold algorithm selects the first value that is greater than $\frac{1}{2}\mathbb{E}_{\mathbf{v}\sim F}[\mathsf{OPT}(\mathbf{v})]$, which is 4. The expected value of this policy is $\frac{1}{2}6 + \frac{1}{4}8 + \frac{1}{8}10 = 6.25$, which is indeed more than half the expected maximum value of 8.

A nice feature of fixed-threshold algorithms is that they have a natural economic interpretation in the context of markets. Imagine that the decision-maker is selling a good. A potential buyer arrives at each round, and the value v_t represents the buyer's value for the good. Then the fixed-threshold policy chooses to trade with the first buyer whose willingness to pay exceeds a fixed threshold τ. We can therefore interpret τ as a posted price! The prophet inequality then says that posting a fixed price and selling to the first buyer willing to purchase achieves at least half the expected welfare of a welfare-maximizing auction.

Theorem 30.8. *The* fixed-threshold *algorithm with* $\tau = \frac{1}{2}\mathbb{E}_{\mathbf{v}\sim F}[\mathsf{OPT}(\mathbf{v})]$ *is 2-competitive.*

Proof We will prove the result using the economic interpretation of fixed-threshold algorithms where τ is a posted price on an item for sale. If the item is sold to buyer t, then this generates revenue τ for the seller and a net utility of $v_t - \tau$ for buyer t. Writing R for the expected revenue and u_t for the expected net utility of buyer t, over the realization of v_t we have that

$$\mathbb{E}_{\mathbf{v}\sim F}[\mathsf{ALG}(\mathbf{v})] = R + \sum_t u_t. \tag{30.2}$$

We will consider the revenue and the sum of utilities separately. Notice that since the fixed-threshold algorithm only ever accepts values greater than τ, there is a chance that it does not accept any prize at all. Let q be the probability that the algorithm accepts any prize. Then the expected revenue is precisely

$$R = q\tau. \tag{30.3}$$

Now consider the net utility obtained in round t. The fixed-threshold algorithm will select value v_t precisely if (a) the algorithm has not selected any earlier value, and (b) $v_t > \tau$. Since case (a) depends only on the values $v_1, \ldots, v_{t-1}$ (and, in particular, does not depend on v_t) these events are independent. When both events occur, the net utility to buyer t is precisely $v_t - \tau$; otherwise it is 0. So, if we write γ_t for the probability that the algorithm reaches round t, and writing $(x)"+$ to denote $\max\{x, 0\}$, we have

$$u_t = \gamma_t \mathbb{E}_{v_t}[(v_t - \tau)^+].$$

With probability $1 - q$ the algorithm does not select any reward and therefore reaches *every* round. That is, $\gamma_t \geq 1 - q$ for all t. Since $(v_t - \tau)^+ \geq 0$, we can conclude (through the linearity of expectation) that

$$\sum_{t \in [n]} u_t \geq (1 - q) \mathbb{E}_{\mathbf{v} \sim F} \left[\sum_{t \in [n]} (v_t - \tau)^+ \right]$$

$$\geq (1 - q) \mathbb{E}_{\mathbf{v} \sim F} \left[\max_{t \in [n]} (v_t - \tau) \right] = (1 - q)\tau \tag{30.4}$$

where the last equality is immediate from the definition of τ. It might seem very lossy to replace the sum with a maximum, since in principle one might imagine that the expected sum of utilities is spread out among many rounds. But it turns out that in the worst examples (such as the one used to prove Theorem 30.6) a single agent contributes all the surplus. Substituting (30.3) and (30.4) into (30.2) completes the proof:

$$\mathbb{E}_{\mathbf{v} \sim F}[\mathsf{ALG}(\mathbf{v})] = R + \sum_t u_t \geq q\tau + (1 - q)\tau = \tau = \frac{1}{2} \mathbb{E}_{\mathbf{v} \sim F}[\mathsf{OPT}(\mathbf{v})]. \qquad \square$$

The choice of threshold we used to obtain our 2-approximation is not unique. As it turns out, setting τ equal to the median of the distribution of the largest reward also leads to a competitive ratio of 2. The proof is a variation of the argument presented here; we explore this further in Exercise 30.4.

Another thing to notice is that our choice of threshold τ – half the expected maximum value – depends on the set of distributions F_t but not on their order. So, the competitive ratio of the threshold algorithm is order-oblivious: it holds even if an adversary is allowed to permute the distributions before the algorithm begins.

30.4 Application: Online Weighted Matching

Up to this point we have seen two different threshold-based approaches to solving stopping problems. For the secretary problem, we observed some initial elements (without accepting any of them) and then set a threshold equal to the highest value seen so far. For the prophet inequality, we used prior knowledge of the distributions to set a threshold in advance. Either way, once the threshold was set we took the first element whose value is above the threshold.

This approach seems simple enough that it is natural to wonder whether it extends to more advanced stochastic optimization tasks. For example, instead of choosing a single element from a sequence, let us revisit the online matching problem from Chapter 2. In that chapter we studied unweighted matching, but we will now consider the weighted version. This might model a housing market: there is a pool of houses on offer, and possible buyers arrive one by one. When a buyer arrives they must either be matched to a house or they will leave the market. The basic stopping problem coincides with the case where there is just one house up for sale. When there are multiple houses, the problem becomes more complicated: the decision-maker must decide not only whether to accept a buyer, but which house they should be matched with upon acceptance.

We can model this as a one-sided matching problem as follows. The market is represented by a graph $G = (B, S, E)$, where B is a set of n buyers and S is a set of m goods for sale. The edges E have weights described by a value function v, where $v(i, j)$ is the weight of edge $(i, j) \in E$. As in Chapter 6, the goods S are present from the beginning, but the buyers B arrive online. In each round t, a buyer from B arrives and can either be matched to a good or left unmatched, and this decision is irrevocable. Each good can be matched to at most a single agent. The goal is to maximize the total value of the resulting match.

As it turns out, the solutions that we have discussed so far for stopping problems extend naturally to matching markets. We will describe each of them in turn.

30.4.1 A Secretary Model of Online Matching

For the secretary variant of the matching problem, the value function v can be arbitrary but the buyers arrive in a uniformly random order. The buyers are $B = \{1, \ldots, n\}$, and they arrive in a uniformly random order described by a permutation σ. That is, $\sigma(t)$ is the buyer that arrives in round t.

We note that this formulation of online bipartite matching with stochastic arrival order is very closely related to the stochastic random permutation model described in Chapter 6. The main difference lies in the matching constraint: in Chapter 6 it is assumed that each vertex on the static side (i.e., each good) can match with many buyers, as dictated by a budget constraint, and for the random permutation model the focus is on settings where the number of buyers matched to each good grows large. In the current section we focus instead on the case where each good can be matched with at most one buyer. This limits an online algorithm's ability to "learn while doing" since a single misallocation can completely block a good from being allocated in the future.

To solve this problem, we return to the case where there is just a single good for sale. Our solution was to wait for n/e rounds and then select the first value greater than all those seen so far. It will be helpful to consider the following equivalent formulation of that solution. On each round $t > n/e$, consider the optimal *offline* solution for the part of the input sequence seen so far. This is an easy problem to solve: choose the highest value among $\{v_1, \ldots, v_t\}$. Our online policy then accepts v_t if and only if it was chosen as the solution to this offline problem. This is clearly equivalent to our solution to the secretary problem: each v_t solves the offline problem in round t precisely when it is the largest value seen so far.

With this interpretation in hand, it is now natural to generalize to the matching problem. For each round $t \geq \lceil n/e \rceil$, write $B_t \subseteq B$ for the first t buyers to arrive. We consider the maximum weighted matching μ_t between the goods S and the buyers B_t. We will then match the most recently arrived buyer to her assigned good in μ_t, if possible. That is, we do that if this good is still available in the market. Otherwise the buyer is left unmatched. See Algorithm 30.5.

Example 30.9. There are four buyers, $\{1, 2, 3, 4\}$, and three items, $\{a, b, c\}$. The value function is given by $v(1, a) = 3$, $v(2, a) = 4$, $v(2, b) = 2$, $v(3, b) = 2$, $v(4, b) = 3$, and $v(4, c) = 2$. All other values are 0 (or, equivalently, no other edges are present in the set E). The optimal matching is $\mu = \{(2, a), (3, b), (4, c)\}$, with total value 8.

Algorithm 30.5 e-Competitive algorithm for matching secretaries

---

1: Let $A = S$, $\mu = \emptyset$
2: **for** $t \in \{\lceil n/e \rceil, \dots, n\}$ **do**
3:     Let $B_t = \{\sigma(1), \dots, \sigma(t)\}$.
4:     Let μ_t be the maximum weighted matching between B_t and S.
5:     **if** $\mu_t(\sigma(t)) \in A$ **then**
6:         Add $(\sigma(t), \mu_t(\sigma(t)))$ to μ
7:         Remove $\mu_t(\sigma(t))$ from A
8:     **end if**
9: **end for**
10: Return matching μ

In this example $\lceil n/e \rceil = 2$, so the algorithm will begin matching on round 2. Suppose the order of arrival is $(1, 4, 3, 2)$. The optimal matching with buyers 1 and 4 is $\mu_2 = \{(1, a), (4, b)\}$. So, in round 2, buyer 4 is provisionally matched to item b. As item b is still available in round 2 (along with all other items), we accept this match and add $(4, b)$ to our final matching μ. Note that buyer 1 is not (and will never be) matched in μ.

In round 3 agent 3 arrives. The optimal matching with buyers 1, 3, and 4 is $\mu_3 = \{(1, a), (3, b), (4, c)\}$. So buyer 3 is provisionally matched to item b. But b is unavailable (since it has already been matched to 4), so buyer 3 is left unmatched. Finally, agent 2 arrives in round 4. The optimal matching for all buyers matches agent 2 to item a, as described above. Item a is still available, so this provisional match is accepted and $(2, a)$ is added to our final matching. The matching returned by the algorithm is therefore $\mu = \{(2, a), (4, b)\}$, which has a total value of 6.

Theorem 30.10. *Algorithm 30.5 is e-competitive (up to lower-order terms) for the secretary-matching problem.*

Proof We prove the theorem in two steps. First, we will show that, on average, the provisional match $(\sigma(t), \mu_t(\sigma(t)))$ considered in each round t of the algorithm has expected value at least $\mathsf{OPT}(\mathbf{v})/n$. Intuitively, this is so because $\mathsf{OPT}(\mathbf{v})/n$ is the average agent's share of the optimal matching, and considering only a subset of the agents should only reduce competition and increase the average value per agent. In the second step, we argue that each of these provisional matches will be accepted with a reasonably high probability. Roughly speaking, this occurs because at most one good is removed in each round, and since we start removing goods only in round n/e, any given good has a low chance of being removed in any given round. Formalizing this intuition requires some careful probabilistic reasoning.

First some notation. For a given matching μ, write $v(\mu) = \sum_{(i,j) \in \mu} v(i, j)$ for its total value. Write μ^* for the overall optimal match, so that $\mathsf{OPT}(\mathbf{v}) = v(\mu^*)$. Given a subset of the agents $T \subseteq B$ and a matching μ, write $\mu|_T = \{(i, j) \in \mu | i \in T\}$ for the matching μ restricted to buyers in T.

The expected value added to the matching in round t depends on the length-t prefix of the arrival order σ. We will imagine revealing this random prefix in

---

644

stages, and analyzing how each stage impacts the matching outcome. First we reveal the set B_t of agents who arrive in the first t steps, but not their order. Note that B_t determines μ_t, the match considered in round t of the algorithm. Also, by the optimality of μ_t, we must have $v(\mu_t) \geq v(\mu^*|_{B_t})$. But since each buyer lies in B_t with probability exactly t/n, we have that $\mathbb{E}_{B_t}[v(\mu^*|_{B_t})] = v(\mu^*) \cdot (t/n)$. Putting this together gives

$$\mathbb{E}_{B_t}[v(\mu_t)] \geq \mathbb{E}_{B_t}[v(\mu^*|_{B_t})] = \mathsf{OPT}(\mathbf{v})\,(t/n).$$

Next we reveal the identity of $\sigma(t)$; i.e., which of the t buyers in B_t arrived last. As each buyer in B_t is equally likely to have arrived last, given B_t, this revelation selects each agent in B_t with probability $1/t$. This means that the expected value of the provisional match constructed in round t of the algorithm is

$$\mathbb{E}_{B_t,\sigma(t)}[v(\sigma(t),\mu_t(\sigma(t)))] - \mathbb{E}_{B_t}[v(\mu_t)]\,(1/t) \geq \mathsf{OPT}(\mathbf{v})/n.$$

Now we need to analyze the probability that this provisional match is accepted by the algorithm, which happens precisely if the matched item $\mu_t(\sigma(t))$ is still available in round t. Write $r = \mu_t(\sigma(t))$ for the node provisionally matched to buyer $\sigma(t)$. For each $\lceil n/e \rceil \leq k < t$, write U_k for the event that node r was matched and became unavailable in round k. Event U_k occurs precisely if μ_k matches r to agent $\sigma(k)$.

Recall that we have up to this point revealed B_t and $\sigma(t)$, but not the order in which the other agents in B_t arrived. We do, however, know that $B_{t-1} = B_t - \{\sigma(t)\}$, and μ_{t-1} depends only on B_{t-1}. So μ_{t-1}, the match considered in round $t-1$, is determined once we reveal $\sigma(t)$. We now reveal the identity of $\sigma(t-1)$, the agent who arrived in round $t-1$. As this is equally likely to be any agent in B_{t-1}, at most one of whom was matched to item r in μ_{t-1}, we have that $\Pr_{\sigma(t-1)}[U_{t-1}] \leq 1/(t-1)$.

We can now repeat this argument. With agent $t-1$ revealed we can infer B_{t-2} and hence μ_{t-2}. We then reveal the identity of $\sigma(t-2)$, which bounds the probability of event U_{t-2}. Continuing in this way, revealing the identity of each buyer $\sigma(k)$ one at a time, we conclude that $\Pr[U_k] \leq 1/k$ for each k, independently.

Node r is still available in round t precisely if none of the events U_k occurs, for each $\lceil n/e \rceil \leq k < t$. Since these events are independent, and each U_k occurs with probability at most $1/k$, node r is still available with probability at least

$$\prod_{k=\lceil n/e \rceil}^{t-1} (1 - 1/k) = (\lceil n/e \rceil - 1)/(t-1) = (\lfloor n/e \rfloor)/(t-1).$$

We conclude that the expected value added to the matching μ in each round t is at least $\mathsf{OPT}(\mathbf{v})\,(1/n)\,(\lfloor n/e \rfloor)/(t-1)$. Summing up over all t rounds, we get

$$\mathbb{E}[v(\mu)] \geq \mathsf{OPT}(\mathbf{v})\,(\lfloor n/e \rfloor/n) \sum_{t=\lfloor n/e \rfloor}^{n-1} (1/t).$$

645

Since $(\lfloor n/e \rfloor / n) \geq 1/e - 1/n$ and $\sum_{t=\lfloor n/e \rfloor}^{n-1} (1/t) \geq \ln(n/\lfloor n/e \rfloor) \geq 1$, we conclude that

$$\mathbb{E}[v(\mu)] \geq (\tfrac{1}{e} - \tfrac{1}{n}) \mathrm{OPT}(\mathbf{v}). \qquad \square$$

30.4.2 Stochastic Model – Matching with Prophets

Next we will turn to a variant of online matching that extends the prophet inequality. The order in which the buyers arrive is arbitrary, so we can say without loss that buyer t arrives in round t. But the value function v is now randomly drawn from a known distribution F. Remember that in the simple prophet inequality we assumed that values are independent across rounds. We will make the same assumption here: values assigned to edges are independent across buyers, but the values of edges incident at the same buyer need not be independent. That is, the values revealed in round t can be arbitrarily correlated with each other, but the values revealed in different rounds are independent.

As with the secretary problem, we will show that our solution to the prophet inequality extends to the matching setting. This requires an appropriate extension of the fixed threshold algorithm. Recall the economic interpretation of the simple prophet inequality, where the fixed threshold is a price and each buyer chooses rationally whether or not to purchase. We will take a similar economic interpretation here. We will assign a threshold τ_j to each item $j \in S$, which we can think of as a price assigned to that good. We then match each incoming buyer t to whichever remaining item she prefers at those prices. That is, buyer t is assigned an item j that maximizes her net utility $v(t,j) - \tau_j$, if any item yields non-negative utility. Any item matched this way is marked as unavailable, and is not considered for future buyers. See Algorithm 30.6. Note that when there is only a single item, this is precisely the fixed-threshold algorithm for the simple prophet inequality.

Algorithm 30.6 Fixed-threshold algorithm for one-sided stochastic matching.

1: Let $\tau_1, \ldots, \tau_m$ be a sequence of fixed thresholds provided as parameters
2: Let $A = S$
3: **for** $t \in \{1, ..., n\}$ **do**
4:     Let $j \in \arg\max_{j \in A}\{v(t,j) - \tau_j\}$
5:     **if** $v(t,j) > \tau_j$ **then**
6:         Add (t,j) to μ
7:         Remove j from A
8:     **end if**
9: **end for**

How shall we set the thresholds? Recall that, in the single-item case, we set τ to half the expected optimum value. We extend this construction in the natural way: for each good j, we set its threshold τ_j to be half the expected value of its match in the optimal matching. That is, writing μ_v^* for the maximum weighted matching when the weight function is v, we will set $\tau_j = \tfrac{1}{2} \cdot \mathbb{E}_v[v(\mu_v^*(j), j)]$. If we apply these thresholds, the fixed-threshold algorithm is 2-competitive.

Example 30.11. There are two buyers $\{1, 2\}$ and two items $\{a, b\}$. The value of each edge is distributed independently and uniformly from $\{1, 3\}$. One can check that the expected optimal match value is 19/4. By symmetry each item contributes half, or 19/8, to this optimal value. So we have $\tau_a = \tau_b = 19/16$, half of each item's contribution.

Consider a run of the fixed threshold algorithm with these thresholds. Since $\tau_a = \tau_b > 1$, each buyer will take an item only if its value is 3. So with probability 1/4, $v(1, a) = v(1, b) = 1$ and buyer 1 takes no item, in which case buyer 2 takes an item with probability 3/4. Otherwise buyer 1 has value 3 for at least one item and takes it, in which case buyer 2 will take the remaining item with probability 1/2. The expected value of the resulting match, over all these cases, is 63/16. This is less than the optimal value of 19/4, but more than half of it.

Theorem 30.12. *The fixed-threshold algorithm is 2-competitive when used with the thresholds described above.*

Proof As with the simple prophet inequality, we will take the economic interpretation, of thresholds as prices and edge values as buyer valuations. The value of a match can therefore be decomposed into its expected revenue R (the sum of payments for items allocated) and the sum of expected net utilities u_t for each buyer t (value minus payment). For each good $j \in S$, write q_j for the probability that j is matched by the end of the algorithm, over all randomness in the value function. Then the total expected revenue generated by the algorithm is $R = \sum_{j \in S} \tau_j q_j$.

Consider now the expected net utility enjoyed by buyer t in round t. Write v_t for the value function v restricted to edges incident with t. Under our economic interpretation, we think of v_t as the valuation of buyer t. Write A_t for the set of items available in round t. Agent t will be allocated whichever item from A_t maximizes $v(t, j) - \tau_j$. This means that u_t is at least the utility obtained by *any* buying strategy that agent t could dream up. To bound u_t, we will analyze a buying strategy that is suboptimal but convenient to analyze. Suppose buyer t fixes some distribution over the items, say λ (where λ_j is the probability assigned to item j). Then buyer t could draw an item j from distribution λ and purchase it if j is available and gives non-negative utility. For any such distribution λ (and remembering that the event $j \in A_t$ is independent of $v(t, j)$),

$$u_t \geq \sum_j \lambda_j (v(t, j) - \tau_j)^+ \Pr[j \in A_t]. \tag{30.5}$$

What distribution λ should we choose? Write $p_{tj}(v_t)$ for the probability that $\mu^*(t) = j$ given v_t. That is, $p_{tj}(v_t)$ represents agent t's belief about her likelihood to be assigned item j in the optimal allocation. As this belief is a probability distribution, we can take $\lambda_j = p_{tj}(v_t)$ in (30.5).[3]

As an aside, at this point the careful reader might be worried about correlation between the event that (t, j) appears in the optimal match, and the event that $j \in A_t$. Importantly, while we are making use of the probability $p_{tj}(v_t)$ in our expression, we are not actually conditioning on the event that t and j

---

[3] It could be that $\sum_j p_{tj}(v_t) < 1$ if agent t is sometimes not allocated any item, in which case we also have $\sum_j \lambda_j < 1$. But this is fine: buyer t will simply choose not to purchase any item with probability $1 - \sum_j \lambda_j$, obtaining utility consistent with (30.5).

will truly be matched, or conditioning this probability on the values revealed before step t. We are thinking of $p_{tj}(v_t)$ as just a number; these values simply define a convex combination of the utilities that agent t could obtain by buying different items.

Returning to the argument, $\Pr[j \in A_t] \geq (1 - q_j)$ since the event that j is assigned before round t is a special case of the event that j is assigned at all. So taking expectations and summing (30.5) gives

$$\sum_t u_t \geq \mathbb{E}_v \left[\sum_t \sum_j (1 - q_j) p_{tj}(v_t)(v(t,j) - \tau_j) \right]$$

$$= \sum_j (1 - q_j) \mathbb{E}_v \left[\sum_t p_{tj}(v_t) v(t,j) \right] - \sum_j (1 - q_j)\tau_j.$$

Here we will use the definition of $p_{tj}(v_t)$. Since $p_{ti}(v_t)$ is precisely the probability that agent t matches to item u_i given type v_t, $\mathbb{E}_v[\sum_t p_{tj}(v_t)v(t,j)]$ is simply the expected value generated by j's match in the optimal matching. But recall that this latter quantity is, by definition, equal to $2\tau_j$. So we conclude that

$$\sum_t u_t \geq \sum_j (1 - q_j)(2\tau_j) - \sum_j (1 - q_j)\tau_j = \sum_j (1 - q_j)\tau_j.$$

Adding the expected revenue to the expected total buyer net utilities, we have

$$\mathbb{E}[\mathsf{ALG}(v)] = R + \sum_t u_t \geq \sum_j q_j\tau_j + \sum_j (1 - q_j)\tau_j = \sum_j \tau_j.$$

As this last summation is simply half the expected optimal match value, we conclude that the algorithm is 2-competitive. $\qquad\square$

30.4.3 Extension: Matching with Prophets on General Graphs

In the previous section we considered a setting with a bipartite graph $G = (B, S, E)$, for a set of static items S and a set of buyers B, who arrive over time. However, in many market scenarios, the items are not static but rather are brought to market by sellers who also arrive over time. This is the case, for example, with jobs and employees in labor markets, and with passengers and drivers in ridesharing platforms. In these settings the one-sided arrival model may be too simplistic. Moreover, some matching markets include agents who can be matched in any way, not necessarily according to a bipartite graph. This includes, for example, students who should be paired into roommates or exchange markets such as pairwise kidney exchange (see Chapter 9). What competitive ratio can be obtained in these scenarios? Does it admit a 2-competitive algorithm? Can the tools developed in previous sections be used in this generalized setting?

Before answering these questions we should clarify our model. The market is now represented by a *general* (not necessarily bipartite) graph $G = (N, E)$, where N is the set of vertices, corresponding to agents in the market. As before, the edges E have weights described by a value function v, where $v(i,j)$ is the weight of edge $(i,j) \in E$. The agents N arrive online, in an arbitrary order, so we can say without loss of generality that agent t arrives in round t. The arrival order is unknown. The value function v is randomly drawn from a known distribution F.

Upon the arrival of agent t, the value $v(j, t)$ is revealed for all agents $j < t$. Consequently, agent t can either be matched to some $j < t$ (in which case t and j are marked as unavailable) or left unmatched (in which case t remains available for future matches). As before, each agent can be matched to at most a single agent, and the goal is to maximize the total value of the resulting match. Note that this generalizes the single-sided online matching problem from the previous section, which corresponds to the special case where the graph is bipartite and all vertices from one side (S) arrive before any of the vertices from the other side (B).

Recall that the 2-competitive algorithm for single-sided online matching from Section 30.4.2 worked by setting thresholds (prices) on goods for sale. In Exercise 30.8 the reader can prove that a natural extension of this pricing approach fails in the more general setting we consider here. We will instead follow a different approach, reminiscent of the algorithm for matching secretaries from Section 30.4.1.

For a given matching μ, recall that $v(\mu) = \sum_{(i,j) \in \mu} v(i, j)$ is its total value and $\mu^*(v)$ is a maximum weighted matching under v. For every edge (i, j), let $x_{ij} = \Pr_{v \sim F}[(i, j) \in \mu^*(v)]$. That is, x_{ij} is the unconditional probability that i and j are matched in $\mu^*(v)$, over the randomness in v.[4] For each agent t, write $E_t \subseteq E$ for the set of edges from t to previous agents, i.e., $E_t = \{(j, t) : j < t\}$. Write $\bar{E}_t$ for all other edges. As in the previous section, the values of edges across different rounds are independent, but the values of edges within a round may be correlated. We write F_{E_t} and $F_{\bar{E}_t}$ for the distribution of values for edges in E_t and $\bar{E}_t$, respectively.

Algorithm 30.7 2-Competitive algorithm for matching prophets in general graphs.

1: Let $A = N$, $\mu = \emptyset$
2: **for** $t \in \{1, \ldots, n\}$ **do**
3:     Let $E_t = \{(j, t) \mid j < t\}$, and let $\bar{E}_t = E \setminus E_t$
4:     Let v_t be the *observed* values of edges in E_t.
5:     *Sample* values $\tilde{v}_{-t}$ for edges in $\bar{E}_t$ (from $F_{\bar{E}_t}$)
6:     Let $\mu_t = \mu^*(v_t, \tilde{v}_{-t})$ be the maximum match with values v_t and $\tilde{v}_{-t}$
7:     Let $j = \mu_t(t)$
8:     **if** $j < t$ and $j \in A$ **then**
9:         With probability $\alpha_j(t)$ (see (30.6)):
10:             Add (j, t) to μ
11:             Remove j and t from A
12:     **end if**
13: **end for**
14: Return matching μ

Consider Algorithm 30.7. Upon the arrival of agent t, we observe the values of edges in E_t, and sample the values of edges in $\bar{E}_t$. Let v_t and $\tilde{v}_{-t}$ be the observed and sampled values, respectively. Importantly, we are sampling not only the values of edges that we have yet to see, but also the values of edges that have already been revealed. We then consider the maximum weighted matching μ_t using values v_t and $\tilde{v}_{-t}$ on the corresponding edges. If agent t is matched in μ_t to some earlier agent j,

---

[4] Note the connection with $p_{tj}(v_t)$ from the proof of Theorem 30.12: $p_{tj}(v_t)$ is the probability that t and j are matched *given* v_t, whereas x_{tj} takes this probability also with respect to v_t, so $x_{tj} = \Pr_{v_t}[p_{tj}(v_t)]$.

and j is still available in the market, we would like to match t and j (and mark them unavailable), but we can do so only with probability

$$\alpha_j(t) = \frac{1}{2 - \sum_{i<t} x_{ij}}. \tag{30.6}$$

We shall soon see that $\alpha_j(t)$ is chosen so that every edge (i, j) is matched with probability precisely $\frac{x_{ij}}{2}$. Note that $\alpha_j(t)$ can be calculated only upon the arrival of t, not before, since it depends on the arrival order up to t.

The attentive reader might notice the similarities that Algorithm 30.7 shares with Algorithm 30.5 for secretary matching. Like Algorithm 30.5, it computes some matching μ_t in round t, with all potential matches – including those that have already become unavailable – and then matches t to its match in μ_t under some conditions. However, there are some notable differences between the algorithms. First, Algorithm 30.7 works in a prophet environment, where the probability distributions of all values is known from the outset. It uses this information when computing μ_t, by sampling values $\tilde{v}_{-t}$ for all edges not incident with t. Second, while Algorithm 30.5 matches t to its match under μ_t *whenever it is available*, this policy is apparently too aggressive in the more general setting. We would like to leave agents available for future matches with higher probability. Algorithm 30.7 accomplishes this by hedging: whenever it considers making a match, it will sometimes randomly abort the execution of that match in order to leave the agents available for future opportunities.

Example 30.13. Consider a triangle graph with three agents, $\{1, 2, 3\}$, and three edges. The value of every edge is uniformly distributed on $[0, 3]$. Clearly, every edge is equally likely to be in the maximum weighted matching; thus $x_{ij} = \frac{1}{3}$ for every edge (i, j). Consider a run of Algorithm 30.7. Upon the arrival of agent 1, nothing happens. Upon the arrival of agent 2, we observe the value $v(2, 1)$ and sample values $v(2, 3), v(1, 3)$. Suppose the observed value is $v(2, 1) = 2$ and the sampled values are $v(2, 3) = 1.5, v(1, 3) = 1.8$. Then, the maximum weighted match consists of $(2, 1)$, and, since 1 is available, we match $(2, 1)$ with probability

$$\alpha_1(2) = \frac{1}{2 - \sum_{i<2} x_{i1}} = \frac{1}{2}.$$

So, with probability $1/2$, the algorithm terminates with match $(2, 1)$ and, with probability $1/2$, we continue to agent 3. Upon the arrival of agent 3, we observe values $v(3, 1), v(3, 2)$ and sample the value $v(1, 2)$. Suppose the observed values are $v(3, 1) = 1.2$, and $v(3, 2) = 0.6$ and the sampled value is $v(1, 2) = 1.1$. Then, the maximum weighted match consists of $(3, 1)$, and, since 1 is available, we match $(3, 1)$ with probability

$$\alpha_1(3) = \frac{1}{2 - \sum_{i<3} x_{i1}} = \frac{1}{2 - \frac{1}{3}} = \frac{3}{5}.$$

So with probability $3/5$, the algorithm terminates with match $(3, 1)$, and with probability $2/5$ the algorithm terminates with the empty matching.

———— **650** ————

We shall soon prove that Algorithm 30.7 is 2-competitive. We first observe that it is well defined; i.e., that the probability calculated in line 9 is at most 1. Indeed,

$$\alpha_j(t) = \frac{1}{2 - \sum_{i<t} x_{ij}} \leq \frac{1}{2 - \sum_i x_{ij}} \leq \frac{1}{2 - 1} = 1,$$

where the last inequality follows from the fact that $\sum_i x_{ij} \leq 1$ since i cannot be matched to more than one agent in a valid matching.

Theorem 30.14. *Algorithm 30.7 is 2-competitive for general matching prophets.*

We shall use the following lemma and corollary in our proof of Theorem 30.14.

Lemma 30.15. *Every edge (i,j) is matched by Algorithm 30.7 with probability equal to precisely $\frac{x_{ij}}{2}$.*

Lemma 30.15 is proved by induction. The reader is invited to prove it in Exercise 30.7.

Corollary 30.16. *For every agent t and $j < t$, the probability that j is available upon t's arrival is $\Pr[j \text{ available at } t] = \frac{1}{2\alpha_j(t)}$.*

Proof Let μ be the matching returned by Algorithm 30.7. Then $\Pr[j$ available at $t] = 1 - \sum_{i<t} \Pr[(i,j) \in \mu] = 1 - \frac{\sum_{i<t} x_{ij}}{2} = \frac{1}{2\alpha_j(t)}$, where the last equality follows by the definition of $\alpha_j(t)$ (see (30.6)) and the one preceding it follows by Lemma 30.15. $\square$

Note that the probability in the above corollary depends only on events that occurred before round t. We are now ready to prove Theorem 30.14.

Proof The expected value of the maximum weighted matching can be written as

$$\mathbb{E}_{v \sim F}[v(\mu^*(v))] = \mathbb{E}_{v \sim F}\left[\sum_t \sum_{j<t} \mathbb{1}\left[(j,t) \in \mu^*(v)\right] v(j,t) \right]$$

$$= \sum_t \mathbb{E}_{v_t \sim F_t}\left[\sum_{j<t} \mathbb{E}_{v_{-t} \sim F_{\bar{E}_t}} [\mathbb{1}[(j,t) \in \mu^*(v)] v(j,t) \right] \quad (30.7)$$

where the second equality follows from the linearity of expectation (note how useful that is!) and the fact that v_t is independent of v_{-t}. Since $v(j,t)$ is fixed given v_t, we can replace the expectation of the indicator variable by the probability of the corresponding event, to give

$$\mathbb{E}_{v \sim F}[v(\mu^*(v))] = \sum_t \mathbb{E}_{v_t \sim F_t}\left[\sum_{j<t} v(j,t) \Pr_{v_{-t} \sim F_{\bar{E}_t}}[(j,t) \in \mu^*(v_t, v_{-t})] \right]. \quad (30.8)$$

Applying the same manipulation with respect to ALG gives

$$\mathbb{E}[v(\text{ALG}(v))] = \sum_t \mathbb{E}_{v_t \sim F_t} \left[\sum_{j<t} v(j, t)\Pr\left[(j, t) \in \mu(v_t, v_{-t})\right] \right], \tag{30.9}$$

where $\mu(v)$ is the matching returned by ALG on input v, and the probability that $(j, t) \in \mu(v_t, v_{-t})$ is over the choice of $v_{-t} \sim F_{\bar{E}_t}$ and any randomness in ALG. Comparing the expressions (30.8) and (30.9), we see that to prove that ALG is 2-competitive it suffices to prove that, for every pair of agents j, t and every v_t,

$$\Pr\left[(j, t) \in \mu(v_t, v_{-t})\right] = \frac{1}{2} \Pr_{v_{-t} \sim F_{\bar{E}_t}} \left[(j, t) \in \mu^*(v_t, v_{-t})\right]. \tag{30.10}$$

When is (j, t) matched under ALG? First, (j, t) should belong to the maximum weighted matching for values $(v_t, \tilde{v}_{-t})$. This event depends only on the randomness of $\tilde{v}_{-t}$. Second, j should be available upon t's arrival. This event depends on the randomness of the algorithm (both in round t and in earlier steps) and on v_{-t}, but *not* on $\tilde{v}_{-t}$. Therefore, these two events are independent. Conditioned on these two independent events, ALG matches (j, t) with probability $\alpha_j(t)$. It follows that

$$\Pr\left[(j, t) \in \mu(v_t, v_{-t})\right] = \Pr_{\tilde{v}_{-t} \sim F_{\bar{E}_t}} \left[(j, t) \in \mu^*(v_t, \tilde{v}_{-t})\right] \Pr[j \text{ available at } t] \, \alpha_j(t).$$

By the corollary following Lemma 30.15, we have that $\Pr[j$ available at $t]\alpha_j(t) = \frac{1}{2}$. Therefore

$$\Pr\left[(j, t) \in \mu(v_t, v_{-t})\right] = \frac{1}{2} \Pr_{\tilde{v}_{-t} \sim F_{\bar{E}_t}} \left[(j, t) \in \mu^*(v_t, \tilde{v}_{-t})\right]$$

$$= \frac{1}{2} \Pr_{v_{-t} \sim F_{\bar{E}_t}} \left[(j, t) \in \mu^*(v_t, v_{-t})\right]$$

where the last inequality follows since v_{-t} and $\tilde{v}_{-t}$ are equally distributed. This establishes (30.10) and therefore concludes the proof. $\qquad\qquad\square$

30.5 Exercises

Exercise 30.1 Extend Theorem 30.5 to show that no algorithm (even one that is not ranking-based) can obtain a better competitive ratio than e for the secretary problem.

Exercise 30.2 Consider the following two-player game, sometimes called the game of Googol. The first player chooses any two distinct positive real numbers, in secret. One of the two numbers is then chosen uniformly at random and shown to the second player. The second player then guesses whether or not the number they were shown is the larger of the two. Show that there is a strategy for the second player that guarantees a win with probability strictly greater than $1/2$. Hint: Suppose the second player uses a threshold strategy. Under what conditions would she win?

Exercise 30.3 Consider a variant of the secretary problem where the objective is to maximize the expected value of the item chosen. Show that the threshold-by-exploration algorithm is e-competitive for this problem, and that no rank-based algorithm can guarantee a better competitive ratio than e. (One can also show that no algorithm of any kind can guarantee a better competitive ratio than e, but this is much more challenging!)

Exercise 30.4 Consider a fixed-threshold algorithm for the prophet inequality where the threshold τ is chosen so that the probability of accepting any item is exactly $1/2$ (possibly by randomizing appropriately at the threshold). Show that the resulting algorithm is 2-competitive. Hint: Use the economic interpretation from Theorem 30.8 and derive bounds on the revenue and buyer surplus.

Exercise 30.5 Consider a variant of the prophet inequality where each value is drawn from a known distribution and then the values arrive in a uniformly random order. This is known as the prophet secretary problem. Show that it is possible to achieve strictly better than a 2-competitive algorithm for this variant. Hint: Consider a threshold algorithm where the threshold changes part of the way through the input sequence.

Exercise 30.6 Consider a variant of the stochastic matching from Section 30.4.2 where each buyer can be assigned up to k items, with total value equal to the sum of the values for individual items. Find a 2-competitive fixed-threshold algorithm for this generalized problem.

Exercise 30.7 Prove Lemma 30.15 from Section 30.4.3. *Hint:* Use induction on the number of agents.

Exercise 30.8 Consider the following algorithm for online matching in bipartite graphs with 2-sided arrivals in a prophet setting. Upon the arrival of a vertex v, the algorithm sets its price p_v to be one half of the expected future contribution (to the optimum matching) of future edges incident to v. It then chooses the edge (u, v) that maximizes $w_{uv} - p_u - p_v$, if any such values are non-negative. Show that this algorithm cannot obtain a better competitive ratio than 4. *Hint:* Consider a star graph with four vertices.

Exercise 30.9 Consider matching in general graphs, as in Section 30.4.3, but where edges arrive dynamically rather than vertices. Suggest a modification to Algorithm 30.7 that gives a competitive ratio of 3 for this setting.

30.6 Bibliographic Notes

The secretary problem first appeared in print in Martin Gardner's 1960 Scientific American column [6], but originated much earlier (see [5] for an entertaining historical review). The prophet inequality was first established in [9], and in [11] it was shown that this guarantee can be obtained by a simple threshold rule. The threshold rule used in this chapter was proposed in [8], and the proof presented here is adapted from [10].

The e-competitive algorithm for secretary matching is due to [7]. The 2-competitive algorithm for single-sided prophet matching was studied in [3] and [1]. The generalization to general graphs in Section 30.4.3 appeared in [2] and is based on an online contention resolution scheme developed in [4].

References

[1] Duutting, Paul, Feldman, Michal, Kesselheim, Thomas, and Lucier, Brendan. 2020. Prophet inequalities made easy: Stochastic optimization by pricing non-stochastic inputs. *SIAM J. Comput.,* **49**(3), 540–582.

[2] Ezra, Tomer, Feldman, Michal, Gravin, Nick, and Tang, Zhihao Gavin. 2022. Prophet inequality for vertex and edge arrival models. *Math. Oper. Res.,* **47**(2), 878–898

[3] Feldman, Michal, Gravin, Nick, and Lucier, Brendan. 2015. Combinatorial auctions via posted prices. Pages 123–135 of: *Proc. SODA.* SIAM.

[4] Feldman, Moran, Svensson, Ola, and Zenklusen, Rico. 2016. Online contention resolution schemes. Pages 1014–1033 of: *Proc. SODA.* SIAM.

[5] Ferguson, T. S. 1989. Who solved the secretary problem? *Statistical Science,* **4**(3), 282–296.

[6] Gardner, Martin. 1966. *New Mathematical Diversions from Scientific American.* Simon and Schuster. Reprint of the original column published in February 1960 with additional comments.

[7] Kesselheim, Thomas, Radke, Klaus, Tönnis, Andreas, and Vöcking, Berthold. 2013. An optimal online algorithm for weighted bipartite matching and extensions to combinatorial auctions. Pages 589–600 of: *Proc. ESA.* Lecture Notes in Computer Science, vol. 8125. Springer.

[8] Kleinberg, Robert, and Weinberg, S. Matthew. 2019. Matroid prophet inequalities and applications to multi-dimensional mechanism design. *Games and Economic Behavior,* **113**, 97–115.

[9] Krengel, Ulrich, and Sucheston, Louis. 1978. On semiamarts, amarts, and processes with finite value. *Advances in Probability,* **4**(197–266), 1–5.

[10] Lucier, Brendan. 2017. An economic view of prophet inequalities. *SIGecom Exchanges,* **16**(1), 24–47.

[11] Samuel-Cahn, Ester, 1984. Comparison of threshold stop rules and maximum for independent nonnegative random variables. *Annals of Probability,* **12**(4), 1213–1216.

CHAPTER THIRTY-ONE

Exploration and Persuasion

Aleksandrs Slivkins

How to incentivize self-interested agents to explore when they prefer to exploit?

Consider a population of self-interested agents that make decisions under uncertainty. They *explore* to acquire new information and *exploit* this information to make good decisions. Collectively they need to balance these two objectives, but their incentives are skewed toward exploitation. The reason is that exploration is costly, but its benefits are spread over many agents in the future.

Incentivized exploration addresses this issue via strategic communication. Consider a benign "principal" which can communicate with the agents and make recommendations but cannot force the agents to comply. Moreover, suppose the principal can observe the agents' decisions and the outcomes of these decisions. The goal is to design a communication and recommendation policy which (i) achieves a desirable balance between exploration and exploitation, and (ii) incentivizes the agents to follow recommendations. What makes it feasible is *information asymmetry*: the principal knows more than any one agent, as it collects information from many. It is essential that the principal does not fully reveal all its knowledge to the agents.

Incentivized exploration combines two important problems in, respectively, machine learning and theoretical economics. First, if agents always follow recommendations, the principal faces a *multi-armed bandit* problem: essentially, to design an algorithm that balances exploration and exploitation. Second, interaction with a single agent corresponds to *Bayesian persuasion*, where a principal leverages information asymmetry to convince an agent to take a particular action. We provide a brief but self-contained introduction to each problem through the lens of incentivized exploration, solving a key special case of the former as a sub-problem of the latter.

Our motivation comes from the economic design of recommendation systems, a core part of modern market design, particularly in online markets.[1]

---

[1] Sections 31.6–31.8 are based on [30, Chapter 11]

31.1 Motivation and Problem Formulation

Our motivation comes from recommendation systems. Users there of consume information from previous users, and produce information for the future. For example, a decision to dine in a particular restaurant may be based on existing reviews, and may lead to some new subjective observations about this restaurant. This new information can be consumed either directly (via a review, photo, tweet, etc.) or indirectly through aggregations, summarizations, or recommendations, and can help others make similar choices in similar circumstances in a more informed way. This phenomenon applies very broadly to the choice of a product or experience, be it a movie, hotel, book, home appliance, or the object virtually any other consumer choice. Similar issues, albeit with higher stakes, arise in health and lifestyle decisions such as adjusting exercise routines or selecting a doctor or a hospital. Collecting, aggregating, and presenting users' observations is a crucial value proposition of numerous businesses in the modern economy.

When self-interested individuals (*agents*) engage in the information-revealing decisions discussed above, individual and collective incentives are misaligned. If a social planner were to direct the agents, she would trade off exploration and exploitation so as to maximize the social welfare. In the absence of such a social planner, each agent's incentives are typically skewed in favor of exploitation. This is so because agents tend to be myopic in their decisions, and (even when they are somewhat forward-looking) they prefer to side-step the costs of exploration and instead benefit from exploration done by others. Therefore, the society as a whole may suffer from an insufficient amount of exploration. In particular, if a given alternative appears suboptimal given the information available so far, however sparse and incomplete, then this alternative may remain unexplored forever.

Let us consider a simple example in which the agents fail to explore. Suppose there are two actions $a \in \{1, 2\}$ with deterministic rewards μ_1, μ_2 that are initially unknown. Each μ_a is drawn independently from a known Bayesian prior such that $\mathbb{E}[\mu_1] > \mathbb{E}[\mu_2]$. Agents arrive sequentially: each agent chooses an action, observes its reward, and reveals it to all subsequent agents. Then the first agent chooses action 1 and reveals μ_1. If $\mu_1 > \mathbb{E}[\mu_2]$ then all future agents also choose action 1. So, action 2 never gets chosen, even though it may be better. This is particularly wasteful if the prior assigns a large probability to the event $\{\mu_2 \gg \mu_1 > \mathbb{E}[\mu_2]\}$.

The problem of ***incentivized exploration*** asks how to incentivize the agents to explore. We consider a *principal* who cannot control the agents but can communicate with them, e.g., recommend an action and observe the outcome later on. Such a principal would typically be implemented via a website, either one dedicated to recommendations and feedback collection (e.g., Yelp, Waze) or one that actually provides the product or experience being recommended (e.g., Netflix, Amazon). While the principal would often be a for-profit company, its goal for our purposes would typically be well aligned with the social welfare.

We posit that the principal creates incentives *only* via communication, rather than via monetary incentives such as rebates or discounts. What makes this feasible is *information asymmetry*: the principal collects observations from the past agents and therefore has more information than any one agent. Being aware of this information asymmetry, agents realize that they may benefit from the algorithm's advice. In particular, they may be incentivized to follow the principal's recommendations, even if these recommendations sometimes include exploration.

Incentivizing exploration is a non-trivial task even in the simple example described above, and even if there are only two agents. This is *Bayesian persuasion*, a well-studied problem in theoretical economics. When rewards are noisy, incentivized exploration is non-trivial even when incentives are not an issue. This is the case of *multi-armed bandits*, a well-studied problem in machine learning. Incentivized exploration addresses both problems simultaneously.

Problem formulation. Let us put forward a concrete problem formulation, which we will consider throughout this chapter. While idealized, it captures the essence of incentivized exploration. There are T rounds and two possible actions, denoted, respectively, $t \in [T]$ and $a \in \{1, 2\}$. The actions are also referred to as *arms*; we use these terms interchangeably. In each round t, the principal chooses a message msg_t from some fixed universe Ω_{msg}. Then a new agent arrives, call it agent t, observes this message, chooses an arm a_t, and collects a reward $r_t \in [0, 1]$ for this arm. The action and the reward are observed by the principal but not by the other agents.

Problem protocol. Incentivized exploration

In each round $t = 1, 2, 3, \ldots, T$:

1. Principal chooses its message $\text{msg}_t \in \Omega_{\text{msg}}$.
2. Agent t arrives, observes msg_t, and chooses an arm $a_t \in \{1, 2\}$.
3. (Agent's) reward $r_t \in [0, 1]$ is realized.
4. Chosen arm a_t and reward r_t are observed by the principal.

A given round reveals a reward r_t for the chosen arm and no other information. In particular, the reward for the other arm – had this arm been chosen by the agent – is not revealed. This is precisely what necessitates exploration.

The rewards are generated as follows. A mean reward vector $\mu \in [0, 1]^2$ is drawn from a Bayesian prior $\mathcal{P}$ before the game starts; μ_a is the mean reward of each arm $a \in \{1, 2\}$. Each time an arm is chosen, the reward is realized as an independent draw from some fixed distribution specific to this arm. Specifically, there is a parameterized family $(\mathcal{D}_x : x \in [0, 1])$ of reward distributions such that $\mathbb{E}[\mathcal{D}_x] = x$, and the reward distribution for each arm a is defined as $\mathcal{D}_x$ with $x = \mu_a$. The distribution family and the prior $\mathcal{P}$ are known to the principal and the agents, whereas the mean reward vector μ is not known to anybody.

Let $\mu_a^0 = \mathbb{E}[\mu_a]$ denote the prior mean reward for arm a. Without loss of generality, we assume that $\mu_1^0 \geq \mu_2^0$, i.e., arm 1 is weakly preferred according to the prior. We allow *correlated priors*, i.e., random variables μ_1, μ_2 can be correlated. An important special case is *independent priors*, when μ_1, μ_2 are mutually independent. The paradigmatic reward distributions are *deterministic rewards* (when $\mathcal{D}_x$ always returns x) and *Bernoulli rewards* (when $\mathcal{D}_x$ is a Bernoulli distribution).

Agents choose arms so as to maximize their conditional expected rewards. Let us unpack this statement carefully. Each agent t knows the messaging policy and the round in which she arrives. As mentioned above, she knows the prior and the distribution family but not the mean reward vector μ. She does not directly observe anything from the previous rounds, except via the principal's message msg_t. She strives to maximize $\mathbb{E}[r_t]$ given all available information. This task is ill defined unless one specifies what the previous agents do; so, she assumes that all previous agents use the same decision rule. Formally, we define agents' behavior recursively:

$$a_t = \min \left(\underset{\text{arms } a \in \{1,2\}}{\text{argmax}} \ \mathbb{E}[\mu_a \mid \mathcal{E}_{t-1}, \text{msg}_t] \right), \tag{31.1}$$

where $\mathcal{E}_{t-1}$ is the event that (31.1) holds for all previous agents $s < t$. The minimization provides that ties in argmax are always broken in favor of arm 1 (and this is known to the principal and the agents). We posit this tie-breaking rule throughout to simplify the presentation. Note that it only makes exploration more difficult.

During the game, the principal chooses messages $\text{msg}_t \in \Omega_{\text{msg}}$ according to some algorithm called the *messaging policy*. The latter is chosen by the principal before the game, along with the universe Ω_{msg} (as a superset of all possible messages).

The principal's objective is to maximize the total reward $\text{REW} := \sum_{t \in [T]} r_t$; we make this objective more precise later, see (31.2). One could also consider a more basic and immediate objective: sample arm 2. We call this the *pure exploration* objective, as it neglects exploitation. There are several ways to formalize it, e.g., minimize the time horizon T so as to guarantee that arm 2 is sampled at least once.

Preliminaries: conditional expectations. For a more elementary exposition, we allow realized rewards and messages to take finitely many values. Then the notion of conditional expectation simplifies as follows. Let X be a real-valued random variable, and let Y be another random variable with arbitrary (not necessarily real-valued) but finite support $\mathcal{Y}$. The conditional expectation of X given Y is itself a random variable: $\mathbb{E}[X \mid Y] := f(Y)$, where $f(y) = \mathbb{E}[X \mid Y = y]$ for all $y \in \mathcal{Y}$. The conditional expectation given an event E can be expressed as $\mathbb{E}[X \mid E] = \mathbb{E}[X \mid \mathbb{1}_E]$.

We often use the following fact, (a version of) the *law of iterated expectation*.

Fact 31.1. *Suppose X, Y are as above, and a random variable Z is determined by Y and some other random variable Z_0 such that X and Z_0 are independent (e.g., the algorithm's random seed). Then $\mathbb{E}[\mathbb{E}[X \mid Y] \mid Z] = \mathbb{E}[X \mid Z]$.*

31.2 Connection to Multi-Armed Bandits

In the "social planner" version of incentivized exploration, an algorithm directly chooses the arm a_t in each round t and balances exploration and exploitation. This is a well-studied problem called *multi-armed bandits*, or *bandits* for short.

Problem protocol. Multi-armed bandits
In each round $t = 1, 2, 3, \ldots, T$:
    the algorithm chooses an arm $a_t \in \{1, 2\}$ and collects reward $r_t \in [0, 1]$.

Bandit problems arise in recommendation systems as well as many other application domains. The problem name comes from a whimsical gambling scenario in which a gambler faces several identical-looking slot machines, or one-armed bandits. The initial motivation for bandit problems came from the design of "ethical" medical trials, which attain useful scientific data while minimizing harm to the patients.

Prominent modern applications concern the Web: from tuning the look and feel of a website, to choosing which content to display or highlight, to optimizing web search results, to placing ads on webpages. A cluster of applications pertains to economics: a frequent seller (resp., buyer) can optimize prices and the selection of products (resp., offers); a frequent auctioneer (resp., bidder), particularly in ad auctions, can adjust its auction (resp., bids) over time; an online labor market can improve the assignment of tasks, workers, and prices. A computer system can experiment and learn over time rather than rely on a rigid design, so as to optimize the protocols inside the computer, or data center, or communication network.

These applications motivate a rich problem space, with many dimensions along which the models can be made more expressive and closer to reality. To take a few examples: there can be many arms and a known, helpful structure that binds across arms; reward distributions may change over time; the algorithm may observe auxiliary payoff-relevant information before and/or after it chooses an action; the algorithm may be bound by global supply or budget constraints. The model we consider here – with i.i.d. rewards and no "extras" – is the basic version.

A standard performance measure is the *regret*, which compares the algorithm's reward to that of the best arm. Specifically, it measures how much one regrets not knowing the best arm in advance, in expectation over the random rewards:

$$R(T) := R(T \mid \mu) := T \max(\mu_1, \mu_2) - \mathbb{E}[\text{REW}]. \tag{31.2}$$

We think of the mean reward vector μ as a problem instance. Typical results upper-bound regret uniformly (i.e., in the worst case) over all problem instances, as a function of the time horizon T and possibly also of some parameters of the problem instance. For such results, the algorithm does not need to know the prior. Some results consider *Bayesian regret*, i.e., regret in expectation over the Bayesian prior, defined as $R_{\mathcal{P}}(T) := \mathbb{E}_{\mu \sim \mathbb{P}}[R(T \mid \mu)]$.

While the regret tracks cumulative performance over time, instantaneous performance can be measured by the *instantaneous regret* (or *simple regret*) at time t, defined as $R_{\text{inst}}(t) := \max(\mu_1, \mu_2) - \mathbb{E}[r_t]$. That is, $R_{\text{inst}}(t)$ directly tracks how fast the algorithm converges to the best possible reward. Note that $R(T) = \sum_{t \in [T]} R_{\text{inst}}(t)$.

Going back to incentivized exploration, we observe that the messaging policy induces a bandit algorithm. (Indeed, the principal jointly with the agents constitute an algorithm that sequentially chooses actions and observes rewards according to the protocol of multi-armed bandits, and this algorithm's behavior is determined by the messaging policy.) Thus, one can directly compare messaging policies with bandit algorithms, using standard performance measures for the latter.

31.2.1 Optimal Exploration for Two-Armed Bandits

We will optimally solve the "social planner problem" described above, i.e., the two-armed bandit problem with i.i.d. rewards. Along the way, we invoke some of the central ideas from the literature on multi-armed bandits and discuss the types of guarantees for which one is looking (which is somewhat subtle). Our solution can be used as a subroutine for incentivized exploration, as we explain in Section 31.6.

First, let us handle the randomness in rewards by arguing that average rewards are close to their respective means; such arguments are known as *concentration inequalities*. Let $n_{t,a}$ be the number of times that a given arm a has been chosen before round t, and let $\bar{\mu}_{t,a}$ be the average reward of this arm in these rounds. Then

$$\Pr\left[\,|\bar{\mu}_{t,a} - \mu_a| \leq \texttt{conf}_{t,a}\,\right] \geq 1 - 2/T^4, \text{ where } \texttt{conf}_{t,a} := \sqrt{2\log T/n_{t,a}}. \quad (31.3)$$

This holds for any bandit algorithm, as a direct application of the *Azuma–Hoeffding inequality* (a standard, generic, concentration inequality), restated in a notation that is convenient for our purposes. Thus, with high probability it holds that

$$\mu_a \in \left[\,\texttt{LCB}_{t,a},\,\texttt{UCB}_{t,a}\,\right] := \left[\,\bar{\mu}_{t,a} - \texttt{conf}_{t,a},\,\bar{\mu}_{t,a} + \texttt{conf}_{t,a}\,\right] \quad (31.4)$$

for all arms a and all rounds t. The interval in (31.4) has two key properties: it contains μ_a with high probability and it can be computed from data in round t. An interval with these two properties is called a *confidence interval* for μ_a (at time t), and its endpoints are called, respectively, upper and lower *confidence bounds*.

We use a simple algorithm, called $\texttt{AdaptiveRace}$, which alternates the arms until their confidence intervals are disjoint (so that one arm appears better with high confidence). More precisely: we choose an arm uniformly at random in each round t until $\texttt{LCB}_{t,a} > \texttt{UCB}_{t,a'}$, and use arm a forever after.

Theorem 31.2. *Let $\Delta = |\mu_1 - \mu_2|$. For each round t, $\texttt{AdaptiveRace}$ attains*

$$R(t) = O\left(\min\left(\sqrt{t\log T},\,\tfrac{1}{\Delta}\log T\right)\right) \quad \text{and} \quad R_{\text{inst}}(t) = O\left(\sqrt{t^{-1}\log T}\right).$$

Proof The Azuma–Hoeffding inequality mentioned above also implies that

$$|n_{t,a} - t/2| \leq O\left(\sqrt{t\log T}\right) \quad \forall \text{ arms } a, \text{ rounds } t, \quad (31.5)$$

with probability at least $1 - 2\,T^{-4}$. It suffices to perform the analysis conditional on the high-probability event that (31.4) and (31.5) hold. We are interested in the "raw" expressions $R^{\text{raw}}(t) := t\max(\mu_1,\mu_2) - \sum_{s\leq t} r_s$ and $R^{\text{raw}}_{\text{inst}}(t) := \max(\mu_1,\mu_2) - r_t$, whose expectations give, respectively, $\overline{R}(t)$ and $R_{\text{inst}}(t)$.

Let τ be the last round in which we did *not* invoke the stopping rule. In all rounds $t \leq \tau$ the arms' confidence intervals overlap, so

$$\Delta \leq 2\left(\texttt{conf}_{t,a} + \texttt{conf}_{t,a'}\right) = O\left(\sqrt{t^{-1}\log T}\right) \quad \forall \text{ rounds } t \leq \tau. \quad (31.6)$$

The best arm is chosen in all rounds $t > \tau$, so $R^{\text{raw}}_{\text{inst}}(t) \leq O\left(\sqrt{t^{-1}\log T}\right)$ and

$$R^{\text{raw}}(t) \leq \Delta\min(t,\tau) \leq O\left(\sqrt{t\log T}\right).$$

To obtain the gap-dependent regret bound, we observe that (31.6) implies $\tau \leq O(\Delta^{-2}\log T)$, which in turn implies $R^{\text{raw}}(t) \leq \Delta\tau \leq O(\Delta^{-1}\log T)$. $\qquad\square$

Remark 31.3. The significance of regret bounds in bandits typically focuses on the "main terms" in the regret bounds, ignoring the constants and the logarithmic terms (unless the logarithmic term *is* the main term). Thus, we obtain $R(t) \sim \sqrt{t}$ and $R_{\text{inst}}(t) \sim 1/\sqrt{t}$ in the worst case. Moreover, we obtain $R(T) \sim \log T$ when the *gap* $\Delta = |\mu_1 - \mu_2|$ is constant, with a multiplier that scales as $1/\Delta$. All log log T terms can be replaced with $\log t$ via a slightly more involved analysis.

The regret bounds in Theorem 31.2 are optimal, as are the lower bounds presented below (without a proof). These lower bounds are rather subtle to state, and come in two flavors. First, a given upper bound cannot be improved *in the worst case*, i.e., for any algorithm there exists a problem instance that fools this algorithm. In fact, there is a pair of problem instances one of which fools *every* algorithm. Second, the logarithmic regret bound is optimal *for any given problem instance*, provided that the algorithm is at least somewhat good overall.[2]

Theorem 31.4. *Focus on Bernoulli rewards. Fix any bandit algorithm* ALG.

1. *Fix a time horizon T and $\epsilon > c/\sqrt{T}$, for a large enough absolute constant c. Consider problem instances $\mu = (1/2, 1/2 + \epsilon)$ and $\mu = (1/2, 1/2 - \epsilon)$. Then on (at least) one of these instances* ALG *suffers a regret $R(T) \geq \Omega(1/\epsilon)$ and $R_{\text{inst}}(T) \geq \Omega(\epsilon)$.*
2. *Consider $T = \infty$. Suppose for each problem instance and each $\alpha > 0$ there exists a constant C such that $R(t) \leq C t^\alpha$ for all rounds $t \in \mathbb{N}$. Then for any given problem instance there exists a time t_0 such that $R(t) \geq \frac{\mu^*(1-\mu^*)}{\Delta} \log t$ for all rounds $t > t_0$, where $\mu^* = \max(\mu_1, \mu_2)$ and $\Delta = |\mu_1 - \mu_2|$.*

Note that AdaptiveRace adapts its exploration schedule to the observations. This property, called *adaptive exploration*, is necessary to achieve the regret bounds listed in Theorem 31.2. Otherwise one can only achieve regret $R(T) = \tilde{O}(T^{2/3})$ and $R_{\text{inst}}(t) = \tilde{O}(t^{-1/3})$. Two paradigmatic *non*-adaptive algorithms are as follows. ExploreFirst samples each arm for a predetermined number N of rounds and then chooses an arm with a larger average reward and plays it forever after. A more robust version called EpsilonGreedy spreads exploration uniformly: in each round t, with probability ϵ_t the algorithm explores by choosing an arm uniformly at random, and otherwise it exploits by choosing an arm with a larger average reward. One can achieve $R(T) = \tilde{O}(T^{2/3})$ by setting, respectively, $N = T^{2/3}$ and $\epsilon_t = t^{-1/3}$. The proof uses the same technique as Theorem 31.2, so we leave it as an exercise.

There are three techniques that attain optimal regret bounds and extend far beyond the basic case of two-armed bandits. SuccessiveElimination, of which AdaptiveRace is a special case, eliminates an arm from consideration once it appears worse than some other arm with high confidence. UCB1 always chooses an arm with the best upper confidence bound. ThompsonSampling in each round forms a posterior distribution $\mathcal{P}'$ on μ, samples a mean reward vector $\mu' \sim \mathcal{P}'$, and chooses the best arm according to μ'. The first two algorithms are easier to analyze (focusing on a high-probability event, as in Theorem 31.2), whereas ThompsonSampling attains the $R(t) = O(\frac{1}{\Delta} \log t)$ regret bound with an optimal constant factor.

---

[2] Such an assumption is needed to rule out trivial solutions, e.g., that an algorithm that always plays arm 1 is optimal for all instances with best arm 1.

31.3 Connection with Bayesian Persuasion

A single round of incentivized exploration can be seen as a stand-alone game between the principal and the agent. More precisely, let us focus on the pure exploration objective (so we sample arm 2), and consider some round $t > 1$. The principal observes what happened in the previous rounds (the *history*) and chooses a message $\mathrm{msg} \in \Omega_{\mathrm{msg}}$. The agent observes the message, chooses an arm $a_* \in \{1, 2\}$, and collects an expected reward μ_{a_*}. Incentives are misaligned: the agent prefers an arm with a larger reward, whereas the principal prefers arm 2 no matter what. Thus, we can model the principal's reward as u_{a_*}, where the reward vector is $u = (0, 1)$. As the principal's messaging policy is fixed and known, and the past agents' behavior is specified by (31.1), a joint distribution over μ and the histories is well defined and known to both the agent and the principal. The agent's choice simplifies to

$$a_* = \min \left(\underset{\mathrm{arms}\, a \in \{1,2\}}{\mathrm{argmax}}\ \mathbb{E}[\mu_a \mid \mathrm{msg}] \right). \tag{31.7}$$

To make this game more generic, let us posit that the principal observes an initial signal sig from some universe Ω_{sig} of possible signals, and receives reward u_{a_*} from some reward vector $u \in [0, 1]^2$. The triple (sig, μ, u) is drawn from some joint prior $\mathcal{P}$ which is known to both the principal and the agent. During the game, the principal chooses the message $\mathrm{msg} \in \Omega_{\mathrm{msg}}$ given the initial signal sig according to some (possibly randomized) rule called the *messaging policy*. Before the game, the principal chooses the messaging policy and the universe Ω_{msg} (as a superset of all possible messages), so as to maximize its expected reward $\mathbb{E}[u_{a_*}]$. The messaging policy is known to the agent (which is needed to make (31.7) well defined).

This single-round game, called *Bayesian persuasion*, has been well studied in theoretical economics as a simple (yet quite rich) model of persuasion via strategic communication. The principal can neither choose the arms nor modify their payoffs directly. Instead, the principal leverages the initial signal and strategically chooses what information to reveal to the agent.

Problem protocol. Bayesian persuasion

1. The initial signal $\mathrm{sig} \in \Omega_{\mathrm{sig}}$ and reward vectors $\mu, u \in [0, 1]^2$ are drawn: triple (sig, μ, u) is drawn from Bayesian prior $\mathcal{P}$.
2. The principal observes $\mathrm{sig} \in \Omega_{\mathrm{sig}}$, then computes message $\mathrm{msg} \in \Omega_{\mathrm{msg}}$.
3. The agent observes msg, then chooses arm $a_* \in \{1, 2\}$ as per (31.7).
4. The agent receives an expected reward μ_{a_*}, the principal receives a reward u_{a_*}.

Motivating examples come from a variety of domains, in addition to recommendation systems. In a criminal investigation, the evidence can be seen as a "message" from the prosecutor to the judge, and the prosecutor can strategically choose which evidence to request or seek out, so as to maximize the probability of conviction. Product information can be seen as a "message" from the producer to potential consumers, and the producer may be able to strategically choose what tests to perform, what types of statistics to report, or what to offer in a free trial. Several examples concern grading policies: here, a grade is interpreted as a "message" from the grader to the world. To wit, a student's grade is a "message" from the school to potential employers; an employee's performance feedback is a "message" from the employer to the employee; a person's credit score is a "message" from the credit agency to potential lenders. In all these cases, a grading policy can be chosen so as to achieve desirable social effects. Finally, the government chooses what information must be disclosed to the public, and can choose disclosure policies anticipating the strategic response thereto. For example, this could concern disclosing health risks (e.g., those from environment pollution, infectious diseases, or vaccines), product data (especially about foods and medicines), and some aspects of law enforcement strategies (e.g., in policing, tax fraud detection, or wildlife protection).

The basic formulation defined above can be extended in several directions. For example, there can be multiple senders, the sender(s) may observe their own private signals, and messaging policies may be restricted to have a particular shape (e.g., grading policies must assign the same or a higher grade for better achievements).

31.3.1 Optimal Persuasion for a Special Case

We will work out a special case of Bayesian persuasion which is *also* a special case of incentivized exploration (with deterministic rewards and $T = 2$ rounds). We can obtain an optimal solution for this special case, whereas general solutions for incentivized exploration are only approximate. On the technical level, we showcase a fundamental technique from Bayesian persuasion, whereby one directly optimizes over the agent's posterior beliefs rather than over the principal's messaging policies.

We consider Bayesian persuasion with a pure exploration objective:

$$\sup \{ \Pr[a_* = 2] : \text{ messaging policies } \pi \}. \tag{31.8}$$

We assume that the principal has full knowledge of arm 1, i.e., that $\text{sig} = \mu_1$. This is equivalent to incentivized exploration with deterministic rewards, $T = 2$ rounds, and the pure exploration objective. Indeed, then arm 1 is chosen in round $t = 1$, a messaging policy is only used in round $t = 2$, and its input is precisely μ_1.

To make the problem more tractable, we also posit independent priors and that μ_1 has only two possible values: $\mu_1 \in \{v_L, v_H\}$ with $0 \leq v_L < v_H \leq 1$. Since the problem is trivial if $\mu_2^0 \notin (v_L, v_H)$, we focus on the case when $v_L \leq \mu_2^0 \leq \mu_1^0 \leq v_H$. We make these assumptions without further notice in the rest of this subsection.

We solve this problem as follows.

Theorem 31.5. *The supremum in (31.8) equals* $(v_H - \mu_1^0)/(v_H - \mu_2^0)$.

In particular, we achieve a larger $\Pr[a_* = 2]$ compared to full revelation. Indeed, under full revelation ($\text{msg} = \mu_1$) the agent chooses arm 2 if and only if $\mu_1 < \mu_2^0$, and one can calculate that $\Pr[\mu_1 < \mu_2^0] = (v_H - \mu_1^0)/(v_H - v_L)$.

Next, we prove Theorem 31.5. We assume without loss of generality that there are only two possible messages. This follows from Claim 31.9, a general fact proved in the next section.

We are interested in the posterior distribution on μ_1 formed by the agent after observing the message msg; we refer to this distribution as a *belief*. Thus, a belief is a distribution on $\{v_L, v_H\}$ determined by the messaging policy π and the realized message. To simplify the notation, we identify a belief with the probability it assigns to v_H; we call this probability the *scalar belief*. We write

$$B^\pi := \Pr[\mu_1 = v_H \mid \text{msg}] \in [0, 1].$$

Note that B^π is a random variable on $[0, 1]$ whose realization is the scalar belief. We interpret B^π as a distribution over beliefs induced by policy π. Since there are only two possible messages, B^π has a support of size at most 2.

Any distribution B^π is consistent with the prior, in the sense that $\mathbb{E}[B^\pi] = \Pr[\mu_1 = v_H]$. (To prove this, apply Fact 31.1 to the indicator function of $\{\mu_1 = v_H\}$.). A distribution over scalar beliefs with this property is called *Bayes-plausible*.

Let $\mathcal{B}$ be the set of all Bayes-plausible distributions with support size at most 2. In fact, any distribution $B \in \mathcal{B}$ can be realized by some messaging policy.

Claim 31.6. *Any distribution $B \in \mathcal{B}$ equals B^π for some messaging policy π.*

Proof We specify the policy π explicitly. This necessitates additional notation (only for this proof). Fix a distribution $B \in \mathcal{B}$ with over scalar beliefs $\{b_1, b_2\}$. For each $j \in \{1, 2\}$, let $\mathbf{b}_j$ be the belief that corresponds to b_j, i.e., a distribution over $V = \{v_L, v_H\}$ such that $\mathbf{b}_j(v_H) = b_j$ and $\mathbf{b}_j(v_L) = 1 - b_j$. Let $B(\mathbf{b}_j)$ be the probability assigned to this belief by distribution B.

Now we are ready to specify the messaging policy π. It has two possible messages: $\Omega_{\text{msg}} = \{1, 2\}$. For each $v \in V$ and $j \in \{1, 2\}$,

$$\Pr[\text{msg} = j \mid \mu_1 = v] = \mathbf{b}_j(v)B(\mathbf{b}_j)/\Pr[\mu_1 = v]. \qquad \square$$

Henceforth we will optimize directly over $\mathcal{B}$, rather than over the messaging policies.

Let us spell out this maximization problem in more precise terms. Given any scalar belief $b \in [0, 1]$, let $\text{mean}(b) := b\, v_H + (1-b)\, v_L$ denote the corresponding expectation, i.e., the mean reward of arm 1; we call it the *mean belief*. The agent chooses arm 2 if and only if $\text{mean}(b) < \mu_2^0$. For a given messaging policy π, the agent chooses arm 2 with probability $\Pr[\text{mean}(B^\pi) < \mu_2^0]$. Thus, the maximization problem is

$$\sup_{B \in \mathcal{B}} \Pr\left[\text{mean}(B) < \mu_2^0\right]. \tag{31.9}$$

Lemma 31.7. *The supremum in (31.9) equals $(v_H - \mu_1^0)/(v_H - \mu_2^0)$.*

Proof Fix some distribution $B \in \mathcal{B}$ with support $\{b_L, b_H\}$, where $0 \le b_L \le b_H \le 1$, and respective probabilities $\{B_L, B_H\}$. Writing out the formula for Bayes plausibility, we obtain

$$B_L\, b_L + B_H\, b_H = \Pr[\mu_1 = v_H], \tag{31.10}$$

$$B_L\, \text{mean}(b_L) + B_H\, \text{mean}(b_H) = \text{mean}\left(\Pr[\mu_1 = v_H]\right) = \mu_1^0. \tag{31.11}$$

Equation (31.11) was obtained by applying $\text{mean}(\cdot)$ to both sides of (31.11). The two equations are equivalent since $\text{mean}(\cdot)$ is monotone. Equation (31.11) implies that

$$v_L \le \text{mean}(b_L) \le \mu_1^0 \le \text{mean}(b_H) \le v_H.$$

Now, if $\text{mean}(b_\mathrm{L}) \geq \mu_2^0$ then $\Pr\left[\text{mean}(B) < \mu_2^0\right] = 0$. So, without loss of generality we will assume $\text{mean}(b_\mathrm{L}) < \mu_2^0$ from here on. Then $\Pr\left[\text{mean}(B) < \mu_2^0\right] = B_\mathrm{L}$. Thus, the maximization problem in (31.9) can be rewritten as follows:

$$\sup\left\{ B_\mathrm{L} : B \in \mathcal{B}, \ \text{mean}(b_\mathrm{L}) < \mu_2^0 \right\}. \tag{31.12}$$

Equivalently, we can maximize B_L subject to two constraints: Bayes-plausibility, as expressed by (31.11), and $\text{mean}(b_\mathrm{L}) < \mu_2^0$. This is maximized when $\text{mean}(b_\mathrm{L}) \to \mu_2^0$ and $\text{mean}(b_\mathrm{H}) = v_\mathrm{H}$. Substituting this into (31.11), we obtain $B_\mathrm{L} \to (v_\mathrm{H} - \mu_1^0)/(v_\mathrm{H} - \mu_2^0)$. $\qquad\square$

This completes the proof of Theorem 31.5. The supremum in (31.8) and (31.9) is not attained, essentially because the tie-breaking in (31.7) favors arm 1. If the tie-breaking favored arm 2 instead, the supremum would be attained by setting $\text{mean}(b_\mathrm{L}) = \mu_2^0$ in the proof of Lemma 31.7.

31.4 How Much Information to Reveal?

How much information should the principal reveal to the agents? Consider two extremes: revealing the entire history, and recommending an arm without providing any supporting information. The former does not work, and the latter suffices.

Recommendations. We transition from arbitrary messages to recommendations as follows. A *recommendation policy* is a messaging policy whose messages are arms: formally, a message at each round t is $\text{rec}_t \in \{1, 2\}$. Given an arbitrary messaging policy, the induced recommendation policy is one in which rec_t equals the right-hand side of (31.1). Let us argue that the agents choose recommended actions. Formally, we require Bayesian incentive compatibility:

Definition 31.8. Let $\mathcal{E}_{t-1}^{\text{rec}} = \{a_s = \text{rec}_s : s < t\}$ denote the event that recommendations were followed before round t. A recommendation policy is called *Bayesian incentive-compatible (BIC)* if for all rounds t the following property holds:

$$\text{rec}_t = \min\left(\underset{\text{arms } a \in \{1,2\}}{\text{argmax}} \ \mathbb{E}\left[\mu_a \mid \text{rec}_t, \mathcal{E}_{t-1}^{\text{rec}} \right] \right). \tag{31.13}$$

Claim 31.9. *Given any messaging policy, the induced recommendation policy is BIC.*

Proof If a recommendation policy is induced by a messaging policy, event $\mathcal{E}_t^{\text{rec}}$ coincides with event $\mathcal{E}$ from (31.1). For each round t and all arms $a \neq a'$, we immediately obtain a version with msg_t in the conditioning, by definition of rec_t:

$$\begin{aligned} 0 &\leq \mathbb{E}\left(\mu_a - \mu_{a'} \mid \text{msg}_t, \text{rec}_t = a, \mathcal{E}_{t-1} \right), \\ 0 &\leq \mathbb{E}\left(\mu_a - \mu_{a'} \mid \text{rec}_t = a, \mathcal{E}_{t-1} \right) \quad \text{(by (31.14) and Fact 31.1).} \end{aligned} \tag{31.14}$$

Finally, if we have a strict equality in the latter equation, for some $a \neq a'$, then we also have it in the former equation, in which case $\text{rec}_t = 1$ by (31.1). □

The above argument follows a well-known technique from theoretical economics called Myerson's *direct revelation principle*. The conclusion is very strong, since it allows us to focus on BIC recommendation policies without loss of generality. However, it relies on the assumptions of Bayesian rationality and of power to commit that are implicit in our model; see Section 31.8 for discussion thereof.

We are interested only in BIC recommendation policies from here on. By (31.1) and (31.13), all agents comply with recommendations issued by such a policy. Accordingly, it is simply a bandit algorithm with an auxiliary BIC constraint.

Full revelation does not work. Does the principal need to bother to design and deploy a bandit algorithm? What if the principal just reveals the full history and lets the agents choose for themselves? Then the agents, being myopic, would follow a "greedy" bandit algorithm which always "exploits" and never "explores."

Formally, suppose that in each round t, the message msg_t includes the history $H_t := \{(a_s, r_s) : s \in [t-1]\}$. Posterior mean rewards are determined by H_t:

$$\mathbb{E}[\mu_a \mid \text{msg}_t] = \mathbb{E}[\mu_a \mid H_t] \quad \text{for each arm } a.$$

(This follows because msg_t can depend only on H_t and the algorithm's random seed.) Then

$$a_t = \min\left(\underset{\text{arms } a \in \{1, 2\}}{\text{argmax}} \ \mathbb{E}[\mu_a \mid H_t] \right). \tag{31.15}$$

This is (a version of) the greedy bandit algorithm; call it GREEDY.

This algorithm performs very poorly on a variety of problem instances; it suffers from Bayesian regret $\Omega(T)$, whereas bandit algorithms can achieve regret $\tilde{O}(\sqrt{T})$ on all problem instances, as we saw in Section 31.2.1. The root cause of this inefficiency is that GREEDY may never try arm 2. For the special case of deterministic rewards, this happens with probability $\Pr[\mu_1 \leq \mu_2^0]$, since μ_1 is revealed in round 1 and arm 2 is never chosen if $\mu_1 \leq \mu_2^0$; we discussed this case as a "simple example" in Section 31.1. This result (with a different probability) carries over to the general case.

Theorem 31.10. *With probability at least $\mu_1^0 - \mu_2^0$, GREEDY never chooses arm 2.*

Proof In each round t, the key quantity is $Z_t = \mathbb{E}[\mu_1 - \mu_2 \mid H_t]$. Indeed, arm 2 is chosen if and only if $Z_t < 0$. Let τ be the first round when GREEDY chooses arm 2 or $T+1$ if this never happens. We can use martingale techniques to prove that

$$\mathbb{E}[Z_\tau] = \mu_1^0 - \mu_2^0. \tag{31.16}$$

Thus, we obtained (31.16) via a standard application of the optional stopping theorem (it can be skipped by readers who are not familiar with martingales).

We observe that τ is a stopping time relative to $\mathcal{H} = (H_t : t \in [T+1])$ and $(Z_t : t \in [T+1])$ is a martingale relative to $\mathcal{H}$.[3] The optional stopping theorem asserts that $\mathbb{E}[Z_\tau] = \mathbb{E}[Z_1]$ for any martingale Z_t and any bounded stopping time τ. Equation (31.16) follows because $\mathbb{E}[Z_1] = \mu_1^0 - \mu_2^0$.

On the other hand, by Bayes' theorem it holds that

$$\mathbb{E}[Z_\tau] = \Pr[\tau \leq T]\, \mathbb{E}[Z_\tau \mid \tau \leq T] + \Pr[\tau > T]\, \mathbb{E}[Z_\tau \mid \tau > T]. \tag{31.17}$$

Recall that $\tau \leq T$ implies that GREEDY chooses arm 2 in round τ, which in turn implies that $Z_\tau \leq 0$ by the definition of GREEDY. It follows that $\mathbb{E}[Z_\tau \mid \tau \leq T] \leq 0$. Plugging this into (31.17), we find that

$$\mu_1^0 - \mu_2^0 = \mathbb{E}[Z_\tau] \leq \Pr[\tau > T].$$

And $\{\tau > T\}$ is precisely the event that GREEDY never tries arm 2. $\quad\square$

Under some mild assumptions, the algorithm never tries arm 2 *when it is in fact the best arm*, leading to $\Omega(T)$ Bayesian regret.

Corollary 31.11. *Consider independent priors such that* $\Pr[\mu_1 = 1] < (\mu_1^0 - \mu_2^0)/2$. *Pick any* $\alpha > 0$ *such that* $\Pr[\mu_1 \geq 1 - 2\alpha] \leq (\mu_1^0 - \mu_2^0)/2$. *Then* GREEDY *suffers a Bayesian regret equal to at least* $T\left(\frac{\alpha}{2}(\mu_1^0 - \mu_2^0)\Pr[\mu_2 > 1 - \alpha]\right)$.

Proof Let $\mathcal{E}_1$ be the event that $\mu_1 < 1 - 2\alpha$ and GREEDY never chooses arm 2. By Theorem 31.10 and the definition of α, we have $\Pr[\mathcal{E}_1] \geq (\mu_1^0 - \mu_2^0)/2$.

Let $\mathcal{E}_2$ be the event that $\mu_2 > 1 - \alpha$. Under the event $\mathcal{E}_1 \cap \mathcal{E}_2$, each round contributes $\mu_2 - \mu_1 \geq \alpha$ to the regret, so $\mathbb{E}[R(T) \mid \mathcal{E}_1 \cap \mathcal{E}_2] \geq \alpha T$.

Since the event $\mathcal{E}_1$ is determined by the prior on arm 1 and the rewards of arm 2, it is independent of $\mathcal{E}_2$. It follows that

$$\mathbb{E}[R(T)] \geq \mathbb{E}[R(T) \mid \mathcal{E}_1 \cap \mathcal{E}_2]\, \Pr[\mathcal{E}_1 \cap \mathcal{E}_2]$$
$$\geq \alpha T(\mu_1^0 - \mu_2^0)/2\, \Pr[\mathcal{E}_2]. \quad\square$$

Here is a less quantitative but perhaps cleaner implication:

Corollary 31.12. *Consider independent priors. Assume that each arm's prior has a positive density. That is, for each arm* a, *the prior on* $\mu_a \in [0, 1]$ *has a probability density function that is strictly positive on* $[0, 1]$. *Then* GREEDY *suffers a Bayesian regret of at least* $c_\mathcal{P} T$, *where the constant* $c_\mathcal{P} > 0$ *depends only on the prior* $\mathcal{P}$.

31.5 "Hidden Persuasion" for the General Case

We introduce a general technique for Bayesian persuasion, called Hidden Persuasion, which we then use to incentivize exploration. The idea is to *hide a little persuasion in a lot of exploitation*. We define a messaging policy which inputs a signal $\texttt{sig} \in \Omega_{\texttt{sig}}$ and outputs a recommended arm $\texttt{rec} \in \{1, 2\}$. With a given probability ϵ, we recommend what we actually want to happen, as described by the

---

[3] The latter follows from the general fact that the sequence $\mathbb{E}[X \mid H_t]$, $t \in [T+1]$ is a martingale with respect to $\mathcal{H}$ for any random variable X with $\mathbb{E}[|X|] \infty$. It is known as the *Doob martingale* for X.

(possibly randomized) *target function* $a_{\text{trg}} \colon \Omega_{\text{sig}} \to \{1,2\}$. Otherwise we *exploit*, i.e., choose an arm that maximizes $\mathbb{E}[\mu_a \mid \text{sig}]$.

Algorithm 31.1. `HiddenPersuasion` with signal `sig`.

Parameters: probability $\epsilon > 0$, function $a_{\text{trg}} \colon \Omega_{\text{sig}} \to \{1,2\}$.
Input: signal realization $S \in \Omega_{\text{sig}}$.
Output: recommended arm `rec`.
With probability $\epsilon > 0$,   // persuasion branch
    `rec` $\leftarrow a_{\text{trg}}(S)$
else   // exploitation branch
    `rec` $\leftarrow a^*(S) := \min\left(\arg\max_{a \in \{1,2\}} \mathbb{E}[\mu_a \mid \text{sig} = S] \right)$

We are interested in the (single-round) BIC property

$$\text{rec} = \min\left(\underset{\text{arms } a \in \{1,2\}}{\arg\max} \ \mathbb{E}[\mu_a \mid \text{rec}] \right). \tag{31.18}$$

We can prove that `HiddenPersuasion` satisfies this property when the persuasion probability ϵ is sufficiently small that the persuasion branch is offset by exploitation. A key quantity here is a random variable which summarizes the meaning of `sig`:

$$G := \mathbb{E}[\mu_2 - \mu_1 \mid \text{sig}] \qquad \text{(posterior gap)}.$$

Lemma 31.13. `HiddenPersuasion` *with persuasion probability* $\epsilon > 0$ *is BIC, for any target function* a_{trg}, *as long as* $\epsilon < \frac{1}{3} \mathbb{E}[G \cdot \mathbb{1}_{\{G>0\}}]$.

Remark 31.14. A suitable $\epsilon > 0$ exists if and only if $\Pr[G > 0] > 0$. Indeed, if $\Pr[G > 0] > 0$ then $\Pr[G > \delta] = \delta' > 0$ for some $\delta > 0$, so

$$\mathbb{E}[G \cdot \mathbb{1}_{\{G>0\}}] \geq \mathbb{E}[G \cdot \mathbb{1}_{\{G>\delta\}}] = \Pr[G > \delta] \, \mathbb{E}[G \mid G > \delta] \geq \delta\delta' > 0.$$

The rest of this section proves Lemma 31.13. To keep the exposition fairly simple, we assume that the universe Ω_{sig} is finite.[4] We start with an easy observation: for any algorithm, it suffices to guarantee the BIC property when arm 2 is recommended.

Claim 31.15. *Assume (31.18) holds for arm* `rec` $= 2$. *Then it also holds for* `rec` $= 1$.

Proof If arm 2 is never recommended, then the claim holds trivially since $\mu_1^0 \geq \mu_2^0$. Now, suppose both arms are recommended with some positive probability. Then

$$0 \geq \mathbb{E}[\mu_2 - \mu_1] = \sum_{a \in \{1,2\}} \mathbb{E}[\mu_2 - \mu_1 \mid \text{rec} = a] \Pr[\text{rec} = a].$$

Since $\mathbb{E}[\mu_2 - \mu_1 \mid \text{rec} = 2] > 0$ by the BIC assumption, it holds that $\mathbb{E}[\mu_2 - \mu_1 \mid \text{rec} = 1] < 0$. $\qquad\square$

Thus, we need to prove (31.18) for `rec` $= 2$, i.e., that

$$\mathbb{E}[\mu_2 - \mu_1 \mid \text{rec} = 2] > 0. \tag{31.19}$$

---

[4] Otherwise our proof requires a more advanced notion of conditional expectation.

(We note that $\Pr[\mu_2 - \mu_1] > 0$, e.g., because $\Pr[G > 0] > 0$, as per Remark 31.14).

Denote the event $\{\texttt{rec} = 2\}$ by $\mathcal{E}_2$. By Fact 31.1, $\mathbb{E}[\mu_2 - \mu_1 \mid \mathcal{E}_2] = \mathbb{E}[G \mid \mathcal{E}_2]$.[5]

We focus on the posterior gap G from here on. More specifically, we work with expressions of the form $F(\mathcal{E}) := \mathbb{E}[G \cdot \mathbb{1}_{\mathcal{E}}]$, where $\mathcal{E}$ is some event. Proving (31.19) is equivalent to proving that $F(\mathcal{E}_2) > 0$; we prove the latter in what follows.

We will use the following fact:

$$F(\mathcal{E} \cup \mathcal{E}') = F(\mathcal{E}) + F(\mathcal{E}') \quad \text{for any disjoint events } \mathcal{E}, \mathcal{E}'. \tag{31.20}$$

Letting $\mathcal{E}_{\texttt{pers}}$ (resp., $\mathcal{E}_{\texttt{expl}}$) be the event that the algorithm chooses the persuasion branch (resp., exploitation branch), we can write

$$F(\mathcal{E}_2) = F(\mathcal{E}_{\texttt{pers}} \,\&\, \mathcal{E}_2) + F(\mathcal{E}_{\texttt{expl}} \,\&\, \mathcal{E}_2). \tag{31.21}$$

We prove that this expression is non-negative by analyzing the persuasion and exploitation branches separately. For the exploitation branch, the events $\{\mathcal{E}_{\texttt{expl}} \,\&\, \mathcal{E}_2\}$ and $\{\mathcal{E}_{\texttt{expl}} \,\&\, G > 0\}$ are the same by the algorithm's specification. Therefore,

$$
\begin{aligned}
F(\mathcal{E}_{\texttt{expl}} \,\&\, \mathcal{E}_2) &= F(\mathcal{E}_{\texttt{expl}} \,\&\, G > 0) \\
&= \mathbb{E}[G \mid \mathcal{E}_{\texttt{expl}} \,\&\, G > 0] \Pr[\mathcal{E}_{\texttt{expl}} \,\&\, G > 0] \quad \text{(by definition of } F) \\
&= \mathbb{E}[G \mid G > 0] \Pr[G > 0](1 - \epsilon) \quad \text{(by independence)} \\
&= (1 - \epsilon)F(G > 0) \quad \text{(by definition of } F).
\end{aligned}
$$

For the persuasion branch, recall that $F(\mathcal{E})$ is non-negative for any event $\mathcal{E}$ with $G \geq 0$, and non-positive for any event $\mathcal{E}$ with $G \leq 0$. Therefore,

$$
\begin{aligned}
F(\mathcal{E}_{\texttt{pers}} \,\&\, \mathcal{E}_2) &= F(\mathcal{E}_{\texttt{pers}} \,\&\, \mathcal{E}_2 \,\&\, G < 0) + F(\mathcal{E}_{\texttt{pers}} \,\&\, \mathcal{E}_2 \,\&\, G \geq 0) \quad \text{(by (31.20))} \\
&\geq F(\mathcal{E}_{\texttt{pers}} \,\&\, \mathcal{E}_2 \,\&\, G < 0) \\
&= F(\mathcal{E}_{\texttt{pers}} \,\&\, G < 0) - F(\mathcal{E}_{\texttt{pers}} \,\&\, \neg\mathcal{E}_2 \,\&\, G < 0) \quad \text{(by (31.20))} \\
&\geq F(\mathcal{E}_{\texttt{pers}} \,\&\, G < 0) \\
&= \mathbb{E}[G \mid \mathcal{E}_{\texttt{pers}} \,\&\, G < 0] \Pr[\mathcal{E}_{\texttt{pers}} \,\&\, G < 0] \quad \text{(by definition of } F) \\
&= \mathbb{E}[G \mid G < 0] \Pr[G < 0] \epsilon \quad \text{(by independence)} \\
&= \epsilon F(G < 0) \quad \text{(by definition of } F).
\end{aligned}
$$

Putting this together and substituting into (31.21), we have

$$F(\mathcal{E}_2) \geq \epsilon F(G < 0) + (1 - \epsilon)F(G > 0). \tag{31.22}$$

Now, applying (31.20) yet again we see that $F(G < 0) + F(G > 0) = \mathbb{E}[\mu_2 - \mu_1]$. Substituting this back into (31.22) and rearranging, it follows that $F(\mathcal{E}_2) > 0$ whenever

$$F(G > 0) > \epsilon\,(2F(G > 0) + \mathbb{E}[\mu_1 - \mu_2]).$$

In particular, $\epsilon < \frac{1}{3}F(G > 0)$ suffices. This completes the proof of Lemma 31.13.

---

[5] This is the only step in the analysis where it is essential that both the persuasion and exploitation branches (and therefore event $\mathcal{E}_2$) are determined by the signal $\texttt{sig}$.

31.6 Incentivized Exploration via "Hidden Persuasion"

Let us develop the hidden persuasion technique into an algorithm for incentivized exploration. We take an arbitrary bandit algorithm ALG and consider a repeated version of HiddenPersuasion (called RepeatedHP), where the persuasion branch executes one call to ALG. We interpret calls to ALG as exploration. To get started, we include N_0 rounds of "initial exploration," where arm 1 is chosen. The exploitation branch conditions on the history of all previous exploration rounds are

$$\mathcal{S}_t = ((s, a_s, r_s) : \text{all exploration rounds } s < t). \qquad (31.23)$$

Algorithm 31.2. RepeatedHP with bandit algorithm ALG.

Parameters: $N_0 \in \mathbb{N}$, exploration probability $\epsilon > 0$
In the first N_0 rounds, recommend arm 1.　　　　　// initial exploration
In each subsequent round t,
　　With probability ϵ　　　　　　　　　　　　　　　// explore
　　　　call ALG, let rec_t be the chosen arm, feed reward r_t back to ALG.
　　else　　　　　　　　　　　　　　　　　　　　　// exploit
　　　　$\text{rec}_t \leftarrow \min \left(\arg\max_{a \in \{1,2\}} \mathbb{E}[\mu_a \mid \mathcal{S}_t] \right).$　　// $\mathcal{S}_t$ from (31.23)

Remark 31.16. RepeatedHP can be seen as a reduction from bandit algorithms to BIC bandit algorithms. The simplest version always chooses arm 2 in exploration rounds, and (only) provides non-adaptive exploration. For better regret bounds, ALG needs to perform adaptive exploration, as per Section 31.2.

Each round $t > N_0$ can be interpreted as HiddenPersuasion with signal $\mathcal{S}_t$, where the "target function" executes one round of algorithm ALG. Note that rec_t is determined by $\mathcal{S}_t$ and the random seed of ALG, as required by the specification of HiddenPersuasion. Thus, Lemma 31.13 applies, and yields the following corollary in terms of $G_t = \mathbb{E}[\mu_2 - \mu_1 \mid \mathcal{S}_t]$, the posterior gap given signal $\mathcal{S}_t$.

Corollary 31.17. RepeatedHP *is BIC if* $\epsilon < \frac{1}{3} \mathbb{E}\left[G_t \cdot \mathbb{1}_{\{G_t > 0\}} \right]$ *for each time* $t > N_0$.

For the final BIC guarantee, we show that it suffices to focus on $t = N_0 + 1$.

Theorem 31.18. RepeatedHP *with exploration probability* $\epsilon > 0$ *and* N_0 *initial samples of arm 1 is BIC if* $\epsilon < \frac{1}{3} \mathbb{E}\left[G \cdot \mathbb{1}_{\{G > 0\}} \right]$, *where* $G = G_{N_0+1}$.

Proof The only remaining piece is the claim that the quantity $\mathbb{E}\left[G_t \cdot \mathbb{1}_{\{G_t > 0\}} \right]$ does not decrease over time. This holds for any sequence of signals $(\mathcal{S}_1, \mathcal{S}_2, \ldots, \mathcal{S}_T)$ such that each signal $\mathcal{S}_t$ is determined by the next signal $\mathcal{S}_{t+1}$.
　Fix round t. Applying Fact 31.1 twice, we obtain

$$\mathbb{E}[G_t \mid G_t > 0] = \mathbb{E}[\mu_2 - \mu_1 \mid G_t > 0] = \mathbb{E}[G_{t+1} \mid G_t > 0].$$

(The last equality uses the fact that S_{t+1} determines S_t.) Then,

$$\mathbb{E}\left[G_t \cdot \mathbb{1}_{\{G_t>0\}}\right] = \mathbb{E}[G_t \mid G_t > 0]\,\Pr[G_t > 0]$$
$$= \mathbb{E}[G_{t+1} \mid G_t > 0]\,\Pr[G_t > 0]$$
$$= \mathbb{E}\left[G_{t+1} \cdot \mathbb{1}_{\{G_t>0\}}\right]$$
$$\leq \mathbb{E}\left[G_{t+1} \cdot \mathbb{1}_{\{G_{t+1}>0\}}\right].$$

The last inequality holds because $x \cdot \mathbb{1}_{\{\cdot\}} \leq x \cdot \mathbb{1}_{\{x>0\}}$ for any $x \in R$. $\qquad\square$

Remark 31.19. The theorem focuses on the posterior gap G given N_0 initial samples from arm 1. It requires parameters $\epsilon > 0$ and N_0 to satisfy some condition that depends only on the prior. Such parameters exist if and only if $\Pr[G > 0] > 0$ for some N_0. (This is for precisely the same reason as in Remark 31.14.) The latter condition is in fact necessary, as we will see in Section 31.7.

Performance guarantees for RepeatedHP are completely separated from the BIC guarantee, in terms of results as well as proofs. Essentially, RepeatedHP learns at least as fast as an appropriately slowed-down version of ALG. There are several natural ways to formalize this, in line with the standard performance measures for multi-armed bandits. For notation, let $\mathrm{REW}^{\mathrm{ALG}}(n)$ be the total reward of ALG in the first n rounds of its execution, and let $R_{\mathcal{P}}^{\mathrm{ALG}}(n)$ be the corresponding Bayesian regret.

Theorem 31.20. *Consider* RepeatedHP *with exploration probability $\epsilon > 0$ and N_0 initial samples. Let N be the number of exploration rounds $t > N_0$. [6] Then:*

1. *If* ALG *always chooses arm 2,* RepeatedHP *chooses arm 2 at least N times.*
2. *The expected reward of* RepeatedHP *is at least $\frac{1}{\epsilon}\,\mathbb{E}\left[\mathrm{REW}^{\mathrm{ALG}}(N)\right]$.*
3. *Bayesian regret of* RepeatedHP *is $R_{\mathcal{P}}(T) \leq N_0 + \frac{1}{\epsilon}\,\mathbb{E}\left[R_{\mathcal{P}}^{\mathrm{ALG}}(N)\right]$.*

Proof sketch. Part 1 is obvious. Part 3 trivially follows from part 2. The proof of part (ii) invokes Wald's identity and the fact that the expected reward in "exploitation" is at least as large as in "exploration" for the same round. $\qquad\square$

We match the Bayesian regret of ALG up to by factors N_0, $\frac{1}{\epsilon}$ that depend only on the prior. So, we can match the optimal regret for a given prior $\mathcal{P}$ if ALG is optimal for $\mathcal{P}, T$. We achieve the $\tilde{O}(\sqrt{T})$ regret bound for all problem instances, e.g., using AdaptiveRace from Section 31.2. The prior-dependent factors can be arbitrarily large, depending on the prior; we interpret this as the "price of incentives."

31.7 A Necessary and Sufficient Assumption on the Prior

We need to restrict the prior $\mathcal{P}$ so as to give the algorithm a fighting chance to convince some agents to try arm 2. (Recall that $\mu_1^0 \geq \mu_2^0$.) Otherwise the problem is just hopeless. For example, if μ_1 and $\mu_1 - \mu_2$ are independent then samples from arm

---

[6] Note that $\mathbb{E}[N] = \epsilon(T - N_0)$, and $|N - \mathbb{E}[N]| \leq O(\sqrt{T \log T})$ with high probability.

1 have no bearing on the conditional expectation of $\mu_1 - \mu_2$, and therefore cannot possibly incentivize any agent to try arm 2.

We posit that arm 2 *can* appear better after sufficiently many samples of arm 1 are seen. Formally, we consider the posterior gap given n samples from arm 1:

$$G_{1,n} := \mathbb{E}[\mu_2 - \mu_1 \mid \mathcal{S}_{1,n}], \tag{31.24}$$

where $\mathcal{S}_{1,n}$ denotes an ordered tuple of n independent samples from arm 1. We focus on the property that this random variable can be positive:

$$\Pr[G_{1,n} > 0] > 0 \quad \text{for some prior-dependent constant } n = n_{\mathcal{P}} < \infty. \tag{31.25}$$

For independent priors, this property can be simplified to $\Pr[\mu_2^0 > \mu_1] > 0$. Essentially, this is so because $G_{1,n} = \mu_2^0 - \mathbb{E}[\mu_1 \mid \mathcal{S}_{1,n}] \to \mu_2^0 - \mu_1$.

We prove that property (31.25) is necessary for BIC bandit algorithms. Recall that it is sufficient for `RepeatedHP`, as per Remark 31.19.

Theorem 31.21. *Without (31.25), any BIC algorithm never plays arm 2.*

Proof Suppose property (31.25) does not hold. Let `ALG` be a strongly BIC algorithm. We prove by induction on t that `ALG` cannot recommend arm 2 to agent t.

This is trivially true for $t = 1$. Suppose the induction hypothesis is true for some t. Then the decision whether to recommend arm 2 in round $t + 1$ (i.e., whether $a_{t+1} = 2$) is determined by the first t outcomes of arm 1 and the algorithm's random seed. Letting $U = \{a_{t+1} = 2\}$, we have

$$\mathbb{E}[\mu_2 - \mu_1 \mid U] = \mathbb{E}\big[\ \mathbb{E}[\mu_2 - \mu_1 \mid \mathcal{S}_{1,t}]\ \mid U\big] \quad \text{(by Fact 31.1)}$$
$$= \mathbb{E}[G_{1,t} \mid U] \quad \text{(by definition of } G_{1,t})$$
$$\leq 0 \quad \text{(since (31.25) does not hold).}$$

The last inequality holds because the negation of (31.25) implies $\Pr[G_{1,t} \leq 0] = 1$. This contradicts the fact that `ALG` is BIC, and completes the induction proof. $\square$

31.8 Bibliographic Notes

To conclude this chapter, we include citations to relevant publications, survey the "landscape" of incentivized exploration, and place this work in a larger context. A more detailed literature review can be found in [30, Section 11.5].

The technical results in this chapter map to the literature as follows. The results on incentivized exploration in Sections 31.5–31.7 are from [25]. The algorithmic results on bandits presented in Section 31.2 are folklore; the lower bounds trace back to [20] and [2]. The Bayesian persuasion example in Section 31.3 follows the technique from [15]. The inefficiency of `GREEDY` has been folklore for decades. The general impossibility result (Theorem 31.10) first appeared in [30, Chapter 11], and is due to [27].

Incentivized exploration was introduced in [19] and [8]. Our model of incentivized exploration was studied, and largely resolved, in [19], [25], [24], and [28]. Results come in a variety of flavors: to wit, optimal policies for deterministic rewards; "frequentist" regret bounds (as in Theorem 31.2); extension to $K > 2$ arms; performance loss compared to bandits; and exploring all actions that can possibly be explored.

Algorithms come in a variety of flavors, too. In particular, `RepeatedHP` is made more efficient by inserting a third "branch" that combines exploration and exploitation and allows the exploration probability to increase substantially over time. Moreover, `ThompsonSampling`, an optimal bandit algorithm mentioned in Section 31.2, is BIC for independent priors when initialized with enough samples of each arm. Unlike `RepeatedHP`, this algorithm does not suffer from multiplicative prior-dependent blow-up; however, the initial samples should be collected by some other method.

Our model can be made more realistic in three broad directions. First, one can generalize the *exploration* problem in all the ways that one can generalize multi-armed bandits. In particular, `RepeatedHP` generalizes well, because it inputs a generic exploration algorithm `ALG` [24]. However, this approach does not scale to "structured" exploration problems with exponentially many actions or policies. In [29] this issue was addressed for incentivized reinforcement learning, via a different technique.

Second, one can generalize the *persuasion* problem in our model in all the ways that one can generalize Bayesian persuasion. Prior work has considered repeated games and misaligned incentives [24], heterogenous agents [13], partially known agents' beliefs [25], [13], and unavoidable information leakage [3], [4].

Third, one can relax the standard (yet strong) economic assumptions that the principal is committed to the messaging policy and that the agents optimize their Bayesian-expected rewards. The latter assumption rules out generic issues such as risk aversion, probability matching, or approximate reasoning, as well as problem-specific issues such as aversion to being singled out for exploration, or reluctance to follow a recommendation without supporting evidence. In [14] near-optimal regret was achieved under weaker assumptions: all that was needed was to specify how agents respond to fixed datasets and to allow a flexible "frequentist" response thereto.

Related but technically different models of incentivized exploration feature time-discounted utilities [7], monetary incentives [10], [9], continuous information flow [8], and the coordination of costly "exploration decisions" which are separate from "payoff-generating decisions" [18], [22], [23]. GREEDY (full revelation) works well for heterogenous agents under strong assumptions on the structure of rewards and diversity of agent types [17], [5], [26], [1].

Incentivized exploration is closely related to two prominent subareas of theoretical economics. *Information design* [6], [15] studies the design of information disclosure policies and incentives that they create. One fundamental model is Bayesian persuasion [16]. *Social learning* [11], [12] studies self-interested agents that interact and learn over time in a shared environment.

Multi-armed bandits have been studied since the 1950s in economics, operations research, and computer science, with a big surge in the last two decades coming mostly from machine learning. This vast literature is covered in various books; the most recent ones are [21] and [30].

Acknowledgements

The author is grateful to Ian Ball, Brendan Lucier, and David Parkes for careful reading of the manuscript and valuable suggestions.

References

[1] Acemoglu, Daron, Makhdoumi, Ali, Malekian, Azarakhsh, and Ozdaglar, Asuman. 2019. Learning from reviews: The selection effect and the speed of learning. *Econometrica,* accepted. Working Paper available since 2017.

[2] Auer, Peter, Cesa-Bianchi, Nicolò, Freund, Yoav, and Schapire, Robert E. 2002. The nonstochastic multiarmed bandit problem. *SIAM J. Comput.*, **32**(1), 48–77. Preliminary version in *Proc. 36th IEEE FOCS*, 1995.

[3] Bahar, Gal, Smorodinsky, Rann, and Tennenholtz, Moshe. 2016. Economic recommendation systems. In: *Proc. 16th ACM Conference on Electronic Commerce*.

[4] Bahar, Gal, Smorodinsky, Rann, and Tennenholtz, Moshe. 2019. Social learning and the innkeeper's challenge. Pages 153–170 of: *Proc, ACM Conference on Economics and Computation*.

[5] Bastani, Hamsa, Bayati, Mohsen, and Khosravi, Khashayar. 2021. Mostly exploration-free algorithms for contextual bandits. *Management Science*, **67**(3), 1329–1349. Working Paper available on `arxiv.org` since 2017.

[6] Bergemann, Dirk, and Morris, Stephen. 2019. Information design: A unified perspective. *Journal of Economic Literature*, **57**(1), 44–95.

[7] Bimpikis, Kostas, Papanastasiou, Yiangos, and Savva, Nicos. 2018. Crowdsourcing exploration. *Management Science*, **64**(4), 1477–1973.

[8] Che, Yeon-Koo, and Hörner, Johannes. 2018. Recommender systems as mechanisms for social learning. *Quarterly Journal of Economics*, **133**(2), 871–925. Working Paper since 2013, entitled "Optimal design for social living."

[9] Chen, Bangrui, Frazier, Peter I., and Kempe, David. 2018. Incentivizing exploration by heterogeneous users. Pages 798–818 of: *Proc. Conference on Learning Theory*.

[10] Frazier, Peter, Kempe, David, Kleinberg, Jon M., and Kleinberg, Robert. 2014. Incentivizing exploration. Pages 5–22 of: *Proc. ACM Conference on Economics and Computation*.

[11] Golub, Benjamin, and Sadler, Evan D. 2016. Learning in social networks. In: Bramoullé, Yann, Galeotti, Andrea, and Rogers, Brian, eds., *The Oxford Handbook of the Economics of Networks*. Oxford University Press.

[12] Hörner, Johannes, and Skrzypacz, Andrzej. 2017. Learning, experimentation, and information design. Pages 63–98 of: Honoré, Bo, Pakes, Ariel, Piazzesi, Monika, and Samuelson, Larry, eds., *Advances in Economics and Econometrics: 11th World Congress*, vol. 1. Cambridge University Press.

[13] Immorlica, Nicole, Mao, Jieming, Slivkins, Aleksandrs, and Wu, Steven. 2019. Bayesian exploration with heterogenous agents. Pages 751–761 of: *Proc. The Web Conference (formerly known as* WWW*)*.

[14] Immorlica, Nicole, Mao, Jieming, Slivkins, Aleksandrs, and Wu, Steven. 2020. Incentivizing exploration with selective data disclosure. In: *Proc. ACM Conference on Economics and Computation*. Working Paper available at https://arxiv.org/abs/1811.06026.

[15] Kamenica, Emir. 2019. Bayesian persuasion and information design. *Annual Review of Economics*, **11**(1), 249–272.

[16] Kamenica, Emir, and Gentzkow, Matthew. 2011. Bayesian persuasion. *American Economic Review*, **101**(6), 2590–2615.

[17] Kannan, Sampath, Morgenstern, Jamie, Roth, Aaron, Waggoner, Bo, and Wu, Zhiwei Steven. 2018. A smoothed analysis of the greedy algorithm for the linear contextual bandit problem. In: *Advances in Neural Information Processing Systems*.

[18] Kleinberg, Robert D., Waggoner, Bo, and Weyl, E. Glen. 2016. Descending price optimally coordinates search. Pages 23–24 of: *Proc. 17th ACM Conference on Economics and Computation*.

[19] Kremer, Ilan, Mansour, Yishay, and Perry, Motty. 2014. Implementing the "Wisdom of the Crowd." *J. Political Economy*, **122**(5), 988–1012.

[20] Lai, Tze Leung, and Robbins, Herbert. 1985. Asymptotically efficient adaptive allocation rules. *Advances in Applied Mathematics*, **6**, 4–22.

[21] Lattimore, Tor, and Szepesvari, Csaba. 2020. *Bandit Algorithms*. Cambridge University Press. Versions available at https://banditalgs.com/ since 2018.

[22] Liang, Annie, and Mu, Xiaosheng. 2018. Overabundant information and learning traps. Pages 71–72 of: *Proc. ACM Conference on Economics and Computation*.

[23] Liang, Annie, Mu, Xiaosheng, and Syrgkanis, Vasilis. 2018. Optimal and myopic information acquisition. Pages 45–46 of: *Proc. ACM Conference on Economics and Computation*.

[24] Mansour, Yishay, Slivkins, Aleksandrs, Syrgkanis, Vasilis, and Wu, Steven. 2021. Bayesian exploration: Incentivizing exploration in Bayesian games. *Operations Research,* **17**(2). Available at https://arxiv.org/abs/1602.07570.

[25] Mansour, Yishay, Slivkins, Aleksandrs, and Syrgkanis, Vasilis. 2020. Bayesian incentive-compatible bandit exploration. *Operations Research*, **68**(4), 1132–1161.

[26] Raghavan, Manish, Slivkins, Aleksandrs, Vaughan, Jennifer Wortman, and Wu, Zhiwei Steven. 2018. Greedy algorithm almost dominates in smoothed contextual bandits. Revised and resubmitted in *Siam Journal on Computing*. Preliminary version published in *Proc. COLT 2018 (Conf. on Learning Theory*.

[27] Sellke, Mark. 2019. Personal communication.

[28] Sellke, Mark, and Slivkins, Aleksandrs. 2022. The price of incentivizing exploration: A characterization via thompson sampling and sample complexity. *Operations Research,* accepted. Preliminary version in *Proc. ACM EC 2021 (ACM Conf. on Economics and Computation)*. Available at https://arxiv.org/abs/2002.00558.

[29] Simchowitz, Max, and Slivkins, Aleksandrs. 2021. Incentives and exploration in reinforcement learning. Working Paper, available at https://arxiv.org/abs/2103.00360.

[30] Slivkins, Aleksandrs. 2019. Introduction to multi-armed bandits. *Foundations and Trends® in Machine Learning*, vol. 12, 1–286. Now Publishers. Also available at https://arxiv.org/abs/1904.07272.

CHAPTER THIRTY-TWO

Fairness in Prediction and Allocation

Jamie Morgenstern and Aaron Roth

32.1 Introduction

Many high-stakes decisions that are now aided by machine learning can be viewed as *allocation* problems. We will often have some *good* (such as a job or a loan) or *bad* (such as incarceration) to distribute amongst a population. People on at least one side of the problem will have preferences over the other side that are based on qualities that are not directly observable (e.g., banks want to give loans to the creditworthy; courts want to incarcerate the guilty or those likely to repeat their offenses). The machine learning task is to make predictions about those qualities from observable attributes. It is natural that when we make high-stakes decisions, we will be concerned about *unfairness* – the potential for the system as a whole (of which a machine learning algorithm or statistical model may play only a relatively small role) to disproportionately favor some people over others, perhaps for reasons more related to their demographics than features relevant for the task at hand. And we note at the outset that these considerations are not hypothetical: statistical models are currently being used to inform bail and parole decisions, hiring and compensation decisions, lending decisions, and an increasingly extensive collection of high-stakes tasks, and there are now an enormous number of cases of systemic decision-making that would be called sexist or racist – at least if the decisions had been made by a human being.

But what should we make of such decision making when it is carried out by an algorithm that was derived by optimizing an apparently neutral objective function, like classification error? The first thing we need to understand is why we might expect machine learning to exacerbate unfair decision making in the first place. After all, at its heart, machine learning usually corresponds to simple, principled optimization. Typically, the process of machine learning will start by gathering a dataset consisting of various measured *features* for each person. For example, in the recidivism-prediction problem that is often used to inform whether prisoners should be released on parole, features might include basic demographics (e.g., age, sex), together with information about criminal history, such as the number of previous arrests and convictions for violent and non-violent offences. It is also necessary to specify something that we wish to predict, called the *label* – importantly, something that we can measure. For example, in a recidivism-prediction setting, the goal is to predict whether inmates will commit a violent crime within (e.g.) 18 months of being released – but because this is not directly observable, the label is often taken to be a proxy variable such as whether the individual was *arrested* for a violent crime. And bias of the sort we are trying to avoid can creep in to the final decision making rule via the data, and via the optimization process itself in both obvious and non-obvious ways.

First, lets consider the labels that we are trying to predict. In the criminal-recidivism application, are arrests an equally good proxy for crime in all populations? Perhaps not: if police are more likely to stop black people than white people, all things being equal, then the effect of using arrest labels as proxies for unmeasured criminality will be that black people in the dataset will in aggregate appear to be a higher risk population than they would if we could measure the actual variable of interest. And of course there is no reason to expect that applying machine learning techniques will somehow remove these human biases which have crept into the dataset via the labeling process: machine learning at best replicates the patterns already in the data.

But the problem goes beyond that, and bias can creep into machine learning even if the labels are correctly recorded in the data. It is enough that two different populations are statistically different in the sense that features correlate differently with the label, depending on the population. Consider, for example, a college admissions problem in which we seek to identify talented students from their high school records. Suppose there are two populations, one of which attends well resourced suburban high schools, and the other of which attends poorly resourced city high schools. One feature that we may have available to us in a college application is how many advanced placement (AP) science courses a student has taken. For students from the well resourced high schools, which offer many AP science courses, this might be an informative predictor of student talent. But amongst students from the poorly resourced high schools – which offer many fewer, or perhaps even no AP courses, this feature is much less predictive (because ordinary and talented students alike do not take AP courses, since none are available). It may be that the distribution of talent is the same in both high schools – and even that, in isolation, talent is equally predictable within both populations – but predictable using different models. Yet if we insist on selecting a single model for both populations,[1] optimizing for overall error will result in finding the model that better fits the majority population, simply because error on the majority population contributes more to overall error by virtue of their numbers. In this case (because for the wealthy students, taking no AP classes is a negative signal) this will result in penalizing students who have not taken AP classes, which will have the effect of reducing admission rate on the population from under-resourced schools.

32.1.1 What is "Fairness" in Classification?

We have discussed informally how "unfairness" might creep into statistical models learned from data – but if we want to quantify it and think about how to eliminate it, we need to be much more precise. So what should "fairness" entail in a limited

---

[1] As we must if we do not want to explicitly use group membership as a feature in our decision making process – something that is explicitly illegal in many settings such as lending and insurance.

setting such as binary classification? Here we will intentionally start with a narrowly specified version of the problem, in which things such as the data distribution are taken as exogenously given properties of the world, and the only object of study is the statistical model that we train from the data itself. Later in the chapter we will expand the scope of our analysis to account for the second-order effects of the choices that we make in defining a classification technology. We will focus on the simplest possible setting, removing many of the difficulties that arise in more realistic settings. For example, we will assume that there are only two disjoint groups of interest, which we will denote by $g \in \{0, 1\}$. This could denote any binary distinction made by e.g., biological sex, race, or class. This avoids (important) complications that arise when there are many – potentially intersecting – groups for whom we care about fairness. We will also implicitly assume that the labels recorded in the data are the true labels, i.e. that our data is not contaminated with the sort of proxy label bias we discussed above. We will find that, even in this simplified setting, there are already thorny issues to deal with.

Definition 32.1 (Data distribution). We model individuals as being sampled from *data distributions* $\mathcal{D}_g$ which may depend on their group g. The distributions $\mathcal{D}_g$ have support over $X \times \{0, 1\}$, where X represents an abstract *feature space*, and Y represents some binary outcome of interest.

In the above, we imagine that the feature space X is the same for both populations and does not encode group membership g, which we handle separately (because we wish to study the question of whether decision making should condition on g or not). We write $\gamma \in [0, 1]$ to represent the fraction of the overall population that group 0 represents, and thus $1 - \gamma$ is the fraction of the overall population that group 1 represents. We write $\mathcal{D}$ to denote the distribution over the entire population of both groups, defined as follows. The distribution $\mathcal{D}$ is supported on $\{0, 1\} \times X \times \{0, 1\}$, corresponding to triples (g, x, y) of group membership, features, and labels. To sample from $\mathcal{D}$, we:

1. let $g = 0$ with probability γ (otherwise $g = 1$),
2. sample $(x, y) \sim \mathcal{D}_g$,
3. output the triple (g, x, y).

The fact that the distributions $\mathcal{D}_0$ and $\mathcal{D}_1$ may differ allows us to model the unavoidable fact that distinct populations will have different statistical properties (without modeling for now the source of those differences, such as, e.g., the difference in high school resources as discussed above).

The prediction problem is to learn some rule $h \colon \{0, 1\} \times X \to \{0, 1\}$ to predict the unknown label y as a function of the observable features x, and possibly the group label g.

Definition 32.2 (Unconstrained error minimization). The overall error rate of a hypothesis h is

$$\text{error}(h) = \Pr_{(g,x,y)\sim\mathcal{D}}[h(g, x) \neq y].$$

The error rate of a hypothesis h on a group g is

$$\text{error}_g(h) = \Pr_{(x,y)\sim\mathcal{D}_g} [h(g,x) \neq y].$$

We denote by h^* the *Bayes-optimal classifier* – i.e. the classifier that martials all available statistical information to optimally predict the label:

$$h^*(g,x) = \begin{cases} 1 & \text{if } \Pr[y=1|x,g] \geq 1/2, \\ 0 & \text{otherwise.} \end{cases}$$

Observe that the Bayes-optimal classifier is error-optimal both overall and on each group in isolation:

$$\text{error}(h^*) \leq \text{error}(h), \quad \text{error}_g(h^*) \leq \text{error}_g(h)$$

for all h and for all g.

Perhaps the most immediately obvious definition of fairness in classification is that our deployed classifier h should not make explicit use of group membership. This is a moral analogue of the goal of "anonymity" discussed as a fairness objective in Chapter 4. Here we are not making decisions in a way that is entirely independent of the individual (since in our setting, individuals are not identical but are distinguished by their features). However, we are asking that individuals who are identical with respect to their "relevant" features x should be treated in the same way, independently of their group membership g.

Definition 32.3 (Group independence).   A classifier h is group independent if it does not make decisions as a function of group membership. In other words, if for all $x \in X$,

$$h(0,x) = h(1,x).$$

This is an appealing requirement at first sight, but it is not obviously desirable in isolation (although we will return to it in a dynamic model in Section 32.3). Consider the following toy example.

Example 32.4.   Suppose that we have a majority population $g = 0$ with proportion $\gamma = 2/3$ and a minority population $g = 1$. There is a single binary feature: $X = \{0,1\}$. The distribution $\mathcal{D}_0$ is uniform over $\{(0,0),(1,1)\}$ (i.e., the label is perfectly correlated with the feature) and $\mathcal{D}_1$ is uniform over $\{(0,1),(1,0)\}$ (i.e., the label is perfectly anti-correlated with the feature).

The Bayes-optimal classifier h^* is group dependent and has $\text{error}(h^*) = 0$. But the error-optimal group-independent classifier is $h(x) = x$, i.e., it fits the majority population and has $\text{error}_0(h) = 0$, $\text{error}_1(h) = 1$, and $\text{error}(h) = 1 - \gamma = 1/3$. Here (in any setting in which higher error on a population corresponds to harm), requiring group independence has harmed the minority population without changing how the classifier behaves on the majority population and without decreasing its overall performance.

As Example 32.4 demonstrates, attempting to enforce fairness by prohibiting a classifier from using certain inputs ("fairness through blindness") can backfire, and a more promising way forward is to approach fairness by enunciating what properties of the outputs are undesirable. Doing this correctly can be tricky, and is context dependent. In the following, we go through the exercise of articulating the rationale for several popular formalizations of "statistical fairness." These differ in spirit from the notion of "envy-freeness," introduced as a measure of fairness in Chapter 4, in that we do not necessarily have the aim of giving every individual what they want: instead, these measures are concerned with how different measures of the *mistakes* made by the classifier are distributed across populations. Notions like envy-freeness are not appropriate when the designer's goal is explicitly to distribute some *bad* such as incarceration: the incarcerated will always prefer not to be incarcerated, but committing ahead of time to incarcerate nobody (or everybody – the only two deterministic envy-free solutions) is likely to be at odds with society's objectives.

32.1.1.1 Thinking about Fairness Constraints

Any statistical estimation procedure will inevitably make errors, and, depending on the setting, those errors can cause personal harms. For example, in a criminal justice application in which we are making decisions about incarceration, we may judge that the individuals who are harmed the most are those who should *not* have been incarcerated (say, because they are innocent) but are mistakenly incarcerated. These kinds of errors can be cast as *false positives*. In contrast, in settings in which we are allocating a good – say, when making a hiring decision or admitting students to college – we may judge that the individuals who are most harmed are those who should have received the good (e.g., because they were qualified for the job) but were mistakenly denied it. These kinds of errors can be cast as *false negatives*. A sensible and popular approach to fairness questions is to ask that the harms caused by the mistakes of a classifier not be disproportionately borne by one population. This approach motivates error-rate balance constraints.

Definition 32.5 (Error rate balance). A hypothesis h satisfies false-positive rate balance if

$$\Pr_{(x,y)\sim\mathcal{D}_0} [h(x) = 1|y = 0] = \Pr_{(x,y)\sim\mathcal{D}_1} [h(x) = 1|y = 0].$$

It satisfies false negative rate balance if

$$\Pr_{(x,y)\sim\mathcal{D}_0} [h(x) = 0|y = 1] = \Pr_{(x,y)\sim\mathcal{D}_1} [h(x) = 0|y = 1].$$

If h satisfies both conditions we say that it satisfies error-rate balance. These definitions have natural approximate relaxations; rather than requiring exact equality, we can require that the difference in false-positive or false-negative rates across populations should not exceed some threshold ϵ.

Of course, not all statistical estimators are directly used to take action: a (currently) more common case occurs when statistical estimators are used to inform some downstream decision – often made by a human being – that will involve many sources of information. In such cases, we cannot directly attribute harms that result from an eventual decision to mistakes made by the classification technology, and so it is difficult to ask that the "harms" due to the mistakes in classification be equally borne by all populations. For these mid-stream statistical estimators, we might instead ask that the predictions they make be *equally informative* for both populations. In other words, the *meaning of the inference that we can draw about the true label from the prediction should be the same for both populations.*

Definition 32.6 (Informational balance). A hypothesis h satisfies positive informational balance if

$$\Pr_{(x,y)\sim\mathcal{D}_0}[y = 1|h(x) = 1] = \Pr_{(x,y)\sim\mathcal{D}_1}[y = 1|h(x) = 1].$$

It satisfies negative informational balance if

$$\Pr_{(x,y)\sim\mathcal{D}_0}[y = 1|h(x) = 0] = \Pr_{(x,y)\sim\mathcal{D}_1}[y = 1|h(x) = 0].$$

If h satisfies both conditions, we say that it satisfies informational balance. Just as with error-rate balance, we can easily define an approximate relaxation parameterized by an error tolerance ϵ.

We could continue and come up with additional fairness desiderata, but this will be plenty for this chapter.

32.2 The Need to Choose

We have enunciated two distinct – and reasonable – notions of balance: error-rate balance and informational balance. Which of these (if any) should we impose on our statistical models? Or perhaps there is no need to choose; both conditions are reasonable, so why not ask for both?

It turns out that doing so is simply impossible, under generic conditions on the prediction problem. An important parameter for understanding this issue will be the *base rate* in each population g, which is simply the proportion of the population that has a label of 1.

Definition 32.7 (Base rate). The base rate of population g is

$$B_g = \Pr_{(x,y)\sim\mathcal{D}_g}[y = 1].$$

The next observation we can make is that the statistical quantities used to define error-rate balance and informational balance are conditional probabilities that are Bayes duals of one another – that is, they are directly related to each other via Bayes' rule.

Claim 32.8 (Bayes' rule). *In our present context, Bayes' rule state that*

$$\Pr_{(x,y)\sim\mathcal{D}_g}[y = 1|h(x) = 0] = \frac{\Pr_{(x,y)\sim\mathcal{D}_g}[h(x) = 0|y = 1]\Pr_{(x,y)\sim\mathcal{D}_g}[y = 1]}{\Pr_{(x,y)\sim\mathcal{D}_g}[h(x) = 0]}.$$

We now give some shorthand for false-positive and false-negative rates, the quantities that will be of interest to us:

$$\mathrm{FP}_g(h) = \Pr_{(x,y)\sim\mathcal{D}_g}[h(x) = 1|y = 0], \quad \mathrm{FN}_g(h) = \Pr_{(x,y)\sim\mathcal{D}_g}[h(x) = 0|y = 1].$$

Note that the quantity appearing in the denominator of the Bayes' rule statement, $\Pr_{(x,y)\sim\mathcal{D}_g}[h(x) = 0]$, can be expanded out by observing that there are two ways in which a classifier $h(x)$ can predict 0. Either the true label is 1 and the classifier makes an error (a false negative), or the true label is 0 and the classifier is correct, i.e., it did not make a false positive error. In other words:

$$\Pr_{(x,y)\sim\mathcal{D}_g}[h(x) = 0] = B_g \, \mathrm{FN}_g(h) + (1 - B_g)(1 - \mathrm{FP}_g(h)).$$

We can now rewrite the right-hand side of Bayes' rule as follows:

$$\Pr_{(x,y)\sim\mathcal{D}_g}[y = 1|h(x) = 0] = B_g \left(\frac{\mathrm{FN}_g(h)}{B_g \, \mathrm{FN}_g(h) + (1 - B_g)(1 - \mathrm{FP}_g(h))} \right). \quad (32.1)$$

Observe that if h satisfies informational balance, the left-hand side of the equation is equal across groups, and therefore the right-hand side must be as well:

$$B_0 \left(\frac{\mathrm{FN}_0(h)}{B_0 \, \mathrm{FN}_0(h) + (1 - B_0)(1 - \mathrm{FP}_0(h))} \right)$$
$$= B_1 \left(\frac{\mathrm{FN}_1(h)}{B_1 \, \mathrm{FN}_1(h) + (1 - B_1)(1 - \mathrm{FP}_1(h))} \right)$$

Now suppose that h also satisfies error-rate balance (i.e., $\mathrm{FP}_0(h) = \mathrm{FP}_1(h)$ and $\mathrm{FN}_0(h) = \mathrm{FN}_1(h)$). When can it be the case that the above equality holds? By inspection, there are only two ways. Either it could be that the base rates are equal: $B_0 = B_1$. In this case, the left-hand side is identical to the right-hand side. Or, it could be that the classifier is perfect. Then, the two sides are equal even if the base rate is not, because $\mathrm{FN}_g(h) = 0$ and so both sides evaluate to 0. But these are the only two cases. These observations combine to give a basic impossibility result.

Theorem 32.9. *For any two groups on which the base rates are unequal ($B_0 \neq B_1$), any hypothesis h that simultaneously achieves error-rate balance and informational balance must be perfect – i.e., must be such that* $\mathrm{error}(h) = 0$.

This is an impossibility result because:

1. The first hypothesis of the theorem – that base rates are unequal – is true in almost every interesting problem, and
2. The conclusion of the theorem – that prediction is perfect – is unobtainable in almost every interesting problem.

The correct interpretation is therefore that we must almost always settle for a hypothesis that either fails to satisfy error-rate balance or fails to satisfy informational balance – in other words, we are forced to choose amongst the fairness desiderata that we discussed in Section 32.1.1.1.

This basic fact is quite intuitive if we reflect on what 32.1 is telling us. To compute the conditional probability $\Pr_{(x,y)\sim\mathcal{D}_g}[y = 1|h(x) = 0]$, we first start with our *prior* belief that $y = 1$, before we see the output of the classifier. But this is just the base rate B_g. Then, after we see the output of the classifier, we must update our prior belief to form our posterior belief, based on the strength of the evidence that we have observed. Equation 32.1 shows us that the proper way to do this is to multiply our prior belief by the Bayes factor

$$\left(\frac{\mathrm{FN}_g(h)}{B_g\,\mathrm{FN}_g(h) + (1 - B_g)(1 - \mathrm{FP}_g(h))} \right).$$

But the Bayes factor – i.e., the strength of the evidence – is determined by the false-positive and false-negative rates of our classifier!

Thus, the impossibility result is telling us no more than the following. If we have two groups, and we start with different prior beliefs about their labels (because the base rates differ) then, if we are to have identical posterior beliefs about their labels after we see a given classifier output, it must be that the classifier provides evidence of different strengths for the two groups. Or, equivalently, if we have a classifier that provides evidence of the same strength for both groups then, if we started out with different prior beliefs about the groups, we will continue to have different posterior beliefs about the group after seeing the output of the classifier. This is why informational balance is necessarily at odds with error-rate balance.

But we need not panic – this is ok! Remember that our normative justification for error-rate balance applied in settings in which the classification algorithm was actually making decisions itself, whereas our normative justification for informational balance applied in settings in which the algorithm was informing downstream decision making. But it does mean that we must give thought, when we design algorithms with a desire for "fairness," to how the algorithm is going to be used; different use cases call for different notions of fairness, and the safe approach of having every algorithm satisfy them all is impossible.

32.3 Fairness in a Dynamic Model

How should we proceed after observing the impossibility result from Section 32.2? The message seemed to be that we should be thoughtful and choose amongst different fairness constraints in different settings, but how precisely should we go about choosing? In this section we go through a case study of one reasonable method:

1. Model the upstream and downstream effects of choices made by selecting a particular classification technology,
2. Enunciate a societal goal that you can evaluate within this larger system, and
3. Study which constraints on the classification technology are helpful or harmful in achieving that goal.

32.3.1 A Toy Criminal Justice Model

We will derive a simple model using the language of criminal justice, in part because this is the setting in which the conflict between of error-rate balance and informational balance has been most fiercely debated. In this model, our "societal goal" will be to minimize overall crime. But the reader can map our simple model onto a lending or college admissions setting, in which the corresponding societal goals will correspond to minimizing default or maximizing preparation. We stress at the outset that this is a toy model that plainly fails to capture many important aspects of criminal justice. The point is to set up the simplest possible mathematical scenario that:

1. Allows us to consider all the kinds of classification technologies that we have discussed so far (Bayes-optimal classifiers, group independence, error-rate balance, and informational balance), in a setting in which they are in tension because of Theorem 32.9, and
2. Allows us to shed light on the incentives engendered by imposing different fairness constraints, and how those interact with system-wide goals.

With these aims in mind, we proceed.

The impossibility result in Theorem 32.9 begins with the premise that different populations have different *base rates* – i.e., different proportions of positive labels. But when data points correspond to people, as they do when deploying classification technologies in criminal justice settings, base rates are just aggregates over lots of individual decisions. To model how these individual decisions are made, we will think of individuals as rational decision makers, who make a binary decision (crime versus no crime) by weighting their expected utility to be conditioned on both choices, and making the decision that corresponds to the higher expected utility. In this sense, we model people as being identical to one another. However, they differ in the opportunities available to them: we model individuals as having some *outside-option value* (or *legal employment opportunity*) that is drawn from a distribution that may be specific to their group g, thereby modeling the fact that different populations may have different legal opportunities available to them (eventually making crime relatively more appealing to some people than others).

Definition 32.10 (Outside-option distributions). Each individual from group g has an *outside-option value* v drawn independently from a real-valued distribution $v \sim \mathcal{D}_g$, which may differ by group.

Individuals will take an action $a \in \{C, N\}$ (crime or no crime). If they decide not to commit a crime, they obtain their outside-option value. If they decide to commit a crime, they obtain value I. (We could equally well have I be drawn from a group-dependent distribution, but for simplicity we will let it be a fixed value here). They will also experience some penalty P if they are incarcerated, which will occur with some probability that depends on their decision and on the classification technology that society ends up deploying, on which we will elaborate shortly. As a function of their action a, we obtain a "signal," i.e., some noisy information about what action they took. We can view this as an abstraction of the "evidence" that a crime was committed: allowing the evidence to be noisy takes into account both that criminals can go free for lack of evidence and that innocent people can end up being jailed because of misleading evidence. As we shall see, it is also from this noise that the risk of stereotyping based on group membership g arises.

Definition 32.11 (Signal distributions). An individual who takes action a generates a *signal* s drawn independently from a real-valued distribution $s \sim \mathcal{Q}_a$.

For the sake of intuition, it is helpful to imagine that larger signals correspond to stronger evidence of guilt and vice versa. This would be the case if for example $\mathcal{Q}_C$ first-order stochastically dominates $\mathcal{Q}_D$ – but we won't actually need to make this assumption. Note however that we *are* making a crucial assumption here: namely, that signals depend *only* on the action that an individual takes, and in particular are conditionally independent of their group given their action. This assumption need not hold in practice, if for example evidence is gathered by a method that itself encodes bias.

There will be some classification technology (an extremely reduced-form representation of the criminal justice system generally) that, for each individual, takes as input the signal s that they generated and then makes an incarceration decision – possibly as a function of their group membership g.

Definition 32.12 (Incarceration rule). An incarceration rule $h\colon \mathbb{R} \times \{0, 1\} \to \{0, 1\}$ takes as input a signal s and a group membership g and outputs an incarceration decision $h(s, g)$, where $h(s, g) = 1$ corresponds to incarceration.

Note that an incarceration rule fixes a false-positive rate and a false-negative rate across the two populations. For each group g:

$$\mathrm{FP}_g(h) = \Pr_{s \sim \mathcal{Q}_N} [h(s, g) = 1], \quad \mathrm{FN}_g(h) = \Pr_{s \sim \mathcal{Q}_C} [h(s, g) = 0].$$

Once an incarceration rule h is fixed, we can speak about the expected payoff of the actions of an agent who has outside-option value v and is a member of group g. Such an agent's payoff for choosing $a = C$ is

$$u(g, v, h, C) = I - P \Pr_{s \sim \mathcal{Q}_C} [h(s, g) = 1] = I - P(1 - \mathrm{FN}_g(h)).$$

In other words, the agent immediately gets a payoff I for choosing to commit a crime, but then receives a penalty P in the event that they are incarcerated, which occurs exactly when we do *not* have a false negative.

Similarly, the agent's payoff for choosing $a = N$ is

$$u(g, v, h, N) = v - P \Pr_{s \sim \mathcal{Q}_N} [h(s, g) = 1] = v - P\,\mathrm{FP}_g(h).$$

In other words, the agent immediately gets a payoff equal to their outside-option value v when they do not commit a crime, but receive a penalty P in the event that they are incarcerated, which occurs exactly when we *do* have a false positive.

Thus, in our model, an individual will commit a crime when $u(g, v, h, C) \geq u(g, v, h, N)$, which by rearranging the expressions occurs exactly when

$$v \leq I + P(\mathrm{FP}_g(h) + \mathrm{FN}_g(h) - 1).$$

Finally, this allows us to bring the model full circle and compute the base rates $B_g(h)$ in each population, which in our model are a function of the deployed classification technology h. We have that the base rate in population g is

$$B_g(h) = \Pr_{v \sim \mathcal{D}_g} [v \leq I + P(\mathrm{FP}_g(h) + \mathrm{FN}_g(h) - 1)],$$

which is just the cumulative distribution function (CDF) of the outside-option distribution $\mathcal{D}_g$ evaluated at $I + P(\mathrm{FP}_g(h) + \mathrm{FN}_g(h) - 1)$.

We pause here to make a couple of observations.

1. First, because the outside-option distributions $\mathcal{D}_0$ and $\mathcal{D}_1$ are not equal, in general, the base rates $B_0(h)$ and $B_1(h)$ will also not be equal. Thus we are in a setting in which the impossibility result from Theorem 32.9 applies.
2. Because signal distributions are conditionally independent of group membership, conditional on actions, we can equalize false-positive and false-negative rates across groups simply by selecting an incarceration rule that ignores group membership – i.e., an h such that, for all s, $h(s, 0) = h(s, 1)$.
3. On the other hand, from Bayes' rule, we know that

$$\Pr[a = C | s, g] = B_g(h) \left(\frac{\Pr_{\mathcal{Q}_C}[s]}{B_g(h) \Pr_{\mathcal{Q}_C}[s] + (1 - B_g(h)) \Pr_{\mathcal{Q}_N}[s]} \right),$$

which depends on g exactly because base rates will differ across groups. In other words, when base rates differ, group membership really does give statistically informative information about whether an individual has committed a crime or not, because it affects prior beliefs and therefore posterior beliefs. Therefore, the incarceration rule h that *minimizes overall classification error* – i.e., that is most likely to incarcerate the guilty and release the innocent – will not be independent of group membership, and therefore will not equalize false-positive and false-negative rates.

Thus we have established a model in which the selection of a classifier feeds back into the decisions of individuals, which in turn affects base rates, which in turn affects what an informative classifier must do – but we have found ourselves back where we started, in which attempts to equalize harm will lead to decisions that are differently informative across populations and vice versa.

In this model, however, we can enunciate different goals compared with what we could ask for in a static model. For example, because base rates now depend dynamically on our choice of incarceration rule h, we can ask what properties h should have if we wish to *minimize crime rates*. For example, we might ambitiously hope that some incarceration rule h^* would result in simultaneously minimizing crime rates across both populations, i.e.,

$$h^* \in \arg\min_h B_0(h), \quad h^* \in \arg\min_h B_1(h).$$

So how should we do this? And is it even possible to simultaneously minimize base rates across two different populations, with different outside-option distributions? First, recall that the base rate $B_g(h)$ for population g is simply the CDF of the distribution $\mathcal{D}_g$ evaluated at $I + P(\mathrm{FP}_g(h) + \mathrm{FN}_g(h) - 1)$. We can therefore think about how to minimize the crime rate within each population without needing to understand much about the particularities of the distributions $\mathcal{D}_g$, because CDFs are monotone. Therefore, to minimize the base rate, we need to minimize $I + P(\mathrm{FP}_g(h) + \mathrm{FN}_g(h) - 1)$ and, in this expression, only two of the parameters are under our control and neither of them depends on $\mathcal{D}_g$. Therefore we can find an h^* that minimizes the crime rate $B_g(h)$ on population g by solving

$$h^*(\cdot, 0) = \arg\min_{h(\cdot, 0)} \mathrm{FP}_0(h) + \mathrm{FN}_0(h), \quad h^*(\cdot, 1) = \arg\min_{h(\cdot, 1)} \mathrm{FP}_1(h) + \mathrm{FN}_1(h).$$

Note that this is not the same thing as minimizing overall error, because we are not weighting false-positive and false-negative rates by base rates.

Because signal distributions depend only on the action a taken by an individual, and not (directly) on group membership, the two minimization problems above must have exactly the same solution. The result is that the optimal incarceration rule h^* must be group independent – i.e., it must hold that, for all s, $h^*(s, 0) = h^*(s, 1)$. Recall that this also implies that the optimal solution equalizes the false-positive and false-negative rates across the populations. Thus we obtain the following theorem.

Theorem 32.13. *For any set of outside-option distributions $\mathcal{D}_0, \mathcal{D}_1$ and for any set of signal distributions $\mathcal{Q}_C, \mathcal{Q}_N$, there is a classifier h^* that simultaneously minimizes crime rates across both groups:*

$$h^* \in \arg\min_h B_0(h), \quad h^* \in \arg\min_h B_1(h)$$

and h^* has the following properties.

1. *h^* is independent of group membership g (even though g is statistically informative). In other words, for every s,*

$$h^*(s, 0) = h^*(s, 1).$$

2. *h^* equalizes the false-positive and false-negative rates across groups:*

$$\mathrm{FP}_0(h^*) = \mathrm{FP}_1(h^*), \quad \mathrm{FN}_0(h^*) = \mathrm{FN}_1(h^*)$$

in other words it satisfies error-rate balance.

32.3.2 Interpreting Theorem 32.13

As we have already observed, when base rates differ across groups (as they do in this setting), Bayes' rule tells us that the best classifier, from the point of view of minimizing the number of mistaken predictions will make decisions as a function of group membership. Thus, the classifier h^* in our model that is best from the perspective of minimizing crime rates is doing something that seems odd at first sight: it is *intentionally* committing not to make decisions as a function of an informative variable g, and is instead only making decisions as a function of s. How can this be?

The answer sheds some light on why we view stereotyping – i.e., using group membership to inform our decision making – as unfair in the first place. Although g is a statistically informative variable, it is immutable and not under the control of the individual. On the other hand, the signal s *is* under the control of the individual, via their choice of action. Hence, by basing our decisions on g, we are distorting individual incentives – essentially reducing the disincentive that individuals from populations with higher base rates have with regard to committing crimes in the first place. If we used the classifier optimized purely for predictive performance, we would convict individuals from the population with reduced access to legal opportunities based on evidence that we would view as insufficiently strong to convict individuals from the higher-opportunity population. This in turn would increase the crime rate in the lower-opportunity population by increasing the false-positive rate, thereby distorting the incentives of the criminal justice system. In our model, minimizing crime rates is about correctly setting the incentives of the criminal justice system – and the way to provide equal incentives to both populations is to commit to ignoring immutable individual characteristics. In other words, stereotyping or racial profiling (i.e., making statistical inferences on the basis of immutable group characteristics) can be statistically justified in a static model, but in a dynamic model it serves to distort incentives in a way that has pernicious effects in equilibrium.

We have also confirmed our intuition (within this model, of course) that it is error-rate balance that matters *when our classifier is being used to make utility-relevant decisions for people.* On the other hand, if our statistical model is being used merely to *inform* future decisions then we probably want something more like informational balance. Here, the *signal s* plays the role of the statistical instrument used to inform future decisions. Theorem 32.13 crucially relies on the fact that the signal distributions $\mathcal{Q}_C$, $\mathcal{Q}_N$ are equally informative about an agent's actions, independently of the group g to which the agent belongs. This is what allowed the equal treatment of *signals* to correctly incentivize agents across groups; if the signal distributions had not been equally informative for members of both groups then the downstream conclusion would also have failed to hold. This suggests that if we find ourselves in the position of designing a statistical model that serves the role of the signal then we should strive for (some analogue of) informational balance.

32.4 Preserving Information Before Decisions

In Section 32.1.1.1 we argued on normative grounds that when we are *taking actions* in consequential domains in which our errors lead to personal harms then we might want to deploy decision rules that optimize error, subject to error-rate balance constraints; in Section 32.3 we rigorously justified this in a particular dynamic model. Currently, however, most statistical models are not deployed to directly take action themselves, but rather to inform some downstream decision making task. This is the case, e.g., with criminal-recidivism prediction tools, which have obtained scrutiny within the algorithmic fairness literature: they are used to inform bail and parole decisions, but those decisions are ultimately made by a human judge with access to other information as well. When this is the case, we might perhaps be better served by asking that our statistical models preserve enough information about each group g that it is possible to implement the error-optimal decision rule, subject to some fairness constraint such as error-rate balance, downstream at the actual decision making process. What information is needed?

As we already observed, a sufficient statistic for computing the error-optimal classifier (i.e., the "Bayes-optimal classifier") on any distribution over points is the conditional label expectation: $f(x, g) = \mathbb{E}_{\mathcal{D}_g}[y|x]$. Here we briefly observe that this is also a sufficient statistic for computing the error-optimal classifier subject to error-rate balance constraints. Observe that we can write the error rate of a binary classifier as

$$\text{error}(h) = \mathbb{E}[h(x)(1 - \mathbb{E}[y|x]) + (1 - h(x))\mathbb{E}[y|x]].$$

Note that minimizing error(h) is equivalent to minimizing $\mathbb{E}[h(x)(1 - 2\mathbb{E}[y|x])]$. Thus we can describe the error-optimal classifier subject to error-rate balance constraints as the solution to

$$\text{Minimize}_h \quad \mathbb{E}[h(x)(1 - 2\mathbb{E}[y|x])]$$

$$\text{s.t.} \quad \mathbb{E}_{\mathcal{D}_0}[h(x)|y = 0] = \mathbb{E}_{\mathcal{D}_1}[h(x)|y = 0], \quad\quad (\lambda_1)$$

$$\mathbb{E}_{\mathcal{D}_0}[1 - h(x)|y = 1] = \mathbb{E}_{\mathcal{D}_1}[1 - h(x)|y = 1]. \tag{λ_2}$$

This is a linear program over the set of distributions over hypotheses h. Let λ_1 and λ_2 be the optimal dual solution to this linear program. By Lagrangian duality, we have that the error-optimal classifier subject to error-rate balance constraints is a minimizer of

$$\mathbb{E}\Big[h(x)\Big((1 - 2\mathbb{E}[y|x]) + \lambda_1(1 - \mathbb{E}[y|x])(\mathbb{1}[g = 0] - \mathbb{1}[g = 1])$$
$$+ \lambda_2(\mathbb{E}[y|x](\mathbb{1}[g = 1] - \mathbb{1}[g = 0]))\Big)\Big].$$

In other words, the optimal such classifier h^* must satisfy:

$$h^*(x, g) = \begin{cases} 1 & \text{if } g = 0 \text{ and } (2 + \lambda_1 + \lambda_2)\mathbb{E}_{\mathcal{D}_0}[y|x] > 1 + \lambda_1, \\ 0 & \text{if } g = 0 \text{ and } (2 + \lambda_1 + \lambda_2)\mathbb{E}_{\mathcal{D}_0}[y|x] < 1 + \lambda_1, \\ 1 & \text{if } g = 1 \text{ and } (2 - \lambda_1 - \lambda_2)\mathbb{E}_{\mathcal{D}_1}[y|x] > 1 - \lambda_1, \\ 0 & \text{if } g = 1 \text{ and } (2 - \lambda_1 - \lambda_2)\mathbb{E}_{\mathcal{D}_1}[y|x] < 1 - \lambda_1. \end{cases}$$

(If none of these conditions is satisfied, the optimal classifier may need to randomize). From this we learn that the optimal classifier h^* remains a thresholding on the conditional label expectation, even under error-rate balance constraints. Therefore, to allow a downstream decision maker to deploy an optimal classifier subject to error-rate balance, it continues to suffice that our statistical estimator f should correctly encode the conditional label expectations: $f(x, g) = \mathbb{E}_{\mathcal{D}_g}[y|x]$.

On the other hand, it is not hard to see that if we must learn a *binary* model h (e.g., by thresholding $\mathbb{E}_{\mathcal{D}_g}[y|x]$ or via any other method) then in most cases we will have destroyed the information needed to implement the optimal classifier h^* satisfying error-rate balance downstream. Similarly, modifying the statistical estimator $f(x, g)$ in such a way that it deviates from $f(x, g) = \mathbb{E}_{\mathcal{D}_g}[y|x]$ will generically preclude us from being able to implement the optimal classifier h^* subject to error-rate balance downstream. This suggests a general rule of thumb:

> Constraints such as error-rate balance should be applied at the very end of decision making pipelines, at the moment when actions are taken that have the potential to harm people. At the intermediate stages of decision making pipelines, we should strive to capture statistical information about the population that is as accurate as possible (ideally $\mathbb{E}_{\mathcal{D}_g}[y|x]$), because failing to do this harms not only accuracy but also our ability to usefully impose fairness constraints downstream.

How should we think about realizing this rule of thumb? In general, we cannot hope to learn $\mathbb{E}_{\mathcal{D}_g}[y|x]$ from data, because if X is a large feature space then we will see each particular feature vector x only infrequently, and so we will have only a few or maybe no samples of the conditional label distributions that are conditional on x. At best we can hope to learn some "good" proxy $\bar{f}(x, g)$. But what makes a good proxy? In the following, for simplicity we will assume that g is encoded in the feature vector x so that we may write simply $f(x)$ and $\mathbb{E}[y|x]$.

Suppose we are given a function f that purports to represent conditional label distributions: $\bar{f}(x) = \mathbb{E}[y|x]$. How can we attempt to falsify this assertion? Here is one family of tests. Consider any subset $S \subseteq X$ of the feature space. If $\bar{f}(x) = \mathbb{E}[y|x]$, then we will have

$$\mathbb{E}[y|x \in S] = \mathbb{E}[\bar{f}(x)|x \in S].$$

If $\bar{f}$ fails to satisfy this condition on any set S then this certifies that f does not correctly represent the conditional label distribution. Moreover, this is a condition that we can easily test (approximately) from data, because, for any set S with sufficiently large probability in the underlying distribution $\mathcal{D}$, we can estimate conditional expectations accurately from sample quantities. Suppose we have some very large collection G of such sets S: $G \subseteq 2^X$. This would parameterize a suite of statistical tests aimed at falsifying the conjecture that $\bar{f}$ correctly encoded the conditional label distribution, and we could ask that estimators $\bar{f}$ are produced that pass every statistical test in this suite – i.e., that satisfy $\mathbb{E}[y|x \in S] = \mathbb{E}[\bar{f}(x)|x \in S]$ simultaneously for every $S \in G$. At the very least we can check from data whether our classifiers satisfy these conditions. Can we find other classifiers that satisfy them as well? We can phrase this as an optimization problem:

$$\min_{\bar{f}} \max_{S \in G} \left| \mathbb{E}[y|x \in S] - \mathbb{E}[\bar{f}(x)|x \in S] \right|.$$

There is a solution $\bar{f}$ that obtains optimal objective value 0 – i.e., the true conditional label distribution – and so the only question is whether we can efficiently find some $\bar{f}$ that does well according to this objective.

Remarkably, it turns out that we can, although the details of how we do this are beyond the scope of this chapter (but see the references for further reading). We call ϵ-approximate solutions to this problem ϵ-*multiaccurate* estimators $\bar{f}$ with respect to the collection of groups G.

Definition 32.14. A statistical estimator $\bar{f} : X \to \mathbb{R}$ is ϵ-multiaccurate with respect to a collection of groups $G \in 2^X$ if, for every $S \in G$.

$$\left| \mathbb{E}[y|x \in S] - \mathbb{E}[\bar{f}(x)|x \in S] \right| \le \epsilon.$$

There are efficient algorithms that learn approximately multiaccurate estimators for any collection of sets G, with sufficiently large measure, from datasets that have size only polynomial in $1/\epsilon$ and $\log|G|$. The logarithmic dependence on $|G|$ means that we can learn estimators that pass an exponentially large number of "sanity check" statistical tests – one for each of the groups $S \in G$.

Multiaccuracy is one of a family of "informational balance" constraints that it is sensible to ask mid-stream statistical estimators to satisfy. This family of constraints can be generalized by enlarging the set of statistical tests that we insist that our estimator $\bar{f}$ should satisfy, each aimed at falsifying the conjecture that $\bar{f}$ correctly encodes the conditional label expectations. In addition to enlarging the collection of sets G that define our tests, we can ask that $\bar{f}$ shoud pass similar statistical tests over sets S that are defined not just by the features x but also by our predictions $\bar{f}(x)$ – this leads to a notion of statistical balance called *multi-calibration*. We can also ask for statistical tests based not just on the expectations of label distributions but on variances and other higher moments. Or we can ask that our statistical estimators be indistinguishable from the true conditional label distribution with respect to the actions taken by some well-defined set of downstream decision makers who are informed by our predictions. All these measures can be not only checked but also guaranteed by learning procedures that have only small amounts of data, logarithmic in $|G|$, which allows us to ask for consistency with respect to an exponentially large collection of sets G. If we consider the sets in G as themselves representing demographic groups g that we wish to protect, multiaccuracy give us a way to think about enforcing statistical fairness constraints over large collections of carefully defined and potentially overlapping groups; this can save us from the need to anticipate, ahead of time, every group g for which we might desire, for example, error-rate balance in some downstream classification task.

32.5 Bibliographic Notes

The importance of error-rate balance and informational balance were dramatically brought to the public consciousness in a 2016 *ProPublica* article [1] investigating bias in the COMPAS recidivism prediction tool that was used to inform bail and parole decisions in a number of US jurisdictions. The impossibility result that we derived in Section 32.2 was originally proven in [2]. A similar result for real-valued predictors was proven [18]. The dynamic model from Section 32.3 corresponds to the "baseline model" in [12], wherein the model is generalized in various ways, including to cover the case in which signal distributions *do* depend on group membership and the case in which the observation of signal distributions is mediated by a third party with its own incentives (e.g., the police). That the conditional label distribution is a sufficient statistic for the optimal classifier subject to error-rate balance constraints has been observed in several publications, including [8] and [3]. The idead of multiaccuracy and multicalibration were proposed [9]. The paper [13] generalized the notion of multicalibration from means to variances and other higher moments of the label distribution. In [7] further generalize this idea was further generalized and "multivalid" statistical estimators of different sorts were defined, including multivalid prediction intervals which can obtain tight 95% coverage intervals over large numbers of intersecting demographic groups. In [22], a multicalibration-like notion of consistency was defined with respect to a class of downstream decision makers. It is also possible to define analogues of error-rate balance with respect to large collections of overlapping groups G, just as multiaccuracy and multicalibration provide analogues of informational balance in this setting; see [17]. For a fuller popular treatment of the issues discussed in this chapter, see [16]. Here we have focused on statistical estimation problems – although these are related sometimes to allocation problems, we have ignored capacity or supply constraints. We refer the reader to [5], [4], [21], and [6] for discussions of fairness in allocation problems with capacity constraints. There are also other papers that study related fairness desiderata in game-theoretic settings: we refer the reader to [14], [10], [20], [11], [19], and [15] for other work in this style.

References

[1] Angwin, Julia, Larson, Jeff, Mattu, Surya, and Kirchner, Lauren. 2016. Machine bias. *ProPublica*, **23**, 2016.

[2] Chouldechova, Alexandra. 2017. Fair prediction with disparate impact: A study of bias in recidivism prediction instruments. *Big Data*, **5**(2), 153–163.

[3] Corbett-Davies, Sam, Pierson, Emma, Feller, Avi, Goel, Sharad, and Huq, Aziz. 2017. Algorithmic decision making and the cost of fairness. Pages 797–806 of: *Proc. 23rd ACM SIGKDD International Conference on Knowledge Discovery and Data Mining.*

[4] Donahue, Kate, and Kleinberg, Jon. 2020. Fairness and utilization in allocating resources with uncertain demand. Pages 658–668 of: *Proc. Conference on Fairness, Accountability, and Transparency.*

[5] Elzayn, Hadi, Jabbari, Shahin, Jung, Christopher, Kearns, Michael, Neel, Seth, Roth, Aaron, and Schutzman, Zachary. 2019. Fair algorithms for learning in allocation problems. Pages 170–179 of: *Proc. Conference on Fairness, Accountability, and Transparency.*

[6] Finocchiaro, Jessie, Maio, Roland, Monachou, Faidra, Patro, Gourab K., Raghavan, Manish, Stoica, Ana-Andreea, and Tsirtsis, Stratis. 2021. Bridging machine learning and mechanism design towards algorithmic fairness. Pages 489–503 of: *Proc. 2021 ACM Conference on Fairness, Accountability, and Transparency.*

[7] Gupta, Varun, Jung, Christopher, Noarov, Georgy, Pai, Mallesh M., and Roth, Aaron. 2021. Online multivalid learning: Means, moments, and prediction intervals. *arXiv preprint arXiv:2101.01739.*

[8] Hardt, Moritz, Price, Eric, and Srebro, Nathan. 2016. Equality of opportunity in supervised learning. Pages 3323–3331 of: *Proc. 30th International Conference on Neural Information Processing Systems.*

[9] Hébert-Johnson, Úrsula, Kim, Michael, Reingold, Omer, and Rothblum, Guy. 2018. Multicalibration: Calibration for the (computationally-identifiable) masses. Pages 1939–1948 of: *Proc. International Conference on Machine Learning.*

[10] Hu, Lily, and Chen, Yiling. 2018. A short-term intervention for long-term dairness in the labor market. International World Wide Web Conference Committee.

[11] Hu, Lily, Immorlica, Nicole, and Vaughan, Jennifer Wortman. 2019. The disparate effects of strategic manipulation. Pages 259–268 of: *Proc. Conference on Fairness, Accountability, and Transparency.*

[12] Jung, Christopher, Kannan, Sampath, Lee, Changhwa, Pai, Mallesh M., Roth, Aaron, and Vohra, Rakesh. 2020. Fair prediction with endogenous behavior. Pages 677–678 of: Biró, Péter, Hartline, Jason, Ostrovsky, Michael, and Procaccia, Ariel D., eds., *Proc. 21st ACM Conference on Economics and Computation.*

[13] Jung, Christopher, Lee, Changhwa, Pai, Mallesh M., Roth, Aaron, and Vohra, Rakesh. 2021. Moment multicalibration for uncertainty estimation. In: *Proc. 34th Annual Conference on Learning Theory.*

[14] Kannan, Sampath, Kearns, Michael, Morgenstern, Jamie, Pai, Mallesh, Roth, Aaron, Vohra, Rakesh, and Wu, Zhiwei Steven. 2017. Fairness incentives for myopic agents. Pages 369–386 of: *Proc. 2017 ACM Conference on Economics and Computation.*

[15] Kannan, Sampath, Niu, Mingzi, Roth, Aaron, and Vohra, Rakesh. 2021. Best vs. all: equity and accuracy of standardized test score reporting. *arXiv preprint arXiv:2102.07809.*

[16] Kearns, Michael, and Roth, Aaron. 2019. *The Ethical Algorithm: The Science of Socially Aware Algorithm Design.* Oxford University Press.

[17] Kearns, Michael, Neel, Seth, Roth, Aaron, and Wu, Zhiwei Steven. 2018. Preventing fairness gerrymandering: Auditing and learning for subgroup fairness. Pages 2564–2572 of: *Proc. International Conference on Machine Learning.*

[18] Kleinberg, Jon M., Mullainathan, Sendhil, and Raghavan, Manish. 2017. Inherent trade-offs in the fair determination of risk scores. Pages 43:1–43:23 of: Papadimitriou, Christos H., ed., *Proc. 8th Innovations in Theoretical Computer Science Conference.*

[19] Liu, Lydia T., Wilson, Ashia, Haghtalab, Nika, Kalai, Adam Tauman, Borgs, Christian, and Chayes, Jennifer. 2020. The disparate equilibria of algorithmic decision making when individuals invest rationally. Pages 381–391 of: *Proc. 2020 Conference on Fairness, Accountability, and Transparency.*

[20] Milli, Smitha, Miller, John, Dragan, Anca D., and Hardt, Moritz. 2019. The social cost of strategic classification. Pages 230–239 of: *Proc. Conference on Fairness, Accountability, and Transparency.*

[21] Sinclair, Sean R., Jain, Gauri, Banerjee, Siddhartha, and Yu, Christina Lee. 2020. Sequential fair allocation of limited resources under stochastic demands. *arXiv preprint arXiv:2011.14382.*

[22] Zhao, Shengjia, Kim, Michael P., Sahoo, Roshni, Ma, Tengyu, and Ermon, Stefano. 2021. Calibrating predictions to decisions: A novel approach to multiclass calibration. *arXiv preprint arXiv:2107.05719.*

Index

acceptability graph, 285
action, 615
additive valuation, 594
adverse selection, 626
agent, 614
algorithm
  greedy, 51
  online, 50
  random, 52
allocation problem, 92
ascending auction, 579
assignment, 362
assignment game, 450
assortative matching, 436, 444
asymptotic incentive compatibility, 368
  of pseudomarkets, 368
auction, 93

Bayesian persuasion, 662
Bayesian regret, 659
best edge, 267
bipartite graph, 4
bipartite preference profile, *see* preference
  profile, bipartite
Birkhoff–von Neumann theorem, 362, 601
block
  matching with salaries, 83
  set of contracts, 86
blocking pair, 4, 9, 11, 17, 285, 601
b-blocking, 266
bounded search tree algorithms, 297
budget, 362
bundle, 375

capacity function, 3
cardinal property, 91
centralized market, 428
cheapest bundle property, 364
cheapest purchase property, 364

choice function, 85
Choo and Siow formula, 560
clock auction, 161
combinatorial choice domain, 243
combinatorial choice function, 243
combinatorial choice model, 243
combinatorial demand correspondence, 243
combinatorial demand model, 243
competitive ratio, 51
complementary slackness, 134
complete preference profile, *see* preference
  profile, complete
congestion, 476
connected graph, 272
constraints, 377
consumer surplus, 100
contract, 615
contract theory, 614
convex duality, 552, 556, 558
coordinate descent, 565
core, 4
  matching with salaries, 83
costly signaling, 471

data reduction rules, 295
decentralized market, 428
deferred acceptance, 602
deferred acceptance algorithm, 6, 7
descending clock auction, 170
dictator, 96
dictatorial social choice function, 105
differentiable economics, 591
direct-revelation mechanism, 103
dominant strategy, 103
  implementation, 103
dominant-strategy equilibrium, 103
dominant-strategy incentive compatible, 14,
  103
domination, 266

downward distortion, 621
dual program, 556
duality, 134

EGAL-SMI-DEC, 287
EGAL-SRI-DEC, 287
EGAL-SRTI-DEC, 287
L-edge-choosable graph, 276
L-edge-coloring of a graph, 276
k-edge-choosable graph, 276, 656
efficiency, 369
    of pseudomarkets, 370
efficient outcome, 94
egalitarian cost, 287
egalitarian stable matching, *see* matching,
        egalitarian stable
empirical model, 531
    random utility model, 531
    school choice, 533
endowment, 92
entropy, 559
envy-freeness, 94, 375
envy-freeness of pseudomarkets, 375
equilibrium, 362
estimation using final matches
    many-to-one matching, 537
    one-to-one matching, 535
    stability, 534
estimation using rank-order lists, 543
    manipulated reports, 545
    truthful reports, 543
ex ante justified envy, 601
ex ante stable, 601
ex post regret, 594, 606
ex post stability, 440
exchange economy, 92
exhausted, state of worker, 291
existence of pseudomarket equilibria, 363
exploding offers, 432
extended entropy, 563

favor, 290
feasibility, 362
feasible payoff profile, 450
feasible profile for the matching μ, 450
finite distributive lattice, 19
$F(\mathcal{P})$, 294
firm-optimal matching, 10
firm not matched to capacity, 11
first–last property, 268
fixed pair, 294
fixed-parameter algorithms, 294

$\gamma(F(\mathcal{P}))$, 294

$\gamma(\mu)$, 287
$\hat{\gamma}$, 295
generalized entropy, 559, 562
gradient descent, 566
guaranteed payoff, 622
Gumbel distribution, 559

heterosexual marriage market, 552
hidden actions, 614
hidden information, 614

identification, 552, 556, 559, 567
implementable allocation function, 628
incentivized exploration, 656
incomplete preference profile, *see* preference
        profile, incomplete
INDEPENDENT SET, 287
individual rationality, 396, 601
individual stability, 258
individual-rationality violation, 606
individually rational
    matching with salaries, 83
    set of contracts, 86
induced-value theory, 512
information asymmetry, 654
interim stability, 440
iterative proportional fitting procedure (IPFP),
        565

join operation, 19
joint surplus, 553, 555, 557, 562, 563
joint surplus function, 552, 567

Karush–Kuhn–Tucker optimality conditions,
        554
kernel, 295
kernelization algorithms, 295
Király's approximation algorithm, 290

lack of justified envy, 377
Lagrangian optimization, 597
Lagrangian relaxation, 135
large market, 366
lattice, 19
    canonical finite distributive, 26
Legendre–Fenchel transform, 558
limited liability, 617
linear constraints, 377
linear contract, 623
Logit, 553, 560, 563, 564

man-optimal stable matching, 270
many-to-one property, 278
market clearing, 363

matched to capacity, 11
matching, 285, 450
  egalitarian stable, 287
  perfect, 285
  stable, 285
b-matching, 11, 265
matching function, 560
matching patterns, 553
Matsubara formalism, i, 3, 23, 37, 66, 90, 107,
    109, 130, 155, 180, 201, 217, 219, 238, 264,
    283, 303, 323, 343, 361, 381, 402, 428, 448,
    467, 484, 509, 511, 530, 552, 573, 575, 591,
    614, 635, 655, 676
MAX-SMTI, 286
MAX-SMTI-DEC, 288
MAX-SMTI-TF, 290
maximal matching, 9, 51
maximum likelihood estimator, 561
maximum-score method, 564
mechanism, 101
  for hidden-information models, 627
meet operation, 19
messages, 101
messaging policy, 658
moment-matching estimator, 561
monotone contract, 618
monotone convex hidden-action problem, 618
moral hazard, 615
multi-armed bandits, 658
multiple-unit demand, 375

neural network, 591
firm not matched to capacity, 11

obvious strategy-proofness, 577
online algorithm, 50
open offers, 432
optimal matching, 564, 567
optimal partner, 7
optimal transport, 552
ordinal property, 91
ordinal strategy-proofness, 602
outside option, 363, 615

parametric model, 560
Pareto
  dominated, 94
  efficiency, 369
  optimal, 94
  weakly optimal, 94
perfect matching, 4, *see* matching, perfect
perfectly transferable utility, 552, 553
pessimal partner, 7
Poisson process, 567

Poisson regression, 563
pre-arranged matches, 431
preference aggregation rule, 96
preference profile, 285
  bipartite, 286
  complete, 285
  incomplete, 285
preference relation, 90
preference signaling, 470
price, 362
primal program, 555, 559
principal, 614
principal-agent framework, 614
priorities, 377
promoted worker, 290
proper edge-coloring of a graph, 276
pseudomarket equilibrium, 362
pseudomarket mechanism, 365
pseudomarket representation of efficient
    assignments, 372
public goods, 98
pure strategy, 58

quality signaling, 471
quasilinear utility, 92

random mechanism, 440
random permutation model, 138
random priority, 371, 602
random serial dictatorship, 602
random utility model, 531
randomized matching, 601
rank, 285
realm of possibilities, 7, 10
regret, 659
RegretNet, 594
regular distribution, 366
regular economy, 367
revealed preference, 245
revealed strict preference, 245
revenue-optimal auction, 593
risk aversion, 617
rotation, 18, 22
rural hospital theorem, 11

screening, 626
separability, 552, 556
separation lemma, 374
sheepskin effect, 479
signaling, 467
simultaneous multiple-round auction, 159
single-unit demand, 362
Sinkhorn's algorithm, 565
social choice environment, 101

social welfare function, 98
SMI, 286
SMTI, 286
SRI, 286
SRTI, 286
STABLE MARRIAGE, 285
STABLE ROOMMATES, 285
stability, 377, 554, 601
stability and strategy-proofness: impossibility
    of, 602
stability violation, 604
stable b-matching, 266
    instance, 266
stable matching, 5, 266, 448, 532, *see also*
    matching, stable
    instance, 265
    lattice, 19
    set of contracts, 86
stochastic dominance, 440
strategy, 103
strategy-proofness, 103, 365
strategy-proofness of pseudomarkets, 366
substitutability, 86
surplus, 616

technology, 615
tie, 285
token money, 362
types, 556, 559, 566

unit-demand valuation, 594

unobserved heterogeneity, 552, 555, 558, 560,
    567
unrestricted preference domain, 105
upper bound, 19
    least, 19
utilitarian solution, 99
utility function, 91, 92
utility possibility set, 99

$V(F(\mathcal{P}))$, 294
$V^r(\mathcal{P})$, 294
$V^u(\mathcal{P})$, 294
valid contract, 616
    with limited liability, 617
valid mechanism, 627
value of a game, 59
Vickrey auction, 165
virtual surplus for hidden-information model,
    630
virtual value for hidden-information model,
    630

WARSPrio, 254
weak axiom of revealed preference, 246
weak axiom of revealed strict priority, 254
welfare theorem, first, 370
welfare theorem, second, 372
woman-optimal stable matching, 270
worker-optimal matching, 10

zero-sum game, 58